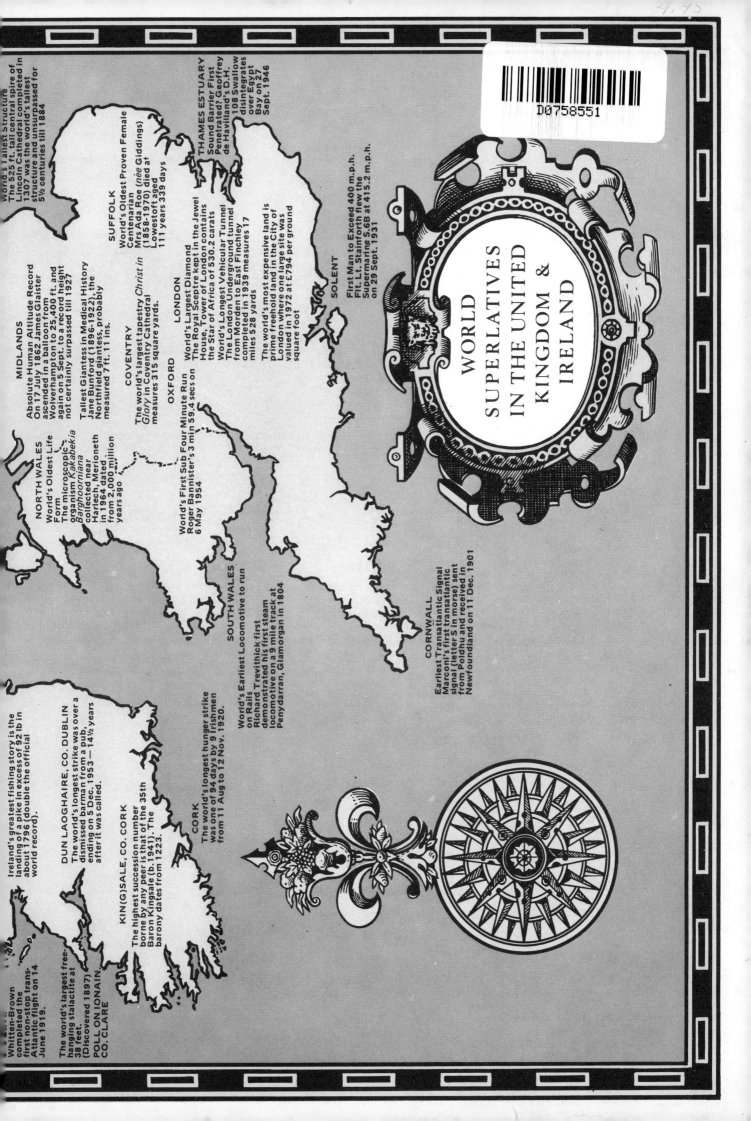

WORLD SUPERLATIVES IN THE UNITED KINGDOM & IRELAND

World's Tallest Structure
The 525 ft. tall central spire of Lincoln Cathedral completed in 1307 was the world's tallest structure and unsurpassed for 5½ centuries till 1884

SUFFOLK
World's Oldest Proven Female Centenarian
Mrs Ada Roe (née Giddings) (1858-1970) died at Lowestoft aged 111 years 339 days

THAMES ESTUARY
Sound Barrier First Penetrated? Geoffrey de Havilland's D.H. 108 Swallow disintegrates over Egypt Bay on 27 Sept. 1946

MIDLANDS
Absolute Human Altitude Record
On 17 July 1862 James Glaister ascended in a balloon from Wolverhampton to 25,400 ft. and again on 5 Sept. to a record height not certainly surpassed till 1927

Tallest Giantess in Medical History
Jane Bunford (1896-1922), the Northfield giantess, probably measured 7 ft. 11 ins.

COVENTRY
The world's largest tapestry *Christ in Glory* in Coventry Cathedral measures 315 square yards.

LONDON
World's Largest Diamond
The Royal Sceptre kept in the Jewel House, Tower of London contains the Star of Africa of 530.2 carats

World's Longest Vehicular Tunnel
The London Underground tunnel from Morden to East Finchley completed in 1939 measures 17 miles 528 yards

The world's most expensive land is prime freehold land in the City of London where one large site was valued in 1972 at £794 per ground square foot

OXFORD
World's First Sub Four Minute Run
Roger Bannister's 3 min 59.4 secs on 6 May 1954

SOLENT
First Man to Exceed 400 m.p.h.
Flt. Lt. Stainforth flew the Supermarine S.6B at 415.2 m.p.h. on 29 Sept. 1931

NORTH WALES
World's Oldest Life Form
The microscopic organism *Kakabekia Barghoorniana* collected near Harlech, Merioneth in 1964 dated from 2,000 million years ago

SOUTH WALES
World's Earliest Locomotive to run on Rails
Richard Trevithick first demonstrated his first steam locomotive on a 9 mile track at Penydarran, Glamorgan in 1804

CORNWALL
Earliest Transatlantic Signal
Marconi's first transatlantic signal (letter S in morse) sent from Poldhu and received in Newfoundland on 11 Dec. 1901

Whitten-Brown completed the first non-stop trans-Atlantic flight on 14 June 1919.

The world's largest free-hanging stalactite at 38 feet.
(Discovered 1897)
POLL ON IONAIN, CO. CLARE

Ireland's greatest fishing story is the landing of a pike in excess of 92 lb in about 1796 (double the official world record).

DUN LAOGHAIRE, CO. DUBLIN
The world's longest strike was over a dismissed barman from a pub ending on 5 Dec. 1953 — 14½ years after it was called.

KIN(G)SALE, CO. CORK
The highest succession number borne by any peer is that of the 35th Baron Kingsale (b.1941). The barony dates from 1223.

CORK
The world's longest hunger strike was one of 94 days by 9 Irishmen from 11 Aug to 12 Nov. 1920.

Standard Book Number SBN: 900424 06 0
Copyright 1972 by Guinness Superlatives Limited

Standard Book Number SBN: 900424 12 5
Australian Edition
Standard Book Number SBN: 900424 07 9
South African Edition
© 1972 by Guinness Superlatives Limited
World Copyright Reserved
Nineteenth Edition

Note.
In keeping with the standardization sought by the Booksellers' Association,
The Library Association and The Publishers' Association,
editions have been designated thus:—

Edition	Published		Edition	Published	
First Edition	October	1955	Eleventh Edition	November	1964
Second Edition	October	1955	Twelfth Edition	November	1965
Third Edition	November	1955	Thirteenth Edition	October	1966
Fourth Edition	January	1956	Fourteenth Edition	October	1967
Fifth Edition	October	1956	Fifteenth Edition	October	1968
Sixth Edition	December	1956	Sixteenth Edition	October	1969
Seventh Edition	November	1958	Seventeenth Edition	October	1970
Eighth Edition	November	1960	Eighteenth Edition	October	1971
Ninth Edition	April	1961	Nineteenth Edition	October	1972
Tenth Edition	November	1962			

Note.
No back numbers are now available. Orders for current editions published overseas
will willingly be passed on to the publishers concerned. The date indicates the first year
an edition was established in the country concerned.

Guinness Book of World Records 1956 Casebound U.S.A.
Guinness Book of World Records 1962 Paperback U.S.A.
Le Livre des Extrêmes 1962 Casebound French
Guinness Rekord bog Først og Størst Sidst og Mindst 1967 Casebound Danish
Guinness Das Buch Der Rekorde 1967 Paperback German
Guinness Rekord bok Først og Størst Sist og Minst 1967 Casebound Norwegian
Guinness Korega Sekai Ichi 1968 Paper (2 vols.) Japanese
Enciclopedia Guinness de Superlativos Mundiales 1968 Paperback Spanish
Il Guinness dei Primati 1968 Italian
Guinnessin Ennätysten Kirja 1968 Casebound Finnish
Guinness Rekord bok Först och Störst 1968 Casebound Swedish
Het Groot Guinness Rekord Boek 1971 Casebound Dutch
Guinnessova kniha rekordu 1973 Paperback Czech
Note: A Hebrew language edition has been contracted for 1973 (Hardback)

Layout and illustrations by DENZIL REEVES

Printed by
Redwood Press Limited
Trowbridge, Wiltshire, England
Made and Printed in Great Britain

 GUINNESS SUPERLATIVES LIMITED, 2 CECIL COURT, LONDON ROAD, ENFIELD, MIDDX.

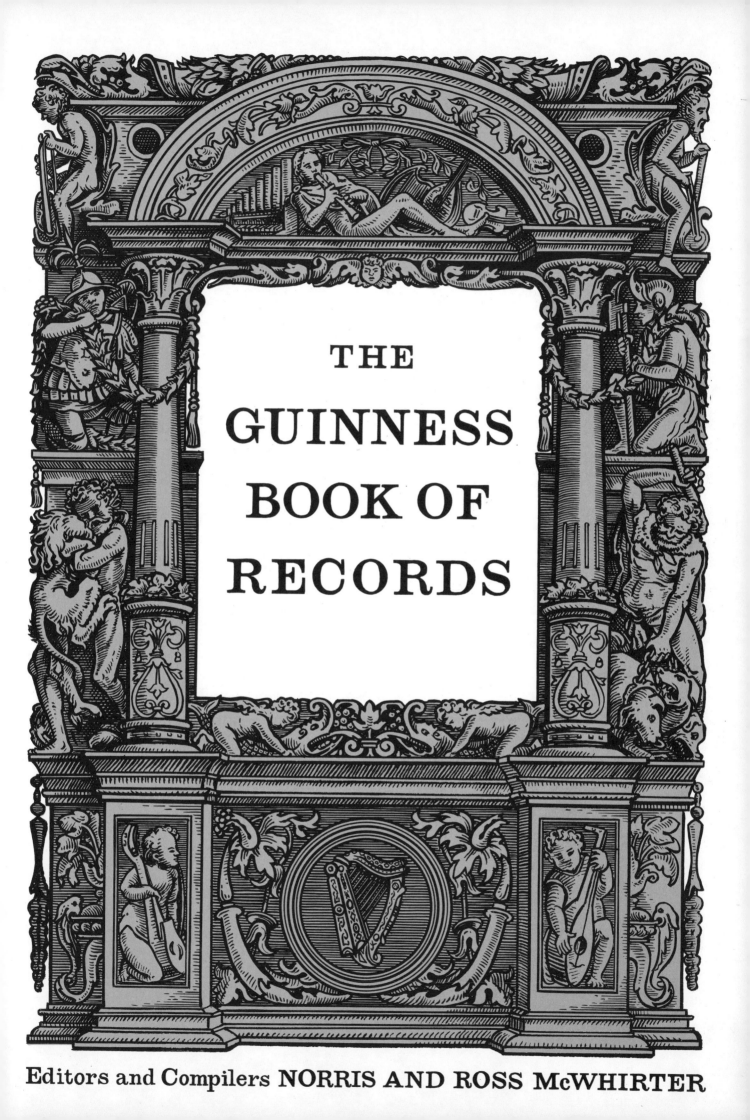

THE
GUINNESS
BOOK OF
RECORDS

Editors and Compilers **NORRIS AND ROSS McWHIRTER**

ACKNOWLEDGEMENTS

Ian Allen & Co.
The Alpine Club
American Telephone & Telegraph Co.
J. W. Arblaster, Esq., A.I.M.
The Automobile Association
T. Banner, Esq.
James Bond
The Brewers' Society
The British Broadcasting Corporation
British European Airways
British Medical Association
British Museum (Natural History)
British Mycological Society
British Overseas Airways Corporation
British Rail
British Transport Commission
British Travel
British Waterworks Association
A. W. Bulley, Esq.
Burkes' Peerage Ltd.
Henry G. Button, Esq.
Central Electricity Generating Board
Central Office of Information
Dr. A. J. C. Charig
The Chemical Society
Chicago Daily News
Church Commissioners
Conchological Society of Great Britain and Ireland
County Councils Association
Clerk of Dail Eireann
Department of Employment and Productivity
Eldon Pothole Club
Fédération Aéronautique Internationale
Fédération Internationale de l'Automobile
Fédération Internationale des Hôpitaux
George Fisher, Esq.
Frank L. Forster
Fortune
Dr. Francis C. Fraser
The Fur Trade Information Centre
General Motors Corporation
General Post Office
Geological Survey and Museum
The Gramophone Co. Ltd.
Greater London Council
W. T. Gunston, Esq., *Flight International*
John I. Haas Inc.
A. Herbert, Esq. (New Zealand)
Michael E. R. R. Herridge, Esq.
The Home Office
Imperial War Museum
The Inland Waterways Association
Institut International des Châteaux Historiques
Institute of Strategic Studies
International Association of Volacanology
International Civil Aviation Organization
The Kennel Club
D. G. King-Hele, Esq., F.R.S.
Kline Iron and Steel Company
Frank W. Lane, Esq.
Dr. L. S. B. Leakey
The Library of Congress, Washington, D.C.
Lloyd's Register of Shipping
London Transport Board
J. Lyons & Co. Ltd.
Marconi's Wireless Telegraph Co. Ltd.
The late T. L. Marks, Esq., O.B.E., T.D.
Prof. K. G. McWhirter, M.A., M.SC.
Meteorological Office
Mertopolitan Police
Ministry of Agriculture, Fisheries and Food
Ministry of Defence
Ministry of Housing and Local Government
Ministry of Labour
Ministry of Public Buildings and Works
Ministry of Social Security
Ministry of Technology
Alan Mitchell, Esq.
Miss Carole Mortimer
The Museums Association
Music Research Bureau
Mational Aeronautics and Space Administration
National Coal Board

National Geographic Society
National Maritime Museum
National Physical Laboratory
The New York Times
Mrs. Susann Palmer
The Patent Office Library
Photo Dealer Magazine
Port of New York Authority
Ransomes and Rapier Ltd.
Registrar General's Annual Report and Statistics Review
Registrar General's Office, Edinburgh
Jean Reville, Esq.
Rolls-Royce Ltd.
Royal Astronomical Society
Royal Botanic Gardens
Royal College of Surgeons of England
Royal Geographic Society
Royal National Life-boat Institution
Royal Norwegian Embassy
Sampson Low, Marston & Co. Ltd.
Dr. Albert Schwartz
B.A.Seaby Ltd
Cdr. T.R. Shaw, R.N.
Siems und Halske Aktiengesellschaft
Société Nationale des Chemins de Fer Français
Statutory Publications Office
John W. R. Taylor, Esq.
Time-Life International Inc.
The Treasury
Trinity House
U.N.E.S.C.O.
U.N. Statistical Office
United States Department of Agriculture
United States Department of the Interior
Water and Water Engineering
Gerry L. Wood, Esq., F.Z.S.
World Meteorological Organization
World Record Breakers Association
Zoological Society of London
Zoological Society of Philadelphia
Also to Mrs. Barbara Anderson, Mrs. Sally Bennett, Mrs. Christine Bethlehem, Mrs. Rosemary Bevan, Signa. Wendy Cirillo, Mrs. Pamela Croome, Miss Trüdy Doyle, Mlle. Béatrice Frei, Harold C. Harlow, Esq., Miss Tessa Hegley, E. C. Henniker, Esq., Mrs. Angela Hoaen, David F. Hoy, Esq., Mrs. Eileen Jackson, Mrs. Jane Mayo, G. M. Nutbrown, Esq., Mrs. Margaret Orr-Deas, Peter B. Page, Esq., Geoffrey Potter, Esq., John Rivers, Esq., Mrs. Judith Sleath, Mrs. Anne Symonds, Andrew Thomas, Esq. (Associate Editor 1964-68), Tony Thomas, Esq., Miss Hilary Tippett, Mrs. Winnie Ulrich, Miss Diana Wilford.

CONTENTS

All Sports
Angling
Archery
Association Football (see Football)
Athletics (see Track and Field)
Badminton
Baseball
Basketball
Beagling (see Fox Hunting)
Billiards
Bobsleigh
Bowling (Ten Pin)
Bowls
Boxing
Bridge (see Contract Bridge)
Bullfighting
Canoeing
Card Playing
Caving
Chess
Coursing
Cricket
Croquet
Cross-Country Running
Curling
Cycling
Darts
Diving (see Swimming)
Equestrian Sports
Eton Fives (see Fives)
Fencing
Fishing (see Angling)
Fives
Football (Association)
Football (Gaelic)
Football (Rugby League)
Football (Rugby Union)
Fox Hunting
Gaelic Football (see Football)
Gambling
Gliding
Golf
Greyhound Racing
Gymnastics
Handball (Court and Field)
Harness Racing (see Trotting)
Hockey
Horse Racing
Hurling
Ice Hockey
Ice Skating
Ice Yachting
Jai Alai (see Pelota Vasca)

Judo (Jiu-Jitsu)
Karate
Lacrosse
Lawn Tennis
Lugeing (see Bobsleigh)
Modern Pentathlon
Motorcycling
Motor Racing
Mountaineering
Netball
Olympic Games
Orienteering
Pelota Vasca (Jai Alai)
Pigeon Racing
Polo
Power Boat Racing
Rackets
Real Tennis (see Tennis)
Rodeo
Roller Skating
Rowing
Royal Tennis (see Tennis)
Rugby Fives (see Fives)
Rugby League (see Football)
Rugby Union (see Football)
Sailing (see Yachting)
Sculling (see Rowing)
Shooting
Show Jumping (see Equestrian Sports)
Skating (Ice) (see Ice Skating)
Skating (Roller) (See Roller Skating)
Ski-ing
Snooker
Speedway
Squash Rackets
Surfing
Swimming
Table Tennis
Tennis (Real or Royal)
Tiddlywinks
Tobogganing (see Bobsleigh)
Track and Field Athletics
Trampolining
Trotting and Pacing
Tug of War (see Athletics)
Volleyball
Walking
Water Polo
Water Ski-ing
Weightlifting
Wrestling
Yachting

FOREWORD

By the Rt. Hon. The Earl of Iveagh

When we first brought out this book, some seventeen years ago, we did so in the hope of providing a means for the peaceful settling of arguments about record performances in this record-breaking world in which we live. We realise, of course, that much joy lies in the argument, but how exasperating it can be if there is no final means of finding the answer.

In the event, we have found that the interest aroused by this book has exceeded our wildest expectations. We have now produced more than 7,000,000 copies, and eleven editions in the United States. Translations into Czech, Danish, Dutch, French, Finnish, German, Hebrew, Italian, Japanese, Norwegian, Spanish and Swedish and special editions for Australia and Southern Africa are showing the universality of its appeal. Whether the discussion concerns the smallest fish ever caught, the most expensive wine, the greatest weight lifted by a man, the furthest reached in space, the world's most successful racehorse, or—an old bone of contention—the longest river in the world, I can but quote the words used in introducing the first edition, "How much heat these innocent questions can raise: Guinness, in producing this book, hopes that it may assist in resolving many such disputes, and may, we hope, turn heat into light".

Iveagh

Chairman
Arthur Guinness, Son & Co., Ltd.
St. James's Gate Brewery, Dublin
Park Royal Brewery, London   October 1972

PREFACE

This nineteenth Edition has been completely re-set and re-illustrated.

The book is compiled as a result of many hundreds of experts answering highly specific enquiries which have in turn resulted from the leads provided by press cuttings, articles and correspondence from many of the world's 227 countries. We cannot overstress the fact that records are, almost by definition, highly perishable. Accordingly would-be record breakers should not rely on old editions nor indeed in some cases on the current edition, without at least consulting the Stop Press.

The title is essentially confined to the chronicling of *measurable* superlatives and thus we do not opine on the prettiest woman, the most beautiful sound or the most formidable mother-in-law, only the woman with the greatest girth or the organ (or indeed the mother-in-law) generating the most decibels.

Norris McWhirter

Editors and compilers

Ross McWhirter

October 1972   Guinness Superlatives Limited, 2 Cecil Court, London Road, Enfield, Middlesex.

1 THE HUMAN BEING

1. DIMENSIONS

TALLEST GIANTS

The height of human giants is a subject on which accurate information is frequently obscured by exaggeration and commercial dishonesty. The only admissible evidence on the true height of giants is that collected in recent years under impartial medical supervision.

The Biblical claim that Og, the Amorite king of Bashan and Gilead in *c.* 1450 B.C., stood 9 Hebrew cubits (13 feet 2½ inches) is based solely on the length of his basalt sarcophagus or "iron bedstead". The assertion that Goliath of Gath (*c.* 1060 B.C.) stood 6 cubits and a span (9 feet 6½ inches) suggests a confusion of units or some over-zealous exaggeration by the Hebrew chroniclers. The Jewish historian Flavius Josephus (born in A.D. 37 or 38, died after A.D. 93) and some of the manuscripts of the Septuagint (the earliest Greek translation of the Old Testament) attribute to Goliath the more credible height of 4 Greek cubits and a span (6 feet 10 inches).

Extreme mediaeval data, taken from bone measurements, invariably refer to specimens of extinct whale, giant cave bear, mastodon, woolly rhinoceros or other prehistoric non-human remains.

Paul Topinard (1830-1911), a French anthropometrist, stated that the tallest man who ever lived was Daniel Mynheer Cajanus (1714-49) of Finland, standing 283 centimetres (9 feet 3.4 inches). In 1872 his right femur, now in Leyden Museum, in the Netherlands, was measured by Prof. Carl Langer of Germany and indicated a height of 222 centimetres (7 feet 3.4 inches). Pierre Lemolt, a member of the French Academy, reported in 1847 that Ivan Stepanovich Lushkin (1811-44), a drum major in the Russian Imperial Regiment of Guards at Preobrazhenskiy, measured 3 arshin 9¼ vershok (8 feet 3¾ inches) and was "the tallest man that has ever lived in modern days". However, his left femur and tibia, which are now in the Museum of the Academy of Sciences in Leningrad, U.S.S.R., indicate a height of 7 feet 10¼ inches.

Circus giants and others who are exhibited are normally under contract not to be measured and are,

almost traditionally, billed by their promoters at heights up to 18 inches in excess of their true heights. There are many notable examples of this, and 23 instances were listed in the *Guinness Book of Records* (14th edition). The acromegalic giant Eddie Carmel (b. Tel Aviv, Israel, 1938), formerly "The Tallest Man on Earth" of Ringling Bros. and Barnum & Bailey's Circus (1961-68) is allegedly 9 feet 0⅝ inches tall (weighing 535 lb., 38 st. 3 lb.), but photographic evidence suggests that his true height is about 7 feet 6 inches.

An extreme case of exaggeration concerned Siah Khān ibn Kashmir Khān (b. 1913) of Bushehr (Bushire), Iran. Prof. D. H. Fuchs showed photographs of him at a meeting of the Society of Physicians in Vienna, Austria, in January 1935, claiming that he was 320 centimetres (10 feet 6 inches) tall. Later, when Siah Khān entered the Imperial Hospital in Teheran for an operation, it was revealed that his actual height was 220 centimetres (7 feet 2.6 inches).

World Modern opinion is that the tallest recorded man of whom there is irrefutable evidence was Robert Pershing Wadlow, born at 6.30 a.m. on 22 Feb. 1918 in Alton, Illinois, U.S.A. Weighing 8½ lb. at birth, his abnormal growth began almost immediately. His height progressed as follows:

Age in Years	Height	Weight in lb.	Age in Years	Height	Weight in lb.
5	5'4"	105	15	7'8"	355
8	6'0"	169	16	7'10½"	374
9	6'2½"	180	17	8'0½"	315*
10	6'5"	210	18	8'3½"	–
11	6'7"	–	19	8'5½"	480
12	6'10½"	–	20	8'6¾"	–
13	7'1¾"	255	21	8'8¼"	491
14	7'5"	301	22.4†	8'11"	439

* *Following severe influenza and infection of the foot.*
† *Wadlow was still growing during his terminal illness.*

Dr. C. M. Charles, Associate Professor of Anatomy at Washington University's School of Medicine in St. Louis, Missouri, measured Robert Wadlow at 272 centimetres (8 feet 11.1 inches) in St. Louis on 27

The world's tallest living man—Don Koehler of the U.S.A. at 8 feet 2 inches.

June 1940. Wadlow died 18 days later, at 1.30 a.m. on 15 July 1940, in Manistee, Michigan, as a result of cellulitis of the feet aggravated by a poorly fitted brace.

He was buried in Oakwood Cemetery, Alton, Illinois in a coffin measuring 10 feet 9 inches in length, 32 inches wide and 30 inches deep. His greatest recorded weight was 491 lb. (35 stone 1 lb.), on his 21st birthday. He weighed 439 lb. (31 stone 5 lb.) at the time of his death. His shoes were size 37AA (18½ inches long) and his hands measured 12¾ inches from the wrist to the tip of the middle finger.

The only other men for whom heights of 8 feet or more have been reliably reported are the seven listed below. In each case gigantism was followed by acromegaly, a disorder which causes an enlargement of the nose, lips, tongue, lower jaw, hands and feet, due to renewed activity by the already swollen pituitary gland, which is located at the base of the brain.

John F. Carroll (1932-69) of Buffalo, New York State, U.S.A. (a) 8 feet 7¾ inches (263.5 centimetres).
John William Rogan (1871-1905), a Negro of Gallatin, Tennessee, U.S.A. (b) 8 feet 6 inches (259.1 centimetres).
Don Koehler (b. 1929-*fl.* 1972) of Denton, Montana, U.S.A. (c) 8 feet 2 inches (248.9 centimetres).
Väinö Myllyrinne (1909-63) of Helsinki, Finland (d) 8 feet 1.2 inches (247 centimetres).
Gabriel Estavão Monjane (b. 1944) of Monjacaze, Mozambique (e) 8 feet 1 inch (246.3 centimetres).
"Constantine" (1872-1902) of Reutlingen, West Germany (f) 8 feet 0.8 inch (246 centimetres).
Sulaimān 'Alī Nashnush (b. 1943) of Tripoli, Libya (g) 8 feet 0.4 inch (245 centimetres).

(a) *Severe kypho-scoliosis (two dimensional spinal curvature). The figure represents his height with assumed normal spinal curvature, calculated from a standing height of 8 feet 0 inches, measured on 14 Oct. 1959. His standing height was 7 feet 8¼ inches shortly before his death.*
(b) *Measured in a sitting position. Unable to stand owing to ankylosis (stiffening of the joints through the formation of adhesions) of the knees and hips.*
(c) *He has a twin sister who is 5 feet 9 inches tall.*

(d) *Stood 7 feet 3½ inches at the age of 21 years. Experienced a second phase of growth in his late thirties and may have stood 8 feet 3 inches at one time.*
(e) *Abnormal growth started at the age of 10, following a head injury. Some kypho-scoliosis. Present height c. 7 feet 10 inches. A height of 8 feet 6 inches is claimed.*
(f) *Height estimated, as both legs were amputated after they turned gangrenous. He claimed a height of 259 centimetres (8 feet 6 inches).*
(g) *Operation to correct abnormal growth in Rome in 1960 was successful.*

A table of the tallest giants of all-time in the 31 countries with men taller than 7 feet 4 inches (223.5 cms.) was listed in the 15th edition of the *Guinness Book of Records* (1968) at page 9.

The claim that Sa'īd Muhammad Ghazi (b. 1909) of Alexandria, Egypt (now the United Arab Republic) attained a height of 8 feet 10 inches in February 1941 is now considered unreliable. Photographic evidence suggests his height was more nearly 7 feet 10½ inches, though he may have reached 8 feet at the time of his death.

England The tallest Englishman ever recorded was William Bradley (1788-1820), born in Market Weighton, in the East Riding of Yorkshire. He stood 7 feet 9 inches. John Middleton (1578-1623), the famous Childe of Hale, in Lancashire, was claimed to be 9 feet 3 inches. Hat pegs were accurately but inconclusively measured in October 1969 to be 12 feet 9 inches above the present floor of his cottage. James Toller (1795-1819) of St. Neots, near Huntingdon, was alleged to be 8 feet 6 inches but was actually 7 feet 6 inches. Albert Brough (1871-1919), a publican of Nottingham, reached a height of 7 feet 7½ inches. Frederick Kempster (1889-1918) of Bayswater, London, was reported to have measured 8 feet 4½ inches at the time of his death, but photographic evidence suggests that his height was 7 feet 8½ inches. He measured 234 centimetres (7 feet 8.1 inches) in 1913. Henry Daglish, who stood 7 feet 7 inches, died in Upper Stratton, Wiltshire, on 16 March 1951, aged 25. The much-publicized Edward (Ted) Evans (1924-58) of Englefield Green, Surrey, was reputed to be 9 feet 3 inches but actually stood 7 feet 8½ inches. The tallest fully mobile man now living in Great Britain is Christopher Paul Greener (b. New Brighton, Cheshire, 21 Nov. 1943) of Hayes, Kent,

One of the world's three living 8-footers—Sulamein Ali Nashnush of Libya at 8 feet 0.4 inches.

The world's tallest wedding story being enacted at St. Martin-in-the-Fields, London in June 1871, when the bride and bridegroom aggregated 14 ft. 8 ins. (see below).

who measures 7 feet 4¾ inches. Terence Keenan (b. 1942) of Rock Ferry, Birkenhead, Cheshire measures 7 feet 6 inches, but is unable to stand erect owing to a leg condition. His abnormal growth began at the age of 17 when he was only 5 feet 4 inches tall.

Scotland The tallest Scotsman, and the tallest recorded "true" (non-pathological) giant, was Angus Macaskill (1825-63), born on the island of Berneray, in the Sound of Harris, in the Outer Hebrides. He stood 7 feet 9 inches and died in St. Ann's, on Cape Breton Island, Nova Scotia, Canada. Lambert Quételet (1796-1874), a Belgian anthropometrist, considered that a Scotsman named MacQuail, known as "the Scotch Giant", stood 8 feet 3 inches. He served in the famous regiment of giants of Frederick William I (1688-1740), King of Prussia. His skeleton, now in the Staatliche Museum zu Berlin, East Germany, measures 220 centimetres (7 feet 2.6 inches). Sam McDonald (1762-1802) of Lairg in Sutherland, was reputed to be 8 feet tall but actually stood 6 feet 10 inches. The tallest Scotsman now living is George Gracie (b. 1938) of Forth, Lanarkshire. He stands 7 feet 3 inches and weighs 28 stone. His brother Hugh (b. 1941) is 7 feet 0½ inch.

Wales The tallest Welshman ever recorded was George Auger (1886-1922), born in Cardiff, Glamorgan. He stood 7 feet 7 inches and died in New York City, N.Y., U.S.A.

Ireland The tallest Irishman was Patrick Cotter O'Brian (1760-1806), born in Kinsale, County Cork. He died at Hotwells, Clifton, Bristol. He said that he was 8 feet 7¾ inches at the age of 26, but his actual living height was 7 feet 10.86 inches, calculated from measurements of his long bones made by Dr. Edward Fawcett, Professor of Anatomy at University College, Bristol, on 3 March 1906, after his coffin had been accidentally exposed during excavation work.

The tallest Irishman now living is believed to be Jim Cully (b. 1926) of Tipperary, a former boxer and wrestler. He stands 7 feet 2 inches.

Isle of Man The tallest Manxman ever recorded was Arthur Caley

(b. 16 Nov. 1829) of Sulby. He was variously credited with heights of 8 feet 2 inches and 8 feet 4 inches, but actually stood 7 feet 6 inches. He died at Clyde, New Jersey, U.S.A., on 12 Feb. 1889 aged 60.

TALLEST GIANTESSES

World All-time Giantesses are rarer than giants but their heights are still spectacular. The tallest woman in medical history was the acromegalic giantess Jane ("Ginny") Bunford, born on 26 July 1895 at Bartley Green, Northfield, Birmingham. Her abnormal growth started at the age of 11 following a head injury, and on her 13th birthday she measured 6 feet 6 inches. Shortly before her death on 1 April 1922 she stood 7 feet 7 inches tall, but she had a severe curvature of the spine and would have measured about 7 feet 11 inches with assumed normal curvature. Her skeleton, now preserved in the Anatomical Museum in the Medical School at Birmingham University, has a mounted height of 7 feet 4 inches. Archaeologists announced on 10 Feb. 1972 the discovery of the remains of a mediaeval giantess reputedly 8 feet 3 inches in the Laga mountains near Abruzzi, Italy. Anna Hanen Swan (1846-88) of Nova Scotia, Canada, was billed at 8 feet 1 inch but actually measured 7 feet 5½ inches. In London on 17 June 1871 she married Martin van Buren Bates (1845-1919) of Whitesburg, Letcher County, Kentucky, U.S.A., who stood 7 feet 2½

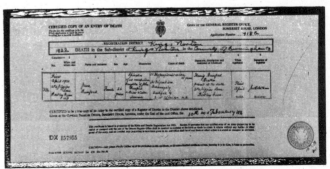

Death Certificate of Jane Bunford—the tallest woman in medical history from Bartley Green, Birmingham. She stood 7 ft 11 ins.

11

inches. Ella Ewing (1875-1913) of Goring, Missouri, U.S.A., was billed at 8 feet 2 inches and reputedly measured 6 feet 9 inches at the age of 10 (*cf.* 6 feet 5 inches for Robert Wadlow at this age). She measured 7 feet 4½ inches at the age of 23 and may have attained 7 feet 6 inches before her death.

Living The tallest living woman is believed to be a eunuch-oidal giantess named Tiliya (b. 1947) who lives in the village of Saidpur in Bihar State, north-eastern India. She stands 7 feet 5 inches tall. In Nov. 1971 a height of 7 feet 2¾ inches was reported for Mildred Tshakayi (b. 1946), a Rhodesian bush dweller. The tallest woman recently living was believed to be Delores Ann Johnson, *née* Pullard (b. 13 August 1946), a negress from De Quincy, Louisiana, U.S.A. She measured 6 feet 10 inches in March 1961 and grew to 7 feet 5 inches by October 1964. She reportedly wore size 52 dresses and size 23 shoes and weighed 435 lb. (31 stone 1 lb.). At the time of her death in Houston, Texas on 19 May 1971 she was credited with a height of 8 feet 2 inches, but her true stature was 7 feet 5½ inches.

SHORTEST DWARFS
The strictures which apply to giants apply equally to dwarfs, except that exaggeration gives way to under-statement. In the same way as 9 feet may be regarded as the limit towards which the tallest giants tend, so 23 inches must be regarded as the limit towards which the shortest mature dwarfs tend (*cf.* the average length of new-born babies is 18 to 20 inches). In the case of child dwarfs the age is often enhanced by their agents or managers.

The shortest type of dwarf is an ateliotic dwarf, known as a midget. In this form of dwarfism the skeleton tends to remain in its infantile state. Midgets seldom grow to more than 40 inches tall. The most famous midget in history was Charles Sherwood Stratton, *alias* "General Tom Thumb", born on 11 Jan. 1832 in Bridgeport, Connecticut, U.S.A. He measured 25 inches at the age of 5 months and grew to only 70 centimetres (27.6 inches) by the age of 13½. He was 30½ inches tall at the age of 18 and 35 inches at 30. He stood 40 inches tall at the time of his death from apoplexy on 15 July 1883.

Another celebrated midget was Józef ('Count') Boru-walaski (b. November 1739) of Poland. He measured only 8 inches long at birth, growing to 14 inches at the age of one year. He stood 17 inches at 6 years, 21 inches at 10, 25 inches at 15, 35 inches at 25 and 39 inches at 30. He died near Durham, England, on 5 Sept. 1837, aged 97.

World The shortest mature human of whom there is independent evidence was Pauline Musters ('Princess Pauline'), a Dutch midget. She was born at Ossen-drecht, on 26 Feb. 1876 and measured 12 inches at birth. At the age of 9 she was 55 centimetres (21.65 inches) tall and weighed only 1½ kilogrammes (3 lb. 5 oz.). She died, at the age of 19, of pneumonia, with meningitis, her heart weakened from alcoholic excesses, on 1 March 1895 in New York City, N.Y., U.S.A. Although she was billed at 19 inches, she was measured shortly before her death and was found to be 59 centimetres (23.2 inches) tall. A *post mortem* examination showed her to be exactly 24 inches (her body was slightly elongated after death). Her mature weight varied from 7½ lb. to 9 lb. and her "vital statistics" were 18½-19-17.

The Italian girl Caroline Crachami, born in Palermo, Sicily, in 1815, was only 20.2 inches tall when she died in London in 1824, aged 9. At birth she measured 7 inches long and weighed 1 lb. Her skeleton, measuring 19.8 inches, is now part of the Hunterian collection in the Museum of the Royal College of Surgeons, London.

Male The shortest recorded adult male dwarf was Calvin Phillips, born on 14 Jan. 1791 in Bridgewater, Massachusetts, U.S.A. He weighed 2 lb. at birth and stopped growing at the age of 5. When he was 19 he measured 26½ inches tall and weighed 12 lb. with his clothes on. He died two years later, in April 1812, from progeria, a rare disorder characterised by dwarfism and premature senility.

William E. Jackson, *alias* "Major Mite", born on 2 Oct. 1864 in Dunedin, New Zealand, measured 9 inches long and weighed 12 oz. at birth. In November 1880 he stood 21 inches and weighed 9 lb. He died in New York City, N.Y., U.S.A., on 9 Dec. 1900, when he measured 27 inches.

Another notable case was Max Taborsky, *alias* "Prince Kolibri", born in Vienna, Austria, in January 1863. He measured 35 centimetres (13.8 inches) at birth and stopped growing at the age of 9. When he died, aged 25, in 1888, he stood 69 centimetres (27.2 inches) tall and weighed 5 kilogrammes (11 lb.).

United Kingdom The shortest mature human ever recorded in Britain is believed to be Miss Jean Carpenter (b. 21 Dec. 1929), a rachitic dwarf of Charford, Worcestershire, who stands 29 inches tall and weighs 30 lb. Her mother is 5 feet 9 inches tall. Hopkins Hopkins (1737-54) of Llantrisant, Glamorgan, South Wales was 31 inches. Hopkins, who died from progeria (see above) weighed 19 lb. at the age of 7 and 13 lb. at the time of his death. There are an estimated 2,000 people of severely restricted growth living in Britain today.

The famous 'Sir' Geoffrey Hudson (b. 1619) of Oakham, Rutland, was reputedly 18 inches tall at the age of 30, but this extreme measurement is not borne out in portraits which show he was then about 3 feet 6 inches. At the time of his death in London in 1682 he measured 3 feet 9 inches.

Ireland The shortest recorded Irish adult dwarf was Mrs. Catherine Kelly (b. in August 1756), known as "the Irish fairy", who stood 34 inches tall and weighed 22 lb. She died in Norwich, Norfolk, on 15 Oct. 1785. David Jones (b. 28 April 1903) of Lisburn, County Antrim, Northern Ireland, reputedly measured 26 inches at the time of his death on 1 April 1970 aged 66. But as he weighed 4 stone (56 lb.), his height was probably nearer 36 inches.

Most variable stature Adam Rainer, born in Graz, Austria, in 1899, measured 1.18 metres (3 feet 10.45 inches) at the age of 21. But then he suddenly started growing upwards at a rapid rate, and by 1931 he had reached 2.18 metres (7 feet 1¾ inches). He became so weak as a result that he was bed-ridden for the rest of his life. He died on 4 March 1950 aged 51.

RACES
Tallest The tallest race in the world is the Tutsi (also called Batutsi, Watutsi, or Watussi), Nilotic herdsmen of Rwanda and Burundi, Central Africa whose males average 6 feet 1 inch, with a maximum of 7 feet 6 inches. The Tehuelches of Patagonia, long regarded as of gigantic stature (*i.e.* 7 to 8 feet), have in fact an average height (males) of 5 feet 10 inches with a maximum of just over 2 metres (6 feet 6¾ inches). A tribe with an average height of more than 6 feet was discovered in the inland region of Passis Manua of New Britain in December 1956. In May 1965 it was reported that the Crahiacoro Indians in the border district of the states of Mato Grosso and Pará, in Brazil, are exceptionally tall—certainly with an average of more than 6 feet. A report in May 1966 specifically attributed great stature to the Kran-hacacore Indians of the Xingu region of the Mato Grosso. In December 1967 the inhabitants of Barbuda, Leeward Islands were reported to have an average height in excess of 6 feet. The tallest people in

Members of the world's tallest ethnic group—the Tutsi or Watutsi performing a traditional tribal dance

Europe are the Montenegrins of Yugoslavia, with a male average of 5 feet 10 inches, (in the town of Trebinje the average height is 6 feet), compared with the men of Sutherland, at 5 feet 9½ inches. In 1912 the average height of the men living in Balmaclellan, Kirkcudbrightshire was reported to be 179 centimetres (5 feet 10.4 inches).

Shortest The world's shortest known race is the negrito Onge tribe, of whom only 22 (12 men, 10 women) survived on Little Andaman Island in the Indian Ocean by May 1956. Few were much more than 4 feet. The smallest pygmies are the Mbuti, with an average height of 4 feet 6 inches for men and 4 feet 5 inches for women, with some groups averaging only 4 feet 4 inches for men and 4 feet 1 inch for women. They live in the forests near the river Ituri in the Congo (Kinshasa), Africa. In June 1936 there was a report, not subsequently substantiated, that there was a village of dwarfs numbering about 800 in the Hu bei (Hupeh) province of Central China between Wu han and Lishan in which the men were all less than 4 feet tall and the women slightly taller. In October 1970 a tribe of pygmies, reportedly measuring only 1 metre (3 feet 3.4 inches) tall, was discovered in the border area of Bolivia, Brazil and Peru.

WEIGHT

Heaviest The heaviest recorded human of all time was the
Heavyweights 6-foot 0½-inch tall Robert Earl Hughes (b. 4 June
World 1926) of Monticello, Illinois, U.S.A. An 11¼ lb. baby,
Men he weighed 14½ stone at six years, 27 stone at ten, 39 stone at 13, 49½ stone at 18, 64 stone at 25 and 67½ stone at 27. His greatest recorded weight was 1,069 lb. (76 stone 5 lb.) in February 1958, and he weighed 1,041 lb. (74 stone 5 lb.) at the time of his death. His claimed waist of 122 inches, his chest of 104 inches and his upper arm of 40 inches were also the greatest on record. He died of uraemia (a condition caused by retention of urinary matter in the blood) in a trailer at Bremen, Indiana, on 10 July 1958, aged 32, and was buried in Binville Cemetery, near Mount Sterling, Illinois, U.S.A. His coffin, a converted piano case measuring 7 feet by 4 feet 4 inches and weighing more than half a ton, had to be lowered by crane. It was once claimed by a commercial interest that Hughes had weighed 1,500 lb. (107 st. 2 lb.)—a 40 per cent exaggeration.

Johnny Alee (1853–87) of Carbon (now known as Carbonton) North Carolina, U.S.A. is reputed to have weighed 1,132 lb. (80 stone 12 lb.) at the time of his death, but the accuracy of this report has not yet been fully substantiated. He died from a heart attack after plunging through the flooring of his log cabin, which had been his "prison" for 19 years.

The only other men for whom weights of 800 lb. (57 stone 2 lb.) or more have been reliably reported are the 7 listed below:

	lb.	Stone	lb.
Mills Darden (1798-1857) U.S.A. (7 ft. 6 in.)	1,020	72	12
John Hanson Craig (1856-94) U.S.A. (6 ft. 5 in.)	907 (a)	64	11
Arthur Knorr (1914-60) U.S.A. (6 ft. 1 in.)	900 (b)	64	4
Toubi (b. 1946) Cameroon	857½	61	3½
T. A. Valenzuela (1895-1937) Mexico (5 ft. 11 in.)	850	60	10
David Maquire (1904-fl. 1935) U.S.A. (5 ft. 10 in.)	810	57	12
William J. Cobb (b. 1926) U.S.A. (6 ft. 0 in.)	802 (c)	57	4

(a) *Won $1,000 in a "Bonny Baby" contest in New York City in 1858.* (b) *Gained 300 lb. in the last 6 months of his life.* (c) *Reduced to 232 lb. (16 stone 8 lb.) by July 1965.*

Michael Walker (b. 1934) was treated for obesity and drug-induced bulimia (morbid desire to overeat) in a caravan outside the Ben Taub Hospital, Houston, Texas in December 1971. Reports on his weight varying between 800 lb. (57 st. 2 lb.) and 900 lb. (64 st. 4 lb.) were received. A business partner in the company which exhibited him claimed that in the summer of 1971 he had reached a peak of 1,100 lb. (78 st. 8 lb.).

Women The heaviest woman ever recorded was a negress whose name was not recorded. She died in Baltimore, Maryland, U.S.A., on 4 Sept. 1888. Her weight was stated to be 850 lb. (60 stone 10 lb.).

A more reliable and better documented case was that of Mrs. Flora Mae (or May) Jackson (*née* King), a 5 ft. 9 in. negress born in 1930 at Shugualak, Mississippi, U.S.A. She weighed 10 lb. at birth, 267 lb. (19 stone 1 lb.) at the age of 11, 621 lb. (44 stone 5 lb.) at 25 and 840 lb. (60 stone) shortly before her death in Meridian, Florida, on 9 Dec. 1965. She was known in show business as "Baby Flo".

Great Britain The heaviest recorded man in Great Britain was
Men William Campbell, who was born in Glasgow in 1856 and died on 16 June 1878, when a publican at High Bridge, Newcastle upon Tyne, Northumberland. He was 6 feet 3 inches tall and weighed 53 stone 8 lb., with an 85-inch waist and a 96-inch chest. His coffin weighed 1,500 lb. He was "a man of considerable

A meeting between Britain's heaviest and tallest men—George MacAree (5 ft. 10½ ins. and 37 stone) and Christopher Greener (7 ft. 5 ins. and 20 stone)

intelligence and humour". The only other British man with a recorded weight of more than 50 stone (700 lb.) was the celebrated Daniel Lambert (1770-1809) of Leicester. He stood 5 feet 11 inches tall, weighed 52 stone 11 lb. shortly before his death and had a girth of more than 92 inches.

The highest weight attained by any man living in Britain today was that of Arthur Armitage (born a 5 lb. baby on 28 June 1929) of Knottingley, Yorkshire, who scaled 40 stone 6 lb. (566 lb.) in his clothes on 15 Feb. 1970. He is 5 feet 9 inches tall and his vital statistics were 76-80-80. By March 1972 he had reduced by dieting (600 calories per day) to 18 stone 2 lb. (254 lb.).

George MacAree (b. 24 Dec. 1923) of Newham, London, who scaled 37 stone 8 lb. on 2 March 1972 is now the heaviest man in Britain. He is 5 feet 10½ inches tall and has vital statistics of 72½-71-80.

Women The heaviest recorded woman in Great Britain was Miss Nellie Lambert (b. 3 April 1894) of Leicester, who weighed 40 stone 3 lb. at the age of 19 years. She stood 5 feet 3 inches tall, with a waist of 88 inches and 26-inch upper arm. She claimed to be a great-granddaughter of Daniel Lambert (see above). The heaviest woman living in Britain today is Miss Jean Renwick (b. 1939) of Brixton, London, who weighed 40 stone 2 lb. (height 5 feet 3½ inches) in January 1972. She was recently reported to be dieting.

Ireland The heaviest Irishman is reputed to have been Roger Byrne, who was buried in Rosenallis, County Laoighis (Leix), on 14 March 1804. He died in his 54th year and his coffin and its contents weighed 52 stone. Another Irish heavyweight was Lovelace Love (1731-66), born in Brook Hill, County Mayo. He weighed "upward of 40 stone" at the time of his death.

Heaviest twins The heaviest twins in the world are the McCreary twins (b. 1948), farmers of Hendersonville, North Carolina, U.S.A., who in March 1970 weighed 660 lb. (47 stone 2 lb.) and 640 lb. (45 stone 10 lb.). Their names are Bill and Ben.

Lightest lightweights *World* The lightest adult human on record was Lucia Zarate (b. San Carlos, Mexico 2 Jan. 1863, d. October 1889), an emaciated Mexican ateliotic dwarf of 26½ inches, who weighed $2\frac{1}{8}$ kilogrammes (4.7 lb.) at the age of 17. She "fattened up" to 13 lb. by her 20th birthday. At birth she weighed 2½ lb. The lightest adult ever recorded in the United Kingdom was Hopkins Hopkins (Shortest dwarfs, see p. 12).

The thinnest recorded adults of normal height are those suffering from Simmonds' Disease (Hypophyseal cachexia). Losses up to 65 per cent. of the original body-weight have been recorded in females, with a "low" of 45 lb. (3 stone 3 lb.). In cases of anorexia nervosa, weights of under 5 stone (70 lb.) have been reported. Edward C. Hagner (1892-1962), *alias* Eddie Masher (U.S.A.) is alleged to have weighed only 48 lb. (3 stone 6 lb.) at a height of 5 feet 7 inches. He was also known as "the Skeleton Dude". In August 1825 the biceps measurement of Claude-Ambroise Seurat (b. 10 April 1797, d. 6 April 1826) of Troyes, France was 4 inches and the distance between his back and his chest was less than 3 inches. According to one report he stood 5 feet 7½ inches and weighed 78 lb. (5 stone 8 lb.) but in another account was described as 5 feet 4 inches and only 36 lb. (2 stone 8 lb.). It was recorded that the American exhibitionist Rosa Lee Plemons (b. 1873) weighed 27 lb. at the age of 18.

Slimming The greatest recorded slimming feat was that of William J. Cobb (b. 1926), *alias* 'Happy Humphrey', a professional wrestler of Macon, Georgia, U.S.A. It was reported in July 1965 that he had reduced from 802 lb. (57 stone 4 lb.) to 232 lb. (16 stone 8 lb.), a loss of 570 lb. (40 stone 10 lb.), in 3 years. His waist measurement declined from 101 inches to 44 inches.

The U.S. circus fat lady Mrs. Celesta Geyer (b. 1901), *alias* Dolly Dimples, reduced from 553 lb. to 152 lb. in 1950—51, a loss of 401 lb. in 14 months. Her vital statistics diminished *pari passu* from 79-84-84 to a *svelte* 34-28-36. Her book "How I lost 400 lbs." was not a best-seller because of the difficulty of would-be readers identifying themselves with the dressmaking problems of losing more than 28 stone when 4 feet 11 inches tall. In December 1967 she was reportedly down to 110 lb. (7 stone 12 lb.). The speed record for slimming was established by Paul M. Kimelman, 21 of Pittsburgh, Pennsylvania, U.S.A., who from 25 Dec. 1966 to August 1967 went on a crash diet of 300 to 600 calories per day to reduce from 427 lb. (30 stone 7 lb.) to 130 lb. (9 stone 4 lb.). In his prime he wore size 56 trousers into one leg of which he can now step easily.

Arthur Armitage (see col. 1) reportedly lost 12 stone in 6 weeks in November-December 1970 when reducing from 40 stone towards his target of 16 stone.

Weight gaining A probable record for gaining weight was set by Arthur Knorr (b. 17 May 1914), who died on 7 July 1960, aged 46, in Reseda, California, U.S.A. He gained 300 lb. (21 stone 6 lb.) in the last 6 months of his life and weighed 900 lb. (64 stone 4 lb.) when he died. Miss Doris James of San Francisco, California U.S.A. is alleged to have gained 325 lb. (23 stone 3 lb.) in the 12 months before her death in August 1965, aged 38, at a weight of 675 lb. (48 stone 3 lb.) She was only 5 feet 2 inches tall.

Man *(Homo sapiens)* is a species in the sub-family Homininae of the family Hominidae of the super-family Hominoidea of the sub-order Simiae (or Anthropoidea) of the order Primates of the infra-class Eutheria of the sub-class Theria of the class Mammalia of the sub-phylum Vertebrata (Craniata) of the phylum Chordata of the sub-kingdom Metazoa of the animal kingdom.

2. ORIGINS

EARLIEST MAN
SCALE OF TIME
If the age of the Earth-Moon system (latest estimate at least 4,700 million years) is likened to a single year, Handy Man appeared on the scene at about 8.35 p.m. on 31 December, Britain's earliest known inhabitants arrived at about 11.32 p.m., the Christian era began about 13 seconds before midnight and the life span of a 113-year-old man (see page 16) would be about three-quarters of a second. Present calculations indicate that the Sun's increased heat, as it becomes a "red giant", will make life insupportable on Earth in about 10,000 million years. Meanwhile there may well be colder epicycles. The period of 1,000 million years is sometimes referred to as an aeon.

World The earliest known primates appeared in the Palaeocene period of about 70,000,000 years ago. The sub-order of higher primates, called Simiae (or Anthropoidea), evolved from the catarrhine or old-world sect nearly 30,000,000 years later in the Lower Oligocene period. During the Middle and Upper Oligocene the super-family Hominoidea emerged. This contains three accepted families, *viz* Hominidae (bipedal, ground-dwelling man or near man), Pongidae (brachiating forest apes) and Oreopithecidae, which includes *Apidium* of the Oligocene and *Oreopithecus* of the early Pliocene. Opinion is divided on whether to treat gibbons and their ancestors as a fourth full family (Hylobatidae) or as a sub-family (Hylobatinae) within the Pongidae. Some consider that Proconsulidae should also comprise a family, although others regard the genus *Proconsul,* who lived on the open savannah, as part of another sub-family of the Pongidae.

Earliest Hominid There is a conflict of evidence on the time during which true but primitive Hominidae were evolving. Fossil evidence indicates that it was some time during the Upper Miocene (about 10,000,000 to 12,000,000 years ago). The characteristics of the Hominidae, such as a large brain, very fully distinguish them from any of the other Hominoidea. Evidence published in August 1969 indicated that the line of descent of *Ramapithecus,* from the north-eastern Indian sub-continent, was not less than 10,000,000 years old and that of *Australopithecus,* from Eastern Africa possibly 6,000,000 years old.

Earliest Genus Homo The earliest known true member of the genus *Homo* was found between 6 Dec. 1960 and 1963 by Dr. Louis Seymour Bazett Leakey (b. 7 Aug. 1903 at Kabete, Kenya) Hon. Director of the Kenya National Museum's Centre for Pre-History and Palaeontology, in Nairobi, and his wife Mary in Bed I in the Olduvai Gorge, Tanganyika (now part of Tanzania). These remains have been determined by stratigraphic, radio-metric and fission-track dating to have existed between 1,750,000 and 2,300,000 years ago. They were first designated *"pre-Zinjanthropus"* but in March 1964 were renamed Handy Man *(Homo habilis),* to differentiate them from the more primitive Nut-cracker Man *(Zinjanthropus boisei),* an East African australopithecine who was contemporary with Handy Man throughout Bed I and the greater part of Bed II times. Handy Man was about 4 feet tall.

In August 1965 a fragment of a *humerus* bone from a hominine upper arm was found near Kanapoi, Kenya, by Professor Bryan Patterson, the vertebrate palaeontologist of the Museum of Comparative Zoology at Harvard University, Cambridge, Massachusetts, U.S.A. It was announced in Dec. 1971 that this bone dates from about 2,500,000 years ago.

Earliest Homo sapiens The earliest recorded remains of the species *Homo sapiens,* variously dated from 300,000 to 450,000 years ago in the Middle Pleistocene, were discovered on 24 Aug. 1965 by Dr. Lászlo Vértes in a limestone quarry at Vértesszöllös, about 30 miles west of Budapest, Hungary. The remains, designated *Homo sapiens palaeo-hungaricus,* comprised an almost complete occipital bone, part of a skull with an estimated cranial capacity of nearly 1,400 cubic centimetres (85 cubic inches).

Earliest man in the Americas date from at least 50,000 B.C. and "more probably 100,000 B.C." according to Dr. Leakey after the examination of some hearth stones found in the Mojave Desert, California and announced in October 1970. The earliest human relic is a skull found in the area of Los Angeles, California dated in December 1970 to be from 22,000 B.C.

British Isles The earliest known inhabitants of the British Isles who belonged to the genus *Homo* were Clactonian man (probably fewer than 200 of them), one of whose middens was discovered in Aug. 1969 by Dr. John Waechter in the Lower Gravels of the Barnfield Pit at Swanscombe, Kent, together with some of their discarded choppers made of flint cores and blunted flake tools. They probably lived in the Thames valley area during the first third of the Great Interglacial 500,000-475,000 B.C. The oldest human remains ever found in Britain are pieces of a brain case from a specimen of *Homo sapiens fossilis,* believed to be a woman, recovered in June 1935 and March 1936 by Dr. Alvan T. Marston from the Boyn Hill terrace in the Barnfield Pit, near Swanscombe, northern Kent. This find is attributed to Acheulian man, type *III* or *IV*, dating from the warm Hoxnian interglacial period, about 250,000 years ago.

The mandible found in the Red Crag at Foxhall, near Ipswich, in 1863, but subsequently lost in the United States, has been claimed as a Clactonian relic and thus possibly anything up to 100,000 years older than Swanscombe man.

No remains from the Mesolithic period *(ante* 3500 B.C.) have yet been found but a site at Portland Bill is expected to yield some.

3. LONGEVITY

No single subject is more obscured by vanity, deceit, falsehood and deliberate fraud than the extremes of human longevity. Extreme claims are generally made on behalf of the very aged rather than by them.

Many hundreds of claims throughout history have been made for persons living well into their second century and some, insulting to the intelligence, for people living even into their third. Centenarians surviving beyond their 110th year are in fact of the extremest rarity and the present absolute limit of proven human longevity does not yet admit of anyone living to celebrate a 114th birthday.

It is highly significant that in Sweden, where alone proper and thorough official investigations follow the death of every allegedly very aged citizen, none has been found to have surpassed 110 years. The most reliably pedigreed large group of people in the world, the British peerage, has, after ten centuries, produced only one peer who reached even his 100th birthday. However, this is possibly not unconnected with the extreme draughtiness of many of their residences.

Scientific research into extreme old age reveals that the correlation between the claimed density of centenarians in a country and its regional illiteracy is 0.83 ±0.03. In late life, very old people often tend to advance their ages at the rate of about 17 years per decade. This was nicely corroborated by a cross analysis of the 1901 and 1911 censuses of England and Wales. Early claims must necessarily be without the elementary corroboration of birth dates. England was among the earliest of all countries to introduce compulsory local registers (Sept. 1538) and official birth registration (1 July 1837), which was made fully compulsory only in 1874. Even in the United States, where in 1971 there were reputed to be 12,642 centenarians, 45 per cent. of births occurring between 1890 and 1920 were unregistered.

Several celebrated super-centenarians are believed to have been double lives (father and son, brothers with the same names or successive bearers of a title). The most famous example is Christian Jakobsen Drackenberg allegedly born in Stavanger, Norway on 18 Nov. 1626 and died in Aarhus, Denmark aged seemingly 145 years 326 days on 9 Oct. 1772. A number of instances have been commercially sponsored, while a fourth category of recent claims are those made for political ends, such as the 100 citizens of the Russian Soviet Federative Socialist Republic (population about 132,000,000 at mid-1967) claimed in March 1960 to be between 120 and 156. From data on documented centenarians, actuaries have shown that only one 115-year life can be expected in 2,100 million lives (cf. world population was estimated to be 3,730 million at mid-1972).

The height of credulity was reached on 5 May 1933, when a news agency solemnly filed a story from China with a Peking date-line that Li Chung-yun, the "oldest man on Earth", born in 1680, had just died aged 256 years (sic). Currently the most extreme case of longevity claimed in the U.S.S.R. is 167 years for Shirali "Baba" Muslimov of Barzavu, Azerbaijan, reputedly born on 26 Mar. 1805. It was reported in 1954 that in the Abkhasian Republic of Georgia,

U.S.S.R., 2.58 per cent of the population was aged over 90—25 times the proportion in the U.S.A. In 1972 there were an estimated 25,000 centenarians living in the world.

Sylvester Magee died at Marcon County General Hospital, Columbia, Mississippi, U.S.A. on 15 Oct. 1971 at a claimed age of 130 years 139 days. Though illiterate, he alleged that a family bible destroyed in a fire in 1966 showed that he was born at a now disappeared village called Carpet, North Carolina on 29 May 1841. It was claimed on his behalf that, though he fought and was twice wounded at the Civil War seige of Vicksburg in 1863, being an "impressed" slave the Army kept no records of the service for which he drew Veteran's benefits. He flew in a jet plane in February and divorced in April 1971.

Mythology often requires immense longevity; for example Larak the god-King lived, according to Sumerian mythology, 28,800 years and Dumuzi even longer. The most extreme biblical claim is that for Methuselah at 969 years (Genesis V, verse 27).

Oldest authentic centenarian World The greatest authenticated age to which a human has ever lived is 113 years 124 days in the case of Pierre Joubert, a French-Canadian bootmaker. He was born in Charlesbourg, Québec Province, Canada, on 15 July 1701, son of Pierre Joubert (b. 1670) and Magdeleine Boesmier, and died in Québec on 16 Nov. 1814. His longevity was the subject of an investigation in 1870 by Dr. Tache, Official Statistician to the Canadian Government, and the proofs published are irrefutable. The following national records can be taken as authentic:

AUTHENTICATED NATIONAL LONGEVITY RECORDS

	Years	Days		Born	Died
Canada (a)	113	124	Pierre Joubert	15 July 1701	16 Nov. 1814
United States (b)	113	1	John B. Salling	15 Mar. 1846	16 Mar. 1959
Morocco	>112		El Hadj Mohammed el Mokri (Grand Vizier)	1844	16 Sept. 1957
United Kingdom (c)	111	339	Ada Roe (née Giddings)	6 Feb. 1858	11 Jan. 1970
Ireland	111	327	The Hon. Katherine Plunket	22 Nov. 1820	14 Oct. 1932
South Africa (d)	111	151	Johanna Booyson	17 Jan. 1857	16 June 1968
Czechoslovakia	111	+	Marie Bernatkova	22 Oct. 1857	fl. Oct. 1968
Channel Islands	110	321	Margaret Ann Neve (née Harvey)	18 May 1792	4 April 1903
Yugoslavia	110	150+	Demitrius Philipovitch	9 Mar. 1818	fl. Aug. 1928
Japan (e)	110	114	Yoshigiku Ito	3 Aug. 1856	26 Nov. 1966
Australia (f)	110	39	Ada Sharp (Mrs.)	6 April 1861	15 May 1971
Netherlands	110	5	Baks Karnebeek (Mrs.)	2 Oct. 1849	7 Oct. 1959
France	109	309	Marie Philoméne Flassayer	13 June 1844	18 April 1954
Italy	109	179	Rosalia Spoto	25 Aug. 1847	20 Feb. 1957
Scotland	109	14	Rachel MacArthur (Mrs.)	26 Nov. 1827	10 Dec. 1936
Norway	109	+	Marie Olsen (Mrs.)	1 May 1850	fl. May 1959
Tasmania	109	+	Mary Ann Crow (Mrs.)	2 Feb. 1836	1945
Germany (g)	108	128	Luise Schwatz	27 Sept. 1849	2 Feb. 1958
Portugal	108	+	Maria Luisa Jorge	7 June 1859	fl. July 1967
Finland	107	+	Marie Anderson	3 Jan. 1829	1936
Belgium	106	267	Marie-Joseph Purnode (Mrs.)	17 April 1843	9 Nov. 1949
Austria	106	231	Anna Migschitz	3 Feb. 1850	1 Nov. 1956
Sweden	106	98	Emma Gustaffsson (Mrs.)	18 June 1858	14 Sept. 1964
Spain (h)	106	14	Jose Palido	15 Mar. 1866	29 Mar. 1972
Malaysia	106	+	Hassan Bin Yusoff	14 Aug. 1865	fl. Jan. 1972
Isle of Man	105	221	John Kneen	12 Nov. 1852	9 June 1958

(a) *Mrs. Ellen Carroll died in North River, Newfoundland, Canada on 8 December 1943, reputedly aged 115 years 49 days.*
(b) *Mrs. Betsy Baker (née Russell) was allegedly born 20 August 1842 in Brington, Northamptonshire, and died in Tecumseh, Nebraska, U.S.A. on 24 October 1955, reputedly aged 113 years 65 days. The 67-year-old son of Mrs. Tatzumbie Dupea, a Piute Indian at the Good Hope Convalescent Center, Los Angeles claimed that her birthday on 26 July 1969 was not her 112th but her 120th. Sarah Collins, d. 3 May 1971 was allegedly born in slavery 116 years before.*
(c) *London-born Miss Isabella Shepheard was allegedly 115 years old when she died at St. Asaph, Flintshire, North Wales, on 20 Nov. 1948, but her actual age was believed to have been 109 years 90 days. Charles Alfred Nunez Arnold died in Liverpool on 15 Sept. 1941 reputedly aged 112 years 66 days based on a*

baptismal claim (London, 10 Nov. 1829).
(d) *Mrs. Susan Johanna Deporter of Port Elizabeth, South Africa, was reputedly 114 years old when she died on 4 August 1954. Mrs. Sarah Lawrence, Cape Town, South Africa was reputedly 112 on 3 June 1968.*
(e) *A man named Nakamura of Kamaishi, northern Japan, was reported to have died on 4 May 1969 aged 116 years 329 days.*
(f) *Reginald Beck of Sydney, New South Wales, Australia was allegedly 111 years old when he died on 13 April 1928.*
(g) *Friedrich Sadowski of Heidelberg reputedly celebrated his 111th birthday on 31 October 1936. Franz Joseph Eder d. Spitzburg 3 May 1911 allegedly aged 116.*
(h) *Juana Ortega Villarin, Madrid, Spain, was allegedly 112 in February 1962. Ana Maria Parraga of Murcia was reportedly 107 in Nov. 1969.*

In the face of the above data the claim published in the April 1961 issue of the Soviet Union's *Vestnik Statistiki* ('Statistical Herald') that there were 224 male and 368 female Soviet citizens aged in excess of 120 recorded at the census of 15 Jan. 1959, indicates

a reliance on hearsay rather than evidence. Official Soviet insistence on the unrivalled longevity of the country's citizenry is curious in view of the fact that the 592 persons in their unique "over 120" category must have spent at least the first 78 years of their prolonged lives under Tsarism. It has recently been suggested that the extreme ages claimed by some men in Georgia, U.S.S.R., are the result of attempts to avoid military service when they were younger, by assuming the identities of older men.

Great Britain The oldest living Briton among an estimated population of 1,300 (1,130 women and 170 men) centenarians is Miss Alice Stevenson (b. Piccadilly, London 10 July 1861) now living at Brambleacres Old People's Home, Worcester Road, Sutton, Surrey.

Most reigns The greatest number of reigns during which any English subject could have lived is ten. A person born on the day (11 April) that Henry VI was deposed in 1471 had to live to only the comparatively modest age of 87 years 7 months and 6 days to see the accession of Elizabeth I on 17 Nov. 1558. Such a person could have been Thomas Carn of London, born 1471 and died 28 Jan. 1578 in his 107th year.

4. REPRODUCTIVITY

MOTHERHOOD

Most children
World The greatest number of children produced by a mother in an independently attested case is 69 by the first wife of Fyodor Vassilet, a peasant of the Moscow Jurisdiction, Russia, who, in 27 confinements, gave birth to 16 pairs of twins, 7 sets of triplets and 4 sets of quadruplets. Most of the children attained their majority. Mme. Vassilet (1816-72) became so renowned that she was presented at the court of Tsar Alexander II.

Currently the highest reliably reported figure is a 32nd child born on 11 Nov. 1970 to Maria Addolorata Casalini (b. 1929) of Brindisi, Italy. She was married at 17 and so far has had, in 23 confinements, two sets of quadruplets, one of triplets, one of twins and 19 single births. Only 15 children survive.

Great Britain The British record is probably held by Mrs. Elizabeth Greenhill (d. 1681) of Abbot's Langley, Hertfordshire. It is alleged that she gave birth to 39 children (32 daughters and 7 sons), all of whom attained their majority. She was married at 16, had a world record 38 confinements and died reputedly aged 64. Her last son Thomas (d. c. 1740) became surgeon to the 10th Duke of Norfolk and was the author of the "Art of Embalming" (1705). According to an inscription on a gravestone in Conway Church cemetery, Caernarvonshire, North Wales, Nicholas Hookes (d. 27 March 1637) was the 41st child of his mother Alice Hookes, but further details are lacking.

Great Britain's champion mothers of today are believed to be Mrs. Margaret McNaught, 49 of Balsall Heath, Birmingham (12 boys and 10 girls, all single births) and Mrs. Mable Constable, 52 of Long Itchington, Warwickshire who also has had 22 children including a set of triplets and two sets of twins.

Oldest mother
World Medical literature contains extreme but unauthenticated cases of septuagenarian mothers. The oldest recorded mother of whom there is certain evidence is Mrs. Ruth Alice Kistler (née Taylor), formerly Mrs. Shepard, of Portland, Oregon, U.S.A. She was born at Wakefield, Massachusetts, on 11 June 1899 and gave birth to a daughter, Suzan, at Glendale, near Los Angeles, California, on 18 Oct. 1956, when her age was 57 years 129 days. The incidence of quinquagenarian births varies widely with the highest known rate in Albania (nearly 5,500 per million).

Great Britain The oldest British mother reliably recorded is Mrs. Winifred Wilson (née Stanley) of Eccles, Lancashire. She was born in Wolverhampton on 11 Nov. 1881 or 1882 and had her tenth child, a daughter Shirley, on 14 Nov. 1936, when aged 54 or 55 years and 3 days.

The only surviving portrait of Britain's most prolific woman—Elizabeth Greenhill, mother of 39

At Southampton on 10 Feb. 1916, Mrs. Elizabeth Pearce gave birth to a son when aged 54 years 40 days. It is believed that live births to quinquagenarian mothers occur only twice in each million births in England and Wales.

Ireland The oldest Irish mother recorded was Mrs. Mary Higgins of Cork, County Cork (b. 7 Jan. 1876) who gave birth to a daughter, Patricia, on 17 March 1931 when aged 55 years 69 days.

Descendants In polygamous countries, the number of a person's descendants can become incalculable. The last Sharifian Emperor of Morocco, Moulay Ismail (1672-1727), known as "The Bloodthirsty", was reputed to have fathered a total of 548 sons and 340 daughters.

Capt. Wilson Kettle (b. 1860) of Grand Bay, Port aux Basques, Newfoundland, Canada, died on 25 Jan. 1963, aged 102, leaving 11 children by two wives, 65 grandchildren, 201 great-grandchildren and 305 great-great-grandchildren, a total of 582 living descendants. Mrs. Johanna Booyson (see page 16), of Belfast, Transvaal, was estimated to have 600 living descendants in South Africa in January 1968.

Mrs. Sarah Crawshaw (d. 25 Dec. 1844) left 397 descendants, according to her gravestone in Stones Methodist Church, Ripponden, Halifax, Yorkshire.

Multiple great grandparents Theoretically a great-great-great-great-grandparent is a possibility, though in practice countries in which young mothers are common generally have a low expectation of life. Mrs. Ella M. Prince of the U.S.A., who died, aged 91, on 29 May 1970, had three great-great-great-grandchildren among her 60 living descendants, while Hon. General Walter Washington Williams (1855-1959) of Houston, Texas, U.S.A., was reportedly several times a great-great-great-grandfather. On 8 Oct. 1971 Mrs. Mary Williams (allegedly born 18 Mar. 1856) died at Forest Park, Atlanta, Georgia. She reportedly left, among 192 living descendants, 7 great-great-great-great-great-grandchildren. This was most probably a confusion with her leaving five generations, since an age of 115 and seven successive generations producing children at an average interval of 16 years strains all credence.

MULTIPLE BIRTHS

Quindecaplets It was announced by Dr. Gennaro Montanino of Rome that he had removed the foetuses of 10 girls and 5 boys from the womb of a 35-year-old housewife on 22 July 1971. A fertility drug was responsible for this unique and unsurpassed instance of quindecaplets.

Nonuplets With multiple births, as with giants and centenarians, exaggeration is the rule. Since 1900 two cases of nonuplets, five cases of octuplets, 19 cases of septuplets and at least 23 cases of sextuplets have been reported. Mrs. Geraldine Broderick, 29, gave birth to 5 boys (two still-born) and 4 girls—the only certain nonuplets—at the Royal Hospital, Sydney, Australia on 13 June 1971. The last survivor, Richard (12 oz.) died on the sixth day. Archbishop Etstathios of Salonika, Greece (d. 1150) once alluded to a woman in the Peloponese, named Geyfyra, who produced nine surviving nonuplets. Jamaica has the highest incidence of multiple births (i.e. triplet and upward) at 4 per 1,000.

Octuplets The only confirmed case of live-born octuplets was the four boys and four girls born to Señora María Teresa Lopez de Sepulveda, aged 21, in a nursing home in Mexico City, Mexico, between 7 p.m. and 8 p.m. on 10 March 1967. They had an aggregate weight of 9 lb. 10 oz. and ranged between 1 lb. 3 oz. down to 14 oz. All the boys were named José and all the girls Josefina. They all died within 14 hours.

There have been four unconfirmed reports of octuplets since 1900: to Señora Enriquita Ruibi at Tampico, Mexico, in 1921; seven boys and one girl to Mme. Tam Sing at Kwoom Yam Sha, China, in June 1934; a case near Tientsin, China, on 29 Sept. 1947 (one baby died); and still-born babies to Señora Celia Gonzalez at Bahía Blanca, Argentina, on 2 May 1955.

Septuplets There have been 7 confirmed cases of septuplets since 1900: still-born babies to Britt Louise Ericsson, aged 34, in Uppsala, Sweden, in August 1964; five girls and two boys to Mme. Brigitte Verhaeghe-Denayer in Brussels, Belgium, on 25 March 1966 (all the babies died soon afterwards); four girls and three boys to Mrs. Sandra Cwikielnik in Boston, Massachusetts, U.S.A., on 1 Oct. 1966 (one was born dead and the others died within minutes); a still-born set in Sweden in 1966; a case from Addis Ababa, Ethiopia in March 1969 of seven babies to Mrs. Verema Jusuf of whom two died immediately, a set to Mrs. Garcelia Caldeson Avilia of Santiago, Chile on 6 Nov. 1971 and a set (none survived) in Santa Clara, Cal. on 17 Mar. 1972.

Sextuplets Among sextuplet births, the case of Mrs. Philip Speichinger provided the earliest irrefutable evidence in the person of a surviving daughter, Marjorie Louise of Mendon, Missouri, U.S.A., born on 9 Aug. 1936. The other five children were still-born. Mrs. Alinicia Parker (née Bushnell) was always cited as last survivor of the sextuplets reputedly born on 15 Sept. 1866 to Mrs. James B. Bushnell in Chicago, Illinois, U.S.A. She died, aged 85, in Warsaw, New York State, U.S.A., on 27 March 1952. The birth was registered by Dr. James Edwards but, for obscure reasons, was unrevealed until about 1912. The other children were identified as Lucy (died at 2 months), Laberto (died at 8 months), Norberto (died in 1934), Alberto (died in Albion, N.Y., in c. 1940) and Mrs. Alice Elizabeth Hughes (née Bushnell) who died in Flagstaff, Arizona, on 2 July 1941. From the sextuplets born to Maria Garcia wife of an Indian farmer in Michoacán State, Mexico, on 7 Sept. 1953, three (one boy and two girls) are reputedly still living. A woman living in a remote village in the Faridpur district of East Pakistan allegedly gave birth to six sons on 11 Nov. 1967.

Mrs. Sheila Ann Thorns (née Manning) (b. Birmingham 2 Oct. 1938) of Northfield, Birmingham, England, gave birth by Caesarean section to sextuplets at the New Birmingham Maternity Hospital on 2 Oct. 1968. In order of birth they were Lynne (2 lb. 6 oz., died 22nd), Ian (2 lb. 13 oz., died 13th), Julie (3 lb. 1 oz.), Susan (2 lb. 11 oz.), Roger (2 lb. 10 oz.) and Jillian (died after one hour). A seventh child did not develop beyond the third month of this pregnancy which had been induced by a fertility drug. A second set of British sextuplets were delivered, after

use of a fertility drug, of Mrs. Rosemary Letts (née Egerton) (b. Watford, 1946) of Chorleywood, Hertfordshire by Caesarean section at University College Hospital, London on 15 Dec. 1969. One girl was still-born but the others Cara Dawn (2 lb. 13 oz.), Sharon Marie (2 lb. 9 oz.), Joanne Nadine (2 lb. 7 oz.), Gary John (1 lb. 11½ oz.) and Tanya Odile (2 lb. 1 oz.) survived.

Quintuplets The earliest quintuplets in which all survived were: Emilie (died 6 Aug. 1954, aged 20), Yvonne (now in a convent), Cécile (now Mrs. Phillipe Langlois), Marie (later Mrs. Florian Houle died 28 Feb. 1970) and Annette (now Mrs. Germain Allard), born in her seventh pregnancy to Mrs. Oliva Dionne, aged 25, at Corbeil, near Callander, Ontario, Canada, on 28 May 1934 (aggregate weight 13 lb. 6 oz. with an average of 2 lb. 11 oz.).

Quintuplets were recorded in Wells, Somerset on 5 Oct. 1736 where four boys and a girl were all christened. Quins (three boys and two girls) were born to Mrs. Elspet Gordon of Rothes, Morayshire, Scotland in 1858 but all died within 12 hours, and at Over Darwen, Lancashire on 24 April 1786 Mrs. Margaret Waddington produced five girls (three still-born) weighing a total of 2 lb. 12 oz.

Quins were born to Mrs. Irene Mary Hanson, (née Brown) 33, of Rayleigh, Essex at the Queen Charlotte's Maternity Hospital, Hammersmith, London on 13 Nov. 1969. They are Joanne Lesley (2 lb. 7 oz.) Nicola Jane (2 lb. 13 oz.), Julie Anne (2 lb. 15 oz.) Sarah Louise (3 lb. 7 oz.) and Jacqueline Mary (2 lb 6½ oz.). A fertility drug was used.

Heaviest It was reported that quintuplets weighing 25 lb. were born on 7 June 1953 to Mrs. Lui Saulien of Chekiang province, China. A weight of 25 lb. was also reported for girl quins born to Mrs. Kamalammal in Pondicherry, India, on 30 Dec. 1956. All died shortly afterwards.

Quadruplets The heaviest quadruplets ever recorded were Brucina
Heaviest Paula (5 lb. 7 oz.), Clifford (5 lb. 0 oz.), Stanford (4 lb. 15 oz.) and Stacey Lynn (4 lb. 7 oz.), totalling 19 lb. 13 oz., born by Caesarean section to Mrs. Ruth Becker, aged 28, between 5.15 a.m. and 5.18 a.m. on 3 Aug. 1962 at the Vancouver General Hospital in Vancouver, British Columbia, Canada.

United The earliest recorded quadruplets to have all survived
Kingdom in the United Kingdom were the Miles quads, born at St. Neots, Huntingdon, on 28 Nov. 1935—Ann (now Mrs. Robert Browning), Ernest, Paul and Michael (total weight 13 lb. 15½ oz.). Sarah Coe, one of the quads born to Mrs. Henry Coe of Cambridge on 6 Oct. 1766 was reportedly still alive 42 years later in 1808. The other three died at 2, 15 and 20 months respectively. Quadruplets reputedly survived birth near Devil's Bridge, Cardiganshire, Wales in 1856 only to die of cholera later in the same year. The heaviest set recorded were David John (5 lb. 7 oz.), Thelma Susan (4 lb. 1 oz.), Anthony James (5 lb. 1 oz.) and Beverley Margaret (3 lb. 14 oz.), totalling 18 lb. 7 oz. born on 14 Dec. 1957 to Mrs. Mary Bennett (née Wilson) 37, in the East End Maternity Hospital, Stepney, London. The lightest were Yana (3 lb. 8 oz.), Edward (3 lb. 3½ oz.), Lucille (3 lb. 8 oz.) and Christopher (2 lb. 7½ oz.), totalling 12 lb. 11 oz. born to Mrs. Phoebe Meacham (née Buckley) (b. 1928) of Leigh-on-Sea in Rochford Hospital, Essex, on 3 Jan. 1962.

Ireland The first surviving quadruplets born in Ireland were those born on 23 Jan. 1965 to Mrs. Eileen O'Connell aged 36, of Pallasgreen, County Limerick, in the Limerick Regional Hospital. On 31 Jan. 1965 they were weighed: Catherine Mary (2 lb. 2 oz.), Gerard Michael (3 lb. 6 oz.), John Paul (3 lb. 11 oz.) and Margaret Anne (3 lb. 0 oz.).

The world's longest-lived triplets, the octogenarian Luteys, born in Cornwall, England in 1891

Triplets
Heaviest There is an unconfirmed report of triplets (two boys and a girl) weighing 26 lb. 6 oz. born to a 21-year-old Iranian woman reported on 18 March 1968. Three boy triplets weighing 23 lb. 1 oz. were born in the Yarrawonga District Hospital, Victoria, Australia on 8 Aug. 1946. They weighed 7 lb. 13 oz., 7 lb. 12 oz. and 7 lb. 8 oz. The heaviest recorded triplets born in the United Kingdom, were Timothy Stuart (7 lb. 3 oz.), Martin James (6 lb. 10 oz.) and Guy Thomas (8 lb. 11 oz.) born at 9.0 a.m. to 9.10 a.m. on 21 Feb. 1972 to Mrs. Elizabeth A. Parker aged 31 of Buxton, Derbyshire in the Stepping Hill Hospital, Stockport, Cheshire. They aggregated 22 lb. 8 oz.

Most The greatest reported number of sets of triplets born to one woman is 15 (*cf.* 7 to Mme. Vassilet, page 17) to Maddalena Granata (1839-*fl.*1886) of Nocera Superiore, Italy.

Oldest The oldest known surviving triplets in the world are Richard Henry, John James and Catherine Vivian (now Mrs. Ellis) Lutey born in Carfury, Cornwall on 24 April 1891.

Twins
Heaviest The heaviest recorded twins were two boys, the first weighing 17 lb. 8 oz. and the second 18 lb. This was reported in a letter from Derbyshire in *The Lancet* of 6 Dec. 1884. A more reliable recent case is that of John and Jane Haskin weighing 14 lb. and 13¾ lb. born to Mrs. J. P. Haskin on 20 Feb. 1924 in Fort Smith, Arkansas, U.S.A.

Lightest The lightest recorded birthweight for a pair of surviving twins has been 2 lb. 8 oz. in the case of Stephen (19 oz.) and Adrian (21 oz.) delivered of Mrs. Isobel McAdam at the Isle of Thanet District Hospital, Margate, Kent on 16 July 1971.

Oldest The chances of identical twins both reaching 100 are said to be one in 1,000 million. The oldest recorded twins were Gulbrand and Bernt Morterud, born at Nord Odal, Norway, on 20 Dec. 1858. Bernt died on 1 Aug. 1960 in Chicago, Illinois, U.S.A. aged 101, and his brother died at Nord Odal on 12 Jan. 1964, aged 105. Twin sisters, Mrs. Vassilka Dermendjhieva and Mrs. Vassila Yapourdjieva of Sofia, Bulgaria allegedly celebrated their joint 104th birthday on 27 Sept. 1966.

"Siamese" Conjoined twins derived the name "Siamese" from the celebrated Chang and Eng Bunker, born at Maklong, Thailand (Siam), on 11 May 1811. They were joined by a cartilaginous band at the chest and married in April 1843 the Misses Sarah and Adelaide Yates and fathered ten and twelve children respectively. They died within three hours of each other on 17 Jan. 1874, aged 62. There is no genealogical evidence for the existence of the much-publicized Chalkhurst twins, Mary and Aliza, of Biddenden, Kent, allegedly born in c. 1550 (not 1100). Daisy and Violet Hilton, born in Brighton, Sussex on 5 Feb. 1908, were joined at the hip. They died in Charlotte, North Carolina, U.S.A., on 5 Jan. 1969 aged 60. The earliest successful separation of Siamese twins was performed on Prisna and Napit Atkinson (b. May 1953 in Thailand) by Dr. Dragstedt at the University of Chicago on 29 March 1955.

BABIES
Largest The heaviest normal new-born child recorded in
World modern times was a boy weighing 11 kilogrammes (24 lb 4 oz.), born on 3 June 1961 to Mrs. Saadat Cor of Cegham, Southern Turkey. There is an

19

unconfirmed report of a woman giving birth to a 27 lb. baby in Essonnes, a suburb of Corbeil, central France, in June 1929. A deformed baby weighing 29¼ lb. was born in May 1939 in a hospital at Effingham, Illinois, U.S.A.

United Kingdom The greatest recorded live birth weight in the United Kingdom is 21 lb. for a child born on Christmas Day, 1852. It was reported in a letter to the *British Medical Journal* (1 Feb. 1879) from a doctor in Torpoint, Cornwall. The only other reported birth weight in excess of 20 lb. is 20 lb. 2 oz. for a boy born to a 33-year-old schoolmistress in Crewe, Cheshire, on 12 Nov. 1884. A baby of 33 lb. was reportedly born to a Mrs. Lambert of Wandsworth Road, London *c.* 1930 but its measurements indicate a weight of about 17 lb. The *British Medical Journal* reported in February 1935 the case of a boy aged 2 years 9 months who weighed 7 stone 2½ lb.

Ireland The heaviest baby recorded in Ireland was Anthony Michael Kinch, weighing 17 lb. 3 oz., who was born on 13 June 1950 to Mrs. Mary Kinch, aged 34, of Bray, County Wicklow.

Most Bouncing Baby The most bouncing baby on record is Elias Daou (b. Suniani, Ghana on 12 Oct. 1969). At the age of 22 months Elias weighed 4 st. 5½ lb., his circumference was 91 cm. (35¾ inches).

Smallest The lowest birth weight for a surviving infant, of which there is definite evidence, is 10 oz. in the case of Marion Chapman, born on 5 June 1938 in South Shields, County Durham. She was 12¼ inches long. By her first birthday her weight had increased to 13 lb. 14 oz. She was born unattended and was nursed by Dr. D. A. Shearer, who fed her hourly through a fountain pen filler. Her weight on her 21st birthday was 7 stone 8 lb. The smallest viable baby reported from the United States has been Jacqueline Benson born at Palatine, Illinois on 20 Feb. 1936, weighing 12 oz.

A weight of 8 oz. was reported on 20 March 1938 for a baby born prematurely to Mrs. John Womack, after she had been knocked down by a lorry in East Louis, Illinois, U.S.A. The baby was taken alive to St. Mary's Hospital, but further information is lacking. On 23 Feb. 1952 it was reported that a 6 oz. baby only 6½ inches long lived for 12 hours in a hospital in Indianapolis, Indiana, U.S.A. A twin was still-born. English law has accepted pregnancies with extremes of 174 days (*Clark v. Clark*, 1939) and 349 days (*Hadlum v. Hadlum*, 1949).

Longest pregnancy The longest pregnancy reported is one of 389 days for a woman aged 25 in Woking Maternity Hospital, Surrey, England (*Lancet*, 3 Dec. 1954). The baby, weighing 7 lb. 14 oz., was still-born. The average pregnancy is 273 days. The longest pregnancy for a live-born baby was one of 381 days attributed to Mrs. Christine Houghton, 28, of Walberton, Sussex on 22 May 1971. The baby, Tina, weighed 7 lb. 7 oz.

5. PHYSIOLOGY AND ANATOMY

BONES

Longest The thigh bone or *femur* is the longest of the 206 bones in the human body. It constitutes usually 27½ per cent. of a person's stature, and may be expected to be 19¾ inches long in a 6-foot-tall man. The longest recorded bone was the femur of the German giant Constantine, who died in Mons, Belgium, on 30 March 1902, aged 30 (see page 10). It measured 76 centimetres (29.9 inches). The femur of Robert Wadlow, the tallest man ever recorded, measured approximately 29½ inches.

Smallest The *stapes* or stirrup bone, one of the three auditory ossicles in the middle ear, is the smallest human bone, measuring from 2.6 to 3.4 millimetres (0.10 to 0.17 of an inch) in length and weighing from 2.0 to 4.3 milligrammes (0.03 to 0.065 of a grain). Sesamoids are not included among human bones.

MUSCLES

Largest Muscles normally account for 40 per cent. of the body weight and the bulkiest of the 639 muscles in the human body is the *gluteus maximus* or buttock muscle, which extends the thigh.

Smallest The smallest muscle is the *stapedius*, which controls the *stapes* (see above), an auditory ossicle in the middle ear, and which is less than 1/20th of an inch long.

Smallest waists Queen Catherine de Medici (1519–89) decreed a waist measurement of 13 inches for ladies of the French court. This was at a time when females were more diminutive. The smallest recorded waist among women of normal stature in the 20th century is a reputed 13 inches in the case of the French actress Mlle. Polaire (1881-1939) and Mrs. Ethel Granger (b. 12 April 1905) of Peterborough who reduced from a natural 22 inches over the period 1929-1939.

Largest chest measurements The largest chest measurements are among endo-morphs (those with a tendency toward globularity). In the extreme case of Hughes (see page 13) this was reportedly 124 inches but in the light of his known height and weight a figure of 104 inches would be more supportable. George MacAree (see Britain's heaviest man) has a chest measurement of 72½ inches. Among muscular subjects (mesomorphs), chest measurements above 56 inches are extremely rare. The largest such chest measurement ever recorded was that of Angus Macaskill (1825–63) of Berneray, Scotland (see page 11), who may well have been the strongest man who ever lived. His chest must have measured 65 inches at his top weight of 37½ stone.

BRAIN

Largest The brain has 1.5×10^{10} cells each containing 10^{10} macromolecules. Each cell has 10^4 interconnections with other cells. After the age of 18 the brain loses some 10^3 cells per day but the macromolecular contingent of each cell is renewed 10^4 times in a normal life span. The brain of an average adult male (*i.e.* 30–59 years) weighs 1,410 grammes (2 lb. 13.21 oz.) falling to 1,030 grammes (2 lb. 12.83 oz.). The heaviest brain ever recorded was that of Ivan Sergey-vich Turgenev (1818-83), the Russian author. His brain weighed 2,012 grammes (4 lb. 6.96 oz.). The brain of Oliver Cromwell (1599-1658) reputedly weighed 2,222 grammes (4 lb. 14.8 oz.), but the size of his head in portraits does not support this extreme figure. The brain of Lord Byron, who died in Greece in 1824 aged 36, reportedly weighed 6 Neopolitan pounds (1,924 grammes or 4 lb. 3.17 oz.), but this also included a certain amount of blood. In January 1891 the *Edinburgh Medical Journal* reported the case of a 75-year-old man in the Royal Edinburgh Asylum whose brain weighed 1,829 grammes (4 lb. 0.5 oz.).

Smallest The brain of Anatole France (1844-1924), the French writer, weighed only 1,017 grammes (2 lb. 4 oz.) without the membrane, but there was some shrinkage due to old age. His brain probably weighed *c.* 1,130 grammes (2 lb. 7.78 oz.) at its heaviest.

Brains in extreme cases of microcephaly may weigh as little as 300 grammes (10.6 oz.) (*cf.* 20 oz. for the adult male gorilla, and 16-20 oz. for other anthropoid apes).

Longest necks The maximum measured extension of the neck by the successive fitting of copper coils, as practised by the Padaung or Mayan people of Burma, is 15¾ inches.

From the male viewpoint the practice serves the dual purpose of enhancing the beauty of the female and ensuring fidelity. The neck muscles can become so atrophied that the removal of the support of the coils can produce asphyxiation.

Commonest illness The commonest illness in the world is coryza (acute nasopharyngitis) or the common cold. Only 4,600,000 working days were reportedly lost as a result of this illness in Great Britain between mid 1968 and mid 1969, since absences of less than three days are not reported. The greatest reported loss of working time in Britain is from bronchitis, which accounted for 37,490,000, or 11.39 per cent., of the total of 329,000,000 working days lost in the same period.

DISEASE

Commonest The commonest disease in the world is dental caries or tooth decay. In Great Britain 13 per cent. of people have lost all their teeth before they are 21 years old. During their lifetime few completely escape its effects. Infestation with pinworm *(Enterobius vermicularis)* approaches 100 per cent. in some areas of the world.

Rarest Medical literature periodically records hitherto undescribed diseases. The only recorded case of congenital agammaglobulinaemia was reported from Houston, Texas in February 1972. Of once common diseases, rabies (hydrophobia) was last contracted in Britain in 1922 and last recorded in 1964. Kuru, or laughing sickness, afflicts only the Fore tribe of eastern New Guinea and is 100 per cent. fatal. The rarest fatal diseases in England and Wales have been those from which the last deaths (all males) were all recorded more than 40 years ago—yellow fever (1930), cholera nostras (1928) and bubonic plague (1926).

Most and least infectious The most infectious of all diseases is the pneumonic form of plague, with a mortality rate of about 99.99 per cent. Leprosy transmitted by *Mycobacterium leprae* is the least infectious of communicable diseases.

Highest morbidity Rabies in humans has been regarded as uniformly fatal when associated with the hydrophobia symptom. A 25-year-old woman Candida de Sousa Barbosa of Rio de Janeiro, Brazil, was believed to be the first ever survivor of the disease in November 1968. In 1969 all 515 cases reported were fatal.

Most notorious carrier The most notorious of all typhoid carriers has been Mary Mallon, known as Typhoid Mary, of New York City, N.Y., U.S.A. She was the source of the 1903 outbreak, with 1,300 cases. Because of her refusal to leave employment, often under assumed names, involving the handling of food, she was placed under permanent detention from 1915 until her death in 1938.

Most Bee Stings The greatest number of bee stings sustained by any surviving human subject is 2,443 by Johannes Relleke, at the Gwaii River in the Wankie District of Rhodesia, on 28 Jan. 1962.

Touch sensitivity The extreme sensitivity of the fingers is such that a vibration with a movement of 0.02 of a micron can be detected. On 12 Jan. 1963 the Soviet newspaper *Izvestiya* reported the case of a totally blindfolded girl, Rosa Kulgeshova, who was able to identify colours by touch alone. Later reports confirmed in 1970 that under rigorous test conditions this claimed ability totally disappeared.

Most fingers Voight records a case of someone with 13 fingers on each hand and 12 toes on each foot.

Richard Latter of Kent, England (1831-1914) whose beard was reputed to be of the world record length of 18 feet

Longest finger nails The longest recorded finger nails were reported from Shanghai in 1910, in the case of a Chinese priest who took 27 years to achieve nails up to 22¾ inches in length. Probably the longest nails now grown are those of Ramesh Sharma of Delhi, whose nails on his left hand now aggregate 52½ inches after 10 years, with his best at 15 inches. Human nails normally grow from cuticle to cutting length in from 117 to 138 days.

Longest hair The longest recorded hair was that of Swami Pandarasannadhi, the head of the Thiruvadu Thurai monastery in India. His dead matted hair was reported in 1949 to be 26 feet in length.

Longest beard The longest beard preserved was that of Hans N. Langseth (b. 1846 in Norway) which measured 17½ feet at the time of his death in 1927 after 15 years residence in the United States. The beard was presented to the Smithsonian Institution, Washington, D.C. in 1967. Richard Latter (b. Pembury, Kent, 1831) of Tunbridge Wells, Kent, who died in

21

1914 aged 83, reputedly had a beard 18 feet long but contemporary independent corroboration is lacking and photographic evidence indicates this figure was exaggerated. The beard of the bearded lady Janice Deveree (b. Bracken Co., Kentucky, U.S.A., 1842) was measured at 14 inches in 1884.

Longest moustache The longest moustache on record is that of Masuriya Din (b. 1908), a Brahmin of the Partabgarh district in Uttar Pradesh, India. It grew to an extended span of 8 feet 6 inches between 1949 and 1962, and costs £13 per annum in upkeep. The longest moustache in Great Britain is that of Mr. John Roy (b. 14 Jan. 1910), licensee of the "Cock Inn" at Beazely End, near Braintree, Essex. It attained a span of 44 inches between 1939 and 9 Nov. 1971 when measured on the *Magpie* T.V. programme.

Blood groups The preponderance of one blood group varies greatly from one locality to another. On a world basis Group O is the most common (46 per cent.), but in some areas, for example London and Norway, Group A predominates.

The full description of the commonest sub-group in Britain is O MsNs, P+, Rr, Lu(a−), K−, Le(a−b+), Fy(a+b+), Jk(a+b+), which occurs in one in every 270 people.

The rarest blood group on the ABO system, one of nine systems, is AB, which occurs in less than three per cent. of persons in the British Isles. The rarest type in the world is a type of Bombay blood (sub-type A-h) found so far only in a Czechoslovak nurse in 1961 and in a brother and sister in New Jersey, U.S.A. reported in February 1968. The American male has started a blood bank for himself.

Richest Natural Resources Joe Thomas of Detroit, Michigan, U.S.A. was reported in August 1970 to have the highest known count of Anti-Lewis B, the rare blood antibody. A U.S. biological supply firm pays him $1,500 per quart—an income of $12,000 (£4,615) per annum. The Internal Revenue regard this income as a taxable liquid asset.

Champion blood donor Joseph Elmaleh (b. 1915) of Marseilles, France, donated on 22 May 1968 his 597th pint of blood making a total of 74 gallons 5 pints since 1931. A 50-year-old haemophiliac Warren C. Jyrich required 2,400 pints of blood when undergoing open heart surgery at the Michael Reese Hospital, Chicago, U.S.A., in December 1970.

Largest vein The largest vein in the human body is the cardiac vein known as the vena cava.

Most alcoholic subject It is recorded that a hard drinker named Vanhorn (1750-1811), born in London, averaged more than four bottles of ruby port per day for the 23 years 1788 to his death aged 61 in 1811. The total of his "empties" was put at 35,688.

The United Kingdom's legal limit for motorists is 80 milligrammes of alcohol per 100 millilitres of blood. The hitherto recorded highest figure in medical literature of 600 mg. per 100 ml. was submerged when the late Mr. Michael Spring, 41, of Derby was found to have a level of 605 mg. by a pathologist after a fatal road accident on 7 Jan. 1972.

Longest coma The longest duration of human unconsciousness was 32 years 99 days endured by Karoline Karlsson (b. Mönsterås, Sweden in 1862) from 25 Dec. 1875 to 3 April 1908. She died on 6 April 1950 aged 88. The longest recorded coma of any person still living is that of Elaine Esposito (b. 3 Dec. 1934) of Tarpon Springs, Florida, U.S.A. She has never stirred since an appendicectomy on 5 Aug. 1941, when she was six, in Chicago, Illinois, U.S.A. She was still living in 1969.

Fastest reflexes The results of experiments carried out in 1943 have shown that the fastest messages transmitted by the nervous system travel at 265 m.p.h. With advancing age impulses are carried 15 per cent. more slowly.

BODY TEMPERATURE

Highest In Kalow's case (*Lancet*, 31 Oct. 1970) a woman following halothane anaesthesia ran a temperature of 112° F (44.4° C). She recovered after a procainamide infusion. Marathon runners in hot weather attain 105.8° F (41° C).

A temperature of 115° F was recorded in the case of Christopher Legge in the Hospital for Tropical Diseases, London, on 9 Feb. 1934. A subsequent examination of the thermometer disclosed a flaw in the bulb, but it is regarded as certain that the patient sustained a temperature of more than 110° F.

Lowest The lowest body temperature ever recorded for a living person was 60.8° F (16.0° C) in the case of Vickie Mary Davis (b. 25 Dec. 1953) of Milwaukee, Wisconsin, when she was admitted to the Evangelical Hospital, Marshalltown, Iowa, U.S.A., on 21 Jan. 1956. The house in which she had been found unconscious on the floor was unheated and the air temperature had dropped to −24° F (−31° C). Her temperature returned to normal (98.4° F or 36.9° C) after 12 hours and may have been as low as 59° F (15.0° C) when she was first found.

Heart stoppage The longest recorded heart stoppage is 3 hours in the case of a Norwegian boy, Roger Arntzen, in April 1962. He was rescued, apparently drowned, after 22 minutes under the waters of the River Nideelv, near Trondheim.

The longest recorded interval in a *post mortem* birth was one of at least 80 minutes in Magnolia, Mississippi, U.S.A. Dr. Robert E. Drake found Fanella Anderson, aged 25, dead in her home at 11.40 p.m. on 15 Oct. 1966 and he delivered her of a son weighing 6 lb. 4 oz. by Caesarean operation in the Beacham Memorial Hospital on 16 Oct. 1966.

Largest stone The largest stone or vesical calculus reported in medical literature was one of 13 lb. 14 oz. (6,294 grammes) removed from an 80-year-old woman by Dr. Humphrey Arthure at Charing Cross Hospital, London, on 29 Dec. 1952.

Earliest influenza An epidemic bearing symptoms akin to influenza was first recorded in 412 B.C. by Hippocrates (c. 460-c. 375 B.C.). The earliest description of an epidemic in Great Britain was in the *Chronicle of Melrose* in 1173 although the term influenza was not introduced until 1743 by John Huxham (1692-1768) of Plymouth, Devon.

Earliest duodenal ulcer The earliest description in medical literature of duodenal ulcer was made in 1746 by Georg Erhard Hamberger (1696-1755).

Earliest slipped disc The earliest description of a prolapsed intervertebral cartilage was by George S. Middleton and John H. Teacher of Glasgow, Scotland, in 1911.

Pill-taking It is recorded that among hypochondriacs Samuel Jessup (b. 1752), a wealthy grazier of Heckington, Lincolnshire, has never had a modern rival. His consumption of pills from 1794 to 1816 was 226,934, with a peak annual total of 51,590 in 1814. He is also recorded as having drunk 40,000 bottles of medicine before death overtook him at the surprisingly advanced age of 65.

Most tattoos Vivian "Sailor Joe" Simmons, a Canadian tattoo artist, had 4,831 tattoos on his body. He died in Toronto on 22 Dec. 1965 aged 77. Britain's most tattooed man is Arthur (Eddy) Noble (b. 1924) of Newcastle, who filled in his last gaps with 114 more tattoos in 1970 making a total of more than 400. Britain's most tattooed woman is Rusty Field (b. 1944) of Aldershot, Hampshire, who after 11 years under the needle, is nearing totality.

Hiccoughing The longest recorded attack of hiccoughs was that afflicting Jack O'Leary of Los Angeles, California, U.S.A. It was estimated that he "hicked" more than 160,000,000 times in an attack which lasted from 13 June 1948 to 1 June 1956, apart from a week's respite in 1951. His weight fell from 9 stone 12 lb. to 5 stone 4 lb. People sent 60,000 suggestions for cures of which only one apparently worked—a prayer to St. Jude, the patron saint of lost causes. The infirmary at Newcastle upon Tyne is recorded to have admitted a young man from Long Witton, Northumberland on 25 March 1769 suffering from hiccoughs which could be heard at a range of more than a mile.

Sneezing The most chronic sneezing fit ever recorded was that of June Clark, aged 17, of Miami, Florida, U.S.A. She started sneezing on 4 Jan. 1966, while recovering from a kidney ailment in the James M. Jackson Memorial Hospital, Miami. The sneezing was stopped by electric "aversion" treatment on 8 June 1966, after 155 days. The highest speed at which expelled particles have been measured to travel is 103.6 m.p.h.

Snoring
Loudest Research at the Ear, Nose and Throat Department of St. Mary's Hospital, London, published in November 1968, shows that a rasping snore can attain a loudness of 69 decibels.

Yawning In Lee's case, reported in 1888, a fifteen-year-old female patient yawned continuously for a period of five weeks.

SWALLOWING
The worst known case of compulsive swallowing was reported in the *Journal of the American Medical Association* in December 1960. The patient, who complained only of swollen ankles, was found to have 258 items in his stomach, including a 3-lb. piece of metal, 26 keys, 3 sets of rosary beads, 16 religious medals, a bracelet, a necklace, 3 pairs of tweezers, 4 nail clippers, 39 nail files, 3 metal chains and 88 assorted coins.

Coins The most extreme recorded case of coin swallowing was revealed by Sedgefield General Hospital, County Durham, on 5 Jan. 1958, when it was reported that 366 halfpennies, 26 sixpences, 17 threepences, 11 pennies and four shillings (424 coins valued at £1 17s. 5d.), plus 27 pieces of wire totalling 5 lb. 1 oz., had been extracted from the stomach of a 54-year-old man.

Sword The longest length of sword able to be "swallowed" by a practised exponent, after a heavy meal, is 27 inches. Perhaps the greatest exponent is Alex Linton, born on 25 Oct. 1904 in Boyle, County Roscommon, Ireland. He stands 5 feet 3 inches tall and has "swallowed" four 27-inch blades at one time. He now lives in Sarasota, Florida, U.S.A.

DENTITION
Earliest The first deciduous or milk teeth normally appear in infants at five to eight months, these being the mandibular and maxillary first incisors. There are many records of children born with teeth, the most famous example being Prince Louis Dieudonné, later Louis XIV of France, who was born with two teeth on 5 Sept. 1638. Molars usually appear at 24 months, but in 1956 Bellevue Hospital in New York City, N.Y., U.S.A., reported a molar in a one-month-old baby, Robert R. Clinton.

Most Cases of the growth in late life of a third set of teeth

have been recorded several times. A reference to an extreme case in France of a fourth dentition, known as Lison's case was published in 1896. A triple row of teeth was noted in 1680 by Albertus Hellwigius.

Most dedicated dentist Brother Giovanni Battista Orsenigo of the Ospedale Fatebenefratelli, Rome, Italy, a religious dentist, conserved all the teeth he extracted in three enormous cases during the time he exercised his profession from 1868 to 1904. In 1903 the number was counted and found to be 2,000,744 teeth.

OPTICS
Smallest visible object The resolving power of the human eye is 0.0003 of a radian or an arc of one minute (1/60th of a degree), which corresponds to 100 microns at 10 inches. A micron is a thousandth of a millimetre, hence 100 microns is 0.003937, or less than four thousandths, of an inch. The human eye can, however, detect a bright light source shining through an aperture only 3 to 4 microns across.

Colour sensitivity The unaided human eye, under the best possible viewing conditions, comparing large areas of colour, in good illumination, using both eyes, can distinguish 10,000,000 different colour surfaces. The most accurate photo-electric spectrophotometers possess a precision probably only 40 per cent as good as this.

Colour blindness The most extreme form of colour blindness, mono-chromatic vision, is very rare. The highest recorded rate of red-green colour blindness is in Czechoslovakia and the lowest rate among Fijians and Brazilian Indians.

VOICE
Highest and lowest The highest and lowest recorded notes attained by the human voice before this century were a C in *alt-altissimo* (C^{iv}) by Lucrezia Agujari (1743-83), noted by the Austrian composer Wolfgang Amadeus Mozart (1756-91) in Parma, northern Italy, in 1770, and an A_1 (55 cycles per second) by Kaspar Foster (1617-73). Since 1950 singers have achieved high and low notes far beyond the hitherto accepted extremes. However, notes at the bass and treble extremities of the register tend to lack harmonics and are of little musical value. Frl. Marita Günther, trained by Alfred Wolfsohn, has covered the range of the piano from the lowest note, A_{11}, to C^v. Of this range of 7¼ octaves, six octaves are considered to be of musical value. Mr. Roy Hart, also trained by Wolfsohn, has reached notes below the range of the piano. The highest note being sung by a tenor is G in *alt-altissimo* by Louis Lavelle, coached by Mr. S. Pleeth, in *Lovely Mary Donelly*. The lowest note put into song is a D_{11} by the singer Tom King, of King's Langley, Hertfordshire. The highest note called for in singing was an f^{iv}#, which occurred twice in Zerbinetta's Recitative and Aria in the first (1912) version of the opera *Ariadne auf Naxos* by Richard Georg Strauss (1864-1949). It was transposed down a tone in 1916.

Greatest range The normal intelligible outdoor range of the male human voice in still air is 200 yards. The *silbo*, the whistled language of the Spanish-speaking Canary Island of La Gomera, is intelligible across the valleys, under ideal conditions, at five miles. There is a recorded case, under freak acoustic conditions, of the human voice being detectable at a distance of 10½ miles across still water at night. It was said that Mills Darden (see page 13) could be heard 6 miles away when he shouted at the top of his voice.

Lowest detectable sound The intensity of noise or sound is measured in terms of power. The power of the quietest sound that can be detected by a person of normal hearing at the most sensitive frequency of *c*. 2.750 Hz is 1.0×10^{-16} of a watt per square centimetre. One tenth of the logarithm (to the base of 10) of the ratio of the power of a noise to this standard provides a unit termed a decibel. Noises above 150 decibels will cause immediate permanent deafness, while a noise of 30 decibels is negligible.

Highest detectable pitch The upper limit of hearing by the human ear has long been regarded as 20,000 Hz (cycles per second), although children with asthma can often detect a sound of 30,000 cycles per second. It was announced in February 1964 that experiments in the U.S.S.R. had conclusively proved that oscillations as high as 200,000 cycles per second can be heard if the oscillator is pressed against the skull.

OPERATIONS

Longest The most protracted operations are those involving brain surgery. Such an operation lasting up to 31 hours was performed on Victor Zazueta, 19, of El Centro at San Diego Hospital, California by Dr. John F. Alksne and his team on 17-18 Jan. 1972.

Oldest subject The greatest recorded age at which a person has been subjected to an operation is 111 years 105 days in the case of James Henry Brett, Jr. (b. 25 July 1849, d. 10 Feb. 1961) of Houston, Texas, U.S.A. He underwent a hip operation on 7 Nov. 1960. The oldest age established in Britain was the case of Miss Mary Wright (b. 28 Feb. 1862) who died during a thigh operation at Boston, Lincolnshire on 22 April 1971 aged 109 years 53 days.

Youngest subject The youngest reported subject in a heart operation has been identified only as "Hamish". He underwent such an operation at the Royal Alexandra Hospital, Sydney, Australia on 15 April 1971 at the age of two days.

Heart The first human heart transplant operation was performed on Louis Washkansky, aged 55, at the Groote Schuur Hospital, Cape Town, South Africa, between 1.00 a.m. and 6 a.m., on 3 Dec. 1967, by a team of 30 headed by Prof. Christiaan Neethling Barnard (b. Beaufort West, South Africa, 8 Oct. 1922). The donor was Miss Denise Ann Darvall, aged 25. Washkansky died on 21 Dec. 1967. The longest surviving heart transplant patient has been the American negro Harry Lewis (b. 1923), who received his replacement heart in August 1968. He entered the 39th month of his second life in November 1971. Britain's longest-surviving heart transplant patient has been Mr. Charles Hendrick who died in Guy's Hospital of a lung infection on 31 Aug. 1969—107 days after his operation.

Earliest appendicectomy The earliest recorded successful appendix operation was performed in 1736 by Claudius Amyand (1680-1740). He was Serjeant Surgeon to King George II (reigned 1727-60).

Longest in iron lung The longest survival in an "iron lung" is 22 years since 1950 by Mrs. Mary Ann Hough (b. 1923) of Hillsborough, San Francisco, California.

Earliest anaesthesia The earliest recorded operation under general anaesthesia was for the removal of a cyst from the neck of James Venable by Dr. Crawford Williamson Long (1815-78), using diethyl ether $(C_2H_5)_2O$, in Jefferson, Georgia, U.S.A., on 30 March 1842. The earliest use of an anaesthetic in Great Britain was by Robert Liston (see also below) at the University College Hospital, London on 21 Dec. 1846 for an amputation on a man.

Fastest amputation The shortest time recorded for the amputation of a limb in the pre-anaesthetic era was 33 seconds through a patient's thigh by Robert Liston (1794-1847) of Edinburgh, Scotland. This feat caused his assistant the loss of three fingers from his master's saw.

Surgical instruments The largest surgical instruments are robot retractors used in abdominal surgery introduced by Abbey Surgical Instruments of Chingford, Essex in 1968 and weighing 11 lb. Some bronchoscopic forceps measure 60 cms. (23½ inches) in length. The smallest is Elliot's eye trephine, which has a blade 0.078 of an inch in diameter.

Highest I.Q. On the Terman index for Intelligence Quotients, 150 represents "genius" level. The indices are sometimes held to be immeasurable above a level of 200 but a figure of 210 has been attributed to Kim Ung-Yong of Seoul, South Korea (b. 7 March 1963). He composed poetry and spoke four languages (Korean, English, German and Japanese), and performed integral calculus at the age of 4 years 8 months on television in Tokyo on "The World Surprise Show" on 2 Nov. 1967. Both his parents are University professors and were both born at 11 a.m. on 23 May 1934. Research into past geniuses at Stanford University, California, U.S.A., has produced a figure of "over 200" for John Stuart Mill (United Kingdom) (1806-73), who began to learn ancient Greek at the age of three. A similar rating has also been attributed to Johann Wolfgang von Goethe (1749-1832) of Frankfurt am Main, West Germany. More than 20 per cent. of the 15,000 members of the international Mensa society have an I.Q. of 161 or above on the Cattell index which is equivalent to 142 on the Terman index.

Human memory Mehmed Ali Halici of Ankara, Turkey on 14 Oct. 1967 recited 6,666 verses of the Koran from memory in six hours. The recitation was followed by six Koran scholars. Rare instances of eidetic memory—the ability to re-project and hence 'visually' recall material—are known to science.

The greatest number of places of π The greatest number of places to which Pi has been memorised is 750 by David Richard Spencer (b. 10 Dec. 1952) of Powell River, British Columbia, Canada. He desisted in going further on making the disconcerting discovery that two sources disagreed on the 512th place.

Calculating ability Herbert B. de Grote of Mexico City, Mexico has been attested to have extracted the 13th root of a 100-digit number by an algorithm of his own invention in 23 minutes in a test in Chicago, Illinois on 5 Oct. 1970. His answer was 46,231,597. No comparable feat has been recorded.

Sleeplessness Researches indicate that on the Circadian cycle for the majority peak efficiency is attained between 8 p.m. and 9 p.m. and the low point comes at 4 a.m. The longest recorded period for which a person has voluntarily gone without sleep, while under medical surveillance, is 282 hours 55 minutes (11 days 18 hours 55 minutes) by Mrs. Bertha Van Der Merwe, aged 52, a housewife of Cape Town, South Africa, ending on 13 Dec. 1968.

It was reported that Toimi Artturinpoika Silvo, a 54-year-old port worker of Hamina, Finland, stayed awake for 32 days 12 hours from 1 March to 2 April 1967. He walked 17 miles per day and lost 33 lb. in weight. Mr. Eustace Rushworth Burnett (b. 1880) of Hose, Leicestershire, claimed to have lost all desire to sleep in 1907 and that he never again went to bed. He died in January 1965, 58 years later, aged 85.

Motionlessness The longest that a man has voluntarily remained motionless is 4½ hours by Private (1st Class) William A. Fuqua of Fort Worth, Texas, U.S.A. He is a male mannequin or "fashioneer" in civil life earning up to $1,300 (£541) per hour for his ability to "freeze". The job is hazardous for it was reported in November 1967 that he was stabbed in the back by a man "proving" to his wife that he was only a dummy.

The man able to extract 13th roots by mental arithmetic—Herbert de Grote

Fastest talker Few people are able to speak articulately at a sustained speed above 300 words per minute. The fastest broadcaster has been regarded as Jerry Wilmot, the Canadian ice hockey commentator in the post World War II period. Raymond Glendenning (b. Newport, Monmouth, 25 Sept. 1907) of the B.B.C. once spoke 176 words in 30 seconds while commentating on a greyhound race. In public life the highest speed recorded is a 327 words per minute burst in a speech made in December 1961 by John Fitzgerald Kennedy (1917-63), then President of the United States. In October 1965 it was reported that Peter Spiegel, 62, of Essen, West Germany, achieved 908 syllables in one minute at a rally of shorthand writers.

Dr. Charles Hunter of Rochdale, Lancashire, England on 14 Dec. 1968 demonstrated an ability to recite the 262 words of the soliloquy *To Be or Not To Be* from Shakespeare's *Hamlet* (Act III, Scene 1) in 41 secs. or at a rate of 383 words per minute. In March 1968 he covered the first 50 words in 7.2 secs. (a rate of 416.6 words per minute).

Fasting Most humans experience considerable discomfort after an abstinence from food for even 12 hours but this often passes off after 24-28 hours. Records claimed without unremitting medical surveillance are of little value.

The longest period for which anyone has gone without food is 382 days by Angus Barbieri (b. 1940) of Tayport, Fife, who lived on tea, coffee, water, soda water and vitamins in Maryfield Hospital, Dundee, Angus, from June 1965 to July 1966. His weight declined from 33 stone 10 lb. to 12 stone 10 lb. Dr. Stephen Taylor, 43, of Mount Roskill, New Zealand, fasted 40 days with only a glass of water per day in a political protest in 1970.

Hunger strike The longest recorded hunger strike was one of 94 days by John and Peter Crowley, Thomas Donovan, Michael Burke, Michael O'Reilly, Christopher Upton, John Power, Joseph Kenny and Seán Hennessy in Cork Prison, Ireland, from 11 Aug. to 12 Nov. 1920. These nine survivors (Joseph Murphy died on the 76th day) owed their lives to expert medical attention. The longest recorded hunger strike with forcible feeding in a British gaol is 375 days by Ronald Barker, 28, in Lincoln Jail and Armley Prison, Leeds from 23 Jan. 1970. He was protesting his innocence of a robbery in Louth, Lincolnshire in which he was found uninvolved in a re-trial at Northamptonshire Assizes on 2 Feb. 1971. The feeding was done with "Complan" by tube orally.

Most voracious fire-eater The hardest blowing fire-eater is Kjell Swing (Sweden), who can produce a flame 6½ feet long.

Underwater The world record for voluntarily staying under water is 13 minutes 42.5 seconds by Robert Foster, aged 32, an electronics technician of Richmond, California, who stayed under 10 feet of water in the swimming pool of the Bermuda Palms Motel at San Rafael, California, U.S.A., on 15 March 1959. He hyperventilated with oxygen for 30 minutes before his descent. His longest breath-hold without oxygen was 5 mins. 40 secs. It must be stressed that record-breaking of this kind is *extremely* dangerous.

Human salamanders The highest dry-air temperature endured by naked men in the U.S. Air Force experiments in 1960 was 400° F, and for heavily clothed men 500° F. Steaks require only 325° F. Temperatures of 140° C (284° F) have been found quite bearable in *Sauna* baths.

g forces The acceleration g, due to gravity, is 32 feet 1.05 inches per second per second at sea-level at the Equator. A *sustained* acceleration of 31 g was withstood for 5 seconds by R. Flanagan Gray, aged 39, at the U.S. Naval Air Development Center in Johnsville, Pennsylvania, in 1959. This makes the bodyweight of a 185 lb. (13 stone 3 lb.) man seem like 5,700 lb. (2.54 tons). The highest value endured in a dry capsule is 25 g. The highest g value endured on a water-braked rocket sled is 82.6 g for 0.04 of a second by Eli L. Beeding Jr. at Holloman Air Force Base, New Mexico, U.S.A., on 16 May 1958. He was put in hospital for 3 days. A man who fell off a 185-foot cliff (before 1963) has survived a *momentary* g of 209 in decelerating from 68 m.p.h. to stationary in 0.015 of a second.

Isolation The longest recorded period for which any volunteer has been able to withstand total deprivation of all sensory stimulation (sight, hearing and touch) is 92 hours, recorded in 1962 at Lancaster Moor Hospital, Lancashire.

Extra-sensory perception The highest consistent performer in tests to detect powers of extra-sensory perception is Pavel Stepánek (Czechoslovakia) known in parapsychological circles as "P.S.". His performance on nominating hidden white or green cards from May 1967 to March 1968 departed from a chance probability yielding a Chi^2 value corresponding to $P < 10^{-50}$ or odds of more than 100 octillion to one against the achievement being one of chance. One of the two appointed referees recommended that the results should not be published. The highest published scores in any E.S.P. test were those of a 26-year-old female tested by Prof. Bernard F. Reiss of Hunter College, New York in 1936. In 74 runs of 25 guesses each she scored one with 25 all correct, two with 24 and an average of 18.24 instead of the random 5.00. Such a result would depart from chance probability by a factor $> 10^{700}$.

Most durable ghosts Ghosts are not immortal and, according to the *Gazeteer of British Ghosts,* seem to deteriorate after 400 years. The most outstanding exception to their normal 'half-life' is the ghost of a Roman centurion that still reportedly haunts Strood, Mersea Island, Essex after 15½ centuries. The book's author, Peter Underwood, states that Britain has more reported ghosts per square mile than any other country with Borley Rectory near Long Melford, Suffolk the site of unrivalled activity between 1863 and its destruction by fire in 1939.

2 ANIMAL AND PLANT KINGDOMS

Note—Guinness Superlatives Ltd. has newly published a specialist volume entitled *The Guinness Book of Animal Facts and Feats.* This work treats the dimensions and performances of all the Classes of the Animal Kingdom in greater detail giving also the sources and authorities for much of the material in this chapter.

Largest and heaviest The largest and heaviest animal in the world, and probably the biggest creature which has *ever* existed, is the Blue or Sulphur-bottom whale (*Balaenoptera musculus*), also called Sibbald's rorqual. The largest accurately measured specimen on record was a female taken near the South Shetlands in March 1926 which measured 33.27 metres (109 feet 4¼ inches) in length. Another female measuring 96¾ feet brought into the shore station at Prince Olaf, South Georgia in *c.* 1931 was calculated to have weighed 163.7 tons, inclusive of blood, judging by the number of cookers that were filled by the animal's blubber, meat and bones. The total weight of the whale was believed to have been 174 tons.

In November 1947 a weight of 190 tons was reported for a 90¾ foot Blue whale weighed piecemeal by the Russians during the first cruise of the "Slava" whaling fleet in the Antarctic, but this figure was a misprint and should have read 140 tons. On the principle that the weight should vary as the cube of linear dimensions, a 100 foot Blue whale in good condition should weigh about 160 tons, but in the case of pregnant females the weight could be as much as 190-200 tons.

Tallest The tallest living animal is the Giraffe (*Giraffa camelopardalis*), which is now found only in the dry savannah and semi-desert areas of Africa south of the Sahara. The tallest ever recorded was a Masai bull (*G. camelopardalis tippelskirchi*) shot in Kenya before 1930 which measured 19 feet 3 inches between pegs (tip of forehoof to tip of "false" horn with neck erect) and must have stood about 19 feet when alive. It was thus 4½ feet taller than a London double-decker bus. Less credible heights of up to 23 feet have been claimed.

The first giraffe ever seen in England was a six-month-old cow of the Nubian race (*G.c. camelopardalis*) presented to George IV (1762-1830) by Mohammed Ali, Pasha of Egypt. The 9 foot 2 inches tall animal arrived in London in August 1827.

Longest The longest animal ever recorded is the giant jellyfish *Cyanaea arctica*, which is found in the north-western Atlantic Ocean. One specimen washed up in Massachusetts Bay, Mass., U.S.A., in *c.* 1865 had a bell diameter of 7½ feet and tentacles measuring 120 feet, thus giving a theoretical tentacular span of some 245 feet.

Smallest The smallest of all free-living organisms are pleuro-pneumonia-like organisms (P.P.L.O.) of the *Mycoplasma.* One of these, *Mycoplasma laidlawii,* first discovered in sewage in 1936, has a diameter during its early existence of only 100 millimicrons, or 0.000004 of an inch. Examples of the strain known as H.39 have a maximum diameter of 300 millimicrons and weigh an estimated 1.0×10^{-16} of a gramme. Thus a 174-ton blue whale would weigh 1.77×10^{23} or 177,000 trillion times as much.

Longest lived Few creatures live longer than humans. It would appear that tortoises are the longest lived animals. The greatest authentic age recorded for a tortoise is 152-plus years for a male Marion's tortoise (*Testudo sumeirii*) brought from the Seychelles to Mauritius in 1766 by the Chevalier de Fresne, who presented it to the Port Louis army garrison. This specimen (it went blind in 1908) was accidentally killed in 1918. When the famous Royal Tongan tortoise "Tu'malilia" (believed to be a specimen of *Testudo radiata*) died on 19 May 1966 it was reputed to be over 200 years old, having been presented to the then King of Tonga by Captain James Cook (1728-79) on 22 Oct. 1773, but this record lacks proper documentation.

Fastest The fastest reliably measured speed of any animal is 106.25 m.p.h. for the Spine-tailed swift (*Chaetura caudacuta*) reported from the U.S.S.R. in 1942. In 1934 ground speeds ranging from 171.8 to 219.5 m.p.h. were recorded by stop-watch for spine-tailed swifts over a 2-mile course in the Cachar Hills of north-eastern India, but scientific tests since have revealed that this species of bird cannot be seen at a distance of 1 mile, even with standard binoculars. This bird is the fastest moving living creature and has a blood temperature of 112.5° F (44.7° C). Speeds even higher than a "free fall" maximum of 185 m.p.h. have been ascribed to the Peregrine falcon (*Falco peregrinus*) in a stoop, but in recent experiments in which miniature air speedometers were fitted, the maximum recorded diving speed was 82 m.p.h.

Rarest The best claimant to the title of the world's rarest land animal is probably the tenrec *Dasogale fontoynonti*, which is known only from the type specimen collected in eastern Madagascar and now preserved in the Paris Museum of Natural History.

Commonest It has been estimated that man shares the earth with about 3,000,000,000,000,000,000,000,000, 000,000,000 (3,000 quintillion or 3×10^{33}) other living things. Of these, more than 75 per cent are bacteria, namely 2,200 quintillion or 2.2×10^{33}.

Fastest growth The fastest growth in the Animal Kingdom is that of the Blue whale calf (see above). A barely visible ovum weighing a fraction of a milligramme (0.000035 of an ounce) grows to a weight of *c.* 26 tons in 22¾ months, made up of 10¾ months gestation and the first 12 months of life. This is equivalent to an increase of 30,000 million-fold.

Largest egg The largest egg of any living animal is that of the whale-shark (*Rhineodon typus*). One egg case measured 12 inches by 5.5 inches by 3.5 inches was picked up by the shrimp trawler "Doris" on 29 June 1953 at a depth of 31 fathoms (186 feet) in the Gulf of Mexico 130 miles south of Port Isabel, Texas, U.S.A. The egg contained a perfect embryo of a whale-shark 13.78 inches long.

Greatest size difference between sexes The largest female deep-sea angler fish of the species *Ceratias holboelki* on record weighed half a million times as much as the smallest known parasitic male. It has been suggested that this fish would make an appropriate emblem for the Women's Lib. Movement.

Largest eye The giant squid *Architeuthis sp.* has the largest eye of any living animal. The ocular diameter may exceed 38 cm. (15 inches), compared to 10-12 centimetres (3.93 to 4.71 inches) for the largest Blue whales.

1. MAMMALS (*Mammalia*)

Largest and heaviest World For details of the Blue whale (*Balaenoptera musculus*) see page 26. Further information: the tongue and heart of a 27.6 m (90 feet 8 inches) long female Blue whale taken by the Salva whaling fleet in the Antarctic on 17 March 1947 weighed 4.22 tons and 1,540 lb. respectively.

British waters The largest blue whale ever recorded in British waters was probably an 88 foot specimen killed near the Buneveneader station in Harris in the Outer Hebrides, Scotland in 1904. In Sept. 1750 a Blue whale allegedly measuring 101 feet in length ran aground in the River Humber estuary. Another specimen stranded on the west coast of Lewis, Outer Hebrides, Scotland in *c.* 1870 was credited with a length of 105 feet, but the carcase was cut up by the local people before the length could be verified. In both cases the length was probably exaggerated or taken along the curve of the body instead of in a straight line from the tip of the snout to the notch in the flukes. Four blue whales have been stranded on British coasts since 1913. The last occurrence (*c.* 60 feet) was at Wick, Caithness, Scotland on 15 Oct. 1923.

Blue whales inhabit the colder seas and migrate to warmer waters in the winter for breeding. Observations made in the Antarctic in 1947-48 showed that a Blue whale can maintain a speed of 20 knots (23 m.p.h.) for ten minutes when frightened. It has been

The Giraffe of which the tallest example measured 19 feet, which is 4 feet 6 inches higher than a London double decker bus

calculated that a 90 foot blue whale travelling at 20 knots would develop 520 horsepower. New-born calves measure 6.5 to 8.6 m (21 feet 3½ inches to 28 feet 6 inches) in length and weigh up to 3,000 kg. (2.95 tons).

It has been estimated that there were 100,000 blue whales living throughout the oceans in 1930, but that only 7,500 survived (6,500 in the Southern Hemisphere) in 1971.

Deepest dive The greatest *recorded* depth to which a whale has dived is 620 fathoms (3,720 feet) by a 47 foot bull sperm whale (*Physeter catodon*) found with its jaw entangled with a submarine cable running between Santa Elena, Ecuador and Chorillos, Peru on 14 Oct. 1955. At this depth the whale withstood a pressure of 1,680 lb. per square inch of body surface. On 25 August 1969 a Sperm whale was killed 100 miles south of Durban after it had surfaced from a dive lasting 1 hour 52 minutes, and inside its stomach were found two small sharks which had been swallowed about an hour earlier. These were later identified as *Scymnodon sp.*, a species found only on the sea floor. At this point from land the depth of water is in excess of 1,646 fathoms (10,476 feet) for a radius of 30-40 miles, which now suggests that the Sperm whale sometimes may descend to a depth of over 10,000 feet when seeking food.

Largest on land The largest living land animal is the African bush elephant (*Loxodonta africana africana*). The average adult bull stands 10 feet 6 inches at the shoulder and weighs 5.6 tons. The largest specimen ever recorded was a bull shot 48 miles north-west of Macusso, Angola on 13 Nov. 1955. Lying on its side this elephant measured 13 feet 2 inches in a projected line from the highest point of the shoulder to the base of the forefoot, indicating that its standing height must have been about 12 feet 6 inches. Other measurements included an over-all length of 33 feet 2 inches (tip of extended trunk to tip of extended tail) and a maximum bodily girth of 19 feet 8 inches. The weight was estimated at 24,000 lb. (10.7 tons). On 6 March 1959 the mounted specimen was put on display in the rotunda of the U.S. National Museum in Washington, D.C., U.S.A. (see also Shooting, Chapter XII). Another outsized bull elephant known as "Zhulamati" (Taller than the Trees), reputed to stand over 12 feet at the shoulder, was shot in the *Gonare* Zhou area of Nuanetsi, south-eastern Rhodesia in 1967 in mysterious circumstances.

The largest wild mammal in the British Isles, excluding the wild pony (*Equus caballus*) is the Red deer (*Cervus elephus*). A full-grown stag stands 3 feet 8 inches at the shoulder and weighs 230-250 lb. The heaviest ever recorded was probably a stag weighing 462 lb. killed in Glenmore Deer-forest, Inverness, Scotland in 1877. The heaviest park red deer on record was a stag weighing 476 lb. (height at shoulder 4 feet 6 inches) killed at Woburn, Bedfordshire in 1836. The wild population in 1968 was estimated at 180,000 to 185,000.

Tallest The tallest mammal is the giraffe (*Giraffa camelopardalis*). For details see page 26.

Smallest The smallest recorded mammal is Savi's white-**land** toothed pygmy shrew (*Suncus etruscus*), also called the Etruscan shrew, which is found along the coast of the northern Mediterranean and southwards to Cape Province, South Africa. Mature specimens have a head and body length of 36-52 mm. (1.32-2.04 in.), a tail length of 24-29 mm. (0.94-1.14 in.) and weigh between 1.5 and 2.5 grammes (0.052 and 0.09 oz.). The smallest mammal found in the British Isles is the European pygmy shrew (*Sorex minutus*). Mature specimens have a head and body length of 43-64 mm. (1.69-2.5 in.), a tail length of 31-46 mm. (1.22-1.81 in.) and weigh between 2.4 and 6.1 grammes (0.084 and 0.213 oz.).

Marine The smallest totally marine mammal is the Sea otter (*Enhydra lutris*), which is found in coastal waters off California, western Alaska and the Komandorskie and Kurile Islands in the Bering Sea. Adult specimens measure 120-156 cm. (47.24-61.5 in.) in total length and weigh 25-38.5 kg. (55-81.4 lb.).

Rarest The rarest placental mammal in the world is now the Javan rhinoceros (*Rhinoceros sondaicus*). In mid-1970 there were an estimated 28 in the Udjung-Kulon (also called Oedjoeng Kuelon) Reserve of 117 square miles at the tip of western Java, Indonesia, but there may also be a few left in the Tenasserim area on the Thai-Burmese border. Among sub-species, there are believed to be only a dozen specimens of the Javan tiger (*Leo tigris sondaica*) left in the wild, all of them in east Java. The rarest marine mammals are the three species which have been recorded only once. These are: Hose's Sarawak dolphin (*Lagenodelphis hosei*), which is known only from the type specimen collected at the mouth of the Lutong River, Barama, Borneo in 1895; the New Zealand beaked whale (*Tasmacetus shepherdi*), which is known only from the type specimen cast up on Ohawe Beach, New Zealand in 1936; and Longman's beaked whale (*Mesoplodon pacificus*), which is known only from a skull discovered on a Queensland beach in 1926.

The rarest British land mammal is the Pine marten (*Martes martes*), which is found in the highlands of Scotland, particularly in Coille na Glas, Leitire, Ross and Cromarty, and thinly distributed in North Wales and the Scottish border country. The largest specimens measure up to 34 inches from nose to tip of tail (tail 6-9 inches) and weigh up to 4 lb. 6 oz.

Fastest The fastest of all land animals over a short distance **World** (*i.e.* up to 600 yards) is the Cheetah or Hunting leopard (*Acinonyx jubatus*) of the open plains of East Africa, Iran, Turkmenia and Afghanistan, with a probable maximum speed of 60-63 m.p.h. over suitably level ground. Speeds of 71, 84 and even 90 m.p.h. have been claimed for this animal, but these figures must be considered exaggerated. Tests in London in 1937 showed that on an oval greyhound track over 345 yards a female cheetah's average speed over three runs was 43.4 m.p.h. (*cf.* 43.26 m.p.h. for the fastest racehorse), but this specimen was not running flat out. The fastest land animal over a sustained distance (*i.e.* 1,000 yards or more) is the Pronghorn antelope (*Antilocapra americana*) of the western United States. Specimens have been observed to travel at 35 m.p.h. for 4 miles, at 42 m.p.h. for 1 mile and 55 m.p.h. for half a mile. On 14 Aug. 1936 at Spanish Lake, in Lake County, Oregon a hardpressed buck was timed by a car speedometer at 61 m.p.h. over 200 yards.

Britain The fastest British land mammal over a sustained distance is the Roe deer (*Capreolus capreolus*), which can cruise at 25-30 m.p.h. for more than 20 miles, with occasional bursts of up to 40 m.p.h. On 19 Oct. 1970 a frightened runaway Red deer (*Cervus elephus*) registered a speed of 42 m.p.h. on a police radar trap as it charged through a street in Stalybridge, Cheshire.

Slowest The slowest moving land mammal is the Ai or Three-toed sloth (*Bradypus tridactylus*) of tropical America. The usual ground speed is 6 to 8 feet a minute (0.068 to 0.098 m.p.h.), but one mother sloth, speeded up by the calls of her infant, was observed to cover 14 feet in one minute (0.155 m.p.h.). In the trees this speed may be increased to 2 feet a second (1.36 m.p.h.) (*cf.* these figures with the 0.03 m.p.h. of the common garden snail and the 0.17 m.p.h. of the giant tortoise).

Longest No mammal can match the extreme proven age of 113 **lived** years attained by Man (*Homo sapiens*) (see page 16). It is probable that the closest approach is over 90 years by the Killer whale (*Orcinus orca*). A bull with distinctive physical characteristics known as "Old Tom" was seen every winter from 1843 to 1930 in Twofold Bay, Eden, New South Wales, Australia.

The longest lived land mammal, excluding Man, is the Asiatic elephant (*Elephas maximus*). The greatest age that has been verified with reasonable certainty is an estimated 69 years in the case of a cow named "Jessie", who arrived at Taronga Park Zoo in Sydney, New South Wales, Australia in 1882. She was destroyed on 26 Sept. 1939. Her age on arrival was believed to have been 12, but may have been as high as 20. An elephant's life span is indicated by the persistence of its teeth, which generally wear out around the 50-55th year.

Highest The highest living mammal in the world is probably **living** the Yak (*Poephagus grunniens*), the wild ox of Tibet, which has occasionally been found at an altitude of 20,000 feet in the Himalayas.

Largest The largest herds on record were those of the **herds** Springbok (*Antidorcas marsupialis*) during migration across the plains of the western parts of southern Africa in the 19th century. In 1849 John Fraser (later Sir John Fraser) saw a *trekbokken* that took three days to pass through the settlement of Beaufort West, Cape Province. Another herd seen moving near Nels Poortje, Cape Province in 1888 was estimated to contain 100,000,000 head.

Longest and The longest of all mammalian gestation periods is that **shortest** of the Asiatic elephant (*Elephas maximus*), with an **gestation** average of 609 days or just over 20 months and a **periods** maximum of 760 days—more than two and a half times that of a human. The gestation period of the American opossum (*Didelphis marsupialis*), also called the Virginian opossum, is normally 12 to 13 days but may be as short as eight days.

The gestation periods of the rare Water opossum or Yapok (*Chironectes minimus*) of Central and northern South America (average 12-13 days) and the Eastern native cat (*Dasyurus viverrinus*) of Australia (average 12 days) may also be as short as 8 days.

Largest litter The greatest recorded number of young born to a *wild* mammal at a single birth is 32 (not all of which survived) in the case of the Common tenrec (*Centetes ecaudatus*) found in Madagascar and the Comoro Islands. The average litter size is thirteen to fourteen. In March 1961 a litter of 32 was also reported for a House mouse (*Mus musculus*) at the Roswell Park Memorial Institute in Buffalo, N.Y., U.S.A. (average litter size 13-21) (see also Chapter 9 Agriculture Prolificacy records—pigs).

Fastest breeder The Streaked tenrec (*Hemicentetes semispinosus*) of Madagascar is weaned after only 5 days, and females are capable of breeding 3-4 weeks after birth.

Heaviest brain The Sperm whale (*Physeter catodon*) has the heaviest brain of any living animal. The brain of a 49 foot bull processed aboard the Japanese factory ship *Nissin Maru No. I* in the Antarctic on 11 Dec. 1949 weighed 9.2 kg. (20.24 lb.), compared with 6.9 kg. (15.38 lb.) for a 90 foot Blue whale. The heaviest brain recorded for an elephant is 16.5 lb. in the case of an Asiatic bull.

CARNIVORES

Largest Land World The largest living terrestrial carnivore is the Kodiak bear (*Ursus arctos middendorffi*), which is found on Kodiak Island and the adjacent Afognak and Shuyak islands in the Gulf of Alaska, U.S.A. The average adult male has a nose to tail length of 8 feet (tail about 4 inches), stands 52 inches at the shoulder and weighs between 1,050 and 1,175 lb. In 1894 a weight of 1,656 lb. was recorded for a male shot at English Bay, Kodiak Island, whose *stretched* skin measured 13 feet 6 inches from the tip of the nose to the root of the tail. This weight was exceeded by a male in the Cheyenne Mountain Zoological Park, Colorado Springs, Colorado, U.S.A. which scaled 1,670 lb. at the time of its death on 22 Sept. 1955.

Weights in excess of 1,600 lb. have also been reported for the Polar bear (*Ursus maritimus*), but the average adult male weighs 850-900 lb. and measures 7¾ feet nose to tail. In 1960 a polar bear allegedly weighing 2,210 lb. before skinning was shot at the polar entrance to Kotzebue Sound, north-west Alaska. In April 1962 the 11 feet 1½ inch tall mounted specimen was put on display at the Seattle World Fair, Washington, U.S.A.

Britain The largest land carnivore found in Britain is the Common badger (*Meles meles*). The average adult boar measures 2 feet 6 inches in overall length and weighs 25-30 lb. The heaviest ever recorded was a boar weighing 68 lb. killed at Ampleforth, Yorkshire on 10 Feb. 1942.

Sea The largest toothed mammal ever recorded is the Sperm whale (*Physeter catodon*), also called the cachalot. The average adult bull measures 47 feet in length and weighs about 33 tons. The largest accurately measured specimen on record was a 20.7 m (67 feet 11 inches) bull captured near the Kurile Islands in the north-west Pacific by a Russian whaling fleet during the summer of 1950. The whale was not weighed, but it must have scaled about 78 tons. On 25 June 1903 a measurement of 68 feet was reported for a bull killed 60 miles west of Shetland and landed at the Norrona whaling station, but the measurement was believed to have been taken over the curve of the body instead of in a straight line. Eleven cachalots have been stranded on British coasts since 1913. The largest, a bull measuring 61 feet 5 inches, was washed

A group of the largest members of the cat family—long furred Siberian tigers

ashore at Birchington, Kent on 18 Oct. 1914. Another bull measuring 60 feet was stranded at North Roe, Shetland on 30 May 1958.

Smallest The smallest living toothed carnivore is the Least weasel (*Mustela rixosa*), also called the Dwarf weasel, which is circumpolar in distribution. Four races are recognised, the smallest of which is *M.r. pygmaea* of Siberia. Mature specimens have an overall length of 177-207 mm. (6.96-8.14 inches) and weigh between 35 and 70 grammes (1¼ and 2½ oz.).

Largest feline The largest member of the cat family (Felidae) is the long-furred Siberian tiger (*Leo tigris altaica*), also called the Amur or Manchurian tiger. Adult males average 10 feet 4 inches in length (nose to tip of extended tail), stand 39-42 inches at the shoulder and weigh about 585 lb. The heaviest specimen on record was one shot by a German hunter near the Amur river in *c.* 1933 which weighed 350 kg. (770 lb.). In 1970 the total wild population, now strictly protected, was estimated at 160-170 animals.

The average adult African lion (*Leo leo*) measures 9 feet overall, stands 36-38 inches at the shoulder and weighs 400-410 lb. The heaviest wild specimen on record was one weighing 690 lb. shot just outside Hectorspruit in the eastern Transvaal, South Africa in 1936. In July 1970 a weight of 826 lb. was reported for an 11-year-old black-maned lion named "Simba" at Colchester Zoo, Essex. In 1953 a weight of 750 lb. was recorded for an 18-year-old male liger (a lion-tigress hybrid) living in Bloemfontein Zoological Gardens, South Africa.

Smallest The smallest member of the cat family is the Rusty-spotted cat (*Felis rubiginosa*) of southern India and Ceylon. The average adult male has an overall length of 25-28 inches (tail 9-10 inches) and weighs about 3 lb.

PINNIPEDS (Seals, Sea-lions and Walruses)

Largest World The largest of the 32 known species of pinniped is the Southern elephant seal (*Mirounga leonina*), which inhabits the sub-Antarctic islands. Adult bulls average 16½ feet in length (tip of inflated snout to the extremities of the outstretched tail flippers), 12 feet in maximum bodily girth and weigh about 5,000 lb. (2.18 tons). The largest accurately measured specimen on record was a bull killed in Possession Bay, South Georgia on 28 February 1913 which measured 21 feet 4 inches after flensing (original length about 22½ feet) and probably weighed at least 4 tons. There are old records of bulls measuring 25, 30 and even 35 feet, but these figures must be considered exaggerated.

British The largest pinniped among British fauna is the Grey seal (*Halichoerus grypus*), also called the Atlantic seal, which is found mainly on the western coasts of Britain. Adult bulls have been recorded up to 9 feet 6 inches in length and 700 lb. in weight.

Smallest The smallest pinniped is the Baikal seal (*Pusa sibrica*) of Lake Baikal, a large freshwater lake in southern Siberia, U.S.S.R. Adult specimens measure about 4 feet 6 inches from nose to tail and weigh about 140 lb.

Fastest and The highest speed recorded for a pinniped is 25 m.p.h.
deepest for a Californian sea lion (*Zalophus californianus*). The deepest diving pinniped is the Weddell seal (*Laptonychotes weddelli*), which is found along the Antarctic mainland and neighbouring islands. In March 1966 a large bull with a depth-gauge attached to it recorded a dive of 600 m. (1,968 feet) in McMurdo Sound. At this depth the seal withstood a pressure of 875 lb. per square inch of body area. The Harp seal (*Pagophilus groenlandicus*), also called the Greenland seal, may also dive deeper than 1,000 feet.

Longest A female Grey seal (*Halichoerus grypus*) shot at
lived Shunni Wick on Shetland Island on 23 April 1969 was believed to be "at least 46 years old" based on a count of dental annuli.

Rarest The Caribbean or West Indian monk seal (*Monachus tropicalis*) has not been recorded since 1962 when a single specimen was sighted on the beach of Isla Mujueres off the Yucatan Peninsula, Mexico, and the species is now believed to be on the verge of extinction.

BATS
Largest The only flying mammals are bats (order Chiroptera),
World of which there are about 1,000 living species. That with the greatest wing span is probably the Kalong (*Pteropus niger*), a fruit bat found in Indonesia. It has a wing span of up to 170 cm. (5 feet 7 inches) and weighs up to 900 grammes (31.7 oz.).

Some unmeasured specimens of *Pteropus neohibernicus*, another fruit bat found in New Guinea, may possibly reach 6 feet in wing span.

Britain The largest native British bat is the Noctule or Great bat (*Nyctalus noctula*). Mature specimens have a wing span of 353-387 mm. (13.89-15.23 inches) and weigh up to 40 grammes (1.4 oz.). The largest bat found in Britain is the very rare Large mouse-eared bat (*Myotis myotis*). Mature specimens have a wing span of 355-450 mm. (13.97-17.71 inches) and weigh up to 45 grammes (1.58 oz.).

Smallest The smallest known species of bat is the rare Tiny
World pipistrelle (*Pipistrellus nanulus*), found in West Africa. It has a wing span of about 152 mm. (6 inches) and weighs about 2.5 grammes (0.088 oz.), which means it rivals the Etruscan pygmy shrew (*Suncus etruscus*) for the title of "smallest living mammal".

Britain The smallest native British bat is the Pipistrelle (*Pipistrellus pipistrellus*). Mature specimens have a wing span of 200-230 mm. (7.87-9.05 inches) and weigh between 5½ and 7½ grammes (0.19-0.26 oz.).

Fastest The greatest speed attributed to a bat is 32 m.p.h. in the case of a Free-tailed or Guano bat (*Tadarida mexicana*) which flew 31 miles in 58 minutes. This speed is closely matched by the Noctule bat (*Nyctalus noctula*) and the Long-winged bat (*Miniopterus schreibersi*), both of which have been timed at 31 m.p.h.

Rarest The rarest native British bat is Bechstein's bat (*Myotis*
Britain *bechsteini*), which is confined to a small area in southern England, with the New Forest as the main centre of population. There have been about a dozen

records since 1900. In January 1965 fifteen specimens of the Grey long-eared bat (*Plecotus austriacus*) were discovered in the roof of the Nature Conservancy's Research Station at Furzebrook, Dorset. Up to then this species, which is found all over Europe, had only been recorded once in Britain (Hampshire, 1875).

Longest lived The greatest age reliably reported for a bat is "at least 24 years" for a female Little brown bat (*Myotis lucifugus*) found on 30 April 1960 in a cave on Mount Aeolis, East Dorset, Vermont, U.S.A. It had been banded at a summer colony in Mashpee, Massachusetts on 22 June 1937.

Highest Because of their ultrasonic echolocation bats have the
detectable most acute hearing in the animal world. Vampire bats
pitch (*Desmodontidae*) and fruit bats (*Pteropodidae*) can hear frequencies as high as 150,000 cycles per second (*cf.* 15,000 cycles per second for the average adult human).

PRIMATES
Largest The largest living primate is the Eastern lowland gorilla (*Gorilla gorilla graueri*), which inhabits the lowlands of the eastern part of the Upper Congo (Zaïre) and south-western Uganda. An average adult bull stands 5 feet 8 inches tall, measures 58-60 inches around the chest and weighs 360-400 lb. The average adult female stands about 4 feet 7 inches and weighs 170-210 lb. The greatest height (crown to heel) reliably recorded for a gorilla is 6 feet 2 inches for a bull of the Mountain race (*Gorilla g. beringei*) shot in the eastern Congo in *c.* 1921. The heaviest gorilla ever kept in captivity was a bull of the mountain race named "Mbongo", who died in San Diego Zoological Gardens, California, U.S.A. on 15 March 1942. During an attempt to weigh him shortly before his death the platform scales "fluctuated from 645 pounds to nearly 670". This specimen measured 5 feet 7½ inches in height and 69 inches around the chest.

Smallest The smallest known primate is the Lesser mouse lemur (*Microcebus murinus*) of Madagascar. Adult specimens have a head and body length of 125-150 mm. (4.9-5.9 inches) and a tail of about the same length. The weight varies from 45 to 85 grammes (1.58-2.99 oz.).

Longest lived The greatest irrefutable age reported for a primate (excluding humans) is 50 years 3 months for a male chimpanzee (*Pan troglodytes*) named "Heine" at Lincoln Park Zoological Gardens, Chicago, Illinois, U.S.A. He arrived there on 10 June 1924 when aged about 3 years and died on 10 September 1971.

Strength In 1924 "Boma", a 165 lb. male chimpanzee at Bronx Zoo, New York, N.Y., U.S.A. recorded a right-handed pull (feet braced) of 847 lb. on a dynamometer (*cf.* 210 lb. for a man of the same weight). On another occasion an adult female chimpanzee named "Suzette" (estimated weight 135 lb.) at the same zoo registered a right-handed pull of 1,260 lb. while in a rage.

MONKEYS
Largest The largest member of the monkey family is the Mandrill (*Mandrillus sphinx*) of equatorial West Africa. Adult males have an average head and body length of 24-30 inches and weigh 55-70 lb. The greatest reliable weight recorded for a mandrill is 54 kg. (119 lb.) for a specimen which had a head and body length of 36 inches, but unconfirmed weights up to 130 lb. have been reported.

Smallest The smallest known monkey is the Pygmy marmoset (*Cebuella pygmaea*) of Ecuador, northern Peru and western Brazil. Mature specimens have a maximum total length of 304 mm. (12 inches), half of which is tail, and weigh from 49 to 80 grammes (1.7 to 2.81 oz.), which means it rivals the mouse lemur for the title of the smallest living primate (see page 30).

Rarest The rarest monkey is the Hairy-eared mouse lemur (*Cheirogaleus trichotis*) of Madagascar which, until fairly recently, was known only from the type specimen and two skins. In 1966, however, a live example was found on the east coast near Mananara.

Longest lived The greatest reliable age reported for a monkey is *c.* 46 years for a male mandrill (*Mandrillus sphinx*) named "George" of London Zoological Gardens, who died on 14 March 1916. He had originally been imported into Europe in 1869.

Most and most intelligent Of sub-human primates, chimpanzees appear to have the most superior intelligence. Lemurs have less learning ability than any monkey or ape and, in some tests, are inferior to dogs and even pigeons.

RODENTS
Largest The world's largest rodent is the Capybara (*Hydrochoerus hydrocharis*), also called the carpincho or water hog, which is found in tropical South America. Mature specimens have a head and body length of 3¼ to 4½ feet and weigh up to 150 lb. Britain's largest rodent is now the Coypu (*Myocastor coypus*), also known as the Nutria, which was introduced from Argentina by East Anglian fur-breeders in 1927. In 1937 four escaped from a nutria-farm near Ipswich, Suffolk.

Adult males measure 30-36 inches in length (including short tail) and weigh up to 28 lb. in the wild state (40 lb. in captivity).

Smallest The smallest rodent is probably the Old World harvest mouse (*Microymys minutus*), of which the British form measures up to 135 mm. (5.3 inches) in total length and weighs between 4.2 and 10.2 grammes (0.15 to 0.36 of an ounce). In June 1965 it was announced that an even smaller rodent had been discovered in the Asian part of the U.S.S.R. (probably a more diminutive form of *M. minutus*), but further information is lacking.

Rarest The rarest rodent in the world is believed to be the James Island rice rat (*Oryzomys swarthi*), also called Swarth's rice rat. Four specimens were collected on this island in the Galapagos group in 1906, and it was not heard of again until January 1966 when the skull of a recently dead animal was found.

Longest lived The greatest reliable age reported for a rodent is 22 years for an Indian crested porcupine (*Hystrix indica*) which died in Trivandrum Zoological Gardens, south-western India in 1942.

INSECTIVORES
Largest The largest insectivore is the Moon rat (*Echinosorex gymnurus*), also known as Raffles gymnure, which is found in Burma, Thailand, Malaysia, Sumatra and Borneo. Mature specimens have a head and body length of 265-445 mm. (10.43-17.52 inches), a tail measuring 200-210 mm. (7.87-8.26 inches) and weigh up to 1,400 grammes (3.08 lb.).

Smallest The smallest insectivore is Savi's white-toothed shrew (see Smallest mammal, page 28).

Longest lived The greatest reliable age recorded for an insectivore is 6½ years for a Haitian solenodon (*Solenodon paradoxus*) which died in Leipzig Zoological Gardens, Germany in 1950.

ANTELOPES
Largest The largest of all antelopes is the rare Lord Derby eland (*Taurotragus derbianus*), also called the Giant eland, of West and north-central Africa, which may

The largest member of the deer family—the Alaskan moose

surpass 2,000 lb. The Common eland (*T. oryx*) of East and South Africa has the same shoulder height of up to 5 feet 10 inches, but is not quite so massive, although there is one record of a 5 feet 5 inches bull shot in Nyasaland (now Malawi) in *c.* 1937 which weighed 2,078 lb.

Smallest The smallest known antelope is the Royal antelope (*Neotragus pygmaeus*) of West Africa. Mature specimens measure 10-12 inches at the shoulder and weigh only 7-8 lb., which is the size of a large Brown hare (*Lepus europaeus*). The slender Swayne's dik-dik (*Madoqua swaynei*) of Somalia, East Africa weighs only 5-6 lb. when adult, but this species stands about 13 inches at the shoulder.

Rarest The rarest antelope is probably Jentink's duiker (*Cephalopus jentinki*), also known as the Black-headed duiker, which is found only in a restricted area of tropical West Africa. Its total population may be anything from a few dozen to possibly a few hundred.

DEER
Largest The largest deer is the Alaskan moose (*Alces alces gigas*). A bull standing 7 feet 8 inches at the withers and weighing an estimated 1,800 lb. was shot on the Yukon River in the Yukon Territory, Canada in Sept. 1897. Unconfirmed measurements up to 8½ feet at the withers and estimated weights up to 2,600 lb. have been claimed. The record antler span is 78½ inches.

Smallest The smallest deer, and the smallest known ruminant, is the Lesser Malayan chevrotain or Mouse deer (*Tragulus javinicus*) of south-eastern Asia. Adult specimens measure 8-10 inches at the shoulder and weigh 6-7 lb.

Rarest The rarest deer in the world is Fea's muntjac (*Muntiacus feae*), which is known only from two specimens collected on the borders of Tennasserim, Lower Burma and Thailand.

TUSKS
Longest The longest recorded elephant tusks (excluding prehistoric examples) are a pair from the eastern Congo (Zaïre) preserved in the National Collection of Heads and Horns kept by the New York Zoological Society in Bronx Park, New York City, N.Y., U.S.A. The right tusk measures 11 feet 5½ inches along the outside curve and the left 11 feet. Their combined weight is 293 lb. A single tusk of 11 feet 6 inches has been reported, but further details are lacking.

Heaviest The heaviest recorded tusks are a pair in the British Museum of Natural History, London which were collected from an aged bull shot at the foot of Mount

Kilimanjaro, Kenya in 1897. They were sent to London for auction in 1901. The tusks were measured in 1955, when the first was found to be 10 feet 2½ inches long, weighing 226½ lb., and the other 10 feet 5½ inches, weighing 214 lb., giving a combined weight of 440½ lb. The tusks, when fresh, were reportedly 236 lb. and 225 lb. giving a combined weight of 461 lb. A single tusk with an alleged weight of 117 kilogrammes (258 lb.) collected in Dahomey, West Africa was exhibited at the Paris Exposition of 1900.

HORNS

Longest The longest recorded animal horn was one measuring 81¼ inches on the outside curve, with a circumference of 18¼ inches, found on a specimen of domestic Ankole cattle (*Bos taurus*) near Lake Ngami, Botswana (formerly Bechuanaland).

Wild animal The longest horns grown by a wild animal are those of the Pamir argali (*Ovis poli*), also called Marco Polo's argali, a wild sheep found in the mountains of Soviet Central Asia. One of these has been measured at 75 inches along the front curve, with a maximum circumference of 16 inches.

Rhinoceros The longest recorded anterior horn of a rhinoceros is one of 62¼ inches found on a female southern race White rhinoceros (*Ceratotherium simum simum*) shot in South Africa in *c.* 1848. The interior horn measured 22¼ inches. There is also an unconfirmed record of an anterior horn measuring 81 inches.

Blood temperatures The highest mammalian blood temperature is that of the Domestic goat (*Capra hircus*) with an average of 103.8° F (39.9° C), and a normal range of from 101.7° to 105.3° F (38.7° to 40.7° C). The lowest mammalian blood temperature is that of the Spiny anteater (*Tachyglossus aculeatus*), a monotreme found in Australia and New Guinea, with a normal range of 72° to 87° F (22.2° to 24.4° C). The blood temperature of the Golden hamster (*Mesocricetus auratus*) sometimes falls as low as 38.3° F (3.5° C) during hibernation, and an extreme figure of 29.6° F (1.4° C) has been reported for a myotis bat (family Vespertilionidae) during a deep sleep.

Most valuable furs The highest-priced animal pelts are those of the Sea otter (*Enhydra lutris*), also known as the Kamchatka beaver, which fetched up to $2,700 (then £675) before their 55-year-long protection started in 1912. The protection ended in 1967, and at the first legal auction of sea otter pelts at Seattle, Washington, U.S.A. on 31 January 1968 Neiman-Marcus, the famous Dallas department store, paid $9,200 (then £3,832) for four pelts from Alaska. On 30 Jan. 1969 a New York company paid $1,100 (£457) for an exceptionally fine pelt from Alaska. On 26 Feb. 1969 forty selected pelts of the mink-sable cross-breed "Kojah" from the Piampiano Fur Ranch, Zion, Illinois, U.S.A. realised $2,700 (£1,125) in New York City. In May 1970 a Kojah coat costing $125,000 (£52,083) was sold by Neiman-Marcus to Welsh actor Richard Burton for his wife.

Ambergris The heaviest piece of ambergris on record was a 1,003 lb. lump recovered from a Sperm whale (*Physeter catadon*) taken in Australian waters on 3 Dec. 1912 by a Norwegian whaling fleet. It was later sold in London for £23,000.

MARSUPIALS

Largest The largest of all marsupials is the Red kangaroo (*Macropus rufus*) of southern and eastern Australia. Adult males or "boomers" stand 6-7 feet tall, weigh 150-175 lb. and measure up to 8 feet 11 inches in a straight line from the nose to the tip of the extended tail. The Great grey kangaroo (*Macropus giganteus*) of eastern Australia and Tasmania is almost equally as large, and there is an authentic record of a boomer

measuring 8 feet 8 inches from nose to tail (9 feet ? inches along the curve of the body) and weighing 200 lb. The skin of this specimen is preserved in the Australian Museum, Sydney, New South Wales.

Smallest The smallest known marsupial is the Kimberley planigale (*Planigale subtilissima*), which is found only in the Kimberley district of Western Australia. Adult males have a head and body length of 44.5 mm. (1.75 inches), a tail length of 51 mm. (2 inches) and weigh about 4 grammes (0.141 oz.). Females are smaller than males.

Rarest The rarest marsupial is probably the little-known Thylacine (*Thylacinus cynocephalus*), also known as the Tasmanian wolf or tiger, which is now confined to the remoter parts of south-western Tasmania. The last thylacine held in captivity was caught in a trapper's snare in the Florentine Valley a few miles west of Mountain Field Park in 1933 and was exhibited at Hobart Zoo for a few months before it died. On 2 January 1957 it was reported that one had been kept in sight for two minutes and photographed by a helicopter pilot, Captain J. Ferguson, on Birthday Bay Beach, 35 miles south-west of Queenstown. Experts who examined the photograph, however, declared that the animal was a dog. In 1961 a young male was accidentally killed at Sandy Cape on the west coast, and in December 1966 the traces of the lair in which a female and pups had been living were found by zoologists in the boiler of a wrecked ship near Mawbanna on the west coast. On 3 Nov. 1969 the tracks of a thylacine were positively identified in the Cradle Mountain National Park, and other definite sightings have been made since in the Cardigan river area on the north-west coast and the Tooms Lake region.

Highest and longest jumps The greatest measured height cleared by a hunted kangaroo is 10 feet 6 inches over a pile of timber. During the course of a chase in January 1951 a female Red kangaroo (*Macropus rufus*) made a series of bounds which included one of 42 feet. There is also an unconfirmed report of a Great grey kangaroo (*M. conguru*) jumping nearly 13.5 metres (44 feet 8½ inches) on the flat.

HORSES AND PONIES

Largest The heaviest horse ever recorded was a 19½-hand (6 feet 6 inches) pure-bred Belgian stallion named "Brooklyn Supreme" (foaled 12 April 1928) owned by Ralph Fogleman of Callender, Iowa, U.S.A. who weighed 3,200 lb. (1.42 tons) shortly before his death on 6 Sept. 1948 aged 20. The heaviest horse living in Britain today is "Saltmarsh Silver Crest" (foaled 1955), an 18¼-hand (6 feet 1 inch) champion Percheron stallion owned by George E. Sneath of Money Bridge near Pinchbeck, Lincolnshire. He weighed 2,772 lb. in 1967.

The tallest horse ever recorded was "Firpon" which stood 21-hands 1 inch (7 feet 1 inch) and weighed 2,976 lb. He died on a ranch in Argentina on 14 Mar. 1972. The tallest horse recently living in Britain was "Wandle Robert", a Shire gelding owned by Young and Company's Brewery Ltd., Wandsworth, London. He stood 18 hands 1½ inches (6 feet 1½ inches) and weighed 2,360 lb. He died on 11 April 1972.

Smallest The smallest breed of horse are those bred by Julio Falabella at the El Peludo Ranch, Argentina. Adult specimens range from under 12 inches to 42 inches at the shoulder and weigh up to 150 lb. The smallest breed of pony is the Shetland pony, which usually measures 8-10 hands (32-40 inches) and weighs 275-385 lb. In March 1969 a measurement of 3½ hands (14 inches) was reported for a "miniature" Shetland pony named "Midnight", owned by Miss Susan Perry of Worths Circus, Melbourne, Victoria, Australia.

Oldest The greatest reliable age recorded for a horse is 52 years for a 17 hands (5 feet 8 inches) light draught-horse named "Monty", owned by Mrs. Marjorie Cooper of Albury, New South Wales, Australia, who died on 25 Jan. 1970. He was foaled in Wodonga, New South Wales in 1917. The jaws of this horse are now preserved in the School of Veterinary Science at Melbourne University. On 1 Nov. 1969 a mare named "Nellie" died of a heart attack on a farm near Danville, Missouri, U.S.A. reputedly foaled in March 1916 and then aged 53½, but this claim has not yet been fully substantiated. The greatest reliable age recorded for a pony is 54 years for a stallion owned by a farmer in Central France which was still alive in 1919. In June 1970 a Welsh pony living on a farm near Pebbles Bay, Gower Peninsula, South Wales was reported to be 66 years old, but this claim lacks proper documentation.

Strongest The greatest load hauled by a pair of draught horses
draught (probably Shires) was 50 logs comprising 36,055 board-feet of timber (=53.8 tons) on a sledge litter across snow at the Nester Estate, Ewen, Ontonagon County, Michigan, U.S.A. in 1893. In a test at Liverpool Road, Islington, London on 25 Feb. 1924 an 8-year-old draught-horse "Umber" moved a 2 ton 9½ cwt. cart carrying 16 tons of iron on stone setts.

DOGS

Largest The heaviest breed of domestic dog (*Canis familiaris*) is the St. Bernard. The heaviest recorded example was "Schwarzwald Hof Duke", owned by Dr. A.M. Bruner of Oconomowoc, Wisconsin, U.S.A. He was whelped on 8 Oct. 1964 and weighed 295 lb. (21 stone 1 lb.) on 2 May 1969, dying three months later aged 4 years 10 months. The largest St. Bernard ever weighed in Britain was one named "Brandy", owned by Miss Gwendoline L. White of Chinnor, Oxfordshire. He weighed 18 stone 7 lb. (259 lb.) on 11 Feb. 1966, dying 23 days later aged 6½ years. "Montmorency of Hollesley", also known as "Monty", an Old English mastiff owned by Mr. Randolph Simon of Wilmington, Sussex, was also of comparable size. He was whelped on 1 May 1962 and weighed 18 stone 7 lb. in July 1969. In April 1970 his weight was estimated to be 19 stone. He was put to sleep in April 1971 aged 8 years 11 months. The heaviest dog living in Britain today is believed to be a St. Bernard named "Corna-Garth Wildfire", also known as "Shandy", owned by Mr. Charles Langley of Southery, Norfolk and whelped on 30 May 1966. In May 1971 he weighed 18 stone 1 lb. (253 lb.).

Tallest The world's tallest breed of dog is the Irish wolf-hound. The extreme recorded example was "Broadbridge Michael", owned by Mrs. Mary Beynon of Sutton-at-Hone, Kent. He stood 39½ inches at the shoulder in 1928 when aged two years. The tallest dog now living in Britain is "Simon", a five-year-old Great Dane owned by Mr. Terry Hoggarth of North Wingfield, near Chesterfield, Derbyshire, who stands 38½ inches at the shoulder and weighs 16 stone 5 lb. (229 lb.).

Smallest The smallest breed of dog is the Chihuahua from Mexico. New-born pups average 3½-4½ oz. and weigh 2-4 lb. when fully grown, but some "miniature" specimens weigh only 16 oz. The smallest British breed is the Yorkshire terrier, one of which named "Cody Queen of Dudley" was reported in July 1968 to have weighed only 20 oz. at 16 months. In January 1971 a full-grown white toy poodle named "Giles", owned by Mrs. Sylvia Wyse of Bucknall, Staffordshire, stood 4½ inches at the shoulder and weighed 13 oz. Shortly afterwards he was exported to Canada.

Oldest Authentic records of dogs living over 20 years are extremely rare, but even 34 years has been accepted by one authority. The greatest reliable age recorded for a dog is 27 years 3 months for a black Labrador

'Shandy'—Britain's heaviest living dog

gun-dog named "Adjutant", who was whelped on 14 August 1936 and died on 20 Nov. 1963 in the care of his lifetime owner, James Hawkes, a gamekeeper at the Revesby Estate, near Boston, Lincolnshire. Less reliable is a claim of 28 years for an Irish terrier which died in 1951.

Rarest The rarest breed of dog is the Löwchen ("Little Lion"), of which only 52 (45 in Britain, five in West Germany and two in Majorca) were reported in Oct. 1971. The Chinese crested dog (now extinct in China) is also extremely rare. In 1971 the world population was estimated at 55-60 (22 in Britain).

Fastest The fastest breed of untrained dog is the Saluki, also called the Arabian gazelle hound or Persian greyhound. Speeds up to 43 m.p.h. have been claimed, but tests in the Netherlands have shown that it is not as fast as the present-day greyhound which has attained a measured speed of 41.7 m.p.h. on a track.

Largest The largest recorded litter of puppies is one of 23
litter thrown on 11 February 1945 by "Lena", a foxhound bitch owned by Commander W.N. Ely of Ambler, Pennsylvania, U.S.A. On 9 February 1895 a St. Bernard bitch named "Lady Millard", owned by a Mr. Thorpe of Northwold, Norfolk, produced a litter of 21.

Most The greatest sire of all time was the champion
prolific greyhound "Low Pressure", nicknamed "Timmy", whelped in September 1957 and owned by Mrs. Bruna Amhurst of Regent's Park, London. From December 1961 until his death on 27 November 1969 he fathered 2,414 registered puppies, with at least 600 others unregistered.

Most The breed with the most Kennel Club registrations in
popular 1971 was the Alsatian with 13,857. In 1972, Cruft's Dog Show (founded in 1886 for terriers only) had an entry of 6,633, compared with the record entry of 10,650 dogs in 1936 before entrants were restricted to prize winners.

Most In January 1956 Miss Mary de Pledge of Bracknell,
expensive Berkshire, turned down an offer of £10,500 from an American-dog-breeder for her 3½-year-old champion pekingese "Caversham Ku-Ku of Yam". The highest price ever paid for a dog is £2,000 by Mrs. A.H. Hempton in December 1929 for the champion greyhound "Mick the Miller" (whelped in Ireland in June 1926 and died 1939). In 1947 a figure of £2,000 was also quoted for a champion English bulldog sold to an American breeder, but further details are lacking.

The world's strongest dog—Nelson who pulled 3,260 lb. in 1971

"Top dog" The greatest altitude attained by an animal is 1,050 miles by the Samoyed husky bitch fired as a passenger in Sputnik II on 3 Nov. 1957. The dog was variously named "Kudryavka" (feminine form of "Curly"), "Limonchik" (diminutive of lemon), "Malyshka", "Zhuchka" or by the Russian breed name for husky, "Laika".

Highest and longest jump It has been claimed that a male bouvier or Flanders cattle dog weighing 140 lb. has been trained to scale a 16 foot wall at Stormville, New York, U.S.A. in 1971.

Strongest The greatest load ever shifted by a dog is 3,260 lb. pulled over 15 feet in under 90 secs. in accordance with international rules by a champion Newfoundland dog "Newfield's Nelson" aged 6½ and weighing 164 lb. on 10 Oct. 1970 at Bethell, Washington, U.S.A. owned by Mr. and Mrs. Allen A. Wolman. The record time for the annual 15 mile dog sled race at Whitehorse, Yukon Territory, Canada is 59 mins. 33 secs. by the driver "Charlie", 33 in March 1969.

Ratting The greatest ratter of all time was Mr. James Searle's bull terrier bitch "Jenny Lind", who killed 500 rats in 1 hour 30 minutes at "The Beehive", Old Crosshall Street, Liverpool on 12 July 1853. Another bull terrier named "Jacko", owned by Mr. Jemmy Shaw, was credited with killing 1,000 rats in 1 hour 40 minutes, but the feat was performed over a period of ten weeks in batches of 100 at a time. The last 100 were accounted for in 5 minutes 28 seconds in London on 1 May 1862.

Tracking The greatest tracking feat on record was performed by a Doberman named "Sauer", trained by Detective-Sergeant Herbert Kruger. In 1925 he tracked a stock-thief 100 miles across the Great Karroo, South Africa by scent alone. In Jan. 1969 an Alsatian bitch was reported to have followed her master 745 miles from Brindisi to Milan, Italy in four months. The dog's owner had left her behind when he went on a visit. An alsatian's sense of smell is one million times better than man's.

CATS

Heaviest The heaviest domestic cat *(Felis catus)* on record was probably a female tabby named "Gigi" (1959-72), owned by Miss Ann Clark of Carlisle, Cumberland. The weight of this cat normally fluctuated between 37 and 40 lb., but in April 1970 she weighed 42 lb. and had a maximum bodily girth of 37 inches. The average weight for an adult cat is 11 lb.

Oldest Cats are longer-lived animals than dogs and there are a number of authentic records over 20 years. The oldest cat ever recorded was probably the tabby "Puss", owned by Mrs. T. Holway of Clayhidon, Devon who celebrated his 36th birthday on 28 November 1939. A more recent and better-documented case was that of the female tabby "Ma", owned by Mrs. Alice St. George Moore of Drewsteignton, Devon. She was put to sleep on 5 November 1957 aged 34. According to the American Feline Society a cat living in Hazleton, Pennsylvania celebrated its 37th birthday on 1 November 1958 but it was later discovered by the Society that two or more cats were involved. The oldest cat living in Britain today is believed to be a ginger tom named "Sandy" (b. 7 June 1943), owned by Mrs. Elsie Emmett of Isleworth, Middlesex, who is 29. "Flip", a black and white female Manx owned by Mrs. Rosemary Morley of Brighton, Sussex celebrated her 27th birthday in November 1971 (a female tabby named "Buncle", also owned by Mrs. Morley, died on 13 February 1971 aged 26 years 2 months).

Largest litter The largest live litter ever recorded was one of 13 kittens born on 13 April 1969 to "Boccaccio Blue Danielle", a one-year-old blue-pointed Siamese cat owned by Mrs. Helen J. Coward of Klemzig, South Australia. In July 1970 a litter of 19 kittens (four incompletely formed) was reportedly born by Caesarean section to "Tarawood Antigone", a brown Burmese owned by Mrs. Valerie Gane of Church Westcote, Kingham, Oxfordshire, but this claim has not yet been fully substantiated.

Most prolific A cat named "Dusty", aged 17, living in Bonham, Texas, U.S.A., gave birth to her 420th kitten on 12 June 1952.

Greatest fall On 7 March 1965 "Pussycat", a tom owned by Miss Anne Walker of Maida Vale, London slipped and fell 120 feet from the balcony of his mistress' 11th storey flat. The cat landed unhurt.

"Thumper", a 2½-year-old tabby owned by Mrs. Reg Buckett of Westminster, London was rescued from a lift shaft on 29 March 1964 after being trapped for 52 days.

Richest and most valuable Dr. William Grier of San Diego, California, U.S.A. died in June 1963 leaving his entire estate of $415,000 to his two 15-year-old cats "Hellcat" and "Brownie". When the cats died in 1965 the money went to the George Washington University in Washington, D.C. In 1967 Miss Elspeth Sellar of Grafham, Surrey turned down an offer of 2,000 guineas (£2,100) from an American breeder for her champion copper-eyed white Persian tom "Coylum Marcus" (b. 28 March 1965).

Rarest breed The rarest of the 52 recognised breeds of cat in Britain is the Red self Persian or Long-haired red self.

Ratting and mousing A five-month-old tabby kitten named "Peter" living at Stonehouse railway station, Gloucestershire, killed 400 rats during a four-week period in June-July 1938. Many of the kitten's victims seemed almost as large as itself. The greatest mouser on record was a tabby named "Mickey", owned by Shepherd & Sons Ltd. of Burscough, Lancashire which killed more than 22,000 mice during 23 years with the firm. He died in November 1968.

Cat population The largest cat population is that of the U.S.A. with 28,000,000. Of Britain's cat population of 6,000,000, an estimated 100,000 are "employed" by the Civil Service.

RABBITS

Largest The largest breed of domestic rabbit (*Oryctolagus cuniculus*) is the Flemish giant, which has an average toe to toe length of 36 in. when fully extended and weighs 12-14 lb. The heaviest recorded specimen was

A marabou stork which rivals the albatross for the longest wing span of any bird.

a male named "Floppy" who weighed 25 lb. shortly before his death in June 1963 aged eight. In May 1971 a weight of 25 lb. was also reported for a four-year-old Norfolk Star named "Chewer", owned by Mr. Edward Williams of Attleborough, Norfolk.

Oldest The greatest reliable age recorded for a domestic rabbit is 18 years for a doe which was still alive in 1947. A buck rabbit named "Blackie" owned by Mrs. H. H. Chivers of Brixham, Devon died on 13 March 1971 aged 16 years 3 months.

Most prolific The most prolific domestic breed is the Norfolk Star. Females produce 9 to 10 litters a year, each containing about 10 young (*cf.* five litters and three to seven young for the wild rabbit).

2. BIRDS (*Aves*)

Largest The largest living bird is the North African ostrich
Ratite (*Struthio camelus camelus*), which is found in reduced numbers south of the Atlas Mountains from Upper Senegal and Niger across to the Sudan and central Ethiopia. Male examples of this flightless or ratite bird have been recorded up to 9 feet in height and 345 lb. in weight.

Carinate The heaviest flying bird or carinate is the Kori bustard or Paauw (*Otis kori*) of East and South Africa. Cock birds weighing up to 40 lb. have been shot in South Africa, and one enormously fat specimen killed in the western Transvaal in *c.* 1892 with a wing span of 8 ft. 4 in. was estimated to weigh 54 lb. The Mute swan (*Cygnus olor*), which is resident in Britain, also exceeds 40 lb. on occasion, and there is a record from Poland of a cob weighing 22.5 kg. (49.5 lb.). The heaviest flying bird of prey is the Andean condor (*Vultur gryphus*). Adult males average 20-25 lb., but one specimen shot on San Gallan Island off the coast of Peru in 1919 weighed 26½ lb.

Largest The Wandering albatross (*Diomedea exulans*) of the
wing span southern oceans has the largest wing span of any living bird, adult males averaging 10 feet 2 inches with wings tightly stretched. The largest recorded specimen was a male measuring 11 feet 10 inches caught by banders in Western Australia in *c.* 1957, but some unmeasured birds may reach or possibly just exceed 12 feet. This size is closely matched by the Andean condor (*Vultur gryphus*). Adult males commonly have a wing span of 9 feet 3 inches, and some specimens exceed 10 feet. One bird killed in the Ilo Valley, southern Peru in

c. 1714 allegedly measured 12 feet 3 inches, but this figure must be considered excessive. In extreme cases the wing span of the Marabou stork (*Leptoptilus crumeniferus*) may also exceed 10 feet (average span 9 feet), and there is an unconfirmed record of 13 feet 4 inches for a specimen shot in Central Africa in the 1930s. In August 1939 a wing span of 12 feet was recorded for a Mute swan (*Cygnus olor*) named "Guardsman" (d. 1945) at the famous swannery at Abbotsbury, near Weymouth, Dorset. The average span is 8½-9 feet.

Smallest The smallest bird in the world is the bee hummingbird
World (*Mellisuga helenae*), also known as Helena's hummingbird or "the fairy hummer", found in Cuba. An average adult male has a wing-span measurement of 28.4 mm. (1.11 in.), a total length of 58 mm. (2.28 in.) and weighs about 2 grammes (0.070 oz.). This means it is lighter than a Sphinx moth which weighs about 0.080 oz. Adult females are slightly larger than males. The bee hummingbird (*Acestruta bombus*) of Ecuador is about the same size as *M. helenae*, but is slightly heavier.

United The smallest resident British bird is the Goldcrest
Kingdom (*Regulus regulus*), also known as the Golden-crested wren or Kinglet. Adult specimens measure 90 mm. (3.5 in.) in total length and weigh between 3.8 and 4.5 grammes (0.108 and 0.127 oz.). The rare Firecrest (*Regulus ignicapillus*) is of almost equal diminutiveness.

Most The most abundant species of bird is the chicken, the
abundant domesticated form of the wild Red jungle fowl (*Gallus gallus*) of south-east Asia. There are believed to be about 3,500,000,000 in the world, or nearly one chicken for every member of the human race. The fowl stock in Britain was estimated at 190,000,000 in 1971, producing 270,000,000 chicks annually. The most abundant species of wild bird is believed to be the Starling (*Sturnus vulgaris*) with an estimated world population of well over 1,000,000,000. The most abundant, and also the smallest, of all sea birds is Wilson's petrel (*Oceanites oceanicus*).

The most abundant species of bird ever recorded was the Passenger pigeon (*Ectopistes migratoria*) of North America. It has been estimated that there were between 5,000,000,000 and 9,000,000,000 of these birds before 1840. Thereafter the birds were killed in vast numbers, and the last recorded specimen, a female named "Martha", died in Cincinnati Zoological Gardens, Ohio, U.S.A. at 1 p.m. Eastern standard time on 1 Sept. 1914 aged about 12 years. The mounted specimen is now on display in the U.S. National Museum, Washington, D.C.

United Kingdom The commonest wild breeding birds in Great Britain are the Blackbird (*Turdus merula*) and the Chaffinch (*Fringilla coelebs*), both of which have an estimated population of 10,000,000. It was estimated in 1967 that 250,000 pigeon fanciers owned an average of 40 racing pigeons per loft, making a population of *c*. 10,000,000 in Great Britain.

Rarest World Perhaps the best claimants to this title would be the ten species last seen in the 19th century but still just possibly extant. They are the New Caledonian lorikeet (*Vini diadema*) (New Caledonia *ante* 1860); the Himalayan mountain quail (*Ophrysia superciliosa*) (eastern Punjab, 1868); Forest Spotted Owlet (*Athene blewitti*) (Central India, *c*. 1872); the Samoan wood rail (*Pareudiastes pacificus*) (Savaii, Samoa, 1873); the Fiji bar-winged rail (*Rallina poecilopterus*) (Ovalau and Viti Levu, 1890); the Kona "finches" (*Psittirostrata flaviceps* and *P. palmeri*) (Kona, Hawaii, 1891 and 1896); the Akepa (*Loxops coccinea*) (Oahu, Hawaii, 1893); the Kona "finch" (*Psittirostrata kona*) (Kona, Hawaii, 1894) and the Mamo (*Drepanis pacifica*) (Hawaii, 1898). The Puerto Rican nightjar (*Caprimulgus ruficollis*), believed extinct since 1888, was rediscovered in 1962, and the Ivory-billed woodpecker (*Campephilus principalis*) has been confirmed as surviving since 1963.

United Kingdom There are 36 species of bird (8 of them unconfirmed) which have been recorded only once in the British Isles. That which has not recurred for the longest period is the black-capped petrel (*Pterodroma hasitata*), also known as the Diablotin. A specimen was caught alive on a heath at Southacre, near Swaffham, Norfolk in March or April 1850. The most tenuously established British bird is now the Snowy owl (*Nyctea scandiaca*), now found only on Fetlar in the Shetland Islands. In 1971 only one pair was observed.

Longest lived The greatest irrefutable age reported for any bird is 68 years in the case of a female European eagle-owl (*Bubo bubo*) which was still alive in 1899. Other records which are regarded as *probably* reliable include 73 years (1818-91) for a Greater sulphur-crested cockatoo (*Cacatua galerita*); 72 years (1797-1869) for an African grey parrot (*Psittacus erithacus*); 70 years (1770-1840) for a Mute swan (*Cygnus olor*) and 69 years for a Raven (*Corvus corax*). An Egyptian vulture (*Neophron percnopterus*) which died in the menagerie at Schönbrunn, Vienna, Austria in 1824 was stated to have been 118 years old, but the menagerie was not founded until 1752. On 22 March 1968 an Asiatic white crane (*Megalornis leucogeranus*) died in the National Zoological Gardens, Washington, D.C., U.S.A. after spending 61 years 8 months 25 days in captivity.

Fastest flying The fastest flying bird is the spine-tailed swift (*Chaetura caudacuta*). For details see page 26.

The bird which presents the hunter with the greatest difficulty is the Spur-wing goose (*Plectropterus gambiensis*), with a recorded air speed of 88 m.p.h. in level flight.

The fastest recorded wing beat of any bird is that of the hummingbird (*Heliactin cornuta*) of tropical South America with a rate of 90 beats a second. Large vultures (family Vulturidae) can soar for hours without beating their wings, but sometimes exhibit a flapping rate as low as one beat per second.

Fastest swimmer The fastest swimming bird is the Gentoo penguin (*Pygoscelis papua*). In January 1913 a small group were timed at 10 metres a second (22.3 m.p.h.) under

water near the Bay of Isles, South Georgia. This is a respectable flying speed for some birds.

Longest flights The greatest distance covered by a ringed bird during migration is 14,000 miles by an Arctic tern (*Sterna paradisaea*), which was banded as a nestling on 5 July 1955 in the Kandalaksha Sanctuary on the White Sea coast and was captured alive by a fisherman 8 miles south of Fremantle, Western Australia on 16 May 1956.

Highest flying The celebrated example of a skein of 17 Egyptian geese (*Alopochen aegptiacus*) photographed by an astronomer at Dehra Dun, northern India on 17 Sept. 1919 as they crossed the sun at an estimated height of between 11 and 12 miles (58,080-63,360 ft.), has been discredited by experts.

The highest acceptable altitude recorded for a bird is 8,200 metres (26,902 ft.) for a small number of Alpine choughs (*Pyrhocorax graculus*) which followed the successful British expedition led by Col. John Hunt up Mount Everest in May 1953, but their take-off point may have been as high as 20,000 feet. On three separate occasions in 1959 a radar station in Norfolk picked up flocks of small passerine night migrants flying in from Scandinavia at heights up to 21,000 feet. They were probably Warblers (*Sylviidae*), Chats (*Turnidae*) and Flycatchers (*Muscicapidae*).

Most airborne The most "airborne" of all birds is the common swift (*Apus apus*) which remains aloft for at least nine months of the year.

Most acute vision Tests have shown that under favourable conditions the Long-eared owl (*Asio otus*) and the Barn owl (*Tyto alba*) can swoop on targets from a distance of 6 feet or more in an illumination of only 0.00000073 of a foot candle (equivalent to the light from a standard candle at a distance of 1,170 ft.). This acuity is 50-100 times as great as that of human night vision. In good light and against a contrasting background a Golden eagle (*Aquila chrysaetos*) can detect an 18-inch long hare at a range of 2,150 yards (possibly even 2 miles).

Eggs Largest The largest egg produced by any living bird is that of the ostrich (*Struthio camelus*). The average example measures 6-8 inches in length, 4 to 6 inches in diameter and weighs 3.63 to 3.88 lb. (equal to the volume of two dozen hen's eggs). It requires about 40 minutes for boiling. The shell is one-sixteenth of an inch thick and can support the weight of an 18 stone (252 lb.) man. The largest egg laid by any bird on the British list is that of the Mute swan (*Cygnus olor*), which measures from 4.3 to 4.9 inches in length and between 2.8 and 3.1 inches in diameter. The weight is 12-13 oz.

Smallest The smallest egg laid by any bird is that of the bee hummingbird (*Mellisuga helenae*), the world's smallest bird (see page 35). A specimen collected at Boyate, Santiago de Cuba on 8 May 1906 and later presented to the U.S. National Museum, Washington, D.C., U.S.A. measures 11.4 mm. (0.45 in.) in length, 8 mm. (0.32 in.) in diameter and weighs 0.5 grammes (0.176 oz.). The smallest egg laid by a bird on the British list is that of the Goldcrest (*Regulus regulus*), which measures 12.2-14.5 mm. (0.48-0.57 in.) in length and between 9.4 and 9.9 mm. (0.37 and 0.39 in.) in diameter.

Incubation Longest and shortest The longest incubation period is that of the Wandering albatross (*Diomedea exulans*), with a normal range of 75 days to 82 days. The shortest incubation period is probably that of the Hawfinch (*Coccothraustes coccothraustes*), which is only 9-10 days. The idlest of cock birds are hummingbirds (family Trochilidae), among whom the hen bird does 100 per cent of the incubation, whereas the female Common

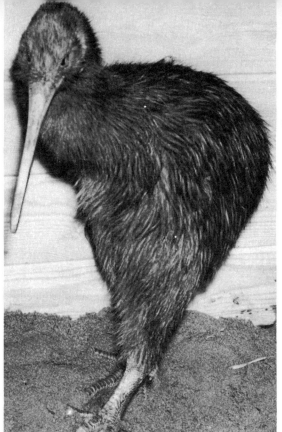

The kiwi from New Zealand in which species the female delegates the entire incubation process to the male.

by Mrs. Lyn Logue of Golders Green, London, which has won the "Best talking parrot-like bird" title at the National Cage and Aviary Bird Show in London for the seven years 1965-71. Prudle was taken from a nest in a tree about to be felled at Jinja, Uganda in 1958.

3. REPTILES *(Reptilia)*
(Crocodiles, snakes, turtles, tortoises and lizards.)

Largest and heaviest The largest reptile in the world is the Estuarine or Salt-water crocodile (*Crocodylus porosus*) of southeast Asia, northern Australia, New Guinea, the Philippines and the Solomon Islands. Adult bulls average 12-14 feet in length and scale about 1,100 lb. In 1823 a notorious man-eater measuring 27 feet in length and weighing an estimated 2 tons was shot at Jala Jala on Luzon Island in the Philippines after terrorising the neighbourhood for many years. Its skull, the largest on record if we exclude fossil remains, is now preserved in the Museum of Comparative Zoology at Harvard University, Cambridge, Massachusetts, U.S.A. Another outsized example with a reputed length of 33 feet and a maximum bodily girth of 13 feet 8 inches was shot in the Bay of Bengal in 1840, but the dimensions of its skull (preserved in the British Museum of Natural History, London) suggest that it must have come from a crocodile measuring about 24 feet. In April 1966 an estuarine crocodile measuring 20 feet 9 inches in length and weighing more than a ton was shot at Liaga, on the south-east coast of Papua.

Smallest The smallest known species of reptile is believed to be *Sphaerodactylus parthenopiom*, a tiny gecko found only on the island of Virgin Gorda, one of the British Virgin Islands, in the West Indies. It is known only from 15 specimens, including some gravid females found between 10 and 16 Aug. 1964. The three largest females measured 18 mm. (0.71 in.) from snout to vent, with a tail of approximately the same length. It is possible that another gecko, *Sphaerodactylus elasmorhynchus*, may be even smaller. The only known specimen was an apparently mature female with a snout-vent length of 17 mm. (0.67 in.) and a tail the same measurement found on 15 March 1966 among the roots of a tree in the western part of the Massif de la Hotte in Haiti. A species of dwarf chameleon, *Evoluticauda tuberculata* found in Madagascar, and known only from a single specimen, has a snout-vent length of 18 mm. (0.71 in.) and a tail length of 14 mm. (0.55 in.). Chameleons, however, are more bulky than geckos, and it is not yet known if this specimen was fully grown.

The smallest reptile found in Britain is the Viviparous or Common lizard (*Lacerta vivipara*). Adult specimens have an overall length of 108-178 mm. (4.25-7in.).

Fastest The highest speed measured for any reptile on land is 18 m.p.h. for a Six-lined racerunner (*Cnemidophorus sexlineatus*) pursued by a car near McCormick, South Carolina, U.S.A. in 1941. The highest speed claimed for any reptile in water is 22 m.p.h. by a frightened Pacific leatherback turtle (see below).

Lizards Largest The largest of all lizards is the Komodo monitor or Ora (*Varanus komodoensis*), a dragonlike reptile found on the Indonesian islands of Komodo, Rintja, Padar and Flores. Adult males average 8 feet in length and weigh 175-200 lb. Lengths up to 23 feet (*sic*) have been quoted for this species, but the largest specimen to be accurately measured was a male presented to an American zoologist in 1928 by the Sultan of Bima which taped 3.05 metres (10 ft. 0.8 in.). In 1937 this animal was put on display in St. Louis Zoological Gardens, Missouri, U.S.A. for a short period. It then measured 10 ft. 2 in. in length and weighed 365 lb.

kiwi (*Apteryx australis*) leaves this entirely to the male for 75 to 80 days.

Feathers **Longest** The longest feathers grown by any bird are those of the cock Long-tailed fowl or Onagadori (a strain of *Gallus gallus*) bred at Kochi in Shikoku, Japan which have tail coverts measuring up to 20 feet in length.

Most In a series of "feather counts" on various species of bird a Whistling swan (*Cygnus columbianus*) was found to have 25,216 feathers. A Ruby-throated hummingbird (*Archilochus colubris*) had only 940, although hummingbirds have more feathers per area of body surface than any other living bird.

Earliest and latest cuckoo It is unlikely that the Cuckoo (*Cuculus canorus*) has ever been *heard and seen* in Britain earlier than 10 March, on which date one was observed in Devon in 1884 and another in Wiltshire in 1938. The two latest dates are 16 Dec. 1912 at Anstey's Cove, Torquay, Devon and 26 Dec. 1897 or 1898 in Cheshire.

DOMESTICATED BIRDS
Turkey Heaviest The greatest *live* weight recorded for a Turkey (*Meleagris gallapavo*) is 70 lb., reported in December 1966 for a White Holland stag named "Tom" owned by a breeder in California, U.S.A. The U.S. record for a dressed bird is 68½ lb. in 1953. The British record for a *clean plucked* turkey is 65 lb. 4 oz. for a Triple Six stag shown at the International Poultry Show in London on 14 Dec. 1971. It was bred and reared by Hugh Arnold of British United Turkeys Ltd. at Hockenhull Hall Farm, Tarvin, Cheshire and weighed about 68 lb. when alive. Turkeys were introduced into Britain *via* Germany from Mexico in 1549.

Longest lived The budgerigar has an average life span of 6 to 8 years. A specimen named "Pretty Boy" (hatched Nov. 1948), owned by Mrs. Anne Dolan of Loughton, Essex, died on 25 February 1972 aged 23 years 3 months. The largest caged budgerigar (*Melopsittacus undulatus*) population is probably that of the United Kingdom with an estimated 3½-4 million. In 1956 the population was about 7 million. This small parakeet is found wild in Australia.

Most talkative The world's most talkative bird is a male African grey parrot (*Psittacus erythacus*) named "Prudle", owned

Oldest The greatest age recorded for a lizard is more than 54 years for a male Slow worm (*Anguis fragilis*) kept in the Zoological Museum in Copenhagen, Denmark from 1892 until 1946.

Chelonians
Largest The largest of all chelonians is the Pacific leatherback turtle (*Dermochelys coriacea schlegelii*). The average adult measures 6-7 feet in overall length (length of carapace 4-5 ft.) and weighs between 660 and 800 lb. The greatest weight reliably recorded is 1,908 lb. for a specimen captured off Monterey, California, U.S.A. in 1961 which is now on permanent display at the Wharf Aquarium, Fisherman's Wharf, Monterey. The largest chelonian found in British waters is the Atlantic leatherback turtle (*Dermochelys coriacea coriacea*). One weighing 997 lb. and measuring more than 7 feet in length was caught by a French fishing trawler in the English Channel on 8 May 1958, and another specimen reportedly weighing 1,345 lb. was caught by a fishing vessel in the North Sea on 6 Oct. 1951.

The largest living tortoise is *Geochelone gigantea* of Aldabra Island in the Indian Ocean. Adult males sometimes exceed 500 lb. in weight, and a specimen weighing 900 lb. was collected in 1847.

Longest
lived Tortoises are the longest lived of all vertebrates. (See Animal Kingdom Records above). Other reliable records over 100 years include a Common box tortoise (*Testudo carolina*) of 138 years and a European pond-tortoise (*Emys orbicularis*) of 120+ years. The greatest proven age of a continuously observed tortoise is 116+ years for a Mediterranean spur-thighed tortoise (*Testudo graeca*) which died in Paignton Zoo, Devon in 1957. On 19 May 1966 the death was reported of "Tu'imalilia" or "Tui Malela", the famous but much battered Madagascar radiated tortoise (*Testudo radiata*) reputedly presented to the King of Tonga by Captain James Cook in 1773, but this record lacks proper documentation.

Slowest
moving Tests on a giant tortoise (*Geochelone gigantea*) in Mauritius show that even when hungry and enticed by a cabbage it cannot cover more than 5 yards in a minute (0.17 m.p.h.) on land. Over longer distances its speed is greatly reduced.

SNAKES
Longest The longest (and the heaviest) of all snakes is the
World Anaconda (*Eunectes murinus*) of tropical South America. The largest accurately measured anaconda on record was probably a specimen shot on the upper Orinoco River, eastern Colombia in 1944 which later recovered and escaped. Another anaconda killed on the lower Rio Guaviare, in south-eastern Colombia in November 1956 reportedly measured 10.25 metres (33 feet 7½ inches), but nothing of this snake was preserved. In 1912 a Reticulated python (*Python reticulatus*) measuring 10 metres (32 feet 9½ in.) was killed near a mining camp on the north coast of Celebes in the Malay Archipelago. An African rock python (*Python sebae*) measuring 9.81 metres (32 ft. 2¼ in.) was killed in the grounds of a school at Bingerville, Ivory Coast in 1932. The longest snake ever kept in a zoo was probably "Colossus", a female reticulated python (*Python reticulatus*), who died of reptilian tuberculosis on 15 April 1963 in the Highland Park Zoological Gardens, Pittsburgh, Pennsylvania, U.S.A. She measured 28 feet 6 inches on 15 Nov. 1956 and was probably at least 29 feet at the time of her death. Her maximum girth before a feed was measured at 36 inches on 2 March 1955 and she weighed 320 lb. (22 stone 12 lb.) on 12 June 1957. A long-standing reward of $5,000 (now £1,923) offered by the New York Zoological Society in Bronx Park, New York City, U.S.A. for the skin or vertebral column of a snake measuring more than 30 feet has never been collected.

The giant tortoise (Geochelone gigantea) from Aldabra Island, Indian Ocean, with a smaller relative. Males may weigh up to 900 lb.

British The longest snake found in Britain is the Grass snake (*Natrix natrix*), which is found throughout southern England, parts of Wales and in Dumfries-shire, Scotland. One female killed in the New Forest, Hampshire, measured 1.7 metres (5 ft. 6.9 in.).

Shortest The shortest known snake is the thread snake (*Leptotyphlops bilineata*), which is found on the islands of Martinique, Barbados and St. Lucia in the West Indies. It has a maximum recorded length of 11.9 centimetres (4.7 in.).

Heaviest The heaviest snake is the anaconda (*Eunectes murinus*) (see above). The 37½ foot specimen shot in eastern Colombia in 1944 probably weighed nearly 1,000 lb. The heaviest venomous snake is the Eastern diamond-back rattlesnake (*Crotalus adamanteus*) of the south-eastern United States. One specimen measuring 7 ft. 9 in. in length weighed 34 lb. Less reliable lengths up to 8 ft. 9 in. and weights up to 40 lb. have been reported. A 15 ft. 7 in. King cobra (*Ophiophagus hannah*) captured alive on Singapore Island and presented to Raffles Museum weighed 26½ lb.

The longest venomous snake in the world, the Hamadryad of South East Asia. This specimen at 16½ feet is 4 feet longer than the average.

Venomous The longest venomous snake in the world is the King
Longest and cobra (*Ophiophagus hannah*), also called the Hama-
Shortest dryad, of south-east Asia and the Philippines. A specimen collected near Fort Dickson in the state of Negri Sembilan, Malaya in April 1937 grew to 18 feet 9 inches in London Zoo. The shortest venomous snake is probably Peringuey's adder (*Bitis peringueyi*) of south-west Africa which has a maximum recorded length of 12 inches.

Oldest The greatest irrefutable age recorded for a snake is 34 years 1 month in the case of an Indian python

(*Python molurus*) at Philadelphia Zoological Gardens, Philadelphia, Pennsylvania, U.S.A. which was still alive on 1 Jan. 1971.

Fastest moving The fastest moving land snake is probably the slender Black mamba *(Dendroaspis polylepis)*. On 23 April 1906 an angry black mamba was timed at a speed of 7 m.p.h. over a measured distance of 47 yards near Mbuyuni on the Serengeti Plains, Kenya. Stories that black mambas can overtake galloping horses (maximum speed 43.26 m.p.h.) are wild exaggerations, though a speed of 15 m.p.h. may be possible for short bursts over level ground. The British grass snake (*Natrix natrix*) has a maximum speed of 4.2 m.p.h.

Most venomous Authorities differ on which of the world's 300 venomous snakes possesses the most toxic venom. That of the Tiger snake (*Notechis scutatus*) of southern Australia is perhaps matched by the Javan krait (*Bungarus javincus*), and more likely by the Beaked sea snake (*Enhydrina schistosa*) of the Indo-Pacific region. The beaked sea snake has a minimal lethal dose for Man of only 1.5 mg. (1/22,000th of an ounce). It is estimated that between 30,000 and 40,000 people die from snakebite each year, 75 per cent of them in densely populated India. Burma has the highest mortality rate with 15.4 deaths per 100,000 population per annum.

Britain The only venomous snake in Britain is the Adder (*Vipera berus*). Since 1890 nine people have died after being bitten by this snake, including five children. The most recently recorded death was on 13 May 1957 when a 14-year-old boy was bitten on the right hand at Carey Camp, near Wareham, Dorset and died three hours later. The longest specimen recorded was one of 38 inches killed on Walberswick Common, Suffolk on 8 July 1971.

Longest fangs The longest fangs of any snake are those of the Gaboon viper (*Bitus gabonica*) of tropical Africa. In a 6 ft. long specimen they measured 50 mm. (1.96 in.). On 12 Feb. 1963 a Gaboon viper bit itself to death in the Philadelphia Zoological Gardens, Philadelphia, Pennsylvania, U.S.A. Keepers found the dead snake with its fangs deeply embedded in its own back.

4. AMPHIBIANS *(Amphibia)*

Largest World The largest species of amphibian is the Chinese giant salamander (*Megalobatrachus davidianus*), which lives in the cold mountain streams and marshy areas of north-eastern, central and southern China. The average adult measures 1 metre (39.37 in.) in total length and weighs 11-13 kg. (24.2 to 28.6 lb.). One huge individual collected in Kweichow (Guizhou) Province in southern China in the early 1920s measured 5 feet in total length and weighed nearly 100 lb. The Japanese giant salamander (*Megalobatrachus japonicus*) is slightly smaller, but one captive specimen weighed 40 kg. (88 lb.) when alive and 45 kg. (99 lb.) after death, the body having absorbed water from the aquarium.

Britain The largest British amphibian is the Warty or Great crested newt (*Triturus cristatus*). One specimen collected at Hampton, Middlesex measured 16.2 cm. (6.37 in.) in total length, and another one collected at Dunbar, East Lothian, Scotland weighed 10.6 grammes (0.37 oz.).

Newt The largest newt in the world is the Pleurodele or Ribbed newt (*Pleurodeles waltl*), which is found in Morocco and on the Iberian Peninsula. Specimens measuring up to 40 cm. (15.74 in.) in total length and weighing over 1 lb. have been reliably reported.

Frog World The largest known frog is the rare Goliath frog (*Rana goliath*) of Cameroun and Spanish Guinea, West Africa. A female weighing 3,306 grammes (7 lb.

4.5 oz.) was caught in the rapids of the River Mbia, Spanish Guinea on 23 Aug. 1960. It had a snout-vent length of 34 cm. (13.38 in.) and measured 81.5 cm. (32.08 in.) overall with legs extended. In December 1960 another giant frog known locally as "agak" or "carn-pnag" and said to measure 12-15 inches snout to vent and weigh over 6 lb. was reportedly discovered in central New Guinea, but further information is lacking. In 1969 a new species of giant frog was discovered in Sumatra.

Britain The largest frog found in Britain is the *introduced* Marsh frog (*Rana r. ridibunda*). Adult males have been measured up to 9.6 cm. (3.77 in.) snout to vent, and adult females up to 12.6 cm. (4.96 in.), the weight ranging from 60 to 95 grammes (1.7 oz. to 3 oz.).

Tree frog The largest species of tree frog is *Hyla vasta*, found only on the island of Hispaniola (Haiti and the Dominican Republic) in the West Indies. The average snout-vent length is about 9 cm. (3.54 in.), but a female collected from the San Juan River. Dominican Republic, in March 1928 measured 14.3 cm. (5.63 in.).

Toad World The most massive toad in the world is probably the Marine toad (*Bufo marinus*) of tropical South America. An enormous female collected on 24 Nov. 1965 at Miraflores Vaupes, Colombia and later exhibited in the Reptile House at Bronx Zoo, New York City, U.S.A. had a snout-vent length of 23.8 cm. (9.37 in.) and weighed 1,302 grammes (2 lb. 11¼ oz.) at the time of its death in 1967.

Britain The largest toad found in Britain is the Common toad (*Bufo vulgaris*). An adult female of 10.2 cm. (3.94 in.) in length has been recorded.

Smallest World The smallest species of amphibian is believed to be the arrow-poison frog *Sminthillus limbatus*, found only in Cuba. Adult specimens have a snout-vent length of 8.5-12.4 mm. (0.33-0.48 in.).

Britain The smallest amphibian found in Britain is the Palmate newt (*Triturus helveticus*). Adult specimens measure 7.5-9.2 cm. (2.95-3.62 in.) in total length and weigh up to 2.39 grammes (0.083 oz.). The Natterjack or Running toad (*Bufo calamita*) has a maximum snout-vent length of only 8 cm. (3.14 in.), but it is a bulkier animal.

Newt The smallest newt in the world is believed to be the Striped newt (*Notophthalmus perstriatus*) of the south-eastern United States. Adult specimens average 51 mm. (2.01 in.) in total length.

Tree frog The smallest tree frog in the world is the Least tree frog (*Hyla ocularis*), found in the south-eastern United States. It has a maximum snout-vent length of 15.8 mm. (0.62 in.).

Toad The smallest toad in the world is the sub-species *Bufo taitanus beiranus*, first discovered in *c.* 1906 near Beira, Mozambique, East Africa. Adult specimens have a maximum recorded snout-vent length of 24 mm. (0.94 in.).

Salamander The smallest species of salamander is the Pygmy salamander (*Desmognathus wrighti*), which is found only in Tennessee, North Carolina and Virginia, U.S.A. Adult specimens measure from 37 to 50.8 mm. (1.45 to 2.0 in.) in total length.

Longest lived The greatest authentic age recorded for an amphibian is about 55 years for a male Japanese giant salamander (*Megalobatrachus japonicus*) which died in the aquarium at Amsterdam Zoological Gardens on 3 June 1881. It was brought to Holland in 1829, at which time it was estimated to be three years old.

Highest and lowest The greatest altitude at which an amphibian has been found is 8,000 metres (26,246 ft.) for a Common toad (*Bufo vulgaris*) collected in the Himalayas. This species has also been found at a depth of 340 metres (1,115 ft.) in a coal mine.

Most poisonous The most active known poison is the batrachotoxin derived from the skin secretions of the Kokoi (*Phyllobates latinasus*), an arrow-poison frog found in north-western Colombia, South America. Only about 1/100,000th of a gramme (0.0000004 oz.) is sufficient to kill a man.

Longest jump Frog The record for three consecutive leaps is 32 feet 3 inches by a 2-inch-long South African sharp-nosed frog (*Rana oxyrhyncha*) named "Leaping Lena" (later discovered to be a male) on Green Point Common, Cape Town on 16 Jan. 1954. At the annual Calaveras County Jumping Frog Jubilee at Angels Camp, California, U.S.A. in May 1955 another male of this species made an unofficial *single* leap of over 15 feet when being retrieved for placement in its container.

5. FISHES (*Pisces, Bradyodonti, Selachii, Marsipoli*)

Largest Marine World The largest fish in the world is the rare plankton-feeding Whale shark (*Rhineodon typus*), which is found in the warmer areas of the Atlantic, Pacific and Indian Oceans. It is not, however, the largest marine animal, since it is smaller than the larger species of whales (mammals). In 1919 a whale shark measuring 59 feet in length and weighing an estimated 90,000 lb. (42.4 tons) was trapped in a bamboo stake-trap at Koh Chik, in the Gulf of Siam. The largest carnivorous fish (excluding plankton eaters) is the rare Great white shark (*Carcharodon carcharias*), also called the "Man-eater", which is found mainly in tropical and sub-tropical waters. In June 1930 a specimen measuring 37 feet in length was found trapped in a herring weir at White Head Island, New Brunswick, Canada. Another great white shark which ran aground in False Bay, near the Cape of Good Hope, South Africa many years ago reportedly measured 43 feet, but further information is lacking. The longest of the bony or "true" fishes (Pisces) is the Russian sturgeon (*Acipenser huso*), also called the Beluga, which is found in the temperate areas of the Adriatic, Black and Caspian Seas but enters large rivers like the Volga and the Danube for spawning. Lengths up to 8 metres (26 ft. 3 in.) have been reliably reported, and a gravid female taken in the estuary of the Volga in 1827 weighed 1,474.2 kg. (3,250½ lb.) or 1.44 tons. The heaviest bony fish in the world is the Ocean sunfish (*Mola mola*), which is found in all tropical, sub-tropical and temperate waters. On 18 Sept. 1908 a huge specimen was accidentally struck by the S.S. *Fiona* off Bird Island about 40 miles from Sydney, New South Wales, Australia and towed to Port Jackson. It measured 14 feet between the anal and dorsal fins and weighed 4,928 lb. (2.24 tons).

Britain The largest fish ever recorded in the waters of the British Isles was a Basking shark (*Cetorhinus maximus*) measuring 40 feet in length and 25 feet in maximum girth killed off Mutton Island, Galway Bay, western Ireland. It weighed an estimated 14 tons. The largest bony fish found in British waters is the ocean sunfish (*Mola mola*). A specimen measuring 6 ft. 6 in. between the anal and dorsal fins and weighing 672 lb. was washed ashore at Kessingland near Lowestoft, Suffolk on 19 Dec. 1948.

Largest Freshwater World The largest fish which spends its whole life in fresh or brackish water is the European catfish or Wels (*Silurus glanis*). In September 1918 a specimen measuring nearly 11 feet in length and weighing 256.7 kilogrammes (564.74 lb.) was caught in the Desna River, six miles from Chernigou in the Ukraine,

U.S.S.R. Another one caught in the Dnieper River near Kremenchug, U.S.S.R. allegedly weighed 300 kg. (660 lb.), but further details are lacking. The Arapaima (*Arapaima gigas*), also called the Pirarucu, found in the Amazon and other South American rivers and often claimed to be the largest freshwater fish, averages 6½ feet and 150 lb. The largest "authentically recorded" measured 8 ft. 1½ in. in length and weighed 325 lb. It was caught in the Rio Negro, Brazil in 1836.

Britain The largest fish ever caught in a British river was a Common sturgeon (*Acipenser sturio*) weighing 460 lb. taken in the Esk, Yorkshire in 1810. Another one allegedly weighing "over 500 lb." was caught in the Severn at Lydney, Glos. on 1 June 1937 and sent to Billingsgate, London, but further details are lacking. Larger specimens have been taken at sea—notably one weighing 700 lb. and 10 ft. 5 in. long netted by the trawler *Ben Urie* off the Orkneys and landed at Aberdeen on 18 Oct. 1956.

Smallest Marine The smallest recorded marine fishes are the Marshall Islands goby (*Eviota zonura*) measuring 12 to 16 millimetres (0.47 to 0.63 in.) and *Schindleria praematurus* from Samoa, measuring 12 to 19 millimetres (0.47 to 0.74 in.), both in the Pacific Ocean. Mature specimens of the latter fish, which was not described until 1940, have been known to weigh only 2 milligrammes, equivalent to 17,750 to the ounce—the lightest of all vertebrates and the smallest catch possible for any fisherman. The smallest British marine fish is the Diminutive or Scorpion goby (*Gobios scorpoides*) of the English Channel which measures 20 to 25 millimetres (0.78 to 0.98 in.) in length.

Freshwater The shortest known fish, and the shortest of all vertebrates, is the Dwarf pygmy goby (*Pandaka pygmaea*), a colourless and nearly transparent fish found in the streams and lakes of Luzon in the Philippines. Adult males measure only 7.5 to 9.9 millimetres (0.28 to 0.38 in.) in length and weigh 4 to 5 milligrammes (0.00014 to 0.00017 oz.).

Fastest The Sailfish (*Isiophorus platypterus*) is generally considered to be the fastest species of fish, although the practical difficulties of measurement make data extremely difficult to secure. A figure of 68.18 m.p.h. (100 yards in 3 seconds) has been cited for one off Florida, U.S.A. The Swordfish (*Xiphias gladius*) has also been credited with very high speeds, but the evidence is based mainly on bills that have been found deeply embedded in in ships' timbers. A speed of 50 knots (57.6 m.p.h.) has been calculated from a penetration of 22 inches by a bill into a piece of timber, but 30 to 35 knots (35 to 40 m.p.h.) is the most conceded by some experts. Speeds in excess of 35 knots (40 m.p.h.) have also been attributed to the Marlin (*Tetrapturus sp.*), the Wahoo (*Acanthocybium solandri*), the Great blue shark (*Prionace glauca*) and the Bonefish (*Albula vulpes*), and the Bluefin tuna (*Thunnus thynnus*) has been scientifically clocked at 43.4 m.p.h. in a 20-second dash. The Four-winged flying fish (*Cypselurus heterurus*) may also exceed 40 m.p.h. during its rapid rush to the surface before take-off (the average speed in the air is about 35 m.p.h.). Record flights of 42 seconds, 36 feet in altitude and 1,200 feet length have been recorded in the tropical Atlantic.

Longest lived Aquaria are of too recent origin to be able to establish with certainty which species of fish can fairly be regarded as the longest lived. Early indications are that it is the Lake sturgeon (*Acipenser fulvescens*). One specimen 6 ft. 7 in. long caught in the Lake Winnebago region, Wisconsin, U.S.A. was believed to be 82 years old based on a count of the growth rings (*annuli*) in the marginal ray of the pectoral fin. Another lake sturgeon 6 ft. 9 in. long and weighing

215 lb. caught in the Lake of the Woods, Kenora, Ontario, Canada on 15 July 1953 was believed to be 150 years old based on a growth ring count, but this extreme figure has been questioned by some authorities. A figure of 150 years has also been attributed to the Mirror carp (*Cyprinus carpion*), but the greatest authoritatively accepted age is "more than 50 years". Other long-lived fish include the European sterlet (*Acipenser ruthenus*) with 69 years, the European catfish (*Silurus glanis*) with 60+ years, the European freshwater eel (*Anguilla anguilla*) with 55 years and the American eel (*Anguilla chrisypa*) with 50 years.

Oldest goldfish The exhibition life of a Goldfish (*Carassius auratus*) is normally about 17 years, but much greater ages have been reliably reported. On 22 Aug. 1970 Mrs. I. M. Payne of Dawlish, Devon announced that her pet goldfish had just celebrated its 34th birthday. There is also a record of a goldfish living in a water-butt for 40 years.

Shortest lived There are several contenders for the title of shortest-lived fish. One of them is the Transparent or White goby (*Latrunculus pellucidus*), which hatches, grows, reproduces and dies in less than a year. Other "annuals" include the Top minnow (*Gambusia holbrookii*), the Sea horse (*Hippocampus husonius*), the Dwarf pygmy goby (*Pandaka pygmaea*) and the Ice fishes (family Chaenichthyidae) of the Antarctic.

Deepest The greatest depth from which a fish has been recovered is 7,130 metres (23,392 ft.) for a 6¾ in. long brotulid of the genus *Bassogigas*, sledge-trawled by the Royal Danish research vessel *Galathea* in the Sunda Trench, south of Java, in September 1951. Dr. Jacques Piccard and Lieutenant Don Walsh, U.S. Navy, reported they saw a sole-like fish about 1 foot long (tentatively identified as *Chascanopsetta lugubris*) from the bathyscaphe *Trieste* at a depth of 35,802 feet in the Challenger Deep (Mariana Trench) in the western Pacific on 24 Jan. 1960. This sighting, however, has been questioned by some authorities, who still regard the brotulids of the genus *Bassogigas* as the deepest-living vertebrates.

Most eggs The Ocean sunfish (*Mola mola*) produces up to 300,000,000 eggs, each of them measuring about 0.05 in. in diameter. The egg yield of the guppy *Lebistes reticulatus* is usually only 40-50, but one female measuring 1¼ inches in length had only four in her ovaries.

Most venomous The most venomous fish in the world are the Stonefish (family Synanceidae) of the tropical waters of the Indo-Pacific. Direct contact with the spines of their fins, which contain a strong neurotoxic poison, often proves fatal.

Most electric The most powerful electric fish is the Electric eel (*Electrophorus electricus*), which is found in the rivers of Brazil, Columbia, Venezuela and Peru. An average sized specimen can discharge 400 volts at 1 ampere, but measurements up to 650 volts have been recorded.

6. STARFISHES *(Asteroida)*

Largest The largest of the 1,600 known species of starfish is probably the five-armed *Evasterias echinosomo* of the North Pacific. One specimen collected by a Russian expedition in the flooded crater of a volcano in Broughton Bay, Semushir, one of the Kurile Islands in June 1970 measured 96 cm. (37.79 in.) in total diameter and weighed more than 5 kg. (11 lb.). The largest starfish found in British waters is the northern sun star (*Solaster endeca*), which has been measured up to 40 cm. (15.74 in.) in total diameter.

Smallest The smallest recorded starfish is the North Pacific deep-sea species *Leptychaster propinquus*, which has

a maximum total diameter of 18.3 mm. (0.72 in.). The smallest starfish found in British waters is the Cushion starfish (*Asterrina gibbosa*), which has a maximum total diameter of 60 mm. (2.36 in.).

Deepest The greatest depth from which a starfish has been recovered is 7,630 metres (25,032 ft.) for a specimen of *Eremicaster tenebrarius* collected by the Galathea Deep Sea Expedition in the Kermadec Trench in the central Pacific in 1951.

7. ARACHNIDS *(Arachnida)*

SPIDERS (Order Araneae)

Largest World The world's largest known spider is the bird-eating spider (*Theraphosa leblondi*) of northern South America. A male specimen with a leg span of 10 inches when fully extended and a body length of 3½ inches was collected at Montagne la Gabrielle, French Guiana in April 1925. It weighed nearly 2 ounces. The heaviest spider ever recorded was a female "tarantula" of the genus *Lasiodora* collected at Manaos, Brazil in 1945. It measured 9½ inches across the legs and weighed almost 3 ounces.

Britain Of the 610 known British species of spider covering an estimated population of over 500,000,000,000,000, the Cardinal spider (*Tegenaria parietina*) has the greatest leg span, males sometimes exceeding 5 inches (length of body up to 19 mm. or 0.75 in.). This spider is found only in southern England. The well-known "Daddy Longlegs" spider (*Pholcus phanlangoides*) rarely exceeds 3 inches in leg span, but one outsized specimen collected in England measured 6 inches across. The heaviest spider found in Britain is probably the orb weaver *Araneus quadratus* (formerly called *Araneus reaumuri*). An *average-sized* specimen collected in October 1943 weighed 1.174 grammes (0.041 oz.) and measured 15 millimetres (0.58 in.) in body length.

Smallest World The smallest known spider is *Microlinypheus bryophilus* (family Argiopedae), discovered in Lorne, Victoria, Australia in January 1928. Adult males have a body length of 0.6 millimetres (0.023 in.) and adult females 0.8 mm. (0.031 in.). The smallest spider found in Britain is the money spider *Glyphesis cottonae*, which is confined to a swamp near Beaulieu Road Station, New Forest, Hants and Thurley Heath, Surrey. Adult specimens of both sexes have a body length of 1 mm. (0.039 in.).

Largest webs The largest webs are the aerial ones spun by the tropical orb weavers of the genus *Nephila*, which have been measured up to 18 ft. 9¾ in. in circumference. The smallest webs are spun by spiders like *Glyphesis cottonae*, etc. which are about the size of a postage stamp.

Most venomous The most venomous spider in the world is probably *Latrodectus mactans* of the Americas, which is better known as the "black widow" in the United States. Females of this species (the much smaller males are harmless) have a bite capable of killing a human being, but deaths are rare. The Funnel web spider (*Atrax robustus*) of Australia, the Jockey spider (*Latrodectus hasseltii*) of Australia and New Zealand, the Button spider (*Latrodectus indistinctus*) of South Africa, the Podadora (*Glyptocranium gasteracanthoides*) of Argentina and the Brown recluse spider (*Loxosceles reclusa*) of the central and southern United States have also been credited with fatalities.

Rarest The most elusive of all spiders are the primitive atypical tarantulas of the genus *Liphistius*, which are found in south-east Asia. The most elusive spider in Britain is the handsome crimson and black Lace web eresus spider (*Eresus niger*), found in Hampshire, Dorset and Cornwall, which is known only from eight specimens (seven males and one female). In the early

1950s a specimen was reportedly seen at Sandown on the Isle of Wight, but it escaped.

Fastest The highest speed recorded for a spider on a level surface is 1.73 feet per second (1.17 m.p.h.) in the case of a specimen of *Tegenaria atrica*.

Longest lived The longest lived of all spiders are the primitive *Mygalomorphae* (tarantulas and allied species). One mature female tarantula collected at Mazatlan, Mexico in 1935 and estimated to be 12 years old at the time, was kept in a laboratory for 16 years, making a total of 28 years. The longest-lived British spider is probably the purse web spider (*Atypus affinis*). One specimen was kept in a greenhouse for nine years.

8. CRUSTACEANS (*Crustacea*)

(Crabs, lobsters, shrimps, prawns, crayfish, barnacles, water fleas, fish lice, woodlice, sandhoppers, kril, etc.)

Largest World The largest of all crustaceans (although not the heaviest) is the giant spider crab (*Macrocheira kaempferi*), also called the stilt crab, which is found in deep waters off the south-eastern coast of Japan. Mature specimens usually have a 12-14 inches wide body and a claw-span of 8-9 feet, but unconfirmed measurements up to 19 feet have been reported. A specimen with a claw span of 12 feet 1½ inches weighed 14 lb.

The largest species of lobster, and the heaviest of all crustaceans, is the American or North Atlantic lobster (*Homarus americanus*). One weighing 42 lb. 7 oz. and measuring 4 feet from the end of the tail-fan to the tip of the claw was caught by the smack *Hustler* in a deep-sea trawl off the Virginia Capes, Virginia, U.S.A. in 1934 and is now on display in the Museum of Science, Boston, Massachusetts. Another specimen allegedly weighing 48 lb. was caught off Chatham, New England, U.S.A. in 1949.

Britain The largest crustacean found in British waters is the common or European lobster (*Homarus vulgarus*), which averages 2-3 lb. in weight. On 17 Aug. 1967 a lobster weighing 14½ lb. was caught by a skin-diver off St. Ann's Head, Pembrokeshire, Wales. It is now mounted in the bar of the Amroth Arms, Amroth, Pembrokeshire. The largest crab found in British waters is the Edible or great crab (*Cancer pagurus*). In 1895 a crab measuring 11 inches across the shell and weighing 14 lb. was caught off the coast of Cornwall.

Smallest The smallest known crustaceans are water fleas of the genus *Alonella*, which may measure less than 0.25 mm. (0.0098 in.) in length. They are found in British waters. The smallest known lobster is the Cape lobster (*Homarus capensis*) of South Africa which measures 10-12 cm. (3.93-4.72 in.) in total length. The smallest crabs in the world are the pea crabs (family Pinnotheridae). Some species have a shell diameter of only 0.25 in., including *Pinnotheres pisum* which is found in British waters.

Longest lived The longest lived of all crustaceans is the American lobster (*Homarus americanus*). Very large specimens may be as much as 50 years old.

Deepest The greatest depth from which a crustacean has been recovered is 9,790 metres (32,119 ft.) for an amphiopod (order Amphiopoda) collected by the Galathea Deep Sea Expedition in the Philippine Trench in 1951. The marine crab *Ethusina abyssicola* has been taken at a depth of 14,000 feet.

9. INSECTS (*Insecta*)

Heaviest World The heaviest insect in the world is the Goliath beetle *Goliathus giganteus* of equatorial Africa. One specimen measuring 14.85 cm. (5.85 in.) in length

(jaw to tip of abdomen) and 10 cm. (3.93 in.) across the back weighed 3.52 ounces. The longhorn beetles *Titanus giganteus* of South America and *Xinuthrus heros* of the Fiji Islands are also massive insects, and both have been measured up to 15 cm. (5.9 in.) in length. The heaviest insect found in Britain is the rare Great silver water-beetle (*Hydrophilus piceus*) of southern England. One example measuring 48 mm. (1.88 in.) in length and 22 mm. (0.86 in.) across the back weighed 9 grammes (0.255 oz.).

Longest The longest insect in the world is the tropical stick-insect *Pharnacia serratipes*, females of which have been measured up to 33 cm. (12.99 in.) in body length. The longest known beetle (excluding antennae) is the Hercules beetle (*Dynastes hercules*) of Central and South America, which has been measured up to 18 cm. (7.08 in.), but over half of this length is accounted for by the "prong" from the thorax. The longhorn beetle *Batocera wallacei* of New Guinea has been measured up to 26.7 cm. (10.5 in.), but 19 cm. (7.5 in.) of this was antenna. The longest beetle found in Britain is the Stag beetle (*Lucanus cervus*), now found only in Hampshire and Berkshire. One measuring 3 inches in total length was captured at Priest Hill, Caversham, Berkshire in June 1969.

Smallest World The smallest insects recorded so far are the "Hairy-winged" beetles of the family Trichopterygidae and the "battledore-wing fairy flies" (parasitic wasps) of the family Mymaridae. They measure only 0.2 mm. (0.008 in.) in length, and the fairy flies have a wing span of only 1 mm. (0.04 in.). This makes them smaller than some of the protozoa (single-celled animals). The male bloodsucking banded louse (*Enderleinellus zonatus*), ungorged, and the parasitic wasp *Caraphractus cinctus* may each weigh as little as 0.005 milligrammes, or 567,000 to an ounce. The eggs of the latter each weigh 0.0002 milligrammes, or 14,175,000 to the ounce.

Fastest flying Experiments have proved that the widely publicised claim by an American entomologist in 1926 that the Deer bot-fly (*Cephenemyia pratti*) could attain a speed of 818 m.p.h. (*sic*) was wildly exaggerated. Acceptable modern experiments have now established that the highest maintainable air-speed of any insect, including the deer bot-fly, is 24 m.p.h., rising to a maximum of 36 m.p.h. for short bursts. A relay of bees (maximum speed 11 m.p.h.) would use only a gallon of nectar in cruising 4,000,000 miles at an average speed of 7 m.p.h.

Longest lived The longest-lived insects are queen termites (*Isoptera*), which have been known to lay eggs for up to 50 years.

Loudest The loudest of all insects is the male cicada (family Cicadidae). At 7,400 pulses per minute its tymbal organs produce a noise (officially described by the United States Department of Agriculture as "Tsh-ee-EEEE-e-ou") detectable more than a quarter of a mile distant. The only British species is the very rare Mountain cicada (*Cicadetta montana*), which is confined to the New Forest area in Hampshire.

Southern-most The farthest south at which any insect has been found is 77° S (900 miles from the South Pole) in the case of a springtail (order Collembola).

Largest locust swarm The greatest swarm of Desert locusts (*Schistocerea gregaria*) ever recorded was one covering an estimated 2,000 square miles observed crossing the Red Sea in 1889. Such a swarm must have contained about 250,000,000,000 insects weighing about 500,000 tons.

Fastest wing beat The fastest wing beat of any insect under natural conditions is 62,760 a minute by a tiny midge of the genus *Forcipomyia*. In experiments with truncated

Part of a swarm of locusts—such swarms may involve up to 250,000,000,000 insects. Inset An individual desert locust.

wings at a temperature of 37° C (98.6° F) the rate increased to 133,080 beats per minute. The muscular contraction-expansion cycle in 0.00045 or 1/2,218th of a second, further represents the fastest muscle movement ever measured.

Slowest wing beat The slowest wing beat of any insect is 300 a minute by the swallowtail butterfly (*Papilo machaon*). Most butterflies beat their wings at a rate of 460 to 636 a minute.

Largest ants The largest ant in the world is the Driver ant (*Dinoponera grandis*) of Africa, workers of which measure up to 33 mm. (1.31 in.) in length. The largest of the 27 species found in Britain is the Wood ant (*Formica rufa*), males reaching 9 mm. (0.35 in.) and queens 11 mm. (0.43 in.). The smallest is the Thief ant (*Solenopsis fugax*), whose workers measure 1.5-3 mm. (0.059-0.18 in.).

Bush-cricket
Largest The bush-cricket with the largest wing span is the New Guinean grasshopper *Siliquofera grandis* with female examples measuring more than 10 inches. *Pseudophyllanax imperialis*, found on the island of New Caledonia in the south-western Pacific has antennae measuring up to 8 inches. The largest bush-cricket found in Britain is *Tettigonia viridissima*, which normally has a body length of 1¼ inches. In August 1953 a female measuring 77 mm. (3.03 in.) in body, length (including ovipositor) was caught in a sand pit at Grays, Essex and later presented to London Zoological Gardens. The largest of the 14 true grasshoppers found in Britain is *Mecostethus grossus*, females of which measure up to 39 mm. (1.53 in.) in body length.

Dragonflies
Largest The largest dragonfly in the world is *Tetracanthagyne plagiata* of north-eastern Borneo, which is known only from a single specimen preserved in the British Museum of Natural History, London. This dragonfly has a wing span of 19.4 cm. (7.63 in.) and an overall length of 10.8 cm. (4.25 in.). The largest dragonfly found in Britain is the Golden-ringed dragonfly (*Cordulegaster boltoni*), which has been measured up to 84 mm. (3.3 in.) in overall length and may have a wing span of more than 100 mm. (3.93 in.). The

smallest British dragonfly is the Scarce ischnura (*Ischnura pumilio*), which has a wing span of 33 mm. (1.3 in.).

Flea jump
Longest The champion jumper among fleas is the common flea (*Pulex irritans*). In one American experiment carried out in 1910 a specimen allowed to leap at will performed a long jump of 13 inches and a high jump of 7¾ inches. In jumping 130 times its own height a flea subjects itself to a force of 200 g. Siphonapterologists recognise 1,830 varieties.

BUTTERFLIES AND MOTHS (order Lepidoptera)

Largest
World The largest known butterfly is the giant birdwing *Troides victoriae* of the Solomon Islands in the south-western Pacific. Females may have a wing span exceeding 12 inches and weigh over 5 grammes (0.176 oz.). The largest moth in the world is the Hercules emperor moth (*Coscinoscera hercules*) of tropical Australia and New Guinea. Females measure up to 10½ inches across the outspread wings and have a wing area of up to 40.8 square inches. The rare Owlet moth (*Thysania agrippina*) of Brazil has been measured up to 30 cms. (11.81 in.) in wing span, and the Atlas moth (*Attacus atlas*) of south-east Asia up to 28 cm. (11.02 in.), but both these species are less bulky than *C. hercules*.

Britain The largest of the 21,000 species of insect found in Britain is the very rare Death's head hawk moth (*Acherontia atropos*), females of which have a body length of 60 mm. (2.36 in.), a wing span of up to 133 mm. (5.25 in.) and weigh about 1.6 grammes (0.065 oz.). The largest butterfly found in Britain is the Monarch butterfly (*Danaus plexippus*), also called the Milkweek or Black-veined brown butterfly, a rare vagrant which breeds in the southern United States and Central America. It has a wing span of up to 5 inches and weighs about 1 gramme (0.04 oz.). The largest *native* butterfly is the Swallowtail (*Papilo machaon*), females of which have a wing span of 7-10 cm. (2.75-3.93 in.). This species is now confined to a small area of the Norfolk Broads.

Britain's largest native butterfly the Swallowtail, found in Cambridgeshire and Norfolk. It may have a span of up to 3½ inches.

Smallest
World The smallest of the 140,000 known species of Lepidoptera is the moth *Nepticula microtheriella*, which has a wing span of 3-4 mm. (0.11-0.15 in.) and a body length of 2 mm. (0.078 in.). It is found in Britain. The world's smallest known butterfly is the dwarf blue (*Brephidium barberae*) of South Africa. It has a wing span of 14 mm. (0.55 in.). The smallest butterfly found in Britain is the Small blue (*Cupido minimus*), which has a wing span of 19-25 mm. (0.75-1.0 in.).

Rarest The rarest of all butterflies (and the most valuable) is the giant birdwing *Troides allottei*, which is found only on Bougainville in the Solomon Islands. A specimen was sold for £750 at an auction in Paris on 24 Oct. 1966. The rarest *native* British butterflies are probably the large blue (*Maculinea arion*), now found only in north Cornwall, and the Swallowtail (*Papilo*

43

Most acute sense of smell
machaon), which is now restricted to a small area of the Norfolk Broads. Britain's rarest moth is the Tree-lichen Beauty (*Briophila algae*), one specimen of which was captured in Manchester in July 1858.

The most acute sense of smell exhibited in nature is that of the male True silkworm moth (*Bombyx mori*) which, according to German experiments in 1961, can detect the sex signals of the female at the almost unbelievable range of 11 kilometres (6.8 miles) upwind. This scent has been identified as one of the higher alcohols ($C_{16}H_{29}OH$), of which the female carries less than 0.0001 mg.

10. CENTIPEDE (*Chilopoda*)

Longest
The longest known species of centipede is the 46-legged Giant scolopender (*Scolopendra gigantea*) of the rain forests of Central and South America. Specimens have been reliably measured up to 26.5 cm. (10.43 in.) in length and 2.54 cm. (1 in.) in diameter. The longest centipede found in Britain is *Haplophilus subterraneus*, which measures up to 70 mm. (2.75 in.) in length and 1.4 mm. (0.005 in.) across the body.

Shortest
The shortest recorded centipede is an unidentified species which measures only 5 mm. (0.19 in.). The shortest centipede found in Britain is *Lithobius dubosequi*, which measures up to 9.5 mm. (0.374 in.) in length and 1.1 mm. (0.043 in.) across the body.

Most legs
The centipede with the greatest number of legs is *Himantarum gabrielis* of southern Europe which has 171-177 pairs when adult.

Fastest
The fastest centipede is probably *Scutiger coleoptrata* of southern Europe which can travel at a rate of 50 cm. (19.68 in.) a second or 4.47 m.p.h.

11. MILLIPEDES (*Diplopoda*)

Longest
The longest known species of millipede are *Graphidostreptus gigas* of Africa and *Scaphistostreptus seychellarum* of the Seychelles in the Indian Ocean, both of which have been measured up to 28 cm. (11.02 in.) in length and 2 cm. (0.78 in.) in diameter. The longest millipede found in Britain is *Cylindroiulus londinensis* which measures up to 50 mm. (1.96 in.).

Shortest
The shortest millipede in the world is the British species *Polyxenus lagurus*, which measures 2.1-4.0 mm. (0.082-0.15 in.) in length.

Most legs
The greatest number of legs reported for a millipede is 355 pairs (710 legs) for an unidentified South African species.

12. SEGMENTED WORMS (*Annelida* or *Annulata*)

Longest
The longest known species of earthworm is *Megascolides australis*, first discovered in Brandy Creek, southern Gippsland, Victoria, Australia in 1868. An average-sized specimen measures 4 feet in length (2 feet when contracted) and nearly 7 feet when *naturally* extended. The longest accurately measured *Megascolides* on record was one collected before 1930 in southern Gippsland which measured 7 feet 2 inches in length and over 13 feet when naturally extended. The eggs of this worm measure 2-3 inches in length and 0.75 inches in diameter. In November 1967 a specimen of the African giant earthworm *Microchaetus rappi* (=*M. microchaetus*) measuring 11 feet in length and 21 feet when naturally extended was found on the road between Alice and King William's Town, Eastern Cape Province, South Africa. The *average* length of this species, however, is 3 feet 6 inches and 6-7 feet when naturally extended. The

The longest known species of segmented worm—the *Megascolides australis*, first discovered in Australia in 1868.

longest segmented worm found in Britain is *Lumbricus terrestris*, which has been reliably measured up to 35 cm. (13.78 in.) when naturally extended.

Shortest
The shortest known segmented worm is *Chaetogaster annandalei*, which measures less than 0.5 mm. (0.0019 in.) in length.

13. MOLLUSCS (*Mollusca*)

(Squids, octopuses, shellfish, snails, etc.)

Largest squid
The heaviest of all invertebrate animals is the Atlantic giant squid (*Architeuthis sp.*). The largest specimen ever recorded was one measuring 55 feet in total length (head and body 20 feet, tentacles 35 feet) captured on 2 Nov. 1878 after it had run aground in Thimble Tickle Bay, Newfoundland, Canada. It weighed an estimated 2 tons. In October 1887 a giant squid (*Architeuthis longimanus*) measuring 57 feet in total length was washed up in Lyall Bay, New Zealand, but 49 feet of this was tentacle. The largest squid ever recorded in British waters was one found at the head of Whalefirth Voe, Shetland on 2 Oct. 1949 which measured 24 feet in total length.

Largest octopus
The largest known octopus is the Common Pacific octopus (*Octopus apollyon*). One specimen trapped in a fisherman's net in Monterey Bay, California, U.S.A. had a radial spread of over 20 feet and scaled 110 lb., and a weight of 125 lb. has been reported for another individual. In 1874 a radial spread of 32 feet was reported for an octopus (*Octopus hongkongensis*) speared in Illiuliuk Harbour, Unalaska Island, Alaska, U.S.A., but the body of this animal only measured 12 inches in length and it probably weighed less than 20 lb. The largest octopus found in British waters is the Common octopus (*Octopus vulgaris*), which has been measured up to 7 feet in radial spread and may weigh more than 10 lb.

Most ancient mollusc
The longest existing living creature is *Neopilina galatheae*, a deep-sea worm-snail which had been believed extinct for about 320,000,000 years. In 1952, however, specimens were found at a depth of 11,400 feet off Costa Rica by the Danish research vessel *Galathea*. Fossils found in New York State, U.S.A., Newfoundland, Canada, and Sweden show that this mollusc was also living about 500,000,000 years ago.

SHELLS

Largest
The largest of all existing bivalve shells is the marine Giant clam (*Tridacna derasa*), which is found on the

Indo-Pacific coral reefs. A specimen measuring 43 inches by 29 inches and weighing 579½ lb. (over a quarter of a ton) was collected from the Great Barrier Reef in 1917, and is now preserved in the American Museum of Natural History, New York City, N.Y., U.S.A. The largest bivalve shell found in British waters is the Fan mussel (*Pinna fragilis*). One specimen found at Tor Bay, Devon measured 37 centimetres (14.56 in.) in length and 20 centimetres (7.87 in.) in breadth at the hind end.

Smallest The smallest bivalve shell found in British waters, and one of the smallest in the world, is *Neolepton skysi,* which measures less than 16 millimetres (0.629 in.) in length. This species is only known from a few specimens collected off Guernsey in the Channel Islands in 1894.

Rarest The most highly prized of all molluscan shells in the hands of conchologists is the three-inch long White-tooth cowrie (*Cypraea leucodon*), which is found in the deep waters off the Philippines. Only three examples are known, including one in the British Museum of Natural History, London. The highest price ever paid for a sea shell is £1,350 in a sale at Sotheby's, London, on 4 March 1971 for one of the four known examples of *Conus bengalensis.* The four-inch long shell was trawled by fishermen off north-western Thailand in December 1970.

Longest lived The longest lived of all molluscs is probably the Freshwater mussel (*Margaritan margaritifera*) which has been credited with a potential maximum longevity of 100 years. The Giant clam (*Tridacna derasa*) lives about 30 years.

SNAILS

Largest The largest known species of snail is the sea hare *Tethys californicus,* which is found in coastal waters off California, U.S.A. The average weight is 7 to 8 lb., but one specimen scaled 15 lb. 13 oz. The largest known land snail is the African giant snail (*Achatina fulica*), which has been recorded up to 10¾ inches in overall length and 1 lb. 2 oz. in weight. The largest land snail found in Britain is the Roman or Edible snail (*Helix pomatia*), which measures up to 4 inches in overall length and weighs up to 3 oz. The smallest British land snail is *Punctum pygmaeum,* which has a shell measuring 0.023-0.035 of an inch by 0.047-0.059 of an inch.

14. RIBBON WORMS *(Nermertina* or *Rhynchopods)*

Longest The longest of the 550 recorded species of ribbon worms, also called nemertines (or nemerteans), is the "Boot-lace worm" (*Lincus longissimus*), which is found in the shallow waters of the North Sea. A specimen washed ashore at St. Andrews, Fifeshire, Scotland in 1864 after a severe storm measured more than 180 feet in length, making it easily the longest recorded worm of any variety.

15. JELLYFISHES *(Scyphozoa* or *Scyphomedusia)*

Largest and smallest The largest jellyfish is *Cyanea arctica.* For details see page 26.

The largest coelenterate found in British waters is the rare "Lion's mane" jellyfish (*Cyanea capillata*), which is also known as the Common sea blubber. One specimen measured at St. Andrew's Marine Laboratory, Fifeshire, Scotland had a bell diameter of 91 centimetres (35.82 in.) and tentacles stretching over

45 feet. Some true jellyfishes have a bell diameter of less than 20 millimetres (0.78 in.).

Most venomous The most venomous coelenterates are the box jellies of the genera *Chiropsalmus* and *Chironex* of the Indo-Pacific region, which carry a neuro-toxic venom similar in strength to that found in the Asiatic cobra. These jellyfish have caused the deaths of at least 60 people off the coast of Queensland, Australia in the past 25 years.

16. SPONGES *(Parazoa, Porifera* or *Spongida)*

Largest The largest known sponge is the barrel-shaped Logger-head sponge (*Spheciospongia vesparium*) of the West Indies and the waters off Florida, U.S.A. Single individuals measure up to 3 ft. 6 in. in height and 3 ft. in diameter. Neptune's cup or goblet (*Poterion patera*) of Indonesia grows up to 4 feet in height, but it is not such a bulky animal. In 1909 a Wool sponge (*Hippospongia canaliculatta*) measuring 6 feet in circumference was collected off the Bahama Islands. When first taken from the water it weighed between 80 and 90 lb., but after it had been dried and relieved of all excrescences it scaled 12 lb. (this sponge is now preserved in the U.S. National Museum, Washington, D.C., U.S.A.).

Smallest The smallest known sponge is the widely distributed *Leucosolenia blanca,* which measures 3 millimetres (0.11 in.) in height when fully grown.

Deepest Sponges have been recovered from depths of up to 18,500 feet (3.5 miles).

17. EXTINCT ANIMALS

Longest World The first dinosaur to be scientifically described was *Megalosaurus* ("large lizard"), a 20-foot long bipedal theropod, in 1824. A lower jaw and other bones of this animal had been found before 1818 in a slate quarry at Stonesfield, near Woodstock, Oxfordshire. It stalked across what is now southern England about 130,000,000 years ago. The word "dinosaur" ("fear-fully great lizard") was not used for such reptiles until 1842. The longest recorded dinosaur was *Diplodocus* ("double-beam"), an attentuated sauropod which ranged over western North America about 150,000,000 years ago. A composite skeleton of three individuals excavated near Split Mountain, Utah between 1909 and 1922 and mounted in the Carnegie Museum of the Natural Sciences in Pittsburgh, Pennsylvania measures 87½ feet in total length (neck 22 ft., body 15 ft., tail 50 ft. 6 in.)—nearly the length of three London double-decker buses—and 11 ft. 9 in. at the pelvis (the highest point on the body). This animal weighed a computed 10.56 metric tons in life.

Britain Britain's longest dinosaur was the sauropod *Cetio-saurus* ("whale lizard"), which lived in what is now England about 165,000,000 years ago. It measured up to 60 feet in total length and weighed over 15 tons. The bones of this dinosaur were first discovered in the No. 1 Brickyard at the New Peterborough Brick Co., Peterborough, Northamptonshire in May 1898 and subsequently in Oxfordshire.

Heaviest The heaviest of all prehistoric animals, and the heaviest land vertebrate of all time, was *Brachiosaurus* ("arm lizard"), which lived in East Africa (Rhodesia and Tanzania) and Colorado and Oklahoma, U.S.A. between 135,000,000 and 165,000,000 years ago. A complete skeleton excavated near Tendaguru Hill, southern Tanganyika (Tanzania) in 1909 and

Berlin, Germany measures 74 feet 6 inches in total length and 21 feet at the shoulder. This reptile weighed a computed 78.26 metric tons in life, but isolated bones have since been discovered in East Africa which indicate that some specimens may have weighed as much as 100 tons and measured over 90 feet in total length.

Largest predator It is now known that some carnosaurs were even larger than the 6¾ ton 47 foot *Tyrannosaurus*. In 1930 the British Museum Expedition to East Africa dug up the pelvic bones and part of the vertebrae of another huge carnosaur at Tendaguru Hill which must have measured about 54 feet in total length when alive. During the summers of 1963-65 a Polish-Mongolian expedition discovered the remains of a carnosaur in the Gobi Desert which had 8 ft. 6 in. long forelimbs! It is not yet known, however, whether the rest of this dinosaur was built on the same colossal scale.

Most brainless *Stegosaurus* ("plated reptile"), which measured up to 30 feet in total length and weighed 1¾ tons, had a walnut-sized brain weighing only 2½ ounces, which represented 0.004 of one per cent of its bodyweight (*cf.* 0.074 of 1 per cent for an elephant and 1.88 per cent for a human). It roamed widely across the Northern Hemisphere about 150,000,000 years ago.

Largest dinosaur eggs The largest known dinosaur eggs are those of *Hypselosaurus priseus*, a 30 ft. long sauropod which lived about 80,000,000 years ago. Some specimens found in the valley of the Durance near Aix-en-Provence, southern France in October 1961 would have had, uncrushed, a length of 12 inches and a diameter of 10 inches.

Largest flying creature The largest flying creature was probably the winged reptile *Pteranodon ingens*, a dynamic soarer which glided over what is now the State of Kansas, U.S.A. about 80,000,000 years ago. It had a wing-span of up to 27 feet and weighed an estimated 40 lb.

Largest marine reptile The largest marine reptile ever recorded was *Kronosaurus queenslandicus*, a short-necked pliosaur which swam in the seas around what is now Australia about 100,000,000 years ago. It measured up to 55 feet in length and had an 11½ foot long skull.

Largest crocodile The largest known crocodile was *Phobosuchus* ("horror crocodile"), which lived in the lakes and swamps of what are now the States of Montana and Texas, U.S.A. about 75,000,000 years ago. It measured up to 50 feet in total length and had a 6 ft. long skull. The gavial *Rhamphosuchus*, which lived in what is now northern India about 7,000,000 years ago, also reached a length of 50 feet, but it was not so bulky.

Largest chelonians The largest prehistoric marine turtle was probably *Archelon ischyros*, which lived in the shallow seas over what are now the states of South Dakota and Kansas, U.S.A. about 80,000,000 years ago. An almost complete skeleton with a carapace (shell) measuring 6 ft. 6 in. in length was discovered in August 1895 near the south fork of the Cheyenne River in Custer County, South Dakota. The skeleton, which has an overall length of 11 ft. 4 in. (20ft. across the outstretched flippers) is now preserved in the Peabody Museum of Natural History at Yale University, New Haven, Connecticut, U.S.A. This specimen is estimated to have weighed 6,000 lb. (2.7 tons) when it was alive. In 1914 the fossil remains of another giant marine turtle (*Cratochelone berneyi*) which must have measured at least 12 feet in overall length when alive were discovered at Sylvania Station, 20 miles west of Hughenden, Queensland, Australia.

The largest prehistoric tortoise was *Colossochelys atlas*, which lived in what is now northern India between 7,000,000 and 12,000,000 years ago. The fossil remains of a specimen with a carapace 5 ft. 5 in. long (7 ft. 4 in. over the curve) and 2 ft. 11 in. high were discovered near Chandigarh in the Siwalik Hills in 1923. This animal had a nose to tail length of 8 feet and is computed to have weighed 2,100 lb. when it was alive.

Longest snake The longest prehistoric snake was the python-like *Gigantophis garstini*, which inhabited what is now Egypt about 50,000,000 years ago. Parts of a spinal column and a small piece of jaw discovered at El Faiyum indicate a length of about 42 feet.

Largest amphibian The largest amphibian ever recorded was the alligator-like *Eogyrinus* which lived between 280,000,000 and 345,000,000 years ago. It measured nearly 15 feet in length.

Largest fish The largest fish ever recorded was the great shark (*Carcharodon megalodon*), which lived between 1,000,000 and 25,000,000 years ago. In 1909 the American Museum of Natural History undertook a restoration of the jaws of this giant shark, basing the size on 4 inch long fossil teeth, and found that the jaws measured 9 feet across and had a gape of 6 feet. The length of this fish was estimated at 80 feet. Other fossil teeth measuring up to 6 inches in length and weighing 12 ounces have since been discovered near Bakersfield, California, U.S.A.

Largest insect The largest prehistoric insect was the dragonfly *Meganeura monyi*, which lived between 280,000,000 and 325,000,000 years ago. Fossil remains (*i.e.* impressions of wings) discovered at Commentry, central France, indicate that it had a wing span reaching up to 70 centimetres (27.5 inches).

Most southerly The most southerly creature yet found is a freshwater salamander-like amphibian *Labyrinthodont*, represented by a 2½-inch piece of jawbone found near Beardmore Glacier, Antarctica, 325 miles from the South Pole, dating from the early Jurassic of 200,000,000 years ago. This discovery was made in December 1967.

Largest bird The largest prehistoric bird was the Elephant bird (*Aepyornis maximus*), also known as the "Roc bird", which lived in southern Madagascar. It was a flightless bird standing 9-10 feet in height and weighing nearly 1,000 lb. Aepyornis also had the largest eggs of any known animal. One example preserved in the British Museum of Natural History, London measures 33¾ inches round the long axis with a circumference of 28½ inches, giving a capacity of 2.35 gallons—seven times that of an ostrich egg. A more cylindrical egg preserved in the Academie des Sciences, Paris, France measures 12⅞ by 15⅜ inches and probably weighed about 27 lb. with its contents. This bird may have survived until *c.* 1660. The flightless moa *Dinornis giganteus* of North Island, New Zealand was taller, attaining a height of over 13 feet, but it only weighed about 500 lb. In May 1962 a single fossilised ankle joint of an enormous flightless bird was found at Gainsville, Florida, U.S.A.

The largest prehistoric bird actually to fly was probably the condor-like *Teratornis incredibilis* which lived in what is now North America about 100,000,000 years ago. Fossil remains discovered in Smith Creek Cave, Nevada in 1952 indicate it had a wing span of 5 metres (16 ft. 4¼ in.) and must have weighed nearly 50 lb. A wing span measurement of 5 metres has also been reported for another flying bird named *Ornithodesmus latidens*, which flew over what is now Hampshire and the Isle of Wight about 90,000,000 years ago. Another gigantic flying bird named *Osteodontornis orri*, which lived in what is now the State of California, U.S.A. about 20,000,000 years ago, had a wing span of 16 feet and was

A reconstruction of the extinct flightless Moa of New Zealand which weighed ¼ ton and stood over 13 feet tall.

The heaviest single tusk on record is one weighing 330 lb. with a maximum circumference of 35 inches now preserved in the Museo Archeologico, Milan, Italy. It measures 11 feet 9 inches in length. The heaviest recorded mammoth tusks are a pair in the Peabody Museum of Archaeology and Ethnology at Harvard University, Cambridge, Massachusetts, U.S.A. which have a combined weight of 498 lb. and measure 13ft. 9in. and 13ft. 7in. respectively.

Horns
Longest The prehistoric Giant deer (*Megaceros giganteus*), which lived in northern Europe and northern Asia as recently as 50,000 B.C., had the longest horns of any known animal. One specimen recovered from an Irish bog had greatly palmated antlers measuring 14 feet across.

18. PROTISTA AND MICROBES

PROTISTA
Protista were first discovered in 1676 by Anton van Leeuwenhoek of Delft (1632–1723), a Dutch microscopist. Among Protista characteristics common to both plants and animals are exhibited. The more plant-like are termed Protophyta (protophytes) and the more animal-like are placed in the phylum Protozoa (protozoans).

Largest The largest protozoans which are known to have existed were the now extinct Nummulites, which each had a diameter of 0.95 of an inch. The largest existing protozoan is *Pelomyxa palustris*, which may attain a length of up to 0.6 of an inch.

Smallest The smallest of all free-living organisms are pleuropneumonia-like organisms (P.P.L.O.) of the *Mycoplasma*. For fuller details see page 26. The smallest of all protophytes is *Micromonas pusilla*, with a diameter of less than 2 microns.

Fastest
moving The protozoan *Monas stigmatica* has been measured to move a distance equivalent to 40 times its own length in a second. No human can cover even seven times his own length in a second.

Fastest
reproduction The protozoan *Glaucoma*, which reproduces by binary fission, divides as frequently as every three hours. Thus in the course of a day it could become a "six greats grandparent" and the progenitor of 510 descendants.

Densest The most densely existing species in the animal kingdom is the sea water dinoflagellate *Gymnodinium breve*, which exists at a density of 240,000,000 per gallon of sea water in certain conditions of salinity and temperature off the coast of Florida, U.S.A.

BACTERIA
Largest The largest of the bacteria is the sulphur bacterium

probably even heavier. It was related to the pelicans and storks. The albatross-like *Gigantornis eaglesomei*, which flew over what is now Nigeria between 34,000,000 and 58,000,000 years ago, has been credited with a wing span of 20 feet on the evidence of a single fossilised breastbone.

Largest
mammal The largest prehistoric mammal, and the largest land mammal ever recorded, was *Baluchitherium* (=*Indricotherium, Paraceratherium, Aceratherium, Thaumastotherium, Aralotherium* and *Benaratherium*), a long-necked hornless rhinoceros which lived in Europe and central and western Asia between 20,000,000 and 40,000,000 years ago. It stood up to 17 ft. 9 in. to the top of the shoulder hump (27 feet to the crown of the head), measured 27-28 feet in length and probably weighed at least 20 tons. The bones of this gigantic browser were first discovered in 1907-08 in the Bugti Hills in east Baluchistan, Pakistan.

Tusks
Longest The longest tusks of any prehistoric animal were those of the straight-tusked elephant *Hesperoloxodon antiquus germanicus,* which lived in what is now northern Germany about 2,000,000 years ago. The average length in adult bulls was 5 metres (16 ft. 4¾ in.). A single tusk of a woolly mammoth (*Mammonteus primigenius*) preserved in the Franzens Museum at Brno, Czechoslovakia measures 5.02 metres (16 ft. 5½ in.) along the outside curve. In *c.* August 1933, a single tusk of an Imperial mammoth (*Archidiskodon imperator*) measuring 16+ feet (anterior end missing) was unearthed near Post, Gorza County, Texas, U.S.A. In 1934 this tusk was presented to the American Museum of Natural History in New York City, N.Y., U.S.A.

Earliest of their type

Type	Scientific name and year of discovery	Location	Estimated years before present
Ape	*Aegyptopitherus zeuxis* (1966)	Fayum, U.A.R.	28,000,000
Primate	tarsier-like	Indonesia	70,000,000
	lemur	Madagascar	70,000,000
Social insect	*Sphecomyrma freyi* (1967)	New Jersey, U.S.A.	100,000,000
Bird	*Archaeopteryx lithographica* (1861)	Bavaria, W. Germany	140,000,000
Mammal	shrew-like (1966)	Thaba-ea-Litau, Lesotho	190,000,000
Reptiles	*Hylonomus, Archerpeton, Protoclepsybrops, Romericus*	all in Nova Scotia	290,000,000
Amphibian	*Ishthyostega* (first quadruped)	Greenland	350,000,000
Spider	*Palaeostenzia crassipes*	Aberdeenshire, Scotland	370,000,000
Insect	*Rhyniella proecursor*	Aberdeenshire, Scotland	370,000,000
Vertebrates	Agnathans (Jawless fish)	near Leningrad, U.S.S.R.	480,000,000
Mollusc	*Neophilina galatheae* (1952)	off Costa Rica	500,000,000
Crustacean	*Karagassiema* (12 legged)	Sayan Mts., U.S.S.R.	*c.* 650,000,000

Beggiatoa mirabilis, which is from 16 to 45 microns in width and which may form filaments several millimetres long.

Highest In April 1967 the U.S. National Aeronautics and Space Administration reported that bacteria had been recently discovered at an altitude of 135,000 feet (25.56 miles).

Longest lived The oldest deposits from which living bacteria are claimed to have been extracted are salt layers near Irkutsk, U.S.S.R., dating from about 600,000,000 years ago. The discovery, not accepted internationally, of their survival was made on 26 Feb. 1962 by Dr. H. J. Dombrowski of Freiberg University, West Germany.

Toughest The bacterium *Micrococcus radiodurans* can withstand atomic radiation of 6.5 million röntgens or 10,000 times that fatal to the average man.

VIRUSES
Largest The largest true viruses are the brick-shaped pox viruses (*e.g.* smallpox, vaccina, orf etc.) measuring *c.* 250 × 300 millimicrons (mμ) or 0.0003 of a millimetre.

Smallest Of more than 1,000 identified viruses, the smallest is the potato spindle tuber virus measuring less than 20 mμ in diameter.

Sub viral infective agents Evidence was announced from the Institute of Research on Animal Diseases at Compton, Berkshire, in January 1967 for the existence of a form of life more basic than both the virus and nucleic acid. It was named SF or Scrapie factor, from the sheep disease. If proven this will become the most fundamental replicating particle known. Its diameter is believed to be not more than 7 millionths of a millimetre. Having now been cultured, it has been allocated back to its former status of an ultra-virus.

19. PLANT KINGDOM (*Plantae*)

Earliest life World If one accepts the definition of life as the ability of an organism to make replicas of itself by taking as building materials the simpler molecules in the medium around it, life probably appeared on Earth about 3,200 million years ago. In April 1969 such a dating was reported for minute spherical bluish fluorescent organisms measuring up to 0.000008 of an inch in diameter found in Swaziland, Southern Africa. The oldest known living life-form was announced in December 1970 by Drs. Sanford and Barbara Siegel of Harvard University, U.S.A., to be a microscopic organism, similar in form to an orange slice, first collected near Harlech, Merionethshire, Wales in 1964. It has been named *Kakabekia barghoorniana* and has existed from 2,000 million years ago.

United Kingdom The oldest micro-fossils found in Great Britain are those suggestive of blue-green algae mucilage identified in pre-Cambrian chert pebbles from north-west Scotland announced in April 1970. The age of the rock antedates the oldest Torridonian rocks of 935 million years and may derive from the fossiliferous Greenland sediments as old as 1,700 million years.

Earliest flower The oldest fossil of a flowering plant with palm-like imprints was found in Colorado, U.S.A., in 1953 and dated about 65,000,000 years old.

Largest forest World The largest afforested areas in the world are the vast coniferous forests of the northern U.S.S.R., lying mainly between latitude 55° N. and the Arctic Circle. The total wooded areas amount to 2,700,000,000 acres (25 per cent. of the world's forests), of which 38 per cent. is Siberian larch. The U.S.S.R. is 34 per cent. afforested.

Great Britain The largest forest in England is Kielder Forest (72,336 acres), in Northumberland. The largest forest in Wales is the Coed Morgannwg (Forest of Glamorgan) (42,555 acres). Scotland's most extensive forest is the Glen Trool Forest (51,376 acres) in Kirkcudbrightshire. The United Kingdom is 7 per cent. afforested.

PLANT
Rarest Plants thought to be extinct are rediscovered each year and there are thus many plants of which specimens are known in but a single locality. The flecked pink spurred coral-root (*Epipogium aphyllum*) is usually cited as Britain's rarest orchid, having been unrecorded between 1931 and 1953. The rose purple Alpine coltsfoot (*Homogyne alpina*), recorded by Don prior to 1814 in the mountains of Clova, Angus, Scotland, was not again confirmed until 1951. The only known location of the adder's-tongue spearwort (*Ranunculus ophioglossifolius*) in the British Isles is the Badgeworth Nature Reserve, Gloucestershire (see page 53). There were only two or three plants of the Lady's Slipper orchid (*Cyripedium calceolus*) in a single locality in 1971.

Commonest World The most widely distributed flowering plant in the world is *Cynodon dactylon*, a toothed grass found as far apart as Canada, Argentina, New Zealand, Japan and South Africa.

British The most widely distributed plant in Great Britain appears to be Ribwort plantain.

Northernmost The yellow poppy (*Papaver radicatum*) and the Arctic willow (*Salix arctica*) survive, the latter in an extremely stunted form, on the northernmost land (83° N.).

Southernmost The most southerly plant life recorded is seven species of lichen found in 1933-34 by the second expedition of Rear-Admiral Richard E. Byrd, U.S. Navy, in latitude 86° 03′ S. in the Queen Maud Mountains, Antarctica. The southernmost recorded flowering plant is the carnation (*Colobanthus crassifolius*), which was found in latitude 67° 15′ S. on Jenny Island, Margaret Bay, Graham Land (Palmer Peninsula), Antarctica.

Highest The greatest altitude at which any flowering plant has been found is 20,130 feet in the Himalaya for *Stellaria decumbens*.

Deepest roots The greatest recorded depth to which roots have penetrated is a calculated 150 feet in the case of a species of *Acacia*, probably *Acacia giraffae*, in a borehole on Okapanje Farm, about 60 miles east of Windhoek, in South West Africa, reported in 1948.

TREES
World's largest living thing The most massive living thing on Earth is the biggest known California big tree (*Sequoiadendron giganteum*) named the "General Sherman", standing 272 feet 4 inches tall, in the Sequoia National Park, California, U.S.A. It has a true girth of 79.1 feet (at 5 feet above the ground). The "General Sherman" has been estimated to contain the equivalent of 600,120 board feet of timber, sufficient to make 40 five-roomed bungalows. The foliage is blue-green, and the red-brown tan bark may be up to 24 inches thick in parts. In 1968 the official published figure for its estimated weight was "2,145 tons" (1,915 long tons).

The seed of a "big tree" weighs only 1/6,000th of an ounce. Its growth at maturity may therefore represent an increase in weight of over 250,000 million fold.

Tallest World The world's tallest known species of tree is the coast redwood (*Sequoia sempervirens*), now found only

The world's tallest tree—a 367.8 foot tall coast redwood discovered in Humboldt County, California in 1964—33½ inches taller than St. Paul's Cathedral, London.

unverified. The tallest specimen now known is c. 310 feet (see above). The most probable claimant was thus a coast redwood of 367 feet 8 inches, felled in 1873 near Guernville, California, U.S.A., thus being the same height as the Howard Libbey Tree as originally measured.

Great Britain The tallest tree in Great Britain is a Douglas fir (*Pseudotsuga taxifolia*) at Powis Castle, Montgomery-shire, Wales, measured at 180 feet in 1970. The tallest in England is a Wellingtonia (*Sequoiadendron giganteum*) measured at 165 feet in February 1970 at Endsleigh, Devon. The tallest measured in Scotland is the Grand fir (*Abies grandis*) at Strone' Cairndow, Argyllshire, planted in 1876, and 175 feet when measured in May 1969 and now estimated to be at least two feet taller.

Ireland The tallest tree in Ireland is a Sitka spruce (*Picea sitchensis*) 162 feet tall at Shelton Abbey, County Wicklow. The Sitka spruce, planted in 1835, at Curraghmore, now 160 feet tall, will soon surpass the Shelton Abbey specimen.

Greatest girth **World** The Santa Maria del Tule Tree, in the state of Oaxaca, in Mexico is a Montezuma cypress (*Taxodium mucronatum*) with a girth of 112—113 feet (1949) at a height of 5 feet above the ground. A figure of 204 feet in circumference was reported for the European chestnut (*Castanea sativa*) known as the "Tree of the 100 Horse" (Castagno di Cento Cavalli) on the edge of Mount Etna, Sicily, Italy in 1770.

Britain's greatest oaks The largest-girthed living British oak is one at Chirk, Denbighshire measuring 40 feet 2 inches (April 1971). It may however be a pollard. The largest "maiden" oak is the Majesty Oak at Fredville, Kent, with a girth of 37 feet 5 inches.

OLDEST
World The oldest recorded living tree is a bristlecone pine (*Pinus longaeva*) designated WPN—114, growing at 10,750 feet above sea-level on the north-east face of Wheeler Peak (13,063 feet) in eastern Nevada, U.S.A. During studies in 1963 and 1964 it was found to be about 4,900 years old. The oldest dated California big tree (*Sequoiadendron giganteum*) is a 3,212-year-old stump felled in 1892, but larger standing specimens are estimated to be between 3,500 and 4,000 years as in the case of the "General Sherman" tree from a ring count from a core drilled in 1931. Dendrochronologists estimate the *potential* life-span of a bristlecone pine at nearly 5,500 years, but that of a "big tree" at perhaps 6,000 years. Ring count dating extends back to 5,150 B.C. by examination of fallen bristlecone pine wood. Such tree-ring datings have led archaeologists to realize that some radiocarbon datings could be 1,000 years or more too young.

growing indigenously near the coast of California from just across the Oregon border south to Monterey.

The tallest example is now believed to be the Howard Libbey Tree in Redwood Creek Grove, Humboldt County, California announced at 367.8 feet in 1964 but discovered to have an apparently dead top and re-estimated at 366.2 feet in 1970. The nearby tree announced to a Senate Committee by Dr. Rudolf W. Becking on 18 June 1966 to be 385 feet proved on re-measurement to be no more than 311.3 feet tall. It has a girth of 44 feet. The tallest non-sequoia is a Douglas fir at Quinault Lake Park trail, Washington, U.S.A. of c. 310 feet.

All-time The identity of the tallest tree of all-time has never been satisfactorily resolved. In 1872 a mountain ash (*Eucalyptus regnans*) found in Victoria, Australia, measured 435 feet from its roots to the point where the trunk had been broken off by its fall. At this point the trunk's diameter was 3 feet, so the overall height was probably at least 500 feet. Its diameter was 18 feet at 5 feet above the ground. Another specimen, known as the "Baron Tree", was reported to be 464 feet in 1868. Modern opinion tends to the view that the highest accurately measured Australian "big gum" tree is one 346 feet tall felled near Colac, Victoria, in 1890. Claims for a Douglas fir (*Pseudotsuga taxifolia*) of 417 feet with a 77-foot circumference felled in British Columbia in 1940 remain

TALLEST TREES IN GREAT BRITAIN AND IRELAND—BY SPECIES

		ft.			ft.
Alder (Italian)	Westonbirt, Gloucester	90	Larch (Japanese)	Blair Castle, Perthshire	121
Alder (Common)	Sandling Park, Kent	85	Lime	Duncombe Park, Yorkshire	154
Ash	Duncombe Park, Yorkshire	148	Metasequoia	Savill Gardens, Windsor, Berkshire	57
Beech	Yester House, East Lothian	142	Monkey Puzzle	Endsleigh, Devon	86
Cedar	Petworth House, Sussex	132	Oak (Common)	Fountains Abbey, Yorkshire	120
Chestnut (Horse)	Petworth House, Sussex	125	Oak (Sessile)	Whitfield House, Hereford	135
Chestnut (Sweet)	Godinton Park, Kent	118	Oak (Red)	West Dean, Sussex	115
Cypress (Lawson)	Endsleigh, Devon	126	Pine (Corsican)	Stanage Park, Radnor	147
Cypress (Monterey)	Tregothnan, Cornwall	120	Plane	Carshalton, Surrey	125
Douglas Fir	Powis Castle, Montgomery	180	Poplar (Black Italian)	Fairlawne, Kent	140
Elm (Wych)	Rossie Priory, Nr. Dundee	128	Poplar (Lombardy)	Marble Hill, Twickenham	118
Elm (Jersey)	Wilton, Wiltshire	121	Silver Fir	Dupplin Castle, Perthshire	154
Eucalyptus (Blue Gum)	Glengarriff, Co. Cork	140	Spruce (Sitka)	Murthly, Perth	174
Grand Fir	Strone, Argyllshire	177	Sycamore	Drumlanrig Castle, Dumfries-shire	112
Ginkgo	Linton Park (Maidstone), Kent	93	Tulip-tree	Taplow House, Buckingham	119
Hemlock (Western)	Benmore, Argyllshire	157	Walnut	Laverstoke Park, Hampshire	82
Holly	Staverton Thicks, Suffolk	74	Wellingtonia	Endsleigh, Devon	165
Hornbeam	Durdans, Epsom, Surrey	105	Yew	Midhurst, Sussex	85
Larch (European)	Parkhatch, Surrey	142			

Great Britain Of all British trees that with the longest life is the yew (*Taxus baccata*), for which a maximum age well in excess of 1,000 years is usually conceded. The oldest known is the Fortingall Yew near Aberfeldy, Perthshire, part of which still grows. In 1777 this tree was over 50 feet in girth and it cannot be much less than 1,500 years old today.

Earliest The earliest species of tree still surviving is the maiden-hair tree (*Ginkgo biloba*) of Chekiang, China, which first appeared about 160,000,000 years ago, during the Jurassic era. It was "re-discovered" by Kaempfer (Netherlands) in 1690 and reached England c. 1754. It has been grown in Japan since c. 1100 where it is known as *Yin Kou*.

Fastest growing Discounting bamboo, which is not botanically classified as a tree, but as a woody grass, the fastest growing tree is *Eucalyptus deglupta*, which has been measured to grow 35 feet in 15 months in New Guinea. The youngest recorded age for a tree to reach 100 feet is 7 years for *E. regnans* in Rhodesia and for 200 feet is 40 years for a Monterey pine in New Zealand.

Slowest growing The speed of growth of trees depends largely upon conditions, although some species, such as box and yew, are always slow-growing. The extreme is represented by a specimen of Sitka spruce which required 98 years to grow to 11 inches tall, with a diameter of less than one inch, on the Arctic tree-line. The growing of miniature trees or *bonsai* is an oriental cult mentioned as early as c. 1320.

Most spreading The greatest area covered by a single clonal growth is that of the wild box huckleberry (*Gaylussacia brachyera*), a mat-forming evergreen shrub first reported in 1796. A colony covering 8 acres was discovered in 1845 near New Bloomfield, Pennsylvania. Another colony, covering about 100 acres, was "discovered" on 18 July 1920 near the Juniata River, Pennsylvania. It has been estimated that this colony began 13,000 years ago.

Most expensive The highest price ever paid for a tree is $51,000 (then £18,214) for a single Starkspur Golden Delicious apple tree from near Yakuma, Washington, U.S.A., bought by a nursery in Missouri in 1959.

WOOD

Heaviest The heaviest of all woods is black ironwood (*Olea laurifolia*), also called South African ironwood, with a specific gravity of up to 1.49, and weighing up to 93 lb. cu. ft. The heaviest British wood is boxwood *(Buxus sempervivens)* with an extreme of 64 lb./cu. ft.

Lightest The lightest wood is *Aeschynomene hispida*, found in Cuba, which has a specific gravity of 0.044 and a weight of only 2¾ lb. per cubic foot. The wood of the balsa tree (*Ochroma pyramidale*) is of very variable density—between 2½ and 24 lb. per cubic foot. The density of cork is 15 lb. per cubic foot.

BAMBOO

Tallest The tallest recorded species of bamboo is *Dendrocalamus giganteus*, native to southern Burma. It was reported in 1904 that there were specimens with a culm-length of 30 to 35 metres (100 to 115 feet) in the Botanic Gardens at Peradeniya, Ceylon.

Fastest growing Some species of the 45 genera of bamboo have attained growth rates of up to 36 inches per day (0.00002 m.p.h.), on their way to reaching a height of 100 feet in less than three months.

BLOOMS

Largest World The mottled orange-brown and white parasitic stinking corpse lily (*Rafflesia arnoldi*) has the largest of all blooms. These attach themselves to the cissus vines of the jungle in south-east Asia and measure up to 3 feet across and ¾ of an inch thick, and attain a weight of 15 lb.

The largest known inflorescence is that of *Puya raimondii*, a rare Bolivian plant with an erect panicle (diameter 8 feet) which emerges to a height of 35 feet. Each of these bears up to 8,000 white blooms (see also Slowest-flowering plant, below).

The world's largest blossoming plant is the giant Chinese wisteria at Sierra Madre, California, U.S.A. It was planted in 1892 and now has branches 500 feet long. It covers nearly an acre, weighs 225 tons and has an estimated 1,500,000 blossoms during its blossoming period of five weeks, when up to 30,000 people pay admission to visit it.

Great Britain The largest bloom of any indigenous British flowering plant is that of the wild white water lily (*Nymphaea alba*), which measures 6 inches across. Other species bear much larger inflorescences.

Smallest flowering plant The smallest of all flowering plants are duckweeds, seen on the surface of ponds. Of these the rootless *Wolffia punctata* has fronds only 1/50th to 1/35th of an inch long. Another species, *Wolffia arrhiza*, occurs in Great Britain but rarely, if ever, flowers there. The smallest plant regularly flowering in Britain is the chaffweed (*Cetunculus minimus*), a single seed of which weighs 0.00003 of a gramme.

Slowest flowering plant The slowest flowering of all plants is the rare *Puya raimondii*, the largest of all herbs, discovered in Bolivia in 1870. The panicle emerges after about 150 years of the plant's life. It then dies. (See also above under Largest blooms.)

Longest daisy chain A team from Hardwicke School, Hardwicke, Aylesbury, Buckinghamshire, completed a daisy chain 289 feet long on 3 May 1972.

LEAVES

Largest World The largest leaves of any plant belong to the raffia palm (*Raphia raffia*) of the Mascarene Islands, in the Indian Ocean, and the Amazonian bamboo palm (*R. toedigera*) of South America, whose leaf blades may measure up to 65 feet in length with petioles up to 13 feet.

The largest undivided leaf is that of *Alocasia macrorrhiza*, found in Sabah, East Malaysia. One found in 1966 measured 9 feet 11 inches long and 6 feet 3½ inches wide, and had an area of 34.2 square feet on one side.

Great Britain The largest leaves to be found in outdoor plants in Great Britain are those of *Gunnera manicata* from Brazil with leaves 6 to 10 feet across on prickly stems 5 to 8 feet long.

FRUIT

Most and least nutritive An analysis of the 38 commonly eaten fruits shows that the one with by far the highest calorific value is avocado (*Persea drymifolia*), with 1,200 calories per lb. That with the lowest value is rhubarb (*Rheum rhaponticum*), which is 94.9 per cent. water, with 80 calories per lb. The fruit with the highest percentage of invert sugar by weight is plantain or cooking banana (*Musa paradisiaca*) with 25.3 per cent., and that with the lowest is rhubarb, with 0.4 of one per cent. Apple (*Malus pumila*) and quince (*Cydonia oblonga*) are the least proteinous, at 0.3 of one per cent.

ORCHID

Largest The largest of all orchids is *Grammatophyllum speciosum*, native to Malaysia. A specimen recorded in Penang, West Malaysia, in the 19th century had 30 spikes up to 8 feet tall and a diameter of more than 40 feet. The largest orchid flower is that of *Selenipedium caudatum*, found in tropical areas of America. Its petals are up to 18 inches long, giving it a maximum outstretched diameter of 3 feet. The flower is, however, much less bulky than that of the stinking corpse lily (see Largest blooms, above).

Tallest The tallest of all orchids is the terrestrial tree-orchid (*Angraecum infundibulare*), which grows in the swamps of Uganda to a height of 12 feet.

Smallest The smallest orchid plant is believed to be *Notylia norae,* found in Venezuela. The smallest orchid flower is that of *Bulbophyllum minutissium,* found in Australia.

Highest priced The highest price ever paid for an orchid is 1,150 guineas (£1,207.50), paid by Baron Schröder to Sanders of St. Albans for an *Odontoglossum crispum* (variety *pittianum*) at an auction by Protheroe & Morris of Bow Lane, London, on 22 March 1906.

Longest seaweed Claims made that seaweed off Tierra del Fuego, South America, grows to 600 and even to 1,000 feet in length have gained currency. More recent and more reliable records indicate that the longest species of seaweed is the Pacific giant kelp (*Macrocyctis pyrifera*), which does not exceed 195 feet in length. It can grow 45 centimetres (17¾ inches) in a day. The

Britain's largest recorded beetroot—a 24 lb monster grown by Mr R. G. Arthur (see table).

RECORD DIMENSIONS AND WEIGHTS FOR FRUIT, VEGETABLES AND FLOWERS GROWN IN THE UNITED KINGDOM

Most data subsequent to 1958 comes from the annual *Garden News* Giant Vegetable and Fruit Contest.

Apple	3 lb. 1 oz.	V. Loveridge	Ross-on-Wye, Herefordshire	1965
Artichoke	8 lb.	A. R. Lawson	Tollerton, Yorkshire	1964
Beetroot	24 lb.	R. G. Arthur	Longlevens, Gloucestershire	1971
Broad Bean	23 ⅜ inches	T. Currie	Jedburgh, Roxburghshire	1963
Broccoli	28 lb. 14¾ oz.	J. T. Cooke	Funtington, Sussex	1964
Brussels Sprout[1]	7 lb. 10 oz.	J. Marsh	Whitfield, Kent	1966
Cabbage[2]	69 lb. 8 oz.	P. Hayes	Uttoxeter, Staffordshire	1965
Carrot[3]	7 lb. 5 oz.	R. Clarkson	Freckleton, Lancashire	1970
Cauliflower	52 lb. 11½ oz.	J. T. Cooke	Funtington, Sussex	1966
Celery	27 lb. 8 oz.	E. E. Allen	Heston, Middlesex	1970
Cucumber	10 lb. 2 oz. (indoor)	W. Hodgson	Birkenhead, Cheshire	1967
	4 lb. 14 oz. (outdoor)	M. Housden	Efford Hill, Hampshire	1966
Dwarf Bean	14½ inches	E. E. Jenkins	Shipston-on-Stour, Warwickshire	1970
Gourd	196 lb.	J. Leathes	Herringfleet Hall, Suffolk	1846
Kale	12 ft. tall	B. T. Newton	Mullion, Cornwall	1950
Leek	9 lb. 4 oz.	E. E. Jenkins	Shipston-on-Stour, Warwickshire	1968
Lemon	1 lb. 12 oz. (girth 15 inches)	T. P. Matthews	Iver Heath, Buckinghamshire	1969
Lettuce	16 lb. 2¼ oz.	J. T. Cooke	Funtington, Sussex	1966
Mangold	46 lb.	D. Bolland	Spalding, Lincolnshire	1964
Marrow[4]	60 lb.	A. V. Bishop	Snailwell, Cambridgeshire	1963
Mushroom[5]	54 inches circum.	—	Hasketon, Suffolk	1957
Onion	5 lb. 13 oz.	W. Taylor	Leicester	1965
Parsnip[6]	9 lb. 4 oz. (31 inches long)	P. C. Richardson	Heighington, Lincolnshire	1962
Pea Pod	10 ⅛ inches	T. Currie	Jedburgh, Roxburghshire	1964
Pear	1 lb. 12¼ oz.	A. Bratton	Shifnal, Shropshire	1966
Potato[7]	7 lb. 1 oz.	J. H. East	Spalding, Lincolnshire	1963
Pumpkin[8]	204 lb. 8 oz.	F. H. Smith	Coventry, Warwickshire	1970
Radish	16 lb. 8 oz.	E. E. Allen	Heston, Middlesex	1966
Red Cabbage	33 lb. 2 oz.	A. Bratton	Ryton, Shropshire	1963
Rhubarb	5 feet 1 inches	A. C. Setterfield	Englefield, Reading, Berkshire	1968
Runner Bean	33¾ inches	A. Bratton	Ryton, Shropshire	1966
Savoy	38 lb. 8 oz.	W. H. Neil	Retford, Nottinghamshire	1966
Shallot	1 lb. 7 oz.	H. H. May	Inkpen, Berkshire	1962
Strawberry[9]	6 oz.	K. M. Muir	Clacton, Essex	1968
Sugar Beet	21 lb.	L. Hawcroft	Holme-on-Spalding Moor, Yorkshire	1971
Sunflower	15 feet 2 inches tall	Mrs. J. A. Hawkins	Capel, Surrey	1969
Swede[10]	32 lb. 8 oz.	R. T. Leeson	Irchester, Northamptonshire	1963
Tomato	3 lb.	B. Austin	Uttoxeter, Staffordshire	1964
Tomato Plant	20 ft. tall, 34 lb. fruit	—	Southport, Lancashire	1957
Tomato Truss	10 lb. 4 oz.	A. L. Smith	Hove, Sussex	1971
Turnip[11]	33 lb. 8 oz.	R. Speight	Cowplain, Hampshire	1963

1 A Brussels Sprout plant measuring 7 feet tall was grown by D. J. Tredrea at Hassocks, Sussex in 1965—66.
2 A 75 lb. cabbage has been reported (since 1930) from Bolton, Lancashire. The Swalwell, County Durham cabbage of 1865 grown by R. Collingwood reputedly weighed 123 lb.
3 One of 7 lb. 7 oz. (15 inches long) reported grown by Police Sgt. Alfred Garwood of Blidworth, Nottinghamshire in November 1970.
4 A 96 lb. marrow has been reported from Suffolk.
5 Same size reported by J. Coombes at Mark, Somerset on 28 July 1965.
6 50 inches long: G. Chesterton near Wyberton, Lincolnshire, April 1959.

7 One weighing 18 lb. 4 oz. reported dug up by Thomas Siddal in his garden in Chester on 17 Feb. 1795. A yield of 1,242 lb. 14 oz. from 6 plants reported on 28 Sept. 1969 by J. T. Cooke (see Broccoli above).
8 One weighing 245 lb. grown by M. Jean Giraud of France reported in 1968. 5 of 298 lb. (biggest 82 lb.) on one plant by George F. Ould, Feniton, Devon in Oct. 1970.
9 A berry weighing 6.35 oz. was gathered in Oberentfelden, Switzerland in June 1971.
10 One weighing 39 lb. 8 oz. claimed by E. R. Reay of Gaitsgill Hall, Dalston, Cumberland in 1940 (unratified).
11 A 73 lb. turnip was reported in December 1768, and one of 34 lb. grown by J. Orr of Preesall, Lancashire in November 1970.

51

longest of the 700 species of seaweed recognized around the coasts of Britain is the brown seaweed *Corda filum* which grows up to a length of 20 feet.

Mosses The smallest of mosses is the pygmy moss (*Ephemerum*), and the longest is the brook moss (*Fontinalis*), which forms streamers up to 3 feet long in flowing water.

FUNGUS

Largest The largest recorded ground fungus was a specimen of the giant puff ball (*Calvatia gigantea*) which was 5 feet 3 inches long, 4 feet 5 inches wide and 9½ inches high. It was discovered in New York State, U.S.A., in 1884.

The largest officially recorded tree fungus was a specimen of *Oxyporus (Fomes) nobilissimus*, measuring 56 inches by 37 inches and weighing at least 300 lb., found by J. Hisey in Washington State, U.S.A., in 1946. The largest recorded in the United Kingdom is an ash fungus (*Fomes fraxineus*) measuring 50 inches by 15 inches wide, found by the forester A. D. C. LeSueur on a tree at Waddesdon, Buckinghamshire, in 1954.

Largest rose tree A "Lady Banks" rose tree at Tombstone, Arizona, U.S.A., has a trunk 40 inches thick, stands 9 feet high and covers an area of 5,380 square feet, supported by 68 posts and several thousand feet of iron piping. This enables 150 people to be seated under the arbour. The original cutting came from Scotland in 1884.

Largest rhododendron The largest species of rhododendron is the scarlet *Rhododendron arboreum*, examples of which reach a height of 60 feet at Mangalbaré, Nepal.

Largest aspidistra The aspidistra (*Aspidistra elatior*) was introduced to Britain as a parlour palm from Japan and China in 1822. The biggest aspidistra in the world is one 49¾ inches tall and grown by George Munns at Perth University, Western Australia and measured in January 1972.

Largest vines The largest recorded grape vine was one planted in 1842 at Carpinteria, California, U.S.A. By 1900 it was yielding more than 9 tons of grapes in some years, and averaging 7 tons per year. It died in 1920. Britain's largest vine (1898–1964) was at Kippen, Stirling with a girth, measured in 1956, of 5 feet. England's largest vine is the Great Vine, planted in 1768 at Hampton Court, Greater London. Its girth is 38 inches, with branches up to 110 feet long and an average yield of 1,200 lb.

Tallest hedge World The world's tallest hedge is the Meikleour beech hedge in Perthshire, Scotland. It was planted in 1746 and has now attained a trimmed height of 85 feet. It is 600 yards long.

Yew The tallest yew hedge in the world is in Earl Bathurst's Park, Cirencester, Gloucestershire. It was planted in 1720, runs for 130 yards, reaches 35 feet and takes 30 man-days to trim.

Box The tallest box hedge is one 35 feet in height at Birr Castle, Offaly, Ireland.

Largest cactus The largest of all cacti is the saguaro (*Cereus giganteus* or *Carnegieia gigantea*), found in Arizona, New Mexico and California, U.S.A., and Sonora, Mexico. The green fluted column is surmounted by candelabra-like branches rising to a height of 53 feet in the case of a specimen found in 1950 near Madrona, New Mexico. They have waxy white blooms which are followed by edible crimson fruit. A cardon cactus in Baja California, Mexico was reputed to reach 58 feet and a weight of 9 tons.

Most poisonous toadstool The yellowish-olive death cap (*Amanita phalloides*) is regarded as the world's most poisonous fungus. It is found in England. From six to fifteen hours after

The "tallest aspidistra in the world", a 49½ inch specimen grown in Perth, Western Australia.

tasting, the effects are vomiting, delirium, collapse and death. Among its victims was Cardinal Giulio de' Medici, Pope Clement VII (b. 1478) on 25 Sept. 1534.

The Registrar General's Report states that between 1920 and 1950 there were 39 fatalities from fungus poisoning in the United Kingdom. As the poisonous types are mostly *Amanita* varieties, it is reasonable to assume that the deaths were predominantly due to *Amanita phalloides.* The most recent fatality was probably in 1960.

FERNS

Largest The largest of all the more than 6,000 species of fern is the tree fern (*Alsophila excelsa*) of Norfolk Island, in the South Pacific, which attains a height of up to 80 feet.

Smallest The world's smallest ferns are *Hecistopteris pumila*, found in Central America, and *Azolla caroliniana*, which is native to the United States.

SEED

Largest The largest seed in the world is that of the double coconut or Coco de Mer (*Lodoicea seychellarum*), the single-seeded fruit of which may weigh 40 lb. This grows only in the Seychelles Islands, in the Indian Ocean.

Smallest The smallest seeds are those of *Epiphytic* orchids, at 35,000,000 to the ounce (*cf.* grass pollens at up to 6,000,000,000 grains per ounce). A single plant of the American ragweed can generate 8,000,000,000 pollen grains in five hours.

Most viable The most viable of all known seeds are those of the Arctic Lupin (*Lupinus arcticus*) found in frozen silt at Miller Creek in the Yukon, Canada in July 1954. They were germinated in 1966 and dated by the radio carbon method to at least 8,000 B.C. and more probably to 13,000 B.C.

GRASS

Longest The tallest of the 160 grasses found in Great Britain is the common reed (*Phragmites communis*), which reaches a height of 9 feet 9 inches.

Shortest The shortest grass native to Great Britain is the very rare sand bent (*Mibora minima*) from Anglesey, which has a maximum growing height of under 6 inches.

Hay fever The highest recorded grass pollen count in Britain was one of 720 (mean number of grains per cubic metre of air noon to noon) near London on 15—16 June 1964. A figure of 1,460 for plane tree pollen was recorded on 9 May 1970. The lowest counts are nil.

orst weeds The most intransigent weed is the mat-forming water weed *Salvinia auriculata,* found in Africa. It was detected on the filling of Kariba Lake in May 1959 and within 11 months had choked an area of 77 sq. miles rising by 1963 to 387 sq. miles. The world's worst land weeds are regarded as purple nut sedge, Bermuda grass, barnyard grass, junglerice, goose grass, Johnson grass, Guinea grass, cogon grass and lantana. The most damaging and widespread cereal weeds in Britain are the wild oats *Avena fatua* and *A. ludoviciana.* Their seeds can withstand temperatures of 240° F. for 15 minutes and remain viable.

Ten-leafed clover A certified ten-leafed clover (*Trifolium pratense*) found by Phillipa Smith in Woodborough, Nottinghamshire in 1966 was exhibited on the *Magpie* T.V. programme on 8 July 1971.

20. PARKS, ZOOS, AQUARIA AND OCEANARIA

PARKS
Largest World The world's largest park is the Wood Buffalo National Park in Alberta, Canada (established 1922), which has an area of 11,172,000 acres (17,560 square miles).

Britain The largest National Park in Great Britain is the Lake District National Park which has an area of 866 square miles. The largest private park in the United Kingdom is Woburn Park (3,000 acres), near Woburn Abbey, the seat of the Dukes of Bedford. The largest common in the United Kingdom is Llansantffraed Cwmdauddwr (28,819 acres) in Radnorshire, Wales.

Smallest The world's smallest nature reserve is believed to be the Badgeworth Nature Reserve (346 square yards), near Cheltenham, Gloucestershire. Owned by the Society for the Promotion of Nature Reserves, it is leased to the Gloucestershire Trust for Nature Conservation to protect the sole site in the British Isles of the adder's-tongue spearwort (*Ranunculus ophioglossifolius*).

The smallest park in the world is Mill Ends Park on a safety island on S.W. Front Avenue, Portland, Oregon, U.S.A. It measures 452.4 square inches (*cf.* this page of 96.9 square inches) and was designated in 1948 at the behest of the city journalist Dick Fagan (d. 1969) for snail races and as a colony for leprechauns.

ZOOS
Largest game reserve It has been estimated that throughout the world there are some 500 zoos with an estimated annual attendance of 330,000,000. The largest zoological preserve in the world has been the Etosha Reserve, South West Africa established in 1907 with an area which grew to 38,427 square miles. In 1970 it was announced that the Kaokoveld section of 26,000 square miles had been de-proclaimed in the interests of the 10,000 Ovahimba and Ovatjimba living in the area.

Largest collection The largest collection in any zoo is that in the Zoological Gardens of West Berlin, Germany. At 1 Jan. 1972 the zoo had a total of 12,653 specimens from 2,399 species. This total included 1,057 mammals (230 species), 2,801 birds (746 species), 575 reptiles (289 species), 148 amphibians (67 species), 2,863 fishes (782 species) and 5,209 invertebrates (285 species).

The giant panda Chi Chi the most valuable animal ever exhibited in the London Zoo.

Oldest The earliest known collection of animals was that set up by Wu-Wang, the first Emperor of the famous Chou Dynasty in China, about 1050 B.C. This 'Park of Intelligence' contained tigers, deer, rhinoceroses, birds, snakes, tortoises and fish. The oldest known zoo is that at Schönbrunn, Vienna, Austria, built in 1752 by the Holy Roman Emperor Franz I for his wife Maria Theresa. The oldest privately owned zoo in the world is that of the Zoological Society of London, founded in 1826. Its collection, housed partly in Regent's Park, London (36 acres) and partly at Whipsnade Park, Bedfordshire (541 acres, opened 1931) is the most comprehensive in the United Kingdom. At the stocktaking on 31 Dec. 1971 there were a total of 9,051 specimens including 1,884 mammals (308 species), 2,567 birds, (684 species), 499 reptiles (216 species), 396 amphibians (46 species), 2,544 fish (311 species), and 1,161 invertebrates (120 species). The record annual attendances are 3,031,571 in 1950 for Regent's Park and 756,758 in 1961 for Whipsnade. The most valuable animal is Chi-Chi the Giant Panda (*Ailuropoda melanoleuca*). She was captured in China on 4th July 1957 when aged probably six months.

Largest aquarium The world's largest aquarium is the John G. Shedd Aquarium on 12th Street and Grant Park, Chicago, Illinois, U.S.A., completed in November 1929 at a cost of $3,250,000 (now £1,354,166). The total capacity of its display tanks is 375,000 gallons, with reservoir tanks holding 1,665,000 gallons. Exhibited are 10,000 specimens from 350 species. Salt water is brought in road and rail tankers from Key West, Florida, and a tanker barge from the Gulf of Mexico. The record attendances are 78,658 in a day on 21 May 1931, and 4,689,730 visitors in the single year of 1931.

OCEANARIA
Earliest and largest The world's first oceanarium is Marineland of Florida, opened in 1938 at a site 18 miles south of St. Augustine, Florida, U.S.A. Up to 5,800,000 gallons of sea-water are pumped daily through two major tanks, one rectangular (100 feet long by 40 feet wide by 18 feet deep) containing 375,000 gallons and one circular (233 feet in circumference and 12 feet deep) containing 330,000 gallons. The tanks are seascaped, including coral reefs and even a shipwreck. The salt water tank at the Marineland of the Pacific, Palos Verdes Peninsula, California, U.S.A. is 251½ feet in circumference and 22 feet deep, with a capacity of 530,000 gallons. The total capacity of this whole oceanarium is 1,830,000 gallons.

3 THE NATURAL WORLD

THE EARTH

The Earth is not a true sphere, but flattened at the poles and hence an ellipsoid. The polar diameter of the Earth (7,899.809 miles) is 25.576 miles less than the equatorial diameter (7,926.385 miles). The Earth also has a slight ellipticity of the equator since its long axis (about longitude 37° W) is 174 yards greater than the short axis. The greatest departures from the reference ellipsoid are a protuberance of 266 feet in the area of New Guinea and a depression of 371 feet south of Ceylon, in the Indian Ocean.

The greatest circumference of the Earth, at the equator, is 24,901.47 miles, compared with 24,859.75 miles at the meridian. The area of the surface is estimated to be 196,937,600 square miles. The period of axial rotation, i.e. the true sidereal day, is 23 hours 56 minutes 4.0996 seconds, mean time.

The mass of the Earth is 5,882,000,000,000, 000,000,000 tons and its density is 5.517 times that of water. The volume is an estimated 259,875,424,000 cubic miles. The Earth picks up cosmic dust but estimates vary widely with 40,000 tons a day being the upper limit. Modern theory is that the Earth has an outer shell or lithosphere about 25 miles thick, then an outer and inner rock layer or mantle extending 1,800 miles deep, beneath which there is an iron-nickel core at an estimated temperature of 3,700° C. and at a pressure of 24,500 tons per square inch or 3,400 kilobars. If the iron-nickel core theory is correct, iron must be by far the most abundant element in the Earth.

1. NATURAL PHENOMENA

EARTHQUAKES

Greatest It is estimated that each year there are some 500,000
World detectable seismic or micro-seismic disturbances of which 100,000 can be felt and 1,000 cause damage.

Using the comparative scale of Mantle Wave magnitudes (defined in 1968), the world's largest earthquake since 1930 has been the cataclysmic Alaska, U.S.A., or Prince William Sound earthquake (epicentre Latitude 61° 10′ N., Longitude 147° 48′ W.) of 28 March 1964 with a magnitude of 8.9. The Kamchatka, U.S.S.R., earthquake (epicentre Lat. 52° 45′ N., Long. 159° 30′ E.) of 4 Nov. 1952 and the

shocks around Lebu, south of Concepción, Chile of 22 May 1960 are both now assessed at a magnitude 8.8. Formerly the largest earthquake during th period had been regarded as the submarine sho (epicentre Lat. 39° 30′ N., Long. 144° 30′ E.) abo 100 miles off the Sanriku coast of north-easter Honshū, Japan on 2 March 1933 estimated at 8.9 the Gutenberg-Richter scale (1956). It is possible th the earthquake in Lisbon, Portugal, on 1 Nov. 175 would have been accorded a magnitude of betwee 8¾ and 9 if seismographs, invented in 1853, had bee available to record traces. The first of the three shoc was at 9.40 a.m. and lasted for between 6 and minutes. Lakes in Norway were disturbed. The energ of an earthquake of magnitude 8.9 is about 5.6×10 ergs, which is equivalent to an explosion of 14 megatons (140,000,000 tons of trinitrotolue $[C_7H_5(NO_2)_3]$ called T.N.T.).

Worst The greatest loss of life occurred in the earthquake
death roll Shensi Province, China, on 23 Jan. 1556, when a estimated 830,000 people were killed. The greate material damage was in the earthquake on th Kwanto plain, Japan, at 11.58 a.m. (local time) of 1 Sept. 1923 (magnitude 8.2, epicentre in Lat. 35° 1 N., Long. 139° 30′ E.). In Sagami Bay the sea-botto

A scene in Alaska 15 months after the most cataclysmic earthqua yet measured on 28 March 1964.

54

in one area sank 1,310 feet. The official total of persons killed and missing in the *Shinsai* or great 'quake and the resultant fires was 142,807. In Tōkyō and Yokohama 575,000 dwellings were destroyed. The cost of the damage was estimated at £1,000 million (now more than £3,000 million).

The East Anglian or Colchester earthquake at 9.18 a.m. on 22 Apr. 1884 (epicentres Lat. 51° 48′ N., Long. 0° 53′ E., and Lat. 51° 51′. N., Long. 0° 55′ E.) caused damaged estimated at £10,000 to 1,200 buildings, and the death of a child at Rowhedge. Langenhoe Church was wrecked. Windows and doors were rattled over an area of 53,000 square miles and the shock was felt in Exeter and Ostend, Belgium. The most marked since 1844 and the worst since instruments have been in use (*i.e.* since 1927) occurred in the Midlands at 3.43 p.m. on 11 Feb. 1957, showing a strength of between five and six on the Davison scale. The strongest Scottish tremor occurred at Inverness at 10.45 p.m. on 13 Aug. 1816, and was felt over an area of 50,000 square miles. The strongest Welsh tremor occurred in Swansea at 9.45 a.m. on 27 June 1906 (epicentre Lat. 51° 38′. N., Long 4° W.). It was felt over an area of 37,800 square miles.

Ireland No earthquake with its epicentre in Ireland has ever been instrumentally measured, though the effects of remoter shocks have been felt. However, there was a shock in August 1734 which damaged 100 dwellings and five churches.

VOLCANOES
The total number of known active volcanoes in the world is 455 with an estimated 80 more that are submarine. The greatest active concentration is in Indonesia, where 77 of its 167 volcanoes have erupted within historic times.

Greatest eruption The total volume of matter discharged in the eruption of Tambora, a volcano on the island of Sumbawa, in Indonesia, 5-7 April 1815, has been estimated at 36.4 cubic miles. The energy of this eruption was 8.4×10^{26} ergs. The volcano lost about 4,100 feet in height and a crater seven miles in diameter was formed. This compares with a probable 15 cubic miles ejected by Santoríni and 4.3 cubic miles ejected by Krakatoa (see below). The internal pressure causing the Tambora eruption has been estimated at 46,500,000 lb. per square inch or more than 20,000 tons per square inch.'

Greatest explosion The greatest volcanic explosion in historic times was the eruption in *c.* 1470 B.C. of Thíra (Santoríni), a volcanic island in the Aegean Sea. It is highly probable that this explosion destroyed the centres of the Minoan civilization in Crete, about 80 miles away, with a *tsunami* 165 feet high. Evidence was published in December 1967 of an eruption that spewed lava over 100,000 square miles of Oregon, Idaho, Nevada and northern California about 3,000,000 years ago.

The greatest explosion since Santoríni occurred at 9.56 a.m. (local time), or 2.56 a.m. G.M.T., on 27 Aug. 1883, with an eruption of Krakatoa, an island (then 18 square miles) in the Sunda Strait, between Sumatra and Java, in Indonesia. A total of 163 villages were wiped out, and 36,380 people killed by the wave it caused. Rocks were thrown 34 miles high and dust fell 3,313 miles away 10 days later. The explosion was recorded four hours later on the island of Rodrigues, 2,968 miles away, as "the roar of heavy guns" and was heard over 1/13th part of the surface of the globe. This explosion has been estimated to have had about 26 times the power of the greatest H-bomb test detonation but was still only a fifth part of the Santoríni cataclysm (see above).

Highest Extinct The highest extinct volcano in the world is Cerro Aconcagua (22,834 feet) on the Argentine side of the Andes. It was first climbed on 14 Jan. 1897 and was the highest summit climbed anywhere until 12 June 1907.

Dormant The highest dormant volcano is Volcán Llullaillaco (22,058 feet), on the frontier between Chile and Argentina.

Active The highest volcano regarded as active is Volcán Antofalla (20,013 feet), in Argentina, though a more definite claim is made for Volcán Guayatiri or Guallatiri (19,882 feet), in Chile, which erupted in 1959.

Northernmost and southernmost The northernmost volcano is Beeren Berg (7,470 feet) on the island of Jan Mayen (71° 05′ N.) in the Greenland Sea. It erupted on 20 Sept. 1970 and the island's 39 male inhabitants had to be evacuated. It was possibly discovered by Henry Hudson in 1607 or 1608, but definitely visited by Jan Jacobsz May (Netherlands) in 1614. It was annexed by Norway on 8 May 1929. The most southerly known active volcano is Mount Erebus (12,450 feet) on Ross Island (77° 35′ S.), in Antarctica. It was discovered on 28 Jan. 1841 by the expedition of Captain (later Rear-Admiral Sir) James Clark Ross, R.N. (1800-1862), and first climbed at 10 a.m. on 10 March 1908 by a British party of five, led by Professor (later Lieut.-Col. Sir) Tannatt William Edgeworth David (1858-1934).

Largest crater The world's largest *caldera* or volcano crater is that of Mount Aso (5,223 feet) in Kyūshū, Japan, which measures 17 miles north to south, 10 miles east to west and 71 miles in circumference. The longest lava flows known as *pahoehoe* (twisted cord-like solidifications) are 60 miles in length in Iceland.

GEYSERS
World's tallest The Waimangu geyser, in New Zealand, erupted to a height in excess of 1,000 feet in 1909, but has not been active since it erupted violently in 1917. Currently the world's tallest active geyser is the "Giant", discovered in 1870 in what is now the Yellowstone National Park, Wyoming, U.S.A., which erupts at intervals varying from 7 days to 3 months, throwing a spire 200 feet high at a rate of 580,000 gallons per hour. The *Geysir* ("gusher") near Mount Hekla in south-central Iceland, from which all others have been named, spurts, on occasions, to 180 feet.

OCEANS
Largest The area of the Earth covered by the sea is estimated to be 139,670,000 square miles, or 70.92 per cent. of the total surface. The mean depth of the hydrosphere was once estimated to be 12,450 feet, but recent surveys suggest a lower estimate, of 11,660 feet. The total weight of the water is estimated to be 1.3×10^{18} tons, or 0.022 per cent. of the Earth's total weight. The volume of the oceans is estimated to be 308,400,000 cubic miles compared with only 8,400,000 cubic miles of fresh water.

The largest ocean in the world is the Pacific. Excluding adjacent seas, it represents 45.8 per cent. of the world's oceans and is about 63,800,000 square miles in area. The shortest navigable trans-Pacific distance from Guayaquil, Ecuador to Bangkok, Thailand is 10,905 miles.

Most southerly The most southerly part of the oceans is 85° 34′ S., 154° W., at the snout of the Robert Scott Glacier, 305 miles from the South Pole, in the Pacific sector of Antarctica.

Deepest The deepest part of the ocean was first discovered in 1951 by H.M. Survey Ship *Challenger* in the Marianas Trench in the Pacific Ocean. The depth was measured by sounding and by echo-sounder and published as 5,960 fathoms (35,760 feet). Subsequent visits to the

55

Challenger Deep have resulted in claims by echo-sounder only, culminating in one of 6,033 fathoms (36,198 feet) by the U.S.S.R.'s research ship *Vityaz* in March 1959. A metal object, say a pound ball of steel, dropped into water above this trench would take nearly 63 minutes to fall to the sea-bed 6.85 miles below. The average depth of the Pacific Ocean is 14,000 feet.

Sea temperature The temperature of the water at the surface of the sea varies from–2° C (28.5° F) in the White Sea to 35.6° C (96° F) in the shallow areas of the Persian Gulf in summer. A freak geo-thermal temperature of 56° C (132.8° F) was recorded in February 1965 by the survey ship *Atlantis II* near the bottom of Discovery Deep (7,200 feet) in the Red Sea. The normal sea temperature in the area is 22° C (71.6° F).

Remotest spot from land The world's most distant point from land is a spot in the South Pacific, approximately 48° 30' S., 125° 30' W., which is about 1,660 miles from the nearest points of land, namely Pitcairn Island, Ducie Island and Cape Dart, Antarctica. Centred on this spot, therefore, is a circle of water with an area of about 8,657,000 square miles—about 7,000 square miles larger than the U.S.S.R., the world's largest country (see Chapter 10).

Largest sea The largest of the world's seas (as opposed to oceans) is the South China Sea, with an area of 1,148,500 square miles. The Malayan Sea comprising the waters between the Indian Ocean and the South Pacific, south of the Chinese mainland covering 3,144,000 square miles is not now an entity accepted by the International Hydrographic Bureau.

Largest gulf The largest gulf in the world is the Gulf of Mexico, with an area of 580,000 square miles and a shoreline of 3,100 miles from Cape Sable, Florida, U.S.A., to Cabo Catoche, Mexico.

Largest bay The largest bay in the world is the Bay of Bengal, with a shoreline of 2,250 miles from south-eastern Ceylon to Pagoda Point, Burma. Its mouth measures 1,075 miles across. Great Britain's largest bay is Cardigan Bay which has a 140 mile long shoreline and measures 72 miles across from the Lleyn Peninsula, Caernarvonshire to St. David's Head, Pembrokeshire in Wales.

Highest seamount The highest known submarine mountain, or sea-mount is one discovered in 1953 near the Tonga Trench, between Samoa and New Zealand. It rises 28,500 feet from the sea bed, with its summit 1,200 feet below the surface.

STRAITS

Longest The longest straits in the world are the Malacca Straits between West Malaysia (formerly called Malaya) and Sumatra, in Indonesia, which extend for 485 miles.

Broadest The broadest straits in the world are the Mozambique Straits between Mozambique and Madagascar, which are at one point 245 miles across.

Narrowest The narrowest navigable straits are those between the Aegean island of Euboea and the mainland of Greece. The gap is only 45 yards wide at Chalkis. The Seil Sound, Argyllshire, Scotland, narrows to a point only 20 feet wide where a bridge joins the island of Seil to the mainland and is thus said to span the Atlantic.

HIGHEST WAVES

The highest officially recorded sea wave was measured by Lt. Frederic Margraff U.S.N. from the U.S.S. *Ramapo* proceeding from Manila, Philippines, to San Diego, California, U.S.A., on the night of 6-7 Feb. 1933, during a 68-knot (78.3 m.p.h.) gale. The wave was computed to be 112 feet from trough to crest. A stereophotograph of a wave calculated to be

24.9 metres (81.7 feet) high was taken from th U.S.S.R.'s diesel-electric vessel *Ob'* in the Sout Pacific Ocean, about 600 kilometres (370 mile south of Macquarie Island, on 2 April 1956. Th highest instrumentally measured wave was one 7 feet high, recorded by the British ship *Weathe Adviser* on station Juliette, in the North Atlantic a noon on 17 Feb. 1968. Its length was 1,150 feet an its period was 15 seconds. It has been calculated c the statistics of the Stationary Random Theory tha one wave in more than 300,000 may exceed th average by a factor of 4.

On 9 July 1958 a landslip caused a wave to was 1,740 feet high along the fiord-like Lituya Ba Alaska, U.S.A.

Seismic wave The highest recorded *tsunami* (often wrongly called tidal wave), was one of 220 feet which appeared o Valdez, south-west Alaska, after the great Princ William Sound earthquake of 28 March 196 *Tsunami* (a Japanese word which is singular an plural) have been observed to travel at 490 m.p. Between 479 B.C. and 1967 there were 286 instanc of devastating *tsunami*.

CURRENTS

Greatest The greatest current in the oceans of the world is th Antarctic Circumpolar Current, which was measure in 1969 in the Drake Passage between South Americ and Antarctica to be flowing at a rate of 9,500 millic cubic feet per second—nearly treble that of the Gu Stream. Its width ranges from 185 to 620 miles an has a surface flow rate of ¾ of a knot.

Strongest The world's strongest currents are the Saltstraumen the Saltfjord, near Bodø, Norway, which reach 15 knots (18.0 m.p.h.). The flow rate through the 50 foot wide channel surpasses 500,000 cusecs (cub feet per sec.). The fastest current in British territori waters is 10.7 knots in the Pentland Firth between th Orkney Islands and Caithness.

GREATEST TIDES

World The greatest tides in the world occur in the Bay c Fundy, which separates Nova Scotia, Canada, fro the United States' north-easternmost state of Mair and the Canadian province of New Brunswicl Burncoat Head in the Minas Basin, Nova Scotia, ha the greatest mean spring range with 47.5 feet, and a extreme range of 53.5 feet.

United Kingdom The place with the greatest mean spring range in Grea Britain is Beachley, on the Severn, with a range c 40.7 feet, compared with the British Isles' average c 15 feet. Prior to 1933 tides as high as 28.9 feet abov and 22.3 feet below datum (total range 51.2 fee were recorded at Avonmouth though an extrem range of 52.2 feet for Beachley was officiall accepted. In 1883 a freak tide of greater range wa reported from Chepstow, Monmouthshire.

Ireland The greatest mean spring tidal range in Ireland is 17. feet at Mellon, Limerick, on the banks of the Riv Shannon.

ICEBERGS

Largest The largest iceberg on record was an Antarctic tabula 'berg of over 12,000 square miles (208 miles long an 60 miles wide and thus larger than Belguim) sighte 150 miles west of Scott Island, in the South Pacifi Ocean, by the U.S.S. *Glacier* on 12 Nov. 1956. Th 200-foot-thick Arctic ice island T.1 (140 squar miles) was discovered in 1946, and was still bein plotted in 1963.

Most southerly Arctic The most southerly Arctic iceberg was sighted in th Atlantic in 30° 50' N., 45° 06' W., on 2 June 1934 The tallest on record was one calved off north-wes Greenland with 550 feet above the surface. Th southernmost iceberg reported in British home waters was one sighted 60 miles from Smith's Knoll, on the Dogger Bank, in the North Sea.

Most The most northerly Antarctic iceberg was a remnant
northerly sighted in the Atlantic by the ship *Dochra* in Latitude
Antarctic 26° 30′ S., Longitude 25° 40′ W., on 30 April 1894.

LAND

There is satisfactory evidence that at one time the Earth's land surface comprised a single primeval continent of 80 million square miles, now termed Pangaea, and that this split about 190,000,000 years ago, during the Jurassic period, into two super-continents, termed Laurasia (Eurasia, Greenland and Northern America) in the north and Gondwanaland (Africa, Arabia, India, South America, Oceania and Antarctica) and named after Gondwana, India. The South Pole was apparently in the area of the Sahara as recently as the Ordovician period of *c.* 450 million years ago.

2. STRUCTURE AND DIMENSIONS

ROCKS

The age of the Earth is generally considered to be within the range of 4600 ± 100 million years, by analogy with directly measured ages of meteorites and of the moon. However, no rocks of this great age have yet been found on the Earth since geological processes have presumably destroyed the earliest record.

Oldest The greatest recorded age for any reliably dated rock
World is 3800 ± 50 million years for the Amitsoq Gneiss from the Godthaab area of West Greenland, as measured by the rubidium-strontium method by workers at Oxford University. A date of 3550 million years has been reported for the Morton Gneiss of Minnesota, U.S.A., measured by the uranium-lead method by American workers, whilst a number of dates in the general range 3200-3400 million years have been reported from Africa, India and the U.S.S.R.

Britain A considerable proportion of the Lewisian Complex of the Northwest Mainland of Scotland and of the Outer Hebrides has been proved to be 2800-2900 million years old by measurements using the rubidium-strontium and uranium-lead methods.

Largest The largest exposed rocky outcrop is the 1,237 foot high Mount Augustus (3,627 feet above sea-level), discovered on 3 June 1858, 200 miles east of Carnarvon, Western Australia. It is an up-faulted monoclinal gritty conglomerate 5 miles long and 2 miles across and thus twice the size of the celebrated monolithic arkose Ayer's Rock (1,100 feet), 250 miles south-west of Alice Springs, in Northern Territory, Australia.

CONTINENTS
Largest Only 29.08 per cent., or an estimated 57,270,000 square miles, of the Earth's surface is land, with a mean height of 2,480 feet above sea-level. The Eurasian land mass is the largest, with an area (including islands) of 21,053,000 square miles.

Smallest The smallest is the Australian mainland, with an area of about 2,940,000 square miles, which, together with Tasmania, New Zealand, New Guinea and the Pacific Islands, is described sometimes as Oceania. The total area of Oceania is about 3,450,000 square miles, including West Irian (formerly West New Guinea), which is politically in Asia.

Land There is an as yet unpinpointed spot in the
remotest Dzoosotoyn Elisen (desert), northern Sinkiang,
ɔm the sea China, that is more than 1,500 miles from the open
World sea in any direction. The nearest large town to this

The largest exposed rock in the world, Mount Augustus, Western Australia, discovered in 1858.

point is Wulumuchi (Urumchi) to its south.

Great Britain The point furthest from the sea in Great Britain is a point near Meriden, Warwickshire, England, which is 72½ miles equidistant from the Severn Bridge, the Dee and Mersey estuaries and the Welland estuary in the Wash. The equivalent point in Scotland is in the Forest of Atholl, Perthshire, 40½ miles equidistant from the head of Loch Leven, Inverness Firth and the Firth of Tay.

Peninsula The world's largest peninsula is Arabia, with an area of about 1,250,000 square miles.

ISLANDS
Largest Discounting Australia, which is usually regarded as a
World continental land mass, the largest island in the world is Greenland (part of the Kingdom of Denmark), with an area of about 840,000 square miles. There is some evidence that Greenland is in fact several islands overlayed by an ice-cap.

Great Britain The mainland of Great Britain (Scotland, England and Wales) is the eighth largest in the world, with an area of 84,186 square miles. It stretches 603½ miles from Dunnet Head in the north to Lizard Point in the south and 287½ miles across from Porthaflod, Pembrokeshire, Wales to Lowestoft, Suffolk. The island of Ireland (32,594 square miles) is the 20th largest island in the world.

LARGEST OFF-SHORE ISLANDS

	Sq. Miles	Name	County	Max. Dimension
Scotland	825.2	Lewis with Harris	Ross and Cromarty, and Inverness-shire	61¼ miles
Wales	278.08	Anglesey	Anglesey	23 miles
England	147.34	Isle of Wight	Hampshire	22¼ miles
Republic of Ireland	56.83	Achill Island	County Mayo	14¼ miles
N. Ireland	5.31	Rathlin Island	County Antrim	4¾ miles

Freshwater The largest island surrounded by fresh water is the Ilha de Marajó (1,553 square miles), in the mouth of the River Amazon, Brazil. The world's largest inland island (*i.e.* land surrounded by rivers) is Ilha do Bananal, Brazil. The largest island in a lake is Manitoulin Island (1,068 square miles) in the Canadian (Ontario) section of Lake Huron. This island itself has on it a lake of 41.09 square miles called Manitou Lake, in which there are several islands. The largest lake island in Great Britain is Inchmurrin in Loch Lomond with an area of 284 acres.

Remotest The remotest island in the world is Bouvet Øya
World (formerly Liverpool Island), discovered in the South
Uninhabited Atlantic by J. B. C. Bouvet de Lozier on 1 Jan. 1739, and first landed on by Capt. George Norris on 16 Dec. 1825. Its position is 54° 26′ S., 3° 24′ E. This uninhabited Norwegian dependency is about 1,050 miles from the nearest land–the uninhabited Queen Maud Land coast of eastern Antarctica.

Inhabited The remotest inhabited island in the world is Tristan

The Shetland Islet of Out Stack to the north of Muckle Flugga, the most northerly chip of the United Kingdom. It is further north than Southern Greenland.

da Cunha, discovered in the South Atlantic by Tristao da Cunha, a Portuguese admiral, in March 1506. It has an area of 38 square miles (habitable area 12 square miles) and was annexed by the United Kingdom on 14 Aug. 1816. The island's population was 235 in August 1966. The nearest inhabited land is the island of St. Helena, 1,320 miles to the north-east. The nearest continent, Africa, is 1,700 miles away.

British The remotest of the British islets is Rockall 191 miles west of St. Kilda, allocated to the County of Inverness in 1971. This 70 foot high rock measuring 83 feet across was not formally annexed until 18 Sept. 1955. The remotest British island which has ever been inhabited is North Rona which is 44 miles from the next nearest land at Cape Wrath and the Butt of Lewis. It was evacuated *c.* 1844. Muckle Flugga, off Unst, in the Shetlands, was the northernmost inhabited until the lighthouse was made automatic in 1970. Unst had a 1971 population of 1,129 and is in a latitude north of southern Greenland.

Newest The world's newest island is a volcanic one about 100 feet high, which began forming in 1970 south of Gatukai Island in the British Solomon Islands, south-west Pacific.

Greatest archipelago The world's greatest archipelago is the 3,500-mile-long crescent of more than 3,00 islands which forms Indonesia.

Northern-most land The most northerly land is Kaffeklubben Øyen (the Coffee Club Island) off the north-east of Greenland, 440 miles from the North Pole, discovered by Dr. Lange Koch in 1921, but determined only in June 1969 to be in Latitude 83° 40′ 6″.

Largest atoll The largest atoll in the world is Kwajalein in the Marshall Islands, in the central Pacific Ocean. Its slender 176-mile-long coral reef encloses a lagoon of 1,100 square miles. The atoll with the largest land area is Christmas Island, in the Line Islands, in the central Pacific Ocean. It has an area of 184 square miles. Its two principal settlements, London and Paris, are 4 miles apart.

Longest reef The longest reef in the Great Barrier Reef off Queensland, north-eastern Australia, which is 1,260 geographical miles in length. Between 1959 and 1969 a large section between Cooktown and Townsville was destroyed by the proliferation of the Crown of Thorns starfish *(Acanthaster planci)*.

MOUNTAINS

Highest World An eastern Himalayan peak of 29,028 feet above sea-level on the Tibet-Nepal border (in an area first designated Chu-mu-lang-ma on a map of 1717) was discovered to be the world's highest mountain in 1852 by the Survey Department of the Government of India, from theodolite readings taken in 1849 and 1850. In 1860 its height was computed to be 29,002 feet. The 5½-mile peak was named Mount Everest after Sir George Everest, C.B. (1790-1866), formerly Surveyor-General of India. After a total loss of 11

lives since the first reconnaissance in 1921, Evere was finally conquered at 11.30 a.m. on 29 May 195 (For details of ascents, see under Mountaineering Chapter 12.) The mountain whose summit is farthe from the Earth's centre is the Andean peak Chimborazo (20,561 feet), 98 miles south of th equator in Ecuador, South America. The highe mountain on the equator is Volcán Gayambe (19,28 feet), Ecuador in, Long. 83°.

The highest insular island in the world is Mt. Sukarı (Carstensz Pyramide) (17,096 feet) in West Iri (formerly New Guinea), Indonesia.

In *The Guinness Book of Records* (seventh edition) a uniq table of the highest points in 220 countries and oth territories was published. Some additional data and amen ments appeared in the 8th, 9th, 10th and 11th editions.

Highest U.K. and Ireland The highest mountain in the United Kingdom is B Nevis (4,406 feet, excluding the 12-foot cairn), 4 miles south-east of Fort William, Inverness-shir Scotland higher than England's highest point, Scaf climbed before 1720 and it was not discovered to higher than Ben Macdhui (4,300 feet) until 1870. 1830 Bens Macdhui and Nevis (Gaelic, Beinn Nibhei were respectively quoted as 4,418 feet and 4,358 fe

There is some evidence that, before being grou down by the ice-cap, mountains in the Loch Bà ar of the Island of Mull were 15,000 feet above sea-lev

There are 577 peaks and tops over 3,000 feet in t whole British Isles and 165 peaks and 136 tops Scotland higher than England's highest point, Scaf Pike. The highest mountain off the mainland is Sgù Alasdair (3,309 feet) on Skye named after Alexand (in Gaelic Alasdair) Nicolson, who made the fi ascent in 1873.

Highest unclimbed Excluding subsidiary summits, the highest separa unclimbed mountain in the world is Gasherbrum (26,090 feet) in the Karakoram, followed by Kar bachen (25,925 feet) in the Himalaya. These rar respectively, 15th and 19th in height in the world.

Largest The world's tallest mountain measured from submarine base (3,280 fathoms) in the Hawaii Trough to peak is Mauna Kea (Mountain White) the Island of Hawaii, with a combined height 33,476 feet, of which 13,796 feet are above sea-lev Another mountain whose dimensions, but not heig exceed those of Mount Everest is the Hawaiian pe of Mauna Loa (Mountain Long) at 13,680 feet. T axes of its elliptical base, 15,000 feet below sea-lev have been estimated at 74 miles and 53 miles. should be noted that Cerro Aconcagua (22,834 fe is more than 38,800 feet above the 16,000 foot de Pacific abyssal plain or 42,834 feet above t Peru-Chile Trench which is 180 miles distant in t South Pacific.

Greatest ranges The world's greatest land mountain range is t Himalaya-Karakoram, which contains 96 of t world's 109 peaks of over 24,000 feet. The greatest all mountain ranges is, however, the submari mid-Atlantic Ridge, which is 10,000 miles long a 500 miles wide, with its highest peak being Mou Pico in the Azores, which rises 23,615 feet from t ocean floor (7,615 feet above sea-level).

Greatest plateau The most extensive high plateau in the world is t Tibetan Plateau in Central Asia. The average altitu is 16,000 feet and the area is 77,000 square miles.

Highest halites Along the northern shores of the Gulf of Mexico 725 miles there exist 330 subterranean "mountain of salt, some of which rise more than 60,000 fe from bed rock and appear as the low salt domes fi discovered in 1862.

HIGHEST POINTS IN THE GEOGRAPHICAL COUNTIES OF THE UNITED KINGDOM AND THE REPUBLIC OF IRELAND.

Numbers in brackets indicate the order of the counties with the highest point.

ENGLAND

40 Geographical counties	Height in feet	Location
Bedfordshire	798	Dunstable Downs
Berkshire	974	Walbury Hill
Buckinghamshire	857	In Halton Woods, Halton Hill
Cambridgeshire and Isle of Ely	478	300 yards south of the Hall, Great Chishill
Cheshire	1,908	Black Hill
Cornwall	1,375	Brown Willy
Cumberland (1)	3,206[1]	SCAFELL PIKE
Derbyshire (9)	2,088	Kinder Scout
Devon (10)	2,038	High Willhays
Dorset	908	Pilsdon Pen
Durham, County (6)	2,449	Near Burnhope Seat
Essex	480	In High Wood, nr. Langley
Gloucestershire	1,083	Cleeve Cloud
Hampshire (inc. Isle of Wight)	937	Pilot Hill, nr. Ashmansworth
Herefordshire (7)	2,306	Black Mountains
Hertfordshire	802	Hastoe
Huntingdon and Peterborough	c.267	South of Stamford
Kent	824	Westerham (old fort trig. point)
Lancashire (4)	2,631	Old Man of Coniston
Leicestershire	912	Bardon Hill, nr. Coalville
Lincolnshire	550	Normanby-le-Wold
London, Greater	809	33 yds. S.E. of "Westerham Height", (a house) on the Kent-G.L.C. boundary
Monmouthshire (8)	2,228	Chwarel-y-Fan
Norfolk	329	Roman Camp, Sheringham
Northamptonshire	734	Arbury Hill
Northumberland (3)	2,676	The Cheviot
Nottinghamshire	652	S. side of Herrods Hill
Oxfordshire	835	Portobello
Rutland	646	West of Oakham
Shropshire	1,772	Brown Clee Hill
Somerset	1,705	Dunkery Beacon
Staffordshire	1,684	Oliver Hill
Suffolk	420	Rede
Surrey	965	Leith Hill
Sussex	919	Blackdown Hill
Warwickshire	854	Ilmington Downs
Westmorland (2)	3,118	Helvellyn
Wiltshire	964	Milk Hill and Tan Hill
Worcestershire	1,394	Worcestershire Beacon
Yorkshire (5)	2,591	Mickle Fell

[1] *Formerly 3,210 feet.*

SCOTLAND   33 Geographical counties

Aberdeenshire (2)	4,296	Ben Macdhui (shared with Banffshire)
Angus (7)	3,504	Glas Maol
Argyll (6)	3,766	Bidean nam Bian
Ayrshire	2,565	Kirriereoch Hill
Banffshire (2)	4,296	Ben Macdhui (shared with Aberdeenshire)
Berwickshire	c, 1,730	Meikle Says Law (slopes of)
Bute	2,868	Goat Fell, Arran
Caithness	2,313	Morven
Clackmannanshire	2,363	Ben Cleugh (Clach) (Ochils)
Dumfries-shire	2,696	White Coomb
Dumbarton (10)	3,092	Ben Vorlich
East Lothian	1,755	Meikle Says Law
Fife	1,713	West Lomond
Inverness-shire (1)	4,406	BEN NEVIS
Kincardineshire	2,555	Mount Battock (on Angus border)
Kinross-shire	1,630	Innerdouny Hill (Ochils)
Kirkcudbrightshire	2,770	Merrick
Lanarkshire	2,455	Culter Fell
Midlothian	2,137	Blackhope Scar
Moray	2,329	Càrn A 'Ghille Chearr
Nairnshire	2,162	Càrn-Glas-Choire
Orkney	1,570	Ward Hill, Hoy
Peebles-shire	2,756	Broad Law (shared with Selkirkshire)
Perthshire (4)	3,984	Ben Lawers
Renfrewshire	1,713	Hill of Stake (on Ayrshire border)
Ross and Cromarty (5)	3,880	Carn Eige (on Inverness-shire border)
Roxburghshire	2,433	Nr. Auchope Cairn (on English border)
Selkirkshire	2,756	Broad Law (shared with Peebles-shire)
Shetland	1,486	Ronas Hill, Northmavine
Stirlingshire (9)	3,192	Ben Lomond
Sutherland (8)	3,273	Ben More Assynt
West Lothian	1,023	The Knock
Wigtownshire	1,051	Craigairie Fell

WALES   12 Geographical counties

Anglesey	720	Caer y Twr
Breconshire (3)	2,906	Pen-y-Fan (Cader Arthur)
Caernarvonshire (1)	3,560	SNOWDON (Y WYDDFA)
Cardiganshire	2,468	Plynlimon
Carmarthenshire (6)	2,500+	Carmarthen Fan Foel
Denbighshire (4)	2,713	Moel Sych (shared with Montgomery-shire)
Flintshire	1,820	Moel Fammau
Glamorgan	1,969	Cefnfford
Merionethshire (2)	2,972	Aran Fawddwy, nr. Bala
Montgomeryshire (4)	2,713	Moel Sych (shared with Denbighshire)
Pembrokeshire	1,760	Foel Cumcerwyn
Radnorshire	2,166	In Radnor Forest

NORTHERN IRELAND (6 Counties)

Antrim	1,817	Trostàn
Armagh	1,894	Slieve Gullion
Down (1)	2,796	SLIEVE DONARD
Fermanagh	2,188	Cuilcagh
Londonderry	2,240	Sawel Mountain
Tyrone	2,240	Sawel Mountain

REPUBLIC OF IRELAND (26 Counties)

Carlow (6)	2,610	Mount Leinster
Cavan	2,188	Cuilcagh
Clare	1,746	Glennagalliagh
Cork	2,321	Knockboy
Donegal	2,466	Errigal
Dublin	2,475	Kippure
Galway	2,395	Benbaun
Kerry (1)	3,414	CARRANTUOHILL
Kildare	1,248	Cupidstown Hill
Kilkenny	1,703	Brandon
Leitrim	2,113	Truskmore
Leix	1,734	Arderin
Limerick (3)	3,018	Galtymore
Longford	916	Cornhill
Louth	1,935	Slieve Foye
Mayo (5)	2,688	Mweelrea
Meath	911	Canbane East
Monaghan	1,255	Slieve Beagh
Offaly	1,734	Arderin
Roscommon	1,284	Corry Mountain
Sligo	2,113	Truskmore
Tipperary (3)	3,018	Galtymore
Waterford (8)	2,609	Knockmealdown
Westmeath	855	Mullaghmeen
Wexford (6)	2,610	Mount Leinster
Wicklow (2)	3,039	Lugnaquillia

Sand dunes The world's highest measured sand dunes are those in the Saharan sand sea of Isaouane-N-Tiferine of east central Algeria in Lat. 26° 42′ N, Long. 6° 43′ E. They have a wavelength of nearly 3 miles and attain a height of 430 metres (1,410 feet).

DEPRESSIONS

Deepest
World The deepest depression so far discovered is beneath the Hollick-Kenyon Plateau in Marie Byrd Land, Antarctica, where, at a point 5,900 feet above sea-level, the ice depth is 14,000 feet, hence indicating a bed rock depression 8,100 feet below sea-level. The greatest submarine depression is a large area of the floor of the north west Pacific which has an average depth of 15,000 feet.

The deepest exposed depression on land is the shore surrounding the Dead Sea, 1,291 feet below sea-level. The deepest point on the bed of this lake is 2,600 feet below the Mediterranean. The deepest part of the bed of Lake Baykal in Siberia, U.S.S.R., is 4,872 feet below sea-level.

Great The lowest lying area in Great Britain is in the Holme
Britain Fen area of the Great Ouse, in northern Huntingdon and Peterborough, at nine feet below sea-level. The deepest depression in England is the bed of part of Windermere, 94 feet below sea-level, and in Scotland the bed of Loch Morar, 987 feet below sea-level.

Largest The largest exposed depression in the world is the Caspian Sea basin in the Azerbaydzhani, Russian, Kazakh and Turkmen Republics of the U.S.S.R. and northern Iran (Persia). It is more than 200,000 square miles, of which 143,550 square miles is lake area. The preponderant land area of the depression is the Prikaspiyskaya Nizmennost', lying around the northern third of the lake and stretching inland for a distance of up to 280 miles.

RIVERS

The river systems of the world are estimated to contain 55,000 cubic miles of fresh water.

Longest The two longest rivers in the world are the Amazon
World *(Amazonas)*, flowing into the South Atlantic, and the Nile *(Bahr-el-Nil)* flowing into the Mediterranean. Which is the longer is a matter of definition rather than measurement.

The true source of the Amazon was discovered in 1953 to be a stream named Huarco, rising near the summit of Cerro Huagra (17,188 ft.) in Peru. This stream progressively becomes the Toro then the Santiago then the Apurímac, which in turn is known as the Ene and then the Tambo before its confluence with the Amazon prime tributary the Ucayali. The length of the Amazon from this source to the South Atlantic *via* the Canal do Norte was measured in 1969 to be 4,007 miles (usually quoted to the rounded off figure of 4,000 miles).

If, however, a vessel navigating down river turns to the south of Ilha de Marajó through the straits of Breves and Boiuci into the Pará, the total length of the watercourse becomes 4,195 miles. The Pará is not however a tributary of the Amazon, being hydrologically part of the basin of the Tocantins.

The length of the Nile watercourse, as surveyed by M. Devroey (Belgium) before the loss of a few miles of meanders due to the formation of Lake Nasser, behind the Aswan High Dam, was 4,145 miles. This course is the hydrologically acceptable one from the source in Ruanda of the Luvironza branch of the Kagera feeder of the Victoria Nyanza *via* the White Nile *(Bahr-el-Jebel)* to the delta.

Ireland The longest river in Ireland is the Shannon, which is longer than any river in Great Britain. It rises 258 feet above sea-level, in County Cavan, and flows

through a series of loughs to Limerick. It is 240 mi long, including the 56-mile long estuary to Lo Head. The basin area is 6,060 square miles.

Great Britain The longest river in Great Britain is the Severn, whi empties into the Bristol Channel and is 220 mil long. Its basin extends over 4,409 square miles. It ris in south-western Montgomeryshire, in Wales a flows through Shropshire, Worcestershire a Gloucestershire. The longest river wholly in Engla

A statue marking one of the disputed sources of England's longest river—the 215 mile long Thames.

is the Thames, which is 215 miles long to the Nore. remotest source is at Seven Springs, Gloucestershi whence the River Churn joins the other head wate The source of the Thames proper is Trewsbury Mea Coate, Cirencester, Gloucestershire. The basin me sures 3,841 square miles. The longest river who in Wales is the Towy, with a length of 64 miles. It ris in Cardiganshire and flows out into Carmarthen Ba The longest river in Scotland is the Tay, with Dund Angus, on the shore of the estuary. It is 117 miles lo from the source of its remotest head-stream, t Tummel, and has the greatest volume of any river Great Britain, with a flow of up to 49,000 cubic fe per second. Its basin extends over 1,961 square mil

Greatest flow The greatest flow of any river in the world is that the Amazon, which discharges an average 4,200,000 cusecs into the Atlantic Ocean, rising more than 7,000,000 cusecs in full flood. The low 900 miles of the Amazon average 300 feet in dep

Largest basin The largest river basin in the world is that drained
and longest the Amazon (4,195 miles). It covers about 2,720,0
tributary square miles. It has about 15,000 tributaries a subtributaries, of which four are more than 1,0 miles long. These include the Madeira, the longest all tributaries, with a length of 2,100 miles, which surpassed by only 14 rivers.

Longest The longest sub-tributary is the Pilcomayo (1,0
sub-tributary miles long) in South America. It is a tributary of t Paraguay (1,500 miles long), which is itself a tribut of the Parana (2,500 miles).

Submarine In 1952 a submarine river 250 miles wide, known
river the Cromwell current, was discovered flowing ea ward 300 feet below the surface of the Pacific f 3,500 miles along the equator. Its volume is 1,0 times that of the Mississippi.

Subterranean In August 1958 a crypto-river was tracked by rad
river isotopes flowing under the Nile with a mean annu flow six times greater—560,000 million cubic meti (20 million million cubic feet).

Longest The world's longest estuary is that of the Ob', in t
estuary northern U.S.S.R., at 450 miles.

Largest delta The world's largest delta is that created by the Ganga (Ganges) and Brahmaputra in Bangla Desh (formerly East Pakistan) and West Bengal, India. It covers an area of 30,000 square miles.

RIVER BORES

World The bore on the Ch'ient'ang'kian (Hang-chou-fe) in eastern China is the most remarkable in the world. At spring tides the wave attains a height of up to 25 feet and a speed of 13 knots. It is heard advancing at a range of 14 miles. The bore on the Hooghly branch of the Ganges travels for 70 miles at more than 15 knots. The annual downstream flood wave on the Mekong sometimes reaches a height of 46 feet. The greatest volume of any tidal bore is that of the Canal do Norte (10 miles wide) in the mouth of the Amazon.

Great Britain The most notable river bore in the United Kingdom is that on the River Severn, which attained a measured height of 9¼ feet on 15 Oct. 1966 downstream of Stonebench, and a speed of 13 m.p.h. It travels 21 miles from Awre to Gloucester.

Fastest rapids The fastest rapids which have ever been navigated are the Lava Falls on the River Colorado in the United States. At times of flood these attain a speed of 30 m.p.h. (26 knots) with waves boiling up to 12 feet high.

WATERFALLS

Highest The highest waterfall in the world is the Angel Falls, in Venezuela, on a branch of the River Carrao, an upper tributary of the Caroní with a total drop of 3,212 feet—the longest single drop is 2,648 feet. It was discovered in 1935 by a United States pilot named Jimmy Angel (died 8 Dec. 1956), who crashed nearby.

United Kingdom The tallest waterfall in the United Kingdom is Eas-Coul-Aulin, in the parish of Eddrachillis, Sutherland, Scotland, with a drop of 658 feet. England's highest fall is Caldron (or Cauldron) Snout, on the Tees, with a fall of 200 feet, in 450 feet of cataracts, but no sheer leap. It is at the junction of Durham, Westmorland and Yorkshire. The highest Welsh waterfall is the Pistyll Rhaiadr (240 feet), on the River Rhaiadr, in southern Denbighshire.

Ireland The highest falls in Ireland are the Powerscourt Falls (350 feet), on the River Dargle, County Wicklow.

Greatest On the basis of the average annual flow, the greatest waterfall in the world is the Guaira (374 feet high), known also as the Salto dos Sete Quedas, on the Alto Paraná River between Brazil and Paraguay. Although attaining an average height of only 110 feet, its estimated annual average flow over the lip (5,300 yards wide) is 470,000 cubic feet per second. The amount of water this represents can be imagined by supposing that it was pouring into the dome of St. Paul's Cathedral—it would fill it completely in three-fifths of a second. It has a peak flow of 1,750,000 cubic feet per second. The seven cataracts of the Stanley Falls in the Congo (Kinshasa) have an average annual flow of 600,000 cubic feet per second.

Widest The widest waterfalls in the world are the Khône Falls (50 to 70 feet high) in Laos, with a width of 6.7 miles and a flood flow of 1,500,000 cubic feet per second.

Longest fjords and sea lochs
World The world's longest fjord is the Nordvest fjord arm of the Scoresby Sund in eastern Greenland, which extends inland 195 miles from the sea. The longest of Norwegian fjords is the Sogne Fjord, which extends 183 kilometres (113.7 miles) inland from Sygnefest to the head of the Lusterfjord arm at Skjolden. It averages barely 3 miles in width and has a deepest point of 4,085 feet. If measured from Huglo along the Bømlafjord to the head of the Sørfjord arm at Odda, the Hardengerfjorden can also be said to extend 183

kilometres (113.7 miles). The longest Danish fjord is the Limfjorden (100 miles long).

Great Britain Scotland's longest sea loch is Loch Fyne, which extends 42 miles inland into Argyllshire.

LAKES AND INLAND SEAS

Largest
World The largest inland sea or lake in the world is the Kaspiskoye More (Caspian Sea) in the southern U.S.S.R. and Iran (Persia). It is 760 miles long and its total area is 143,550 square miles. Of the total area some 55,280 square miles (38.6%) is in Iran, where it is named the Darya-ye-Khazar. Its maximum depth is 980 metres (3,215 feet) and its surface is 92 feet below sea-level. Its estimated volume is 21,500 cubic miles of saline water. Since 1930 it has diminished 15,000 square miles in area with a fall of 62 feet, while the shore line has retreated more than 10 miles in some places.

Freshwater lake
World The freshwater lake with the greatest surface area is Lake Superior, one of the Great Lakes of North America. The total area is 31,800 square miles, of which 20,700 square miles are in Minnesota, Wisconsin and Michigan, U.S.A. and 11,100 square miles in Ontario, Canada. It is 600 feet above sea-level. The freshwater lake with the greatest volume is Baykal (see Deepest lake, below) with an estimated volume of 5,750 cubic miles.

United Kingdom The largest lake in the United Kingdom is Lough Neagh (48 feet above sea-level) in Northern Ireland. It is 18 miles long and 11 miles wide and has an area of 147.39 square miles. Its extreme depth is 102 feet.

Great Britain The largest lake in Great Britain, and the largest inland loch in Scotland is Loch Lomond (23 feet above sea-level), which is 22.64 miles long and has a surface area (including islands) of 32.81 square miles. It is situated in the counties of Stirling and Dunbarton and its greatest depth is 623 feet. The longest lake is Loch Ness which measures 22.75 miles. The largest lake in England is Windermere, in the county of Westmorland. It is 10½ miles long and has a surface area of 5.69 square miles. Its greatest depth is 219 feet in the northern half. The largest *natural* lake in Wales is Llyn Tegid, with an area of 1.69 square miles, although it should be noted that the largest lake in Wales is that formed by the reservoir at Lake Vyrnwy, where the total surface area is 1,120 acres.

Republic of Ireland The largest lough in the Republic of Ireland is Lough Corrib in the counties of Mayo and Galway. It measures 27 miles in length and is 7 miles across at its widest point with a total surface area of 41,616 acres (65.0 square miles).

Lake in a lake The largest lake in a lake is Manitou Lake (41.09 square miles) on Manitoulin Island (1,068 square miles) in the Canadian part of Lake Huron.

DEEPEST LAKES

World The deepest lake in the world is Ozero (Lake) Baykal in central Siberia, U.S.S.R. It is 620 kilometres (385 miles) long and between 20 and 46 miles wide. In 1957 the Olkhon Crevice was measured to be 1,940 metres (6,365 feet) deep and hence 4,872 feet below sea-level.

Great Britain The deepest lake in Great Britain is the 12-mile-long Loch Morar, in Inverness-shire. Its surface is 30 feet above sea-level and its extreme depth 1,017 feet. England's deepest lake is Wast Water (258 feet), in Cumberland.

HIGHEST LAKES

World The highest steam-navigated lake in the world is Lago Titicaca (maximum depth 1,214 feet), with an area of about 3,200 square miles (1,850 square miles in Peru, 1,350 square miles in Bolivia), in South America. It is

130 miles long and is situated at 12,506 feet above sea-level. There is a small unnamed lake north of Mount Everest by the Changtse Glacier, Tibet, at an altitude of 20,230 feet above sea-level.

United Kingdom The highest lake in the United Kingdom is the 1.9 acre Lochan Buidhe at 3,600 feet above sea-level in the Cairngorm Mountains, Scotland. England's highest is Broad Crag Tarn (2,746 feet above sea-level) on Scafell, Cumberland, and the highest in Wales is a pool above Llyn y Fign (c. 2,540 feet), 8 miles east of Dolgellau, Merionethshire.

Longest glaciers It is estimated that 6,020,000 square miles, or about 10.4 per cent of the Earth's land surface, is permanently glaciated. The world's longest known glacier is the Lambert Glacier, discovered by an Australian aircraft crew in Australian Antarctic Territory in 1956—57. It is up to 40 miles wide and, with its upper section, known as the Mellor Glacier, it measures at least 250 miles in length. With the Fisher Glacier limb, the Lambert forms a continuous ice passage about 320 miles long. The longest Himalayan glacier is the Siachen (47 miles) in the Karakoram range, though the Hispar and Biafo combine to form an ice passage 76 miles long.

Greatest avalanches The greatest avalanches, though rarely observed, occur in the Himalaya but no estimates of their volume have been published. It was estimated that 3,500,000 cubic metres (120,000,000 cubic feet) of snow fell in an avalanche in the Italian Alps in 1885. (See also Disasters, end of Chapter 11.)

DESERT

Largest Nearly an eighth of the world's land surface is arid with a rainfall of less than 25 cms. (9.8 in.) per annum. The Sahara Desert in N. Africa is the largest in the world. At its greatest length it is 3,200 miles from east to west. From north to south it is between 800 and 1,400 miles. The area covered by the desert is about 3,250,000 square miles. The land level varies from 436 feet below sea-level in the Qattâra Depression, United Arab Republic (formerly Egypt), to the mountain Emi Koussi (11,204 feet) in Chad. The diurnal temperature range in the western Sahara may be more than 80 degrees F. or 45 degrees C.

GORGE

Largest The largest gorge in the world is the Grand Canyon on the Colorado River in north-central Arizona, U.S.A. It extends from Marble Gorge to the Grand Wash Cliffs, over a distance of 217 miles. It varies in width from 4 to 13 miles and is up to 7,000 feet deep.

Deepest The deepest visible canyon in the world is Hell's Canyon, dividing Oregon and Idaho, U.S.A. It plunges 7,900 feet from the Devil Mountain down to the Snake River. The deepest submarine canyon yet discovered is one 25 miles south of Esperance, Western Australia, which is 6,000 feet deep and 20 miles wide.

CAVES

Largest World The largest known underground chamber in the world is the Big Room of the Carlsbad Caverns (1,320 feet deep) in New Mexico, U.S.A. It is 4,270 feet long and reaches 328 feet in height and 656 feet in width. The largest cavern in Britain is a cavern about 2,500 feet long, discovered on 13 April 1966 under Mynydd-dhu, a hill in Carmarthenshire, Wales. It contains stalagmites 12 feet tall and a waterfall with a drop of 100 feet.

The most extensive cave system in the world is said to be the Flint Ridge Cave system, discovered in 1799 in Kentucky, U.S.A. Its total length is reputed to be more than 150 miles, but it contains only 72.9 miles of actual mapped passageway. The longest cave system in Great Britain is Ogof Ffynnon Ddu,

Breconshire in South Wales, in which 20.3 miles of passages have so far been surveyed.

DEEPEST CAVES BY COUNTRIES

These depths are subject to continuous revisions.

Feet below Entrance		
4,300	Gouffre de la Pierre Saint-Martin, Pyrenees	France/Spain
3,750	Gouffre Berger, Sornin Plateau, Vercors	France
2,906	Spulga della Preta, Lessinische Alps	Italy
2,427	Hölloch, Moutatal, Schwyz	Switzerland
2,329	Gruberhorn Höhle, Hoher Göll, Salzburg	Austria
2,099	Sniezna, Tatra	Poland
2,040	Gouffre de Faour Dara	Lebanon
2,006	Sotano del San Agustin	Mexico
1,969	Gouffre Juhue	Spain
1,885	Ragge favreraige	Norway
1,770	Abisso Vereo, Istria	Yugoslavia
1,690	Anou Boussouil, Djurdjura	Algeria
>1,300	Provetina, Mount Astraka	Greece
1,184	Neff's Cave, Utah	U.S.A.
1,115	Izvorul Tausoarelor, Rodna	Romania
850	Ogof Ffynnon Du, Breconshire	Wales
653	Oxlow Cavern, Giant's Hole, Derbyshire	England
527	Growling Swallet Cave, Tasmania	Australia
330	Pollnagollum-Poulelva, County Clare	Ireland

LONGEST CAVE SYSTEMS BY COUNTRIES

These surveyed lengths are subject to continuous revision.

Miles		
72.9	Flint Ridge Cave System, Kentucky	U.S.A.
67.2	Hölloch, Schwyz	Switzerland
32.74	Sistema Cavernavio de Cuyaguatega	Cuba
*26.10	Eisriesenwelt, Werfen, Salzburg	Austria
22.74	Peschtschera Optimistitshcheskaya, Pololien	U.S.S.R.
22.48	Complejo Palomera-Dolencias, Burgos	Spain
20.3	Ogof Ffynnon Du, Breconshire	Wales
17.00	Postojnska Jama, Slovenia	Yugoslavia
15.98	Réseau de la Dent de Crolles	France
13.67	Baradla Barlang-Jaskyna Domica, Magyarország	Hungary
12.5	Lancaster Hole—Easegill Caverns, Westmorland	England
7.39	Poulnagollum-Poulelva Caves, County Clare	Ireland
>6	Mullamullang Cave	Australia

Longest ice caves, discovered in 1879. Now rank as eighth longest known.

Longest stalactite The longest known stalactite in the world is wall-supported column extending 195 feet from roof to floor in the Cueva de Nerja, near Málaga, Spain. The rather low tensile strength of calcite (calcium carbonate) precludes very long free-hanging stalactites, but one of 38 feet exists in the Poll an Ionai cave in County Clare, Ireland.

Tallest stalagmite The tallest known stalagmite in the world is La Grande Stalagmite in the Aren Armand cave, Lozère, France, which has attained a height of 98 feet from the cave floor. It was found in September 1897.

SEA CLIFFS

Highest The location of the highest sea cliffs in the world has yet to be established. These may be in north-west Greenland. Coastal terrain at Dexterity Fjord, north-east Baffin Island rises to 4,000 feet. The highest cliffs in the British Isles are those on the north coast of Achill Island, in County Mayo, Ireland, which are 2,192 feet sheer above the sea at Croaghan. The highest cliffs in the United Kingdom are the 1,300 feet Conachair cliffs on St. Kilda, Scotland (1,397 feet). England's highest cliffs are at Countisbury, North Devon, where they drop 900 feet.

NATURAL BRIDGE

Longest The longest natural bridge in the world is the Landscape Arch in the Arches National Monument, Utah, U.S.A. This natural sandstone arch spans 291 feet and is set about 100 feet above the canyon floor. In one place erosion has narrowed its section to six feet.

3. WEATHER

The meteorological records given below necessarily relate largely to the last 125 to 145 years, since data before that time are both sparse and unreliable. Reliable registering thermometers were introduced as recently as c. 1820.

Palaeo-entomological evidence is that there was a southern European climate in England c. 90,000 B.C.

while in *c.* 6,000 B.C. the mean summer temperature reached 67° F, or 6 deg. F higher than the present. The earliest authentic British weather records relate to the period 26–30 Aug. 55 B.C. The earliest reliably known hot summer was in A.D. 664 during our driest ever century and the earliest known severe winter was that of A.D. 763-4. In 1683-84 there was frost in London from November to April. Frosts were recorded during August in the period 1668–89.

Progressive extremes The world's extremes of temperature have been noted progressively thus:

127.4°F	Ouargla, Algeria	27 Aug. 1884
130°F	Amos, California, U.S.A.	17 Aug. 1885
130°F	Mammoth Tank, California, U.S.A.	17 Aug. 1885
134°F	Death Valley, California, U.S.A.	10 July 1913
136.4°F	Al 'Aziziyah (el-Azizia), Libya*	13 Sept. 1922

* Obtained by the U.S. National Geographic Society but not officially recognized by the Libyan Ministry of Communications.

A reading of 140° F at Delta, Mexico, in August 1953 is not now accepted because of over-exposure to roof radiation. The official Mexican record of 136.4° F at San Luis, Sonora on 11 Aug. 1933 is not internationally accepted.

A freak heat flash reported from Coimbra, Portugal, in September 1933 to have caused the temperature to rise to 70° C (158° F) for 120 seconds is apocryphal.

Lowest Screen Temperatures

−73° F	Floeberg Bay, Ellesmere Is., Canada		1852
−90.4° F	Verkhoyansk, Siberia, U.S.S.R.	3 Jan.	1885
−90.4° F	Verkhoyansk, Siberia, U.S.S.R.	5 & 7 Feb.	1892
−90.4° F	Oymyakon, Siberia, U.S.S.R.	6 Feb.	1933
−100.4° F	South Pole, Antarctica	11 May	1957
−102.1° F	South Pole, Antarctica	17 Sept.	1957
−109.1° F	Sovietskaya, Antarctica	2 May	1958
−113.3° F	Vostok, Antarctica	15 June	1958
−113.8° F	Sovietskaya, Antarctica	19 June	1958
−117.4° F	Sovietskaya, Antarctica	25 June	1958
−122.4° F	Vostok, Antarctica	7–8 Aug.	1958
−124.1° F	Sovietskaya, Antarctica	9 Aug.	1958
−125.3° F	Vostok, Antarctica	25 Aug.	1958
−126.9° F	Vostok, Antarctica	24 Aug.	1960

Most equable temperature The location with the most equable recorded temperature over a short period is Garapan, on Saipan, in the Mariana Islands, Pacific Ocean. During the nine years from 1927 to 1935, inclusive, the lowest temperature recorded was 19.6° C (67.3° F) on 30 Jan. 1934 and the highest was 31.4° C (88.5° F) on 9 Sept. 1931, giving an extreme range of 11.8 deg. C (21.2 deg. F). Between 1911 and 1966 the Brazilian off-shore island of Fernando de Noronha had a minimum temperature of 18.6° C (65.5° F) on 17 Nov. 1913 and a maximum of 32.0° C (89.6° F) on 2 March 1965, an extreme range of 13.4 deg. C (24.1 deg. F).

Humidity and discomfort Human comfort or discomfort depends not merely on temperature but on the combination of temperature, humidity, radiation and wind-speed. The United States Weather Bureau uses a Temperature-Humidity Index, which equals two-fifths of the sum of the dry and wet bulb thermometer readings plus 15. When the THI reaches 75 in still air, at least half of the people will be uncomfortable while at 79 few, if any, will be comfortable. When the index reaches 86 inside a Federal building in Washington, D.C., everybody may be sent home. A reading of 92 (shade temperature 119° F, relative humidity 22%) was recorded at Yuma, Arizona, U.S.A., on 31 July 1957, but even this must have been surpassed in Death Valley, California, U.S.A.

Greatest temperature ranges The greatest recorded temperature ranges in the world are around the Siberian "cold pole" in the eastern U.S.S.R. Olekminsk has ranged 189 deg. F from -76° F to 113° F and Verkhoyansk (67° 33′ N., 133° 23′ E.) has ranged 192 deg. F from -94° F (unofficial) to 98° F.

The greatest temperature variation recorded in a day is 100 deg. F (a fall from 44° F to -56° F) at Browning, Montana, U.S.A., on 23–24 Jan. 1916. The most freakish rise was 49 deg. F in 2 minutes at Spearfish, South Dakota, from -4° F at 7.30 a.m. to 45° F at 7.32 a.m. on 22 Jan. 1943. The British record is 50.9 deg. F (34.0° F to 84.9° F) in 9 hours at Rickmansworth, Hertfordshire, on 29 Aug. 1936.

Longest freeze The longest recorded unremitting freeze (maximum temperature 32° F and below) in the British Isles was one of 34 days at Moor House, Westmorland, from 23 Dec. 1962 to 25 Jan. 1963. This was almost certainly exceeded at the neighbouring Great Dun Fell, where the screen temperature never rose above freezing during the whole of January 1963. Less rigorous early data includes a frost from 5 Dec. 1607 to 14 Feb. 1608 and a 91 day frost on Dartmoor, Devon in 1854–5.

Upper atmosphere The lowest temperature ever recorded in the atmosphere is −143° C (−225.4° F) at an altitude of about 50 to 60 miles, during noctilucent cloud research above Kronogård, Sweden, from 27 July to 7 Aug. 1963. A jet stream moving at 408 m.p.h. at 154,200 feet (29.2 miles) was recorded by Skua rocket above South Uist, Outer Hebrides, Scotland on 13 Dec. 1967.

Deepest permafrost The greatest recorded depth of permafrost is 1.5 kilometres (4,921 feet) reported in April 1968 in the basin of the River Lena, Siberia, U.S.S.R.

Most intense rainfall Difficulties attend rainfall readings for very short periods but the figure of 1.23 inches in one minute at Unionville, Maryland, U.S.A., at 3.23 p.m. on 4 July 1956, is regarded as the most intense recorded in modern times. The cloudburst of "near two foot . . . in less than a quarter of half an hour" at Oxford on the afternoon of 31 May (Old Style) 1682 is regarded as unacademically recorded. The most intense rainfall in Britain recorded to modern standards has been 2.0 inches in 12 minutes at Wisbech, Cambridgeshire on 28 June 1970.

Falsest St. Swithin's Days The legend that the weather on St. Swithin's Day, celebrated on 15 July since A.D. 912, determines rainfall for the next 40 days is one which has long persisted. There was a brilliant 13½ hours sunshine in London on 15 July 1924, but 30 of the next 40 days were wet. On 15 July 1913 there was a 15-hour downpour, yet it rained on only nine of the subsequent 40 days in London

Lightning The visible length of lightning strokes varies greatly. In mountainous regions, when clouds are very low, the flash may be less than 300 feet long. In flat country with very high clouds, a cloud-to-earth flash sometimes measures four miles, though in extreme cases such flashes have been measured at 20 miles. The intensely bright central core of the lightning channel is extremely narrow. Some authorities suggest that its diameter is as little as half an inch. This core is surrounded by a "corona envelope" (glow discharge) which may measure 10 to 20 feet in diameter.

The speed of a lightning discharge varies from 100 to 1,000 miles per second for the downward leader track, and reaches up to 87,000 miles per second (nearly half the speed of light) for the powerful return stroke. In Britain there is an average of six strikes per square mile per annum, and an average of 4,200 per annum over Greater London alone. Every few million strokes there is a giant discharge, in which the cloud-to-earth and the return lightning strokes flash from the top of the thunder clouds. In these "positive giants" energy of up to 3,000 million joules (3×10^{16} ergs) is sometimes recorded. The temperature reaches about 30,000° C, which is more than five times greater than that of the surface of the Sun.

Highest waterspout The highest waterspout of which there is a reliable record was one observed on 16 May 1898 off Eden,

New South Wales, Australia. A theodolite reading from the shore gave its height as 5,014 feet. It was about 10 feet in diameter. A waterspout moved around Tor Bay, Devon on 17 Sept. 1969 which was according to press estimates 1,000 feet in height.

Cloud extremes The highest standard cloud form is cirrus, averaging 27,000 feet and above, but the rare nacreous or mother-of-pearl formation sometimes reaches nearly 80,000 feet. The lowest is stratus, below 3,500 feet. The cloud form with the greatest vertical range is cumulo-nimbus, which has been observed to reach a height of nearly 68,000 feet in the tropics. Noctilucent "clouds", e.g. over Hampshire on 30 June 1950, are believed to pass at a height of over 60 miles.

Best and worst British summers According to Prof. Gordon Manley's survey over th period 1728 to 1970 the best (i.e. driest and hottes British summer was that of 1949 and the worst (i. wettest and coldest) that of 1879. The mean tempe ature for June, July and August 1911 at Shanklin, Is of Wight was, however, 2.5 deg. F. higher than 1949 at 64.9° F.

Most recent White Christmas and Frost Fair London has experienced seven "White" Christma Days since 1900. These have been in 1906, 191 (slight), 1923 (slight), 1927, 1938, 1956 (slight) an 1970. These were more frequent in the 19th centur and even more so before the change of calendar 1752. The last of the nine recorded Frost Fairs hel on the Thames was in Dec. 1813 to 26 Jan. 1814.

WEATHER RECORDS

World Records	United Kingdom & Ireland
Highest Shade Temperature: 136.4° F Al' Aziziyah, Libya, 13.9.1922	100.5° F (38° C), Tonbridge, Kent, 22.7.1868[1]
Lowest Screen Temperature: −126.9° F, Vostok, Antarctica, 24.8.1960[2]	−17° F (−27.2° C), Braemar, Aberdeenshire, Scotlan 11.2.1895[3]
Greatest Rainfall (24 hours): 73.62 in., Cilaos, La Réunion, Indian Ocean, 15-16.3.1952[4]	11.00 in., Martinstown, Dorset, 18–19.7.1955
(Month) 366.14 in., Cherrapunji, Assam, India, July 1861	56.54 in., Llyn Llydau, Snowdon, Caernarvonshi October 1909
(12 Months): 1,041.78 in., Cherrapunji, Assam, 1.8.1860- 31.7.1861	257.0 in., Sprinkling Tarn, Cumberland, in 1954[5]
Greatest Snowfall[6] (12 Months): 1,014.5 in. At 5,400 ft. on Mt. Rainier, Washington State, U.S.A. 1970-71.	60 in., Upper Teesdale and Denbighshire Hills, 1947
Maximum Sunshine:[7] 97%+ (over 4,300 hours), eastern Sahara, annual average	78.3% (382 hours), Pendennis Castle, Falmou Cornwall, June 1925
Minimum Sunshine: Nil at North Pole-for winter stretches of 186 days	Nil in a month at Westminster, London, in Decem 1890[8]
Barometric Pressure (Highest): 1,083.8 mb. (32.00 in.), Agata, Siberia, U.S.S.R. (alt 862 ft.), 31.12.1968	1,054.7 mb. (31.15 in.), Aberdeen, 31.1.1902
(Lowest): 877mb. (25.91 in.), about 600 miles north- west of Guam, Pacific Ocean, 24.9.1958	925.5 mb. (27.33 in.), Ochtertyre, near Crie Perthshire, 26.1.1884
Highest Surface Wind-speed:[9] 231m.p.h., Mt. Washington (6,288 ft.), New Hampshire, U.S.A., 12.4.1934	144 m.p.h. (125 knots), Coire Cas ski lift (3,525 fee Cairn Gorm, Inverness-shire, 6.3.1967[10]
Thunder-Days (Year):[11] 322 days, Bogor (formerly Buitenzorg), Java, Indonesia (average, 1916−19)	38 days, Stonyhurst, Lancashire, 1912 a Huddersfield, Yorkshire, 1967
Hottest Place (Annual mean):[12] Dallol, Ethiopia, 94° F (34.4° C) (1960−66).	Penzance, Cornwall, and Isles of Scilly, both 52.7° (11.5° C), average 1931-60
Coldest Place (Annual mean): Pole of Cold (78° S., 96° E.), Antarctica, −72° F (16 deg. F lower than the Pole)	Braemar, Aberdeenshire, 43.7° F (6.5° C), avera 1931-60
Wettest Place (Annual mean): Mt. Wai-'ale'ale (5,080 ft.), Kauai, Hawaii, 486.1 inches (average, 1920−58). About 335 rainy days per year	Styhead Tarn (1,600 ft.), Cumberland, 172.9 in.
Driest Place (Annual mean): Calama, in the Desierto de Atacama, Chile	Great Wakering, Essex 19.2 in. (1916−1950)[13]
Longest Drought: c 400 years to 1971, Desierto de Atacama, Chile	73 days, Mile End, London, 4.3 to 15.5.1893[14]
Most Rainy Days (Year): Bahia Felix, Chile, 348 days in 1916	Ballynahinch Galway, 309 days in 1923
Heaviest Hailstones:[15] 1.67 lb. (7½ in. diameter, 17½ in. circumference), Coffeyville, Kansas, U.S.A., 3.9.1970.	5 oz., Horsham, Sussex, 5.9.1958
Longest Fogs (Visibility less than 1,000 yards): Fogs persist for weeks on the Grand Banks, Newfoundland, Canada, and the average is more than 120 days per year	London, 26.11 to 1.12.1948 (4 days 18 hours) Londo 5.12 to 9.12.1952 (4 days 18 hours)
Windiest Place: The Commonwealth Bay, George V Coast, Antarctica, where gales reach 200 m.p.h.	Tiree, Argyllshire (89 ft.); annual average 17.4 m.p.h.

1 The shade temperature in London on 8 July 1808 may have reached this figure.
2 Vostok is 11,500 feet above sea-level. The coldest permanently inhabited place is the Siberian village of Oymyakon (63° 16' N., 143° 15' E.), in the U.S.S.R., where the temperature reached −96° F in 1964.
3 The −23° F at Blackadder, Berwickshire on 4 Dec. 1879, and the −20° F at Grantown-on-Spey on 24 Feb. 1955, were not standard exposures. The −11° F reported from Buxton, Derbyshire on 11 Feb. 1895 was not standard. The lowest official temperature in England is −6° F (−21.1° C) at Bodiam, Sussex on 20 Jan. 1940, at Ambleside, Westmorland on 21 Jan. 1940 and at Houghall, Durham on 5 Jan. 1941 and 4 March 1947.
4 This is equal to 7,435 tons of rain per acre. Elevation 1,200 metres (3,937 feet).
5 The record for Ireland is 154.4 in. near Derriana Lough, County Kerry, in 1948.
6 The record for a single snow storm is 175.4 in. at Thompson Pass, Alaska, on 26—31 Dec. 1955, and, for 24 hours, 76 in. at Silver Lake, Colorado, U.S.A., on 14—15 April 1921. London's earliest recorded snow was on 25 Sept. 1885, and the latest on 27 May 1821. Less reliable reports suggest snow on 12 Sept. 1658 and on 12 June 1791.
7 St. Peterburg, Florida, U.S.A. recorded 768 consecutive sunny days from 9 Feb. 1967 to 17 March 1969.
8 The south-eastern end of the village of Lochranza, Isle of

Arran, Bute is in shadow of mountains from 18 Nov. 8 Feb. each winter.
9 The highest speed yet measured in a tornado is 280 m.p. at Wichita Falls, Texas, U.S.A., on 2 April 1958.
10 The figure of 177.2 m.p.h. at R.A.F. Saxa Vord, Unst, the Shetlands, Scotland, on 16 Feb. 1962, was n recorded with standard equipment. There were gales great severity on 15 Jan. 1362 and 26 Nov. 1703.
11 Between Lat. 35° N. and 35° S. there are some 3,2 thunderstorms each 12 night-time hours, some of whi can be heard at a range of 18 miles.
12 In Death Valley, California, U.S.A., maximum temp atures of over 120° F were recorded on 43 consecut days—6 July to 17 Aug. 1917. At Marble Bar, Weste Australia (maximum 121° F), 160 consecutive days wi maximum temperatures of over 100° F were rec ded—31 Oct. 1923 to 7 April 1924. At Wyndha Western Australia, the temperature reached 90° F more on 333 days in 1946.
13 The lowest rainfall recorded in a single year was 9.29 at one station in Margate, Kent, in 1921.
14 The longest drought in Scotland was one of 38 days Port William, Wigtownshire on 3 Apr. to 10 May 1938.
15 Much heavier hailstones are sometimes reported. The are usually not single but coalesced stones. An 8½- stone was reported at Bicester, Oxfordshire, on 11 M 1945.

64

4 THE UNIVERSE AND SPACE

LIGHT-YEAR—that distance travelled by light (speed 186,282.42±0.06 miles per second or 670,616,722.8 m.p.h., *in vacuo*) in one tropical (or solar) year (365.24219878 mean solar days at January 0, 12 hours Ephemeris time in A.D. 1900) and is 5,878,500,600,000 miles. The unit was first used in March 1888.

MAGNITUDE—a measure of stellar brightness such that the light of a star of any magnitude bears a ratio of 2.511886 to that of a star of the next magnitude. Thus a fifth magnitude star is 2.511886 times as bright, while one of the first magnitude is exactly 100 (or 2.511886^5) times as bright, as a sixth magnitude star. In the case of such exceptionally bright bodies as Sirius, Venus, the Moon (magnitude −11.2) or the Sun (magnitude −26.7), the magnitude is expressed as a minus quantity.

PROPER MOTION—that component of a star's motion in space which, at right angles to the line of sight, constitutes an apparent change of position of the star in the celestial sphere.

The universe is the entirety of space, matter and anti-matter. An appreciation of its magnitude is best grasped by working outward from the Earth, through the Solar System and our own Milky Way galaxy, to the remotest extra-galactic nebulae.

METEOROIDS

Meteor shower Meteoroids are mostly of cometary origin. A meteor is the light phenomenon caused by the entry of a meteoroid into the Earth's atmosphere. The greatest meteor "shower" on record occurred on the night of 16-17 Nov. 1966, when the Leonid meteors (which recur every 33¼ years) were visible between western North America and eastern U.S.S.R. It was calculated that meteors passed over Arizona, U.S.A., at a rate of 2,300 per minute for a period of 20 minutes from 5 a.m. on 17 Nov. 1966.

METEORITES

Largest World When a meteoroid penetrates to the Earth's surface, the remnant is described as a meteorite. The largest known meteorite is one found in 1920 at Hoba West, near Grootfontein in South West Africa. This is a block about 9 feet long by 8 feet broad, weighing 132,000 lb. (59 tons). The largest meteorite exhibited by any museum is the "Tent" meteorite, weighing 68,085 lb. (30.4 tons), found in 1897 near Cape York, on the west coast of Greenland, by the expedition of Commander (later Rear-Admiral) Robert Edwin Peary (1856-1920). It was known to the Eskimos as the Abnighito and is now exhibited in the Hayden Planetarium in New York City, N.Y., U.S.A.

The largest piece of stony meteorite recovered is a piece of the Norton County meteorite which fell in Nebraska, U.S.A. on 18 Feb. 1948. The greatest amount of material recovered from any non-metallic meteorite is from the Allende fall of more than 1 ton in Chihuahua, Mexico on 8 Feb. 1969.

There was a mysterious explosion of about 35 megatons in Latitude 60° 55′ N., Longitude 101° 57′ E., in the basin of the Podkamennaya Tunguska river, 40 miles north of Vanavara, in Siberia, U.S.S.R., at 00 hours 17 minutes 11 seconds U.T. on 30 June 1908. The energy of this explosion was about 10^{24} ergs and the cause has been variously attributed to a meteorite (1927), a comet (1930), a nuclear explosion (1961) and to anti-matter (1965). This devastated an area of about 1,500 square miles and the shock was felt as far as 1,000 kilometres (more than 600 miles) away.

United Kingdom and Ireland The heaviest of the 22 meteorites known to have fallen on the British Isles since 1795 was one weighing at least 102 lb. (largest piece 17 lb. 6 oz.), which fell at 4.12 p.m. on 24 Dec. 1965 at Barwell, Leicestershire. Scotland's largest recorded meteorite fell in Strathmore, Perthshire, on 3 Dec. 1917. It weighed 22¼ lb. and was the largest of four stones totalling 29 lb. 6 oz. The largest recorded meteorite to fall in Ireland was the Limerick Stone of 65 lb., part of a shower 106 lb. which fell near Adare, County Limerick, on 10 Sept. 1813. The larger of the two recorded meteorites to land in Wales was one weighing 28 oz., of which a piece weighing 25½ oz. went through the roof of the Prince Llewellyn Hotel in Beddgelert, Caernarvonshire, shortly before 3.15 a.m. on 21 Sept. 1949.

Largest craters Aerial surveys in Canada in 1956 and 1957 brought to light a gash, or astrobleme, 8½ miles across near Deep Bay, Saskatchewan, possibly attributable to a very old and very oblique meteorite. U.S.S.R. scientists reported in Dec. 1970 an astrobleme with a 60 mile diameter and a maximum depth of 1,300 feet in the basin of the River Popigai. There is a possible crater-like formation 275 miles in diameter on the eastern shore of the Hudson Bay, where the Nastapoka Islands are just off the coast.

The largest proven crater is the Coon Butte or Barringer crater, discovered in 1891 near Canyon Diablo, Winslow, northern Arizona, U.S.A. It is 4,150 feet in diameter and now about 575 feet deep, with a parapet rising 130 to 155 feet above the surrounding plain. It has been estimated that an iron-nickel mass

65

with a diameter of 200 to 260 feet, and weighing about 2,000,000 tons, gouged this crater in c. 25,000 B.C., with an impact force equivalent to an explosion of 30,000,000 tons of trinitrotuluenc ($C_7H_5O_6N_3$), called T.N.T.

Evidence published in 1963 discounted a meteoric origin for the crypto-volcanic Vredefort Ring (diameter 26 miles), to the south-west of Johannesburg, South Africa, but this has now been re-asserted. The New Quebec (formerly the Chubb) "Crater", first sighted on 20 June 1943 in northern Ungava, Canada, is 1,325 feet deep and measures 6.8 miles round its rim.

Tektites The largest tektite of which details have been published has been of 3.2 kilogrammes (7.04 lb.) found c. 1932 at Muong Nong, Saravane Province, Laos and now in the Paris Museum.

AURORA

Most frequent Polar lights, known as Aurora Borealis or Northern Lights in the northern hemisphere and Aurora Australis in the southern hemisphere, are caused by electrical solar discharges in the upper atmosphere and occur most frequently in high latitudes. The maximum auroral frequencies, of up to 240 displays per year, have occurred in the Hudson Bay area of northern Canada. The extreme height of auroras has been measured at 1,000 kilometres (620 miles), while the lowest may descend to 45 miles.

Southernmost "Northern Lights" Displays occur 90 times a year (on average) in the Orkneys, 25 times a year in Edinburgh, seven times a year in London, and once a decade in southern Italy. On 25 Sept. 1909 a display was witnessed as far south as Singapore (1° 25′ N.). The greatest auroral displays over the United Kingdom in recent times occurred on 24-25 Oct. 1870 and 25-26 Jan. 1938.

Us

THE MOON

The Earth's closest neighbour in space and only natural satellite is the Moon, at a mean distance of 238,855 statute miles centre to centre or 233,812 miles surface to surface. Its closest approach (perigee) and most extreme distance away (apogee) measured surface to surface are 216,420 and 247,667 miles respectively or 221,463 and 252,710 miles measured centre to centre. It has a diameter of 2,159.9 miles in the plane of the sky and has a mass of 7.23×10^{19} tons with a mean density of 3.34. The average orbital speed is 2,287 m.p.h.

The first direct hit on the Moon was achieved at 2 minutes 24 seconds after midnight (Moscow time) on 14 Sept. 1959, by the Soviet space probe *Lunik II*

The shore of the Quebec crater discovered in Northern Ungava, Canada which measures 6¾ miles round its rim.

near the *Mare Serenitatis*. The first photographi images of the hidden side were collected by th U.S.S.R.'s *Lunik III* from 6.30 a.m. on 7 Oct. 1959 from a range of up to 43,750 miles, and transmitte to the Earth from a distance of 470,000 kilometre (292,000 miles). The first "soft" landing was made b: the U.S.S.R.'s *Luna IX,* launched at about 11 a.m G.M.T. on 31 Jan. 1966. It landed in the area of th Ocean of Storms (*Oceanus Procellarum*) at 18 hour 45 minutes 30 seconds G.M.T. on 3 Feb. 1966.

"Blue Moon" Owing to sulphur particles in the upper atmospher from a forest fire covering 250,000 acres betwee Mile 103 and Mile 119 on the Alaska Highway i northern British Columbia, Canada, the Moon too on a bluish colour, as seen from Great Britain, on th night of 26 Sept. 1950. The Moon also appeared blu after the Krakatoa eruption of 27 Aug. 1883 (see pag 55) and on other occasions.

Crater Largest Only 59 per cent. of the Moon's surface is directl visible from the Earth because it is in "capture rotation", *i.e.* the period of revolution is equal to th period of orbit. The largest wholly visible crater is th walled plain Bailly, towards the Moon's South Pol which is 183 mile across, with walls rising to 14,00 feet. The Orientale Basin, partly on the averted sid measures more than 600 miles in diameter.

Deepest The deepest crater is the Newton crater, with a floc estimated to be between 23,000 and 29,000 fee below its rim and 14,000 feet below the level of th plain outside. The brightest directly visible spot o the Moon is *Aristarchus*.

Highest mountains As there is no water on the Moon, the heights c mountains can be measured only in relation t lower-lying terrain near their bases. The highest luna mountains were, until 1967, thought to be in th Leibnitz and Doerfel ranges, near the lunar Sout Pole with a height of some 35,000 feet. On th discovery from Lunar Orbiter spacecraft of evidenc that they were merely crater rims, the names hav been withdrawn. Currently it is believed that such a elevation would be an exaggerated estimate for an feature of the Moon's surface.

Temperature extremes When the Sun is overhead, the temperature on th lunar equator reaches 243° F. (31 deg. F. above th boiling point of water). By sunset the temperature 58° F., but after nightfall it sinks to −261° F.

Moon rocks The age attributed to the oldest of the moon rock brought back to Earth by the *Apollo XV* crew on Aug. 1971 was the "genesis rock" aged 4,200 millio years. It was picked up at Spur Crater on th Apennine Front on 1 August.

THE SUN

Distance extremes The Earth's 66,690 m.p.h. orbit of 584,000,000 mil around the Sun is elliptical, hence our distance fro the Sun varies. The orbital speed varies between 65,600 m.p.h. (minimum) and 67,800 m.p.h. The average distance of the Sun is 92,955,840 miles.

The closest approach (perihelion) is 91,395,000 miles and the farthest departure (aphelion) is 94,513,300 miles. The Solar System is revolving around the centre of the Milky Way once in each 225,000 years, at a speed of 481,000 m.p.h. and has a velocity of 42,500 m.p.h. relative to stars in our immediate region such as Vega, towards which it is moving.

Temperature and dimensions The Sun has an internal temperature of about 20,000,000° K., a core pressure of 500,000,000 tons per square inch and uses up 4,000,000 tons of hydrogen per second, thus providing a luminosity of 3 $\times$ 10^{27} candlepower, or 1,500,000 candlepower per square inch. The Sun has the stellar classification of a "yellow dwarf" and, although its density is only 1.41 times that of water, its mass is 333,430 times as much as that of the Earth. It has a mean diameter of 865,370 miles. The Sun with a mass of 1.961 $\times$ 10^{27} tons represents more than 99 per cent. of the total mass of the Solar System.

Sun-spots
Largest To be visible to the *protected* naked eye, a Sun-spot must cover about one two-thousandth part of the Sun's hemisphere and thus have an area of about 500,000,000 square miles. The largest recorded Sun-spot occurred in the Sun's southern hemisphere on 8 April 1947. Its area was about 7,000 million square miles, with an extreme longitude of 187,000 miles and an extreme latitude of 90,000 miles. Sun-spots appear darker because they are more than 1,500 deg. C. cooler than the rest of the Sun's surface temperature of 5,660° C. The largest observed solar prominence was one measuring 70,000 miles across its base and protruding 300,000 miles, observed on 4 June 1946.

Most frequent In October 1957 a smoothed Sun-spot count showed 263, the highest recorded index since records started in 1755 (*cf.* previous record of 239 in May 1778). In 1943 a Sun-spot lasted for 200 days from June to December.

ECLIPSES
Earliest recorded The earliest extrapolated eclipses that have been identified are 1361 B.C. (lunar) and 2136 B.C. (solar). For the Middle East only, lunar eclipses have been extrapolated to 3450 B.C. and solar ones to 4200 B.C. No centre of the path of totality for a solar eclipse crossed London for the 575 years from 20 March 1140 to 3 May 1715. The most recent occasion when a line of totality of a solar eclipse crossed Great Britain was on 29 June 1927, and the next instance may just clip the Cornish coast on 11 Aug. 1999. On 30 June 1954 a total eclipse was witnessed in Haroldswick, Unst, Shetland Islands but the line of totality was to the north of territorial waters.

Longest duration The maximum possible duration of an eclipse of the Sun is 7 minutes 31 seconds. The longest actually occurring since 13 June A.D. 717 was on 20 June 1955 (7 minutes 8 seconds), seen from the Philippines. The longest possible in the British Isles is 5½ minutes. Those of 15 June 885 and 3 May 1715 were both nearly 5 minutes, as will be the eclipse of 2381. An annular eclipse may last for 12 minutes 24 seconds. The longest totality of any lunar eclipse is 104 minutes. This has occurred many times.

Most and least frequent The highest number of eclipses possible in a year is seven, as in 1935, when there were five solar and two lunar eclipses; or four solar and three lunar eclipses, as will occur in 1982. The lowest possible number in a year is two, both of which must be solar, as in 1944 and 1969.

COMETS
Earliest recorded The earliest records of comets date from the 7th century B.C. The speeds of the estimated 2,000,000 comets vary from 700 m.p.h. in outer space to 1,250,000 m.p.h. when near the Sun. The successive appearances of Halley's Comet have been traced to 466 B.C. It was first depicted in the Nuremburg Chronicle of A.D. 684. The first prediction of its return by Edmund Halley (1656-1742) proved true on Christmas Day 1758, 16 years after his death. Its next appearance should be at 9.9 (*viz.* at 9.30 p.m.) February 1986, 75.81 years after the last, which was on 19 April 1910.

Closest approach On 1 July 1770, Lexell's Comet, travelling at a speed of 23.9 miles per second (relative to the Sun), came within 1,500,000 miles of the Earth. However, the Earth is believed to have passed through the tail of Halley's Comet, most recently on 19 May 1910.

Largest Comets are so tenuous that it has been estimated that even the head of one rarely contains solid matter much more than *c.* 1 kilometre in diameter. In the tail 10,000 cubic miles contain less than a cubic inch of solid matter. These tails, as in the case of the Great Comet of 1843, may trail for 200,000,000 miles.

Shortest period Of all the recorded periodic comets (these are members of the Solar System), the one which most frequently returns is Encke's Comet, first identified in 1786. Its period of 1,206 days (3.3 years) is the shortest established. Not one of its 48 returns (up to May 1967) has been missed by astronomers. Now increasingly faint, it is expected to "die" by Feb. 1994. The most frequently observed comets are Schwassmann-Wachmann I, Kopff and Oterma, which can be observed every year between Mars and Jupiter.

Longest period At the other extreme is the comet 1910a, whose path was not accurately determined. It is not expected to return for perhaps 4,000,000 years.

PLANETS
Largest Planets (including the Earth) are bodies which belong to the Solar System and which revolve round the Sun in definite orbits. Jupiter, with an equatorial diameter of 88,070 miles and a polar diameter of 82,720 miles, is the largest of the nine major planets, with a mass 317.83 times, and a volume 1,293 times that of the Earth. It also has the shortest period of rotation with a "day" of only 9 hours 50 minutes 30.003 seconds in the equatorial zone.

Smallest Of the nine major planets, Mercury is the smallest with a diameter of 3,033 miles and a mass only 0.0555 of that of the Earth or 326 trillion tons. Mercury, which orbits the Sun at an average distance of 35,983,100 miles, has a period of revolution of 87.9686 days so giving the highest average speed in orbit of 107,030 m.p.h.

Hottest The U.S.S.R. probe *Venera 7* recorded a temperature of 474° C. (885° F.) on the surface of Venus on 17 Dec. 1970. The surface temperature of Mercury has now been calculated to be 421° C. (790° F.) on its daylight side at perihelion (28,566,000 miles). The planet with a surface temperature closest to Earth's average figure of 59° F. is Mars with a value of 55° F. for the sub-solar point at a mean solar distance of 141,636,000 miles.

Coldest The coldest planet is, not unnaturally, that which is the remotest from the Sun, namely Pluto, which has an estimated surface temperature of −420° F. (40 deg. F. above absolute zero). Its mean distance from the Sun is 3,675,300,000 miles and its period of revolution is 248.62 years. Its diameter is about 3,400 miles (*c.* 5,450 Km.) and has a mass about one twentieth of that of the Earth. Pluto was first recorded by

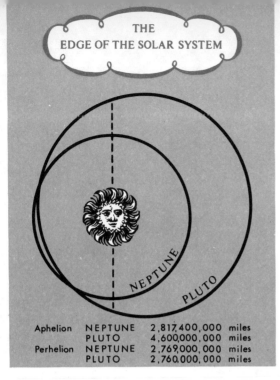

THE EDGE OF THE SOLAR SYSTEM

The edge of the Solar System showing how on occasions Neptune is remoter than Pluto. Pluto is, however, at times 1,780 million miles more remote from the sun than Neptunes farthest

Aphelion	NEPTUNE	2,817,400,000	miles
	PLUTO	4,600,000,000	miles
Perihelion	NEPTUNE	2,769,000,000	miles
	PLUTO	2,760,000,000	miles

Clyde William Tombaugh (b. 4 Feb. 1906) at Lowell Observatory, Flagstaff, Arizona, U.S.A., on 18 Feb. 1930 from photographs taken on 23 and 29 January. Because of its orbital eccentricity Pluto will move closer to the Sun than Neptune between 21 Jan. 1979 and 14 Mar. 1999.

Nearest The fellow planet closest to the Earth is Venus, which is, at times, about 25,700,000 miles inside the Earth's orbit, compared with Mars's closest approach of 34,600,000 miles outside the Earth's orbit. Mars, known since 1965 to be cratered, has temperatures ranging from 85° F. to −130° F. but in which infusorians of the *genus* Colpoda *could* survive.

Surface features Mariner 9 photographs have revealed a canyon in the Tithonias Lacus region of Mars which is 62 miles wider and 4,000 feet deeper than the 13 mile wide 5,500 foot deep Grand Canyon on Earth. The volcanic pile Nix Olympica is 305 miles across with a 40 mile wide crater probably 19,500 feet high.

Brightest and faintest Viewed from the Earth, by far the brightest of the five planets visible to the naked eye (Uranus at magnitude 5.7 is only marginally visible) is Venus, with a maximum magnitude of −4.4. The faintest is Pluto, with a magnitude of 14.

Densest and least Dense Earth is the densest planet with an average figure of 5.517 times that of water, whilst Saturn has an average density only about one eighth of this value or 0.705 times that of water.

Conjunctions The most dramatic recorded conjunction (coming together) of the other seven principal members of the Solar System (Sun, Moon, Mercury, Venus, Mars, Jupiter and Saturn) occurred on 5 Feb. 1962, when 16° covered all seven during an eclipse in the Pacific area. It is possible that the seven-fold conjunction of September 1186 spanned only 12°. The next notable conjunction will take place on 5 May 2000.

SATELLITES

Most Of the nine major planets, all but Mercury, Venus and Pluto have natural satellites. The planet with the most is Jupiter, with four large and eight small moons. The Earth is the only planet with a single satellite. The distance of the Solar System's 32 known satellites from their parent planets varies from the 5,818 miles of *Phobos* from the centre of Mars to the 14,730,000 miles of Jupiter's ninth satellite (Jupiter IX).

Largest and smallest The largest satellite is *Ganymede* (Jupiter III) with a diameter of 3,450 miles and a mass 2.11 times that of

our Moon. The smallest is Mars's outer "moon" *Deimos* discovered on 18 Aug. 1877 by Asaph Hall (U.S.) with a major axis of 8.4 miles and a minor one of 7.5 miles.

Largest asteroids In the belt which lies between Mars and Jupiter, there are some 45,000 (only 3,100 charted) minor planets or asteroids which are, for the most part, too small to yield to diameter measurement. The largest and first discovered (by Piazzi at Palermo, Sicily on 1 Jan. 1801) of these is *Ceres,* with a diameter of 480 miles. The only one visible to the naked eye is *Vesta* (diameter 260 miles) discovered on 29 March 1807 by Dr Heinrich Wilhelm Olbers (1758-1840), a German amateur astronomer. The closest measured approach to the Earth by an asteroid was 485,000 miles, in the case of *Hermes* on 30 Oct. 1937. It was announced in Dec. 1971 that the orbit of *Toro* (disc. 1964), though centered on the Sun, is also in resonance with the Earth-Moon system. Its nearest approach to Earth is 9,600,000 miles.

STARS

Largest and most massive Of those measured, the star with the greatest diameter is the "red giant" *Epsilon Aurigae B* at 1,800 million miles. This star is so vast that our own Solar System of the Sun and the six planets out as far as Saturn could be accommodated inside this hot vacuum. The *Alpha Herculis* aggregation, consisting of a main star and a double star companion, is enveloped in a cold gas. This system, visible to the naked eye, has a diameter of 170,000 million miles. The fainter component of Plaskett's star discovered by J. S. Plaskett from the Dominion Astrophysical Observatory, Victoria, British Columbia, Canada c. 1920 is the most massive star known with a mass c. 55 times that of the Sun.

Smallest The smallest known star is LP 327-186, a "white dwarf" with a diameter only half that of the Moon, 100 light-years distant and detected in May 1962 from Minneapolis, Minnesota, U.S.A. The claim that LP 768-500 is even smaller at <1000 miles is not widely accepted. Some pulsars or neutron stars may however have diameters of only 10−20 miles.

Oldest The Sun is estimated to be about 7,500 million years old and our galaxy between 10,000 million and 12,000 million years old.

Farthest The Solar System, with its Sun, nine principal planets, 32 satellites, asteroids and comets, was discovered in 1921 to be about 27,000 light-years from the centre of the lens-shaped Milky Way galaxy (diameter 100,000 light-years) of about 100,000 million stars. The most distant star in our galaxy is therefore about 75,000 light-years distant.

Nearest Excepting the special case of our own Sun, the nearest star is the very faint *Proxima Centauri,* which is 4.2 light-years (25,000,000,000,000 miles) away. The nearest star visible to the naked eye is the southern hemisphere star *Alpha Centauri,* or *Rigil Kentaurus* (4.33 light-years), with a magnitude of 0.1.

Brightest Sirius A (*Alpha Canis Majoris*), also known as the Dog Star, is the brightest star in the heavens, with an apparent magnitude of −1.58. It is in the constellation *Canis Major* and is visible in the winter months of the northern hemisphere, being due south at midnight on the last day of the year. Sirius A is 8.7 light-years away and has a luminosity 26 times as much as that of the Sun. It has a diameter of 1,500,000 miles and a mass of 4,580,000,000,000, 000,000,000,000,000 tons.

Most and least luminous If all stars could be viewed at the same distance, the most luminous would be the apparently faint variable *S. Doradûs,* in the Greater Magellanic Cloud (*Nebecula Major*), which can be 300,000 to 500,000 times brighter than the Sun, and has an absolute magnitude of −8.9. The faintest star detected visually is a very red star 30 light-years distant in *Pisces*, with one two-millionth of the Sun's brightness.

Coolest A 16th magnitude star with a surface temperature of only about 425° C. (800° F.) was detected in *Cygnus* in 1965.

Densest The limit of stellar density is at the neutron state, when the atomic particles exist in a state in which there is no space between them. Theoretical calculations call for a density of 4.7×10^{15} grammes per cubic centimetre (75,000 million tons per cubic inch) in the innermost core of a pulsar.

Brightest super-nova Super-novae, or temporary "stars" which flare and then fade, occur perhaps five times in 1,000 years. The brightest "star" ever seen by historic man is believed to be the super-nova close to *Zeta Tauri*, visible by day for 23 days from 4 July 1054. The remains, known as the "Crab" Nebula, now appear to have a diameter of about 3×10^{13} miles and are still expanding at a rate of 800 miles per second so indicating a diameter of 1.3×10^{14} miles now. It is about 4,100 light-years away, indicating that the explosion actually occurred in about 3000 B.C.

Constellations The largest of the 89 constellations is *Hydra* (the Sea Serpent), which covers 1,302.844 square degrees and contains at least 68 stars visible to the naked eye (to 5.5 mag.). The constellation *Centaurus* (Centaur), ranking ninth in area embraces however at least 94 such stars. The smallest constellation is *Crux Australis* (Southern Cross) with an area of 68.477 square degrees compared with the 41,252.96 square degrees of the whole sky.

Stellar planets Planetary companions, with a mass of less than 7 per cent. of their parent star, have been found to 61 *Cygni* (1942), Lalande 21185 (1960) *Krüger 60, Ci 2354, BD + 20° 2465* and one of the two components of 70 Ophiuchi. Barnard's Star (Munich 15040) was discovered to have a planet in April 1963 with 1.1 times the mass of Jupiter and a second planet more recently with 0.8 times this mass.

Listening operations ("Project Ozma") on the *Tau Ceti* and *Epsilon Eridani* were maintained from 4 April 1960 to March 1961, using an 85-foot radio telescope at Deer Creek Valley, Green Bank, West Virginia, U.S.A. The apparatus was probably insufficiently sensitive for any signal from a distance of 11 light-years to be received. Monitoring has been conducted from Gorkiy, U.S.S.R. since 1969.

THE UNIVERSE

According to Einstein's Special Theory time dilatation effect (published in 1905), time actually runs more slowly for an object as its speed increases. However time speeds up for an object as it moves away from a body exerting gravitational force. During their mission the crew of the Apollo VIII circum-lunar space flight aged a net 300 microseconds more than earthlings. No formal overtime claim was lodged.

Outside the Milky Way galaxy, which possibly moves around the centre of the local super-cluster of 2,500 neighbouring galaxies at a speed of 1,350,000 m.p.h., there exist 1,000,000 million other galaxies. These range in size up to 200,000 light-years in diameter. The nearest heavenly body outside our galaxy is its satellite body the Large Magellanic Cloud near the Southern Cross, at a distance of 160,000 light-years. In 1967 it was suggested by the astronomer G. Idlis (U.S.S.R.) that the Magellanic Clouds were detached from the Milky Way by another colliding galaxy, now in *Sagittarius*, about 3,800,000 years ago.

Farthest visible object The remotest heavenly body often visible to the naked eye is the Great Galaxy in *Andromeda* (Mag. 3.47). This is a rotating nebula in spiral form, and its distance from the Earth is about 2,200,000

The great spiral in Andromeda—the most distant object visible to the naked eye

light-years, or about 13,000,000,000,000,000,000 miles. It is just possible however that, under ideal seeing conditions, Messier 33, the Spiral in Triangulum (Mag. 5.79), is visible to the naked eye at a distance of 2,300,000 light-years.

Heaviest Galaxy In April 1971 the heaviest galaxy was found to be 41C 31:04 (a "binary" system) with a mass 45 times that of the Milky Way, thus indicating a figure of 12,000 sextillion tons (1.2×10^{40} tons).

Quasars In November 1962 the existence of quasi-stellar radio sources ("quasars" or QSO's) was established. No satisfactory model has yet been constructed to account for the immensely high luminosity of bodies apparently so distant and of such small diameter. The diameter of 3C 446 is only about 90 light-days, but there are measurable alterations in brightness in less than one day. It is believed to be undergoing the most violent explosion yet detected, since it has increased 3.2 magnitudes or 20-fold in less than one year.

"Pulsars" The discovery of the first pulsating radio source or "pulsar" CP 1919 was announced from the Mullard Radio Astronomy Observatory, Cambridge, England, on 29 Feb. 1968. The fastest so far discovered is NP 0532 in the Crab Nebula with a pulse of 33 milli-seconds. The now accepted model is that it is a rotating neutron star of immense density.

Remotest object The greatest distance yet ascribed to a radio detected and visibly confirmed body is that claimed for the quasar designated 4C 05.34, identified from the Kitt Peak National Observatory, Arizona, U.S.A., and announced in May 1970. Though the Symposium on Relativistic Astrophysics in New York City, U.S.A., concluded in January 1967 that quasars "have no agreed distance from the Earth", a figure of at least 13,000 million light-years has been ascribed to quasars exhibiting a lesser red shift than the extreme figure of 2.87 measured for this body. PKS 0237−23 announced in March 1967 is the most luminous of observed heavenly bodies.

Proponents of the oscillation theory of cosmology believe that the Universe is between 15 and 20,000 million years advanced on the expanding phase of an 80,000 million year expansion-contraction cycle. The number of previous cycles, if any, is not determinable.

ROCKETRY AND MISSILES

Earliest experiments The origin of the rocket dates from war rockets propelled by a charcoal-saltpetre-sulphur gunpowder, made by the Chinese as early as *c.* 1100. These early rockets became known in Europe by 1258. The pioneer of military rocketry in Britain was Col. Sir William Congreve, Bt., M.P. (1772-1828), Comptroller of the Royal Laboratory, Woolwich and Inspector of Military Machines, whose "six-pound rocket" was developed to a range of 2,000 yards by 1805 when used by the Royal Navy against Boulogne, France.

The first launching of a liquid-fuelled rocket (patented 14 July 1914) was by Dr. Robert Hutchings Goddard (1882-1945) of the United States, at Auburn, Massachusetts, U.S.A., on 16 March 1926, when his rocket reached an altitude of 41 feet and travelled a distance of 184 feet. The U.S.S.R.'s earliest rocket was the semi-liquid fuelled GIRD-IX tested on 17 Aug. 1933.

Longest ranges The longest range achieved in a ground-to-surface rocket test is 9,000 miles by a U.S. *Atlas,* measuring 85 feet long and weighing 120 tons, fired across the South Atlantic from Cape Canaveral (now Cape Kennedy), Florida, U.S.A., to a point 1,000 miles south-east of the Cape of Good Hope, South Africa, on 20 May 1960. The flight lasted about 53 minutes. On 16 March 1962, Nikita Khrushchyov, then the Soviet Prime Minister, claimed in Moscow that the U.S.S.R. possessed a "global rocket" with a range of about 19,000 miles, *i.e.* more than the Earth's semi-circumference and therefore capable of hitting any target from either direction.

Most powerful World It has been suggested that the U.S.S.R. manned spacecraft booster which blew up at Tyuratam in the summer (? July) of 1969 had a thrust of 10 to 14 million lb. No further details have been released by the U.S.S.R. nor by the U.S. ELINT (Electronic Intelligence Section).

The most powerful rocket that has been publicized is the *Saturn V,* used for the Project Apollo 3-man lunar exploration mission, on which development began in January 1962, at the John F. Kennedy Space Center, Merritt Island, Florida, U.S.A. The rocket is 363 feet 8 inches tall, with a payload of 107,500 lb. in the case of Apollo 15, and gulps 13.4 tons of propellant per second for 2½ minutes (2,005 tons). Stage I (S-IC) is 138 feet tall and is powered by five Rocketdyne F-1 engines, using liquid oxygen (LOX) and kerosene, each delivering 1,514,000 lb. thrust. Stage II (S-II) is powered by five LOX and liquid hydrogen Rocketdyne J-2 engines with a total thrust of 1,141,453 lb., while Stage III (designated S-IVB) is powered by a single 228,290 lb. thrust J-2 engine. The whole assembly generates 175,600,000 horse-power and weighs up to 6,582,000 lb. (2,938 tons) fully loaded in the case of Apollo 14. It was first launched on 9 Nov. 1967, from Cape Kennedy, Florida.

Highest velocity The first space vehicle to achieve the Third Cosmic velocity sufficient to break out of the Solar System was *Pioneer 10* (see page 71). The Atlas SLV-3C launcher with a modified Centaur D second stage Thiokol Te-364-4 third stage left the Earth at an unprecedented 31,700 m.p.h. on 2 Mar. 1972.

Ion rockets Speeds of up to 100,000 m.p.h. are envisaged for rockets powered by an ion discharge. It was announced on 13 Jan. 1960 that caesium vapour discharge had been maintained for 50 hours at the Lewis Research Center in Cleveland, Ohio, U.S.A. Ion rockets were first used in flight by the U.S.S.R.'s Mars probe *Zond II,* launched on 30 Nov. 1964.

ARTIFICIAL SATELLITES
The dynamics of artificial satellites were first propounded by Sir Isaac Newton (1642-1727) in his *Philosophiae Naturalis Principia Mathematica* ("Mathematical Principles of Natural Philosophy"), begun in March 1686 and first published in the summer of 1687. The first artificial satellite was successfully put into orbit at an altitude of 142/588

The historic nose cone of Vostok I in which the late Col. Gagarin became the first spaceman in 1961

miles and a velocity of more than 17,500 m.p.h. from Tyuratam, a site located 170 miles east of the Aral Sea on the night of 4 Oct. 1957. This spherical satellite *Sputnik* ("Fellow Traveller") *I,* officially designated "Satellite 1957 Alpha 2", weighed 83.6 kilogrammes (184.3 lb.), with a diameter of 58 centimetres (22.8 inches), and its lifetime is believed to have been 92 days, ending on 4 Jan. 1958. It was designed under the direction of Dr. Sergey Pavlovich Korolyov (1906-1966).

Earliest successful manned satellite The first successful manned space flight began at 9.07 a.m. (Moscow time), or 6.07 a.m. G.M.T., on 12 April 1961. Cosmonaut Flight Major (later Colonel) Yuriy Alekseyevich Gagarin (born 9 March 1934) completed a single orbit of the Earth in 89.34 minutes in the U.S.S.R.'s space vehicle *Vostok* ("East") *I* (10,417 lb.). The take-off was from Tyuratam in Kazakhstan, and the landing was 108 minutes later near the village of Smelovka, near Engels, in the Saratov region of the U.S.S.R. The maximum speed was 17,560 m.p.h. and the maximum altitude 327 kilometres (203.2 miles). Major Gagarin, invested a Hero of the Soviet Union and awarded the Order of Lenin and the Gold Star Medal, was killed in a jet plane crash near Moscow on 27 March 1968.

First woman in space The first and only woman to orbit the Earth was Junior Lieutenant (now Lieut.-Col.) Valentina Vladimirovna Tereshkova, now Mme. Nikolayev (b. 6 March 1937), who was launched in *Vostok VI* from Tyuratam, U.S.S.R., at 9.30 a.m. G.M.T. on 16 June 1963, and landed at 8.16 a.m. on 19 June, after a flight of 2 days 22 hours 46 minutes, during which she completed over 48 orbits (1,225,000 miles) and passed momentarily within 3 miles of *Vostok V.*

First In flight fatality Col. Vladimir Mikhailovich Komarov (b. 16 March 1927) was launched in *Soyuz* ("Union") *I* at 00.35 a.m. G.M.T. on 23 April 1967. The spacecraft was in orbit for about 25½ hours but he impacted on the final descent due to parachute failure and was thus the first man indisputedly known to have died during space flight.

First "walk" in space The first person to leave an artificial satellite during orbit was Lt.-Col. Aleksey Arkhipovich Leonov (b. 30 May 1934), who left the Soviet satellite *Voshkod II* at about 8.30 a.m. G.M.T. on 18 March 1965. Lt.-Col. Leonov was "in space" for about 20 minutes, and for 12 minutes 9 seconds he "floated" at the end of a line 5 metres (16 feet) long.

Longest manned space flight The longest space flight has been that of Cdr. Georgy Timofeyevitch Dobrovolskiy, Test Engineer Viktor Nikolayevitch Patsàyev and Fl. Eng. Vladislav Volkov in Soyuz XI lasting 23 days 18 hours 15 mins., on 6-29 June 1971. The crew died of hypoxia 30 minutes before landing in Kazakhstan, when the capsule suffered a hatch-sealing failure. Captain James Arthur Lovell, U.S.N., has the overall duration record award from Earth between 4 Dec. 1965 and his return from his fourth mission, the abortive *Apollo XIII* flight on 17 Mar. 1970, with 715 hours 4 minutes 57 seconds.

Astronauts
Oldest and youngest The oldest of the 57 people in space has been Col. Georgiy T. Beregovoiy who was 47 years and 6 months when launched in *Soyuz 3* on 26 Oct. 1968. The youngest was Major Gherman Stepanovich Titov aged 25 years 11 months when launched in *Vostok II* on 6 Aug. 1961.

Longest lunar mission The longest duration of any manned lunar orbit was the Apollo XV's command module *Endeavour,* which set a record of manned lunar orbit with 6 days 1 hour 13 mins. during a mission of 12 days 7 hours 12 mins. from 26 July to 7 Aug. 1971.

Duration record on the Moon The crew of Apollo XVI's lunar exploration module *Orion,* manned by Capt. John Watts Young U.S.N., 41 and Lt.-Col. Charles M. Duke, Jnr., 36, was on the lunar surface for 71 hours 2 mins. on 22-24 Apr.

1972. The crew collected a record 245 lb. of rock and soil during their 20 hrs. 15 mins. "extra-vehicular activity"

First Extra-terrestrial vehicle The first wheeled vehicle landed on the Moon was *Lunokhod I* which began its travels on 17 Nov. 1970. It moved a total of 10.54 kilometres (6.54 miles) on gradients up to 30 degrees in the Mare Imbrium and did not become non-functioning until 4 Oct. 1971. The lunar speed and distance record was set by the Apollo XVI Rover with 11 m.p.h. and 18.4 miles.

Most expensive project The total cost of the U.S. manned space programme up to and including the lunar mission of *Apollo XVII* has been estimated to be \$25,541,400,000 or (£9,823,150,000).

Accuracy record The most accurate recovery from space was the splashdown of *Gemini IX* on 6 June 1966 only 769 yards from the *U.S.S. Wasp* in the Western Atlantic (27° 52′ N., 75° 0′ 24″ W.).

PROGRESSIVE ROCKET ALTITUDE RECORDS

Height in Miles	Rocket	Place	Launch Date
0.71 (3,762 ft.)	A 3-inch rocket	near London, England	April 1750
1.24 (6,460 ft.)	Rheinhold Tiling [1] (Germany) solid fuel rocket	Osnabrück, Germany	April 1931
nearly 3	OR-2 liquid fuel (U.S.S.R.)	U.S.S.R.	17 Aug. 1932
8.1	U.S.S.R. "Stratosphere" rocket	U.S.S.R.	1935
52.46	A.4 rocket (Germany)	Peenemünde, Germany	3 Oct. 1942
c. 85	A.4 rocket (Germany)	Heidelager, Poland	early 1944
118	A.4 rocket (Germany)	Heidelager, Poland	mid 1944
244	V-2/W.A.C. Corporal (2-stage) Bumper No. 5 (U.S.A.)	White Sands, N.M., U.S.A.	24 Feb. 1949
250	M.104 *Raketa* (U.S.S.R.)	? Tyuratam, U.S.S.R.	1954
682	Jupiter C (U.S.A.)	Cape Canaveral (now Cape Kennedy), Florida, U.S.A.	20 Sept. 1956
>2,700	Farside No. 5 (4-stage) (U.S.A.)	Eniwetok Atoll	20 Oct. 1957
70,700	Pioneer I-B Lunar Probe (U.S.A.)	Cape Canaveral (now Cape Kennedy), Florida, U.S.A.	11 Oct. 1958
215,300,000*	Luna I or Mechta (U.S.S.R.)	Tyuratam, U.S.S.R.	2 Jan. 1959
242,000,000*	Mars I (U.S.S.R.)	U.S.S.R.	1 Nov. 1962
1,800,000,000 [2]	Pioneer 10 (U.S.A.) (see page 70)	Cape Kennedy, Florida U.S.A.	2 Mar. 1972

*   *Apogee in solar orbit.*
[1]   *There is some evidence that Tiling may shortly after have reached 9,500 m. (5.90 miles) with a solid fuel rocket at Wangerooge, East Friesian Islands, West Germany.*
[2]   *This distance will be reached by 1980 on its way to passing out of the Solar System's gravitational field.*

ROCKETRY AND SPACE RECORDS

	Earth Orbits	Moon Orbits	Solar Orbits
Earliest Satellite	Sputnik I, 4 Oct. 1957	Luna X, 31 March 1966	Luna 1, 2 Jan. 1959
Earliest Planetary Contact	Sputnik I rocket–burnt out 1 Dec. 1957	Luna II hit Moon, 13 Sept. 1959	Venus III hit Venus, 1 Mar. 1966
Earliest Planetary Touchdown	Discoverer XIII capsule, landed 11 Aug. 1960	Luna IX soft landed on Moon 3 Feb. 1966	Venus VII soft landed on Venus 15 Dec. 1970
Earliest Rendezvous and Docking	Gemini 8 and Agena 8, 16 March 1966	Apollo X and LEM 4 docked 23 May 1969	None
Earliest Crew Exchange	Soyuz IV and V, 14-15 Jan. 1969	Apollo X and LEM 4, 18 May 1969	None
Heaviest Satellite	30.44 tons, Apollo IV, 9 Nov. 1967	30.34 tons, Apollo XV, 26 July 1971	13.60 tons, Apollo X rocket, 18 May 1969
Lightest Satellite	1.47 lb. each, Tetrahedron Research Satellites (TRS), 2 and 3, 9 May 1963	150 lb., Interplanetary Monitoring Probe 6, 19 July 1967	13 lb., Pioneer IV, 3 March 1959
Longest First Orbit	42 days, Apollo XII rocket, 14 Nov. 1969	720 minutes, Lunar Orbiter 4, 4 May 1967	636 days, Mariner 6 (Mars Probe), 25 Feb 1969
Shortest First Orbit	86 minutes 30.6 seconds, Cosmos 169 (rocket), 17 July 1967	114 minutes, LEM 9 ascent stage (Apollo XV), 2 Aug. 1971	195 days, Mariner 5 (Venus Probe), 14 June 1967
Longest Expected Lifetime	)1 million years, Vela 12, 8 April 1970	Unlimited, IMP 6 (see above), 19 July 1967	All unlimited
Nearest First Perigee, Pericynthion or Perihelion	63 miles, Cosmos 169 rocket, 17 July 1967	10 miles, LEM 6 ascent stage (Apollo XII), 20 Nov. 1969	50,700 miles Apollo IX rocket, 3 Mar 1969
Furthest First Apogee, Apcynthion or Aphelion	535,522 miles, Apollo XII rocket, 14 Nov. 1969	4,900 miles, IMP 6 (see above), 19 July 1967	162,900,000 miles Mariner 6 (Mars Probe), 25 Feb 1969

The highest and lowest speeds in solar orbit are by Apollo IX rocket and Mariner 6 (see above), respectively.
NOTE: *The largest artificial satellite measured by volume has been Echo II (diameter 135 feet), weighing 565 lb., launched into orbit (642/816 miles) from Vandenberg Air Force Base, California, U.S.A., on 25 Jan. 1964. It was an inflated sphere, comprising a 535 lb. balloon, whose skin was made of Mylar plastic 0.00035 of an inch thick, bonded on both sides by aluminium alloy foil 0.00018 of an inch thick, together with equipment. Echo II was the brightest of artificial satellites (its magnitude was about −1) and it has been claimed that it became the man-made object seen by more people than any other. Its lifetime was 1,960 days until it burned up on 7 June 1969.*

5 THE SCIENTIFIC WORLD

1. ELEMENTS

All known matter in the Solar System is made up of chemical elements. The total of naturally-occurring elements so far detected is 94, comprising, at ordinary temperature, two liquids, 11 gases and 81 solids. The so-called "fourth state" of matter is plasma, when negatively-charged electrons and positively-charged ions are in flux.

Lightest and heaviest sub-nuclear particles The number of fundamental sub-nuclear particles catered for by the 1964 Unitary Symmetry Theory, or SU(3), was 34. The SU(6) system caters for 91 particles, while the later SU(12) system caters for an infinite number, some of which are expected to be produced by higher and higher energies, but with shorter and shorter lifetimes and weaker and weaker interactions. By 1971 some 400 particles and resonances had been recorded. Of SU(3) particles the one with the highest mass is the omega minus, announced on 24 Feb. 1964 from the Brookhaven National Laboratory, near Upton, Long Island, New York State, U.S.A. It has a mass of $1,672.5\pm0.5$ Mev and a lifetime of 1.3×10^{10} of a second. Of all sub-atomic concepts only the neutrino calls for masslessness. There is experimental proof that the mass, if any, of an electron neutrino, first observed in June 1956, cannot be greater than one ten-thousandth of that of an electron, which itself has a rest mass of $9.10956(\pm0.00005) \times 10^{-28}$ of a gramme, i.e. it has a weight of less than 1.07×10^{-31} of a gramme.

Fastest particles A search for the existence of super-luminary particles, named tachyons (symbol T^+ and T^-), with a speed in vacuo greater than c. the speed of light, was instituted in 1968 by Dr. T. Alvager and Dr. M. Kriesler of Princeton University, U.S.A. Such particles would create the conceptual difficulty of disappearing before they exist. Quarks and anti-quarks (q and q̄) have similarly evaded proof of detection.

Commonest The commonest element in the Universe is hydrogen, which has been calculated to comprise 90 per cent. of all matter and over 99 per cent. of matter in interstellar space.

Most and least isotopes The element with the most isotopes is the colourless gas xenon (Xe) with 30 and that with the least is hydrogen with only 3 confirmed isotopes. The

metallic element with the most is platinum (Pt) with 29 and that with the least is lithium (Li) with 5. Of stable and naturally-occurring isotopes, tin (Sn) has the most with 10 whilst 20 elements exist in Nature only as single nuclides.

GASES

Lightest Hydrogen, a colourless gas discovered in 1766 by the Hon. Henry Cavendish (1731-1810), a British millionaire, is less than 1/14th the weight of air, weighing only 0.005611 of one lb. per cubic foot, or 89.8 milligrammes per litre.

Heaviest The heaviest elemental gas is radon, the colourless isotope Em 222 of the gas emanation, which was discovered in 1900 by Friedrich Ernst Dorn (1848-1916) of Germany, and is 111.5 times as heavy as hydrogen. It is also known as niton and emanates from radium salts.

Melting and boiling points Of all substances, helium has the lowest boiling point ($-268.94°$ C.). This element, which is at normal **Lowest** temperatures a colourless gas, was discovered in 1868 by Sir Joseph Norman Lockyer, K.C.B. (1836-1920) working with Sir Edward Frankland, K.C.B. (1825-99) and the French astronomer Pierre Jules Cesar Janssen (1824-1907) working independently. Helium was first liquefied in 1908 by Heike Kamerlingh Onnes (1853-1926), a Dutch physicist. Liquid helium, which exists in two forms, can be solidified only under pressure of 26 atmospheres. This was first achieved on 26 July 1926 by Wilhemus H. Keesom (b. Netherlands 1876). At this pressure helium will melt at $-272°$ C.

Highest Of the elements that are gases at normal temperatures, chlorine has the highest melting point ($-101.0°$ C.) and the highest boiling point ($-34.1°$ C.). This yellow-green gas was discovered in 1774 by the German-born Karl Wilhelm Scheele (1742-86) of Sweden.

Rarest The Earth's atmosphere weighs an estimated 5,075,000,000,000,000 tons, of which nitrogen constitutes 78.09 per cent. by volume in dry air. The heavy hydrogen isotope tritium exists in the atmosphere to an extent of only 5×10^{-23} of one per cent. by volume.

METALS

Lightest The lightest of all metals is lithium (Li), a light golden brown (*in vacuo*) metal, discovered in 1817 by Johan August Arfvedson (1792-1841) of Sweden. It has a density of 0.5333 of a gramme per cubic centimetre or 33.29 lb. per cubic foot. The isotope Li 6 (7.56 per cent. of naturally-occurring lithium) has a density of only 0.4616 g./cu. cm. compared with 0.5391 for Li 7.

Densest The densest of all metals and hence the most effective possible paperweight is osmium (Os), a grey-blue metal of the platinum group, discovered in 1804 by Smithson Tennant (1761-1815) of the United Kingdom. It has a density at 20° C. of 22.59 grammes per cubic centimetre or 1,410 lb. per cubic foot. A cubic foot of uranium would weigh 220 lb. less than a cubic foot of osmium. During the period 1955-70 iridium was thought by some inorganic chemists to be the densest metal but it has a density of 22.56.

Melting and boiling points
Lowest Excluding mercury, which is liquid at normal temperatures, caesium (Cs), a silvery-white metal discovered in 1860 by Robert Wilhelm von Bunsen (1811-99) and Gustav Robert Kirchhoff (1824-87) of Germany, has the lowest metallic melting point at 28.5° C. (83.3° F.).

Excluding mercury, which vaporizes at 356.66° C., the metal which vaporizes at the lowest temperature and hence has the lowest boiling point is caesium with a figure of 669° C. (1236° F.).

Highest The highest melting point of any pure element is that of tungsten or wolfram (W), a grey metal discovered in 1783 by the Spanish brothers, Juan José d'Elhuyar and Fausto d'Elhuyar (1755-1833). It melts at 3417° C, ±10 deg. C.

The most refractory substances known are the tantalum carbide ($TaC_{0.88}$), a black solid, and the hafnium carbide ($HfC_{0.95}$), which melt at 4010° C. ±75 deg. C. and 3960° C. ±20 deg. C. respectively.

Expansion The highest normal linear thermal expansion of a metal is that of caesium which at 20° C., is 9.7×10^{-5} of a cm. per cm. per one degree C. The trans-uranic metal plutonium will, however, expand and contract by as much as 8.9 per cent. of its volume when being heated to its melting point of 639.5° C. ±2 deg. C.

The lowest linear expansion is that of the alloy invar, containing 35 per cent. nickel, the remainder being iron, with one per cent. carbon and manganese. This has a linear thermal expansion of 9×10^{-7} of an inch per inch per one degree C. at ordinary temperatures. It was first prepared *c.* 1930 by Charles Edouard Guillaume (b. Switzerland 1861, d. 1938).

Highest ductility The most malleable, or ductile, of metals is gold. One ounce (avoirdupois) of gold can be drawn in the form of a continuous wire thread (diameter 2×10^{-4} of an inch) to a length of 43 miles. A cubic inch can be beaten into a leaf five-millionths of an inch thick, so as to cover nearly 1,400 square feet. It has been estimated that all the gold mined since A.D. 1500 could be stored in a vault with dimensions of 55 × 55 × 55 feet.

Highest tensile strength The material with the highest known UTS (ultimate tensile strength) is sapphire whisker (Al_2O_3) at 6.2×10^6 lb. in.^{2}. This is equivalent to a whisker of the thickness of a human hair (an as yet unachieved 70 microns) which could support a weight of 621 lb. Amorphous boron has a maximum cohesive strength of 3.9×10^6 lb. in.^{2} and thus theoretically a wire 189.4 miles long could be suspended without parting.

Rarest The fourteen of the fifteen "rare earth" or "lanthanide" elements which have naturally-occurring isotopes (this includes lutetium) have now been separated into metallic purity exceeding 99.9%. The highly radioactive element promethium (Pm) has been produced artificially with a purity exceeding only 99.8%. The radioactive elements 43 (technetium) and 61 (promethium) were chemically separated from pitch-blende ore in 1961 and 1968 respectively. Because of their relatively short half-lives their existence in Nature is due entirely to the "spontaneous fission" radioactive decay of uranium.

The rarest naturally-occurring element is astatine (element 85) first produced artificially in 1940 and identified in Nature three years later. It has been calculated that only 0.3 of a gramme exists in the Earth's crust to a depth of 10 miles.

The isotope polonium 213 (Po 213) is, however, rarer by a factor of 5×10^{10} which is equivalent to one atom in 3.5×10^{37}.

Several of the trans-uranium elements have been produced on an atom-to-atom basis so that at any one moment only single atoms of these elements may have existed.

Commonest Though ranking behind oxygen (46.60 per cent.) and silicon (27.72 per cent.) in abundance, aluminium is the commonest of all metals constituting 8.13 per cent. by weight of the Earth's crust.

Most magnetic and non-magnetic The most highly magnetic material, at ordinary temperatures, known is a cobalt-copper-samerium compound $Co_3 Cu_2 Sm$ with a coercive force of 10,500 oersted. The most non-magnetic alloy yet discovered is 963 parts of copper to 37 parts of nickel.

Newest The newest trans-uranium element, number 105, was synthesised in the HILAC heavy-ion linear accelerator in the Lawrence Radiation Laboratory, University of California, Berkeley, California, U.S.A. by an American-Finnish team led by Dr. Albert Ghiorso. The element, for which the name "hahnium" has been proposed, was first produced on the 5th March 1970 with a mass of 260 and a half-life of 1.6 seconds.

Attempts initiated in November 1968 at Berkeley, California, U.S.A. to find traces of elements 110 (eka-platinum) to 114 (eka-lead) have so far proved inconclusive. U.S.S.R. claims to have detected elements 108 and 114 in the Earth's crust have not been substantiated. Element 110 was apparently recorded by the Physics Department of Bristol University, England on emulsion plates sent aloft in a balloon 25 miles above Palestine, Texas, U.S.A. in September 1968, but the evidence must be regarded as being very tenuous. The heaviest isotope for which there is definite evidence is that of mass 262 of element 105 (Hahnium 262) synthesised by Ghiorso and others and announced in 1971.

Dr. Glenn Theodore Seaborg (b. 19 April 1912), Chairman of the United States Atomic Energy Commission, estimated in June 1966 that elements up to 126 would be produced by the year 2000.

Most expensive substance In October 1968 the U.S. Atomic Energy Commission announced that minuscule amounts of californium 252 (Element 98) were on sale at $100 for a tenth of a microgramme. A fanciful calculation would indicate that the price of an ingot weighing 1 lb. (if such were available) would at this rate have been £189,000 million or more than double the entire national wealth of the United Kingdom. It was announced in August 1970 that by using Am 243 and Cm 244, the price might be reduced to *only* $10 per microgramme.

The world's largest and most expensive bottle of perfume—2 litres of Chanel No. 5 which retails in Britain for £350

Longest and shortest half-lives The half-life of a radio-active substance is the period taken for its activity to fall to half of its original value. The highest theoretical figure is $>2 \times 10^{18}$ years for bismuth 209, while the shortest is 2.4×10^{-21} of a second for helium 5.

Purest The purest metal yet achieved is the grey-white metal germanium by the zone refining technique, first mooted in 1939 and published by William G. Pfann of Bell Laboratories, U.S.A. in 1952. By 1967 a purity of 99.99999999 per cent. had been achieved, which has been likened to one grain of salt in a freight car-load of sugar.

Hardest substances Prof. Naoto Kawai of Osaka University, Japan announced in June 1967 the production by dint of a pressure of 150 tonnes/cm.^{2} (5,300,000 p.s.i.) of a single crystal of 1 part silica, 1 part magnesium and 4 parts oxygen which was "twice as hard as diamond".

Plastics The plastic with best temperature resistance is modified polymide which can withstand temperatures of up to $500°$ C. ($930°$ F.) for short periods. The plastics with the greatest tensile strength are polyvinyl alcoholic fibres which have been tested to 1.5×10^5 lb./in.^{2}.

SMELLIEST SUBSTANCE
The most pungent of the 17,000 smells so far classified is 4-hydroxy-3-methoxy benzaldehyde or vanillaldehyde. This can be detected in a concentration of 2×10^{-8} of a milligramme per litre of air. Thus 9.7×10^{-5} (about one ten-thousandth) of an ounce completely volatilized would still be detectable in an enclosed space with a floor the size of a full-sized football pitch (360 feet $\times$ 300 feet) and a roof 45 feet high. Only 2.94 ounces would be sufficient to permeate a cubic mile of the atmosphere. The most evil smelling substance must be a matter of opinion but ethyl mercaptan (C_2H_5SH) and butyl seleno-mercaptan (C_4H_9SeH), are powerful claimants, each with a smell reminiscent of a combination of rotting cabbage, garlic, onions and sewer gas.

Most expensive perfume The costliest perfume in the world is "Adoration", manufactured by Nina Omar of Puerto Real, Cadiz, Spain, and distributed in the United States at a retail price of $185 (£77) per half-ounce. Its most expensive ingredient is a very rare aromatic gum from Asia. The biggest and most expensive bottle of perfume sold is the two litre (3.52 pints) size of Chanel No. 5, from France introduced on 1 Aug. 1961. It retails in Great Britain at £350 per bottle.

Sweetest substance The sweetest naturally-occurring substance is exuded from the red serendipity berry (*Dioscoreophyllum cumminsii*) from Nigeria, which was announced in September 1967 to be 1,500 times as sweet as sucrose. The chemical 1-n-propoxy-2-amino-4-nitro-

benzene was determined by Verkade in 1946 to b 5,600 times as sweet as 1 per cent. sucrose.

Bitterest substance The bitterest known substance is Bitrex, th proprietary name for benzyldiethyl (2:6-xylylcarba moyl methyl) ammonium benzoate ($C_{28}H_{34}N_2O_3$) first reported from Macfarlan Smith Ltd. o Edinburgh, Scotland. This can be detected in solutio at a concentration of one part in 20,000,000 and i thus about 200 times as bitter as quinine sulphat ($[C_{22}H_{24}N_2O_2]_2, H_2SO_4 2H_2O$).

Strongest acid The strength of acids and alkalis is measured on th pH scale. The pH of a solution is the logarithm to th base 10 of the reciprocal of the hydrogen-io concentration in gramme ions per litre. The stronges simple acid is perchloric acid ($HClO_4$). Assessed o its power as a hydrogen-ion donor, the most powerft acid is a solution of antimony pentafluoride i fluosulphonic acid ($SbF_5 + FSO_3H$).

Strongest alkali The strength of alkalis is expressed by pH values risin above the neutral 7.0. The strongest bases are causti soda or sodium hydroxide (NaOH), caustic potash c potassium hydroxide (KOH) and tetramethylan monium hydroxide ($N[CH_3]_4OH$), with pH values c 14 in normal solutions. True neutrality, pH 7, occu in pure water at $22°$ C.

Most powerful fuel The greatest specific impulse of any rock propulsion fuel combination is 435 lb. f. sec. per l produced by lithium fluoride and hydrogen. Th compares with a figure of 300 for liquid oxygen an kerosene.

POISON
Quickest The barbiturate thiopentone, if given as a larg intracardiac injection, will cause permanent cessatio of respiration in one to two seconds.

Most potent The rikettsal disease, Q-fever can be instituted by *single* organism but is only fatal in 1 in 1,000 case Effectually the most poisonous substance y discovered is the toxin of the bacterium *Pasteurel tularensis*. About 10 organisms can institu tulaeremia variously called alkali disease, Franc disease or deerfly fever, and this is fatal in 50 to 8 cases in 1,000.

Most powerful nerve gas The nerve gas Sarin or GB (isopropylmethylphosph nofluoridate), a lethal colourless and odourless ga has been developed since 1945 in the United Stat and is reputedly 30 times as toxic as phosge ($COCl_2$) used in World War I. In the early 195 substances known as V-agents, notably VX, 10 tim more toxic than GB, were developed at the Chemic Defence Experimental Establishment, Porton Dow Wiltshire, which are lethal at 1 milligramme per ma

Most powerful drugs The most potent and, to an addict, the mo expensive of all naturally-derived drugs is heroi which is a chemically-processed form of opium fro the juice of the unripe seed capsules of the whi poppy (*Papaver somniferum*). An ounce, whi suffices for up to 1,800 hypodermic shots or "fixes may fetch up to $9,000 (£3,460) in the United State or a 70,000 per cent. profit over the raw materi price in Turkey. It has been estimated that an addi who has no income is impelled to steal $40,000 (£15,384) worth of goods per annum to keep him herself in "fixes". The United States had, accordi to President Nixon, 180,000 heroin addicts by 197 compared with the United Kingdom's estimate 6,000. The most potent analgesic drug is Etorphine M-99, announced in June 1963 by Dr. Kenneth Bentley (b. 1925) and D. G. Hardy of Reckitt & So Ltd. of Hull, Yorkshire, with almost 10,000 times t potency of morphine.

The full range of champagne bottle sizes—quarter bottle to Nebuchadnezzar

2. DRINK

The strength of spirituous liquor is gauged by degrees proof. In the United Kingdom proof spirit is that mixture of ethyl alcohol (C_2H_5OH) and water which at 51° F. weighs 12/13ths of an equal measure of distilled water. Such spirit in fact contains 57.06 per cent. alcohol by volume, so that pure or absolute alcohol is 75.254° over proof (O.P.). A "hangover" is due to toxic congenerics such as amyl alcohol ($C_5H_{11}OH$).

Most alcoholic Absolute (or 100%) alcohol is 75.254 degrees over proof (U.K.) or 100° O.P. (U.S.). The strongest alcoholic spirits produced are unmarketable raw rums and vodkas at 97.2% alcohol by volume at 60° F. or 70° O.P. (U.K.) or 95.3° O.P. (U.S.). Polish White Spirit vodka produced for the Polish State Spirits Monopoly is 79.8% alcohol and 40° O.P. (U.K.) or 59.9° O.P. (U.S.). Royal Navy rum, introduced in 1692, was also 40° O.P. (79.8%) before 1948 but was reduced to 4.5° U.P. (under proof) or 54.7% alcohol by volume, before its abolition on 31 July 1970.

BEER
Strongest The world's strongest beer is Thomas Hardy's Ale brewed in July 1968 by Dorchester Brewery, Dorset with 10.15 per cent. alcohol by weight and 12.58 per cent. by volume. The strongest regularly brewed nationally distributed beer in Britain is Gold Label Barley Wine brewed by Tennant Bros. of Sheffield, a subsidiary of Whitbread & Co. Ltd. It has an alcoholic content of 8.6 per cent. by weight and 10.6 per cent. by volume.

Weakest The weakest liquid ever marketed as beer was a sweet ersatz beer which was brewed in Germany by Sunner, Colne-Kalk, in 1918. It had an original gravity of 1,000.96° and a strength 1/30th that of the weakest beer now obtainable in the United Kingdom.

WINE
Most expensive The highest price ever paid for a bottle of wine of any size is £3,538 for a Jeroboam of *Château Mouton Rothschild* 1929 sold by the Rt. Hon. Michael Noble M.P., Minister for Trade at Parke-Bernet Galleries, New York City on 23 May 1972. This bottle contained the equivalent of *five* normal bottles and was thus equivalent to about £115 per glass or £10 a sip.

A bottle of *Château Lafite* Rothschild 1946 was sold at auction by Mr Michael Broadbent of Christie's in San Francisco, California on 26 May 1971, and was bought by Laurence H. Bender, 25 on behalf of Hublein's for $5,000 (then £2,083.33). This thus worked out at an even higher price of £86.80 per fluid ounce.

Most expensive liqueurs The most expensive liqueur in France is the orange-flavoured *Le Grand Marnier Coronation*. Owing to excise duties, *Elixir Végétale de la Grande Chartreuse* which is 24 degrees O.P. is sold only by special order in miniature bottles of 2.8 fluid oz. at 90p per bottle in the United Kingdom. This liqueur has been produced since 1757, by Carthusian monks from a recipe of 1605, which reputedly contains 130 herbs including *Arnica montana*. Ancient *Chartreuse* (before 1903) has been known to fetch more than £15 per litre bottle. An 1878 bottle was sold in 1954 for this price.

Most expensive spirits The most expensive spirit is *Grande Fine Champagne Arbellot* 1749 brandy, retailed at Fauchon, Paris, at 667 francs (then £48.25) per bottle. *Hennessy Extra* retails in Britain for £15.25 a bottle.

Largest bottles The largest bottle normally used in the wine and spirit trade is the Jeroboam (equal to 4 bottles of champagne or, rarely, of brandy) and the Double Magnum (equal, since c. 1934, to 6 bottles of claret, more rarely red Burgundy). A complete set of champagne bottles would consist of a ¼ bottle, through the ½ bottle, bottle, magnum, Jeroboam, Rehoboam, Methuselah, Salmanazer and Balthazar, to the Nebuchadnezzar, which has a capacity of 16 litres (28.16 pints), and is equivalent to 20 bottles. In May 1958 a 5-foot-tall sherry bottle with a capacity of 20½ Imperial gallons was blown in Stoke-on-Trent, Staffordshire. This bottle, with the capacity of 131 normal bottles, was named an "Adelaide".

Smallest bottles The smallest and meanest bottles of liquor sold are the Thistle bottles of Scotch whisky marketed by The Cumbrae Supply Co. of Glasgow. They contain 24 minims or $1/20$ of a fluid ounce and retail for 10p.

Champagne cork flight The longest distance for a champagne cork to fly from an untreated and unheated bottle 4 feet from level ground is 73 feet 10½ inches popped by the author A.D. Beaty D.F.C. at Hever, Kent on 20 July 1971.

3. GEMS *and other Precious Materials*

PRECIOUS STONE RECORDS

	Largest	Largest Cut Stone	Other Records
Diamond (pure crystallized carbon)	3,106 metric carats (over 1¼lb.)−*The Cullinan*, found by Capt. M.F. Wells 26 Jan. 1905 in the Premier Mine, Pretoria, South Africa.	530.2 metric carats. Cleaved from *The Cullinan* in 1908, in Amsterdam by Jak Asscher and polished by Henri Koe known as *The Star of Africa* No. 1 and now in the Royal Sceptre.	Diamond is the *hardest* known naturally-occurring substance, being 90 times as hard as the next hardest mineral, corundum (Al_2O_3). The peak hardness value on the Knoop scale is 8,400 compared with an average diamond of 7,000. The rarest colours for diamond are blue (record−44.4 carat *Hope* diamond) and pink (record−24 carat presented by Dr. John Thoburn Williamson to H.M. The Queen in 1958). Auction record: $1,050,000 (£437,500) for a 69.42 carat stone bought by Cartier and sold to Richard Burton (at $1,200,000 (£500,000) for Elizabeth Taylor on 24 Oct. 1969. The largest uncut diamond is *The Star of Sierra Leone* found at Kono on 14 Feb. 1972 weighing 969.8 carats.
Emerald (green beryl) $[Be_3Al_2(SiO_3)_6]$	125lb. (up to 15¾ inches long and 9¾ inches in diameter) from a Ural, U.S.S.R. mine.	2,680 carat unguent jar carved by Dionysio Miseroni in the 17th century owned by the Austrian Government. 1,350 carat of *gem* quality, the *Devonshire* stone from Muso, Columbia.	An 11,000 carat emerald was reported to have been found by Charles Kempt and J. Botes at Letaba, northern Transvaal, South Africa 16 Oct. 1956.
Sapphire (blue corundum) (Al_2O_3)	2,302 carat stone found at Anakie, Queensland, Australia, in *c.* 1935, now a 1,318 carat head of President Abraham Lincoln (1809-65).	1,444 carat *Black Star Sapphire of Queensland* carved in 1953-55 into a bust of General Dwight David Eisenhower (1890-1969).	*Note*: both the sapphire busts are in the custody of the Kazanjian Foundation of Los Angeles, California, U.S.A.
Ruby (red corundum) (Al_2O_3)	3,421 carat broken stone reported found in July 1961 (largest piece 750 carats).	1,184 natural gem stone of Burmese origin.	Since 1955 rubies have been the world's most precious gem attaining a price of up to £4,000 per carat by 1969. The ability to make corundum prisms for laser technology up to over 1 inches in length must now have a bearing on the gem market.

RECORDS FOR OTHER PRECIOUS MATERIALS

	Largest	Where Found	Notes On Present Location, etc.
Pearl (Molluscan concretion)	14lb. 1oz. 9½in. long by 5½in. in diameter−*Pearl of Lao-tze*	At Palawan, Philippines, 7 May 1934 in shell of giant clam.	In a San Francisco bank vault. It is the property since 1936 of Wilburn Dowell Cobb and was valued at $3,500,000 in 1939.
Opal $(SiO_2.nH_2O)$	Any stone: 220 troy oz. (yellow-orange). Gem stone: 17,700 carats (*Olympic Australis*)	Anda Mooka, South Australia, Jan 1970. Coober Pedy, South Australia, Aug 1956.	The Anda Mooka specimen was unearthed by a bulldozer.
Crystal (SiO_2)	Any stone: 70 tons (piezo-quartz crystal). Ball: 106¾lb. $12\frac{7}{8}$ in. diameter, the *Warner* sphere	Kazakhstan, U.S.S.R., Sept 1958. Burma, (originally a 1,000 lb. piece).	Note: There is a single rock crystal of 1,728 lb. placed in the Ural Geological Museum, Sverdlovsk, U.S.S.R., November 1968. U.S. National Museum in Washington, D.C.
Topaz $[(Al_2SiO_4)_4(F,OH)_2]$	Any stone: 596 lb. Gem stone: 7,725 carats	Minas Gerais, Brazil.	American Museum of Natural History, New York City, since 1951. Also at the American Museum of Natural History.
Amber (Coniferous fossil resin)	33 lb. 10 oz.	Reputedly from Burma acquired in 1860.	Bought by John Charles Bowring (d.1893) for £300 in Canton, China. Natural History Museum, London, since 1940.
Jade $[NaAl(Si_2O_6)]$	Sub-marine boulder of 5 short tons (valued at $180,000)	Off Monterey, California. Landed 5 June 1971.	Reputedly worth $50,000. Jadeite can be virtually any colour. The less precious nephrite is $[Ca_2(Mg,Fe)_5(OH)_2(Si_4O_{11})_2]$
Marble (Metamorphosed $CaCO_3$)	90 tons (single slab)	Quarried at Yule, Colorado, U.S.A.	A piece of over 45 tons was dressed from this slab for the coping stone of the Tomb of the Unknown Soldier in Arlington National Cemetery, Virginia, U.S.A.
Nuggets−Gold (Au)	7,560 oz. (472½ lb.) (reef gold) *Holtermann Nugget*	Beyers & Holtermann Star of Hope Gold Mining Co., Hill End, N.S.W., Australia, 19 Oct. 1872.	The purest large nugget was the *Welcome Stranger*, found at Tarnagulla, near Moliagul, Victoria, Australia, which yielded 2,248 troy oz. of pure gold from 2,280¼ oz.
Silver (Ag)	2,750 lb. troy	Sonora, Mexico	Appropriated by the Spanish Government before 1821.

Other Gems Records:
Largest Stone of Gem Quality:
A 520,000 carat (2 cwt. 5 lb.) aquamarine $(Be_3Al_2[SiO_3]_6)$ found near Marambaia, Brazil in 1910. Yielded over 200,000 carats of gem quality cut stones.

Rarest:
Taaffeite $(Be_4Mg_4Al_{15}O_{32})$ first discovered in Dublin, Ireland, in November 1945. Only two of these pale mauve stones known−the larger is of 0.84 of a carat.

Densest Gem Mineral:
Stibotantalite $[(SbO)_2(Ta,Nb)_2O_6]$ a rare brownish-yellow mineral found in San Diego County, California, has a density of 7.46. The alloy platiniridium has a density of more than 22.0.

4. TELESCOPES

Earliest Although there is evidence that early Arabian scientists understood something of the magnifying power of lenses, their first use to form a telescope has been attributed to Roger Bacon (*c.* 1214-92) in England. The prototype of modern refracting telescopes was that completed by Johannes Lippershey for the Dutch government on 2 Oct. 1608.

Largest Refractor The largest refracting (*i.e.* magnification by lenses) telescope in the world is the 62-foot-long 40-inch telescope completed in 1897 at the Yerkes Observatory, Williams Bay, Wisconsin, and belonging to the University of Chicago, Illinois, U.S.A. The largest in the British Isles is the 28-inch at the Royal Greenwich Observatory completed in 1894.

Reflector World The largest operational telescope in the world is the 6 metre (236.2 inch) sited on Mount Semirodriki, near Zelenchukskaya in the Caucasus Mountains, U.S.S.R., at an altitude of 6,830 feet. The mirror, weighing 70 tons, was completed in November 1967 and assembled by October 1970. The overall weight of the 80-foot long assembly is 850 tons. Being the most powerful of all telescopes its range, which includes the location of objects down to the 25th magnitude, represents the limits of the observable Universe. Its light-gathering power would enable it to detect the light from a candle at a distance of 15,000 miles.

United Kingdom The largest reflector in the British Isles is the Isaac Newton 98.2-inch reflector at the Royal Greenwich Observatory, Herstmonceux Castle, Sussex. It was built in Newcastle upon Tyne, Northumberland, weighs 92 tons, cost £641,000 and was inaugurated on 1 Dec. 1967.

Radio Earliest The world's first fully steerable radio telescope is the Mark I telescope at the University of Manchester Department of Radio Astronomy, Nuffield Radio Astronomy Laboratories, Jodrell Bank, Macclesfield, Cheshire, on which work began in September 1952. The 750-ton 250-foot diameter bowl of steel plates and 180-foot-high supports weigh 2,000 tons. Its cost is believed to have been about £750,000 when it was completed in 1957.

Largest steerable dish The world's largest trainable dish-type radio telescope is the 328 foot diameter, 3,000 ton assembly at the Max Planck Institute for Radio Astronomy of Bonn in the Effelsberger Valley, West Germany; it became operative in May 1971. The cost of the installation begun in November 1967 was £14,200,000. The Manchester University Mark V radio telescope at Meiford, Montgomeryshire will have a diameter of 400 feet and is due for completion at a cost of some £5 million in 1975.

Largest Dish The world's largest dish radio telescope is the partially-steerable ionospheric assembly built over a natural bowl at Arecibo, Puerto Rico, completed in November 1963 at a cost of about $9,000,000 (£3.75 million). The dish has a diameter of 1,000 feet and covers 18½ acres. Its sensitivity is being raised by a factor of 2,000 and its range to 15,000 million light-years by the fitting of new aluminium plates at a cost of $7 million. The RATAN-600 radio telescope being built in the Northern Caucasus, U.S.S.R. will have a dish 1,968.5 feet in diameter.

Largest World The first $3 million instalment for the building of the world's largest and most sensitive radio telescope was included by the National Science Foundation in their federal budget for the fiscal year 1973. The instrument termed the VLA (Very Large Array) will be

The world's largest steerable dish telescope in the Effelsberger Valley, W. Germany

Y-shaped with each arm 13 miles long with 27 mobile antennae on rails. The site selected will be 50 miles west of Socorro in the Plains of San Augustin, New Mexico and the completion date will be 1979 to 1981 at a total cost of $74 million (£28.4 million).

The British Science Research Council 5 kilometre radio telescope at Lord's Bridge, Cambridgeshire and Isle of Ely to be operated by the Mullard Radio Astronomy Observatory of Cambridge University will utilize eight mobile 42-foot rail-borne computer-controlled dish aerials, which will be equivalent to a single steerable dish 5 kilometres in diameter. The project, to be operational before the end of 1973, will cost more than £2,100,000.

Solar The world's largest solar telescope is the 480-foot-long McMath telescope at Kitt Peak National Observatory near Tucson, Arizona, U.S.A. It has a focal length of 300 feet and an 80-inch heliostat mirror. It was completed in 1962 and produces an image measuring 33 inches in diameter.

Observatory Highest The highest altitude observatory in the world is the Mauna Kea Observatory, Hawaii at an altitude of 13,824 feet, opened in 1969. The principal instrument is an 88-inch (224 cm.) telescope.

Oldest The earliest astronomical observatory in the world is the Chomsong-dae built in A.D. 632 in Kyongju, South Korea and still extant.

Planetaria World The ancestor of the planetarium is the rotatable Gottorp Globe, built by Andreas Busch in Denmark between 1654 and 1664 to the orders of Duke Frederick III of Holstein's court mathematician Olearius. It is 34.6 feet in circumference, weighs nearly 3½ tons and is now preserved in Leningrad, U.S.S.R. The stars were painted on the inside. The earliest optical installation was not until 1923 in the Deutsches Museum, Munich, by Zeiss of Jena, Germany. The world's largest planetarium, with a diameter of 85 feet, is the Washington Planetarium and Space Center in Washington D.C. The total construction cost was $5 million.

United Kingdom The United Kingdom's first planetarium was opened at Madame Tussaud's, Marylebone Road, London, on 19 March 1958. Accurate images of 8,900 stars are able to be projected on the 70-foot high copper dome.

5. PHOTOGRAPHY

It is estimated that the total expenditure on photography in the U.S.A. in 1970 was $3,802,176,896 (£1,657 million) and that 70,135,000 still cameras

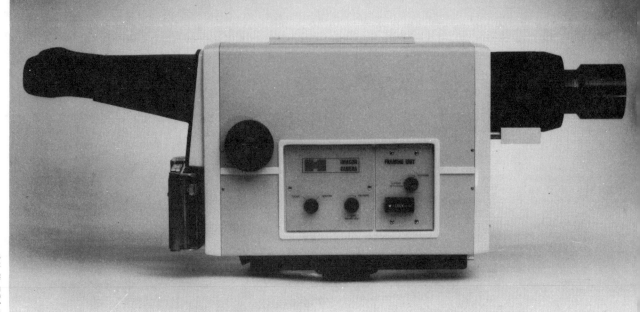

The world's fastest camera, capable of taking 60,000,000 exposures per second

and 8,275,000 cine cameras were in use.

CAMERAS

Earliest The earliest photograph was taken in the summer of 1826 by Joseph Nicéphore Niépce (1765-1833), a French physician and scientist. It showed the courtyard of his country house at Gras, near St. Loup-de-Varennes. It probably took eight hours to expose and was taken on a bitumen-coated polished pewter plate measuring 8 inches by 6½ inches. The earliest photograph taken in England was one of a diamond-paned window in Laycock (or Lacock) Abbey, Wiltshire, taken in 1835 by William Henry Fox Talbot (1800-1877), the inventor of the negative-positive process. This was bought by the Johannesburg City Council for £480 in November 1970. The world's earliest aerial photograph was taken in 1858 by Gaspard Félix Tournachon (1820-1910), *alias* Nadar, from a balloon near Villacoublay, on the outskirts of Paris, France.

Largest The largest camera ever built was the Anderson Mammoth camera, built in Chicago, Illinois, U.S.A., in 1900. When extended, it measured 9 feet high, 6 feet wide and 20 feet long. Its two lenses were a wide-angle Zeiss with a focal length of 68 inches and a telescope Rapid Rectilinear of 120 inches focal length. Exposures averaged 150 seconds and 15 men were required to work it.

Smallest Apart from cameras built for intra-cardiac surgery and espionage, the smallest camera generally marketed is the Japanese Kiku 16 Model II, which measures $2\frac{3}{8}$ inches $\times$ 1 inch $\times$ $\frac{5}{8}$ of an inch.

Fastest A paper on a camera of highly limited application with a time resolution of 1.0×10^{-11} of a second has been published by Butslov *et al.* of the U.S.S.R. Academy of Sciences. In June 1969 a camera from the U.S.S.R. was demonstrated at the N.P.L., Teddington, London with "events" moving across image tubes at 167 million m.p.h. or one quarter of the speed of light. Britain's fastest camera is the E.12 image tube camera announced by the Optical Group of the Atomic Weapons Research Establishment at Aldermaston, Berkshire in January 1966, with a rate of 60,000,000 exposures per second. The camera is marketed under the title of TE.12 by Telford Products Ltd., of Greenford, Middlesex, and Imacon

by John Hadland (P.I.) Ltd., of Bovingdon, Hertfordshire.

Most expensive The most expensive "amateur" roll-film cameras in the world are the F-1 35 mm system by Canon Amsterdam N.V. of Schiphol, Netherlands. The 40 lenses offered range from the Fish Eye 7.5 mm F5.6 to the FL 1200 mm F11, while the accessories available number 180.

Fastest Lens The world's fastest lens is the Canon X 200 mm. F0.56 mirror lens used for X-Ray work. The fastest lens available in Television Cameras is the Canon F0.65.

Largest print The largest photographic print ever produced was an enlargement of a hand-drawn map of Europe, measuring over 4,000 square feet, made for the British Broadcasting Corporation by the Newbold Wells Organisation Limited of London. In 1964 this company produced the largest colour transparency, a hand-coloured transparency of the London sky-line, measuring 212 feet long by 12½ feet high, for the Vickers stand at the Sydney Exhibition in Australia.

X-ray Largest The largest X-ray ever made was of a 17-foot long Mercedes 280 SL car using Agfa-Gevaert Structurix D4 film and a 50-hour exposure in September 1959.

6. NUMEROLOGY

In dealing with large numbers, scientists use the notation of 10 raised to various powers to eliminate a profusion of noughts. For example, 19,160,000,000,000 miles would be written 1.916×10^{13} miles. Similarly, a very small number, for example 0.0000154324 of a grain, would be written 1.5432×10^{-5} of a grain. Of the prefixes used before numbers the smallest is "atto-" from the Danish *atten* for 18, indicating a trillionth part (10^{-18}) of the unit, and the highest is "tera-" (Greek, *teras*=monster), indicating a billion (10^{12}) fold.

NUMBERS

Highest The highest generally accepted named number is the centillion, which is 10 raised to the power 600, or one followed by 600 noughts. Higher numbers are named in linguistic literature the most extreme of which is the milli-millimillillion (10 raised to the power 6,000,000,000) devised by Rudolf Ondrejka. The number Megiston written with symbol ⑩ is a number too great to have any physical meaning. The highest named number outside the decimal notation is the Buddhist *asankhyeya,* which is equal to 10^{140} or 100 tertio-vigintillions (British system) or 100 quinto-quadragintillions (U.S. system).

The number 10^{100} (10,000 sexdecillion) is designated a Googol. This was invented by Dr. Edward Kasner (U.S.) (d. 1955). Ten raised to the power of a Googol is described as a Googolplex. Some conception of the magnitude of such numbers can be gained when it is said that the number of atoms in some models of the observable Universe does not exceed 10^{85}. Factorial 10^{85} approximates to 10 to the power of $43 + 85 \times 10^{85}$

The largest number to have become sufficiently well-known in mathematics to have been named after its begetter is the larger of the two Skewes numbers which is 10 to the power 10 to the power 10 to the power 3, obtained by Prof. Stanley Skewes, M.A., Ph.D., now of Cape Town University, South Africa, and published in two papers of 1933 and 1955 concerning the occurrence of prime numbers.

Prime numbers A prime number is any positive integer (excluding 1) having no integral factors other than itself and unity, *e.g.* 2, 3, 5, 7 or 11. The lowest prime number is thus 2. The highest known prime number is $2^{19937}-1$, received by the American Mathematical Society on 18 March 1971 and calculated on an I.B.M. 360/91 computer in 39 mins. 26.4 secs. by Dr. Bryant Tuckerman at Yorktown Heights, New York.

Perfect numbers A number is said to be perfect if it is equal to the sum of its divisors other than itself, *e.g.* $1 + 2 + 4 + 7 + 14 = 28$. The lowest perfect number is $6 (1 + 2 + 3)$. The highest known and the 24th so far discovered, is $(2^{19937}-1) \times 2^{19936}$ which has 12,003 digits.

Most primitive The lowest limit in enumeration among primitive peoples is among the Yancos, an Amazon tribe who cannot count beyond *poettarrarorincoaroac,* which is their word for "three". The Temiar people of West Malaysia (formerly called Malaya) also stop at three. Investigators have reported that the number "four" is expressed by a look of total stupefaction indistinguishable from that for any other number higher than three. It is said that among survivors of the Aimores, naked nomads of Eastern Brazil, there is no apparent word for "two".

Most accurate and most inaccurate version of "pi" The greatest number of decimal places to which *pi* (π) has been calculated is 500,000 by the French mathematicians Jean Guilloud and Michele Dichampt of the *Commissariat* à l'Energie Atomique published on 26 Feb. 1967. The published value to 500,000 places was 3.141592653589793 ... (omitting the next 499,975 places) ... 5138195242. In 1897 the State legislature of Indiana came within a single vote of declaring that pi should be *de jure* 3.2.

Earliest measures The earliest known measure of weight is the *beqa* of the Amratian period of Egyptian civilization *c.* 3,800 B.C. found at Naqada, United Arab Republic. The weights are cylindrical with rounded ends from 188.7 to 211.2 grammes and are the basis of the English troy ounce. The unit of length used by the megalithic tomb-builders in Britain *c.* 2300 B.C. appears to have been 2.72±0.003 feet.

TIME MEASURE
Longest The longest measure of time is the *kalpa* in Hindu chronology. It is equivalent to 4,320 million years. In astronomy a cosmic year is the period of rotation of the Sun around the centre of the Milky Way galaxy, *i.e.* about 225,000,000 years. In the Late Cretaceous Period of *c.* 85 million years ago the Earth rotated faster so resulting in 370.3 days per year.

Shortest Owing to variations in the length of a day, which is estimated to be increasing irregularly at the average rate of about two milliseconds per century due to the Moon's tidal drag, the second has been redefined. Instead of being 1/86,400th part of a mean solar day, it has, since 1960, been reckoned as 1/31,556, 925.9747th part of the solar (or tropical) year at A.D. 1900, January 0 to 12 hours, Ephemeris time. In 1958 the second of Ephemeris time was computed to be equivalent to 9,192,631,770±20 cycles of the radiation corresponding to the transition of a caesium 133 atom when unperturbed by exterior fields. In a nano-second or a milli-micro second (1.0×10^{-9} of a second) light travels 11.7 inches.

SMALLEST UNITS
The shortest unit of length is the atto-metre which is 1.0×10^{-16} of a centimetre. The smallest unit of area is a "shed", used in sub-atomic physics and first mentioned in 1956. It is 1.0×10^{-48} of a square centimetre. A "barn" is equal to 10^{24} "sheds". The reaction of a neutrino occurs over the area of 1×10^{-43} of a square centimetre.

7. PHYSICAL EXTREMES
TEMPERATURES
Highest The highest man-made temperatures yet attained are those produced in the centre of a thermonuclear fusion bomb, which are of the order of 300,000,000 to 400,000,000° C. Of controllable temperatures, the highest effective laboratory figure reported is 50,000,000° C. for 2/100ths of a second by Prof. Lev A. Artsimovich at Tokamuk in the U.S.S.R. in 1969. At very low particle densities even higher figures are obtainable. Prior to 1963 a figure of 3,000 million °C. was reportedly achieved in the U.S.S.R. with Ogra injection-mirror equipment.

Lowest The lowest temperature reached is 5×10^{-7} degree Kelvin, achieved by Professor A. Abragam (b. 1914) in collaboration with M. Chapellier, M. Goldman, and Vu Hoang Chau at the Centre d'Etudes Nucléaires, Saclay, France, in 1969. Absolute or thermodynamic temperatures are defined in terms of ratios rather than as differences reckoned from the unattainable absolute zero, which on the Kelvin scale is −273.15° C. or −459.67° F. Thus the lowest temperature ever attained is 1 in 1.8×10^9 of the melting point of ice (0° C. or 273.15K or 32° F.).

Highest pressures The highest sustained laboratory pressures yet reported are of 5,000,000 atmospheres (32,800 tons per square inch), achieved in the U.S.S.R. and announced in October 1958. Using dynamic methods and impact speeds of up to 18,000 m.p.h., momentary pressures of 75,000,000 atmospheres (490,000 tons per square inch) were reported from the United States in 1958.

Highest vacuum The highest (or 'hardest') vacuums obtained in scientific research are of the order of 1.0×10^{-16} of an atmosphere. This compares with an estimated pressure in inter-stellar space of 1.0×10^{-19} of an atmosphere. At sea-level there are 3×10^{19} molecules per cubic centimetre in the atmosphere, but in inter-stellar space there are probably less than 10 per cubic centimetre.

Fastest centrifuge The highest man-made rotary speed ever achieved is 1,500,000 revolutions per second, or 90,000,000 revolutions per minute, on a steel rotor with a diameter of about 1/100th of an inch suspended in a vacuum in an ultra-centrifuge installed in March 1961 in the Rouss Physical Laboratory at the University of Virginia in Charlottesville, Virginia, U.S.A. This work is led by Prof. Jesse W. Beams. The edge of the rotor is travelling at 2,500 m.p.h. and is subject to a stress of 1,000,000,000 g.

Microscopes Most powerful Electron microscopes have now reached the point at which individual atoms are distinguishable. In March 1958 the U.S.S.R. announced an electronic point projector with a magnification approaching X 2,000,000, in which individual atoms of barium and molecules of oxygen can be observed. In 1970 a resolution of 0.88 of an Ångström unit diameter was achieved by Dr. K. Yada (Japan) using a Hitachi Model HU-11B. In February 1969 it was announced from Pennsylvania State University, U.S.A., that the combination of the field-ion microscope invented by their Prof. Erwing W. Müller in 1956 and a spectrometer enabled single atoms to be identified.

Smallest The smallest high power microscope in the world is the 2,000 X 18 oz. McArthur microscope measuring 4 X 2½ X 2 inches. It provides immersion dark ground, phase contrast, polarising and incident illumination and is produced at Landbeach, Cambridge, England.

Electron microscope The most powerful electron microscope in the world is the 3,500 kV installation at the National Scientific Research Centre, Toulouse, France which reached testing stage in October 1969. The high voltage generator and accelerator fill a cylinder 15 feet in diameter and 30 feet high. Its six lenses form a column 3 feet by 11 feet and weigh 20 tons.

Highest note The highest note yet attained is one of 60,000 megahertz (GHz) (60,000 million vibrations per second), generated by a "laser" beam striking a sapphire crystal at the Massachusetts Institute of Technology in Cambridge, Massachusetts, U.S.A., in September 1964. This is 3,000,000 times as high in pitch as the upper limit of adult human audibility.

Loudest noise The loudest noise created in a laboratory is 210 decibels or 400,000 acoustic watts reported by N.A.S.A. from a 48 foot steel and concrete horn at Huntsville, Alabama, U.S.A. in October 1965. Holes can be bored in solid material by this means.

Quietest place The "dead room", measuring 35 feet by 28 feet, in the Bell Telephone System laboratory at Murray Hill, New Jersey, U.S.A., is the most anechoic room in the world, eliminating 99.98 per cent. of reflected sound.

Finest balance The most accurate balance in the world is the Q01 quartz fibre decimicro balance made by L. Oertling Ltd. of Orpington, Kent, England which has a read-out scale on which one division corresponds to 0.0001 of a milligramme. It can weigh to an accuracy of 0.0002 of a milligramme which is equivalent to little more than one third of the weight of ink on this full stop.

Lowest viscosity The California Institute of Technology, U.S.A. announced on 1 Dec. 1957 that there was no measurable viscosity, *i.e.* perfect flow, in liquid helium II, which exists only at temperatures close to absolute zero ($-273.15°$ C. or $-459.67°$ F.).

Lowest friction The lowest coefficient of static and dynamic friction of any solid is 0.02, in the case of polytetrafluoro-ethylene ($[C_2F_4]_n$), called P.T.F.E.—equivalent to wet ice on wet ice. It was first manufactured in quantity by E.I. du Pont de Nemours & Co. Inc. in 1943, and is marketed from the U.S.A. as Teflon. In the United Kingdom it is marketed by I.C.I. as Fluon.

At the University of Virginia (see above, Fastest centrifuge) a 30 lb. rotor magnetically supported has been spun at 1,000 revolutions per second in a vacuum of 10^{-6} mm. of mercury pressure. It loses only one revolution per second per day, thus spinning for years.

Most powerful electric current The most powerful electric current generated is that from the Zeus capacitor at the Los Alamos Scientific Laboratory, New Mexico, U.S.A. If fired simultaneously the 4,032 capacitors would produce for a few micro-seconds twice as much current as that generated elsewhere on Earth.

Most powerful adhesive The most powerful adhesive known is epoxy resin, which, after being supercooled to $-450°$ F., can withstand a shearing pull of 8,000 lb. per square inch.

Most powerful particle accelerator The 1.24 mile diameter proton synchrotron at the National Accelerator Laboratory at Weston, Illinois, U.S.A. is the largest and most powerful "atom-smasher" in the world. An energy of 200 GeV was attained on 1 Mar. 1972. The plant cost $250 million. The construction of the CERN II 1.37 mile diameter proton synchrotron on the French-Swiss border at Megrin near Geneva was authorized on 19 Feb. 1971 and should attain 300 GeV by 1979.

The £32 million CERN intersecting storage rings (ISR) project, started on 27 Jan. 1971, using two 28 GeV proton beams, is designed to yield the equivalent of 1,700 GeV in its centre of mass experiments.

World's largest bubble chamber The largest bubble chamber in the world is at the Argonne National Laboratory, Illinois, U.S.A. It is 12 feet in diameter and contains 5,330 gallons of liquid hydrogen at a temperature of $-247°$ C. A 30,000 litre chamber (6,600 gallons) is being built at CERN, near Geneva.

Strongest magnet The heaviest magnet in the world is one measuring 200 feet in diameter, with a weight of 36,000 tons, for the 10 GeV synchrophasotron in the Joint Institute for Nuclear Research at Dubna, near Moscow, U.S.S.R. The largest super-conducting magnet is a niobium-zirconium magnet, weighing 15,675 lb., completed in June 1966 by Avco Everett Research Laboratory, Massachusetts, U.S.A. It produces a magnetic field of 40,000 gauss and the windings are super-cooled with 6,000 litres of liquid helium.

Strongest magnetic field The strongest recorded magnetic fields are ones of 10 megagaus, fleetingly produced by explosive flux compression devices reported in Sept. 1968. The first megagauss field was announced also from the United States in March 1967.

The strongest steady magnetic field yet achieved is one of 255,000 gauss in a cylindrical bore of 1.25 inches, using 10 megawatts of power, called the "1J" magnet designed by D. Bruce Montgomery, which was put into operation at the Francis Bitter National Magnet Laboratory at Massachusetts Institute of Technology in 1964.

Most Powerful Sound System The World's most powerful Sound System is that installed at the Ontario Motor Speedway, California in July 1970. It has an output of 30,800 watts, connectable to 355 horn speaker assemblies and thus able to communicate the spoken word to 230,000 people above the noise of 50 screaming racing cars.

WIND TUNNELS

World The world's largest wind tunnel is a low-speed tunnel with a closed test section measuring 40 feet by 80 feet, built in 1944 at the Ames Research Center, Moffett Field, California, U.S.A. The tunnel encloses 800 tons of air and cost approximately $7,000,000 (now £2,916,666). The maximum volume of air that can be moved is 60,000,000 cubic feet per minute. The most powerful is the 216,000 h.p. installation at the Arnold Engineering Test Center at Tullahoma, Tennessee, U.S.A. opened in September 1956. The highest Mach number attained with air is Mach 27 at the works of the Boeing Company in Seattle, Washington State, U.S.A. For periods of micro-seconds, shock Mach numbers of the order of 30 have been attained in impulse tubes at Cornell University, Ithaca, New York State, U.S.A.

United Kingdom The largest wind tunnel in the United Kingdom is the transonic installation at the Aircraft Research Association at Bedford, with a working area 9 feet × 8 feet, and a tunnel power of 25,000 h.p. (18.5 Mw). This machine is capable of producing Mach 1.4, which is equivalent to 1,065 m.p.h. at sea level.

Finest cut Biological specimens embedded in epoxy resin can be sectioned by a glass knife microtome under ideal conditions to a thickness of 1/875,000th of an inch or 290 Ångström units.

Brightest light The brightest steady artificial light sources are "laser" beams with a luminosity exceeding the Sun's 800,000 candles per square inch by a factor well in excess of 1,000. In May 1969 the U.S.S.R. Academy of Sciences announed blast waves travelling through a luminous plasma of inert gases heated to 90,000° K. The flare-up for up to 3 micro-seconds shone at 50,000 times the brightness of the Sun *viz.* 40,000 million candles per square inch. Of continuously burning sources, the most powerful is a 200 kW high-pressure xenon arc lamp of 600,000 candlepower, reported from the U.S.S.R. in 1965. The most powerful searchlight ever developed was one produced during the 1939-45 war by the General Electric Company Ltd. at the Hirst Research Centre in Wembley, Greater London. It had a consumption of 600 kW and gave an arc luminance of 300,000 candles per square inch and a maximum beam intensity of 2,700,000,000 candles from its parabolic mirror (diameter 10 feet).

Most powerful "laser" beams The first illumination of another celestial body was achieved on 9 May 1962, when a beam of light was successfully reflected from the Moon by the use of an optical "maser" (microwave amplification by stimulated emission of radiation) or "laser" (light amplification by stimulated emission of radiation) attached to a 48-in. telescope at Massachusetts Institute of Technology, Cambridge, Massachusetts, U.S.A. The spot was estimated to be 4 miles in diameter on the Moon. A "maser" light flash is focused into liquid nitrogen-cooled ruby crystal. Its chromium atoms are excited into a high energy state in which they emit a red light which is allowed to escape only in the direction desired. The device was propounded in 1958 by Dr. Charles Hard Townes (born 1915) of the U.S.A. Such a flash for 1/5,000th of a second can bore a hole through a diamond by vaporization at 10,000° C., produced by 2×10^{23} photons.

COMPUTERS

World The world's most powerful computer is the Control Data Corporation CDC 7600 first delivered in January 1969. It can perform 36 million operations in one second and has an access time of 27.5 nano-seconds. It has two internal memory cores of 655,360 and 5,242,880 characters (6 bits per character) supplemented by a Model 817 disc file of 800 million characters. Commercial deliveries have been scheduled from 1972 at a cost of $9 to $15 million (£3¾ to £6¼ million) depending on peripherals. The most capacious storage device is the Ampex Terabit Memory which can store 2.88×10^{12} bits.

United Kingdom The largest computer built in the United Kingdom is the £2,800,000 Ferranti "Atlas I". The largest of these was installed in 1964 in the Atlas Computer Laboratory of the Science Research Council, Chilton, Didcot, Berkshire. This machine can perform 500,000 arithmetic operations in a second and 25,000,000 9 digit multiplications in two minutes. It has a capacity of 7,077,888 bits.

Computer Reference Number The most extravagant reference number yet reported from a computerized payment counterfoil is one of 43 digits in the case of a householder's insurance paid in July 1971 by the playwright Alan Melville for his home in Brighton, Sussex, England. The number was 1.37 quintillion times larger than the entire population of the world at that date.

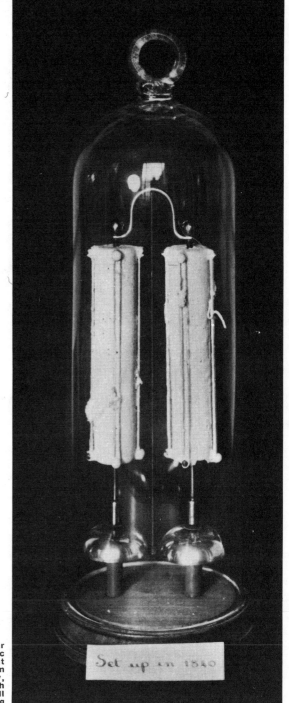

The 132 year old electric battery at Clarendon Laboratory, Oxford which is still operating

Longest Lived Electric Battery A battery kept in the Clarendon Laboratory, University of Oxford, has been causing a suspended bob to be electrostatically attracted a few times a second alternately by two small bells since 1840 when it was made by the London firm of scientific apparatus makers Watkins and Hill. It produces about 2 kV at 10^{-8} A and is an example of the so-called "dry column" associated with the names of Marechaux, de Luc, Behrens and Zamboni. The only known use of this form of battery in this century was for an infra-red viewer in the 1939-45 war.

Most durable light The electric light bulb was invented in New York City, U.S.A. in 1860 by Heinrich (later Henry) Goebel (1818-93) of Springe, Germany. The average bulb lasts for 750 to 1,000 hours. There is some evidence that a carbide filament bulb burning in the Fire Department, Livermore, South Alameda County, California has been burning since 1901.

6 THE ARTS AND ENTERTAINMENTS

1. PAINTING

Earliest Evidence of Palaeolithic art was first found in 1834 at Chaffaud, Vienne, France by Brouillet when he recognised an engraving of two deer on a piece of flat bone from the cave, dating to about 20,000 B.C. The number of stratigraphically-dated examples of cave art is very limited. The oldest known dated examples came from La Ferrassie, near Les Eyzies in the Périgord, where large blocks of stone engraved with animal figures and symbols were found in the Aurignacian II layer (*c.* 25,000 B.C.); similarly engraved blocks and with traces of paint possibly representing a cervid (a deer-like form) came from the Aurignacian III layer (*c.* 24,000 B.C.).

LARGEST

World
All time *Panorama of the Mississippi,* completed by John Banvard (1815-91) in 1846, showing the river scene for 1,200 miles in a strip probably 5,000 feet long and 12 feet wide, was the largest painting in the world, with an area of more than 1.3 acres. The painting is believed to have been destroyed when the rolls of canvas, stored in a barn at Cold Spring Harbor, Long Island, New York State, U.S.A., caught fire shortly before Banvard's death on 16 May 1891.

Existing The largest painting now in existence is probably *The Battle of Gettysburg,* completed in 1883, after 2½ years of work, by Paul Philippoteaux (France) and 16 assistants. The painting is 410 feet long, 70 feet high and weighs 5.36 tons. It depicts the climax of the Battle of Gettysburg, in southern Pennsylvania, U.S.A., on 3 July 1863. In 1964 the painting was bought by Joe King of Winston-Salem, North Carolina, U.S.A. after being stored by E.W. McConnell in a Chicago warehouse since 1933.

"Old
Master" The largest "Old Master" is *Il Paradiso,* painted between 1587 and 1590 by Jacopo Robusti, *alias* Tintoretto (1518-94), and his son Domenico on Wall "E" of the Sala del Maggior Consiglio in the Palazzo Ducale (Doge's Palace) in Venice, Italy. The work is 22 metres (72 feet 2 inches) long and 7 metres (22 feet 11½ inches) high and contains more than 100 human figures.

United
Kingdom The largest painting in the United Kingdom is the giant oval *Triumph of Peace and Liberty* by Sir James Thornhill (1676-1734), on the ceiling of the Painte Hall in the Royal Naval College, Greenwich, Londor It measures 106 feet by 51 feet and took 20 year (1707-1727) to complete.

MOST VALUABLE

World The "Mona Lisa" (*La Gioconda*) by Leonardo d Vinci (1452-1519) in the Louvre, Paris, was assesse for insurance purposes at the highest ever figur of $100,000,000 (then £35.7 million) for its move f(exhibition in Washington, D.C., and New York Cit) N.Y., U.S.A., from 14 Dec. 1962 to 12 March 196: However, insurance was not concluded because th cost of the closest security precautions was less tha that of the premiums. It was painted in *c.* 1503-0 and measures 77 × 53 centimetres or 30.5 × 20. inches. It is believed to portray Mona (short f(Madonna) Lisa Gherardini, the wife of Francesco d(Giocondo of Florence, who disliked it and refused t pay for it. Francis I, King of France, bought th painting for his bathroom for 4,000 gold florins (no equivalent to £225,000) in 1517.

HIGHEST PRICE

Auction
price
World The highest price ever bid in a public auction for an painting is £2,310,000 for *Portrait of Juan de Parej* also known as *The Slave of Velázquez,* painted i Rome in 1649 by Diego Rodríguez de Silva Velá quez (1599-1660) and sold on 27 Nov. 1970 at tl salerooms of Christie, Manson & Woods, London t the Wildenstein Gallery, New York. The painting ha been sold at Christie's at auction in 1801 for 3 guineas (£40.95). It was in the possession of the Ear of Radnor from May 1811 until 1970.

Art Auction
Sale
Highest
Total The highest total ever achieved for a single auction (works of art is £3,638,825 by a sale of 27 paintings b old Masters at the salerooms of Messrs. Christi Manson and Woods, London on 25 June 1971. Th highest price in the sale was paid for *The Death c Acteon* by Titian (£1,680,000).

By British
artist The highest auction price for any painting by a Britis artist is £220,000 for *A Cheetah with two Indians* b George Stubbs, R.A. (1724-1806) at Sotheby's on 1 March 1970. It was sold by the Trustees of Sir Georg Pigot's Will Trust to Thomas Agnew & Sons Ltd. c

82

Painting

behalf of City Art Gallery, Manchester. The painting measures 71 × 107 inches and was painted c. 1765.

Miniature portrait The highest price ever paid for a portrait miniature is the £65,100 given by an anonymous buyer at a sale held by Messrs. Christie, Manson and Woods, London on 8 June 1971 for a miniature of Frances Howard, Countess of Essex and Somerset by Isaac Oliver, painted c. 1605. This miniature, sent for auction by Lord Derby, measured 5⅛ inches in diameter.

Modern painting The highest price paid for a modern painting is $1,550,000 (£645,833) paid by the Norton Simon Foundation of Los Angeles, California, U.S.A. at the Parke-Bernet Galleries, New York City on 9 Oct. 1968 for *Le Pont des Arts* painted by Pierre Auguste Renoir (1841-1919) of France in 1868. Renoir sold the picture to the Paris dealer Durand-Ruel for about £16.

Living artist **World** The highest price paid for paintings in the lifetime of the artist is $1,950,000 (£812,500) paid for the two canvases *Two Brothers* (1905) and *Seated Harlequin* (1922) by Pablo Diego José Francisco de Paula Juan Nepomuceno Crispín Crispiano de la Santisima Trinidad Ruiz y Picasso (b. 25 Oct. 1881) of Spain. This was paid by the Basle City Government to the Staechelin Foundation to enable the Basle Museum of Arts to retain the painting after an offer of $2,560,000 (£1,066,666) had been received from the United States in December 1967. The highest price for a single work for a living artist is the £200,000 paid by the Cleveland Museum, Ohio, for his *Bottle, Glass and Fork* (painted in 1912) on 22nd March 1972. The painting was offered for a second time at Messrs. Christie, Manson and Woods but, even though the bidding reached £294,000, it was withdrawn after failing to reach the reserve price.

Over a period of two years (1968-70) a total sum of £4,460,663 was made at auctions of Picasso's work. Numerically this represented only 1/70th of his total output. Therefore it can be estimated that his life-time's *oeuvre* is worth more than £300,000,000 of which his own collection is worth an estimated £30,000,000.

British The highest price for any painting by a living British artist is £26,000 for a painting of a Pope in "convulsive hysteria" by Francis Bacon, completed in 1953, sent in anonymously and bought by Lefevre Gallery at auction at Sotheby's in 1970.

Pop Art The highest price for an item of Pop Art was for "Big Painting No. 6" (1965) by Roy Lichtenstein (U.S.) which was sold for $79,200 (then £33,000) at Parke-Bernet, New York City on 18 Nov. 1970.

The Ansidei Madonna sold for £70,000 in 1885—the highest price of any 19th Century painting (see table)

Drawing The highest price ever attached to any drawing is £804,361 for the cartoon *The Virgin and Child with St. John the Baptist and St. Anne,* measuring 54¼ inches by 39¼ inches, drawn in Milan, probably in 1499-1500, by Leonardo da Vinci (1452-1519) of Italy, retained by the National Gallery in 1962. Three United States bids of over $4,000,000 (then £1,428,570) were reputed to have been made for the cartoon.

Most prolific painter Antoine Joseph Wiertz (1806-1865) of Belgium painted 131 canvases 50 feet wide and 30 feet high, totalling over 4.5 acres. This is believed to be the greatest area covered by any painter of note.

Largest gallery The world's largest art gallery is the Winter Palace and the neighbouring Hermitage in Leningrad, U.S.S.R. One has to walk 15 miles to visit each of the 322 galleries, which house nearly 3,000,000 works of art and archaeological remains.

Oldest and youngest R.A. The oldest ever Royal Academician has been (Thomas) Sidney Cooper C.V.O., who died on 8 Feb. 1902 aged 98 years 136 days, having exhibited 266

HIGHEST-PRICED PAINTINGS—PROGRESSIVE RECORDS

Price	Equivalent 1970 Price	Painter, title, sold by and sold to	Date
£6,500	£52,000	Antonio Correggio's *The Magdalen Reading* (in fact spurious) to Elector Freidrich Augustus II of Saxony.	1746
£8,500	£68,000	Raphael's *The Sistine Madonna* to Elector Friedrich Augustus II of Saxony.	1759
£16,000	£73,600	Van Eyck's *Adoration of the Lamb*, 6 outer panels of Ghent altarpiece by Edward Solby to the Government of Prussia.	1821
£24,600*	£162,400	Murillo's *The Immaculate Conception* by estate of Marshall Soult to the Louvre (against Czar Nicholas I) in Paris.	1852
£70,000	£560,000	Raphael's *Ansidei Madonna* by the 8th Duke of Marlborough to the National Gallery.	1885
£100,000	£800,000	Raphael's *The Colonna Altarpiece* by Sedelmeyer to J. Pierpoint Morgan.	1901
£102,880	£823,000	Van Dyck's *Elena Grimaldi-Cattaneo* (portrait) by Knoedler to Peter Widener (1834-1915).	1906
£102,880	£680,000	Rembrandt's *The Mill* by 6th Marquess of Lansdowne to Peter Widener.	1911
£116,500	£770,000	Raphael's smaller *Panshanger Madonna* by Joseph (later Baron) Duveen (1869-1939) to Peter Widener.	1913
£310,400	£2,050,000	Leonardo da Vinci's *Benois Madonna* to Czar Nicholas II in Paris.	1914
£821,429*	£1,215,000	Rembrandt's *Aristotle Contemplating the Bust of Homer* by estate of Mr. and Mrs. Alfred W Erickson to New York Metropolitan Museum of Art.	1961
£1,785,714	£2,155,000	Leonardo da Vinci's *Ginevra de' Benci* (portrait) by Prince Franz Josef II of Liechtenstein to National Gallery of Art, Washington, D.C., U.S.A.	1967
£2,310,000*		Velázquez's *Portrait of Juan de Pareja* by the Earl of Radnor to the Wildenstein Gallery, New York.	1970

*Indicates price at auction, otherwise prices were by private treaty.

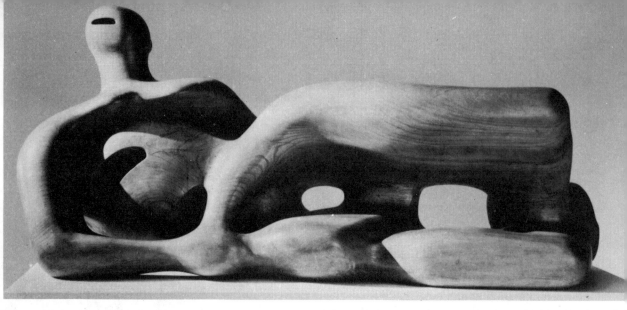

The only sculpture sold for six figures in the lifetime of the sculptor—Henry Moore's 'Reclining Figure' in wood

paintings over the record span of 67 consecutive years (1833-1902). The youngest ever R.A. has been Mary Moser (later Mrs. Hugh Lloyd), who was elected on the foundation of the Royal Academy in 1768 when aged 24.

Youngest exhibitor at R.A. The youngest ever exhibitor at the Royal Academy of Arts Annual Summer Exhibitions is Lewis Melville ("Gino") Lyons (b. 30 April 1962) at their 199th exhibition in 1967 when aged just over 5 years. His picture "Trees and Monkeys" was hung in Gallery IX having been accepted on 7 May 1967. The previous record had been set by Sir Edwin H. Landseer (1802-73) at the age of 13 in 1815.

Shortest apprenticeship Mr. T. Dempster-Jones, of Buckley, Flintshire, had one of his first pictures, *Death-bed of H.M.S. Conway* accepted for the Royal Academy's Summer Exhibition of 1961—only one year after he had begun to paint.

Endurance record The marathon record for painting is 60 hours by 60 students of the St. Albans College of Art, Hertfordshire on a 3 mile long roll of cartridge paper on 1-3 July 1971.

MURALS
Earliest The earliest known murals on man-made walls are those at Catal Hüyük in southern Anatolia, Turkey, dating from *c.* 5850 B.C.

Largest The world's largest mural is *The March of Humanity,* a mural of 54 panels, covering 48,000 square feet, by David Alfaro Siqueiros, which was unveiled in 1968 in the Olimpico Hotel, Mexico City, Mexico. A rainbow mural stretching nearly 300 feet up the sides of the Hilton Rainbow Hotel, Waikiki, Honolulu was completed in 1968.

Largest mobile The largest mobile in the world is one measuring 45 feet by 17 feet and weighing 600 lb., suspended in December 1957 in the main terminal building of the John F. Kennedy International Airport (formerly Idlewild), Long Island, New York State, U.S.A. It was created by Alexander Calder (b. 1898), who invented this art form in 1930 as a reaction to sculptures or "stabiles". The heaviest of all mobiles is *Spirale,* weighing 4,000 lb., outside the U.N.E.S.C.O. headquarters in Paris, France. The word "mobile" was coined by Marcel Duchamp in 1932.

Largest mosaic The world's largest mosaic is on the walls of the central library of the Universidad Nacional Autónomao de México, Mexico City. There are four walls, the two largest measuring 12,949 square feet each representing the pre-Hispanic past.

MUSEUMS
Oldest The oldest museum in the world is the Ashmolean Museum in Oxford, built in 1679.

Largest The largest museum in the world is the America Museum of Natural History on 77th to 81st Stree and Central Park West, New York City, N.Y., U.S.A. Founded in 1874, it comprises 19 interconnecte buildings with 23 acres of floor space. The large museum in the United Kingdom is the Briti Museum (founded in 1753), which was opened to th public in 1759. The main building in Bloomsbur London, was built in 1823 and has a total floor area 17.57 acres.

2. SCULPTURE

Earliest World The earliest known examples of sculpture are th so-called Venus figurines from Aurignacian site dating to *c.* 25,000-22,000 B.C., *e.g.* the famou Venus of Willendorf from Austria and the Venus Brassempouy (Landes, France).

Britain The earliest British art object is an engraving of horse's head on a piece of rib-bone from Robin Hoc Cave, Creswell Crag, Derbyshire. It dates from th Upper Palaeolithic period (*c.* 15,000 to 10,000 B.C. The earliest Scottish rock carving from Lagalocha Argyllshire dates from pre-3,000 B.C.

Most expensive World The highest price ever paid for a sculpture is th $380,000 (£158,333) given at Sotheby's New Yo salerooms, Parke-Bernet, on 5 May 1971 for Edg Degas' (1834-1917) bronze *Petite Danseuse de Qua orze Ans,* executed in an edition of about 12 casts 1880.

Living sculptor The highest price paid for the work of a living sculpt is the $260,000 (£100,000) given at Sotheby Parke-Bernet Galleries, New York on 1 March 197 for the wooden carving *Reclining Figure* by Henr Moore, O.M., C.H. (b. Castleford, Yorkshire, 30 Ju 1898).

Largest The world's largest sculptures are the mounted figur of Jefferson Davis (1808-89), Gen. Robert Edwa Lee (1807-70) and Gen. Thomas Jonathan ("Ston wall") Jackson (1824-63), covering 1.33 acres on th face of Stone Mountain, near Atlanta, Georgia. The are 20 feet higher than the more famous Rushmo sculptures. When completed the world's largest scul ture will be that of the Indian chief Tashunca-Uitc known as Crazy Horse, of the Oglala tribe of th Dakota or Nadowessioux (Sioux) group. He is beli ved to have been born in about 1849, and he died Fort Robinson, Nebraska, on 5 Sept. 1877. Th sculpture was begun on 3 June 1948 near Mou Rushmore, South Dakota, U.S.A. A projected 56 feet high and 641 feet long, it will require the remov of 5,800,000 tons of stone and is the life work of on man, Korczak Ziolkowski. The work will take until least 1978.

Language

Ground figures In the Nazca Desert, south of Lima, Peru there are straight lines (one 5 miles long), geometric shapes and plants and animals drawn on the ground by still unknown persons for an unknown purpose.

Hill figures The largest human hill carving in Britain is the "Long Man" of Wilmington, Sussex, 226 feet in length. The oldest of all White Horses in Britain is the Uffington White Horse in Berkshire, dating from the late Iron Age (*c.* 150 B.C.) and measuring 374 feet from nose to tail and 120 feet from ear to heel.

3. LANGUAGE

Earliest Anthropologists have evidence that the truncated pharanx of Neanderthal man precluded his speaking anything akin to a modern language any more than an ape or a modern baby. Cro Magnon man of 40,000 B.C. had however developed an efficient vocal tract. Clay tablets of the neolithic Danubian culture discovered in Dec. 1966 at Tartaria, Moros River, Romania have been dated to the fifth or fourth millennium B.C. The tablets bear symbols of bows and arrows, gates and combs. In 1970 it was announced that writing tablets bearing an early form of the Elamite language dating from 3,500 B.C. had been found in south-eastern Iran. The scientist Alexander Marshack (U.S.) maintains that marked Upper Palaeolithic artifacts, such as a Cro Magnon bone from 30,000 B.C. in the Musée des Antiquités Nationales, outside Paris with 69 marks with 24 stroke changes, are not random but of possibly lunar or menstrual cycle significance.

Oldest words in English Recent research indicates that several river names in Britain date from pre-Celtic times (*ante* 550 B.C.). These include Ayr, Hayle and Nairn. This ascendant, Indo-Germanic tongue, which was spoken from *c.* 3000 B.C. on the Great Lowland Plain of Europe, now has only fragments left in Old Lithuanian, from which the modern English word *eland* derives. The word *land* is traceable to the Old Celtic *landa*, a heath and therefore must have been in use on the continent before the Roman Empire grew powerful in the 6th century B.C.

Commonest language Today's world total of languages and dialects still spoken is about 5,000 of which some 845 come from India. The language spoken by more people than any other is Northern Chinese, or Mandarin, by an estimated 615,000,000 people at mid-1972. The so-called national language (*guoyu*) is a standardized form of Northern Chinese as spoken in the Peking area. This was alphabetized into *zhuyin zimu* of 39 letters in 1918. In 1958 the *pinyin* system, using a Latin alphabet, was introduced. The next most commonly spoken language and the most widespread is English, by an estimated 340,000,000 in mid-1972. English is spoken by 10 per cent. or more of the population in 29 sovereign countries.

In Great Britain and Ireland there are six indigenous tongues: English, Scots Gaelic, Welsh, Irish Gaelic, Manx and Romany (Gipsy). Of these English is, of course, predominant, while Manx has almost followed Cornish (whose last fluent speaker, John Davey, died in 1891) into extinction. By 1972 there remained only Mr. Edward (Ned) Maddrell (b. 20 Aug. 1877) of Glen Chass, Port St. Mary, Isle of Man, whose mother tongue is Manx. In the Channel Islands, apart from Jersey and Guernsey *patois,* there survive words of Sarkese, in which a prayer book was published in 1812. A movement exists to revive the use of Cornish.

Most complex The following extremes of complexity have been noted: Chippewa, the North American Indian language of Minnesota, U.S.A., has the most verb forms with up to 6,000; Tillamook, the North American Indian language of Oregon, U.S.A., has the most

Central Bougainville, the terrain of the Rotakas people who manage on an eleven-letter alphabet

prefixes with 30; Tabassaran, a language in Daghestan, U.S.S.R., uses the most noun cases with 35, while Eskimaux use 63 forms of the present tense and simple nouns have as many as 252 inflections. In Chinese the *Chung-wên Ta Tz'û-tien* dictionary lists 49,905 characters. The fourth tone of "i" has 84 meanings, varying as widely as "dress", "hiccough" and "licentious". The written language provides 92 different characters for "i⁴". The most complex written character in Chinese is that representing the sound of thunder which has 52 strokes and is somewhat surprisingly pronounced *ping.* The most complex in current use consists of 36 strokes representing a blocked nose and less surprisingly pronounced *nang.*

Rarest and commonest sounds The rarest speech sound is probably the sound written ř in Czech which occurs in very few languages and is the last sound mastered by Czech children. The *l* sound in Arabic as in *Allah* is seemingly unique as it occurs in no other word in the language. The commonest sound is the vowel *a* (as in the English father); no language (even Wishram) is known to be without it.

Most and least regular verbs Esperanto was devised in 1887 without irregular verbs and is now estimated (by text book sales) to have a million speakers. Swahili has a strict 6-class pattern of verbs and no verbs which are irregular to this pattern. According to the more daunting grammars published in West Germany, English has 194 irregular verbs though there are arguably 214.

Vocabulary The English language contains about 490,000 words plus another 300,000 technical terms, the most in any language, but it is doubtful if any individual uses more than 60,000. Written English contains about 10,000 words, while spoken English among the better educated has about 5,000 words.

ALPHABET
Oldest The development of the use of an alphabet in place of pictograms occurred in the Sinaitic world between 2000 and 1700 B.C. This northern Semitic language developed the consonantal system based on phonetic and syllabic principles. Its "O" has remained unchanged and is thereby the oldest of all letters in the 65 alphabets now in use.

Longest and shortest The language with most letters is Cambodian with 74, and Rotakas least with 11 (just a, ƀ, e, g, i, k, ó, p, ř, t and u). Amharic has 231 formations from 33 basic syllabic forms, each of which has seven modifications, so this Ethiopian language cannot be described as alphabetic.

Most and least consonants and vowels The language with most consonants is the Caucasian mountain language Ubyx, with 80 and that with least is Rotakas, spoken in central Bougainville Island with only 6 consonants. The language with the most

85

The Readymix symbol on the Nullarbor Plain taken from 31,000 feet.

vowels is Sedang, a central Vietnamese language with 55 distinguishable vowel sounds and those with the least are those with two such as the Caucasian languages Abuza and Kabardian. The Hawaiian word for "certified" has 8 consecutive vowels—hooiaioia.

Largest letter The largest permanent letters in the world are the giant 600 foot letters spelling READYMIX on the ground in the Nullarbor near East Balladonia, Western Australia. This was constructed in Dec. 1971. In sky-writing (normally at *c.* 8,000 feet) a seven letter word may stretch for six miles in length and can be read from 50 miles. The world's earliest example was over Epsom racecourse, Surrey on 30 May 1922 when Cyril Turner "spelt out" "London Daily Mail" from an S.E.5A biplane.

Greatest linguist The most accomplished linguist ever known was Cardinal Giuseppe Caspar Mezzofanti (b. 17 Sept. 1774 at Bologna, d. 1849), the former chief keeper of the Vatican library in Rome, Italy. He could translate 114 languages and 72 dialects, and spoke 39 languages fluently, 11 others passably and understood 20 others along with 37 dialects. The claims made on behalf of Prof. Rasmus Christian Rask (1787-1832) of Copenhagen in 1837 have proved highly exaggerated. The greatest living linguist is probably Georges Schmidt (b. Strasbourg, France in 1915) of the United Nations Translation Department in New York City, U.S.A. who can speak fluently in 30 languages and can translate 66.

Longest chemical name The longest chemical term is that describing tryptophan synthetase A protein, which has the formula $C_{1289}H_{2051}N_{343}O_{375}S_8$ and the 1,913 letter name:

Methionylglutaminylarginyltyrosylglutamylserylleu-cylphenylalanylalanylglutaminylleucyllysylglutamyl-arginyllysyglutamylglycylalanylphenylalanylvalylpro-lylphenylalanylvalylthreonylleucylglycylaspartylpro-lylglycylisoleucylglutamylglutaminylserylleucyllysyli-soleucylaspartylthreonylleucylisoleucylglutamylalanyl-glycylalanylaspartylalanylleucylglutamylleucylglycyli-soleucylprolylphenylalanylserylaspartylprolylleucyl-alanylaspartylglycylprolylthreonylisoleucylgluta-minylasparaginylalanylthreonylleucylarginylalanyl-phenylalanylalanylalanylglycylvalylthreonylprolyl-alanylglutaminylcysteinylphenylalanylglutamylmethi-onylleucylalanylleucylisoleucylarginylglutaminyllysyl-histidylprolylthreonylisoleucylprolylisoleucylglycyl-leucylleucylmethionyltyrosylalanylaspraginylcucyl-valylphenylalanylasparaginyllysylglycylisoleucylaspar-tylglutamylphenylalanyltyrosylalanylglutaminylcy-steinylglutamyllysylvalylglycylvalylaspartylserylvalyl-leucylvalylalanylaspartylvalylprolylvalylglutaminyl-glutamylserylalanylprolylphenylalanylarginylgluta-minylalanylalanylleucylarginylhistidylasparaginyl-valylalanylprolylisoleucylphenylalanylisoleucylcy-steinylprolylprolylaspartylalanylaspartylalanylas-partylleucylleucylarginylglutaminylisoleucylalanyl-seryltyrosylglycylarginylglycyltyrosylthreonyltyrosyl-leucylleucylserylarginylalanylglycylvalylthreonylgly-cylalanylglutamylasparaginylarginylalanylalanyl-leucylprolylleucylasparaginylhistidylleucylvalylalanyl-lysylleucyllysylglutamyltyrosylasparaginylalanyl-alanylprolylprolylleucylglutaminylglycylphenylalanyl-glycylisoleucylserylalanylprolylaspartylglutaminyl-valyllysylalanylalanylisoleucylaspartylalanylglycyl-alanylalanylglycylalanylisoleucylserylglycylseryl-alanylisoleucylvalyllysylisoleucylisoleucylglutamyl-glutaminylhistidylasparaginylisoleucylglutamylprolyl-glutamyllysylmethionylleucylalanylalanylleucyllysyl-valylphenylalanylvalylglutaminylprolylmethionyllysyl-alanylalanylthreonylarginylserine.

Longest words World The longest word ever to appear in literature occur in *The Ecclesiazusae,* a comedy by Aristophane (448-380 B.C.). In the Greek it is 170 letters lon but transliterates into 182 letters in English, thus lopadotemachoselachogaleokranioleipsanodrimhy potrimmatosilphioparaomelitokatakechymenokich lepikossyphophattoperisteralektryonoptekephalli kigklopeleiolagoiosiraiobaphetraganopterygon. Th term describes a fricassee of 17 sweet and sou ingredients including mullet, brains, honey, vinega pickles, marrow and ouzo (a Greek drink laced wit anisette).

English The longest word in the Oxford English Dictionar is floccipaucinihilipilification (alternatively spelt i hyphenated form with "n" in seventh place), wit 29 letters, meaning "the action of estimating a worthless", first used in 1741, and later by Si Walter Scott (1771-1832). Webster's Third Inter national Dictionary lists among its 450,000 entrie pneumonoultramicroscopicsilicovolcanoconiosis (4! letters), the name of a miners' lung disease.

The nonce word used by Dr. Edward Strothe (1675-1737) to describe the spa waters at Bristc was aequeosalinocalcalinoceraceoaluminosocuprec vitriolic of 52 letters.

The longest regularly formed English word i praetertranssubstantiationalistically (37 letters) used by Mark McShane in his novel *Untimel Ripped,* published in 1963. The medical tern hepaticocholangiocholecystenterostomies (3! letters) refers to the surgical creations of ne communications between gallbladders and hepati ducts and between intestines and gallbladders. Th longest in common use is disproportionableness (2 letters).

Longest palindromic words The longest known palindromic word is *saippuakaup pias* (15 letters), the Finnish word for soap-seller. Th longest in the English language are *evitative* an *redivider* (each nine letters), while another nine-lette word, *Malayalam,* is a proper noun given to th language of the Malayali people in Kerala, southern India. The nine-letter brand name Rotavator i becoming accepted to describe a horticultural culti vating machine. The contrived chemical term *detar trated* has 11 letters, as does *kinnikinnik* (sometime written *kinnik-kinnik,* a 12-letter palindrome), th word for the dried leaf and bark mixture which wa smoked by the Cree Indians of North America. Som baptismal fonts in Greece and Turkey bear th circular 25 letter inscription ΝΙΨΟΝ ΑΝΟΜΗΜΑΤΑ ΜΗ ΜΟΝΑΝ ΟΨΙΝ meaning "wash (my) sins no only (my) face". This appears at St. Mary's Church Nottingham, St. Paul's, Woldingham, Surrey an other churches. The longest palindromic compositio devised is one of 242 words by Howard Bergeson o Oregon, U.S.A. It begins "Deliver no evil, avi diva . . . and hence predictably ends . . . avid diva, liv on reviled.

Most frequently used letters In English the most frequently used letters are according to a survey carried out by Mr. Arthur Ha of St. John's Preparatory School, Northwood, Lor don, e, t, a, o, i, n, s, h, r, d, l, m, u, w, g, c, f, y, p, b, v k, j, q, x and z. The most frequent initial letters ar found by indexers to be s, e, p, a, t, b, m, d, r, f and h

Commonest words In written English the most frequently used words ar in order: the, of, and, to, a, in, that, is, I, it, for *and* as The most used in conversation is I.

Most meanings The most over-worked word in English is the wor *jack* which has 10 main substantive uses with 4 sub-uses and two verbal uses.

LONGEST WORDS IN VARIOUS LANGUAGES

French	Anticonstitutionnellement (25 letters) –anticonstitutionally.
Croatian	Prijestolenaslijeduikovice (26 letters) –wife of an heir apparent.
Italian	Precipitevolissimevolmente (26 letters) –as fast as possible.
Russian	Dyeryevopyeryerabatyvayushchego (31 letters representing 23 Cyrillic letters) –of the timber processing (Genitive singular).
Japanese	Ryāgū-no-otohime-no-motoyui-no-kirihanshi (35 letters) –a seaweed, literally of small pieces of the paper hair streamers of the underwater princess.
Dutch	Rijksluchtvaartdienstweerschepenpersoneel (41 letters) –Government aviation department weather ship personnel.
Hungarian	Legmegengedelmeskedhetetlenségeskeidetekért (43 letters) because of your continued greatest disobedience.
German	Lebensmittelzuschusseinstellungskommissionsvorsitzenderstellvertreter (69 letters) –Deputy-president of the Food Rationing winding up Commission.
Swedish	Spårvagnsaktiebolagsskensmutsskjutarefackföreningspersonalbeklädnadsmagasinsförrådsförvaltaren (94 letters) –Manager of the depot for the supply of uniforms to the personnel of the track cleaners' union of the tramway company

Most homophones The most homophonous sound in English is *rōz* which has 8 meanings: roes (deer); roes (fish); rose (flower); rose (watering can); rose (past tense of rise); rows (boats); rows (of houses) or rhos (plural of the Greek letter).

Most accents Accents were introduced in French in the reign of Louis XIII (1601-43). The word with most accents is hétérogénéité, meaning heterogeneity. An atoll in the Pacific Ocean 320 miles E.S.E. of Tahiti is named Héréhérétué.

Worst tongue twisters The most difficult tongue twister in the only anthology of its type *Anthology of British Tongue-Twisters* by Ken Parkin of Teesside, is deemed by the author to be "The sixth sick sheik's sixth sheep's sick"—especially when spoken quickly.

Perhaps the most difficult in the world is the Xhosa (from Transkei, South Africa) for "The skunk rolled down and ruptured its larynx" Iqaqa laziqikaqika kwaze kwaqhawaka uqhoqhoqha. The last word contains three "clicks". A European rival is the vowelless *Strch prst skrz krk*, the Czech for "stick a finger in the throat".

Longest abbreviation The longest known abbreviation is S.O.M.K.H.P.-B.K.J.C.S.S.D.P.M.W.D.T.B., the initials of the Sharikat Orang-Orang Melayu Kerajaan Hilir Perak Berkerjasama-Serkerjasama Kerana Jimat Chermat Serta Simpanan Dan Pinjam Meminjam Wang Dengan Tanggongan Berhad. This is the Malay name for the Lower Perak Malay Government Servants' Co-operative Thrift and Loan Society Limited, in Telok Anson, Perak State, West Malaysia (formerly Malaya). The abbreviation for this abbreviation is not recorded.

Longest anagrams The longest non-scientific English words which can form anagrams are the 16-letter transpositions "interlaminations" *and* "internationalism" and "conservationists" *and* "conversationists".

Shortest holo-alphabetic sentence The contrived headline describing the annoyance of an eccentric in finding inscriptions on the side of a fjord in a rounded valley as "Cwm fjord-bank glyphs vext quiz" represents the ultimate in containing all 26 letters in 26 letters.

Longest sentence The longest sentence in classical western literature is one in *Les Misérables* by Victor Marie Hugo (1802-85) which runs to 823 words punctuated by 93 commas, 51 semi-colons and 4 dashes. A sentence of 958 words appears in "Cities of the Plain" by the French author, Marcel Proust (1871-1922), while some authors such as James Joyce (1882-1941) appear to eschew punctuation altogether. The Report of the President of Columbia University 1942-43 contained a sentence of 4,284 words. The first 40,000 words of *The Gates of Paradise* by George Andrzeyevski (Panther) appear to lack any punctuation.

Most Prepositions with which to end The sentence that has the most prepositions with which to end describes the protest of a child against an Australian bed-time story-book thus "Mummy why did you bring that book which I didn't want to be read to out of from about Down Under up for?"

PLACE-NAMES

Longest World The official name for Bangkok, the capital city of Thailand, consists of the Thai words Krungt'ep ("city of the divine messenger"), plus a long list of Pali titles, as proclaimed at the city's foundation in 1782. A *shortened version* of this name is Krungtepmahanakornbowornratanakosinmahintarayudhayamahadilokpopnoparatanarajthaniburiromudomrajniwesmahasatarnamornpimarnavatarsatitsakatattiyavisanukamprasit (158 letters). The longest place-name now in use in the world is Taumatawhakatangihangakoauauotamatea (turipukakapikimaungahoronuku) pokaiwhenuakitanatahu, the unofficial 85-letter version of the name of a hill (1,002 feet above sea-level) in the Southern Hawke's Bay district of North Island, New Zealand. This Maori name means "the place where Tamatea, the man with the big knee who slid, climbed and swallowed mountains, known as Traveller, played on his flute to his loved one". The official version has 57 letters (1 to 36 and 65 to 85).

United Kingdom The longest place-name in the United Kingdom is the concocted 58-letter name Llanfairpwllgwyngyllgogerychwyrndrobwllllantysiliogogogoch, which is translated: "St. Mary's Church in a hollow by the white hazel, close to the rapid whirlpool, by the red cave of St. Tysilio". This is the name given to a village in Anglesey, Wales, but the official name consists of only the first 20 letters. The longest genuine Welsh place-name listed in the Ordnance Survey Gazetteer is Lower Llanfihangel-y-Creuddyn (26 letters), a village near Aberystwyth, Cardiganshire.

England The longest single word (unhyphenated) place-name in England is Blakehopeburnhaugh, a hamlet between Burness and Rochester in Northumberland, of 18 letters. The hyphenated Sutton-under-Whitestonecliffe, Yorkshire has 27 letters on the Ordnance Survey but with the insertion of 'the' and the dropping of the final 'e' 29 letters in the Post Office List. The longest multiple name is North Leverton with Habbelsthorpe (30 letters), Nottinghamshire, while the longest parish name is Saint Mary le More and All Hallows with Saint Leonard and Saint Peter, Wallingford (68 letters) in Berkshire formed on 5 Apr. 1971.

Scotland The longest single word place-names in Scotland are Claddochknockline, with a population of 18 in 1961, on the island of North Uist, in the Outer Hebrides and the nearby Claddochbaleshare both with 17 letters. The statutory name for Kirkcudbrightshire (18 letters) is however County of Kirkcudbright. A 12-acre loch nine miles west of Stornoway on Lewes is named Loch Airidh Mhic Fhionnlaidh Dhuibh (31 letters).

Ireland The longest place-name in Ireland is Muckanagheder-dauhaulia (22 letters), 4 miles from Costello in Carris Bay, County Galway. The name means "soft place between two seas".

Shortest The shortest place names in the world are the French village of Y (population 143), so named since 1241; the Norwegian village of Å (pronounced "Aw"), U in the Caroline Islands, Pacific Ocean; and the Japanese town of Sosei which is alternatively called Aioi or O-o or even O. There was once a 6 in West Virginia, U.S.A. The shortest place-names in Great Britain are the two-lettered villages of Ae (population 199 in 1961) in Dumfriesshire and Oa on the island of Islay off western Scotland. In the Shetland Islands there are skerries called Ve and two stacks called Aa. The island of Iona was originally I. The River E flows into the southern end of Loch Mhór, Inverness-shire. The shortest place-name in Ireland is Ta (or Lady's Island) Lough, a sea-inlet off the coast of County Wexford. Tievelough, in County Donegal, is also called Ea.

Earliest The earliest recorded British place-name is Belerion, the Penwith peninsula of Cornwall, referred to as such by Pytheas of Massalia in *c.* 308 B.C. The earliest reference to Britain was as *Pretanic* (implying an earlier *Qrtanic*). The oldest name among England's 41 counties is Kent, first mentioned in its Roman form of Cantium (from the Celtic *canto,* meaning a rim, *i.e.* a coastal district) from the same circumnavigation by Pytheas. The youngest is Lancashire, first recorded in the 12th century. The earliest mention of England is the form *Angelcynn,* which appeared in the Anglo-Saxon Chronicle in A.D. 880.

Commonest The commonest place-name in England and Wales is Newtown or New Town, with 129 entries in the 1961 Census Gazetteer, and Newton with 47. The British place-name most widely used overseas is Richmond, Yorkshire, which has given its name, according to a list compiled by Mr. David Ball, to 43 other villages, towns and cities, including examples in 20 of the 50 states of the U.S.A.

PERSONAL NAMES

Earliest The earliest personal name which has survived is uncertain. Some experts believe that it is En-lil-ti, a word which appears on a Sumerian tablet dating from *c.* 3000 B.C., recovered before 1936 from Jamdat Nasr, 40 miles south-east of Baghdad, Iraq. Other antiquarians regard it purely as the name of a deity, Lord of the air, and claim that the names Lahma and Lahamu, Sumer gods of silt, are older still. N'armer, the father of Men (Menes), the first Egyptian Pharaoh, dates from about 2900 B.C. The earliest known name of any resident of Britain is Divitiacus, King of the Suessones, the Gaulish ruler of the Kent area *c.* 75 B.C. under the name Prydhain.

Longest The longest name used by anyone is Adolph Blaine
World Charles David Earl Frederick Gerald Hubert Irvin John Kenneth Lloyd Martin Nero Oliver Paul Quincy Randolph Sherman Thomas Uncas Victor William Xerxes Yancy Zeus Wolfeschlegelsteinhausenberger-dorff, Senior, who was born at Bergedorf, near Hamburg, Germany, on 29 Feb. 1904. On printed forms he uses only his eighth and second Christian names and the first 35 letters of his surname. The full version of the name of 590 letters appeared in the 12th edition of *The Guinness Book of Records.* He now lives in Philadelphia, Pennsylvania, U.S.A., and has shortened his surname to Mr. Wolfe+590, Senior.

The longest Christian or given name on record i Napuamahalaonaonekawehiwehionakuahiweaner awawakehoonkakehoaalekeeaonanainananiakeao Hawaiikawao (94 letters) in the case of Miss Dawn N Lee so named in Honolulu, Hawaii, U.S.A. in February 1967. The name means "The abundant, beautiful blossoms of the mountains and valleys begin to fill th air with their fragrance throughout the length an breadth of Hawaii".

Most The daughter of Arthur Pepper of West Derby
Christian Lancashire, born on 19 Dec. 1882, was christened
names Ann Bertha Cecilia Diana Emily Fanny Gertrud Hypatia Inez Jane Kate Louisa Maud Nora Opheli Quince Rebecca Starkey Teresa Ulysis Venu Winifred Xenophen Yetty Zeus Pepper.

United The longest surname in the United Kingdom was th
Kingdom six-barrelled one borne by the late Major L.S.D.O.F (Leone Sextus Denys Oswolf Fraudati filius Tollemache-Tollemache de Orellana Plantagene Tollemache Tollemache, who was born in 1884 an died of pneumonia in France on 20 Feb. 1917. O non-repetitive surnames, the last example of five-barrelled one was that of the Lady Carolin Jemima Temple-Nugent-Chandos-Brydges-Grenvill (1858-1946). The longest single English surname i Featherstonehaugh, correctly pronounced on occa sions (but improbably on the correct occasion Featherstonehaw or Festonhaw or Fessonhay o Freestonhugh or Feerstonhaw or Fanshaw.

Scotland In Scotland the surname nin (feminine of mac Achinmacdholicachinskerray (29 letters) wa recorded in an 18th century parish register.

Shortest in There exist among the 42,500,000 names on th
Britain Ministry of Social Security index four examples of one-lettered surname. Their identity has not bee disclosed, but they are "E", "J", "M" and "X" Two-letter British surnames include By and On.

Commonest The commonest surname in the world is the Chines
World name Chang which is borne, according to estimates by between 9.7% and 12.1% of the Chinese popula tion, so indicating even on the lower estimate tha there are at least some 75,000,000 Changs—mor than the entire population of all but 7 of the 14: other sovereign countries of the world.

English The commonest surname in the English-speakin world is Smith. There are 671,550 nationally insure Smiths in Great Britain, of whom 7,081 are plai John Smith and another 22,550 are John (plus one c more given names) Smith. Including uninsure persons, there are over 800,000 Smiths in Englan and Wales alone, of whom 90,000 are called A. Smith There were an estimated 1,678,815 Smiths in th United States in 1964.

"Macs" There are, however, estimated to be 1,600,00 persons in Britain with M', Mc or Mac (Gaelic "so of") as part of their surnames. The commonest o these is Macdonald which accounts for about 55,00 of the Scottish population.

The most common forenames in Britain would appea from C.V. Appleton's study of a very large sampl from the latest available birth registers at Somerse House, London to be Tracey or Tracie for girls an Paul for boys. In the period 1196-1307 William wa the commonest boy's name but since 1340 to recen times this had been John.

Most The palm for the most determined attempt to be las
contrived in the local telephone directory must be awarded to
name Mr. Zeke Zzzypt of Chicago, Illinois, U.S.A. H outdid the previous occupant who was a mere Mr Zyzzy Zzyryzxxy. In September 1970 Mr. Zerc

Zzyzz (rhymes with "fizz") was ousted by Mr. Vladimir Zzzyd (rhymes with outdid) in the Miami directory.

THE WRITTEN WORD

Smallest handwriting The smallest writing achieved is a density of 85 letters per square millimetre with an engraving tool on metal by Dr. Anto Leikola of Helsinki, Finland.

In 1968 Mr. C. N. Swift of Edgbaston, Birmingham, England, wrote the Lord's Prayer 25 times on a piece of paper half the size of a standard United Kingdom postage stamp, *i.e.* 22 millimetres (0.87 of an inch) by 18 millimetres (0.71 of an inch), with a density of nearly 37 letters per square millimetre.

TEXTS

Oldest The oldest known written text is the pictograph expression of Sumerian speech (see Earliest Language, p. 85). The earliest known vellum document dates from the 2nd century A.D.; it contains paragraphs 10 to 32 of Demosthenes' *De Falsa Legatione*. Demosthenes died in the 4th century B.C.

Oldest printed The oldest surviving printed work is a Korean scroll or *sutra* from wooden printed blocks found in the foundations of the Pulguk Sa pagoda, Kyongju, Korea, on 14 Oct. 1966. It has been dated no later than A.D. 704.

Mechanically printed It is generally accepted that the earliest mechanically printed book was the 42-line Gutenberg Bible, printed at Mainz, Germany, in *c.* 1455 by Johann Henne zum Gensfleisch zur Laden, called "zu Gutenberg" (*c.* 1398-*c.* 1468). Recent work on water marks published in 1967 indicates a copy of a surviving printed Latin grammar was made from paper made in *c.* 1450. The earliest exactly dated printed work is the Psalter completed on 14 Aug. 1457 by Johann Fust (*c.* 1400-1466) and Peter Schöffer (1425-1502), who had been Gutenberg's chief assistant. The earliest printing in Britain was an Indulgence dated 13 Dec. 1476, issued by Abbot Sant of Abingdon, Berkshire, and printed by William Caxton (*c.* 1422-1491).

Largest The largest book in the world is *The Little Red Elf*, a story in 64 verses by William P. Wood, who designed, constructed and printed the book. It measures 7 feet 2 inches high and 10 feet across when open. The book is at present on show in a case at the Red Elf Cave, Ardentinny near Dunoon. The largest art book ever produced was one 210 centimetres (82.7 inches) high and 80 centimetres (31.5 inches) wide, first shown in Amsterdam, in the Netherlands, in May 1963. It contained five "pages", three the work of Karel Appel (b. 1921), an abstract painter, and two with poems by Hugo Claus. The price was $5,255 (now £2,177).

Largest publication The largest publication in the world is the 1,200 volume set of *British Parliamentary Papers* of 1800-1900 by Irish University Press in 1967-1971. A complete set weighs 3¼ tons, costs £25,000 and would take 6 years to read at 10 hours per day. The production involved the death of 34,000 Indian goats and £15,000 worth of gold ingots. Further volumes are planned.

New Testament Smallest The smallest New Testament ever produced was published by David Bryce of Glasgow in 1895. It is printed on the thinnest India paper, with a total of 520 pages, its dimensions are: 15 × 17 × 7.5 millimetres thick.

The smallest book printed in metal type as opposed to any micro-photographic process is one printed for the Gutenberg Museum, Mainz, West Germany. It measures 3.5 millimetres by 3.5 millimetres (0.13 of an inch square) and consists of the Lord's Prayer in seven languages.

The world's smallest New Testament printed in moveable type

Most valuable The most valuable printed books are the three surviving perfect vellum copies of the Gutenberg Bible, printed in Mainz, Germany, in *c.* 1455 by Gutenberg (see above). The United States Library of Congress copy, bound in three volumes, was obtained in 1930 from Dr. Otto Vollbehr, who paid about $330,000 (now £137,500) for it. During 1970 a paper edition in the hands of the New York book dealer, Hans Peter Kraus, was privately bought for $2,500,000 (£1,041,666).

Broadsheet The highest price ever paid for a broadsheet has been $404,000 (£168,333) for one of the 16 known copies of *The Declaration of Independence,* printed in Philadelphia in 1776 by Samuel T. Freeman & Co., and sold to a Texan in May 1969.

Longest novel The longest important novel ever published is *Les hommes de bonne volonté* by Louis Henri Jean Farigoule (b. 26 Aug. 1885), *alias* Jules Romains, of France, in 27 volumes in 1932—46. The English version *Men of Good Will* was published in 14 volumes in 1933—46 as a "novel-cycle". The novel *Tokuga-Wa Ieyasu* by Sohachi Yamaoka has been serialized in Japanese daily newspapers since 1951. When completed it will run to 40 volumes.

Encyclopaedias Earliest The earliest known encyclopaedia was compiled by Speusippas (*post* 408–*c.* 388 B.C.) a nephew of Plato, in Athens *c.* 370 B.C. The earliest encyclopaedia compiled by a Briton was *Liber exerptionum* by the Scottish monk Richard (d. 1173) at St. Victor's Abbey, Paris *c.* 1140.

Most comprehensive The most comprehensive present day encyclopaedia is the *Encyclopaedia Britannica,* first published in Edinburgh, Scotland, in December 1768. A group of booksellers in the United States acquired reprint rights in 1898 and complete ownership in 1899. In 1943 the *Britannica* was given to the University of Chicago, Illinois, U.S.A. The current 24-volume edition contains 28,380 pages, 34,696 articles and 2,247 other entries, 36,674,000 words and 22,670 illustrations. It is now edited in Chicago and in London. There are 10,326 contributors.

Largest The largest encyclopaedia ever compiled was the *Great Standard Encyclopaedia* of Yung-lo ta tien of 22,937 manuscript chapters (370 still survive), written by 2,000 Chinese scholars in 1403-08.

Largest dictionary The largest dictionary now published is the 12-volume Royal quarto *The Oxford English Dictionary* of 15,487 pages published between 1884 and 1928 with a first supplement of 963 pages in 1933 with a further 2-volume supplement, edited by R.W. Burchfield, due in 1974. The work contains 414,825 words, 1,827,306 illustrative quotations and reputedly 227,779,589 letters and figures.

Manuscripts Highest price The highest price ever paid for any manuscript is £100,000, paid in December 1933 by the British Museum, London, to the U.S.S.R. Government for the manuscript Bible *Codex Sinaiticus* originally from the Monastery of St. Catherine on Mt. Sinai, Egypt (now the United Arab Republic). It consists of 390 of the original 730 leaves, measuring 16 inches by 28 inches, of the book, dictated in Greek and written by three scribes in about A.D. 350 and rescued from a waste paper basket in May 1844 by Lobegott Friedrich Konstantin von Tischendorf (1815-74), a German traveller and Biblical critic. The highest price at auction is 1,100,000 Francs (then £94,933 incl. tax) paid by H.P. Krauss, the New York dealer, at the salerooms of Rheims et Laurin, Paris on 24 June 1968 for the late 13th-century North Italian illuminated vellum Manuscript of the Apocrypha.

BIBLE

Oldest The oldest known Bible is the Yonan manuscript of the complete New Testament, written in Syriac-Aramaic (still spoken in Malonia Syria) in about A.D. 350 and presented to the United States Library of Congress in Washington, D.C., on 27 March 1955. The longest of the Dead Sea scrolls is the Temple Scroll measuring 28 feet which first became available for study in June 1967. The earliest Bible printed in English was one edited by Miles Coverdale, Bishop of Exeter (c. 1488-1569), printed in 1535 at Marberg in Hesse, Germany.

Longest and shortest books The longest book in the Bible is the Book of Psalms, while the longest prose book is the Book of the Prophet Isaiah, with 66 chapters. The shortest is the Third Epistle of John, with 294 words in 14 verses. The Second Epistle of John has only 13 verses but 298 words.

Longest Psalm, verse sentence and name Of the 150 Psalms, the longest is the 119th, with 176 verses, and the shortest is the 117th, with two verses. The shortest verse in the English language version of the Bible is verse 35 of Chapter XI of the Gospel according to St. John, consisting of the two words "Jesus wept". The longest is verse 9 of Chapter VIII of the Book of Esther, which extends to a 90-word description of the Persian empire. The total number of letters in the Bible is 3,566,480. The total number of words depends on the method of counting hyphenated words, but is usually given as between 773,692 and 773,746. The word "and" appears 46,399 times. The longest personal name in the Bible is Maher-shalal-hash-baz, the symbolic name of the second son of Isaiah (Isaiah, Chapter VIII, verses 1 and 3). The caption of Psalm 22, however, contains a title sometimes rendered Al-'Ayyeleth Hash-Shahar (20 letters).

MOST PROLIFIC WRITERS

The most prolific writer for whom a word count has been published was Charles Hamilton, *alias* Frank Richards (1875-1961), the Englishman who created Billy Bunter. At his height in 1908 he wrote the whole of the boys' comics *Gem* (founded 1907) and *Magnet* (1908-1940) and most of two others, totalling 80,000 words a week. His lifetime output was at least 72,000,000 words. He enjoyed the advantages of the use of electric light rather than candlelight and of being unmarried.

Novels The Belgian writer Georges Simenon (b. Georges Sim in Liège on 13 Feb. 1903), creator of Inspector Maigret, writes a novel of 200 pages in 8 days actual writing and in February 1969 completed his 200th under his own name of which 74 were about Inspector Maigret. He has also written 300 other novels under 19 other pen-names since 1919. These are published in 31 countries in 43 languages and have sold more than 300,000,000 copies. He hates adverbs and has had his children's playroom soundproofed. Since 1931 the British novelist John Creasey (b. 1908) has, under his own name and 13 *aliases,* written 564 books totalling more than 40,000,000 words. The authoress with the greatest total of published books is Miss Ursula Harvey Bloom (Mrs. A.C.G. Robinson), with 420 full-length works, starting in 1922 with *The Great Beginning* and including the best

sellers *The Ring Tree* (novel) and *The Rose of Norfol* (non-fiction).

Short stories The highest established count for published shor stories is 3,500 in the case of Michael Hervey (bor London, 1914) of Henley, New South Wales, Aus tralia. Aided by his wife Lilyan Brilliant, he has als written 60 detective novels and 80 stage and tele vision plays. The most prolific short story writer i Britain is Herbert Harris (born 1911) of Leatherhead Surrey, with nearly 3,000 published in Britain and i 28 other countries.

Fastest novelist The world's fastest novelist has been Erle Stanle Gardner (1889-1970) of the U.S.A., the mystery write who created Perry Mason. He dictated up to 10,00 words per day and worked with his staff on as many a seven novels simultaneously. His sales on 140 title reached 170 million by his death. The British novelis John Creasey (see above) has an output of 15 to 2 novels per annum, with a record of 22. He once wrot two books in a week with a half-day off. The mos translated British writer has been Enid Blyton wit 128 languages.

Writer and playwright Edgar Wallace (1875-1932 began his play *On the Spot* on a Friday and finished i by lunchtime on the following Sunday. This include the stage directions and, unusually, after the produc tion the prompt copy was identical to his origina The shortest time in which he wrote a novel was in th case of *The Three Oaks Mystery* which he started on Tuesday and delivered typed to his publishers on th following Friday.

The world's "slowest" author, Sir Harold Hartley

Longest literary gestation Brig.-Gen. Sir Harold Hartley, G.C.V.O., C.H., C.B.E M.C., F.R.S. (b. 3 Sept. 1878) made an agreemer with Oxford University Press to publish "Studies i the History of Chemistry" on 22 Feb. 1901. Th book appeared in April 1971—more than 70 year later.

Highest paid writer The highest rate ever offered to a writer was $30,00 (now £12,500) to Ernest Miller Hemingwa (1899-1961) for a 2,000-word article on bullfightin by *Sports Illustrated* in January 1960. This was a rat of $15 (£6.25) per word. In 1958 a Mrs. Debora Schneider of Minneapolis, Minnesota, U.S.A., wrot 25 words to complete a sentence in a competition fc the best blurb for Plymouth cars. She won from abou 1,400,000 entrants the prize of $500 (£208) ever month for life. On normal life expectations she wi collect $12,000 (£5,000) per word. No know anthology includes Mrs. Schneider's deathless pros

Top selling author It was announced on 13 March 1953 that 672,058,00 copies of the works of Marshal Iosif Vissarionovic Dzhugashvili, *alias* Stalin (1879-1953), had been so or distributed in 101 languages.

Among writers of fiction, sales alone of ove

The world's oldest authoress, Mrs Alice Pollock aged 102

300,000,000 have been claimed for Georges Simenon (see above) and for the British authoress Dame Agatha Christie (born Agatha Mary Clarissa Miller), now Lady Mallowan (formerly Mrs. Archibald Christie) (b. Torquay, Devon 15 Sept. 1890). Her paperback sales of 80 novels in the United Kingdom alone are 1½ million per annum.

Britain's most successful writer of text books is the ex-schoolmaster Ronald Ridout (b. 23 July 1916) who between 1950 and 1971 had 259 books published with sales of 43,500,000. His *The First English Workbook* has sold 3,493,000 copies.

Oldest authoress The oldest authoress in the world is Mrs. Alice Pollock (*née* Wykeham-Martin) b. 2 July 1868) of Haslemere, Surrey, whose book "Portrait of My Victorian Youth" (Johnson Publications) was published in March 1971 when she was aged 102 years 8 months.

Youngest The youngest recorded commercially-published author is Janet Aitchison of Reigate, Surrey, who wrote *The Pirates' Tale* when aged 5½ years. It was published in a Puffin Book Children's Magazine by Penguin in April 1969 when she was 6½.

POETS LAUREATE

Youngest and oldest The youngest Poet Laureate was Laurence Eusden (1688-1730), who received the bays on 24 Dec. 1718, at the age of 30 years and 3 months. The greatest age at which a poet has succeeded is 73 in the case of William Wordsworth (1770-1850) on 6 April 1843. The longest lived Laureate was John Masefield, O.M., who died on 12 May 1967, aged 88 years 345 days. The longest which any poet has worn the laurel is 41 years 322 days, in the case of Alfred (later the 1st Lord) Tennyson (1809-92), who was appointed on 19 Nov. 1850 and died in office on 6 Oct. 1892.

Longest poem The longest poem ever written was the *Mahabharata* which appeared in India in the period *c.* 400 to 150 B.C. It runs to 220,000 lines and nearly 3,000,000 words.

The longest poem ever written in the English language is *Poly-Olbion* or *A Chorographicall Description of Tracts, Rivers, Mountains, Forests, etc.*, written in Alexandrines in 30 books, comprising nearly 100,000 lines, by Michael Drayton (1563-1631) between 1613 and 1622.

Shortest poem The shortest poem in the *Oxford Dictionary of Quotations* is *On the Antiquity of Microbes* and consists of the 3 words "Adam, Had 'em".

Most Successful Sloganeer "Think Mink" invented by John Gasnick in 1929 has sold in metal, celluloid and ribbon 50 million since 1950. His *"Cross at the Green... not in Between Enterprises"* of New York City has sold 55 million buttons, badges and tabs and 40 million other pieces.

BEST SELLERS

World The world's best seller is the Bible, portions of which have been translated into 1,315 languages. This compares with 222 languages by Lenin. It has been estimated that between 1800 and 1950 some 1,500,000,000, were printed of which 1,100,000,000 were handled by Bible Societies. The total production of Bibles or parts of the Bible in the United States in the year 1963 alone was reputed to be 50,000,000.

It has been reported that 800,000,000 copies of the red-covered booklet *Quotations from the Works of Mao Ze dong* were sold or distributed between June 1966, when possession became virtually mandatory in China, and November 1970. The name of Mao Tse-tung (b. 26 Dec. 1893) means literally "Hair Enrich-East".

Non-fiction The total disposal through non-commercial channels by Jehovah's Witnesses of the 190 page hard bound book *The Truth That Leads to Eternal Life* published by the Watchtower Bible and Tract Society of Brooklyn, New York, published on 8 May 1968, reached 46 million in 67 languages by February 1972.

The commercially best selling non-fiction book is *The Common Sense Book of Baby and Child Care* by Dr. Benjamin McLane Spock (b. 2 May 1903) of New Haven, Connecticut, U.S.A. It was first published in New York in May 1946 and the total sales were 19,076,822 by December 1965 and probably over 23,000,000 by 1970. Dr. Spock's book was written with a ball-point pen and typed by his wife, a silk heiress.

The total sales of *Aircraft Recognition* by R.A. Saville-Smith (published 1941) have surpassed 7 million.

Slowest seller The accolade for the world's slowest selling book (known in U.S. publishing as slooow-sellers) probably belongs to David Wilkin's Translation of the New Testament into Coptic published by Oxford University Press in 1716 in 500 copies. Selling an average of one each 139 days it was in print for 191 years.

Frontispiece of the world's slowest seller—The New Testament in Coptic

91

Fiction The novel with the highest sales has been *Peyton Place* (first published in 1956) by Mrs. Grace de Repentigny Metalious (1924-64) of the United States, with a total of 11,919,660 copies by November 1970. Six million were sold in the first six months. In the United Kingdom the highest print order has been 3,000,000 by Penguin Books Ltd. for their paperback edition of *Lady Chatterley's Lover*, by D.H. (David Herbert) Lawrence (1885-1930). The total sales to January 1968 were 3,600,000 copies.

Post-cards The world's first post-cards were issued in Vienna on 1 Oct. 1869. Pin-up girls came into vogue in 1914 having been pioneered in 1900 by Raphaël Kirchner (1876-1917). The most expensive on record were ones made in ivory for an Indian prince which involved the killing of 60 elephants.

LARGEST PUBLISHERS
World The largest publisher in the world is the United States Government Printing Office in Washington, D.C., U.S.A. The Superintendents of Documents Division dispatches more than 150,000,000 items every year. The annual list of new titles and annuals is about 6,000.

United Kingdom The U.K. published a record 33,489 book titles in 1970 of which a record 9,977 were reprints. The highest figure for new titles was 23,563 in 1971.

LARGEST PRINTERS
World The largest printers in the world are R.R. Donnelly & Co. of Chicago, Illinois, U.S.A. The company, founded in 1864, has plants in seven main centres, turning out $200,000,000 (£83,300,000) worth of work per year from 180 presses, 125 composing machines and more than 50 binding lines. Nearly 18,000 tons of inks and 450,000 tons of paper and board are consumed every year.

Print order The print order for the 46th Automobile Association Handbook (1970-71) was 5,130,000 copies. The total print since 1908 has been 53,510,000. It is currently printed by web offset by Petty & Sons of Leeds.

Largest cartoon The largest cartoon ever published was one covering two floors (35 feet by 30 feet) on a building opposite the United Nations Headquarters in New York City, N.Y., U.S.A., depicting the enslavement by the U.S.S.R. of eight Eastern European nations.

Longest lived strip The most durable newspaper comic strip has been the Katzenjammer Kids (Hans and Fritz) created by Rudolph Dirks and first published in the United States in 1897 and currently drawn by Joe Musial. The most read is believed to be "Peanuts" by Charles M. Schulz (b. 1922) which since 1950 has grown to be syndicated to 1,000 U.S. newspapers with a total readership of 90,000,000.

LETTERS
Longest Physically the longest letter ever written was one of 3,696 feet 10 inches in length. It was written on an adding machine roll by Miss Terry Finch of Southsea, Hampshire to her boyfriend Sergeant Jerry Sullivan of Texas, U.S.A. and posted on 11 June 1969.

A letter of 325,000 words by Anton van Dam of Arnhem, Netherlands to his pen pal Clementi (now Mrs. H. Randolph Holder) between 24 June 1940 and 15 July 1945 is believed to be the most voluminous.

To an editor The longest recorded letter to an editor was one of *Longest* 13,000 words (a third of a modern novel) written to the editor of the *Fishing Gazette* by A.R.I.E.L. and published in 7-point type spread over two issues in 1884.

Most Britain's, and seemingly the world's, most indefatigable writer of letters to the editors of newspapers is Raymond L. Cantwell, 52 of Oxford, who since 194 has had more than 12,000 letters published in print o on the air. His peak production has been 425 in 3 hours non-stop in aid of charity.

Shortest The shortest correspondence on record was tha between Victor Marie Hugo (1802-85) and his pub lisher Hurst and Blackett in 1862. The author was o holiday and anxious to know how his new novel *Le Misérables* was selling. He wrote "?". The reply wa "!".

SIGNATURES
Earliest Not counting attested crosses in a few charters of th early Norman kings ostensibly affixed by their ow hands, the earliest English sovereign whose hand writing is known to have survived is Henry I (1207-72). The earliest signature to have survived i that of Richard II (dated 26 July 1386). The Magn Carta does not bear even the mark of King Joh (reigned 1199-1216), but carries his seal. In 1932 a attested cross of William I (reigned 1066-87) was sol in London.

Most expensive The highest price ever paid on the open market for single autograph letter signed is $51,000 (no £19,615), paid in 1927 for a letter written by th Gloucestershire-born Button Gwinnett (1732-77 one of the three men from Georgia to sign the Unite States' Declaration of Independence in Philadelphi on 4 July 1776. Such an item would probably attrac bids of $250,000 (£104,163) today. If one of the si known signatures of William Shakespeare (1564 1616) were to come on the market or a new one wa discovered the price would doubtless set a record There is no known surviving signature of Christophe Marlowe (1564-1593).

CROSSWORDS
First The earliest crossword was one with 32 clues invente by Arthur Wynne (b. Liverpool, England, d. 1945 and published in the *New York World* on 21 De 1913. The first crossword published in a Britis newspaper was one furnished by C.W. Shepherd in th *Sunday Express* of 2 Nov. 1924.

Largest The largest crossword ever published is one wit 3,185 clues across and 3,149 clues down, compiled b Robert M. Stilgenbauer of Los Angeles in 7½ years o spare time between 15 May 1938 and publication i 1949. Despite the 125,000 copies distributed not on copy has been returned worked out or even partiall worked out. The largest crosswords regularly pub lished are of 1,694 squares compiled by Lenna Fosselins for the Swedish monthly *Chansen*.

Fastest solution The fastest recorded time for completing *The Time* crossword under test conditions is 3 minutes 45. seconds by Roy Dean, 43, of Bromley, Kent in th B.B.C. "Today" radio studio on 19 Dec. 1970.

Slowest solution In May 1966 *The Times* of London received a announcement from a Fijian woman that she had ju succeeded in completing their crossword No. 673 i the issue of 4 April 1932.

MAP
Oldest The oldest known map is the Turin Papyrus, showin the layout of an Egyptian gold mine, dated abou 1320 B.C.

Christmas cards The greatest number of personal Christmas cards sen out is believed to be 40,000 in 1969 by President an Mrs. Nixon to friends and others, some of whom mus have been unilateral acquaintances.

LIBRARIES
Largest World The largest library in the world is the United State Library of Congress (founded on 24 April 1800), o Capitol Hill, Washington, D.C. On 30 June 1969 i

The circular Reading Room at the British Museum, London—Britain's largest library

contained more than 59,000,000 items, including 14,846,000 books and pamphlets. The two buildings cover six acres and contain 327 miles of book shelves.

The Lenin State Library in Moscow, U.S.S.R., claims to house more than 20,000,000 books, but this total is understood to include periodicals.

The largest non-statutory library in the world is the New York Public Library (founded 1895) on Fifth Avenue with a floor area of 525,276 square feet. The main part of its collection is in a private research library which has 4,662,326 volumes on 80 miles of shelves, 9,000,000 manuscripts, 120,000 prints, 150,000 gramophone records, and 275,000 maps. There are also 81 tax-supported branch libraries with 3,231,696 books. The central research library is open until the civilized hour of 10 p.m. on every day of the year.

United Kingdom The largest library in the United Kingdom is that in the British Museum, London. It contains more than 9,000,000 books, about 115,000 manuscripts and 101,000 charters on 158 miles of shelf. There are spaces for 370 readers in the domed Reading Room, built in 1854. The largest public library in the United Kingdom will be the new Birmingham Public Library with a floor area of 230,000 square feet or more than 5¼ acres; seating for 1,200 people and an ultimate reference capacity for 1,500,000 volumes on 31 miles of shelving. The oldest public library in Scotland is in Kirkwall, Orkney, founded in 1683.

Overdue books It was reported on 7 Dec. 1968 that a book checked out in 1823 from the University of Cincinnati Medical Library on Febrile Diseases (London, 1805 by Dr. J. Currie) was returned by the borrower's great-grandson Richard Dodd. The fine calculated to be $22,646 (£9,435) was waived.

NEWSPAPERS

Most It has been estimated that the total circulation of newspapers throughout the world averaged 320,000,000 copies per day in 1966. The country with the greatest number is the U.S.S.R., with 7,967 in 1966. Their average circulation in 1966 was 110,400,000.

The United States had 1,749 English language daily newspapers at 1 Jan. 1968. They had a combined net paid circulation of 61,397,000 copies per day at 30 Sept. 1966. The peak year for U.S. newspapers was 1910, when there were 2,202. The leading newspaper readers in the world are the people of Sweden, where 515 newspapers were sold for each 1,000 of the population in 1967-68. The U.K. figure was 488.

Oldest World The oldest existing newspaper in the world is the Swedish official journal *Post och Inrikes Tidningar*, founded in 1644. It is published by the Royal Swedish Academy of Letters. The oldest existing commercial newspaper is the *Haarlems Dagblad/ Oprechte Haarlemsche Courant*, published in

Haarlem, in the Netherlands. The *Courant* was first issued as the *Weeckelycke Courante van Europa* on 8 Jan. 1656 and a copy of issue No. 1 survives.

United Kingdom The oldest continuously produced newspaper in the United Kingdom is *Berrow's Worcester Journal* (originally the *Worcester Post Man*), published in Worcester. It was traditionally founded in 1690 and has appeared weekly since June 1709. The oldest newspaper title is that of the *Stamford Mercury* dating back to at least 1714 and traditionally to 1695. The oldest daily newspaper in the United Kingdom is *Lloyd's List*, the shipping intelligence bulletin of Lloyd's, London, established as a weekly in 1726 and as a daily in 1734. The *London Gazette* (originally the *Oxford Gazette*) was first published on 16 Nov. 1665. In November 1845 it became the most expensive daily newspaper ever sold in the United Kingdom, priced at 2s. 8d. per copy. The oldest Sunday newspaper in the United Kingdom is *The Observer*, first issued on 4 Dec. 1791.

Largest The most massive single issue of a newspaper was the 7½lb. *New York Times* of Sunday 10 Oct. 1971. It comprised 15 sections with a total of 972 pages, including about 1,200,000 lines of advertising.

The largest page size ever used has been 51 inches by 35 inches for *The Constellation*, printed in 1859 by George Roberts as part of the Fourth of July celebrations in New York City, N.Y., U.S.A. The *Worcestershire Chronicle* was the largest British newspaper. A surviving issue of 16 Feb. 1859 measures 32¼ inches by 22½ inches. The largest page size of any present newspaper is 30 inches by 22 inches in *The Nantucket Inquirer and Mirror*, published every Friday in Nantucket, on Nantucket Island, Massachusetts, U.S.A.

The smallest recorded page size has been 3½ inches by 4½ inches, as used in *Diario di Roma*, an issue of which dated 28 Feb. 1829 survives.

HIGHEST CIRCULATION
The first newspaper to achieve a circulation of 1,000,000 was *Le Petit Journal*, published in Paris, France, which reached this figure in 1886, when selling at 5 centimes (now about ½p) per copy.

World The claim exercised for the world's highest circulation is that by the *Ashashi Shimbun* (founded 1879) of Japan with a figure which attained more than 10,000,000 copies in October 1970. This, however, has been achieved by totalling the figures for editions published in various centres with a morning figure of 6,100,000 and an evening figure of 3,900,000. The highest circulation of any single newspaper in the world is that of the Sunday newspaper *The News of the World*, printed in Bouverie Street, London. Single issues have attained a sale of 9,000,000 copies, with an estimated readership of more than 19,000,000. The paper first appeared on 1 Oct. 1843, averaged 12,971 copies per week in its first year and surpassed the million mark in 1905. To provide sufficient pulp for the 1,500 reels used per week, each measuring 5 miles long, more than 780,000 trees have to be felled each year. The latest sales figure is 6,085,680 copies per issue (average for 1 July to 31 Dec. 1971), with a last published estimated readership of 16,208,000.

Daily World The highest circulation of any daily newspaper is that of the U.S.S.R. government organ *Izvestia* (founded in Leningrad on 12 March 1917 as a Menshevik news sheet and meaning "Information") with a figure of 8,670,000 in March 1967. The daily tabloid *Pionerskaya Pravda* had an average circulation of 9,181,000 copies per issue in 1966. This is the news organ of the Pioneers, a Communist youth organization founded in 1922.

93

United Kingdom The highest daily net sale of any newspaper in the United Kingdom is that of *The Daily Mirror*, founded in London in 1903. A print of 7,161,704 was sold out on 3 June 1953. The latest sales figure is 4,388,446 (for July-December 1971), with an estimated readership of 13,767,000.

Evening The highest circulation of any evening newspaper is that of *The Evening News*, established in London in 1881. The average daily net sale reached 1,752,166 in the first six months of 1950. The latest figure is 1,876,182 copies per issue (average for 1 July to 31 Dec. 1971), with an average readership of 2,644,000.

"Earliest" newspaper The first newspaper to be published in the world each day is sometimes said to be the *Fiji Times* because it is closest to the international date-line.

Most read The newspaper which achieves the closest to a saturation circulation is *The Sunday Post*, established in Glasgow in 1914. In 1971 its total estimated readership of 2,947,000 represented more than 79 per cent. of the entire population of Scotland aged 15 and over.

PERIODICALS
Largest circulation **World** The largest circulation of any weekly periodical has been that of *This Week Magazine*, produced in the United States to circulate with 43 newspapers which find it uneconomical to run their own coloured Sunday magazine section. The circulation reached 11,889,211 copies at 31 March 1967. In its 30 basic international editions *The Reader's Digest* (established February 1922) circulates more than 29,000,000 copies monthly, in 13 languages, including a United States edition of 17,750,000 copies (average for July to December 1971) and a United Kingdom edition (established 1939) of 1,500,000 copies.

United Kingdom Britain's oldest periodical is *Lancet* first published in 1823.

The highest circulation of any periodical in the United Kingdom is that of *The Radio Times* (instituted in September 1923). The average weekly sale for July-December 1971 was 3,434,787 copies. The highest sale of any issue was 9,778,062 copies for the Christmas issue of 1955. The materials used include 885 tons of paper, 9½ tons of ink and 355 miles of stapling wire per issue.

Annual *Old Moore's Almanack* has been published annually since 1697, when it first appeared as a broadsheet, by Dr. Francis Moore (1657-1715) of Southwark, London to advertise his "physiks". The annual sale certified by its publishers W. Foulsham & Co. Ltd. of Slough, England is 1,150,000 copies and its aggregate sale must well exceed 100,000,000 copies.

ADVERTISING RATES
The highest price asked for advertising space *pro rata* is $98,200 (£35,071) for a four-colour centre-spread in *This Week*. The highest price for a single page has been $84,100 (£35,060) for a four-colour back cover in *Life* magazine (circulation 8½ million per week) from Jan. 1969 to Jan. 1971.

The highest expenditure ever incurred on a single advertisement in a periodical is $950,000 (£395,833) by Uniroyal Inc. for a 40-page insert in the May 1968 issue of the U.S. edition of *The Reader's Digest*. The British record is about £50,000 for a 12-page colour supplement by Woolworths in the *Radio Times* of 18 Nov. 1971. The colour rate for a single page in the *Radio Times* is £5,800.

Longest editorship The longest editorship of any national newspaper has been more than 59 years by C. P. Scott (1846-1932) of the (then *Manchester*) Guardian, who was appointed aged 25 in 1872 and died on 1 Jan. 1932. The Irish record for editorship of a national newspaper

was set by Hector Legge, editor of the *Sund-Independent* from 13 Oct. 1940 to 31 Oct. 1970—years 2 weeks.

Most durable feature The longest lasting feature in the British press fro one pen is *Your Stars* by Edward Lyndoe. It has r since 1 Oct. 1933.

4. MUSIC

INSTRUMENTS
Oldest The world's oldest surviving musical notation is heptonic scale deciphered from a clay tablet by I Duchesne-Guillemin in 1966-67. The tablet has be dated to *c.* 1800 B.C. and was found at a site Nippur, Sumer, now Iraq. Musical history is, howeve able to be traced back to the 3rd millennium B.c when the yellow bell (*huang chung*) had a recogniz standard musical tone in Chinese temple music. It possible that either a flute or a mouth bow is t object depicted in a painting from the Magdaleni period (*c.* 18,000 B.C.) in the Trois Frères Caves the Pyrenees. Rock-gongs probably existed ev earlier.

Earliest piano The earliest pianoforte in existence is one built Florence, Italy, in 1720 by Bartolommeo Cristof (1655-1731) of Padua, and now preserved in t Metropolitan Museum of Art New York City.

Organ Largest **World** The largest and loudest musical instrument ev constructed is the now only partially functior Auditorium Organ in Atlantic City, New Jerse U.S.A. Completed in 1930, this heroic instrument h two consoles (one with seven manuals and anoth movable one with five), 1,477 stop controls a 33.112 pipes ranging from $^3/_{16}$ of an inch to 64 feet length. It is powered with blower motors of 3 horsepower, cost $500,000 (now £208,333) and h the volume of 25 brass bands, with a range of sev octaves. The Grand organ at Wannamaker's Sto Philadelphia, installed in 1911, was enlarged until 1930 it had 6 manuals and 30,067 pipes includin 64-foot Gravissima.

The world's largest church organ is that in Pass Cathedral, Germany. It was completed in 1928 D. F. Steinmeyer & Co. It has 16,000 pipes a five manuals.

United Kingdom The largest organ in the United Kingdom is th installed in Liverpool Cathedral in 1926, with o five-manual and one four-manual console, and 9,7 pipes.

Loudest stop The loudest organ stop in the world is the Ophiclei stop of the Grand Great in the Solo Organ in t Atlantic City Auditorium (see above). It is operat by a pressure of 100 inches of water (3½lb. per squa inch) and has a pure trumpet note of ear-splitti volume, more than six times the volume of t loudest locomotive whistles.

Organ marathon The longest organ recital ever sustained was one 43¼ hours at Handsworth College Chapel, Birmi ham, England, by the Rev. Ian Yates on 9-11 M 1970. The record for playing an electric organ 64 hours by James A. Barron at the Sundale Shopp Complex, Southport, Queensland, Australia 16-19 Nov. 1971. An entirely non-stop record of hours was set by Jeremy Cody, aged 15, from 10- April 1971 at Pontypridd, Glamorgan.

Harmonium marathon The longest recorded non-stop harmonium marath is 72 hours by Iain Stinson and John Whiteley, bc of the Royal Holloway College at Englefield Gre Surrey on 6-9 Feb. 1970.

Brass instrument The largest recorded brass instrument is a tu standing 7½ feet tall, with 39 feet of tubing and a b

Largest 3 feet 4 inches across. This contrabass tuba was constructed for a world tour by the band of John Philip Sousa (1854-1932), the United States composer, in *c.* 1896-98, and is still in use. This instrument is now owned by Mr. Ron Snyder (G.B.).

Longest alphorn The longest Swiss alphorn, which is of wooden construction, is 26½ feet long and was constructed before June 1968 in Maine, U.S.A. by Dr. Allison.

Stringed instrument *Largest* The largest stringed instrument ever constructed was a pantaleon with 270 strings stretched over 50 square feet, used by George Noel in 1767.

ost players The greatest number of musicians required to operate a single instrument was the six required to play the gigantic orchestrion, known as the Apollonican, built in 1816 and played until 1840.

Largest guitar The largest and presumably also the loudest playable guitar in the world is one 8 feet 10 inches tall, weighing 80 lb. and with a volume of 16,000 cubic inches (*c.f.* the standard 1,024 cubic inches) built by The Harmony Company of Chicago and completed in April 1970.

Largest **ouble bass** The largest bass viol ever constructed was an octobass 10 feet tall, built in *c.* 1845 by J. B. Vuillaume (1798-1875) of France. Because the stretch was too great for any musician's finger-span, the stopping was effected by foot levers. It was played in London in 1851.

Violin *st valuable* The highest recorded auction price for a violin is the £84,000 paid by W. E. Hill & Son, London, at Sotheby's on 3 June 1971 for the Lady Anne Blunt Stradivarius, made in 1721. On this valuation the "Messie" Stradivarius in the Ashmolean Museum at Oxford, England, is now worth some £200,000.

Smallest The smallest fully-functional violin is one 5½ inches overall, constructed by Mr. T.B. Pollard of Rock Ferry, Birkenhead, Cheshire, England.

gest drum The largest drum in the world is the Disneyland Big Bass Drum with a diameter of 10 feet 6 inches and a weight of 450 lb. It was built in 1961 by Remo Inc. of North Hollywood, California, U.S.A. and is mounted on wheels and towed by a tractor.

ORCHESTRAS

Most The greatest number of professional orchestras maintained in one country is 94 in West Germany. The total number of symphony orchestras in the United States, including "community" orchestras, was estimated to be 1,436 including 30 major and 66 metropolitan ones (as of August 1970).

Largest The vastest orchestra ever recorded were those assembled on Band Day at the University of Michigan, U.S.A. In some years between 1958 and 1965 the total number of instrumentalists reached 13,500. On 17 June 1872, Johann Strauss the younger (1825-99) conducted an orchestra of 2,000, supported by a choir of 20,000, at the World Peace Jubilee in Boston, Massachusetts, U.S.A. The number of violinists was more than 350.

Greatest ttendance The greatest attendance at any classical concert was 90,000 for a presentation by the New York Philharmonic Orchestra, conducted by Leonard Bernstein, at Sheep Meadow in Central Park, New York City, N.Y., U.S.A., on 1 Aug. 1966.

p Festival The greatest estimated attendance at a Pop Festival has been 400,000 for the Woodstock Music and Art Fair at Bethel, New York State, U.S.A. on 15-17 Aug. 1969. According to one press estimate "at least 90 per cent." were smoking marijuana. The attendance at the third Pop Festival at East Afton Farm, Freshwater, Isle of Wight, England on 30 Aug. 1970 was claimed by its promoters, Fiery Creations, also to be 400,000.

Highest and lowest notes The extremes of orchestral instruments (excluding the organ) range between the piccolo or octave flute, which can reach e^v or 5,274 cycles per second, and the sub-contrabass clarinet, which can reach C_{11} or 16.4 cycles per second. The highest note on a standard pianoforte is c^v (4,186 cycles per second), which is also the violinist's limit. In 1873 a sub double bassoon able to reach $B_{111}\#$ or 14.6 cycles per second was constructed but no surviving specimen is known. The extremes for the organ are g^{vi} (the sixth G above middle C) (12,544 cycles per sec.) and C_{111} (8.12 cycles per sec.) obtainable from ¾-inch and 64-foot pipes respectively.

COMPOSERS

Most prolific The most prolific composer of all time was probably Georg Philipp Telemann (1681-1767) of Germany. He composed 12 complete sets of services (one cantata every Sunday) for a year, 78 services for special occasions, 40 operas, 600 to 700 orchestral suites, 44 Passions, plus concertos and chamber music. The most prolific symphonist was Johann Melchior Molter (*c.* 1695-1765) of Germany who wrote 169. Joseph Haydn (1732-1809) of Austria wrote 104 numbered symphonies some of which are regularly played today.

Most rapid Among composers of the classical period the most prolific was Wolfgang Amadeus Mozart (1756-91) of Austria, who wrote 600 operas, operettas, symphonies, violin sonatas, divertimenti, serenades, motets, concertos for piano and many other instruments, string quartets, other chamber music, masses and litanies, of which only 70 were published before he died, aged 35. His opera *The Clemency of Titus* (1791) was written in 18 days and three symphonic masterpieces, *Symphony No. 39 in E flat major, Symphony in G minor* and the *Jupiter Symphony in C,* were reputedly written in the space of 42 days in 1788. His overture *Don Giovanni* was written in full score at one sitting in Prague in 1787 and finished on the day of its opening performance.

National anthems The oldest national anthem is the *Kimigayo* of Japan, in which the words date from the 9th century. The anthem of Greece constitutes the first four verses of the Solomos poem, which has 158 verses. The shortest anthems are those of Japan, Jordan and San Marino, each with only four lines. The anthems of Bahrain and Qatar have no words at all.

Longest rendering "God Save the King" was played non-stop 16 or 17 times by a German military band on the platform of Rathenau Railway Station, Brandenburg, on the morning of 9 Feb. 1909. The reason was that King Edward VII was struggling inside the train with the uniform of a German Field-Marshal before he could emerge.

Longest symphony The longest of all symphonies is the orchestral symphony No. 3 in D minor by Gustav Mahler (1860-1911) of Austria. This work, composed in 1895, requires a contralto, a women's and a boys' choir and an organ, in addition to a full orchestra. A full performance requires 1 hour 34 minutes, of which the first movement alone takes 45 minutes. The Symphony No. 2 (the Gothic, now renumbered as No. 1), composed in 1919-22 by Havergal Brian, has been performed only twice, on 24 June 1961 and 30 Oct. 1966. The total *ensemble* included 55 brass instruments, 31 wood wind, six kettledrummers playing 22 drums, four vocal soloists, four large mixed choruses, a children's chorus and an organ. The symphony is continuous and required, when played as a recording on 27 Nov. 1967, 100 minutes. Brian has written an even vaster work based on **Shelley's**

"Prometheus Unbound" lasting 4 hours 11 mins. but the full score has been missing since 1961. He wrote 27 symphonies, 4 grand operas and 7 large orchestral works between 1948 when he was 72 and 1968.

Longest piano composition The longest continuous non-repetitive piece for piano ever composed has been the Opus Clavicembalisticum by Kaikhosru Shapurji Sorabji (b. 1892). The composer himself gave it its only public performance on 1 Dec. 1930 in Glasgow, Scotland. The work is in 12 movements with a theme and 49 variations and a Passacaglia with 81 and a playing time of 2¾ hours.

The longest piano piece of any kind is *Vexations* by Erik Satie (France) which consists of a 180-note composition which on the composer's orders must be repeated 840 times such that the whole lasts 18 hours 40 minutes. Its first reported public performance in September 1963 in the Pocket Theater, New York City required a relay of ten pianists. The *New York Times* critic fell asleep at 4 a.m. and the audience dwindled to six masochists. Richard Toop, played the first solo rendition in London on 10-11 Oct. 1967 in 25 hours.

Longest silence The most protracted silence in a modern composition is one entitled *4 minutes 33 seconds* in a totally silent *opus* by John Cage (U.S.A.). Commenting on this trend among young composers, Igor Fyodorovich Stravinsky (1882-1971) said that he looked forward to their subsequent compositions being "works of major length".

HIGHEST PAID MUSICIANS

Pianist The highest-paid concert pianist was Ignace Jan Paderewski (1860-1941), Prime Minister of Poland from 1919 to 1921, who accumulated a fortune estimated at $5,000,000 (now about £1,800,000), of which $500,000 (£180,000) was earned in a single season in 1922-23. He once received $33,000 (£11,800) for a concert in Madison Square Garden, New York City, the highest fee ever paid for a single performance.

Singers Of great fortunes earned by singers, the highest on record are those of Enrico Caruso (1873-1921), the Italian tenor, whose estate was about $9,000,000 (£3,750,000), and the Italian-Spanish coloratura soprano Amelita Galli-Curci (1889-1963), who received about $3,000,000 (£1,250,000). In 1850, up to $653 (now £272) was paid for a single seat at the concerts given in the United States by Johanna ("Jenny") Maria Lind, later Mrs. Otto Goldschmidt (1820-87), the "Swedish Nightingale". She had a range from go to e^{111}, of which the middle register is still regarded as unrivalled.

Violinist The Austrian-born Fritz Kreisler (1875-1962) is reputed to have received more than £1,000,000 in his career.

Drummer The most highly paid drummer, or indeed "side man" of any kind, is Bernard ("Buddy") Rich (b. 1917) in the band of Harry James, at more than $75,000 (£31,250) per annum.

OPERA

Longest The longest of commonly performed operas is *Die Meistersinger von Nurnberg* by Wilhelm Richard Wagner (1813-83) of Germany. A normal uncut performance of this opera as performed by the Sadler's Wells company between 24 Aug. and 19 Sept. 1968 entailed 5 hours 15 minutes of music. *William Tell* by Rossini, never now performed uncut, would according to the *tempi* require some 7 or more hours if performed in full.

Ginetta La Bianca—the world's youngest opera star in her debut rôle in the Barber of Seville in 1950

Aria The longest single aria, in the sense of an opera solo, is Brünnhilde's immolation scene in Wagne *Götterdämmerung*. A well-known recording of th has been precisely timed at 14 minutes 46 seconds.

Cadenza The longest recorded cadenza in operatic histo occured in *c.* 1815, when Crevilli, a tenor, sang t two words *felice ognora* ("always happy") as cadenza for 25 minutes in the Milan Opera Hou Italy.

Opera houses **Largest** The largest opera house in the world is the Metropo itan Opera House, Lincoln Center, New York Cit N.Y., U.S.A., completed in September 1966 at a co of $45,700,000 (£16,320,000). It has a capacity 3,800 seats in an auditorium 451 feet deep. The sta is 234 feet in width and 146 feet deep. The talle opera house is one housed in a 42-storey building Wacker Drive in Chicago, Illinois, U.S.A.

Most tiers The Teatro della Scala (La Scala) in Milan, Ital shares with the Bolshoi Theatre in Moscow, U.S.S.I the distinction of having the greatest number of tie Each has six, with the topmost in Moscow bei termed the Galurka.

Opera Singers Youngest and Oldest The youngest opera singer in the world has be Jeanette Gloria La Bianca, born in Buffalo, New Yo on 12 May 1934, who made her debut as Rosina *The Barber of Seville* at the Teatro dell'Opera, Ror on 8 May 1950 aged 15 years 361 days. Ginetta Bianca was taught by Lucia Carlino and managed Angelo Carlino. Giacomo Lauri-Volpi (Spain) gave public performance on 26 Jan. 1972 aged 79.

BELLS

Heaviest World The heaviest bell in the world is the Tsar Kolokol, ca in 1733 in Moscow, U.S.S.R. It weighs 193 tor measures 22 feet 8 inches in diameter and over 19 fe high, and its greatest thickness is 24 inches. The bell cracked, and a fragment, weighing about 11 tor broken from it. The bell has stood on a platform the Kremlin, in Moscow, since 1836.

The heaviest bell in use is the Mingoon bell, weighi 87 tons, in Mandalay, Burma, which is struck by teak boom from the outside. The heaviest swingi bell in the world is the Kaiserglock in Colog Cathedral, Germany, which was recast in 1925 at tons. The heaviest change ringing peal in the world the 13 bells, weighing 16½ tons, in Liverpo Cathedral of which the tenor alone weighs 82 cwt.

United Kingdom The heaviest bell hung in the United Kingdom "Great Paul" in St. Paul's Cathedral, London. It w cast in 1881, weighs 16 tons 14 cwt. 2 quarters 19 and has a diameter of 9 feet 6½ inches. "Big Ben", t hour bell in the clock tower of the House

Commons, was cast in 1858 and weighs 13 tons 10 cwt. 3 quarters 15 lb. The heaviest peal is the 13 with a tenor bell weighing 72 cwt. donated by Bishop Grandison (1327-1369) to Exeter Cathedral.

The heaviest bell ever cast in England and the heaviest tuned bell in the world is the bourdon bell of the Laura Spelman Rockefeller Memorial carillon in Riverside Church, New York City, N.Y., U.S.A. It weighs 18 tons 5 cwt. 1 quarter 18 lb. and is 10 feet 2 inches in diameter.

Oldest The oldest bell in the world is reputed to be that
World found in the Babylonian Palace of Nimrod in 1849 by Mr. (later Sir) Austen Henry Layard (1817-94). It dates from *c.* 1000 B.C.

United The oldest *dated* bell in England is that hung in St.
Kingdom Chad's, Claughton, in the parish of Hornby with Claughton, Lancashire. It weighs about 2½ cwt., is 21¼ inches in diameter and 16½ inches high. Still in perfect condition and in regular use, it is dated 1296. A claim that the church bell at Enborne, Berkshire dates from *c.* A.D. 1260 is accepted by some experts.

CARILLON

Largest The largest carillon in the world is the Laura Spelman Rockefeller Memorial carillon in Riverside Church, New York City, N.Y., U.S.A. It consists of 72 bells with a total weight of 102 tons.

Heaviest The heaviest carillon in the United Kingdom is in St. Nicholas Church, Aberdeen, Scotland. It consists of 48 bells, the total weight of which is 25 tons 8 cwt. 2 quarters 13 lb. The bourdon bell weighs 4 tons 9 cwt. 3 quarters 26 lb. and the carillon comprises four octaves, less the bottom semi-tone.

BELL RINGING

Eight bells have been rung to their full "extent" (a complete "Bob Major" of 40,320 changes) only once without relays. This took place in a bell foundry at Loughborough, Leicestershire, beginning at 6.52 a.m. on 27 July 1963 and ending at 00.50 a.m. on 28 July, after 17 hours 58 minutes. The peal was composed by Kenneth Lewis of Altrincham, Cheshire, and the eight ringers were conducted by Robert B. Smith, aged 25, of Marple, Cheshire. Theoretically it would take 37 years 355 days to ring 12 bells (maximus) to their full extent of 479,001,600 changes.

SONG

Oldest The oldest known song is the *chadouf* chant, which has been sung since time immemorial by irrigation workers on the man-powered treadwheel Nile water mills (or *saqiyas*) in Egypt (now the United Arab Republic). The English song *Sumer is icumen in* dates from *c.* 1240.

Top songs The most frequently sung songs in English are *Happy*
of all time *Birthday to You* (based on the original *Good morning to all*), by Mildred and Patty S. Hill of New York (published in 1936 and in copyright until 1996); *For He's a Jolly Good Fellow* (originally the French *Malbrouk*), known at least as early as 1781, and *Auld Lang Syne* (originally the Strathspey *I fee'd a Lad at Michaelmass*), some words of which were written by Robert Burns (1759-96). *Happy Birthday* was sung in space by the Apollo IX astronauts on 8 March 1969.

Top selling Sales of three non-copyright pieces are known to have
sheet music exceeded 20,000,000 namely *The Old Folks at Home, Listen to the Mocking Bird* (1855) and *The Blue Danube* (1867). Of copyright material the two top-sellers are *Let Me Call You Sweetheart* (1910, by Whitson Friedman) and *Till We Meet Again* (1918, by Egan Whiting) each with some 6,000,000 by 1967.

Most The longest song sung on one note is *Ein Ton*, written
onotonous in 1859 by Peter Cornelius (1824-74) of Germany.

The single note (the B above middle C) is repeated 80 times for 30 bars.

Most In terms of sales of single records, the most successful
successful of all song writers have been John Lennon and Paul
song writers McCartney (see also Gramophone, Fastest sales, p. 100) of the Beatles. Between 1962 and 1 Jan. 1970 they together wrote 30 songs which sold more than 1,000,000 records each.

HYMNS

Earliest There are believed to be more than 500,000 Christian hymns in existence. "Te Deum Laudamus" dates from about the 5th century, but the earliest exactly datable hymn is the French one "Jesus soit en ma teste et mon entendement" from 1490, translated into the well-known "God be in my head" in 1512.

Longest and The longest hymn is "Hora novissima tempora
shortest pessima sunt; vigilemus" by Bernard of Cluny (12th century), which runs to 2,966 lines. In English the longest is "The Sands of Time are sinking" by Mrs. Anne Ross Cousin, *née* Cundell (1824-1906), which is in full 152 lines, though only 32 lines in the Methodist Hymn Book. The shortest hymn is the single verse in Long Metre "Be Present at our Table, Lord", anonymous but attributed to "J. Leland".

Most prolific Mrs. Frances (Fanny) Jan Van Alstyne, *née* Crosby
hymnists (1820-1915), of the U.S.A., wrote more than 8,000 hymns although she had been blinded at the age of 6 weeks. She is reputed to have knocked off one hymn in 15 minutes. Charles Wesley (1707-88) wrote about 6,000 hymns. In the seventh (1950) edition of *Hymns Ancient and Modern* the works of John Mason Neale (1818-66) appear 56 times.

Longest The Cambridge University Student Methodist Society
hymn-in sang through the 984 hymns in the Methodist Hymn Book in 45 hours 42 minutes, and completed 1,000 hymns with 16 more requests in 88 minutes on 7-9 Feb. 1969 in the Wesley Church, Cambridge.

5. THEATRE

Origins Theatre in Europe has its origins in Greek drama performed in honour of a god, usually Dionysus. The earliest amphitheatres date from the 5th century B.C. The largest of all known *orchestras* is one at Megalopolis in central Greece, where the auditorium reached a height of 75 feet and had a capacity of 17,000.

Oldest The oldest indoor theatre in the world is the Teatro
World Olimpico in Vicenza, Italy. Designed in the Roman style by Andrea di Pietro, *alias* Palladio (1508-80), it was begun three months before his death and finished in 1582 by his pupil Vicenzo Scamozzi (1552-1616). It is preserved today in its original form.

The Permanent Set at The Theatre Olimpico Vicenza, Italy

United Kingdom The earliest London theatre was James Burbage's "The Theatre", built in 1576 near Finsbury Fields, London. The oldest theatre still in use in the United Kingdom is the Theatre Royal, Bristol. The foundation stone was laid on 30 Nov. 1764, and the theatre was opened on 30 May 1766 with a "Concert of Music and a Specimen of Rhetorick". The City Varieties Music Hall, Leeds was a singing room in 1762 and so claims to outdate the Theatre Royal. Actors were legally rogues and vagabonds until the passing of an act (5 Geo. IV C.38) in 1824. The first honour for work on the stage was to Henry Irving (1838-1905), b. John Henry Brodribb, who was knighted in 1895. The earliest Dame was Geneviève Ward made D.B.E. in 1921. The first stage peer has been Sir Laurence Kerr Olivier (b. 22 May 1907), created a life Baron on 13 June 1970.

Largest World The world's largest building used for theatre is the National People's Congress Building (*Ren min da hui tang*) on the west side of Tian an men Square, Peking, China. It was completed in 1959 and covers an area of 12.9 acres. The theatre seats 10,000 and is occasionally used as such as in 1964 for the play "The East is Red". The largest regular theatre in the world is Radio City Music Hall in Rockefeller Center, New York City, N.Y., U.S.A. It seats more than 6,200 people and the average annual attendance is more than 8,000,000. The stage is 144 feet wide and 66 feet 6 inches deep, equipped with a revolving turntable 43 feet in diameter and three elevator sections, each 70 feet long.

The greatest seating capacity of any regular theatre in the world is that of the "Chaplin" (formerly the "Blanquita") in Havana, Cuba. It was opened on 30 Dec. 1949 and has 6,500 seats.

United Kingdom The highest capacity theatre is the Odeon, Hammersmith, West London, with 3,485 seats in 1972. The largest theatre stage in the United Kingdom is the Opera House in Blackpool, Lancashire. It was re-built in July 1939 and has seats for 2,975 people. Behind the 45-foot-wide proscenium arch the stage is 110 feet high, 60 feet deep and 100 feet wide, and there is dressing room accommodation for 200 artists.

Smallest The smallest regularly operated professional theatre in the United Kingdom is the Little Theatre, Tobermory, Isle of Mull, Scotland with a capacity of 36 seats.

Largest amphi-theatre The largest amphitheatre ever built is the Flavian amphitheatre or Colosseum of Rome, Italy, completed in A.D. 80. Covering 5 acres and with a capacity of 87,000, it has a maximum length of 612 feet and maximum width of 515 feet.

Longest runs World The longest run of any show at one theatre anywhere in the world was by the play *The Drunkard*, written by W. H. Smith and "a gentleman". First produced, as a moral lesson, in 1844 by Phineas Taylor Barnum (1810-91), a United States showman, it was not performed commercially again until it was revived on 6 July 1933 at the Theatre Mart in Los Angeles, California, U.S.A. From that date it ran continuously, one show a night, for 7,510 performances, until 3 Sept. 1953. Starting on 7 Sept. 1953, a new musical adaptation of *The Drunkard*, called *The Wayward Way*, started to play alternate nights with the original version. On 17 Oct. 1959 it played its 9,477th and final time. It was seen by more than 3,000,000 people. The producer, Miss Mildred Ilse, was with the play throughout. In Britain, the Brighton Corporation's variety show *Tuesday Night at the Dome* reached its 1,200th performance in 24 years on 1 Dec. 1970.

Broadway The Broadway record is 3,213 performances of *Life with Father* at the Empire, which opened on 8 Nov.

1937 and closed at the end of 1947. The Broadw record for musicals was set by *Fiddler on the Roc* which opened on 22 Sept. 1964 and reached a reco 3,195th performance on 20 May 1972. The o Broadway show *The Fantasticks* achieved its 4,750 performance on 30 Sept. 1971.

London The longest continuous run of any show at o theatre in the United Kingdom is by *The Mousetr* by Dame Agatha Mary Clarissa Christie, D.B.E. (*n* Miller, now Lady Mallowan) (b. Torquay, Devon, Sept. 1890) at the Ambassadors Theatre (capaci 453). This thriller opened on 25 Nov. 1952, and h its 8,000th performance on 28 Feb. 1972. On 19 Au 1969 a power failure caused one performance to missed. So far 137 actors have played its 8 roles, wh A. Huntley Gordon has been the stage manager sin the start.

The longest-running musical show ever performed Britain was *The Black and White Minstrel Show*, musical variety presentation which opened at t Victoria Palace, London, on 25 May 1962, w performed *twice* nightly and continued until 24 M 1969 reaching 4,354 performances. The total atte dance had been recorded at 5,614,077. One chor girl claims a pedometer strapped to a leg registered miles in one night. It reopened as *Magic of t Minstrels* on 24 Nov. 1969 and reaches its 2,000 performance on 13 Dec. 1972.

One-man show The longest run of any one-man show has been 3 performances of *Comedy To Night* by James You at the Ulster Group Theatre, Belfast from 7 Apr. 19 to 22 Mar. 1970. He was on stage for 2 hours minutes.

Shortest runs World The shortest run on record was that of *The Intima Revue* at the Duchess Theatre, London, on 11 Mar 1930. Anything which could go wrong did. Wi scene changes taking up to 20 minutes apiece, t management scrapped seven scenes to get the fina on before midnight. The run was described as "hal performance". Even this fractional first night w surpassed by *As You Like It* by William Shakespea (1564-1616) at the Shaftesbury Theatre, London, 1888. On the opening night the fire curtain was l down, jammed, and did not rise again that night ever again on this production.

Broadway Of the many Broadway shows for which the openi and closing nights coincided, the most costly w *Kelly*, a musical costing $700,000 (then £250,00 which underwent the double ceremony on 6 Fe 1965.

Longest play The Oberammergau *Passionsspiel* ("Passion Play" performed every ten years since 1633, was performe with 125 speaking parts, 102 times in 1970, ea performance occupying 5½ hours or 8½ hours inclu ing intervals. The audience for this 37th presentatio ending on 30 September was 530,000. The 15 century Cornish Cycle of Mystery Plays was revived English in July 1969, at the earthwork theatre, S Piran's Round, Piran, near Perranporth, Cornwall, t the Drama Department of Bristol University. Thr parts, *Origo Mundi, Passio,* and *Resurrectio,* ran fo 12 hours with two intermissions.

Shakespeare The first all amateur company to have staged all 37 Shakespeare's plays was The Southsea Shakespea Actors, Hampshire, England, when in October 196 they presented *Cymbeline*. The director throughou was Mr. K. Edmonds Gateley. Eleven members Leeds Polytechnic Union Drama Society, Yorkshi completed a dramatic reading of all the plays, 15 sonnets and five narrative poems in 53 hours 1 minutes on 28-30 Apr. 1971. The longest is *Richa III*.

Longest chorus line The world's longest permanent chorus line is that formed by the Rockettes in the Radio City Music Hall, which opened in December 1932 in New York City, U.S.A. The 36 girls dance precision routines across the 144 foot-wide stage. The whole troupe, which won the *Grand Prix* in Paris in July 1937, is 46 strong, but 10 girls are always on alternating vacation or are undergoing repairs. The troupe is sometimes augmented to 64.

6. GRAMOPHONE

Origins The gramophone (phonograph) was first described on 30 April 1877 by Charles Cros (1842-88), a French poet and scientist. The first successful machine was constructed by Thomas Alva Edison (1847-1931) of the U.S.A., who gained his first patent on 19 Feb. 1878. It was on 15 Aug. 1877 that he shouted "Mary had a little Lamb". The first practical hand-cranked foil cylinder phonograph was manufactured in the United States by Chichester Bell and Charles Sumner Tainter in 1886.

The country with the greatest number of record players is the United States, with a total of more than 60,000,000 by mid-1969. A total of more than half a billion dollars (now £192 million) is spent annually on 500,000 juke boxes in the United States.

World sales of records for 1968 have been estimated at 1,141 million. In the United States retail sales of discs and tapes reached $1,660 million in 1970 of which $1,017 million was for L.P.'s and $77 million for cassettes.

The peak year for value in U.K. sales of records was 1971 with £43,485,000 for 120,524,000 records.

OLDEST RECORD
The oldest record in the British Broadcasting Corporation's gramophone library is a record made by Emile Berliner (b. Berlin, 1851) of himself reciting the Lord's Prayer. It was made in 1884. Berliner invented the flat disc to replace the cylinder in 1888.

The B.B.C. library, the world's largest, contains over 750,000 records, including 5,250 with no known matrix.

Earliest jazz records The earliest jazz record made was *Indiana* and *The Dark Town Strutters Ball*, recorded for the Columbia label in New York City, N.Y., U.S.A., on or about 30 Jan. 1917, by the Original Dixieland Jazz Band, led by Dominick (Nick) James La Rocca (1889-1961). This was released on 31 May 1917. The first jazz record to be released was the O.D.J.B.'s *Livery Stable Blues* (recorded 24 Feb.), backed by *The Dixie Jass Band One-Step* (recorded 26 Feb.), released by Victor on 7 March 1917.

Most successful solo recording artist On 9 June 1960 the Hollywood Chamber of Commerce presented Harry Lillis (*alias* Bing) Crosby, Jr. (b. 2 May 1904 at Tacoma, Washington) with a platinum disc to commemorate a sale of 200,000,000 records from the 2,600 singles and 125 albums he had recorded. On 15 Sept. 1970 he received a second platinum disc for selling 300,650,000 discs with Decca. It was then estimated that his global life-time sales on 88 labels in 28 countries totalled, according to his royalty reports, 362,000,000. His first commercial recording was *"I've Got the Girl"* recorded on 18 Oct. 1926 (master number W142785 (Take 3) issued on the Columbia label). The greatest collection of Crosbiana by Mr. Bob Roberts of Chatham, Kent includes 1,677 records.

Most successful group The singers with the greatest sales of any group have been the Beatles. This group from Liverpool, Lancashire, comprised George Harrison, M.B.E. (b. 25 Feb. 1943), John Ono (formerly John Winston) Lennon, M.B.E. (b. 9 Oct. 1940), James Paul McCartney, M.B.E. (b. 18 June 1942) and Richard Starkey, M.B.E., *alias* Ringo Starr (b. 7 July 1940). Between February 1963 and September 1970 their sales were estimated at more than 133 million (74 million singles, 3 million E.P.s and 56 million albums) which represented more than 420 million in singles' equivalents. The 40,000 strong Beatles Fan Club closed down on 31 March 1972.

GOLDEN DISCS
Earliest The earliest recorded piece eventually to aggregate a total sale of a million copies were performances by Enrico Caruso (b. Naples, Italy, 1873, and d. 2 Aug.

Osamu Mina-
gawa—the
youngest ever
Golden Disc
winner

1921) of the aria *Vesti la giubba (On with the Motley)* from the opera *I Pagliacci* by Ruggiero Leoncavallo (1858-1919), the earliest version of which was recorded with piano on 12 Nov. 1902. The first single recording to surpass the million mark was Alma Gluck's *Carry me back to old Virginny* on the Red Seal Victor label on the 12-inch single faced (later backed) record 74420. The first actual golden disc was one sprayed by R.C.A. Victor for presentation to the U.S. trombonist and band-leader Alton 'Glenn' Miller (1904-44) for his *Chattanooga Choo Choo* on 10 Feb. 1942.

Most The only *audited* measure of million-selling records within the United States, is certification by the Recording Industry Association of America (R.I.A.A.) introduced in 1958. By their yardstick on U.S. sales, Presley has 10 Golden Discs with an additional 11 for million *dollar* sales (based on one third of list price plus sales of tapes). The champions for R.I.A.A. awards are The Beatles with 21 for singles which sold more than 1 million *copies* and 17 for L.P.s each of which sold more than $1 million worth by 1 Sept. 1970. The Beatles' global total of million-selling titles was believed to stand at 59 by 1 Jan. 1971. The singer with the most golden discs claimed is Elvis Aron Presley (b. Tupelo, Mississippi, U.S.A., 8 Jan. 1935). By 1 Jan. 1972 he had 101 golden discs (78 for singles, 1 E.P. and 7 for L.P.s), which are said to mark each sale of each 1,000,000 copies and each million dollar sale among his 65 best-selling records. His total global sales were estimated at 160,000,000 discs by that date representing 300 million singles equivalents.

Youngest The youngest age at which an artist has achieved sales of 1,000,000 copies of a record is 6 years by Osamu Minagawa of Tōkyō, Japan for his single *Kuro Neko No Tango (Black Cat Tango)* released on 5 Oct. 1969.

Most recorded song Two songs have each been recorded between 900 and 1,000 times in the United States alone—*St. Louis Blues*, written in 1914 by W.C. (William Christopher) Handy (b. Florence, Alabama 1873 and d. 1958), and *Stardust*, written in 1927 by Hoagland ("Hoagy") Carmichael (b. Bloomington, Indiana, 22 Nov. 1899).

Most recordings Miss Lata Mangeshker (b. 1928) between 1948 and 1971 has reportedly recorded not less than 20,000 solo, duet and chorus backed songs in 20 Indian languages. She frequently has 5 sessions in a day.

Biggest sellers The greatest seller of any gramophone record to date

is *White Christmas* by Irving Berlin (b. Israel Bailin, a Tyumen, Russia, 11 May 1888). First recorded i 1941, it became the first ever record to reach 9 figure (100,000,000) sales in 1970. The top-selling "pop record has been *Rock Around the Clock* by Willia John Clifton Haley, Jr. (b. Detroit, Michigan, Marc 1927) and the Comets, recorded on 12 April 195 with sales of 16,000,000 by January 1972. Th top-selling British record of all-time is *I Want to Hol Your Hand* by the Beatles with world sales c 11,000,000, including 5,000,000 in the Unite States.

Best-sellers' charts Radio Luxembourg's "Top Twenty" Sunday nigh programme, launched in the autumn of 1948, was th first *programme* based on current selling strengt though best-selling lists had been appearing in th U.S. periodical *Billboard* since 1941. The longest sta in the British charts has been by Frank Sinatra's *M Way* released in 1969 which on 23 Oct. 197 celebrated its 120th consecutive week. The longes stay in the L.P. charts in the U.S.A. has been 49 weeks from late in 1958 to July 1968 by th Columbia album *Johnny's Greatest Hits* (Johnn Mathis). The longest in the U.K. has been *Sound c Music* (sound track) with 344 weeks to 13 May 197

Top-selling L.P. The best-selling L.P. is the 20th Century Fox albu *Sing We now of Christmas*, issued in 1958 an re-entitled *The Little Drummer Boy* in 1963. Its sale were reported to be more than 13,000,000 by 1 Ja 1972. The first British L.P. to sell 1,000,000 copie was *With the Beatles* (Parlophone), from Novembe 1963 to January 1964 in the United States and t September 1965 in Britain. The top-selling Britis L.P. is *Sergeant Pepper's Lonely Hearts Club Band* b the Beatles with more than 7,000,000 to 1 Jan. 197

Top-selling L.P. sound track The all-time best-seller among long-playing records c musical film shows is *The Sound of Music* sound trac album, released by R.C.A Victor in U.S.A. on 2 Marc and in Britain on 9 April 1965, with more tha 14,000,000 to 1 Jan. 1972. In Britain it was No. 1 i the L.P. Charts for 69 weeks.

Top-selling classical L.P. The first classical long-player to sell a million was performance featuring the pianist Harvey Lava (Van) Cliburn, Jr. (b. Kilgore, Texas, 12 July 1934) c the *Piano Concerto No. 1* by Pyotr Ilyich Tcha kovsky (1840-93) (more properly rendered Chay kovskiy) of Russia. This recording was made in 195 and sales reached 1,000,000 by 1961, 2,000,000 b 1965 and about 2,500,000 by January 1970.

Longest L.P. set The longest long-playing record is the 137-disc set o the complete works of William Shakespear (1564-1616). The recordings, which were made i 1957-1964, cost £260.62½ per set, and are by th Argo Record Co. Ltd., London, S.W.3. The Vienn Philharmonic's playing of Wagner's "The Ring covers 19 L.P.s, was eight years in the making an requires 14½ hours playing time.

Fastest selling L.P.s The fastest selling record of all time is *John Fitzgeral Kennedy—A Memorial Album* (Premium Albums), a L.P. recorded on 22 Nov. 1963, the day of M Kennedy's assassination, which sold 4,000,000 copie at 99 cents (then 35p) in six days (7-12 Dec. 1963 thus ironically beating the previous speed record se by the satirical L.P. *The First Family* in 1962-63. Th fastest selling British record has been the Beatle double album *The Beatles* (Parlophone) with "nearl 2 million" in its first week in November 1968.

Advance sales The greatest advance sale was 2,100,000 for *Can Buy Me Love* by the Beatles, released in the Unite States on 16 March 1964. The Beatles also equalle their British record of 1,000,000 advance sales, set b *I want to Hold Your Hand* (Parlophone transferred t Apple Aug. 1968) on 29 Nov. 1963, with this sam

record on 20 March 1964. The U.K. record for advance sales of an L.P. is 750,000 for the Parlophone album *Beatles for Sale* released on 4 Dec. 1964.

Highest fee The highest fee ever paid to recording artists for a single performance is $189,000 (then £67,500), paid to The Beatles for a performance in the William A. Shea Stadium baseball park, New York City, N.Y., U.S.A., on 23 Aug. 1966.

Longest Silence Silent records (Hush Label) were first placed on juke boxes at the University of Detroit, U.S.A. in January 1959. The longest programme of sponsored silence was one of 6 hours on Station WS00 of Sault Ste. Marie, Michigan on 1 Jan. 1971.

7. CINEMA

EARLIEST

Origins The greatest impetus in the development of cinematography came from the inventiveness of Etieene Jules Marey (1830-1903) of France.

Earliest silent showings The earliest demonstration of a celluloid cinematograph film was given at Lyon (Lyons), France on 22 March 1895 by Auguste Marie Louis Nicolas Lumière (1862-1954) and Louis Jean Lumière (1864-1948), the French brothers. The first public showing was at the Indian Salon of the Hotel Scribe, on the Boulevard des Capucines, in Paris, on 28 Dec. 1895. The 33 patrons were charged 1 franc each and saw ten short films, including *Baby's Breakfast, Lunch Hour at the Lumière Factory* and *The Arrival of a Train*. The same programme was shown on 20 Feb. 1896 at the Polytechnic Institute in Regent Street, London.

Earliest 'Talkie' The earliest sound-on-film motion picture was demonstrated by Joseph Tycocinski-Tykociner of the University of Illinois, U.S.A. in June 1922. The event is more usually attributed to Dr. Lee de Forest (1873-1961) in New York City, N.Y., U.S.A., on 13 March 1923. The first all-talking picture was *Lights of New York*, shown at The Strand, New York City, on 6 July 1928.

Highest production Japan annually produces most full length films, with 607 films of 1,500 metres (4,921 feet) or more completed in 1967, compared with 367 films of 3,400 metres (11,155 feet) or more approved by the censor in India in 1969. This compares, however, with Japan's production of 1,000 films in 1928. The average seat price in Japan is 70 yen (7p). In the United Kingdom 90 feature films of 72 or more minutes duration were registered in the year ending 31 Dec. 1971.

Highest cinema-going The people of Taiwan go to the cinema more often than those of any other country in the world with an average of 66 attendances per person in 1967. The Soviet Union has the most cinemas in the world, with 146,400 in 1969 including those projecting only 16 mm. film. The number of cinemas in the U.K. declined from 4,542 in 1953 to 1,527 at 31 March 1971. The average weekly admissions declined from 24,700,000 in 1953 to 3,250,000 in 1971.

Most cinema seats The Falkland Islands have more cinema seats per total population than any other country in the world, with 250 seats for each 1,000 inhabitants. The Central African Republic has 2 cinemas and hence one seat for 3,000 people. Excluding "captive" projectionists, the most persistent voluntary devotee of a film has been Mrs. Myra Franklin (b. 1919) of Cardiff, Wales, who saw *The Sound of Music* more than 900 times.

CINEMAS

Largest World The largest open-air cinema in the world is in the British Sector of West Berlin, Germany. One end of the Olympic Stadium, converted into an amphitheatre, seats 22,000 people.

United Kingdom The United Kingdom's largest cinema is the Odeon Theatre, Hammersmith, London, with 3,485 seats.

Oldest The earliest cinema was the "Electric Theatre", part of a tented circus in Los Angeles, California, U.S.A. It opened on 2 April 1902. The oldest building designed as a cinema is the Biograph Cinema in Wilton Road, Victoria, London. It was opened in 1905 and originally had seating accommodation for 500 patrons. Its present capacity is 700.

Most expensive film The most expensive film ever made is the 5 hour 57 min. long *War and Peace,* the U.S.S.R. government adaptation of the masterpiece of Tolstoy produced by Sergei Bondarchuk (b. 1921) over the period 1962-67. The total cost has been officially stated to be more than £40,000,000. More than 165,000 uniforms had to be made. The re-creation of a Napoleonic battle involved 12,000 men and 800 horses on a location near Smolensk in 1964. The greatest number of "extras" used in a film is more than 20,000 Red Army soldiers, at 3 roubles (£1.38) per month, in the joint Hollywood-Columbia, Paramount-Mosfilms production *Waterloo*, filmed in the Ukraine on a $33 million (£13¾ million) budget and released in 1970.

Most expensive film rights The highest price ever paid for film rights is $5,500,000, paid on 6 Feb. 1962 by Warner Brothers for *My Fair Lady*, which cost $17,000,000 thus making it the most expensive musical film then made.

Longest film The longest film ever shown is *The Human Condition*, directed in three parts by Masaki Kobayashi of Japan. It lasts 8 hours 50 minutes, excluding two breaks of 20 minutes each. It was shown in Tōkyō in October

THE ARTS AND ENTERTAINMENTS

1961 at an admission price of 250 yen (24½p). The longest film ever released was **** by Andy Warhol which lasted 24 hours. It proved, not surprisingly, except reportedly to its creator, a commercial failure and was withdrawn and re-released in 90-minute form as *The Loves of Ondine*.

Longest title The longest film title is: *Persecution and Assassination of Jean-Paul Marat as performed by the Inmates of the Asylum of Charenton under the direction of the Marquis de Sade,* first distributed by United Artists in March 1967.

Highest box office gross The film which has had the highest world gross earnings (amount paid by cinema owners) is *The Sound of Music* (released in February 1965) which reached $112,481,000 (£46,867,000) by September 1969 having cost 20th Century Fox $8,100,000 to produce. In the U.S. *Gone With the Wind* reasserted its former lead with $74,200,000 by January 1972. The fastest-earning film has been *Goldfinger,* the third in the series of films based on stories of James Bond (Agent 007 in the Secret Service) by Ian Lancaster Fleming (1908-64). The fastest return ever was $36,647,251 (£14.1 million) for another Ian Fleming epic *Diamonds Are Forever* in the 31 days from 17 Dec. 1971. It also set a British record for a single cinema with £34,866 at the Odeon, Leicester Square, London (1,983 seats) in January 1972.

Highest earning by an actor The greatest earnings by any film star for one film is expected to be that of Elizabeth Taylor in *Cleopatra* (1963). Her undisputed share of the earnings is $3,000,000 (then £1,071,400) and could eventually reach $7,000,000 (now £2,692,300).

OSCARS

Most Walter (Walt) Elias Disney (1901-1966) won more "Oscars"—the awards of the United States Academy of Motion Picture Arts and Sciences, instituted on 16 May 1929 for 1927-28—than any other person. His total was 35 from 1931 to 1969. The only actress to win three Oscars in a starring rôle has been Miss Katharine Hepburn, formerly Mrs. Ludlow Ogden Smith (b. Hartford, Conn., 9 Nov. 1909) in *Morning Glory* (1932-3), *Guess Who's Coming to Dinner* (1967) and *The Lion in Winter* (1968). Oscars are named after Mr. Oscar Pierce of Texas, U.S.A. The films with most awards have been *Ben Hur* (1959) with 11, followed by *West Side Story* (1961) with 10. The film with the highest number of nominations was *All About Eve* (1950) with 14.

Newsreels The world's most durable newsreel commentator has been Bob Danvers Walker (b. Cheam, Surrey, 11 Oct. 1906), who commentated for Pathé "Gazette" from June 1940 until its demise in February 1970.

8. RADIO BROADCASTING

Origins The earliest description of a radio transmission system was written by Dr. Mahlon Loomis (U.S.A.) (b. Fulton County, N.Y., 21 July 1826) on 21 July 1864 and demonstrated between two kites more than 14 miles apart at Bear's Den, Loudoun County, Virginia in October 1866. He received U.S. patent No. 129,971 entitled Improvement in Telegraphing on 20 or 30 July 1872. He died in 1886.

Earliest patent The first patent for a system of communication by means of electro-magnetic waves, numbered No. 12039, was granted on 22 June 1896 to the Italian-Irish Marchese Guglielmo Marconi (1874-1937). A public demonstration of wireless transmission of speech was, however, given in the town square of Murray, Kentucky, U.S.A. in 1892 by Nathan B. Stubblefield. He died destitute on 28 March 1928. The first permanent wireless installation was at The

A scene from The Sound of Music which has led the world all-time box-office rankings

Needles on the Isle of Wight, Hampshire, by Marconi Wireless Telegraph Co., Ltd., in November 1896.

Earliest broadcast World The world's first advertised broadcast was made on 2 Dec. 1906 by Prof. Reginald Aubrey Fessenden (1868-1932) from the 420-foot mast of the National Electric Signalling Company at Brant Rock, Massachusetts, U.S.A. The transmission included the *Largo* by George Friedrich Händel (1685-1759) of Germany. Fessenden had achieved the broadcast of highly distorted speech as early as November 1900.

United Kingdom The first experimental broadcasting transmitter in the United Kingdom was set up at the Marconi Works in Chelmsford, Essex, in December 1919, and broadcast a news service in February 1920. The earliest regular broadcast of entertainment was made from the Marconi transmitter "2 MT" at Writtle, Essex, on 14 Feb. 1922.

Transatlantic transmissions The earliest transatlantic wireless signals (the letter S in Morse Code) were sent by Marconi from a 10-kilowatt station at Poldhu, Cornwall, and received by Percy Wright Paget and G. S. Kemp at St. John's Newfoundland, Canada, on 11 Dec. 1901. Human speech was first heard across the Atlantic in November 1915 when a transmission from the U.S. Navy station at Arlington, Virginia was received by U.S. radio-telephone engineers on the Eiffel Tower, Paris.

Most stations The country with the greatest number of radio broadcasting stations is the United States, where there were 6,980 authorized broadcast stations in 1971 of which 4,346 were AM (Amplitude modulation) and 2,634 FM (Frequency modulation).

Radio sets There were an estimated 620,000,000 radio sets in use throughout the world in 1970, equivalent to 9 for each 1,000 people. Of the U.S. total of 333 million for the end of 1970, 85,000,000 were in cars. The equivalent United Kingdom figure is not now available as sound licences were abolished on 1 Feb. 1971. The last figure was 2,074,034 for December 1970.

Longest The longest B.B.C. broadcast was the reporting of the Coronation of Queen Elizabeth II on 2 June 1953. It began at 10.15 a.m. and finished at 5.30 p.m., after 7 hours 15 minutes. This was well surpassed by Radio Station ELBC, Monrovia, on 23 Nov. 1961 when a transmission of 14 hours 20 minutes was devoted to the coverage of the Queen's visit to Liberia.

Most durable B.B.C. programmes The most durable B.B.C. radio series is *The Week's Good Cause* beginning on 24 Jan. 1926. The longest running record programme is *Desert Island Discs* which began on 29 Jan. 1942 and on which programme the only guests to be thrice stranded have been Arthur Bowden Askey, O.B.E. (b. 6 June 1900) and Robertson Hare (b. 17 Dec. 1891). The *Desert Island* programme has been presented since its inception by Roy Plomley who also devised the idea. The longest running solo radio feature is *Letter from America* by (Alfred) Alistair Cooke (b. 20 Nov. 1908), first commissioned as a series of 13 talks on 6 March 1946. The longest running comedy show has been *The Clitheroe Kid* started in 1958, which entered its 14th successive year in 1971.

Recording artists The most intensive recorded recording session was one in the B.B.C. Belfast studios in which Harry Stamper was required to record 56 character parts in 2½ days on 27 Feb.-1 Mar. 1971.

9. TELEVISION

Invention The invention of television, the instantaneous viewing of distant objects, was not an act but a process of successive and inter-dependent discoveries. The first commercial cathode ray tube was introduced in 1897 by Karl Ferdinand Braun (1850-1918), but was not linked to "electric vision" until 1907 by Boris Rosing of Russia in St. Petersburg (now Leningrad). The earliest public demonstration of television was given on 26 Jan. 1926 by John Logie Baird (1888-1946) of Scotland, using a development of the mechanical scanning system suggested by Paul Nipkov in 1884. A patent application for the Iconoscope (Number 2,141,059) had been filed on 29 Dec. 1923 by Vladimir Kosma Zworykin (born in Russia on 30 July 1889, became a U.S. citizen in 1924), and a short range transmission of a model windmill had been made on 13 June 1925 by C. Francis Jenkins in Washington, D.C., U.S.A. The first experimental transmission in Britain was on 30 Sept. 1929. Public transmissions on 30 lines were made from 22 Aug. 1932 until 11 Sept. 1935.

Earliest service The world's first high definition (*i.e.* 405 lines) television broadcasting service was opened from Alexandra Palace, London, N.22, on 2 Nov. 1936, when there were about 100 sets in the United Kingdom. The Chief Engineer was Mr. Douglas Birkinshaw. A television station in Berlin, Germany, made a low definition (180 line) transmission from 22 Mar. 1935. The transmitter burnt out in Aug. 1935.

Transatlantic transmission The earliest transatlantic transmission by satellite was achieved at 1 a.m. on 11 July 1962, *via* the active satellite *Telstar I* from Andover, Maine, U.S.A., to Pleumeur Bodou, France. The picture was of Mr. Frederick R. Kappel, chairman of the American Telephone and Telegraph Company, which owned the satellite. The first "live" broadcast was made on 23 July 1962. The earliest satellite transmission was one of 2,700 miles from California to Massachusetts, U.S.A., *via* the satellite *Echo I*, on 3 May 1962–the letters M.I.T.

Most sets In 1971 the total estimated number of television transmitters in use or under construction was 6,400 serving 270,500,000 sets (75 for each 1,000 of the world population). Of these, about 92,700,000 were estimated to be in use in the United States where 96 per cent. of the population is reached. The number of colour sets in the U.S.A. has grown from 200,000 in 1960 to 31,300,000 by January 1971. The number of licences current in the United Kingdom was 16,672,000 on 1 Feb. 1972 of which 1,527,000 were for colour sets.

Greatest audience The greatest number of viewers for a televised event is an estimated 600,000,000 for the live and recorded transmissions of man's first lunar landing with the *Apollo XI* mission on 20-21 July 1969. This total was reportedly matched by the viewership of the landing of the nearly disastrous *Apollo XIII* space mission on 17 April 1970.

Largest T.V. prizes World The greatest amount won by an individual in T.V. prizes was $264,000 (then £94,286) by Teddy Nadler on quiz programmes in the United States up to September 1958. In March 1960 he failed a test to become a census enumerator because of his inability to distinguish between east and west. His comment was, reportedly, "Those maps threw me". In Australia, where T.V. prizes were not subject to income tax, the most successful contestant has been Barry O. Jones, a schoolteacher of Windsor, Victoria, who won $A52,620 (then £21,012 sterling) between June 1960 and June 1966.

United Kingdom The largest T.V. prize won in the U.K. is £5,580 by Bernard Davis, aged 33, on Granada T.V.'s "Twenty-one" quiz programme, reached on 24 Sept. 1958.

Most successful appeal The greatest amount raised by any B.B.C. T.V. or Radio Appeal was £1,500,000, raised as a result of an appeal by Richard Samuel Attenborough, C.B.E. (b. Cambridge, 29 Aug. 1923) on behalf of the fund for the East Pakistan Cyclone Disaster of 12-13 Nov. 1970.

LARGEST CONTRACTS

World The largest T.V. contract ever signed was one for $34,000,000 (£14,166,666) in a three-year no-option contract between Dino Paul Crocetti (b. 7 June 1917) otherwise Dean Martin, and N.B.C.

Dean Martin was acclaimed in September 1968 as the top-earning show-business personality of all-time with $5,000,000 (over £2 million) in a year. Television's highest-paid interviewer has been Garry Moore (b. Thomas Garrison Morfit on 31 Jan. 1915), who was earning $43,000 (£15,357) a week in 1963, equivalent to $2,236,000 (nearly £800,000) per year.

United Kingdom The largest contract in British television was one of a reported £9,000,000, inclusive of production expenses, signed by Tom Jones (b. Thomas Jones Woodward, 7 June 1940) of Treforest, Glamorgan, Wales in June 1968 with ABC-TV of the United States and ATV in London for 17 one-hour shows per annum from January 1969 to January 1974.

Hourly The world's highest paid television performer based on an hourly rate is Perry Como (b. Pierino Como, Canonsburg, Pennsylvania, U.S.A., on 18 May 1912) who began as a barber. In May 1969 he signed a contract with N.B.C. to star in four one-hour video specials at $5,000,000 (£2,083,333) or at the rate of £8,680.55 per minute. The contract requires him to provide supporting artistes.

Longest telecast The longest pre-scheduled telecast on record was a non-stop transmission of *The Forsyte Saga* lasting 23 hours 50 mins. on the U.S. station XYZ in November 1971.

Most durable B.B.C. programme The longest running T.V. programme on B.B.C. is *Panorama* which was first transmitted, first introduced by Patrick Murphy, on 11 Nov. 1953. The News has been featured since 23 March 1938.

Earliest T.V. critic The first man in the world appointed to be a T.V. critic and correspondent was Leonard Marsland Gander (b. 27 June 1902) by the London *Daily Telegraph* in 1935–the year before the B.B.C.'s 405 line transmissions. He retired in July 1970 after spanning 35 years with T.V. and 44 years with radio.

Biggest sale The greatest number of episodes of any T.V. programme ever sold has been 1,144 episodes of "Coronation Street" by Granada Television to CBKST Saskatoon, Saskatchewan, Canada on 31 May 1971. This constituted 22 days 5 hours continuous viewing.

7 THE WORLD'S STRUCTURES

EARLIEST STRUCTURES

World The earliest known human structure is a rough circle of loosely piled lava blocks found in 1960 on the lowest cultural level at the Lower Palaeolithic site at Olduvai Gorge in Tanganyika (now part of Tanzania). The structure was associated with artifacts and bones and may represent a work-floor, dating to *circa* 1,750,000 B.C. (see Chapter 1, Earliest Man). The earliest evidence of *buildings* yet discovered is that ot 21 huts with hearths or pebble-lined pits and delimited by stake holes found in October 1965 at the Terra Amata site in Nice, France originally dated to 300,000 B.C. but now thought to be more likely belonging to the Acheulian culture of 120,000 years ago. Excavation carried out between 28 June and 5 July 1966 revealed one hut with palisaded walls with axes of 49 feet and 20 feet.

United Kingdom A rudimentary platform of birch branches, stones and wads of clay thrown down on the edge of a swamp at Star Carr, south of Scarborough, Yorkshire, may possibly represent the earliest man-made "dwelling" yet found in Britain (Mesolithic, *circa* 7650 B.C.). Remains of the earliest dated stone shelter and cooking pit were discovered in 1967 on the Isle of Portland, Dorset (Mesolithic, *c.* 5200 B.C.). The rock shelter on Oldbury Hill, ¾ of a mile south-west of Ightham, Kent, is believed to have been occupied by the Mousterian people before the onset of the La Glaciation of the Ice Age, *c.* 80,000 B.C.

Ireland The carbon dating of the earliest known house Ireland at Ballynagilly, County Tyrone was annou ced in 1970 to be 3675 B.C. ± 50. It is made of woo

1. BUILDINGS FOR WORKING

LARGEST BUILDINGS

Manufacturing The largest ground area covered by any building in t world is the main assembly building at the Boei Company's works at Everett, Washington Sta U.S.A. It encloses a floor area of 1,565,000 squa feet (36.0 acres). Construction was begun in Augu 1966 and parts were in use by late 1967. The buildi constructed for the manufacture of Boeing 747 j airliners, has a maximum height of 115 feet and ha capacity of 200 million cubic feet.

Scientific The most capacious scientific building in the world the Vehicle Assembly Building (VAB) at Complex 3 the selected site for the final assembly and launchi of the Apollo moon spacecraft on the Saturn rocket, at the John F. Kennedy Space Center (KS on Merritt Island, near Cape Kennedy (formerly Ca Canaveral), Florida, U.S.A. It is a steel-fram building measuring 716 feet in length, 518 feet width and 525 feet high. The building contains fo bays, each with its own door 460 feet high. Constru tion began in April 1963 by the Ursum Consortiu Its floor area is 343,500 square feet (7.87 acres) a its capacity is 129,482,000 cubic feet. The buildi was "topped out" on 14 April 1965 at a cost $108,700,000 (£45.3 million).

Administrative The largest ground area covered by any offi building is that of the Pentagon, in Arlington Coun Virginia, U.S.A. Built to house the U.S. Defer Department's offices, it was completed on 15 Ja 1943 and cost an estimated $83,000,000 (nc £34,583,000). Each of the outermost sides of t Pentagon is 921 feet long and the perimeter of t building is about 1,500 yards. The five storeys of t building enclose a floor area of 6,500,000 square fe During the day 29,000 people work in the buildi The telephone system of the building has over 44,0 telephones connected by 160,000 miles of cable a its 220 staff handle 280,000 calls a day. T

The Terra Amata site at Nice, France, where the earliest known buildings were found in 1966

Buildings for Working

restaurants, six cafeterias and ten snackbars and a staff of 675 form the catering department of the building. The corridors measure 17 miles in length and there are 7,748 windows to be cleaned.

Commercial The largest commercial or office buildings in the world are The World Trade Center in New York City, U.S.A. with a total of 9,000,000 square feet (206.6 acres) of rentable space.

Single office
Largest in U.K. The largest single office in the United Kingdom is that of the West Midlands Gas Board at Solihull, Warwickshire, built by Spooners (Hull) Ltd. in 1962. It now measures 753 feet by 160 feet (2.77 acres) in one open plan room accommodating 2,170 clerical and managerial workers.

TALLEST BUILDINGS
World The tallest inhabited building in the world is the Port of New York Authority's World Trade Center with twin towers of 110 storeys, standing 1,353 feet tall. Work started in August 1966 on Barclay and Liberty Streets, Lower West Side, Manhattan Island, New York City, N.Y., U.S.A. and the North Tower was topped out on 14 Dec. 1970, having surpassed the Empire State Building on 21 Oct. 1970. The total cost is estimated at $650,000,000 (£270.8 million). A 365-foot antenna tower will bring the total height of the North Tower to 1,718 feet. Completion will be in 1973. Each tower will have 21,800 windows and 104 elevators. The World Trade Center will be overtopped by the Sears Tower, the national headquarters of Sears Roebuck & Co. in Wacker Drive, Chicago, Illinois. It will have 109 storeys, rising to 1,451 feet and be due for completion in 1974. Its gross area will be 4,400,000 square feet (101.0 acres).

The maximum sway allowed for in a 150 m.p.h. hurricane would be 11 inches.

Most storeys The World Trade Center (see above) has 110 storeys—eight more than the Empire State Building. The projects for the 1,300-foot Schaumburg Planet Corporation Building with a 250-foot antenna and the 1,610-foot Barrington Space Needle, Barrington, Illinois, call for 113 and 120 storeys respectively.

United Kingdom The tallest office block in Britain is The National Westminster tower block in Bishopsgate, City of London due to be topped out in 1972, it will be 600 feet above street level.

HABITATIONS
Greatest altitude The highest inhabited buildings in the world are those in the Chilean sulphur-mining village of Aucanquilca, at an altitude of 17,500 feet above Amincha (see also Chapter 11). During the 1960-61 Himalayan High Altitude Expedition, the "silver hut", a prefabricated laboratory, was inhabited for four months in the Ming Bo Valley at 18,765 feet. In April 1961, however, a 3-room dwelling was discovered at 21,650 feet on Cerro Llullaillaco (22,058 feet), on the Argentine-Chile border, believed to date from the late pre-Columbian period c. 1480.

Northernmost The most northerly habitation in the world is the Danish scientific station set up in 1952 in Pearyland, northern Greenland, over 900 miles north of the Arctic Circle. Eskimo hearths dated to before 1,000 B.C. were discovered in Pearyland in 1969. The U.S.S.R. and the United States have maintained research stations on ice floes in the Arctic. The U.S.S.R.'s "North Pole 15" which drifted 1,250 miles passed within 1¼ miles of the North Pole in December 1967.

Southernmost The most southerly permanent human habitation is the United States' Scott-Amundsen I.G.Y. (International Geophysical Year) base 800 yards from the South Pole.

The world's tallest inhabited building with 110 storeys, standing 1,353 feet tall—the twin towers of the World Trade Center, Manhattan, New York City

EMBASSIES
Largest The largest embassy in the world is the U.S.S.R. embassy on Bei Xiao Jie, Peking, China, in the north-eastern corner of the Northern walled city. The whole 45-acre area of the old Orthodox Church mission (established 1728), now known as the *Bei guan,* was handed over to the U.S.S.R. in 1949. The largest in Great Britain is the United States of America Embassy in Grosvenor Square, London. The Chancery Building, completed in 1960, alone has 600 rooms for a staff of 700, on seven floors with a usable floor area of 255,000 square feet (5.85 acres).

PLANTS
Atomic The largest atomic plant in the world is the Savannah River Project, near Aiken, South Carolina, U.S.A., extending 27 miles along the river and over a total area of 315 square miles. The plant, comprising 280 permanent buildings, cost $1,400 million (£583 million). Construction was started in February 1951 and by September 1952 the labour force had reached 38,500. The present operating strength is 8,500.

Underground The world's largest underground factory was the Mittelwerk Factory, near Nordhausen in the Kohnstein Hills, south of the Harz Mountains, Germany. It was built with concentration camp labour during World War II and had a floor area of 1,270,000 square feet and an output of 900 V-2 rockets per month.

Tallest chimneys The world's tallest chimney is the $5.5 million International Nickel Company's stack 1,250 feet 9 inches tall at Copper Cliff, Sudbury, Ontario, Canada, completed in 1970. It was built by The M. W. Kellogg Company and the diameter tapers from 116.4 feet at the base to 51.8 feet at the top. It weighs 38,390 tons and became operational in 1971. The tallest chimney in Great Britain is one of 850 feet at Drax Power Station, Yorkshire, begun in 1966 and topped out on 16 May 1969. It was built by Holst & Co. Ltd. of Watford, Hertfordshire.

Cooling towers The largest cooling towers in the United Kingdom are the Ferrybridge "C" power station, Yorkshire, type measuring 375 feet tall and 300 feet across the base. Each of the first 24 of the eventual 38 of this type throughout the country cost £340,000.

105

LARGEST HANGARS

World The world's largest hangar is the Goodyear Airship hangar at Akron, Ohio, U.S.A. which measures 1,175 feet long, 325 feet wide and 200 feet high. It covers 364,000 square feet (8.35 acres) and has a capacity of 55,000,000 cubic feet. The world's largest single fixed-wing aircraft hangar is the Lockheed-Georgia engineering test center at Marietta, Georgia measuring 630 feet by 480 feet (6.94 acres) completed in 1967.

The largest group of hangars in the world is at the U.S. Air Force Base near San Antonio, Texas, U.S.A. These, including covered maintenance bays, cover 23 acres.

United Kingdom The largest hangar building in the United Kingdom is the Britannia Assembly Hall at the Bristol Aeroplane Company's works at Filton, Bristol. The overall width of the Hall is 1,054 feet and the overall depth of the centre bay is 420 feet. It encloses a floor area of 7½ acres. The cubic capacity of the Hall is 33,000,000 cubic feet. The building was begun in April 1946 and completed by September 1949.

Largest Fair Hall The largest fair hall in the world is that in Hanover, West Germany completed on 1 Apr. 1970 at a cost of 55 million DMk (£6½ million) with dimensions of 1,180 feet by 885 feet and a floor area of 877,500 square feet.

GRAIN ELEVATOR

The world's largest single-unit grain elevator is that operated by the C-G-F-Grain Company at Wichita, Kansas, U.S.A. Consisting of a triple row of storage tanks, 123 on each side of the central loading tower or "head house", the unit is 2,717 feet long and 100 feet wide. Each tank is 120 feet high, with an inside diameter of 30 feet, giving a total storage capacity of 20,000,000 bushels of wheat. The largest collection of elevators in the world is at Thunder Bay, Ontario, Canada, on Lake Superior with a total capacity of 3,300 million bushels.

GARAGES

Largest The largest garage in Britain is that completed in September 1961 for the Austin Motor Works at Longbridge, near Birmingham. It has nine storeys and cost £500,000. It has a capacity of 3,300 cars. The United Kingdom's largest underground garage is Normand Ltd.'s Park Lane Garage, London, W.1, extending over nearly seven acres, 350 yards long by 96 yards wide with a capacity of 1,100 cars. It was opened on 15 Oct. 1962 at a cost of £1,051,915. The

Britain's largest motorway service area at Leigh Delamere on the M.4 near Chippenham, Wiltshire

air can be changed six times per hour. The Ea corridor to Marble Arch tube station is 534 yards, more than three-tenths of a mile, long.

Private The largest private garage ever built was one for 1(cars at the Long Island, New York mansion of Willia Kissam Vanderbilt (1849-1920).

Filling station The largest filling station of 36,000 in the Unit Kingdom is the Esso service area on the M4 at Lei Delamere, Wiltshire, opened on 3 Jan. 1972. It has petrol and diesel pumps and extends over 43 acres. cost £650,000 has a staff of 280 and can service million vehicles a year.

SEWAGE WORKS

Largest World The largest single full treatment sewage works in th world is the West-Southwest Treatment Plant, open in 1940 on a site of 501 acres in Chicago, Illino U.S.A. It serves an area containing 2,940,000 peop It treated an average of 685,000,000 gallons of wast per day in 1971. The capacity of its sedimentatic and aeration tanks is 1,125,000 cubic metres.

United Kingdom The largest full treatment works in Britain a probably in Europe are the G.L.C. Crossness Pla with a tank capacity of 338,000 cubic metres, resident population of 1,600,000 and an average dai flow of 103 million Imperial gallons. This will overtaken in Sept. 1973 by the G.L.C. Beckton Wor which when extended will serve a 2,966,000 popu tion and handle a daily flow of 207 million gallons i tank capacity of 757,000 cubic feet.

WAREHOUSES

Largest World The world's largest warehouse is the Eurostore, bu by the Garoner warehousing firm on a 240-acre si near Le Bourget, in north-east Paris, France. T building provides 5,400,000 square feet (124 acre of floor-space.

United Kingdom The largest in the United Kingdom is the tobac warehouse at Stanley Dock, Liverpool, with storeys giving a total floor space of 36 acres, and frontage of 625 feet.

Glasshouse The largest glasshouse in the United Kingdom is o 826 feet long and 348 feet wide, covering 6.5 acres Brough, East Yorkshire, completed in 1971. A to of 420 tons of glass was used in glazing it.

2. BUILDINGS FOR LIVING

WOODEN BUILDINGS

Oldest The oldest wooden building in the world is t Temple of Horyu (Horyu-ji), built at Nara, Japan, A.D. 708-715. The largest wooden building in t world, the nearby Daibutsuden, built in 1704-1 measures 285.4 feet long, 167.3 feet wide and 153 feet tall.

Largest The municipal building occupied by the Departme of Education in Wellington, New Zealand built 1876 has the largest floor area of any wood building with 101,300 square feet.

CASTLES

Earliest World Castles in the sense of unfortified manor hous existed in all the great early civilizations, includi that of ancient Egypt from 3,000 B.C. Fortifi castles in the more accepted sense only existed mu later. The oldest in the world is that at Gomdan, in t Yemen, which originally had 20 storeys and dat from before A.D. 100.

British Isles The oldest stone castle extant in Great Britain Richmond Castle, Yorkshire, built in c. 1075. Ir Age relics from the first century B.C. or A.D. ha been found in the lower levels of the Dover Castle sit

Buildings for Living

Ireland The oldest Irish castle is Ferrycarrig near Wexford dating from *c.* 1180. The oldest castle in Northern Ireland is Carrickfergus Castle, County Antrim, which dates from before 1210.

Largest The largest ancient castle in the world is the Qila
World (Citadel) at Halab (Aleppo) in Syria. It is oval in shape and has a surrounding wall 1,230 feet long and 777 feet wide. It dates, in its present form, from the Humanid dynasty of the 10th century A.D Fort George, Ardersier, Inverness-shire, built in 1748-1769 measures 2,100 feet in length and has an average width of 620 feet. The total site covers 42½ acres.

Thickest The most massive keep in the world was that
walls belonging to the 13th-century château at Coucy-le-Château-Auffrique, in the Department of L'Aisne, France. It was 177 feet high, 318 feet in circumference and had walls over 22½ feet in thickness. It was levelled to its foundations by the Germans in 1917. The walls of Babylon north of Al Hillah, Iraq, built in 600 B.C., were up to 85 feet in thickness. The walls of part of Dover Castle, Kent, measure 20 feet in thickness. The largest Norman keep in Britain is that of Colchester Castle measuring 152½ feet by 111½ feet.

United The largest castle in the British Isles and the largest
Kingdom inhabited castle in the world is the Royal residence of
and Ireland Windsor Castle at New Windsor, Berkshire. It is primarily of 12th century construction and is in the form of a parallelogram 1,890 feet by 540 feet. The overall dimensions of Carisbrooke Castle (450 feet by 360 feet), Isle of Wight, if its earthworks are included, are 1,350 feet by 825 feet. The largest castle in Scotland was the unfinished Doune Castle, Perthshire, built *c.* 1425. The most capacious of all Irish castles is Carrickfergus (see above) in Antrim but that with the most extensive fortifications is Trim Castle, County Meath, built in *c.* 1205 with a curtain wall 485 yards long.

PALACES

Largest The largest palace in the world is the Imperial Palace
World (*Gu gong*) in the centre of Peking (*Bei jing*, the northern capital), China, which covers a rectangle 1,050 yards by 820 yards, an area of 177.9 acres. The outline survives from the construction of the third Ming emperor Yong le of 1307-20, but due to constant re-arrangements most of the intra-mural buildings are 18th century. These consist of 5 halls and 17 palaces of which the last occupied by the last Empress was the Palace of Accumulated Elegance (*Chu xia gong*) until 1924.

Residential The largest residential palace in the world is the Vatican Palace, in the Vatican City, an enclave in Rome, Italy. Covering an area of 13½ acres, it has 1,400 rooms, chapels and halls, of which the oldest date from the 15th century.

United The largest palace in the United Kingdom in Royal
Kingdom use is Buckingham Palace, London, so named after its site, bought in 1703 by John Sheffield, the 1st Duke of Buckingham and Normanby (1648-1721). Buckingham House was reconstructed in the Palladian style between 1835 and 1836, following the design of John Nash (1752-1835). The 610-foot-long East Front was built in 1846 and refaced in 1912. The Palace, which stands in 39 acres of garden, has 600 rooms including a ballroom 111 feet long.

The largest ever Royal palace has been Hampton Court Palace, Greater London, acquired by Henry VIII from Cardinal Wolsey in 1525 and greatly enlarged by the King and later by William III, Anne and George I, whose son George II was its last resident monarch. It covers 4 acres of a 669 acre site.

Largest moat The world's largest moats are those which surround the Imperial Palace in Peking (see above). From plans

Colchester Castle. It has the largest Norman keep in Britain

drawn by French sources it appears to measure 54 yards wide and have a total length of 3,600 yards.

Throne The oldest Throne Room in existence is in the
rooms restored Bronze Age palace of Knossos, Crete dating to the Middle Minoan III or Late Minoan I phase of the Great Palaces (*c.* 1500 B.C.).

FLATS

Largest The largest block of flats in Britain is Dolphin Square, London, covering a site of 7½ acres. The building occupies the four sides of a square enclosing gardens of about three acres. Dolphin Square contains 1,220 separate and self-contained flats, an underground garage for 300 cars with filling and service station, a swimming pool, eight squash courts, a tennis court and an indoor shopping centre. It cost £1,750,000 to build in 1936 but was sold to Westminster City Council for £4,500,000 in January 1963. Its nine storeys house 3,000 people.

The Hyde Park development in Sheffield, Yorkshire, comprises 1,322 dwellings and an estimated population of 4,675 persons. It was built between 1959 and 1966.

Tallest The tallest block of flats in the world are Lake Point
World Towers of 70 storeys, and 645 feet in Chicago, Illinois, U.S.A.

Britain The tallest residential blocks in the United Kingdom are the two tower blocks in the Barbican in the City of London, E.C.2, which have between 39 and 41 levels of flats and rise to a height of 417 feet above the street. The first tower was topped out in May 1971.

HOTELS

Largest The world's largest hotel is the Hotel Rossiya in
World Moscow, U.S.S.R., with 3,200 rooms providing accommodation for 6,000 guests, in three buildings, each of 14 storeys completed in December 1967. The largest hotel in a single building is the Conrad Hilton (formerly the Stevens) on Michigan Avenue, Chicago, Illinois, U.S.A. Its 25 floors contain 2,600 (originally 3,000) guest rooms. It would thus take more than seven years to spend one night in each room of the hotel. The hotel employs about 2,000 people, of whom more than 70 are telephone operators and supervisors, and 72 are lift operators. The laundry of the hotel, with 195 employees, handles 535 tons of flat work each month.

The largest hotel building in the world, on the basis of volume, is the Waldorf Astoria, on Park Avenue, New York City, N.Y., U.S.A. It occupies a complete block of 81,337 square feet (1.87 acres) and reaches a maximum height of 625 feet 7 inches. The Waldorf Astoria has 47 storeys and 1,900 guest rooms and maintains the largest hotel radio receiving system in the world. The Waldorf can accommodate 10,000 people at one time and has a staff of 1,700. The restaurants have catered for parties up to 6,000 at a time. The coffee-makers' daily output reaches 1,000 gallons. The electricity bill is about $360,000 (£150,000) each year.

United Kingdom The greatest capacity of any hotel in the United Kingdom is that of the Regent Palace Hotel, Piccadilly Circus, London (opened on 20 May 1915). It has 1,140 rooms accommodating 1,670 guests. The total staff numbers 1,200. The largest hotel is the Grosvenor House Hotel, Park Lane, London, which was opened in 1929. It is of 8 storeys covering 2½ acres and caters for more than 100,000 visitors per year in 470 rooms. The Great Room is the largest hotel room in Great Britain measuring 181 feet by 131 feet with a height of 23 feet. Banquets for 1,500 are frequently handled.

Tallest The world's tallest hotel is the 34-storey Ukrania in Moscow, U.S.S.R., which, including its tower, is 650 feet tall. The highest hotel rooms in the world are those on the topmost 50th storey of the 509-foot-tall Americana Hotel, opened on 24 Sept. 1962 on 7th Avenue at 52nd Street, New York City, N.Y., U.S.A. Britain's tallest hotel is the 33-storey London Hilton (328 feet tall), completed in Park Lane, London, W.1, in 1962. It was opened on 17 April, 1963.

Most expensive The world's costliest hotel is the Mauna Kea Beach Hotel on Hawaii Island, U.S.A., which was built at a cost of $15,000,000 (£6,250,000) and has only 154 rooms. This implies a construction and amenity cost of more than £40,600 per room.

Daily Charge The Presidential Suite (8 rooms) in the New York Hilton cost $500 (then £178.50) in 1963. The most expensive hotel suites in Britain are the luxury suites in the London Hilton, Park Lane, London, W.1. Some suites are 90 guineas (£94.50) per night in 1972.

SPAS
The largest spa in the world measured by number of available hotel rooms is Vichy, Allier, France, with 14,000 rooms. Spas are named after the watering place in the Liège province of Belgium where hydropathy was developed from 1626. The highest French spa is Baréges, Hautes-Pyrénées, at 4,068 feet above sea level.

HOUSING
Largest estate The largest housing estate in the United Kingdom is the 1,670-acre Becontree Estate, on a site of 3,000 acres in Barking and Redbridge, Greater London, built between 1921 and 1929. The total number of homes is 26,822, with an estimated population of nearly 90,000.

New towns Of the 23 new towns being built in Great Britain that with the largest eventual planned population will be Milton Keynes, Buckinghamshire, with 250,000 by 1992.

Largest house World The largest private house in the world is the 250-room Biltmore House in Asheville, North Carolina, U.S.A. It is owned by George and William Cecil, grandsons of George Washington Vanderbilt II (1862-1914). The house was built between 1890 and 1895 in an estate of 119,000 acres, at a cost of $4,100,000 (now £1,708,333) and now valued at $55,000,000 with 12,000 acres. The most expensive private house ever built is La Cuesta Encunada at San Simeon, California, U.S.A. It was built in 1922-39 for William Randolph Hearst (1863-1951), at a total cost of more than $30,000,000 (then £6,120,000). It has more than 100 rooms, a 104-foot-long heated swimming pool, an 83-foot-long assembly hall and a garage for 25 limousines. The house required 60 servants to maintain it.

United Kingdom The largest house in the United Kingdom is Wentworth Woodhouse, near Rotherham, Yorkshire, for-

A row of houses which cost £138 each at Longridge, Lancashire

merly the seat of the Earls Fitzwilliam. The main pa of the house, built over 300 years ago, has more th 240 rooms with over 1,000 windows, and its princi facade is 600 feet long. The Royal residence, Sar ringham House, Norfolk, has been reported to ha 365 rooms. The largest house in Ireland is Castleto in County Kildare, formerly owned by Lord Care Scotland's largest house is Hopetoun House, W Lothian, built between 1696 and 1756 with a w facade 675 feet long.

Stately home most visited The most visited stately home in the United Kingd is Beaulieu, Hampshire, owned by Lord Montagu Beaulieu with 503,380 visitors in 1971. The figu for Woburn Abbey, Bedfordshire, owned by the Du of Bedford, have not been published since 1963 b reached 470,000 as early as 1961.

Smallest The smallest house in Britain is the 19th-centu fisherman's cottage on Conway Quay, Caernarve shire, North Wales. It has a 72-inch frontage, is 1 inches high and has two tiny rooms and a staircase.

Most expensive The most expensive private house in Britain Ramsbury Manor, Wiltshire, which was bought by American property dealer as a residence for a pri including the 460-acre grounds, of reporte £650,000 in May 1965. The house itself, which da from c. 1660, cost £275,000.

Cheapest housing The cheapest housing in Britain and the old building society property consists of Nos. 4 to Higher Road, Longridge, Lancashire built w pooled money and labour by a group of quarrymer a cost of £138 3s. 6d. each in the 1790's.

3. BUILDINGS FOR ENTERTAINMENT

STADIUMS
Largest World The world's largest stadium is the Strahov Stadium Praha (Prague), Czechoslovakia. It was completed 1934 and can accommodate 240,000 spectators mass displays of up to 40,000 Sokol gymnasts.

Football The largest football stadium in the world is t Maracaña Municipal Stadium in Rio de Janei Brazil, where the football ground has a norm capacity of 205,000, of whom 155,000 may seated. A crowd of 199,854 was accommodated the World Cup final between Brazil and Uruguay 16 July 1950. A dry moat, 7 feet wide and over 5 fo deep, protects players from spectators and vice ver Britain's most capacious football stadium is Hampd Park, Glasgow opened on 31 Oct. 1903 and on surveyed to accommodate 184,000 compared w the present licensed limit of 135,000 (see also belo

Covered The largest covered stadium in the world is Empire Stadium, Wembley, London, opened in Ap 1923. It was the scene of the 1948 Olympic Gam and the final of the 1966 World Cup. In 1962-63

capacity under cover was increased to 100,000, of whom 45,000 may be seated. The original cost was £1,250,000. The Azteca Stadium, Mexico City, Mexico, opened in 1968, has a capacity of 107,000 of whom nearly all are under cover.

Roofed The transparent acryl glass "tent" roof over the Munich Olympic Stadium, West Germany measures 914,940 square feet (21.0 acres) in area resting on a steel net supported by masts.

Indoor The world's largest completed indoor stadium is the Harris County Sports Stadium, or Astrodome, in Houston, Texas, U.S.A. opened in April 1965. It has a capacity of 45,000 for baseball and 66,000 (maximum) for boxing. The domed stadium covers 9½ acres and is so large that an 18-storey building could be built under the roof (208 feet high). The total cost was $38,000,000 (£15,830,000). The architects of the $150 million Superdome due to be completed in New Orleans, Louisiana by mid-1974 say that the Astrodome could fit comfortably inside it. Its capacity will be 103,402. The dome will rise 280 feet.

United Kingdom The highest capacity stadium in the United Kingdom is that at Hampden Park, Glasgow, which accommodated a football crowd of 149,547 on 17 April 1937.

Largest ballroom The largest ballroom in the United Kingdom is the Orchid Ballroom, Purley, Surrey. The room is over 200 feet long and 117 feet wide, and has a total floor area of 23,320 square feet. When laid out for dance championships, the floor of the Earl's Court Exhibition Hall is 256 feet in length. The Empress Ballroom, Blackpool, Lancashire, when used for dances, can accommodate 4,500 couples.

Amusement resort The world's largest amusement resort is Disney World in 27,443 acres of Orange and Osceola counties, near Orlando in central Florida. It was opened on 23 Oct. 1971.

Holiday Camps The largest of the 8 major holiday camps in Britain is that at Filey, Yorkshire opened by Butlins Ltd. It extends over 500 acres and can house 11,000 residents.

Miniature Village The largest miniature village in the world is Legoland on a 8¼ acre site at Billund, Denmark opened in June 1968 and now attended by 750,000 visitors a year. It is built of 9 million Lego bricks and has 30,000 lights at night.

RESTAURANTS
Highest The highest restaurant in Great Britain is the Ptarmigan Observation Restaurant at 3,650 feet above sea-level on Cairngorm (4,084 feet) near Aviemore, Inverness-shire, Scotland.

NIGHT CLUBS
Oldest The oldest night club (*boîte de nuit*) is "Le Bal des Anglais" at 6 Rue des Anglais, Paris 5*me*, France. It was founded in 1843.

Largest The largest night club in the world is that in the Imperial Room of the Concord Hotel in the Catskill Mountains, New York State, U.S.A., with a capacity of 3,000 patrons. In the more classical sense the largest night club in the world is "The Mikado" in the Akasaka district of Tōkyō, Japan, with a seating capacity of 2,000. It is "manned" by 1,250 hostesses, some of whom earn an estimated £4,800 per annum. Long sight is essential to an appreciation of the floor show.

Loftiest The highest night club will be that on the 52nd storey of the Antigone Building, now under construction, in Montparnasse, Paris, at 187 metres (613.5 feet) above street level.

An artist's impression of the world's largest dome—the Louisiana Superdome now being built in New Orleans, U.S.A. The Astrodome at Houston, Texas would fit comfortably inside it.

Lowest The lowest night club is the "Minus 206" in Tiberias, Israel, on the shores of the Sea of Galilee. It is 206 metres (676 feet) below sea-level. An alternative candidate is "Outer Limits", opposite the Cow Palace, San Francisco, California which was raided for the 151st time on 1 Aug. 1971. It has been called both "The Most Busted Joint" and "The Slowest to Get the Message".

PLEASURE BEACH
Largest The largest pleasure beach in the world is Virginia Beach, Virginia, U.S.A. It has 28 miles of beach front on the Atlantic and 10 miles of estuary frontage. The area embraces 255 square miles and 134 hotels and motels.

Longest pleasure pier The longest pleasure pier in the world is Southend Pier at Southend-on-Sea in Essex. It is 1.33 miles in length. It was built in 1889, with final extensions made in 1929. It is decorated with more than 75,000 lamps.

FAIRS
Earliest The earliest major international fair was the Great Exhibition of 1851 in the Crystal Palace, Hyde Park, London which in 141 days attracted 6,039,195 admissions.

Largest The largest fair ever held was the New York World's Fair, covering 1,216½ acres of Flushing Meadow Park, Queens Borough, Long Island, New York, U.S.A. The fair was open at times between 20 April 1939 and 21 Oct. 1940 and there were 25,817,265 admissions and an attendance of 51,607,037 for the 1964-65 Fair there.

Record attendance The record attendance for any fair was 65,000,000 for Expo 70 held on an 815-acre site at Osaka, Japan from March to 13 Sept. 1970. It made a profit of more than £11,000,000.

Big Wheel The original Ferris Wheel, named after its constructor, George W. Ferris (1859-96), was erected in 1893 at the Midway, Chicago, Illinois, U.S.A., at a cost of $300,000 (now £125,000). The wheel was 250 feet in diameter, 790 feet in circumference, weighed 1,070 tons, and carried 36 cars each seating 40 people, making a total of 1,440 passengers. The structure was removed in 1904 to St. Louis, Missouri, and was eventually sold as scrap for $1,800 (now £750). In 1897 a Ferris Wheel with a diameter of 300 feet was erected for the Earls Court Exhibition, London. It had ten 1st-class and 30 2nd-class cars. The largest wheel now operating is the Riesenrad in the Prater Park, Vienna, Austria with a diameter of 197 feet. It was built by the British engineer Walter Basset in 1896 and carried 15 million people in its first 75 years.

Fastest switchback The world's fastest gravity switchback has been the "Bobs" in the Belle Vue Amusement Park, Manchester, Lancashire. The cars attained a peak speed of 61

109

m.p.h. The track was 862 yards 2 inches long with a maximum height of 76 feet. It had been imported from the U.S.A. in 1929.

PUBLIC HOUSES

Largest
World
The largest beer-selling establishment in the world is the Mathäser, Bayerstrasse 5, München (Munich), West Germany, where the daily sale reaches 84,470 pints. It was established in 1829, was demolished in World War II and re-built by 1955 and now seats 5,500 people. The through-put at the Dube beer halls in the Bantu township of Soweto, Johannesburg, South Africa may, however, be higher on some Saturdays when the average consumption of 6,000 gallons (48,000 pints) is far exceeded.

United Kingdom
The largest public house in the United Kingdom is The Swan at Yardley, Birmingham. It has eight bars with a total drinking area of 13,852 square feet. The sale of beer is equivalent to 31,000 bottles per week. The pub can hold well over 1,000 customers and 320 for banqueting. The permanent staff totals 60 with seven resident. The Swan is owned by Allied Breweries and administered by Ansells Limited.

Smallest
The smallest pub in the United Kingdom is "The Smith's Arms" in Godmanstone, Dorset, which is only 10 feet wide and 4 feet high at the eaves. It has a licence granted personally by Charles II (reigned 1660-85).

Highest
The highest public house in the United Kingdom is the Tan Hill Inn in Yorkshire. It is 1,732 feet above sea-level, on the moorland road between Reeth in Yorkshire and Brough in Westmorland. The White Lady Restaurant, 2,550 feet up on Cairngorm (4,084 feet) near Aviemore, Inverness-shire, Scotland, is the highest licensed restaurant.

Oldest
There are various claimants to the title of the United Kingdom's oldest inn. The foremost claimants include "The Angel and Royal" (*c.* 1450) at Grantham, Lincolnshire, which has cellar masonry dated 1213; the "George" (early 15th century) at Norton St. Philip, Somerset; "The George and Vulture" off Lombard Street, in the City of London, first mentioned in 1175; the oldest inn in Wales the Skirrid Mountain Inn, Llanvihangel Crucorney, Monmouthshire recorded in 1110; and "The Trip to Jerusalem" in Nottingham, with foundations believed to date back to 1070. An origin as early as A.D. 560 has been claimed for Ye Olde Ferry Boat Inn at Holywell, Huntingdonshire. There is some evidence that it ante-dates the local church, built in 980, but the earliest documents are not dated earlier than 1100. There is evidence that the Bingley Arms, Bardsey, near Leeds, Yorkshire, restored and extended in 1738, existed as the Priest's Inn according to Bardsey Church records dated 905.

Longest name
The English pub with the longest name was the 39 letter "The Thirteenth Mounted Cheshire Rifleman Inn" at Stalybridge, Cheshire. The word "Mounted" is now omitted making "The London, Chatham and Dover Railway Tavern" (37 letters), the champion. The man who visited most pubs with *varied* names in Britain is Mr. Stanley House, whose total is over 1,800.

Shortest name
There are two public houses in the United Kingdom with a name of only two letters: the "C.B." Hotel, Arkengarthdale, near Richmond, Yorkshire and the "M.C." Bar in Hawkhill, Dundee reopened by the University Medical Society in 1972.

Commonest name
The commonest pub name in Britain is "Crown", often coupled with the Rose, of which there are some 1,099 examples—169 more than the total of "Red Lions."

The pub with the longest name The London Chatham and Dover Railway Tavern in Cabul Road, London S.W.11.

Longest bars
World
The longest permanent bar with beer pumps is that built in 1938 at the Working Men's Club, Mildura, Victoria, Australia. It has a counter 287 feet in length served by 32 pumps. Temporary bars have been erected of greater length. The Falstaff Brewing Corp. put up a temporary bar 336 feet 5 inches in length on Wharf St., St. Louis, Missouri, U.S.A., on 22 June 1970.

United Kingdom
The longest bar in the United Kingdom with beer pumps is the French Bar (198 feet 5½ inches) at Butlin's Holiday Camp, Filey, Yorkshire. It has 20 beer pumps, 12 tills and stillage for 30 barrels, and is operated by 30 barmaids, 20 floor waiters and 20 other hands. The Grand Stand Bar at Galway Racecourse, Ireland completed in 1955, measures 210 feet.

Wine cellar
The largest wine cellars in the world are at Paarl, those of the Ko-operative Wijnbouwers Vereeniging, known as K.W.V. near Cape Town, in the centre of the wine-growing district of South Africa. They cover an area of 25 acres and have a capacity of 30,000,000 gallons. The largest blending vats have a capacity of 45,700 gallons and are 17 feet high, with a diameter of 26 feet.

4. MAJOR CIVIL ENGINEERING STRUCTURES

TALLEST STRUCTURES

World Completed
The tallest structure in the world is a stayed television transmitting tower 2,063 feet tall, between Fargo and Blanchard, North Dakota, U.S.A. It was built at a cost of about $500,000 (£208,000) for Channel 11 of KTHI-TV, owned by the Pembina Broadcasting Company of North Dakota, a subsidiary of the Polaris Corporation from Milwaukee, Wisconsin, U.S.A. The tower was erected in 30 days (2 Oct. to 1 Nov. 1963) by 11 men of the Kline Iron and Steel Company of Columbia, South Carolina, U.S.A., who designed and fabricated the tower. The cage elevator in the centre rises to 1,948 feet. The tower is built to allow for a sway of up to 13.9 feet in a wind gusting to 120 m.p.h. and is so tall that anyone falling off the top would no longer be accelerating just before hitting the ground.

Uncompleted
Work was begun in July 1970 on a tubular steel guyed T.V. tower near Plock, north-west Poland, which will rise to 2,100 feet. The structure, designed by Jan Polak, will weigh 550 tons and is due for completion in 1974.

United Kingdom The tallest structure in the United Kingdom is the Independent Television Authority's mast at Belmont, north of Horncastle, Lincolnshire, completed in 1965 to a height of 1,265 feet with 7 feet added by meteorological equipment installed in September 1967. It serves Anglia T.V. and was severely threatened by the icing on 21 March 1969 which two days earlier felled the 1,265-foot Emley Moore mast in Yorkshire, which was replaced in 1971 by the 1,080 foot self-supporting concrete tower.

TALLEST TOWERS

World The tallest self-supporting tower (as opposed to a guyed mast) in the world is the 1,749-foot-tall tower at Ostankino, Greater Moscow, U.S.S.R., topped out in May 1967. It is of reinforced concrete construction and weighs over 22,000 tons. A three-storey restaurant revolves at the 882-foot level and there is a balcony at 1,050 feet. In a high wind the T.V. antennae may sway up to 26 feet but the restaurant only 3.14 inches. The tower was designed by N. V. Nikitin.

The tallest tower built before the era of television masts is the Eiffel Tower, in Paris, France, designed by Alexandre Gustav Eiffel (1832-1923) for the Paris exhibition and completed on 31 March 1889. It was 300.51 metres (985 feet 11 inches) tall, now extended by a T.V. antenna to 1,052 feet 4 inches, and weighs 6,900 tons. The maximum sway in high winds is 5 inches. The whole steel edifice which has 1,792 steps, took 2 years, 2 months and 2 days to build and cost 7,799,401 francs 31 centimes. The 352nd suicide committed from the tower had occurred by 1 Jan. 1970.

The architects André and Jean Polak put forward a design in February 1969 for a tower 2,378.6 feet (725 metres) in height to be erected at La Défense in Paris.

United Kingdom The tallest tower in the United Kingdom is the Post Office Tower, opened on 8 Oct. 1965 in Maple Street, off Tottenham Court Road, London, W.1. It is 580 feet tall to the top of the concrete structure and 620 feet to the top of the lattice mast.* The weight of the tower and its foundations has been estimated at 13,000 tons.

The 525 foot spire of Lincoln Cathedral which was unsurpassed as man's tallest building for over 5½ centuries from 1307 till 1884

* The fastest times recorded for racing up the 814 steps to the top observation floor are:—Male: Norman Harrison (Imperial College, London) 4 mins. 21.4 secs. on 6 Feb. 1970. Female: Hillary Tanner (Hull University) 6 mins. 39 secs. on 12 Feb. 1971. Competition is limited to students.

TALLEST STRUCTURES IN THE WORLD—PROGRESSIVE RECORDS

Height in feet	Structure	Location	Material	Building or Completion Dates
204	Djoser step pyramid (earliest Pyramid)	Saqqâra, Egypt	Tura limestone	c. 2650 B.C.
294	Pyramid of Meidun	Meidun, Egypt	Tura limestone	c. 2600 B.C.
c. 336	Snefru Bent pyramid	Dahshûr, Egypt	Tura limestone	c. 2600 B.C.
342	Snefru North Stone pyramid	Dahshûr, Egypt	Tura limestone	c. 2600 B.C.
480.9[1]	Great Pyramid of Cheops (Khufu)	El Gizeh, Egypt	Tura limestone	c. 2580 B.C.
525[2]	Lincoln Cathedral, Central Tower	Lincoln, England	lead sheathed wood	c. 1307-1548
489[3]	St. Paul's Cathedral	London, England	lead sheathed wood	1315-1561
465	Minster of Notre Dame	Strasbourg, France	Vosges sandstone	1420-1439
502[4]	St. Pierre de Beauvais	Beauvais, France	lead sheathed wood	-1568
475	St. Nicholas Church	Hamburg, Germany	stone and iron	1846-1874
485	Rouen Cathedral	Rouen, France	cast iron	1823-1876
513	Köln Cathedral	Cologne, West Germany	stone	-1880
555	Washington Memorial	Washington, D.C., U.S.A.	stone	1848-1884
985.9[5]	Eiffel Tower	Paris, France	iron	1887-1889
1,046	Chrysler Building	New York City, U.S.A.	steel and concrete	1929-1930
1,250[6]	Empire State Building	New York City, U.S.A.	steel and concrete	1929-1930
1,572	KWTV Television Mast	Oklahoma City, U.S.A.	steel	Nov. 1954
1,610[7]	KSWS Television Mast	Roswell, New Mexico, U.S.A.	steel	Dec. 1956
1,619	WGAN Television Mast	Portland, Maine, U.S.A.	steel	Sept. 1959
1,676	KFVS Television Mast	Cape Girardeau, Missouri, U.S.A.	steel	June 1960
1,749	WTVM & WRBL TV Mast	Columbus, Georgia, U.S.A.	steel	May 1962
1,749	WBIR-TV Mast	Knoxville, Tennessee, U.S.A.	steel	Sept. 1963
2,063	KTHI-TV Mast	Fargo, North Dakota, U.S.A.	steel	Nov. 1963
c. 2,100	Polish T.V. Service Tower	Plock, Poland	galvanised steel	1970-1974

1 *Original height. With loss of pyramidion (topmost stone) height now 449 ft. 6 in.*
2 *Fell in a storm.*
3 *Struck by lightning and destroyed 4 June 1561.*
4 *Fell April 1573, shortly after completion.*
5 *Original height. With addition of T.V. antenna in 1957, now 1,052 ft. 4 in.*
6 *Original height. With addition of T.V. tower on 1 May 1951 now 1,472 ft.*
7 *Fell in gale in 1960.*

5. BRIDGES

OLDEST

World Arch construction was understood by the Sumerians as early as 3200 B.C. but the oldest surviving bridge in the world is the slab stone single arch bridge over the River Meles in Smyrna (now Izmir), Turkey, which dates from *c.* 850 B.C.

Britain The clapper bridges of Dartmoor and Exmoor (*e.g.* the Tarr Steps over the River Barle, Exmoor, Somerset) are thought to be of prehistoric types although none of the existing examples can be certainly dated. They are made of large slabs of stone placed over boulders. The Romans built stone bridges in England and remains of these have been found at Corbridge (Roman, Corstopitum), Northumberland dating to the 2nd century A.D.; Chester, Northumberland and Willowford, Cumberland. Remains of a very early wooden bridge have been found at Ardwinkle, Northamptonshire.

LONGEST

Cable suspension
World The world's longest single span bridge is the Verrazano-Narrows Bridge stretching across the entrance to New York City harbour from Richmond, Staten Island to Brooklyn. Work on the $305,000,000 (then £109 million) project began on 13 Aug. 1959 and the bridge was opened to traffic on 21 Nov. 1964. It measures 6,690 feet between anchorages and carries two decks, each of six lanes of traffic. The centre span is 4,260 feet and the tops of the main towers (each 690 feet tall) are 1⅝ inches out of parallel, to allow for the curvature of the Earth. The traffic in the first 12 months was 17,000,000 vehicles, and is rising towards 48,000,000 with the completion of the second deck. The bridge was designed by Othmar H. Ammann (1879-1965), a Swiss-born engineer.

The Mackinac Straits Bridge between Mackinaw City and St. Ignace, Michigan, U.S.A., is the longest suspension bridge in the world measured between anchorages (8,344 feet) and has an overall length, including viaducts of the bridge proper measured between abutment bearings, of 19,203 feet 4 inches. It was opened in November 1957 (dedicated 28 June 1958) at a cost of $100 million (then £35,700,000) and has a main span of 3,800 feet.

Detailed plans have been published for the building of a $333 million (£138.7 million) suspension bridge

The world's longest cantilever span—the Quebec Bridge measuring 1,800 feet

with a central span of 1,300 metres (4,265 feet) across the Akashi Straits, west of Kobe, Japan. It will have an overall length of 4,900 metres (16,076 feet or 3.04 miles), including all main and side spans. The distance between the main anchors will be 8,530 feet and the cables will be 126 centimetres (50 inches) in diameter. Even longer main spans are planned for completion in 1976 across the Humber Estuary (4,625 feet), a bridge of 4,600 feet across Tōkyō Bay, Japan, and one of even 9,000 feet, with piers 400 feet deep, across the Messina Straits, Italy. A progressive list of the world's longest spans covering the period 219 B.C. to date appeared in the 18th edition.

United Kingdom The longest span bridge in the United Kingdom is the Firth of Forth Road Bridge with a main channel span of 3,300 feet and side spans of 1,340 feet each, opened on 4 Sept. 1964. The main towers each stand 512 feet high. It is the sixth longest span in the world and cost £11,000,000 excluding the approaches.

Cantilever
World The Quebec Bridge (Pont de Québec) over the St Lawrence River in Canada has the longest cantilever truss span of any in the world—1,800 feet between the piers and 3,239 feet overall. It carries a railway track and 2 carriageways. Begun in 1899, it was finally opened to traffic on 3 Dec. 1917 at a cost of 87 lives, and $Can.22,500,000 (then £4,623,000).

United Kingdom The longest cantilever bridge in the United Kingdom is the Forth Bridge. Its two main spans are 1,710 feet long. It carries a double railway track over the Firth of Forth 150 feet above the water level. Work commenced in November 1882 and the first test trains crossed on 22 Jan. 1890 after an expenditure of £3 million. It was officially opened on 4 March 1890. Of the 4,500 workers who built it, 57 were killed in various accidents.

Longest steel arch
World The longest steel arch bridge in the world is the Bayonne Bridge over the Kill Van Kull, which has connected Bayonne, New Jersey, to Staten Island, New York, since its completion in November 1931. Its span is 1,652 feet 1 inch—25 inches longer than the Sydney Harbour Bridge, Australia (see below).

United Kingdom The longest steel arch bridge in the United Kingdom is the Runcorn-Widnes bridge from Widnes, Lancashire, to Runcorn, Cheshire, opened on 21 July 1961. It has a span of 1,082 feet and a total length including approaches of 3,489 feet.

Largest steel arch The largest steel arch bridge in the world is the Sydney Harbour Bridge in Sydney, New South Wales,

An artist's impression of the Humber Suspension Bridge which when completed will have the world's longest span. The towers will be out of parallel to allow for the curvature of the Earth

LONGEST BRIDGE SPANS IN THE WORLD—BY TYPE

Type	feet	metres	Location	Built
Cable Suspension	4,260	1,298.4	Verrazano-Narrows, New York, N.Y., U.S.A.	1964
Cantilever Truss	1,800	548.6	Quebec Railway Bridge, Quebec, Canada	1917
Steel Arch	1,652	503.6	Bayonne (Kill Van Kull), New York, N.Y., U.S.A.	1931
Covered Bridge	1,282	390.8	Hartland, New Brunswick, Canada	
Continuous Truss	1,232	375.5	Astoria, Columbia River, Oregon, U.S.A.	1966
Cable-Stayed	1,148	350.0	Duisberg-Nuenkamp, West Germany	1970
Chain Suspension	1,114	339.5	Florianopolis, Santa Catarina, Brazil	1926
Concrete Arch	1,000	304.8	Gladesville, Sydney, Australia	1964
Plate and Box Girder	984	300.0	Rió Niterói, Rio de Janeiro, Brazil	1972
Stone Arch	295	89.9	Plauen, East Germany	1903

Australia. Its main arch span is 1,650 feet long and it carries two electric overhead railway tracks, eight lanes of roadway, a cycleway and a footway, 172 feet above the waters of Sydney Harbour. It took seven years to build and was officially opened on 19 March 1932 at a cost of $A9,500,000 (then £7,600,000). Its total length is 3,770 feet excluding complex viaducts.

Floating bridge *Longest* The longest floating bridge in the world is the Second Lake Washington Bridge, Seattle, Washington State, U.S.A. completed in 1963. Its total length is 12,596 feet and its floating section measures 7,518 feet (1.42 miles). It was built at a total cost of $15,000,000 (£6,250,000) and completed in August 1963.

Railway bridge *Longest* The longest railway bridge in the world is the Huey P. Long Bridge, Metairie, Louisiana, U.S.A. with a railway section 22,996 feet (4.35 miles) long. It was completed on 16 Dec. 1935 with a longest span of 790 feet. The longest railway bridge in Britain is the second Tay Bridge (11,653 feet), joining Fife and Angus, opened on 20 June 1887. Of the 85 spans, 74 (length 10,289 feet) are over the waterway.

HIGHEST

World The highest bridge in the world is the bridge over the Royal Gorge of the Arkansas River in Colorado, U.S.A. It is 1,053 feet above the water level. It is a suspension bridge with a main span of 880 feet and was constructed in 6 months, ending on 6 Dec. 1929. The highest railway bridge in the world is the single track span at Fades, outside Clermont-Ferrand, France. It was built in 1901-09 with a span of 472 feet and is 430 feet above the River Sioule.

United Kingdom The highest railway bridge in the United Kingdom was the Crumlin Viaduct, Monmouthshire, completed in June 1857 to a height of 200 feet.

WIDEST

The world's widest long-span bridge is the Sydney Harbour Bridge (160 feet wide). The Crawford Street Bridge in Providence, Rhode Island, U.S.A., has a width of 1,147 feet. The River Roch is bridged for a distance of 1,460 feet where the culvert passes through the centre of Rochdale, Lancashire.

Deepest undations The deepest foundations of any structure are those of the 3,323-foot-span Ponte de Salazar, which was opened on 6 Aug. 1966, at a cost of £30,000,000, across the Rio Tejo (the River Tagus), in Portugal. One of the 625-foot-tall towers extends 260 feet down.

Longest viaduct The world's longest viaduct is the second Lake Ponchartrain Causeway, completed on 23 March 1969, joining Lewisberg and Metairie, Louisiana, U.S.A. It has a length of 126,055 feet (23.87 miles). It cost $29,900,000 (£12.45 million) and is 228 feet longer than the adjoining First Causeway completed in 1956. The longest railway viaduct in the world is the rock-filled Great Salt Lake Railroad Trestle, carrying the Southern Pacific Railroad 11.85 miles across the Great Salt Lake, Utah, U.S.A. It was opened as a pile and trestle bridge on 8 March 1904, but converted to rock fill in 1955-60.

AQUEDUCTS

World Longest Ancient The greatest of ancient aqueducts was the Aqueduct of Carthage in Tunisia, which ran 141 kilometres (87.6 miles) from the springs of Zaghouan to Djebel Djougar. It was built by the Romans during the reign of Publius Aelius Hadrianus (A.D. 117-138). By 1895, 344 arches still survived. Its original capacity has been calculated at 7,000,000 gallons per day. The triple-tiered aqueduct Pont du Gard, built in A.D. 19 near Nîmes, France, is 160 feet high. The tallest of the 14 arches of Aguas Livres Aqueduct, built in Lisbon, Portugal, in 1748 is 213 feet 3 inches.

The 3-tier Roman aqueduct, Pont du Gard, near Nîmes, France

Modern The world's longest aqueduct, in the modern sense of a water conduit, is the Colorado River Aqueduct in south-eastern California, U.S.A. The whole system, complete with the aqueduct conduit, tunnels and syphons, is 242 miles long and was completed in 1939. The California Aqueduct. (completion due 1973) will be 444 miles long.

United Kingdom The longest aqueduct in the United Kingdom is the Pontcysyllte in Denbighshire, Wales, on the Frankton to Llantisilio branch of the Shropshire Union Canal. It is 1,007 feet long, has 19 arches up to 121 feet high and crosses the valley of the Dee. It was designed by Thomas Telford (1757-1834) of Scotland, and was opened for use in 1803.

6. CANALS

EARLIEST

World Relics of the oldest canals in the world, dated by archaeologists to 5000 B.C., were discovered near Mandali, Iraq early in 1968.

Britain The first canals in Britain were undoubtedly cut by the Romans. In the Midlands the 11-mile-long Fossdyke Canal between Lincoln and the River Trent at Torksey was built in about A.D. 65 and was scoured in 1122. Part of it is still in use today. Though Exeter Canal was cut as early as 1564-68, the first wholly artificial major navigation canal in the United Kingdom was the Bridgewater canal, dug in 1759-61. It ran from Worsley to Manchester, Lancashire. Parts of the Sankey Canal from St. Helens to Widnes, Lancashire, were however, dug before the Bridge-water Canal.

LONGEST

World The longest canalized system in the world is the Volga-Baltic Canal opened in April 1965. It runs 1,850 miles from Astrakhan up the Volga, *via* Kuybyshev, Gor'kiy and Lake Ladoga, to Leningrad, U.S.S.R. The longest canal of the ancient world has been the Grand Canal of China from Peking to Hangchou. It was begun in 540 B.C. and not completed until the 13th century by which time it extended for 1,107 miles. Having been allowed by 1950 to silt up to the point that it was in no place more than 6 feet deep, it is reported to have been reconstructed.

The Beloye More (White Sea) Baltic Canal from Belomorsk to Povenets, in the U.S.S.R., is 141 miles long with 19 locks. It was completed with the use of forced labour in 1933 and cannot accommodate ships of more than 16 feet in draught.

The world's longest big ship canal is the still in-operative (since June 1967) Suez Canal in the United Arab Republic, opened on 16 Nov. 1869. The canal was planned by the French diplomatist Count Ferdinand de Lesseps (1805-94) and work began on 25 April 1859. It is 100.6 miles in length from Port Said lighthouse to Suez Roads, 60 metres (197 feet) wide and dredged to 34 feet.

United Kingdom The longest inland waterway in the United Kingdom is the Grand Union Canal Main Line from Brentford Lock Junction, Middlesex, to Langley Mill, a total distance of 167⅜ miles. The Grand Union System was originally 255 miles long when nine canals, including the Grand Junction, were amalgamated in 1929. The voyage along the whole length of the Grand Union Canal, Main Line, would involve the negotiation of 169 locks.

Largest seaway The world's longest artificial seaway is the St. Lawrence Seaway (189 miles long) along the New York State-Ontario border from Montreal to Lake Ontario, which enables 80 per cent. of all ocean-going ships, and bulk carriers with a capacity of 26,000 tons, to sail 2,342 miles from the North Atlantic, up the St. Lawrence estuary and across the Great Lakes to Duluth, Minnesota, U.S.A., on Lake Superior (602 feet above sea-level). The project cost $470,000,000 (then £168 million) and was opened on 25 April 1959.

Irrigation canal The longest irrigation canal in the world is the Karakumskiy Kanal, stretching 528 miles from Haun-Khan to Ashkhabad, Turkmenistan, U.S.S.R. In Sept. 1971 the "navigable" length was reported to have reached 280 miles. The length of the £370 million project will reach 870 miles by 1975.

LOCKS

Largest World The world's largest locking system is the Miraflores lock system in the Panama Canal, opened on 15 Aug. 1914. The two lower locks are 1,050 feet long, 110 feet wide and have gates 82 feet high, 65 feet long and 7 feet thick, with doors weighing 652 to 696 tons each. The largest liner ever to transit was S.S. *Bremen* (51,730 gross tons), with a length of 899 feet, a beam of 101.9 feet and a draught of 48.2 feet, on 15 Feb. 1939. The swimmer Albert H. Oshiver was charged a toll of 45 cents in Dec. 1962.

The world's largest single lock is that connecting the

The world's deepest lock—the Wilson Dam measuring 100 feet in depth with twin leaf gates weighing 1,400 tons, on the Tennessee River

Schelde with the Kanaaldok system at Zandvliet, we[st] of Antwerp, Belgium. It is 500 metres (1,640 fee[t] long and 187 feet wide and is an entrance to a[n] impounded sheet of water 18 kilometres (11.2 mile[s]) long.

United Kingdom The largest lock on any canal system in the Unite[d] Kingdom is the Eastham Large Lock, Eastha[m] Cheshire, on the Manchester Ship Canal. It can hand[le] craft up to 600 feet long and 80 feet beam.

Deepest The world's deepest lock is the Wilson dam lock [at] Muscle Shoals, Alabama, U.S.A. on the Tenness[ee] River completed in Nov. 1959. It can raise or low[er] barges 100 feet and has twin-leaf gates weighing 1,4[00] tons.

Longest flight The world's highest lock elevator is at Arzwiller-Sai[nt] Louis in France. The lift was completed in 1969 [to] replace 17 locks on the Marne-Rhine canal system. [It] drops 146 feet over a ramp 383.8 feet long on a 4[1] degree gradient.

The longest flight of locks in the United Kingdom [is] on the Worcester and Birmingham Canal at Tar[d]bigge, Worcestershire, where a 2½-mile-long flight [of] 30 consecutive locks raises the canal level 217 feet.

Largest cut The Gaillard Cut (known as "the Ditch") on th[e] Panama Canal is 270 feet deep between Gold Hill a[nd] Contractor's Hill with a bottom width of 300 feet. [In] one day in 1911 as many as 333 dirt trains ea[ch] carrying 357 tons left this site. The total amount [of] earth excavated for the whole Panama Canal w[as] 8,910,000 tons, which total will be raised by t[he] widening of the Gaillard Cut to 500 feet. In 19[69] there were a record 14,807 transits.

7. DAMS

Earliest The earliest dam ever built was the Sadd al-Kafar[a] seven miles south-east of Helwan, United Ar[ab] Republic. It was built in the period 2950 to 2750 B.[C]. and had a length of 348 feet and a height of 37 feet.

Most massive Measured by volume, the largest dam in the world [is] the Fort Peck Dam, completed in 1940 across th[e] Missouri River in Montana, U.S.A. It contai[ns] 125,628,000 cubic yards of earth and rock fill, and [is] 21,026 feet (3.98 miles) long and up to 251 feet hig[h]. It maintains a reservoir with a capacity of 19.1 milli[on] acre-feet. Work started in December 1967 on th[e] Tarbela Dam across the River Indus, in the Sind, We[st] Pakistan. The total expenditure on the 485-foot-ta[ll] 9,000-foot-long construction is expected to rea[ch] $815 million (£339.6 million) by completion in 19[?]

114

including the $623 million contract awarded to the Impregilo Consortium. The total volume of the dam will be 186,000,000 cubic yards.

Largest concrete The world's largest concrete dam, and the largest concrete structure in the world, is the Grand Coulee Dam on the Columbia River, Washington State, U.S.A. Work on the dam was begun in 1933, it began working on 22 March 1941 and was completed in 1942 at a cost of $56 million. It has a crest length of 4,173 feet and is 550 feet high. It contains 10,585,000 cubic yards of concrete, and weighs about 19,285,000 tons. The hydro-electric power plant (now being extended) will have a capacity of 9,771,000 kilowatts.

Highest The highest dam in the world is the Grande Dixence in Switzerland, completed in September 1961 at a cost of 1,600 million Swiss francs (£151,000,000). It is 932 feet from base to rim, 2,296 feet long and the total volume of concrete in the dam is 7,792,000 cubic yards. The earth fill Nurek dam on the Vakhsh-Amu Darya river, U.S.S.R. will be 1,017 feet high, have a crest length of 2,280 feet and a volume of 75,900,000 cubic yards. The concrete Ingurskaya dam in western Georgia, U.S.S.R., is planned to have a final height of 988 feet, a crest length of 2,240 feet and a volume of 3,920,000 cubic yards.

Longest The longest river dam in the world is the Hirakud Dam on the Mahanadi River, near Sambalpur, Orissa, India completed in 1956. It consists of a main concrete and masonry dam (3,768 feet), an Earth Dam (11,980 feet), the Left Dyke (five sections of 32,275 feet) and the Right Dyke (35,500 feet), totalling 15.8 miles altogether.

The longest sea dam in the world is the Afsluitdijk stretching 20.195 miles across the mouth of the Zuider Zee in two sections of 1.553 miles (mainland of North Holland to the Isle of Wieringen) and 18.641 miles from Wieringen to Friesland. It has a sea-level width of 293 feet and a height of 24 feet 7 inches.

United Kingdom The most massive (5,630,000 cubic yards), the highest (240 feet) and longest high dam (2,050 feet crest length) in the United Kingdom is the Scammonden Dam, West Riding of Yorkshire, begun in November 1966 and completed in the summer of 1970. This rock fill dam carries the M62 on its crest and was built by Sir Alfred McAlpine's. The cost of the project together with the 6½-mile motorway was £8,400,000. There are longer low dams or barrages of the valley cut-off type notably the Hanningfield Dam, Essex, built from July 1952 to August 1956 to a length of 6,850 feet and a height of 64.5 feet. The Llyn Brianne Dam in Carmarthenshire, also rock fill, will reach 300 feet in 1972 thus surpassing the concrete Clywedog Dam (built April 1964-April 1968), Montgomeryshire, of 237 feet as the highest in the United Kingdom.

LARGEST RESERVOIR
World The largest man-made is Bratsk Lake on the Angara river, U.S.S.R., with a volume of 137,214,000 acre-feet. The dam was completed in 1964. A volume of 149,000,000 acre-feet was quoted for Kariba Lake, Zambia-Rhodesia in 1959 but is now more reliably estimated at 130,000,000 acre-feet. The Volta Lake, Ghana, which filled behind the Akosombo dam from May 1964 to late 1968, also often referred to as the world's largest man-made lake, has a capacity of 120,000,000 acre-feet.

The completion in 1954 of the Owen Falls Dam near Jinja, Uganda, across the northern exit of the White Nile from the Victoria Nyanza marginally raised the level of that lake by adding 166,000,000 acre-feet, and technically turned it into a reservoir with a surface area of 17,169,920 acres (26,828 square miles).

The most grandiose reservoir project mooted is the Xingu-Araguaia river plan in central Brazil for a reservoir behind a dam at Ilha da Paz with a volume of 780,000 million cubic yards extending over 22,800 square miles. A dam at Obidos on the Amazon would produce a 744-mile-long back-up and a 68,400-square-mile reservoir at an estimated cost of $3,000 million (£1,250 million).

United Kingdom The largest wholly artificial reservoir in the United Kingdom is the Queen Mary Reservoir, built from August 1914 to June 1925, at Littleton, near Staines, with an available storage capacity of 8,130 million gallons and a water area of 707 acres. The length of the perimeter embankment is 20,766 feet (3.93 miles). Of valley cut-off type reservoirs the most capacious is Llyn Celyn, North Wales with a capacity of 17,800,000,000 gallons. The capacity of Hawes-water, Westmorland, was increased by 18,660 million gallons by the building in 1929-41 of a 1,540-foot-long concrete buttress dam 120 feet high. The natural surface area was trebled to 1,050 acres. The deepest reservoir in Europe is Lock Morar, in Inverness-shire, Scotland, with a maximum depth of 1,017 feet (see also Chapter 3).

Largest polder The largest of the five great polders in the old Zuider Zee, Netherlands, will be the 149,000 acre (232.8 square miles) Markerwaard. Work on the 66-mile-long surrounding dyke was begun in 1957. The water area remaining after the erection of the 1927-32 dam is called IJssel Meer, which will have a final area of 487.5 square miles.

Largest levees The most massive earthworks ever carried out are the Mississippi levees begun in 1717 but vastly augmented by the U.S. Federal Government after the disastrous floods of 1927. These extend for 1,732 miles along the main river from Cape Girardeau, Missouri, to the Gulf of Mexico and comprise more than 1,000 million cubic yards of earthworks. Levees on the tributaries comprise an additional 2,000 miles.

8. TUNNELS

LONGEST
Water supply **World** The world's longest tunnel of any kind is the New York City West Delaware water supply tunnel begun in 1937 and completed in 1945. It has a diameter of 13 feet 6 inches and runs for 85.0 miles from the Rondout Reservoir into the Hillview Reservoir, in the northern part of Manhattan Island, New York City, N.Y., U.S.A.

United Kingdom The longest water supply tunnel in the United Kingdom is the Thames water tunnel from Hampton-on-Thames to Walthamstow, Greater London, completed in 1960 with a circumference of 26 feet 8 inches and a length of 18.8 miles.

RAILWAY
World The world's longest main-line tunnel is the Simplon II Tunnel, completed after 4 years' work on 16 Oct. 1922. Linking Switzerland and Italy under the Alps, it is 12 miles 559 yards long. Over 60 were killed boring this and the Simplon I (1898-1906), which is 22 yards shorter. Its greatest depth below the surface is 7,005 feet.

Subway tunnel The world's longest continuous vehicular tunnel is the London Transport Executive underground railway line from Morden to East Finchley, *via* Bank. In use since 1939, it is 17 miles 528 yards long and the diameter of the tunnel is 12 feet and the station tunnels 22.2 feet.

United Kingdom The United Kingdom's longest main-line railway tunnel is the Severn Tunnel (4 miles 628 yards), linking Gloucestershire and Monmouthshire, completed with 76,400,000 bricks between 1873 and 1886.

ROAD

World The longest road tunnel is the tunnel 7.2 miles long under Mont Blanc (15,771 feet) from Pèlerins, near Chamonix, France, to Entrèves, near Courmayeur in Valle d'Aosta, Italy, on which work began on 6 Jan. 1959. The holing through was achieved on 14 Aug. 1962 and it was opened on 16 July 1965, after an expenditure of £22,800,000. The 29½-foot-high tunnel with its carriage-way of two 12-foot lanes is expected to carry 600,000 vehicles a year. There were 23 deaths during tunnelling.

Sub- The world's longest sub-aqueous road tunnel is the
aqueous Kanmon Tunnel, completed in 1958, which runs 6.15 miles from Shimonseki, Honshū, to Kyūshū, Japan. The 33.6 mile long Seikan Tunnel, 460 feet beneath the sea-bed of the Tsugaru Strait between Tappi Saki, Honshū, and Fukushima, Hokkaidō, Japan, is due to be completed by 1977 at a cost of £240 million. Tests started on the sub-aqueous section (14.5 miles) in 1963 and construction in April 1971.

Channel On 8 July 1966 the United Kingdom and French
tunnel governments reached agreement on a Channel Tunnel for electric trains. It would run in two passages, each of 35.6 miles, 21 miles being sub-aqueous, between Westenhanger, near Dover, Kent, and Sangatte, near Calais. The project, now known as the "Chunnel", was first mooted in 1802. It will cost more than £350,000,000, if proceeded with.

United The longest road tunnel in the United Kingdom is the
Kingdom Mersey Tunnel, joining Liverpool, Lancashire, and Birkenhead, Cheshire. It is 2.13 miles long, or 2.87 miles including branch tunnels. Work was begun in December 1925 and it was opened by H.M. King George V on 18 July 1934. The total cost was £7¾ million. The 36-foot-wide 4-lane roadway carries nearly 7½ million vehicles a year. The first tube of the second Mersey Tunnel was opened on 24 June 1971.

Largest The largest diameter road tunnel in the world is that blasted through Yerba Buena Island, San Francisco, California, U.S.A. It is 76 feet wide, 58 feet high and 540 feet long. More than 35,000,000 vehicles pass through on its two decks every year.

HYDRO-ELECTRIC

World The longest hydro-electric tunnel in the world will be the 51.5-mile-long Orange-Fish Rivers Tunnel, South Africa, begun in 1967 at an estimated cost of £250 million. A 30-mile-long tunnel joining the River Arpa with Lake Sevan at an altitude of 6,500 feet in the Armenian Mountains, U.S.S.R. was also reported under construction in 1967.

United The longest in the United Kingdom is that at Ben
Kingdom Nevis, Inverness-shire, which has a mean diameter of 15 feet 2 inches and a length of 15 miles. It was begun in June 1926 and was holed through into Loch Treig on 3 Jan. 1930.

BRIDGE-TUNNEL

The world's longest bridge-tunnel system is the Chesapeake Bay Bridge-Tunnel, extending 17.65 miles from the Delmarva Peninsula to Norfolk, Virginia, U.S.A. It cost $200,000,000 (then £71.4 million) and was completed after 42 months and opened to traffic on 15 April 1964. The longest bridged section is Trestle C (4.56 miles long) and the longer tunnel is the Thimble Shoal Channel Tunnel (1.09 miles).

CANAL TUNNELS

Longest The world's longest canal tunnel is that on the Rove
World canal between the port of Marseilles, France and the

river Rhône, built in 1912-27. It is 4.53 miles long, 7▯ feet wide and 50 feet high, involving 2¼ million cub▯ yards of excavation.

United The longest of the 49 canal tunnels in the Unite
Kingdom Kingdom is the Standedge Tunnel in the West Ridi▯ of Yorkshire on the Huddersfield Narrow Canal bu▯ from 1794 to 4 April 1811. It measures 3 miles 13▯ yards in length and was closed on 21 Dec. 1944. T▯ Huddersfield Narrow Canal is also the highest in t▯ United Kingdom, reaching a height at one point ▯ 638 feet above sea-level.

Tunnelling The world's record for rapid tunnelling was set on ▯
record March 1967 in the 8.6-mile-long Blanco Tunnel, Southern Colorado when the "mole" (giant bori▯ machine) crew advanced the 10-foot diameter hea▯ ing 375 feet in one day.

9. SPECIALISED STRUCTURES

SEVEN WONDERS OF THE WORLD

The Seven Wonders of the World were first designat▯ by Antipater of Sidon in the 2nd century B.C. Th▯ included the Pyramids of Gîza, built by three Four▯ Dynasty Egyptian Pharaohs, Hwfw (Khufu Cheops), Kha-f-Ra (Khafre, Khefren or Chephre▯ and Menkaure (Mycerinus) near El Gîza (El Gize▯ south-west of El Qâhira (Cairo) in Egypt (now t▯ United Arab Republic). The Great Pyramid ("H▯ izon of Khufu") was built in c. 2580 B.C. Its origi▯ height was 480 feet 11 inches (now, since the loss ▯ its topmost stone or pyramidion, reduced to 4▯ feet 6 inches) with a base line of 756 feet and th▯ originally covering slightly more than 13 acres. It h▯ been estimated that a work force of 4,000 required ▯ years to manoeuvre into position the 2,300,0▯ limestone blocks averaging 2½ tons each, totalli▯ about 5,750,000 tons and a volume of 90,700,0▯ cubic feet.

Of the other six wonders only fragments remain ▯ the Temple of Artemis (Diana) of the Ephesians, b▯ in c. 350 B.C. at Ephesus, Turkey (destroyed by ▯ Goths in A.D. 262), and of the Tomb of K▯ Mausolus of Caria, built at Halicarnassus, n▯ Bodrum, Turkey, in c. 325 B.C. No trace remains ▯ the Hanging Gardens of Semiramis, at Babylon, I▯ (c. 600 B.C.); the 40-foot-tall marble, gold and iv▯ statue of Zeus (Jupiter), by Phidias (5th century B.▯ at Olympia, Greece (lost in a fire at Istanbul); ▯ 117-foot-tall statue by Charles of Lindos of the fig▯ of the god Helios (Apollo), called the Colossus ▯ Rhodes (sculptured 292-280 B.C., destroyed by ▯ earthquake in 224 B.C.); or the 400-foot-tall lig▯ house built by Soscratus of Cnidus during the ▯ century B.C. (destroyed by earthquake in A.D. 13▯ on the island of Pharos (Greek, *pharos*=lighthou▯ off the coast of El Iskandarîya (Alexandria), Eg▯ (now the United Arab Republic).

PYRAMIDS

Largest The largest pyramid, and the largest monument e▯ constructed, is the Quetzalcóatl at Cholula de R▯ dahia, 63 miles south-east of Mexico City, Mexic▯ is 177 feet tall and its base covers an area of nearly ▯ acres. Its total volume has been estimated ▯ 4,300,000 cubic yards, compared with 3,360,▯ cubic yards for the Pyramid of Cheops (see abo▯ The pyramid-building era here was between the ▯ and 12th centuries A.D.

Oldest The oldest known pyramid is the Djoser step pyra▯ at Saqqâra, Egypt constructed to a height of 204 ▯ of Tura limestone in c. 2650 B.C. The oldest N▯ World pyramid is that on the island of La Vent▯ south-eastern Mexico built by the Olmec peopl▯ 800 B.C. It stands 100 feet tall with a base diamete▯ 420 feet.

Specialised Structures

TALLEST FLAGSTAFF

World The tallest flagstaff ever erected was that outside the Oregon Building at the 1915 Panama-Pacific International Exposition in San Francisco, California, U.S.A. Trimmed from a Douglas fir, it stood 299 feet 7 inches in height and weighed 45 tons. The tallest unsupported flag pole in the world is a 220-foot-tall metal pole weighing 28,000 lb. erected in 1955 at the U.S. Merchant Marine Academy in King's Point, New York, U.S.A. The pole, built by Kearney-National Inc., tapers from 24 inches to 5½ inches at the jack.

United Kingdom The tallest flagstaff in the United Kingdom is a 225-foot-tall Douglas fir staff at Kew, London. Cut in Canada, it was shipped across the Atlantic and towed up the River Thames on 7 May 1958, to replace the old 214-foot-tall staff of 1919.

Tallest totem pole The tallest totem pole in the world is one 160 feet tall in McKinleyville, California, U.S.A. It weighs 57,000 lb. (25.4 tons), was carved from a 500-year-old tree and was erected in May 1962.

MONUMENTS

Tallest The world's tallest monument is the stainless steel Gateway to the West Arch in St. Louis, Missouri, U.S.A., completed on 28 Oct. 1965 to commemorate the westward expansion after the Louisiana Purchase of 1803. It is a sweeping arch spanning 630 feet and rising to the same height of 630 feet, and costing $29,000,000 (£12,083,000). It was designed in 1947 by Eero Saarinen (died 1961).

The tallest monumental column in the world is that commemorating the battle of San Jacinto (21 April 1836), on the bank of the San Jacinto river near Houston, Texas, U.S.A. General Sam Houston (1793-1863) and his force of 743 Texan troops killed 630 Mexicans (out of a total force of 1,600) and captured 700 others, for the loss of nine men killed and 30 wounded. Constructed in 1936-39, at a cost of $1,500,000 (now £625,000), the tapering column is 570 feet tall, 47 feet square at the base, and 30 feet square at the observation tower, which is surmounted by a star weighing 196.4 tons. It is built of concrete, faced with buff limestone, and weighs 31,384 tons.

Prehistoric Largest Britain's largest megalithic prehistoric monuments are the 28½-acre earthworks and stone circles of Avebury, Wiltshire, rediscovered in 1646. This is believed to be the work of the Beaker people of the later Neolithic period of c. 1700 to 1500 B.C. The whole work is 1,200 feet in diameter with a 40-foot ditch around the perimeter. The largest trilithons exist at Stonehenge, to the south of Salisbury Plain, Wiltshire, with single sarsen blocks weighing over 45 tons and requiring over 550 men to drag them up a 9° gradient. The dating of the ditch was in 1969 revised to 2180 B.C.±105.

Largest earthwork The greatest prehistoric earthwork in Britain is Wansdyke, originally Woden's Dyke, which ran 86 miles from Portishead, Somerset to Inkpen Beacon and Ludgershall, south of Hungerford, Berkshire. It is believed to have been built by the pre-Roman Wessex culture. The most extensive single site earthwork is the Dorset Cursus near Gussage St. Michael, dating from c. 1900 B.C. The workings are 6 miles in length, involving an estimated 250,000 cubic yards of excavations. The largest of the Celtic hill-forts is that known as Mew Dun, or Maiden Castle, two miles south-west of Dorchester, Dorset. It covers 115 acres and was abandoned shortly after A.D. 43.

Largest mound The largest artificial mound in Europe is Silbury Hill, 6 miles west of Marlborough, Wiltshire, which involved the moving of an estimated 670,000 tons of chalk to make a cone 130 feet high with a base of 5½ acres. Prof. Richard Atkinson in charge of the 1968 excavations showed that it is based on an innermost

The world's tallest monument during construction in St Louis, Missouri. The London Post Office Tower could stand underneath its 630-foot high arch.

central mound, similar to contemporary round barrows, and may be dated to c. 2200 B.C. The largest long barrow in England is that inside the Neolithic camp and Iron Age Hill-fort at Maiden Castle (see above). It originally had a length of 1,800 feet and had several enigmatic features such as a ritual pit with pottery, limpet shells and animal bones. In 1934-37 the remains of a man of 25-35 was discovered, who had been hacked to pieces after death. The longest long barrow containing a megalithic chamber is that at West Kennet (c. 2200 B.C.), near Silbury, measuring 385 feet in length.

Youngest Ancient Monument Of all the ancient monuments scheduled in Great Britain, the youngest is Fort Wallington, near Portsmouth, Hampshire. It was begun in 1860, when a French invasion was thought possible, and was not completed until 1870.

OBELISKS (Monolithic)

Oldest The longest an obelisk has remained *in situ* is that at Heliopolis (now Masr-el-Gedîda) United Arab Republic (Egypt), erected by Senusret I c. 1750 B.C.

Largest The largest standing obelisk in the world is that in the Piazza of St. John in Lateran, Rome, erected in 1588. It came originally from the Circus Maximus (erected A.D. 357) and before that from Heliopolis, Egypt (erected c. 1450 B.C.). It is 110 feet in length and weighs 450 tons. The largest obelisk in the United Kingdom is Cleopatra's Needle on the Embankment, London, which is 68 feet 5½ inches tall and weighs 186.36 tons. It was towed up the Thames from Egypt on 20 Jan. 1878.

Largest tomb The largest tomb in the world is that of Emperor Nintoku (died c. A.D. 428) south of Osaka, Japan. It measures 1,594 feet long by 1,000 feet wide by 150 feet high.

Largest ziqqurat The largest surviving ziqqurat (from the verb *zaqaru*, to build high) or stage-tower is the Ziqqurat of Ur (now Muqqayr, Iraq) with a base 200 feet by 150 feet built to at least three storeys of which the first and part of the second now survive to a height of 60 feet. It was built by the Akkadian King Ur-Nammu (c. 2113-2006 B.C.) to the moon god Nanna covering 30,000 sq. feet.

STATUES

Tallest The tallest free-standing statue in the world is that of "Motherland", an enormous female figure on Mamayev Hill, outside Volgograd, U.S.S.R., designed

117

The world's longest breakwater system at Long Beach, California, U.S.A.

in 1967 by Yevgenyi Vuchetich, to commemorate victory in the Battle of Stalingrad (1942-43). The statue from its base to the tip of the sword clenched in her right hand measures 270 feet.

Longest Near Bamiyan, Afghanistan there are the remains of the recumbent Sakya Buddha, built of plastered rubble, which was "about 1,000 feet" long and is believed to date from the 3rd or 4th century A.D.

LARGEST DOME

World The world's largest dome is the "Astrodome" of the Harris County Sports Stadium, in Houston, Texas, U.S.A. It has an outside diameter of 710 feet and an inside diameter of 642 feet. (See page 109 for further details.) The largest dome of ancient architecture is that of the Pantheon, built in Rome in A.D. 112, with a diameter of 142½ feet.

Britain The largest dome in Britain is that of the Bell Sports Centre, Perth, Scotland with a diameter of 222 feet, designed by D. B. Cockburn and constructed in Baltic whitewood by Muirhead & Sons Ltd. of Grangemouth, Stirlingshire.

Tallest columns The tallest columns (as opposed to obelisks) in the world are the sixteen 82-foot-tall pillars in the Palace of Labour in Torino (Turin), Italy, for which the architect was Pier Luigi Nervi (born 21 June 1891). They were built of concrete and steel in only 8 days. The tallest load-bearing stone columns in the world are those measuring 69 feet in the Hall of Columns of the Temple of Amun at Al Karnak, the northern part of the ruins of Thebes, the Greek name for the ancient capital of Upper Egypt (now the United Arab Republic). They were built in the 19th dynasty in the reign of Rameses II in c. 1270 B.C.

HARBOUR WORKS

Longest jetty The longest deep water jetty in the world is the Quai Hermann du Pasquier at Le Havre, France, with a length of 5,000 feet. Part of an enclosed basin, it has a constant depth of water of 32 feet on both sides.

Longest pier The world's longest pier is the Dammam Pier at El
World Hasa, Saudi Arabia, on the Persian Gulf. A rock-filled causeway 4.84 miles long joins the steel trestle pier 1.80 miles long, which joins the Main Pier (744 feet long), giving an overall length of 6.79 miles. The work was begun in July 1948 and completed on 15 March 1950.

United Kingdom The longest pier in Great Britain is the Bee Ness Jetty, completed in 1930, which stretches 8,200 feet along the west bank of the River Medway, 5 to 6 miles below Rochester, at Kingsnorth, Kent.

Longest The world's longest breakwater system is that whic
breakwater protects the Ports of Long Beach and Los Angele
World California, U.S.A. The combined length of the fou breakwaters is 43,602 feet (8.26 miles) of which th Long Beach section, built between 1941 and Fe ruary 1949, is the longest at 13,350 feet (2.53 miles The North breakwater at Tuticorin, Madras Provinc Southern India on which construction began in 196 will extend when complete to 13,589 feet.

United The longest breakwater in the United Kingdom is th
Kingdom North Breakwater at Holyhead, Anglesey, which 9,860 feet (1.86 miles) in length and was complete in 1873.

LARGEST DRY DOCK

World The largest dry dock in the world is the Belfa Harbour Commission and Harland and Wolff buildin dock at Belfast, Northern Ireland. It has bee excavated by Wimpey's to a length of 1,825 feet and width of 305 feet and can accommodate tankers c 1,000,000 d.w.t. Work was begun on 26 Jan. 196 and completed on 30 Nov. 1969 and involved th excavation of 400,000 cubic yards. See also Large crane.

Work started at Nagasaki, Japan on 16 Sept. 1970 o a building dock capable of taking a tanker c 1,200,000 d.w.t. for Mitsubishi Heavy Industries C at a cost of £32,000,000

LARGEST FLOATING DOCKS

Sectional The largest floating docks ever constructed are th United States Navy's advanced base sectional dock (A.B.S.D.). These consist of 10 sectional units givin together an effective keel block length of 827 feet an clear width of 140 feet, with a lifting capacity c 71,000 tons. One designated AFDB 3 at Green Cov Springs, Florida, U.S.A. has a nominal lifting capacit of 80,000 tons.

Single unit The largest single unit floating dock is Admiralt Floating Dock (AFD) 35, which was towed from th Royal Navy's dockyard in Malta to the Cantieri Nava Santa Maria of Genoa, Italy, in May 1965. It has lifting capacity of 65,000 tons and an overall lengt of 857 feet 8 inches. It had been towed to Malta fro Bombay, India, where it was built in 1947.

LIGHTHOUSES

Brightest The lighthouse with the most powerful light in th
World world is Créac'h d'Ouessant lighthouse, established i 1638 and last altered in 1939 on l'Ile d'Ouessan Finistère, Brittany, France. It is 163 feet tall and, i times of fog, has a luminous intensity of up t

Specialised Structures

500,000,000 candelas.

The lights with the greatest visible range are those 1,092 feet above the ground on the Empire State Building, New York City, N.Y., U.S.A. Each of the four-arc mercury bulbs has a rated candlepower of 450,000,000, visible 80 miles away on the ground and 300 miles away from aircraft. They were switched on on 31 March 1956.

United Kingdom The lighthouse in the United Kingdom with the most powerful light is the shorelight Orfordness, Suffolk. It has an intensity of 7,500,000 candelas. The Irish light with the greatest intensity is Aranmore on Rinrawros Point, County Donegal.

Tallest The world's tallest lighthouse is the steel tower 348 feet tall near Yamashita Park in Yokohama, Japan. It has a power of 600,000 candles and a visibility range of 20 miles.

Remotest The most remote Trinity House lighthouse is The Smalls, about 16 sea miles (18.4 statute miles) off the Pembrokeshire coast. The most remote Scottish lighthouse is Sule Skerry, 35 miles off shore and 45 miles north-west of Dunnet Head, Caithness. The most remote Irish light is Blackrock, about 9 miles off the Mayo coast.

WINDMILLS
Earliest The earliest recorded windmills are those used for grinding corn in Iran (Persia) in the 7th century A.D. The earliest known in England was the post-mill at Bury St. Edmunds, Suffolk, recorded in 1191. The oldest Dutch mill is the towermill at Zedden, Gelderland built in *c.* 1450. The oldest working mill in England is the post-mill at Outwood, Surrey, built in 1665, though the Ivinghoe Mill in Pitstone Green Farm, Buckinghamshire, dating from 1627, has been restored.

Largest The largest Dutch windmill is the Dijkpolder in Maasland built in 1718. The sails measure 95¾ feet from tip to tip. The tallest windmill in the Netherlands is De Walvisch in Schiedam built to a height of 108 feet in 1794. The largest conventional windmill in England is a disused one at Sutton, Norfolk.

WATERWHEEL
Largest World The largest waterwheel in the world is the Mohammadieh Noria wheel at Hama, Syria with a diameter of 131 feet dating from Roman times. The Lady Isabella wheel at Laxey, Isle of Man is the largest in the British Isles and was built in Lancashire for draining a lead mine and completed on 27 Sept. 1854, has a circumference of 228 feet, a diameter of 72½ feet and an axle weighing 9 tons.

Barns The largest barn in Britain is one at Manor Farm, Cholsey, near Wallingford, Berkshire. It is 303 feet in length and 54 feet in breadth (16,362 square feet). The Ipsden Barn, Oxfordshire, is 385½ feet long but 30 feet wide (11,565 square feet).

The longest tithe barn in Britain is one measuring 268 feet long at Wyke Farm, near Sherborne, Dorset.

NUDIST CAMP
Largest The first nudist camps were established in Germany in 1912. The largest such camp in the world was that at l'Île du Levant, southern France, which had up to 15,000 *adeptes* before most of it was taken over for defence purposes by the French Navy in 1965. Currently Naked City, Rose Lawn, Indiana covers 386 acres catering for up to 8,400 customers on pageant days.

LONGEST WALL
World The Great Wall of China, completed during the reign of Shih Huang-ti (246-210 B.C.), is 1,684 miles in

The largest conventional windmill in England (now disused) at Sutton Norfolk

length, with a height of from 15 to 39 feet and up to 32 feet thick. Its erection is the most massive construction job ever undertaken by the human race. It runs from Shanhaikuan, on the Gulf of Pohai, to Chiayukuan in Kansu and was kept in repair up to the 16th century.

Britain The longest of the Roman Walls built in Britain was the 15-20-foot-tall Hadrian's Wall, built in the period A.D. 122-126. It ran across the Tyne-Solway isthmus of 74½ miles from Bowness-on-Solway, Cumberland, to Wallsend-on-Tyne, Northumberland, and was abandoned in A.D. 383.

LONGEST FENCE
The longest fence in the world is the dingo-proof fence enclosing the main sheep areas of Queensland, Australia. The wire fence is 6 feet high, one foot underground and stretches for 3,437 miles.

DOORS
Largest World The largest doors in the world are the four in the Vertical Assembly Building near Cape Kennedy, Florida, with a height of 460 feet (see page 104).

The largest doors in the United Kingdom are those to the Britannia Assembly Hall, at Filton, Bristol. The doors are 1,035 feet in length and 67 feet high, divided into three bays each 345 feet across. The largest simple hinged door in Britain is that of Ye Old Bull's Head, Beaumaris, Anglesey, Wales, which is 12 feet wide and 30 feet high.

Oldest The oldest doors in Britain are those of Hadstock Church, Essex, which date from *c.* 1040 and exhibit evidence of Danish workmanship.

LARGEST WINDOWS
The largest sheet of glass ever manufactured was one of 50 square metres (538.2 square feet), or 20 metres (65 feet 7 inches) by 2.5 metres (8 feet 2½ inches), exhibited by the Saint Gobain Company in France at the *Journées Internationales de Miroiterie* in March 1958. The largest windows in the world are the three in the Palace of Industry and Technology at Rondpoint de la Défense, Paris, with an extreme width of 218 metres (715.2 feet) and a maximum height of 50 metres (164 feet).

LONGEST STAIRS
The world's longest stairs are reputedly at the Mår power station, Øverland, western Norway. Built of wood, these are 4,101 feet in length, rising in 3,875 steps at an angle of 41 degrees inside the pressure shaft. The length of a very long, now discontinuous, stone stairway in the Rohtang Pass, Manali, Kulu, Northern India, is still under investigation.

TALLEST FIRE ESCAPE
The world's tallest mobile fire escape is a 250-foot-tall turntable ladder built in 1962 by Magirus, a West German firm.

LARGEST MARQUEE
World The largest tent ever erected was one covering an area of 188,368 square feet (4.32 acres) put up by the firm of Deuter from Augsburg, West Germany, for the 1958 "Welcome Expo" in Brussels, Belgium.

Britain The largest marquee in Britain is one made by Piggot Brothers in 1951 and used by the Royal Horticultural Society at their annual show (first held in 1913) in the grounds of the Royal Hospital, Chelsea, London. The marquee is 310 feet long X 480 feet wide, and consists of 18¾ miles of 36-inch-wide canvas covering a ground area of 148,800 square feet. A tent 390 feet long was erected in one lift by the Army at the 1970 Colchester Tattoo in Kings Head Meadow with 135 men.

LARGEST VATS
The largest vats in the United Kingdom are those used in cider brewing by H. P. Bulmer & Company. Their standard oak vats hold 60,000 gallons and reinforced concrete vats hold up to 100,000 gallons. Largest of all is Apollo XI, a lined steel vat with a capacity of 1,100,000 gallons and a diameter of 60 feet at Hereford.

The world's largest fermentation vessel is the giant stainless steel container, No. 26M, built by the A.P.V. Co. Ltd. of Crawley, Sussex, for the Guinness Brewery, St. James's Gate, Dublin, Ireland. This has a nominal capacity of 8,000 standard barrels, or 2,304,000 Imperial pints, and dimensions of 63 feet long by 28 feet 9 inches wide by 29 feet 7 inches high.

ADVERTISING SIGNS
Largest The greatest advertising sign ever erected was the electric Citroën sign on the Eiffel Tower, Paris. It was switched on on 4 July 1925, and could be seen 24 miles away. It was in six colours with 250,000 lamps and 56 miles of electric cables. The letter "N" which terminated the name "Citroën" between the second and third levels measured 68 feet 5 inches in height. The whole apparatus was taken down after 11 years in 1936.

The world's largest neon sign was that owned by the Atlantic Coast Line Railroad Company at Port Tampa, Florida, U.S.A. It measured 387 feet 6 inches long and 76 feet high, weighed 175 tons and contained about 4,200 feet of red neon tubing. It was demolished on 19 Feb. 1970. Broadway's largest billboard in New York City is 11,426 square feet in area—equivalent to 107 feet by 107 feet. Britain's largest illuminated sign is the word PLAYHOUSE extending 90 feet across the frontage of the new theatre in Leeds, Yorkshire opened in 1970.

The world's largest working sign was that in Times Square at 44 & 45th Streets, New York City, U.S.A., in 1966. It showed two 42½-foot-tall "bottles" of Haig Scotch Whisky and an 80-foot-long "bottle" of Gordon's Gin being "poured" into a frosted glass. The world's tallest free-standing advertising sign is the 188-foot tall, 93-foot-wide Stardust Hotel sign at Las Vegas, Nevada, U.S.A. completed in February 1968. It uses 25,000 light bulbs and 2,500 feet of neon tubing and has letters up to 22 feet tall.

Highest World The highest advertising sign in the world is the "R.C.A." on the Radio Corporation of America Building in Rockefeller Plaza, New York City, U.S.A. The top of the 25-foot-tall illuminated letters is 822 feet above street level.

United Kingdom The highest advertising sign in the United Kingdom was the revolving name board of the contractor "Peter Lind" on the Post Office Tower, London (see Towers). The illuminated letters were 12 feet tall and 563 to 575 feet above the street.

LARGEST GASHOLDER
World The world's largest gasholder is that at Fontain l'Evêque, Belgium, where disused mines have been adapted to store up to 500 million cubic metres (17,650 million cubic feet) of gas at ordinary pressure. Probably the largest conventional gasholder is that at Wien-Simmering, Vienna, Austria, completed in 1968, with a height of 274 feet 8 inches and a capacity of 10.59 million cubic feet.

United Kingdom The largest gasholder ever constructed in the United Kingdom is the East Greenwich Gas Works No. 2 Holder built in 1891 with an original capacity for 12,200,000 cubic feet. As reconstructed its capacity is 8.9 million cubic feet with a water tank 303 feet in diameter and a full inflated height of 148 feet. The No. 1 holder (capacity 8.6 million cubic feet) has a height of 200 feet. The River Tees Northern Gas Board's 1,186-foot-deep underground storage in use since January 1959 has a capacity of 330,000 cubic feet.

TALLEST FOUNTAIN
World The world's tallest fountain is the "Delacorte Geyser" in Welfare Park, Manhattan, New York City which can attain a height of 600 feet. It was installed in June 1969 at a cost of $350,000 (£145,833) and given to the City by George T. Delacorte, founder of the Dell Publishing Company.

United Kingdom The tallest fountain in the United Kingdom is the Emperor Fountain at Chatsworth, Bakewell, Derbyshire. When first tested on 1 June 1844, it attained the then unprecedented height of 260 feet. Since the war it has not been played to more than 250 feet and rarely beyond 180 feet.

Bonfire Largest The largest Guy Fawkes bonfire constructed was one using 150 tons of timber and 1,500 tyres built to a height of 75 feet by The First Company of Torrington Cavaliers in Torrington, Devon for 5 Nov. 1971.

CEMETERIES
The world's largest cemetery is that in Leningrad, U.S.S.R., which contains over 500,000 of the 1,300,000 victims of the German army's siege of 1941-42. The largest cemetery in the United Kingdom is Brookwood Cemetery, Brookwood, Surrey. It is owned by the London Necropolis Co. and is 500 acres in extent with 224,952 interments to June 1972.

CREMATORIA
Earliest The oldest crematorium in Britain is one built in 1879 at Woking, Surrey. The first legal cremation took place there on 20 March 1885.

Largest The largest crematorium in the world is at the Nikolo-Arkhangelskoye Cemetery, East Moscow completed to a British design in March 1972. It has seven twin furnaces and several Halls of Farewell for atheists. Britain's largest is The Enfield Crematorium, Middlesex which extends over 40 acres and also carries out most cremations.

The headgear above a hole in the earth that is deeper than Everest is high—the 5.69 mile deep Baden No. 1 well, Oklahoma, U.S.A.

10. BORINGS

DEEPEST

World Man's deepest penetration into the Earth's crust is the Baden No. 1 gas wildcat well, Beckham County, Oklahoma, U.S.A. After 546 days drilling the Loffland Brothers Drilling Co. reached 30,050 feet (5.69 miles) on 29 Feb. 1972. The hole temperature at the bottom was 420° F. A conception of the depth of this hole can be gained by the realization that it was sufficient in depth to lower the Empire State Building down it 24 times.

The most recent in a succession of announcements of intentions to drill down 15 kilometers (49,213 feet) from the U.S.S.R. was in February 1972 from the Baku Scientific Research Institute. A depth of 21,620 feet has been reached at the Kura River valley site in Southern Azerbaijan. The target here remains 48,000 feet (9.09 miles).

PROGRESSIVE RECORDS IN DEEP DRILLING

Depth in ft.	Location	Date
475	Duck Creek, Ohio (brine)	1841
550	Perpignan, France (artesian)	1849
5,735	Schladebach, Germany	1886
6,570	Schladebach, Germany	1893
7,230	Schladebach, Germany	1909
8,046	Olinda, Calif.	1927
8,523	Big Lake, W. Texas	1928
9,280	Long Beach, Calif.	1929
9,753	Midway, Calif.	1930
10,030	Rinconfield, Calif.	1931
10,585	Vera Cruz, Mexico	1931
10,944	Kettleman Hills, Calif.	1933
11,377	Belridge, Calif.	1934
12,786	Gulf McElroy, W. Texas	1935
15,004	Wasco, Calif.	1938
15,279	Pecos County, W. Texas	1944
16,246	S. Coles Levee, Calif.	1944
16,655	Brazos County, Texas	1945
16,668	Miramonte, Calif.	1946
17,823	Caddo County, Oklahoma	1947
18,734	Ventura County, Calif.	1949
20,521	Sublette County, Wyoming	1949
21,482	Bakersfield, Calif.	1953
22,570	Plaquemines, Louisiana	1956
25,340	Pecos County, W. Texas	1958
25,600	St. Bernard Parish, Louisiana	1970
28,500	Pecos County, W. Texas	1972
30,050	Beckham County, Oklahoma	1972

United Kingdom The deepest oil well in the United Kingdom is the British Petroleum well drilled to a depth of 9,355 feet at Tetney Lock, near Cleethorpes, Lincolnshire, in 1963. A depth of 19,171 feet was attained at an undisclosed site in the U.K. North Sea fields in 1970.

OIL FIELDS

The largest oil field in the world is that at Oktyabr'skiy, U.S.S.R., which extends over 1,800 square miles (60 miles by 30 miles). It has been asserted that the Groningen gas field in the Netherlands is the largest discovered. It was estimated in 1968 that the United Kingdom's segment of the North Sea gas field contains 2.5×10^{13} cubic feet of almost pure methane of which the Leman Field (discovered April 1966), operated by the Shell-Esso-Gas Council-Amoco group, accounts for about half.

Greatest gusher The most prolific wildcat recorded is the 1,160-foot-deep Lucas No. 1, at Spindletop, about 3 miles north of Beaumont, Texas, U.S.A., on 10 Jan. 1901. The gusher was heard more than a mile away and yielded 800,000 barrels during the 9 days it was uncapped. The surrounding ground subsequently yielded 142,000,000 barrels.

Greatest flare The greatest gas fire was that which burnt at Gassi Touil in the Algerian Sahara from noon on 13 Nov. 1961 to 9.30 a.m. on 28 April 1962. The pillar of flame rose 450 feet and the smoke 600 feet. It was eventually extinguished by Paul Neal ("Red") Adair, aged 47, of Austin, Texas, U.S.A., using 550 lb. of dynamite. His fee was understood to be about $1,000,000 (then £357,000).

WATER WELLS

Deepest World The world's deepest water bore is the Stensvad Water Well 11-W1 of 7,320 feet drilled by the Great Northern Drilling Co. Inc. in Rosebud County, Montana, U.S.A. in October-November 1961. The Thermal Power Co. geothermal steam well begun in Sonora County, California in 1955 is now down to 9,029 feet.

United Kingdom The deepest well in the United Kingdom is a water table well 2,842 feet deep in the Staffordshire coal measures at Smestow. The deepest artesian well in Britain is that at the White Heather Laundry, Stonebridge Park, Willesden, London, N.W.10, bored in 1911 to a depth of 2,225 feet.

Largest Hand-dug The largest hand-dug well was one 100 feet in circumference and 109 feet deep dug in 1877-8 at Greensburg, Kansas, U.S.A.

MINES

Earliest The earliest known mining operations were in the Ngwenya Hills of the Hhohho District of northwestern Swaziland where haematite (iron ore) was mined for body paint c. 41,000 B.C. The earliest known mines in England are the Neolithic flint mines at Church Hill, Findon, Sussex dated to 3390 B.C. ±150.

Deepest World The world's deepest mine is the East Rand Proprietary Mine at Boksburg, Transvaal, South Africa. In November 1959 a depth of 11,246 feet (2.13 miles) below the ground and 5,875 feet below sea-level was first attained. Mining does not now proceed below 10,788 feet where the rock temperature is two degrees cooler at 124° F. The deepest terminal below any vertical mine shaft in the world is No. 3 sub-vertical main shaft on the Western Deep Levels Mine reaching 9,783 feet below the surface. The longest vertical shaft is No. 3 Ventilation Shaft at the mine which measures 9,673 feet in one continuous hole. The longest sub-incline shaft is the

The site of Cornwall's deepest ever tin mine at Dolcoath near Camborne

Angelo Tertiary at E.R.P.M. (see above) with a length of 6,656 feet (1.26 miles).

United Kingdom The all-time record depth is 4,132 feet in the Arley Seam of the Parsonage Colliery, Leigh, Lancashire in Feb. 1949. The record in Scottish coalmines was 3,093 feet in the Michael Colliery, Barncraig, Fife, reached in August 1939. The deepest present mine workings are the Hem Heath Colliery (Moss Seam), Trentham, Staffordshire, England at 3,300 feet. The deepest in Scotland is the Great Seam at Monkton Hall Colliery, Millerhill, Midlothian, at 2,930 feet. The deepest shaft in England was No. 2 shaft at Wolstanton Colliery, Stoke-on-Trent, Staffordshire, at 3,434 feet and the deepest in Scotland was Monkton Hall No. 1, Midlothian at 3,054 feet. The deepest Cornish tin mine was Dolcoath mine, near Camborne. The Williams shaft was completed in 1910 to 550 fathoms (3,300 feet) from adit or approximately 3,600 feet from the surface. A shaft in the Cleveland Potash Ltd. mine at Boulby, Yorkshire which reached 3,300 feet by March 1972 will surpass 3,700 feet.

GOLDMINES

Largest area The largest goldmining area in the world is the Witwatersrand gold field extending 30 miles east and west of Johannesburg, South Africa. Gold was discovered there in 1886 and by 1944 more than 45 per cent. of the world's gold was mined there by 320,000 Bantu and 44,000 Europeans. Currently 74 per cent. of the free world's supply comes from this area which now has a total labour force of 650,000.

Largest World The largest goldmine in area is the East Rand Proprietary Mines Ltd., whose 8,785 claims cover 12,100 acres. The largest, measured by volume extracted, is Randfontein Estates Gold Mine Co. Ltd. with 170 million cubic yards—enough to cover Manhattan Island to a depth of 8 feet. The main tunnels if placed end to end would stretch a distance of 2,600 miles.

United Kingdom The largest goldmine in Britain was Gwynfyngdd, Merionethshire, Wales, where gold was discovered in 1834 and which was worked from 1864 till 1961. Alluvial gold deposits are believed to have been worked in the Wicklow Mountains, Ireland, as early as 1800 B.C.

Richest The richest goldmine has been Crown Mines with nearly 45 million ounces and still productive. The richest in yield per year was West Driefontein which averaged more than 2½ million ounces per year until disrupted in November 1968 by flooding. The only large mine in South Africa yielding more than one ounce per ton milled is Free State Geduld.

Iron The world's largest iron-mine is at Lebedinsky, U.S.S.R., in the Kursk Magnetic Anomaly which has altogether an estimated 20,000 million tons of rich (45-65 per cent.) ore and 10,000,000 million tons of poorer ore in seams up to 2,000 feet thick. The world's greatest reserves are, however, those of Brazil estimated to total 58,000 million tons, or 35 per cent. of the world's total surface stock.

Copper Historically the world's most productive copper mine has been the Bingham Canyon Mine (see below) belonging to the Kennecott Copper Corporation with over 9,000,000 short tons in the 65 years 1904-69. Currently the most productive is the Chuquicamata mine of the Anaconda Company 150 miles north of Antofagasta, Chile with 334,578 short tons in 1966.

The world's largest underground copper mine is at El Teniente, 50 miles south-east of Santiago, Chile, with more than 200 miles of underground workings and an annual output of nearly 11,000,000 tons of ore.

Silver, lead and zinc The world's largest lead, zinc and silver mine is the Sullivan Mine at Kimberley, British Columbia, Canada, with 248 miles of tunnels. The mines at Broken Hill, New South Wales, Australia, found September 1883, produce annually 2,300,000 tons of ore, from which is extracted some 10 per cent. of the world's output of lead. The world's largest zinc smelter is the Cominco Ltd. plant at Trail, British Columbia, Canada which has an annual capacity of 263,000 tons of zinc and 800 tons of cadmium.

Spoil heap The world's largest artificial heap is the sand dump of the Randfontein Estates Gold Mines, South Africa which comprises 42 million tons of crushed ore and rock waste and has a volume six times that of the Great Pyramid. The largest colliery tip in Great Britain covers 114 acres (maximum height 130 feet) with 18 million tons of slag at Cutacre Clough, Lancashire.

QUARRIES

Largest World The world's largest excavation is the Bingham Canyon Copper Mine, 30 miles south of Salt Lake City, Utah, U.S.A. From 1906 to mid-1969 the total excavation has been 2,445 million long tons over an area of 2.0 square miles to a depth of 2,280 feet. This is five times the amount of material moved to build the Panama Canal. Three shifts of 900 men work round the clock with 38 electric shovels, 62 locomotives hauling 1,268 wagons and 18 drilling machines for the 28 tons of explosive used daily. The average daily extraction is 96,000 tons of one per cent. ore and 225,000 tons of overburden.

The world's deepest open pit is the Kimberley Open Mine in South Africa, dug over a period of 43 years (1871 to 1914) to a depth of nearly 1,200 feet and with a diameter of about 1,500 feet and a circumference of nearly a mile, covering an area of 36 acres. Three tons (14,504,566 carats) of diamonds were extracted from the 21,000,000 tons of earth dug out. The inflow of water has now made the depth 845 feet to the water surface. The "Big Hole" was dug by pick and shovel.

United Kingdom The largest quarry in Britain is Imperial Chemical Industries Ltd.'s Tunstead Quarry, near Buxton, Derbyshire. The working face is 1½ miles long and 120 feet high.

Largest stone The largest mined slab of quarried stone is one measuring 68 feet by 14 feet by 14 feet, weighing about 1,590 tons, at Ba'labakk (Baalbeck), in the Lebanon. The largest able to be moved from the mine were slabs of 805 tons for the trilithon of the nearby Temple of Jupiter.

8 THE MECHANICAL WORLD

1. SHIPS

EARLIEST BOATS
The earliest known vessel which is still sea-worthy is a 102-foot-long sailing vessel dated to the Egyptian sixth dynasty from *c.* 2420 B.C. Oars found in bogs at Magle Mose, Sjaelland, Denmark and Star Carr, Yorkshire, England, have been dated to *c.* 8000 B.C.

Earliest power The earliest experiments with marine steam engines date from those on the river Seine, France, in 1775. Propulsion was first achieved when in 1783 the Marquis Jouffroy d'Abbans ascended a reach of the river Saône near Lyons, France, in the 180-ton paddle steamer *Pyroscaphe.*

The tug *Charlotte Dundas* was the first successful power-driven vessel. She was a paddle-wheel steamer built in Scotland in 1801-02 by William Symington (1763-1831), using a double-acting condensing engine constructed by James Watt (1736-1819). The earliest regular steam run was by the *Clermont*, built by Robert Fulton (1765-1815), a U.S. engineer, which maintained a service from New York to Albany from 17 Aug. 1807.

Oldest steam vessel The oldest steamer is believed to be the *Skibladner* (206 gross tons), which was built in Motala, Sweden, in 1856 and sank on Lake Mjøsa, Norway, in February 1967 but was raised and refitted for re-commission. Mr. G. H. Pattinson's 40-foot steam launch, raised from Ullswater in 1962 and now on Lake Windermere, may date from a year or two earlier.

Earliest turbine The first turbine ship was the *Turbinia*, built in 1894 at Wallsend-on-Tyne, Northumberland, to the design of the Hon. Sir Charles Algernon Parsons, O.M., K.C.B. (1854-1931). The *Turbinia* was 100 feet long and of 44½ tons displacement with machinery consisting of three steam turbines totalling about 2,000 shaft horsepower. At her first public demonstration in 1897 she reached a speed of 34.5 knots (39.7 m.p.h.).

Atlantic crossings **Earliest** The earliest crossing of the Atlantic by a power vessel, as opposed to an auxiliary engined sailing ship, was a 22-day voyage begun in April 1827, from Rotterdam, Netherlands, to the West Indies by the *Curaçao.* She was a wooden paddle boat of 438 registered tons,

built in Dundee, Angus, in 1826 and purchased by the Dutch Government for the West Indian mail service. The earliest Atlantic crossing entirely under steam (with intervals for desalting the boilers) was by H.M.S. *Rhadamanthus* from Plymouth to Barbados in 1832. The earliest crossing of the Atlantic under continuous steam power was by the condenser-fitted packet ship *Sirius* (703 tons) from Queenstown (now Cóbh), Ireland, to Sandy Hook, N.Y., U.S.A., in 18 days 10 hours on 4-22 April 1838.

Fastest World The fastest Atlantic crossing was made by the *United States* (then 51,988, now 38,216 gross tons), flagship of the United States Lines Company. On her maiden voyage between 3 and 7 July 1952 from New York City, N.Y., U.S.A., to Le Havre, France, and Southampton, England, she averaged 35.59 knots, or 40.98 m.p.h., for 3 days 10 hours 40 minutes (6.36 p.m. G.M.T. 3 July to 5.16 a.m. 7 July) on a route of 2,949 nautical miles from the Ambrose Light Vessel to the Bishop Rock Light, Isles of Scilly, Cornwall. During

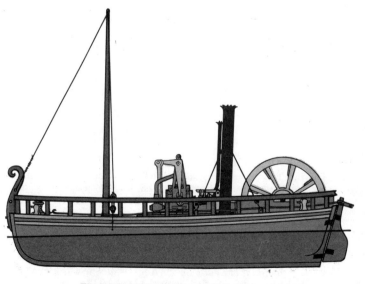

The tug Charlotte Dundas. 1801 the first successful power-driven vessel

The one time largest liner in the world—the Mauretania which plied the Atlantic from 1907 to 1935

PROGRESSIVE LIST OF WORLD'S LARGEST AND LONGEST LINERS

Gross Tonnage	Name	Propulsion	Overall Length in Feet	Dates
1,340	Great Western (U.K.)	Paddle wheels	236	1838–1856
1,862	British Queen (U.K.)	Paddle wheels	275	1839–1844
2,360	President (U.K.)	Paddle wheels	268	1840–1841
3,270	Great Britain (U.K.)	Single screw	322	1845–1937
4,690	Himalaya (U.K.)	Single screw	340	1853–1927
18,914[1]	Great Eastern (U.K.)	Paddles and screw	692	1858–1888
10,650	City of New York (later Harvard, Pittsburgh) (U.S.)	Twin screw	528	1888–1923
17,274	Oceanic (U.K.)	Twin screw	705	1899–1914
20,904	Celtic (U.K.)	Twin screw	700	1901–1928
21,227	Cedric (U.K.)	Twin screw	700	1903–1932
23,884	Baltic (U.K.)	Twin screw	726	1904–1933
31,550	Lusitania (U.K.)	4 screws	790	1907–1915
31,938	Mauretania (U.K.)	4 screws	787	1907–1935
45,300	Olympic (U.K.)	Triple screw	892	1911–1935
46,300	Titanic (U.K.)	Triple screw	882	1912–1912
52,022	Imperator (Germany) (later Berengaria [U.K.])	4 screws	919	1913–1938
54,282[2]	Vaterland (Germany) (later Leviathan [U.S.])	4 screws	950	1914–1938
56,621	Bismarck (Germany) (later Majestic [U.K.] and H.M. Troopship Caledonia)	4 screws	954	1922–1936
79,280[3]	Normandie (France) (later U.S.S. Lafayette)	4 screws	1,029	1935–1946
80,774[4]	Queen Mary (U.K.) (later sold to U.S. interests)	4 screws	1,019	1936–
83,673[5]	Queen Elizabeth (U.K.) (later sold to U.S., then Hong Kong interests)	4 screws	1,031	1940–
66,348	France (France)	4 screws	1,035	1961–

[1] Originally 22,500 tons.
[2] Listed as 59,957 gross tons under U.S. registration, 1922–31, but not internationally accepted as such.
[3] Gross tonnage later raised by enclosure of open deck space to 83,423 gross tons.
[4] Later 81,237 gross tons.
[5] Later 82,998 gross tons.

this run, on 6-7 July 1952, she steamed the greatest distance ever covered by any ship in a day's run (24 hours)—868 nautical miles, hence averaging 36.17 knots (41.65 m.p.h.). Her maximum speed is 41.75 knots (48 m.p.h.) on a full power of 240,000 shaft horse-power. The s.h.p. figure was only revealed by the U.S. Defense Department in 1968.

British The fastest crossing of the Atlantic by a British ship is 3 days 15 hours 48 minutes by the Cunard liner *Queen Mary* in September 1946 on a 2,710-mile voyage from Halifax, Nova Scotia, Canada, to Southampton at an average of 30.86 knots (35.54 m.p.h.). On her 2,938-mile crossing from the Ambrose Light to Bishop Rock on 10-14 Aug. 1938, she averaged 31.69 knots (36.49 m.p.h.) for 3 days 20 hours 42 minutes.

Submerged The fastest disclosed submerged Atlantic crossing is 6 days 11 hours 55 minutes by the U.S. nuclear-powered submarine *Nautilus*, which travelled 3,150 miles from Portland, Dorset, to New York City, N.Y., U.S.A., arriving on 25 Aug. 1958.

Most crossings Between 1856 and June 1894 Captain Samuel Brooks (1832-1904) crossed the North Atlantic 690 times—equal to 2,437,712 statute miles. In 1850-51 he had sailed in the brig *Bessie* as an Able Bodied seaman round The Horn to Panama coming home to Liverpool as her master. His life-time sailing distance was at least 2,513,000 miles.

Pacific crossing The fastest crossing of the Pacific Ocean (Yokohama, Japan to San Francisco, U.S.A.) is 8 days 35 minutes achieved by the 14,114-ton diesel cargo liner *Italy Maru* in August 1967.

EXTREMITIES REACHED

Northern-most The farthest north ever attained by a surface vessel is 86° 39′ N. in 47° 55′ E. by the drifting U.S.S.R. icebreaker *Sedov* on 29 Aug. 1939. She was locked in the Arctic ice floes from 23 Oct. 1937 until freed on 13 Jan. 1940.

Southern-most The farthest south ever reached by a ship was achieved on 3 Jan. 1955, by the Argentine icebreaker *General San Martin* in establishing the General Belgrano Base, Antarctica, on the shores of the Weddell Sea at 78° S., 39° W., 830 miles from the South Pole.

PASSENGER LINERS

Largest The world's longest and largest active liner (66,348 gross tons) is the *France*, built at St. Nazaire, owned by the Compagnie Générale Transatlantique. She measures 1,035 feet 2 inches overall and made her official maiden voyage from Le Havre, France, to New York City, N.Y., U.S.A., on 3 Feb. 1962, and cost £29,000,000. Britain's largest liner is R.M.S. *Queen Elizabeth 2* of 65,863 gross tons and an overall length of 963 feet, completed for the Cunard Line Ltd. in 1969. She set a "turn round" record of 8 hours 3 mins. at New York on 17 May 1972.

Largest ever The R.M.S. *Queen Elizabeth* (finally 82,998 but formerly 83,673 gross tons), of the Cunard fleet, was the largest passenger vessel ever built and had the largest displacement of any liner in the world. She had an overall length of 1,031 feet and is 118 feet 7 inches in breadth and was powered by steam turbines which developed 168,000 h.p. Her last passenger voyage ended on 15 Nov. 1968. In 1970 she was removed to Hong Kong to serve as a floating marine university and renamed *Seawise University*. On 9 Jan. 1972 she caught fire and was gutted.

WARSHIPS

Battleships Largest World The largest battleships in the world are now the U.S.S. *Iowa* (completed 22 Feb. 1943) and U.S.S. *Missouri* (completed 11 June 1944), each of which has a full load displacement of 57,950 tons and mounts nine 16-inch and 20 5-inch guns. The U.S.S. *New Jersey* (57,216 tons full load displacement) is, however, longer than either by nine inches, with an overall length of 888 feet. She was the last battleship of active service in the world and was de-commissioned on 17 Dec. 1969.

The last moments of the greatest battleship ever built—Japan's 72,809 ton Musashi

Largest The Japanese battleships *Yamato* (completed on 16
all-time Dec. 1941 and sunk in the Bungo Strait off Kyūshū,
Japan, by U.S. planes on 7 April 1945) and *Musashi*
(sunk in the Philippine Sea by 11 bombs and 16
torpedoes on 24 Oct. 1944) were the largest battleships ever constructed, each with a full load displacement of 72,809 tons. With an overall length of 863
feet, a beam of 127 feet and a full load draught of 35½
feet, they mounted nine 460 mm. (18.1 inch) guns in
three triple turrets. Each gun weighed 162 tons and
was 75 feet in length, firing a 3,200 lb. projectile.

Britain Britain's largest ever and last battleship was H.M.S.
Vanguard with a full load displacement of 51,420
tons, overall length 814 feet, beam 108½ feet, with a
maximum draught of 36 feet. She mounted eight
15-inch and 16 5.25-inch guns. A shaft horse-power
of 130,000 gave her a sea speed of 29½ knots (34
m.p.h.). The *Vanguard* was laid down in John Brown
& Co. Ltd.'s yard at Clydebank, Dunbartonshire, on
20 Oct. 1941, launched on 30 Nov. 1944 and
completed on 25 April 1946. She was sold for scrap in
August 1960 for £500,000 having cost a total of
£14,000,000.

Largest The largest guns ever mounted in any of H.M. ships
guns were the 18-inch pieces in the light battle cruiser
(later aircraft carrier) H.M.S. *Furious* in 1917. In
1918 they were transferred to the monitors H.M.S.
Lord Clive and *General Wolfe.* The thickest armour
ever carried was in H.M.S. *Inflexible* (completed
1881), measuring 24 inches.

AIRCRAFT CARRIERS
Largest The warship with the largest full load displacement in
World the world is the aircraft carrier U.S.S. *Nimitz* at

An artist's impression of the world's largest ever aircraft
carrier—the U.S.S. Nimitz launched in April 1972 which will
have a full load displacement of 95,100 tons

95,100 tons. She was launched in April 1972 and will
be commissioned in Sept. 1973. U.S.S. *Enterprise*
is, however, 1,101½ feet long and thus 65½ feet
longer. U.S.S. *Nimitz,* which will have a speed well in
excess of 30 knots, will cost $536,000,000 (£223.3
million). She will be followed by a sister ship U.S.S.
Eisenhower, which will be only 9½ feet shorter than
the *Enterprise.*

Britain Britain's largest ever aircraft carrier is H.M.S. *Ark
Royal,* completed on 25 Feb. 1955, with a full load
displacement of 50,786 tons (previously 53,340
tons), 845 feet overall, 166 feet wide, maximum
draught 36 feet, with a full complement of 2,640 and
a capacity of 30 naval jet aircraft and 6 helicopters.
Her 152,000 shaft horse-power give her a maximum
speed of 31.5 knots (36.27 m.p.h.).

Most deck The pilot who has made the greatest number of deck
landings landings is Capt. Eric M. Brown, C.B.E., D.S.C.,
A.F.C., R.N. with 2,407. Capt. Brown, who retired in
1970, flew a record 325 types of aircraft during his
career and also set a world record with 2,721 catapult
launchings.

Most The Fleet Escort Ships (formerly cruisers) with the
powerful greatest fire power are the three Albany class ships
cruiser U.S.S.'s *Albany, Chicago* and *Columbus* of 13,700

The world's most powerful cruiser—the 13,700 ton U.S.S.
Albany which carries 12, surface to air and anti-submarine
missiles

tons and 673 feet overall. They carry 2 twin Talos and
2 twin Tartar surface-to-air missiles and an 8-tube
Asroc launcher. The Royal Navy's largest ever cruiser
H.M.S. *Belfast* displacing 10,000 tons, is now moored
on exhibition above Tower Bridge, London.

Fastest The highest speed attained by a destroyer was 45.02
destroyer knots (51.84 m.p.h.) by the 3,750-ton French destroyer *Le Terrible* in 1935. She was powered by four
Yarrow small tube boilers and two geared turbines
giving 100,000 shaft horse-power. She was removed
from the active list at the end of 1957.

Fastest The world's fastest warship is H.M.C.S. *Bras d'Or,* the
warship 180-ton 150.8-foot-long Canadian Navy Hydrofoil
commissioned in 1967. On 17 July 1969 outside
Halifax harbour, Nova Scotia she attained 61 knots
(70.2 m.p.h.).

SUBMARINES
Largest The world's largest submarines are believed to be the
18 nuclear-powered U.S.S.R. "Y" Class submarines
with a submerged displacement of 9,000 tons and an
overall length of 426.5 feet. The largest submarines
built for the Royal Navy are the four atomic-powered
nuclear missile R class boats with a surface displacement of 7,500 tons and 8,400 tons submerged, a
length of 425 feet, a beam of 33 feet and a draught of
30 feet.

Fastest The world's fastest submarines are the 35-knot U.S. Navy's tear-drop hulled nuclear vessels of the *Skipjack* class. They have been listed semi-officially as capable of a speed of 45 knots (51.8 m.p.h.) submerged. In November 1968 the building of attack submarines with submerged speeds in the region of 50 knots was approved for the U.S. Navy.

Deepest The greatest depth recorded by a true submarine was 8,310 feet by the Lockheed *Sea Quest* off California, U.S.A., on 29 Feb. 1968. The 51-foot-long *Aluminaut* launched by the Reynolds Metals Co. on 2 Sept. 1964 is designed for depths of up to 15,000 feet but is prevented from descending below 6,250 feet by prohibitive insurance costs. The U.S. Navy's nuclear-powered NR-1 being built by General Dynamics Inc. will be able to operate at a "very great" but classified depth which is assumed to be lower than the published figure of 20,000 feet for the first 7-man Deep Submergence Search Vehicle DSSV due in service in 1973.

Largest fleet The largest submarine fleet in the world is that of the U.S.S.R. Navy or *Krasni Flot,* which numbers 401 boats, of which 83 (18 ballistic missile armed) are nuclear-powered and 318 conventional. The U.S. Navy has 41 nuclear submarines in service.

TANKERS

Largest The world's largest tanker is the *Nisseki Maru* of 366,518 tons deadweight and 1,137 feet 7½ inches length overall built by Ishikawajima-Harima Heavy Industries Co. Ltd. at Kure, Japan, launched in April 1971 and completed on 10 Sept. 1971. She is 178 feet 9½ inches in the beam and draws 88 feet 7 inches. She is powered by a set of I.H.I. steam turbines delivering 39,450 s.h.p. at 90 revs. per minute giving 15 knots. The even larger *Globtik Tokyo* of 477,000 tons deadweight and 1,243 feet 5 inches length overall is scheduled for delivery by the same yard at a cost of £11.5 million in February 1973. She will be 203 feet 5 inches in the beam, will draw 91 feet 10 inches and will be powered by an I.H.I. turbine set rated at 44,385 s.h.p.

Longest The longest ships in the world of any kind are the Esso class tankers, which have a length of 1,141 feet 1 inch—106 feet longer than the world's longest ever liner, *France.* They have a deadweight tonnage of 253,000 tons, a gross registered tonnage of 127,150 and a beam of 170 feet 2 inches. Some idea of this length can be conveyed by the thought that it would take a golfer, standing on the stem, a full-blooded drive and a chip shot to reach the stern. The largest vessels launched in a United Kingdom shipyard are those of this class, the first of which was, on 2 May 1969, the *Esso Northumbria* launched for Esso Petroleum at the yard of Swan Hunter and Tyne Shipbuilders. She is 110 feet longer than the *Queen Elizabeth.*

CARGO VESSELS

Largest The largest vessel in the world capable of carrying dry cargo is *La Loma* (129,961 gross) (U.K.). She is 1,069 feet 8 inches in length and has a beam of 170 feet 8 inches. The world's largest ore carrier is the *Niizuru Maru* of 165,196 deadweight tons which made her maiden voyage in Oct. 1971.

Fastest built During the Second World War "Liberty ships" of prefabricated welded steel construction were built at seven shipyards on the Pacific coast of the United States, under the management of Henry J. Kaiser (1882-1967). The record time for assembly of one ship of 7,200 gross tons (10,500 tons deadweight) was 4 days 15½ hours. In January 1968, 900 Liberty ships were still in service.

The world's most powerful tug—the 17,500h.p. Oceanic

Largest cable ship The world's largest cable-laying ship is the Americ[an] Telephone & Telegraph Co.'s German-built *Lo[ng] Lines* (11,200 gross tons), completed by Deutsc[he] Werft of Hamburg in April 1963, at a cost [of] £6,800,000. She has a fully-laden displacement [of] 17,000 tons, measures 511 feet 6 inches overall and [is] powered by twin turbine electric engines.

Largest whale factory The largest whale factory ship is the U.S.S.R[.] *Sovietskaya Ukraina* (32,034 gross tons), with[a] summer deadweight of 46,000 tons, completed [in] October 1959. She is 714.6 feet in length and 94 fe[et] 3 inches in the beam.

Most powerful tug World The world's largest and most powerful tugs are t[he] two 17,500 i.h.p. *Oceanic* class boats of 2,046 gr[oss] tons, 284 ft. 5 in. overall, a beam of 46 ft. 11 in. [a] speed of 22 knots and a range 20,000 miles. T[he] largest ship ever to take another in tow is S.S. *Ardl[...]* the 214,180 deadweight ton tanker which towed S[...] *British Architect* (22,729 gross tons) 73 miles in t[he] China Sea on 16 June 1970.

British The most powerful tug ever built for a British owne[r] m.t. *Lloydsman* completed in June 1971 for Unit[ed] Towing Limited of Hull at the Victoria shipyard [of] Robb Caledon Shipbuilders Ltd., Leith. She is rat[ed] at 16,000 h.p. with a bollard pull of 115 tons.

Fastest tow H.M.S. *Scylla* (Cdr. A.F.C. Wemyss O.B.E., R.[N.]) towed her sister ship, H.M.S. *Penelope,* in the Weste[rn] Mediterranean on 25 Sept. 1970 with an 11-i[nch] mile-long nylon rope (breaking strain 165 tons) a[t a] speed of 24 knots. The £10,000 Viking Ny[lon] Braidline hawser, made by British Ropes, stretch[ed] 38% to 7,325 feet.

Largest car ferry The world's largest car and passenger ferry is t[he] 502-foot-long *Finlandia* (8,100 gross tons), delive[red] by Wärtsilä Ab. of Helsinki in May 1967, for serv[ice] between Helsinki and Copenhagen with Finska A[ng]fartygs Ab. She can carry 321 cars and up to 1,2[...]

The fastest tow ever recorded—H.M.S. Scylla (on the horizon) towed H.M.S. Penelope through the Mediterrane[an] at 24 knots

passengers and achieved a speed of 22 knots (25 m.p.h.) during trials.

Largest hydrofoil The world's largest naval hydrofoil is the 212-foot-long *Plainview* (310 tons full load), launched by the Lockheed Shipbuilding and Construction Co. at Seattle, Washington, U.S.A., on 28 June 1965. She has a service speed of 50 knots (57 m.p.h.). A larger hydrofoil, carrying 150 passengers and 8 cars at 40 knots to ply the Göteborg-Ålborg crossing, came into service in June 1968. It was built by Westermoen Hydrofoil Ltd. of Mandal, Norway.

Most powerful icebreaker The world's most powerful icebreaker and first atomic-powered ship has been the U.S.S.R.'s 18 knot 44,000 s.h.p. *Lenin* (16,000 gross tons), which was launched at Leningrad on 2 Dec. 1957 and began her maiden voyage on 18 Sept. 1959. In 1971-2 mystery surrounded her continued existence. She is or was 439¾ feet long and 90½ feet in the beam. In March 1970 the U.S.S.R. announced the building of a more powerful atomic-powered icebreaker to be named *Arctika*, able to go through ice 7 feet thick at 4 knots.

The largest *converted* icebreaker has been the 1,007-foot-long S.S. *Manhattan* (43,000 s.h.p.), which was converted by the Humble Oil Co. into a 150,000-ton icebreaker with an armoured prow 69 feet 2 inches long. She made a double voyage through the North-West Passage in arctic Canada from 24 Aug. to 12 Nov. 1969. The North-West Passage was first navigated in 1906.

Largest dredger The world's largest dredger is one reported to be operating in the lower Lena basin in May 1967, with a rig more than 100 feet tall and a cutting depth of 165 feet. The pontoon is 750 feet long. The largest dredging grabs in the world are those of 635 cubic feet capacity built in 1965 by Priestman Bros. Ltd. of Hull, Yorkshire for the dredging pontoon *Biarritz*.

Most successful trawler The greatest tonnage of fish ever landed from any British trawler in a year is 4,169 tons in 1969 from the freezer stern trawler *Lady Parkes* owned by Boston Deep Sea Fisheries Ltd. (est. 1894).

Wooden ship The heaviest wooden ship ever built was H.M. Battleship *Lord Clyde* at 7,750 tons. She was completed at Pembroke Dock, Wales, on 2 June 1866. She measured 280 feet in length and was sold in 1875.

SAILING SHIPS

Largest The largest sailing vessel ever built was the *France II* (5,806 gross tons), launched at Bordeaux in 1911. The *France II* was a steel-hulled, five-masted barque (square-rigged on four masts and fore and aft rigged on the aftermost mast). Her hull measured 418 feet overall. Although principally designed as a sailing vessel with a stump topgallant rig, she was also fitted with two steam engines. She was wrecked in 1922. The only 5 masted full-rigged ship ever built was the *Preussen*, built in 1902, of 5,548 gross tons and 410 feet overall.

Largest junks The largest junk on record was the sea-going *Cheng Ho* of c. 1420, with a displacement of 3,100 tons and a length variously estimated at from 300 feet to 440 feet.

A river junk 361 feet long, with treadmill-operated paddle-wheels, was recorded in A.D. 1161. In c. A.D. 280 a floating fortress 600 feet square, built by Wang Chün on the Yangtze, took part in the Chin-Wu river war. Modern junks do not, even in the case of the Chiangsu traders, exceed 170 feet in length.

Longest day's run under sail The longest day's run by any sailing ship was one of 465 nautical miles (535.45 statute miles) by the clipper *Champion of the Seas* (2,722 registered tons) of the Liverpool Black Ball Line running before a

north-westerly gale in the south Indian Ocean under the command of Capt. Alex. Newlands. The elapsed time between the fixes was 23 hours 17 minutes giving an average of 19.97 knots.

Greatest speed The highest recorded speed by a sailing ship is 22 knots (25.3 m.p.h.) in 4 consecutive watches, by *Lancing* (ex *La Péreire*) when "running her easting down" on a passage to Melbourne in 1890/91. She was the last 4 masted full-rigged ship (36 sails) and at 405 feet the longest. Her main and mizzen masts were 203 feet from keelson to truck with yards 98 ft. 9 ins. across.

Slowest voyage Perhaps the slowest passage on record was that of the *Red Rock* (1,600 tons), which was posted missing at Lloyd's of London after taking 112 days for 950 miles across the Coral Sea from 20 Feb. to 12 June 1899, at an average speed of less than 0.4 of a knot.

Largest sails The largest spars ever carried were those in H.M. Battleship *Temeraire*, completed at Chatham, Kent, on 31 Aug. 1877. The fore and main yards measured 115 feet in length. The mainsail contained 5,100 feet of canvas, weighing 2 tons, and the total sail area was 25,000 square feet. At 8,540 tons the *Temeraire* was the largest brig ever built. The main masts of H.M.S. *Achilles*, *Black Prince* and *Warrior* all measured 175 feet from truck to deck.

Largest propeller The largest ship's propeller will be one of 30 feet 2 inches diameter from blade tip to blade tip built for the 477,000-ton tanker *Globtik Tokyo* due to be delivered in February 1973.

Largest Dracones The largest Dracones (flexible plastic containers used for bulk transport of liquids) ever built were completed by Frankenstein and Sons (Manchester) Ltd., in July 1962. They are 300 feet in length and can transport 1,200 tons (250,000 gallons) of water.

Deepest anchorage The deepest anchorage ever achieved is one of 24,600 feet in the mid-Atlantic Romanche Trench by Capt. Jacques-Yves Cousteau's research vessel *Calypso*, with a 5½-mile-long nylon cable, on 29 July 1956.

Largest Oil Rigs The largest oil drilling rigs are those under construction for the Humble Oil & Refinery Co. for their Santa Barbara Channel, California oil field. Each four-legged structure will tower 775 feet and weigh more than 20,000 tons.

Largest wreck The largest ship ever wrecked has been the Japanese-built, Royal Dutch/Shell owned, 206,600-ton (deadweight) tanker *Marpessa* after a tank explosion when sailing in ballast from Rotterdam, 50 miles northwest of Dakar, Senegal on 15 Dec. 1969. She was 1,067 feet 5 inches long. The largest vessel ever to be wrecked in British waters has been the 965-foot-long tanker, *Torrey Canyon*, of 61,275 tons gross and 118,285 tons deadweight, which struck the Pollard Rock of the Seven Stones Reef between the Isles of Scilly and Land's End, Cornwall, England, at 08.50 on 18 March 1967. The resultant oil pollution from some 30,000 tons of Kuwait crude was "on a scale which had no precedent anywhere in the world". In an attempt to fire the remaining oil, the ship was bombed to virtual destruction on 28−30 March 1967.

Oldest wreck The oldest vessel regarded as salvageable in British waters is the carrack *Mary Rose* of 1509, which sank off Ryde, Isle of Wight in 1545. On 18 Sept. 1970 a 4 cwt. 8-foot-long breech-loader was recovered from her hull, which appears to have been preserved in a blue clay layer of the sea bed.

Greatest Roll The ultimate in rolling was recorded in heavy seas off Coos Bay, Oregon, U.S.A. on 13 Nov. 1971, when the U.S. Coast Guard motor lifeboat *Intrepid* made a 360 degree roll.

THE MECHANICAL WORLD

Guinness Superlatives has now published automotive records in much greater detail in the more specialist publication "Car Facts and Feats" (price £2.20) and obtainable from any good bookshop or, if in difficulties, from the address in the front of this volume.

2. ROAD VEHICLES

COACHING

Before the advent of the McAdam road surfaces in *c.* 1815 coaching was slow and hazardous. The zenith was reached on 13 July 1888 when J. Selby, Esq., drove the "Old Times" coach 108 miles from London to Brighton and back with 8 teams and 14 changes in 7 hours 50 minutes to average 13.79 m.p.h. Four-horse carriages could maintain a speed of 21¼ m.p.h. for nearly an hour.

MOTOR CARS

Earliest automobiles — *Model* The earliest automobile of which there is record is a two-foot-long steam-powered model constructed by Ferdinand Verbiest (d. 1687) a Belgian Jesuit priest, and described in his *Astronomia Europaea*. His model of 1668 was possibly inspired either by Giovanni Branca's description of a steam turbine, published in his *La Macchina* in 1629, or by writings on "fire carts" during the Chu dynasty (*c.* 800 B.C.) in the library of the Emperor Khang-hi of China, to whom he was an astronomer during the period *c.* 1665-80. A 3-wheeled model steam locomotive was built at Redruth, Cornwall by William Murdoch (1754-1839) in 1785-6.

Passenger-carrying The earliest mechanically-propelled passenger vehicle was the first of two military steam tractors, completed at the Paris Arsenal in 1770 by Nicolas-Joseph Cugnot (1725-1804). This reached 2¼ m.p.h. Cugnot's second, larger tractor, completed in May 1771, today survives in the *Conservatoire Nationale des Arts et Métiers* in Paris. Britain's first steam carriage carried eight passengers on 24 Dec. 1801 and was built by Richard Trevithick (1771-1833) at Cambourne, Cornwall.

Internal combustion The first true internal-combustion engined vehicle was that built by the Londoner Samuel Brown whose 4 h.p. two cylinder engined carriage climbed Shooters Hill, Blackheath, Kent in 1824.

Earliest petrol-driven cars The first successful petrol-driven car, the Motor-wagen, built by Karl-Friedrich Benz (1844-1929) of Karlsruhe, ran at Mannheim, Germany, in late 1885. It was a 5 cwt. 3-wheeler reaching 8-10 m.p.h. Its single cylinder chain-drive engine (bore 91.4 mm., stroke 160 mm.) delivered 0.85 h.p. at 200 r.p.m. It was patented on 29 Jan. 1886. Its first 1 kilometre road test was reported in the local newspaper, the *Neue Badische Landeszeitung*, of 4 June 1886, under the heading "Miscellaneous". Two were built in 1885 of which one has been preserved in "running order" at the Deutsche Museum, Munich since 1959.

Earliest British cars In Britain Frank Hedges Butler (1856-1928) built a twin cylinder petrol-engined tricycle automobile in 1887 but the earliest successful British cars were the 3-wheeled air-cooled 2 h.p. Wolseley built in 1895 by Herbert (the first and last Lord) Austin (1866-1941) and John H. Knight's Surrey-built 3-wheeler of July of the same year. The first car to run on an English road was an 1894 3½ h.p. twin-cylinder Panhard-Levassor built in France, driven in June 1895 by the Hon. Evelyn Henry Ellis (1843-1913).

Oldest The oldest internal-combustion engine car seen on British roads has been the Danish "Hammel". Designed by Albert Hammel, who took out the original patents in 1886, it was completed in 1887. In 1954 it completed the London-to-Brighton run in 12½ hours, averaging 4½ m.p.h. The engine is a twin-cylinder,

128

The world's most expensive number plate—the £3,300 RR

horizontal water-cooled four-stroke with a capac of 2,720 c.c., bore and stroke 104.5 mm.×160 m and a compression ratio of 3.5:1.

Most durable The automotive writer Boyd Eugene Taylor Atlanta, Georgia, U.S.A. in 1956 surpassed 1,000,000 mile mark in his 1936 Ford two-door c The "clock" on its 11th trip round showed (1 milli and) 37,000 miles.

Earliest registrations The world's first plates were probably introduced the Parisian police in France in 1893. Registrati plates were introduced in Britain in 1903. original A1 plate was secured by the 2nd Earl Rus (1865-1931) for his 12 h.p. Napier. This plate, wil in September 1950 to Mr. Trevor T. Laker Leicester, was sold in August 1959 for £2,500 of charity. The Rolls-Royce bearing the registrati plate RR1 was sold by tender to R. H. Owen Ltd. the executors of Mr. Sydney Black on 22 July 19 for £10,800—£3,300 more than the price of the Sil Shadow to which the number plate was affixed.

FASTEST CARS

Rocket engined The highest speed attained by any wheeled la vehicle is 631.368 m.p.h. over the first measu kilometre of *The Blue Flame*, a liquid natu gas-powered 4-wheeled vehicle driven by Gary Ga lich on the Bonneville Salt Flats, Utah, on 23 C 1970. Momentarily Gabelich exceeded 650 m.p The tyres were made by Goodyear. The car powered by a liquid natural gas/hydrogen perox rocket engine delivering 22,000 lb.s.t. maximum thus theoretically capable of 900 m.p.h.

Jet The highest speed attained by any jet-engined ca 613.995 m.p.h. over a flying 666.386 yards by 34-foot 7-inch long 9,000 lb. *Spirit of Americ Sonic I*, driven by Norman Craig Breedlove (b. March 1938, Los Angeles) on Bonneville Salt Fl Tooele County, Utah, U.S.A., on 15 Nov. 1965. car was powered by a General Electric J79 GE-3 engine, developing 15,000 lb. static thrust at sea-le

Wheel-driven The highest speed attained by a wheel-driven ca 429.311 m.p.h. over a flying 666.386 yards Donald Malcolm Campbell, C.B.E. (1921-67) British engineer, in the 30-foot-long *Bluebird*, wei ing 9,600 lb., on the salt flats at Lake Eyre, So Australia, on 17 July 1964. The car was powered Bristol-Siddeley 705 gas-turbine engine develop 4,500 s.h.p. Its peak speed was *c.* 440 m.p.h. It rebuilt in 1962, after a crash at about 360 m.p.h. 16 Sept. 1960.

Piston engine The highest speed attained by a piston-engined ca 418.504 m.p.h. over a flying 666.386 yards Robert Sherman Summers (born 4 April 19 Omaha, Nebraska) in *Goldenrod* at Bonneville Flats on 12 Nov. 1965. The car, measuring 32

long and weighing 5,500 lb., was powered by four fuel-injected Chrysler Hemi engines (total capacity 27,924 c.c.) developing 2,400 b.h.p.

Production The world's fastest and most powerful production car (more than 25 examples produced within 12 months) ever produced was the German Porsche 4.9 litre Type 917 built in 1970 and 1971. It had a flat 12-cylinder air-cooled 4.99 litre engine developing 600 b.h.p. at 8,600 r.p.m. A Type 917L reached a speed calculated to be 238 m.p.h. during practice on the Le Mans Mulsanne straight on 18 Apr. 1971.

LARGEST

World Of cars produced for private road use, the largest has been the Bugatti "Royale", type 41, known in Britain as the "Golden Bugatti", of which only six (not seven) were made at Molsheim, France by the Italian Ettore Bugatti, and some survive. First built in 1927, this machine has an 8-cylinder engine of 12.7 litres capacity, and measures over 22 feet in length. The bonnet is over 7 feet long. The longest present-day limousine is the Stageway Coaches Inc. 10 door Travelall 18 seat model announced in 1970 and measuring 25 feet 4½ inches overall. (For cars not intended for private use, see Largest engines.)

An 8 door Travelall Coach—the world's longest limousine. A 10 door version is becoming available.

Widest The widest standard production car is the U.S.S.R.'s Zil 114, measuring 6 feet 8.3 inches across. The Rolls-Royce Phantom VI is 6 feet 7 inches wide.

MOST EXPENSIVE

The most expensive car to build has been the U.S. Presidential 1969 Lincoln Continental Executive delivered to the U.S. Secret Service on 14 Oct. 1968. It has an overall length of 21 feet 6.3 inches with a 13-foot 4-inch wheel-base and with the addition of two tons of armour plate weighs 5.35 tons (12,000 lb.). The estimated research, development and manufacture cost was $500,000 (then £208,000) but it is rented at $5,000 (now £1,923) per annum. Even if all four tyres were shot out it can travel at 50 m.p.h. on inner rubber-edged steel discs.

The most expensive standard car now available is the 19-foot 10-inch-long 7-seat Rolls-Royce Phantom VI (V8, 6,230 c.c. engine) with coachwork by Park Ward at £14,145 ($36,777) including purchase tax. The cost of a 4.9 litre Series 2 Porsche Type 917 *ex* works with import duty and purchase tax would have been more than £37,000 but none were imported. The all-time dollar record was a Bugatti Royale in 1931 for $55,000 (then £14,850).

Vintage The greatest price paid for any vintage car has been $65,000 (then £27,000) for a 1905 Rolls-Royce paid in U.S.A. in January 1969. A bid for $70,000 (then £25,000) was refused for a 1932 Dusenberg, reserved at $75,000, by Mr. Joe Kaufman at Auburn, Indiana on 6 Sept. 1971. The greatest collection of vintage cars is the William F. Harrah Collection of 1,440, estimated to be worth more than $3 million (£1¼ million), at Reno, Nevada, U.S.A. Mr. Harrah is still looking for a Chalmer's Detroit 1909 Tourabout, an

The Mercedes 600 Pullman—the world's longest production model with an overall length of 20 feet 5½ inches

Owen car of 1910-12 and a Nevada Truck of 1915.

Most inexpensive The cheapest car of all-time was the U.S. 1908 Brownicker for children, but designed for road use, which sold for $150 (then £30 17s. 3d.). The Kavan of 1905, also of U.S. manufacture, was listed at $200 (then £41 3s.). The early models of the King Midget cars were sold in kit form for self-assembly for as little as $100 (then £24 16s.) as late as 1948.

Longest production The longest any car has been in production is 42 years (1910-52), including wartime interruptions, in the case of the "Flat Twin" engined Jowett produced in Britain. The Ford Model T production record of 15,007,033 cars (1908-1927) was surpassed by the Volkswagen "Beetle" series when their 15,007,034th car came off the production line on 17 Feb. 1972.

LARGEST ENGINES

Cars are compared on the basis of engine capacity. Distinction is made between those designed for normal road use and machines specially built for track racing and outright speed records.

All-time record The largest car ever built is the "Quad Al", constructed in 1965 in California, U.S.A. Intended for drag racing, the car has four-wheel drive and is powered by four V12 Allison V-1710 aircraft engines with a total capacity of 112,088 c.c., developing 12,000 b.h.p. It was first exhibited in January 1966 at the San Mateo Auto Show in California but is unable to move under its own power.

The largest car ever used was the "White Triplex", sponsored by J. H. White of Philadelphia, Pennsylvania, U.S.A. Completed early in 1928, after two years' work, the car weighed about 4 tons and was powered by three Liberty V12 aircraft engines with a total capacity of 81,188 c.c., developing 1,500 b.h.p. at 2,000 r.p.m. It was used to break the world speed record but crashed at Daytona, Florida on 13 Mar. 1929.

The largest racing car was the "Higham Special", which first raced in 1923 at Brooklands driven by its owner Count Louis Vorow Zborowski, the younger (k. 1924). It was powered by a V12 Liberty aircraft engine with a capacity of 27,059 c.c., developing 400 to 500 b.h.p. at 2,000 r.p.m. John Godfrey Parry Thomas renamed the car "Babs" and used it to break the land speed record. The car was wrecked, and Thomas killed, during an attempt on this record at Pendine Sands, Carmarthenshire, Wales, on 3 March 1927.

Production car The highest engine capacity of a production car was 13½ litres (824 cubic inches), in the case of the U.S. Pierce-Arrow 6-66 Raceabout of 1912-18, the U.S. Peerless 6-60 of 1912-14 and the Fageol of 1918. The largest currently available is the V8 engine of 500.1 cubic inches (8,195 c.c.), developing 235 b.h.p. net, used in the 1972 Cadillac Fleetwood Eldorado.

One of the buses of the first municipal omnibus service in the world, at Eastbourne in 1903

Petrol consumption The world record for fuel economy on a closed circuit course (one of 14.08 miles) was set by R. J. 'Bob' Greenshields, C. A. 'Skeeter' Hargrave, Jan Evans and Earl Elmqvist in a highly modified 1956 Austin Healey in the annual Shell Research Laboratory contest at Wood River, Illinois on 19 Sept. 1970 with 302.7 ton miles per U.S. gallon and 145.5 miles on one U.S. gallon. These figures are equivalent to 324.57 ton miles and 174.7 miles on an Imperial gallon.

On 24 Aug. 1969 a 4-seat 600 c.c. Reliant Regal 3-wheeler driven by Brian Lodwick plus an R.A.C. observer, described as 'large', achieved 103.6 miles on one gallon at Mallory Park, Leicestershire.

The best recorded figure in an unmodified 4-wheeled car using pump petrol is 96.59 m.p.g. by a Fiat 500 driven on an out and home course from Cheltenham to Evesham, Gloucestershire, England, by W. (Featherfoot Joe) Dembowski on 1 July 1965.

BUSES

Earliest The first municipal motor omnibus service in the world was inaugurated on 12 April 1903 between Eastbourne railway station and Meads, Sussex, England.

Longest The longest buses in the world are the 65-foot-long articulated buses for 160 passengers built by Bus Bodies (S.A.) Ltd. of Port Elizabeth, South Africa for use in Johannesburg.

Longest route The longest regularly scheduled bus route is the Greyhound "Supercruiser" Miami, Florida to San Francisco, California route over 3,240 miles in 81 hours 50 minutes (average speed of travel 39.59 m.p.h.). The total Greyhound fleet numbers 5,500 buses.

Largest trolleybuses The largest trolleybuses in the world are the articulated vehicles put into service in Moscow, U.S.S.R., in May 1959, with a length of 57 feet and a capacity of 200.

Most massive vehicle The most massive vehicle ever constructed is the Marion eight-caterpillar crawler used for conveying

Saturn V rockets to their launching pads at the John F. Kennedy Space Center, Florida (see Chapter Most powerful rocket). It measures 131 feet 4 inch by 114 feet and cost $12,300,000 (then £5,125,00 for two. The loaded train weight is 8,036 tons. windscreen wipers with 42-inch blades are the world largest. Two were built.

Largest lorry The world's largest lorry is the M-200 Lectra Ha built by Unit Rig and Equipment Co. of Fort Wort Texas with a capacity of 200 tons. It is powered by 1,650 h.p. diesel and twin 750 h.p. electric motors. is 43 feet long and 20 feet high.

The most powerful British-engined prime mover is t Rotinoff Tractor Super Atlantic with a 400 b.h. Rolls-Royce engine. In May 1958, one of these haul the first of 12 atomic power station heat-exchange at Bradwell, Essex. The gross train weight was 3 tons. The Aveling Barford Sn 35 Dump Truck is fitt with a 450 b.h.p. engine.

Longest vehicle The longest vehicle in the world was the 572-foo long, 54-wheeled U.S. Army Overland Train Mk. built by R. G. Le Tourneau Inc. of Longview, Texa U.S.A. Its gross weight was 400 tons and it had a to speed of 20 m.p.h. from four engines with a combin s.h.p. of 4,680, which required a capacity of 6,5 Imperial gallons of fuel. Despite a cost of $3,755,00 it was sold for scrap for $47,900 (£18,425) in 197

Largest bulldozers The world's largest bulldozer is the Caterpillar S D9G with a 24 foot dozer blade weighing 84.8 ton The largest road grader in the world is the 25.0 ton foot 5 inch long CMI Corporation Autograde 55 wi a 325 h.p. engine.

Largest Dumper Truck The world's largest dumper truck is the Euclid In R-210 Hauler announced on 31 Aug. 1971. Th 111.6 ton 8 wheeled vehicle measuring 35 feet lon 25 feet wide and 16 feet 11 ins. high costs $500,0 (£192,307).

Largest tractor The most powerful tractor in the world is the 142 ton K-205 Pacemaker with a 1,260 horse-pow rating. It is built by R. G. Le Tourneau, Inc., Longview, Texas, U.S.A.

The world's longest bus—65 foot long articulated bus operating in South Africa

Largest taxi fleet The largest taxi fleet was that of New York City, which amounted to 29,000 cabs in October 1929, compared with the 1969 figure of 11,500.

Fastest caravan The world record for towing a caravan in 24 hours is 1,689 miles (average speed 70.395 m.p.h.) by a Ford Zodiac Mk. IV towing a Sprite Major 5-berth caravan, 16 feet long and weighing 14½ cwt., at Monza Autodrome near Milan, Italy, on 15-16 Oct. 1966. The drivers were Ian Mantle, John Risborough and Michael Bowler, all of Great Britain.

Longest motor caravan journey The longest motor caravan tour on record is one of 68,000 miles carried out in a 1966 Commer Highwayman through 69 sovereign countries between 27 Dec. 1966 and 20 Oct. 1971 by Sy Feldman, his wife Christine, and two sons, Greg and Tim.

Round Britain motoring *The Guinness Book of Records does not publish place to place or rally records made on public roads due to public policy unless these are under the aegis of H.M. Armed Forces, the R.A.C. or the Police.*

On 7-11 May 1971 an R.A.F. team of Corporals Peter Mitchell and Ken Jones, and Junior Technician John Housley from Leuchars, Fife, completed 3,542 miles in 97¾ hours in a rally round the coast of Great Britain in a 1961 Mark 2, 2.4 Jaguar.

Britain's biggest road hog (see largest load)

LOADS

Heaviest and largest The heaviest road loads moved in the United Kingdom have been 305.5 ton generator inner cores moved both by Pickfords Heavy Haulage Ltd and Robert Wynn & Sons Ltd. for the C.E.G.B. to various power stations since 25 June 1971 when Pickfords hauled the first to Dungeness "B" Station, Kent. The longest load moved on British roads has been a 171 foot long Carbon dioxide absorber column, by Pickfords from Lindhouse Works to Glasgow Docks in May 1971. The bulkiest load moved was a 212 ton cracking tower 111½ feet long with a diameter of 78½ feet for a distance of 17 miles by Wynn's from Birkenhead to the Shell Refinery, Stanlow Cheshire. By 1976 it is anticipated that loads of up to 600 tons will be being moved on British roads.

Tallest The tallest load ever conveyed by road comprised two 98-foot-tall cableway towers, each weighing 70 tons, which were taken 25 miles from Ohakuri to Aratiatia, New Zealand, in June 1961. The loads were carried on a 68-wheel trailer, towed by a 230 h.p. Leyland Buffalo tractor, for George Dale and Son Ltd.

Amphibious vehicle The only trans-Atlantic crossing by an amphibious vehicle was achieved by Ben Carlin (U.S.A.) in an amphibious jeep called "Half-Safe". He completed the cross channel leg on 24 Aug 1951.

Mr J. Lord the only Driving Test Examiner to test more than 40,000 people

Longest skid marks The longest recorded skid marks on a public road have been those 950 feet long left by a Jaguar car involved in an accident on the M1 near Luton, Bedfordshire, on 30 June 1960. Evidence given in the High Court case *Hurlock v. Inglis and others* indicated a speed "in excess of 100 m.p.h." before the application of the brakes. The skid marks made by the jet-powered *Spirit of America,* driven by Craig Breedlove, after the car went out of control at Bonneville Salt Flats, Utah, U.S.A., on 15 Oct. 1964, were nearly 6 miles long.

Largest tyres The world's largest tyres are the 4000-57 OR tyre built in 1971 by Bridgestone Tyre Co. of Japan which have a diameter of 11 feet 10 inches and weigh 7,275 lb. (3.24 tons).

"L" test Most failures The record for persistence in taking the Ministry of Transport's Learners' Test is held by Mrs. Miriam Hargrave, 62, of Wakefield, Yorkshire, who failed her 39th driving test in eight years on 29 April 1970. She triumphed at her 40th attempt on 3 Aug. 1970. The examiner was alleged not to have known about her previous 39 tests.

Most Durable Examiner The most durable examiner has been Mr. Jack Lord of Allestree, near Derby who in 33 years (1935-1968) survived 40,639 tests. The only examinee to defeat his acutely developed sense of self-preservation was a driver (woman) who impaled her Straight 8 Buick on a tramway standard in Grimsby in 1937.

Oldest driver In a survey by the U.S. Social Security Administration of 300 centenarians in 1968 it was discovered that one, identified as a Mr. Dring, drove his car to work every day. Britain's oldest recorded driver was the Rev. Wilfred Lionel de Buckenhold Thorold of Petersfield, Hampshire, who was banned in June 1971

The 100 year old Mr. Dring (U.S.) who in 1969 was driving to work daily

131

from further driving without a test when aged 98. The oldest age at which anyone has passed the then Ministry of Transport driving test was on 20 September 1969 at Sutton-in-Derwent, Yorkshire, when Mr. Arther Daniel passed at his second attempt aged 85. The highest year number ever displayed on a Veteran Motorist's badge was "75" by Walter Herbert Weake, who started his accident free career in 1894 and drove daily until his death in 1969, aged 91.

MOTORCYCLES

Earliest The earliest internal combustion-engined motorized bicycle was a wooden-framed machine built in 1885 by Gottlieb Daimler (1834-1900) of Germany. It had a top speed of 12 m.p.h. and developed one-half of one horse-power from its single cylinder 264 c.c. engine at 700 r.p.m. The earliest factory which made motorcycles in quantity was opened in 1894 by J. Hildebrand and A. Wolfmüller at München (Munich), Bavaria, Germany. In its first two years this factory produced over 1,000 machines, each having a water-cooled 1,488 c.c. twin-cylinder engine developing about 2.5 b.h.p. at 600 r.p.m.

Fastest road machine The fastest standard motorcycle ever produced is the Dunstall Norton Commando powered by a twin-cylinder 810 c.c. engine developing 70 b.h.p. at 7,000 r.p.m. and capable of 135 m.p.h.

Fastest racing machine The fastest racing motorcycle ever has been the 748 c.c. 105 b.h.p. Kawasaki 3-cylinder 2-stroke produced in Dec. 1971 and capable of 185 m.p.h. (see also Motorcycle racing, Chapter 12). Of British machines the fastest ever were the 741 c.c. 3-cylinder B.S.A. Rocket 3 and Triumph Trident racers used in the "Daytona 200" on 14 March 1971. They developed 84 b.h.p. and were capable of 170 m.p.h.

Largest The largest motorcycle ever put into production was the 1,301 c.c. in-line 4-cylinder Henderson, manufactured in the United States in the period 1926-29.

Most expensive The most expensive motorcycles in current production are the Harley-Davidson FLHB and FLHFB Super Sports Electra Glide machines, made in the U.S.A., with an engine capacity of 1,213 c.c. Extensively used for highway patrol work by State Police Departments, they weigh 661 lb. and sell for £1,395 in the United Kingdom (May 1972).

The most expensive British-made motorcycle in current production is the 810 c.c. Dunstall Norton Commando with a front disc brake. It retailed at £980 in May 1972.

BICYCLES

Earliest Though there were many velocipedes before that time, the term bicycle was first used in 1868. The earliest portrayal of such a vehicle is in a stained glass window, dated 1642, in Stoke Poges Church, Buckinghamshire, depicting a man riding a hobby horse or celeripede.

The first machine propelled by cranks and pedals, with connecting rods, was that invented in 1839 by Kirkpatrick Macmillan (1810-78) of Dumfries. It is now in the Science Museum, South Kensington, London.

Penny-Farthing record The record for riding from Land's End to John o'Groats on Ordinary Bicycles, more commonly known in the 1870's as Penny-Farthings, is 13 days (123½ hours riding) by Brian Thompson, 34 in 1970.

Longest The longest tandem "bicycle" ever built is the 31-man 50 foot long trigintapede built in Queanbeyan, Australia in November 1971.

Smallest The world's smallest rideable bicycle is a 5½ inch high 3 inch wheel model made and ridden by Alfred G.

Bert Tabb, 88, over-taking on the world's smal-lest bicycle

Tabb (b. 5 Mar. 1883) of Kidderminister, Worceste shire.

Largest tricycle The largest tricycle ever made was one manufactur in 1897 for the Woven-Hose and Rubber Company Boston, Massachusetts, U.S.A. Its side wheels were feet in diameter and it weighed nearly a ton. It cou carry eight riders.

Tallest unicycle The tallest unicycle ever mastered is one 32 feet ta ridden by Steve McPeak of Seattle Pacific Colleg U.S.A., in 1969. McPeak set a duration record whe on 26 Nov. 1968 he completed a 2,000 mile journe from Chicago, Illinois to Las Vegas, Nevada, U.S.A. 6 weeks on a 13-foot unicycle. He covered 80 miles c some days.

LAWN MOWER

Largest The widest gang mower on record is one of overlapping sections manufactured by Lloyds & C of Letchworth Ltd., Hertfordshire, England used b The Jockey Club to mow 2,500 acres on Newmark Heath. Its cutting width is 41 feet 6 inches and has capacity, with a 15 m.p.h. tractor, of up to 70 acr per hour.

Longest lawnmower journey In an endurance trial over 306.6 miles from Washin ton, D.C. to New York City on 9-21 Sept. 1971 thr Gravely machines (a 12 h.p. walking model, an 8 h. lawn tractor and a 16.5 h.p. riding tractor) ea covered 144.1 miles mowing 47 per cent of the tim

3. RAILWAYS

EARLIEST

Railed trucks were used for mining as early as 1550 Leberthal, Alsace and by Ralph Allen from Comb Down to the River Avon in 1731, but the fir self-propelled locomotive ever to run on rails was tha built by Richard Trevithick (1771-1833) and demo strated over 9 miles with a 10-ton load and 7 passengers in Penydaren, Glamorgan, on 21 Fe 1804. The earliest established railway to have steam-powered locomotive was the Middleton Co liery Railway, set up by an Act of 1758 runni between Middleton Colliery and Leeds Bridge, Yor shire. This line went over to the use of stea locomotives, built by Matthew Murray, in 1812. Th Stockton and Darlington colliery line, County Du ham, which ran from Shildon through Darlington Stockton, opened on 27 Sept. 1825. The 7-to *Locomotion I* (formerly *Active*) could pull 48 tons a speed of 15 m.p.h. It was designed and driven b George Stephenson (1781-1848). The first regul steam passenger run was inaugurated over a one mi section (between Bogshole Farm and South Stree on the 6¼-mile track between Canterbury and Wh stable, Kent, on 3 May 1830 hauled by the engine *Invicta*. The first electric railway was Werner von Siemen's 300-yard-long Berlin electric tramway opened for the Berlin Trades' Exhibition on 31 May 1879.

FASTEST

Electric The world rail speed record is held jointly by two French Railway electric locomotives, the CC7107 and the BB9004. On 28 and 29 March 1955, hauling three carriages of a total weight of 100 tons, they each achieved a speed of 205.6 m.p.h. The runs took place on the 1,500-volt D.C. Bordeaux-Dax line, from Facture to Morcenx, and the top speed was maintained by the drivers, H. Braghet and J. Brocca, for 2 kilometres (1.24 miles). The CC7107 weighs 106 tons and has a continuous rating of 4,300 h.p. at 1,500 volts, but developed 12,000 h.p. over the timing stretch. The BB9004 weighs 81 tons and has a continuous rating of 4,000 h.p.

Steam The highest speed ever recorded by a steam locomotive was 126 m.p.h. over 440 yards by the 167.1 ton L.N.E.R. 4-6-2 No. 4468 *Mallard* (later numbered 60022), which hauled seven coaches weighing 240 tons gross, near Essendine, down Stoke Bank, between Grantham, Lincolnshire, and Peterborough on 3 July 1938. Driver Duddington was at the controls with Fireman T. Bray.

Fastest regular run The fastest point-to-point schedule in the world is that of the "New Tokaido" service of the Japanese National Railways from Osaka to Okayama, inaugurated on 15 Mar. 1972. The train covers 112.03 miles in exactly 1 hour. The maximum speed is being raised from 130.5 to 159 m.p.h. The 60-ton 12-car

Trevithick's engine — the first self-propelled railway engine from 1804

unit has motors generating 8,880 kW on a single-phase 25,000 volt A.C. system.

The fastest regular run on British Rail is over the 140-mile 47-chain stretch from Crewe to Watford Junction in 101½ minutes giving an average of 83.1 m.p.h. The prototype British Rail APT (Advanced Passenger Train) 125 m.p.h. diesel started trials in June 1972 for service in May 1975.

LONGEST NON-STOP

The world's longest daily non-stop run is that of the "Florida Special" from New York City to Miami (1,377 miles) of which the 936 mile stretch from Washington D.C. to Winter Haven contains only conditional stops. The longest run on British Rail without any advertised stop is the "Night Aberdonian", which runs from King's Cross, London to Inverkeith, Scotland, a distance of 406¼ miles.

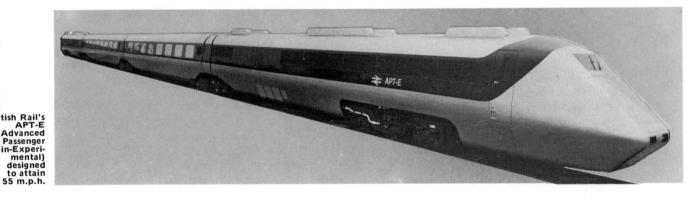

tish Rail's APT-E Advanced Passenger in-Experi- mental) designed to attain 55 m.p.h.

PROGRESSIVE RAILWAY SPEED RECORDS

Speed m.p.h	Engine	Place	Date
29.1	The *Rocket* (Stephenson's and Booth's 0-2-2)	Liverpool—Manchester	8 Oct. 1829
36	The *Northumbrian*	from Parkside, Newton-le-Willows	15 Sept. 1830
56¾	Grand Junction Rly., 2-2-2 *Lucifer*	Madeley Bank, Staffordshire	13 Nov. 1839
c.85 [1]	Atmospheric railway (Frank Elrington)	Dun Laoghaire-Dalkey, Co. Dublin	19 Aug. 1843
74½	Great Western Rly., 8 ft. single 4-2-2 *Great Britain*	Wootton Bassett, Wiltshire	11 May 1845
74½	Great Western Rly., 8 ft. single 4-2-2 *Great Western*	Wootton Bassett, Wiltshire	1 June 1846
78	Great Western Rly., 8 ft. single 4-2-2 *Great Britain*	Wootton Bassett, Wiltshire	11 May 1848
81.8	Bristol & Exeter Rly., 9 ft. single 4-2-4 tank No. 41	Wellington Bank, Somerset	June 1854
89.48	Crompton No. 604 engine	Champigny Pont sur Yvonne, France	20 June 1890
98.4 [2]	*Philadelphia & Reading Rly., Engine 206*	*Skillmans to Belle Mead, New Jersey*	*July 1890*
102.8 [2]	N.Y. Central & Hudson River Rly.*Empire State Express No 999*	*Grimesville, N.Y., U.S.A.*	*9 May 1893*
112.5 [2] [3]	N.Y. Central & Hudson River Rly. *Empire State Express No. 999*	*Crittenden West. N.Y., U.S.A.*	*11 May 1893*
102	*Pennsylvania Railroad*	*Landover to Anacosta, U.S.A.*	*Aug. 1895*
90.0	Midland Rly., 7 ft. 9 in. single 4-2-2	Melton Mowbray—Nottingham	Mar. 1897
130 [2]	*Burlington Route*	*Siding to Arion, Iowa, U.S.A.*	*Jan 1899*
101.0	Siemens und Halske Electric	near Berlin	1901
120.0 [2] [4]	*Savannah, Florida and Western Rly. mail train*	*Screven, Florida, U.S.A.*	*1 Mar 1901*
124.89	Siemens und Halske Electric	Marienfeld-Zossen, nr. Berlin	6 Oct. 1903
128.43	Siemens und Halske Electric	Marienfeld-Zossen, nr. Berlin	23 Oct. 1903
130.61	Siemens und Halske Electric	Marienfeld-Zossen, nr. Berlin	27 Oct. 1903
99-100 [5]	Great Western Rly., 4-4-0 *City of Truro* (Steam Record only)	Wellington Bank, Somerset	9 May 1904
143.0	Kruckenberg (propeller-driven)	Karstädt-Dergenthin, Germany	21 June 1931
150.9	Co-Co S.N.C.F. No. 7121	Dijon-Beaune, France	21 Feb. 1953
205.6	Co-Co S.N.C.F. No. 7107	Facture-Morcenx, France	28 Mar. 1955
205.6	Bo-Bo S.N.C.F. No. 9004	Facture-Morcenx, France	29 Mar. 1955
235	*L'Aérotrain (jet aero engines)*	Gometz le Chatel-Limours, France	4 Dec. 1967

[1] Speed attributed to runaway compressed air train. No independent timings.
[2] Not internationally regarded as authentic.
[3] Later alleged to be unable to attain 82 m.p.h. on this track when hauling 4 coaches.

[4] 5 miles in 2½ minutes to a stop, hence fictitious.
[5] Previously unauthenticated at 102.3 m.p.h.

MOST POWERFUL

World The world's most powerful compound type steam locomotive was No. 700, a triple articulated or triplex 2-8-8-8-4, the Baldwin Locomotive Co. 6-cylinder engine built in 1916 for the Virginian Railway. It had a tractive force of 166,300 lb. working compound and 199,560 lb. working simple. In 1918 this railway operated a 4-cylinder compound 2-10-10-2 engine, built by the American Locomotive Co., with a starting (*i.e.* working simple) tractive effort of 176,000 lb. Probably the heaviest train ever hauled by a single engine was one of 15,300 tons made up of 250 freight cars stretching 1.6 miles by the *Matt H. Shay* (No. 5014), a 2-8-8-8-2 engine which ran on the Erie Railroad from May 1914 until 1929.

PERMANENT WAY

The longest stretch of continuous four track main line in the United Kingdom is between St. Pancras, London, and Glendon North Junction, Northamptonshire, and is 75 miles in length.

Longest straight The longest straight in the world is on the Commonwealth Railways Trans Australian line over the Nullarbor Plain from Mile 496 between Nuringa and Loongana, Western Australia, to Mile 793 between Ooldea and Watson, South Australia, 297 miles dead straight although not level. The longest straight on British Rail is the 18 miles between Selby and Kingston-upon-Hull, Yorkshire.

Longest electric line The world's longest stretch of electrified line is the 3,240 miles between Moscow and Irkutsk in Siberia, U.S.S.R., completed in late 1960.

Widest The widest gauge in standard use is 5 feet 6 inches. This width is used in India, Pakistan, Ceylon, Spain, Portugal, Argentina and Chile. In 1885 there was a lumber railway in Oregon, U.S.A., with a gauge of 8 feet.

HIGHEST

World The highest standard gauge (4 feet 8½ inches) track in the world is on the Central Railway of Peru (owned by the Peruvian Corporation Ltd.) at La Cima, where a branch siding rises to 15,844 feet above sea-level. The highest point on the main line is 15,688 feet in the Galera tunnel.

Great Britain The highest point on the British Rail system is at the pass of Druimnachdar on the Perth-Inverness border, where the track reaches an altitude of 1,484 feet above sea-level. The highest railway in Britain is the Snowdon Mountain Railway, which rises from Llanberis to 3,493 feet above sea-level, just below the summit of Snowdon (Yr Wyddfa). It has a gauge of 2 feet 7½ inches.

Lowest The lowest point on British Rail is in the Severn Tunnel—144 feet below sea-level.

STEEPEST GRADIENTS

World The world's steepest standard gauge gradient by adhesion is 1:11. This figure is achieved by the Guatemalan State Electric Railway between the River Samala Bridge and Zunil.

Great Britain The steepest sustained adhesion-worked gradient on a main line in the United Kingdom is the two-mile Lickey incline of 1:37.7 in Worcestershire. From the tunnel bottom to James Street, Liverpool, on the former Mersey Railway, there is a stretch of 1:27; just south of Ilfracombe, Devon, two miles of 1:36; and between Folkestone Junction and Harbour a mile of 1:30.

Shallowest The shallowest gradient posted on the British Rail system is one indicated as 1 in 13,707 between Pirbright Junction and Farnborough, Hampshire. This could, perhaps, also be described as England's most obtuse summit.

BUSIEST

Rail system The world's most crowded rail system is the Tōk service of the Japanese National Railways, which 1970 carried 6,129,000 passengers daily. Professio pushers are employed to squeeze in passengers befo the doors can be closed. Among articles lost in 19 were 419,929 umbrellas, 172,106 shoes, 250,6 spectacles and hats and also assorted false teeth a artifical eyeballs.

Station The world's busiest stations are Tōkyō Cent Japan, which in 1970, handled 2,600 trains, a Shinjuku, 2,200,000 passengers daily. The busi railway junction in Great Britain is Clapham Juncti on the Southern Region of British Rail, with o 2,070 trains passing through each 24 hours.

STATIONS

Largest World The world's largest railway station is Grand Cent Terminal, Park Avenue and 43rd Street, New Yc City, N.Y., U.S.A., built 1903-13. It covers 48 ac on two levels with 41 tracks on the upper level and on the lower. On average more than 550 trains a 180,000 people per day use it, with a peak of 252,2 on 3 July 1947.

United Kingdom The largest railway station in extent on the Brit Rail system is the 17-platform Clapham Junctic London, covering 27¾ acres and with a total face 11,185 feet. The station with the largest number platforms is Waterloo, London (24½ acres), with main line and two Waterloo and City Line platforr with a total face of 15,352 feet. Victoria Station (2 acres) with 17 platforms has, however, a total fa length of 18,412 feet. The oldest station in Britair Liverpool Road Station, Manchester, first used 15 Sept. 1830.

Highest The highest station in the world on standard gau railways is Ticlio, at 15,685 feet above sea-level, the Central Railway of Peru, in South America. T highest passenger station on British Rail is Corro Inverness-shire, at an altitude of 1,347 feet abc sea-level.

Waiting rooms The world's largest waiting rooms are those in Peki Station, Chang'an Boulevard, Peking, China, open in September 1959, with a capacity of 14,000.

Longest platform The longest railway platform in the world is t Kharagpur platform, Bihar, India, which measu 2,733 feet in length. The State Street Center subw platform staging on "The Loop" in Chicago, Illino U.S.A., measures 3,500 feet in length.

The longest platform in the British Rail system is t 1,981-foot-long platform at Colchester, Essex.

Britain's longest platform at Colchester Station, Essex

Seven Sisters station on the Victoria Line—part of the world's most extensive underground railway system

Longest freight train The longest and heaviest freight train on record was one about 4 miles in length consisting of 500 coal cars with three 3,600 h.p. diesels pulling and three more pushing on the Iaeger, West Virginia to Portsmouth, Ohio stretch of 157 miles on the Norfolk and Western Railway on 15 Nov. 1967. The total weight was nearly 42,000 tons.

Greatest load The heaviest single piece of freight ever conveyed by rail was a 1,230,000-lb. (549.2-ton) 106-foot-tall hydrocracker reactor which was carried from Birmingham, Alabama, to Toledo, Ohio, U.S.A., on 12 Nov. 1965.

The heaviest load carried by British Rail was a 122-foot-long boiler drum, weighing 275 tons, which was carried from Immingham Docks to Killinghome, Lincolnshire in September 1968.

Greatest mileage The greatest mileage covered with a weekly roving ticket on British Rail is 8,662 miles between 2 Jan. and 9 Jan. 1972 by Peter Higson and Roderic Marten, both aged 16.

Dearest season ticket The most expensive annual season ticket issued by British Rail is a 1st class weekly return between London (Euston) and Inverness for £1,250.00 issued to Mr. Henry E. Williamson.

UNDERGROUND RAILWAYS

Most extensive The most extensive and oldest (opened 10 Jan. 1863) underground railway system in the world is that of the London Transport Executive, with 257 miles of route, of which 80 miles is bored tunnel and 24 miles is "cut and cover". This whole Tube system is operated by a staff of 20,000 serving 278 stations. The 500 trains comprising 4,350 cars carried 654,000,000 passengers in 1971. The greatest depth is 192 feet at Hampstead. The record for touring all 277 stations was 15 hours precisely by Leslie R. V. Burwood on 3 Sept. 1968. The record for the Paris Metro's 270 stations (7 closed) is 11 hours 13 minutes by Alan Paul Jenkins of Bushey, Hertfordshire on 30 Aug. 1967.

Busiest The busiest subway in the world is the New York City Transit Authority (opened on 27 Oct. 1904) with a total of 237.22 miles of track and 2,081,810,464 passengers in 1970. The stations are closer set and total 475. The previous peak number carried was 2,051,400,973 in 1947. The record for travelling the whole system is 22 hours 11½ minutes by Morgan Chu and 6 others on 3 Aug. 1967.

Model railway The record run for a model train was set at Nuremburg, West Germany in 1971 when the Fleischmann *Black Elephant* HO gauge engine pulled a 62 axle train 1,053 actual miles. The run was equivalent, at scale, to 11,600 miles averaging 123.9 m.p.h.

MONORAIL

Highest speed The highest speed ever attained on rails is 3,090 m.p.h. (Mach 4.1) by an unmanned rocket-powered sled on the 6.62-mile-long captive track at the U.S. Air Force Missile Development Center at Holloman, New Mexico, U.S.A., on 19 Feb. 1959. The highest speed reached carrying a chimpanzee is 1,295 m.p.h.

The highest speed attained by a tracked hovercraft is 235 m.p.h. by the jet-powered *L'Aérotrain*, invented by Jean Bertin (see Progressive speed table page 133).

Speeds as high as Mach 0.8 (608 m.p.h.) are planned in 1973 from The Onsoku Kasotai (sonic speed sliding vehicle), a wheelless rocket-powered train running on rollers designed by Prof. H. Ozawa (Japan) and announced in March 1968.

4. AIRCRAFT

Note—The use of the Mach scale for aircraft speeds was introduced by Prof. Acherer of Zürich, Switzerland. The Mach number is the ratio of the velocity of a moving body to the local velocity of sound. This ratio was first employed by Dr. Ernst Mach (1838-1916) of Vienna, Austria in 1887. Thus Mach 1.0 equals 760.98 m.p.h. at sea-level at 15° C. and is assumed, for convenience, to fall to a constant 659.78 m.p.h. in the stratosphere, *i.e.* above 11,000 metres (36,089 feet).

EARLIEST FLIGHTS

World The first controlled and sustained power-driven flight occurred near the Kill Devil Hills, Kitty Hawk, North Carolina, U.S.A., at 10.35 a.m. on 17 December 1903, when Orville Wright (1871-1948) flew the 16 h.p. chain-driven *Flyer 1* at an airspeed of 30-35 m.p.h., a ground speed of less than 8 m.p.h. and an altitude of 8-12 feet for 12 seconds, watched by his brother Wilbur (1867-1912) and five coastguards. Both the brothers, from Dayton, Ohio, were bachelors because, as Orville put it, they had not the means to "support a wife as well as an aeroplane". The plane is now in the Smithsonian Institution, Washington, D.C.

The first man-carrying powered aeroplane to fly, but not entirely under its own power, was the monoplane with a hot-air engine built by Félix Du Temple de la Croix (1823-90), a French naval officer, and piloted by a young sailor who made a short hop after taking off, probably down an incline, at Brest, France, in *c.* 1874. The first hop by a man-carrying aeroplane entirely under its own power was made when Clément Ader (1841-1925) of France flew in his *Eole* for about 50 metres (164 feet) at Armainvilliers, France, on 9 Oct. 1890.

British Isles The first officially recognised flight in the British Isles was made by "Colonel" Samuel Franklin Cody (1861-1913) of the U.S.A., who flew 1,390 feet in his own biplane at Farnborough, Hampshire, on 16 Oct. 1908. Horatio Frederick Phillips (1845-1926) almost certainly covered 500 feet in his Philips II *"Venetian blind"* aeroplane at Streatham, in 1907. The first British citizen to fly was Griffith Brewer (1867-1948), as a passenger of Wilbur Wright, on 8 Oct. 1908 at Auvours, France.

Cross-Channel The earliest cross-Channel flight by an aeroplane was made on 25 July 1909, when Louis Blériot (1872-1936) of France flew his *Blériot XI* monoplane, powered by a 23 h.p. Anzani engine, 26 miles from Les Baraques, France, to a meadow near Dover Castle, England, in 36½ minutes after taking off at 4.41 a.m.

Jet-engined Proposals for jet propulsion date back to Captain Marconnet (1909) of France, and to the turbojet proposals of Maxime Guillaume in 1921. The earliest test bed run was that of the British Power Jets Ltd.'s experimental W.U. (Whittle Unit) on 12 April 1937, invented by Flying Officer (now Air Commodore Sir) Frank Whittle (b. Coventry, 1 June 1907), who had applied for a patent on jet propulsion in 1930. The first flight by an aeroplane powered by a turbojet engine was made by the Heinkel He 178, piloted by Flug Kapitan Erich Warsitz, at Marienehe, Germany, on 27 Aug. 1939. It was powered by a Heinkel S3B engine (834 lb. s.t. as installed with long tail-pipe) designed by Dr. Hans 'Pabst' von Ohain and first tested in August 1937.

The first British jet flight occurred when Fl. Lt. P. E. G. "Jerry" Sayer, O.B.E., flew the Gloster-Whittle E.28/39 (wing span 29 feet, length 25 feet 3 inches) fitted with a 860 lb. s.t. Whittle W-1 engine for 17 minutes at Cranwell, Lincolnshire, on 15 May 1941. The second prototype attained 466 m.p.h.

Supersonic flight The first supersonic flight was achieved on 14 Oct. 1947 by Capt. (now Brig.-Gen.) Charles ("Chuck") E. Yeager, U.S.A.F. (b. 13 Feb. 1923), over Edwards Air Force Base, Muroc, California, U.S.A., in a U.S. Bell XS-1 rocket plane ("Glamorous Glennis"), with Mach 1.015 (670 m.p.h.) at an altitude of 420,000 feet.

TRANS-ATLANTIC
The first crossing of the North Atlantic by air was made by Lt-Cdr. (later Rear Admiral) Albert Cushing Read (1887-1967) and his crew (Stone, Hinton, Rodd, Rhoads and Breese) in the 84 knot Curtiss flying-boat NC-4 of the U.S. Navy from Trepassey Harbour, Newfoundland, *via* the Azores, to Lisbon, Portugal, on 16 to 27 May 1919. The whole flight of 3,936 miles originating from Rockaway Air Station, Long Island, N.Y. on 8 May required 53 hours 58 minutes, terminating at Plymouth, England, on 31 May.

First non-stop The first non-stop trans-Atlantic flight was achieved from 4.13 p.m. G.M.T. on 14 June 1919, from Lester's Field, St. John's Newfoundland, 1,960 miles to Derrygimla bog near Clifden, County Galway, Ireland, at 8.40 a.m. G.M.T., 15 June, when the pilot Capt. John William Alcock, D.S.C. (1892-1919), and the navigator Lt. Arthur Whitten-Brown (1886-1948) flew across in a Vickers *Vimy*, powered by two 360 h.p. Rolls-Royce *Eagle VIII* engines. Both men were created K.B.E. on 21 June 1919 when Alcock was aged 26 years 286 days and won the *Daily Mail* prize of £10,000.

First solo The 79th man to achieve a trans-Atlantic flight but the first to do so solo was Capt. (later Col.) Charles Augustus Lindberg (b. 4 Feb. 1902, Detroit) who took off in his 220 h.p. Ryan monoplane "Spirit of St. Louis" at 12.52 p.m. G.M.T. on 20 May 1927 from Roosevelt Field, Long Island, New York State, U.S.A. He landed at 10.21 p.m. G.M.T. on 21 May 1927 at Le Bourget airfield, Paris, France. His flight of 3,610 miles lasted 33 hours 29½ minutes and he won a prize of $25,000 (then £5,300).

Fastest The present New York—Paris trans-Atlantic record is 3 hours 19 minutes 44.5 seconds by a General Dynamics/Convair B-58A *Hustler* "Firefly", piloted by Major William R. Payne, U.S.A.F., on 26 May 1961. The 3,626 miles were covered at an average of 1,089 m.p.h. The B-58 was withdrawn from operational service in January 1970.

The fastest time between New York and London is 4 hours 36 minutes 30.4 seconds by Lt.-Cdr. Brian Davies, 35, and Lt.-Cdr. Peter M. Goddard, R.N., 32, of No. 892 Squadron, Royal Navy, on 11 May 1969, flying a McDonnell Douglas F-4K. *Phantom II* with Rolls-Royce *Spey* engines. Lt.-Cdr. Goddard was participating in the *Daily Mail* trans-Atlantic air race, which he won (prize £5,000) with an overall time of 5 hours 11 minutes 22 seconds from the top of the Empire State Building, New York, to the top of the Post Office Tower, London.

CIRCUMNAVIGATION
Earliest The earliest flight around the world was completed by two U.S. Army Air Service Douglas aircraft "Chicago" (Lt. Lowell H. Smith and Lt. Leslie P. Arnold) and "New Orleans" (Lt. Erik H. Nelson and Lt. John Harding) on 28 Sept. 1924 at Seattle,

Washington, U.S.A. The 175-day flight of 26,1• miles began on 24 April 1924 and involved 57 "ho and a flying time of 351 hours 11 minutes. The aircraft had interchangeable wheels and floats. T earliest solo flight round the world was made from to 22 July 1933 by Wiley Hardeman P (1899-1935) (U.S.A.) in the Lockheed *Vega* "Winr Mac" starting and finishing at Floyd Bennett Fie New York City, U.S.A. He flew the 15,596 mi east-about in 7 days 18 hours 49 minutes—in 10 ho with a flying time of 115 hours 36 minutes.

Fastest The fastest circumnavigation of the globe w achieved by three U.S.A.F. B-52 *Stratofortresses*, l by Maj.-Gen. Archie J. Old, Jr., chief of the U.S. 15 Air force. They took off from Castle Air Force Ba Merced, California, at 1 p.m. on 16 Jan. and fle eastwards, arriving 45 hours 19 minutes later at Mar Air Force Base, Riverside, California, on 18 Ja 1957, after a flight of 24,325 miles. The plan averaged 525 m.p.h. and were refuelled four times flight by KC-97 aerial tankers.

Earliest Solo Circum-polar flight Capt. Elgen M. Long, 44 completed at San Francis International Airport the first ever solo polar circu navigation in his Piper Navajo in 215 hours a 38,896 miles, flying from 5 Nov. to 3 Dec. 1971. T cabin temperature sank to -40° F. over Antarctica.

A reader's snap of Alcock and Brown about to embark on th first ever trans-Atlantic non-stop flight

LARGEST AIRCRAFT
Heaviest and Most Powerful The greatest weight at which an aeroplane has take off is 820,700 lb. (366.38 tons), achieved by th prototype Boeing Model 747-200 (747B) commerci transport at Edwards Air Force Base, California, November 1970. The basic aeroplane weighe 320,000 lb. (142.9 tons), the remaining weig representing fuel, flight test equipment and a artificial payload of sand and water. The 747B has wing span of 195 feet 8 inches, is 231 feet 4 inch long. It is structurally capable of accepting 4 Pratt Whitney JT9D-7W turbofans, giving a total thrust 188,000 lb.

Largest wing span The aircraft with the largest wing span ever co structed was the $40 million Hughes H.2 *Hercul* flying-boat, which was raised 70 feet into the air in test run of 1,000 yards, piloted by Howard Hughe off Long Beach Harbor, California, U.S.A., on 2 No 1947. The eight-engined 190-ton aircraft had a wir span of 320 feet and a length of 219 feet. The Harbc Commission have served notice on Hughes Tool C to remove the plane, known as the "Spruce Goose from its hangar by 4 Mar. 1973.

Most Powerful From Oct. 1971 the 4 Pratt & Whitney JT 9D-7 turbofans gave a total thrust of 188,000 lb. s.t., s

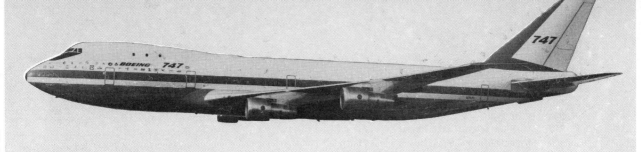

surpassing the 186,000 lb. s.t. of the 6 engined North American XB-70A *Valkyrie*.

Lightest The lightest aeroplane ever flown is the Whing Ding II, a single seat biplane designed and built by R.W. Hovey of Sangus, California and first flown in Feb. 1971. It has a wing span of 17 feet and an empty weight of 120 lb. and a loaded weight of 310 lb. It is powered by a 14 h.p. McCulloch Go-Kart engine, driving a pusher propeller and has a maximum speed of 50 m.p.h. and a range of 20 miles on half a gallon of fuel. The pilot sits on an open seat. A second Whing Ding II was completed in Spring 1972.

Smallest The smallest aeroplane ever flown is the Stits *Skybaby* biplane, designed, built and flown by Ray Stits at Riverside, California, U.S.A., in 1952. It was 9 feet 10 inches long, with a wing span of 7 feet 2 inches, and weighed 452 lb. empty. It was powered by an 85 h.p. Continental C85 engine giving a top speed of 185 m.p.h.

BOMBERS

Heaviest The world's heaviest bomber is the eight-jet swept-wing Boeing B-52H *Stratofortress*, which has a maximum take-off weight of 488,000 lb. (217.86 tons). It has a wing span of 185 feet and is 157 feet 6¾ inches in length, with a speed of over 650 m.p.h. The B-52 can carry 12 750-lb. bombs under each wing and 84 500-lb. bombs in the fuselage giving the total bomb load of 60,000 lb. or 26.78 tons. The ten-engined Convair B-36J, weighing 183 tons, had a greater wing span, at 230 feet, but is no longer in service. It had a top speed of 435 m.p.h.

Fastest The world's fastest operational bombers are the French Dassault *Mirage IV*, which can fly at Mach 2.2 (1,450 m.p.h.) at 36,000 feet, and the American General Dynamics FB-111A, which also flies above Mach 2. Under development is a swing-wing Tupolev bomber known to N.A.T.O. as "Backfire", which has an estimated over-target speed of Mach 2.25-2.5 and a range of 4,600 feet. The fastest Soviet bomber is the Tupolev Tu-22 "Blinder", with an estimated speed of Mach 1.4 (925 m.p.h.) at 36,000 feet.

AIRLINERS

Largest The highest capacity jet airliner is the Boeing 747, **World** "Jumbo Jet", first flown on 9 Feb. 1969, which by November 1970 had set a record for gross take-off weight with 820,700 lb. (366.38 tons) (see Heaviest aircraft) and has a capacity of from 362 to 490 passengers with a cruising speed of 595 m.p.h. Its wing span is 195.7 feet and its length 231.3 feet. It entered service on 21 Jan. 1970.

United The heaviest United Kingdom airliner in service is the *Kingdom* B.A.C. Super VC10, which first flew on 7 May 1964. It weighs 335,000 lb. (149.5 tons) and is 171.7 feet long, with a wing span of 146.2 feet. The largest ever British aircraft was the prototype Bristol Type 167 *Brabazon,* which had a maximum take-off weight of 129.4 tons but a wing span of 230 feet and a length of 177 feet. This eight-engined aircraft first flew on 4 Sept. 1949. The *Concorde* (see column 2) will have a maximum take-off weight of 385,000 lb. (171.8 tons).

rgest Cargo The largest cargo compartment of any aircraft is the **mpartment** 3,900 cubic feet of the Super Guppy ZO1 which was

put into service in Sept. 1971. The compartment is more than 25 feet in diameter.

Fastest The world's fastest airliner in service is the Convair **World** CV-990 *Coronado,* one of which flew at 675 m.p.h. at 22,500 feet (Mach 0.97) on 8 May 1961. Its maximum cruising speed is 625 m.p.h. A Douglas DC-8 Series 40, with Rolls-Royce Conway engines, exceeded the speed of sound in a shallow dive on 21 Aug. 1961. Its true air speed was 667 m.p.h. or Mach 1.012 at a height of 40.350 feet. The U.S.S.R.'s Tu-144 supersonic airliner, with a capacity of 121 passnegers, first flew on 31 Dec. 1968. Its design speed is Mach 2.35 (1,553 m.p.h.) with a ceiling of 65,000 feet and it "went" supersonic on 5 June 1969. It first exceeded Mach 2 on 26 May 1970, and attained 1,565.8 m.p.h. (Mach 2.37) at 59,000 ft. in late December 1971. The 288 foot long scale mock up of the planned Mach 2.7 Boeing SST which cost $10,680,000 was sold to Marks O Morrison for $31,119 on 18 Feb. 1972.

Britain The fastest British airliner in service is the three-engined Hawker Siddeley *Trident 1C* which has reached 627 m.p.h. (Mach 0.9) in level flight and 667 m.p.h. (Mach 0.96) in a shallow dive at 24,000 feet. The supersonic BAC/Aérospatiale *Concorde,* first flown on 2 March 1969, with a capacity of 128 passengers, is expected to cruise at 1,320–1,450 m.p.h. It flew at Mach 1.05 on 10 Oct. 1969 and exceeded Mach 2 for the first time on 4 Nov. 1970.

Scheduled The longest scheduled non-stop flight is the Buenos **flights** Aires, Argentina to Madrid, Spain stage of 6,462 *Longest* statute miles, by Aerolíneas Argentinas and Iberia inaugurated on 7 Aug. 1967. The Boeing 707-320B requires 11½ hours.

Shortest The shortest scheduled flight in the world is that by Loganair between the Orkney Islands of Westray and Papa Westray which has been flown since September 1967. Though scheduled for 2 minutes, in favourable wind conditions it is accomplished in 70 seconds.

HIGHEST SPEED

Official The official air speed record is 2,070.102 m.p.h. by **record** Col. Robert L. Stephens and Lt.-Col. Daniel André (both U.S.A.F.) in a Lockheed YF-12A near Edwards Air Force Base, California, U.S.A., on 1 May 1965.

Air- The fastest fixed-wing aircraft in the world is the U.S. **launched** North American Aviation X-15A-2, which flew for **record** the first time (after conversion) on 28 June 1964 powered by a liquid oxygen and ammonia rocket propulsion system. Ablative materials on the airframe have once enabled a temperature of 3,000° F. to be withstood. The landing speed was 210 knots (241.8 m.p.h.) momentarily. The highest speed attained was 4,520 m.p.h. (Mach 6.70) when piloted by Major William J. Knight, U.S.A.F. (b. 1930), on 3 Oct. 1967. An earlier version piloted by Joseph A. Walker (1920-66), reached 354,200 feet (67.08 miles) also over Edwards Air Force Base, California, U.S.A., on 22 Aug. 1963. The programme was suspended after the final flight of 24 Oct. 1968.

Fastest jet The world's fastest jet aircraft is the U.S.A.F. Lockheed SR-71 reconnaissance aircraft (a variant of the YF-12A) which was first flown on 22 Dec. 1964 and is reportedly capable of attaining a speed of

137

2,200 m.p.h. and an altitude ceiling of close to 100,000 feet. The SR-71 has a span of 55.6 feet and a length of 107.4 feet and weighs 170,000 lb. (75.9 tons) at take-off. Its reported range is 2,982 miles at Mach 3 at 78,750 feet. Only 23 are believed to have been built and 9 had been lost by April 1969. The fastest Soviet jet aircraft in service is the Mikoyan MiG-23 fighter (code name "Foxbat") with a speed of Mach 3.2 (2,110 m.p.h.) It is armed with air-to-air missiles.

Fastest biplane The fastest recorded biplane was the Italian Fiat C.R.42B, with a 1,010 h.p. Daimler-Benz DB601A engine, which attained 323 m.p.h. in 1941. Only one was built.

Fastest piston-engined aircraft The fastest speed at which a piston-engined aeroplane has ever been measured was for a cut-down privately owned Hawker *Sea Fury* which attained 520 m.p.h. in level flight over Texas, U.S.A., in August 1966 piloted by Mike Carroll (k. 1969) of Los Angeles. The official record for a piston-engined aircraft is 482-462 m.p.h. over Edwards AFB, California by Darryl C. Greenamyer, 33 (U.S.) in a modified Grumman F8F-2 *Bearcat* on 16 Aug. 1969. The Republic XF-84M prototype U.S. Navy fighter which flew on 22 July 1955 had a claimed top speed of 670 m.p.h.

Fastest propeller-driven aircraft The Soviet Tu-114 turboprop transport is the world's fastest propeller-driven aeroplane. It has achieved average speeds of more than 545 m.p.h. carrying heavy payloads over measured circuits. It is developed from the Tupolev Tu-95 bomber, known in the West as the "Bear", and has 14,795-horse-power engines.

Largest propeller The largest aircraft propeller ever used was the 22 feet 7½ inches diameter Garuda propeller, fitted to the Linke-Hofmann R II built in Breslau, Germany, which flew in 1919. It was driven by four 260 h.p. Mercédès engines and turned at only 545 r.p.m.

ALTITUDE

Official record The official world altitude record by an aircraft which took off from the ground at Podnoskovnoe under its own power is 113,891 feet (21.57 miles) by Lt.-Col. Georgiy Mosolov (U.S.S.R.) in a Mikoyan E-66A aircraft, powered by one turbojet and one rocket engine, on 28 April 1961. Major R. W. Smith of the U.S. Air Force reached an unofficial record height of 118,860 feet (22.15 miles) in a Lockheed NF-104A over Edwards Air Force Base, California, U.S.A., early in November 1963.

DURATION

The flight duration record is 64 days, 22 hours, 19 minutes and 5 seconds, set up by Robert Timm and John Cook in a Cessna 172 "Hacienda". They took off from McCarran Airfield, Las Vegas, Nevada, U.S.A., just before 3.53 p.m. local time on 4 Dec. 1958, and landed at the same airfield just before 2.12 p.m. on 7 Feb. 1959. They covered a distance equivalent to six times around the world.

AIRPORTS

Largest World The world's largest airport is the Dulles International Airport, Washington, D.C., U.S.A., which extends over an area of 9,880 acres (15.59 square miles). The largest international airport terminal is that at John F. Kennedy International Airport (opened as Idlewild in July 1948) on Long Island, New York, U.S.A. Terminal City covers an area of 840 acres. Work was started in December 1968 on Fort Worth/Dallas Regional Airport, Texas, a 17,000 acre complex for completion at a cost of $500 million (£192 million) by June 1973. The four terminals will have 65 gates.

United Kingdom Sixty-three airline companies from 50 countries operate scheduled services into London (Heathrow) Airport (2,765 acres), and during 1971 there were a total number of 273,425 air transport movements handled by a staff of 48,576 employed by the various companies and the British Airports Authority. T total number of passengers, both incoming a outgoing, was 16,332,442 in 1971. The most flig in a day was 947 on 30 July 1971 and the larg number of passengers yet handled in a day was 71,6 on the same day. Aircraft fly to 94 countries.

Busiest The world's busiest airport is the Chicago Int national Airport, O'Hare Field, Illinois, U.S.A., wit total of 628,013 movements (569,199 air carr movements) in 1970. This represents a take-off landing every 50.2 seconds.

The busiest landing area is, however, Bien Hoa Base, South Vietnam, which handled more th 1,000,000 take-offs and landings in 1970. T world's largest "helipad" is An Khe, South Vietna which services U.S. Army and Air Force helicopte

Highest and lowest The highest airport in the world is El Alto, near Paz, Bolivia, at 13,599 feet above sea-level. Lada airstrip in Kashmir has, however, an altitude 14,270 feet. The highest landing ever made is 6,0 metres (19,947 feet) on Dhaulagri in the Ne Himalaya by a highwing monoplane, named Y supplying the 1960 Swiss Expedition. The low landing field is El Lisan on the east shore of the De Sea, 1,180 feet below sea-level, but the low international airport is Schiphol, Amsterdam, at feet below sea-level.

LONGEST RUNWAY

World The longest runway in the world is one of 7 miles length (of which 15,000 feet is concreted) at Edwa Air Force Base on the bed of Rogers Dry Lake Muroc, California, U.S.A. The whole test cen airfield extends over 65 square miles. In an emergen an auxiliary 12-mile strip is available along the bed the Dry Lake. The world's longest civil airpo runway is one of 15,510 feet (2.95 miles) Salisbury, Rhodesia, completed in 1969.

United Kingdom The longest runway available normally to civil aircr in the United Kingdom is No. 1 at London (Heat row) Airport, measuring 12,799 feet (2.42 miles).

HELICOPTERS

Fastest rotating wing A Bell YUH-1B Model 533 compound resear helicopter, boosted by two auxiliary turbojet engine attained an unofficial speed record of 316.1 m.p. over Arlington, Texas, U.S.A., in April 1969. T world's speed record for a pure helicopter, subject official confirmation, is 220.8 m.p.h. by a Sikors S-67 Blackhawk, flown by test pilot Kurt Canno between Milford and Branford, Connecticut, U.S. on 19 Dec. 1970. In Nov. 1971 a Lockheed AH-56 Cheyenne reportedly flew at 266 m.p.h.

Largest The world's largest helicopter is the Soviet Mil V- ("Homer"), also known as the V-12, which set up international record by lifting a payload of 88,636 (39.5 tons) to a height of 7,398 feet on 6 Aug. 196 It is powered by four 6,500 h.p. turboshaft engin and has an estimated span of 219 ft. 10 ins, over rotor tips with a fuselage length of 121 feet a weighs 103.3 tons.

Highest The altitude record for helicopters is 36,027 feet Jean Boulet in a Stud-Aviation S.E.3150 *Alouette* at Brétigny,sur-Orge, France on 13 June 1958. claim was made for a U.S. Sikorsky CH-54B (James Church) at 36,122 ft. on 4 Nov. 1971. The highe landing has been at 23,000 feet below the South-Ea face of Everest in a rescue sortie in May 1971.

FLYING-BOAT

The fastest flying-boat ever built has been the Mart XP6M-1, the U.S. Navy 4 jet engined minelayer flow in 1955-59 with a top speed of 646 m.p.h. Sept. 1946 the Martin Caroline *Mars* flying boat set pay load record of 68,327 lb. Two Mars flying boa

The world's largest helicopter — the U.S.S.R's Mil V-12

are still working as forest fire protection water bombers in British Columbia.

AIRSHIPS

Earliest The earliest flight of an airship was by Henri Giffard from Paris in his hydrogen 88,000 cu. ft. 144 foot long rigid airship on 24 Sept. 1852. The earliest British airship was a 20,000 cu. ft. 75 foot long craft built by Stanley Spencer whose maiden flight was from Crystal Palace, London on 22 September 1902. The only airship now based in Britain is the 202,700 cu. ft., 192½ foot long *Europa* built at Cardington, Bedfordshire by the Goodyear Tyre & Rubber Co. which first flew on 8 Mar. 1972.

Largest The largest rigid airship ever built was the German
Rigid *Graf Zeppelin II* (LZ130), with a length of 803 feet
World and a capacity of 7,063,000 cubic feet. She made her maiden flight on 14 Sept. 1938 and in May and August 1939 made radar spying missions in British air space. She was dismantled in April 1940.

British The largest British airship was the R101 built by the Royal Airship Works, Cardington, Bedfordshire which first flew on 29 Oct. 1929. She was 777 feet in length and had a capacity of 5,500,000 cubic feet. She crashed near Beauvais, France, killing 48 aboard on 5 Oct. 1930.

Non-rigid The largest non-rigid airship ever constructed was the U.S. Navy ZPG 3-W. It had a capacity of 1,516,300 cubic feet, was 403.4 feet long and 85.1 feet in diameter, with a crew of 21. She first flew on 21 July 1958, but crashed into the sea in June 1960.

Greatest The most people ever carried in an airship was 207 in
Passenger the U.S. Navy *Akron* in 1931. The transatlantic
Load record is 117 by the German *Hindenberg* in 1937.

BALLOONS

Distance The record distance travelled is 3,052.7 kilometres
record (1,896.9 miles) by H. Berliner (Germany) from Bitterfeld, Germany, to Kirgishan in the Ural Mountains, Russia, on 8-10 Feb. 1914. The official duration record is 87 hours by H. Kaulen (Germany) set on 13-17 Dec. 1913.

Largest The largest balloon ever to fly is the 800-foot-tall balloon built by G. T. Schjeldahl for the U.S.A.F., first tested on 18 July 1966. It was used for a Martian re-entry experiment by N.A.S.A. 130,000 feet above Walker AFB, New Mexico, U.S.A., on 30 Aug. 1966. Its capacity is 260 million cubic feet.

Human- The earliest successful attempt to fly over half a mile
powered with a human-powered aircraft was made by John C.
flight Wimpenny, who flew 993 yards at an average altitude

of 5 feet (maximum 8 feet) and an average speed of 19.5 m.p.h. in a pedal-cranked propeller-driven aircraft called "Puffin I" at Hatfield, Herts., on 2 May 1962.

HOVERCRAFT

Earliest The inventor of the ACV (air-cushion vehicle) is Sir Christopher Sydney Cockerell, C.B.E., F.R.S. (b. 4 June 1910), a British engineer who had the idea in 1954, published his Ripplecraft Report 1/55 on 25 Oct. 1955 and patented it on 12 Dec. 1955. The earliest patent relating to an air-cushion craft was applied for in 1877 by John I. Thornycroft (1843-1928) of Chiswick, London. The first flight by a hovercraft was made by the 4-ton Saunders Roe SR-N1 at Cowes on 30 May 1959. With a 1,500-lb. thrust Viper turbojet engine, this craft reached 68 knots in June 1961. The first hovercraft public service was run across the Dee Estuary by the 60-knot 24-passenger Vickers-Armstrong VA-3 between July and September 1962.

Largest The largest is the £1,500,000 Westland SR-N4, *Mountbatten*, weighing 168 tons, first run on 4 Feb. 1968. It has a top speed of 77 knots powered by 4 Bristol Siddeley Marine Proteus engines with 19-foot propellers. It carries 34 cars and 174 passengers and is 130 feet 2 inches long with a 76-foot 10-inch beam.

Longest The longest hovercraft journey was one of 5,000
flight miles through eight West African countries between 15 Oct. 1969 and 3 Jan. 1970 by the British Trans-African Hovercraft Expedition. The longest non-stop journey on record is one of 550 miles lasting 33 hours by a Denny Mark II piloted by Sir John Onslow from Poole, Dorset to Fleetwood, Lancashire on 4-5 July 1968.

MODEL AIRCRAFT
The world record for altitude is 26,929 feet by Maynard L. Hill (U.S.A.) on 6 Sept. 1970 using a radio-controlled model. The speed record is 213.71 m.p.h. by V. Goukoune and V. Myakinin with a motor piston radio-controlled model at Klementyeva, U.S.S.R., on 21 Sept. 1971. The best British performance is 101.5 m.p.h. by an unsponsored home-built 7.9 c.c engined model of 32-inch wing span by John Crampton at Dunsfold, Surrey on 20 Oct. 1968.

5. POWER PRODUCERS

LARGEST POWER PLANT
World The world's largest power station is the U.S.S.R.'s hydro-electric station at Krasnoyarsk on the river Yenisey, Siberia, U.S.S.R. with a power of 6,096,000 kW. Its third generator turned in March 1968 and the twelfth became operative in December 1970. The turbine hall, completed in June 1968, is 1,378 feet long. The turbine hall at the Volga-V.I. Lenin Power Plant, Kuybyshev is more than 2,100 feet long. The underground turbine hall at the Canadian Churchill Falls (5,255,000 kW) installation is 972 feet long.

The largest non-hydro-electric generating plant in the world is the 2,500,000 kW Tennessee Valley Authority installation at Paradise, Kentucky, U.S.A. with an annual consumption of 8,150,000 tons of coal. It cost $189,000,000 (then £78,750,000).

United The power stations with the greatest installed capa-
Kingdom city in the United Kingdom are Ferrybridge "C" near Pontefract, Yorkshire, which reached full power of 2,000 MW in December 1967, and which with the Ferrybridge "A" and "B" forms a 2,430 MW complex. A single station in Longannet, Fife, Scotland began building up towards a delivery of 2,400 MW in 1971. A 3,960 MW station is under construction at Drax, Yorkshire, the first half of which (3 X 660 MW sets) will be completed in 1973.

The largest hydro-electric plant in the United Kingdom is the North of Scotland Hydro-electricity Board's Power Station at Loch Sloy, Dunbartonshire. The installed capacity of this station is 130,450 kW or 175,000 h.p. The Ben Cruachan Pumped Storage Scheme was opened on 15 Oct. 1965 at Loch Awe, Argyll, Scotland. It has a capacity of 400,000 kW and cost £24,000,000.

Biggest black-out The greatest power failure in history struck seven north-eastern U.S. States and Ontario, Canada, on 9-10 Nov. 1965. About 30,000,000 people in 80,000 square miles were plunged into darkness. Only two were killed. In New York City the power failed at 5.27 p.m. Supplies were eventually restored by 2 a.m. in Brooklyn, 4.20 a.m. in Queens, 6.58 a.m. in Manhattan and 7 a.m. in the Bronx.

ATOMIC POWER

Earliest The world's first atomic pile was built in a disused squash court at the University of Chicago, Illinois, U.S.A. It went "critical" at 3.25 p.m. on 2 Dec. 1942.

Largest The world's largest atomic power station is the 1,180 MW plant at Wylfa, Anglesey which was completed in Feb. 1971. It will be overtaken by Hinkley Point "B" (1973) Hartlepool, Durham (1974), and Heysham, Lancashire (1976) all at 1320 MW. The largest atomic plant scheduled in the United States is the Spring City, Tennessee Unit 1 and Unit 2 (1,169 MW) due to be completed for T.V.A. in 1976 or 1977.

LARGEST REACTOR
The largest single atomic reactor in the world is the 873 MW Westinghouse Electric Corporation pressurized water type reactor installed at Indian Point No. 2 Station, New York, U.S.A. which became operative in 1969.

TIDAL POWER STATION
The world's first major tidal power station is the *Usine marèmotrice de la Rance,* officially opened on 26 Nov. 1966 at the Rance estuary in the Golfe de St. Malo, Britanny, France. It was built in five years, at a cost of 420,000,000 francs (£34,685,000), and has a net annual output of 544,000,000 kWh. The 880-yard barrage contains 24 turbo alternators. This harnessing of the tides has imperceptibly slowed the Earth's rate of revolution. The $1,000 million (£416 million) Passamaquoddy project for the Bay of Fundy in Maine, U.S.A., and New Brunswick, Canada, is not expected to be operative before 1978. The first ever tidal power station was the Dee Hydro Station, Cheshire with a capacity of 635 kW which began producing in October 1913.

LARGEST BOILER
The largest boilers ever designed are those ordered in the United States from The Babcock & Wilc Company (U.S.A.) with a capacity of 1,330 MW involving the evaporation of 9,330,000 lb. of ste per hour. The largest boilers now being installed in t United Kingdom are the three 660 MW units for t Drax Power Station (see page 139) designed a constructed by Babcock & Wilcox Ltd.

LARGEST GENERATOR
Generators in the 2,000,000 kW (or 2,000 MW) ra are now in the planning stages both in the U.K. a the U.S.A. The largest under construction is one 1,300 MW by the Brown Boveri Co. of Switzerla for the Tennessee Valley Authority.

LARGEST TURBINES
The largest turbines under construction are the rated at 820,000 h.p. with an overload capacity 1,000,000 h.p., 32 feet in diameter with a 401-t runner and a 312½-ton shaft for the Grand Cou "Third Powerplant" (see page 115).

GAS TURBINE
The largest gas turbine in the world is that installed the Krasnodar thermal power station in August 19 with a capacity of 100,000 kW. It was built Leningrad, U.S.S.R.

LARGEST PUMP TURBINE
The world's largest integral reversible pump-turbin that made by Allis-Chalmers for the $50,000,0 Taum Sauk installation of the Union Electric Co. St. Louis, Missouri, U.S.A. It has a rating 240,000 h.p. as a turbine and a capacity of 1,100,0 gallons per minute as a pump. The Tehach Pumping Plant, California will in 1972 pu 18,300,000 gallons per minute over 1,700 feet up.

SOLAR POWER PLANT
The largest solar furnace in the world is the Labo toire de l'Energie Solaire, at Mont Louis in the easte Pyrenees, France. Its parabolic reflector, 150 feet diameter, is the largest mirror in the world a concentrates the Sun's rays to provide a temperatu of 5,432° F. In April 1958 it was announced tl Soviet scientists had designed a solar power stati for the Ararat Valley, Armenia, U.S.S.R., using 1,3 moving mirrors, totalling 5 acres in area, to provi 2,500,000 kW hours in a year. The U.S. Air Fo solar furnace at Cloudcroft, New Mexico, U.S.A., a parabolic mirror 108 feet in diameter and a f mirror 154 feet square, yielding temperatures of 8,500° F.

LARGEST GAS WORKS
The flow of natural gas from the North Sea diminishing the manufacture of gas by the carboni tion of coal and the re-forming process using pet

THE WORLD'S LARGEST HYDRO-ELECTRIC GENERATING PLANTS
(Progressive List)

Kilowattage	First Operational	Location	River
38,400	1898	De Cew Falls No. 1 (old plant)	Welland Canal
132,500	1905	Ontario Power Station	Niagara
403,900	1922	Sir Adam Beck No. 1 (formerly Queenston-Chippawa)	Niagara
524,000[1]	1967	Guri, Venezuela	Caroní
1,641,000	1942	Beauharnois, Quebec, Canada	St. Lawrence
2,025,000[2]	1941	Grand Coulee, Washington State, U.S.A.	Columbia
2,100,000	1955	Volga-V.I. Lenin Station, Kuybyshev, U.S.S.R.	Volga
2,543,000	1958	Volga-22nd Congress Station, Volgograd, U.S.S.R.	Volga
4,500,000	1961	Bratsk, U.S.S.R.	Angara
6,096,000	1967	Krasnoyarsk, U.S.S.R.	Yenisey
6,400,000	–	Sayano-Shushensk, U.S.S.R.	Yenisey
c. 20,000,000	–	Lower Lena, near Verkoyansk, U.S.S.R.	Lena

[1] *Ultimate Kilowattage will be 6,500,000 kW.*
[2] *Ultimate long-term planned kilowattage will be 9,771,000 kW with the completion of the "Third Powerplant" (capacity 7,200,000 kW).*

leum derivatives. Britain's largest ever gasworks covering 300 acres were at Beckton, Essex. Currently the most productive gasworks are at the oil re-forming plant at East Greenwich, London, with an output of 420.5 million cubic feet per day.

MOST POWERFUL JET ENGINE

The world's most powerful jet engine was the General Electric GE4/J5 turbojet which attained a thrust of 69,900 lb., with after-burning, on 13 Nov. 1969. The Pratt & Whitney JT 90D-X turbofan first run on 15 Jan. 1972 has a thrust of 62,000 lb. at 23° F. The thrust of the Thiokol XLR99-RM-2 rocket motor in each of the three experimental U.S.X-15 aircraft was 56,880 lb. at sea-level, reaching 70,000 lb. at peak altitudes. The Rolls-Royce RB 211-22B powered the Lockheed L-1011-1 'Tristar', from April 1972 and develops 42,000 lb. The -22X version (45,000 lb.) may be developed for the L-1011-2.

6. ENGINEERING

OLDEST MACHINERY

World The earliest machinery still in use is the *dâlu*—a water raising instrument known to have been in use in the Sumerian civilization which originated *c.* 3,500 B.C. in Lower Iraq.

Britain The oldest piece of machinery operating in the United Kingdom is the snuff mill driven by a water wheel at Messrs. Wilson & Co.'s Sharrow Mill in Sheffield, Yorkshire. It is known to have been operating in 1797 and more probably since 1730.

LARGEST PRESS

The world's two most powerful production machines are forging presses in the U.S.A. The Loewy closed-die forging press, in a plant leased from the U.S. Air Force by the Wyman-Gordon Company at North Grafton, Massachusetts, U.S.A. weighs 9,469 tons and stands 114 feet 2 inches high, of which 66 feet is sunk below the operating floor. It has a rated capacity of 44,600 tons, and went into operation in October 1955. The other similar press is at the plant of the Aluminium Company of America at Cleveland, Ohio. There has been a report of a press in the U.S.S.R. with a capacity of 75,000 tonnes (73,800 tons), at Novo Kramatorsk. The most powerful press in Great Britain is the closed-die forging and extruding press installed in 1967 at the Cameron Iron Works, near Edinburgh, Scotland. The press is 92 feet tall (27 feet below ground) and exerts a force of 30,000 tons.

LATHE

The world's largest lathe is the 72-foot-long 385-ton giant lathe built by the Dortmunder Rheinstahl firm of Wagner in 1962. The face plate is 15 feet in diameter and can exert a torque of 289,000 ft./lb. when handling objects weighing up to 200 tons.

EXCAVATOR

The world's largest excavator is the 33,400 h.p. Marion 6360 excavator, weighing 12,500 tons. This vast machine can grab 241 tons in a single bite in a bucket of 85 cubic yards capacity.

DRAGLINE

World The Ural Engineering Works at Ordzhonikidze, U.S.S.R., completed in March 1962, has a dragline known as the ES-25(100) with a boom of 100 metres (328 feet) and a bucket with a capacity of 31.5 cubic yards. The world's largest walking dragline is the Bucyrus-Erie 4250W with an all-up weight of 12,000 tons and a bucket capacity of 220 cubic yards on a 310-foot boom. This machine, the world's largest mobile land machine is now operating on the Central Ohio Coal Company's Muskingum site in Ohio, U.S.A.

Part of the world's longest pipeline — the Trans Canada

United Kingdom The largest dragline excavator in Britain is "Big Geordie", the Bucyrus-Erie 1550W 6250 gross h.p., weighing 3,000 tons with a forward mast 160 feet high. On open-cast coal workings at Widdrington, Northumberland in February 1970, it proved able to strip 100 tons of overburden in 65 seconds with its 65 cubic yard bucket on a 265-foot boom. It is operated by Derek Crouch (Contractors) Ltd. of Peterborough.

BLAST FURNACE

The world's largest blast furnace is the No. 3 Blast Furnace at the Nippon Steel Corporation's Kimitsu Steel Works completed in April 1971. It has a daily pig iron production capacity of 10,000 tons.

Largest forging The largest forging on record is one 53 feet long weighing 396,000 lb. (176.79 tons) forged by Bethlehem Steel for the Tennessee Valley Authority nuclear power plant at Brown Ferry, Alabama, U.S.A. in Nov. 1969.

LONGEST PIPELINES

Oil The longest crude oil pipeline in the world is the Interprovincial Pipe Line Company's installation from Edmonton, Alberta, to Buffalo, New York State, U.S.A., a distance of 1,775 miles. Along the length of the pipe 13 pumping stations maintain a flow of 6,900,000 gallons of oil per day. In Britain the longest commercial oil pipeline, 242 miles from the Thames to the Mersey, is owned by Chevron, Mobil, Petrofina, Shell-Mex and B.P., and Texaco. It was opened on 19 March 1969 at a cost of £8½ million.

The eventual length of the Trans-Siberian Pipeline will be 2,319 miles, running from Tuimazy through Omsk and Novosibirsk to Irkutsk. The first 30-mile section was opened in July 1957.

Natural gas The longest natural gas pipeline in the world is the TransCanada Pipeline which by mid-1971 had 3,769 miles of pipe up to 36 inches in diameter. The mileage will be increased to 4,464 miles, some of it in 42-inch pipe, by mid-1973. A system 5,625 miles in length, with a 3,500-mile trunk from northern Russia to Leningrad, is under construction in the U.S.S.R., for completion by 1976.

Largest Cat Cracker The world's largest catalyst cracker is the American Oil Company's installation at the Texas City Refinery, Texas, U.S.A., with a capacity of 3,322,000 gallons per day.

An example of a Pilgrim nut—the world's largest nuts used to secure propellors to ships

Largest nut The largest nuts ever made weigh 29.5 cwt. (1.48 tons) each and have an outside diameter of 43½ inches and a 26 inch thread. Known as the Pilgrim Nuts, they are manufactured by Doncaster Moorside Ltd. Of Oldham, Lancashire, for securing propellers.

TRANSFORMER
The world's largest single phase transformers are rated at 1,500,000 kVa of which 8 are in service with the American Electric Power Service Corporation. Of these five stepdown from 765 to 345 kV. Britain's largest transformer is one rated at 700,000 kVa at Longannet, Fife, Scotland, completed in January 1970.

HIGHEST ROPEWAY OR TELEPHERIQUE
World The highest and longest aerial ropeway in the world is the Teleférico Mérida (Mérida téléphérique) in Venezuela, from Mérida City (5,379 feet) to the summit of Pico Espejo (15,629 feet), a rise of 10,250 feet. The ropeway is in four sections, involving 3 car changes in the 8 mile ascent in one hour. The fourth span is 10,070 feet in length. The two cars work on the pendulum system—the carrier rope is locked and the cars are hauled by means of three pull ropes powered by a 230 h.p. motor. They have a maximum capacity of 45 persons and travel at 32 feet per second (21.8 m.p.h.). The longest single span ropeway is the 13,500-foot-long span from The Coachella Valley to Mt. San Jacinto (10,821 feet), California, U.S.A., inaugurated on 12 Sept. 1963. The largest cable cars in the world are those at Squaw Valley, California, U.S.A., with a capacity of 121 persons built by Carrosseriewerke A.G. of Aarburg, Switzerland, and first run on 19 Dec. 1968. The breaking strain on the 7,000-foot cable is 279 tons.

Great Britain Britain's longest cabin lift is that at Llandudno, Caernarvonshire, Wales opened in June 1969. It has 42 cabins with a capacity of 1,000 people per hour and is 5,320 feet in length.

PASSENGER LIFTS
Fastest World The fastest domestic passenger lifts in the world are those fitted in the 100-storey, 1,107-foot-tall John Hancock Building in Chicago, Illinois, U.S.A. They operate at a speed of 1,600 feet per minute. Much higher speeds are achieved in the winding cages of

mine shafts. A hoisting shaft 6,800 feet deep, owned by Western Deep Levels Ltd. in South Africa, winds at speeds of up to 40.9 m.p.h. (3,595 feet per minute)

United Kingdom The longest lift in the United Kingdom is one 930 feet long inside the B.B.C. T.V. tower at Bilsdale, West Moor, North Riding, Yorkshire built by J. L. Eve Construction Co. Ltd. It runs at 130 feet/min. The longest fast lifts are the two 15-passenger cars in the Post Office Tower, Maple Street, London W1 which travel 540 feet up at up to 1,000 feet/min.

LONGEST ESCALATORS
The longest escalators of the 235 on the London Underground system are those at Leicester Square which measure 175½ feet comb to comb. Escalators were introduced at Earl's Court station, London, on 3 Oct. 1911.

The world's longest "moving sidewalk" is the Speed-walk Passenger Conveyor System at San Francisco Airport, California, U.S.A., comprising two conveyors measuring 450 feet each, and each with a capacity of 7,200 passengers per hour. It was opened on 20 May 1964.

The longest "travolators" in Great Britain are the pair of 360 feet and 375 feet in tandem at Terminal No. 3 London Airport, installed by Fletcher, Sutcliffe and Wild of Horbury, Leeds, Yorkshire in March-May 1970.

FASTEST PRINTER
The world's fastest printer is the Radiation Inc electro-sensitive system at the Lawrence Radiation Laboratory, Livermore, California. High speed recording of up to 30,000 lines each containing 120 alphanumeric characters per minute is attained by controlling electronic pulses through chemically impregnated recording paper which is rapidly moving under closely spaced fixed styli. It can thus print the wordage of the whole Bible (773,692 words) in 65 seconds—3,333 times as fast as the world's fastest typist.

TRANSMISSION LINES
Longest The longest span between pylons of any power line in the world is that across the Sogne Fjord, Norway

142

between Rabnaberg and Flatlberg. Erected in 1955, by the Whitecross Co. Ltd. of Warrington, England, as part of the high-tension power cable from Refsdal power station at Vik, it has a span of 16,040 feet and a weight of 12 tons. In 1967 two further high tensile steel/aluminium lines 16,006 feet long, and weighing 33 tons, manufactured by Whitecross and B.I.C.C. (see below), were erected here. The longest in Britain are the 5,310-foot lines built by J. L. Eve Co. across the Severn with main towers each 488 feet high.

Highest The world's highest are those across the Straits of Messina, with towers of 675 feet (Sicily side) and 735 feet (Calabria) and 11,900 feet apart. The highest lines in Britain are those made by British Insulated Callender's Cables Ltd. at West Thurrock, Essex, which cross the Thames estuary suspended from 630-foot-tall towers at a minimum height of 250 feet, with a 130-ton breaking load. They are 4,500 feet in length.

Highest voltages The highest voltages now carried are 765,000 volts A.C. in the United States since 1969. The Swedish A.S.E.A. Company is experimenting with a possible 1,000,000 volt D.C. transmission line.

LONGEST CONVEYOR BELT
The world's longest single flight conveyor belt is one of 9 miles installed near Uniontown, Kentucky, U.S.A. by Cable Belt Ltd. of Camberley, Surrey. It has a weekly capacity of 140,000 short tons of coal on a 42-inch-wide 800 ft./min. belt and forms part of a 12½ mile long system. The longest installation in Great Britain is also by Cable Belt Ltd. and of 5½ miles at Longannet Power Station, Fife, Scotland.

LONGEST WIRE ROPE
The longest wire rope ever spun in one piece was one measuring 46,653 feet (8.83 miles) long and $3\frac{1}{8}$ inches in circumference, with a weight of 28½ tons, manufactured by British Ropes Ltd. of Doncaster, Yorkshire.

CLOCKS
Oldest The earliest mechanical clock, that is one with an escapement, was completed in China in A.D. 725 by I Hsing and Liang Ling-tsan.

The oldest surviving working clock in the world is one dating from 1386, or possibly earlier, at Salisbury Cathedral, Wiltshire, which was restored in 1956. Earlier dates, ranging back to c. 1335, have been attributed to the weight-driven clock in Wells Cathedral, Somerset, but only the iron frame is original. A model of Giovanni de Dondi's heptagonal astronomical clock of 1348-64 was completed in 1962.

Largest World The world's most massive clock is the Astronomical Clock in Beauvais Cathedral, France, constructed between 1865 and 1868. It contains 90,000 parts and measures 40 feet high, 20 feet wide and 9 feet deep. The Su Sung clock, built in China at K'aifeng in 1088-92, had a 20-ton bronze armillary sphere for 1½ tons of water. It was removed to Peking in 1126 and was last known to be working in its 40-foot-high tower in 1136.

United Kingdom The largest clock in the United Kingdom was on the Singer Sewing Machine factory at Clydebank, Dunbartonshire, Scotland. It had four faces, each 26 feet in diameter, the minute hand was 12 feet 9 inches long and the hour hand 8 feet 9 inches. It was built in 1882, re-modelled in 1926 and operated until 5 p.m. on 5 March 1963. The largest clock face constructed in Britain is the Synchronome turret clock (diameter 60 feet) exhibited at Earl's Court, London, in March 1959. The largest clock wheel in the world is the World Time Clock installed at 120 Cheapside, London, E.C.2. It has a diameter of 10 feet and enables the zone times in the major cities of the world to be read off. This was commissioned by J. Henry Schro-

The Salisbury Cathedral faceless clock dating from the 14th Century and only tells the time by chimes

der Wagg & Co. Ltd., from Martin Burgess.

Public clocks The largest four-faced clock in the world is that on the building of the Allen-Bradley Company of Milwaukee, Wisconsin, U.S.A. Each face has a diameter of 40 feet 3½ inches with a minute hand 20 feet in overall length. The tallest four-faced clock in the world is that of the Williamsburgh Savings Bank in Brooklyn, New York City, N.Y., U.S.A. It is 430 feet above street level.

Longest stoppage The longest stoppage of Big Ben, Palace of Westminster, London since the first tick on 31 May 1859 has been 8 hours in 1900 due to a snow-storm. In 1945 a host of starlings slowed the minute hand by 5 minutes.

Most accurate The most accurate and complicated clock in the world is the Olsen clock, installed in the Copenhagen Town Hall, Denmark. The clock, which has more than 14,000 units, took 10 years to make and the mechanism of the clock functions in 570,000 different ways. The celestial pole motion of the clock will take 25,753 years to complete a full circle and is the slowest moving designed mechanism in the world. The clock is accurate to 0.5 of a second in 300 years.

Most expensive The highest auction price for any portable English clock is £16,000 for an ebony bracket clock made by Thomas Tompian (c. 1639-1713) sold at the salerooms of Sotheby & Co., London on 22 May 1972.

WATCHES
Oldest The oldest watch (portable clock-work time-keeper) is one made of iron by Peter Henlein (or Hele) in Nürnberg (Nuremberg), Bavaria, Germany, in c. 1504 and now in the Memorial Hall, Philadelphia, Pennsyl-

The most expensive standard watch in the world La Grand Complication, which has a stop watch perpetual calendar and moon phases among its 12 operations. (see below)

vania, U.S.A. The earliest wrist watches were those of Jacquet-Droz and Leschot of Geneva, Switzerland, dating from 1790.

Most expensive Excluding watches with jewelled cases, the most expensive standard men's wrist watch is the Swiss *Grande Complication* by Audemars-Piguet which retails for $25,000 (£9,615). On 1 June 1964, a record £27,500 was paid for the Duke of Wellington's watch made in Paris in 1807 by Abraham Louis Bréguet, at the salerooms of Sotheby & Co., London, by the dealers Messrs. Ronald Lee for a Portuguese client.

Smallest The smallest watches in the world are produced by Jaeger Le Coultre of Switzerland. Equipped with a 15-jewelled movement they measure just over half-an-inch long and three-sixteenths of an inch in width. The movement, with its case, weighs under a quarter of an ounce.

TIME MEASURER

Most accurate **World** The most accurate time-keeping devices are the twin atomic hydrogen masers installed in 1964 in the U.S. Naval Research Laboratory, Washington, D.C. They are based on the frequency of the hydrogen atom's transition period of 1,420,450,751,694 cycles per second. This enables an accuracy to within one second per 1,700,000 years.

United Kingdom The most accurate measurer in the United Kingdom is the 14-foot-long rubidium resonance Standard Atomic Clock at the National Physical Laboratory, Teddington, Greater London, devised by Dr. Louis Essen, O.B.E. and Mr. J.V.L. Parry and completed in 1962. It is accurate to within one second in 1,000 years.

RADAR INSTALLATIONS

Largest The largest of the three installations in the U.S. Ballistic Missile Early Warning System (B.M.E.W.S.) is that near Thule, in Greenland, 931 miles from the North Pole, completed in 1960 at a cost of $500,000,000 (now £208.3 million). Its sister stations are one at Cape Clear, Alaska, U.S.A.. completed in July 1961, and a $115,000,000 (now £47.9 million) installation at Fylingdales Moor, Yorkshire, completed in June 1963. A fourth station is being built on an Indian Ocean island site. A 187-mast installation has been erected at Orfordness, Suffolk for the U.S.A.F. and R.A.F.

Smallest tubing The smallest tubing in the world is made by Accles and Pollock, Ltd. of Oldbury, Worcestershire. It is of pure nickel with an outside diameter of 0.0005 of an inch and was announced on 9 Sept. 1963. The average human hair measures from 0.002 to 0.003 of an inch

in diameter. The tubing, which is stainless, can used for the artificial insemination of bees and for t medical process of "feeding" nerves, and weighs on 5 oz. per 100 miles.

LARGEST CRANE

World The crane with the world's greatest lifting capacity the Goliath crane installed at Harland and Wolff shipbuilding dock, Belfast, Northern Ireland, in 196 The crane spans 460 feet and has a working safe load of 840 tons, but on a test lifted 1,050 tons. It w built to the design of Krupper-Ardelt of Wilhelm haven, West Germany. A 32-wheeled gantry hydraul crane with a span of 95 feet with a capacity of 2,00 short tons (1,785.7 tons) by R. A. Hanson Co. Inc. installed at the Grand Coulee Third Powerplan Washington, U.S.A. The highest crane reported is mobile crane, owned by Van Twist N.V. of Dor recht, Netherlands, of 350 tons capacity whic overtopped a 540-foot-high high-tension power pyl during its erection on the bank of the River Scheld near Antwerp, Belgium in March 1970.

The world's tallest mobile crane at work on a high lift at the 594 foot Euromast, Rotterdam.

Hoisting tackle The greatest weight lifted by hoisting tackle is 70 tons by the Fluor Corporation of Los Angeles California, U.S.A., in the case of an Isomax reactor 9 feet in length at Shuaiba, Kuwait, on 26 Aug. 1968.

Floating crane The world's most powerful floating crane is the Dutc vessel *Taklift I* (2,370 tons gross) completed in 196 It is capable of lifting objects as heavy as 800 tons.

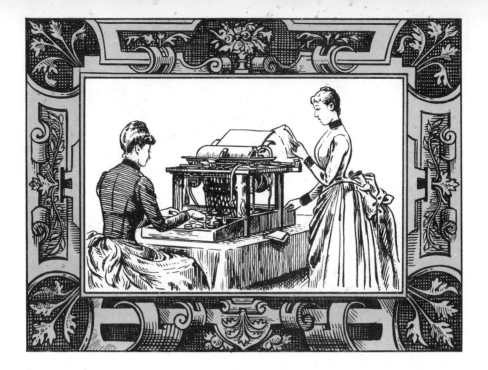

9 THE BUSINESS WORLD

1. COMMERCE

OLDEST INDUSTRY
Agriculture is often described as "the oldest industry in the world", whereas in fact there is no evidence that it was practised before *c.* 7000 B.C. The oldest known industry is flint knapping, involving the production of chopping tools and hand axes, dating from about 1,750,000 years ago.

OLDEST COMPANY
World The oldest company in the world is the Faversham Oyster Fishery Co., referred to in the Faversham Oyster Fishing Act 1930, as existing "from time immemorial", *i.e.* from before 1189.

Britain The Royal Mint has origins going back to A.D. 287. The Whitechapel Bell Foundry of Whitechapel Road, London, E.1, has been in business since 1570. The oldest retail business in Britain is the Cambridge bookshop Messrs. Bowes & Bowes, which, though under various ownership, has traded under this name since 1581. R. Durtnell & Sons, builders, of Brasted, Kent, has been run by the same family since 1591. The first bill of adventure signed by the English East India Co., was dated 21 Mar. 1601.

GREATEST ASSETS
World The business with the greatest amount in physical assets is the Bell System, which comprises the American Telephone and Telegraph Company, with headquarters at 195 Broadway, New York City, N.Y., U.S.A., and its subsidiaries. The group's total assets on the consolidated balance sheet at 31 Dec. 1971 were valued at $54,547,929,000 (£20,979 million). The plant involved included 100,366,000 telephones. The number of employees was 1,000,600. The shareholders at 1 Jan. 1971 numbered more than those of any other company, namely 3,009,768. A total of 20,109 attended the Annual Meeting in April 1961, thereby setting a world record. The total of operating revenues and other income in 1971 was $18,949,000,000 (£7,228 million). The first company to have assets in excess of $1 billion was the United States Steel Corporation with $1,400 million (then £287.73 million) at the time of its creation by merger in 1900.

United Kingdom The enterprise in the United Kingdom, excluding banks, with the greatest capital employed is the Electricity Council and the Electricity Boards in England and Wales with £5,084,000,000 in 1971. This ranks third in the western world to Standard Oil and General Motors.

The manufacturing company with the greatest total assets employed is Imperial Chemical Industries, Ltd., with £1,774,000,000, as at 31 Dec. 1971. Its staff and payroll then totalled 202,000. The company, which has more than 400 U.K. and overseas subsidiaries, was formed on 7 Dec. 1926 by the merger of four concerns—British Dyestuffs Corporation Ltd.; Brunner, Mond & Co. Ltd.; Nobel Industries Ltd. and United Alkali Co. Ltd. The first chairman was Sir Alfred Moritz Mond (1868-1930), later the 1st Lord Melchett.

The net assets of The "Shell" Transport and Trading Company Ltd., at 31 Dec. 1971, were valued at £1,557,771,574. Of this, £1,553,738,400 represented a 40 per cent. holding of the net assets of the Royal Dutch/Shell Group, which stands at £3,884,346,000. Group companies have 185,000 employees. "Shell" Transport was formed in 1897 by Marcus Samuel (1853-1927), later the 1st Viscount Bearsted.

Greatest sales The first company to surpass the $1 billion (U.S.) mark in annual sales was the United States Steel Corporation in 1917. Now there are 65 corporations with sales exceeding £1,000 million (43 U.S., 17 European and 5 Japanese). The list is headed by General Motors (see Motor car manufacturer) with sales in 1971 of $28,263,918,443 (£10,870 million).

Greatest profit and loss The greatest net profit ever made by one company in a year is $2,125,606,440 (now £8,175 million) by General Motors Corporation of Detroit in 1965. The greatest loss ever sustained by a commercial concern in a year is $431.2 million (£179.6 million) by Penn Central Transportation Co. in 1970—a rate of $13.67 (£5.69) per second. The year 1971 however, had a better start when the 1970 January and February loss figure of $73.1 million (£30.45 million) was "surpassed" with a loss of $66.3 million (£27.62 million) for the two opening months. The top profit earner in the United Kingdom in 1971 was British Petroleum with

£466.5 million and the biggest loss maker was Chrysler United Kingdom Ltd. which lost £10,020,000.

Most efficient The major United Kingdom company with highest return on capital in 1971 was Tampimex Oil Products, a London-based oil distributing company which showed a net profit of £909,000 or 146.4% on a capital employed of £779,000.

Biggest work force The greatest payroll of any civilian organization in the world is that of the United States Post Office with 716,782 on 1 July 1971. The biggest employer in the United Kingdom is the Post Office with 417,006 employees on 1 Jan. 1972.

ADVERTISING AGENTS
The largest advertising agency in the world is J. Walter Thompson Co. Ltd., which in 1971 had total billings of $779,000,000 (£299.6 million).

Biggest advertiser The world's biggest advertiser is Unilever, the Anglo-Dutch group formed on 2 Sept. 1929 whose origins go back to 21 June 1884. The group has more than 500 companies in more than 70 countries and employs 324,000 people, mainly in the production of foods, detergents and toiletries. The advertising bill for over 1,000 branded products was £110,000,000 in 1971.

Aircraft manufacturer The world's largest aircraft manufacturer is the Boeing Company of Seattle, Washington, U.S.A. The corporation's sales totalled $3,040,000,000 (£1,169 million) in 1971, and it had 56,300 employees and assets valued at $2,464,424,000 (£947 million) at 31 Dec. 1971. Cessna Aircraft Company of Wichita, Kansas, U.S.A., produced 3,859 civil aircraft (41 models) in the year 1971, with total sales of $168 million (£64.61 million). The company has produced more than 99,000 aircraft since Clyde Cessna's first was built in 1911. Their record year was 1965-66 with 7,922 aircraft completed.

AIRLINES
Largest The largest airline in the world is the U.S.S.R. State airline "Aeroflot", so named since 1932. This was instituted on 9 Feb. 1923, with the title of Civil Air Fleet of the Council of Ministers of the U.S.S.R., abbreviated to "Dobrolet". It operates 1,300 aircraft over about 373,000 miles of routes, employs 400,000 people and carried 74,000,000 passengers in 1970 to 57 countries. The commercial airline carrying the greatest number of passengers in 1971 was United Air Lines of Chicago, Illinois, U.S.A. (formed 1931) with 26,048,293 passengers. The company had 46,552 employees and a fleet of 381 jet planes. The commercial airline serving the greatest mileage of routes is Air France, with 258,000 miles of unduplicated routes in 1971. In 1971 the company carried 6,386,882 passengers. In March 1972 the British European Airways Group were operating a fleet of 140 aircraft, with 12 on order. BEA employed 27,470 staff and carried 11,000,000 passengers in 1971.

Oldest The oldest commercial airline is Koninklijke-Luchtvaart-Maatschappij N.V. (KLM) of the Netherlands, which opened its first scheduled service (Amsterdam-London) on 17 May 1920, having been established in 1919. One of the original constituents of B.O.A.C., Aircraft Transport and Travel Ltd., was founded in 1918 and merged into Imperial Airways in 1924, and one of the holding companies of S.A.S., Det Danske Luftfartselskab, was established on 29 Oct. 1918 but operated a scheduled service only between August 1920 and 1946.

Aluminium producer The world's largest producer of aluminium is Alcan Aluminium Limited, of Montreal, Quebec, Canada. With its affiliated companies, the company had an output of 1,865,000 short tons (1,665,000 U.K.

The world's largest aluminium works at Arvida, Canada

tons) and record consolidated revenues of U $1,449,000,000 (£557 million) in 1971. The co pany's principal subsidiary, the Aluminum Compa of Canada, Ltd., owns the world's largest aluminiu smelter, at Arvida, Québec, with a capacity 458,500 short tons (409,375 U.K. tons) per annu

Art auctioneering The largest and oldest firm of art auctioneers in t world is Messrs. Sotheby and Co., of New Bo Street, London founded in 1744. The turnover 1970 was £45,211,484 including £15,981,007 tu over in their Parke-Bernet Galleries in New York Ci The highest total of any single art sale has be $5,852,250 (£2,438,437) paid at Parke-Bernet 25 Feb. 1970 for 73 impressionist and mode paintings.

Bicycle factory The 54-acre plant of Raleigh Industries Ltd. Nottingham is the largest factory in the wo producing complete bicycles. The company empl 10,000 and in 1972 has targets to make 800,0 wheeled toys and 1.7 million bicycles.

Book shop The world's largest book shop is that of W. & G. Fo Ltd., of London W.C.2. First established in 1904 i small shop in Islington, the company is now 119-125 Charing Cross Road. The area on one sit 75,825 sq. ft. The largest single display of books one room in the world is in the Norrington Room Blackwell's Bookshop, Broad Street, Oxford. T subterranean adjunct was opened on 16 June 19 and contains 160,000 volumes on 2½ miles shelving in 10,000 square feet of selling space.

BREWER
Oldest The oldest brewery in the world is the Weihenstep Brewery, Freising, near Munich, West German founded in A.D. 1040.

Largest World The largest single brewer in the world is Anheus Busch, Inc. in St. Louis, Missouri, U.S.A. In 1971 t company sold 24,308,794 U.S. barrels, equivalent 6,779 million Imperial pints, the greatest annu volume ever produced by a brewing company. T company's St. Louis plant covers 95 acres and ha capacity of 9,300,000 U.S. barrels.

Europe The largest brewery in Europe is the Guinn Brewery at St. James's Gate, Dublin, Ireland, whi extends over 58.03 acres. The business was found in 1759.

United Kingdom The largest brewing company in the United Kingdo is Bass Charrington Ltd. with 9,206 public hous 1,204 off-licences and 124 hotels. The company l net assets of £344,007,000, 58,248 employees (inc ding bar-staff) and controls 20 breweries. Their sales figure of £385,004,000 for the year ending 30 Sept. 1971 was however, surpassed by Allied Breweries Ltd. with £434 million for the same period.

Greatest exports The largest exporter of beer, ale and stout in the world is Arthur Guinness, Son & Co. Ltd., of Dublin, Ireland. Exports of Guinness from the Republic of Ireland in the 52 weeks ending 18 Dec. 1971 were 1,210,490 bulk barrels (bulk barrel = 36 Imperial gallons), which is equivalent to 1,915,501 half pint glasses per day.

ickworks The largest brickworks in the world is the London Brick Company plant at Stewartby, Bedford. The works, established in 1898, now cover 221 acres and produce 17,000,000 bricks and brick equivalent every week.

Building ntractors The largest construction company in the United Kingdom is George Wimpey & Co. Ltd. (founded 1880), of London, who undertake building, civil, mechanical, electrical and chemical engineering work. With assets of £102,000,000 and over 30,000 employees, the turnover of work was £250,000,000 in 29 countries in 1971.

Building societies The largest building society in the world is the Halifax Building Society of Halifax, Yorkshire. It was established in 1853 and has total assets exceeding £2,400,000,000. It has 4,951 employees and 225 branches and 900 agencies. The oldest building society in the world is the Chelmsford and Essex Society, established in July 1845.

Chemist hop chain The largest chain of chemist shops in the world is Boots the Chemists, which has 1,400 retail branches. The firm was founded by Jesse Boot (b. Nottingham, 1850), later the 1st Baron Trent, who died in 1931.

Chemical company The world's largest chemical company is Imperial Chemical Industries Ltd. (see Greatest Assets, U.K. company above).

Chocolate factory The world's largest chocolate factory is that built by Hershey Foods Inc. of Hershey, Pennsylvania, U.S.A., in 1905. In 1971 sales were $401,879,817 (£154,569,160) and the payroll was over 8,000 employees.

DEPARTMENT STORES

World The largest department store chain, in terms of number of stores, is J.C. Penney Company, Inc., founded in Wyoming, U.S.A., in 1902. The company operates almost 2,000 retail units in the U.S.A., Belgium and Italy, with net selling space of 45.4 million sq. ft. Its turnover was $4,812,238,548 (£1,723 million) in the year ending 29 Jan. 1972, the sixteenth consecutive year of record sales.

United Kingdom The largest department store in the United Kingdom is Harrods Ltd. of Knightsbridge, London, S.W.1 named after Henry Charles Harrod, who opened a grocery in Knightsbridge Village in 1849. It has a total selling floor space of 19 acres, employs 5,300 people and had a total of 10,920,000 transactions in 1971.

Most profitable The department store with the fastest-moving stock in the world is the Marks & Spencer premier branch, known as "Marble Arch" at 458 Oxford Street, London, W.1. The figure of £250 worth of goods per square foot of selling space per year is believed to have become an understatement when the selling area was raised to 72,000 sq. ft. in October 1970. The Company has 250 branches in the U.K. and operates on over 5 million sq. ft. of selling space.

Games ufacturer The largest company manufacturing games is Parker Bros. Inc. of Salem, Massachusetts, U.S.A. The company's top-selling line is the real estate game "Monopoly", acquired in 1935. More than

One of the nearly 2,000 department stores in J. C. Penney's world's largest chain.

65,000,000 sets were sold by January 1972. The daily print of "money" is equivalent to 215,000,000 "dollars", thus exceeding the dollar output of the U.S. Treasury. The most protracted non-stop "Monopoly" session was one of 127½ hours by 4 students of Dundee University in April 1972. At the Power House Youth Club, Birmingham in May 1972, Eric Foxall and Gary Davis played for 86 hours, John Raddon also completed the same time against a series of opponents.

Distillery The world's largest distilling company is Distillers Corporation-Seagrams Limited of Canada. Its sales in the year ending 31 July 1971 totalled U.S. $1,512,246,000, (£581 million), of which $1,219,018,000 (£468 million) were from sales by Joseph E. Seagram & Sons, Inc. in the United States. The group employs about 15,000 people, including about 8,000 in the United States.

The largest of all Scotch whisky distilleries is Carsebridge at Alloa, Clackmannanshire, Scotland, owned by Scottish Grain Distillers Limited. This distillery is capable of producing more than 12,000,000 proof gallons per annum. The largest establishment for blending and bottling Scotch whisky is owned by John Walker & Sons Limited at Kilmarnock, Ayrshire, with a potential annual output of 120,000,000 bottles. "Johnnie Walker" is the world's largest-selling brand of Scotch whisky. The largest malt Scotch whisky distillery is the Tomatin Distillery, Inverness-shire, established at 1,028 feet above sea level in 1897, with an annual capacity well in excess of 2 million proof gallons. The world's largest-selling brand of gin is Gordon's.

General merchandise The largest general merchandising firm in the world is Sears, Roebuck and Co. (founded by Richard W. Sears in Redwood North railway station, Minnesota in 1886) of Chicago, Illinois, U.S.A. The net sales were $10,006,145,548 (£3,849 million) in the year ending 31 Jan. 1972 when the corporation had 864 retail stores and 2,507 catalogue, retail and telephone sales offices and independent catalogue merchants, and total assets valued at $8,312,355,925 (£3,197 million).

Grocery stores The largest grocery chain in the world is The Great Atlantic and Pacific Tea Company, Inc., of New York City, N.Y., U.S.A. At 27 Feb. 1971 the company owned 4,427 stores, including more than 3,000 supermarkets. It operates 24 bakeries, and laundries for the uniforms of its 115,000 employees. The total sales, including subsidiary companies, for the 52 weeks ending 27 Feb. 1971 were $5,664 million (£2,360 million).

Hotelier The top revenue-earning hotel business is Holiday Inns Inc., with a 1971 revenue of $707,876,910 (£272 million), from 1,371 inns (200,464 rooms) at 31 Dec. 1971 in 21 countries. The business was founded by Charles Kemmons Wilson with his first inn in Summer Avenue, Memphis, Tennessee in 1952. Services include spiritual counselling for potential suicides.

Hilton form the largest luxury hotel group in the world. Hilton Hotels Corporation operates 39 hotels, with 30,809 rooms, in the continental U.S.A.; Hilton International Co. operates 54 hotels in 37 countries (51 cities), with 18,133 rooms. In 1971, Hilton Hotels Corporation had an operating revenue of more than $210,000,000 (£80 million) and 20,000 employees. Hilton International Co. had an operating revenue of $222,753,577 and 20,000 employees. The original corporation was founded by Conrad Nicholson Hilton (b. 25 Dec. 1887) who started in 1919 with the Mobley Hotel in Cisco, Texas. In May 1967, Hilton International Co. became a wholly-owned subsidiary of Trans World Airlines Inc.

The 12 storey Holiday Inns' hotel at Plymouth, Devon, a member of the world's top revenue-earning hotel chain

INSURANCE COMPANIES

World The company with the highest volume of insurance in force in the world is the Prudential Insurance Company of America of Prudential Plaza, Newark, New Jersey, U.S.A. The life assurance in force as at 1 Jan. 1971 was $91,119,263,748 (£35,045 million), which amount is £851 million greater than the United Kingdom's peak National Debt. The total amount of insurance issued in 1970 was $11,674,250,863 (£4,490 million).

United The largest insurance company in the United King-
Kingdom dom is the Prudential Assurance Co. Ltd. At 1 Jan. 1972 the total funds were £2,487,166,000 and the total amount assured was £10,009,737,885.

Largest The largest life assurance policy ever written was one
life policy of $10,800,000 (£4,500,000) reported on 18 March 1969 taken out by Mr Michael Davis, 34 from Hollywood, California, U.S.A., chairman of NEBA International Inc., a chain of sandwich stands. His annual premium is $92,200 (£38,000).

Marine The greatest insured value of any ship lost has been
insurance the $16.5 million (then £5.89 million) on the *Torrey Canyon* in 1967. The greatest loss withstood on the London market was $10.8 million (£4.5 million) on the *Marpessa* though the loss on the *Andrea Doria* in 1956 was £3.93 million (then $11.0 million). The cost of the repairs to the U.S.S. *Guittaro,* the nuclear submarine flooded on 15 May 1969 while fitting out at Mare Island, San Francisco, cost $25 million (£10.42 million). The Cunard liner QE2 was insured (builder's value only) on its sea trials in 1969 for £25.5 million ($61.2 million).

Highest The highest pay-out on a single life has been some $14
pay-out million (nearly £6 million) to Mrs. Linda Mullendore, wife of an Oklahoma rancher, reported on 14 Nov. 1970. Her murdered husband had paid $300,000 in premiums in 1969.

Mineral The world's largest mineral firm is Source Perrier,
water near Nîmes, France with an annual production of more than 1,400,000,000 bottles, of which more than 330,000,000 come from the single spring near Nîmes, and 500,000,000 from Contrexeville. The net profits for the year 1971 were 28,212,562.85 francs (£2,054,000). The French drink about 40 litres (70.4 pints) of mineral water per person per year.

MOTOR CAR MANUFACTURER

The largest manufacturing company in the world is General Motors Corporation of Detroit, Michigan, U.S.A. During its peak year of 1971 world wide sales totalled $28,263,918,443 (£10,870 million) inclu-

ding 7,779,225 cars and trucks. Its assets at 31 D 1971 were valued at $18,241,900,040 (£7,015 m lion). Its total 1971 payroll was $8,015,071,5 (£3,082 million) to an average of 773,352 employe The greatest total of dividends ever paid for one y was $1,509,740,939 (£629 million) by Gene Motors for 1965.

The largest manufacturer was the British Leyla Motor Corporation, with 1,070,144 vehicles pr uced. The company is the United Kingdom's larg exporter with record direct exports valued at £4 million in 1970/71. The Austin-Morris 1100/13 was the best-selling car in 1971 with U.K. sales 132,150 units representing 10.3 per cent. of market.

Largest plant The largest single automobile plant in the world is Volkswagenwerk, Wolfsburg, West Germany, w more than 60,000 employees turning out up to 5,0 cars daily. The surface area of the factory building 353½ acres and that of the whole plant 1,730 ac with 45 miles of rail sidings.

Oil Company The world's largest oil company is the Standard
Largest Company (New Jersey), with 143,000 employees a assets valued at $20,315,249,000 (£7,813 million) 1 Jan. 1972.

Oil refineries The world's largest refinery is the Pernis refinery
Largest the Netherlands, operated by the Royal Dutch/Sh Group of companies with a capacity of 25,000,0 long tons. The largest oil refinery in the Uni Kingdom is the Esso Refinery at Fawley, Hampsh Opened in 1921 and much expanded in 1951, it ha capacity of 19,000,000 tons per year. The to investment on the 1,300-acre site is more th £140,000,000.

Paper mills The world's largest paper mill is that established 1936 by the Union Camp Corporation at Savann Georgia, U.S.A., with an output of 903,124 sh tons (806,361 long tons). The largest paper mill in United Kingdom is the Bowater Paper Corporat Ltd.'s Kemsley Mill near Sittingbourne, Kent wit complex covering an area of 2,500 acres (sq. miles) and a capacity in excess of 300,000 tor year.

Pop-corn The largest pop-corn plant in the world is Cla
plant Cereal Products Ltd., (instituted 1933) of Dagenha Essex, which in 1971-72 produced an unrival 21,000,000 packets of "Butter Kist".

Public The world's largest public relations firm is Hill a
relations Knowlton, Inc. of 150 East 42nd Street, New Y City, N.Y., U.S.A. The firm employs a full-time st

of more than 325 and also maintains offices of wholly-owned subsidiary companies in Brussels, Frankfurt, Geneva, London, Paris, Milan, Rome and Tōkyō.

Publishing The publishing company generating most revenue is Time Inc. of New York City with $606.8 million (£233.3 million) in 1971 of $130 million from *Time* magazine. Britain's largest publisher is the International Publishing Corporation Ltd., (now merged with Reed Paper Group) with a turnover of £162 million in 1971.

staurateurs The largest restaurant chain in the world is that operated by F.W. Woolworth and Co. with 2,074 throughout six countries. The largest restaurateurs in the United Kingdom are Trust House-Forte who have a total staff of 50,000 and turned over £141,100,000 in 1970/71.

BANQUET
Greatest The greatest banquet ever staged was that by Presi-
World dent Loubet, President of France, in the gardens of
Outdoors the Tuileries, Paris, on 22 Sept. 1900. He invited every one of the 22,000 mayors in France and their deputies. With the Gallic *penchant* for round numbers, the event has always been referred to as "le banquet des 100,000 maires".

Indoors The largest banquet ever held has been one for 10,158 at a $15 a plate dinner in support of Mayor Richard J. Daley of Chicago at McCormick Place Convention Hall on the Lake, Chicago on 3 March 1971.

The menu for the main 5½ hour banquet at the Imperial Iranian 2500th Anniversary gathering at Persepolis in October 1971 (see Party, greatest) was probably the most expensive ever compiled. It comprised quail eggs stuffed with Iranian caviar, a mousse of crayfish tails in Nantua sauce, stuffed rack of roast lamb, with a main course of roast peacock stuffed with *foie gras,* fig rings and raspberry sweet champagne sherbet, with wines including *Château Lafite-Rothschild* 1945 @ £40 per bottle from the cellars of Maxime, Paris.

eat Britain Britain's largest banquet was one catered for by J. Lyons & Co. Ltd., at Olympia, London, on 8 Aug. 1925. A total of 8,000 guests were seated at 5 miles of tables, served by 1,360 waitresses, supported by 700 cooks and porters. The occasion was a War Memorial fund-raising effort by Freemasons. Of the 86,000 glasses and plates used, 3,500 were broken. The world's largest tea party was one for 25,000 on the Gaslight Coke Company's annual sports day at East Ham, Greater London, in 1939, with Lyons again catering.

hipbuilding In 1971 there were 24,859,701 gross tons of ships, excluding sailing ships, barges and vessels of less than 100 tons, launched throughout the world, excluding the U.S.S.R. and China (mainland). Japan launched 11,992,495 gross tons (48.2 per cent. of the world total), the greatest tonnage launched in peacetime by any single country. The United Kingdom ranked fourth, behind also Sweden and West Germany, with 1,238,692 gross tons.

The world's leading shipbuilding firm in 1971 was the Ishikawajima-Harima Co. of Japan, which launched 49 merchant ships of 2,229,128 gross tons from five shipyards.

Physically the largest shipyard in the United Kingdom is Harland and Wolff Ltd. of Queen's Island, Belfast, which covers some 250 acres.

Shipping The largest shipping owner and operator in the world
line is the Royal Dutch/Shell Group (see page 145). The Group on 31 Mar. 1972 owned and managed 189 ships of 10,215,001 deadweight tons and had on charter on the same date a total of 251 ships of 16,989,254 deadweight tons. Many of the vessels of

this combined fleet of 440 ships of 27,204,255 d.w.t. were mammoth tankers.

Shoe shop The largest shoe shop in the world is that of Lilley & Skinner, Ltd. at 356/360 Oxford Street, London, W.1. The shop has a floor area of 76,000 square feet, spread over four floors. With a total staff of more than 350 people it offers, in ten departments, a choice of 250,000 pairs of shoes. Every week, on average, over 45,000 people visit this store.

LARGEST SHOPPING CENTRE
The world's largest shopping centre is the Lakewood Shopping Center in Lakewood, California, built on a 165 acre site with parking for 12,500 cars. The total selling space is 2,191,000 sq. ft. (50.2 acres). The Center has 140 stores and services and a mall 2,640 ft. in length. The Woodfield Shopping Centre, Schaumburg, Illinois will be increased to 2,203,454 square feet by September 1973 on the current 191 acre site.

Largest store The world's largest store is R.H. Macy & Co. Inc. at Broadway and 34th Street, New York City, N.Y., U.S.A. It has a floor space of 46.2 acres, and 11,000 employees who handle 400,000 items. Macy's have an average of 150,000 customers a day who make 4,500,000 transactions a year. The sales of the company and its subsidiaries exceeded $1,000,000,000 (£385 million) in 1971/72. Mr. Rowland Hussey Macy's sales on his first day at his fancy goods store on 6th Avenue, on 27 Oct. 1858, were recorded as $11.06 (now £4.61).

Largest The largest supermarket building in the United
supermarket Kingdom is the Woolco One-Stop Shopping Centre
U.K. opened in Bournemouth, Hampshire on 29 Oct. 1968. Currently it has an area of 114,000 square feet and parking space for 1,250 cars.

Soft drinks The world's top-selling soft drink is Coca-Cola with over 110,000,000 bottles per day at the end of 1971 in more than 130 countries. Coke was invented by Dr. John S. Pemberton of Atlanta, Georgia in 1886 and The Coca-Cola company was formed in 1892. The fastest bottling line is the plant at Tama, Tōkyō, Japan, which can fill, crown and pack bottles of Coca-Cola at the rate of 90,000 per hour.

STEEL COMPANY
The world's largest steel company is the United States Steel Company, with sales of $4,963,200,000 (£1,908 million) in 1971. The company had an average of 183,940 employees, and net assets valued at $5,282,800,000 (£2,031 million) at 31 Dec. 1971. The largest producer of steel by weight is Japan's largest company Nippon Steel Corp., whose sales were £1,499 million.

United The largest single British plant is the Port Talbot
Kingdom works of the British Steel Corporation, Glamorgan-shire, which stretch over a distance of 4½ miles, with an area of 2,600 acres. The total number employed at this plant is 13,500 and its capacity is 3,000,000 tons.

Largest The largest steelworks in the world is the Bethlehem
steelworks Steel Corporation's plant at Sparrow's Point, Mary-
World land, U.S.A. with an annual ingot steel capacity of more than 9,000,000 short tons or 8,030,000 long tons.

Tobacco The world's largest tobacco company is the British-
company American Tobacco Company Ltd. (founded 1902), of London. The group's net assets were £832,800,000 at 30 Sept. 1971. The sales for 1970/1971 were £1,632,640,000. The group has more than 140 factories and 120,000 employees.

Toy The world's largest toy manufacturer is Mattel Inc. of
manufacturer Hawthorne, Los Angeles, U.S.A. founded in 1945. Its

149

sales in 1971 were $272,358,000 (£104.7 million).

Toy shop
World The world's biggest toy store is F.A.O. Schwarz, 745 Fifth Avenue at 58th Street, New York City, N.Y., U.S.A. with 50,000 sq. ft. on three floors. Schwarz have 16 branch stores with a further 150,000 sq. ft.

United Kingdom Britain's biggest toy shop is that of Hamley of Regent Street Ltd., founded in 1760 in Holborn and removed to Regent Street, London, W.1, in 1901. It has selling space of 20,000 square feet on 8 floors and up to 250 employees during the Christmas season.

Vintners The oldest champagne firm is Ruinart Père et Fils founded in 1729. The oldest cognac firm is Augier Frères & Co., established in 1643.

Fisheries The highest recorded catch of fish was 59,540,000 tons in 1967. Peru had the largest share with 9,223 million metric tons of the 1969 total of 52,986 million metric tons or 17.4%, comprising mostly anchoveta. The United Kingdom's highest figure was 1,187,000 tons in 1948. The world's largest fish-mongers are MacFisheries, a subsidiary of Unilever Ltd., with 303 retail outlets as at March 1972.

Landowners The world's largest landowner is the United States Government, with a holding of 761,301,000 acres (1,189,000 square miles), including 527,000 acres outside the U.S. The total value was $78,813,000,000 (£30,312 million). The United Kingdom's greatest ever private landowner was the 3rd Duke of Sutherland, George Granville Sutherland-Leveson-Gower, K.G. (1828-92), who owned 1,358,000 acres in 1883. Currently the largest landowner in Great Britain is the Forestry Commission (instituted 1919) with 2,900,000 acres. The longest tenure is that by St. Paul's Cathedral of land at Tillingham, Essex, given by King Ethelbert before A.D. 616. Currently the landowner with the largest acreage is the 8th Duke of Buccleuch (b. 1894) with 336,000 acres.

LAND VALUES
Highest Currently the most expensive land in the world is that in the City of London. Prime freehold attained £500 per square foot in mid-1972. The 600-foot National Westminster Bank on a 2¼-acre site off Bishopsgate will become the world's highest valued building. At rents of £10 per square foot on 500,000 net square feet and on 18 years purchase, it will, by 1972, be worth £90 million. The value of the whole site of 6½ acres will be £225,000,000. On 1 Feb. 1926 a parcel of land of 1,275 square feet was bought by the One Wall Street Realty Corporation for $1,000 (then £206) per square foot. In February 1964 a woman paid $510 (£212.50) for a triangular piece of land measuring 3 inches by 6½ inches by 5¾ inches at a tax lien auction in North Hollywood, California, U.S.A.— equivalent to $365,182,470 (£152.1 million) per acre. The real estate value per square metre of the four topmost French vineyards has not been recently estimated.

Lowest The historic example of low land values is the Alaska Purchase of 30 March 1867, when William Henry Seward (1801-72), the United States Secretary of State, agreed that the U.S. should buy the whole territory from the Russian Government of Czar Alexander II for $7,200,000 (now £3,000,000), equivalent to 1.9 cents per acre. When Willem Verhulst bought Manhattan Island, New York, *ante* June in 1626, by paying the Brooklyn Indians (Canarsees) with trinkets and cloth valued at 60 guilders (equivalent to $39 or £16.25), he was buying land now worth up to $425 (£177) per square foot for 0.2 of a cent per acre—a capital appreciation of 9,000 million-fold.

The world's largest toy shop — Schwarz of 5th Avenue, New York City

Greatest auction The greatest ever auction was that at Anchorag Alaska on 11 Sept. 1969 for 179 tracts totallin 450,858 acres of the oil-bearing North Slope, Alask An all-time record bid of $72,277,133 for a 2,56 acre lease was made by the Amerada Hess Corp ration—Getty Oil consortium. This £30,115,472 bi indicated a price of $28,233 (£11,763) per acre.

Highest rent The highest recorded rentals are about £17 per squal foot for office accommodation in the prime areas c the City of London, in mid-1972.

Companies The number of companies on the register in Gre Britain at 1 Jan. 1972 was 577,231 of which 16,68 were public and the balance private companies.

Most directorships The world record for directorships was set in Sep ember 1959 by Harry O. Jasper, a London real esta financier, with 451. If he had attended all the Annual General Meetings this would have involve him, in normal office hours, in an A.G.M. every hours 33 minutes.

STOCK EXCHANGES
The oldest Stock Exchange in the world is that Amsterdam, in the Netherlands, founded in 160 There were 126 throughout the world as of 13 Jun 1972.

Most markings The highest number of markings received in one da on the London Stock Exchange is 32,665 after th 1959 General Election on 14 Oct. 1959. The recor for a year is 4,396,175 "marks" in the year ending 3 March 1960. There were 9,356 securities (gilt-edge 1,228, company 8,128) quoted on 31 March 196 Their total nominal value was £46,528 millio (gilt-edged £25,805 million, company £20,723 mi lion) and their market value was £131,679 millio (gilt-edged £18,459 million, company £113,220 mi lion).

The greatest overall daily movement occurred o 24 Feb. 1955, when the market value of Unite Kingdom Ordinary shares fell by about £200,000,00 or 3.8 per cent.

The highest figure of *The Financial Times* Industri Ordinary share index (1 July 1935=100) was 543. on 19 May 1972. The lowest figure was 49.4 in 194 The greatest rise in a day has been 20.5 points t 352.2 on Budget Day on 30 March 1971.

Highest and lowest par values The highest denomination of any share quoted in th world is a single share in F. Hoffmann—La Roche Basel is worth £17,250. The record for the Lond

Stock Exchange is £100 for preference shares in Baring Brothers & Co. Ltd., the bankers. The lowest unit of quotation is one penny, in the case of the stock of City of San Paulo Improvements and Freehold Land Co. Ltd. and the capital shares in the Acorn Securities Co., Ltd.

U.S.records The highest index figure on the Dow Jones average (instituted 8 Oct. 1896) of selected industrial stocks at the close of a day's trading was 995.15 on 9 Feb. 1966, when the average of the daily "highs" of the 30 component stocks was 1,001.11. The old record trading volume in a day on the New York Stock Exchange of 16,410,030 shares on 29 Oct. 1929, the "Black Tuesday" of the famous "crash" was unsurpassed until April 1968. The Dow Jones industrial average, which had reached 381.17 on 3 Sept. 1929, plunged 48.31 points in the day, on its way to the Depression's lowest point of 41.22 on 8 July 1932. The total lost in security values was $125,000 million (now £48,076 million). World trade slumped 57 per cent. from 1929 to 1936. The greatest paper loss in a year was $62,884 million (£24,186 million) in 1969. The record daily increase of 28.40 on 30 Oct. 1929 was beaten on 16 Aug. 1971, when the index increased 32.93 points to 888.95. That day's trading was also a record 31,730,960 shares. The largest transaction on record "share-wise" was on 14 Mar. 1972 for 5,245,000 shares of American Motors at $7.25 each. The dollar value for one block was $76,135,026 for 730,312 shares of American Standard Class A Preferred shares at $104.25 a share. The largest deal "value-wise" was for two 2,000,000 blocks of Greyhound shares at $20 each sold to Goldman Sachs and Saloman Brothers.

Largest issue The American Telegraph & Telphone Co. offered $1,375 million's worth of shares in a rights offer on 27,500,000 shares of convertible preferred stock on the New York market on 2 June 1971. The largest offering on the London Stock Exchange by a United Kingdom company was the £40 million of loan stock by I.C.I. in December 1970.

Greatest appreciation It is not possible to state categorically which shares have enjoyed the greatest appreciation in value. Spectacular "growth stocks" include the International Business Machines Corporation (IBM), in which 100 shares, costing $5,250 (now £2,019) in July 1932, grew to 13,472 shares with a market value of $4,230,000 (then £1,762,500) on 28 March 1969. In addition $233,100 were paid in dividends. The greatest aggregate market value of any corporation is $35.5 billion, assuming a closing price of $314 multiplied by the 113,116,613 shares extant on 28 March 1969. In the United Kingdom an investment of £100 in Drage's Ltd. in 1951 would have been realizable at £108,000 in 1962. The same amount invested in 1947 in the late Mr. Jack Cotton's Mansion House Chambers Co. would have been worth £200,000 in City Centre Properties stock by 1964.

Largest investment house The largest investment company in the world, and also once the world's largest partnership (124 partners, 61,200 stockholders at 31 Dec. 1971) is Merrill, Lynch, Pierce, Fenner & Smith Inc. (founded 6 Jan. 1914, went public in 1971) of New York City, U.S.A. It has 21,177 employees, 273 offices and 1,800,000 separate accounts. The firm is referred to in the United States stock exchange circles as "We" or "We, the people" or "The Thundering Herd". The company's assets totalled $2,867,558,000 at 31 Dec. 1971.

Largest bank The International Bank for Reconstruction and Development (founded 27 Dec. 1945), the United Nations "World Bank" at 1818 H Street N.W., Washington, D.C., U.S.A., has an authorized share capital of $27,000 million (£10,384 million). There were 117 members with a subscribed capital of

The head-quarters of the world's largest private bank—the Bank of America in San Francisco

$24,046,300,000 (£9,248 million) at 1 Jan. 1972. The International Monetary Fund in Washington, D.C., U.S.A. has 120 members with total quotas of $28,807,800,000 (£11,079 million) at 29 Feb. 1972. The private bank with the greatest deposits is the Bank of America National Trust and Savings Association, of San Francisco, California, U.S.A., with $29,073,301,000 at 31 Dec 1971. Its total resources as at 31 Dec. 1971 were $33,985,906,000. Barclays Bank (with Barclays Bank International and other subsidiary companies) had nearly 5,000 branches in 40 countries (over 3,150 in the United Kingdom) in December 1971. Deposits totalled £6,683,392,000 and assets £7,884,828,000 as at 31 Dec. 1971. The largest bank in the United KIngdom is the National Westminster with total assets of £6,648,489,000 and 3,500 branches as at 1 Jan. 1972.

Largest bank building The largest bank building in the world is the 813-foot-tall Chase Manhattan Building, completed in May 1961 in New York City, N.Y., U.S.A. It has 64 storeys and contains the largest bank vault in the world, measuring 350 feet × 100 feet × 8 feet and weighing 879 tons. Its six doors weigh up to 40 tons apiece but each can be closed by the pressure of a forefinger. The 60-storey First National Bank of Chicago, completed in 1969, is 850 feet tall.

2.MANUFACTURED ARTICLES

Guinness Superlatives Ltd. publishes fine art books in colour on English and Irish Glass; Pottery and Porcelain; English Furniture (2 Volumes); Antique Firearms; Edged Weapons, Militaria and British Gallantry Decorations, obtainable on order from the publishers or from any good book shop.

Antique Largest The largest antique ever sold has been London Bridge in March 1968. The sale was made by Mr. Ivan F. Luckin of the Court of Common Council of the Corporation of London to the McCulloch Corporation of Los Angeles, California, U.S.A. for $2,460,000 (then £1,029,000). The 10,000 tons of elevational stonework were re-assembled at Lake Havasu City, Arizona and "re-dedicated" on 10 Oct. 1971.

Armour The highest price paid for a suit of armour is £25,000, paid in 1924 for the Pembroke suit of armour, made at Greenwich in the 16th century, for the Earl of Pembroke.

Largest beds In Bruges, Belgium, Philip, Duke of Burgundy had a bed 12½ feet wide and 19 feet long erected for the perfunctory *coucher officiel* ceremony with Princess Isabella of Portugal in 1430. The largest bed in Great Britain is the Great Bed of Ware, dating from *c.* 1580, from the Crown Inn, Ware, Hertfordshire, now preserved in the Victoria and Albert Museum, London. It is 10 feet 8½ inches wide, 11 feet 1 inch long and 8 feet 9 inches tall. The largest standard bed currently marketed in the United Kingdom is the London Bedding Centre's "King Size" bed, 7 feet wide by 7 feet long, with 1,600 springs, sold for £170.

Heaviest beds The world's most massive beds are waterbeds which first became a vogue in California, U.S.A. in 1970 when merchandised by Michael V. Zamoro, 53. When filled, king-sized versions measuring 8 feet square will weigh more than 14 cwt. (1,568 lb.) and are more advisably used on the ground floor.

Beer Mats The world's largest collection of beer mats is owned by Leo Pisker of Vienna, who has more than 40,000 different mats. The largest collection of purely British mats is 5,300 by Colin White of Godalming, Surrey.

Largest candle The world's biggest candle is Western Candle Ltd.'s 50 foot high, 18 foot diameter by U.S. Highway 30, near Scappose, Oregon, completed on 9 May 1971.

CARPETS AND RUGS

Earliest The earliest carpet known is a white bordered black hair pelt from Pazyryk, U.S.S.R. dated to the 5th century B.C. now preserved in Leningrad. The earliest known in Britain were some depicted at the court of Edward IV *c.* 1480.

Largest Of ancient carpets the largest on record was the gold-enriched silk carpet of Hashim (dated A.D. 743) of the Abbasid caliphate in Baghdad, Iraq. It is reputed to have measured 180 feet by 300 feet.

The world's largest carpet now consists of 88,000 square feet (over two acres) of maroon carpeting in the Coliseum exhibition hall, Columbus Circle, New York City, N.Y., U.S.A. This was first used for the International Automobile Show on 28 April 1956.

Most expensive The most magnificent carpet ever made was the Spring carpet of Khusraw made for the audience hall of the Sassanian palace at Ctesiphon, Iraq. It was about 7,000 square feet of silk, gold thread and encrusted with emeralds. It was cut up as booty by a Persian army in A.D. 635 and from the known realization value of the pieces must have had an original value of some £80,000,000.

It was reported in March 1968 that a 16th century Persian silk hunting carpet was sold "recently" to an undisclosed U.S. museum by a member of the Rothschild family for "about $600,000" (£205,000).

Most finely woven The most finely woven carpet known is one with more than 2,490 knots per square inch from a fragment of an Imperial Mughal prayer carpet of the 17th century now in the Altman collections in the Metropolitan Museum of Art, New York City.

Chair *Largest* The world's largest chair is claimed to be an American ladderback outside Hayes and Kane furniture store, Bennington, Vermont, U.S.A. 19 feet 1 inch tall and weighing 2,200 lb.

Christmas present *Most expensive* The most expensive Christmas present listed in any store's catalogue has been in the 1971 Neiman-Marcus, Dallas, Texas, offering of a "Fortress of the Freeway" for $845,300 (£325,115). This Total Transportational Security Environment features anti-theft device hood ornament, closed-circuit dual-lens infra-red scanning camera, infra-red periscope, 360° vision indestructable cockpit bubble, telephoto peri-

scope, radar, dual-exhaust anti-pollution device, hig way signal markers, signals "Stop"—"Too Close marine prop, retractable tyres, tank-tracks, lou speakers to warn off passing motorists, multi-le terrain stabilizer, safety air bumpers and padd safety bumpers—absolutely one of a kind.

CIGARS

Largest The largest cigar in existence is one 5 feet 4½ inch long and 10½ inches in diameter made by Abrahan Gluckstein, London and now housed at the Northu brian University Air Squadron. The largest standa cigar in the world is the 9¾-inch-long "Partag Visible Immensas". The Partagas factory in Havan Cuba, manufactures special gift cigars 50 centimet (19.7 inches) long, which retail in Europe for mc than £5 each.

Most expensive The world's most expensive regular cigar has been t "Partagas Visible Immensas". This used to be retail in the United States for $7.50 (£3.12½). The mc expensive cigars imported into Britain, where t duty is £5.48½ per lb., are the Montecristo 'A', whi normally retail for £1.36½ each.

Most voracious cigar smoker The only man to master the esoteric art of smoking full-sized cigars simultaneously whilst whistli talking or giving bird imitations is Mr. Simon Ar vitch of Oakland, California, U.S.A.

CIGARETTES

Consumption The heaviest smokers in the world are the people the United States, where about 533,000 milli cigarettes (an average of nearly 4,000 per adult) we consumed at a cost of more than $10,000 milli (£3,846 million) in 1971. The peak consumption the United Kingdom was 3,020 cigarettes per adult 1970. The peak volume was 243,100,000 lb. in 196 compared with 204,000,000 lb. in 1971, wh 122,400 million cigarettes were sold.

In the United Kingdom 68 per cent. of adult men a 44 per cent. of adult women smoke. Nicotine relea acetylcholine in the brain, so reducing tension a increasing resolve. It has thus been described as anodyne to civilization.

Most expensive The most expensive cigarettes in the world are t gold-tipped "Royal Dragoons", made by Simon A of Cairo, in the United Arab Republic (forme Egypt). They have been retailed in the Unit Kingdom for more than 5p each.

Most popular The world's most popular cigarette has been t "Winston", a filter cigarette made by the R Reynolds Tobacco Co., which sold 82,000 million them in 1969. The largest selling British cigarette 1971 was W.D. & H.O. Wills' "Players No. 6."

Longest and shortest The longest cigarettes ever marketed were "He Plays", each 11 inches long and sold in packets of f in the United States in about 1930, to save tax. T shortest were "Lilliput" cigarettes, each 1¼ incl long, made in Great Britain in 1956.

Earliest absention The earliest recorded case of a man giving up smoki was on 5 April 1679 when Johan Kastu, Sheriff Turku, Finland wrote in his diary "I quit smoki tobacco". He died one month later.

Cigarette lighter *Most Expensive* The most expensive cigarette lighter in the worlc made by Alfred Dunhill Ltd. of St. James's, Lond S.W.1. and costing £2,750. It is made of two-to bark textured 18 ct. gold, scattered with a fringe 200 brilliant-cut diamonds.

Largest collection The world's largest collection of cigarettes is that Robert E. Kaufman, M.D., of 950 Park Avenue, N York City 28, N.Y., U.S.A. In March 1972 he h 6,404 different kinds of cigarettes from 159 co

tries. The oldest brand represented is "Lone Jack", made in the U.S.A. in *c.* 1885. Both the longest and shortest (see above) are represented.

Cigarette packets The world's largest collection of cigarette packets is that of Niels Ventegodt of Frederiksberg Allé 13A, Copenhagen, Denmark. He had 46,188 different packets from 202 countries by March 1972. The countries supplying the largest numbers were the United Kingdom (6,258) and the United States (3,734). The earliest is the Finnish "Petit Canon" packet for 25, made by Tollander & Klärich in 1860. The rarest is the Latvian 700-year-anniversary (1201-1901) Riga packet, believed to be unique.

Cigarette cards The earliest known and most valuable cigarette card is that bearing the portrait of the Marquess of Lorne published in the United States *c.* 1879. The only known specimen is in the Metropolitan Museum of Art, New York City. The earliest British example appeared in 1883 in the form of a calendar issued by Allen & Ginter, of Richmond, Virginia, trading from Holborn Viaduct, London. The largest known collection is that of Mr. Edward Wharton-Tigar (b. 1913) of London with a collection of more than 500,000 cigarette and trade cards in about 25,000 sets.

Clock Most expensive The highest price ever paid for a longcase or "Grandfather" clock is £16,800 at the London salerooms of Messrs. Christie, Manson & Woods on 16 March 1972, for an English example with a walnut case and a movement made by Joseph Knibb, *c.* 1675. It stands 6 feet 5 inches high, and was purchased by Mr. Ronald A. Lee, a London dealer specialising in horological works of art.

Largest curtain The largest curtain ever built has been the bright orange 4-ton 250,000-sq.-ft. curtain suspended across the Rifle Gap, Grand Hogback, Colorado, U.S.A. by the Bulgarian-born sculptor Christo, 36 (*né* Javacheff) in the summer of 1971.

Dinner service The highest price ever paid for a silver dinner service is £207,000 for the Berkeley Louis XV Service of 168 pieces, made by Jacques Roettiers between 1736 and 1738, sold at the salerooms of Sotheby & Co., London, in June 1960.

FABRICS
Most expensive The most expensive fabric obtainable is an evening-wear fabric 40 inches wide, hand embroidered and sequinned on a pure silk ground in a classical flower pattern. It has 194,400 tiny sequins per yard, and is designed by Alan Hershman of London; it costs £105 per yard.

Finest cloth The finest of all cloths is Shahtoosh (or Shatusa), a brown-grey wool from the throats of Indian goats. It is sold by Nieman-Marcus of Dallas, Texas, U.S.A., at $18.50 (£7.71p) per square foot and is both more expensive and finer than Vicuña. A simple hostess gown in Shahtoosh costs up to $5,000 (£1,923).

LARGEST FIREWORK
The most powerful firework obtainable is the Bouquet of Chrysanthemums *hanabi*, marketed by the Marutamaya Ogatsu Fireworks Co. Ltd., of Tōkyō, Japan. It is fired to a height of over 3,000 feet from a 36-inch calibre mortar. Their chrysanthemum and peony flower shells produce a spherical flower with "twice-thrice changing colours", 2,000 feet in diameter. The largest firework produced in Britain is one fired from Brock's 25-inch, 22 cwt. mortar. The shell weighs 200 lb. and is 6½ feet in circumference and was first used in Lisbon in 1886. The last firing was in London on 8 June 1946 for the World War II Victory Celebration which was the most elaborate show of aerial pyrotechny ever fired. Brock's Fireworks Ltd. of Hemel Hempstead, Hertfordshire was established before 1720.

FLAGS
Oldest The oldest national flag in the world is that of Denmark (a large white cross on a red field), known as the Dannebrog ("Danish Cloth"), dating from 1219, adopted after the Battle of Lindanissa in Estonia, now part of the U.S.S.R. The crest in the centre of the Austrian flag has its origins in the 11th century. The origins of the Iranian flag, with its sword-carrying lion and sun, are obscure but "go beyond the 12th century".

Largest The largest flag in the world is the "Stars and Stripes" displayed annually on the Woodward Avenue side of J.L. Hudson Company store in Detroit, Michigan, U.S.A. The flag, 104 feet by 235 feet and weighing 1,500 lb., was unfurled on 14 June 1949. The 50 stars are each 5½ feet high and each stripe is 8 feet deep. The largest Union Flag (or Union Jack) was one of 11,720 square feet (144 by 80 feet) used at a military tattoo in the Olympic Stadium, West Berlin in September 1967. The largest flag *flown* from a public building in Britain is a Union Flag measuring 36 feet

153

by 18 feet, flown on occasions from the Victoria Tower of the Palace of Westminster, London.

Largest float The largest float used in any street carnival is the 200-foot-long dragon *Sun Loon* used in Bendigo, Victoria, Australia. It has 65,000 mirror scales. Six men are needed to carry its head alone.

FURNITURE

Most expensive The highest price ever paid for a single piece of furniture is 165,000 guineas (£173,250) at auction at Christies, London on 24 June 1971, for a Louis XVI *bureau plat* by Martin Carlin in 1778 and once belonging to the Empress Marie-Freodorovna in 1784, sold by the estate of Mrs. Anna Thompson Dodge and bought by Mr. Henri Sabet of Teheran, Iran. It is 51½ inches wide, 30 inches deep and 30 inches high in veneered pale tulipwood with a tooled and guilded black leather top and 14 Sèvres porcelain plaques in ormolu frames.

Oldest British The oldest surviving piece of British furniture is a three-footed tub with metal bands found at Glastonbury, Somerset, and dating from between 300 and 150 B.C.

Gold plate The world's highest auction price for a single piece of gold plate is £40,000 for a 20 oz. 4 dwt. George II teapot made by James Ker for the King's Plate horse race for 100 guineas at Leith, Scotland in 1736. The sale was by Christie's of London on 13 Dec. 1967 to a dealer from Boston, Massachusetts, U.S.A.

Hat Most expensive The highest price ever paid for a hat is 165,570 francs (inc. tax) (£14,032) by Moët et Chandon at an auction by Maîtres Liery, Rheims et Laurin on 23 April 1970 for one last worn by Emperor Napoleon I (1769-1821) on 1 Jan. 1815.

Jade The highest price paid for jade has been £42,000 for a Chinese spinach green screen emblematic of the Four Seasons sold by auction at Christie's, London on 16 July 1963.

Largest jig-saw The largest jig-saw ever made is believed to be one of 10,400 pieces, measuring 15 feet by 10 feet, made in 1954, at the special request of a man from Texas, U.S.A., by Ponda Puzzle Products, Limited, of St. Leonard's-on-Sea, Sussex.

Matchbox labels The oldest match label is that of John Walker, Stockton-on-Tees, County Durham, England in 1827. Collectors of labels are phillumenists, of bookmatch covers philliberumenists and of matchboxes cumyxaphists. The world's longest and perhaps dullest set is one in the U.S.S.R. comprising 600 variations on interior views of the Moscow Metro.

Sheerest nylon The lowest denier nylon yarn ever produced is the 6-denier used for stockings exhibited at the Nylon Fair in London in February 1956. The sheerest stockings normally available are 9-denier. An indication of the thinness is that a hair from the average human head is about 50 denier.

Paperweight The highest price ever paid for a paperweight is £8,500 at Sotheby & Co., London on 16 March 1970 for a Clichy lily-of-the-valley weight.

Penknife Most blades The penknife with the greatest number of blades is the Year Knife made by the world's oldest firm of cutlers, Joseph Rodgers & Sons Ltd., of Sheffield, England, whose trade mark was granted in 1682. The knife was built in 1822 with 1,822 blades but now has 1,972 to match the year of the Christian era until A.D. 2000, beyond which there will be no further space. It was acquired by Britain's largest hand tool manufacturers, Stanley Works (Great Britain) Ltd. of Sheffield, in 1970.

A replica of the priceless 2,000 year old Portland vase

Pipe Most expensive The most expensive smoker's pipe is the Charata *Summa cum Laude* straight-grain briar root pip available in limited numbers in New York City ᵢ $2,500 (£970).

Longest In the Braunschweig Museum, Germany, there exhibited an outsize late 19th century pipe, 15 feet ᵢ length, the bowl of which can accommodate 3 lb. ᵢ tobacco.

Porcelain and pottery The highest price ever paid for a single piece ᵢ porcelain is £220,500 at auction at the salerooms ᵢ Christie's, London, on 5 June 1972, for a 14 century Chinese porcelain wine jar in blue and whi with a red underglaze decoration, 13½ inches hig previously used as an umbrella stand. The mo priceless example of the occidental ceramic art usually regarded as the Portland Vase which dat from late in the first century B.C. or 1st century A.ᵢ It was made in Italy and was in the possession of tl Barberini family in Rome from at least 1642. It w. eventually bought by the Duchess of Portland in 179 but smashed while in the British Museum in 1847.

Pistols Most expensive The highest price ever paid for antique firearms £43,050 by Frank Partridge & Sons, Bond Stree London for a garniture of a flintlock rifle and a pair ᵢ pistols, inlaid with gold and silver, and accessorie made between 1798 and 1809 by Nicolas Boutet ᵢ Versailles, gunsmith to Emperor Napoleon I. The sa was at Christie, Manson and Woods Ltd. of Londc on 8 July 1970.

Largest rope The largest rope ever made was a coir fibre launchir rope with a circumference of 47 inches, made in 185 for the British liner *Great Eastern* by John and Edwi Wright of Birmingham. It consisted of four strand each of 3,780 yarns.

SHOES

Most expensive The most expensive standard shoes obtainable are tl alligator shawl-tongued custom golf shoe, Style 559 made by Brocton Footwear Inc. of Massachusett U.S.A., which retail for $200 (£76.92) per pair.

Largest Excluding cases of elephantiasis, the largest shoes ev sold are a pair size 42 built for the giant Harle Davidson of Avon Park, Florida, U.S.A.

Silver The highest price ever paid for a single piece of silver is £78,000 at Christie's of London on 1 July 1970 for a unique Charles I silver inkstand, hallmarked for 1639, weighing 172 oz. It had been sold also at Christie's on 5 June 1893 for £446.

The highest price for English Silver is £56,000 paid by the London dealer Wartski for the Brownlow James II Tankards at Christie's, London, on 20 Nov. 1968. This pair made in 1686 was in mint condition and weighed nearly 7½ lb. It has been calculated that they appreciated at the rate of 75p per hour since they were sold by Lord Astor for £17,000 in 1963.

Apostle spoons The highest price ever paid for a set of 13 apostle spoons is $30,000 (£10,700), paid by the Clark Institute of Williamstown, Massachusetts, U.S.A. There are only six other complete sets known.

Stuffed bird The highest price ever paid for a stuffed bird is £9,000. This was given in the salerooms of Messrs. Sotheby & Co., London by the Iceland Natural History Museum for a specimen of the Great Auk (*Alca impennis*) in summer plumage, which was taken in Iceland *c.* 1821; this particular specimen stood 22½ inches high. The Great Auk was a flightless North Atlantic seabird, which was finally exterminated on Eldey, Iceland in 1844, becoming extinct through hunting. The last British sightings were at Co. Waterford in 1834 and St. Kilda *c.* 1840.

Sword The highest price recorded for a European sword is £21,000 paid at Sotheby's on 23 March 1970 for a swept hilt rapier 48½ inches long made by Israel Schuech in 1606 probably for Elector Christian II or Duke Johann Georg of Saxony. The hilt is inset with pearls and semi-precious stones. It should be noted that prices as high as £60,000 have been reported in Japan for important swords by master Japanese swordsmiths such as the incomparable 13th century master Masamune.

Most expensive snuff The most expensive snuff obtainable in Britain is "Café Royale" sold by G. Smith and Sons (inst. 1869) of 74, Charing Cross Road, London. It sells at 86p per oz.

The world's largest teapot — sufficient for a tea party of 290.

Snuff box The highest price ever paid for a snuff box is the 825,570 frans inc. tax (£61,609) given in a sale held by Maîtres Ader and Picard at the Palais Galliera in Paris for a gold and lapis lazuli example by J. A. Meissonnier (d. 1750), dated Paris 1728. This is the only signed example of a snuff box by Meissonnier to have survived although he is known to have been one of the most patronised of French 18th-century goldsmiths. It was made for Marie-Anne de Vaviere-Neubourg, wife of Charles II of Spain. It measures 84 x 29 millimetres. It was sent for sale by the executors of the estate of the late D. David Weill, and was purchased by Messrs. Wartski of Regent Street, London.

TAPESTRY

Earliest The earliest known examples of tapestry weaved linen are three pieces from the tomb of Thutmose IV, the Egyptian Pharaoh and dated to 1483-1411 B.C.

Largest The largest single piece of tapestry ever woven is "Christ in Glory", measuring 74 feet 8 inches by 38 feet, designed by Graham Vivian Sutherland, O.M. (b. 24 Aug. 1903) for an altar hanging in Coventry Cathedral, Warwickshire. It cost £10,500 and was delivered from Pinton Frères of Felletin, France, on 1 March 1962.

Longest Embroidery The longest of all embroideries is the famous Bayeux *Telle du Conquest, dite tapisserie de la reine Mathilde*, a hanging 19½ inches wide by 231 feet in length. It depicts events of the period 1064-66 in 72 scenes and was probably worked in Canterbury, Kent, in *c.* 1086. It was "lost" from 1476 until 1724.

Most expensive The highest price paid for a set of tapestries is £200,000 for four Louis XV pieces at Sotheby & Co., London on 8 Dec. 1967.

Table cloth The world's largest table cloth is one 60 yards long by 2½ yards wide woven in linen in Belfast in January 1972 for King Bhumibol of Thailand whose titles include Brother of the Moon and Half-Brother of the Sun.

Earliest tartan The earliest evidence of tartan is the so-called Falkirk tartan, found stuffed in a jar of coins in Bells Meadow, north of Callendar Park, Scotland. It is of a dark and light brown pattern and dates from *c.* A.D. 245. The earliest reference to a specific named tartan has been to a Murray tartan in 1618.

Largest teapot The largest recorded teapot is one of 9 gallons capacity (290 cups) with a girth of 4 feet 9½ inches, weighing 47 lb. made at Corsham, Wiltshire, in July 1971.

Largest wig The largest wig yet made is that by Jean Leonard, owner of a salon in Copenhagen, Denmark. It is intended for bridal occasions, made from 24 tresses, measures nearly 8 feet in length and costs £416.

Most expensive wreath The most expensive wreath on record was that sent to the funeral of President Kennedy in Washington, D.C. on 25 Nov. 1963 by the civic authority of Paris. It was handled by Interflora Inc. and cost $1,200 (now £460). The only rival was a floral tribute sent to the Mayor of Moscow in 1970 by Umberto Farmichello, general manager of Interflora which is never slow to scent an opportunity. The largest wreath on record is a Christmas wreath 61 ft. 4 in. in diameter weighing 750 lb. built for the Park Plaza, Oshkosh, Wisconsin, U.S.A. in November 1971.

Writing paper The most expensive writing paper in the world is that sold by Cartier Inc. on Fifth Avenue, New York City at $1,904 (£793) per 100 sheets with envelopes. It is of hand made paper from Finland with deckle edges and a "personalized" portrait watermark. Second thoughts and mis-spellings are costly.

3. AGRICULTURE

ORIGINS

It has been estimated that only 21 per cent. of the world's land surface is cultivable and that of this only two-fifths is cultivated. The earliest attested evidence of cultivated grain is that from Jarmo, Iraq, dated *c.* 6750 B.C. The earliest evidence of animal husbandry comes from sheep at Zawi Chemi Shanidar, Iraq, dating from *c.* 8800 B.C. The order in which animals have been domesticated appears to be: Sheep (*c.* 8800 B.C.); dog (*c.* 7700 B.C. *e.g.* at Star Carr, Yorkshire); goat (at Jarmo and Jericho, *c.* 6500 B.C.); pig (at Jarmo, *c.* 6500 B.C.) and cattle (at Banahilk, northen Iraq, before 5000 B.C.). Reindeer may have been domesticated as early as *c.* 18000 B.C. but definite evidence is still lacking.

FARMS

Earliest The earliest dated British farming site is a neolithic one, enclosed within the Iron Age hill-fort at Hembury, Devon, excavated during 1934-5 and now dated to *c.* 3140 B.C.

Largest The largest farms in the world are collective farms in
World the U.S.S.R. These have been reduced in number from 235,500 in 1940 to only 36,000 in 1969 and have been increased in size so that units of over 60,000 acres are not uncommon.

Britain The largest farms in the British Isles are Scottish hill farms in the Grampians. The largest arable farm is that of Elveden, Suffolk, farmed by the Earl of Iveagh. Here 11,356 acres are farmed on an estate of 23,000 acres, the greater part of which was formerly derelict land. The 1970 production included 833,602 gallons of milk, 2,190 tons of grain and 7,790 tons of sugar beet. The livestock includes 3,344 cattle, 948 ewes and 3,537 pigs.

Largest The world's largest single wheat field was probably
wheat field one of more than 35,000 acres, sown in 1951 near Lethbridge, Alberta, Canada.

Largest The largest hop field in the world is one of 710 acres
hop field at Toppenish, Washington State, U.S.A. It is owned by John I. Haas, Inc., the world's largest hop growers, with hop farms in British Columbia (Canada), California, Idaho, Oregon and Washington, with a total net area of 3,065 acres.

Cattle The world's largest cattle station was Alexandria
station Station, Northern Territory, Australia, selected in 1873 by Robert Collins, who rode 1,600 miles to reach it. It has 66 wells, a staff of 90 and originally extended over 7,207,608 acres—more than the area of the English counties of Yorkshire, Devon, Norfolk and Cambridgeshire put together. The present area is 6,500 square miles which is stocked with 58,000 shorthorn cattle. Until 1915 the Victoria River Downs Station, Northern Territory, was over three times larger, with an area of 22,400,000 acres (35,000 square miles).

Sheep The largest sheep station in the world is Common-
station wealth Hill, in the north-west of South Australia. It grazes between 70,000 and 90,000 sheep in an area of 3,640 square miles (2,329,006 acres) *i.e.* larger than the combined area of Norfolk and Suffolk.

The largest sheep move on record occurred when 27 horsemen moved a mob of 43,000 sheep 40 miles from Barealdine to Beaconsfield Station, Queensland, Australia, in 1886.

Mushroom The largest mushroom farm in the world is the Butler
farm County Mushroom Farm, Inc., founded in 1937 in a disused limestone mine near West Winfield, Pennsylvania, U.S.A. It now has 900 employees working underground, in a maze of galleries 110 miles long,

Members of a 32 strong litter of pigs on the starboard side

producing about 32,000,000 lb. (14,285 tons) mushrooms per year.

Turkey farm Europe's largest turkey farm is that of Berna Matthews, Ltd., at Weston Longville, Norfolk, wi up to 300 workers tending 160,000 turkeys.

CROP YIELDS

Wheat Crop yields for highly tended small areas are of litt significance. The greatest recorded wheat yield 169.9 bushels (91 cwt.) per acre from 27.7 acres 1964 by Yoshino Brothers Farms at Quincy, Was ington State, U.S.A. The British record is 71.4 cw per acre (variety Viking) on a field of 9.453 acres by F. Oliver, near Doncaster, Yorkshire in 1962.

Barley A yield of 64¾ cwt. per acre of variety Pallas w reported in 1962 from a field of 20 acres by Colon K. C. Lee of Blaco Hill Farm, Mattersey, ne Doncaster, Yorkshire.

DIMENSIONS AND PROLIFICACY

Cattle Of heavyweight cattle the heaviest on record was Hereford-Shorthorn named "Old Ben", owned b Mike and John Murphy of Miami, Indiana, U.S.A When he died at the age of 8, in February 1910, l had attained a length of 16 feet 2 inches from nose tail, a girth of 13 feet 8 inches, a height of 6 feet inches at the forequarters and a weight of 4,720 l (42.1 cwt.). The stuffed and mounted steer is di played in Highland Park, Kokomo, Indiana, as prod to all who would otherwise have said "there ain't n such animal". The British record is the 4,480 lb. (4 cwt.) of "The Bradwell Ox" owned by Willia Spurgin of Bradwell, Essex. He was 15 feet from no to tail and had a girth of 11 feet.

The highest recorded birthweight for a calf is 225 l (16 stone 1 lb.) from a British Friesian cow Rockhouse Farm, Bishopston, Swansea, Glamorga shire, in 1961.

On 25 April 1964 it was reported that a cow name "Lyubik" had given birth to seven calves at Mogile U.S.S.R. A case of five live calves at one birth w reported in 1928 by T. G. Yarwood of Mancheste Lancashire. The life-time proificacy record is 30 the case of a cross-bred cow owned by G. Page Warren Farm, Wilmington, Sussex, which died November 1957, aged 32. A cross-Hereford calved 1916 and owned by A. J. Thomas of West Hoc Farm, Marloes, Pembrokeshire, Wales, produced h 30th calf in May 1955 and died in May 1956, aged 4

Pigs The heaviest pig ever recorded in Britain was one of 12 cwt. 66 lb. (1,410 lb.)., bred by Joseph Lawton of Astbury, Cheshire. In 1774 it stood 4 feet 8½ inches in height and was 9 feet 8 inches long. The highest recorded weight for a piglet at weaning (8 weeks) is 81 lb. for a boar, one of nine piglets farrowed on 6 July 1962 by the Landrace gilt "Manorport Ballerina 53rd", *alias* "Mary", and sired by a Large White named "Johnny" at Kettle Lane Farm, West Ashton, Trowbridge, Wiltshire.

The highest recorded number of piglets in one litter is 34, thrown on 25-26 June 1961 by a sow owned by Aksel Egedee of Denmark. In February 1955 a Wessex sow owned by Mrs. E. C. Goodwin of Paul's Farm, Leigh, near Tonbridge, Kent, had a litter of 34, of which 30 were born dead. A litter of 32 piglets (26 live born) was thrown in February 1971 by a British saddleback owned by Mr. R. Spencer of Toddington, Gloucestershire. In September 1934 a Large White sow, owned by Mr. H. S. Pedlingham, died after having farrowed 385 piglets in 22 litters in 10 years 10 months.

Sheep The highest recorded birthweight for a lamb in Britain is 26 lb., in the case of a lamb delivered on 9 Feb. 1967 by Alan F. Baldry from a ewe belonging to J. L. H. Arkwright of Winkleigh, Devonshire. A case of eight lambs at a birth was reported by D. T. Jones of Priory Farm, Monmouthshire, in June 1956, but none lived.

Egg-laying The highest authenticated rate of egg-laying by a hen is 361 eggs in 364 days by a Black Orpington in an official test at Taranki, New Zealand, in 1930. The U.K. record is 353 eggs in 365 days in a National Laying Test at Milford, Surrey in 1957 by a Rhode Island Red owned by W. Lawson of Welham Grange, Retford, Nottinghamshire. In January 1957 a battery pullet owned by Mr. Thomas Whitwell of Goodies Farm, Firbank, Westmorland, laid 16 eggs in six days.

The largest egg reported is one of 16 ounces, with double yolk and double shell, laid by a white Leghorn at Vineland, New Jersey, U.S.A., on 25 Feb. 1956. The largest in the United Kingdom was one of 8¼ ounces, laid by "Daisy", owned by Peter Quarton, aged 8, at Lodge Farm, Kexby Bridge, near York, in March 1964.

MILK YIELDS
Cows The world lifetime record yield of milk is 334,292 lb. (149.2 tons) at 3.4 per cent. butter fat by the U.S. Holstein cow "College Ormsby Burke" which died at Fort Collins, Colorado in August 1966. The greatest yield of any British cow was that given by the British Friesian "Manningford Faith Jan Graceful", owned by R. and H. Jenkinson of Oxfordshire. This cow yielded 326,451 lb. (145.7 tons) before she died in November 1955, aged 17½ years. The greatest recorded yield for one lactation (365 days) is 45,081 lb. (20.13 tons) by R.A. Pierson's British Friesian "Bridge Birch" in England in 1947-48. The British record for milk yield in a day is 198¼ lb. by R.A. Pierson's British Friesian "Garsdon Minnie" in 1948.

Milking The hand milking record for cows is 17 lb. 11 oz. in two minutes from two cows by Manuel Dutra of Stockton, California at the Cow Palace, San Francisco, California, U.S.A., on 27 Oct. 1970. Dutra, known as a fierce competitor, proclaimed "I credit my cows with the victory".

Goats The highest recorded milk yield for any goat is 6,661 pints in 365 days by "Malpas Melba", owned by Mr. J. R. Egerton of Bramford, East Anglia, in 1931.

SHEEP SHEARING
The highest recorded speed for lamb shearing in a working day was that of Steve Morrell who machine-sheared 585 lambs (average 65 per hour) in 9 hours at Ashburton, New Zealand on 29 Dec. 1971. The blade (*i.e.* hand-shearing) record in a 9-hour working day is 350, set in 1899. The female record is held by Mrs. Pamela Warren, aged 21, who machine-sheared 337 Romney Marsh ewes and lambs at Puketutu, near Piopio, North Island, New Zealand on 25 Nov. 1964.

Britain British records for 9 hours have been set at 555 by Roger Poyntz-Roberts (300) and John Savery (255) on 9 June 1971 (sheep caught *by* shearers), and 610 by the same pair (sheep caught *for* shearers) in July 1970. In a shearing marathon by the Kingsbridge Young Farmer's Club, four men machine-shore 776 sheep in 24 hours on 4-5 June 1971.

LIVESTOCK PRICES
The highest nominal value ever placed on a bull is $1,050,000 (then £375,000), implicit in the $350,000 paid on 22 Jan. 1967 for a one-third share in the Aberdeen-Angus bull "Newhouse Jewror Eric", aged 7, by the Embassy Angus Farm of Mississippi, U.S.A.

The highest price ever paid for a bull in Britain is 60,000 guineas (£63,000), paid on 5 Feb. 1963 at Perth, Scotland, by Jock Dick, co-manager of Black Watch Farms, for "Lindertis Evulse", an Aberdeen-Angus owned by Sir Torquil and Lady Munro of Lindertis, Kirriemuir, Angus, Scotland. This bull failed a fertility test in August 1963 when 20 months old thus becoming the world's most expensive piece of beef.

Cow The highest price ever paid for a cow is Can. $62,000 (£23,890) for the Holstein-Friesian "Oak Ridges Royal Linda" by Mr. E. L. Vesley of Lapeer, Michigan, U.S.A. at the Oak Ridges, Canada dispersal sale on 12 Nov. 1968.

Sheep The highest price ever paid for a sheep is $A27,200 (£12,920) for a Merino ram from John Collins & Sons, Mount Bryan, South Australia by L.W. Gare & Sons of Burra, South Australia at Adelaide in Sept. 1970.

The British auction record is £5,000 paid by J. and A. Stoddart for a Scottish Blackface ram lamb owned by Ben Wilson, at Lanark in October 1963.

The highest price ever paid for wool is 1,800 Australian pence ($A15 or £6.98) per lb. for a bale from 120 selected sheep of the Hillcrest Merino stud, bought for Illingworth, Morris & Co. of Shipley, Yorkshire, at an auction at Goulbourn, New South Wales, Australia, on 3 Dec. 1964.

Pig The highest price ever paid for a pig is $10,200 (now £3,920), paid in 1953 for a Hampshire boar "Great Western" by a farm at Byron, Illinois, U.S.A. The U.K. record is 3,300 guineas (£3,465), paid by Malvern Farms for the Swedish Landrace gilt "Bluegate Ally 33rd" owned by Davidson Trust in a draft sale at Reading on 2 March 1955.

Horse The highest price ever given for a farm horse is £9,500, paid for the Clydesdale stallion "Baron of Buchlyvie" by William Dunlop at Ayr, Scotland, in December 1911.

Donkey Perhaps the lowest ever price for livestock was at a sale at Kuruman, Cape Province, South Africa in 1934 where donkeys were sold for less than 2p each.

Turkey The highest price ever paid for a turkey is $990 (then £353) for a 33 lb. stag bird bought at the Arkansas State Turkey Show at Springdale, Arkansas, U.S.A. on 3 Dec. 1955.

Ivetta, the Brown Swiss cow which broke all career records for butter-fat production

BUTTER FAT

The world record lifetime yield is 13,607 lb. from 308,569 lb. by the U.S. Brown Swiss cow "Ivetta" (1954-71) in the herd of W. E. Naffziger at Pekin, Illinois, U.S.A. in 4,515 days. The British record butter fat yield in a lifetime is 12,144 lb. by the Friesian "Lavenham Wallen 87th" (b. 30 Nov. 1946, d. 17 Oct. 1967), owned by Mr. John Lindley of Nowers Farm, Wellington, Somerset. The world's lactation (365 days) record is 1,866 lb. by the U.S. Holstein-Friesian "Princess Breezewood R.A. Patsy" while the British record is 1,799 lb. (33,184 lb. milk at 5.42 per cent.) by A. Drexler's British Friesian "Zenda Bountiful" at Manor Farm, Kidlington, Oxfordshire, in the year ending 3 March 1953. This is sufficient to produce 2,116 lb. of butter. The United Kingdom record for butter fat in one day is 9.30 lb. (79 lb. milk at 11.8 per cent.) by Queens Letch Farms' Guernsey Cow "Thisbe's Bronwen of Trewollack".

CHEESE

The most active cheese-eaters are the people of France, with an annual average in 1969 of 29.98 lb. per person. The world's biggest producer is the United States with a factory production of 998,800 tons in 1970. The U.K. cheese consumption in 1970 was 11.4 lb. per head.

Oldest The oldest and most primitive cheeses are the Arabian *kishk,* made of the dried curd of goats' milk. There are today 450 named cheeses of 18 major varieties, but many are merely named after different towns and differ only in shape or the method of packing. France has 240 varieties.

Most The most expensive of all cheeses is the small goat
expensive cheese Crottin de Chavignol, from the Berri area of France, which is marketed in Paris, at times, for 30 francs per kilogramme (£1.12½ per lb.). Britain's most costly cheeses are Blue Cheshire and Windsor Red both at 45p per lb. In the U.S. Roquefort may cost more than $4 (£1) per lb. retail.

Largest The largest cheese ever made was a cheddar of 34,591 lb. (15.44 tons), made in 43 hours on 20-22 Jan. 1964 by the Wisconsin Cheese Foundation for exhibition at the New York World's Fair, U.S.A. It

was transported in a specially designed refrigera▮ tractor trailer "Cheese Mobile" 45 feet long.

Longest The longest sausage ever recorded was one 3,124 f
sausage long, made on 29 June 1966 by 30 butchers ▮ Scunthorpe, Lincolnshire. It was made from 6½ c▮ of pork and 1½ cwt. of cereal and seasoning.

Piggery The world's largest piggery is the Sljeme pig unit Yugoslavia which is able to process 300,000 pigs i▮ year. Even larger units may exist in Romania ▮ details are at present lacking.

Cow shed The longest cow shed in Britain is that of ▮ Yorkshire Agricultural Society at Harrogate. I▮ 456 feet in length with a capacity of 686 cows. ▮ National Agricultural Centre, Kenilworth, Warwi▮ shire, completed in 1967, has, however, capacity 782 animals.

Foot-and- The worst outbreak of foot-and-mouth disease
mouth Great Britain was that from Shropshire on 25 C
disease 1967 to 25 June 1968 in which there were 2,3▮ outbreaks and 429,632 animals slaughtered at a dir▮ and consequential loss of £150,000,000. The o▮ break of 1871, when farms were much smal▮ affected 42,531 farms. The disease first appeared Great Britain at Stratford near London in Aug 1839.

Ploughing The world championship (instituted 1953) has b▮ staged in 15 countries and won by ploughmen of ei▮ nationalities of which the United Kingdom has b▮ most successful with 6 champions. The only man take the title three times has been Hugh Barr▮ Northern Ireland in 1954-55-56.

The fastest recorded time for ploughing an a (minimum 32 right-hand turns and depth 9 inches 17 minutes 52.5 seconds by Mervyn Ford usin▮ six-furrow 14-inch Ransomes plough towed by Roadless 114 four-wheel drive tractor at Bow▮ Farm, Ide, Exeter, Devon on 25 Sept. 1970.

The greatest recorded acreage ploughed in 24 hour 84.1 acres by five farmers of the Exeter and Dist▮ Young Farmers' Club near Ide, Exeter, Devon 25-26 Sept. 1970.

10 HUMAN ACHIEVEMENTS

1. ENDURANCE AND ENDEAVOUR

LUNAR CONQUEST

Neil Alden Armstrong (b. Wapakoneta, Ohio, U.S.A. of Scoto-Irish and German ancestry, on 5 Aug. 1930), command pilot of the Apollo XI mission, became the first man to set foot on the Moon on the Sea of Tranquillity at 02.56 and 20 seconds G.M.T. on 21 July 1969. He was followed out of the Lunar Module *Eagle* by Col. Edwin Eugene Aldrin, Jr. U.S.A.F. (b. Montclair, New Jersey, U.S.A. of Swedish, Dutch and British ancestry, on 20 Jan. 1930), while the Command Module *Columbia* piloted by Lt.-Col. Michael Collins U.S.A.F. (b. Rome, Italy, of Irish and pre-Revolutionary American ancestry, on 31 Oct. 1930) orbited above.

Eagle landed at 20.17 hrs. 42 secs. G.M.T. on 20 July and lifted off at 17.54 G.M.T. on 21 July, after a stay of 21 hours 36 minutes. The Apollo XI had blasted off from Cape Kennedy, Florida at 13.32 G.M.T. on 16 July and was a culmination of the U.S. space programme, which, at its peak, employed 376,600 people and attained in the year 1966-67 a peak budget of $5,900,000,000 (£2,460 million).

ALTITUDE

Man The greatest altitude attained by man was when the crew of the ill-fated Apollo XIII were at apocynthion (*i.e.* their furthest point from the Moon) 158 miles above its far surface and 248,655 miles above the Earth's surface at 1.21 a.m. B.S.T. on 15 April 1970. The crew were Capt. James Arthur Lovel, U.S.N. (b. Denver, Colorado 30 Aug. 1931), Frederick Wallace Haise Jr. (b. Cleveland Ohio 25 Mar. 1928) and John L. Swigert Jr. (b. Biloxi, Miss. 14 Nov. 1933).

Woman The greatest altitude attained by a woman is 231 kilometres (143.5 miles) by Jnr. Lt. (now Lt. Col.) Valentina Vladimirovna Tereshkove-Nikolayev (b. 6 Mar. 1937) of the U.S.S.R., during her 48-orbit flight in *Vostok VI* on 16 June 1963. (See also Chapter 4.) The record for an aircraft is 24,336 metres (79,842 feet) by Natalia Prokhanova (U.S.S.R.) (b. 1940) in an E-33 jet, on 22 May 1965.

SPEED

Man The fastest speed at which any human has travelled is 24,791 m.p.h. when the Command Module of Apollo X carrying Col. Thomas P. Stafford U.S.A.F. (b. Weatherford, Okla. 17 Sept. 1930), and Cdrs.

Eugene Andrew Cernan (b. Chicago 14 Mar. 1934) and John Watts Young, U.S.N. (b. San Francisco 24 Sept. 1930), reached this maximum value at the 400,000-foot (75¾-mile) altitude interface on its trans-Earth return flight on 26 May 1969. It was widely but incorrectly reported that the stricken Apollo XIII attained the highest recorded speed on its return on 17 April 1970. Its maximum value was in fact 24,689.2 m.p.h.

Woman The highest speed ever attained by a woman is 17,470 m.p.h. by Jnr. Lt. (now Lt. Col.) Valentina Vladimirovna Tereshkova-Nikolayev (b. 6 March 1937) of the U.S.S.R. in *Vostok VI* on 16 June 1963. The highest speed ever achieved in an aeroplane is 1,429.2 m.p.h. by Jacqueline Cochran (Mrs. Floyd Bostwick-Odlum) (U.S.A.), in an F-104G1 *Starfighter* jet over Edwards Air Force Base, California, U.S.A., on 11 May 1964. The first woman in Britain to fly at over 1,000 m.p.h. was Flt. Off. Jean Oakes, who flew at 1,125 m.p.h. in an R.A.F. Lightning Mark 4 on 6 Sept. 1962.

LAND SPEED

Man The highest speed ever achieved on land is 650 m.p.h. momentarily during the 627.287 m.p.h. run of *The Blue Flame* driven by Gary Gabelich (b. San Pedro, California, 29 Aug. 1940) on Bonneville Salt Flats, Utah, U.S.A., on 23 Oct. 1970 (see Mechanical World, page 128). The car built by Reaction Dynamics Inc. of Milwaukee, Wisconsin, is designed to withstand stresses up to 1,000 m.p.h. while the tyres have been tested to speeds of 850 m.p.h.

Woman The highest land speed recorded by a woman is 335.070 m.p.h. by Mrs. Lee Ann Breedlove (*née* Roberts) (born 1937) of Los Angeles, California, U.S.A., driving her husband's *Spirit of America–Sonic I* (see page 129) over the timing kilometre on the Bonneville Salt Flats, Utah, U.S.A., on 4 Nov. 1965.

WATER SPEED

Unofficial The highest speed ever achieved on water is 328 m.p.h. by Donald Malcolm Campbell, C.B.E. (1921-67) of the U.K., on his last and fatal run in the turbo-jet engined 2¼ ton *Bluebird* K7, on Coniston Water, Lancashire, England, on 4 Jan. 1967.

PROGRESSIVE HUMAN ALTITUDE RECORDS

Metres	Feet	Pilot	Vehicle	Place	Date
25	84	Jean François Pilâtre de Rozier (France)	Hot Air Balloon (tethered)	Fauxbourg, Paris	15 & 17 Oct. 17
64	210	J. F. Pilâtre de Rozier (France)	Hot Air Balloon (tethered)	Fauxbourg, Paris	19 Oct. 17
80	262	J. F. Pilâtre de Rozier (France)	Hot Air Balloon (tethered)	Fauxbourg, Paris	19 Oct. 17
99	325	de Rozier and Girand de Villette (France)	Hot Air Balloon (tethered)	Fauxbourg, Paris	19 Oct. 17
c. 100	c. 330	de Rozier and the Marquis François-Laurent d'Arlandes (1742-1809) (France)	Hot Air Balloon (free flight)	La Muette, Paris	21 Nov. 17
c. 600	c. 2,000	Dr. Jácques-Alexandre-César Charles (1746-1823) and Ainé Robert (France)	Charlière Hydrogen Balloon	Tuileries, Paris	1 Dec. 17
c. 2 750	c. 9,000	J.-A.-C. Charles (France)	Hydrogen Balloon	Nesles, France	1 Dec. 17
c. 4 000	c. 13,000	James Sadler (G.B.)	Hydrogen Balloon	Manchester	May 17
c. 6 100	c. 20,000	E. G. R. Robertson (U.K.) and Loest (Germany)	Hydrogen Balloon	Hamburg, Germany	18 July 18
7 000	22,965	Joseph Louis Gay-Lussac (France)	Hydrogen Balloon	Paris	15 Sept. 18
c. 7 620	c. 25,000	Charles Green, Edward Spencer (G.B.)	Coal Gas Balloon Nassau	Vauxhall, London	24 July 18
7 740	25,400[1]	James Glaisher (U.K.)	Hydrogen Balloon	Wolverhampton	17 July 18
8 520	27,950	H. T. Sivel, J. E. Crocé-Spinelli, Gaston Tissandier (only survivor)	Coal Gas Balloon Zénith	La Villette, Paris	15 April 18
9 615	31,500	Prof. A. Berson (Germany)	Hydrogen Balloon Phoenix	Strasbourg, France	4 Dec. 18
10 800	35,433	Prof. Berson and Dr. R. J. Süring (Germany)	Hydrogen Balloon Preussen	Berlin, Germany	30 June 1
11 145	36,565	Sadi Lecointe (France)	Nieuport Aircraft	Issy-les-Moulineaux, France	30 Oct. 19
12 945	42,470[2]	Capt. Hawthorne C. Gray (U.S.A.)	Hydrogen Balloon	Scott Field, Illinois	4 May 19
12 945	42,470	Capt. Hawthorne C. Gray (U.S.A.)	Hydrogen Balloon	Scott Field, Illinois	4 Nov. 19
13 157	43,166	Lt. Apollo Soucek (U.S.A.)	U.S. Navy Wright Apache	Washington, D.C.	4 June 19
15 837	51,961	Prof. Auguste Piccard and Paul Kipfer (Switzerland)	F.N.R.S. I Balloon	Augsburg	27 May 19
16 196	53,139	Piccard & Dr. Max Cosyns (Belgium)	F.N.R.S. I Balloon	Dübendorf, nr. Zürich	18 Aug. 1
18 500	60,695[3]	G. Profkoviev, F. N. Birnbaum and K. D. Godunov (U.S.S.R.)	Army Balloon U.S.S.R.	Moscow, U.S.S.R.	30 Sept. 1
18 665	61,237	Lt.-Col. T. G. W. Settle, U.S.N. and Major Chester L. Fordney, U.S.M.C.	Hydrogen Balloon Century of Progress	Akron, Ohio	20 & 21 Nov. 19
22 000	72,178[4]	Raul F. Fedoseyenko, A. B. Vasienko and E. D. Ususkin (U.S.S.R.)	Osaviakhim Balloon	Moscow, U.S.S.R.	30 Jan. 19
22 066	72,395	Capts. Orvill A. Anderson and Albert W. Stevens (U.S. Army—Air Corps)	U.S. Explorer II Helium Balloon	Rapid City, South Dakota, U.S.A.	11 Nov. 19
24 230	79,494	William Barton Bridgeman (U.S.A.)	U.S. Douglas D558-II Skyrocket	California, U.S.A.	15 Aug. 19
25 370	83,235	Lt.-Col. Marion E. Carl, U.S.M.C.	U.S. Douglas D558-II Skyrocket	California, U.S.A.	21 Aug. 19
c. 28 350	c. 93,000	Major Arthur Murray (U.S.A.F.)	U.S. Bell X-1A Rocket 'plane	California, U.S.A.	4 June 19
38 465	126,200	Capt. Iven C. Kincheloe, Jnr. (U.S.A.F.)	U.S. Bell X-2 Rocket 'plane	California, U.S.A.	7 Sept. 19
41 605	136,500	Major Robert M. White (U.S.A.F.)	U.S. X-15 Rocket 'plane	California, U.S.A.	12 Aug. 19
51 694	169,600	Joseph A. Walker (U.S.A.)	U.S. X-15 Rocket 'plane	California, U.S.A.	30 Mar. 19

Kilometres	Statute Miles				
327	203.2	Flt.-Major Yuriy A. Gagarin (U.S.S.R.)	U.S.S.R. Vostok I Capsule	Oribital flight	12 April 19
408	253.5	Col. Vladimir M. Komarov, Lt. Boris B. Yegorov and Konstantin P. Feoktistov	U.S.S.R. Voskhod I Capsule	Oribital flight	12 Oct. 19
497.6	309.2	Col. Pavel I. Belyayev and Lt.-Col. Aleksey A. Leonov (U.S.S.R.)	U.S.S.R. Voskhod II Capsule	Oribital flight	18 Mar. 19
763.4	474.4	Cdr. John Watts Young, U.S.N. and Major Michael Collins, U.S.A.F.	U.S. Gemini X Capsule	Orbital flight	19 July 19
1 369.0	850.7	Cdr. Charles Conrad, Jr. U.S.N. and Lt.-Cdr. Richard F. Gordon, Jr., U.S.N.	U.S. Gemini XI Capsule	Orbital flight	14 Sept. 19
377 347	234,473	Col. Frank Borman, U.S.A.F., Capt. James Arthur Lovell Jr. U.S.N. and Major William A. Anders, U.S.A.F.	U.S. Apollo VIII Command Module	Circum-lunar flight	25 Dec. 19
399 814	248,433	Cdr. Eugene Andrew Cernan U.S.N. and Col. Thomas P. Stafford U.S.A.F.	U.S. Apollo X Lunar Module	Circum-lunar flight	22 May 19
389 920	242,285[5]	Neil Alden Armstrong, Col. Edwin Eugene Aldrin, Jr. and Lt.-Col. Michael Collins U.S.A.F.	U.S. Apollo XI	Circum-lunar flight and first Moon landing	21-22 July 19
400 187	248,655	Capt. James Arthur Lovell Jr. U.S.N., Frederick Wallace Haise Jr. and John L. Swigert Jr.	U.S. Apollo XIII	Abortive lunar landing mission	15 April 19

1 Glaisher, with Henry Coxwell, claimed 37,000 feet (11 275 metres) from Wolverhampton on 5 Sept. 1862. Some writers accept 30,000 feet (9 145 metres).
2 Neither of Gray's altitudes were official records because he had to parachute on his first descent and he landed dead from his second

3 None surived the ascent.
4 All died on descent.
5 Note. This historic space flight did not establish an altitude rec but has been included for reference only.

ascent to an identical height.

PROGRESSIVE ABSOLUTE HUMAN SPEED RECORDS

The progression of the **voluntary** human speed record is listed below. It is perhaps noteworthy that the petrol-engined car at no time featured in this compilation.

Speed Km./h.	m.p.h.	Person and Vehicle	Place	Date
<40	<25	Running	—	ante 6500 B
>40	>25	Sledging	Southern Finland	c. 6500 B
>55	>35	Ski-ing	Fenno-Scandia	c. 3000 B
>55	>35	Horse-riding	Anatolia, Turkey	c. 1400 B
<80	<50	Ice Yachts (earliest patent)	Netherlands	A.D. 16
95	56¾	Grand Junction Railway 2-2-2 Lucifer	Madeley Banks, Staffs., England	13 Nov. 18
119	74.5[1]	Great Western Railway 4-2-2 Great Britain	Wootton Bassett, Wiltshire, England	11 May 18
119.8	74.5	Great Western Railway 2-2-2 8 ft. single Great Western	Wootton Bassett, Wiltshire, England	1 June 18
125.5	78	Great Western Railway 4-2-2 8 ft. single Great Britain	Wootton Bassett, Wiltshire, England	11 May 18
131.6	81.8	Bristol & Exeter Railway 4-2-4 tank 9 ft. single No. 41	Wellington Bank, Somerset, England	June 18
141.3	87.8	Tommy Todd, downhill skier	La Porte, California, U.S.A.	Mar. 18
144	89.48	Crompton No. 604 engine	Champigny-Pont sur Yonne, France	20 June 18
144.8	90.0	Midland Railway 4-2-2 7 ft. 9 in. single	Ampthill, Bedford, England	Mar. 18

162.5	101.0	Siemens und Halske electric engine	near Berlin, Germany	1901
201	124.89	Siemens und Halske electric engine	Marienfeld-Zossen, near Berlin	6 Oct. 1903
206.7	128.43	Siemens und Halske electric engine	Marienfeld-Zossen, near Berlin	23 Oct. 1903
210.2	130.61	Siemens und Halske electric engine	Marienfeld-Zossen, near Berlin	27 Oct. 1903
c.257.5	c. 150	Frederick H. Marriott, Stanley Steamer *Rocket* (fl. 1957)	Ormond Beach, Florida, U.S.A.	26 Jan. 1907
>338	>210	World War I fighters in dives including Martinsyde F.4's and Nieuport *Nighthawks*	over England and Flanders	1918—19
339	210.64	Sadi Lecointe (France) Nieuport-Delage 29	Villesauvage, France	25 Sept. 1921
341	211.91	Sadi Lecointe (France) Nieuport-Delage 29	Villesauvage, France	21 Sept. 1922
392.64	243.94	Brig.-Gen. William Mitchell (U.S.Army (1879-1936)) Curtiss R-6.	Detroit, Michigan	18 Oct. 1922
435.3	270.5	Lt. Alford Joseph Williams (U.S.N.), Curtiss R.2 C-1	Mitchell Field, Long Is., N.Y.	4 Nov. 1923
441.3	274.2	Lt. A. Brown (U.S.N.), Curtiss H.S. D-12	Mitchell Field, Long Is., N.Y.	4 Nov. 1923
448.15	278.47[2]	Adj. Chef Florentin Bonnet (France) Bernard-Ferbois V-2	Istres, France	11 Dec. 1924
457	284	Fg. Off. Sidney Norman Webster A.F.C. Supermarine S.5	Calshot, Hampshire	14 July 1927
>482	>300	Flt. Lt. Sidney Norman Webster, A.F.C. Supermarine S.5	Venice, Italy	26 Sept. 1927
504.67	313.59	Major Mario de Bernardi (Italy) Macchi M-52	Venice, Italy	4 Nov. 1927
519.1	322.6[3]	Lt. Alford J. Williams (U.S.N.) Kirkham-Williams	Mitchell Field, Long Is., N.Y.	7 Nov. 1927
561	348.6	Col. Mario de Bernardi (Italy) Macchi M-52 R	Venice, Italy	30 Mar. 1928
582	362	Capt. Guiseppe Motta Macchi 67	Lago di Garda, Italy	22 Aug. 1929
>595.4	>370	Fg. Off. Henry Richard D. Waghorn, A.F.C. and Fg. Off. Richard Llewellyn Roger Atcherley (1904-70) (later Air Marshal Sir, K.B.E., C.B., A.F.C*) Supermarine S.6's	Solent, Hampshire, England	7 Sept. 1929
603	375	Lt. Ariosti Nevi Macchi 72	Desenzaro, Italy	July 1931
634	394	Lt. Ariosti Nevi Macchi 72	Desenzaro, Italy	Aug. 1931
668.2	415.2	Flt. Lt. (later Wing Cdr.) George Hedley Stainforth, A.F.C. Supermarine S.6B	Lee-on-Solent, England	29 Sept. 1931
692.529	430.32[4]	W.O. Francesco Agello (Italy) Macchi-Castoldi 72	Lago di Garda, Italy	10 April 1933
>700	>434.96[5]	Col. Mario Bernasconi (Italy) Macchi-Castoldi 72	Desenzaro, Italy	18 April 1934
710.07	441.22	Sec. Lt. Francesco Agello (Italy) Macchi-Castoldi 72	Lago di Garda, Italy	23 Oct. 1934
746.64	463.94[2]	Flug kapitan Hans Dieterle (Germany) Heinkel He. 100V-8	Oranienburg, E. Germany	30 Mar. 1939
782	486	Flug kapitan Fritz Wendel (Germany) Messerschmitt 209 V-1	Augsburg, E. Germany	26 April 1939
.845	c.525	Heinkel 176 test flight	Peenemünde, Germany	3 July 1939
920.2	571.78	Flugkapitan Heinz Dittmar Me. 163V-1	Peenemünde, Germany	July—August 1941
1,004	623.85	Flugkapitan Heinz Dittmar Me. 163V-1	Peenemünde, Germany	2 Oct. 1941
1,005	624.62	Unnamed test pilot—possibly Gerd Linter Me.262V-12	Insterburg, Germany	July 1944
1,050	c. 652	Franz Rösle Me.163B	Brandis, Germany	March—April 1945
1,030—1,060	c. 640—660	Geoffrey Raoul de Havilland, O.B.E., (1910-46) D.H. 108 *Swallow*	Egypt Bay, Kent, England	27 Sept. 1946
1,050.3	652.6	Cdr. Turner F. Caldwell, U.S.N., Douglas *Skystreak* D-558-I	Muroc Dry Lake, California	20 Aug. 1947
1,051.5	653.4	Major (later Lt.-Col.) Marion E. Carl, U.S.M.C., Douglas *Skystreak* D-558-I	Muroc Dry Lake, California	25 Aug. 1947
1,078	670	Capt. Charles E. Yeager, U.S.A.F., Bell XS-1 *Glamorous Glennis* (Mach 1.015)	Muroc Dry Lake, California	14 Oct. 1947
1,556	967	Capt. Charles E. Yeager, U.S.A.F., Bell XS-1	Muroc Dry Lake, California	1948
1,826.6	1,135	William Barton Bridgeman, Douglas *Skyrocket* D-558-II	Muroc Dry Lake, California	June 1951
1,900.6	1,181	William Barton Bridgeman, Douglas *Skyrocket* D-558-II	Muroc Dry Lake, California	11 June 1951
1,965.0	1,221	William Barton Bridgeman, Douglas *Skyrocket* D-558-II	Muroc Dry Lake, California	June 1951
1,992.3	1,238	William Barton Bridgeman, Douglas *Skyrocket* D-558-II	Muroc Dry Lake, California	7 Aug. 1951
2,013.2	1,241	William Barton Bridgeman, Douglas *Skyrocket* D-558-II	Muroc Dry Lake, California	Dec. 1951
2,047.0	1,272	Albert Scott Crossfield, Douglas *Skyrocket* D-558-II	Muroc Dry Lake, California	14 Oct. 1953
2,137.2	1,328	Albert Scott Crossfield, Douglas *Skyrocket* D-558-II	Muroc Dry Lake, California	20 Nov. 1953
2,594.2	1,612	Major Charles E. Yeager, Bell X-1A	Muroc Dry Lake, California	12 Dec. 1953
3,112.4	1,934	Lt.-Col. Frank K. Everest, Jr. Bell X-2	Muroc Dry Lake, California	23 July 1956
3,369.9	2,094	Capt. Milburn G. Apt, Bell X-2	Muroc Dry Lake, California	27 Sept 1956
3,397.3	2,111	Joseph A. Walker, North American X-15	Muroc Dry Lake, California	12 May 1960
3,534.1	2,196	Joseph A. Walker, North American X-15	Muroc Dry Lake, California	4 Aug. 1960
3,661.1	2,275	Major Robert M. White, North American X-15	Muroc Dry Lake, California	7 Feb. 1961
4,675.1	2,905	Major Robert M. White, North American X-15	Muroc Dry Lake, California	7 Mar. 1961
3,260	c. 17,560	Flt. Maj. Yuriy Alekseyevich Gagarin, *Vostok 1*	Earth orbit	12 April 1961
3,257	17,558	Cdr. Walter Marty Schirra, Jr. U.S.N., *Sigma 7*	Earth orbit	3 Oct. 1962
3,325	c. 17,600	Air Eng. Col. Vladimir Mikhaylovich Komarov, Lt. Boris Borisovich Yegorov and Konstantin Petrovich Feoktistov, *Voskhod I*	Earth orbit	12 Oct. 1964
8,565	c. 17,750	Col. Pavel Ivanovich Belyayev and Lt. Col. Aleksey Arkhipovich Leonov, *Voskhod II*	Earth orbit	18 Mar. 1965
8,876	17,943	Cdr. Charles Conrad, Jr., Lt-Cdr. Richard F. Gordon, Jr., U.S.N. *Gemini XI*	Earth orbit	14 Sept. 1966
8,988	24,226	Col. Frank Borman, U.S.A.F., Capt. James Arthur Lovell, Jr., U.S.N., Major William A. Anders, U.S.A.F. *Apollo VIII*	Trans-lunar injection	21 Dec. 1968
9,834	24,752	Col. Frank Borman, U.S.A.F., Capt. James Arthur Lovell, Jr., U.S.N., Major William A. Anders, U.S.A.F. *Apollo VIII*	Re-entry after lunar orbit	27 Dec. 1968
9,897	24,791	Cdrs. Eugene Andrew Cernan and John Watts Young, U.S.N. and Col. Thomas P. Stafford, U.S.A.F. *Apollo X*	Re-entry after lunar orbit	26 May 1969

[1] A speed of 85 m.p.h. (137 Km./h.) was claimed by Frank Elrington in a run-away compressed air railway from Kingstown (now Dún Laoghaire) to Dalkey, County Dublin on 19 Aug. 1843. It was, however, self-timed.
[2] Average of 4 runs, individual runs not officially published.
[3] Self-timed unofficial run.
[4] Earlier runs at 421.58 m.p.h., 678.477 Km./h. and 424.17 m.p.h., 682.637 Km./h.
[5] Unofficial single run.

Official The official record is 285.213 m.p.h. (average of two 1 mile runs) by Lee Taylor, Jr. (b. 1934) of Downey, California, U.S.A., in the hydroplane *Hustler* on Lake Guntersville, Alabama, U.S.A., on 30 June 1967.

Propeller driven The world record for propeller-driven craft is 200.42 m.p.h. held by Roy Duby (U.S.A.) in his Rolls-Royce-engined hydroplane on Lake Guntersville, Alabama, U.S.A., on 17 April 1962.

TRAVELLING

Most travelled man The man who has visited more countries than anyone is J. Hart Rosdail (b. 1915) of Elmhurst, Illinois, U.S.A. Since 1934 he has visited 144 of the 148 sovereign countries and 76 of the 80 non-sovereign territories of the world making a total of 219. He estimates his mileage as 1,170,000 miles by February 1972. The only sovereign countries which he has not visited are China (Mainland), Cuba, North Korea and North Vietnam.

The most countries visited by a disabled person is 119 by Lester Nixon of Sarasota, Florida, U.S.A. who is confined to a wheelchair.

Flying The greatest number of flying hours claimed is more than 40,000 by the light aircraft pilot Max. A. Conrad (b. 1903) of the U.S.A., who began his flying career

Gipsy Moth IV in which Sir Francis Chichester made the first single stop solo circumnavigation of the world.

on 13 March 1928. Capt. Charles Blair (Pan America World Airways) logged 35,000 flying hours and mor than 10,000,000 miles including 1,450 Atlanti crossings up to July 1969. Capt. Gordon R. Buxto surpassed 8,000,000 miles in 22,750 flying hours i 38 years to 22 May 1966. He retired as Senic B.O.A.C. captain, aged 60, having passed all medical:

Space The most travelled man in space is Capt. James Arthu Lovell, Jr. U.S.N. (b. Cleveland, Ohio, 25 Mar. 1928 with 715 hours 4 mins. 57 secs. and an estimate mileage of 7,270,000.

Cross-Channel record The record for travelling the 214 miles between Par (Arc de Triomphe) and London (Marble Arch) is 4 minutes 44 seconds by Sqn. Ldr. Charles G. Maugha R.A.F. (b. 1924), by motorcycle, helicopter an Hunter jet aircraft on 22 July 1959, so winning th *Daily Mail* award.

MARINE CIRCUMNAVIGATION RECORDS *(Compiled by Sq. Ldr. D.H. Clarke DFC AFC.)*

A true circumnavigation entails passing through two antipodal points (which are at least 12,429 statute miles apart).

CATEGORY	VESSEL	NAME	START DATE AND PLACE	FINISH DATE AND DURATION
Earliest	*Vittoria* Expedition of Fernão de Magalhães, c. 1480-1521	Juan Sebastion de Eleano (d.1526) and 17 crew including Andrews of Bristol (first Briton)	Guadalquivir, Spain 20 Sept. 1519	6 Sept. 1521 30,700 miles
Earliest British	*Golden Hind* (ex *Pelican*) 100 tons	Francis Drake (c. 1540-1596) (Knighted 4 April 1581).	Plymouth, 13 Dec. 1577	26 Sept. 1580
Earliest Woman	*La Bordeuse*	Crypto-female valet of M. de Commerson		1764
Earliest Solo	*Spray* 36¾ foot gaff yawl	Capt. Joshua Slocum, 51, (U.S.) (a non-swimmer)	Newport, Rhode Island, U.S.A. *via* Magellan Straits, 24 Apr. 1895	3 July 1898 46,000 miles
Earliest Solo Eastabout *via* Cape Horn	*Lehg II* 31¼ foot Bermuda Ketch	Vito Dumas (Argentina)	Buenos Aires, 27 June 1942	7 Sept. 1943 (272 days)
Smallest Boat	*Trekka* 20½ foot Bermuda Ketch	John Guzzwell (G.B.)	Victoria B.C., 10 Sept. 1955 Westabout *via* Panama	12 Sept. 1959 (4 years 2 days)
Earlist Submarine	*U.S.S. Triton*	Capt. Edward L. Beach U.S.N. plus 182 crew	New London, Connecticut 16 Feb. 1960	10 May 1960 30,708 miles
Earliest Solo with One Stop Over	*Gipsy Moth IV* 53 ft. Bermuda Yawl	Sir Francis Chichester K.B.E. (b.1901)	Plymouth to Sydney 27 Aug. 1966	Sydney to Plymouth 28 May 1967 29,626 miles
Earliest non-stop Solo	*Suhaili* 32.4 foot Bermuda Ketch	Robin Knox-Johnston C.B.E. (b.1928)	Falmouth, 14 June 1968 (unaided repairs at Otago, N.Z.)	22 Apr. 1969 (313 days)
Fastest Solo	*Victress* 40 foot Trimaran	Lt-Cdr. Nigel C.W. Tetley R.N. (South Africa)	Plymouth, 16 Sept. 1968	Tied the Knot in 179 days
Earliest non-stop Solo Westabout	*British Steel* 59 foot ketch (largest solo)	Charles 'Chay' Blyth C.B.E., B.E.M. (b.1940)	The Hamble 18 Oct. 1970	6 Aug. 1971 292 days

TRANS ATLANTIC MARINE RECORDS *(Compiled by Sq. Ldr. D.H. Clarke DFC AFC.)*

Earliest Trimaran	John Mikes + 2 crew (U.S.)	*Non Pareil*, 25 ft.	New York (4 June)	Southampton	43 days	1868
Earliest Solo Sailing	Alfred Johnson (Denmark)	*Centennial* 20 ft.	Nova Scotia	Wales	46 days	187
Earliest Woman Sailing	Mrs Joanna Crapo (Scotland)	*New Bedford* 20 ft.	Chatham, Mass.	Newlyn, Cornwall	51 days	187
Earliest Single-handed race	J.W. Lawlor (U.S)	*Sea Serpent* 15 ft.	Boston (17 June)	Coverack, Cornwall	47 days	189
Earliest Rowing	George Harbo and Frank Samuelson (U.S.)	*Richard K. Fox* 18¹/₃ft.	New York City (6 June)	Isles of Scilly (1 Aug.)	55 days	189
Fastest Solo Sailing West-East	J.V.T. McDonald (G.B.)	*Inverarity* 38 ft.	Nova Scotia	Ireland	16 days	192
Earliest Canoe (with sail)	E. Romer (Germany)	*Deutches Sport* 19½ ft.	Cape St. Vincent (17 Apr.)	St. Thomas, West Indies	58 days	192
Fastest Solo Sailing East-West (Shortest Route)	Cdr. R.D. Graham R.N. (G.B.)	*Emanuel* 30 ft.	Bantry, Ireland	St. John's, Newfoundland	24.35 days	193
Earliest Woman Solo-Sailing	Mrs Ann Davison (G,B.)	*Felicity Ann* 23 ft.	Plymouth (18 May 1952)	Miami, Florida (13 Aug. 1953)	454 days	195
Smallest East-West	John Riding (G.B.)	*Sjø Åg* 12 ft.	Plymouth, July 1964	Newport, Rhode Is. (17 Aug. 1965)	403 days	196
Smallest West-East	William Verity (U.S.)	*Nonoalca* 12 ft.	Ft. Lauderdale, Florida	Tralee, Kerry (12 July)	68 days	196
Earliest Rowing (G.B.)	Capt. John Ridgway M.B.E. Sgt. Charles Blyth B.E.M. (G.B.)	*English Rose III* 22 ft.	Cape Cod (4 June)	Inishmore (3 Sept.)	91 days	196
Fastest Crossing Sailing (Trimaran)	Eric Tabarly (France) +2 crew	*Pen Duick IV* 63 ft.	Tenerife	Martinique	251.4 miles/ day (10 days 12 hrs).	196
Fastest Solo East-West (Northern)	Geoffrey Williams (G.B.)	*Sir Thomas Lipton* 57 ft.	Plymouth (1 June)	Brenton Reef (27 June)	25.85 days	196
Fastest Solo Rowing East-West	Sidney Genders, 51 (G.B.)	*Khaggavisana* 19¾ ft.	Sennen Cove, Cornwall	Miami, Florida *via* Antigua (27 June)	37.3 miles/ day	197
Earliest Solo Rowing East-West	John Fairfax (G.B.)	*Britannia* 22 ft.	Las Palmas (20 Jan.)	Ft. Lauderdale, Florida (19 July)	180 days	196
Fastest Solo East-West (Southern)	Sir Francis Chichester K.B.E. (G.B.)	*Gipsy Moth V* 57 ft.	Portuguese Guinea	Nicaragua	171.9 miles/ day (22.4 days)	197
Earliest Solo Rowing West-East	Tom McClean (Ireland)	*Super Silver* 20 ft	St John's, Newfoundland (17 May)	Black Sod Bay, Ireland (27 July)	70.7 days	196

U.S.S. Triton — the first submarine to circumnavigate the world submerged.

POLAR CONQUESTS

North Pole The claims of neither of the two U.S. Arctic explorers, Dr. Frederick Albert Cook (1865-1940) nor Civil Engineer Robert Edwin Peary, U.S.N. (1856-1920) in reaching the North Pole is subject to positive proof. Cook, accompanied by the Eskimos, Ah-pellah and Etukishook, two sledges and 26 dogs, struck north from a point 60 miles north of Svartevoeg, on Axel Heibert Is., Canada, 460 miles from the Pole on 21 March 1908, allegedly reaching Lat. 89° 31' N. on 19 April and the Pole on 21 April. Peary, accompanied by his negro assistant, Matthew Alexander Henson (1866-1955) and the four Eskimos, Ooqueah, Egingwah, Seegloo, and Ootah (1875-1955), struck north from his Camp Bartlett (Lat. 87° 44' N.) at 5 a.m. on 2 April 1909. After travelling another 134 miles, he allegedly established his final camp, Camp Jessup, in the proximity of the Pole at 10 a.m. on 6 April and marched a further 42 miles quartering the sea-ice before turning south at 4 p.m. on 7 April. Peary's longest claimed 3-day march for a record 163 geographical miles must be regarded as highly improbable. Cook's comparative maximum claim was for 68 geographical miles in 3 days.

The earliest indisputable attainment of the North Pole over the sea-ice was at 3 p.m. (Central Standard Time) on 19 April 1968 by Ralph Plaisted (U.S.) and three companions after a 42-day trek in four Skidoos (snow-mobiles). Their arrival was independently verified 18 hours later by a U.S. Air Force weather aircraft.

Arctic crossing The first crossing of the Arctic sea-ice was achieved by the British Trans-Arctic Expedition which left Point Barrow, Alaska on 21 Feb. 1968 and arrived at the Seven Island Archipelago north-east of Spitzbergen 464 days later on 29 May 1969 after a haul of 3,620 statute miles. The team was Wally Herbert (leader), 34, Major Ken Hedges, 34, R.A.M.C., Allan Gill, 38, and Dr. Roy Koerner, 36 (glaciologist), and 40 huskies. This was the longest sustained journey ever made on polar pack ice.

South Pole The first ship to cross the Antarctic circle (Lat. 66° 30' S.) was the *Resolution* (462 tons), under Capt. James Cook (1728-79), on 17 Jan. 1773. The first person to sight the Antarctic *mainland*—on the best available evidence and against claims made for British and Russian explorers—was Nathaniel Brown Palmer (U.S.) (1799-1877). On 17 Nov. 1820 he sighted the Orleans Channel coast of the Palmer Peninsular from his 45 ton sloop *Hero*.

The South Pole was first reached on 14 Dec. 1911 by a Norwegian party, led by Capt. Roald Amundsen (1872-1928), after a 53-day march with dog sledges from the Bay of Whales, to which he had penetrated in the *Fram*. Olav Olavson Bjaaland, the first to arrive,

was the last survivor, dying in June 1961, aged 88. The others were the late Helmer Hanssen, Sverre H. Hassell and Oskar Wisting.

Antarctic crossing The first crossing of the Antarctic continent was completed at 1.47 p.m. on 2 March 1958, after a 2,158-mile trek lasting 99 days from 24 Nov. 1957, from Shackleton Base to Scott Base *via* the Pole. The crossing party of twelve was led by Dr. (now Sir) Vivian Ernest Fuchs (born 11 Feb. 1908).

Longest sledge journey The longest polar sledge journey was one of 3,720 statute route miles in 476 days by the British Trans-Arctic Expedition from 21 Feb. 1968 to 10 June 1969 (see above).

MOUNTAINEERING

Highest by man The conquest of the highest point on Earth, Mount Everest (29,028 feet) was first achieved at 11.30 a.m. on 29 May 1953, by Edmund Percival Hillary (New Zealand) and the Sherpa Tenzing Norkhay (see Mountaineering, Chapter 12).

Highest by women The greatest altitude attained by a woman mountaineer is 26,223 feet by Miss Setsuko Watanabe, 31 (Japan) on Everest in May 1970. The highest mountain summit reached by women is Qungur I (Kongur Tiube Tagh) (*c.* 25,146 feet), climbed in 1961 by Shierab and another (unnamed) Tibetan woman.

GREATEST OCEAN DESCENT

The record ocean descent was achieved in the Challenger Deep of the Marianas Trench, 250 miles south-west of Guam, in the Pacific Ocean, when the Swiss-built U.S. Navy bathyscaphe *Trieste*, manned by Dr. Jacques Piccard (b. 1914) (Switzerland), and Lt. Donald Walsh, U.S.N., reached the ocean bed 35,802 feet (6.78 miles) down, at 1.10 p.m. on 23 Jan. 1960 (but see also Chapter 3). The pressure of the water was 16,883 lb. per square inch (1,085.3 tons per square foot), and the temperature 37.4° F. The descent required 4 hours 48 minutes and the ascent 3 hours 17 minutes.

Deep sea diving The world's record depth for a salvage observation chamber is that established by the Admiralty salvage ship *Reclaim* on 28 June 1956. In an observation chamber measuring 7 feet long and 3 feet internal diameter, Senior Com. Boatswain (now Lt.-Cdr.) G.A.M. Wookey, M.B.E., R.N., descended to a depth of 1,060 feet in Oslo Fjord, Norway.

SALVAGING

Deepest The deepest salvaging operation ever carried out was on the wreck of the S.S. *Niagara*, sunk by a mine in 1940, 438 feet down off Bream Head, Whangarei, North Island, New Zealand. All but 6 per cent. of the £2,250,000 of gold in her holds was recovered in 7 weeks. The record recovery was that from the White Star Liner *Laurentic*, which was torpedoed in 114 feet of water off Malin Head, Donegal, Ireland, in 1917, with £5,000,000 of gold ingots in her Second Class baggage room. By 1924, 3,186 of the 3,211 gold bricks had been recovered with immense difficulty.

Largest vessel The largest vessel ever salvaged was the U.S.S. *Lafayette*, formerly the French liner *Normandie* (83,423 tons), which keeled over during fire-fighting operations at the West 49th Street Pier, New York Harbour, U.S.A., on 9 Feb. 1942. She was righted in October 1943, at a cost of $4,500,000 (then £1,250,000), and was broken up at Newark, New Jersey, beginning September 1946.

Most expensive The most expensive salvage operation ever conducted was that by the U.S. Navy off Palomares, southern Spain, for the recovery of a 2,800 lb. 20 megaton H-bomb, dropped from a crashing B-52 bomber, at a cost of $30,000,000 (£12.5 million). A fleet of 18

OCEAN DESCENTS—PROGRESSIVE RECORDS

Feet	Vehicle	Divers	Location	Date
c. 245	Steel Sphere	Ernest Bazin (France)	Belle Île	1
c. 830	Diving Bell	Balsamello Bella Nautica (Italy)		1
c. 1,650	Hydrostat	Hartman		1
1,426	Bathysphere	Dr. Charles William Beebe (1887-1962) and Dr. Otis Barton (b.1901) (U.S.A.)	S.E. Bermuda	11 June 1
2,200	Bathysphere	Dr. C. W. Beebe and Dr. O. Barton (U.S.A.)	S.E. Bermuda	22 Sept. 1
2,510	Bathysphere	Dr. C. W. Beebe and Dr. O. Barton (U.S.A.)	S.E. Bermuda	11 Aug. 1
3,028	Bathysphere	Dr. C. W. Beebe and Dr. O. Barton (U.S.A.)	S.E. Bermuda	15 Aug. 1
7,850	Converted U-boat	Heinz Sellner (Germany) (unwitnessed)	Murmansk	Aug. 1
4,500	Benthoscope	Dr. Otis Barton (U.S.A.)	off Santa Cruz, California	16 Aug. 1
5,085	Bathyscaphe F.N.R.S. 3	Lt-Cdr. Georges S. Houet and Lt. Pierre-Henri Willm (France)	off Toulon	12 Aug. 1
6,890	Bathyscaphe F.N.R.S. 3	Lt-Cdr. G. S. Houet and Lt. P.-H. Willm (France)	off Cap Ferrat	14 Aug. 1
10,335	Bathyscaphe Trieste	Prof. Auguste and Dr. Jaques Piccard (Switzerland)	Ponza Is.	30 Sept. 1
13,287	Bathyscaphe F.N.R.S. 3	Lt-Cdr. G.S. Houet and Eng. Off. P.-H. Willm (France)	off Dakar, Senegal	15 Feb. 1
18,600	Bathyscaphe Trieste	Dr. J. Piccard (Swiss) and Andreas B. Rechnitzer (U.S.A.)	Marianas Trench	14 Nov. 1
24,000	Bathyscaphe Trieste	Dr. J. Piccard (Swiss) and Lt. D. Walsh, U.S.N.	Marianas Trench	7 Jan. 1
35,802	Bathyscaphe Trieste	Dr. J. Piccard (Swiss) and Lt. D. Walsh, U.S.N.	Marianas Trench	23 Jan. 1

DEEP DIVING—PROGRESSIVE RECORDS

BREATH-HOLDING

It must be noted that competitive breath-held diving is an extremely dangerous activity and is the cause of several fatalities in most years.

Feet	Divers	Location	Date
c. 50	Mother-of-pearl divers	Mediterranean	c. 3,300 B
c. 120	Sponge and oyster divers (limit)	Ceylon and elsewhere	c. 1,000 B
c. 200	Stotti Georghios (Greece)	Adriatic	1
198	Jaques Mayol (France)	off Freeport, Grand Bahama	July 1
212½	P.O. Robert Croft, U.S.N.	Floridian coast, U.S.A.	8 Feb. 1
#125	Evelyn Patterson (Zambia)	off Freeport, Grand Bahama	1
217½	P.O. Robert Croft, U.S.N.	off Ft. Lauderdale, U.S.A.	19 Dec. 1
231	Jacques Mayol (France)	Mediterranean	14 Jan. 1
240	P.O. Robert Croft, U.S.N.	Floridian coast, U.S.A.	12 Aug. 1
242.7	Enzio Maiorca (Italy)		1
249.3	Jacques Mayol (France)	off Japanese coast	
250	Enzio Maiorca (Italy)	Syracuse, Sicily	11 Aug. 1

BREATHING AIR

Feet	Divers	Location	Date
162[1]	Alexander Lambert (U.K.)	Point Gando, Grand Canary Is.	1
190[1]	Greek and Swedish divers	off Patras, Greece	1
210[1]	Lt. G. C. C. Damant, R.N.	Loch Striven, Scotland	1
274[2]	Chief Gunner S. J. Drellifsak, U.S.N.	from U.S.S. Walke	9 Oct. 1
304[2]	F. Crilley, W.F. Loughman, F.C.L. Nielson, U.S.N.	off Hawaii	1
344[2]	Diver Hilton, R.N.	British waters	1
307[3]	Frederick Dumas (France)	Mediterranean	1
†396[3]	Lt. Maurice Farques (France)	Mediterranean	1
††400[3]	Hope Root (U.S.A.)	U.S. waters	1
350[3]	Jean Clarke-Samazen	off Santa Catalina, U.S.A.	Aug. 1
#320[3]	Katherine Troutt (Australia)	Sydney Heads, Australia	7 Sept. 1
355[3]	Hal D. Watts and Herb Johnson (U.S.A.)	off Loo Key, Fla., U.S.A.	4 Sept. 1
380[3]	Hal D. Watts and Arthur J. Muns (U.S.A.)	off Miami Beach, U.S.A.	3 Sept. 1
#325[3]	Margarete (Kitty) Geissler (b. West Germany)	off Freeport, Grand Bahama	27 Oct. 1
437[3]	John J. Gruener and R. Neal Watson (U.S.A.)	off Freeport, Grand Bahama	14 Oct. 1

BREATHING GAS MIXTURES

Feet	Divers	Location	Date
420[4]	M. G. Nohl (U.S.A.)	Lake Michigan, U.S.A.	1 Dec. 1
440[5]	R. M. Metzger and Claude Conger, U.S.N.	Portsmouth, N.H., U.S.A.	22 June 1
†528[5]	A. Zetterström (Sweden)	Baltic	7 Aug. 1
451[4]	P.O.'s Wilfred H. Bollard and W. Soper, R.N.	Loch Fyne, Argyllshire, Scotland	26 Aug. 1
540[4]	P.O. W. H. Bollard, R.N.	Loch Fyne, Argyllshire, Scotland	28 Aug. 1
550	Diver John E. Johnsone	Hauriki Gulf, N.Z.	1
600[4]	Sen. Bnsn. George A. M. Wookey, M.B.E., R.N.	Oslo Fjord, Norway	13 Oct. 1
728[6]	Hannes Keller (Switzerland) and Kenneth MacLeish (U.S.A.)	Lake Maggiore, Italy	30 June 1
*1,000[6]	H. Keller (Switzerland) and Peter Small.† (U.K.)	off Santa Catalina, U.S.A.	3 Dec. 1
**1,025[4]	U.S. Navy Aquanauts		Feb. 1
**1,100[4]	Carl Deckman (Int. Underwater Contractors, Inc.)	Murray Hill, N.J. U.S.A.	12 Mar. 1
**1,197[4]	Ralph W. Brauer (U.S.A.) and René Veyrunes (France)	Comex Chamber, Marseille, France	27 June 1
**1,500[4]	John Bevan and Peter Sharphouse (U.K.)	Alverstoke, Hampshire	11 Mar. 1
**1,706	Patrice Chemin and Bernard Reuiller (France)	Comex Chamber, Marseille, France	19 Nov. 1

Female record.
† Died on the ascent.   * Emerged from a diving bell.
†† Died on the descent. ** Simulated chamber dive.

[1] Surface supplied, helmet.
[2] Surface supplied, flexible dress.
[3] Scuba (self-contained underwater breathing apparatus).

[4] Oxygen-helium.
[5] Oxygen-hydrogen.
[6] Oxygen-helium plus an addi

---

ships and 2,200 men took part between 17 Jan. and 7 Apr. 1966. A CURV (Cable-controlled Underwater Research Vehicle) was flown from California and, directed by the 2 man submarine Alvin, retrieved the bomb from a depth of 2,850 feet.

Highest award The highest salvage award ever paid out was £575,000 to the salvors of the S.S. Toledo (4,581 gross tons), stranded off Karachi, West Pakistan, in July 1952.

MINING DEPTHS

Greatest penetration Man's deepest penetration made into the ground is in the East Rand Proprietary Mine in Boksburg, Transvaal. In November 1959 a level of 11,246 feet or 2.13 miles below ground level was attained in a pilot winze

in the Hercules section. The rock temperature at t depth was 126° F. Incline shafts to a planned dep of 12,000 feet are being worked at Western De Levels mine, Klerksdorp, South Africa.

Shaft sinking record The one month (31 days) world record is 1,251 f for a standard shaft 26 feet in diameter at Buff fontein Mine, Transvaal, South Africa, in Ma 1962. The British record is 336 feet in 31 days January 1961 at the No. 2 shaft of Kelling Colliery, Knottingley, Yorkshire.

RUNNING

Mensen Ehrnst (1799-1846) or Norway is reputed have run from Istanbul, Turkey, to Calcutta, in W

Bengal, India, and back in 59 days in 1836, so averaging an improbable 94.2 miles per day. The greatest non-stop run recorded is 121 miles 440 yards in 22 hours 27 minutes by Jared R. Beads, 41, of Westport, Maryland in October 1969. The 24-hour running record is 159 miles 562 yards (6 marathons plus 3,532 yards) by Wally H. Hayward, 45 (South Africa) at Motspur Park, Surrey on 20-21 Nov. 1954. The best distance by a 19th century "wobbler" was 150 miles 395 yards by Charles Rowell in New York City in February 1882.

-day races The greatest distance covered by a man in six days (*i.e.* the 144 permissible hours between Sundays in Victorian times) was 623¾ miles by George Littlewood (England), who required only 139 hours 1 min. for this feat in December 1888 at the old Madison Square Gardens, New York City, U.S.A.

Greatest mileage The greatest life-time mileage recorded by any runner is 151,740 miles by Ken Baily of Bournemouth, England up to 21 June 1972.

Longest race The longest race ever staged was the 1929 Transcontinental Race (3,665 miles) from New York City, N.Y., to Los Angeles, California, U.S.A. The Finnish-born Johnny Salo (killed 6 Oct. 1931) was the winner in 79 days, from 31 March to 17 June. His elapsed time of 525 hours 57 minutes 20 seconds gave a running average of 6.97 m.p.h.

Hottest run The traverse of the 120-mile-long Death Valley, California in both directions was uniquely accomplished by Paul Pfau with ground temperatures reaching 140° F. on 22-24 Jan. (30½ elapsed hours) for the southbound and on 3-5 March 1971 (26 hours 10 minutes) for the northbound traverse.

WALKING

Non-Stop The greatest distance ever walked literally non-stop is 230.8 miles in 68½ hours near Napier, New Zealand on 11-14 Sept. 1971, by John Sinclair, 54, of Great Britain.

World Chief Warrant Officer Philippe Latulippe of Canada walked 256.54 miles at Ottawa, Canada on 24-27 April 1972 in 81 hours 55 minutes.

British Lt.-Col. Richard Crawshaw O.B.E. T.D. (b. 1917), M.P. for Toxteth, Liverpool walked 255.84 miles in 76 hours 10 mins. round the 1.64 mile long Aintree Motorcycle track near Liverpool, Lancashire on 21-24 April 1972 in support of N.S.P.C.C. fund raising. He had six brief stops.

The longest officially controlled walking race was that of 3,415 miles from New York to San Francisco, U.S.A., from 3 May to 24 July 1926, won by A. L. Monteverde aged 60, occupying 79 days 10 hours 10 minutes. In 1909 Edward Payson Weston walked 7,495 miles on a trans-continental and return walk in 181 days.

North America coast to coast John Lees, 27 of Brighton, England between 13 Apr. and 6 June 1972, walked 2,876 miles across the U.S.A. from City Hall, Los Angeles to City Hall, New York City in 53 days 12 hours 15 minutes (average 53.746 miles a day). This betters the time of 54 days (average 53.29 miles a day) for *running* the distance completed by John Bull (South Africa) in May 1972.

Walking backwards The greatest ever exponent of reverse pedestrianism has been Plennie L. Wingo of Abilene, Texas, who started on his 8,000 mile trans-continental walks on 15 Apr. 1931 from Fort Worth, Texas to Istanbul, Turkey. His best distance in a day (12½ hours) was 45 miles.

SWIMMING

The greatest recorded distance ever swum is 1,826 miles down the Mississippi, U.S.A. by Fred P. Newton, 27, from 6 July to 29 Dec. 1933. He was 742 hours in the water between Ford Dam near Minneapolis and Carrollte Ave., New Orleans, Louisiana. The water temperature fell to 47° F. and Newton used olive oil and axle grease.

The longest duration swim ever achieved was one of 168 continuous hours, ending on 24 Feb. 1941, by the legless Charles Zibbelman, *alias* Zimmy (b. 1894) of the U.S.A., in a pool in Honolulu, Hawaii, U.S.A.

The greatest distance covered in a continuous swim is 288 miles by Clarence Giles from Glendive to Billings, Montana in the Yellowstone River in 71 hours 3 mins. on 30 June to 3 July 1939.

The longest duration swim by a woman was 87 hours 27 minutes in a pool by Mrs. Myrtle Huddleston of New York City, N.Y., U.S.A., in 1931.

Longest on a raft The longest recorded survival alone on a raft is 133 days (4½ months) by Second Steward Poon Lim (born Hong Kong) of the U.K. Merchant Navy, whose ship, the S.S. *Ben Lomond,* was torpedoed in the Atlantic 750 miles off the Azores at 11.45 a.m. on 23 Nov. 1942. He was picked up by a Brazilian fishing boat off Salinas, Brazil, on 5 April 1943 and was able to walk ashore. In July 1943, he was awarded the B.E.M.

The longest intentional single-handed voyage on a raft was one of 7,450 miles by William Willis (born in Germany, 1893) of the U.S.A., who arrived at Upolu, Western Samoa, on 12 Nov. 1963, accompanied by two cats, on his steel-hulled trimaran raft *Age Unlimited* (32 by 20 feet), after a 130-day voyage across the Pacific Ocean. He had been cast off 50 miles off Callao, Peru, on 5 July 1963.

CYCLING

The duration record for cycling on a track is 168 hours (7 days) by Syed Muhammed Nawab, aged 22, of Lucknow, India, in Addis Ababa, Ethiopia, in 1964. The monocycle duration record is 11 hours 21 minutes (83.4 miles) by Raymond Le Grand at Maubeuge, France, on 12 Sept. 1955. The longest cycle tour on record is one of 135,000 miles by Mishreelal Jaiswal (b. 1924) of India, through 107 countries from 1950 to 5 April 1964, ending in San Francisco, California, U.S.A. He wore out five machines.

MARRIAGE AND DIVORCE

Most The greatest number of marriages accumulated in the monogamous world is 19 by Glynn de Moss Wolfe (U.S.) (b. 1908) who married for the 19th time since 1930 his 17th wife Gloria, aged 23, on 22 Feb. 1969. His total number of children is, he says, 31. In 1955 he was reputedly worth $500,000 but recently testified to be living on welfare. The most often marrying millionaire was Thomas F. Manville (1894-1967) who contracted his 13th marriage to his 11th wife Christine Erdlen, aged 20, in New York City, U.S.A., on 11 Jan. 1960 when aged 65. His shortest marriage (to his seventh wife) effectively lasted only 7½ hours. His fortune came from asbestos, none of which he could take with him.

Mrs. Beverly Nina Avery, then aged 48, a barmaid from Los Angeles, California, U.S.A., set a monogamous world record in October 1957 by obtaining her sixteenth divorce from her fourteenth husband, Gabriel Avery. She alleged outside the court that five of the 14 had broken her nose.

Reports in April 1959 that Francis Van Wie, a conductor on the street-cars of the San Francisco

Britain's oldest bridegroom — the 98 year old Edward Simpson

Municipal Railway, California, U.S.A., had married his 18th wife, one Minnie Reardon, were later revised when it was discovered that some of his earlier marriages were undissolved. The widely publicized story of Bora Mičić, 44, of Milesevo, Boznia who reputedly married 79 times and divorced 78 times between 1944 and 1970, is not regarded as authentic by Yugoslav diplomatic sources.

Britain Seven times married individuals in Britain include Sir Francis Cook Bt. (b. 1907) and Mr. Lionel Birch.

Oldest Bride and Bridegroom The oldest bridegroom on record was Ralph Cambridge, 105, who married Mrs. Adriana Kapp, 70, at Knysna, South Africa on 30 Sept. 1971. The British record was set by Edward Simpson, 98, who married Mrs. Eva Midwinter, 82, at Swindon, Wilts. on 8 Dec. 1971.

The British record for collective age is 187 years by Alfred Caple, 91, and Kate Benson, Britain's oldest bride at 96 married in Stoke Newington, London, on 3 Aug. 1971.

Longest engagement The longest engagement on record is one of 67 years between Octavio Guillen, 82 and Adriana Martinez, 82. They finally took the plunge in June 1969 in Mexico City, Mexico.

Longest Marriage *World* The longest recorded marriage is one of 86 years between Sir Temulji Bhicaji Nariman and Lady Nariman from 1853 to 1940 resulting from a cousin marriage when both were five. Sir Temulji (b. 3 Sept. 1848) died, aged 91 years 11 months, in August 1940 at Bombay. Probably the longest marriage now existing is that between Edd (105) and Margaret (99) Hollen (U.S.) who celebrated their 83rd anniversary on 7 May 1972. They were both living in June 1972. They were married in Kentucky on 7 May 1889.

Britain James Frederick Burgess (born 3 March 1861, died 27 Nov. 1966) and his wife Sarah Ann, *née* Gregory (born 11 July 1865, died 22 June 1965) were married on 21 June 1883 at St. James's, Bermondsey, London, and celebrated their 82nd anniversary in 1965.

Most married James and Mary Grady of Illinois, U.S.A. ha⋅ married each other 27 times as a protest against th existence of divorce in the period 1964-69. They ha⋅ married in 25 different States, 3 times in a da (16 Dec. 1968), twice in an hour and twice ⋅ television.

Mass ceremony The largest mass wedding ceremony was one of 7⋅ couples officiated over by Sun Myung Moon of th Holy Spirit Association for the Unification of Wor Christianity in Seoul, South Korea in October 197 The response to the question "Will you swear to lo⋅ your spouse for ever?" is "Ye".

Eating out The world champion for eating out is Fred E. Magel Chicago, Illinois, U.S.A. who since 1928 has dined more than 34,509 restaurants in 60 nations as⋅ restaurant grader (to Nov. 1971). He asserts the mo⋅ expensive is Voisins, Park Avenue, New York Cit U.S.A. where a solo lunch cost him $26.50 (mo than £11) and the one serving the largest helpings⋅ Zehnder's Hotel, Frankenmuth, Michigan, U.S.A. ⋅ Magel's favourite dishes are South African ro⋅ lobster and mousse of fresh English strawberries.

Party giving The most expensive private party ever thrown w⋅ that of Mr. and Mrs. Bradley Martin of Troy, N.⋅ U.S.A. staged at the Waldorf Hotel, Manhattan February 1897. The cost to the host and hostess w⋅ estimated to be $369,200 in the days when doll⋅ were made of gold.

Toast-masters The Guild of Professional Toastmasters (found⋅ 1962) has only 12 members. Its founder and Pre⋅ dent, Ivor Spencer, has listened to 21,670 speeches 7 May 1969, including one in excess of 2 hours by t maudlin victim of a retirement luncheon. The Gu⋅ also elects the most boring speaker of the year, but ⋅ professional reasons, does not publicize the winne⋅ name. Red coats were introduced by the earli⋅ professional William Knight-Smith (d. 1932) *c.* 19⋅

Working week The longest working week (maximum possible 1⋅ hours) is up to 139 hours at times by some housem⋅ and registrars in some hospitals. This peak value w⋅ alleged by Dr. Adrian Cox at the Norfolk a⋅ Norwich Hospital in November 1971.

Working career The longest recorded working career in one job⋅ Britain was that of Miss Polly Gadsby who start⋅ work with Archibald Turner & Co. of Leicester at ⋅ age of 9. In 1932, after 86 years service, she was sti⋅

Polly Gadsby, who worked for 86 years with a Leiceste⋅ elastic company until her death in 1932.

her bench wrapping elastic aged 95. Mr. Ernest Turner of Ramsgate, Kent has been working since 1886 (minding sheep at 2s. 6d. a week) and in January 1972 was a canteen cleaner for Volkswagen aged 93. His son, a retired old age pensioner, has to get up at 6.30 a.m. every morning to drive 'my dad' to work.

Longest pension Miss Millicent Barclay, daughter of Col. William Barclay was born posthumously on 10 July 1872 and became eligible for a Madras Military Fund pension to continue until her marriage. She died unmarried on 26 Oct. 1969 having drawn the pension for every day of her life of 97 years 3 months.

MISCELLANEOUS ENDEAVOURS

Apple peeling The longest single unbroken apple peel on record is one of 1,568½ inches (130 ft. 8½ ins.) peeled by Frank Freer (U.S.) in 8 hours at Wolcott, N.Y., on 17 Oct. 1971. The apple was 15 inches in diameter.

Apple picking The greatest recorded performance is 235.8 U.S. bushels (228.5 Imperial bushels) picked in 8 hours by Harold Oaks, 21, at his father's ranch, Hood River, Oregon, U.S.A. on 2 Oct. 1971.

Coal carrying The record time for the annual "World Coal Carrying Championship" over the uphill 1,080 yards course at Ossett cum Gawthorpe, Yorkshire, England with a 112 lb. sack is 4 minutes 36 seconds by Tony Nicholson, 26, of Penrith, Cumberland on 3 Apr. 1972. The non-stop distance record carrying 1 cwt. is 12¼ miles in 3 hours 40 minutes from Perranporth to Cambourne, Cornwall by E. John Rapson on 4 April 1953.

Bag-pipes The longest duration pipe has been one of 50 hours by William Donaldson, Donald Grant, John Lovie and William Wotherspoon of Aberdeen University on 21-23 April 1969. The comment of some local inhabitants after the "lang blaw" was "Thank God there's nae smell".

Balancing on one foot The longest recorded duration for balancing on one foot is 5½ hours by Olof Hedlund, 19, at Skelleftea, Sweden on 3 Feb. 1972. The disengaged foot may not be rested on the standing foot nor may any sticks be used for support or balance.

Balloon racing The largest balloon release on record has been one of 100,000 helium balloons at the opening of "Transpo 72" at Dallas Airport, Washington D.C. on 27 May 1972. The longest authenticated balloon flight is one of 1,200 miles from Grantham Football Ground, Lincolnshire (released by Mr. R. Fenn on 31 Aug. 1971) and found near Skelleftea, Northern Sweden on 24 Oct. 1971.

Ballooning (Hot Air) The world's endurance and distance records for hot-air ballooning are 8 hrs. 30 mins. by Matt. Wiedertehr, 42, in an AX-5 from St. Paul, Minnesota 255 miles to Bankston, Iowa on 29 Mar. 1972. The altitude record is 31,500 feet by Karl H. Stefan, 54 on 19 June 1971. The record-holder for hot-air ballooning records is Ray Munro with 34 F.A.I. ratified records. On 1 Feb. 1970 he flew 158.34 miles across the Irish Sea in 4 hours 52 mins. He also has 50 honorary citizenships.

Ball punching Ron Renaulf (Australia) equalled his own world duration ball punching record of 125 hours 20 minutes at 10.20 p.m. on 31 Dec. 1955, at the Esplanade, Southport, Queensland, Australia.

Band marathons The longest recorded "blow-in" is 8 hours by the Harwich Grange Brass Band at Dovercourt, Essex on 14 Aug. 1971. Each bandsman was allowed 5 minutes per hour to regain his wind. The record for a one-man band is 7 hours (no breaks) by Johnny Magoo on drums, harmonica and stylaphone at Strood, Kent on 22 May 1971.

Barrel jumping The greatest number of barrels jumped by a skater is 17 (total length 28 feet 8 inches) by Kenneth LeBel at the Grossinger Country Club, New York State, U.S.A., on 9 Jan. 1965.

Bed of nails The duration record for lying on a bed of nails (needle-sharp 6-inch nails 2 inches apart) is 25 hours 20 minutes by Vernon C. Craig (Komar, the Hindu *fakir*) at Wooster, Ohio, U.S.A. 22-23 July 1971. Much longer durations are claimed by uninvigilated *fakirs*—the most extreme case being *Silki* who claimed 111 days in Sao Paulo, Brazil ending on 24 Aug. 1969. The greatest weight borne on a bed of nails is also by Komar with 4 persons aggregating 992 lb.

167

(70 st. 12 lb.) standing on him in Honolulu, Hawaii on 7 Feb. 1972.

Bed-pushing The longest recorded push of a normally sessile object is of 604 miles in the case of a wheeled hospital bed by a team of 12 from Box Hill High School, Victoria, Australia on 19-24 Aug. 1972.

Bed race The record time for the annual Knaresborough Bed Race (established 1966) in Yorkshire is 15 mins. 54 secs. for the 2½ mile course across the River Nidd by the Leeds Regional Hospital Board team, from a field of 34, on 5 June 1971.

Best man The world's champion "best man" is Mr. Wally Gant, a bachelor fishmonger from Wakefield, Yorkshire, who officiated for the 50th time since 1931 in December 1964.

Big wheel riding The endurance record for riding a Big Wheel is 14 days 21 hours by David Trumayne, 22, at Ramsgate, Kent ending on 8 June 1969. He completed 62,207 revolutions. Richard Ford, 30, sat for 20 days 16½ hours in a 40-foot Ferris Wheel in San Francisco, California in January 1971. It did not, however, revolve at night.

Body jump The greatest number of "bodies" cleared in a motorcycle ramp jump is 41 by Sgt.-Maj. Thomas Gledhill, B.E.M., 41, of the Royal Artillery Motorcycle Display Team on a 441 c.c. B.S.A. Victor G.P. at Woolwich, Greater London on 4 June 1971. The 41st man was Capt. Tony Scarisbrick. Tony Yeates cleared 84 feet (*equivalent* to 55 men) at Swindon in 1970.

Bomb defusing The highest reported number of unexploded bombs defused by any individual is 8,000 by Werner Stephan in West Berlin, Germany, in the 12 years from 1945 to 1957. He was killed by a small grenade on the Grunewald blasting site on 17 Aug. 1957.

Bond signing The greatest feat of bond signing was that performed by L. E. Chittenden (d. 1902), the Registrar of the United States Treasury. In 48 hours (20-22 March 1863) he signed 12,500 bonds worth $10,000,000 (now £4,166,666), which had to catch a steam packet to England. He suffered years of pain and the bonds were never used.

Boomerang throwing The earliest mention of a word similar to *boomerang* is *wo-mur-rang* in Collins *Acct. N.S. Wales Vocab.* published in 1798. The earliest certain account of a returning boomerang (term established, 1827) was in 1831 by Major (later Sir Thomas) Mitchell.

The longest measured throws for a return type are ones of 90 yards with an orbital perimeter of 250 yards with a 6 oz. vulcanized fibre boomerang by Bob

Bob Burwell of Australia, Champion boomerang thrower

and Jack Burwell of Slack's Creek, Queensland. Nov. 1971 Jeff Lewry (Australia) threw well pas⟨ steward at 85½ yards at Palmerston, New Zeala⟨ with a 16 inch boomerang.

Brick carrying The record for the annual Narrogin Brick Carry⟨ contest in Western Australia (instituted in 1960) 40.0 miles by Ronald D. Hamilton on 10 Oct. 19⟨ The 8 lb. 12 oz. wire-cut semi-pressed brick has to carried in a downward position with a nomina⟨ ungloved hand. The feminine record for a 7¾ lb. br⟨ is 1.6 miles by Pat McDougall, aged 16, but Jeane⟨ Bartlett of Swindon, Wiltshire carried 8 lb. 13¾ oz. brick more than 1.49 miles on 4 J⟨ 1969.

Bricklaying The world record for bricklaying was established⟨ 1937 by Joseph Raglon of East St. Louis, Illinc⟨ U.S.A., who, supported by assistants, placed 3,4⟨ bricks in 60 minutes of foundation-work—at a rate⟨ nearly 58 a minute.

The record for constructional bricklaying was⟨ when J. E. Bloxham, of Stratford-upon-Avon, E⟨ land laid a 13½-foot wall of 5,188 bricks in 7 hours⟨ minutes with two assistants on 28 May 1960. It v⟨ also reported that Mr. C. Hull of Sheffield, Yorksh⟨ laid 860 bricks in 60 minutes on 24 Nov. 1924.

Brick throwing The greatest reported distance for throwing a st⟨ dard 5 lb. building brick is 135 feet 8 inches⟨ Robert Gardner at Stroud, Gloucestershire, Engla⟨ in the annual contest on 18 July 1970.

Burial alive The longest recorded burial alive is one of 100 d⟨ ending on 17 Sept. 1968 in Skegness by Mrs. Em⟨ Smith of Ravenshead, Nottinghamshire, Engla⟨ The male record is 78 days by Bill Kearns, 36,⟨ South Hiendley, Yorkshire, from 21 June to 7 Se⟨ 1969.

The record in a "regulation" size coffin is 242 ho⟨ 58 minutes by Tim Hayes of Cóbh, Ireland from⟨ May to 2 June 1971 14 feet down in Naas, ⟨ Kildare. His coffin was 6 feet 3 inches long, 14 inc⟨ deep and 21 inches wide at the shoulder tapering⟨ 12 inches at the ankle.

Clapping The duration record for continuous clapping is⟨ hours 6 minutes by Nicholas Willey, 18 and Chris⟨ pher Floyd, 17 of Canford School, Dorset, Engla⟨ on 13-14 Dec. 1968. They sustained an average⟨ 140 claps per minute and an audibility range of⟨ least 100 yards.

Club swinging Bill Franks set a world record of 17,280 revoluti⟨ (4.8 per second) in 60 minutes at Webb's Gymnasiu⟨ Newcastle, N.S.W., Australia on 2 Aug. 1934.⟨ Dobrilla swung continuously for 144 hours at Co⟨ N.S.W. finishing on 15 Sept. 1913.

Coal shovelling The record for filling a half-ton hopper with coa⟨ 56.6 seconds by D. Coghlan of Reefton, New Zeal⟨ on 3 Jan. 1969.

Commuter Most durable Bruno Leuthardt commuted 370 miles each day⟨ the 11 years 1957-67 from Hamburg to teach in⟨ Bodelschwingh School, Dortmund, West Germa⟨ He was late only once due to the 1962 Hamb⟨ floods.

Competition winnings The largest individual competition prize win⟨ record is $307,500 (then £109,821) by Herber⟨ Idle, 55, of Chicago in an encyclopaedia contest⟨ by Unicorn Press Inc. on 20 Aug. 1953.

The highest value first prize offered in Britain⟨ been a £21,000 cash alternative to a $50,000 N⟨ York spending spree offered by Soft Blue B⟨ Luxury Margarine in a contest which closed

Endurance and Endeavour

30 Nov. 1971. It was won by Mrs. Susan B. Jenkins of Kirby, Lancashire, who took the cash.

DANCING
The largest dance ever staged was that put on by the Houston Livestock Show at the Astro Hall, Houston, Texas, U.S.A. on 8 Feb. 1969. The attendance was more than 16,500 with 4,000 turned away.

Marathon dancing must be distinguished from dancing mania, which is a pathological condition. The worst outbreak of dancing mania was at Aachen, Germany, in July 1374, when hordes of men and women broke into a frenzied dance in the streets which lasted for hours till injury or complete exhaustion ensued.

The most severe marathon dance staged as a public spectacle in the U.S.A. was one lasting 3,780 hours (22 weeks 3½ days) completed by Callum L. deVillier, 24 and Vonny Kuchinski, 20 at Sommerville, Massachusetts, U.S.A. from 28 Dec. 1932 to 3 June 1933. In the last two weeks the rest allowance was cut from 15 minutes per hour to only 3 minutes while the last 52½ hours were continuous. The prize of $1,000 was equivalent to less than 26½ cents per hour.

Ballet Among the world's greatest ballet dancers, Vatslav Fomich Nijinsky (1890-1950), a Russian-born Pole, was alone in being credited with being able to achieve the *entrechat dix*—crossing and uncrossing the feet 10 times in a single elevation. This is not believed by physical education experts since no high jumper can stay off the ground for more than 1 second and no analysable film exists.

Most turns The greatest number of spins called for in classical ballet choreography is the 32 *fouettés en tournant* in "Swan Lake" by Pyotr Ilych Chaykovskiy (Tschaikovsky) (1840-1893). Miss Rowena Jackson, of New Zealand, achieved 121 such turns at her class in Melbourne, Victoria, Australia, in 1940.

Most curtain calls The greatest recorded number of curtain calls ever received by ballet dancers is 89 by Dame Peggy Arias, D.B.E. *née* Hookham (born Reigate, Surrey, 18 May 1919), *alias* Margot Fonteyn, and Rudolf Hametovich Nureyev (born in a train near Ufa, U.S.S.R., 17 Mar. 1939) after a performance of "Swan Lake" at the Vienna Staatsoper, Austria, in October 1964.

Ballroom The individual continuous world record for ballroom
Marathon dancing is 106 hours 5 minutes 10 seconds by Carlos Sandrini in Buenos Aires, Argentina, in September 1955. Three girls worked shifts as his partner.

Champions The world's most successful professional ballroom dancing champions have been Bill Irvine, M.B.E. and Bobby Irvine, M.B.E., who have been undefeated as World Professional Champions since 1960.

Charleston The Charleston duration record is 25 hours by Tom Garrett, 23, at Pensacola, Florida, U.S.A. on 8-9 Oct. 1971.

Flamenco The fastest flamenco dancer ever measured is Solero de Jerez aged 17 who in Brisbane, Australia in Sept. 1967 in an electrifying routine attained 16 heel taps per second or a rate of 1,000 a minute.

Go-go The duration record for go-go dancing (Boogoloo or Reggae) is 108 hours (with 5 minute breaks each hour) by Jane Berins, 16, of Glinton, Peterborough on 24-28 March 1970.

Jiving The duration record for non-stop jiving is 40 hours by Gordon Lightfoot and Kathleen Fowler at Penrith, on 22-24 April 1960. Breaks of 3½ minutes per hour were permitted for massage. This time was equalled by Terry Ratcliffe, aged 16, and Christina Woodcroft,

Trevor Mitchell who set the world drumming record with 170 hours (7 days 2 hours)

aged 17, at Traralgon, Victoria, Australia, from 10.15 p.m. on 28 May to 2.13 p.m. on 30 May 1965.

Limbo The lowest height for a bar under which a clothed limbo dancer has passed is 6½ inches by Teresa Marquis of St. Lucia, West Indies, at the Guinness Distribution Depot, Grosvenor Road, Belfast, Northern Ireland on 15 April 1970. Her vital statistics are 34-24-36.

Twist The duration record for the twist is 102 hours by Mrs. Cathie Harvey (then Mrs. Cathy Connelly) at the Theatre Royal, Tyldesley, Lancashire ending on 29 Nov. 1964. She had 5 minutes time out per hour and 20 minutes every 4 hours.

Most expensive course The world's most expensive dance course has been the "Lifetime Executive Course" of Arthur Murray (b. Murray Teichmann, 4 April 1895) in the United States. It came after the Lifetime Course ($7,300) and the $9,000 "Gold Medal Course" and cost $12,000, making a total of $28,300 or now equivalent to £11,791.

Modern The longest recorded dancing marathon (50 minutes per hour) in modern style is one of 74½ hours by Julia Reece and Vic Jones at the Starlight Ballroom, Crawley, Sussex on 9-12 July 1970.

Dance band The most protracted session for a dance band is one of 321 hours (13 days 9 hours) by the Black Brothers of West Germany at Bonn ending on 2 Feb. 1968. Never less than a quartet were in action during the marathon.

Disc-jockey The longest continuous period of acting as a disc-jockey is 506 hours by Robert Airbright, 20, at the Sighthill Community Centre, Edinburgh, Scotland on 4 to 25 June 1971. L.P.'s are limited to 50% of total playing time. Jnr. Tech. Peter Jackson R.A.F. played 3,200 singles without rest periods for 144 hours on the Leeming Forces Network, Yorkshire ending on 14 Apr. 1972.

Drumming The world's duration drumming record is 171 hours 2 mins. by Trevor Mitchell, 20 at Oswald Hotel, Scunthorpe, Lincolnshire on 31 July to 7 Aug. 1971. He had a 5 minute rest allowance per hour.

169

Ducks and Drakes The best accepted ducks and drakes (stone-skipping) or Gerplunking record is 17 skips by Cdr. E. F. Tellefson U.S.N. of Mackinac Island, Michigan, U.S.A. in 1932. The modern video-tape verified record is a 13 skipper (7 plinkers and 6 pitty-pats) by Rolf Anselm in the Open Championship at Mackinac on 2 July 1971.

Egg and spoon racing David Smith and Peter Dilley of Chigwell, Essex completed a local 20-mile fresh egg and dessert spoon marathon in 5 hours 25 minutes on 27 July 1969.

Egg-shelling Two kitchen hands, Harold Witcomb and Gerald Harding shelled 1,050 dozen eggs in a 7¼ hour shift at Bowyers, Trowbridge, Wiltshire on 23 Apr. 1971. Both are blind.

Egg throwing The longest recorded distance for throwing a fresh hen's egg without breaking is 303 ft. 6 ins. at their 119th exchange by Rauli Rapo and Markku Kuikka at Rilhimäki, Finland on 28 Oct. 1971.

Jack Gently escaping from a strait-jacket when suspended 135 feet above the ground

Escapology The most renowned of all escape artists has been Ehrich Weiss *alias* Harry Houdini (1874-1926), who pioneered underwater escapes from locked, roped and weighted containers while handcuffed and shackled with irons. Jack Gently performed an escape from a straight jacket when suspended from a crane 135 feet from the ground for A.T.V. on 16 Aug. 1971.

Face-slapping The face-slapping contest duration record was set in Kiev, U.S.S.R., in 1931, when a draw was declared between Vasiliy Bezbordny and Goniusch after 30 hours.

Ferret legging Record durations for keeping a ferret down a pair of trousers with ankle ties are unsatisfactory owing to reports of the ferrets being tranquilized. The competitors are abusing the National Health Services in applications for free anti-tetanus injections.

Frisbee throwing Competitive Frisbee throwing began in 1958. The longest throw over level ground on record is one of 285 feet by Robert F. May in San Francisco on 2 July 1971.

Grave digging It is recorded that Johann Heinrich Karl Thiem sexton of Aldenburg, Germany, dug 23,311 grav during a 50-year career. In 1826 his understudy d *his* grave.

Guitar playing The longest recorded solo guitar playing marathon one of 93 hours by Peter Baco, 21, in Winnipe Canada in July 1970.

Gun running The record for the Royal Tournament naval gun r competition (instituted 1900, with present rules sin 1919) is 2 minutes 48.0 seconds by the Fleet Air Ar Gun Crew at Earl's Court, London in 1971. The bar alone weighs 8 cwt. The wall is 5 feet high and t chasm 28 feet across. This F.A.A. team trained l CPO R. Wilson, achieved an unofficial 2 mi 42.4 secs. in a practice run at Lee-on-the-Soler Hampshire in 1971.

Hair-dressing The world record for non-stop barbering is 80 hou (610 heads) by Rolf Elfso at Engelen, Stockhol: Sweden on 27-30 Nov. 1970. During the same ma: thon Gabino Padron dried and blow-waved 4 customers in 51 hours. The world's most expensi men's hairdresser is Tristan of Hollywood, Californ U.S.A. who charges any "client" $100 (£41.66) their first visit. This consists of a "consultatio followed by "remedial grooming". "Mr. Richar (the late Richard McGarth) cut, set and styled hair f 80 hours at Raymond's Salon, Colchester, Essex 8-11 Oct. 1971.

Handbell ringing The longest recorded handbell ringing recital was o of 10 hours 10 minutes by 10 ringers of the Cha Handbell Ringers, Kent playing in unison with minute breaks between pieces and 5 minute brea each hour on 13 May 1972.

Hand-shaking The world record for handshaking was set up I Theodore Roosevelt (1858-1919), President of t U.S.A., who shook hands with 8,513 people at a Ne Year's Day, White House Presentation in Washingto D.C., U.S.A. on 1 Jan. 1907. Outside public life t record has become meaningless because aspirar merely arrange circular queues and shake the sar hands repetitively.

HIGH DIVING
The highest regularly performed dive is that professional divers from La Quebrada ("the break the rocks") at Acapulco, Mexico, a height of 118 fe The leader of the 25 divers in the exclusive Club Clavadistas is Raúl Garcia (b. 1928). The base roc 21 feet out from the take-off, necessitate a leap of feet out. The water is 12 feet deep.

On 18 May 1885, Sarah Ann Henley, aged 24, jump from the Clifton Suspension Bridge, which crosses t Avon, England. Her 250-foot fall was slightly cush ned by her voluminous dress and petticoat acting a parachute. She landed, bruised and bedraggled, in t mud on the Gloucestershire bank and was carried hospital by four policemen. On 11 Feb. 1968 Jeffr Kramer, 24, leapt off the George Washington Brid 250 feet above the Hudson River, New York Ci N.Y. and survived. Of the 436 (to 13 Dec. 19: people who have made suicide dives from the Gold Gate Bridge, San Francisco, Califonia, U.S.A. sir 1937, four have survived. On 10 July 1921 stuntman named Terry leapt from a seaplane into t Ohio River at Louisville, Kentucky. The alleg altitude was 310 feet.

Samuel Scott (U.S.A.) is reputed to have made a d of 497 feet at Pattison Fall (now Manitou Falls) Wisconsin, U.S.A. in 1840, but this would ha entailed an entry speed of 86 m.p.h. The actual hei; was probably 165 feet.

Hitch-hiking The title of world champion hitch-hiker is claimed Devon Smith who from 1947 to 1971 thumbed li

"Captain" Alfred Schneider who simultaneously mastered 40 caged lions.

totalling 291,000 miles. In 1957 he covered all the then 48 U.S. states in 33 days. It was not till his 6,013th 'hitch' that he got a ride in a Rolls Royce.

The hitch-hiking record for the 873 miles from Land's End, Cornwall, to John o' Groats, Caithness, Scotland, is 29 hours by J. F. Hornsey on 12-13 Aug. 1971. The time before the first 'hitch' on the first day is excluded. This time was equalled in the reverse direction by Bernard Atkins, aged 18, of Donington, Lincolnshire in 11 lifts on 28 July 1966. The fastest time recorded for the round trip is 77 hours 20 minutes by Christine Elvery, 20 and Gwendolen Sherwin, 20, of which 61 hours 20 minutes was travelling on 24-27 March 1969.

Hiking The longest recorded hike is one of 18,500 miles through 14 countries from Singapore to London by David Kwan, aged 22, which occupied 81 weeks from 4 May 1957, or an average of 32 miles a day.

Hoop rolling In 1968 it was reported that Zolilio Diaz (Spain) had rolled a hoop 600 miles from Mieres to Madrid and back in 18 days.

House of cards The greatest number of storeys achieved in building houses of cards is 34 in the case of a tower using 7 packs by R. F. Gompers of the University of Kent, Canterbury on 3 May 1971. The highest claim authenticated by affidavit for a 7 or 8 card per storey "house" is 27 storeys by Joe Whitlam of Barnsley, Yorkshire on 28 Feb. 1972.

Human cannonball The record distance for firing a human from a cannon is 175 feet in the case of Emanuel Zacchini in the Ringling Bros. and Barnum & Bailey Circus, Madison Square Garden, New York City, U.S.A., in 1940. His muzzle velocity was 145 m.p.h. On his retirement the management were fortunate in finding that his daughter Florinda was of the same calibre.

Juggling The only juggler in history able to juggle—as opposed to "shower"—10 balls or eight plates was the Italian Enrico Rastelli, who was born in Samara, Russia, on 19 Dec. 1896 and died in Bergamo, Italy, on 13 Dec. 1931.

Kissing The most prolonged osculatory marathon in cinematic history is one of 185 seconds by Regis Toomey and Jane Wyman in *You're In the Army Now* released in 1940.

Kite-flying The greatest reported height attained by kites is 35,530 feet by a train of 19 flown near Portage by 10 Gary, Indiana high school boys on 13 June 1969. The

flight took 7 hours and was assessed by telescopic triangulation. The longest recorded flight is one of 44½ hours by Patrick Dunlop, 15 of San Diego, California on 3 Apr. 1972.

Knitting The longest recorded knitting marathon is one of 90 hours by Mrs. Janice Marwick (with 5-minute time out allowances per hour), at Pukekohe, New Zealand on 30 Aug.-3 Sept. 1971. The world's most prolific hand-knitter of all time has been Mrs. Gwen Matthewman (b. 1927) of Featherstone, Yorkshire, who retired on 31 Dec. 1970. In her last year she knitted 615 garments involving 438 lb. 14 oz. (7,022 oz.) of wool (equivalent to the fleece of 57 sheep). She had been timed to average 108 stitches per minute in a 30-minute test. Her technique has been filmed by the world's only Professor of Knitting—a Japanese. The finest recorded knitting is a piece of 2,464 stitches per square inch by Douglas Milne of Mount Florida, Glasgow, Scotland in May 1969.

Knot-tying The non-stop knot-tying marathon record is 76,504 links of a drummer's chain knot in ¾ inch tarred sisal robe in 50½ hours by four members of the 9th Beds. (Biggleswade) Scout Troop on 29-31 May 1969.

Leap frogging Fifteen members of the International Budo Association, Dinnington, Yorkshire covered 40 miles in 6,764 leaps on a 440 yards track on 25 Mar. 1972. An average of more than 40 leaps per lap was maintained.

Lightning most times struck The only living man in the world to be struck by lightning 4 times is Park Ranger Roy "Dooms" C. Sullivan (U.S.), the human lightning conductor of Virginia. Dooms' attraction for lightning began in 1942 (lost big toe nail), and was resumed in July 1969 (lost eye brows), in July 1970 (left shoulder seared) and, he hopes, finally on 16 April 1972 (hair set on fire).

Lion-taming The greatest number of lions mastered and fed in a cage by an unaided lion-tamer was 40, by "Captain" Alfred Schneider in 1925. Clyde Raymond Beatty (1903-65) handled more than 40 "cats" (mixed lions and tigers) simultaneously. Twenty-one lion-tamers have died of injuries since 1900. The youngest legally licensed animal trainer is Carl Ralph Scott Norman (Captain Carl) of Cardforth, Yorkshire (b. 23 Mar. 1968) who was licensed under the Performing Animals (Regulation) Act, 1925 on 13 Mar. 1970 aged 1 year 11 months.

The world's youngest licensed animal trainer "Captain Carl"

Log rolling The most protracted log rolling contest on record was one in Chequamegon Bay, Ashland, Wisconsin, U.S.A., in 1900, when Allan Stewart dislodged Joe Oliver from a 24-inch diameter log after 3 hours 15 minutes birling.

Message in a bottle The longest voyage recorded for a message in a bottle was one of 25,000 miles, from the Pacific to the shore of the island of Sylt in the North Sea on 3 Dec. 1968. The bottle had been dropped on 27 May 1947.

Morse The highest recorded speed at which anyone has received morse code is 75.2 words per minute—over 17 symbols per second. This was achieved by Ted R. McElroy of the United States in a tournament at Asheville, North Carolina, U.S.A. on 2 July 1939.

Needle threading The record number of strands of cotton threaded through a number 13 needle (eye ½ inch by $\frac{1}{16}$ of an inch) in 2 hours is 3,795 by Miss Brenda Robinson of the College of Further Education, Chippenham, Wiltshire on 20 March 1971.

Omelette making The greatest number of two-egg omelettes made in 30 minutes is 105 (26mins. 25 secs.) by Clement Raphael Freud (b. 1924) at The Victoria, Nottingham on 15 July 1971. The world's largest omelette occurred at Key West, Florida on 14 Oct. 1971 when a lorry carrying 60,000 eggs overturned and caught fire.

Pancake tossing Roy Woodward of the Preston Venture Scouts Unit, Wembley, London succeeded in tossing a pancake 2,105 times at Ealing on 15 Feb. 1972.

PARACHUTING

Earliest descent The earliest demonstration of a quasi-parachute was by Sébastien Lenormand of Lyons, France, with a conical canopy from an observation tower in Montpellier, France, in 1783. The first successful parachute jump from a balloon was by André-Jacques Garnerin (1769-1823) from 2,230 feet over Monceau Park, Paris, on 22 Oct. 1797. The earliest descent from an aeroplane was that of Captain Albert Berry, U.S. Army, over St. Louis, Missouri, on 1 March 1912. The first free fall from an aircraft was by Leslie LeRoy Irvin (1895-1966) at McCook Field near Dayton, Ohio, U.S.A. on 19 April 1919.

Longest delayed drop
Male The longest delayed drop and the greatest altitude for any parachute descent was achieved by U.S.A.F. doctor Captain Joseph W. Kittinger Jr. D.F.C., aged 32, over Tularosa, New Mexico, U.S.A. on 16 Aug. 1960. He stepped out of a balloon at 102,200 feet for a free fall of 84,700 feet (16.04 miles) lasting 4 minutes 38 seconds, during which he reached a speed of 614 m.p.h., despite a stabilizing drogue. He experienced a temperature of -94° F. His 28-foot parachute opened at 17,500 feet and he landed after a total time of 13 minutes 45 seconds. The step by the gondola door was inscribed "This is the highest step in the world".

The British record for a group delayed drop is 39,183 feet (7.43 miles) (from 41,383 feet) by 5 R.A.F. Parachute Jumping Instructors over Boscombe Down, Wiltshire on 16 June 1967. They were Sq.-Ldr. J. Thirtle; Flt.-Sgt. A. K. Kidd and Sgts. L. Hicks, P. P. Keane and K. J. Teesdale.

Female The women's delayed drop record is 46,250 feet (8.76 miles) by O. Komissarova (U.S.S.R.) on 21 Sept. 1965.

Biggest Free Fall 'Star' The world record for the greatest number of free falling parachutists to form a hand-holding circle is 24 over Perris Valley, California (70 seconds of manoeuvre from 14,500 feet) on 16 Jan. 1972.

172

The greatest achievement yet in free-falling is the formation of a 24-man star (see Column One below).

Highest escape The greatest altitude from which a successful parachute *escape* has been made from an aircraft is from a *Canberra* jet bomber by Flt.-Lt. John de Salis, aged 29, of Southampton, and Fg. Off. Patrick Lowe, aged 23, of Potters Bar, Hertfordshire, over Monyash Derbyshire, on 9 April 1958. Their plane exploded at 56,000 feet (10.60 miles) and they fell free in a temperature of -70° F. to a height of 10,000 feet at which altitude their parachutes were automatically opened. The longest descent recorded was one by Lt.-Col. William H. Rankin, U.S.M.C., from a Chance Vought F8U *Crusader* jet fighter at 47,000 feet on 2 July 1959. His "descent" through a thunderstorm over North Carolina took 40 minutes instead of the expected 11 minutes because of violent upward air currents.

Heaviest load The greatest single load ever dropped by parachute 50,450 lb. (22.52 tons) of steel plates from a U.S. Air Force C-130 *Hercules* with 6 'chutes near El Centro California on 28 Jan. 1970. The largest parachute made is a U.S. Air Force cargo parachute with 100-foot diameter, reported in September 1964.

Most descents The greatest number of parachute jumps is over 5,000 by Lt.-Col. Ivan Savkin (U.S.S.R.) (b. 1913), who reached 5,000 on 12 Aug. 1967. Since 1935 he has spent 27 hours in free fall, 587 hours floating and has dropped 7,800 miles. The British record was set by Sq.-Ldr. Charles Agate, A.F.C. (b. March 1905) of the R.A.F., who totalled 1,601 descents with packed parachutes between 1939 and 1946. The speed record is 81 jumps in 8 hours 22 minutes by Michael Davis 24, and Richard Bingham, 25, at Columbus, Ohio, U.S.A., on 26 June 1966.

Longest fall without a parachute The greatest altitude from which anyone has bailed out without a parachute and survived is 22,000 feet. This occurred in January 1942, when Lt. (now Lt.-Col.) I. M. Chisov (U.S.S.R.) fell from an Ilyushin 4 which had been severely damaged. He struck the ground a glancing blow on the edge of a snow-covered ravine and slid to the bottom. He suffered a fractured pelvis and severe spinal damage. It is estimated that the human body reaches 99 per cent. of its low level terminal velocity after falling 1,880 feet which takes 13 to 14 seconds. This is 117-125 m.p.h. at normal atmospheric pressure in a random posture, but up to 185 m.p.h. in a head down position.

Vesna Vulovic, 23 a Jugoslavenski Aerotransport hostess, survived when her D.C.-9 blew up at 33,330 feet over the Czechoslovak village of Česká Kamenice on 26 Jan. 1972. She was found inside a section of tail unit.

The British record is 18,000 feet by Flt.-Sgt. Nicholas Stephen Alkemade, aged 21, who jumped from a blazing R.A.F. *Lancaster* bomber over Germany on 23 March 1944. His headlong fall was broken by a fir tree and he landed without a broken bone in an 18-inch snow bank.

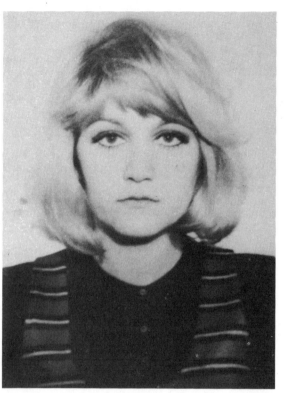

Miss Vesna Vulović — who survived ?ling 33,330 feet from a ?sintegrated airliner.

Highest landing The record landing height for parachute jumps is 23,405 feet by 10 U.S.S.R. parachutists onto the summit of Lenina Peak reported in May 1969. Four of the ten were killed.

Highest tower jump The highest jump ever achieved from a building is from the top of the 1,984-foot-tall KTUL-TV tower at Tulsa, Oklahoma, U.S.A. by Herb. Schmidt on 4 Oct. 1970.

Most northerly The most northerly parachute jump was made in 89° 30' N. on the polar ice cap on 31 March 1969 by Ray Munro, 47, of Lancaster, Ontario, Canada. His eyes were frozen shut instantly in the temperature of −39° F.

Piano-playing The longest piano-playing marathon has been one of 1,091 hours (45 days 11 hours) playing 22 hours every day from 11 Oct. to 24 Nov. 1970 by James Crowley, Jr., 30 at Scranton, Pennsylvania, U.S.A. The British record is 195 hours 17 minutes (with 5 minute breaks each hour) set in Manchester by Michael George, 24, of Heaton Norris, Cheshire, ending on 24 July 1969.

The women's world record is 133 hours (5 days 13 hours) by Mrs. Marie Ashton, aged 40, in a theatre in Blyth, Northumberland, on 18-23 Aug. 1958.

Piano smashing The record time for demolishing an upright piano and passing the entire wreckage through a circle 9 inches in diameter is 2 minutes 26 seconds by six men representing Ireland led by Johnny Leydon of Sligo, at Merton, Surrey, England on 7 Sept. 1968. The fastest time in which an upright piano has been sawn in half is 28 mins. 29 secs. by a team of four at the Highland Games, Dronfield Woodhouse, Derbyshire on 3 July 1971, using an Eclipse all-purpose saw.

Pillar box standing The record number of people to pile on top of a pillar box (6 square foot oval top) is 29, all students of the City of London College, Moorgate, in Finsbury Circus, London, E.C.2 on 21 Oct. 1970.

Pilot *Youngest* The youngest age at which anyone has ever qualified as a military pilot is 15 years 5 months in the case of Sgt. Thomas Dobney (b. 6 May 1926) of the R.A.F. He had understated his age (14 years) on entry.

Pipe smoking The duration record for keeping a pipe (3.3 grammes of tobacco) continously alight with only an initial match is 253 minutes 28 seconds by Yrjö Pentikäinen of Kuopio, Finland on 15-16 March 1968.

Plate spinning The greatest number of plates spun simultaneously is 44 by Holley Gray, on the *Blue Peter* T.V. show at the B.B.C. T.V. Centre, London on 31 Jan. 1972.

Pogo Stick Jumping Stephen Newman, 12 of Great Haywood near Stafford, completed 11,052 jumps on 27 June 1971.

Pole-squatting There being no international rules, the "standards of living" atop poles vary widely. The record squat is 8 months by Kenneth Gidge, an unemployed (or resting) actor in a hut on a 30 foot pole at Peabody, Mass. U.S.A. ending on 21 Dec. 1971.

The British record is 32 days 14 hours by John Stokes, aged 32, of Moseley, in a barrel on a 45-foot pole in Birmingham, ending on 27 June 1966. This is claimed as a world record for a barrel.

Modern records do not, however, compare with that of St. Daniel (A.D. 409-493), called Stylites (Greek, *stylos*=pillar), a monk who spent 33 years 3 months on a stone pillar in Syria. This is probably the oldest of all human records.

Pond bailing Elaborate rules exist for bailing a village pond with a No 1 size sewing thimble. The record of 57 gallons in 12 hours was set at the Memorial Pond, Castle Cary, Dorset on 31 July 1971.

Pop group The duration record for a 5-man pop-playing group is 122 hours 32 minutes at Portsmouth Polytechnic on 14-19 Feb. 1972. The group at no time, despite power cuts, sank below a quartet.

Pram pushing The greatest distance covered in pushing a pram in 24 hours is 272.8 miles on a track by a 20 strong team from Brisbane Boys's College, Toowong, Queensland on 18-19 Mar. 1972. A 249.5 mile pram-pushing 'safari' was completed at altitudes up to 7,000 feet by 4 Round Table teams from Nairobi and Thika, Kenya on 8-9 Jan. 1972. A team of 10 with an adult "baby" from Y.M.C.A., St. Austell, Cornwall covered 200.2 miles on 27-28 Apr. 1972.

Fastest "psych-iatrist" The world's fastest "psychiatrist" was the osteopath Dr. Albert L. Weiner of Erlton, New Jersey, U.S.A., who dealt with up to 50 patients a day in four treatment rooms. He relied heavily on narcoanalysis, muscle relaxants and electro-shock treatments. In December 1961 he was found guilty on 12 counts of manslaughter from using unsterilized needles.

Pub-crawling The world's champion pub-crawler is the abstemious Mr. Barry Cameron-Lunn of New Zealand. In Britain alone he has visited more than 12,500 pubs up to April 1972.

Quiz league The largest and oldest (established 1959) quiz league in the world is the Merseyside Quiz League, England with 82 teams and five major trophies.

Quoit throwing The world's record for rope quoit throwing is an unbroken sequence of 4,002 pegs by Bill Irby, Snr. of Australia in 1968.

Riding in armour The longest recorded ride in full armour is one of 145 miles from Wednesfield to London *via* Birmingham and Oxford in 6 days by Kenneth Quicke in Aug. 1956.

Riveting The world's record for riveting is 11,209 in 9 hours by J. Moir at the Workman Clark Ltd. shipyard, Belfast, Northern Ireland, in June 1918. His peak hour was his seventh with 1,409, an average of nearly 23½ per minute.

Rocking-chair The longest recorded duration of a "Rockathon" is 150 hours 18 minutes by Rande Dahl, 18 at the Seattle Sea Fair, Washington, U.S.A. ending on 30 July 1971.

Rolling pin The record distance for a woman to throw a 2 lb. rolling pin is 140 feet 4 inches by Sheri Salyer at Stroud, Oklahoma on 18 July 1970. The British record is 135 feet 2 inches by Marilyn Roberts at Eastbourne, Sussex on 16 June 1971.

Rope tricks Will Rogers (1879-1935) of the United States demonstrated an ability to rope three separate objects with 3 lariats at a single throw.

Longest safari The world's longest safari was one mounted in Africa by Peter Parnwell of Johannesburg, South Africa. It lasted 365 days, embraced 37 African countries and territories and extended over 30,000 miles.

Scooter riding The greatest distance covered by a team (18 boys, 7 girls) in 24 hours is 276.5 miles by the Wagga Wagga Methodist Youth Fellowship, N.S.W., Australia on 2-3 April 1971.

See-saw The most protracted session for see-sawing is one of 384 hours (16 days) by Ed. Garcia, 18 and Steve Pontes, 17 of San Leandro, California, U.S.A. on 29 Nov. to 8 Dec. 1971. Total time out was only 6 hours 39 minutes or 1.73 per cent. The "constant motion" record is 200 hours by Tom Adamo and Bob Rowell at Manassa, Va., U.S.A. from 16 Aug. 1971.

Sermon The longest sermon on record was delivered by Clinton Locy of West Richland, Washington, U.S.A., in February 1955. It lasted 48 hours 18 minutes and ranged through texts from every book in the Bible. A congregation of eight was on hand at the close. From 31 May to 10 June 1969 the Dalai Lama, the exiled ruler of Tibet, completed a sermon on Tantric Buddhism for five to seven hours per day to total 60 hours in India.

Sewing machines The fastest time recorded for sewing down a piece of tape 9 yards long with a treadle machine is 4 minutes 41.4 seconds by Harry Walgate at the Joint Reading Round Table, Berkshire on 19 Nov. 1969.

Shaving The fastest barber on record is Gerry Harley, who shaved 130 men in 60 minutes at The Plough, Gillingham, Kent on 1 April 1971. In an attempt to set a marathon he ran out of volunteer subjects.

Sheaf tossing The world's best performance for tossing an 8 lb. sheaf is 56 feet by C. R. Wiltshire of Geelong, Victoria, Australia in 1956. Contests date from 1914.

Shoe-shining In this category (limited to Boy Scouts (aged 11 to 13) and Cubs) 4 scouts shined 707 pairs of shoes in 18 hours in Lincoln on 8 Apr. 1972. They were S. Quincy, P. Gadd, A. Doyle and A. Taylor.

Fastest shorthand The highest recorded speeds ever attained under championship conditions are: 300 words per minute (99.64 per cent. accuracy) for five minutes and 350 w.p.m. (99.72 per cent. accuracy, that is, two insignificant errors) for two minutes by Nathan

Mrs June Meader, the only current holder of a 230 w.p.m. shorthand Pitman's Certificate.

Behrin (U.S.A.), in New York in December 192 Behrin (b. 1887) used the Pitman system invented 1837. Morris I. Kligman of New York current claims to be the world's fastest shorthand writer 300 w.p.m. He has taken 50,000 words in five hou and transcribed them in under five hours. Mr. G. Bunbury of Dublin, Ireland held the unique distin tion of writing at 250 w.p.m. for 10 minutes 23 Jan. 1894. The record for the Gregg system w held by Mr. Leslie Bear at 220 w.p.m. He retired editor of Hansard in Feb. 1972.

Currently the fastest shorthand writer in Britain June Swan (Mrs. Kenneth Meader) of North Finchl with a Pitman's Certificate for 230 w.p.m.

In the British Isles only five shorthand writers ha passed the official Pitman test at 250 w.p.m. for fi minutes:

Miss Edith Ulrica Pearson of London, on 30 June 1927.
Miss Emily Doris Smith of London, on 22 March 1934.
Miss Beatrice W. Solomon of London, in March 1942.
Mrs. Audrey Boyes (*née* Bell) of Finchley, London, in 195

Shouting The greatest number of wins in the national tov criers' contest is eight by Herbert T. Waldron of Gre Torrington, Devon. He won every year from 1957 1965, except for 1959. (See also Longest-rang voice, Chapter I.) In a test in November 1970 Richa Smith (b. 1947), the 1969 and 1970 champio registered 97 decibels.

Showering The most prolonged continuous shower bath record is one of 174 hours by David Hoffman at t University, Gary, Indiana from 21-27 Jan. 1972. T feminine record is 98 hours 1 minute by Paula Glen 18 and Margaret Nelson, 20 in Britain on 24 No 1971.

Singing The longest recorded solo singing marathon is one 48 hours and 880 songs by Jerry Cammarata Nathan's, Times Square, New York City on 12- June 1972. The longest recorded group marathon w performed by five students (at least four singing any one time) from Chippenham College of Furth Education, Wiltshire, who sang for 36 hours 5 mir on 10-12 Mar. 1972.

Skipping The greatest number of turns ever performed without a break is variously reported as 32,089 and 32,809 by J.P. Hughes of Melbourne, Victoria, Australia, in 3 hours 10 minutes on 26 Oct. 1953.

Other records made without a break:

Most turns in one jump	5 by Katsumi Suzuki, Tōkyō, early 1968.
Most turns in 1 minute	286 by J. Rogers, Melbourne, 10 Nov. 1937.
	and T. Lewis, Melbourne, 16 Sept. 1938.
Most turns in 2 hours	22,806 by Tom Morris, Sydney, 21 Nov. 1937.
Double turns	2,001 by K. Brooks, Brisbane, January 1955.
Treble turns	70 by J. Rogers, Melbourne, 17 Sept. 1951.
Duration	1,264 miles by Tom Morris, Brisbane‘ Cairns, Queensland 1967.

Slinging The greatest distance recorded for a sling-shot is 1,147 feet 4 inches using a 34-inch-long sling and a 7½ ounce stone by Melvyn Gaylor on Newport Golf Course, Shide, Isle of Wight on 25 Sept 1970.

moke ring blowing The highest recorded number of smoke rings formed from a single pull of a cigarette is 86 by Robert Reynard, 46 of George and Pilgrims’ Inn, Glastonbury, Somerset, on 1 Jan. 1972.

nakes and Ladders The longest recorded game of Snakes and Ladders has been one of 68¼ hours by a team of (4 always in play) 6 students from the Scottish College of Textiles on 12-15 Jan. 1972.

Snow Shoeing The fastest time recorded for covering a mile is 5 mins 18.6 secs. by Clifton Cody (U.S.) at Somersworth, New Haven, on 19 Feb. 1939.

“Space Hopping” A longest marathon claimed is one of 144 miles 452 yards in 41 hours by a team of 12 in a S.C.A.S. team at R.A.F. St. Athan, Barry, Glamorgan, Wales on 10-12 Dec. 1971.

Spinning The duration record for spinning a clock balance wheel by hand is 5 minutes 26.8 seconds by Philip Ashley, aged 16, of Leigh, Lancashire, on 20 May 1968.

Spitting The greatest distance achieved at the annual classic at Raleigh, Mississippi is 25 feet 10 inches by Don Snyder, 22, set in August 1970. He achieved 31 feet 6 inches at the Mississippi State University on 21 Apr. 1971. Distance is dependent on the quality of salivation, absence of cross wind and the co-ordination of the quick hip and neck snap. The record for projecting a melon seed is 37 feet 4 inches by Frank Ganger at the “World” Championships at Pardeeville, Wisconsin on 11 Sept. 1971. Serious spitters wear 12-inch boots so practice spits can be measured without a tape.

Stilt-walking The highest stilts ever successfully mastered were more than 21 feet from the ankle to the ground by the late Albert Yelding (“Harry Sloan”) 1901-1971 of Great Yarmouth, Norfolk. Hop stringers use stilts up to 15 feet. In 1892 M. Garisoain of Bayonne stilt-walked the last 8 kilometres into Biarritz in 42 minutes to average 7.1 m.p.h. In 1891 Sylvain Dornon stilt-walked from Paris to Moscow *via* Vilno in 50 stages for the 1,830 miles. Another source gives his time as 58 days.

Stretcher bearing The longest recorded carry of a stretcher case with a 10 stone “body” is 29.1 miles in 10 hours by a team of 8 from the 4th Ealing Company, London W.13 on 4 Dec. 1971.

Sub-mergence The longest submergence in a frogman’s suit is 100 hours 3 minutes by Mrs. Jane Lisle Baldasare, aged 24, at Pensacola, Florida, U.S.A., ending on 24 Jan. 1960. Mrs. Baldasare also holds the feminine underwater distance record at 14 miles. Her ex-husband, Fred Baldasare, aged 38, set the underwater distance record of 42 miles in his France-England Channel crossing of 18 hours 1 minute ending 10-11 July 1962.

Suggestion boxes The most prolific example on record of the use of any suggestion box scheme is that of Mr John Drayton of Pontypool, Monmouthshire, who plied British Rail with a total of 25,000 suggestions.

Swinging Jim Anderson and Lyle Hendrickson completed a 100 hour marathon on a swing at the Seattle Sea Fair, Washington, U.S.A. on 1 Aug. 1971.

Switchback riding The world endurance record for rides on on a roller coaster is 465 circuits of the John Collins Pleasure Park switchback at Barry Island, Glamorgan by ·a group of four men and two girls. The test lasted 31 hours, with two brief breaks, on 15-16 Aug. 1968.

Tailoring The highest speed at which a three-piece man’s suit has been made is 84 minutes including measuring and pressing by Wallis and Linnell Ltd. of Kettering, Northamptonshire on 18 Dec. 1969 on the occasion of a retirement presentation to Mr. Ernie Earl after 50 years service.

Talking The world record for non-stop talking is 138 hours (5 days 18 hours) by Victor Villimas of Cleveland, Ohio, U.S.A. in Leeds, Yorkshire, England, from 25-31 Oct. 1967. The longest continuous political speech on record was one of 29 hours 5 minutes by Gerard O’Donnell in Kingston-upon-Hull, Yorkshire, on 23-24 June 1959. The longest recorded lecture was one of 45 hours on “The Christian Faith and its Response” by the Rev. Roger North, 26, at Hartley Victoria Methodist College, Manchester on 15-17 May 1971.

A feminine non-stop talking record was set by Mrs. Alton Clapp of Greenville, North Carolina, U.S.A., in August 1958, with 96 hours 45 minutes 11 seconds. In the U.S.A. such contests have been referred to as “gab fests”.

T-bone dive The so-called T-bone dives by motor cycles off ramps over parked cars are measured by the number of cars but, owing to their variable size, distance is more significant. Gary Davis and Rex Blackwell both cleared 21 Datsun cars taking off at 85 m.p.h. in 138 foot jumps at Ontario, California, U.S.A. in March 1972. Evel Knievel, who jumped over 19 regular-size and compact cars (129 feet), disputes that more than 17 cars were cleared by Blackwell-Davis ahead of their take-offs.

Teeth-pulling The man with the “strongest teeth in the world” is John Massis of Belgium, who in 1969 demonstrated the ability to pull a 36-ton train along rails with a bit in his teeth.

TIGHTROPE WALKING
The greatest 19th century tightrope walker was Jean François Gravelet, *alias* Charles Blondin (1824-1897), of France, who made the earliest crossing of the Niagara Falls on a 3-inch rope, 1,100 feet long, 160 feet above the Falls on 30 July 1855. He also made a crossing with Harry Colcord, pick-a-back on 15 Sept. 1860. Though this is difficult to believe, Colcord was his agent.

Endurance The world tightrope endurance record is 214 hours by Henri Rochetain (b. 1926) of France on a wire 4,950 feet long, 550 feet above La Seuge river at Le Puy, France, on 13-21 Aug. 1966. The feminine record is 34 hours 15 minutes by Francine Pary, aged 17, on a wire 50 feet high at Toulouse, France, in February 1957.

Longest The longest walk by any funambulist was achieved by Henri Rochetain (b. 1926) of France on a wire 3,790 yards long slung across a gorge at Clermont Ferrand, France on 13 July 1969. He required 3 hours 20 minutes to negotiate the crossing.

Chester Peek successfully negotiating a 60 foot tunnel of fire.

High-wire act *Highest* The greatest drop beneath any high wire act was over the 750-foot-deep Tallulah Gorge, Georgia, U.S.A. where, on 18 July 1970, Karl Wallenda, 66, walked 821 feet in 616 steps with a 35 lb. pole in 17 minutes including pauses for two headstands. The highest altitude high-wire act was that of the Germans Alfred and Henry Traber on a 520-foot rope stretched from the Zugspitze (9,738 feet) to the Western Peak, Bavaria, Germany, during July and August 1953.

Tree-climbing The fastest tree-climbing record is one of 36 seconds for a 90-foot pine by Kelly Stanley (Canada) at the Toowoomba Show, Queensland, Australia in 1968.

Tree-sitting The duration record for sitting in a tree is 55 days from 10 a.m. 22 July to 10 a.m. 15 Sept. 1930 by David William Haskell (b. 1920) on a 4-foot by 6-foot platform up a backyard walnut tree in Wilmar (now Rosemund) California, U.S.A.

Tunnel of fire The longest tunnel of fire (petrol-soaked hoops of straw) negotiated by a trick motorcyclist is one of 60 feet by Chester Peek at Puyallup Raceway Park, Washington State, U.S.A., on 27 Feb. 1972.

TYPEWRITING

Fastest The highest recorded speeds attained with a ten-word penalty per error on a manual machine are:

One Minute: 170 words, Margaret Owen (U.S.A.) (Underwood Standard), New York, 21 Oct. 1918.
One Hour: 147 words (net rate per minute), Albert Tangora (U.S.A.) (Underwood Standard), 22 Oct. 1923.

The official hour record on an electric machine is 9,316 words (40 errors) on an I.B.M. machine, giving a net rate of 149 words per minute, by Margaret Hamma, now Mrs. Dilmore (U.S.A.), in Brooklyn, New York City, N.Y., U.S.A. on 20 June 1941.

In an official test in 1946 Stella Pajunas now Mrs. Garnand attained a speed of 216 words per minute on an I.B.M. machine.

Slowest Chinese typewriters were so complex that even the most skilled operator could not select characters from the 1,500 offered at a rate of more than 11 words a minute. The Hoang typewriter first produced in 1962 now has 5,850 Chinese characters. The keyboard is 2 feet wide and 17 inches high.

Longest The world duration record for typewriting on an electric machine is 150 hours by David J. Carnochan, 22, of the University College London Union from

noon on 24 Feb. to 6 p.m. 2 March 1970. His brea[ ] were 70 minutes less than the permitted 5 minutes p[ ] hour.

The longest duration typing marathon on a manu[ ] machine is 120 hours 15 minutes by Mike Howell, 23-year-old blind office worker from Greenfiel[ ] Oldham, Lancashire on 25-30 Nov. 1969 on [ ] Olympia manual typewriter in Liverpool. In aggreg[ ] ting 561,006 strokes he performed a weight mov[ ] ment of 2,482 tons plus a further 155 tons on movi[ ] the carriage for line spacing. On an electric machi[ ] the total figure would have been 565 tons.

Most travelled typewriter The world's most travelled typewriter is the Und[ ] wood Noiseless portable (rebuilt 1938) of Britai[ ] most famous sportswriter, Peter Wilson of the *Dai[ ] Mirror*. It has accompanied him in covering 45 spo[ ] in 51 countries and 60 trans-Atlantic flights for [ ] years (1935-1972).

Walking on hands The duration record for walking on hands is 871 mil[ ] by Johann Hurlinger, of Austria, who in 55 dai[ ] 10-hour stints, averaged 1.58 m.p.h. from Vienna [ ] Paris in 1900.

Wall of death The greatest endurance feat on a wall of death was [ ] hours 4 minutes by the motorcyclist Louis [ ] "Speedy" Babbs on a 32-foot diameter silo, refuellir[ ] in motion, at the Venice Amusement Pier, Californ[ ] on 11 Oct. 1929. In 1934 Babbs performed 1,0[ ] consecutive loop the loops sitting side-saddle in [ ] 18-foot diameter globe at Ocean Park Pier, Californ[ ] U.S.A. In a life of stunting, Babbs, who proclaim[ ] "Stuntmen are not fools", has broken 56 bones.

Whip cracking The longest stock whip ever "cracked" (*i.e.* the er[ ] made to travel above the speed of sound—760 m.p.h[ ] is one of 55 feet by "Saltbush" Bill Mills of Australi[ ]

Wood-cutting The world record for cutting six "shoes" to ascer[ ] and sever the top of a 16-foot high 15-inch diamet[ ] log is the 1 minute 31 seconds set by the Tasmani[ ] axeman, Doug Youd (born 1938). His brother R[ ] felled a tree 12 inches in diameter in 1961 in 1 minu[ ] 52.3 seconds.

The world record for sawing (hand-bucking) throug[ ] a 32-inch log is 1 minute 26.4 seconds by Paul [ ] Searls, aged 46, in Seattle, Washington State, U.S.[ ] on 5 Nov. 1953. The world record for double-hande[ ] sawing through an 18-inch white pine log is 10 [ ]

176

seconds by Bill Donnelly and Ernie Hogg at South-land, South Island, New Zealand, on 4 Dec. 1955, equalled by N. J. Thorburn and M. Reed at Whangarei, New Zealand, on 3 March 1956. Donnelly and Hogg sawed through a 20-inch white pine log in 12.9 seconds at Invercargill, New Zealand, on 11 Feb. 1956. The 24-inch white pine record is 18.8 seconds by Denis Organ and Graham Sanson at Stratford, North Island, New Zealand on 27 Nov. 1965.

Yo-yo The yo-yo originates from a Filipino jungle fighting weapon recorded in the 16th century weighing 4 lb. with a 20-foot cord. The word means "come-come". The craze was started by Louis Marx (U.S.A.) in

1929. The most difficult modern yo-yo trick is the double-handed cross-over loop the loop. Art Pickles of Shere, Surrey, the 1933-53 world champion once achieved 1,269 consecutive loop the loops. The individual continuous endurance record is 17 hours 4 minutes by Chet Brooks on the KRCR Radio Station, California, U.S.A. on 7-8 Apr. 1972.

Largest circus The world's largest permanent circus is Circus Circus Las Vegas, Nevada, U.S.A. opened on 18 Oct. 1968 at a cost of $15,000,000 (£6,250,000). It covers an area of 129,000 square feet capped by a 90-foot-high tent-shaped flexiglass roof. The new Moscow Circus, completed in 1968, has a seating capacity of 3,200.

The following circus acrobatic feats represent the greatest performed, either for the first time or, if marked with an asterisk, uniquely. A "mechanic" is a safety harness.

Flying Trapeze	Earliest Act	Jules Léotard (France)	Circus Napoléon, Paris	12 Nov. 1859
	Double back somersault	Eddie Silbon	Paris Hippodrome	1879
	Triple back somersault (female)	Lena Jordan (Latvia) to Lew Jordan (U.S.A.)	Sydney, Australia	April 1897
	Triple back somersault (male)	Ernest Clarke to Charles Clarke	Publiones Circus, Cuba	1909
	Triple and a half back somersault	Tony Steel to Lee Strath Marilees	Durango, Mexico	30 Sept. 1962
	Quadruple back somersault (in practice)	*Ernest Clarke to Charles Clarke	Orrin Bros. Circus, Mexico City, Mexico	1915
	Triple back somersault (bar to bar, practice)	Edmund Ramat and Raoul Monbar	Various	1905-10
	Head to head stand on swinging bar (no holding)	*Ed. and Ira Millette (née Wolf)	Various	1910-20
Horse back	Running leaps on and off	*26 by "Poodles" Hanneford	New York	1915
	Three-high column without "mechanic"	*Willy, Baby and Rene Fredianis	Nouveau Cirque, Paris	1908
	Double back somersault mounted	(John or Charles) Frederic Clarke	Various	c. 1905
	Double back somersault from a 2-high to a trailing horse with "mechanic"	Aleksandr Sergey	Moscow Circus	1956
Fixed Bars	Pass from 1st to 3rd bar with a double back somersault	Phil Shevette, Andres Atayde	Woods Gymnasium, New York, European tours	1925-27
	Triple fly-away to ground (male)	Phil Shevette	Folies Bergère, Paris	May 1896
	Triple fly-away to ground (female)	Loretto Twins, Ora and Pauline	Los Angeles	1914
Giant Spring Board	Running forward triple back somersault	John Cornish Worland, (1855-1933) of the U.S.A.	St. Louis, Missouri	1874
Risley (Human Juggling)	Back somersault feet to feet	Richard Risley Carlisle (1814-74) and son (U.S.A.)	Theatre Royal, Edinburgh	Feb. 1844
Acrobatics	Quadruple back somersault to a chair	Sylvester Mezzetti (voltiger) to Butch Mezzetti (catcher)	New York Hippodrome	1915-17
Aerialist	One arm swings 125 (no net) 32 feet up	Vicky Unus (La Toria) (U.S.A.)	Ringling Bros., Barnum & Bailey circuit	Nov. 1962
Teeter Board	Seat to seat triple back somersault	The 5 Draytons		1896
Wire-Juggling	16 hoops (hands and feet)	Ala Naito (Japan) (female)	Madison Square Garden, N.Y.	1937
Low Wire (7 feet)	Feet to feet forward somersault	Con Colleano	Empire Theatre, Johannesburg	1923
		Ala Naito (Japan) (female)	Madison Square Garden, N.Y.	1937
High Wire (30-40 feet)	Four high column (with mechanic)	*The Solokhin Brothers (U.S.S.R.)	Moscow Circus	1962
	Three layer, 7 man pyramid	Great Wallendas (Germany)	U.S.A.	1961
Ground Acrobatics	Stationary double back somersault	Francois Gouleau (France)		1905
	Four high column	The Picchianis (Italy)		1905
	Five high pyramids	The Yacopis (Argentina) with 3 understanders, 3 second layer understanders, 1 middle-man, 1 upper middleman and a top mounter	Ringling Bros., Barnum & Bailey circuit	1941

RICHEST
Billionaire
Daniel K.
Ludwig (U.S.)
now regarded
as the world's
richest
businessman
who has
pioneered
ship-welding,
mammoth
tankers and
who is the
world's
largest orange
producer

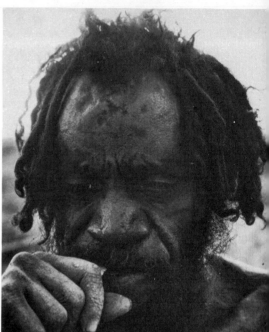

POOREST
One of the
last 20-25 re-
maining Aust-
ralian Aborig-
ines Pintibus
whose entire
collective
wealth could
be valued at
less than £5

WEALTH AND POVERTY

Richest rulers The Kingdom of Saudi Arabia derived an annual income of about $560,000,000 (then £200 million) from oil royalties in 1964, but the Royal Family's share was understood to be not more than £25,000,000. The Shaikh of Abu Dhabi, Zaid ibn Sultan Zaid al Nahayyan (b. 1917), has become extremely wealthy since the Murban oilfield began yielding in 1963, and by 1966 Abu Dhabi was estimated to have an income of $67,000,000 (then £23.9 million) which if divided equally would result in an income of $3,350 per head. Before World War II the income of Maj.-Gen. H. H. Maharajadhiraj Raj Rajeshwar Sawai Shree Yeshwant Rao Holkar Bahadur, G.C.I.E. (1908-61), the Maharaja of Indore, was estimated to be as high as £25,000,000 per annum. The state incomes of the 279 surviving rulers of India's 554 Princely States granted in 1947 were cut off in September 1970. It had been estimated that the Nizam of Hyderabad (1886-1967) was worth nearly £900 million at the time of his death.

The man with once the highest income in the world was H. H. Shaikh Sir Abdullah as-Salim as-Sabah, G.C.M.G., C.I.E. (1895-1965), the 11th Amir of Kuwait, with an estimated £2,600,000 per week or £135 million a year.

Private citizen There are currently five proclaimed dollar billionaires (a billion dollars is £383,771,930) in the United States. The dictum of one of them, Jean Paul Getty (b. Minneapolis, Minnesota, 15 Dec. 1892), that, "if you can count your millions, you are not a billionaire" might be extended to saying that the millions are not intended to be countable. The other accepted living billionaires are Howard Robard Hughes (b. Houston, Texas 24 Dec. 1905); John Donald MacArthur (b. Pittston, Pennsylvania, 1897); Haroldson Lafayette Hunt (b. 1889) of Dallas, Texas and Daniel K. Ludwig (b. South Haven, Mich., June 1897).

Fortune Magazine which in May 1968 assessed Mr. Getty at $1.338 billions and Mr. Hughes at $1.373 billion stated in January 1972 that Mr. Ludwig was richer than either.

Billionaires Probably the only other dollar "billionaires" in the United States have been John Davison Rockefeller, the first (1839-1937), Henry Ford, the first (1863-1947) and Andrew William Mellon (1855-1937). A "billion" dollars is now equivalent to £383,771,930. Rockefeller kept account of his personal expenditure in Ledger No. 1 all his life. He referred to competitors, all of whom he regarded as redundant, as "the dear people".

Centimillionaires and millionaires World *Fortune* Magazine in May 1968 estimated that there were 153 U.S. Centimillionaires (*i.e.* those with disposable assets of more than $100 million). The fastest centimillionaire has been Henry Ross Perot (b. Texarkana, Texas 1930), founder and President of Electronic Data Systems Corporation of Dallas, Texas in 1962. By 1968 his personal fortune was estimated at $320 million (£133,000,000). By December 1969 it was estimated that the value of his stock holding might have reached $1,500 million, but he later said he could raise $100 million from his own resources to buy the release of 1,361 U.S. P.o.W.'s in North Vietnam. It was estimated in 1961 that there were 50,000 millionaires in the United States of whom 13,500 came from the State of California. The 1968 total probably surpassed 100,000 of whom 2 succeeded in paying no taxation.

United Kingdom The wealthiest United Kingdom citizen is believed to be Sir John Reeves Ellerman, 2nd baronet (b. 21 Dec. 1909), a director of Ellerman Lines Ltd., whose father, Sir John Reeves Ellerman, Bt., C.H. (1862-1933), left £36,684,994, the largest will ever proved in the United Kingdom. His fortune estimated to be worth about £500 million. The highest death duties ever paid have been £18,000,000 on the estate of Hugh Richard Arthur Grosvenor, G.C.V.O., D.S.O., the 2nd Duke of Westminster (1879-1953), paid between July 1953 and August 1964.

The greatest will proved in Ireland was that of the 1st Earl of Iveagh (1847-1927), who left £13,486,146.

Millionairesses The world's wealthiest woman was probably Princess Wilhelmina Helena Pauline Maria of Orange-Nassau (1880-1962), formerly Queen of the Netherlands (from 1890 to her abdication, 4 Sept. 1948), with fortune which was estimated at over £200 million. The largest amount proved in the will of a woman in the United Kingdom has been the £4,075,550 (duty paid £3,233,454) of Miss Gladys Meryl Yule, daughter of Sir David Yule, Bt. (1858-1928), in August 1957. Mrs. Anna Dodge (later Mrs. Hugh Dillman) who was born in Dundee, Scotland, died on 3 June

1970 in the United States, aged 103, and left an estate of £40,000,000.

Youngest The youngest person ever to accumulate a millionaire estate was the child film actress Shirley Temple (b. Santa Monica, California 23 April 1928), formerly Mrs. John Agar, Jr., now Mrs. Charles Black, of the U.S.A. Her accumulated wealth exceeded $1,000,000 (then £209,000) before she was 10 years old. Her child actress career spanned 1934-39.

Earliest The earliest recorded self-made millionairess was Mrs. Annie M. Pope-Turnbo Malone (d. 1957), a laundress from St. Louis, Missouri, U.S.A., who in 1905 perfected the permanent straight treatment for those with crinkly hair.

Richest In May 1968 it was estimated that three members of
families the Irish-American Mellon family of the U.S.A., from Omagh, County Tyrone: Mrs. Alisa Mellon Bruce (1902-1969), Paul Mellon (b. 1907) and Richard King Mellon (b. 1900), were each worth between $500 million and $1,000 million (£416.6 million). Another 1968 estimate put the family fortune at more than $3,000 million (about £1,255 million). It has also been tentatively estimated that the combined wealth of the much larger du Pont family of some 2,100 members may be in excess of this figure.

The largest number of millionaires estates in one family in the British Isles is that of the Wills family of the Imperial Tobacco Company, of whom 14 members have left estates in excess of £1,000,000 since 1910. These totalled £55 million, of which death duties (introduced in 1894) have taken over £27,000,000.

Largest The largest recorded dowry was that of Elena Patiño,
dowry daughter of Don Simón Iturbi Patino (1861-1947), the Bolivian tin millionaire, who in 1929 bestowed £8,000,000 from a fortune at one time estimated to be worth £125,000,000.

Greatest Henrietta (Hetty) Howland Green (*née* Robinson)
miser (1835-1916) who kept a balance of over $31,400,000 (then £6.2 million) in one bank alone was so mean that her son had to have his leg amputated because of the delays in finding a *free* medical clinic. She herself lived off cold porridge because she was too mean to heat it and died of apoplexy in an argument over the virtues of skimmed milk. Her estate proved to be of $95 million (then £19 million).

SALARIES AND EARNINGS

Highest In Japan the National Tax Administration Agency
World publishes all identities and earnings of the preceeding year. The 1971 "Number One Man" was Mr Heima Seki, President of Sekihei Seibaku Co. of Sendai-shi with a gross income of Yen 3,890,940,000 (£4,851,546 at Y802.56 per £). Though his company is ostensibly in business for cleaning barley the income was generated by selling forest lard to his own real estate company. The highest salary in the United States is that of the Chairman of the Board and Chief Executive Officer of the General Motors Corporation, of Detroit, Michigan, U.S.A. James Roche (b. 1905) succeeded to this appointment on 30 Oct. 1967. His 1969-70 salary with bonuses was $765,858 (£319,107). The record gain from stock options was that of Ralph Cordiner, Chairman of the General Electric Co., who made a paper profit of $1,262,260 (now £525,941) on options exercised in 1957.

United Britain's highest paid business executive is Mr Richard
Kingdom Tompkins, Chairman of Green Shield the trading stamp company. His service agreement entitled him to 15 per cent. of profits which for the year ending 31 Oct. 1971 would have earned him £390,000. He waived £130,000. On 1972/73 full standard taxation rates it has been calculated that £185,600 of the £260,000 would be payable in income tax and surtax.

In July 1965 it was reported that Mr. Wilfred Harvey, then Chairman of the British Printing Corporation, was eligible under his commission agreement to have drawn £270,000 in 1964-65.

Highest The highest recorded wage in Britain is £290 in a week
wage paid to Jimmy Houston, 43, a stovepipe welder for a 6-day week including two all-night stints on the Isle of Grain, Kent, in 1970.

Highest The highest gross income ever achieved in a single year
income by a private citizen is an estimated $105,000,000 (then £21½ million) in 1927 by the Sicilian born Chicago gangster Alphonse ("Scarface Al") Capone (1899-1947). This was derived from illegal liquor trading and alky-cookers (illicit stills), gambling establishments, dog tracks, dance halls, "protection" rackets and vice. On his business card Capone described himself as a "Second Hand Furniture Dealer". Henry Ford, the first (1863-1947) earned about £25 million per annum at his peak.

Lowest The poorest people in the world are the surviving
incomes Pintibu (or Bindibu) of whom 42 were found in the Northern Territory of Australia in July 1957. They subsist with water from soak holes and by eating rats, lizards and yams. In September 1971 some 20 to 25 were still living. In September 1957 Chinese Government sources admitted that in some areas of the mainland the average annual income of peasants was 42 yuans (£6.90) per head. In 1964 China's average income per head was estimated at £25 per annum and the daily calorie intake at 2,200.

"Golden The most golden "golden handshake" was the
handshake" £83,575 tax-free compensation for loss of office
record received in 1954 by Sir Charles Blampied Colston, C.B.E., M.C., D.C.M. (1891-1969), Chairman and Managing Director of Hoover Ltd. Since the Finance Act of 1960, which made such payments taxable after the first £5,000, the greatest amount ever paid out is believed to be £124,000, which was announced on 29 June 1964 to have been paid to Philip Gordon Walker (b. 9 June 1912), the Managing Director of Albert E. Reed & Co. Ltd. (since renamed Reed International Ltd.) from 1951 until his resignation on 9 July 1963, shortly after the company had been merged with the International Publishing Corporation. After tax he received an estimated £35,000. The largest leaving present recorded in trade union history was one aggregating a reported £25,000 from branches of the Transport and General Workers' Union to its secretary the Rt. Hon. Frank Cousins (b. 1904) in Sept. 1969.

Return The largest amount of cash ever found and returned
of cash to its owners was $240,000 (£85,714) in unmarked $10 (£3.56½) and $20 (£7.13) bills found in a street in Los Angeles, California, U.S.A., by Douglas William Johnston, an unemployed negro, in March 1961. He received many letters, of which 25 per cent. suggested that he was insane.

Greatest The greatest bequest in a life-time of a millionaire
bequests were those of the late John Davison Rockefeller (1839-1937), who gave away sums totalling $750,000,000 (now £312.5 million). The greatest benefactions of a British millionaire were those of William Richard Morris, later the Viscount Nuffield, G.B.E., C.H. (1877-1963), which totalled more than £30,000,000 between 1926 and his death on 22 Aug. 1963. The Scottish-born U.S. citizen Andrew Carnegie (1835-1919) is estimated to have made bene-

factions totalling £70 million during the last 18 years of his life. These included 7,689 church organs and 2,811 libraries. He had started life in a bobbin factory at $1.20 per week.

The largest bequest made in the history of philanthropy was the $500,000,000 (£178,570,000) gift, announced on 12 Dec. 1955, to 4,157 educational and other institutions by the Ford Foundation (established 1936) of New York City, N.Y., U.S.A. The assets of the Foundation had a book value of $2,477,984,000 (now £1,032 million) in 1967.

Best dressed women The longest reign as the "Best Dressed Woman" was 15 years from 1938 to 1953 by the Duchess of Windsor (b. Bessie Wallis Warfield at Blue Ridge Summit, Pennsylvania, 19 June 1896, formerly Mrs. Spencer, formerly Mrs. Simpson). In January 1959 the New York Dress Institute put the Duchess and Mrs. William S. "Babe" Paley beyond annual comparison by elevating them to an ageless "Hall of Fame". Also later elevated was Mrs. Jacqueline Lee Kennedy-Onassis *née* Bouvier (born at Southampton, Long Island, New York, 28 July 1929). Including furs and jewellery, some perennials, such as Mrs. Winston F. C. "Cezee" Guest, Mrs. Paley and Mrs. Gloria Guinness, known as "The Ultimate", are reputed to spend up to $100,000 (£41,666) a year on their wardrobes. Mrs. Henry M. Flagler, the chatelaine of Whitehall, her husband's $300,000 establishment in Palm Beach, Florida, U.S.A. in the era 1902-1914, never wore any dress a second time. Her closets were nonetheless moth proof.

In January 1960 the Institute decided it was politic to list a Top Twelve, not in order of merit, but alphabetically. The youngest winner was Mrs. Amanda Carter Burden, aged 22, a step-daughter of the twice blessed Mr. William Paley (see above), on 13 Jan. 1966. After 1966 rankings were re-established.

GASTRONOMIC RECORDS

Records for eating and drinking by trenchermen do not match those suffering from the rare disease of bulimia (morbid desire to eat) and polydipsia (pathological thirst). Some bulimia patients have to spend 15 hours a day eating, with an extreme consumption of 384 lb. 2 oz. of food in six days by Matthew Daking, aged 12, in 1743 (known as Mortimer's case). Some polydipsomaniacs have been said to be unsatisfied by less than 96 pints of liquid a day. Miss Helge Andersson (b. 1908) of Lindesberg, Sweden was reported in January 1971 to have been drinking 40 pints of water a day since 1922—a total of 87,600 gallons.

The world's greatest trencherman is Edward Abraham ("Bozo") Miller (b. 1909) of Oakland, California, U.S.A. He consumes up to 25,000 calories per day or more than 11 times that recommended. He stands 5 feet 7½ inches tall but weighs from 20 to 21½ stone, with a 57-inch waist. He has been undefeated in eating contests since 1931 (see below). The bargees on the Rhine are reputed to be the world's heaviest eaters with 5,200 calories a day.

While no healthy person has been reported to have succumbed in any contest for eating or drinking non-alcoholic or non-toxic drinks, such attempts, from a medical point of view, must be regarded as *extremely* inadvisable, particularly among young people. Guinness Superlatives will not list any records involving the consumption of more than 2 litres (3.52 Imperial pints) of beer nor any at all involving spirits.

Specific records have been claimed as follows:

Baked Beans 1,220 cold beans one by one with a cocktail stick in 30 mins. by Clifford Pearce at Gerrards Cross, Buckinghamshire on 5 Dec. 1971.

Bananas 50½ in 10 minutes by Steyen Nel, 30 in Port Elizabeth, S. Africa, on 12 July 1970.

Monsieur W. Bley, who set a world speed record for opening oysters.

Beer	Lawrence Hill (b. 1942) of Bolton, Lancashire, drained a 2½-pint Yard of Ale 6½ seconds on 17 Dec. 1964. A 3-pint yard was downed in 10.15 seconds by Jac Boyle, 52, at The Bay Horse, Ormsgill, Barrow-in-Furness, Lancashire on 14 Ma 1971.
	The Oxford University "sconce" record is 12.0 seconds for 2 pints of beer set t the Australian, R. Hawke (University College) in 1955 and Clive Anderso (Magdalen) on 26 Feb. 1967. The record for a single pint is 1.36 seconds t George Purvis in Colchester, Essex on 29 Feb. 1972. The record for 2 litres (3.5 Imperial pints) is 11 seconds by J. H. Cochran (Class of 1925, Princetc University, New Jersey, U.S.A.) in Harry's New York Bar, Paris, on 26 June 193
Beer Upsidedown	2 pints in 44.2 seconds by Ernie Driver at Corby, Northamptonshire on 23 Ja 1972.
Cheese	16 oz. of Cheddar in 4 minutes 30 seconds by John Lombino of Alhambra Hig School, California, U.S.A., on 25 May 1971.
Chicken	27 (2 lb. pullets) by "Bozo" Miller (see above) at Trader Vic's, San Francisco California, U.S.A., in 1963.
Clams	437 in 10 minutes by Joe Gagnon (U.S.) at Everett, Washington, U.S.A. in Janua 1971.
Eggs	(Hard Boiled) 44 in 30 minutes by Georges Grogniet of Belgium on 31 May 195 (Soft Boiled) 25 in 3 minutes 1.8 seconds by Bill (Dink) Hewit, Bethlehem Pennsylvania on 2 Oct. 1971.
Frankfurters	18 (2 oz.) in 5 minutes by Mike Wright, 28 at Dewdrop Inn, Littlehampton, Suss on ?? Dec. 1971.
Gherkins	1 lb. in 1 min. 47.5 secs. by Peter L. Citron in Omaha, Nebraska, U.S.A. on 20 M 1971.
Goldfish (live)	225 by Roger Martinez at St. Mary's University, San Antonio, Texas, U.S.A. 6 Feb. 1970.
Grapes	1 lb. (unpipped) in 65.0 seconds by Leslie Carter, 24 at Bhisworth Fe Northamptonshire, on 20 May 1972.
Haggis	24 oz. haggis in 2 minutes 42 seconds by W. McVeigh at Corby, Northampton 23 Jan. 1972.
Hamburgers	77 at a 2½-hour sitting by Philip Yazdizk (U.S.A.), Chicago, Illinois, U.S.A., 25 April 1955.
Ice Cream	7 lb. 3 oz. (46 2½-oz. scoops) in 30 minutes by Peter Morrow, Brisbar Queensland, Australia on 27 April 1970.
Lemons	12 quarters (3 lemons) whole (including skin and pips) in 162 seconds by Jo Wood at Wakefield Youth Hostel, Yorkshire on 16 April 1971.
Meat	One whole roast ox in 42 days by Johann Ketzler of Munich, Germany in 1880.
Milk	2 pints (1 Imperial quart) in 5.2 seconds by M. Barsby at Corby, Northampton 22 Aug. 1971.
Oysters	500 in 60 minutes by Councillor Peter Jaconelli, Mayor of Scarborough, Yorksh at The Castle Hotel (only 48 minutes 7 seconds required) on 27 Aug. 1972. T official record for opening oysters in 100 in 3 minutes 37 seconds in Paris in 19. by le Champion du Monde des Ecaillers M. Williams Bley.
Pickled Onions	61 in 4 minutes 49 seconds by Ian Davies, 22 at Victoria Hotel, Hanle Stoke-on-Trent on 25 Mar. 1972.
Potatoes	3 lb. in 8 minutes by Arthur L. Warner at Newcastle, N.S.W. on 1 Apr. 1971.
Potato Crisps	30 2-oz. bags in 24 minutes 33.6 seconds, without a drink, by Paul G. Tully Brisbane University in May 1969. The largest single crisp on record is one measur to be 5 inches × 3 inches found at Reeds School, Cobham, Surrey by John Niche 16, on 2 Feb. 1971.
Prunes	130 in 105 seconds by Dave Man at Eastbourne on 16 June 1971.
Ravioli	324 (first 250 in 70 minutes) by "Bozo" Miller (see above) at Rendezvous Roo Oakland, California, U.S.A., in 1963.
Raw Eggs	26 in 9.0 seconds by Leslie Jones on Harlech T.V., Cardiff on 10 Nov. 1970. Dav Taylor at St. Leonards-on-Sea, Sussex ate 16 raw eggs with their shells in 3 minut 20 seconds on 8 Jan. 1970.
Sandwiches	39 (jam "butties" 5 × 3 × ½ inch) in 60 minutes by Paul Hughes, 13 at Ruftwoc School, Kirkby, Liverpool on 16 July 1971.
Sausage Meat	89½ Danish 1 oz. sausages in 6 minutes by Lee Hang in Hong Kong on 3 May 197
Spaghetti	262.6 yards (2.1 lb.) by Tom L. Cresci at Dino's Restaurant, San Diego, California U.S.A. on 20 May 1970. 100 yards in 53.0 secs. by Sian Davis and 3 men at Th Cafe Royal London on 17 June 1972.
Whelks	81 (unshelled) in 15 minutes by William Corfield, 35 at the Helyar Arms, Eas Coker, Somerset on 6 Sept. 1969.

2. HONOURS, DECORATIONS AND AWARDS

onymous record The largest object to which a human name is attached is the super cluster of galaxies known as Abell 7, after the astronomer Dr. George O. Abell of the University of California, U.S.A. The group of clusters has an estimated linear dimension of 300,000,000 light years and was announced in 1961.

ORDERS AND DECORATIONS

Oldest The earliest of the orders of chivalry is the Venetian order of St. Marc, reputedly founded in A.D. 831. The Castilian order of Calatrava has an established date of foundation in 1158. The prototype of the princely Orders of Chivalry is the Most Noble Order of the Garter founded by King Edward III in c. 1348.

Most titles The most titled person in the world is the 18th Duchess of Alba (Albade Termes), Doña María del Rosario Cayetana Fitz-James Stuart y Silva. She is 8 times a duchess, 15 times a marchioness, 21 times a countess and is 19 times a Spanish grandee.

British Rarest The rarest British medal is the Union of South Africa King's Medal for Bravery in Gold. The unique recipient was Francis C. Drake, aged 14, who rescued a child from a deep well at Parys, in the Orange Free State, on 6 Jan. 1943. However, the Queen's Fire Services Medal for Gallantry (instituted in 1954), which can only be won posthumously, has yet to be awarded.

Of War Medals, only three Naval General Service Medals (1793-1840) were issued with seven bars: (Admiral of the Fleet Sir James Gordon G.C.B; Admiral Sir John Hindmarsh K.H; and Gunner Thomas Haines) and only two Military General Service Medals (1793-1814) with 15 bars (James Talbot of the 45th Foot and Daniel Loochstadt of the 60th Foot).

ommonest Of gallantry decorations, the most unsparingly given was the Military Medal, which was awarded to 115,589 recipients between 1916 and 1919. The most frequently awarded decoration in the 1939-45 war was the Distinguished Flying Cross, which was awarded (including bars) 21,281 times.

Most expensive The highest price paid for any United Kingdom decoration is £3,500 for the Victoria Cross won by Able Seaman Edward Robinson at the Relief of Lucknow during the Indian Mutiny of 1858. The purchaser at the auction at Glendining's, London W.1 on 22 Oct. 1970 was Mr. John E. G. Bartholomew, 46, of Windlesham, Surrey.

VICTORIA CROSS

Most bars The only three men ever to have been awarded a bar to the Victoria Cross (instituted 1856) are:-

Surg.-Capt. (later Lt.-Col.) Arthur Martin-Leake, V.C.*, V.D., R.A.M.C. (1874–1953) (1902 and bar 1915).
Capt. Noel Godfrey Chavasse, V.C.*, M.C., R.A.M.C. (1884–1917) (1916 and bar posthumously 14 Sept. 1917).
Second Lieut. (later Capt.) Charles Hazlett Upham, V.C.*, N.Z.M.F. (born 1911) (1941 and bar 1942).

Oldest The greatest reported age at which a man has won the V.C. is 69 in the case of Lieut. (later Capt.) William Raynor of the Bengal Veteran Establishment, in defence of the magazine at Delhi, India, on 11 May 1857. Recent evidence indicates that he was not older than 66.

Youngest The lowest established age for a V.C. is 15 years 100 days for Hospital Apprentice Arthur Fitzgibbon (born at Peteragurh, northern India, 13 May 1845) of the Indian Medical Services for bravery at the Taku Forts in northern China on 21 Aug. 1860. Later, as an assistant surgeon, he was dismissed for insubordination and died in 1879. The youngest living V.C. is

Lance-Corporal Rambahadur Limbu (b. Nepal, 1939) of the 10th Princess Mary's Own Gurkha Rifles. The award, announced on 22 April 1966, was for his courage while fighting in the Bau district of Sarawak, East Malaysia, on 21 Nov. 1965.

Longest lived The longest lived of all the 1,349 winners of the Victoria Cross was Captain (later General Sir) Lewis Stratford Tollemache Halliday, V.C., K.C.B., of the Royal Marine Light Infantry. He was born on 14 May 1870, won his V.C. in China in 1900, and died on 9 March 1966, aged 95 years 299 days. The oldest living V.C. is Maj. Gen. Dudley Graham Johnson, V.C., C.B., D.S.O. and bar, M.C. (b. 13 Feb. 1884), who won his decoration as an Acting Lt.-Col. attached to the 2nd Batt. Royal Sussex Regt. at the Sumbre Canal, France on 4 Nov. 1918. He also received the Queen's South Africa Medal in 1900 aged 16.

The oldest living V.C., Maj. Gen. D. G. Johnson V.C., D.S.O.*, M.C. (b. 1884)

Most awards The two organizations which have won most V.C.s are Eton College (23 this century) and The Church Lads' Brigade with 22.

RECORD NUMBER OF BARS (repeat awards) EVER GAZETTED TO BRITISH GALLANTRY DECORATIONS

*=a bar or repeat award

V.C.*	A first bar has been three times awarded to the Victoria Cross (see above).
D.S.O.***	A third bar has been 16 times awarded to the Distinguished Service Order.
D.S.C.***	A third bar has been uniquely awarded to the Distinguished Service Cross won by Cdr. Norman Eyre Morley, R.N.V.R.
M.C.***	A third bar has been four times awarded to the Military Cross.
D.F.C.**	A second bar has been 54 times awarded to the Distinguished Flying Cross.
A.F.C.**	A second bar has been 12 times awarded to the Air Force Cross.
D.C.M.**	A second bar has been 11 times awarded to the Distinguished Conduct Medal.
C.G.M.*	A first bar has been uniquely awarded to the Conspicuous Gallantry Medal won by C.P.O.A.R. Blore and a second medal to Able Seaman D. Barry.
G.M.*	A first bar has been 25 times awarded to the George Medal.
K.P.M.**	A second bar has been uniquely awarded to the King's/Queen's Police Medal for Gallantry won by Supt. F. W. O'Gormon.
E.M.*	A first bar has twice been awarded to the Edward Medal (1st Class).

Petty Officer W. H. Kelly who was uniquely awarded his fourth D.S.M. during the Battle of the Atlantic in 1944.

D.S.M.*** A third bar has been uniquely awarded to the Distinguished Service Medal won by Petty Officer William Henry Kelly.

M.M.*** A third bar has been uniquely awarded to the Military Medal won by Cpl. Ernest A. Correy.

D.F.M.** A second bar has been uniquely awarded to the Distinguished Flying Medal won by Flt.-Sgt. (now Group Capt.) Donald Ernest Kingaby, D.S.O., A.F.C.

A.F.M.* A first bar has been 8 times awarded to the Air Force Medal.

S.G.M.* A first bar has been uniquely awarded to the Sea Gallantry Medal won by Chief Officer James Whiteley.

B.E.M.* A first bar has been 4 times awarded to the British Empire Medal for Gallantry (as instituted in 1957).

No bars have yet been awarded to the George Cross (G.C.) or the Conspicuous Gallantry Medal (Flying) (C.G.M.). No bars were ever awarded to the now obsolete the Albert Medal in Gold (A.M.), the Albert Medal (A.M.), the Edward Medal (E.M.) or the Empire Gallantry Medal (E.G.M.), which have all been superceded by the G.C.

Most mentions in despatches The record number of "mentions" is 24 by Field Marshal the Rt. Hon. the Earl Roberts, V.C., K.G., K.P., G.C.B., O.M., G.C.S.I., G.C.I.E., V.D. (1832-1914). He was also the only subject with 8 sets of official post-nominal letters.

U.S.S.R. The U.S.S.R.'s highest award for valour is the Gold Star of a Hero of the Soviet Union. Over 10,000 were awarded in World War II. Among the 109 awards of a second star were those to Marshall Iosif Vissariono-vich Dzhugashvili, *alias* Stalin (1879-1953) and Lt.-General Nikita Sergeyevich Khrushchyov (1894-1971). The only war-time triple awards were to Marshal Georgiy Konstantinovich Zhukov, Hon. G.C.B. (b. 1896) (subsequently awarded a fourth Gold Star, unique until Mr. Khrushchyov's fourth award) and the leading air aces Guards' Colonel (now Aviation Maj.-Gen.) Aleksandr Ivanovich Polkyrshkin and Aviation Maj.-Gen. Ivan Nikitaevich Kozhedub.

U.S.A. The highest U.S. decoration is the Congressional Medal of Honor. Five marines received both the Army and Navy Medals of Honor for the same acts in 1918 and 14 officers and men from 1863 to 1915 have received the medal on two occasions.

Most bemedalled The most bemedalled chest is that of H.I.M. Field-Marshal Hailé Selassié, K.G., G.C.B. (Hon.), G.C.M.G. (Hon.) (born, as Ras Tafari Makonnen, on 23 July 1892), Emperor of Ethiopia, who has over 50 medal ribbons worn in up to 14 rows.

TOP SCORING AIR ACES

World   80 Rittmeister Manfred, Freiherr (Baron) von Richthofen (Germany). 352[2] Major Erich Hartman (Germany).

United Kingdom   73[1] Capt. (acting Major) Edward Mannock, V.C., D.S.O.**, M.C.*. 38[3] Wg.-Cdr. (now Air Vice Marshal) James Edgar Johnson, C.B., C.B.E., D.S.O.**, D.F.C.*.

A compilation of the top air aces of 13 combatant nations in World War I and of 22 nations in World War II was included in the 13th edition of *The Guinness Book of Records*.
All except one of the aircraft in this unrivalled total were Soviet combat aircraft on the Eastern Front in 1942–45. The German air ace with most victories against the R.A.F. was Oberleutnant Hans-Joachim Marseille (killed 30 Sept. 1942), who, in 388 actions, shot down 158 Allied aircraft, 151 of them over North Africa.

Recent research suggests that Mannock's total may have been lower than tha Major James Thomas Byford McCudden, V.C., D.S.O., M.C.*, M.M. victories).*
*The greatest number of successes against flying bombs (V.1's) was by Sqn. I Joseph Berry, D.F.C.** (b. Nottingham, 1920, killed 2 Oct. 1944), who brou down 60 in 4 months. The most successful R.A.F. fighter pilot was Sqn. Marmaduke Thomas St. John Pattle, D.F.C.*, of South Africa, with a known t of at least 40.*

Top jet ace The greatest number of kills in jet to jet battles is by Capt. Joseph Christopher McConnell, Jr., U.S.A. (b. Dover, New Hampshire, 30 Jan. 1922) in t Korean war (1950-53). He was killed on 25 A 1954. It is possible that an Israeli ace may ha surpassed this total in the period 1967-70 but t identity of pilots is subject to strict security.

Top woman ace The record score for any woman fighter pilot is 13 Jnr. Lt. Lila Litvak (U.S.S.R.) in the Eastern Fro campaign of 1941-45.

Anti-submarine successes The highest number of U-boat kills attributed to o ship in the 1939-45 war was 13 to H.M.S. *Starl* (Capt. Frederick J. Walker, C.B., D.S.O.***, R.N Captain Walker was in overall command at the sinki of a total of 25 U-boats between 1941 and the time his death on 9 July 1944. The U.S. Destroyer Esc *England* sank six Japanese submarines in the Pac between 18 and 30 May 1944.

Most successful U-boat captain The most successful of all World War II submari commanders was Korvetten-Kapitän (now Kapit zur See) Otto Kretschmer (b. 1911), captain of t U.23 and later the U.99. He sank one Allied destroy and 43 merchantmen totalling 263,682 gross reg tered tons in 16 patrols before his capture on March 1941. He is a Knight's Cross of the Iron Cro with Oakleaves and Swords. In World War I Kapit Leutnant Lothar von Arnauld de la Periere, in t U.35 and U.139, sank 194 allied ships totalling 4, 716 gross tons. The most successful boats were U. which in World War I sank 54 ships of 90,350 g.r.t. a single voyage and 535,900 g.r.t. all told, and U. which sank 53 ships of 318,111 g.r.t. in World War

NOBEL PRIZES

The Nobel Foundation of £3,200,000 was set under the will of Alfred Bernhard Nobel (1833-9 the unmarried Swedish chemist and chemical er ineer, who invented dynamite in 1866. The Nob Prizes are presented annually on 10 Dec., the annive sary of Nobel's death and the festival day of t Foundation. Since the first Prizes were awarded 1901, the highest cash value of the award, in each the six fields of Physics, Chemistry, Medicine a Physiology, Literature, Peace and Economics w £33,000 in 1971.

A portrait of Capt. F. J. Walker C.B., D.S.O.*, R.N., the most successful destroyer of U-boats in the Second World War with a total of 25.**

Honours, Decorations and Awards

MOST AWARDS

By countries The United States has shared in the greatest number of awards (including those made in 1971) with a total of 79, made up of 20 for Physics, 13 for Chemistry, 24 for Medicine-Physiology, 6 for Literature, 14 for Peace and 2 for Economics.

The United Kingdom has shared in 54 awards, comprising 14 for Physics, 15 for Chemistry, 11 for Medicine-Physiology, 6 for Literature and 8 for Peace.

By classes, the United States holds the records for Medicine-Physiology with 24, for Physics with 20 and for Peace with 14; Germany for Chemistry with 21; and France for Literature with 12.

Individuals Individually the only person to have won two Prizes outright is Dr. Linus Carl Pauling (b. 28 Feb. 1901), the Professor of Chemistry since 1931 at the California Institute of Technology, Pasadena, California, U.S.A. He was awarded the Chemistry Prize for 1954 and the Peace Prize for 1962. The only other person to have won two prizes was Madame Marie Curie (1867-1934), who was born in Poland as Marja Sklodowska. She shared the 1903 Physics Prize with her husband Pierre Curie (1859-1906) and Antoine Henri Becquerel (1852-1908), and won the 1911 Chemistry Prize outright. The Peace Prize has been awarded three times to the International Committee of the Red Cross (founded 29 Oct. 1863), of Geneva, Switzerland, namely in 1917, 1944 and in 1963, when it was shared with the International League of Red Cross Societies.

Oldest The oldest prizeman has been Professor Francis Peyton Rous (1879-1970) of the United States. He shared the Medicine Prize in 1966, at the age of 87.

Youngest The yougest laureate has been Professor Sir William Lawrence Bragg, C.H., O.B.E., M.C. (1890-1971), of the U.K., who, at the age of 25, shared the 1915 Physics Prize with his father, Sir William Henry Bragg, O.M., K.B.E. (1862-1942), for work on X-rays and crystal structures. Bragg and also Theodore William Richards (1868-1928) of the U.S.A., who won the 1914 Chemistry prize,carried out their prize work when aged 23. The youngest Literature prizeman has been Joseph Rudyard Kipling (1865-1936) at the age of 41 in 1907. The youngest Peace prize-winner has been the Rev. Dr. Martin Luther King, Jr. (1929-68) of the U.S.A., in 1964.

Greatest reception The greatest ticker-tape reception ever given on Broadway, New York City, N.Y., U.S.A., was that for Lt.-Col. (now Col.) John Herschel Glenn, Jr. (b. 18 July 1921) on 1 March 1962, after his return from his tri-orbital flight. The New York Street Cleaning Department estimated that 3,474 tons of paper descended. This total compared with 3,249 tons for General of the Army Douglas MacArthur (1880-1964) in 1951 and 1,800 tons for Col. Charles Augustus Lindbergh (b. 4 Feb. 1902) in June 1927.

Most statues The world record for raising statues to oneself was set by Generalissimo Dr. Rafael Leónidas Trujillo y Molina (1891-1961), former President of the Dominican Republic. In March 1960 a count showed that there were "over 2,000". The country's highest mountain was named Pico Trujillo (now Pico Duarte). One Province was called Trujillo and another Trujillo Valdez. The capital was named Ciudad Trujillo (Trujillo City) in 1936, but reverted to its old name of Santo Domingo de Guzmán on 23 Nov. 1961. Trujillo was assassinated in a car ambush on 30 May 1961, and 30 May is now celebrated annually as a public holiday. The man to whom most statues have been raised is undoubtedly Vladimir Ilyich Ulyanov, *alias* Lenin (1877-1924), busts of whom have been mass-produced as also in the case of Mao Tse-tung. (b. 26 Dec. 1893) and Hô Chi Minh (1890-1969).

The 5th Baron Penrhyn (1865-1967), the only peer ever to have reached his 102nd year

PEERAGE

Most ancient creation The year 1223 has been ascribed to the premier Irish barony of Kingsale (formerly de Courcy), though on the Order of Precedence the date is listed as 1397. The premier English barony, de Ros, was held until her death on 8 Oct. 1956, by a Baroness in her own right and 26th in her line, dating from 14 Dec. 1264. It was called out of abeyance on 29 Aug. 1958 in favour of a grand-daughter, Mrs. Georgiana Angela Maxwell (born 1933). The earldom of Arundel, a subsidiary title of the Duke of Norfolk, dates from 1139.

Oldest creation The greatest age at which any person has been raised to the peerage is 93 years 337 days in the case of Sir William Francis Kyffin Taylor, G.B.E., K.C. (b. 9 July 1854), who was created Baron Maenan of Ellesmere, County Salop (Shropshire), on 10 June 1948, and died, aged 97, on 22 Sept. 1951, when the title became extinct.

Longest lived peer The longest lived peer ever recorded was the Rt. Hon. Frank Douglas-Pennant, the 5th Baron Penrhyn (b. 21 Nov. 1865), who died on 3 Feb. 1967, aged 101 years 74 days. Currently the oldest peer is the Rt. Hon. Sir John Frederick Whitworth Aylmer, Bt., the 9th Baron Aylmer (b. 23 April 1880). He lives in Canada and his family motto is "Steady". The oldest peeress recorded was the Countess Desmond, who was alleged to be 140 when she died in 1604. This claim is patently exaggerated but it is accepted that she may have been 104. Currently the oldest peeress of parliament is the Countess of Kintore, (Ethel) Sydney Keith, formerly Baird (*née* Keith-Falconer), Dowager Viscountess Stonehaven, born on 20 Sept. 1874.

Youngest peers Twelve Dukes of Cornwall automatically became peers at birth as the eldest son of a Sovereign; and the 9th Earl of Chichester posthumously inherited his father's (killed 54 days previously) earldom at his birth on 14 April 1944.

The youngest age at which a person has had a peerage conferred on them is 7 days old in the case of the Earldom of Chester on H.R.H. the Prince George (later George IV) on 19 Aug. 1762.

Longest and shortest peerages The peer who has sat longest in the House of Lords was Lt.-Col. Charles Henry FitzRoy, O.B.E., the 4th Baron Southampton (b. 11 May 1867), who succeeded to his father's title on 16 July 1872, took his seat on 23 Jan. 1891, 18 months before Mr. W. E. Gladstone's fourth administration began, and died, aged 91, on 7 Dec. 1958, having held the title for 86 years 144 days.

The shortest enjoyment of a peerage was the "split second" by which the law assumes that the Hon. Wilfrid Carlyle Stamp (b. 28 Oct. 1904), the 2nd Baron Stamp, survives his father, Sir Josiah Charles Stamp G.C.B., G.B.E., the 1st Baron Stamp, when both were killed as a result of German bombing of London on 16 April 1941. Apart from this legal fiction, the shortest recorded peerage was one of 30 minutes in the case of Sir Charles Brandon, K.B., the 3rd Duke of Suffolk, who died, aged 13 or 14, just after succeeding his brother, Sir Henry, the 2nd Duke, when both were suffering a fatal illness, at Buckden, Huntingdonshire, on 14 July 1551.

Highest numbering The highest succession number borne by any peer is that of the present 35th Baron Kingsale (John de Courcy, b. 27 Jan. 1941), who succeeded to the 746-year-old Barony on 7 Nov. 1969.

Most creations The largest number of new hereditary peerages created in any year was the 54 in 1296. The record for all peerages (including 40 life peerages) is 55 in 1964. The greatest number of extinctions in a year was 16 in 1923 and the greatest number of deaths was 44 in 1935.

Longest abeyance The longest abeyance of any peerage was that of the barony of Strabolgi, which was called out on 9 May 1916, more than 546 years in abeyance since 10 Oct. 1369.

Most prolific The most prolific peers of all time are believed to be the 1st Earl Ferrers (1650-1717) and the 3rd Earl of Winchilsea (c. 1620-1689) each with 27 legitimate children. In addition, the former reputedly fathered 30 illegitimate children. Currently the peer with the largest family is the Rt. Hon. Bryan Walter Guinness, 2nd Baron Moyne, with 6 sons and 5 daughters.

The most prolific peeress is believed to be Elizabeth (née Barnard), who bore 22 children to her husband Lord Chandos of Sudeley (1642-1714).

BARONETS
Oldest The greatest age to which a baronet has lived is 101 years 188 days, in the case of Sir Fitzroy Maclean, 10th Bt., K.C.B., (1835-1936). He was the last survivor of the Charge of the Light Brigade at Balaclava in the Crimea, Russia, on 25 Oct. 1854.

Most and least creations The largest number of creations this century was 51 in 1919. There were none in 1940 or since 1965.

KNIGHTS
Youngest and oldest The youngest age for the conferment of a knighthood is 214 days for H.R.H. the Prince Albert Edward (later Edward VII) by virtue of his *ex officio* membership of the Order of the Garter (K.G.) consequent upon his creation as Prince of Wales on 8 Dec. 1841. The greatest age for the conferment of a knighthood is 91 years 128 days in the case of Charles Shaw-Lefevre, 1st Viscount Eversley (1794-1888) created G.C.B. (civil) on 30 June 1885.

ORDER OF MERIT
The Order of Merit (instituted on 23 June 1902) is limited to 24 members. Up to 1971 there were 127 awards including only 3 women, plus 9 honorary awards to non-British citizens. The longest lived holder has been the Rt. Hon. Bertrand Arthur William Russell, 3rd Earl Russell, who died on 2 Feb. 1970 aged 97 years 260 days. The oldest recipient was Admiral of the Fleet the Hon. Sir Henry Keppel, G.C.B., O.M. (1809-1904), who received the Order aged 93 years 56 days on 9 Aug. 1902. The youngest recipient has been H.R.H. the Duke of Edinburgh, K.G., K.T., O.M., G.B.E. who was appointed on his 47th birthday on 10 June 1968.

The Duke of Wellington voted £864,000 (worth over £5 million) by unaminous vote of both Houses of Parliament

Most freedoms Probably the greatest number of freedoms ev conferred on any man was 57 in the case of Andre Carnegie (1835-1919), who was born in Dunfermlin Fife but emigrated to the United States in 1848. Th most freedoms conferred upon any citizen of th United Kingdom is 42, in the case of the Rt. Hon. S Winston Leonard Spencer Churchil, K.G., O.M., C.H T.D. (1874-1965).

Most honorary degrees The greatest number of honorary degrees awarded t any individual is 89, given to Herbert Clark Hoov (1874-1964), former President of the United State (1929-33).

Greatest vote The largest monetary vote made by Parliament to subject was the £400,000 given to the 1st Duke c Wellington (1769-1852) on 12 April 1814. H received in all £864,000. The total received by th 1st, 2nd and 3rd Dukes to January 1900 wa £1,052,000.

Who's Who The longest entry in *Who's Who* (founded 1849) wa that of the Rt. Hon. Sir Winston Leonard Spence Churchill, K.G., O.M., C.H., T.D. (1874-1965), wh had 211 lines in the 1965 edition. Apart from thos who qualify for inclusion by hereditary title, th youngest entry has been Yehudi Menuhin, Hor K.B.E. (b. New York City, U.S.A. 22 April 1916), th concert violinist, who first appeared in the 193 edition. The longest entry of the 66,000 entries i *Who's Who in America* is that of Prof. Richar Buckminster Fuller (b. 1895) whose all-time recor of 139 lines compares with the 23 line sketch o President Nixon.

"Time" magazine cover The most frequent subject has been President John son with 41 treatments to the end of 1967. Th youngest subject for a *Time* (first issued 3 Marcl 1923) cover was Charles Augustus Lindbergh, J (b. 22 June 1930), who was kidnapped 1 Mar. 1932 The oldest subject was the veteran sports coach Amo Alonzo Stagg (1862-1965) in the issue of 20 Oct 1958. Summing up his life's work he agreed with th dictum of the Brooklyn baseball manager of 194 "Lippy" Leo Durocher that "Nice guys come last"

Longest obituary The obituary of Thomas Alva Edison (U.S. (1847-1931) occupied 4½ pages in the *New Yor Times* of 19 Nov. 1931.

11 THE HUMAN WORLD

1. POLITICAL AND SOCIAL

The land area of the Earth is estimated at 57,270,000 square miles (including inland waters), or 29.08 per cent. of the world's surface area.

Largest political division The British Commonwealth of Nations, a free association of 32 independent sovereign states together with their dependencies, covers an area of 13,400,000 square miles and had a population estimated to be 930 million in 1972.

COUNTRIES

Total The total number of separately administered territories in the world is 228, of which 148 are independent countries. Of these 24 sovereign and 65 non-sovereign are insular countries. Only 29 sovereign and 3 non-sovereign countries are entirely without a seaboard. Territorial waters vary between extremes of 3 miles (*e.g.* United Kingdom, Australia, France, Ireland and the U.S.A.) up to 200 miles (*e.g.* Argentina, Ecuador, El Salvador and Panama).

Largest The country with the greatest area is the Union of Soviet Socialist Republics (the Soviet Union), comprising 15 Union (constituent) Republics with a total area of 8,649,500 square miles, or 15.0 per cent. of the world's total land area, and a total coastline (including islands) of 66,090 miles. The country measures 5,580 miles from east to west and 2,790 miles from north to south.

The United Kingdom covers 94,221 square miles (including 1,197 square miles of inland water), or 0.16 per cent. of the total land area of the world. Great Britain is the world's eighth largest island, with an area of 84,186 square miles and a coastline 5,126 miles long, of which Scotland accounts for 2,573 miles, Wales 601 miles and England 1,952 miles.

Smallest The smallest independent country in the world is the State of the Vatican City (Stato della Città del Vaticano), which was made an enclave within the city of Rome, Italy on 11 Feb. 1929. It has an area of 44 hectares (108.7 acres).

The world's smallest republic is Nauru, less than 1 degree south of the equator in the Western Pacific, which became independent on 31 Jan. 1968, has an area of 5,263 acres (8.2 square miles) and a population of 7,000 (estimate mid-1969).

The smallest colony in the world is Pitcairn Island with an area of 960 acres (1.5 square miles) and a population of 74 (1 Jan. 1970).

The official residence, since 1834, of the Grand Master of the Order of the Knights of Malta totalling 3 acres and comprising the Villa del Priorato di Malta on the lowest of Rome's seven hills, the 151-foot Aventine, retains certain diplomatic privileges and has accredited representatives to foreign governments and is hence sometimes cited as the smallest state in the world.

On 19 Jan. 1972 the two South Pacific atolls of North and South Minerva (400 miles south of Fiji) were declared to be a sovereign independent Republic under international law by Mr. Michael Oliver formerly of Lithuania.

FRONTIERS

Most The country with the most frontiers is the U.S.S.R., with 12—Norway, Finland, Poland, Czechoslovkia, Hungary, Romania, Turkey, Iran (Persia), Afghanistan, Mongolia, People's Republic of China and North Korea.

Longest The longest continuous frontier in the world is that between Canada and the United States, which (including the Great Lakes boundaries) extends for 3,987 miles (excluding 1,538 miles with Alaska). The frontier which is crossed most frequently is that between the United States and Mexico. It extends for 1,933 miles and there are more than 120,000,000 crossings every year. The Sino-Soviet frontier extends for 4,500 miles with virtually nil crossings.

Most impenetrable boundary The 858-mile-long "Iron Curtain", dividing the Federal Republican (West) and the Democratic Republican (East) parts of Germany, utilises 2,230,000 land mines and 50,000 miles of barbed wire, much of it of British manufacture, in addition to many watch-towers containing detection devices. The whole 270-yard-wide strip occupies 133 square miles of East German territory.

POPULATIONS

World Estimates of the human population of the world depend largely on the component figure for the population of the People's Republic of China (see also below). Her seating in the United Nations on 25 Oct. 1971 may soon result in an improvement of the present unreliability of world estimates. The world total at mid-1972 can be estimated to be 3,782 million, giving an average density of 72.7 people per square mile of land (including inland waters). This excludes Antarctica and uninhabited island groups. The daily increase in the world's population was running at 208,000 in 1972-73. It is estimated that about 245 are born and about 101 die every minute in 1972. The world's population has doubled in the last 50 years and is expected to double again in the next 35 years. It is now estimated that the world's population in the year 2000 will be more than 6,000 million, and probably closer to 7,000 million. The present population "explosion" is of such a magnitude that it has been fancifully calculated that, if it were to continue unabated, there would be one person to each square yard by A.D. 2600, and humanity would weigh more than Earth itself by A.D. 3700. It is estimated that 75,000,000,000 humans have been born and died in the last 600,000 years.

WORLD POPULATION—
Progressive mid-year estimates

Date	Millions	Date	Millions
4000 B.C.	85		
A.D. 1	c. 200-300	1966	3,353
1650	c. 500-550	1967	3,420
1750	750	1968	3,483
1800	960	1969	3,552
1850	1,240	1970	3,632
1900	1,650	1971	3,706
1920	1,862	1972	3,782
1930	2,070	1973	3,860
1940	2,295	2000	6,493*
1950	2,517	2007	7,600**
1960	3,005	2070	25,000**
1965	3,297	2100	48,000**

U.N Forecasts made on medium variants.

**Estimated date of future doublings of the present population.*

Most populous country The largest population of any country is that of the People's Republic of China. Owing to the scarcity of available data, estimates vary considerably, but officials of the United Nations have assumed that the total was about 650,000,000 at mid-1960, increasing to 695,000,000 by mid-1965, and rose to 760,000,000 by mid-1970. According to the Japanese newspaper *Mainichi*, estimates made from Chinese Revolutionary Committee announcements indicate that the Chinese population as of 31 Dec. 1967 was 732 million and hence should have reached over 750,000,000 by mid-1969. Some estimates run considerably higher including one 1971 estimate of 827,000,000.

Colonial The most populous colony in the world is Mozambique, South East Africa with an estimated mid-19 figure of 7,360,000. The capital city of this Portuguese overseas province is Lorenzo Marques.

Least populous The independent state with the smallest population the Vatican City or the Holy See (see Smalle country, page 185), with 880 inhabitants at 1 Ja 1966.

Most densely populated The most densely populated territory in the world the Portuguese province of Macau (or Macao), on t southern coast of China. It has an estimated population of 314,000 (30 June 1970) in an area of 6 square miles, giving a density of 50,645 per squa mile. The population has increased additionally a result of the influx of refugees from the Chine mainland.

The Principality of Monaco, on the south coast France, has a population of 24,000 (estimated June 1970) in an area of 369.9 acres, giving a densi of 41,500 per square mile. This is being relieved marine infilling which will increase her area to 4 acres. Singapore has 2,074,507 (mid-1971 censu people in an inhabited area of 73 square miles.

Of territories with an area of more than 200 squa miles, Hong Kong (398¼ square miles) contai 3,950,802 people (census 9 Mar. 1971), giving t territory a density of 9,920 per square mile. The nam Hong Kong is the transcription of the local pronunci tion of the Peking dialect version of Xiang gang port for incense). About 80 per cent. of the popul tion lives in the urban areas of Hong Kong island a Kowloon, on the mainland, and the density there greater than 200,000 per square mile. At North Poi there are 12,400 people living in 6½ acres, giving unsurpassed spot density of more than 1,200,000 p square mile. In 1959 it was reported that in one hou designed for 12 people the number of occupants w 459, including 104 in one room and 4 living on t roof.

Of countries over 1,000 square miles, the mo densely populated is the Netherlands, with a popul tion of 13,194,000 (estimate 1 July 1971) on 12,97 square miles of land, giving a density of 1,016 peop per square mile. The Indonesian islands of Java a Madura (combined area 51,033 square miles) have population of 73,400,000 (estimate for mid-1969 giving a density of 1,438 per square mile. The Unite Kingdom (94,221 square miles) had an estimate home population of 55,566,000 at 30 June 197 giving a density of 589.7 people per square mile. Th projected population figures for 1980 and 2000 a 59,548,000 and 66,100,000. The population densit for England alone (50,869 square miles) is 959.8 p square mile, while that of south-eastern England more than 1,640 per square mile.

Most sparsely populated Antarctica became permanently occupied by rela of scientists from October 1956. The populatio varies seasonally and reaches 1,500 at times.

BRITISH AND IRISH—LARGEST AND SMALLEST COUNTIES

	By Area (in acres) Largest		Smallest	
England	Yorkshire	3,934,359	Rutland	97,273
Wales	Carmarthen	588,472	Flint	163,707
Northern-Ireland	Tyrone	806,918	Armagh	327,907
Republic of Ireland	Cork	1,843,408	Louth	202,806

Figures for the Republic of Ireland refer to the census of 18 Apr. 1971.

NOTE: *Lanarkshire includes the City of Glasgow (908,000); Antrim includes Belfast County Borough (383,600) and Dublin includes Dublin County Borough (650,153). The largest Welsh town is the City of Cardiff (population 284,000 at 30 June 1970.*

The English county with the longest coastline is Cornwall (320 miles) and that with the longest in Wales is Pembroke-

By Home Population (estimate 30 June 1971)* Largest			
London	7,379,014	Rutland	29,23
Glamorgan	1,252,970	Radnorshire	18,270 Scotlan
Antrim	717,400	Fermanagh	49,87
Dublin county	1,414,415	Longford	28,98

shire with 183 miles. Westmorland has the shortest coastlin with 5½ miles. Of the 91 counties of the United Kingdom a but 28 have a coastline. Fermanagh in Northern Irelan comprises 9.04 per cent. inland water.

† The inclusion of Rockall in the District of Harris in th County of Inverness by Act of Parliament on 10 Feb. 197 made the two points furthest apart in any one county—36 miles.

The world's highest village — Aucanquilca, Chile 17,500 feet above sea level

The least populated territory, apart from Antarctica, is Greenland, with a population of 47,000 (estimate 1 July 1970) in an area of 840,000 square miles, giving a density of about 0.055 of a person per square mile, or one person to every 17.8 square miles. The ice-free area of the island is only 132,000 square miles.

CITIES

Most populous World The most populous city in the world is Tōkyō, the capital of Japan since 1868. The 23 wards (*ku*) of the old City contained 8,807,202 people at December 1971, while Tōkyō-to (Tōkyō Prefecture) had 11,408,000 in its 823.6 square miles at 1 Oct. 1970. The population of this area had surpassed that of Greater London and New York in early 1957 and in January 1962 it became the first urban area in history whose recorded population exceeded 10,000,000. At the census of 1 Oct. 1970, the "Keihin Metropolitan Area" (Tōkyō-Yokohama Metropolitan Area) of 1,081 square miles contained an estimated 14,034,074 people.

In December 1964 the population of Shanghai, in China, was unofficially reported to be 10,700,000. The city proper population figure in the 1957 census was 6,900,000.

The world's largest city not built by the sea or on a river is Mexico City (Ciudad de México), the capital of Mexico, with an estimated population of 7,005,855 at 1 July 1970. Greater Mexico City's population was 8,541,070 (1970 census).

United Kingdom The largest conurbation in Britain is Greater London (established on 1 April 1965), with an estimated home population of 7,379,014 in an area of 396,516 acres (619.5 square miles). The residential population of the City of London (677 acres) is 4,210 compared with 128,000 in 1801.

Largest in area The world's largest town, in area, is Kiruna, in Sweden. Its boundaries have, for fiscal avoidance purposes, been extended to embrace an area of 5,458 square miles. The largest city in the United Kingdom is Greater London with an area of 619.5 square miles.

Smallest hamlet The only hamlet in Great Britain with an official population of one is Gallowhill in the parish of Inveravon, Banffshire, Scotland.

Highest World The highest capital in the world, before the domination of Tibet by China, was Lhasa, at an elevation of 12,087 feet above sea-level. La Paz, the administrative and *de facto* capital of Bolivia, stands at an altitude of 11,916 feet above sea-level. The city was founded in 1548 by Capt. Alonso de Mendoza on the site of an Indian village named Chuquiapu. It was originally called Ciudad de Nuestra Señora de La Paz (City of Our Lady of Peace), but in 1825 was renamed La Paz de Ayacucho, its present official name. Sucre, the legal capital of Bolivia, stands at 9,301 feet above sea-level. The new town of Wenchuan, founded in 1955 on the Chinghai-Tibet road, north of the Tangla range, is the highest in the world at 5,100 metres (16,732 feet) above sea-level. The highest village in the world is the Andean mining village of Aucanquilca, in Chile, at 17,500 feet above sea-level.

Great Britain The highest village in England is Flash, in northern Staffordshire, at 1,518 feet above sea-level. The term "flash" money probably relates to the former wintertime counterfeiting activities of the villagers. The highest in Scotland is Wanlockhead, in Dumfries-shire at 1,380 feet above sea-level.

Oldest World The oldest known walled town in the world is Arīhā (Jericho), in Jordan. Radio-carbon dating on specimens from the lowest levels reached by archaeologists indicate habitation there by perhaps 3,000 people as early as 7800 B.C. The village of Zawi Chemi Shanidar, discovered in 1957 in northern Iraq, has been dated to 8910 B.C. The oldest capital city in the world is Dimashq (Damascus), the capital of Syria. It has been continuously inhabited since *c.* 2500 B.C.

Great Britain The oldest town in Great Britain is often cited as Colchester, the old British Camulodunon, headquarters of Belgic chiefs in the 1st century B.C. However, the place called Ictis, referred to by Pytheas in *c.* 308 B.C., has been identified with Marazion, close to St. Michael's Mount, Cornwall.

Northernmost The world's northernmost town with a population of more than 10,000 is the Arctic port of Dikson, U.S.S.R. in 73° 32' N. The northernmost village is Ny Ålesund (78° 55' N.), a coalmining settlement on King's Bay, Vest Spitsbergen, in the Norwegian territory of Svalbard, inhabited only during the winter season. The northernmost capital is Reykjavík, the capital of Iceland, in 64° 06' N. Its population was estimated to be 81,288 at 1 July 1969. The northernmost permanent human occupation is the base at Alert (82° 31' N.), on Dumb Bell Bay, on the north-east coast of Ellesmere Island, northern Canada.

187

Southern-most The world's southernmost village is Puerto Williams (population about 350), on the north coast of Isla Navarino, in Tierra del Fuego, Chile, about 680 miles north of Antarctica. Wellington, North Island, New Zealand is the southernmost capital city on 41° 17′ S. The world's southernmost administrative centre is Port Stanley (51° 43′ S.), in the Falkland Islands, off South America.

Most remote from sea The largest town most remote from the sea is Wulumuch'i (Urumchi) formerly Tihwa, Sinkiang, capital of the Uighur Autonomous Region of China, at a distance of about 1,400 miles from the nearest coastline. Its population was estimated to be 275,000 at 31 Dec. 1957.

EMIGRATION
More people emigrate from the United Kingdom than from any other country. A total of 299,600 emigrated from the U.K. from mid-1969 to mid-1970 (latest available data). The largest number of emigrants in any one year was 360,000 in 1852, mainly from Ireland in the post-famine period.

IMMIGRATION
The country which regularly receives the most immigrants is the United States, with 358,579 in 1969. It has been estimated that, in the period 1820-1969, the U.S.A. has received 44,789,312 immigrants. The peak year for immigration into the United Kingdom was the 12 months from 1 July 1961 to 30 June 1962, when about 430,000 Common-wealth citizens arrived. The number of immigrants from mid-1969 to mid-1970 was 208,400.

MOST TOURISTS
In 1971 Italy received 33,230,000 foreign visitors—more than any other country except Canada, which in 1970 received 37,735,000, of whom more than 62 per cent. entered and left the same day. In 1971 the United Kingdom received 6,730,000 visitors who spent an estimated £433,500,000.

BIRTH RATE
Highest and lowest Based on latest data available, the highest recorded crude live birth rate is 62 live births per each 1,000 of the population in Guinea (Africans only, based on births reported for the 12-month period preceding the sample survey of 15 Jan. to 31 May 1955). The highest 1968 figure is 52.3 for Swaziland. The rate for the whole world was 33 per 1,000 in 1963-69.

The lowest of the recently available recorded rates is 6.8 in Christmas Island.

The 1971 rate in the United Kingdom was 16.3 per 1,000 (16.1 in England and Wales, 16.6 in Scotland and 20.7 in Northern Ireland), while the 1970 rate for the Republic of Ireland was 21.8 registered births per 1,000.

DEATH RATE
Highest and lowest The highest of the latest available recorded death rates is 40 deaths per each 1,000 of the population in Guinea (Africans only, 12 months preceding 1955 sample survey). The next highest figure is 35 per 1,000 in Burma in 1955 (still latest available). The rate for the whole world was 14 per 1,000 in 1963-69.

The lowest of the latest available recorded rates is 1.3 deaths per 1,000 in Mozambique in 1968. The lowest rate in an independent country in 1967 was 4.1 per 1,000 registered in Iraq and 4.4 in Syria in 1968.

The 1971 rate in the United Kingdom was 11.6 per 1,000 (11.6 in England and Wales, 11.8 in Scotland and 10.6 in Northern Ireland), while the 1970 rate for the Republic of Ireland was 11.5 registered deaths per 1,000. The highest S.M.I. (Standard Mortality

The world's southernmost town — Puerto Williams, Chile - only 680 miles north of Antarctica

Index where the national average is 100) is in Salfor Lancashire with a figure of 133.

NATURAL INCREASE
The highest of the latest available recorded rates natural increase is 55.0 per 1,000 in Kuwait (birt 61.2, deaths 6.2) in 1968. The rate for the who world was 34-14=20 per 1,000 in 1965-70.

The 1971 rate for the United Kingdom was 4.5 p 1,000 (4.5 in England and Wales, 4.8 in Scotlar and 10.1 in Northern Ireland). The figure for th Republic or Ireland was 10.3 per 1,000 in 1970.

There are three territories in which the death ra exceeds the birth rate, and which thus have a rate natural decrease: West Berlin, Germany, 9.9 p 1,000 (birth rate 10.0, death rate 19.9) in 196 East Berlin 1.9 per 1,000 and the Isle of Man 2 per 1,000 (registered births 15.3, registered deat 18.3) in 1969. The lowest rate of natural increase an independent country in 1969 was 0.3 per 1,00 in East Germany (birth rate 14.0 death rate 14.3

Marriage ages The country with the lowest average ages for marriag is India, with 20.0 years for males and 14.5 years f females. At the other extreme is Ireland, with 31.4 f males and 26.5 years for females. In the People Republic of China marriage for men is reportedly n approved before the age of 28.

SEX RATIO
The country with the largest recorded shortage males is the U.S.S.R., with 1,171.6 females to ever 1,000 males at 15 Jan. 1970. The country with th largest recorded woman shortage is Pakistan, wit 900.7 to every 1,000 males at 1 Feb. 1961. The rati in the United Kingdom was 1,052.1 females to ever 1,000 males at 30 June 1966, and is expected to b 1,014.2 per 1,000 by A.D. 2000.

INFANT MORTALITY
Based on deaths before one year of age, the lowest the latest available recorded rates is 9.2 deaths pe 1,000 live births in Gibraltar in 1968, compared wit 12.9 per 1,000 in Sweden in 1967.

The highest recorded infant mortality rate recentl reported has been 259 per 1,000 live births among th indigenous African population of Zambia (the Northern Rhodesia) in the 12 months preceding th sample survey of 30 June 1950. Among most recen estimates the highest is an annual average of 64.2 pe 1,000 for Mexico in 1968. Many countries with rate more than twice as high have apparently ceased t make returns. Among these is Ethiopia, where the infant mortality rate was unofficially estimated to be nearly 550 per 1,000 live births in 1969.

The United Kingdom figure for 1971 was 17.9 per 1,000 live births (England and Wales 17.4, Scotland 19.8, Northern Ireland 22.6). The Republic of Ireland figure for 1970 was 19.2.

LIFE EXPECTATION
There is evidence that life expectation in Britain in the 5th century A.D. was 33 years for males and 27 years for females. In the decade 1890-1900 the expectation of life among the population of India was 23.7 years. The British figure for 1901-1910 was 48.53 years for males and 52.83 years for females.

Based on the latest available data, the highest recorded expactation of life at birth is 71.85 years (male) and 76.54 years (females) both in Sweden in 1969.

The lowest recorded expectation of life at birth is 27 years for both sexes in the Vallée du Niger area of Mali in 1957 (sample survey, 1957-58). The figure for males in Gabon was 25 years in 1960-61.

The latest available figures for England and Wales (1968-70) are 68.5 years for males and 74.7 years for females; for Scotland (1968) 66.92 years for males and 73.05 years for females; for Northern Ireland (1966-68) 68.19 years for males and 73.45 years for females; and for the Republic of Ireland (1960-62) 68.13 years for males and 71.86 years for females.

At the age of 60, the highest recorded expectation of life for males is in Bolivia, with 20.39 years (1949-51). More reliable figures include 18.64 years in Puerto Rico (1959-61), 18.6 years in Iceland (1961-65). The highest recorded figure for females is 21.66 years in Ryukyu Islands (1960), 20.99 years in Puerto Rico (1959-61) and 20.9 years in Iceland (1961-65).

The figures for the United Kingdom for men of 60 is 15.0 years and for women 19.6 years; and for the Republic of Ireland (1960-62) 15.83 years for men and 18.10 years for women.

STANDARDS OF LIVING
National incomes The country with the highest income per person in 1969 was Nauru, with nearly $4,000 (£1,666) per head, followed by Kuwait and the U.S.A. The U.S.A. in 1967 leads on the basis of major industrial countries measured by real product per head at 190 (U.K.=100).

COST OF LIVING
The greatest increase since 1963 (=100) has been in Djakarta, the capital of Indonesia, where the index figure reached 57,712 (food 62,876) by 1968.

In the United Kingdom the official index of retail prices (16 Jan. 1962=100) was 149.0 on 16 March 1971–a rise of 12.0 points or 8.76 per cent. in 12 months.

Capital city Most and least expensive According to data published by the U.N. Statistical Office in June 1970, the world's most expensive capital city in Saigon, South Vietnam (122) and the world's cheapest is Damascus, Syria (69). These indices compare with the cost of living in New York of 100 in 1968. The figure for London is 80.

HOUSING
For comparison, dwelling units are defined as a structurally separated room or rooms occupied by private households of one or more people and having separate access or a common passageway to the street.

The country with the greatest recorded number of private housing units is India, with 79,193,602 occupied in 1960. These contain 83,523,895 private households.

Great Britain comes fourth among reporting countries, with 18,839,000 dwellings (England 16,076,000, Wales 961,000, Scotland 1,802,000) at June 1971. The 1968 figure for Northern Ireland was 435,000. The Republic of Ireland had 687,304 private households in 1966. The record number of permanent houses built has been 425,800 in 1968.

PHYSICIANS
The country with the most physicians is the U.S.S.R., with 550,389 in 1967, or one to every 427 persons. In England and Wales there were 24,775 doctors employed by the National Health Service on 30 Sept. 1970.

The country with the highest proportion of physicians is Israel, where there were 6,312 (one for every 420 inhabitants) in 1967. The country with the lowest recorded proportion is Upper Volta, with 68 physicians (one for every 74,320 people) in 1967.

Dentists The country with the most dentists is the United States, where 115,000 were registered members of the American Dental Association in 1971.

Psychiatrists The country with the most psychiatrists is the United States. The registered membership of the American Psychiatric Association was 18,225 in 1971. The membership of the American Psychological Association was 31,000 in 1971.

HOSPITALS
Largest World The largest medical centre in the world is the District Medical Center in Chicago, Illinois, U.S.A. It covers 478 acres and includes five hospitals, with a total of 5,600 beds, and eight professional schools with more than 3,000 students.

The largest hospital in the world is Danderyd Hospital in northern Stockholm, Sweden. In 1969 it had 12,000 beds.

The largest mental hospital in the world is the Pilgrim State Hospital, on Long Island, New York State, U.S.A., with 12,800 beds. It formerly contained 14,200 beds.

The largest maternity hospital in the world is the Kandang Kerbau Government Maternity Hospital in Singapore. It has 239 midwives, 151 beds for gynaecological cases, 388 maternity beds and an output of 31,255 babies in 1969 compared with the record "birthquake" of 39,856 babies (more than 109 per day) in 1966.

United Kingdom The largest hospitals of any kind in the United Kingdom are the Rainhill Hospital near Liverpool, with 2,250 staffed beds (1972), and St. Bernard's Hospital, Southall, Middlesex, which has 2,267 staffed beds for mental patients (1971).

The largest general hospital in the United Kingdom is the St. James Hospital, Leeds, Yorkshire, with 1,438 available staffed beds.

The largest maternity hospital in the United Kingdom is the Mill Road Maternity Hospital, Liverpool with 206 staffed beds.

The largest children's hospital in the United Kingdom is Queen Mary's Hospital for Children, at Carshalton, Surrey, with 668 staffed beds.

2. ROYALTY AND HEADS OF STATE

Oldest ruling house The Emperor of Japan, Hirohito (born 29 April 1901), is the 124th in line from the first Emperor, Jimmu Tenno or Zinmu, whose reign was traditionally from 660 to 581 B.C., but probably from c. 40 to c. 10 B.C. His Imperial Majesty Muhammad Rizā Shāh Pahlavi of Iran (b. 26 Oct. 1919) claims descent from Cyrus the Great (reigned c. 559-529 B.C.).

Her Majesty Queen Elizabeth II (b. 21 April 1926) represents dynasties historically traceable at least back until the 5th century A.D.; notably that of Elesa of whom Alfred The Great was a 13 greats grandson and the Queen is therefore a 49 greats granddaughter.

REIGNS

Longest The longest recorded reign of any monarch is that of Pepi II, a Sixth Dynasty Pharaoh of ancient Egypt. His reign began in c. 2272 B.C., when he was aged 6, and lasted 91 years. Musoma Kanijo, chief of the Nzega district of western Tanganyika (now part of Tanzania), reputedly reigned for more than 98 years from 1864, when aged 8, until his death on 2 Feb. 1963. The 6th Japanese Emperor Koo-an traditionally reigned for 102 years (from 392 to 290 B.C.), but probably his actual reign was from about A.D. 110 to about A.D. 140. The reign of the 11th Emperor Suinin was traditionally from 29 B.C. to A.D. 71 (99 years), but probably from A.D. 259 to 291. The longest reign in European history was that of King Louis XIV of France, who ascended the throne on 14 May 1643, aged 4 years 8 months, and reigned for 72 years 110 days until his death on 1 Sept. 1715, four days before his 77th birthday.

Currently the longest reigning monarch in the world is King Sobhuza II, K.B.E. (b. July 1899), the *Ngwenyama* (Paramount Chief) of Swaziland, under United Kingdom protection, since December 1899, a: independent since 6 Sept. 1968. Hirohito (s above) has been Emperor in Japan since 25 De 1926.

Shortest The shortest recorded reign was that of the Dauph Louis Antoine, who was technically King Louis X1 of France for the fifteen minutes between t. signature of Charles X (1757-1836) and his ov signature to the act of abdication, in favour of Her V, which was executed at the Château de Rambouill on 2 Aug. 1830.

Highest regnal numbers The highest post-nominal number ever used designate a member of a Royal House was 74 enjoy⸱ by H.S.H. Prince Henry LXXIV Reuss (1798-188(. All male members of this branch of this family a⸱ called Henry and are successively numbered from upwards each century.

The highest British regnal number is 8, used by Hen⸱ VIII (1509-1547), who was the first British user regnal numbers, and by Edward VIII (1936) who di⸱ as H.R.H. the Duke of Windsor K.G., K.T., K.⸱ G.C.B., G.C.S.I., G.C.M.G., G.C.I.E., G.C.V.C G.B.E., I.S.O., M.C. on 28 May 1972. Jacobites lik⸱ to style Henry Benedict, Cardinal York (born 172⸱ the grandson of James II, as Henry IX in respect of ⸱ "reign" from 1777-1807 when he died the la⸱ survivor in the male line of the House of Stuart.

Longest lived 'Royals' The longest life among the Blood Royal of Europe the 96 years 8 months of H.R.H. Princess Anna ⸱ Battenberg, daughter of Nicholas I of Montenegr⸱ who was born 18 Aug. 1874 and died in Switzerlar⸱ 22 Apr. 1971. The greatest age among Europe⸱ Royal Consorts is the 99 years 3 months of H.S.⸱ Princess Marie Felixovna Romanovsky-Krassinsk⸱ who was born 19 Aug. 1872 and died in Paris 7 De⸱ 1971.

BRITISH MONARCHY RECORDS

	KINGS	QUEENS REGNANT	QUEENS CONSORT
Longest Reign or tenure	59 years 96 days[1] George III 1760-1820	63 years 216 days Victoria 1837-1901	57 years 70 days Charlotte 1761-1818 (Consort of George III)
Shortest Reign or tenure	77 days[2] Edward V 1483	13 days Jane July 1553	184 days Anne of Cleves 1540 (4th Consort of Henry VIII)
Longest lived	81 years 239 days George III (b. 1738-d. 1820)	81 years 243 days Victoria (b. 1819-d.1901)	85 years 303 days Mary of Teck (b. 1867-d.1953 (Consort of George V)
Most children (legitimate)[3]	16 Edward I 1272-1307	18[4] Anne (b. 1665-d. 1714)	15 Charlotte (b. 1744-d. 1818) (Consort of George III)
Oldest to start reign or consortship	64 years 10 months William IV 1830-1837	37 years 5 months Mary I 1553-1558	56 years 53 days Alexandra (b. 1844-d.1925) (Consort of Edward VII)
Youngest to start reign or consortship	269 days Henry VI in 1422	6 or 7 days Mary, Queen of Scots in 1542	6 years 11 months Isabella (second consort of Richard II 1396)
Most married	6 times Henry VIII m1509-1547	3 times Mary, Queen of Scots 1542-1567	4 times Catharine Parr (b. c. 1512-d. 1 (sixth consort of Henry VIII)

Notes (Dates are dates of reigns or tenures unless otherwise indicated)
1 James Francis Edward, the Old Pretender, known to his supporters as James III styled his reign from 16 Sept. 1701 until his death 1 Jan. 1766 (i.e. 6⸱ years 109 days)

2 There is the probability that in pre-Conquest times Sweyn 'Forkbeard', the Danish King of England, reigned for only 40 days in 1013-1014.

3 Henry I (1068-1135) in addition to one (possibly two) legitimate sons and a daughter had at least 20 bastard children (9 sons, 11 daughters), and possibl⸱ 22, by six mistresses.

4 None survived infancy. Victoria had nine children all of which survived their infancy.

The highest of regnal numbers was borne by the first user of them Henry VIII and also by Edward VIII here seen at the funeral of his father George V. Sixteen years later he walked also in the funeral procession of his successor George VI.

Head of State oldest and youngest The oldest head of state in the world is Dr. Eamon de Valēra (b. 14 Oct. 1882), President of the Republic of Ireland since 25 June 1959. The youngest head of state is Jean-Claude du Valier, 31 (b. 3 July 1951) President of Haiti.

3. LEGISLATURES

PARLIAMENTS

Oldest The oldest legislative body is the *Alpingi* (Althing) of Iceland, founded in A.D. 930. This body, which originally comprised 39 local chieftains, was abolished in 1800, but restored by Denmark to a consultive status in 1843 and a legislative status in 1874. The Legislative assembly with the oldest continuous history is the Tynwald Court in the Isle of Man, which is believed to have originated more than 1,000 years ago.

Largest The largest legislative assembly in the world is the National People's Congress of the People's Republic of China. The fourth Congress, which met in March 1969, had 3,500 members.

Smallest quorum The House of Lords has the smallest quorum, expressed as a percentage of eligible voters, of any legislative body in the world, namely less than one-third of one per cent. To transact business there must be three peers present, including the Lord Chancellor or his deputy. The House of Commons quorum of 40 M.P.'s, including the Speaker or his deputy, is 20 times as exacting.

Highest paid legislators The most highly paid of all world's legislators are Senators of the United States who receive a basic annual salary of $42,500 (£16,346). Of this, up to $3,000 (£1,153) is exempt from taxation. In addition up to $130,000 (£50,000) per annum is allowed for office help, with a salary limit of $13,345 (£5,132) per assistant per year. Senators also enjoy free travel, telephones, postage, medical care, telegrams (to a limit of $2,000 (£769) per session), flowers and haircuts. They also command very low rates for stationery, filming, speech and radio transcriptions and, in the case of women senators, beauty treatment. When abroad they have access to "counterpart funds" and on retirement to non-contributory benefits.

Longest membership The longest span as a legislator was 83 years by József Madarász (1814-1915). He first attended the Hungarian Parliament in 1832-36 as *ablegatus absentium* (*i.e.* on behalf of an absent deputy). He was a full member in 1848-50 and from 1861 until his death on 31 Jan. 1915.

Filibusters The longest continuous speech in the history of the United States Senate was that of Senator Wayne Morse of Oregon on 24-25 April 1953, when he spoke on the Tidelands Oil Bill for 22 hours 26 minutes without resuming his seat. Interrupted only briefly by the swearing-in of a new senator, Senator Strom Thurmond (South Carolina, Democrat) spoke against the Civil Rights Bill for 24 hours 19 minutes on 28-29 Aug. 1957. The United States national record duration for a filibuster is 38 hours 20 minutes by South Carolina senator J. Ralph Gasque, 55 who began at 12.40 p.m. on 3 Apr. and yielded the floor at 3 a.m. on 5 Apr. 1968. He was opposing a bill regulating the sale of eye-glasses.

ELECTIONS

Largest The largest election ever held was that for the Indian *Lok Sabha* (House of the People) on 1-10 Mar. 1971. About 152,720,000 of the electorate of 272,630,000 chose from 2,785 candidates for 518 seats.

Closest The ultimate in close general elections occurred in Zanzibar (now part of Tanzania) on 18 Jan. 1961, when the Afro-Shirazi Party won by a single seat, after the seat of Chake-Chake on Pemba Island had been gained by a single vote.

Most one-sided North Korea recorded a 100 per cent. turn-out of electors and a 100 per cent. vote for the Worker's Party of Korea in the general election of 8 Oct. 1962. The previous record had been set in the Albanian election of 4 June 1962, when all but seven of the electorate of 889,875 went to the polls—a 99.9992 per cent. turn-out. Of the 889,868 voters, 889,828 voted for the candidates of the Albanian Party of Labour, *i.e.* 99.9955 per cent. of the total poll.

Highest personal majority The highest personal majority was 157,692 from 192,909 votes cast, by H. H. Maharani of Jaipur (born 23 May 1919) in the Indian general election of Feb. 1962.

Communist parties The largest national Communist party outside the Soviet Union (14,254,000 members in 1971) and Communist states has been the Partito Communista Italiano (Italian Communist Party), with a membership of 2,300,000 in 1946. The total was 1,500,000 by 1971. The membership in mainland China was estimated to be 17,000,000 in 1970. The Communist Party of Great Britain, formed on 31 July 1920 in Cannon Street Station Hotel, London, attained its peak membership of 56,000 in December 1942, compared with 28,803 in November 1971. (Latest available figure).

Most parties The country with the greatest number of of political parties is Italy with 73 registered for the elections of 19 May 1968. These included "Friends of the Moon" with one candidate.

Smallest Plebiscite The only persons eligible to vote in the Barrie, Ontario plebiscite of 9 Feb. 1972 on whether or not to have 107 acres converted from a "dry" (*i.e.* temperence) to a "wet" district were Mr and Mrs Harold Frankland. "How we cast our votes is our business," said Mr Frankland, as his wife poured him a long beer. Suspense was ended after the world's shortest count and the only known unanimous vote (2-0) in democratic history. It was a "wet" landslide.

PRIME MINISTERS

Oldest The longest lived Prime Minister of any country is believed to have been Christopher Hornsrud, Prime Minister of Norway from 28 Jan. to 15 Feb. 1928. He was born on 15 Nov. 1859 and died on 13 Dec. 1960, aged 101 years 28 days.

El Hadji Muhammad el Mokri, Grand Vizier of Morocco, died on 16 Sept. 1957, at a reputed age of 116 Muslim (*Hijri*) years, equivalent to 112.5 Gregorian years.

Longest term of office Prof. Dr. António de Oliveirar Salazar, G.C.M.G. (Hon.) (1889-1969) was the President of the Council of Ministers (*i.e.* Prime Minister) of Portugal from 5 July 1932 until 27 Sept. 1968—36 years 84 days. He was superseded 11 days after going into a coma.

UNITED KINGDOM

Parliament The earliest known use of the term "parliament" in an
Earliest official English royal document, in the meaning of a summons to the King's council, dates from 19 Dec. 1241.

The Houses of Parliament of the United Kingdom in the Palace of Westminster, London, had 1,708 members (House of Lords 1,078, House of Commons 630) in June 1972.

Longest The longest English Parliament was the "Pensioners" Parliament of Charles II, which lasted from 8 May 1661 to 24 Jan. 1679, a period of 17 years 8 months and 16 days. The longest United Kingdom Parliament was that of George V, Edward VIII and George VI, lasting from 26 Nov. 1935 to 15 June 1945, a span of 9 years 6 months and 20 days.

Shortest The parliament of Edward I, summoned to Westminster for 30 May 1306, lasted only one day. The parliament of Charles I from 13 April to 5 May 1640 lasted only 22 days. The shortest United Kingdom Parliament was that of George III, lasting from 15 Dec. 1806 to 29 April 1807, a period of only 4 months and 14 days.

Longest sittings The longest sitting in the House of Commons was one of 41½ hours from 4 p.m. on 31 Jan. 1881 to 9.30 a.m. on 2 Feb. 1881, on the question of better Protection of Person and Property in Ireland. The longest sitting of the Lords has been 19 hours 16 mins. from 2.30 p.m. on 29 Feb. to 9.46 a.m. on 1 March 1968 on the Commonwealth Immigrants Bill (Committee stage).

Most Time Consuming Legislation The most profligate use of parliamentary time was on the Government of Ireland Bill of 1893-4, which required 82 days in the House of Commons of which 46 days was in Committee. The record for a standing committee is 57 sittings (248 hours and 4,734 Hansard columns) on the Housing Finance Bill between 25 Nov. 1971 and 27 Mar. 1972.

Divisions The record number of divisions in the House of Commons is 43 in the single session of 20-21 March 1907. The largest division was one of 350-310 on a vote of confidence in 1892.

ELECTORATES

Largest and smallest The largest electorate of all time was the estimated 217,900 for Hendon, Middlesex, now part of Greater London, prior to the redistribution in 1941. The largest electorate for any seat in Great Britain is now Ormskirk, Lancashire with 93,382. In Antrim South, Northern Ireland the figure is 106,440. The smallest electorate of all time was in Old Sarum (number of houses nil, population nil since *c.* 1540) in Wiltshire, with eight electors who returned two members in 1821, thus being 54,475 times as well represented as

the Hendon electorate of 120 years later. There we no contested elections in Old Sarum for the 536 ye from 1295 to 1831. The smallest electorate for a seat is Western Isles with 23,641 electors.

MAJORITIES

Party The largest party majorities were those of t Liberals, with 307 seats in 1832 and 356 seats 1906. In 1931 the Coalition of Conservatives, Lib als and National Labour candidates had a majority 425. The narrowest party majortiy was that of t Whigs in 1847, with a single seat.

The largest majority on a division was one of 463 (4 votes to 1), on a motion of "no confidence" in t conduct of World War II, on 29 Jan. 1942. Since t war the largest majority has been one of 461 (4 votes to 26) on 10 May 1967, during the debate the government's application for Britain to join t European Economic Community (the "Comm Market").

Largest personal All-time The largest individual majority of any Member Parliament was the 62,253 of Sir A. Cooper Rawsc M.P. (Conservative) at Brighton in 1931. He poll 75,205 votes against 12,952 votes for his clos opponent, the Labour Candidate Lewis Colem Cohen, later Lord Cohen of Brighton (1897-196 from an electorate of 128,779. The largest majori of any woman M.P. was 38,823 in the same Gener Election by the Countess of Iveagh (nee´ La Gwendolen Florence Mary Onslow), C.B (1881-1966), the Conservative member f Southend-on-Sea, Essex, from November 1927 October 1935.

Current The largest majority in the 1970 Parliament in 4 433 held by James Kilfedder (Ulster Unionist) Down North where he received 55,679 votes.

Narrowest personal All-time The closest result occurred in the General Election 1886 at Ashton-under-Lyne, Lancashire when t Conservative and Liberal candidates both receiv 3,049 votes. The Returning Officer, Mr. Jam Walker, gave his casting vote for John E.W. Addiso (Con.), who was duly returned while Alexander Rowley (Gladstone-Liberal) was declared unelecte On 13 Oct. 1892 there was a by-election at Cirence ter, Gloucestershire, which resulted in an electio petition after which the number of votes cast for t Conservative and Liberal were found to have be equal. A new election was ordered.

Two examples of majorities of one have occurred. Durham in the 1895 General Election, Matthe Fowler (Lib.) with 1,111 votes defeated the Ho Arthur R.D. Elliott (Liberal-Unionist) (1,110 vote after a recount. At Exeter in the General Election December 1910 a Liberal victory over the Conserva ives by 4 votes was reversed on an election petition a Conservative win by H.E. Duke, K.C. (later the 1 Lord Merrivale) (Unionist) with 4,777 votes to R. St. Maur's (Lib.) 4,776 votes.

The smallest majority since "universal" franchise w one of two votes by Abraham John Flint (b. 190 the National Labour candidate at Ilkeston, Derb shire, on 27 Oct. 1931. He received 17,587 vote compared with 17,585 for G.H. Oliver, D.C. (Labour).

Current The finest economy of effort in getting elected by a member of the 1970 Parliament was a majority of votes by Ernle Money (Conservative) in Ipswic Suffolk with 27,704 votes over Sir Dingle Foot, Q. (Labour) with 27,691.

Most recounts The greatest recorded number of recounts has been 7 in the case of Brighton, Kemptown on 16 Oct. 1964 when Dennis H. Hobden (Labour) won by 7 votes and at Peterborough on 1 Apr 1966 when Sir Harmar Nicholls Bt. (Conservative) won by 3 votes. The counts from the point of view of the loser Michael J. Ward (Labour) went +163, +163; +2, −2, −6, +1, −2, −3.

Fewest votes The smallest number of votes received by any candidate in a parliamentary election since "universal" franchise is 23 in the case of Richard Wort (Independent Conservative) in the Kinross and West Perthshire by-election of 7 Nov. 1963.

Most rapid change of fortune In 1874 Hardinge Stanley Giffard (Con.), later the 1st Earl of Halsbury (1823-1921), received one vote at Launceston, Cornwall. On 3 July 1877 he was returned unopposed for the same seat.

Greatest swing The greatest swing, at least since 1832, was that at Dartford, Kent when on 27 March 1920 Labour turned a Coalition majority of 9,370 to a win of 9,048. This represented a swing of 38.7 per cent. compared with the swing of 26.8 per cent. at Orpington, Kent on 14 March 1962 to the Liberals. In the 1970 General Election an Ulster Unionist majority of 22,986 was turned into a Protestant Unionist majority of 2,679 over the sitting Member by Ian Richard Kyle Paisley. Since there was no Protestant Unionist candidate in 1966 no swing figure is therefore calculable.

Highest poll The highest poll in any constituency since "universal" franchise was 93.42 per cent. in Fermanagh and South Tyrone, Northern Ireland, at the General Election of 25 Oct. 1951, when there were 62,799 voters from an electorate of 67,219. The Anti-Partition candidate, Mr. Cahir Healy (b. 1877), was elected with a majority of 2,635 votes. The highest poll in any constituency in the 1970 General Election was 92.18 per cent. in Fermanagh and South Tyrone. The highest figure in Great Britain was, as in 1966, North Cornwall with 85.11 per cent.

M.P.s Youngest Edmund Waller (1606-1687) was the Member of Parliament for Amersham, Buckinghamshire, in the Parliament of 1621, in which year he was 15. The official returns, however, do not show him as actually having taken his seat until two years later when, in the Parliament of 1623-24, he sat as Member for Ilchester. In 1435 Henry Long (1420-1490) was returned for an Old Sarum seat also at the age of 15. His precise date of birth is unknown. Minors were debarred in law in 1695 and in fact in 1832. Since that time the youngest Member of Parliament has been the Hon. Esmond Cecil Harmsworth (now the 2nd Viscount Rothermere), who was elected for the Isle of Thanet, Kent, on 28 Nov. 1919, when one day short of being 21 years 6 months. The youngest M.P. in 1970 was Miss Bernadette Devlin (b. 23 April 1947) who was elected for Mid Ulster on 17 April 1969 and who made her maiden speech the day before her twenty-second birthday.

Oldest The oldest of all members was Samuel Young (b. 14 Feb. 1822), Nationalist M.P. for East Cavan (1892-1918), who died on 18 April 1918, aged 96 years 63 days. The oldest "Father of the House" in Parliamentary history was the Rt. Hon. Charles Pelham Villiers (b. 3 Jan. 1802), who was the Member for Wolverhampton when he died on 16 Jan. 1898, aged 96. He was a Member of Parliament for 63 years 6 days, having been returned at 16 elections. The longest sitting member in the present Parliament is the Rt. Hon. Sir Robin Turton M.C. (b. 8 Aug. 1903), who has been the Member for Thirsk and Malton since 1929. He attributes his original adoption to the sense of economy of his committee, who, on the death of his uncle, did not wish to waste their "Vote for Turton" posters.

Longest span The longest span of service of any M.P. is 63 years 10 months (October 1900 to September 1964) by the Rt. Hon. Sir Winston Leonard Spencer Churchill, K.G., O.M., C.H., T.D. (1874-1965), with a break only from November 1922 to October 1924. The longest unbroken span was that of C.P. Villiers (see below). The longest span in the Palace of Westminster (both Houses of Parliament) has been 73 years by the 10th Earl of Wemyss, G.C.V.O., who, as Sir Francis Wemyss-Charteris-Douglas, served as M.P. for East Gloucestershire (1841-46) and Haddingtonshire (1847-83) and then took his seat in the House of Lords, dying on 30 June 1914, aged 95 years 330 days.

Earliest women M.P.s The first woman to be elected to the House of Commons was Mme. Constance Georgine Markievicz (née Gore Booth). She was elected as member (Sinn Fein) for St. Patrick's, Dublin, in December 1918. The first woman to take her seat was the Viscountess Astor, C.H. (1879-1964) (b. Nancy Witcher Langhorne at Danville, Virginia, U.S.A.; formerly Mrs. Robert Gould Shaw), who was elected Unionist member for the Sutton Division of Plymouth, Devon, on 28 Nov. 1919, and took her seat three days later.

HOUSE OF LORDS

Oldest Member The oldest member ever was the Rt. Hon. the 5th Baron Penrhyn, who was born on 21 Nov. 1865 and died on 3 Feb. 1967, aged 101 years 74 days. The oldest now is the Rt. Hon. Lord Aylmer (b. 23 March 1880).

Youngest Member The youngest member of the House of Lords is H.R.H. the Prince Charles Philip Arthur George, K.G., the Prince of Wales (b. 14 Nov. 1948). All Dukes of Cornwall, of whom Prince Charles is the 24th, are technically eligible to sit, regardless of age—in his case from his succession on 6 Feb. 1952, aged 3. The 20th and 21st holders, later King George IV (b. 1762) and King Edward VII (b. 1841), were technically entitled to sit from birth. The youngest creation of a life peer under the Peerage Act 1958 has been that of Lord Tanlaw, formerly the Hon. Simon MacKay (b. 30 Mar. 1934) at the age of 37 years and 8 days. However Lady Masham (b. 14 Apr. 1935) was created Baroness Masham of Ilton at the age of 34 years, 261 days.

Longest speech The longest recorded continuous speech in the House of Commons was that of Henry Peter Brougham (1778-1868) on 7 Feb. 1828, when he spoke for 6 hours on Law Reform. He ended at 10.40 p.m. and the report of this speech occupied 12 columns of the next day's edition of *The Times*. Brougham, created the 1st Lord Brougham and Vaux on 22 Nov. 1830, also holds the House of Lords record, also with six hours, on 7 Oct. 1831, speaking on the second reading of the Reform Bill.

The longest post-war speech has been one of 2 hours 37 minutes by Malcolm K. Macmillan (b. 1913), the Labour member for the Western Isles, on 15-16 March 1961.

Greatest parliamentary petition The greatest petition was supposed to be the Great Chartist Petition of 1848 but of the 5,706,000 "signatures" only 1,975,496 were valid. The all time largest was for the abolition of Entertainment Duty with 3,107,080 signatures presented on 5 June 1951.

PREMIERSHIP

Longest term No United Kingdom Prime Minister has yet matched in duration the continuous term of office of Great Britain's first Prime Minister the Rt. Hon. Sir Robert Walpole, K.G., later the 1st Earl of Orford (1676-1745), First Lord of the Treasury and Chancellor of the Exchequer from 3 April 1721 to 12 Feb. 1742. The office was not, however, officially recognised until 1905, since when the longest tenure has been that of Herbert Henry Asquith, later the 1st Earl of Oxford and Asquith (1852-1928), with 8 years 243 days from 8 April 1908 to 7 Dec. 1916. This was 7 days longer than the three terms of Sir Winston Churchill, between 1940 and 1955. The Hon. Sir Thomas Playford, G.C.M.G. (b. 5 July 1896) was State Premier of South Australia from 5 Nov. 1938 to 10 March 1965.

Shortest term The Rt. Hon. Sir James Waldegrave, K.G., 2nd Earl of Waldegrave (1715-63) held office for 5 days from 8-12 June 1757 but was unable to form a ministry. The shortest term of any ministry was that of the 1st Duke of Wellington, K.G., G.C.B., G.C.H. (1769-1852), whose third ministry survived only 22 days from 17 Nov. to 9 Dec. 1834.

Most times The only Prime Minister to have accepted office five times was the Rt. Hon. Stanley Baldwin, later the 1st Earl Baldwin of Bewdley (1867-1947). His ministries were those of 22 May 1923 to 22 Jan. 1924, 4 Nov. 1924 to 5 June 1929, 7 June 1935 to 21 Jan. 1936, from then until 12 Dec. 1936 and from then until 28 May 1937.

Longest lived The oldest Prime Minister of the United Kingdom has been the Rt. Hon. Sir Winston Leonard Spencer Churchill, K.G., O.M., C.H., T.D. (b. 30 Nov. 1874), who surpassed the age of the Rt. Hon. William Ewart Gladstone (1809-98) on 21 April 1963 and died on 24 Jan. 1965, aged 90 years 55 days.

Youngest The youngest of Great Britain's 47 Prime Ministers has been the Rt. Hon. the Hon. William Pitt (b. 28 May 1759), who accepted the King's invitation to be First Lord of the Treasury on 19 Dec. 1783, aged 24 years 205 days. He had previously declined on 27 Feb. 1783, when aged 23 years 275 days.

CHANCELLORSHIP

Longest and shortest tenures The Rt. Hon. Sir Robert Walpole, K.G., later the 1st Earl of Orford (1676-1745), served 22 years 5 months as Chancellor of the Exchequer, holding office continuously from 12 Oct. 1715 to 12 Feb. 1742, except for the period from 16 April 1717 to 2 April 1721. The briefest tenure of this office was 26 days in the case of the Baron (later the 1st Earl of) Mansfield (1705-93), from 11 Sept. to 6 Oct. 1767.

Most appointments The only man with four terms in this office was the Rt. Hon. William Ewart Gladstone (1809-98) in 1852-55, 1859-66, 1873-74 and 1880-82.

SPEAKERSHIP

Longest Arthur Onslow (1691-1768) was elected Mr. Speaker on 23 Jan. 1728, at the age of 36. He held the position for 33 years 54 days, until 18 March 1761.

4. MILITARY AND DEFENCE

WAR

Longest The longest of history's countless wars was the "Hundred Years War" between England and France, which lasted from 1338 to 1453 (115 years), although it may be said that the Holy War, comprising the nine Crusades from the First (1096-1104) to the Ninth (1270-91), extended over 195 years. It has been calculated that in the 3,467 years since 1496 B.C. there have been only 230 years of peace throughout the civilized world.

Last battle on British soil The last pitched land battle in Britain was at Culloden Field, Drummossie Moor, Inverness-shire, on 16 April 1746. The last Clan battle in Scotland was between Clan Mackintosh and Clan MacDonald at Mulroy, Inverness-shire, in 1689. The last battle on English soil was the Battle of Sedgemoor, Somerset, on 6 July

Admiral Sir Harry Rawson, victor of the shortest war on record— 38 minutes.

1685, when the forces of James II defeated t supporters of Charles II's illegitimate son, Jam Scott (formerly called Fitzroy or Crofts), the Duke Monmouth (1649-85). During the Jacobite rising 1745-46, there was a skirmish at Clifton Mo Westmorland, on 18 Dec. 1745, when the Brit forces under Prince William, the Duke of Cumberla (1721-65), brushed with the rebels of Prince Char Edward Stuart (1720-88) with about 12 killed on t King's side and 5 Highlanders. This was a tacti victory for the Scots under Lord George Murray.

Shortest war The shortest war on record was that between t United Kingdom and Zanzibar (now part of Tar ania) from 9.02 to 9.40 a.m. on 27 Aug. 1896. T U.K. battle fleet under Rear-Admiral (later Admi Sir) Harry Holdsworth Rawson (1843-1910) del ered an ultimatum to the self-appointed Sultan Sa' Khalid to evacuate his palace and surrender. This w not forthcoming until after 38 minutes of bombar ment. Admiral Rawson received the Brilliant Star Zanzibar (first class) from the new Sultan Hamud i Muhammad. It was proposed at one time th elements of the local populace should be compell to defray the cost of the ammunition used.

Bloodiest war By far the most costly war in terms of human life w World War II (1939-45), in which the total number fatalities, including battle deaths and civilians of countries, is estimated to have been 54,800,0C assuming 25 million U.S.S.R. fatalities and 7,800,00 Chinese civilians killed. The country which suffere

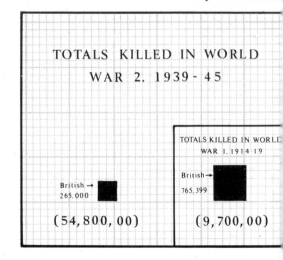

TOTALS KILLED IN WORLD WAR 2. 1939-45

British → 265,000

(54,800,00)

TOTALS KILLED IN WORLD WAR 1. 1914-19

British → 765,399

(9,700,00)

most was Poland with 6,028,000 or 22.2 per cent. of her population of 27,007,000 killed.

In the case of the United Kingdom, however, the heaviest casualties occurred in World War I (1914-18), with 765,399 killed out of 5,500,000 engaged (13.9 per cent.), compared with 265,000 out of 5,896,000 engaged (4.49 per cent.) in World War II. The heaviest total for one day was 21,392 fatalities and 35,493 wounded in the First Battle of the Somme on 1 July 1916. The total casualties in the Third Battle of Ypres (Passchendaele), from 31 July to 6 Nov. 1917, were about 575,000 (238,313 British and 337,000 German). The total death roll from World War I was only 17.7 per cent. of that of World War II, *viz.* 9,700,000.

Most costly Although no satisfactory computation has been published, it is certain that the material cost of World War II far transcended that of the rest of history's wars put together. In the case of the United Kingdom the cost of £34,423 million was over five times as great as that of World War I (£6,700 million) and 158.6 times that of the Boer War of 1899-1902 (£217 million). The total cost of World War II to the Soviet Union was estimated semi-officially in May 1959 at 2,500,000,000,000 roubles (£100,000 million).

Bloodiest civil war The bloodiest civil war in history was the T'ai-p'ing ("Peace") rebellion, in which peasant sympathizers of the Southern Ming dynasty fought the Manchu Government troops in China from 1853 to 1864. The rebellion was led by the deranged Hung Hsiu-ch'üan (poisoned himself in June 1864), who imagined himself to be a younger brother of Jesus Christ. His force was named *T'ai-p'ing T'ien Kuo* (Heavenly Kingdom of Great Peace). According to the best estimates, the loss of life was between 20,000,000 and 30,000,000, including more than 100,000 killed by Government forces in the sack of Nanking on 19-21 July 1864.

Bloodiest battle The battle with the greatest recorded number of fatalities was the First Battle of the Somme from **Modern** 1 July to 19 November 1916, with more than 1,030,000—614,105 British and French and *c.* 420,000 (*not* 650,000) German. The gunfire was heard on Hampstead Heath, London. The greatest battle of World War II and the greatest ever conflict of armour was the Battle of Kursk of 5-22 July 1943 on the Eastern front, which involved 1,300,000 Red Army troops with 3,600 tanks, 20,000 guns and 3,130 aircraft in repelling a German Army Group which had 2,500 tanks. The final investment of Berlin by the Red Army in 1945 is, however, said to have involved 3,500,000 men; 52,000 guns and mortars; 7,750 tanks and 11,000 aircraft on both sides.

Ancient Modern historians give no credence to the casualty figures attached to ancient battles, such as the 250,000 reputedly killed at Plataea (Greeks *v.* Persians) in 479 B.C. or the 200,000 allegedly killed in a single day at Châlons-sur-Marne, France, in A.D. 451. This view is on the grounds that it must have been logistically quite impossible to maintain forces of such a size in the field at that time.

British soil The bloodiest battle fought on British soil was the Battle of Towton, in Yorkshire, on 29 March 1461, when 36,000 Yorkists defeated 40,000 Lancastrians. The total loss has been estimated at between 28,000 and 38,000 killed. A figure of 80,000 British dead was attributed by Tacitus to the battle of A.D. 61 between Queen Boudicca (Boadicea) of the Iceni and the Roman Governor of Britain Suetonius Paulinus, for the loss of 400 Romans in an Army of 10,000. The site of the battle is unknown but may have been near Borough Hill, Daventry, Northamptonshire, or more probably near Hampstead Heath, London. It is improbable that, for such a small loss, the Romans

could have killed more than 20,000 Britons.

GREATEST INVASION

Seaborne The greatest invasion in military history was the Allied land, air and sea operation against the Normandy coasts of France on D-day, 6 June 1944. Thirty-eight convoys of 745 ships moved in on the first three days, supported by 4,066 landing craft, carrying 185,000 men and 20,000 vehicles, and 347 minesweepers. The air assault comprised 18,000 paratroopers from 1,087 aircraft. The 42 available divisions possessed an air support from 13,175 aircraft. Within a month 1,100,000 troops, 200,000 vehicles and 750,000 tons of stores were landed.

Airborne The largest airborne invasion was the Anglo-American assault of three divisions (34,000 men), with 2,800 aircraft and 1,600 gliders, near Arnhem, in the Netherlands, on 17 Sept. 1944.

Last on the soil of Great Britain The last invasion of Great Britain occurred on 12 Feb. 1797, when the Irish-American adventurer General Tate landed at Carreg Gwastad with 1,400 French troops. They surrendered near Fishguard, Pembrokeshire, to Lord Cawdor's force of the Castlemartin Yeomanry and some local inhabitants armed with pitchforks. The U.K. Crown Dependency of the Channel Islands were occupied by German armed forces from 30 June 1940 to 8 May 1945.

Worst sieges The worst siege in history was the 880-day siege of Leningrad, U.S.S.R. by the German Army from 30 Aug. 1941 until 27 Jan. 1944. The best estimate is that between 1.3 and 1.5 million defenders and citizens died. The longest siege in military history was that of Centa which was besieged by the Moors under Mulai Ismail for the 26 years 1674 to 1700.

LARGEST ARMED FORCES
Numerically, the country with the largest regular armed force is the U.S.S.R., with 3,375,000 at mid-1971, compared with the U.S.A.'s 2,700,000 at the same date. The Chinese People's Liberation Army, which includes naval and air services, has 2,900,000 regulars, but there is also a civilian home guard militia claimed to be 200 million strong but regarded by the Institute for Strategic Studies to have an effective element of not more than 5,000,000.

DEFENCE
The estimated level of spending on armaments throughout the world in 1971 was $185,000 million (then £77,000 million). This represents £21 per person per annum, or close to 10 per cent. of the world's total production of goods and services. It was estimated in 1970 that there were 15,400,000 full-time military and naval personnel and 30,000,000 armament workers.

The expenditure on "defence" by the government of the United States in the year ending 30 June 1971 was $78,783 million (£30,301 million), or 7.9 per cent. of the country's gross national product.

The U.S.S.R.'s defence expenditure in 1970 has been estimated to be equivalent to $55,000 million (then £22,900 million) adopting a conversion rate of 0.9 of a rouble to the U.S. dollar. This represents 11 per cent. of Gross National Product. Almost certainly, this does not include space research costs or the research and development budget for advanced weapons systems.

At the other extreme is Andorra, whose defence budget, voted in 1970, amounted to £4.08.

NAVIES
Largest The largest navy in the world is the United States Navy, with a manpower of 623,000 and 212,000 Marines at 30 June 1971. The active strength in 1971

U.S.S. Nimitz — the largest aircraft carrier in the world's largest Navy

included 15 attack and 3 anti-submarine carriers, 99 submarines in commission of which 53 are nuclear-powered, 73 guided missile ships including 8 cruisers, 29 destroyers and 30 frigates, and 133 amphibious assault ships. The total number of ships in commission was 645.

The strength of the Royal Navy in mid-1971 was 2 aircraft carriers, 2 commando ships, 2 assault ships, 1 missile armed cruiser, 9 destroyers (7 with guided missiles), 52 frigates, 8 nuclear (including 4 with *Polaris* missiles) and 17 other submarines and 47 minesweepers. The uniformed strength was 84,600 including Fleet Air Arm and Royal Marines in mid-1971. In 1914 the Royal Navy had 542 warships including 31 battleships with 5 building.

Greatest naval battle The greatest number of ships and aircraft ever involved in a sea-air action was 231 ships and 1,996 aircraft in the Battle of Leyte Gulf, in the Philippines. It raged from 22 to 27 Oct. 1944, with 166 United States and 65 Japanese warships engaged, of which 26 Japanese and 6 U.S. ships were sunk. In addition 1,280 U.S. and 716 Japanese aircraft were engaged. The greatest naval battle of modern times was the Battle of Jutland on 31 May 1916, in which 151 Royal Navy warships were involved against 101 German warships. The Royal Navy lost 14 ships and 6,097 men and the German fleet 11 ships and 2,545 men. The greatest of ancient naval battles was the Battle of Lepanto on 7 Oct. 1571, when an estimated 25,000 Turks were lost in 250 galleys, sunk by the Spanish, Venetian and Papal forces of more than 300 ships in the Gulf of Lepanto, now called Korinthiakós, Kólpos, or the Gulf of Kórinthos (Corinth), Greece.

Greatest evacuation The greatest evacuation in military history was that carried out by 1,200 Allied naval and civil craft from the beachhead at Dunkerque (Dunkirk), France, between 27 May and 4 June 1940. A total of 338,226 British and French troops were taken off.

ARMIES

Largest Numerically, the world's largest army is that of the People's Republic of China, with a total strength of about 2,550,000 in mid-1971. The total size of the U.S.S.R.'s army (including the ground elements of the Air Defence Command) in mid-1971 was estimated at 2,000,000 men, believed to be organized into about 160 divisions with a maximum strength of 10,500 each. The strength of the British Army was 185,300 in mid-1971.

Oldest The oldest army in the world is the 83-strong Swiss Guard in the Vatican City, with a regular foundation dating back to 21 Jan. 1506. Its origins, however, extend back before 1400.

Oldest old soldiers The oldest old soldier of all time was probably Jo B. Salling of the army of the Confederate States America and the last accepted survivor of the U Civil War (1861-65). He died in Kingsport, Tennesse U.S.A., on 16 March 1959, aged 113 years 1 day. T oldest Chelsea pensioner, based only on the eviden of his tombstone, was the 111-year-old Willia Hiseland (b. 6 Aug. 1620, d. 7 Feb. 1732). The la survivor of the Afghan war of 1878-79 was Alfr Hawker, who died on 10 Dec. 1962, aged 104 yea 41 days.

Tallest soldiers The tallest soldier of all time was Väinö Myllyrin (1909-63) who was inducted into the Finnish Arr when he was 7 feet 3 inches and later grew to 8 fe 1¼ inches. The British Army's tallest soldier w Benjamin Crow who was signed on at Litchfield November 1947 when he was 7 feet 1 inch ta Edward Evans (1924-58), who later grew to 7 feet 8 inches, was in the Army when he was 6 feet 10 inch

GUNS

Earliest Although it cannot be accepted as proved, the be opinion is that the earliest guns were constructed North Africa, possibly by Arabs, in *c.* 1250. T earliest representation of an English gun is contain in an illustrated manuscript dated 1326 at Oxfor The earliest anti-aircraft gun was an artillery piece a high angle mounting used in the Franco-Prussi War of 1870 by the Prussians against French balloo

British regimental records The oldest regular regiment in the British Army is t Royal Scots, raised in French service in 1633, thou the Buffs (Royal East Kent Regiment) can trace ba their origin to independent companies in Dutch p as early as 1572. The Coldstream Guards, raised 1650, were, however, placed on the establishment the British Army before the Royal Scots and t Buffs. The oldest armed body in the United Kingdc is the Honourable Artillery Company. Formed frc the Finsbury Archers, it received its charter frc Henry VIII in 1537, and is now the senior regiment the Territorial and Army Volunteer Reserve. T regiment with the greatest number of battle honou is the The Yorkshire and Lancashire Regt. with 55.

TANKS

Earliest The first fighting tank was "Mother" *alias* "l Willie" built by William Foster & Co. Ltd. of Linco and first tested on 12 Jan. 1916. Tanks were fi taken into action by the Machine Gun Corps (Hea Section), which later became the Royal Tank Cor at the battle of Flers, in France, on 15 Sept. 191 The Mark I male tank was armed with a pair of 6-guns and four machine-guns. The Mark I M weighed 28 tons and was driven by a motor deve ping 105 horse-power which gave it a maximu road speed of 4 to 5 m.p.h.

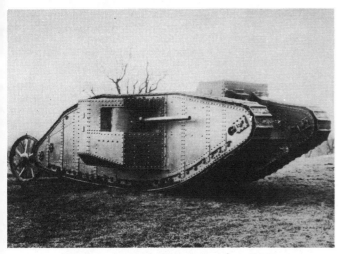

'Mother' — tested in 1916, the earliest fighting tank.

Heaviest The heaviest tank ever constructed was the German Panzer Kampfwagen Maus II, which weighed 189 tons. By 1945 it had reached only the experimental stage and was not proceeded with.

The heaviest operational tank used by any army was the 81.5-ton 13-man French Char di Rupture 3C of 1923. It carried a 155 mm. howitzer and had two 250 h.p. engines giving a maximum speed of 8 m.p.h. On 7, Nov. 1957, in the annual military parade in Moscow, U.S.S.R., a Soviet tank possibly heavier than the German Jagd Tiger II (71.7 tons), built by Henschel, and certainly heavier than the Stalin III, was displayed.

The heaviest British tank ever built is the 76-ton prototype "Tortoise". With a crew of seven and a designed speed of 12 m.p.h., this tank has a width two inches less than that of the operational 65-ton 'Conqueror". The most heavily armed is the 52-ton "Chieftain", put into service in November 1966, with a 120 mm. gun.

Largest The remains of the most massive guns ever constructed were found near Frankfurt am Main, Germany, in 1945. They were "Schwerer Gustav" and "Dora", each of which had a barrel 94 feet 9 inches long, with a calibre of 800 millimetres (31.5 inches), and a breech weighing 108 tons. The maximum charge was 2,000 kilogrammes (4,409 lb) of cordite to fire a shell weighing 4,800 kilogrammes (4.7 tons) a distance of 55 kilometres (34 miles). The maximum projectile was one of 7 tons with a range of 22 miles. Each gun with its carriage weighed 1,323 tons and required a crew of 1,500 men.

During the 1914-18 war the British army used a gun of 18 inches calibre. The barrel alone weighed 125 tons. In World War II the "Bochebuster", a train-mounted howitzer with a calibre of 18 inches, firing a 2,500 lb. shell to a maximum range of 22,800 yards, was used from 1940 onwards as part of the Kent coast defences.

Greatest range The greatest range ever attained by a gun is by the H.A.R.P. (High Altitude Research Project) gun consisting of two 16.5 inch calibre barrels in tandem in Barbados. In 1968 a 200 lb. projectile had been fired to a height of 400,000 feet (75¾ miles).

The famous "Big Bertha" guns, which shelled Paris in World War I, were the "Lange Berta" of which seven were built with a calibre of 21 cm. (8.26 inches), a designed range of 79.5 miles and an achieved range of more than 75 miles.

Mortars The largest mortars ever constructed were Mallets mortar (Woolwich Arsenal, London, 1857), and the "Little David" of World War II, made in the U.S.A. Each had a calibre of 36¼ inches (920 mm.), but neither was ever used in action.

Largest cannon The highest calibre cannon ever constructed is the *Tsar Puchka* (King of Cannons), now housed in the Kremlin, Moscow, U.S.S.R. It was built in the 16th century with a bore of 36 inches (915 mm. and a barrel 17 feet long. It was designed to fire cannon balls weighing 2 tons but was never used. The Turks fired up to seven shots per day from a bombard 26 feet long, with an internal calibre of 42 inches, against the walls of Constantinople (now Istanbul) from 12 April to 29 May 1453. It was dragged by 60 oxen and 200 men and fired a stone cannon ball weighing 1,200 lb.

Military engines The largest military catapults, or onagers, were capable of throwing a missile weighing 60 lb. a distance of 500 yards.

Longest march The longest march in military history was the famous Long March by the Chinese Communists in 1934-35. In 368 days, of which 268 days were of movement, from October to October, their force of 90,000 covered 6,000 miles northward from Kiangsi to Yünnan. They crossed 18 mountain ranges and six major rivers and lost all but 22,000 of their force in continual rear-guard actions against Nationalist Kuomin-tang (K.M.T.) forces.

Most rapid march The most rapid recorded march by foot-soldiers was one of 12 Spanish leagues (42 miles) in 26 hours on 28-29 July 1809, by the Light Brigade under Brigadier-(later Major-) General Robert Craufurd (1764-1812), coming to the relief of Lieut.-Gen. Sir Arthur Wellesley, later Field Marshal the 1st Duke of Wellington (1769-1852), after the Battle of Talavera (Talavera de la Reina, Toledo, Spain) in the Peninsular War.

The longest recorded march by a body of 60 without any fall-outs was one of 14 hours 23 minutes by the London Rifle Brigade on 18-19 April 1914. On 8 April 1922, two officers and 27 other ranks of the London Scottish Regiment covered the 53 miles from London to Brighton in 13 hours 59 minutes, each

The London Rifle Brigade on their 14 hour 23 minute march in April 1914

carrying 46 lb. of equipment, but two men failed to finish.

AIR FORCES

The earliest autonomous air force is the Royal Air Force whose origin began with the Royal Flying Corps (created 13 May 1912); the Air Battalion of the Royal Engineers (1 April 1911) and the Corps of Royal Engineers Balloon Section (1878) which was first operational in Bechuanaland (now Botswana) in 1884.

Largest The greatest Air Force of all time was the United States Army Air Force (now called the U.S. Air Force), which had 79,908 aircraft in July 1944 and 2,411,294 personnel in March 1944. The U.S. Air Force including strategic air forces had 757,000 personnel and 6,000 combat aircraft in mid-1971. The U.S.S.R. Air Force, with about 550,000 men in mid-1971, had 10,000 combat aircraft. In addition, the U.S.S.R.'s Offensive Strategic Rocket Forces had about 350,000 operational personnel in mid-1971. The strength of the Royal Air Force was 111,000 with some 500 combat aircraft in mid 1971.

BOMBS

The heaviest conventional bomb ever used operationally was the Royal Air Force's "Grand Slam", weighing 22,000 lb. and measuring 25 feet 5 inches long, dropped on Bielefeld railway viaduct, Germany, on 14 March 1945. In 1949 the United States Air Force tested a bomb weighing 42,000 lb. at Muroc Dry Lake, California, U.S.A.

Atomic The two atom bombs dropped on Japan by the United States in 1945 each had an explosive power equivalent to that of 20,000 tons (20 kilotons) of trinitrotoluene ($C_7H_5O_6N_3$), called T.N.T. The one dropped on Hiroshima, known as "Little Boy", was 10 feet long and weighed 9,000 lb. The most powerful thermo-nuclear device so far tested is one with a power equivalent to 57,000,000 tons of T.N.T., or 57 megatons, detonated by the U.S.S.R. in the Novaya Zemlya area at 8.33 a.m. G.M.T. on 30 Oct. 1961. The shock wave was detected to have circled the world three times, taking 36 hours 27 minutes for the first circuit. Some estimates put the power of this device at between 62 and 90 megatons. On 9 Aug. 1961, Nikita Khrushchyov, then the Chairman of the Council of Ministers of the U.S.S.R., declared that the Soviet Union was capable of constructing a 100-megaton bomb, and announced the possession of one in East Berlin, Germany, on 16 Jan. 1963. It has been estimated that such a bomb would make a crater 19 miles in diameter and would cause serious fires at a range of from 36 to 40 miles. The atom bomb became inevitable with the meso-thorium experiments of Otto Hahn, Fritz Strassman and Lise Meitner on 17 Dec. 1938. Work started in the U.S.S.R. on atomic bombs in June 1942 although their first chain reaction was not achieved until December 1945 by Dr. Igor Kurchatov. The patent for the fusion or H bomb was filed in the United States on 26 May 1946 by Dr. Janos (John) von Neumann (1903-57), a Hungarian-born mathematician, and Dr. Klaus Emil Julius Fuchs (born in Germany, 1911), the defected physicist.

Largest nuclear arsenal It has been estimated that in 1970 the United States total of 1,054 I.C.B.M.s (Inter-Continental Ballistic Missiles) was surpassed by the U.S.S.R. whose 1971 total has been put at more than 1,300. The greatest S.L.B.M. (Submarine launched Ballistic Missile) armoury was in 1971 that of the United States with 656 compared with 440 in service in the U.S.S.R. Navy. The U.S.S.R.'s arsenal was estimated at 2,300 including 1,300 I.C.B.M.s.

No official estimate has been published of the potential power of the device known as Doomsday, but this far surpasses any tested weapon. A 50,0 megaton cobalt-salted device has been mooted whi could kill the entire human race except those w were deep underground and who stayed there f more than five years.

Largest "conventional" explosion The largest military use of conventional explosive w in tunnels under the German positions on t Messines Ridge, Belgium. These were mined fro January 1916 to June 1917, and packed 416.6 tons ammonal, blastine, guncotton and dynamite. T bombardment which accompanied the detonation 3.10 a.m. on 7 June 1917 was reportedly heard or f in London.

5. JUDICIAL

LEGISLATION AND LITIGATION

STATUTES

Oldest The earliest known judicial code was that of Ki Urnammu during the third dynasty of Ur, Iraq, c. 2145 B.C. The oldest English statute is a section the Statute of Marlborough of 1267, retitled in 19 "The Distress Act, 1267". Some statutes enacted Henry II (d. 1189) and earlier kings are even mc durable as they have been assimilated into t Common Law. An extreme example is Alfr Dooms, c. 43 of c. A.D. 890 which contains t passage "judge thou not one doom to the ri another to the poor".

Longest in the United Kingdom Measured in bulk the longest statute of the Unit Kingdom is the Income Tax and Corporation T Act, 1970, which runs to 540 sections, 15 schedu and 670 pages. It is 1½ inches thick and costs £2.8 However, its 540 sections are surpassed in number the 748 of the Merchant Shipping Act, 1894.

Of old statutes, 31 George III XIV, the Land Tax A of 1791, written on parchment, consists of 780 ski forming a roll 1,170 feet long.

Shortest The shortest statute is the Parliament (Qualificati of Women) Act, 1918, which runs to 27 operati words—"A woman shall not be disqualified by sex marriage from being elected to or sitting or voting a Member of the Common House of Parliament Section 2 contains a further 14 words giving the sh title.

Most It was computed in March 1959 that the total numb of laws on Federal and State statute books in t United States was 1,156,644. The Illinois Sta Legislature only discovered in April 1967 that it h made the sale of cigarettes illegal and punishable b $100 fine for a second offence in 1907.

Earliest English patent The earliest of all known English patents was th granted by Henry VI in 1449 to Flemish-born John Utynam for making the coloured glass required f the windows of Eton College. The peak number applications for patents filed in the United Kingdc in any one year was 63,614 in 1969.

Most protracted litigation The longest contested law suit ever recorded ended Poona, India, on 28 April 1966, when Balasah Patloji Thorat received a favourable judgment on suit filed by his ancestor Maloji Thorat 761 yea earlier in 1205. The points at issue were rights presiding over public functions and precedences religious festivals.

The dispute over the claim of the Prior and Conve of Durham Cathedral to administer the spiritualiti of the diocese during a vacancy in the See grew fier in 1283. It smouldered until 1939, having flared up 1672, 1890 and 1920. In 1939 the Archbishop Canterbury exercised his metropolitan rights a appointed the Dean as guardian of spiritualities

The seven year long trial of Warren Hastings which started in 1788 and ended in 1795.

Durham "without prejudice to the general issue", then 656 years old.

Most inexplicable Statute Certain passages in several Acts have always defied interpretation and the most inexplicable must be a matter of opinion. A Judge of the Court of Session of Scotland has sent the Editors his candidate which reads, "In the Nuts (unground), (other than ground nuts) Order, the expression nuts shall have reference to such nuts, other than ground nuts, as would but for this amending Order not qualify as nuts (unground) (other than ground nuts) by reason of their being nuts (unground)."

Longest British trial The longest trial in the annals of British justice was the Tichborne personation case. The civil trial began on 11 May 1871, lasted 103 days and collapsed on 6 March 1872. The criminal trial went on for 188 days, resulting in a sentence on 28 Feb. 1874 for two counts of perjury (14 years imprisonment and hard labour) on the London-born Arthur Orton, *alias* Thomas Castro (1834-98), who claimed to be Roger Charles Tichborne (1829-54), the elder brother of Sir Alfred Joseph Doughty-Tichborne, 11th Bt. (1839-66). The whole case, during which, miraculously, no juryman fell ill, thus spanned 827 days and cost £55,315. The jury were out for only 30 minutes.

The impeachment of Warren Hastings (1732-1818), which began in 1788, dragged on for seven years until 23 April 1795, but the trial lasted only 149 days. He was appointed a member of the Privy Council in 1814.

Murder The longest murder trial in Britain was that in which Ronald and Reginald Kray (twins), 35, were found guilty of the murder by shooting of George Cornell, 38, at the Blind Beggar public house on 9 Mar. 1966, and by stabbing of Jack "The Hat" McVitie, 38, in Evering Road, Stoke Newington in October 1967. They were sentenced by Mr. Justice Melford Stevenson to imprisonment for not less than 30 years on 5 March 1969 after a 39-day trial at the Old Bailey, London. The costs of the trial were estimated at more than £200,000.

The shortest recorded British murder hearings were *R. v. Murray* on 28 Feb. 1957 and *R. v. Cawley* at Winchester Assizes on 14 Dec. 1959. The proceedings occupied only 30 seconds on each occasion.

Divorce The longest trial of a divorce case in Britain was

Gibbons v. Gibbons and Roman and Halperin. On 19 March 1962, after 28 days, Mr. Alfred George Boyd Gibbons was granted a decree *nisi* against his wife Dorothy for adultery with Mr. John Halperin of New York City, N.Y., U.S.A.

Longest address The longest address in a British court was in *Globe and Phoenix Gold Mining Co. Ltd. v. Amalgamated Properties of Rhodesia.* Mr. William Henry Upjohn, K.C. (1853-1941) concluded his speech on 22 Sept. 1916, having addressed the court for 45 days.

Highest bail The highest amount ever demanded as bail was $46,500,000 (then £16,608,333) against Antonio De Angelis in a civil damages suit by the Harbor Tank Storage Co. filed in the Superior Court, Jersey City, New Jersey, U.S.A. on 16 Jan. 1964. (See also Greatest swindle, page 206.)

Best attended trial The greatest attendance at any trial was that of Major Jesús Sosa Blanco, aged 51, for an alleged 108 murders. At one point in the 12½-hour trial (5.30 p.m. to 6 a.m., 22-23 Jan. 1959), 17,000 people were present in the Havana Sports Palace, Cuba.

The highest bail figure in a British court is £140,000, granted to Manick Banthia at Uxbridge Court, Middlesex on 14 Oct. 1966. The amount involved £30,000 on his own recognizances, a surety of £50,000 and three of £20,000 each. He was charged with an attempt illegally to export £30,000 from London Airport in 60 Bank envelopes. Two other men, Joe Cohen and Amarendra Goswami also charged, had a combined bail of £170,000.

On 2 June 1959 the original bail fixed at Dublin, Ireland, for Dr. Paul Singer, aged 48, managing director of Shanahan's Stamp Auctions Ltd., was £100,000. This was later reduced to £15,000.

Greatest compensation The greatest Crown compensation for wrongful imprisonment was £10,000, paid on 23 Sept. 1931 to T. Boevey Barrett, who had been wrongfully convicted of alleged frauds in 1921. After serving three years' imprisonment in Accra, Ghana, he was granted a free pardon in 1930.

The greatest compensation paid for wrongful imprisonment in the United Kingdom was £6,000, paid in 1929 to Oscar Slater (*né* Leschziner), who had been arraigned for the murder of Miss Marion Gilchrist, aged 83, in Glasgow on 6 May 1909.

GREATEST DAMAGES

The highest damages ever awarded in any court of law were $14,387,674 following upon the crash of a private aircraft at South Lake Tahoe, California, U.S.A. on 21st February 1967, to the sole survivor Ray Rosendin, 45, by the Santa Clara Superior Court on 8th March 1972. Rosendin received $1,069,374 for the loss of both legs and disabling arm injuries; $1,213,129 for the loss of his wife and $10,500,000 punitive damages against Avco-Lyconing Corporation which allegedly violated Federal regulations when it rebuilt the aircraft engine owned by Rosendin Corporation.

Breach of contract The greatest damages ever awarded for a breach of contract were £610,392, awarded on 16 July 1930 to the Bank of Portugal against the printers Waterlow & Sons Ltd., of London, arising from their unauthorized printing of 580,000 five-hundred escudo notes in 1925. This award was upheld in the House of Lords on 28 April 1932. One of the perpetrators, Arthur Virgilio Alves Reis, served 16 years (1930-46) in gaol.

Personal injury The greatest damages ever awarded for personal injury are $3,600,000 (£1,500,000) on 18 Oct. 1970 to Keith Bush, 30, of Ely, Nevada, U.S.A., at Reno, Nevada against General Electric and Westinghouse Air Brake Co. in connection with an industrial accident which left him blind, speechless and paralyzed.

The greatest damages ever awarded for personal injury in a British court were £82,500, awarded to David John Butterworth, 22, of Knutsford, Cheshire, for the "catastrophic injuries" received by him in a road accident involving the collision of two cars in 1969. The award, made in the High Court at Manchester on 13 July 1972 by Mr. Justice Wrangham was jointly against the two drivers, Mr. Alfred Sutton of Sandway, Cheshire, and Peter Frank Dutton now in Australia. Mr. Butterworth, a passenger, suffered severe brain damage.

On 5 Feb. 1960, the Dublin High Court awarded £87,402 damages for motor injuries to Mr. Kevin P. McMorrow, aged 38, of County Leitrim, against his driver Mr. Edward Knott. It is understood that, after an appeal, a settlement was made out of court for £50,000.

Breach of promise The largest sum involved in a breach of promise suit in the United Kingdom was £50,000, accepted in 1913 by Miss Daisy Markham, *alias* Mrs Annie Moss (d. 20 Aug. 1962, aged 76), in settlement against the 6th Marquess of Northampton (b. 6 Aug. 1885).

Defamation The greatest damages for defamation ever awarded in the United Kingdom were £117,000, awarded on 21 July 1961 in *The Rubber Improvement Co. Ltd. v. Associated Newspapers Ltd.* for 51 words which appeared in the *Daily Mail* of 23 Dec. 1958. The company was represented by Colin Duncan, M.C. (now a Q.C.) and Mr. (now Sir) Helenus Patrick Joseph Milmo, Q.C. (b. 24 Aug. 1908), who has since become a judge. After appeal proceedings by both sides this action was settled out of court for a substantially smaller amount.

Divorce The highest award made to the dispossessed party in a divorce suit was $70,000 (then £25,000), awarded to Mr. Demetrus Sophocles Constandinidi against Dr. Henry William Lance for bigamous adultery with his wife Mrs. Julia Constandinidi. She married Dr. Lance after going through a form of divorce in Sioux Falls, South Dakata, U.S.A., on 27 Feb. 1902.

ALIMONY

World The greatest alimony ever paid was $11,550,000 (then £4,125,000), paid by Reuben Hollis Fleet, the

Constance Cornwallis-West, who received a settlement of £13,000 p.a. on the termination of her marriage to the 2nd Duke of Westminster.

United States millionaire aircraft manufacturer, to h second wife Dorothy (*née* Mitchell) in 1945, aft their separation, following "verbal abuse".

Britain The highest alimony awarded in a British court £5,000 per annum, but in 1919 the 2nd Duke Westminster, G.C.V.O., D.S.O. (1879-1953) settle £13,000 per annum upon his first wife, Constan Edwina (*née* Cornwallis-West), C.B.E., later M Lewis.

HIGHEST SETTLEMENT

Divorce The greatest amount ever paid in a divorce settleme is $9,500,000 (£3,393,000), paid by Edward Hudson to Mrs. Cecil Amelia Blaffer Hudson, aged 4 This award was made on 28 Feb. 1963 at t Domestic Relations Court, Houston, Texas, U.S. Mrs Hudson was, reputedly, already wor $14,000,000 (£5,000,000).

Patent case The greatest settlement ever made in a pate infringement suit is $9,250,000 (£3,303,000), paid April 1952 by the Ford Motor Company to t Ferguson Tractor Co. for a claim filed in Janua 1948.

Largest Suit The highest amount of damage ever sought $675,000,000,000,000 (equivalent to the U. Government revenue for 3,000 years) in a suit by M I. Walton Bader brought in the U.S. District Cou New York City on 14 Apr. 1971 against Gener Motors and others for polluting all 50 states.

HIGHEST COSTS

The highest costs in English legal history arose fro the case of the *Société Rateau v. Rolls-Royce,* action concerning the alleged infringement of French patent of 4 Dec. 1939 for an axial flow j engine. Mr Justice Lloyd-Jacob held in April 196 that the patent had not been infringed. Costs we estimated at £325,000.

Income tax The greatest amount paid for information concerni
Highest a case of income tax delinquency was $79,999.
reward (£28,571), paid by the United States Intern Revenue Service to a group of informers. Paymen are limited to 10 per cent. of the amount recoverd as direct result of information laid. Informants are oft low-income accountants or women scorned. The tot of payments in 1965 was $597,731 (then £213,47

Greatest lien The greatest lien ever imposed by the U.S. Intern Revenue Service was one of $21,261,8 (£7,593,500), filed against the California property

John A. T. Galvin in March 1963, in respect of alleged tax arrears for 1954-57.

WILLS

Shortest The shortest valid will in the world is "Vše zene", the Czech for "All to wife", written and dated 19 Jan. 1967 by Herr Karl Tausch of Langen, Hesse, Germany. The shortest will contested but subsequently admitted to probate in English law was the case of *Thorn v. Dickens* in 1906. It consisted of the three words "All for Mother".

Longest The longest will on record was that of Mrs. Frederica Cook (U.S.A.), in the early part of the century. It consisted of four bound volumes containing 95,940 words.

JUDGE

Oldest The oldest recorded active judge was Judge Albert R.
World Alexander (1859-1966) of Plattsburg, Missouri, U.S.A. He was the magistrate and probate judge of Clinton County until his retirement aged 105 years 8 months on 9 July 1965.

Britain The greatest recorded age at which any British judge has sat on a bench was 93 years 9 months in the case of Sir William Francis Kyffin Taylor, G.B.E., K.C. (later Lord Maenan), who was born on 9 July 1854 and retired as presiding judge of the Liverpool Court of Passage in April 1948, having held that position since 1903. The greatest age at which a House of Lords judgment has been given is 92 in the case of the 1st Earl of Halsbury (b. 3 Sept. 1823) in 1916.

Youngest The youngest certain age at which any English judge has been appointed is 31, in the case of Sir Francis Buller (b. 17 March 1746), who was appointed Second Judge of the County Palatine of Chester on 27 Nov. 1777, and Puisne Judge of the King's Bench on 6 May 1778, aged 32 years 1 month. The Hon. Daines Barrington (*c.* 1727-1800) was appointed Justice of the Counties of Merioneth and Anglesey sometime in 1757 and may have been even younger.

Youngest The earliest age at which a barrister has taken silk
Q.C. since 1900 is 33 years 8 months in the case of Mr. (later the Rt. Hon. Sir) Francis Raymond Evershed (1899-1966) in April 1933. He was later Lord Evershed, a Lord of Appeal in Ordinary.

Highest paid It was estimated that Jerry Giesler (1886-1962), an
lawyer attorney in Los Angeles, California, U.S.A., averaged $50,000 (then £17,850) in fees for each case which he handled during the latter part of his career. Currently, the most highly paid lawyer is generally believed to be Louis Nizer of New York City, N.Y., U.S.A.

CRIME AND PUNISHMENT

GREATEST MASS KILLINGS

China The greatest massacre in human history ever imputed is that of 26,300,000 Chinese during the régime of Mao Tse-tung between 1949 and May 1965. This accusation was made by an agency of the U.S.S.R. Government in a radio broadcast on 7 April 1969. The broadcast broke down the total into four periods:—2.8 million (1949-52); 3.5 million (1953-57); 6.7 million (1958-60); and 13.3 million (1961-May 1965). The highest reported death figures in single monthly announcements on Peking radio were 1,176,000 in the provinces of Anhwei, Chekiang, Kiangsu, and Shantung, and 1,150,000 in the Central South Provinces. Po I-po, Minister of Finance, is alleged to have stated in the organ *For a lasting peace, for a people's democracy* "in the past three years (1950-52) we have liquidated more than 2 million bandits". General Jacques Guillermaz, a French diplomat estimated the total executions between February 1951 and May 1952 at between 1 million and 3 million. In April 1971 the Executive

Yuan or cabinet of the implacably hostile government of The Republic of China in Taipei, Taiwan announced its official estimate of the mainland death roll in the period 1949-69 as "at least 39,940,000". This figure, however, excluded "tens of thousands" killed in the Great Proletarian Cultural Revolution, which began in late 1966. The Walker Report published by the U.S. Senate Committee of the Judiciary in July 1971 placed the parameters of the total death roll since 1949 between 32.25 and 61.7 million.

U.S.S.R. The total death roll in the Great Purge, or *Yezhovshchina*, in the U.S.S.R., in 1936-38 has never been published, though evidence of its magnitude may be found in population statistics which show a deficiency of males from before the outbreak of the 1941-45 war. The reign of terror was administered by the *Narodny Kommissariat Vnutrennykh Del* (N.K.V.D.), or People's Commissariat of Internal Affairs, the Soviet security service headed by Nikolay Ivanovich Yezhov (1895-?1939), described by Nikita Khrushchyov in 1956 as "a degenerate". S. V. Utechin, an expert on Soviet affairs, regards estimates of 8,000,000 or 10,000,000 victims as "probably not exaggerations".

Nazi At the S.S. (*Schutzstaffel*) extermination camp
Germany (*Vernichtungslager*) called Auschwitz-Birkenau (Oswiecim-Brzezinka), near Oswiecim (Auschwitz), in southern Poland, where a minimum of 900,000 people (Soviet estimate is 4,000,000) were exterminated from 14 June 1940 to 29 Jan. 1945, the greatest number killed in a day was 6,000. The man who operated the release of the "Zyklon B" cyanide pellets into the gas chambers there during this time was Sergeant Mold. The Nazi (*Nationalsozialistiche Deutsche Arbeiter Partei*) Commandant during the period 1940-43 was Rudolf Franz Ferdinand Höss, who was tried in Warsaw from 11 March to 2 April 1947 and hanged, aged 47, at Oswiecim on 15 April 1947. Erich Koch, the war-time *Gauleiter* of East Prussia and *Reichskommissar* for German-occupied Ukraine, was arrested near Hamburg on 24 May 1949, tried in Warsaw from 20 Oct. 1958 to 9 March 1959 and sentenced to death for his responsibility for, or complicity in, the deaths of 4,232,000 people. The death sentence was later commuted to imprisonment.

Obersturmbannführer (Lt.-Col.) Karl Adolf Eichmann (b. Solingen, West Germany 19 March 1906) of the S.S. was hanged in a small room inside Ramleh Prison, near Tel Aviv, Israel, at just before midnight (local time) on 31 May 1962, for his complicity in the deaths of 5,700,000 Jews during World War II, under the instruction given in April 1941 by Adolf Hitler (1889-1945) for the "Final Solution" (*Endlösung*), *i.e.* the extermination of European Jewry.

Forced No official figures have been published of the death
Labour roll in Corrective Labour Camps in the U.S.S.R., first established in 1918. The total number of such camps was known to be more than 200 in 1946 but in 1956 many were converted to less severe Corrective Labour Colonies. An estimate published in the Netherlands puts the death roll between 1921 and 1960 at 19,000,000. The camps were administered by the *Cheka* until 1922, the O.G.P.U. (1922-34), the N.K.V.D. (1934-1946), the M.V.D. (1946-1953) and the K.G.B. since 1953. Daily intake has been limited to only 2,400 calories since 1961.

Largest The largest syndicate of organized crime is the Mafia
criminal or La Cosa Nostra, which has infiltrated the execu-
organization tive, judiciary and legislature of the United States. It consists of some 3,000 to 5,000 individuals in 24 "families" federated under "The Commission", which has a Sicilian-Jewish axis and an estimated annual turnover in vice, gambling, protection rackets and rigged trading of $30,000 million per annum of which some 25 per cent. is profit. The biggest Mafia

(means *swank* from a Sicilian word for beauty or pride) killing was on 10 Sept. 1931 when the topmost man Salvatore Maranzano, *Il Capo di Tutti Capi,* and 40 allies were liquidated.

Murder rate
Highest The country with the highest recorded murder rate is Equatorial Guinea, with 31.1 registered homicides per each 100,000 of the population in 1967. It has been estimated that the total number of murders in Colombia during *La Violencia* (1945-62) was about 300,000, giving a rate over a 17-year period of more than 48 a day. A total of 592 deaths was attributed to one bandit leader, Teófilo ("Sparks") Rojas, aged 27, between 1948 and his death in an ambush near Armenia on 22 Jan. 1963. Some sources attribute 3,500 slayings to him.

Britain In Great Britain the highest annual total of murders since 1900 has been 242 in 1945, and the lowest 124 in 1937 and 125 in 1958. The murder rate in Britain is running at less than 3.0 per million.

Lowest The country with the lowest officially recorded rate in the world is Spain, with 39 murders (a rate of 1.23 per each million of the population) in 1967, or one murder every 9 days. In the Indian protectorate of Sikkim, in the Himalayas, murder is, however, practcally unknown, while in the Hunza area of Kashmir, in the Karakoram, only one definite case has been recorded since 1900.

MOST PROLIFIC MURDERER
World The greatest number of victims ascribed to an individual has been 610 in the case of Countess Erszebet Báthory (1560-1614) of Hungary. At her trial which began on 2 Jan. 1611 a witness testified to seeing a list of her victims in her own handwriting totalling this number. All were alleged to be young girls from the neighbourhood of her castle at Csejthe where she died on 21 Aug. 1614. She had been walled up in her room for the 3½ years after being found guilty.

Gille de Rays (Raies or Retz) (1404-40) was reputed to have murdered ritually between 140 and 200 kidnapped children. The best estimates put the total of his victims at about 60. He was hanged and burnt at Nantes, France, on 25 Oct. 1440.

The total number of victims of the cannibalistic cave-dwelling Beane family in Galloway, Scotland in the early 17th century is not known but may have run as high as 50 per year. Sawney Beane, head of the family, his wife, 8 sons, 6 daughters and 32 grand-children were taken by an Army detachment to Edinburgh and executed apparently without trial.

The most prolific murderer known in recent criminal history was Herman Webster Mudgett (b. 16 May 1860), better known as H. H. Holmes. It has been estimated that he disposed of some 150 young women "paying guests" in his "Castle" on 63rd Street, Chicago, Illinois, U.S.A. After a suspicious fire on 22 Nov. 1893, the "Castle" was investigated and found to contain secret passages, stairways and a maze of odd rooms, some windowless or padded, containing hidden gas inlets and electric indicators. There was also a hoist, two chutes, a furnace, an acid bath, a dissecting table, a selection of surgical instruments and fragmentary human remains. Holmes was hanged on 7 May 1896, on a charge of murdering his associate, Benjamin F. Pitezel.

Murderess The greatest total of victims ascribed to a recent murderess is 16, together with a further 12 possible victims, making a total of 28. This was in the case of Bella Poulsdatter Sorensen Gunness *née* Grunt (1859-1908) of La Porte, Indiana, U.S.A. Evidence came to light when her farm was set on fire on 28 April 1908, when she herself was found by a jury to

have committed suicide by strychnine poisoning. H victims, remains of many of whom were dug from h hog lot, are believed to comprise two husbands, least eight and possibly 20 would-be suitors lured "Lonely Hearts" advertisements, three women a three children. A claim that Vera Renczi murdered persons in Romania this century lacks authority.

Britain The only man to be arraigned on a charge of ni murders was Peter Thomas Anthony Manuel, aged a New York born Lanarkshire woodworker. He w found guilty, on 29 May 1958, after a 16-day trial Glasgow High Court, of the capital murders of f females and two males. Two other charges were n proceeded with and three other murders were la admitted by him, making a total of twelve. He w hanged at Barlinnie Prison, near Glasgow, at 8 a.m. 11 July 1958. The total number of murders comm ted by "Doctor" William Palmer (b. 1824) of Ru ley, Staffordshire, is not definitely known but was least 13 and most probably 16, the victims havi been poisoned by strychnine or antimony. He w hanged at Stafford on 14 June 1856. Scotland's m prolific known murderer was the Irish-born Willia Burke (1792-1829), who, in partnership with Willia Hare, murdered at least 13 derelicts in Edinbur within 12 months, to sell their corpses. Hare turn King's evidence and Burke was hanged on 28 Ja 1829.

Gang
murders During the period of open gang warfare in Chicag Illinois, U.S.A., the peak year was 1926, when the were 76 unsolved killings. The 1,000th gang murd in Chicago since 1919 occurred on 1 Feb. 1967. On 13 cases have ended in convictions.

Thuggee It has been estimated that at least 2,000,000 India were strangled by Thugs (*burtotes*) during the peri of the Thuggee cult, from 1550 until finally suppre sed in 1852. It was established at the trial of Buhra that he had strangled at least 931 victims with yellow and white cloth strip or *ruhmal* in the Ou district between 1790 and 1830.

Bhagwan, the goddess of the thuggee in the Temple of Bindachun from a sketch made in 1844.

"Smelling out" The greatest "smelling out" recorded in African history occurred before Shaka (1787-1828) and 30,000 Nguni subjects near the River Umhlatuzana, Zululand (now Natal, South Africa) in March 1824. After 9 hours, over 300 were "smelt out" as guilty of smearing the Royal *Kraal* with blood, by 150 witch-finders led by the hideous female *isangoma* Nobela. The victims were declared innocent when Shaka admitted to having done the smearing himself to expose the falsity of the power of his diviners. Nobela poisoned herself with atropine ($C_{17}H_{23}NO_3$), but the other 149 witch-finders were thereupon skewered or clubbed to death.

Suicide The estimated daily total of suicides throughout the world surpassed 1,000 in 1965. The country with the highest recorded suicide rate is Hungary, with 33.1 per each 100,000 of the population in 1969. The country with the lowest recorded rate is Malta with only 1 suicide in 1967.

In England and Wales there were 3,940 suicides in 1970, or an average of nearly 11 per day. In the northern hemisphere April and May tend to be peak months.

CAPITAL PUNISHMENT

Capital punishment was first abolished *de facto* in Liechtenstein in 1798. The death penalty for murder was abolished on a free vote in the House of Commons by a majority of 158 (343-185) on 16 Dec. and a majority of 46 in the House of Lords on 18 Dec. 1969.

Capital punishment in the British Isles dates from A.D. 450, but fell into disuse in the 11th century, only to be revived in the Middle Ages, reaching a peak in the reign of Edward VI (1547-1553), when an average of 560 persons were executed annually at Tyburn alone. The most people executed at one hanging was 24 at Tyburn (Marble Arch, London) in 1571. Even into the 19th century, there were 223 capital crimes, though people were, in practice, hanged for only 25 of these.

Between 1830 and 1955 the largest number hanged in a year was 27 (24 men, 3 women) in 1903. The least was 5 in 1854, 1921 and 1930. In 1956 there were no hangings in England, Wales or Scotland, since when the highest number in any year has been 5.

Last hangings The last public execution in England took place outside Newgate Prison, London at 8 a.m. on 26 May 1868, when Michael Barrett was hanged for his part in the Fenian bomb outrage on 13 Dec. 1867, when 12 were killed outside the Clerkenwell House of Detention, London. The earliest non-public execution was of the murderer Thomas Wells on 13 Aug. 1868. The last public hanging in Scotland was that of the murderer Joe Bell in Perth in 1866. The last in the United States occurred at Owensboro, Kentucky in 1936. The last hangings were those of Peter Anthony Allen (b. 4 Apr. 1943) at Walton Prison, Liverpool, and John Robson Walby (b. 1 April 1940), *alias* Gwynne Owen Evans, at Strangeways Gaol, Manchester both on 13 Aug. 1964. They had been found guilty of the capital murder of John Alan West, on 7 Apr. 1964. The 14th and last woman executed this century was Mrs Ruth Ellis, 28, for the murder of David Blakeley, 25, outside The Magnolia, Hampstead on 10 Apr. 1955. She was executed on 13 July at Holloway.

Last from yard-arm The last naval execution at the yard-arm was the hanging of Marine John Dalliger aboard H.M.S. *Leven* in the River Yangtze, China, on 13 July 1860. Dalliger had been found guilty of two attempted murders.

Last public guillotining The last person to be publicly guillotined in France was the murderer Eugen Weidmann before a large

Ruth Ellis, the last murderess to be hanged in Britain.

crowd at Versailles, near Paris, at 4.50 a.m. on 17 June 1939. Dr. Joseph Ignace Guillotin (1738-1812) died a natural death. He had advocated the use of the machine designed by Dr. Antoine Louis in 1789 in the French constituent assembly.

Youngest Although the hanging of persons under 18 was expressly excluded only in the Children's and Young Person's Act, 1933 (Sec. 33), no person under that age had, in fact, been executed since 1887. Though it has been published widely that a girl of seven was hanged in 1808 and a boy of nine in 1831, the name of neither can be produced. In 1801 Andrew Benning, aged 13, was executed for housebreaking. The youngest persons hanged since 1900 have been 18 years old:—J.H. Clarkson at Leeds on 29 March 1904; Henry Jacoby on 7 Jan. 1922; Bishop in 1925; another case in 1932; James Farrell on 29 March 1949; and Francis Robert George ("Flossie") Forsyth on 10 Nov. 1960.

Oldest The oldest person hanged in the United Kingdom since 1900 was a man of 71 named Charles Frembd (*sic*) at Chelmsford Gaol on 4 Nov. 1914, for the murder of his wife at Leytonstone, Essex. In 1822 John Smith, said to be 80, of Greenwich, London, was hanged for the murder of a woman.

Most attempts The only man in Britain to survive three attempts to hang him was John Lee at Exeter Gaol, Devon, on 23 Feb. 1885. Lee had been found guilty of murdering, on 15 Nov. 1884, Emma Ann Whitehead Keyse of Babbacombe, who had employed him as a footman. The attempts, in which the executioner, James Berry, failed three times to get the trap open, occupied about seven minutes. Sir William Harcourt, the Home Secretary, commuted the sentence to life imprisonment. After release, Lee emigrated to the United States in 1917, was married and lived until 1933. The rope is now owned by Mr. D.A. Dale of Histon, Cambridge. In 1803 it was reported that Joseph Samuels was reprieved in Sydney, Australia after three unsuccessful attempts to hang him in which the rope twice broke.

Slowest The longest delay in carrying out a death sentence in recent history is in the case of Sadamichi Hirasawa (b. 1906) of Tōkyō, Japan, who was sentenced to death in January 1950, after a trial lasting 16 months, on charges of poisoning twelve people with potassium cyanide in a Tōkyō bank. In November 1962 he was transferred to a prison at Sendai, in northern Honshū where he was still awaiting execution in May 1972.

The longest stay on "death row" in the United States has been one of more than 14 years by Edgar Labat, aged 44, and Clifton A. Paret, aged 38, in Angola Penitentiary, Louisiana, U.S.A. In March 1953 they were sentenced to death, after being found guilty of rape in 1950. They were released on 5 May 1967, only to be immediately re-arrested on a local jury indictment arising from the original charge.

Caryl Chessman, aged 39 and convicted of 17 felonies, was executed on 2 May 1960 in the gas chamber at the California State Prison, San Quentin, California, U.S.A. In 11 years 10 months and one week on "death row", Chessman had won eight stays.

EXECUTIONER
The longest period of office of a Public Executioner was that of William Calcraft (1800-1879), who was in office from 1828 to 1871 and officiated at nearly every hanging outside and later inside Newgate Prison, London. The most "suitably qualified" executioner on the Home Office list for the last remaining gallows at Wandsworth Prison, London against possible use for traitors, violent pirates and Royal dockyard arsonists is believed to be Mr. Harry Allen (b. 1918).

BLOODIEST ASSIZES
In the West Country Assizes of 1685 (Winchester to Wells), George Jeffreys, the 1st Baron Jeffreys of Wem (1645-1689), sentenced 330 persons to be hanged, 841 to be transported for periods of ten or more years and larger numbers to be imprisoned and flogged. These sentences followed the Duke of Monmouth's insurrections.

LONGEST SENTENCES
World The longest recorded prison sentence is one of 7,109 years awarded to a pair of confidence tricksters by an Iranian court on 15 June 1969. The duration of sentences are proportional to the amount of the defalcations involved. A sentence of 384,912 years was demanded at the prosecution of Gabriel March Grandos 22 at Palma de Mallorca, Spain on 11 Mar. 1972 for failing to deliver 42,768 letters.

Richard Honeck was sentenced to life imprisonment in the United States in 1899, after having murdered his former schoolteacher. It was reported in November 1963 that Honeck, then aged 84, who was in Menard Petitentiary, Chester, Illinois, was due to be paroled after 64 years in prison, during which time he had received one letter (a four-line note from his brother in 1904) and two visitors, a friend in 1904 and a newspaper reporter in 1963. He was released on 20 Dec. 1963.

United Kingdom On 17 May 1939, William Burkitt, three times acquitted of murder by a jury (1915, 1925 and 1939), was sentenced by Mr. Justice Cassels "to be kept in prison for the rest of your natural life". Burkitt, whose appeal against the sentence failed in 1948, had served 34 years for manslaughter up to 1954, when he was released. He died on 24 Dec. 1956. Mr Justice Chapman at Oxford Assizes in October 1971 jailed the police murderer Arthur William Skingle, 25 for life with the first recommendation that "life should mean for life".

The longest single period served by a reprieved murderer in Great Britain this century was 40 years 11 months by John Watson Laurie, the Goat Fell or Arran murderer, who was reprieved on the grounds of insanity in November 1889 and who died in Perth Penitentiary on 4 Oct. 1930.

The longest prison sentence ever passed under United Kingdom law was one of three consecutive and two concurrent terms of 14 years, thus totalling 42 years, imposed on 3 May 1961 on George Blake (b. Rotter-

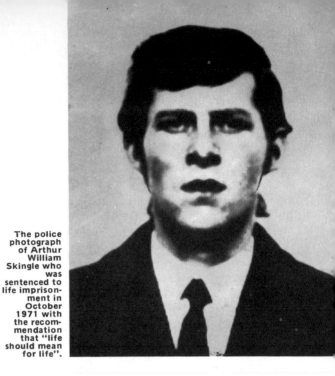

The police photograph of Arthur William Skingle who was sentenced to life imprisonment in October 1971 with the recommendation that "life should mean for life".

dam, 11 Nov. 1922 of an Egyptian-born Jewish British father and a Dutch mother as George Behar) for treachery. Blake, formerly U.K. vice-consul in Seoul, South Korea, has been converted to Communism during 34 months' internment there from July 1950 to April 1953. It had been alleged that his betrayals may have cost the lives of up to 42 United Kingdom agents. He was "sprung" from Wormwood Scrubs Prison, London, W.12, on 22 Oct. 1966.

Miss Myra Hindley was sentenced at Chester Assizes on 6 May 1966 to life imprisonment with a recommendation she should serve at least 30 years for her part with Ian Brady in the "Moors" murders of Edward Evans, 17 and Lesley Ann Downey, 10.

Broadmoor The longest period for which any person has been detained in the Broadmoor hospital for the criminal insane, near Crowthorne, Berkshire, is 76 years in the case of William Giles. He was admitted as an insane arsonist at the age of 11 and died there on 10 March 1962, at the age of 87.

Oldest prisoner The oldest known prisoner in the United States is John Weber, 95, at the Chillicothe Correctional Institute, Ohio who began his 44th year in prison on 29 Oct. 1970.

Greatest mass arrest The greatest mass arrest in the United Kingdom occurred on 17 Sept. 1961, when 1,314 demonstrators supporting the unilateral nuclear disarmament the United Kingdom were arrested for wilfully disregarding the directions of the police and thereby obstructing highways leading to Parliament Square, London, by sitting down.

Lynching The worst year in the 20th century for lynchings in the United States has been 1901, with 130 lynchings (105 Negroes, 25 Whites), while the first year with no reported cases was 1952. The last lynching recorded in Britain was that of Panglam Godolan, a Pakistani and a suspected murderer, in London on 27 Oct. 1958. The last case previous to this was of a kidnapping suspect in Glasgow in 1922.

LONGEST PRISON ESCAPES
The longest recorded escape by a recaptured prisoner was that of Leonard T. Fristoe, 77, who escaped from Nevada State Prison, U.S.A., on 15 Dec. 1923 and was turned in by his son on 15 Nov. 1969 in Compton, California. He had had 46 years of freedom under the name Claude R. Willis. He had killed two sheriff's deputies in 1920. The longest period of freedom achieved by a British gaol breaker is more than 15½ years by Irish-born John Patrick Hannan

who escaped from Verne Open Prison at Portland, Dorset, on 22 Dec. 1955 and was still at large in May 1971. He had served only 1 month of a 21-month term for car-stealing and assaulting two policemen.

Broadmoor The longest escape from Broadmoor was one of 39 years by the Liverpool wife murderer James Kelly, who got away on 28 Jan. 1888, using a pass key made from a corset spring. After an adventurous life in Paris, in New York and at sea he returned in April 1927, to ask for re-admission. After some difficulties this was arranged. He died in 1930.

Greatest gaol break The greatest gaol break in Britain was that from Wandsworth, South London, on 24 June 1961. Eleven men got away, of whom one was immediately recaptured with a broken leg. The other ten were all rounded up within a few days.

ROBBERY

Greatest The greatest robbery on record was that of the Reichbank's reserves by a combine of U.S. military personnel and Germans. Gold bars, 728 in number, valued at £3,518,334 were removed from a caché on Klausenkopf mountainside, near Einsiedel, Bavaria on 7 June 1945 together with six sacks of bank notes of 404,840 U.S. dollars and £405 (possibly forged) from a garden in Oberaer. The book *Gold Is Where You Hide It* by W. Stanley Moss (Andre Deutsch, 1956) named the Town Major of Garmisch-Partenkirken Capt. Robert Mackenzie, *alias* Ben F. Harpman of the Third U.S. Army and the local military governor Captain (later Major) Martin Borg as the instigators. Mackenzie was reputedly sentenced to 10 years after an F.B.I. investigation but Borg vanished from Vitznau, Switzerland on 30 March 1946. In the same area, in which 6 apparently associated murders occurred, 630 cubes of uranium and six boxes of platinum bars and precious stones and 34 forging plates also disappeared. (See, however, Industrial Espionage, column 2.)

Bank On 23 March 1962, 150 *plastiqueurs* of the *Organisation de l'Armée Secrète* (O.A.S.) removed by force 23,500,000 francs (£1,703,000) from the Banque d'Algérie in Oran, Algeria, after the collapse of civil order. The biggest "inside job" was that at the National City Bank of New York, from which the Assistant Manager, Richard Crowe, removed $883,660 (£315,593). He was arrested on 11 April 1949. On 23 Oct. 1969 it was disclosed that $13,193,000 (£5,497,000) of U.S. Treasury bills were inexplicably missing from the Morgan Trust, Wall Street, New York City, U.S.A.

Train The greatest recorded train robbery occurred between about 3.10 a.m. and 3.45 a.m. on 8 Aug. 1963, when a General Post Office mail train from Glasgow, Scotland, was ambushed between Sears Crossing and Bridego Bridge at Mentmore, near Cheddington, Buckinghamshire. The gang escaped with about 120 mailbags containing £2,595,998 worth of bank notes being taken to London for pulping. Only £343,448 had been recovered by 9 Dec. 1966.

Art The greatest recorded art robbery was the theft of eight paintings, valued at £1,500,000, taken during the night of 30-31 Dec. 1966 from the Dulwich College Picture Gallery in London. The haul included three paintings by Peter Paul Rubens (1577-1640), one was by Adam Ehlsheimer (1578-1610), three by Rembrandt van Rijn (1606-69) and one by Gerard Dou (1613-75). Three of the paintings were recovered on 2 Jan. 1967 and the remaining five on 4 Jan. 1967. It is arguable that the value of the *Mona Lisa* at the time of its theft from The Louvre, Paris on 21 Aug. 1911 was greater than this figure. It was recovered in Italy in 1913 and Vicenzo Perruggia was charged with its theft.

Jewels The greatest recorded theft of gem stones occurred on 13 Nov. 1969 in Freetown, Sierra Leone, when an armed gang stole diamonds belonging to the Sierra Leone Selection Trust worth £1,500,000. The haul from Carrington & Co. Ltd. of Regent Street, London, on 21 Nov. 1965 was estimated to be £500,000.

Industrial espionage It has been alleged that about 1966 a division of the American Cyanamid Company lost some papers and vials of micro-organisms through industrial espionage, allegedly organized from Italy, which data had cost them $24,000,000 (then £8.57 million) in research and development. It is arguable that this represents the greatest robbery of all-time.

Greatest kidnapping ransom Historically the greatest ransom paid was that for Atahualpa by the Incas to Francisco Pizarro in 1532-33 at Cajamarca, Peru which constituted a hall full of gold and silver worth in modern money some $170 million (£65 million).

The greatest ransom ever extracted in a kidnapping case in modern times has been 7½ million D.Mk (£900,000) for the return after 19 days of Thomas Albrecht, 49 a West German supermarket owner, on 16-17 Dec. 1971.

Greatest Hijack ransom The highest amount ever paid to hijackers has been £2,000,000 in small denomination notes by the West German government to Popular Front for the Liberation of Palestine representatives 30 miles outside Beirut, Lebanon on 23 Feb. 1972. In return a Lufthansa Boeing 747, hijacked an hour out of New Delhi and bound for Athens which had been forced down at Aden, and its 14 crew members were released.

Largest narcotics haul The heaviest recorded haul of narcotics was made off St. Louis at Rhones, France, where 700 cwt (35 tons) of floating bales containing unprocessed morphine, opium, heroin and hashish, worth £30 million on the retail U.S. market were found being loaded into canoes by 3 men on 25 Feb. 1971. The most valuable ever haul was of 937 lb. of pure heroin worth $106¼ million (£40.8 million) retail seized aboard the 60 ton shrimp boat *Caprice des Temps* at Marseilles, France on 2 Mar. 1972. The captain, Marcel Boucan, 57, tried to commit suicide.

Penal camps The largest penal camp systems in the world were those near Karaganda and Kolyma, in the U.S.S.R., each with a population estimated in 1958 at between 1,200,000 and 1,500,000. The official N.A.T.O. estimate for all Soviet camps was "more than one million" in March 1960. It was estimated in 1966 that the total population of penal camps in China was about 10,000,000.

Devil's Island The largest French penal settlement was that of St. Laurent du Maroni, which comprised the notorious Îles du Diable, Royale and St. Joseph (for incorrigibles) off the coast of French Guiana, in South America. It remained in operation for 99 years from 1854 until the last group of repatriated prisoners, including Théodore Rouselle, who had served 50 years, was returned to Bordeaux on 22 Aug. 1953. It has been estimated that barely 2,000 *bagnard* (ex-convicts) of the 70,000 deportees ever returned. These, however, include the executioner Ladurelle (imprisoned 1921-37), who was murdered in Paris in 1938.

PRISONS

Largest World The largest prison in the world is Kharkov Prison, in the U.S.S.R., which has at times accommodated 40,000 prisoners.

British Isles The largest prison in the United Kingdom is Wormwood Scrubs, West London, with 1,240 cells. The highest prison walls in Great Britain are those of Leicester Prison, measuring 30 feet high.

The largest prison in Scotland is Barlinnie, near Glasgow, with 753 single cells. Ireland's largest prison is Mountjoy Prison, Dublin, with 808 cells.

Smallest The smallest prison in the world is usually cited as that on the island of Sark, in the Channel Islands, which has a capacity of two. In fact the prison on Herm, a neighbouring island, is smaller, with a diameter of 13 feet 6 inches, and must rank with the single person lock-ups such as that at Shenley, Hertfordshire. The smallest prison in England is Oxford Prison (also the oldest, built in c. 1640), with 120 cells. The smallest in Scotland is Penninghame Open Prison, Wigtownshire with accomodation for 63. Ireland's smallest prison is that at Sligo, with 100 cells.

Highest population The highest prison population, including Borstals and detention centres, for England and Wales was the figure for 30 April 1971 of 40,352. In Scotland the average prison population was 5,338 and in Northern Ireland 755 in 1971.

Most secure prison After it became a maximum security Federal prison in 1934, no convict was known to have lived to tell of a successful escape from the prison on Alcatraz ("Pelican") Island in San Francisco Bay, California, U.S.A. A total of 23 men attempted it but 12 were recaptured, 5 shot dead, one drowned and 5 presumed drowned. On 16 Dec. 1962, three months before the prison was closed, one man reached the mainland alive, only to be recaptured on the spot.

Largest bribe An alleged bribe of £30,000,000 offered to Shaikh Zaid ibn Sultan of Abu Dhabi, Trucial Oman, by a Saudi Arabian official in August 1955, is the highest on record. The affair concerned oil concessions in the disputed territory of Buraimi on the Persian Gulf.

Greatest forgery The greatest recorded forgery was the German Third Reich government's forging operation, code name "Bernhard", engineered by Herr Naujocks in 1940-41. It involved £150,000,000 worth of £5 notes.

Greatest swindle The greatest swindle ever perpetrated in commercial history was that of Antonio (Tino) De Angelis (born 1915), a 5 ft. 5 in. 290 lb. ex-hog-cutter from New York City, U.S.A. His Allied Crude Vegetable Oil Refining Corporation (formed 19 Nov. 1955) operated from an uncarpeted office adjoining a converted tank farm in Bayonne, New Jersey. The tanks were rigged with false dipping compartments and were inter-connected such that sea water could be pumped to substitute for phantom salad oil which served as collateral for warehouse receipts. A deficiency of 927,000 short tons of oil valued at $175,000,000 (then £62.5 million) was discovered.

Biggest fraud The largest amount of money named in a fraud case has been £12,707,726 in the Old Bailey, London trial of Ellis Eser Seillon, 60 and Elias Fahimian, 40. A record total of 3,725 documents were involved. They were sentenced on 14 Jan. 1972 by Judge Stanley Price Q.C. to 5 and 4 years respectively.

Passing bad cheques The record for passing bad cheques was set by Frederick Emerson Peters (1886-1959), who, by dint of some 200 impersonations, netted $250,000 (£89,300) with 28,000 bad cheques. Among his many philanthropies was a silver chalice presented to a cathedral in Washington, D.C., U.S.A., also paid for with a bad cheque.

Welfare swindle The greatest welfare swindle yet worked was that of the gypsy Anthony Moreno on the French Social Security in Marseilles. By forging birth certificates and school registration forms, he invented 197 fictitious families and 3,000 children on which he claimed benefits from 1960 to mid-1968. Moreno,

nicknamed "El Chorro" (the fountain), was la reported free of extradition worries and living luxury in his native Spain having absquatulated wi an estimated £2,300,000.

FINES
A fine equivalent to £9.83 million was imposed c Juan Vila Reyes, president of the Barcelona texti machinery manufacturer Matesa, by the Currenc Crime Court, Madrid, Spain on 19 May 1970 f converting export development funds to his own us

Heaviest The heaviest fine ever imposed in the United Kin dom was one of £277,500 plus £3,717 costs, on Hennig & Co. Ltd., the London diamond merchant at Clerkenwell Magistrates' Court, London, on 14 De 1949. The amount was later reduced on appeal.

Rarest prosecution There are a number of crimes in English law for whic there have never been prosecutions. Among uniqu prosecutions are *Rex v. Crook* in 1662 for praemuni and *Rex v. Gregory* for selling honours under th Honours (Prevention of Abuses) Act, 1924, in 193 Maundy Gregory (d. 1941) was the honours broker c Lloyd George's 1919-20 Coalition Government.

It is a specific offence on Pitcairn Island in the Pacif to shout "Sail Ho!" when no vessel is in sight. The fir is 25p, which can be commuted to one day's labo on the public roads (there are no cars) or making a oar for the public boat.

6. ECONOMIC

MONETARY AND FINANCE

Largest budget
World The greatest annual expenditure budgeted by an country has been $229,232 million (£95,500 millior by the United States government for the fiscal yea ending 30 June 1973. The highest budgeted revenu in the United States has been $217,593 millio (£90,666 million) in 1972-3. The estimated revenu receipts of the U.S.S.R. Government in 1969 wer 139,000 million roubles (*officially* equivalent t $148,800 million or £62,000 million).

In the United States, the greatest surplus wa $8,419,469,844 in 1947-48, and the greatest defici was $57,420,430,365 in 1942-43.

United Kingdom The greatest annual budgeted current expenditure o the United Kingdom has been £21,462 million for th fiscal year 1972-73. The highest budgeted curren revenue has been £24,614 million in 1972-73.

The greatest annual surplus achieved wa $8,419,469,844 in 1947-48, and the greatest defici was $57,420,430,365 in 1942-43.

Foreign aid The total net foreign aid given by the United State government between 1 July 1945 and 31 Dec. 197 was $125,061 million (£48,100 million), of whic $4,586 million has gone into Vietnam, Republic o Khmers and Laos. The country which received mos U.S. aid in 1969 was India, with $432,000,000 (£16 million). U.S. foreign aid began with $50,000 t Venezuela for earthquake relief in 1812 and curtaile drastically by vote of the U.S. Senate on 29 Oc 1971.

TAXATION

Most taxed The major national economy with the highest rate o taxation (central and local taxes, plus social securit contribution) is that of France, with 51.2 per cent. o her National Income in 1967 (latest data). The lowes proportion for any advanced national economy i 1967 was 24.1 per cent. in Japan, which also enjoye the highest economic growth rate. In the Unite Kingdom in 1971 current taxation receipts wer 48.7 per cent of G.N.P.

east taxed There is no income tax paid by residents on Lundy Island off North Devon, England. This 1,062.4 acre island issued its own unofficial currency of Puffins and Half Puffins between the Wars.

Highest surtax The country with the most confiscatory marginal rate of income tax is Burma, where the rate is 99 per cent. for annual incomes exceeding 300,000 kyats (pronounced chuts) (£22,540). In November 1969 Premier Ne Win proclaimed "the way of true Socialism—the Burmese way". The second highest marginal rate was in the United Kingdom, where the topmost surtax level was 97.5 per cent. in 1950-51 and 96.25 per cent. in 1965-66. In 1967-68 a "special charge" of up to 9s. (45p) in the £ additional to surtax brought the top rate to 27s. 3d. (136p) in the £. The proposed rate in 1973-74 for earned incomes over £20,000 is 75 per cent. with a surcharge of a further 15 per cent. on any investment income in excess of £2,000 making a rate of 90 per cent. A married man with two children earning £5,000 per year in 1938 would, in March 1970, have to have earned nearly £75,000 to have enjoyed the same standard of living.

ighest and owest rates in United Kingdom Income tax was introduced in Great Britain in 1799 at the standard rate of 2s. (10p) in the £. It was discontinued in 1815, only to be re-introduced in 1842 at the rate of 7d. (3p) in the £. It was at its lowest at 2d. (0.83p) in the £ in 1875, gradually climbing to 1s. 3d. (6p) by 1913. From April 1941 until 1946 the record peak of 10s. (50p) in the £ was maintained to assist in the finances of World War II. Death Duties (introduced in 1894) on millionaire estates began at 8 per cent. (1894-1907) and were raised to a peak of 80 per cent. by 1949.

NATIONAL DEBT

The largest national debt of any country in the world is that of the United States, where the gross federal public debt of the Federal Government reached its peak figure of $429,400,000,000 (£178,916 million), equivalent to $1,834 (£764) per person, in the fiscal year 1971-72. This amount in dollar bills would make a pile 25,421 miles high, weighing 356,150 tons.

The United Kingdom National Debt, which became a permanent feature of Britains economy as early as 1692, was £35,843 million, or £645 per person, at 31 March 1972. This amount placed in a pile of brand new £1 notes would be 2,203.3 miles in height.

Gross National Product The estimated world aggregate of Gross National Products in 1968 exceeded £800,000 million. The country with the largest Gross National Product is the United States, with $1,072.9 billion, that is, more than a trillion dollars for 1970. The estimated G.N.P. of the United Kingdom was £47,935 million in 1971.

National wealth The richest large nation, measured by real Gross National Product per head, has been the U.S.A. since about 1910. The average share of G.N.P. in the U.S.A. was $4,700 (£1.958) in 1970. It has been estimated that the value of all physical assets in the U.S.A. in 1966 was $2,460,000,000,000 or $12,443 (£5,184) per head. The comparative figure for the United Kingdom was £85,423 million at 31 Dec. 1961 (latest available data).

National Savings The highest total of National Savings recorded in a year was £573,549,000 (net receipts) in 1945-46. The highest net receipts in a week were £42,423,000 for the week ending 11 May 1946. The total amount invested was £9,503,200,000 as at 31 March 1972. The greatest withdrawals in a week were £21,208,000 (including interest) in the week ending 23 Dec. 1967. Mr Arthur Ellis of Saltergate, Chesterfield between 1958 and 1970 has won one £250, two £100 and 39

£25 premium bond draw prizes. All his winnings are donated to the local parish church.

GOLD RESERVES

The country with the greatest monetary gold reserve is the United States, whose Treasury had $9,662 million (£3,708 million) on hand on 1 March 1972 The United States Bullion Depository at Fort Knox, 30 miles south-west of Louisville, Kentucky, U.S.A. is the principal Federal depository of U.S. gold. Gold is stored in standard mint bars of 400 troy ounces (439 oz. avoirdupois), measuring 7 inches by $3\frac{5}{8}$ inches by $1\frac{1}{8}$ inches, and each worth $14,000 (£5,833).

The greatest accumulation of gold in the world is now in the Federal Reserve Bank at 33 Liberty Street, New York City, N.Y., U.S.A. The bank has admitted to having had gold valued at $13,000 million (£5,416 million) owned by foreign central banks and stored 85 feet below street level, in a vault 50 feet by 100 feet behind a steel door weighing 89 tons.

United Kingdom The lowest published figure for the sterling area's gold and convertible currency reserves was $298,000,000 (then £74 million) on 31 Dec. 1940. The highest ever figure was the May 1972 figure of £2,744 million (valued at $2.60.57 to the £).

BANK RATE

On 1 Jan. 1972 the highest bank rate in the world was that of Brazil at 20 per cent. and the lowest that of Morocco at 3½ per cent. The lowest that the Bank of England bank rate has ever been is 2 per cent., first from 22 April 1852 to 6 Jan. 1853. The highest ever figure was 10 per cent., first on 9 Nov. 1857, and most recently on 6 Aug. 1914. The highest yearly average was 7.35 per cent. in 1864 (6 per cent. to 9 per cent.). The longest period without a change was the 12 years 13 days from 26 Oct. 1939 to 7 Nov. 1951, during which time the rate stayed at 2 per cent.

PAPER MONEY

Paper money is an invention of the Chinese and, although the date of 119 B.C. has been suggested, the innovation is believed to date from the T'ang dynasty of the 7th century A.D. The world's earliest bank notes were issued by the Stockholms Banco, Sweden, in July 1661. The oldest surviving note is one for 5 dalers dated 6 Dec. 1662. The oldest surviving printed Bank of England note is one for £555 to bearer, dated 19 Dec. 1699 (4½ X 7¾ inches).

Largest and smallest The largest paper money ever issued was the one kwan note of the Chinese Ming dynasty issue of 1368-99, which measured 9 inches by 13 inches. The smallest bank note ever issued was the 5 cent. note of the Chekiang Provincial Bank (established 1908) in China. It measured 55 millimetres (2.16 inches) by 30 millimetres (1.18 inches)

Highest denominations World The highest denomination of paper currency ever authorized in the world are United States gold certificates for $100,000 (£41,666), bearing the head of former President Thomas Woodrow Wilson (1856-1924), issued by the U.S. Treasury in 1934. There also exists in the U.S. Bureau of Engraving and Printing an example of a U.S. Treasury note for $500,000,000 bearing interest coupons for $15,625,000 each 6 months for 14 years at 6¼ per cent.

The highest denomination notes in circulation are U.S. Federal Reserve Bank notes for $10,000 (£4,166). They bear the head of Salmon Portland Chase (1808-73). None has been printed since July 1944 and their circulation fell from 4,600 at 31 Dec. 1941 to only 394 at 30 June 1967 but rose to 1,900 by March 1969. On 15 July 1969 the U.S. Treasury announced that no further notes higher than $100

Britain's largest denomination bank note — a £1,000 note which is no longer legal tender.

Britain's most northerly bank note—a proof of the 19th century One Guines note of the Shetland Islands.

would be issued. By June 1971 only 400 $10,000 bills were in circulation—reputedly mostly around Christmas time in Texas.

United Kingdom Two Bank of England notes for £1,000,000 still exist, dated before 1812, but these were used only for internal accounting. Facsimile million pound notes were reproduced by J. Arthur Rank Productions Ltd. to publicize their film *The Million Pound Note* made in 1954. These were dated 20 June 1903. The highest issued denominations were £1,000 notes, first printed in 1725, discontinued in 1943 and withdrawn on 30 April 1945. A total of 63 of these notes were still unaccounted for up to July 1968 after which no data has been issued by the Bank.

Prior to 1922 there were many issues of banknotes by private banks. The most remote of these were those issued in 1822 by the Shetland Bank in Lerwick, Zetland, (see illustration of a specimen).

The lowest ever denomination Bank of England note was for penny, dated 10 Jan. 1828, which was adapted from a £5 note and doubtless used to adjust an overnight difference. In 1868 it was purchased by the Bank for £1 from the landlord of the "Blue Last", Bell Alley, in the City of London.

Most expensive The highest price paid for a note no longer valid currency is believed to be $3,600 (£1,500), paid in 1900 for the first Ming note (see page 207) ever found. About £3,500 was paid for a £1,000 note signed by Peppiatt in London in 1971.

Highest circulation The highest ever Bank of England note circulation the United Kingdom was 3,826,000,000 on 19 Ap 1972—equivalent to a pile of £1 notes 220.7 mil high.

DEVALUATION
Devaluation was practised by Emperor Nero of Ron (A.D. 54-68), who debased his coinage. Since 194 112 of the world's 120 currencies have devalu including the pound twice, the rouble 3 times and tl Chilean currency 46 times (since 1 Jan. 1949). Tl U.S. dollar has only twice been devalued *vis-à-vis* go (in 1934 and in 1971).

WORST INFLATION
The world's worst inflation occurred in Hungary June 1946, when the 1931 gold pengö was valued 130 trillion (1.3×10^{20}) paper pengös. Notes we issued for szazmillio billion (100 trillion or 10² pengös. Currently the worst inflation is in Braz where the cruzeiro depreciated 42 times, in terms of the United States dollar, between 1 Feb. 1957 (64.8 per $) and March 1967 (2,720 per $). A new cruzeir equivalent to 1,000 old cruzeiros, was introduced c 8 Feb. 1967. In 1966-67 there was a further 21.2 p cent. inflation.

CHEQUES
Largest World The greatest amount paid by a single cheque in tl history of banking was $960,242,000.0 (£342,943,571), paid on 31 Jan. 1961 by the Con nental Illinois National Bank of Chicago, Illino U.S.A. This bank headed a group which bought tl accounts receivable of Sears, Roebuck & Co., whom the cheque was paid.

United Kingdom The largest cheque drawn in Britain was one f £119,595,645, drawn on 24 Jan. 1961 by Laza Brothers & Co. Ltd. and payable to the Nation Provincial Bank, in connection with the takeover the British Ford Motor Company. The rate of chequ clearing was, by May 1971, 1,100,000,000 p annum.

Oldest The oldest surviving English cheque is one drawn c 14 March 1664.

COINS
Oldest World The earliest certainly dated coins are the electru (alloy of gold and silver) staters of Lydia, in As Minor (now Turkey), which were coined in the reig of King Gyges (c. 685-652 B.C.). Primitive uni scribed "spade" money of the Chou dynasty of Chir is now *believed* to date from c. 770 B.C. Countrie without any coins are Paraguay, Laos and Indonesi

British The earliest coins to circulate in Britain were Gall Belgic gold imitations of the Macedonian staters Philip II (359-336 B.C.). The Bellovaci type has bee tentatively dated c. 130 B.C. The earliest da attributed to coins minted in Britain is c. 95 B.C. fe the Westerham type gold stater.

Heaviest The Swedish copper 10 daler coins of 1659 attained weight of up to 43½ lb. Of primitive exchange token the most massive are the holed stone discs, or *F* from the Yap Islands, in the western Pacific Ocea with diameters of up to 12 feet. A medium-sized or was worth one Yapese wife or an 18-foot canoe.

Smallest The smallest coins in the world were the go "pinhead" coins used in Colpata, southern India, in 1800, which weighed as little as one grain, or 480 t the troy ounce. The ⅙₆th silver stater of Ionia c. 6t century B.C. measure 3 × 4½ millimetres.

Highest denomination World The 1654 Indian gold 200 Mohur (£500) coin of tl Mughal Emperor Khurram Shihāb-ud-dīn Muhan mad, Shāh Jahān (reigned 1628-57), is both tl highest denomination coin and that of the greate intrinsic worth ever struck. It weighed 33,600 grains (70 troy oz.) and hence has an intrinsic worth of £875. It had a diameter of 5⅜ inches. The only known example disappeared in Patna, Bihar, India, in c. 1820, but a plaster-cast of this coin exists in the British Museum, London.

British Gold five-guinea pieces were minted from the reign of Charles II (1660-1685) until 1753 in the reign of George II. A pattern 5 guinea piece of George III dated 1777 also exists.

Lowest denomination World The 1 aurar piece of Iceland, had a face value of 0.0114 of a penny in 1971. Quarter farthings (sixteen to the penny) were struck in copper at the Royal Mint, London, in the Imperial coinage for use in Ceylon, in 1839 and 1851-53. The lowest denomination gold coins ever struck are the Kruger gold 3d. pieces struck in South Africa at the behest of Mr. Solly Marks. One is dated 1894 and 215 are dated 1898. They are now worth £250 each.

British There are known to be single examples extant of an Edward VIII 1937 penny, halfpenny and farthing in bronze. These are the most recent examples of unique British coins.

Rarest World More than 100 coins are unique. An example of a unique coin of threefold rarity is one of the rare admixture of bronze with inlaid gold of Kaleb I of Axum (c. 500 A.D.) owned by Richard A. Thorud of Bloomington, Minnesota, U.S.A. Only 700 Axumite coins of any sort are known.

Most expensive World The highest price paid in auction for a single coin is $77,500 (£32,292) for a U.S. 1804 silver dollar, struck in 1834 (sic) of which only seven exist, at Stack's of New York City on 23 Oct. 1970. It was sold by the Massachusetts Historical Society and bought by an anonymous collector. This specimen was spotted by Henry C. Young, a teller, in the ordinary course of his work in the Bank of Pennsylvania in 1850. The two U.S. gold $50 pieces of 1877 in the Smithsonian Institution, Washington, D.C., have been valued at $100,000 (£41,666) each as have the seven surviving examples of the U.S. Brasher Doubloon of 1787. Among the many unique coins that which would attract logically the greatest price on the market would be the unique 1873 dime (U.S. 10 cent piece) with the CC mint mark, since dimes are the most avidly collected series of any coins in the world.

British The highest auction price paid for an English coin is £10,500 paid by the London dealer Spink at the salerooms of Messrs. Glendining and Co. on 17 Oct. 1968 for a gold Edward IV London Noble of the Heavy Coinage period (1461-1464), from the Fishpool Hoard discovered on 22 March 1966. An Irish gold pistole minted in England fetched £13,500 at auction at Sotheby's in June 1972.

Legal tender coins Oldest The oldest legal tender Imperial coins in circulation are the now rare silver shillings (now 5p) and sixpences (now 2½p) of the reign of George III, dated 1816. All gold coinage of or above the least current weight dated onward from 1838 is still legal tender.

Heaviest and highest denomination The gold five-pound (£5) piece or quintuple sovereign is both the highest current denomination coin in the United Kingdom and also, at 616.37 grains (1.4066 oz.), the heaviest. The most recent specimens available to the public are dated 1937, of which only 5,501 were minted.

Lightest and smallest The silver Maundy (new) penny piece is the smallest of the British legal tender coins and, at 7.27 grains (just under 1/60th of an ounce), the lightest. These coins exist for every date since 1822 and are 0.453 of an inch in diameter.

Greatest collection It was estimated in November 1967 that the Lilly coin collection of 1,227 U.S. gold pieces now at the Smithsonian Institution, Washington, D.C., U.S.A., had a market value of $5½ million (£2,290,000). The greatest single coin collection ever amassed in Britain was that of Richard Cyril Lockett (1873-1950) of Liverpool, Lancashire. The collection realized a record of £387,457.

The greatest hoard of gold of unknown ownership ever recovered is one valued at about $3,000,000 (£1,070,000), from the lost $8,000,000 (£2,860,000) carried in 10 ships of a Spanish bullion fleet which was sunk by a hurricane off Florida, U.S.A., on 31 July 1715. The biggest single haul was by the diver Kip Wagner on 30 May 1965.

Largest Treasure Trove The largest hoard of coins ever found in the United Kingdom was the Tutbury hoard, discovered on the bed of the River Dove in Staffordshire in June 1831. It consisted of about 20,000 silver coins of Edward I and Edward II and some of Henry III. The chest is believed to have been deposited in c. 1324-25. The most valuable hoard ever found was one of more than 1,200 gold coins from the reigns of King Richard II to Edward IV, worth more than £500,000, found on 22 March 1966 by John Craughwell, aged 47, at Fishpool, near Mansfield, Nottinghamshire.

Largest mint The largest mint in the world is the U.S. Treasury's mint built in 1965-69 on Independence Mall, Philadelphia, covering 500,000 square feet with an annual capacity on a 3 shift seven day a week production of 8,000 million coins. A single stamping machine can produce coins at a rate of 10,000 per minute.

Greatest hoarders It was estimated in November 1968 that about $22,500 million (£9,375 million) worth of gold is being retained in personal possession throughout the world and that $4,800 million (£2,000 million) of this total is held by the population of France.

Largest pile The tallest column of pennies on record was one 11 feet 10 inches tall containing some 99,600 coins (worth £415) collected for Muscular Dystrophy at the A.B.C. Bowl, North Harrow, London. The pile was pulled over on 27 Feb. 1970. Lower pyramids but of 145,080 pennies (£604 10s.), collected by the licensee Mr. Frank Steele, were "knocked down" in the Coffee House Hotel, Wavertree, Liverpool, for the Royal Wavertree School for Blind Children in January 1969.

TRADE UNIONS

Largest World The world's largest union is the Industrie–Gewerkschaft Metall (Metal Workers' Union) of West Germany, with a membership of 2,312,294 at 1 Jan. 1972. The union with the longest name is probably the F.N.O.M.M.C.F.E.T.M.F., the National Federation of Officers, Machinists, Motormen, Drivers, Firemen and Electricians in Sea and River Transportation of Brazil.

Britain The largest trade union in the United Kingdom is the Transport and General Workers' Union, with 1,643,134 members at 1 Jan 1972.

Oldest The oldest of the 150 trade unions affiliated to the Trade Union Congress (founded 1868) is the National Society of Brushmakers (current membership 2,700) founded in 1747.

Smallest The smallest affiliated union is the Sheffield Wool Shear Workers' Trade Union with a membership of 25. The unaffiliated London Handforged Spoon and Fork Makers' Society instituted in July 1874, has a membership of 6.

LABOUR DISPUTES

Largest The British average of 294 days lost per 1,000 persons employed in the 5 years 1965-69 compares with extremes of 1,574 in Italy, 1,556 in Canada and 4 in Sweden.

The most serious single labour dispute in the United Kingdom was the General Strike of 4-12 May 1926, called by the Trades Union Congress in support of the Miners' Federation. During the nine days of the strike 1,580,000 people were involved and 14,500,000 working days were lost.

During the year 1926 a total of 2,750,000 people were involved in 323 different labour disputes and the working days lost during the year amounted to 162,300,000, the highest figure ever recorded. The figure for 1971 was 13,551,000 working days.

Longest The world's longest recorded strike ended on 4 Jan. 1961, after 33 years. It concerned the employment of barbers' assistants in Copenhagen, Denmark. The longest recorded major strike was that at the plumbing fixtures factory of the Kohler Co. in Sheboygan, Wisconsin, U.S.A., between April 1954 and October 1962. The strike is alleged to have cost the United Automobile Workers' Union about $12,000,000 (£4.3 million) to sustain.

UNEMPLOYMENT

Highest The highest recorded unemployment in Great Britain was on 23 Jan. 1933, when the total of unemployed persons on the Employment Exchange registers was 2,903,065, representing 22.8 per cent. of the insured working population. The highest figure for Wales was 244,579 (39.1 per cent.) on 22 Aug. 1932.

Lowest The lowest recorded peace-time level of unemployment was 0.9 per cent. on 11 July 1955, when 184,929 persons were registered. The peak figure for the total working population in the United Kingdom has been 26,290,000 in September 1966. The figure for September 1971 was 25,485,000.

Largest association The largest single association in the world is the Blue Cross, the U.S.-based medical insurance organization with a membership at 1 Jan. 1971 of 78,715,111. Benefits paid out exceeded $5.30 billion (£2,038 million). The largest association in the United Kingdom is the Automobile Association, with a membership of 4,233,718 on 1 Jan. 1971.

FOOD CONSUMPTION

Calories Of all countries in the world, based on the latest available data, Ireland has the largest available total of calories per person. The net supply averaged 3,450 per day in 1968. The United Kingdom average was 3,180 per day in 1968-69. The highest calorific value of any foodstuff is that of pure animal fat, with 930 calories per 100 grammes (3.5 oz.). Pure alcohol provides 710 calories per 100 grammes.

Protein New Zealand has the highest recorded consumption of protein per person, an average of 107 grammes (3.76 oz.) per day in 1967. The United Kingdom average was 88 grammes (3.10 oz.) per day in 1968-69.

The lowest *reported* figures are 1,720 calories per day in Haiti in 1964-66 and 29 grammes (1.30 oz.) of protein per day in Zaire in 1961-63.

Cereals The greatest consumers of cereal products—flour, milled rice, etc.—are the people of the United Arab Republic, with an average of 501 lb. per person in 1966-67. The United Kingdom average was 160.9 lb. in 1968-69 and the figure for the Republic of Ireland was 210 lb. in 1968.

Starch The greatest eaters of starchy food (e.g. bananas, potatoes, etc.) are the people of Gabon, who consumed 4.02 lb. per head per day in 1964-66. The United

Kingdom average was 9.77 oz. per day in 1970. The average for Ireland was 12.30 oz. in 1967.

Sugar The greatest consumers of sugars are the people of Iceland, with an average of 5.29 oz. per person per day in 1964-66. The lowest consumption is 0.70 oz. per day in Burundi in 1964-66. The United Kingdom average was 5.08 oz. in 1970 and the average in Ireland was 5.04 oz. in 1968.

Meat The greatest meat eaters in the world—figures include offal and poultry—are the people of Uruguay, with an average consumption of 10.93 oz. per person per day in 1964-66. The lowest consumption is 0.16 oz. in Sri Lanka (formerly Ceylon) in 1968. The United Kingdom average was 5.74 oz. in 1970 and the Irish average was 7.34 oz. in 1967.

BEER

Of reporting countries, the nation with the highest beer consumption per person is West Germany, with 30.6 gallons per person in 1970. The equivalent figure for the United Kingdom is 22.2 gallons per person. In the Northern Territory of Australia, however, the annual intake has been estimated to be as high as 50 gallons per person. A society for the prevention of alcoholism in Darwin had to disband in June 1966 for lack of support. The United Kingdom average was 21.6 gallons, or 172.8 pints, per person in 1969. The January 1970 edition of the U.S.S.R. periodical *Sotsialisticheskaya Industria* claimed that the Russians invented beer.

SPIRITS

The freest spirit drinkers are the white population of South Africa, with 1.71 gallons of proof spirit per person per year, and the most abstemious are the people of Belgium, with 2 pints per person. It was estimated in 1969 that 13 per cent. of all males between 20 and 55 years in France were suffering from alcoholism.

Prohibition The longest lasting imposition of prohibition has been 26 years in Iceland (1908-34). Other prohibitions have been U.S.S.R. (1914-24) and U.S.A. (1920-33).

Largest dish The largest menu item in the world is roasted camel prepared occasionally for Bedouin wedding feasts. Cooked eggs are stuffed in fish, the fish stuffed into cooked chickens, the chickens stuffed into a roasted sheep carcass and the sheep stuffed into a whole camel.

Most expensive food The most expensive food is white truffle of Alba which fetches £35 per lb. in the market. Truffles in the Périgard district of France require drought between mid-July and mid-August.

Largest cake The largest cakes ever baked were a six-sided "birthday" cake weighing 25,000 lb., made in August 1962 by Van de Kemp's Holland Dutch Bakers of Seattle, Washington State, U.S.A., for the Seattle World's Fair (the "Century 21 Exposition"), and a 26 foot tall creation of the same weight made for the British Columbia Centennial cut on 20 July 1971.

Longest Loaf The longest loaf ever baked was one of 90 feet (2,600 slices) by United Bakeries of London E.C. in July 1971.

Largest Easter egg The largest Easter egg ever made was one of 550 lb. and £200 worth of chocolate made at the Liverpool College of Crafts and Catering in March 1971.

Largest meat pie The largest meat pie ever baked weighed 5 tons the seventh in the series of Denby Dale (West Riding, Yorkshire) pies, to mark four royal births in 1964. The first was in 1788 to celebrate King George III's return to sanity but the fourth (Queen Victoria's Jubilee, 1887) went a bit "off" and had to be buried in quick-lime.

The Denby Dale Pie of 1964 which had an all up weight of over 7 tons.

Largest pizza pie The largest pizza ever baked was one measuring 11 feet 8 inches by 3 feet 7 inches at Cambridge, New York, U.S.A. on 9 Jan. 1971.

Largest sundae The most monstrous ice cream sundae ever concocted is one of 1,551 lb. by Bob Bercaw of Wooster, Ohio, U.S.A. built on 4 July 1972. It contained 67 flavours and 144 lb. of chocolate fudge syrup.

Largest hamburger The largest hamburger on record is one with buns 12½ feet in circumference and 173lb. of prime beef, 5 gallons of tomato sauce and a gallon of mustard made by McDonald's at Yagoona, Australia on 20 Jan. 1972.

SPICES

Most expensive The most expensive of all spices is Mediterranean saffron (*Crocus sativus*). It takes 96,000 stigmas and therefore 32,000 flowers to make a pound. Packets of 1.9 grains are retailed in the United Kingdom for 8½p—equivalent to £19.50 per oz.

"Hottest" The hottest of all spices is the capsicum hot pepper known as Tabasco, first reported in 1888 by Mr. Edmund McIlhenny on Avery Island, Louisiana, U.S.A.

Rarest condiment The world's most prized condiment is Cà Cuong, a secretion recovered in minute amounts from beetles in North Vietnam. Owing to war conditions, the price rose to $100 (now $38.46) per ounce before supplies virtually ceased.

Sweets The biggest sweet eaters in the world are the people of Britain, with 7.8 oz. of confectionery per person per week in 1971. The figure for Scotland was more than 9 oz. in 1968.

Tea The most expensive tea marketed in the United Kingdom is "Oolong Leaf Bud", specially imported for Fortnum and Mason of Picadilly, London, W.1, where, in 1972, it retailed for £4.40 per lb. It is blended from very young Formosan leaves. In Britain the *per caput* consumption of tea in 1970 was 139.2 oz. followed by Ireland and Libya.

The world's largest tea company is Brooke Bond Liebig Limited (a merger of Brooke Bond Tea Ltd. of London founded 1869 and Liebig's Extract of Meat Co. Ltd. made in May 1968), with a turnover of £246,000,000 in the year ended 30 June 1971. The

company has 40,000 acres of mature plantations in India, Sri Lanka (formerly Ceylon), and East Africa, and ranches in Argentina, Paraguay and Rhodesia extending over 2,663,000 acres and employs over 70,000 people.

Coffee The world's greatest coffee drinkers are the people of Sweden, who consumed 13.29 k.g. (29.27 lb.) of coffee per person in 1969. This compares with 1.59 kg. (3.5 lb.) for the United Kingdom in 1969.

Oldest tinned food The oldest tinned food known was roast beef canned by Donkin, Hall and Gamble in 1823 and salvaged from H.M.S. *Fury* in the Northwest Passage, Canada. It was opened on 11 Dec. 1958.

Recipe The oldest known surviving recipe is one dated 1657 handed down from Bernice Bardolf of the Black Horse Tavern, Barnsley, Yorkshire found buried in September 1969 in the yard of the Alhambra Hotel, Barnsley. Barnsley Bardolf, a variant, is now on the menu.

Fresh water The world's greatest consumers of fresh water are the people of the United States, whose average daily consumption reached 411,200 million gallons in 1970. By 31 Dec. 1967, 40.6 per cent. was fluoridized.

ENERGY
To express the various forms of available energy (coal, liquid fuels and water power, etc., but omitting vegetable fuels and peat), it is the practice to convert them all into terms of coal. On this basis the world average consumption was the equivalent of 1,804 kg. (33.7 cwt.) of coal, or its energy equivalents, per person in 1969.

The highest consumption in the world is in the United States, with an average of 203.3 cwt. per person in 1968. The United Kingdom average was 103.7 cwt. per person in 1971. The lowest recorded average for 1968 was 15.4 lb. per person in Burundi.

MASS COMMUNICATIONS

AIRLINES
The country with the busiest airlines system is the United States, where 107,324 million revenue passenger miles were flown on scheduled domestic and local services in 1971. This was equivalent to an annual trip of 518.4 miles for every one of the inhabitants of the U.S.A. The United Kingdom airlines flew 182,208,000 miles and carried 15,853,000 passengers in 1971. This is equivalent to an annual flight of 103 miles for every person in the United Kingdom.

MERCHANT SHIPPING
The world total of merchant shipping excluding vessels of less than 100 tons gross, sailing vessels and barges was 55,041 vessels of 247,202,634 tons gross on 1 July 1971. The largest merchant fleet in the world as at mid-1971 was that under the flag of Liberia with 38,552,240 tons gross. Liberian registration overtook the United Kingdom Merchant fleet of 21,716,148 tons gross in 1967. The U.K. figure for mid-1971 was 3,785 ships of 27,334,695 tons gross.

Largest and busiest ports Physically, the largest port in the world is New York Harbor, N.Y., U.S.A. The port has a navigable waterfront of 755 miles (460 miles in New York State and 295 miles in New Jersey) stretching over 92 square miles. A total of 261 general cargo berths and 130 other piers give a total berthing capacity of 391 ships at one time. The total warehousing floor space is 18,400,000 square feet (422.4 acres). The world's busiest port and largest artificial harbour is the Rotterdam-Europoort in the Netherlands which covers 38.88 square miles. It handled 32,023 sea-going vessels and about 250,000 barges in 1970. It is able to handle 310 sea-going vessels simultaneously up to

225,000 tons and 65 feet draught. In 1970 225,000,000 tons of seaborne cargo was handled.

RAILWAYS
The country with the greatest length of railway is the United States, with 207,005 miles of track at 1 Jan. 1970.

The farthest anyone can get from a railway on the mainland island of Great Britain is 54 miles in the case of Cape Wrath, Sutherland, Scotland.

The number of journeys made on British Rail in 1971 was 815,500,000, with an average journey of 22.96 miles, compared with the peak year of 1957, when 1,101 million journeys (average 20.51 miles) were made.

ROADS
The country with the greatest length of road is the United States (50 States), with 3,710,299 miles of graded roads at 1 Jan. 1969. The average speed of cars at off-peak times has risen from 45.0 m.p.h. in 1945 to 58.8 m.p.h. by 1966. There is no speed limit in Nevada but only a "careful and prudent" clause.

The country with the greatest number of motor vehicles per mile of road is the United Kingdom, with 221,774 miles of road including 800 miles of motorway at 1 Apr. 1971 and 15,826,000 vehicles in 1971. A total of 36,000,000 vehicles by 2010 has been forecast.

Busiest The highest traffic volume of any point in the world is at the Harbor and Santa Monica Freeways interchange in Los Angeles, California, U.S.A. with a 24-hour average on Fridays of 420,000 vehicles in 1970.

The territory with the highest traffic density in the world is Hong Kong. On 31 May 1970 there were 122,274 motor vehicles on 600 miles of serviceable roads giving a density of 8.64 yards per vehicle. The comparative figure for the United Kingdom is 25 yards.

The greatest traffic density at any one point in the United Kingdom is at Hyde Park Corner, London. The average daytime 8 a.m.-8 p.m. flow in 1970 was 164,338 vehicles every 12 hours. The busiest Thames bridge in 1968 was Putney Bridge, with a 12-hour average of 36,249 vehicles. The greatest reported aggregation of London buses was 38, bumper to bumper, along the Vauxhall Bridge Road on 18 Nov. 1965. Censuses are biennial.

Widest The widest street in the world is the Monumental Axis running for 1½ miles from the Municipal Plaza to the Plaza of the Three Powers in Brasília, the capital of Brazil. The six-lane Boulevard was opened in April 1960 and is 250 metres (273.4 yards) wide. The B Bridge Toll Plaza has 34 lanes (17 in each direction) serving the Bay Bridge, San Francisco, California.

Narrowest The world's narrowest street is St. John's Lane in Rome, with a width of 19 inches. The narrowest street in the United Kingdom is Parliament Street, Exeter, Devon, which at one point measures 26 inches across.

Longest straight road The longest straight road in the United Kingdom was a stretch of 22¾ miles between Bailgate in the City of Lincoln and Broughton Village, Lincolnshire. Part of the Roman road Ermine Street, it now comprises sections of Class I (A.15), Class III and unclassified road, with only two slight deviations of less than 50 feet from the true straight line. Part of the road was closed for an airfield, reducing the straight section to 16½ miles.

Britain's most complex motorway interchange, known as "Spaghetti Junction" at Gravelly Hill north of Birmingham

Longest World The longest motorable road in the world is t Pan-American Highway, which will stretch 13,8: miles from Anchorage, Alaska, to Puerto Mon southern Chile. There remains a gap of 250 mil∙ known as the Darien gap, in Panama and Colomb This was first traversed by two highly modified Ran Rovers of the 1972 British Trans-Americas Expe∙ tion which emerged from the Atrato swamp after weeks.

Most complex interchange The most complex interchange on the British ro system is that at Gravelly Hill, north of Birmingha on the Midland Link road joining the M1 with the M and M6 opened on 24 May 1972. There are 18 rou∙ on 6 levels together with a diverted canal and riv which consumed 26,000 tons of steel, 250,000 to of concrete, 300,000 tons of earth and cost million.

Longest street This title has been accorded to Figueroa Street whi stretches 30 miles from Pasadena at Colorado Blvd. the Pacific Coast Highway, Los Angeles, U.S.A.

Britain The longest designated road in Great Britain is t 404-mile-long A1 from London to Edinburgh. T longest Roman roads were Watling Street, fr∙ Dubrae (Dover) 215 miles through Londinium (L∙ don) to Viroconium (Wroxeter), and Fosse Wa which ran 218 miles from Lindum (Lincoln) throu Aquae Sulis (Bath) to Isca Dumnoniorum (Exete However, a 10-mile section of Fosse Way betwe Ilchester and Seaton remains indistinct. The old∙ roads in Britain are trackways dating from pre-Cel times (i.e. before 550 B.C.) An example is t Ridgeway running across the Berkshire Downs. T commonest street name in Greater London is Pa Road, of which there are 43.

Shortest The shortest High Street in Britain is that at Ash∙ Heath, Hampshire which is 40 yards long.

Longest hill The longest steep hill on any road in the Unit Kingdom is on the road westwards from Lochcarr toward Applecross in Ross and Cromarty, Scotla∙ In 6 miles this road rises from sea-level to 2,054 fe with an average gradient of 1 in 15.4, the steepest pa being 1 in 4.

Highest World The highest pass ever used by traffic is the Bódpo (19,412 feet above sea-level), in western Tibet. It w used in 1929 by a caravan from the Shipki Pass on t trade route to Rudok. The highest carriageable ro in the world is one 1,180 kilometres (733.2 mil∙ long between Tibet and south-western Sinkia∙ completed in October 1957, which takes in passes an altitude up to 18,480 feet above sea-level. Europ∙ highest pass (excluding the Caucasian passes) is t Col de Restefond (9,193 feet) completed in 19∙

with 21 hairpins between Jausiers and Saint-Etienne–de-Tinée, France. It is usually closed between early October and early June. The highest motor road in Europe is the Pico de Veleta in the Sierra Nevada, southern Spain. The shadeless climb of 22.4 miles brings the motorist to 11,384 feet above sea-level and will on the completion of a road on its southern side become also Europe's highest pass.

United Kingdom The highest road in the United Kingdom is the A6293 tarmac extension at Great Dun Fell, Westmorland (2,780 feet) leading to a Ministry of Defence radar installation. A permit is required to use it. The highest classified road in England is the B6293 at Killhope Cross (2,056 feet) on the Cumberland-Durham border near Nenthead. The highest classified road in Scotland is the A93 road over the Grampians through Cairnwell, a pass between Blairgowrie, Perthshire, and Braemar, Aberdeenshire, which reaches a height of 2,199 feet. The highest classified road in Wales is the Rhondda-Afan Inter-Valley road (A4107), which reaches 1,750 feet 2½ miles east of Abergwynfi, Glamorganshire.

Lowest The lowest road in the world is that along the Israeli shores of the Dead Sea, 1,290 feet below sea-level. The lowest in Great Britain are just below sea-level in the Holme Fen area of Huntingdon and Peterborough.

Highest motorway The highest motorway in Great Britain is the trans–Pennine M62, which, at the Windy Hill interchange, reaches an altitude of 1,220 feet. Its 183-foot-deep Dean Head cutting is the deepest roadway cutting in Europe.

Longest viaduct The longest elevated road viaduct in Europe is the 9,680-foot-long Chiswick-Langley section of the M4 motorway in West London. It was completed at a cost of £19,000,000 on 24 March 1965.

Biggest square The Tian an men (Gate of Heavenly Peace) Square in Peking, described as the navel of China, extends over 98 acres.

Traffic jams The worst traffic jams in the world are in Tōkyō, Japan. Only 9 per cent. of the city area is roadway, compared with London (23 per cent.), Paris (25 per cent.), New York (35 per cent.) and Washington, D.C. (43 per cent.). The longest traffic jam reported in Britain was one of 35 miles in length between Torquay and Yarcombe, Devon, on 25 July 1964 and 35 miles on the A30 between Egham, Surrey and Micheldever, Hampshire on 23 May 1970.

Traffic lights Automatic electric traffic lights were introduced into New York City in 1918 and into Great Britain with a one day trial in Wolverhampton on 11 Feb. 1928. They were first permanently operated in Leeds, Yorkshire on 16 March and in Edinburgh, Scotland on 19 March 1928. Semaphore-type traffic signals were set up in Westminster Square, London in 1868. It was not an offence to disobey traffic signals until assent was given to the 1930 Road Traffic bill.

Parking meters The earliest parking meters ever installed were those put in the business district of Oklahoma City, Oklahoma, U.S.A., on 19 July 1935. They were the invention of Carl C. Magee (U.S.A.) and reached London in 1958.

Worst driver It was reported that a 75-year-old *male* driver received 10 traffic tickets, drove on the wrong side of the road four times, committed four hit-and-run offences and caused six accidents, all within 20 minutes, in McKinney, Texas, U.S.A., on 15 Oct. 1966.

Milestone Britain's oldest milestone *in situ* is a Roman stone dating from A.D. 150 on the Stanegate, at Chester-holm, near Badron Mill, Northumberland.

TELEPHONES
There were 272,700,000 telephones in the world at 1 Jan. 1971 as estimated by The American Telephone & Telegraph Co. The country with the greatest number was the United States, with 120,200,000 instruments, equivalent to 583.5 for every 1,000 people, compared with the United Kingdom figure of 14,966,748 (third largest in the world to the U.S.A. and Japan), or 266.8 per 1,000 people, at 31 March 1971. The territory with fewest reported telephones is Pitcairn Island with 30.

The country with the most telephones per head of population is Monaco, with 649.8 per 1,000 of the population at 1 Jan. 1971. The country with the least was Upper Volta with 0.3 of a telephone per 1,000 people at 1 Jan. 1970 (last figure) and Laos with 0.4 at 1 Jan. 1971.

The greatest total of calls made in any country is in the United States, with 152,407 million (779.0 calls per person) in 1970. The lowest recorded figure was Pakistan with 0.3 of a call per person in 1970. The United Kingdom telephone service connected 10,747,000,000 calls in the year 1970-71, an average of 193.7 per person.

The city with most telephones is New York City, N.Y., U.S.A., with 5,904,933 (739 per 1,000 people) at 1 Jan. 1970. In 1970 Washington D.C. reached the level of 1,169 telephones per 1,000 people though in some small areas there are still higher densities such as Beverly Hills, north of Los Angeles with a return of about 1,600 per 1,000.

Longest call The longest telephone connection on record was one of 550 hours from 28 Nov. to 21 Dec. 1966 between co-eds of Ford Hall (7th floor) and the 7th floor of Moore Hall at Kansas State University.

Longest cable The world's longest submarine telephone cable is the Commonwealth Pacific Cable (COMPAC), which runs for more than 9,000 miles from Australia, *via* Auckland, New Zealand and the Hawaiian Islands to Port Alberni, Canada. It cost about £35,000,000 and was inaugurated on 2 Dec. 1963.

POSTAL SERVICES
The country with the largest mail in the world is the United States, whose population posted 95,000 million letters and packages in 1970 when the U.S. Postal Service employed 715,970 people. The United Kingdom total was 13,050 million letters in the year ending 31 March 1971.

The United States also takes first place in the average number of letters which each person posts during one year. The figure was 460 in 1970. The United Kingdom figure was 203.6 per head in 1968-69. Of all

COMPAC, the longest submarine telephone cable in the world — from Australia *via* New Zealand to Canada where it links with the trans-Canadian and trans-Atlantic systems.

countries the greatest discrepancy between incoming and outgoing mail is for the U.S.A. whence in 1969 only 817 million items were mailed in response to 1,397 million items received from foreign sources.

POSTAGE STAMPS

Earliest The earliest adhesive postage stamps in the world were the "Penny Blacks" of the United Kingdom, bearing the head of Queen Victoria, placed on sale on 1 May 1840. A total of 64,000,000 were printed. The national Postal Museum possesses a unique full proof sheet of 240 stamps, printed in April 1840, before the corner letters, plate numbers or marginal inscriptions were added.

Largest The largest postage stamps ever issued were the 1913 Express Delivery stamps of China, which measured 9¾ inches by 2¾ inches. The largest standard postage stamps ever issued were the 10 RLS (ten riyal) airmail stamps issued by the Trucial State of Fujeira (Fujairah) measuring 3¼ by 5¾ inches (18.68 square inches).

Smallest The smallest stamps ever issued were the 10 cents and 1 peso of the Colombian State of Bolívar in 1863-66. They measured 8 millimetres (0.31 0f an inch) by 9.5 millimetres (0.37 of an inch).

Highest and lowest denomination The highest denomination stamp ever issued was a red and black stamp for £100, issued in Kenya in 1925-27. The highest denomination stamp ever issued in the United Kingdom was the £5 orange Victoria stamp issued on 21 March 1882. Owing to inflations it is difficult to determine the lowest denomination stamp but it was probably the 1946 3,000 pengö Hungarian stamp, worth at one time only 1.6×10^{-14}d.

Highest price World The highest price ever paid for a single philatelic item is the $380,000 (£158,333) for two 1d. orange "Post Office" Mauritius stamps of 1847 on a cover bought at H. R. Harmer's Inc., New York City, U.S.A. by Raymond H. Weill Co. of New Orleans, Louisiana for their own account from the Liechtenstein-Dale collection on 21 Oct. 1968. The item was discovered in 1897 in an Indian bazaar by a Mr. Charles Williams who paid less than £1 for it.

Most valuable World There are a number of stamps of which but a single specimen is known. Of these the most celebrated is the one cent black on magenta issued in British Guiana (now Guyana) in February 1856. It was originally bought for six shillings from L. Vernon Vaughan, a schoolboy, in 1873. This is the world's most renowned stamp, for which £A16,000 (£12,774 sterling) was paid in 1940, when it was sold by Mrs. Arthur Hind. It was insured for £200,000, when it was displayed in 1965 at the Royal Festival Hall, London. It was sold on 24 March 1970 by Frederick T. Small by auction at the Siegel Galleries, New York City, U.S.A. for $280,000 (£116,666) by Irwin Weinberg. It was alleged in October 1938 that Hind had, in 1928, purchased and burned his stamp's twin.

Great Britain The highest price paid for stamps in Britain is £28,000 paid on 1 Oct. 1963 for a 1d. orange-red and a 2d. deep blue of Mauritius on an 1847 envelope. The most valuable philatelic piece of Great Britain is the Buccleuch block of 48 (4 × 12) unused Plate 2 imperforate 2d. Blues printed on 21 July 1840. These were found in 1945 by Mr. A. Martin at Dalkeith House, Scotland, and were auctioned, along with some minor pieces, by H. R. Harmer Ltd. for £6,300 in June 1946.

There are three unique British stamps. They are an unissued 1860, 1½d. rosy-mauve error, corner-lettered with an O for a C and an Edward VII 1d. War Office error overprinted "Official", which are both in the royal collection; and an unused 9d. straw of 1862 on azure paper, discovered in 1938. The rarest British

Part of the largest National Stamp Collection in the world, housed at the National Postal Museum in the City of Londo

stamp which is not an error is the King Edward V 6d. dull purple Inland Revenue Official stamp issu and withdrawn on 14 May 1904. Only 11 or 12 a known and one was sold for £3,500 unused in Fe 1967.

Commonest British stamp The most frequently reproduced United Kingdo stamp has been the definitive Elizabeth II 3d. viole issued from 1 Oct. 1953 to 17 May 1965, of whi 19,920 million were issued.

Largest collection The greatest private stamp collection ever auction has been that of Maurice Burrus (d. 1959) of Alsac France, which realised an estimated £1,500,000.

The largest national collection in the world is that the British Museum, London, which has had t General Post Office collection on permanent lo since March 1963. The British Royal collectio housed in 400 volumes, is also believed to be wor more than £1,000,000. The collection of the Unive sal Postal Union (founded 9 Oct. 1874) in Genev Switzerland receives 400 copies of each new issue each member nation but the largest internation collections are those of the Swiss, Swedish, Germa Dutch and U.S.A. (Smithsonian Institution) autho ities.

POSTAL ADDRESSES

Highest numbering The practice of numbering houses began in 1463 the Pont Notre Dame, Paris, France. The highe numbered house in Britain is No. 2,679 Stratfor Road, Solihull, Warwickshire, occupied since 1966 Mr. & Mrs. H. Hughes. The highest numbered house Scotland is No. 2,629 London Road, Mount Verno Glasgow, which is part of the local police station.

Pillar-boxes Pillar-boxes were introduced into Great Britain at t suggestion of the novelist Anthony Trollo (1815-82). The oldest site on which one is still service is one dating from 8 Feb. 1853 in Unic Street, St. Peter Port, Guernsey though the prese box is not the original. The oldest original box Great Britain is another Victorian example at Barn Cross, Holwell, near Bishop's Caundle, Dorset, als dating from probably later in 1853.

Post Offices The Post Office's northernmost post office is Haroldswick, Unst, Shetland Islands. The most sout erly in the British Isles is at Samarès, Jersey. Th oldest is at Sanquhar, Dumfriesshire which was fir referred to in 1763. In England the Post Office Shipton-Under-Wychwood dates back to April 184

TELEGRAMS

The country where most telegrams are sent is the U.S.S.R., whose population sent 357,000,000 telegrams in 1969. The United Kingdom total was 10,450,000 including 2,550,000 sent overseas, in the year ending 31 March 1971.

The world's largest telegraph company is the Western Union Telegraph Company of New York City, N.Y., U.S.A. It had 26,269 employees on 1 Jan. 1969, a total of 11,000 telegraphic offices and agencies and 5,734,792 miles of telegraph channels.

The largest British telegraphic undertaking is Cable and Wireless Ltd., which operates 58,000 nautical miles of ocean cables (including 20,000 miles of telephone cable) and about 300,000 miles of radio circuits. It has a fleet of six cable ships, more than 80 overseas stations and 10,392 employees.

INLAND WATERWAYS

The country with the greatest length of inland waterways is Finland. The total length of navigable lakes and rivers is about 50,000 kilometres (31,000 miles). In the United Kingdom the total length of navigable rivers and canals is 3,940 miles.

Longest navigable river The longest navigable natural waterway in the world is the River Amazon, which sea-going vessels can ascend as far as Iquitos, in Peru, 2,236 miles from the Atlantic seaboard. On a National Geographic Society expedition ending on 10 March 1969, Helen and Frank Schreider navigated downstream from San Francisco, Peru, 3,845 miles up the Amazon, by a balsa raft named *Mamuri* 249 miles to Atalaya, thence 356 miles to Pucallpa by outboard motor dug-out canoe and thence the last 3,240 miles towards Belem in the 30-foot petrol-engined cabin cruiser *Amazon Queen*.

7. EDUCATION

ILLITERACY

Literacy is variously defined as "ability to read simple subjects" and "ability to read and write a simple letter". The looseness of definition and the scarcity of data for some countries preclude anything more than approximations, but the extent of illiteracy among adults (15 years old and over) is estimated to have been 39.3 per cent. throughout the world at the opening of the last decade in 1961. In 1969 a United Nations' estimate put the level at 810 million out of 2,335 million adults or 34.7 per cent. The continent with the greatest proportion of illiterates is Africa, where 81.5 per cent. of adults are illiterate. The latest

Cambridge University's oldest College — Peterhouse founded in 1284.

figure available for the Niger Republic is 99.1 per cent. A U.S.S.R. report published in June 1968, affirms that more than 300 million people in China are still "completely illiterate".

UNIVERSITIES

World Probably the oldest educational institution in the world is the University of Karueein, founded in A.D. 859 in Fez, Morocco. The European university with the earliest date of foundation is that of Naples, Italy, founded in 1224 by charter of Frederick II (1194-1250), Holy Roman Emperor.

United Kingdom The oldest university in the United Kingdom is the University of Oxford, which came into being in c. 1167. The oldest college is quoted as University College (1249), though its foundation is less well documented than that of Merton College in 1264. The earliest college at Cambridge University is Peterhouse, founded in 1284. The largest college at either university is Trinity College, Cambridge. It was founded in 1546. The oldest university in Scotland is the University of St. Andrews, Fife. It was established in 1411.

Trinity College, Cambridge— the largest single college at any British university.

The world's largest university building—the 787 foot tall central building of the Lomonosov State University, Moscow.

Greatest enrolment The university with the greatest enrolment in the world is the University of Calcutta (founded 1857) in India, with more than 196,257 students (internal and external) and 31 professors in 1969. Owing to the inadequacy of the buildings and number of lecturers, the students are handled in three shifts per day. The enrolment at all branches of the State University of New York, U.S.A., was 155,469 in January 1971 and is expected to reach 290,400 by 1974. The University of London had 33,771 full-time students at 31 Oct. 1971.

Largest building The largest university building in the world is the M. V. Lomonosov State University on the Lenin Hills, south of Moscow, U.S.S.R. It stands 240 metres (787.4 feet) tall, has 32 storeys and contains 40,000 rooms. It was constructed in 1949-53.

Richest The richest university in the world is Harvard University in Cambridge, Massachusetts, U.S.A. Its endowments had a book value of $621,795,041 (£259 million) in 1968.

PROFESSORS

Youngest The youngest at which anybody has been elected to a chair in a university is 19 years in the case of Colin MacLaurin (1698-1746), who was admitted to Marischal College, Aberdeen as Professor of Mathematics on 30 Sept. 1717. In 1725 he was made Professor of Mathematics at Edinburgh University on the recommendation of Sir Isaac Newton. In July 1967 Dr. Harvey Friedman, Ph. D., was appointed Assistant Professor of Mathematics at Stanford University, California, U.S.A. aged just 19 years.

Most durable The longest period for which any professorship has been held is 63 years in the case of Thomäs Martyn (1735-1825), Professor of Botany at Cambridge University from 1762 until his death. His father, John Martyn (1699-1768), had occupied the chair from 1733 to 1762.

Senior Wranglers Since 1910 the Wranglers (first class honours students in the Cambridge University mathematical Tripos, part 2) have been placed in alphabetical order only. In 1890 Miss P. G. Fawcett of Newnham was placed "above the Senior Wrangler".

Youngest undergraduate The most extreme recorded cases of undergradua juvenility were those of John Donne (1573-163 who entered Hart Hall, Oxford, aged 11, and Willi Thompson (1824-1907), later Lord Kelvin, O. G.C.V.O., who entered Glasgow University also ag 11.

Longest studentship No central records are kept but the closest approa in Britain to an eternal student appears to be that George A. Goulty of Guildford, Surrey who enter the Southern College of Art, Winchester in 1942 a who, in 1972, after 17 years further education, is Reading University reading for his seventh qualifi tion, a Ph.D.

Oldest student The oldest student enrolled by the Open University Miss Mary Carr of Gosforth, Northumberland, ag 79.

SCHOOLS

Largest World The largest school in the world was the De W Clinton High School in the Bronx, New York Ci N.Y., U.S.A., where the enrolment attained a peak 12,000 in 1934. It was founded in 1897 and now h an enrolment of 6,000.

United Kingdom The school with the most pupils in the Unit Kingdom is Thomas Bennett School, Crawley, Suss with 2,145 in January 1972. The highest figure Scotland is 2,045 at the Portobello Senior Seconda School, Edinburgh as at April 1972.

Oldest in Britain The title of the oldest school in Britain is contested. is claimed that King's School in Canterbury, Ke was a foundation of Saint Augustine, some tir between his arrival in Kent in A.D. 597 and his dea in c. 604.

Oldest old school tie The practice of wearing distinctive neckties beari the colours or registered designs of schools, univ sities, sports clubs, regiments, etc., appears to da from c. 1880. The practice originated in Oxfo University, where boater bands were converted in use as "ribbon ties". The earliest definitive eviden stems from an order from Exeter College for colle ties, dated 25 June, 1880.

Most expensive World The most expensive school in the world is the Oxfo Academy (established 1906) in Pleasantville, N Jersey, U.S.A. It is a private college-preparato boarding school for boys with "academic deficie cies". The school has 15 masters and each of the boys is taught individually in each course. The tuiti fee for the school year is $8,400 (£3,500).

United Kingdom The most expensive school in the United Kingdom Millfield at Street, Somerset, founded by R.J. Meyer in 1937. The termly fees for late entrant pup may amount to £1,300 per annum. The mc expensive girls' school in 1970-71 was Benende Kent (founded 1924) with annual fees of £750.

Smallest In July 1970 it was reported that a school in t Jamma District of India had one pupil and o teacher. Classes were arranged at mutual convenienc

Greatest disenrolment Between June 1966 and March 1967 abou 110,000,000 Chinese schoolchildren over 9 yea were excused attendance to aid the 22,000,000 R Guards (Hongweibing) in prosecuting the "Gre Cultural Revolution".

Most 'O' and 'A' levels Edward Short at St. Kevins Comprehensive Schoc Kirby, Lancashire between June 1967 and June 197 accumulated 11 "O", 11 "A" and 3 "S" levels. H brother Leslie in 1968-71 secured 11 "O", 9 "A" an an "S" level making 46 between them. An anon mous pupil of Marst College, Kingston upon Hull wi an IQ of 161 passed 14 "O", 11 "A" and 1 "S" level 1962-66. Francis L. Thomason of Cleobury Mo

Thomas
Bennett
School,
Crawley,
Sussex, the
school with
more pupils
than any
other in the
U.K.

timer, in Shropshire had by August 1971 accumulated 22 'O', 7 'A' and 1 'S' levels making a total of 30.

Youngest The youngest headmaster of a major public school
Headmaster was Henry Montagh Butler (b. 2 July 1835), appointed Headmaster of Harrow School on 16 Nov. 1859, when aged 24 years 137 days. His first term in office began in January 1860.

8. RELIGIONS

LARGEST
Religious statistics are necessarily highly approximations. The test of adherence to a religion varies widely in rigour, while many individuals, particularly in the East, belong to two or more religions.

Christianity is the world's prevailing religion, with over 985,000,000 adherents in 1971 and probably an additional 150,000,000 Protestants who are not in membership with the Church of their baptism. The total of 175,000,000 practising and 150,000,000 non-practising Protestants is easily outnumbered by the 590,000,000 who have received baptism into the Roman Catholic Church. The largest non-Christian religion is Islam, with about 475,000,000 adherents in 1971.

In the United Kingdom the Anglicans comprise members of the Established Church of England, the Dis-established Church in Wales, the Episcopal Church in Scotland and the Church of Ireland. In 1968 there were 27,756,000 living persons who had been baptized in Anglican churches in the provinces of Canterbury and York. In the same area it is estimated that there were 9,691,000 persons confirmed, of whom nearly 2,000,000 were Easter communicants in 1968. In Scotland the most numerous group is the Church of Scotland (the Presbyterians), which had 1,201,933 members, apart from adherents, at 1 Jan. 1969.

SMALLEST
In New Zealand the 1966 Census revealed 94 religious sects with a single follower each. These included a Millenarian Heretic and an Aesthetic Hedonist. Such followers might alternatively be described as leaders.

Largest The world's largest religious organization is the
clergy Roman Catholic Church, with over 500 million members, 418,000 priests and 946,000 nuns in 1964. The total number of cardinals, patriarchs, metropolitans, archbishops, bishops, abbots and superiors is 2,800. There are about 416,000 churches.

Jews The total of world Jewry was estimated to be 14 million in 1971. The highest concentration was in the United States, with 5,870,000, of whom 1,836,000 were in New York City. The total in Israel was 2,530,000. The total of British Jewry is 450,000, of whom 280,000 are in Greater London, 31,500 in Manchester and Salford, and 13,500 in Glasgow. The total in Tōkyō, Japan, is only 250.

Largest The largest religious structure ever built is Angkor
Temple Wat (City Temple), enclosing 402 acres, in Cambodia, south-east Asia. It was built to the God Vishnu by the Khmer King Suryavarman II in the period 1113-50. Its curtain wall measures 1,400 yards by 1,400 yards and its population, before it was abandoned in 1432, was 80,000.

The Inner Temple of Angkor Wat, which covers 40.9 acres in Cambodia, now called the Khmer Republic.

CATHEDRALS
Largest The world's largest cathedral is the cathedral church
World of the Diocese of New York, St. John the Divine, with a floor area of 121,000 square feet and a volume of 16,822,000 cubic feet. The corner stone was laid on 27 Dec. 1892, and the Gothic building was still uncompleted in 1967. In New York it is referred to as "Saint John the Unfinished". The nave is the longest in the world, 601 feet in length, with a vaulting 124 feet in height.

The cathedral covering the largest area is that of Santa Mariá de la Sede in Sevilla (Seville), Spain. It was built in Spanish Gothic style between 1402 and 1519 and is 414 feet long, 271 feet wide and 100 feet high to the vault of the nave.

The largest Cathedral in the U.K. — the Cathedral Church of Christ, Liverpool.

United Kingdom The largest cathedral in the British Isles is the Anglican Cathedral of Liverpool. Built in modernized Gothic style, work was begun on 19 July 1904, and when completed will have cost over £3,000,000. The building encloses 100,000 square feet and has an overall length of 671 feet. The Vestey Tower is 331 feet high.

Smallest *United Kingdom* The smallest cathedral in use in the United Kingdom (excluding converted parish churches) is St. Asaph in Flintshire, Wales. It is 182 feet long, 68 feet wide and has a tower 100 feet high. Oxford Cathedral in Christ Church (College) is 155 feet long. The nave of the Cathedral of the Isles on the Isle of Cumbrae, Buteshire measures only 40 X 20 feet. The total floor area is 2,124 square feet.

Longest The longest Gothic church in the United Kingdom is Winchester Cathedral, Hampshire, which is 560 feet long (internal length 526 feet).

Longest nave The longest nave in the United Kingdom is that of St. Albans Cathedral, Hertfordshire, which is 285 feet long.

Largest *World* The largest church in the world is the basilica of St. Peter, built between 1492 and 1612 in the Vatican City, Rome.

The length of the church, measured from the apse, is 611 feet 4 inches. The area is 18,110 square yards. The inner diameter of the famous dome is 137 feet 9 inches and its centre is 119 metres (390 feet 5 inches) high. The external height is 457 feet 9 inches.

The elliptical Basilique of St. Pie X at Lourdes, France, completed in 1957 at a cost of £2,000,000 has a capacity of 20,000 under its giant span arches and a length of 659 feet.

The crypt of the underground Civil War Memorial Church in the Guadarrama Mountains, 28 miles from Madrid, Spain, is 853 feet in length. It took 21 years (1937-58) to build, at a reported cost of £140,000,000 and is surmounted by a cross 492 feet tall.

United Kingdom The largest parish church in the United Kingdom Holy Trinity Parish Church, Kingston-upon-Hu Yorkshire. The church exterior is 295 feet long a 104 feet wide, and parts of the transept date fro 1285. The internal area is 26,384 square feet. T parish church of St. Nicholas at Great Yarmout Norfolk, after the addition of the Vestries in 19 reached 25,023 square feet, but was destroyed bombing in 1942. It was rededicated in May 1961.

Smallest *World* The world's smallest church is the Union Church Wiscasset, Maine, U.S.A., with a floor area of 31 square feet (7 feet by 4½ feet). Les Vaubelets Chur in Guernsey has an area of 16 feet by 12 feet, roo for one priest and a congregation of two.

Britain The smallest church in use in England is Bremitha Church, Cowage Farm, Foxley near Malmesbur Wiltshire which measures 12 feet by 12 feet and used for service twice a year. The smallest complet

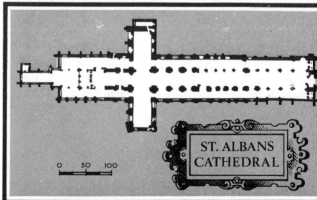

The longest nave in the U.K. at St. Alban's Cathedral, Hertfordshire.

The oldest wooden church in Great Britain and probably the world — St. Andrew's, Greensted, near Ongar, Essex with Saxon timbers dating from A.D. 835 flanking the south porch.

English church in regular use is that at Culbone, Somerset, which measures 35 feet by 12 feet. The smallest Welsh chapel is St. Trillo's Chapel, Rhôs-on-Sea (Llandrillo-yn-Rhos), Denbighshire, measuring only 12 feet by 6 feet. The smallest chapel in Scotland is St. Margaret's, Edinburgh, measuring 16½ feet by 10½ feet, giving an area of 173¼ square feet.

OLDEST
World The earliest known shrine dates from the proto-neolithic Natufian culture in Jericho, where a site on virgin soil has been dated to the ninth millennium B.C. A simple rectilinear red-plastered room with a niche housing a stone pillar believed to be the shrine of a Pre-Pottery fertility cult dating from *c.* 6500 B.C. was also uncovered in Jericho (now Arīhā) in Jordan. The oldest surviving Christian church in the world is Qal'at es Salihige in eastern Syria, dating from A.D. 232. A list of the oldest religious buildings in 43 countries was included in the 11th edition of *The Guinness Book of Records*, at page 117. The oldest wooden church in Great Britain and probably in the world is St. Andrew's, Greensted, near Ongar, Essex dating to A.D. 835 though some of the timbers date to the original building of *c.* A.D. 650.

United The oldest church in the United Kingdom is
Kingdom St. Martin's Church in Canterbury, Kent. It was built in A.D. 560 on the foundations of a 1st century Roman church. The oldest church in Ireland is the Gallerus Oratory, built in *c.* 750 at Ballyferriter, near Kilmalkedar, County Kerry. Britain's oldest nunnery is St. Peter and Paul Minster, on the Isle of Thanet, Kent. It was founded in *c.* 748 by the Abbess Eadburga of Bugga.

TALLEST SPIRES
World The tallest cathedral spire in the world is that of the Protestant Cathedral of Ulm in Germany. The building is early Gothic and was begun in 1377. The tower, in the centre of the west façade, was not finally completed until 1890 and is 528 feet high. The world's tallest church spire is that of the Chicago Temple of the First Methodist Church on Clark Street, Chicago, Illinois, U.S.A. The building consists of a 22-storey skyscraper (erected in 1924) surmounted by a parsonage at 330 feet, a "Sky Chapel" at 400 feet and a steeple cross at 568 feet above street level.

United The highest spire in the United Kingdom is that of the
Kingdom church of St. Mary, called Salisbury Cathedral, Wiltshire. The Lady Chapel was built in the years 1220-25 and the main fabric of the cathedral was finished and consecrated in 1258. The spire was added later, 1334-65, and reaches a height of 404 feet. St. Paul's Cathedral, London, possessed a 489-foot spire, built in 1315, but this was struck by

lightning in June 1561. The height of the present cross above the dome is 365 feet.

Largest The Churchyard beside Walker Parish Church,
Churchyard Newcastle-upon-Tyne, consecrated in 1848, extends over 11 acres.

LARGEST SYNAGOGUES
World The largest synagogue in the world is the Temple Emanu-El on Fifth Avenue at 65th Street, New York City, N.Y., U.S.A. The temple, completed in September 1929, has a frontage of 150 feet on Fifth Avenue and 253 feet on 65th Street. The Sanctuary proper can accommodate 2,500 people, and the adjoining Beth-El Chapel seats 350. When all the facilities are in use, more than 6,000 people can be accommodated.

Great The largest synagogue in Great Britain is the Edgware
Britain Synagogue, Greater London, completed in 1959, with a capacity of 1,630 seats.

Largest The largest mosque ever built was the now ruinous
mosque al-Malawiya mosque of al-Mutawakil in Samarra, Iraq built in A.D. 842-852 and measuring 401,408 square feet (9.21 acres) with dimensions of 784 feet by 512 feet. The world's largest mosque in use is the Jama Masjid (1644-58) in Delhi, India, with an area of more than 10,000 square feet and two 108-foot-tall minarets. The largest mosque will be the Merdeka Mosque in Djakarta, Indonesia, which was begun in 1962. The cupola will be 45 metres (147.6 feet) in diameter and the capacity in excess of 50,000 people.

Tallest The world's tallest minaret is the Qutb Minar, south
minaret of New Delhi, India, built in 1194 to a height of 238 feet.

Tallest The world's tallest pagoda is the 288-foot-tall
pagoda Shwemawdaw in Pegu, Burma. It was restored by April 1954 having been damaged by an earthquake in 1930. The tallest Chinese temple is the 13-storey Pagoda of the Six Harmonies (*Liu he t'a*) outside Hang-chow. It is "nearly 200 feet high".

SAINTS
Most and The shortest interval that has elapsed between the
least rapidly death of a Saint and his canonization was in the case
Canonized of St. Anthony of Padua, Italy, who died on 13 June 1251 and was canonized 352 days later on 30 May 1252. This was one day faster than St. Peter of Verona (1206-52) canonized on 6 April 1253.

The other extreme is represented by St. Bernard of Thiron, for 20 years Prior of St. Sabinus, who died in 1117 and was made a Saint in 1861—744 years later. The Italian monk and painter, Fra Giovanni da Fiesole (*né* Guido di Pietro), called *Il Beato* ("The Blessed") Fra Angelico (*c.* 1400-1455), is still in the first stage of canonization.

POPES
Reign The longest reign of any of the 262 Popes has been
Longest that of Pius IX (Giovanni Maria Mastai-Ferretti), who reigned for 31 years 236 days from 16 June 1846 until his death aged 85, on 7 Feb. 1878.

Shortest Pope Stephen II was elected on 24 March 752 and died two days later, but he is not included in the *Liber pontificalis* or the Catalogue of the Popes. The shortest reign of any genuine Pope is that of Giambattista Castagna (1521-90), who was elected Pope Urban VII on 15 Sept. 1590 and died twelve days later on 27 Sept. 1590.

Oldest It is recorded that Pope St. Agatho (reigned 678-681) was elected at the age of 103 and lived to 106, but recent scholars have expressed doubts. The oldest of recent Pontiffs has been Pope Leo XIII (Vincenzo Gioacchino Pecci), who was born on 2 March 1810,

219

The memorial at Rome to Adrian IV (Nicholas Breakspear) the only Englishman to be elected Pope.

elected Pope at the third ballot on 20 Feb. 1878 and died on 20 July 1903, aged 93 years 140 days.

Youngest The youngest of all Popes was Pope Benedict IX (Theophylact), who had three terms as Pope: in 1032–44; April to May 1045; and 8 Nov. 1047 to 17 July 1048. It would appear that he was aged only 11 or 12 in 1032, though the Catalogue of the Popes admits only to his "extreme youth".

Last non-Italian ex-Cardinal-ate and English Popes The last non-Italian Pope was the Utrecht-born Cardinal Priest Adrian Dedel (1459-1523) of the Netherlands. He was elected on 9 Jan. 1522, crowned Pope Adrian VI on 31 Aug. 1522 and died on 14 Sept. 1523. The last Pope elected from outside the College of Cardinals was Bartolomeo Prignano (1318-89), Archbishop of Bari, who was elected Pope Urban VI on 8 April 1378. The only Englishman to be elected Pope was Nicholas Breakspear (born at Abbots Langley, near Watford, Hertfordshire, in *c.* 1100), who, as Cardinal Bishop of Albano, was elected Pope Adrian IV on 4 Dec. 1154, and died on 1 Sept. 1159.

Last married The first 37 Popes had no specific obligation to celibacy. The last married Pope was Adrian II (867–872). Rodrigo Borgia was the father of at least four children before being elected Pope Alexander VI in 1492.

Slowest election After 31 months without declaring *Habemus Papam* ("We have a Pope"), the cardinals were subjected to a bread and water diet and the removal of the roof of their conclave by the Mayor before electing Teobaldo Visconti (*c.* 1210-76), the Archbishop of Liège, as Pope Gregory X at Viterbo on 1 Sept. 1271. Cardinal Eugenio Maria Guiseppe Giovanni Pacelli (1876-1958), who took the title of Pius XII, was reputedly elected by 61 votes out of 62 at only the third ballot on 2 March 1939, his 63rd birthday.

CARDINALS

Oldest By June 1972 the Sacred College of Cardinals contained 119 declared members compared with 125 a year earlier. The oldest is Cardinal Bishop Paolo Giobbe of Italy (b. 10 Jan. 1880).

Youngest The youngest Cardinal of all time was Giovanni c Medici (b. 11 Dec. 1475), later Pope Leo X, who w made a Cardinal Deacon in March 1489, when aged years 3 months. The youngest in 1971 is Cardin Bishop Stephan Sou Hwan Kim of South Kor (b. 6 May 1922). He was named as a Cardinal in Ap 1969 when aged 46.

BISHOPS

Oldest The oldest serving bishop (excluding Suffragans a Assisants) in the Church of England at 1 July 19 was the Rt. Rev. Cyril Easthaugh, M.C. (b. 22 D 1897), the 34th Bishop of Peterborough.

The oldest Roman Catholic bishop in recent years w Mgr. Alfonson Carinci (b. 9 Nov. 1862), who w titular Archbishop of Seleucia, in Isauria, from 19 until his death on 6 Dec. 1963, at the age of 101 ye 27 days. He had celebrated Mass about 24,800 tim

Bishop Herbert Welch of the United Method Church who was elected a bishop for Japan and Kor in 1916 died on 4 Apr. 1969 aged 106.

Youngest The youngest bishop of all time was Hugnes, who father, the Comte de Vermandois, successfu demanded for him the archbishopric of Reims fro the feeble Pope John X (reigned 914-928), when was only five years old.

The youngest serving bishop (excluding Suffraga and Assistants) in the Church of England at 1 Ja 1971 was the Rt. Rev. Stuart Yarworth Blan (b. 2 Feb. 1918), the 5th Bishop of Liverpool.

Stained glass medallions in Rivenhall Church, Essex believe to date from the first half of the 12th Century.

BISHOPRIC

Longest tenure The longest tenure of any Church of England bishopric is 57 years in the case of the Rt. Rev. Thomas Wilson, who was consecrated Bishop of Sodor and Man on 16 Jan. 1698 and died in office on 7 March 1755. Of English bishoprics the longest tenure, if one excludes the unsubstantiated case of Aethelwulf, reputedly bishop of Hereford from 937 to 1012, are those of 47 years by Jocelin de Bohun (Salisbury) 1142-1189 and Nathaniel Crew or Crewe (Durham) 1674-1721.

STAINED GLASS

Oldest The oldest stained glass in the world represents the Prophets in a window of the cathedral of Augsburg, Bavaria, Germany, dating from *c.* 1050. The oldest datable stained glass in the United Kingdom is represented by 12th century fragments in the Tree of Jesse in the north aisle of the nave of York Minster, dated *c.* 1150, and medallions in Rivenhall Church, Essex which appear to date from the first half of that century. Dates late in the previous century have been attributed to glass in a window of the church at Compton, Surrey and a complete window in St. Mary the Virgin, Brabourne, Kent.

Largest The largest stained glass window is one measuring 300 feet long by 23 feet high at the John F. Kennedy International Airport (formerly Idlewild), Long Island, New York State, U.S.A. The largest single stained glass window in Great Britain is the East window in Gloucester Cathedral measuring 72 feet by 38 feet, set up to commemorate the Battle of Crécy (1346), while the largest area of stained glass is 125 windows, totalling 25,000 square feet in York Minster.

BRASSES

The world's oldest monumental brass is that commemorating Bishop Ysowilpe in St. Andrew's Church, Verden, near Hanover, West Germany, dating from 1231. The oldest in Great Britain is of Sir John D'Abernon at Stoke D'Abernon, near Leatherhead, Surrey, dating from 1277.

PARISHES

Largest and smallest The latest population figures for parishes in the United Kingdom are from the census of 23 April 1961. The most populous parish was the Parish of Kirkby St. Chad, Liverpool, with 52,177 parishioners. Of the nine parishes uninhabited in 1961, Iham Parish, in the diocese of Chichester, Sussex, has had a nil population since 1931.

Longest incumbency The longest incumbency on record is one of 76 years by the Rev. Bartholomew Edwards, Rector of St. Nicholas, Ashill, Norfolk from 1813 to 1889. There appears to be some doubt as to whether the Rev. Richard Sherinton was installed at Folkestone from 1524 or 1529 to 1601. If the former is correct it would surpass the Norfolk record. The parish of Iden, East Sussex had only two incumbents in the 117-year period from 1807 to 1924.

Longest Serving chorister Mr. J. T. Gascoigne (b. 1883) of Newark, Nottinghamshire has been in his local church choir since 1894. He rung the century in in 1900 and has completed 73 years as a bell-ringer.

Oldest parish register The oldest parish registers in England are those of St. James Garlickhythe and St. Mary Bothaw, two old City of London parishes, dating from 1536. Scotland's oldest surviving register is that for Anstruther-Wester, Fife, with burial entries from 1549.

Largest crowd The greatest recorded number of human beings assembled with a common purpose was more than 5,000,000 at the 21-day Hindu festival of Kumbh-Mela, which is held every 12 years at the confluence of the Yamuna (formerly called the Jumna), the Ganges and the invisible "Sarasviti" at Allahabad, Uttar Pradesh, India, on 21 Jan. 1966. According to the Jacob Formula for estimating the size of crowds, the allowance of area per person varies from 4 square feet (tight) to 9½ square feet (loose). Thus such a crowd must have occupied an area of more than 700 acres.

Largest funeral The greatest attendance at any funeral is the estimated 4 million who thronged Cairo, United Arab Republic, for the funeral of President Gamal Abdel Nasser (b. 15 Jan. 1918) on 1 Oct. 1970.

Biggest Demonstrations A figure of 2.7 million was published from China for the demonstration against the U.S.S.R. in Shanghai on 3-4 April 1969 following the border clashes, and one of 10 million for the May Day celebrations of 1963 in Peking.

The devastation caused by the Halifax explosion on 6th December 1917. (see p. 222)

ACCIDENTS AND DISASTERS

WORST IN THE WORLD / WORST FOR THE UNITED KINGDOM

	WORST IN THE WORLD			WORST FOR THE UNITED KINGDOM		
	Death toll	Date	Location	Location	Death toll	Date
Pandemic	75,000,000	1347-1351	The Black Death (bubonic, pneumonic and septicaemic plague)	The Black Death (bubonic, pneumonic and septicaemic plague)	800,000	1347-1350
	21,640,000	1918	Influenza	Influenza	225,000	Sept.-Nov. 1918
Famine	9,500,000[1]	April-Nov. 1918	Northern China	Ireland (famine and typhus)	1,500,000[13]	1846-1851
Flood	3,700,000	Feb. 1877-Sept. 1878	Hwang-ho River, China	Severn Estuary	c. 2,000[14]	20 Jan. 1606
Circular Storm[2]	1,000,000	Aug. 1931	Ganges Delta Islands, Bangladesh	"The Channel Storm"	c. 8,000	26 Nov. 1703
Earthquake	830,000	12-13 Nov. 1970	Shensi Province, China	City of London	1	6 April 1580
		23 Jan. 1556		Rowhedge, Essex	1	22 April 1884
Landslide	200,000	16 Dec. 1920	Kansu Province, China	Pantglas coal tip No. 7, Aberfan, Glamorganshire	144	21 Oct. 1966
Conventional Bombing[3]	135,000	13-15 Feb. 1945	Dresden, Germany	London	1,436	10-11 May 1941
Atomic Bomb	91,223[4]	6 Aug. 1945	Hiroshima, Japan			
Marine (single ship)	c.7,700	30 Jan. 1945	Wilhelm Gustloff (24,484 tons) torpedoed off Danzig by U.S.S.R. submarine S-13	H.M. Troopship Lancastria (16,243 tons) off St. Nazaire	c. 4,000	17 June 1940
Snow Avalanche	c. 5,000[5]	13 Dec. 1941	Huarás, Peru	Lewes, Sussex (snowdrifts)	8	27 Dec. 1836
Panic	c. 4,000	c. 8 June 1941	Chungking (Zhong qing) China air raid shelter	Bethnal Green Tube Station (air raid siren)	173	3 Mar. 1943
Dam Burst	2,209	31 May 1889	South Fork Dam, Johnstown, Pennsylvania	Bradfield Reservoir, Dale Dyke, near Sheffield (embankment burst)	270	11 Mar. 1864
Explosion	1,963[6]	6 Dec. 1917	Halifax, Nova Scotia, Canada	Chilwell, Notts. (explosives factory)	134	1 July 1918
Fire[7] (single building)	1,670	May 1845	The Theatre, Canton, China	Victoria Hall, Sunderland	183[15]	16 June 1883
Mining[8]	1,572	26 April 1942	Honkeiko Colliery, China (coal dust explosion)	Universal Colliery, Senghenydd, Glam., Wales	439	14 Oct. 1913
Riot	c. 1,200	13-16 July 1863	New York City anti-conscription riots	London anti-Catholic Gordon riots	565 (min.)	2-13 June 1780
Crocodiles	c. 900	19-20 Feb. 1945	Japanese soldiers, Ramree Is., Burma			
Fireworks	>800	16 May 1770	Dauphine's Wedding, Seine, Paris			
Tornado	689	18 Mar. 1925	South Central States, U.S.A.	Widecombe, Devon	60[16]	21 Oct. 1638
Railway	543	12 Dec. 1917	Modane, France	Triple collision at Quintins Hill, Dumfries-shire,	227[17]	22 May 1915
Man-eating Tigress[9]	436	1907	Champawat district, India, shot by Col. Jim Corbett			
Hail	246	30 April 1888	Moradabad, Uttar Pradesh, India			
Aircraft (Civil)	162[10]	30 July 1971	Möriota, Japan All Nippon Boeing 727	B.E.A. Trident, Staines, Surrey	118[18]	18 June 1972
Submarine	129	10 April 1963	U.S.S. Thresher off Cape Cod, Massachusetts, U.S.A.	H.M.S. Thetis, during trials, Liverpool Bay	99	1 June 1939
Road[11]	>125	6 Dec. 1965	Two trucks crashed into a crowd of dancers, Sotouboua, Togo	R.M. Cadets, run down by bus, Gillingham, Kent	24	4 Dec. 1951
Mountaineering	40[12]	Dec. 1952	U.S.S.R. Expedition on Mount Everest	On Cairngorm, Scotland (4,084 ft.)	6	21 Nov. 1971
Space Exploration	3	27 Jan. 1967	Apollo oxygen fire, Cape Kennedy, Fla., U.S.A.			
	3	29 June 1971	Soyuz II re-entry over U.S.S.R.			

[1] In 1770 the great Indian famine carried away a proportion of the population estimated as high as one third, hence a figure of tens of millions. The figure for Bengal alone was also probably about 10 million. It has been estimated that more than 5,000,000 died in the post-World War I famine of 1920-21 in the U.S.S.R. The U.S.S.R. government in July 1923 informed Mr. (later President) Herbert Hoover that the A.R.A. (American Relief Administration) had since August 1921 saved 20,000,000 lives from famine and famine diseases.

[2] This figure published in 1972 for the East Pakistan disaster was from Dr. Afzal, Principle Scientific Officer of the Atomic Energy Authority Centre, Dacca. One report asserted that less than half of the population of the 4 islands of Bhola, Charjabbar, Hatia and Ramagati (1961 Census 1·4 million) survived. The most damaging hurricane recorded was the billion dollar Betsy (name now retired) in 1965 with an estimated insurance pay-out of $750 million.

[3] The number of civilians killed by the bombing of Germany has been put variously as 593,000 and "over 635,000". A figure of c. 140,000 deaths in the U.S.A.F. fire raids on Tokyo of 10 Mar. 1945 has been attributed.

[4] United States Casualty Commission figure in 1960 was 79,400, while the Hiroshima Peace Memorial Museum gives a figure of 240,000, excluding later deaths.

[5] A total of 10,000 Austrian and Italian troops is reputed to have been lost in the Dolomite valley of Northern Italy on 13 Dec. 1916 in more than 100 avalanches. The total is probably exaggerated though bodies were still being found in 1952.

[6] Some sources maintain that the final death roll was over 3,000.

[7] Worst ever hotel fire 162 killed Hotel Taeyonkak, Seoul, South Korea 25 Dec. 1971.

[8] The worst gold mining disaster in South Africa was 152 killed due to flooding in the Witwatersrand Gold Mining Co. Gold Mine in 1909.

[9] In the period 1941-42 c. 1,500 Kenyans were killed by a pride of 22 man-eating lions.

[10] Collided in mid-air with an F-86F Sabre, whose pilot escaped. All 155 passengers and 7 crew of the liner were killed.

[11] The worst ever years for road deaths in the U.S.A. and the U.K. have been respectively, 1969 (56,400) and 1941 (9,169). The U.S.'s 2 millionth victim since 1899 will die in Jan. 1973. The world's highest death rate is said to be in Queensland, Australia but global statistics are not available. The greatest pile-up on British roads was on the M6 near Lymm Interchange involving 200 vehicles on 13 Sept. 1971 with 11 dead and 60 injured.

[12] According to Polish sources, not confirmed by the U.S.S.R., 23 died on Mount Fuji, Japan after blizzard and avalanche on 20 Mar. 1972.

[13] Based on the net rate of natural increase between 1841 and 1851, a supportable case for a loss of population of 3 million can be made out if rates of under-enumeration of 25 per cent. (1841) and 10 per cent. (1851) are accepted. Potato rot (Phytophthora infestans) was first reported on 13 Sept. 1845.

[14] Death rolls of 100,000 were reputed in England and Holland in the floods of 1099, 1421 and 1446.

[15] In July 1212, 3,000 were killed in the crush, burned or drowned when London Bridge caught fire at both ends. The death roll in the Great Fire of London of 1666 was only 8. History's first 'fire storm' occurred in the Quebec Yard, Surrey Docks, London during the 300-pump fire in the Blitz on 7-8 Sept. 1940. Dockland casualties were 306 killed.

[16] Killed and injured.

[17] The 213-yard-long troop train was telescoped to 67 yards. Signalmen Meakin and Tinsley were sentenced for manslaughter.

[18] The worst crash by a U.K. operated aircraft was that of the B.O.A.C. Boeing 707 which broke up in midair near Mount Fuji, Japan, on 5 March 1966. The crew of 11

12 SPORTS, GAMES AND PASTIMES

Earliest The origins of sport stem from the time when self-preservation ceased to be the all-consuming human preoccupation. Archery was a hunting skill in mesolithic times (before 20,000 B.C.), but did not become an organized sport until c. A.D. 300, among the Genoese. The earliest dated origin for any sport is c. 3000 B.C. for wrestling, depicted on pre-dynastic murals at Ben Hasan, Egypt (now the United Arab Republic), and also from early Sumerian sources at Kyafefe, Iraq.

Fastest The governing body for aviation, *La Fédération Aéronautique Internationale*, records maximum speeds in lunar flight of up to 24,791 m.p.h. However, these achievements, like all air speed records since 1923, have been para-military rather than sporting. In shooting, muzzle velocities of up to 7,100 feet per second (4,840 m.p.h.) are reached in the case of a U.S. Army Ordnance Department standard 0.30 calibre M1903 rifle. The highest speed reached in a non-mechanical sport is in sky-diving, in which a speed of 185 m.p.h. is attained in a head-down free falling position, even in the lower atmosphere. In delayed drops a speed of 614 m.p.h. has been recorded at high rarefied altitudes. The highest projectile speed in any moving ball game is c. 160 m.p.h. in pelota. This compares with 170 m.p.h. (electronically-timed) for a golf ball driven off a tee.

Slowest In wrestling, before the rules were modified towards "brighter wrestling", contestants could be locked in holds for so long that single bouts could last for up to 11 hours. In the extreme case of the 2 hours 41 minutes pull in the regimental tug o' war in Jubbulpore, India, on 12 Aug. 1889, the winning team moved a net distance of 12 feet at an average speed of 0.00084 m.p.h.

Longest The most protracted sporting test was an automobile duration test of 222,618 miles by Appaurchaux and others in a Ford Taunus. This was contested over 142 days in 1963. The distance was equivalent to 8.93 times around the equator.

The most protracted non-mechanical sporting event is the *Tour de France* cycling race. In 1926 this was over 3,569 miles, lasting 29 days. The total damage to the French national economy of this annual event, now reduced to 23 days, is immense. If it is assumed that one-third of the total working population works for only two-thirds of the time during the currency of *Le Tour* this would account for a loss of more than three-quarters of one per cent. of the nation's annual Gross National Product. In 1970 this was more than £40,000 million, so the loss would have been about £300,000,000.

Shortest Of sports with timed events the briefest recognized for official record purposes is the quick draw in shooting in which electronic times down to 0.02 of a second have been returned in self-draw events.

Most expensive The most expensive of all sports is the racing of large yachts—"J" type boats, last built in 1937, and International 12-metre boats. The owning and racing of these is beyond the means of individual millionaires and is confined to multi-millionaires or syndicates.

Largest crowd The greatest number of live spectators for any sporting spectacle is the estimated 1,000,000 (more than 20 per cent. of the population) who line the route of the annual San Sylvestre road race of 8,600 metres (5 miles 605 yards) through the streets of São Paulo, Brazil, on New Year's night. However, spread over 23 days, it is estimated that more than 10,000,000 see the annual *Tour de France* along the route (see also above).

The largest crowd travelling to any sporting venue is "more than 400,000" for the annual *Grand Prix d'Endurance* motor race on the Sarthe circuit near Le Mans, France. The record stadium crowd was one of 199,854 for the Brazil v. Uruguay match in the Maracanã Municipal Stadium, Rio de Janeiro, Brazil, on 16 July 1950.

Largest field The largest pitch of any ball game is that of polo, with 12.4 acres, or a maximum length of 300 yards and a width, without side boards, of 200 yards.

The world's fastest sport—all over in 21/100th of a second. Bob Munden (U.S.) setting his fast draw record

Most participants The annual Nijmegen Vierdaagse march in the Netherlands over distances up to 50 kilometres (31 miles 120 yards) attracted 16,667 participants in 1968.

Heaviest sportsmen The heaviest sportsman of all-time was the wrestler William J. Cobb of Macon, Georgia, U.S.A., who in 1962 was billed as the 802 lb. (57 st. 4 lb.) "Happy Humphrey". The heaviest player of a ball-game has been Bob Pointer, the U.S. Football tackle formerly on the 1967 Santa Barbara High School team, California, U.S.A. and still playing in 1972 at 480 lb. (34 st. 4 lb.).

Worst disasters The worst sports disaster in recent history was when an estimated 604 were killed after some stands at the Hong Kong Jockey Club racecourse collapsed and caught fire on 26 Feb. 1918. During the reign of Antoninus Pius (A.D. 138-161) the upper wooden tiers in the Circus Maximus, Rome collapsed during a gladiatorial combat killing some 1,112 spectators. Britain's worst sports disaster was when 66 were killed and 145 injured at the Rangers v. Celtic football match at Exit 13 of Ibrox Park stadium, Glasgow on 2 Jan. 1971.

Youngest world record breakers The youngest age at which any person has broken a world record is 12 years 328 days in the case of Karen Yvette Muir (born 16 Sept. 1952) of Kimberley, South Africa, who broke the women's 110 yards backstroke world record with 1 minute 08.7 seconds at Blackpool on 10 Aug. 1965.

Youngest and oldest internationals The youngest age at which any person has won international honours is 8 years in the case of Miss Joy Foster, the Jamaican singles and mixed doubles table tennis champion in 1958. It would appear that the greatest age at which anyone has actively competed for his country is 73 years in the case of Oscar G. Swahn (Sweden), who won a silver medal for shooting in the Olympic Games at Antwerp in 1920.

Youngest and oldest champions The youngest age at which anyone has successful participated in a world title event is 12 years in t case of Bernard Malvoire (France), cox of the winni coxed fours in the Olympic regatta at Helsinki 1952. The youngest individual Olympic winner w Miss Marjorie Gestring (U.S.A.), who took the sprin board diving title at the age of 13 years 9 months the Olympic Games in Berlin in 1936. The greate age at which anyone has held a world title is 60 ye in the case of Pierre Etchbaster, who retired in 195 after 27 years as undefeated world tennis champi from May 1928.

Longest reign The longest reign as a world champion is 27 years Pierre Etchbaster (France) (see above).

The longest reign as a British champion is 41 years the archer Miss Legh who first won the Championsh in 1881 and for the 23rd and final time in 1922.

Greatest earnings The greatest fortune amassed by an individual in sp is an estimated £17,000,000 by the late Sonja He of Norway (1912-1969), the triple Olympic figu skating champion (1928-32-36), when la (1936-56) a professional ice skating promoter starri in her own ice shows and 11 films. The most earn for a single event is the reported $2,500,0 (£1,000,000) each by the boxers Joe Frazier a Muhammad Ali (né Cassius Clay) in their heavyweig world title fight over 15 rounds in Madison Squa Gardens, New York City on 8 March 1971. T works out at £23,148.14 per minute of actu fighting.

Largest following The sport with most participants in Britain is swi ming with 6¾ million. The highest number of pa admissions is 7¾ million for Association Footba which also attracts more than 21 million T.V. view ers.

Most sportsmen According to a report issued in April 197 28,400,000 men and 15,200,000 women are active involved in 209,000 physical culture and spo groups in the U.S.S.R. where there are 6.1 milli track athletes, 5.6 million volleyball players, million footballers and 891,000 weightlifters. T report lists 2,918 stadiums, 430 indoor and 475 o door swimming pools for 791,000 swimmers.

The last of the J Class yachts—H.S. Vanderbilt's 135 ft. 2 long *Ranger* winner of the 1937 America's Cup

The British record blue shark caught by Nigel Sutcliffe off Looe, Cornwall in 1959.

ANGLING

LARGEST SINGLE CATCH

The largest fish ever caught on a rod is an officially ratified man-eating great white shark (*Carcharodon carcharias*) weighing 2,664 lb., and measuring 16 feet 10 inches long, caught on a 130 lb. test line by Alf Dean at Denial Bay, near Ceduna, South Australia, on 21 April 1959. Capt. Frank Mundus (U.S.A.) harpooned a 17-foot-long 4,500 lb. white shark, after a 5-hour battle, off Montauk Point, New York, U.S.A., in 1964.

The largest marine animal ever killed by *hand* harpoon was a blue whale 97 feet in length, killed by Archer Davidson in Twofold Bay, New South Wales, Australia, in 1910. Its tail flukes measured 20 feet across and its jaw bone 23 feet 4 inches. To date this has provided the ultimate in "fishing stories".

SMALLEST CATCH

The smallest full-grown fish ever caught is the *Schindleria praematurus*, weighing 1/14,000 of an ounce (see page 40) found in Samoa, in the Pacific.

Spear fishing The largest fish ever taken underwater was an 804 lb. Giant Black Grouper or Jewfish by Don Pinder of the Miami Triton Club, Florida, U.S.A., in 1955. The British spearfishing record is 89 lb. 0 oz. for an angler fish by J. Brown (Weymouth Association Divers) in 1969.

Casting record The longest freshwater cast ratified under I.C.F. (International Casting Federation) rules is 175.01 metres (574 feet 2 inches) by Walter Kummerow (West Germany), for the Bait Distance Double-Handed 30 gramme event held at Lenzerheide, Switzerland in the 1968 Championships. The British National record is 148.78 m. (488 feet 1 inch) by A. Dickison on the same occasion.

Longest fight The longest recorded individual fight with a fish is 32 hours 5 minutes by Donal Heatley (b. 1938) (New Zealand) with a black marlin (estimated length 20 feet and weight 1,500 lb.) off Mayor Island off Tauranga, North Island on 21-22 Jan. 1968. It towed the 12-ton launch 50 miles before breaking the line.

Rarest fish The burbot or eel-pout, the rarest British freshwater fish, is "almost extinct", so it has been agreed that no record for this species should be published, at least until Nov. 1974, in the interests of conservation.

Championship Records
World The *Confederation Internationale de la Pêche Sportive* Championships were inaugurated in 1954. France has won 6 times and Robert Tesse (France) the individual title in 1959-60-65.

British The British Championship (instituted 1906) has been won seven times by Leeds (1909-10-14-28-48-49-52). Only James H.R. Bazley (Leeds) has ever won the individual title twice (1909-1927). The record catch is 76 lb. 9 oz. by David Burr (Rugby) in the Huntspill, Somerset in 1965. The team record is 136 lb. 15¼ oz. by Sheffield Amalgamated also in the Huntspill in 1955.

WORLD RECORDS (All tackle)

(Sea fish as ratified by the International Game Fish Association to 1 Jan. 1972. Freshwater fish, ratified by *"Field & Stream"*, are marked*)

Species	Weight lb. oz.	Name of Angler	Location	Date	
Amberjack	149 0	Peter Simons	Bermuda	21 June	1964
Barracuda	103 4	C. E. Benet	West End, Bahamas	11 Aug.	1932
Bass (Californian Black Sea)	563 8	James D. McAdam	Anacapa Is., California, U.S.A.	20 Aug.	1968
Bass (Giant Sea)	680 0	Lynn Joyner	Fernandina Beach, Florida, U.S.A.	20 May	1961
*Carp†	55 5	Frank J. Ledwein	Clearwater Lake, Minnesota, U.S.A.	10 July	1952
Cod	98 12	Alphonse J. Bielevich	Isle of Shoals, Massachusetts, U.S.A.	8 June	1969
Marlin (Black)	1,560 0	Alfred C. Glassell, Jr.	Cabo Blanco, Peru	4 Aug.	1953
Marlin (Blue)	845 0	Elliot J. Fishman	St. Thomas, Virgin Is.	4 July	1968
Marlin (Pacific Blue)	1,153 0	Greg. D. Perez	Ritidian Point, Guam	21 Aug.	1969
Marlin (Striped)	465 0	James Black	Mayor Island, New Zealand	27 Feb.	1948
Marlin (White)	161 0	L. F. Hooper	Miami Beach, Florida, U.S.A.	20 Mar.	1938
*Pike (Northern)	46 2	Peter Dubuc	Sacandaga Reservoir, New York State, U.S.A.	15 Sept.	1940
Sailfish (Atlantic)	141 1	Tony Burnand	Ivory Coast, Africa	26 Jan.	1961
Sailfish (Pacific)	221 0	C. W. Stewart	Santa Cruz I., Galapagos Is.	12 Feb.	1947
*Salmon (Chinook)††	92 0	H. Wichmann	Skeena River, British Columbia, Canada	19 July	1959
Sawfish	890 8	Jack Wagner	Fort Amador, Canal Zone	26 May	1960
Shark (Blue)	410 0	Richard C. Webster	Rockport, Massachusetts, U.S.A.	1 Sept.	1960
	410 0	Martha C. Webster	Rockport, Massachusetts, U.S.A.	17 Aug.	1967
**Shark (Mako)	1,061 0	J. B. Penwarden	Mayor Island, New Zealand	17 Feb.	1970
Shark (White or Man-eating)	2,664 0	Alfred Dean	Denial Bay, Ceduna, South Australia	21 April	1959
Shark (Porbeagle)	430 0	Desmond Bougourd	South of Jersey, C.I.	29 June	1969
Shark (Thresher)	922 0	W. W. Dowding	Bay of Islands, New Zealand	21 Mar.	1937

WORLD RECORDS (All tackle) Continued

Species	Weight		Name of Angler	Location	Date	
Shark (Tiger)	1,780	0	Walter Maxwell	Cherry Grove, South Carolina, U.S.A.	14 June	196
*Sturgeon (White)	360	0	Willard Cravens	Snake River, Idaho, U.S.A.	24 April	195
Swordfish	1,182	0	L. E. Marron	Iquique, Chile	7 May	195
Tarpon	283	0	M. Salazar	Lago de Maracaibo, Venezuela	19 Mar.	195
*Trout (Lake)#	63	2	Hubert Hammers	Lake Superior	25 May	195
Tuna (Allison or Yellowfin)	296	0	Edward C. Malnar	San Benedicts Is, Mexico	7 Mar.	197
Tuna (Atlantic Big-eyed)	295	0	Dr. Arsenio Cordeiro	San Miguel, Azores	8 July	196
Tuna (Pacific Big-eyed)	435	0	Dr. Russel V. A. Lee	Cabo Blanco, Peru	17 April	195
Tuna (Bluefin)	1,065	0	Robert G. Gibson	Cape Breton, Nova Scotia, Canada	19 Nov.	197
Wahoo	149	0	John Pirovano	Cat Cay, Bahamas	15 June	196

† A carp weighing 83 lb. 8 oz. was taken (not by rod) near Pretoria, South Africa.

†† A salmon weighing 126 lb. 8 oz. was taken (not by rod) near Petersburg, Alaska U.S.A.

** A 1,295 lb. specimen was taken by two anglers off Natal, South Africa on 17 March

1939 and a 1,500 lb. specimen harpooned inside Durban Harbour, South Africa 1933.

A 102 lb. trout was taken from Lake Athabasca, northern Saskatchewan, Canad on 8 Aug. 1961.

BRITISH ROD-CAUGHT RECORDS (as ratified by the British Record [rod-caught] Fish Committee of the National Anglers' Council)

(Selected from the complete list of about 100 species)

SEA FISH

Species	Weight		Name of Angler	Location	Yea
	lb.	oz.			
Angler Fish	68	2	H. G. T. Legerton	Canvey Island, Essex	196
Bass	18	2	F. C. Borley	Felixstowe Beach, Suffolk	194
Black Bream	6	1	F. W. Richards	The Skerries, Dartmouth	196
Red Bream	7	8	A. F. Bell	Fowey, Cornwall	192
Brill	16	0	A. H. Fisher	Derby Haven, Isle of Man	195
Bull Huss (Greater Spotted Dogfish)	21	3	J. Holmes	Hat Rock, Cornwall	195
Coalfish	26	2	T. J. Trust	Start Point, Devon	197
Cod	46	0½	R. Baird	Firth of Clyde	197
Conger	92	13	P. H. Ascott	Torquay, Devon	197
Dab	2	10¾	A. B. Hare	The Skerries, Dartmouth	196
Dogfish (Lesser Spotted)	4	8	J. Beattie	off Ayr Pier, Ayrshire	196
Dogfish (Spur)	17	1	S. Bates	Deal, Kent	197
Flounder	5	11½	A. G. L. Cobbledick	Fowey, Cornwall	195
Garfish	2	9⅛	A. W. Bodfield	Dartmouth, Devonshire	196
Grey Mullet	10	1	P/O. P. C. Libby	Portland, Dorset	195
Gurnard	11	7¼	C. W. King	Wallasey, Cheshire	195
Gurnard (Red)	3	2	W. S. Blunn	Stoke, nr. Plymouth, Devon	197
Haddock	9	4½	Mrs. L. Morley	Mevagissey, Cornwall	196
Hake	25	5½	Herbert W. Steele	Belfast Lough	196
Halibut	161	12	W. E. Knight	Orkney	196
John Dory	10	12	B. Perry	Porthallow, Cornwall	196
Ling	45	0	H. C. Nicholl	Penzance, Cornwall	191
Lumpsucker	14	3	W. J. Burgess	Felixstowe Beach, Essex	197
Mackerel	5	6½	S. Beasley	N. of Eddystone Lighthouse	196
Megrim	3	10	D. DiCicco	Ullapool, Ross-shire	196
Monkfish	66	0	G. C. Chalk	Shoreham, Sussex	196
Mullet (Red)	3	10	John E. Martel	St. Martin's, Guernsey	196
Plaice	7	15	Ian B. Brodie	Salcombe, Devon	196
Pollack	23	8	G. Bartholomew	Newquay, Cornwall	195
Pouting	5	8	R. S. Armstrong	off Berry Head, Devon	196
Ray (Spotted)	16	3	E. Lockwood	Lerwick Harbour, Shetland	197
Ray (Thornback)	38	0	J. Patterson	Rustington, Sussex	193
Scad	3	4½	D. O. Cooke	Mewstone, Plymouth	197
Allis Shad	3	4½	Bernard H. Sloane	Torquay, Devon	196
Twaite Shad	3	2	T. Hayward	Deal, Kent	194
	3	2	S. Jenkins	Tor Bay, Devon	195
Shark (Blue)	218	0	N. Sutcliffe	Looe, Cornwall	195
Shark (Mako)	500	0	Mrs. J. Yallop	Eddystone Lighthouse	197
Shark (Porbeagle)	430	0	see world record list		
Shark (Thresher)	280	0	H. A. Kelly	Dungeness, Kent	193
Skate (Common)	226	8	R. S. Macpherson	Dury Voe, Shetland	197
Sole	4	1⅞	R. A. Austin	Bordeaux Vale, Guernsey	196
Sting Ray	59	0	J. M. Buckley	Clacton-on-Sea, Essex	195
Three-bearded Rockling	2	13⅛	K. Westaway	Portland Harbour, Dorset	196
Tope	74	11	A. B. Harries	Caldy Island, Pembrokeshire	196
Tunny	851	0	L. Mitchell-Henry	Whitby, Yorkshire	193
Turbot	29	0	G. M. W. Garnsey	The Manacles, Cornwall	196
Greater Weever	2	4	P. Ainslie	Brighton, Sussex	192
Whiting	6	3	Mrs. R. Barrett	Rame Head, Cornwall	197
Wrasse (Ballan)	7	10	B. K. Lawrence	Trevose Head, Cornwall	197

FRESHWATER FISH

It will be noted that seven former "records" achieved between 1923 and 1955 have been discarded because they cannot be substantiated under the existing rules. These are noted as being "open to claim" if a specimen comes up to or over the "minimum qualifying standard".

Species	Weight	Name of Angler	Location	Year
	lb. oz.			
Barbel[1]	13 12	J. Day	Royalty Fishery, Christchurch, Hampshire	1962
Bleak	0 3⅞	D. Pollard	Staythorpe, Notts.	1971
Bream (Common)	12 14	G. J. Harper	Stour, Great Cornard	1971
Bream (Silver)	record open to claim			
Carp	44 0	Richard Walker	Redmire Pool, Herefordshire	1952
Chub	record open to claim			
Crucian Carp	4 6¼	P. H. Oliver	Private lake, Surrey	1970
Dace	1 4¼	J. L. Gasson	Little Ouse, Thetford	1960
Eel	8 10	A. Dart	Hunstrete Lake	1969
Grayling	record open to claim			
Gudgeon	0 4	M. Morris	Susworth Roach Ponds	1971
Gwyniad (Whitefish)	1 4	J. R. Williams	Llyn Tegid, Merionethshire	1965
Loch Lomond Powan	1 5¾	D. J. Warren	Loch Lomond	1970
Perch	4 12	S. F. Baker	Oulton Broad, Suffolk	1962
Pike[3]	record open to claim			
Roach	3 14	W. Penney	Lambeth Reservoir, Molesey, Surrey	1938
	3 14	A. Brown	Pit, near Stamford, Lincolnshire	1964
Rudd	4 8	Rev. E. C. Alston	Mere, near Thetford, Norfolk	1933
"Ruffe"[2]	0 4	B. B. Poyner	River Stour, Warwickshire	1969
Salmon[3]	64 0	Miss G. W. Ballantyne	River Tay	1922
Tench	9 1	John Salisbury	Hemingford Grey, Huntingdonshire	1963
Trout (Brown)[4]	18 2	K. J. Grant	Loch Garry, Inverness-shire	1965
Trout (Rainbow)	10 0¼	M. Parker	From a private lake, King's Lynn	1970
Trout (Sea)	record open to claim			

[1] A 16 lb. 4 oz. Barbel was caught in the close season by R. Beddington in the R. Avon at Christchurch, Hants. in April 1934.
[2] A Pike of allegedly 52 lb. was recovered when Whittlesea Mere, Cambridgeshire and Isle of Ely, was drained in 1851.
[3] The 8th Earl of Home is recorded as having caught a 69¾ lb. specimen in the R. Tweed in 1730. J. Wallace claimed a 67-pounder at Barjarg, Dumfries-shire in 1812.
[4] In 1866 W. C. Muir is reputed to have caught a 39½ lb. specimen in Loch Awe, and in 1816 a 36 lb. specimen was reported from the R. Colne, near Watford, Hertfordshire.

IRISH ANGLING RECORDS (as ratified by the Irish Specimen Fish Committee)

Species	Weight	Name of Angler	Location	Date	
	lb. oz.				
SEA FISH					
Angler Fish	71 8	M. Fitzgerald	Cork (Cóbh) Harbour	5 July	1964
Bass	16 0	Major Ashe Windham	Waterville, Kerry	Aug.	1909
Sea Bream (Red)	9 6	P. Maguire	Valentia, Kerry	24 Aug.	1963
Coalfish	24 7	J. E. Hornibrook	Kinsale, Cork	26 Aug.	1967
Cod	42 0	I. L. Stewart	Ballycotton, Cork		1921
Conger	72 0	J. Greene	Valentia, Kerry	June	1914
Dab	1 12½	Ian V. Kerr	Kinsale, Cork	10 Sept.	1963
Dogfish (Greater Spotted)	19 12	Michael Courage	Bray, Co. Wicklow	6 July	1969
Dogfish (Spur)	16 4	C. McIvor	Strangford Lough, Co. Down	20 June	1969
Flounder	4 3	J. L. McMonagle	Killala Bay, Co. Mayo	5 Aug	1963
Garfish	3 10¼	Evan G. Bazzard	Kinsale, Cork	16 Sept.	1967
Gurnard (Grey)	3 1	Brendan Walsh	Rosslare Bay	21 Sept.	1967
Gurnard (Red)	3 9½	James Prescott	Broadhaven Bay, Co. Mayo	17 July	1968
Gurnard (Tub)	10 8	Clive Gammon	Belmullet, Co. Mayo	18 June	1970
Haddock	10 13½	F. A. E. Bull	Kinsale, Cork	15 July	1964
Hake	25 5½	Herbert W. Steele	Belfast Lough	28 April	1962
Halibut	152 12	E. C. Henning	Valentia, Kerry		1926
John Dory	7 1	Stanley Morrow	Tory Island, Co. Donegal	6 Sept.	1970
Ling	46 8	Andrew J. C. Bull	Kinsale, Cork	26 July	1965
Mackerel	3 6	J. O'Connell	Valentia, Kerry	24 Sept.	1969
Monkfish	69 0	Mons. Michael Fuchs	Westport, Co. Mayo	1 July	1958
Mullet (Grey)	6 12¾	W. H. Connally	Ballycotton Pier, Cork		1971
Plaice	7 0	Ernest Yemen	Portrush, Antrim	28 Sept.	1964
Pollack	19 3	J. N. Hearne	Ballycotton, Cork		1904
Pouting	4 10	W. G. Pales	Ballycotton, Cork		1937
Ray (Blonde)	36 8	D. Minchin	Cork (Cóbh) Harbour	9 Sept.	1964
Ray (Thornback)	37 0	M. J. Fitzgerald	Kinsale, Cork	28 May	1961
Shark (Blue)	206 0	J. L. McMonagle	Achill, Co. Mayo	7 Oct.	1959
Shark (Porbeagle)	365 0	Dr. M. O'Donel Browne	Keem Bay, Achill, Co. Mayo	28 Sept.	1932
Skate (Common)	221 0	T. Tucker	Ballycotton, Cork		1913
Skate (White)	165 0	Jack Stack	Clew Bay, Westport, Co. Mayo	7 Aug.	1966
Sting Ray	51 0	John K. White	Kilfenora Strand, Fenet	8 Aug.	1970
Tope	60 12	Crawford McIvor	Strangford Lough, Co. Down	12 Sept.	1968
Turbot	26 8	J. F. Eldridge	Valentia, Kerry		1915
Whiting	4 8½	Eddie Boyle	Kinsale, Cork	4 Aug.	1969
Wrasse (Ballan)	7 6	Anthony J. King	Killybegs, Donegal	26 July	1964

IRISH ANGLING RECORDS (Continued)

Species

Bream	11 12	A. Pike	River Blackwater, Co. Monaghan	July	188
Carp	18 12	John Roberts	Abbey Lake	6 June	195
Dace	1 2	John T. Henry	River Blackwater, Cappoquin	8 Aug.	196
Eel (River)	5 15	Edmund Hawksworth	River Shannon, Clondra	25 Sept.	196
Perch	5 8	S. Drum	Lough Erne		194
Pike	42 0*	M. Watkins	River Barrow	22 Mar.	196
Roach	2 13½	Lawrie Robinson	River Blackwater, Cappoquin	11 Aug.	19!
Rudd	3 1	A. E. Biddlecombe	Kilglass Lake	27 June	19!
Rudd-Bream hybrid	5 5	W. Walker	Coosan Lough, Garnafailagh, Athlone	5 June	196
Salmon	57 0†	M. Maher	River Suir		18'
Tench	7 13¼	R. Webb	River Shannon, Lanesboro		197
Brown Trout (Lake)	26 2††	William Meares	Lough Ennell	15 July	189
Brown Trout (River)	20 0	Major H. H. Place	River Shannon, Corbally	22 Feb.	19!
Rainbow Trout	8 7	Dr. J. P. C. Purdon	Lough Eyes, Co. Fermanagh	11 Mar.	196
Sea Trout	12 0	T. Regan	River Dargle, Co. Wicklow	3 Oct.	19!

* A Pike in excess of 92 lb. is reputed to have been landed from the Shannon at Portumna, County Galway, in c. 1796.
† A 58 lb. Salmon was reported from the River Shannon in 1872 while one of 62 lb. was taken in a net on the lower Shannon on 27 March 1925.

†† A 35½ lb. Brown Trout is reputed to have been caught at Turlaghvan, near Tuam, August 1738. "Pepper's Ghost", the 30 lb. 8 oz. fish caught by J. W. Pepper Lough Derg in 1860, has now been shown to have been a salmon.

Harry Drake (U.S.A.) holder of the world record for flight shooting for a hand bow with a distance approaching half a mile.

ARCHERY

Earliest references Late Palaeolithic drawings of archers indicate that bows and arrows are an invention of c. 15,000 B.C. Archery developed as an organized sport at least as early as the 4th century A.D. The oldest archery body in the British Isles is the Royal Company of Archers, the Sovereign's bodyguard for Scotland, dating from 1676, though the Ancient Scorton Arrow meeting in Yorkshire was first staged in 1673. The world governing body is the *Fédération Internationale de Tir à l'Arc* (FITA), founded in 1931.

Flight shooting The longest recorded distance ever shot is 1 mile 101 yards 1 foot 9 inches in the unlimited footbow class by the professional Harry Drake of Lakeside, California, U.S.A. at Ivanpah Dry Lake, California on 3 Oct. 1970. Drake also holds the flight records for the handbow at 856 yards 1 foot 8 inches and the crossbow at 1,359 yards 2 feet 5 inches both at Ivanpah Dry Lake on 14-15 Oct. 1967.

The British record is 647 yards 1 foot 11 inches by Alan Webster at York on 20 April 1969.

HIGHEST SCORES

World The world records for FITA Rounds (see below) are: men 1,254 points by Arne Jacobsen (Denmark) in 1971, and women 1,229 points by Miss Irer Szydlowska (Poland) in 1971 and by Emma Ga chenko (U.S.S.R.) at Geneva Switzerland in 1972.

The record for a FITA Double Round is 2,467 poin by Jorma Sandelen (Finland) at Varkaus, Finland c 2-3 Sept. 1969. The feminine record is 2,426 poin by Anna Keunova (U.S.S.R.) at Tallin, U.S.S.R. o 5 June 1972.

British York Round (6 dozen at 100 yards, 4 dozen at 8 yards and 2 dozen at 60 yards).
Single Round, 1,097 J. Ian Dixon at Oxford, o 4 July 1968.
Double Round, 2,138 Roy D. Matthews at Oxfor on 3-4 July 1968.
Hereford (Women) (6 dozen at 80 yards, 4 dozen 60 yards and 2 dozen at 50 yards).
Single Round, 1,090 Mrs. Sandra Simester at Sloug Buckinghamshire, 6 Sept. 1970.
Double Round, 2,143 Mrs. Barbara Strickland Oxford, 29 June 1972.
FITA Round (Men) (3 dozen each at 90, 70, 50 an 30 metres).
Single Round, 1,216 Roy D. Matthews at Warsav Poland, on 19 Sept. 1970.
Double Round, 2,323 Roy D. Matthews at Moscov U.S.S.R., on 27-30 May 1971.
FITA Round (Women's) (3 dozen each at 70, 60, 5 and 30 metres).
Single Round, 1,211 Miss Lynne A. Thomas Warsaw, Poland, on 19-20 Sept. 1970.
Double Round, 2,278 Miss Pauline Edwards at Valle Forge, Pennsylvania, U.S.A., on 13-16 Aug. 1969.

Most titles The greatest number of world titles (instituted 193 ever won by a man is four by H. Deutgen (Sweden) 1947-48-49-50. The greatest number won by woman is seven by Mrs. Janina Spychajow Kurkowska (Poland) in 1931-32-33-34, 1936, 193 and 1947.

The greatest number of British Championships is 1 by Horace A. Ford (b. 1822) between 1849 an 1867, and 23 by Miss B. M. Legh in 188 1886-87-88-89-90-91-92, 1895, 1898-99-190 1902-03-04-05-06-07-08-09, 1913 and 1921-22.

Marathon The highest recorded score over 24 hours by a pair archers is 30,709 during 31 Portsmouth Rounds (6 arrows at 20 yards with a 2 inch diameter 10 ring shot by Barry Davison and Cpl. Bob Pritchard at th Odeon Cinema, Colchester, Essex, on 26-27 Fe 1972.

228

Ron Clarke (Australia) holder of four middle distance running records set between 1965 and 1966.

ATHLETICS

Earliest references Track and field athletics date from the ancient Olympic Games. The earliest accurately known Olympiad dates from 21 or 22 July 776 B.C., at which celebration Coroebus won the foot race. The oldest surviving measurements are a long jump of 23 feet 1½ inches (7.05 metres) by Chionis of Sparta in c. 656 B.C. and a discus throw of 100 cubits by Protesilaus.

Fastest runner Robert Lee Hayes (b. 20 Dec. 1942) of Jacksonville, Florida, U.S.A., was timed at the 60 (6.0 secs.) and 75 yard (7.1 secs.) marks in a 100 yard event at St. Louis, Missouri on 21 June 1963, which indicates

a speed of 27.89 m.p.h. Wyomia Tyus (b. Griffin, Georgia, U.S.A., 29 Aug. 1945) was timed at 23.78 m.p.h. in Kiev, U.S.S.R. on 31 July 1965.

Highest jumper There are several reported instances of high jumpers exceeding the official world record height of 7 feet 6¼ inches. The earliest of these came from unsubstantiated reports of Tutsi tribesmen in Central Africa (see page 12) clearing up to 8 feet 2½ inches, definitely however, from inclined take-offs. The greatest height cleared above an athlete's own head in 17⅝ inches, achieved by Ni Chih-chin of China (Mainland) when clearing 2.29 metres (7 feet 6⅛ inches) in an exhibition at Changsha, Hunan on 8 Nov. 1970. He stands 6 feet 0½ inch tall and was born on 14 April 1942. The greatest height cleared by a woman above her own head is 6 inches by Miroslava Rezkova (Czechoslovakia), standing 5 feet 6½ inches when she jumped 6 feet 0½ inch at Povazka Bystrica, Czechoslovakia on 20 July 1969.

Most Olympic gold medals Ray C. Ewry (U.S.A.) won eight individual Olympic gold medals, three in 1900, three in 1904 and two in 1908. Paavo Johannes Nurmi (Finland) won six individual and three team race gold medals between 1920 and 1928. The greatest number of gold medals won in a single celebration is five by Paavo Nurmi (Finland) in 1924 (1,500 metres, 3,000 metres team, 5,000 metres, cross-country team and individual). The most individual wins is four by Alvin C. Kraenzlein (U.S.A.) in 1900 (60 metres, 110 metres and 200 metres hurdles and long jump). The most wins by a woman is four by Francina E. Blankers-Koen (b. 26 April 1918) of the Netherlands in 1948 (100 and 200 metres, 80 metres hurdles, and the last stage in the 4 × 100 metres relay), and four by Betty Cuthbert (b. 20 April 1938) of Australia in 1956 (100 metres, 200 metres and the last stage in the 4 × 100 metres relay) and 1964 (400 metres).

Most medals The most Olympic medals (of any metal) won by a man is 12 (nine gold and three silver) by Nurmi. The

WORLD RECORDS—MEN

The complete list of World Records for the 54 scheduled men's events (excluding the 6 walking records, see under WALKING) passed by the International Amateur Athletic Federation as at 1 Aug. 1972. *denotes awaiting ratification.

RUNNING

Event	Mins. secs.	Name and Nationality	Place	Date	
100 yards	9.1	Robert Lee Hayes (U.S.A.)	St. Louis, Missouri. U.S.A.	21 June	1963
	9.1	Harry Winston Jerome (Canada)	Edmonton, Alberta, Canada	15 July	1966
	9.1	James Ray Hines (U.S.A.)	Houston, Texas, U.S.A.	13 May	1967
	9.1	Charles Edward Greene (U.S.A.)	Provo, Utah, U.S.A.	15 June	1967
	9.1	John Wesley Carlos (U.S.A.)	Fresno, California, U.S.A.	10 May	1969
220 yards (straight)	19.5	Tommie C. Smith (U.S.A.)	San Jose, California, U.S.A.	7 May	1966
220 yards (turn)	20.0	Tommie C. Smith (U.S.A.)	Sacramento, California, U.S.A.	11 June	1966
440 yards	44.5	John Smith (U.S.A.)	Eugene, Oregon, U.S.A.	26 June	1971
880 yards	1:44.9	James Ronald Ryun (U.S.A.)	Terre Haute, Indiana, U.S.A.	10 June	1966
1 mile	3:51.1	James Ronald Ryun (U.S.A.)	Bakersfield, California, U.S.A.	23 June	1967
2 miles	8:17.8	Emiel Puttemans (Belgium)	Edinburgh, Scotland	21 Aug.	1971
3 miles	12:50.4	Ronald William Clarke, M.B.E. (Australia)	Stockholm, Sweden	5 July	1966
6 miles	26:47.0	Ronald William Clarke, M.B.E. (Australia)	Oslo, Norway	14 July	1965
10 miles	46:37.4	Jerome Drayton	Toronto, Ontario, Canada	6 Sept.	1970
15 miles	1H 12:48.2	Ronald Hill (United Kingdom)	Bolton, Lancashire, England	21 July	1965
100 metres	9.9	James Ray Hines (U.S.A.)	Sacramento, California, U.S.A.	20 June	1968
	9.9	Ronald Ray Smith (U.S.A.)	Sacramento, California, U.S.A.	20 June	1968
	9.9	Charles Edward Greene (U.S.A.)	Sacramento, California, U.S.A.	20 June	1968
	9.9	James Ray Hines (U.S.A.)	Mexico City, Mexico	14 Oct.	1968
	9.9*	Eddie Hart (U.S.A.)	Eugene, Oregon, U.S.A.	1 July	1972
	9.9*	Rey Robinson (U.S.A.)	Eugene, Oregon, U.S.A.	1 July	1972
200 metres (straight)	19.5	Tommie C. Smith (U.S.A.)	San Jose, California, U.S.A.	7 May	1966
200 metres (turn)	19.8	Tommie C. Smith (U.S.A.)	Mexico City, Mexico	16 Oct.	1968
	19.8	Donald O'Riley Quarrie (Jamaica)	Cali, Colombia	3 Aug.	1971
400 metres	43.8	Lee Edward Evans (U.S.A.)	Mexico City, Mexico	18 Oct.	1968
800 metres	1:44.3	Peter George Snell O.B.E. (New Zealand)	Christchurch, New Zealand	3 Feb.	1962
	1:44.3	Ralph D. Doubell (Australia)	Mexico City, Mexico	15 Oct.	1968
	1:44.3*	David Wottle (U.S.A.)	Eugene, Oregon, U.S.A.	1 July	1972
1,000 metres	2:16.2	Jürgen May (East Germany)	Erfurt, East Germany	20 July	1965
	2:16.2	Franz-Josef Kemper (West Germany)	Hanover, West Germany	21 Sept.	1966
1,500 metres	3:33.1	James Ronald Ryun (U.S.A.)	Los Angeles, California, U.S.A.	8 July	1967
2,000 metres	4:56.2	Michel Jazy (France)	St. Maur des Fosses, France	12 Oct.	1966
3,000 metres	7:39.6	Hezekieh Kipchoge Keino (Kenya)	Hälsingborg, Sweden	27 Aug.	1965
5,000 metres	13:16.6	Ronald William Clarke, M.B.E. (Australia)	Stockholm, Sweden	5 July	1966
10,000 metres	27:39.4	Ronald William Clarke, M.B.E. (Australia)	Oslo, Norway	14 July	1965
20,000 metres	58:06.2	Gaston Roelants (Belgium)	Louvain, Belgium	28 Oct.	1966
25,000 metres	1H 15:22.6	Ronald Hill (United Kingdom)	Bolton, Lancashire, England	21 July	1965
30,000 metres	1H 31:30.4	James Noel Carroll Alder (U.K.)	London (Crystal Palace)	5 Sept.	1970
1 hour	12 miles 1,478 yards (20,664 metres)	Gaston Roelants (Belgium)	Louvain, Belgium	28 Oct.	1966

David Wottle (U.S.A.) equalling the World 800 metres record.

HURDLING

120 yards (3′ 6″)	13.0	Rodney Milburn (U.S.A.)	Eugene, Oregon, U.S.A.	25 June	197
220 yards (2′ 6″) (straight)	21.9	Donald Augustus Styron (U.S.A.)	Baton Rouge, Louisiana, U.S.A.	2 April	196
440 yards (3′ 0″)	48.8	Ralph Mann (U.S.A.)	Des Moines, Iowa, U.S.A.	20 June	197
110 metres (3′ 6″)	13.2	Karl Martin Lauer (West Germany)	Zürich, Switzerland	7 July	195
	13.2	Lee Quency Calhoun (U.S.A.)	Bern, Switzerland	21 Aug.	196
	13.2	Earl Ray McCullouch (U.S.A.)	Minneapolis, Minnesota, U.S.A.	16 July	196
200 metres (2′ 6″) (straight)	21.9	Donald Augustus Styron (U.S.A.)	Baton Rouge, Louisiana, U.S.A.	2 April	196
200 metres (2′ 6″) (turn)	22.5	Karl Martin Lauer (West Germany)	Zürich, Switzerland	7 July	195
	22.5	Glen Ashby Davis (U.S.A.)	Bern, Switzerland	20 Aug.	196
400 metres (3′ 0″)	48.1	David Peter Hemery (United Kingdom)	Mexico City, Mexico	15 Oct.	196
3,000 metres Steeplechase	8:22.0	Kerry O'Brien (Australia)	Berlin (West), West Germany	4 July	197

FIELD EVENTS

Event	ft.	ins.	Metres	Name and Nationality	Place	Date	
High Jump	7	6¼	2.29†	Patrick Clifford Matzdorf (U.S.A.)	Berkelev. California. U.S.A.	3 July	197
Pole Vault	18	5¾*	5.63	Robert Seagren (U.S.A.)	Eugene, Oregon, U.S.A.	2 July	197
Long Jump	29	2½	8.90	Robert Beamon (U.S.A.)	Mexico City, Mexico	18 Oct.	196
Triple Jump	57	1	17.40	Pedro Dueros Perez (Cuba)	Cali, Colombia	5 Aug.	197
Shot Putt	71	5½	21.78	James Randel Matson (U.S.A.)	College Station, Texas, U.S.A.	22 April	196
Discus Throw	224	5	68.40	L Jay Silvester (U.S.A.)	Reno, Nevada, U.S.A.	18 Sept.	196
	224	5 *	68.40	Rickard Bruch (Sweden)	Stockholm, Sweden	5 July	197
Hammer Throw	250	8	76.40	Walter Schmidt (Germany)	Lahr, Germany	4 Sept.	197
Javelin Throw	307	9	93.80	Janis Lusis (U.S.S.R.)	Stockholm, Sweden	6 July	197

† Ni Chih-chin (China, Mainland) cleared a non-ratifiable 2.29 (7 feet 6¹/₃ inches) in an exhibition at Changsha, Hunan, China (Mainland), on 8 Nov. 1970.

DECATHLON

8,417 points	William Anthony Toomey (U.S.A.) (1st day: 100m. 10.3s., Long Jump 25′ 5½″, Shot Putt 47′ 2¼″, High Jump 6′ 4″, 400m. 47.1s.)	Los Angeles, California, U.S.A. (2nd day: 110m. Hurdles 14.8s., Discus 152′ 6″, Pole Vault 14′ 0¼″, Javelin 215′ 8″, 1,500m. 4:39.4s.)	10-11 Dec. 1969

THE MARATHON

There is no official marathon record because of the varying severity of courses. The best time over 26 miles 385 yards (standardized in 1924) is 2 hours 08 minute 33.6 seconds (av. 12.24 m.p.h.) by Derek Clayton (b. 1942, at Barrow-in-Furness, England) of Australia, at Antwerp, Belgium, on 30 May 1969.
The best time by a British international is 2 hours 9 minutes 28.0 seconds by Ronald Hill of Bolton United Harriers, at Edinburgh, Scotland on 22 July 1970.
The fastest time by a female is 2 hours 46 minutes 30 seconds (av. 9.53 m.p.h.) by Adrienne Beames (Australia), at Werribee, Victoria, Australia on 31 Aug. 1971 in time trial. Cheryl Bridge née Pedow (U.S.A.) ran 2 hrs. 49 mins. 40.0 secs. at Culver City California on 5 Dec. 1971.

RELAYS

Event	Mins. secs.	Team	Place	Date	
4 × 110 yards (two turns)	38.6	University of Southern California, U.S.A. (Earl Ray McCullouch, Fred Kuller, Orenthal James Simpson, Lennox Miller [Jamaica])	Provo, Utah, U.S.A.	17 June	196
4 × 220 yards and 4 × 200 metres	1:21.7†	Texas Agricultural & Mechanical College (Donald Rogers, Rocklie Woods, Marvin Mills, Curtis Mills)	Des Moines, Iowa, U.S.A.	24 April	197
4 × 440 yards	3:02.8	Trinidad and Tobago (Lennox Yearwood, Kent Bernard, Edwin Roberts, Wendell A. Mottley)	Kingston, Jamaica	13 Aug.	196
4 × 880 yards	7:11.6	Kenyan National Team (Naftali Bon, Hezekiah Nyamau, Thomas Saisi, Robert Ouko)	London (Crystal Palace)	5 Sept.	197
4 × 1 mile	16:02.8	New Zealand Team (Kevin Ross, Anthony Polhill, Richard Taylor, Richard Quax)	Auckland, New Zealand	3 Feb.	197
4 × 100 metres (two turns)	38.2	United States National Team (Charles Edward Greene, Melvin Pender, Ronald Ray Smith, James Ray Hines)	Mexico City, Mexico	20 Oct.	196
4 × 400 metres	2:56.1	United States National Team (Vincent Matthews, Ronald Freeman, G. Lawrence James, Lee Edward Evans)	Mexico City, Mexico	20 Oct.	196
4 × 800 metres	7:08.6	West Germany "A" Team (Manfred Kinder, Walter Adams, Dieter Bogatzki, Franz-Josef Kemper)	Wiesbaden, West Germany	13 Aug.	196
4 × 1,500 metres	14:49.0	France "A" Team (Gerard Vervoort, Claude Nicolas, Michel Jazy, Jean Wadoux)	St. Maur des Fosses, France	25 June	196

† The time of 1:20.7 achieved by University of Southern California (Edesel Garrison, Lee Brown, William Deckard and Donald O'Riley Quarrie) at Fresno, California, U.S.A. 13 May 1972 is not eligible because Quarrie is a Jamaican national.

most won by a woman is seven by Shirley de la Hunty (*née* Strickland) of Australia between 1948 and 1956. The United Kingdom record is four by Guy M. Butler in 1920 and 1924 and for women three by Dorothy Hyman, M.B.E., in 1960 and 1964, and Mrs. Mary Denise Rand, M.B.E. (now Toomey, *née* Bignal), (b. Wells, Somerset 10 Feb. 1940) in 1964.

Most national titles The greatest number of national A.A.A. titles won by one athlete is fourteen individual and two relay titles by Emmanuel McDonald Bailey (b. Williamsville, Trinidad 8 Dec. 1920), between 1946 and 1953.

The greatest number of consecutive title wins is seven by Denis Horgan (Ireland) in the shot putt (1893-99), Albert A. Cooper (2 miles walk, 1932-38), Donald Osborne Finlay, D.F.C., A.F.C. (1909-70) (120 yards hurdles, 1932-38), Harry Whittle (440 yards hurdles, 1947-1953) and Maurice Herriott (3,000 metres steeplechase, 1961-67). The record for consecutive W.A.A.A. titles is eight by Mrs. Judy U. Farr (Trowbridge & District A.C.) (b. 24 Jan. 1942), who won the 1½ mile/2,500 metre walk from 1962-69.

Rod Milburn (U.S.A.) the fastest high hurdler of all time.

Earliest landmarks The first time 10 seconds ("even time") was bettered for 100 yards under championship conditions was when John Owen recorded 9⁴⁄₅ seconds in the United States A.A.U. Championships at Analostan Island, Washington, D.C., U.S.A., on 11 Oct. 1890. The first recorded instance of 6 feet being cleared in the high jump was when Marshall Jones Brooks jumped 6 feet 0¹⁄₈ inch at Marston, near Oxford, England, on 17 March 1876. The breaking of the "4-minute barrier" in the one mile was first achieved by Dr. Roger Gilbert Bannister, C.B.E. (b. Harrow, England 23 March 1929), when he recorded 3 minutes 59.4 seconds on the Iffley Road track, Oxford, at 6.10 p.m. on 6 May 1954.

World record breakers **Oldest** The greatest age at which anyone has broken a world athletics record in a standard Olympic event is 35 years 255 days in the case of Dana Zátopková, *née* Ingrova (b. 19 Sept. 1922) of Czechoslovakia, who broke the women's javelin record with 182 feet 10 inches (55.73 metres) at Prague, Czechoslovakia, on 1 June 1958. On 20 June 1948 Mikko Hietanen (Finland) (b. 22 Sept. 1911) bettered his own world 30,000 metres record with 1 hour 40 minutes 46.4 seconds at Jyvâskylâ, Finland, when aged 36 years 272 days.

Youngest Doreen Lumley (b. September 1921) of New Zealand equalled the world record for the women's 100 yards of 11.0 seconds at Auckland, New Zealand on 11 March 1939, when aged 17 years 6 months.

Bob Seagren (U.S.A.) embraces his coach after raising the world pole vault record to 18ft. 5¾in. at Eugene, Oregon on 2 July 1972.

Most in a day Jesse Owens (U.S.A.) set six world records in 45 minutes at Ann Arbor, Michigan on 25 May 1935 with a 9.4 sec. 100 yards (3.15 p.m.), a 26 ft. 8¼ ins. long jump (3.25 p.m.), a 20.3 sec. 220 yards (and 200 metres) at 3.45 p.m. and a 22.6 sec. 220 yards low hurdles (and 200 metres) at 4.0 p.m.

Professional records Professional records include: 100 yards, 9.3 seconds by Ken Irvine (Australia) at Dubbo, New South Wales, Australia, on 9 March 1963; Mile, 3 minutes 59.7 seconds from scratch by Harold Downes (Australia) in a handicap race at Bendigo, Victoria, Australia, on 9 March 1963; Shot Putt, 64 feet (19.507 metres) by Arthur Rowe (b. 17 Aug. 1936) of Barnsley, Yorkshire, at Keswick, Cumberland, on 6 Aug. 1962.

Shot putt Both hands The greatest combined distance for putting the shot is 106 feet 10½ inches (61 feet 0¾ inch with the right hand and 45 feet 9½ inches left hand) by William Parry O'Brien (b. 28 Jan. 1932) of the U.S.A., at Culver City, California, U.S.A., on 17 Aug. 1962.

Longest tug o'war The longest recorded pull is one of 2 hours 41 minutes between "H" Company and "E" Company of the 2nd

Jan Lusis the world's greatest javelin thrower and U.S.S.R. champion every year since 1963.

231

WORLD RECORDS—WOMEN

The complete list of World Records for the 27 scheduled women's events passed by the International Amateur Athletic Federation as at 1 Aug. 1972. Those marked with an asterisk are awaiting ratification.

RUNNING

Event	Mins. secs.	Name and Nationality	Place	Date	
100 yards	10.0	Chi Cheng (Taiwan, China)	Portland, Oregon, U.S.A.	13 June	197
220 yards (turn)	22.6	Chi Cheng (Taiwan, China)	Los Angeles, U.S.A.	3 July	197
440 yards	52.4	Judith Florence Pollock (nèe Amoore) (Australia)	Perth, Western Australia	27 Feb.	196
800 yards	2:02.0	Dixie Isobel Willis (Australia)	Perth, Western Australia	3 Mar.	196
	2:02.0	Judith Florence Pollock (née Amoore) (Australia)	Stockholm, Sweden	5 July	196
	2:02.0	Madeline Jackson (née Manning) (U.S.A.)	Philadelphia, Pennsylvania, U.S.A.	14 May	196
1 mile	4:35.3	Ellen Tittel (West Germany)	Sittard, Netherlands	20 Aug.	197
60 metres	7.2	Betty Cuthbert (Australia)	Sydney, N.S.W., Australia	21 Feb.	196
	7.2	Irina Robertovna Bochkaryova (née Turova) (U.S.S.R.)	Moscow, U.S.S.R.	28 Aug.	196
100 metres	11.0	Wyomia Tyus (U.S.A.)	Mexico City, Mexico	15 Oct.	196
	11.0	Chi Cheng (Taiwan, China)	Vienna, Austria	18 July	197
	11.0	Renate Stecher (née Meissner) (East Germany)	Berlin (East), East Germany	2 Aug.	197
	11.0	Renate Stecher (née Meissner) (East Germany)	East Berlin, East Germany	31 July	197
	11.0*	Renate Stecher (née Meissner) (East Germany)	Potsdam, East Germany	3 June	197
	11.0*	Eva Gleskova (Czechoslovakia)	Budapest, Hungary	2 July	197
	11.0*	Ellen Strophahl (East Germany)	Potsdam, East Germany	15 June	197
200 metres (turn)	22.4	Chi Cheng (Taiwan, China)	Munich, West Germany	12 July	197
400 metres	51.0	Marilyn Fay Neufville (Jamaica)	Edinburgh, Scotland	23 July	197
	51.0*	Monika Zehrt (East Germany)	Paris, France	4 July	197
800 metres†	1:58.8	Hildegard Falck (néeJanze) (West Germany)	Stuttgart, West Germany	11 July	197
1,500 metres	4:06.9*	Lyudmila Bragina (U.S.S.R.)	Moscow. U.S.S.R.	18 July	197

† *Shin Geum Dan (North Korea) has achieved 1:58.0 at P'yongyang, North Korea, on 5 Sept. 1964; but she was under suspension by the I.A.A.F. at the time of performance.*

HURDLING

Event	Secs.	Name and Nationality	Place	Date	
100 metres (2' 9")	12.5*	Annelie Elrhardt (East Germany)	Potsdam, East Germany	15 June	197
	12.5*	Pamela Ryan (née Kilborn (Australia)	Warsaw, Poland	28 June	197
200 metres (2' 6")	25.7	Pamela Ryan (née Kilborn (Australia)	Melbourne, Australia	25 Nov.	197

FIELD EVENTS

Event	ft.	ins.	Metres	Name and Nationality	Place	Date	
High Jump	6	3½	1.92	Ilona Gusenbower (Austria)	Vienna, Austria	4 Sept.	197
Long Jump	22	5¼	6.84	Heide Rosendahl (West Germany)	Turin, Italy	3 Sept.	197
Shot Putt	67	8¼	20.63	Nadyezhda Chizhova (U.S.S.R.)	Sochi, U.S.S.R.	9 May	197
Discus Throw	215	5	65.48*	Faina Melnik (U.S.S.R.)	Augsberg. W. Germany	24 June	197
Javelin Throw	213	5	65.06	Ruth Fuchs (néeGamm) (East Germany)	Potsdam, East Germany	11 June	197

PENTATHLON (1969 Scoring Tables)

5,406 points	Burglinde Pollak (East Germany) (100m. hurdles 13.3s.; Shot Putt 15.57m. (51' 1"); High Jump 1.75m. (5' 8¾"); Long Jump 6.20m. (20' 4"); 200m. 23.8s.)	Erfurt, East Germany	5-6 Sept. 197

RELAYS

Event	Mins. Secs.	Team	Place	Date	
4 × 110 yards	44.7	Tennessee State University (Diane Hughes, Debbie Wedgeworth, Mattline Render, Iris Davis)	Bakersfield, California, U.S.A.	9 July	197
4 × 220 yards	1:35.8*	Australia (Marian Hoffman, Jennifer Lamy, Raelene Boyle, Pamela Kilborn)	Brisbane, Australia	9 Nov.	196
4 × 440 yards	3:38.8	Atoms Track Club (U.S.A.) (M. McMillan, L. Reynolds, G. Fitzgerald, C. Toussaint)	Bakersfield California	10 July	197
4 × 100 metres	42.8	United States National Team (Barbara Ferrell, Margaret Bailes [née Johnson], Mildrette Netter, Wyomia Tyus)	Mexico City, Mexico	20 Oct.	196
4 × 200 metres	1:33.8	United Kingdom National Team (Maureen Dorothy Tranter, Della P. James, Janet Mary Simpson, Valerie Peat [née Wild])	London (Crystal Palace)	24 Aug.	196
4 × 400 metres	3:28.8*	East Germany (Dagmar Kassling, Helga Seidler Monika Zehrt, Brigitte Rohde.)	Paris, France	5 July	197
4 × 800 metres	8:16.8	West Germany (Ellen Tittel, Sylvia Schenk, Christa Merten, Hildegard Falck)	Lübeck, East Germany	31 July	197

UNITED KINGDOM (NATIONAL) RECORDS—MEN

Event	Mins. Secs.	Name	Place	Date	
100 yards	9.4	Peter Frank Radford	Wolverhampton	28 May	196
220 yards (turn)	20.5	Peter Frank Radford	Wolverhampton	28 May	196
440 yards	45.9	Robbie Ian Brightwell, M.B.E.	London (White City)	14 July	196
880 yards	1:47.2	Christopher Sydney Carter	London (White City)	3 June	196
1 mile	3:55.3*	Peter John Stewart	London (Crystal Palace)	10 June	197
2 miles	8:24.4	Brendan Foster	Edinburgh	21 Aug.	197
3 miles	12:58.2	David Colin Bedford	Stockholm, Sweden	15 June	197
6 miles	26:51.6	David Colin Bedford	Portsmouth, Hampshire	10 July	197
10 miles	46:44.0	Ronald Hill	Leicester	9 Nov.	196
15 miles	1H 12:48.2	Ronald Hill	Bolton, Lancashire	21 July	196
100 metres	10.1*	Brian W. Green	Bratislava, Czechoslovakia	3 June	197
200 metres (turn)	20.5	Peter Frank Radford	Wolverhampton	28 May	196
400 metres	45.3	David Andrew Jenkins	Athens, Greece	27 June	197
800 metres	1:46.1	Colin William Ashburner Campbell	Helsinki, Finland	25 July	197

Ralph Mann (U.S.A.) holder of the world 440 yard hurdles record set in 1970, holding his starting blocks aloft.

Three-legged race The fastest recorded time for a 100 yards three-legged race is 11.0 seconds by Harry L. Hillman and Lawson Robertson at Brooklyn, New York City, N.Y., U.S.A., on 24 April 1909.

Greatest caber toss The 230 lb. Braemar Caber, originally 21 feet in length, defied all comers until it was successfully tossed by George Clark at the Braemar Gathering, Aberdeenshire, Scotland, in September 1951.

INTERNATIONALS

Most The greatest number of full Great Britain internationals won by a British male athlete is 51 by Crawford William Fairbrother, M.B.E. (b. 1 Dec. 1936), the high jumper, from 1957 to mid-1970. The feminine record is 36 full internationals by Rosemary Payne in the discus (see above) and shot.

Oldest and youngest Of full Great Britain (outdoor) internationals the oldest have been Harold Whitlock (b. 16 Dec. 1903) at the 1952 Olympic Games, aged 48 years 218 days, and Mrs. Dorothy Tyler (*née* Odam) (b. 19 March 1920) at the 1956 Olympic Games, aged 36 years 269

Ilona Gusenbauer (Austria) holder of the world women's high jump record at 6ft 3½in.

Battalion of the Sherwood Foresters (Derbyshire Regiment) at Jubbulpore, India, on 12 Aug. 1889. "E" Company won.

The longest recorded pull under A.A.A. Rules (in which lying on the ground or entrenching the feet is not permitted) is one of 8 minutes 18.2 seconds for the first pull between the R.A.S.C. (Feltham) and the Royal Marines (Portsmouth Division) at the Royal Tournament of June 1938.

days. The youngest have been William Land (b. 29 Nov. 1914) *versus* Italy in 1931, aged 16 years 271 days, and Miss Sylvia Needham (b. 28 March 1935) *versus* France in 1950, aged 15 years 166 days. Sonia Lannaman (b. King's Heath, Birmingham of Jamaican parentage, 1956) represented Great Britain *versus* East Germany indoors in East Berlin on 4 Dec. 1970 before she was 15.

Blind 100 yards The fastest time recorded for a 100 yards by a blind man is 11.0 seconds by George Bull, aged 19, of Chippenham, Wiltshire, in a race at the Worcester College for the Blind, on 26 Oct. 1954.

Pancake race record The annual Housewives Pancake Race at Olney, Buckinghamshire, was first mentioned in 1445. The record for the winding 415-yard course is 63.0 seconds, set by Miss Janet Bunker, aged 17, on 7 Feb. 1967. The record for the counterpart race at Liberal, Kansas, U.S.A. is 59.1 seconds by Kathleen West, 19, on 10 Feb. 1970.

Standing high jump The best standing high jump is 5 feet 9¼ inches by Johan Christian Evandt (Norway) at Oslo on 4 March 1962.

Raelene Boyle (Australia) one of the quartette that hold the 4 X 220 yard relay world record.

Event	Time	Name	Place	Date
1,000 metres	2:18.2	John Peter Boulter	London (Crystal Palace)	6 Sept. 196
1,500 metres	3:38.2	Peter John Stewart	London (Crystal Palace)	15 July 197
2,000 metres	5:03.2	David Colin Bedford	London (Crystal Palace)	8 July 197
3,000 metres	7:46.4	David Colin Bedford	Louvain, Belgium	21 June 197
5,000 metres	13:22.2	David Colin Bedford	Edinburgh, Scotland	12 June 197
10,000 metres	27:47.0	David Colin Bedford	Portsmouth, Hampshire	10 July 197
20,000 metres	58:39.0	Ronald Hill	Leicester	9 Nov. 196
25,000 metres	1H 15:22.6	Ronald Hill	Bolton, Lancashire	21 July 196
30,000 metres	1H 31:30.4	James Noel Carroll Alder	London (Crystal Palace)	5 Sept. 197
1 hour	12 miles 1,268 yards	Ronald Hill	Leicester	

HURDLING

Event	Secs.	Name	Place	Date
120 yards/110 metres	13.6	David Peter Hemery	Brno, Czechoslovakia	5 July 196
	13.6*	David Peter Hemery	Warsaw, Poland	13 Sept. 197
200 metres (turn)	23.0	Alan Peter Pascoe	Loughborough, Leicestershire	5 June 196
200 metres/220 yards (straight)	23.3	Peter Burke Hildreth	Imber Court, Surrey	27 Aug. 19
200 metres/220 yards (turn)	23.7	Paul Ashley Laurence Vine	London (White City)	15 July 19
	23.7	John Michael Waller Hogan	London (White City)	9 May 196
400 metres	48.1	David Peter Hemery	Mexico City, Mexico	15 Oct. 196
440 yards	50.2	David Peter Hemery	London (White City)	13 July 196
3,000 metres Steeplechase	8:28.6	David Colin Bedford	London (Crystal Palace)	10 Sept. 19

FIELD EVENTS

Event	ft.	ins.	Metres	Name	Place	Date
High Jump	6	10	2.08	Gordon Albert Miller	London (White City)	18 May 19
	6	9¾	2.08	Michael Campbell	London (Crystal Palace)	6 Aug. 19
	6	9¾	2.08	David J. Livesey	Athens, Greece	27 June 19
Pole Vault	17	1	5.21	Michael Anthony Bull	London (Crystal Palace)	15 July 19
Long Jump	27	0	8.23	Lynn Davies, M.B.E.	Bern, Switzerland	30 June 19
Triple Jump	54	0	16.46	Frederick John Alsop	Tōkyō, Japan	16 Oct. 19
Shot Putt	66	2½	20.18	Geoffrey L. Capes	Helsinki, Finland	25 July 19
Discus Throw	203	2	61.94	William R. Tancred	Loughborough	7 June 19
Hammer Throw	227	2	69.24	Andrew Howard Payne	Solihull, Warwickshire	26 Sept. 19
Javelin Throw	273	9	83.44	David Howard Travis	Zürich, Switzerland	2 Aug. 19

DECATHLON (1962 Scoring Tables)

7,903 points	Peter Gabbett (1st day: 100m. 10.5s., Long Jump 24′ 7¾″ (7.51m.), Shot Putt 43′ 8″ (13.31m.), High Jump 6′ 1¼″ (1.85m.), 400m. 47.4s.)	Kassel, West Germany (2nd day: 110m. Hurdles 15.2s., Discus 151′ 0″ (46,02m.), Pole Vault 13′ 9½″ (4.20m.), Javelin 181′ 10″ (55.42m.), 1500m. 4:39.8s.)	5-6 June 19

RELAYS

Event	Time	Name	Place	Date
4 X 110 yards	40.0	United Kingdom National Team (Peter Frank Radford, Ronald Jones, David Henry Jones, Thomas Berwyn Jones)	London (White City)	3 Aug. 19
4 X 220 yards	1:26.0	London Team (David Henry Jones, Brian Andrew Smouha, Peter Frank Radford, David Hugh Segal)	London (White City)	30 Sept. 19
4 X 440 yards	3:06.5	England Team (Martin John Winbolt-Lewis, John Austin Adey, Peter Warden, Timothy Joseph Michael Graham)	Kingston, Jamaica	13 Aug. 19
4 X 800 metres and 4 X 880 yards†	7:17.4	United Kingdom National Team (Martin Bilham, David Cropper, Michael John Maclean, Peter Miles Browne)	London (Crystal Palace)	7 Sept. 19
4 X 1 mile	16:24.8	Northern Counties Team (Stanley George Taylor, John Paul Anderson, Alan Simpson, Brian Hall)	Dublin, Ireland	17 July 19
4 X 100 metres	39.3	United Kingdom National Team (Joseph William Speake, Ronald Jones, Ralph Banthorpe, Barrie Harrison Kelly)	Mexico City, Mexico	19 Oct. 19
4 X 200 metres	1:24.1	Great Britain (Brian W. Green, Roger Walters, Ralph Banthorpe, Martin E. Reynolds)	Paris, France	2 Oct. 19
4 X 400 metres	3:01.2	United Kingdom National Team (Martin John Winbolt-Lewis, Colin William Ashburner Campbell, David Peter Hemery, John Sherwood)	Mexico City, Mexico	20 Oct. 19
4 X 1,500 metres	15:06.6	Great Britain (Roy C. Young, Walter Wilkinson, Ian Stewart, Adrian P. Weatherhead)	Paris, France	2 Oct. 19

† A U.K. National Team recorded 7:14.6 for 4 X 880 yards at the Crystal Palace,
London, on 22 June 1966, but lap times were illegally communicated to the runners.

UNITED KINGDOM (NATIONAL) RECORDS—WOMEN

Event	Mins. secs.	Name	Place	Date
100 yards	10.6	Heather Joy Young (née Armitage)	Cardiff	22 July 19
	10.6	Dorothy Hyman, M.B.E.	London (White City)	7 July 19
	10.6	Dorothy Hyman, M.B.E.	London (White City)	4 July 19
	10.6	Mary Denise Rand, (now Toomey, née Bignal), M.B.E.	London (White City)	4 July 19
	10.6	Daphne Arden (now Slater)	London (White City)	4 July 19
220 yards (turn)	23.6	Daphne Arden (now Slater)	London (White City)	4 July 19
440 yards	54.1	Deirdre Ann Watkinson	Kingston, Jamaica	8 Aug. 19
880 yards	2:04.2	Anne Rosemary Smith	London (White City)	2 July 19
1 mile	4:37.0	Anne Rosemary Smith	Chiswick, Greater London	3 June 19
100 metres	11.3	Dorothy Hyman, M.B.E.	Budapest, Hungary	2 Oct. 19
	11.3	Dorothy Hyman, M.B.E.	Budapest, Hungary	3 Oct. 19
	11.3	Valerie Peat (née Wild)	Mexico City, Mexico	14 Oct. 19
	11.3*	Anita D. Neil	Tel Aviv, Israel	3 May 19

200 metres	23.2	Dorothy Hyman, M.B.E.	Budapest, Hungary	3 Oct.	1963
	23.2	Margaret A. Critchley	East Berlin	2 Aug.	1970
400 metres	52.1	Lillian Barbara Board, M.B.E.	Mexico City, Mexico	16 Oct.	1968
800 metres	2:01.1	Ann Elizabeth Packer (now Brightwell), M.B.E.	Tōkyō, Japan	20 Oct.	1964
1,500 metres	4:12.7	Rita Ridley (née Lincoln)	Helsinki, Finland	15 Aug.	1971

HURDLING

Event	Secs.	Name	Place	Date	
100 metres	13.2*	Judy A. Vernon	Helsinki, Finland	25 July	1972
200 metres	26.7	Sharon Colyear	London (Crystal Palace)	16 July	1971

FIELD EVENTS

Event	ft.	ins.	Metres	Name	Place	Date	
High Jump	6	0¾	1.85	Barbara Jean Inkpen	Helsinki, Finland	12 Aug.	1971
	6	0¾	1.85	Barbara Jean Inkpen	Munich, West Germany	4 Sept.	1971
Long Jump	22	2¼	6.76	Mary Denise Rand, (now Toomey, née Bignal),M.B.E.	Tōkyō, Japan	14 Oct.	1964
Shot Putt	53	6¼	16.31	Mary Elizabeth Peters	Belfast, Northern Ireland	1 June	1966
Discus Throw	190	4	58.02	Christine Rosemary Payne (née Charters)	Birmingham	3 June	1972
Javelin Throw	182	5	55.60	Susan Mary Platt	London (Chiswick)	15 June	1968

PENTATHLON

4630 points (1971 Tables)	Mary Elizabeth Peters (100m. Hurdles 13.7''., Shot Putt 50' 6¼'' (15.40m.), High Jump 5' 9¾'' (1.77m.) Long Jump 19' 9¾'' (6.04m.), 200m. 24.5s.)	London (Crystal Palace)	6-7 May 1972

RELAYS

Event	Mins. secs.	Name	Place	Date	
4 × 110 yards	45.0	United Kingdom National Team (Anita Doris Neil, Maureen Dorothy Tranter, Janet Mary Simpson, Lillian Barbara Board)	Portsmouth, Hampshire	14 Sept.	1968
4 × 220 yards	1:37.6	London Olympiades A.C. (Della James (now Pascoe) Barbara M. Jones, Lillian Barbara Board, Janet Mary Simpson)	Solihull, Warwickshire	10 June	1967
4 × 100 metres	43.7	United Kingdom National Team (Anita Doris Neil, Maureen Dorothy Tranter, Janet Mary Simpson, Lillian Barbara Board)	Mexico City, Mexico	19 Oct.	1968
4 × 200 metres	1:33.8	(for details see World record)			
4 × 400 metres	3:30.8	Great Britain (Rosemary Olivia Stirling, Patricia Barbara Lowe (now Cropper) Janet Mary Simpson, Lillian Barbara Board, M.B.E.)	Athens, Greece	16 Sept.	1969
4 × 800 metres	8:23.8	Great Britain (Joan F. Allison, Sheila J. Carey (née Taylor), Patricia Barbara Lowe (now Cropper), Rosemary Olivia Stirling)	Paris, France	2 Oct.	1971

BADMINTON

Origins The game was devised *c.* 1863 at Badminton Hall in Gloucestershire, the seat of the Dukes of Beaufort.

International Championships The International Championship or Thomas Cup (instituted 1948) has been won 4 times by Malaya (now part of Malaysia) in 1948-49, 1951-52 and 1954-55, and as Malaysia, by the default of Indonesia in the final in 1966-67 and by Indonesia in 1957-58, 1960-61, 1963-64 and 1970-71.

Most titles Most wins in the All-England Championships (instituted 1899):-

The Ladies International Championship or Uber Cup (instituted 1956) has been most often won by Japan with a fourth win in 1972.

Longest hit Frank Rugani drove a shuttlecock 79 feet 8½ inches in tests at San Jose, California, U.S.A., on 29 Feb. 1964.

Longest games The longest recorded game has been one of 267 hours by 5 players from the Anglia T.V. Badminton Club on 8-19 April, who maintained continuous singles. The longest doubles marathon has been one of 200 hours 5 minutes maintained by 8 players from Whitley Bay Youth Association, Northumberland on 27 May-4 June playing in two teams with 6 hour shifts.

Event	Times	Holder	Dates
Men's Singles	7	Erland Kops (Denmark)	1958, 1960-63, 1965, 1967
Women's Singles	10	Mrs. G. C. K. Hashman (née Judy Devlin) (U.S.A.)	1954, 1957-58, 1960-64, 1966-67

Most titles (*i.e.* including doubles):—

Men	21	G. A. Thomas (later Sir George Thomas, Bt. d. 1972)	from 1903 to 1928
Women	17	Miss M. Lucas (U.K.)	from 1899 to 1910
	17	Mrs. G. C. K. Hashman (née Judy Devlin) (U.S.A.)	from 1954 to 1967

Most internationals Most international appearances:-

	Times	Men	Times	Women
England	100	A. D. Jordan, M.B.E., 1951 to 1970	52	Mrs. W. C. E. Rogers (née Cooley, 1955 to 1969
Ireland	45	K. Carlisle, 1954 to 1970	43	Miss Y. Kelly, 1955 to 1970
Scotland	40	R. S. McCoig, 1956 to 1971	28	Miss C. E. Dunglison, 1956 to 1967
Wales	20	D. Colmer, 1964 to 1970	22	Mrs. L. W. Myers, 1928 to 1939

235

BASEBALL

Earliest game "Baste-Ball" was a pursuit banned at Princeton, New Jersey, U.S.A., as early as 1786. On 4 Feb. 1962, it was claimed in *Nedelya*, the weekly supplement to the Soviet newspaper *Izvestiya*, that "Beizbol" was an old Russian game. The earliest baseball game under the Cartwright rules was at Hoboken, New Jersey, U.S.A., on 19 June 1846, with the New York Nine beating the Knickerbockers 23-1 in 4 innings.

Highest batting average The highest average in a career is .367 by Tyrus Raymond Cobb (1886-1961), the "Georgia Peach" of Augusta, Anniston, Detroit (1905-26) and Philadelphia (1927-28). During his career Ty Cobb made a record 2,244 runs from a record 4,191 hits made during a record 11,429 times at bat in a record 3,033 major league games.

HOME RUNS

Most The highest number of home runs hit in a career is the 714 by George Herman ("Babe") Ruth (1895-1948) of Baltimore-Providence, Boston Red Sox (American League), New York Yankees and Boston (National League), between 1914 and 1935. His major league record for home runs in one year is 60 in 154 games between 15 April and 30 Sept. 1927. Roger Maris (b. 1935) (New York Yankees) hit 61 homers in a 162-game schedule in 1961. Left-hander Joe Baumann of Roswell, New Mexico, hit 72 homers in the minor league in 1954.

Longest The longest home run ever measured was one of 618 feet by Roy Edward Carlyle in a minor league game at Emeryville Ball Park, California, U.S.A., on 4 July 1929. In 1919 "Babe" Ruth hit a 587-foot homer in a Boston Red Sox *v.* New York Giants match at Tampa,

Florida, U.S.A. The longest throw (ball weigh between 5 and 5¼ oz.) is 445 feet 10 inches by Gle Gorbaus on 1 Aug. 1957. The longest throw by woman is 296 feet by Miss Mildred "Babe" Didrikso (later Mrs. George Zaharis) (U.S.) (1914-56) at Jerse City, New Jersey, U.S.A. on 25 July 1931. The fastes time for circling bases is 13.3 seconds by Eva Swanson at Columbus, Ohio, in 1932.

Pitching The first "perfect game" (no hits, no runs) pitched i a World Series was by Don Larsen (New Yor Yankees) with 97 pitches (71 in the strike zone against Brooklyn Dodgers on 8 Oct. 1956.

Highest earnings The greatest earnings of a baseball player $1,091,477 amassed by "Babe" Ruth between 191 and 1938.

Record attendances and receipts The World Series record attendance is 420,784 (games with total receipts of $2,626,973.44, when th Los Angeles (ex-Brooklyn) Dodgers beat the Chicag White Sox 4-2 on 1-8 Oct. 1959. The single gam record is 92,706 for the fifth game (receipt $552,774.77) at the Memorial Coliseum, Lo Angeles, California, on 6 Oct. 1959. The record ne receipts for a series has been $3,018,113 from a pai attendance of 379,670, who saw the Detroit Tiger beat the St. Louis Cardinals 4-3 on 2-10 Oct. 1968 The highest seating capacity in a baseball stadium 74,056 in the Cleveland Municipal Stadium, Ohic U.S.A.

The all-time season record for attendances for bot leagues has been 29,203,589 in 1971.

Highest catch Joe Sprinx (Cleveland Indians) caught a baseba dropped from an airship at 800 feet in July 1931. Th force of the ball broke his jaw.

BASKETBALL

Origins *Ollamalitzli* was a 16th century Aztec precursor o basketball played in Mexico. If the solid rubber ba was put through a fixed stone ring the player wa entitled to the clothing of all the spectators. Moder basketball was devised by the Canadian-born D James A. Naismith (1861-1939) at the Trainin School of the International Y.M.C.A. College Springfield, Massachusetts, U.S.A., in Decembe 1891 and first played on 20 Jan. 1892. The firs public contest was on 11 March 1892. The game now a global activity. The Amateur Basketba Association of England and Wales was founded i 1936.

World Olympic champions The U.S.A. have won the Olympic title since i inception at Berlin in 1936 (7 times with 5 successive victories) and also the 1954 world tit (instituted 1950). Brazil won in 1959 and 1963.

Largest ever gate The Harlem Globetrotters (U.S.A.) played a exhibition to 75,000 in the Olympic Stadium, Wes Berlin, Germany, in 1951. The largest indoor baske ball stadium is the Astrodome, Houston, Texas U.S.A., where 52,693 watched a match on 20 Jar 1968.

Greatest playing record The Harlem Globetrotters set unapproache attendance and scoring records in their silver jubile season of 1951-52. They won 333 games and lost before over 3,000,000 spectators.

The team was founded by the London-born Abraha M. Saperstein (1903-66) of Chicago, Illinois, U.S.A and the first game was played at Hinckley, Illinois, o 7 Jan. 1927. In the 39 seasons to 1965 they wo 8,434 games and lost 322. They have travelled almo 5,000,000 miles, visited 87 countries on si continents, and have been seen by an estimate

236

Chris Greener (7ft 4¾ins.) towering above the rest of England's International Basketball team.

53,000,000 people.

U.S.A. professional records The greatest number of points scored in a career is 30,000 by Wilton ("Wilt the Stilt") Norman Chamberlain (b. 21 Aug. 1936) in the 14 seasons 1959-1972. He stands 7 feet 1¹⁄₁₀ inches tall and weighs 20 st. (280 lb.). He reached 30,003 on 16 Feb. 1972.

Most points scored in a season: Chamberlain scored 4,029 points for the Philadelphia Warriors in the 1961-62 season. Most points scored in a single game: Chamberlain scored 100 points against the New York Knickerbockers at Hershey, Pennsylvania, on 2 March 1962. Most points scored by a team: 173, by Boston Celtics, against Minnesota Lakers (139 points) at Boston, Massachusetts, on 28 Feb. 1959. Most points in a match: 316, between the Philadelphia Warriors (169 points) and the New York Knickerbockers (147 points), as above. The longest reported field goal in a match is 84 feet 11 inches by George Linn, aged 20, of Alabama against North Carolina at Tuscaloosa, Alabama, in January 1955. In 1953 Larry Slinkard at Arlington Heights High School, Illinois, landed a goal from 88 feet.

Non-A.B.A. scoring record Clarence (Bevo) Francis of Rio Grande College, Rio Grande, Ohio, U.S.A., scored 3,964 points (an average of 101 points per game) in the 1953-54 season. This total includes 150 points scored in one game.

Tallest players The tallest player of all time has been Emili Rached of Brazil, who competed in the 1971 Pan American Games when measuring 233 centimetres (7 feet 7⅝ inches). The tallest woman player is Ulyana Semyonova (b. 1950), who plays for T.T.T. Riga, Latvia and stands 6 feet 9½ inches. The tallest British player has been the 7-foot 4¾-inch tall Christopher Greener (see Chapter 1) of L.L.S.K., London whose debut for England was v. France on 17 Dec. 1969.

Most expensive In 1972 Pete Maravich of Louisiana State University signed a 5 year contract with Atlanta Hawks for a reputed $1.5 to $2.0 million.

Most accurate The greatest goal shooting demonstration has been by the professional trick specialist Bunny Levitt (5 feet 4 inches) who in 1935 in Chicago shot 499 consecutive baskets. In 1936 he did 561 in practice. Ted St. Martin of Riverdale, California, "canned" 10,944 throws in 12,099 for a 90.4 per cent average on 30-31 July 1971.

Longest games marathon record The longest recorded basketball marathon with 18 players is of 125 hours by the La Sierra Huddle Group of the Fellowship of Christian Athletes in California from 24-30 March 1972. The longest recorded match between two teams of five without substitutes is 42 hours by 10 students of the College of Education, Bognor Regis, Sussex, on 9-11 June 1972.

Britain The most A.B.B.A. titles (initiated 1936) have been won by the London Central Y.M.C.A. with eight wins in 1957-58, 1960 and 1962-63-64-67-69. The highest score in a final was 98 points by London Polytechnic v. Nottingham Y.M.C.A. in 1954. Four women's titles (instituted 1965) have been won by Malory.

The record score by an England international team is 101-33, when beating Wales at Belfast in 1962.

The highest Championship score in Britain has been 132 points by Aldershot Warriors v. Highbury Hawks (52) on 3 Oct. 1970.

BILLIARDS

Earliest mention The earliest recorded mention of billiards was in a poem by Clément Marot (1496-1544) of France, and it was mentioned in England in 1591 by Edmund Spenser (c. 1552-99). The first recorded public billiards room in England was the Piazza, Covent Garden, London, in the early part of the 19th century. Rubber cushions were introduced in 1835 and slate beds in 1836.

Highest breaks Tom Reece (1873-1953) made an unfinished break of 499,135, including 249,152 cradle cannons (2 points each), in 85 hours 49 minutes against Joe Chapman at Burroughes' Hall, Soho Square, London, between 3 June and 6 July 1907. This was not recognized because press and public were not continuously present. The highest certified break made by the anchor cannon is 42,746 by W. Cook (England) from 29 May to 7 June 1907. The official world record under the then baulk-line rule is 1,784 by Joe Davis, O.B.E. (b. 15 April 1901) in the United Kingdom Championship on 29 May 1936. Walter Lindrum (Australia) made an official break of 4,137 in 2 hours 55 minutes against Joe Davis at Thurston's on 19-20 Jan. 1932, before the baulk-line rule was in force. The amateur record is 702 by Robert Marshall v. Tom Cleary, both of Australia, in the Australian Amateur Championship at Brisbane on 17 Sept. 1953. Davis has an unofficial personal best of 2,502 (mostly pendulum cannons) in a match against Tom Newman (1894-1943) (England) in Manchester in 1930.

Fastest century Walter Lindrum, M.B.E. (1898-1960) of Australia made an unofficial 100 break in 27.5 seconds in Australia on 10 Oct. 1952. His official record is 100 in 46.0 seconds, set in Sydney in 1941.

Most world titles The greatest number of world championship titles (instituted 1870) won by one player is eight by John Roberts, Jnr. (England) in 1870 (twice), 1871, 1875 (twice), 1877 and 1885 (twice). The greatest number of United Kingdom titles (instituted 1934) won by any player is seven (1934-39 and 1947) by Joe Davis (England), who also won four world titles (1928-30 and 1932) before the series was discontinued in 1934. Willie Hoppe (U.S.A.) won 51 "world" titles in the United States variants of the game between 1906 and 1952.

Most amateur titles The record for world amateur titles is four by Robert Marshall (Australia) in 1936-38-51-62. The greatest number of British Amateur Championships (instituted 1888) ever won is eight by Sidney H. Fry (1893 to 1925) and A. Leslie Driffield (1952-54, 1957-59, 1962 and 1967).

Bar billiards marathon The duration record for bar billiards is 90 hours 7 minutes by Dave Baxter, Tony Walter, Keith Baxter, Mike Hurford and Alistair McInnes, at St. Helene Hotel, Guernsey from 30 March to 3 April 1972. In 303 games the score was 1,067,720.

237

In the 19th century in the U.S.A. a tenth pin was added to circumvent the illegality of 9 pin bowling.

BOBSLEIGH

Origins The oldest known sledge is dated *c.* 6500 B.C and came from Heinola, southern Finland. The word toboggan comes from the Micmac American Indian word *tobaakan*. The oldest bobsleigh club in the world is St. Moritz Tobogganing Club, home of the Cresta Run, founded in 1887. Modern world championships were inaugurated in 1924. Four-man bobs were included in the first Winter Olympic Games at Chamonix in 1924 and two-man boblets from the third Games at Lake Placid, U.S.A., in 1932.

Olympic and world titles The Olympic four-man bob title has been won four times by Switzerland (1924-36-56-72). The U.S.A. (1932, 1936), Italy (1956, 1968) and Germany (1952 and (West) 1972) have won the Olympic boblet event twice.

The world four-man bob title has been won nine times by Switzerland (1924-36-39-47-54-55-56-57-71). Italy won the two-man title 13 times (1954-56-57-58-59-60-61-62-63-66-68-69-71). Eugenio Monti (Italy) (b. 1927) has been a member of eleven world championship crews.

TOBOGGANING
Cresta Run The skeleton one-man toboggan dates, in its present form, from 1892. On the 1,325-yard-long Cresta Run at St. Moritz, Switzerland, dating from 1884 speeds of up to 83.8 m.p.h. were reached by Flt.-Lt. (now Sqn. Ldr.) Colin Mitchell (Great Britain) in February 1959. The record from the Junction (2,868 feet) is 43.59 seconds by Nino Bibbia (b. 9 Sept. 1924) of Italy on 16 Jan. 1965. The record from Top (3,981 feet) is 54.67 seconds by Bibbia on 13 Feb. 1965.

The greatest number of wins in the Cresta Run Grand National (inst. 1885) is seven by the 1948 Olympic champion Nino Bibbia (Italy) in 1960-61-62-63-64-66-68. The greatest number of wins in the Cresta Run Curzon Cup (inst. in 1910) is eight by Bibbia in 1950-57-58-60-62-63-64-69 who hence won the Double in 1960-62-63-64.

LUGEING
In lugeing the rider adopts a sitting, as opposed to a prone position. It was largely developed by British tourists at Klosters, Switzerland, from 1883. The first European championships were at Reichenberg, East Germany, in 1914 and the first world championship at Oslo, Norway, in 1953. The International Luge Federation was formed in 1957. Lugeing attracts more than 15,000 competitors in Austria.

Most world titles The most successful rider in the world championship is Thomas Köhler (East Germany), who won the single-seater title in 1962, 1966 and 1967 and shared the two-seater title in 1967 and 1968 (Olympic Otrun Enderlein (East Germany) has won thrice (1965, 1966 and 1967).

Highest speed The fastest luge run is at Krynica, Poland, where speeds of more than 80 m.p.h. have been recorded.

BOWLING (TEN PIN)

Origins The ancient German game of nine-pins was exported to the United States in the early 17th century. In about 1845 the Connecticut and New Haven State Legislatures prohibited the game so a tenth pin was added to evade the ban; but there is some evidence of 10 pins being used in Suffolk about 300 years ago.

In the United States there were 8,922 bowling establishments with 139,483 bowling lanes and 29,500,000 bowlers in 1970-71. The world's largest bowling centre is the Tokyo World Lanes Centre, Japan with 252 lanes. The largest in Europe is the Excel Bowl at Nottingham, England, where the game was introduced in 1960, with 48 lanes on two floors (24 on each floor).

Highest scores The highest individual score for three sanctioned games (possible 900) is 886 by Albert (Allie) Brandt of Lockport, New York, U.S.A., on 25 Oct. 1939. The record for consecutive strikes in sanctioned match play is 29 by Frank Caruana at Buffalo, New York, on 5 March 1924, and 29 by Max Stein at Los Angeles, California, on 8 Oct. 1939. The highest number of sanctioned 300 games is 24 (till 1972) by Elvin Mesger of Sullivan, Missouri, U.S.A. The maximum 900 for a three-game series has been recorded three times in unsanctioned games—by Leo Bentley at Lorain, Ohio, U.S.A., on 26 March 1931; by Joe Sargent at Rochester, New York State, U.S.A., i

1934; and by Jim Margie in Philadelphia, Pennsylvania, U.S.A., on 4 Feb. 1937. Such series must have consisted of 36 consecutive strikes (*i.e.* all pins down with one ball).

The United Kingdom record for a three-game series is 775 by Geoffrey Liddiard at Harrow, Greater London on 3 Oct. 1971. The record score for a single game is 300, first achieved by Albert Kirkham, aged 34, of Burslem, Staffordshire, on 5 Dec. 1965, which has since been equalled on several occasions. The highest score for a woman player is 299 by Mrs. Carole Cuthbert at the Airport Bowl, West London on 16 Mar. 1972.

World Championships The world championships were instituted in 1954. The highest pinfall in the individual men's event is 5,963 (in 28 games) by Ed. Luther (U.S.) at Milwaukee, Wisconsin, in 1971.

Marathon Bill Halstead (U.S.A.) bowled 1,201 games (knocked down 165,959 pins) scoring 1,948 strikes, lifted 130.3 tons and walked 127.2 miles in 151 hours 25 minutes at Tampa, Florida, U.S.A., on 27 Nov. to 3 Dec. 1966. Richard Dewey, 42, bowled 1,206 consecutive games in Kansas City, U.S.A., ending on 25 May 1971.

SKITTLES

The duration record for knocking down skittles (9-pins) is 53 hours (56,191 pins down) by 9 men at the Plymouth Inn alley, Totnes, Devon on 30 June-2 July 1969.

The highest score in 24 hours is 70,872 pins by 12 players from The Bell Inn, Little Addington, Northamptonshire, on 10-11 Sept. 1971.

BOWLS

LAWN

Origins Bowls can be traced back to at least the 13th century in England. The Southampton Town Bowling was formed in 1299. After falling into disrepute, the game was rescued by the bowlers of Scotland who, headed by W. W. Mitchell, framed the modern rules in 1848-49.

World title In the inaugural World Championship held in Sydney, Australia in October 1966 the Singles Title was won by David John Bryant (b. 1931) (England) and the team title (Leonard Cup) by Australia. In the second Championships at Worthing in 1972 the singles was won by Malwyn Evans (Wales) and Scotland won the Leonard Cup.

Most title wins In the annual International Championships (instituted 1903) Scotland have won 23 times to England's 20. The most consecutive wins is five by England from 1958 to 1962 and five by Scotland from 1965 to 1969.

English titles The only man to have won four Singles Titles (instituted 1905) is E. Percy C. Baker (Poole Park, Dorset) in 1932, 1946, 1952 and 1955. He has also shared two pairs wins (1950 and 1962) and a triples win in 1960. The most Pairs Titles (instituted 1912) is four by Worthing, in 1937-38, 1955 and 1957. The Triples Title (instituted 1945) has never been won twice. The Rinks (instituted 1905) have been won three times by Belgrave (Leicester) in 1919, 1922 and 1954 and by Clevedon (Somerset) in 1957, 1968 and 1969. David Bryant, M.B.E., skipped Clevedon to the E.B.A. Triple Title in 1966 and so became the only man ever to have won all four titles. In 1969 he participated in his 8th E.B.A. title win.

Most internationals The greatest number of international appearances by any bowler is 76 reached by Syd Thompson for Ireland in 1972.

John Broughton the 'Father of Boxing' based on a painting by William Hogarth. 1742

BOXING

Earliest references Boxing with gloves was depicted on a fresco from the Isle of Thera, Greece which has been dated 1520 B.C. The earliest prize-ring code of rules was formulated in England on 16 Aug. 1743 by the champion pugilist Jack Broughton (1704-89), who reigned from 1729 to 1750. Boxing, which had, in 1867, come under the Queensberry Rules formulated for John Sholto Douglas, 8th Marquess of Queensberry, was not established as a legal sport in Britain until after the ruling of Mr. Justice Grantham on 24 April 1901, following the death of Billy Smith.

Longest fight The longest recorded fight with gloves was between Andy Bowen of New Orleans (k. 1894) and Jack Burke in New Orleans, Louisiana, U.S.A., on 6-7 April 1893.

The fight lasted 110 rounds and 7 hours 19 minutes from 9.15 p.m. to 4.34 a.m., but was declared a no contest when both men were unable to continue. The longest recorded bare knuckle fight was one of 6 hours 15 minutes between James Kelly and Jack Smith at Melbourne, Australia, on 19 Oct. 1856. The greatest recorded number of rounds is 278 in 4 hours 30 minutes, when Jack Jones beat Patsy Tunney in Cheshire in 1825.

Shortest fight There is a distinction between the quickest knock-out and the shortest fight. A knock-out in 10½ seconds (including a 10-second count) occurred on 26 Sept. 1946, when Al Couture struck Ralph Walton while the latter was adjusting a gum shield in his corner at Lewiston, Maine, U.S.A. If the time was accurately taken it is clear that Couture must have been more than half-way across the ring from his own corner at the opening bell. The shortest fight on record appears to be one at Palmerston, New Zealand on 8 July 1952 when Ross Cleverley (R.N.Z.A.F.) floored D. Emerson (Pahiatua) with the first punch and the referee stopped the contest with a count 7 seconds from the bell. Teddie Barker (Swindon) scored a technical knock-out over Bob Roberts (Nigeria) at the first blow in a welterweight fight at Maesteg, Glamorganshire, Wales, on 2 Sept. 1957. The referee, Joe Brimell, stopped the fight without a count 10 seconds from the bell.

The shortest world heavyweight title fight occurred when Tommy Burns (1881-1955) (*né* Noah Brusso) of Canada knocked out Jem Roche in 1 minute 28 seconds in Dublin, Ireland, on 17 March 1908. The duration of the Clay *v.* Liston fight at Lewiston, Maine, U.S.A., on 25 May 1965 was 1 minute 52 seconds (including the count) as timed from the video tape recordings, despite a ringside announcement giving a time of 1 minute. Charles "Sonny" Liston (b. 1932) died in 1970. The shortest world title fight was when Al McCoy knocked out George Chip in 45 seconds for the middleweight crown in New York on 7 April 1914. The shortest ever British title fight was one of 40 seconds (including the count), when Dave Charnley knocked out David "Darkie" Hughes in a lightweight championship defence in Nottingham on 20 Nov. 1961.

Tallest The tallest boxer to fight professionally was Gogea Mitu (b. 1914) of Romania in 1935. He was 7 feet 4 inches and weighed 23 stone 5 lb. (327 lb.). John Rankin, who won a fight in New Orleans, Louisiana, U.S.A., in November 1967, was reputedly also 7 feet 4 inches.

WORLD HEAVYWEIGHT CHAMPIONS

Longest and shortest reigns The longest reign of any world heavyweight champion is 11 years 8 months and 9 days by Joe Louis (born Joseph Louis Barrow, Lafayette, Alabama, 13 May 1914), from 22 June 1937, when he knocked out James J. Braddock in the eighth round at Chicago, Illinois, U.S.A., until announcing his retirement on 1 March 1949. During his reign Louis made a record 25 defences of his title. The shortest reign was by Primo Carnera (Italy) for 350 days from 29 June 1933 to 14 June 1934. However, if the disputed title claim of Marvin Hart is allowed, his reign from 3 July 1905 to 23 Feb. 1906 was only 235 days.

Heaviest and lightest The heaviest world champion was Primo Carnera (1906-67) of Italy, the "Ambling Alp", who won the title from Jack Sharkey in 6 rounds in New York City, N.Y., U.S.A., on 29 June 1933. He scaled 267 lb. (19 stone 1 lb.), had an expanded chest measurement of 53 inches, the longest reach at 85½ inches (finger tip to finger tip) and also the largest fists with a 14¾-inch circumference. The lightest champion was Robert Prometheus Fitzsimmons (1862-1917), who was born at Helston, Cornwall, and, at a weight of 167 lb. (11 stone 13 lb.), won the title by knocking out James J. Corbett in 14 rounds at Carson City, Nevada, U.S.A., on 17 March 1897.

The greatest differential in a world title fight was 86 lb. between Carnera (267 lb. or 19 stone 1 lb.) and Tommy Loughran (184 lb. or 13 stone 2 lb.) of the U.S.A., when the former won on points at Miami, Florida, U.S.A., on 1 March 1934.

Tallest and shortest The tallest world champion according to measurements by the Physical Director of the Hemingway Gymnasium, Harvard University, was Carnera at 6 foot 5.4 inches. Jess Willard (1881-1968), who won the title in 1915, often stated to be 6 foot 6¼ inches was in fact 6 foot 5¼ inches. The shortest was Tommy Burns (1881-1955) of Canada, world champion from 23 Feb. 1906 to 26 Dec. 1908, who stood 5 feet 7 inches and weighed 12 stone 11 lb.

Oldest and youngest The oldest man to win the heavyweight crown was Jersey Joe Walcott (b. Arnold Raymond Cream, 31 Jan. 1914 at Merchantville, New Jersey, U.S.A.) who knocked out Ezzard Charles on 18 July 1951 in Pittsburgh, Pennsylvania, when aged 37 years 168 days. Walcott was the oldest holder at 38 years 7 months 23 days losing his title to Marciano on 23 Sept. 1952 and in 1953 the oldest challenger. The youngest age at which the world title has been won is 21 years 331 days by Floyd Patterson (b. Waco, North Carolina, 4 Jan. 1935) of the U.S.A. After the

John L Sullivan who spanned the bare knuckle and glove transition and lost his world heavyweight championship fight in 1892.

retirement of Marciano, Patterson won the vacant title by beating Archie Moore in 5 rounds in Chicago, Illinois, U.S.A., on 30 Nov. 1956. He is also the only man ever to regain the heavyweight championship. He lost to Ingemar Johansson (Sweden) on 26 June 1959 but defeated him on 20 June 1960 at the New York Polo Grounds Stadium.

Longest lived The longest lived of any heavyweight champion of the world has been Jess Willard (U.S.A.), who was born 29 Dec. 1881 at St. Clere, Kansas, and died 15 Dec. 1968 at Pacoima, California aged 86 years 351 days.

Earliest title fight The first world heavyweight title fight, with gloves and 3-minute rounds, was that between John Lawrence Sullivan (1858-1918) and "Gentleman" James J. Corbett (1866-1933) in New Orleans, Louisiana, U.S.A., on 7 Sept. 1892. Corbett won in 21 rounds.

Undefeated Only James Joseph (Gene) Tunney (b. Greenwich Village, New York City, 25 May 1898) (1926-1928) and Rocky Marciano (1952-56) *finally* retired as champions, undefeated in the heavyweight division.

WORLD CHAMPIONS (any weight)

Longest and shortest reign Joe Louis's heavyweight duration record of 11 years 252 days stands for all divisions. The shortest reign has been 54 days by the French featherweight Eugène Criqui from 2 June to 26 July 1923. The disputed flyweight champion Emile Pladner (France) reigned only 47 days from 2 March to 18 April 1929, as did also the disputed featherweight champion Dave Sullivan, from 26 Sept. to 11 Nov. 1898.

Youngest and oldest The youngest age at which any world championship has been claimed is 19 years 6 days by Pedlar Palmer (b. 19 Nov. 1876), who won the disputed bantamweight title in London on 25 Nov. 1895. Willie Pep (b. William Papaleo, 20 Nov. 1922), of the U.S.A., won the featherweight crown in New York on his 20th birthday, 22 Nov. 1942. After Young Corbett knocked out Terry McGovern (1880-1918) in two rounds at Hartford, Connecticut, U.S.A., on 28 Nov. 1901, neither was able to get his weight down to nine stone, and the featherweight title was claimed by Abe Attell, when aged only 17 years 251 days. The oldest world champion was Archie Moore (b. Archibald Lee Wright, Collinsville, Illinois on either 13 Dec. 1913 or 1916) (U.S.A.) who was recognized as a light-heavyweight champion up to early 1962 when his title was removed. He was then believed to be between 45 and 48. Bob Fitzsimmons (1862-1917) had the longest career of any official world title-holder with over 32 years from 1882 to 1914. He won his last world title aged 41 years 174 days in San Francisco, California on 25 Nov. 1903. He was an amateur from 1880 to 1882.

Longest fight The longest world title fight (under Queensberry Rules) was that between the lightweights Joe Gans (1874-1910), of the U.S.A., and Oscar Matthew "Battling" Nelson (1882-1954), the "Durable Dane", at Goldfield, Nevada, U.S.A., on 3 Sept. 1906. It was terminated in the 42nd round when Gans was declared the winner on a foul.

Most captures The only boxer to win a world title five times at one weight is "Sugar" Ray Robinson (b. Walker Smith, Jr., in Detroit, 3 May 1920) of the U.S.A., who beat Carmen Basilio (U.S.A.) in the Chicago Stadium on 25 March 1958, to regain the world middleweight title for the fourth time. The other title wins were over Jake LaMotta (U.S.A.) in Chicago on 14 Feb. 1951, Randolph Turpin (United Kingdom) in New York on 12 Sept. 1951, Carl "Bobo" Olson (U.S.A.) in Chicago on 9 Dec. 1955, and Gene Fullmer (U.S.A.) in Chicago on 1 May 1957. The record number of title bouts in a career is 33 or 34 (at bantam and featherweight) by George Dixon (1870-1909), *alias* Little Chocolate, of the U.S.A., between 1890 and 1901;

Greatest weight span The only man to hold world titles at three weights *simultaneously* was Henry ("Homicide Hank") Armstrong (b. 22 Dec. 1912), now the Rev. Harry Jackson, of the U.S.A., at featherweight, lightweight and welterweight from August to December 1938.

Greatest "tonnage" The greatest "tonnage" recorded in any fight is 700 lb., when Claude "Humphrey" McBride (Oklahoma) 340 lb. (24 stone 4 lb.) knocked out Jimmy Black (Houston, Texas), who weighed 360 lb. (25 stone 10 lb.) in the third round. The greatest "tonnage" in a world title fight was 488¾ lb. (34 stone 12¾ lb.) when Carnera (then 259¼ lb.) fought Paolino Uzcuden (229½ lb.) of Spain in Rome on 22 Oct. 1933.

Smallest champion The smallest man to win any world title has been Pascual Perez (b. Mendoza, Argentina, on 4 March. 1926) who won the flyweight title in Tokyo on 26 Nov. 1954 at 7 stone 9 lb. (98 lb.) and 4 foot 11½ inches.

Most k-downs in title fights Vic Toweel (South Africa) knocked down Danny O'Sullivan of London 14 times in 10 rounds in their world bantamweight fight at Johannesburg on 2 Dec. 1950, before the latter retired.

ALL FIGHTS

Largest purse The greatest purse has been $2,500,000, (then £1,041,667) guaranteed to both Joseph "Billy" Frazier (b. South Carolina, U.S.A., 17 Jan. 1944) and Muhammad Ali Haj (formerly Cassius Marcellus Clay 7th) (b. Louisville, Kentucky, U.S.A., 17 Jan. 1942) for their 15-round fight at Madison Square Garden, New York City, on 8 March 1971.

knuckle stake The largest stake ever fought for in this era was $22,500 (then £4,633) in the 27-round fight between Jack Cooper and Wolf Bendoff at Port Elizabeth, South Africa on 29 July 1889.

endances *Highest* The greatest paid attendance at any boxing fight has been 120,757 (with a ringside price of $27.50) for the Tunney *v.* Dempsey world heavyweight title fight at the Sesqui-centennial Stadium, Philadelphia, Pennsylvania, U.S.A., on 23 Sept. 1926. The indoor record is 37,321 at the Clay *v.* Ernie Terrell fight in the Astrodome, Houston, Texas, on 6 Feb. 1967.

Muhammad Ali—the world's highest earning boxer seen in action against Henry Cooper (G.B.)

The highest non-paying attendance is 135,132 at the Tony Zale *v.* Billy Prior fight at Juneau Park, Milwaukee, Wisconsin, U.S.A., on 18 Aug. 1941.

Lowest The smallest attendance at a world heavyweight title fight was 2,434 at the Clay *v.* Liston fight at Lewiston, Maine, U.S.A., on 25 May 1965.

Highest earnings in career The largest known fortune ever made in a fighting career is an estimated $8,000,000 amassed by Muhammad Ali. Including earnings for refereeing and promoting, Jack Dempsey has grossed over $10,000,000 to 1967.

Most knock-outs The greatest number of finishes classed by the rules prevailing as "knock-outs" in a career is 136 by Archie Moore of the U.S.A. The record for consecutive K.O.s is 44, set by Lamar Clark of Utah at Las Vegas, Nevada, U.S.A., on 11 Jan. 1960. He knocked out 6 in one night (5 in the first round) at Bingham, Utah, on 1 Dec. 1958.

Most fights The greatest recorded number of fights in a career is 1,309 by Abraham Hollandersky, *alias* Abe the Newsboy (U.S.A.), in the fourteen years from 1905 to 1918. He filled in the time with 387 wrestling bouts (1905-1916).

Most fights without loss Hal Bagwell, a lightweight, of Gloucester, England, was reputedly undefeated in 183 consecutive fights, of which only 5 were draws, between 10 Aug. 1938 and 29 Nov. 1948. His record of fights in the war-time period (1939-46), is however very sketchy. He never contested a British title.

Greatest weight difference The greatest weight difference recorded in a major bout is 10 stone (140 lb.) between Bob Fitzsimmons (12 stone 4 lb.) and Ed Dunkhorst (22 stone 4 lb.) at Brooklyn, New York City, N.Y., U.S.A., on 30 April 1900. Fitzsimmons won in two rounds.

Longest career The heavyweight Jem Mace, known as "the gypsy" (b. Norwich, 8 April 1831), had a career lasting 35 years from 1855 to 1890, but there were several years in which he had only one fight. He died, aged 79, in Jarrow-on-Tyne on 30 Nov. and was buried in Liverpool on 6 Dec. 1910. Walter Edgerton, the "Kentucky Rosebud", knocked out John Henry Johnson, aged 45, in 4 rounds at the Broadway A.C., New York City, N.Y., U.S.A., on 4 Feb. 1916, when aged 63.

British titles The most defences of a British heavyweight title is 13 by "Bombardier" Billy Wells (1887-1967) from 1911

Hugh Pat Floyd holder of the record span of years for winning an A.B.A. Championship from 1929 to 1946.

to 1919. The only British boxer to win three Lonsd Belts outright has been Henry William Coop O.B.E.(b. Camberwell, London, 3 May 1934), hea weight champion (1959-1969, 1970-71). He reti on 16 Mar. 1971.

Most Olympic gold medals The only amateur boxer ever to win three Olym gold medals is the southpaw László Papp (b. 19? (Hungary), who took the middleweight (1948) a the light-middleweight titles (1952 and 1956). 1 only man to win two titles in one celebration was O Kirk (U.S.A.), who took both the bantam a featherweight titles at St. Louis, Missouri, U.S.A. 1904, when the U.S. won all the titles. In 1908 Gr Britain won all the titles.

A.B.A. TITLES

Most The greatest number of A.B.A. titles won by a boxer is 6 by Joseph Steers at middleweight a heavyweight between 1890 and 1893.

Longest span The greatest span of A.B.A. title-winning per mances is that of the heavyweight H. Pat Floyd, w won in 1929 and gained his fourth title 17 years la in 1946.

Class	Instituted	Wins	Name	Years
Flyweight (8 stone or under)	1920	5	T. Pardoe	1929-33
Bantamweight (8 stone 7 lb. or under)	1884	4	W. W. Allen	1911-12, 1914, 1919
Featherweight (9 stone or under)	1888	5	G. R. Baker	1912-14, 1919, 1921
Lightweight (9 stone 7 lb. or under)	1881	4	M. Wells	1904-7
		4	F. Grace	1909, 1913, 1919-20
Light-Welterweight (10 stone or under)	1951	2	D. Stone	1956-57
		2	R. Kane	1958-59
		2	L./Cpl. B. Brazier	1961-62
		2	R. McTaggart	1963, 1965
Welterweight (10 stone 8 lb. or under)	1920	3	N. Gargano	1954-55-56
Light-Middleweight (11 stone 2 lb. or under)	1951	2	B. Wells	1953-54
		2	B. Foster	1952, 1955
		2	S. Pearson	1958-59
		2	T. Imrie	1966, 1969
Middleweight (11 stone 11 lb. or under)	1881	5	R. C. Warnes	1899, 1901, 1903, 1907, 1
		5	H. W. Mallin	1919-23
		5	F. Mallin	1928-32
Light-Heavyweight (12 stone 10 lb. or under)	1920	4	H. J. Mitchell	1922-25
Heavyweight (any weight)	1881	5	F. Parks	1899, 1901-02, 1905-06

BULLFIGHTING

The first renowned professional *espada* was Francisco Romero of Ronda, in Andalusia, Spain, who introduced the *estoque* and the red muleta *c.* 1700. Spain now has some 190 active matadors. Since 1700, 42 major matadors have died in the ring.

Largest stadiums The world's largest bullfighting ring is the Plaza, Mexico City, with a capacity of 48,000. The largest of Spain's 312 bullrings is Las Ventas, Madrid with a capacity of 28,000.

Most successful matadors The most successful matador measured by bulls killed was Lagartijo (1841-1900), born Rafael Molina, whose lifetime total was 4,867. The longest career of any 20th century *espada* was that of Juan Belmonte (1892-1962) of Spain who survived 29 seasons from 1909-1937, killing 3,000 bulls and being gored 50 times. In 1919 he took part in 109 *corridas*. In 1884 Romano set a record by killing 18 bulls in a day in Seville and in 1949 El Litri (Miguel Báes) set a Spanish record with 114 *novilladas* in a season.

Highest paid The highest paid bullfighter in history is El Cordobés (b. Manuel Benítez Pérez, probably on 4 May 1936, Palma del Rio, Spain), who became a sterling millionaire in 1966, when he fought 111 *corridas* up to 4 October of that year. On 19 May 1968 he received £9,000 for a *corrida* in Madrid. In 1970 he received an estimated £750,000 for 121 fights.

CANOEING

Origins The acknowledged pioneer of canoeing as a sport v John Macgregor, a British barrister, in 1865. T Canoe Club was formed on 26 July 1866.

Most Olympic gold medals Gert Fredriksson of Sweden won the 1,000 met Kayak singles in 1948, 1952 and 1956, the 10,0 metres Kayak singles in 1948 and 1956 and the 1,0 metres Kayak doubles in 1960. With 6 Olympic tit and 3 others (1,000 metres K.1 in 1950 and 1954 a 500 metres K.1 in 1954) his total individual wo titles is 9. The Olympic 1,000 metre record o1 minutes 14.38 seconds represents an average speed 11.51 m.p.h. and a striking rate of 125 strokes minute.

Most British titles The most British Open titles (instituted 1936) e won is 23, of which 11 were individual, by Alist Wilson (Ayrshire Kayak Club) with K.1 500 met 1962-64-65-66; 1,000 metres 1962-64-65-66; 10,0 metres 1963-66-67; K.2 500 metres 1963-68; 1,0 metres 1965; 10,000 metres 1963-66; K.4 1,0 metres 1964-65-66 and K.1 4 × 500 metres Re 1963-64-65-66. David Mitchell (Chester S. & C. won his sixth consecutive British slalom title in 196

The only United Kingdom canoeists to win wo titles have been Paul Farrant (died 18 April 1960) Chalfont Park Canoe Club, who won the canoe slal at Geneva, Switzerland, in August 1959, and A

Emus, who won the canoe sailing at Hayling Island, Hampshire, in August 1961 and on the Boden See (Lake of Constance) in August 1965.

Longest journey The longest journey ever made by canoe is one of 7,200 miles from New York City to Nome, Alaska on the North American river system by paddle and portage by Geoffrey W. Pope and Sheldon Taylor, both 24, from 24 Apr. 1936 to 11 Aug. 1937.

Circum-navigation The first man to circumnavigate Great Britain by canoe is Geoffrey Hunter, 26, who started from and returned to Maidstone Bridge, Kent in 188 days (3 May-7 Nov. 1970). He lost one canoe and had to cling to a buoy for 14 hours in the Solway Firth.

Cross-Channel The singles record for canoeing across the English Channel is 3 hours 36 minutes by David Shankland, aged 29, of Cardiff, in a home-made N.C.K.I. named "Jelly Roll", from Shakespeare Bay, Dover, to Cap Gris-Nez, France, on 21 June 1965. The doubles record is 3 hours 20 minutes 30 seconds by Capt. William Stanley Crook and the late Ronald Ernest Rhodes in their glass-fibre K.2 "Accord", from St.

Margaret's Bay, Dover, to Cap Blanc Nez, France on 20 Sept. 1961.

The record for a double crossing is 14 hours 14 minutes in K.1 canoes by J. McCann, B. Cowburn, Mrs. J. Ledger and Mrs. G. Crow on 18-19 July 1971.

Devizes-Westminster The Senior Class record for the annual Devizes-Westminster Challenge Cup race (instituted 1948) over 125 miles with 77 locks is 19 hours 9 minutes 15 seconds (av. 9 m.p.h.) by T. Shenton and T. Cardale (Royal Marine Canoe Federation) from 96 crews to win the 1972 race. The record for the Junior Class event (held over 4 days) is 16 hours 48 minutes 18 seconds by A. J. Bennett and T. J. Cornish (Pangbourne Canoe Club) in the 1972 race. There are 77 portages and 21 miles of tidal water.

Eskimo rolls The record for Eskimo rolls is 400 in 27 minutes 29 seconds by Terence Russell, 15, of Swanley, Kent at Eltham Baths, Greater London on 18 Dec. 1971. A "hand-rolling" record of 100 rolls in 8 minutes 53 seconds was set in Bedford by Robert Campbell on 29 May 1972.

DOWN STREAM CANOEING

River	Miles			Date	
Rhine	822	Sgt. Charles Kavanagh	Chur, Switzerland to Willemstad, Neths.	13 Feb. 1961	17½ days
Rhine	726	L.Cpl. Peter Salisbury Spr. Simon Chivers	Chur, to Hook of Holland with greater portages	17 Apr –9May 1972	21½ days
Murray	1,300	Phillip Davis, 16, and Robert S. Lodge (15½-foot canoe)	Albury, N.S.W. to Murray Bridge	27 Dec. 1970– 1 Feb. 1971	36 days
Murray	287*	A.Powell (K.1)	Yarrawonga to Swan Hill	28 Dec 1971 –1 Jan 1972	33 hours 49 mins 37.8 secs
Nile	4,000	John Goddard (U.S.), Jean Laporte and André Davy(France)	Kagera to the Delta	Nov.1953–July 1954	9 months
Amazon	4,000	Stephen Z.Bezuk (U.S.) (Kayak)	Atalaya to Belem	21 June-Nov 1970	4½ months

CARD PLAYING

CONTRACT BRIDGE

Earliest references Bridge (a corruption of Biritch) is of Levantine origin, having been played in Greece in the early 1880s. The game was known in London in 1886 under the title of "Biritch" or Russian Whist.

Auction Bridge (highest bidder names trump) was introduced in 1904 but was swamped by the Contract game, which was devised by Harold S. Vanderbilt (U.S.A.) on a Caribbean voyage in November 1925. The new version became a world-wide craze after the

U.S.A. v. Great Britain challenge match between Ely Culbertson (b. Romania, 1891) and Lt-Col. Walter Buller at Almack's Club, London, on 15 Sept. 1930. The U.S.A. won the 54-hand match by 4,845 points.

World titles The World Championship (Bermuda Bowl) has been won most often by Italy's Blue Team (*Squadra Azzura*) (1957-58-59, 1961-62-63, 1965-66-67, 1969), whose team also won the Olympiad in 1964, 1968 and 1972. Three of the Italian players, Massimo D'Alelio, Giorgio Belladonna and Pietro Forquet, were in 12 of these winning teams. The team retired in 1969 but came back to defeat the Dallas Aces (1970-71 World Champions) 338–254 in Las Vegas,

HIGHEST POSSIBLE SCORES (excluding penalties)

Opponents bid 7 of any suit or No Trumps doubled and redoubled and vulnerable

	Opponents make no trick	
Above Line	1st undertrick	400
	12 subsequent undertricks at 600 each	7,200
	All Honours	150
		7,750

Bid 1 No Trump, double and redouble, vulnerable

Below Line	1st trick (40X 4)	160
Above Line	6 over tricks (400 X 6)	2,400
	2nd game of 2-Game Rubber	*350
	All Honours	150
	Bonus for making redoubled contract	50
	(Highest Possible Positive Score)	**3,110**

In Practice, the full bonus of 700 points is awarded after the completion of the second winning game rather than 350 after each game.

243

Perfect deals The mathematical odds against dealing 13 cards of one suit are 158,753,389,899 to 1, while the odds against receiving a "perfect hand" consisting of all 13 spades are 635,013,559,599 to 1. The odds against each of the 4 players receiving a complete suit (a "perfect deal") are 2,235,197,406,895,366,368,301,559,999 to 1. Instances of this are reported frequently but the chances of it happening genuinely are extraordinarily remote—in fact if all the people in the world were grouped in bridge fours, and each four were dealt 120 hands a day, it would require 62×10^{12} years before one "perfect deal" should recur.

A "perfect" perfect deal with the dealer (South) with 13 clubs, round to East with 13 spades was the subject of affidavits by Mrs. E. F. Gyde (dealer), Mrs. Hennion, David Rex-Taylor and Mrs. P. Dawson at Richmond Community Centre, Surrey, on 25 Aug. 1964. This deal, 24 times more remote than a "perfect deal", the second of the rubber, was with a pack not used for the first deal. In view of the fact that there should be 31,201,794 deals with two perfect hands for each deal with four perfect hands and that reports of the latter far outnumber the former, it can be safely assumed that reported occurrences of perfect deals are almost without exception bogus.

Longest session The longest recorded session is one of 180 hours b students at Edinburgh University on 21-28 A 1972.

Most master points In 1971 a new system of Master Points was institut The leading male player in the world was Gior Belladonna (Italy), a member of the Blue team w 1,183 points, followed by six more Italians. T leading Briton was Terence Reese in 16th place w 323 points. The world's leading woman player w Mrs Rixi Markus (G.B.) with 195 points. Britain ha more in the Top Ten.

WHIST

Whist, first referred to in 1529, was the worl premier card game until 1930. The rules we standardized in 1742.

Highest Score No collated records exist but the highest sco notified to the editors have been:- for 24 hands—1 tricks by Mrs. Kathleen Morton of Solihull, Warwi shire in March 1971 and for 32 hands—260 tricks Mrs. Adelaide Stiles at Blagdon, Somerset on 24 N 1971.

Collection of Jokers The largest reported collection of jokers (term fi used in 1885) is one of 1,200 different examples fro 8 countries amassed by Derek Haddon of Willenha Warwickshire.

CAVING

Duration (trogging) The endurance record for staying in a cave is 463 days by Milutin Veljkovič (b. 1935) (Yugoslavia) in the Samar Cavern, Svrljig Mountains, northern Yugo-

slavia from 24 June 1969 to 30 Sept. 1970. T British record is 130 days by David Lafferty, aged of Hampstead, who stayed in Boulder Chamb Gough's Cave, Cheddar Gorge, Somerset, from March to 4 Aug. 1966. He was alone until 1 A when he thought it was 7 July.

PROGRESSIVE WORLD DEPTH RECORDS

Feet	Cave	Cavers	Date	
210	Lamb Lair, near West Harptree, Somerset	John Beaumont (explored)	c. 16	
454	Macocha, Moravia	Joseph Nagel	May	17
742	Grotta di Padriciano, Trieste	Antonio Lindner, Svetina		18
1,079	Grotta di Trebiciano, Trieste	Antonio Lindner	6 April	18
1,293	Nidlenloch, Switzerland	—		19
1,433	Geldloch, Austria	—		19
1,476	Abisso Bertarelli, Yugoslavia	R. Battelini, G. Cesca	24 Aug.	19
1,491	Spluga della Preta, Venezia, Italy	*L.de Battisti	18 Sept.	19
1,775	Antro di Corchia, Tuscany, Italy	E. Fiorentino Club		19
1,980	Trou de Glaz, Isère, France	F. Petzl, C. Petit-Didier	4 May	19
2,389	Gouffre de la Pierre Saint Martin, Basses-Pyrénées, France	*Georges Lépineux	15 Aug.	19
2,428	Gouffre Berger, Sornin Plateau, Vercors, France	J. Cadoux, G. Garby	11 Sept.	19
2,963	Gouffre Berger, Sornin Plateau, Vercors, France	*F. Petzl and 6 men	25 Sept.	19
3,230	Gouffre Berger, Sornin Plateau, Vercors, France	L. Potié, G Garby *et al*	29 July	19
>3,600	Gouffre Berger, Sornin Plateau, Vercors, France	Jean Cadoux and 2 others	11 Aug.	19
>3,600	Gouffre Berger, Sornin Plateau, Vercors, France	*Frank Salt and 7 others	23 Aug.	19
>3,700	Gouffre Berger, Sornin Plateau, Vercors, France	Kenneth Pearce	4 Aug.	19
3,799	Gouffre de la Pierre Saint Martin, Basses-Pyrénées, France	C. Queffélec and 3 others	Aug.	19
3,872	Gouffre de la Pierre Saint Martin, Basses-Pyrénées, France	C. Queffélec and 10 others	Aug.	19
4,300	Gouffre de la Pierre Saint Martin, Basses-Pyrénées, France	Ass. de Rech. Spéléo Internant.	8–11 Nov.	19

*Leader

WORLD'S DEEPEST CAVES

According to the latest available revised measurements, the deepest caves in the world are:-

Feet	Cave	Location
4,300	Gouffre de la Pierre Saint Martin	Basses-Pyrénées, France/Spain
3,750	Gouffre Berger	Sornin Plateau, Vercors, France
3,051	Réseau Trombe	Pyrénées, Haute-Garonne, France
2,872	Spluga della Preta	Lessinische Alps, Italy
2,641	Antro di Corchia	Apuanian Alps, Italy
2,573	Grotta del Monte Cucco	Perugia, Italy

NOTE: *The Provetina Cave, Greece has the world's longest vertical pitch of 1,298 feet. The highest known cave entrance in the world is that of the Rakhiot Cave, Nanga Parbat, Kashmir at 21,860 feet.*

Bobby Fischer J.S.A.) the greatest ster of the 10¹¹⁵ variations of a game of chess.

CHESS

Origins The name chess is derived from the Persian word *shah* (a king or ruler). It is a descendant of the game *Chaturanga*. The earliest reference is from the Middle Persian Karnamak (*c.* A.D. 590-628), though there are grounds for believing its origins are from the 4th century in north west India. It reached Britain in *c.* 1255. The *Fédération Internationale des Échecs* was established in 1924. There were an estimated 7,000,000 competitive players in the U.S.S.R. in 1972.

World champions World champions have been generally recognized since 1886. The longest tenure was 27 years by Dr. Emanuel Lasker (1868-1941) of Germany, from 1894 to 1921. The women's world championship has been most often won by Nona Gaprindashvili (U.S.S.R.) in 1963-66-69-72. Robert J Fischer (b. Chicago, U.S.A. 9 Mar. 1943) is reckoned on the officially adopted Elo System to be the greatest Grandmaster of all-time. He has an I.Q. of 187 and became at 15 the youngest International Grand Master.

itish titles Most British titles have been won by Dr. Jonathan Penrose, O.B.E. (b. 1934) of East Finchley, London with 10 titles in 1958-63, 1966-69. Mrs. Rowena M. Bruce (b. 1919) of Plymouth won 8 titles in 1950-51-54-55 (shared)-59-60-63-66.

Longest games The most protracted chess match on record was one drawn on the 191st move between H. Pilnik (Argentina) and Moshe Czerniak (Israel) at Mar del Plata, Argentina, in April 1950. The total playing time was 20 hours. A game of 21½ hours, but drawn on the 171st move (average over 7½ minutes per move), was played between Makagonov and Chekover at Baku, U.S.S.R., in 1945. A game of 221 moves between Arthur Williams (G.B.) and Kenneth Rogoff (U.S.A.) occurred at Stockholm, Sweden in August 1969 but required only 4 hours 25 minutes.

Marathon The longest recorded session is one of 101 hours between John P. Cameron and Jon Stevens at Ipswich Civic College, Suffolk, England, on 21-25 March 1970. The longest game at "lightning chess" (*i.e.* all moves completed by a player in five minutes) is 60 hours 1 minute by David Freeman and Phillip Luckett of Surrey, England on 29-31 March 1972 with no breaks longer than 3 minutes. At Otago University, New Zealand, Grant Kerr, 20 and Aldis Skuja, 21, played for 73 hours 6 minutes (520 games) against a succession of opponents on 1-4 Aug. 1969.

Slowest Lawrence Grant and Dr. J. Munro MacLennan, the latter now in Sydney, New South Wales, Australia, are still playing a match begun at Aberdeen University on 24 Nov. 1926. They make one move each time they correspond which is most often by an annual Christmas card.

Most opponents Records by chess masters for numbers of opponents tackled simultaneously depend very much on whether or not the opponents are replaced as defeated, are in relays, or whether they are taken on in a simultaneous start. The greatest number tackled on a replacement basis is 400 (379 defeated) by the Swedish master Gideon Ståhlberg (died 26 May 1967) in 36 hours of play in Buenos Aires, Argentina, in 1940. Georges Koltanowski (Belgium, now of U.S.A.) tackled 56 opponents "blindfold" and won 50, drew 6, lost 0 in 9¾ hours at Fairmont Hotel, San Francisco, California, U.S.A., on 13 Dec. 1960.

COURSING

Origins The sport of dogs chasing hares was probably of Egyptian origin in *c.* 3000 B.C. and brought to England by the Normans in 1067. The classic event is the annual Waterloo Cup, instituted at Altcar, near Liverpool, in 1836. A government bill to declare the sport illegal was "lost" owing to the dissolution of Parliament on 29 May 1970.

Most successful dog The most successful Waterloo Cup dog recorded was Colonel North's *Fullerton*, sired by *Greentich*, who tied for first in 1889 and then won outright in 1890-91-92.

The only dogs to win the Victorian Waterloo Cup (instituted 1873) three times have been *Bulwark* in 1906-07-09, at which time it was known as the Australian Waterloo Cup, and *Byamee* in 1953-54-55.

Longest course The longest authenticated course is one of 4 minutes 10 seconds, when Major C. Blundell's *Blackmore* beat *Boldon* in a Barbican Cup decider on 2 March 1934.

CRICKET

Earliest match The earliest evidence of the game of cricket is from a drawing depicting two men playing with a bat and ball dated *c.* 1250. The game was played in Guildford, Surrey, at least as early as 1550. The earliest major match of which the score survives was one in which a team representing England (40 and 70) was beaten by Kent (53 and 58 for 9) by one wicket at the Artillery Ground in Finsbury, London, on 18 June 1744. Cricket was played in Australia as early as 1803.

BATTING

Highest innings The highest recorded innings by any team was one of 1,107 runs by Victoria against New South Wales in an Australian inter-State match at Melbourne, Victoria, on 27-28 Dec. 1926.

England The highest innings made in England is 903 runs for 7 wickets declared, by England in the 5th Test against Australia at the Oval, London, on 20, 22 and 23 Aug. 1938. The highest innings in a county championship match is 887 by Yorkshire *versus* Warwickshire at Edgbaston on 7-8 May 1896.

Lowest The lowest recorded innings is 12 made by Oxford University *v.* the Marylebone Cricket Club (M.C.C.) at Oxford on 24 May 1877, and 12 by Northamptonshire *v.* Gloucestershire at Gloucester on 11 June 1907. On the occasion of the Oxford match, however,

PGH Fender hitter of the fastest ever century in 35 minutes in 1920.

the University batted a man short. The lowest score in a Test match is 26 by New Zealand *v.* England in the 2nd Test at Auckland on 28 March 1955.

The lowest aggregate for two innings is 34 (16 in first and 18 in second) by Border *v.* Natal in the South African Currie Cup at East London on 19 and 21 Dec.1959.

Greatest victory The greatest recorded margin of victory is an innings and 851 runs, when Pakistan Railways (910 for 6 wickets declared) beat Dera Ismail Khan (32 and 27) at Lahore on 2-4 Dec. 1964. The largest margin in England is one of an innings and 579 runs by England over Australia in the 5th Test at the Oval on 20-24 Aug. 1938 when Australia scored 201 and 123 with two men short in both innings. The most one-sided county match was when Surrey (698) defeated Sussex (114 and 99) by an innings and 485 runs at the Oval on 9-11 Aug. 1888.

FASTEST SCORING
The greatest number of runs scored in a day is 721 all out (10 wickets) in 6 hours by the Australians *v.* Essex at Southchurch Park, Southend-on-Sea on the first day on 15 May 1948.

The Test record for runs in a day is 588 at Old Trafford on 27 July 1936 when England put on 398 and India were 190 for 0 in their second innings by the close.

Innings of 200 or more The fastest recorded exhibition of hitting occurred in a Kent *v.* Gloucestershire match at Dover on 20 Aug. 1937, when Kent scored 219 runs for 2 wickets in 71 minutes, at the rate of 156 runs for each 100 balls bowled.

Fastest 50 The fastest 50 ever hit was completed in 8 minutes (1.22 to 1.30 p.m.) and in 11 scoring strokes by Clive C. Inman (b. Colombo, Ceylon, 29 Jan. 1936) in an innings of 57 not out for Leicestershire *v.* Nottinghamshire at Trent Bridge, Nottingham on 20 Aug. 1965.

Century The fastest century ever hit was completed in 35 minutes by Percy George Herbert Fender (b. 22 Aug. 1892), when scoring 113 not out for Surrey *v.* Northamptonshire at Northampton on 26 Aug. 1920. The most prolific scorer of centuries in an hour or less was Gilbert Laird Jessop (1874-1955), with 11 between 1897 and 1913. The fastest Test century was one of 70 minutes by Jack Morrison Gregory (b. 14 Aug. 1895) of New South Wales, for Australia *v.* South Africa in the 2nd Test at Johannesburg on 12 Nov. 1921. Edwin Boaler Alletson (1884-1963) scored 189 runs in 90 minutes for Nottinghamshire *v.* Sussex at Hove on 20 May 1911.

246

Double century The fastest double century was completed in minutes by Gilbert Jessop, (1874-1955) (286) Gloucestershire *v.* Sussex at Hove on 1 June 1903.

Treble century The fastest treble century was completed in minutes by Denis Charles Scott Compton, C.B (b. Hendon, 23 May 1918) of Middlesex, who sco 300 for the M.C.C. *v.* North-Eastern Transvaal Benoni on 3-4 Dec. 1948.

1,000 in May The most recent example of scoring 1,000 runs May was by Charles Hallows (Lancashire) (b. 4 A 1895), who made precisely 1,000 between 5-31 M 1928. Dr.W.G. Grace (9-30 May 1895) and W Hammond (7-31 May 1927) surpassed this feat w 1,016 and 1,042 runs. The greatest number of r made *before the end of May* was by T. W. Hayw with 1,074 from 16 April to 31 May in 1900.

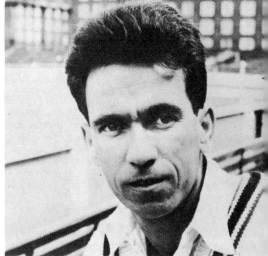

Clive Inman who scored the fastest ever 50 by 11 strokes in 9 minutes in 1965.

Slowest scoring The longest time a batsman has ever taken to open scoring is 1 hour 37 minutes by Thomas Godf Evans (b. Finchley, 18 Aug. 1920) of Kent, w scored 10 not out for England *v.* Australia in t 4th Test at Adelaide on 5-6 Feb. 1947. Richa Gorton Barlow (1850-1919) utilized 2½ hours score 5 not out for Lancashire *v.* Nottinghamshire Nottingham on 8 July 1882. During his innings score remained unchanged for 80 minutes.

The slowest century on record was by Derrick Jo (Jackie) McGlew (b 11 March 1929) of South Afri in the Third Test *v.* Australia at Durban on 25 a 27 Jan. 1958. He required 9 hours 35 minutes f 105, reaching the 100 in 9 hours 5 minutes. T slowest double century recorded is one of 10 hour minutes by Robert Baddeley Simpson (b. 3 Fe 1936) of New South Wales, during an innings of 31 lasting 12 hours 42 minutes, for Australia *v.* Engla in the Fourth Test at Old Trafford on 23, 24 a 25 July 1964.

Highest individual innings The highest individual innings recorded is 499 in hours 40 minutes by Hanif Muhammad (b. Junagad Pakistan, 21 Dec. 1934) for Karachi *v.* Bahawalpur Karachi, Pakistan, on 8, 9 and 11 Jan. 1959. T record for a Test match is 365 not out in 10 hours minutes by Garfield St. Aubrun Sobers (b. Barbado 28 July 1936) playing for the West Indies in the Thi Test against Pakistan at Sabina Park, Kingsto Jamaica, on 27 Feb.-1 March 1958. The England Te record is 364 by Sir Leonard Hutton (b. Fulnec Pudsey, Yorkshire, 23 June 1916) *v.* Australia in t 5th Test at the Oval on 20, 22 and 23 Aug. 1938. T highest score in England is 424 in 7 hours 50 minut by Archibald Campbell MacLaren (1871-1944) f Lancashire *v.* Somerset at Taunton on 15-16 Ju 1895.

Longest innings
The longest innings on record is one of 16 hours 39 minutes for 337 runs by Hanif Muhammad (Pakistan) v. the West Indies in the 1st Test at Bridgetown, Barbados, on 20-23 Jan. 1958. The English record is 13 hours 17 minutes by Hutton (see above).

Least runs in a career
S. Clarke, the Somerset wicket-keeper, played five matches for his county in 1930, scoring no runs in each of his nine innings of which 7 were ducks.

Most runs off an over
The first batsman to score the possible of 36 runs off a six-ball over was Garfield Sobers (Nottingham) off Malcolm Andrew Nash (Glamorgan) at Swansea on 31 Aug. 1968. The ball (recovered from the last hit from the road by a small boy) resides in Nottingham's Museum.

BIGGEST SCORERS

Season
The greatest number of runs ever scored in a season is 3,816 in 50 innings (8 not out) by Denis Compton (Middlesex) in 1947. His batting average was 90.85.

Most runs in a career
The greatest aggregate of runs in a career is 61,237 in 1,315 innings (106 not out) between 1905 and 1934 by Sir John (Jack) Berry Hobbs (1882-1963) of Surrey and England. His career average was 50.65.

Test matches
The greatest number of runs scored in Test matches is 7,626 in 150 innings (20 not out) by Garfield St Aubrun Sobers (b. Bridgetown, Barbados, 28 July 1936) of Barbados and Nottingham playing for the West Indies since 1952-53 and 1972. His average is 58.66.

CENTURIES

Season
The record for the greatest number of centuries in a season is also held by Compton with eighteen in 1947. With their restricted fixture list the Australian record is eight by Sir Donald George Bradman (b. 27 Aug. 1908) in only 12 innings in the 1947-48 season.

Career
The most centuries in a career is 197 by Sir John Hobbs between 1905 and 1934. The Australian record is Sir Donald Bradman's 117 centuries between 1927 and 1949.

Test matches
The greatest number of centuries scored in Test matches is 29 by Sir Donald Bradman (Australia) between 1928 and 1948. The English record is 22 by Walter Hammond (1903-65) of Gloucestershire, between 1927 and 1947, and 22 by Colin Cowdrey (Kent) between 1954-55 and 1971.

Highest averages
The highest recorded seasonal batting average in England is 115.66 for 26 innings (2,429 runs) by Don Bradman (Australia) in England in 1938. The English record is 96.96 by Herbert Sutcliffe (b. 24 Nov. 1894) of Yorkshire, for 42 innings (3,006 runs) in 1931. The world record for a complete career is 95.14 for 338 innings (28,067 runs) by Bradman between 1927 and 1949. The record for Test matches is 99.94 in 80 innings (6,996 runs) by Bradman in 1928-48. The English career record is 56.37 for 500 innings (62 not out) by Kumar Shri Ranjitsinhji (1872-1933), later H.H. the Jam Saheb of Nawanagar, with 24,692 runs between 1893 and 1920.

Double centuries
The only batsman to score double centuries in both innings is Arthur Edward Fagg (b. 18 June 1915), who made 244 and 202 not out for Kent v. Essex at Colchester on 13-15 July 1938.

Longest hit
The longest measured drive is one of 175 yards by Walter (later the Rev.) Fellows (1834-1901) of Christ Church, Oxford University, in a practice on their ground, off Charles Rogers in 1856. J. E. C. Moore made a measured hit of 170 yards 1 foot 5 inches at Griffith, New South Wales, Australia, in February 1930. Peter Samuel Heine (b. 28 June 1929) of the Orange Free State is said to have driven a ball bowled by Hugh Joseph Tayfield (b. 30 Jan. 1929) of Natal for approximately 180 yards at Bloemfontein on 3 Jan. 1955.

Most sixes in an innings
The highest number of sixes hit in an innings is 15 by John Richard Reid, O.B.E. (b. 3 June 1928), in an innings of 296, lasting 3 hours 47 minutes, for Wellington v. Northern Districts in the Plunket Shield Tournament at Wellington, New Zealand, on 14-15 Jan. 1963. The Test record is 10 by Walter Hammond in an innings of 336 not out for England v. New Zealand at Auckland on 31 March and 1 April 1933.

Most sixes in a match
The highest number of sixes in a match is 17 (10 in the first and 7 in the second innings) by William James Stewart (b. 31 Aug. 1934) for Warwickshire v. Lancashire at Blackpool on 29-31 July 1959. His two innings were of 155 and 125.

Most boundaries in an innings
The highest number of boundaries in an innings was 68 (all in fours) by Percival Albert Perrin (1876-1945) in an innings of 343 not out for Essex v. Derbyshire at Chesterfield on 18-19 July 1904.

Most runs off a ball
The most runs scored off a single hit is 10 by Samuel Hill Hill-Wood (1872-1949) off Cuthbert James Burnup (1875-1960) in the Derbyshire v. M.C.C. match at Lord's, London, on 26 May 1900.

GREATEST PARTNERSHIP

World
The record stand for any partnership is the fourth wicket stand of 577 by Gul Muhammad (b. 15 Oct. 1921), who scored 319, and Vijay Samuel Hazare (b. 11 March 1915) (288) in the Baroda v. Holkar match at Baroda, India, on 8-10 March 1947.

England
The highest stand in English cricket, and the world record for a first wicket partnership, is 555 by Percy Holmes (1886-1971) (224 not out) and Herbert Sutcliffe (313) for Yorkshire v. Essex at Leyton on 15-16 June 1932.

Highest score by a No. 11
The highest score by a No. 11 batsman is 163 by Thomas Peter Bromly Smith (1908-67) for Essex v. Derbyshire at Chesterfield in August 1947.

BOWLING

Most wickets
The largest number of wickets ever taken in a season is 304 by Alfred Percy ("Tich") Freeman (1888-1965) of Kent, in 1928. Freeman bowled 1,976.1 overs, of which 423 were maidens, with an average of 18.05 runs per wicket. The greatest wicket-taker in history is Wilfred Rhodes (b. Kirkheaton, Yorkshire, 29 Oct. 1877), who took 4,187 wickets for 69,993 runs (average 16.71 runs per wicket) between 1898 and 1930.

Tests
The greatest number of wickets taken in Test matches is 307 for 6,625 runs (average 21.57) by Frederick Sewards Trueman (b. Scotch Springs, Yorkshire, 6 Feb. 1931), in 67 Tests between June 1952 and June 1965. The lowest bowling average in a Test career (minimum 15 wickets) is 61 wickets for 775 runs (12.70 runs per wicket) by John James Ferris (1867-1900) in 9 Tests (8 for Australia and 1 for England) between 1886 and 1892.

Fastest
The highest measured speed for a ball bowled by any bowler is 93 m.p.h. by Harold Larwood (b. Nuncargate, Notts., 14 Nov. 1904) in 1933. The fastest bowler of all time is regarded by many as Charles Jesse Kortright (1871-1952), who played for Essex from 1889 to 1907. Albert Cotter (1883-1917) of New South Wales, Australia, is reputed to have broken a stump more than 20 times. Wesley Winfield Hall (b. 12 Sept. 1937) of Barbados was timed to bowl at 91 m.p.h. in practice in 1962-63, when playing for Queensland, Australia.

Most consecutive wickets No bowler in first class cricket has yet achieved five wickets with five consecutive balls. The nearest approach was that of Charles Warrington Leonard Parker (1884-1959) (Gloucestershire) in his own benefit match against Yorkshire at Bristol on 10 Aug. 1922, when he struck the stumps with five successive balls but the second was called as a no-ball. The only man to have taken 4 wickets with consecutive balls more than once is Robert James Crisp (b. 28 May 1911) for Western Province v. Griqualand West at Johannesburg on 23-24 Dec. 1931 and against Natal at Durban on 3 March 1934.

Most "hat tricks" The greatest number of "hat tricks" is seven by Douglas Vivian Parson Wright (b. 21 Sept. 1914) on 3 and 29 July, 1937, 18 May 1938, 13 Jan. and 1 July 1939, 11 Aug. 1947 and 1 Aug. 1949. In his own benefit match at Lord's on 22 May 1907, Albert Edwin Trott (Middlesex) took four Somerset wickets with four consecutive balls and then later in the same innings achieved a "hat trick".

Most wickets in an innings The taking of all ten wickets by a single bowler has been recorded many times but only one bowler has achieved this feat on three occasions—Alfred Percy Freeman of Kent, against Lancashire at Maidstone on 24 July 1929, against Essex at Southend on 13-14 Aug. 1930 and against Lancashire at Old Trafford on 27 May 1931. The fewest runs scored off a bowler taking all 10 wickets is 10, when Hedley Verity (1905-43) of Yorkshire dismissed (8 caught, 1 l.b.w., 1 stumped) every Nottinghamshire batsman in 118 balls at Leeds on 12 July 1932. The only bowler to have "cleaned bowled" a whole side out was John Wisden (1826-84) of Sussex, playing for the North v. the South at Lord's in 1850.

Most wickets in a match James Charles Laker (b. Frizinghall, Yorkshire, 9 Feb. 1922) of Surrey took 19 wickets for 90 runs (9-37 and 10-53) for England v. Australia in the 4th Test at Old Trafford on 26-31 July 1956. No other bowler has taken more than 17 wickets in a first class match. Henry Arkwright (1837-66) took 18 wickets for 96 runs in a 12-a-side match, M.C.C. v. Gentlemen of Kent, at Canterbury on 14-17 Aug. 1861. Alfred Percy Freeman (Kent) took ten or more wickets in a match on 140 occasions between 1914 and 1936.

Most wickets in a day The greatest number of wickets taken in a day's play is 17 by Colin Blythe (1879-1917) for 48 runs, for Kent against Northamptonshire at Northampton on 1 June 1907; by Hedley Verity for 91 runs, for Yorkshire v. Essex at Leyton on 14 July 1933; and by Thomas William John Goddard (1900-66) for 106 runs, for Gloucestershire v. Kent at Bristol on 3 July 1939.

Most expensive bowling The greatest number of runs hit off one bowler in one innings is 362, scored off Arthur Alfred Mailey (b. 3 Jan. 1888) in the New South Wales v. Victoria inter-State match at Melbourne on 24-28 Dec. 1926. The greatest number of runs ever conceded by a bowler in one match is 428 by C. S. Nayudu in the Holkar v. Bombay match at Bombay on 4-9 March 1945, when he also made the record number of 917 deliveries.

Most maidens Hugh Joseph Tayfield bowled 16 consecutive 8-ball maiden overs (137 balls without conceding a run) for South Africa v. England at Durban on 25-27 Jan. 1957. The greatest number of consecutive 6-ball maiden overs bowled is 21 (130 balls) by Ragunath G. ("Bapu") Nadkarni (b. 4 April 1932) for India v. England at Madras on 12 Jan. 1964. The English record is 17 overs (105 balls) by Horace L. Hazell (b. 30 Sept. 1909) for Somerset v. Gloucestershire at Taunton on 4 June 1949, and 17 (104 balls) by Graham Anthony (Tony) Richard Lock (b. 5 July 1929) of Surrey, playing for the M.C.C. v. the Governor-General's XI at Karachi, Pakistan, on 31 Dec. 1955. Alfred Shaw (1842-1907) of Nottinghamshire bowled 23 consecutive 4-ball maiden overs (92 balls) for North v. the South at Nottingham in 1876.

Most balls The greatest number of balls sent down by any bowler in one season is 12,234 (651 maidens: 298 wickets) by Alfred Percy Freeman (Kent) in 1933. The most balls bowled in an innings is 588 (98 overs) by Sonny Ramadhin (b. 1 May 1930) of Trinidad, playing for the West Indies in the First Test v. England at Birmingham on 30 May and 1, 3 and 4 June 1957. He took 2 for 179.

Best average The lowest recorded bowling average for a season is one of 8.61 runs per wicket (177 wickets for 1,52- runs) by Alfred Shaw of Nottinghamshire in 1880.

FIELDING

Most catches in an innings The greatest number of catches in an innings is seven by Michael James Stewart (b. 16 Sept. 1932) for Surrey v. Northamptonshire at Northampton on 7 June 1957, and by Anthony Stephen Brown (b. 24 June 1936) for Gloucestershire v. Nottinghamshire at Trent Bridge on 26 July 1966.

In a match Walter Reginald Hammond (1903-65) held a record total of 10 catches (4 in the first innings, 6 in the second) for Gloucestershire v. Surrey at Cheltenham on 16-17 Aug. 1928. The record for a wicket-keeper is 11.

In a season and in a career The greatest number of catches in a season is 78 by Walter Hammond (Gloucestershire) in 1928, and 7- by Michael James Stewart (Surrey) in 1957. The most catches in a career is 1,011 by Frank Edward Woolley (b. 27 May 1887) of Kent in 1906-1938. The Test record is 117 by Michael Colin Cowdrey between 1954-55 and 1971.

Longest throw The longest recorded throw of a cricket ball (5½ oz) is 140 yards 2 feet (422 feet) by R. Percival at Durham Sands Racecourse on Easter Monday, 14 April 1884.

WICKET-KEEPING

In an innings The most dismissals by a wicket-keeper in an innings is eight (all caught) by Arthur Theodore Wallace Grout (1927-68) for Queensland against Western Australia at Brisbane on 15 Feb. 1960. The Test record is six (all caught) by A. T. W. Grout (see above) for the First Australia v. South Africa Test at Johannesburg on 27-28 Dec. 1957; six (all caught) by Denis Lindsay (b. 4 Sept. 1939) of North-Eastern Transvaal, for South Africa v. Australia in the First Test at Johannesburg on 24 Dec. 1966; six (all caught) by John Thomas Murray (b. 1 April 1935) of Middlesex, for England v. India in the second Test at Lord's, London on 22 June 1967.

In a match The greatest number of dismissals by a wicket-keeper in a match is 12 by Edward Pooley (1838-1907) (eight caught, four stumped) for Surrey v. Sussex at the Oval on 6-7 July 1868; nine caught, three stumped by Don Tallon (b. 17 Feb. 1916) of Australia for Queensland v. New South Wales at Sydney on 2-4 Jan. 1939; and also nine caught, three stumped by Hedley Brian Taber (b. 29 April 1940) of New South Wales against South Australia at Adelaide 17-19 Dec. 1968. The record for catches is 11 (seven in the first innings and four in the second) by Arnold Long (b. 18 Dec. 1940), for Surrey v. Sussex at Hove on 18 and 21 July 1964. The Test record for dismissals is 9 (eight caught, one stumped) by Gilbert Roch Andrews Langley of South Australia, playing for Australia v. England in the 2nd Test at Lord's, London, on 22-26 June 1956.

In a season The record number of dismissals for any wicket keeper in a season is 127 (79 caught, 48 stumped) by Leslie Ethelbert George Ames (b. 3 Dec. 1905) of Kent in 1929. The record for the number stumped is 64 by Ames in 1932. The record for catches is 96 by James Graham Binks (b. 5 Oct. 1935) of Yorkshire in 1960.

In a career The highest total of dismissals in a wicket-keeping career is 1,468 (a record 1,215 catches, plus 253 stumpings) by Herbert Strudwick (1880-1970) of Surrey between 1902 and 1927. The most stumpings in a career is 415 by Ames (1926-1951). The Test record is 219 in 91 innings by Godfrey Evans.

Least byes The best wicket-keeping record for preventing byes is that of Archdale Palmer Wickham (1855-1935) when, keeping for Somerset v. Hampshire at Taunton on 20-22 July 1899, he did not concede a single bye in a total of 672 runs. The record for Test matches is no byes in 659 runs by Godfrey Evans for England in the 2nd Test v. Australia at Sydney, New South Wales, on 14, 16, 17 and 18 Dec. 1946.

Most byes The records at the other extreme are those of Philip Harman Stewart-Brown (b. 30 April 1904) of Harlequins, who let through 46 byes in an Oxford University innings of only 188 on 21-23 May 1927 and 48 byes let through by Anthony William Catt of Kent in a Northamptonshire total of 374 at Northampton on 20-22 Aug. 1955.

ENGLISH COUNTY CHAMPIONSHIP
The greatest number of victories has been secured by Yorkshire, with 29 outright wins up to 1968, and one shared with Middlesex in 1949. They have never been lower than 13th (1969 and 1971) on the table. The most "wooden spoons" have been won by Northamptonshire, with ten since 1923. They did not win a single match between May 1935 and May 1939. The record number of consecutive title wins is 7 by Surrey from 1952 to 1958. The greatest number of consecutive appearances for one county is 421 by Joe Vine (1875-1946) of Sussex.

Oldest and youngest county cricketers The youngest player to represent his county was William Wade Fitzherbert Pullen (1866-1937), for Gloucestershire against Middlesex at Lord's on 5 June 1882, when aged 15 years 346 days. The oldest regular County players have been William George Quaife (1872-1951) of Sussex and Warwickshire, who played his last match for Warwickshire against Hampshire at Portsmouth on 27-30 Aug. 1927, when aged 55, and John Herbert King (1871-1946) of Leicestershire, who played his last match for his county against Yorkshire at Leicester on 5-7 Aug. 1925, when aged 54.

Largest crowds The greatest recorded attendance at a cricket match is 350,534 (receipts £30,124) for the Third Test between Australia and England at Melbourne on 1-7 Jan. 1937. For the whole series the figure was a record 933,513 (receipts £87,963). The greatest recorded attendance at a cricket match on one day was 90,800 on the second day of the Fifth Test between Australia and the West Indies at Melbourne on 11 Feb. 1961, when the receipts were £A13,132 (£10,484 sterling). The English record is 159,000 for the Fourth Test between England and Australia at Headingley, Leeds, on 22-27 July 1948, and the record for one day probably a capacity of 46,000 for a match between Lancashire and Yorkshire at Old Trafford on 2 Aug. 1926. The English record for a Test series is 549,650 (receipts £200,428) for the series against Australia in 1953.

Greatest receipts The world record for receipts from a match is £72,882, from the attendance paid by 91,149 at the Second Test between England and Australia at Lord's, London, on 20-25 June 1968. The Test series record is £245,286 paid by 298,631 for the five

England v. Australia Tests of June-August 1968.

Highest benefit The highest "benefit" ever accorded a player is £14,000 for Cyril Washbrook (b. 6 Dec. 1914) in the Lancashire v. Australians match at Old Trafford on 7-10 Aug. 1948.

Most Test appearances The record number of Test appearances is 109 by Michael Colin Cowdrey (England) between 1954-55 and 1971. The highest number of Test captaincies is 41, including 35 consecutive games, by Peter Barker Howard May (b. 31 Dec. 1929) of Cambridge University and Surrey, who captained England from 1955 to 1961 and played in a total of 66 Tests. The most innings batted in Test matches is 179 in 109 Tests by Cowdrey of Kent, playing for England between 1954-55 and 1971. Garfield Sobers (West Indies) holds the record for consecutive Tests, with 80 from April 1955 to April 1971.

Longest match The lengthiest recorded cricket match was the "timeless" Test between England and South Africa at Durban on 3-14 March 1939. It was abandoned after 10 days (8th day rained off) because the boat taking the England team home was due to leave. The lengthiest in England was the 6-day 5th England v. Australia Test on 6-12 Aug. 1930, when rain prevented play on the fifth day.

MINOR CRICKET RECORDS
(where excelling those in First Class Cricket)

Bowling Stephen Fleming bowling for Marlborough College "A" XI, New Zealand v. Bohally Intermediate at Blenheim, New Zealand in Dec. 1967 took 9 wickets in 9 consecutive balls. In February 1931 in a schools match in South Africa Paul Hugo also took 9 wickets with 9 consecutive balls for Smithfield School v. Aliwal North.

Highest individual innings In a Junior House match between Clarke's House and North Town, at Clifton College, Bristol, 22-23-26-7-8 June 1899, A. E. J. Collins (b. India, 1886—k. Flanders, Nov. 1914) scored an unprecedented 628 not out in 6 hours 50 minutes, over five afternoons' batting, carrying his bat through the innings of 836. The scorer, E. W. Pegler, gave the score as "628—plus or minus 20, shall we say".

Fastest individual scoring S. K. Coen (South Africa) scored 50 runs (11 fours and 1 six) in 7 minutes for Gezira v. the R.A.F. in 1942, compared with the First Class record of 8 minutes. Cecil George Pepper hit a century in 24 minutes in a Services match in Palestine in 1943. Cedric Ivan James Smith hit 9 successive sixes for a Middlesex XI v. Harrow and District at Rayners' Lane, Harrow, in 1935. This feat was repeated by Arthur Dudley Nourse, Jr. in a South African XI v. Military Police match at Cairo in 1942-43. Nourse's feat included six sixes in one over.

Highest scoring rate In the match Royal Naval College, Dartmouth v. Seale Hayne Agricultural College in 1923, K. A. Sellar (now Cdr. "Monkey" Sellar, D.S.O., D.S.C., R.N.) and L. K. A. Block (now Judge Block, D.S.C.) were set to score 174 runs in 105 minutes but achieved this total in 33 minutes, so averaging 5.27 runs per minute.

Lowest score There are at least 60 recorded instances of sides being dismissed for 0. A recent instance was in July 1970 when, in a 2nd XI House match at Brentwood School, West dismissed North for 0 with 13 balls.

Greatest stand T. Patten and N. Rippon made a third wicket stand of 641 for Buffalo v. Whorouly at Gapsted, Victoria, Australia, on 19 March 1914.

Wicket-keeping In a Repton School match for Priory v. Mitre, H. W. P. Middleton caught one and stumped eight batsmen in one innings on 10 July 1930.

John Solomon holder of the record number of wins in the Open Croquet championship

CROQUET

Earliest references Croquet, in its present-day form, originated as a country-house lawn game in Ireland in 1852.

Most championships The greatest number of victories in the Open Croquet Championships (instituted at Evesham, Worcestershire, 1867) is ten by John William Solomon (b. 1932) (1953, 1956, 1959, 1961, 1963 to 68). He has also won the Men's Championship on 9 occasions (1951, 1953, 1958 to 60, 1962, 1964-65 and 1971), the Open Doubles (with E. Patrick C. Cotter) on 10 occasions (1954-55, 1958-59, 1961 to 65 and 1969) and the Mixed Doubles once (with Mrs. N. Oddie) in 1954, making a total of 30 titles. Solomon has also won the President's Cup on 8 occasions (1955, 1957 to 59, 1962 to 64 and 1968). He has also been Champion of Champions on all four occasions that this competition was run (1967-70).

Miss Dorothy D. Steel, fifteen times winner of the Women's Championship (1919 to 39), won the Open Croquet Championship four times (1925, 1933, 1935-36). She had also five Doubles and seven Mixed Doubles titles making a total of 31 titles.

Lowest handicap The lowest playing handicap has been that of Humphrey O. Hicks (Devon) with minus 5½. In 1964 the limit was fixed at minus 5, which handicap is held by J. W. Solomon, E. Patrick C. Cotter, H. O. Hicks, G. Nigel Aspinall, Keith F. Wylie, Dr. William P. Ormerod and Dr. Roger W. Bray.

Largest club The largest number of courts at any one club is eleven, at the Sussex County (Brighton) Croquet and Lawn Tennis Club.

CROSS-COUNTRY RUNNING

International championships The earliest recorded international cross-country race took place over 9 miles 20 yards from Ville d'Avray, outside Paris, on 20 March 1898, between England and France (England won by 21 points to 69). The inaugural International Cross-Country Championships took place at the Hamilton Park Racecourse, Glasgow, on 28 March 1903. The greatest margin of victory is 56 seconds or 390 yards by Jack T. Holden (England) at Ayre Racecourse, Scotland, on 24 March 1934. The narrowest win was that of Jean-Claude Fayolle (France) at Ostend, Belgium, on 20 March 1965, when the timekeepers were unable to separate his time from that of Melvyn Richard Batty (England), who was placed second.

The greatest team wins have been those of Engla with a minimum of 21 points (the first six runner finish) on two occasions, at Gosforth Park, Newca upon Tyne, Northumberland. on 22 March 1924, at the Hippodrome de Stockel, Brussels, Belgium, 20 March 1932.

Most wins The greatest number of victories in the Internatio Cross-Country Race is four by Jack Holden (Engla in 1933-34-35 and 1939, and four by Alain Mimo o-Kacha (France) in 1949, 1952, 1954 and 19 England have won 42 times to 1972.

Most appearances The runners of participating countries with the larg number of international championship appearan are:-

Belgium	20	M. Van de Wattyne, 1946-65
Wales	14	D. Phillips, 1922, 1924, 1926-37
England	12	J. T. Holden, 1929-39, 1946
Spain	12	A. L. Amoros, 1951-62
Scotland	11	D. McL. Wright, 1920-30
	11	J. C. Flockhart, 1933-39, 1946-4
France	11	A. Mimoun-o-Kacha, 1949-50, 19 1954, 1956, 1958-62, 1964

English championship The English Cross-Country Championship was in gurated at Roehampton, South London, in 1877. greatest number of individual titles achieved is f by P. H. Stenning (Thames Hare and Hounds) 1877-80 and Alfred E. Shrubb (1878-1964) (Sou London Harriers) in 1901-04. The most success club in the team race has been Birchfield Harri from Birmingham with 27 wins and one tie betwe 1880 and 1953.

Largest field The largest recorded field was one of 1,815 start (1,020 completed the course) at Gosforth Pa Newcastle upon Tyne in the summer of 1916. It v staged by the Northern Command of the Army a was won by Sapper G. Barber in 35 minutes seconds, by a margin of over 40 yards.

CURLING

Origins An early form of the sport is believed to h originated in the Netherlands about 450 years a The first club was formed at Kilsyth, near Glasgow 1510. Organized administration began in 1838 w the formation of the Royal Caledonian Curling Cl the international legislative body based in Edinbur The first indoor ice rink to introduce curling wa Southport in 1879.

The U.S.A. won the first Gordon International Me series of matches, between Canada and the U.S.A. Montreal in 1884. The first Strathcona Cup ma between Canada and Scotland was won by Canad 1903. Although demonstrated at the Winter Oly pics of 1924, 1932 and 1964, curling is not included in the official Olympic programme.

Most titles The most Strathcona Cup wins is seven by Can (1903-09-12-23-38-57-65) against Scotland. The ord for international team matches for the Sco Cup and Silver Broom (instituted 1959) is ten wins Canada, in 1959-60-61-62-63-64-66-68-69-70.

Marathon The longest recorded curling match is one of hours 12 mins. by the Stranraer Curling C at Stranraer Ice Rink, Wigtownshire, Scotland fr 30 Apr.-1 May 1972.

Largest rink The world's largest curling rink is the Big Four Curl Rink, Calgary, Alberta, Canada opened in 1959 cost of $Can2,250,000 (£867,050). Each of the t floors has 24 sheets of ice, accommodating 48 tea of 192 players.

CYCLING

Earliest race The earliest recorded bicycle race was a velocipede race over two kilometres (1.24 miles) at the Parc de St. Cloud, Paris, on 31 May 1868, won by James Moore (G.B.).

cycling Slow bicycling records came to a virtual end in 1965 when Tsugunobu Mitsuishi, aged 39, of Tōkyō, Japan stayed stationary for 5 hours 25 minutes.

Highest speed The highest speed ever achieved on a bicycle is 127.243 m.p.h. by Jose Meiffret (b. April 1913) of France, using a 275-inch gear behind a windshield on a racing car at Freiburg, West Germany, on 19 July 1962. Antonio Maspes (Italy) recorded an unofficial unpaced 10.8 secs. for 200 metres (42.21 m.p.h.) at Milan on 28 Aug. 1962.

The greatest distance ever covered in one hour is 76 miles 604 yards by Leon Vanderstuyft (Belgium) on the Montlhéry Motor Circuit, France, on 30 Sept. 1928. This was achieved from a standing start paced by a motorcycle. The 24-hour record behind pace is 860 miles 367 yards by Hubert Opperman in Australia in 1932.

st world titles The greatest number of world titles for a particular event won since the institution of the amateur championships in 1893 and the professional championships in 1895 are:-

Eddie Merckx (Belgium) who in 1972 equalled Jacques Anquetil's feat of winning the Tour de France in four consecutive years

Amateur Sprint	4	William J. Bailey (U.K.)	1909-10-11, 1913
	4	Daniel Morelon (France)	1966-67, 1969-70
Amateur 100 kms. Paced	7	Leon Meredith (U.K.)	1904-05, 1907-09, 1911, 1913
Amateur Road Race	2	Giuseppe Martano (Italy)	1930, 1932
	2	Gustave Schur (East Germany)	1958-59
Professional Sprint	7	Jeff Scherens (Belgium)	1932-37, 1947
	7	Antonio Maspes (Italy)	1955-56, 1959-62, 1964
Professional 100 kms. Paced	6	Guillermo Timoner (Spain)	1955, 1959-60, 1962, 1964-65
Professional Road Race	3	Alfredo Binda (Italy)	1927, 1930, 1932
	3	Henri (Rik) Van Steenbergen (Belgium)	1949, 1956-57
Women's titles	7	Beryl Burton (G.B.)	1959-60-62-63-66 (pursuits) 1960-67 (Road)
	7	Yvonne Reynders (Belgium)	1961-64-65 (pursuits) 1959-61-63-66 (Road)

WORLD RECORDS — OPEN AIR TRACKS
MEN
Professional unpaced standing start:

Distance	hrs. mins. secs.	Name and nationality	Place	Date	
1 km.	1 08.6	Reginald Hargreaves Harris O.B.E. (U.K.)	Milan	20 Oct.	1952
5 kms.	5 51.6	Ole Ritter (Denmark)	Mexico City	4 Oct.	1968
10 kms.	11 58.4	Ole Ritter (Denmark)	Mexico City	4 Oct.	1968
20 kms.	24 17.4	Ole Ritter (Denmark)	Mexico City	4 Oct.	1968
1 hour	30 miles 214 yards	Ole Ritter (Denmark)	Mexico City	10 Oct.	1968

Professional unpaced flying start:

200 metres	10.8	Antonio Maspes (Italy)	Rome	21 July	1960
500 metres	28.8	Marino Morettini (Italy)	Milan	29 Aug.	1955
1,000 metres	1 02.6	Marino Morettini (Italy)	Milan	26 July	1961

Professional motor-paced:

100 kms.	1 03 40.0	Walter Lohmann (W. Germany)	Wuppertal	24 Oct.	1955
1 hour	58 miles 737 yards	Walter Lohmann (W. Germany)	Wuppertal	24 Oct.	1955

Amateur unpaced standing start:

1 km.	1 02.4[4]	Pierre Trentin (France)	Zürich	15 Nov.	1970
4 kms.	4 37.5[4]	Mogens Frey (Denmark)	Mexico City	17 Oct.	1968
5 kms.	6 01.6	Mogens Frey (Denmark)	Mexico City	5 Oct.	1969
10 kms.	12 23.8	Mogens Frey (Denmark)	Mexico City	5 Oct.	1969
20 kms.	25 00.5	Mogens Frey (Denmark)	Mexico City	5 Oct.	1969
100 kms.	2 19 01.6	Ole Ritter (Denmark)	Rome	19 Sept.	1965
1 hour	29 miles 921 yards	Mogens Frey (Denmark)	Mexico City	5 Oct.	1969

Amateur unpaced flying start:

200 metres	10.61	Omari Phakadze (U.S.S.R.)	Mexico City	22 Oct.	1967
500 metres	27.85	Pierre Trentin (France)	Mexico City	21 Oct.	1967
1,000 metres	1	Luigi Borghetti (Italy)	Mexico City	21 Oct.	1967

251

WOMEN
Amateur unpaced standing start:

1 km.	1 15.1	Irena Kırıchenko (U.S.S.R.)	Yerevan	8 Oct.
3 kms.	4 01.7	Raisa Obdovskaya (U.S.S.R.)	Brno	20 Aug.
5 kms.	7 03.3	Nina Sadovaya (U.S.S.R.)	Irkutsk	2 July
10 kms.	14 27.0	Elsy Jacobs (Luxembourg)	Milan	9 Nov.
20 kms.	28 58.4	Mrs. Beryl Burton, O.B.E. (U.K.)	Milan	11 Oct.
100 kms.	2 44 57.0	Leena Turunen (Finland)	Helsinki	8 Sept.
1 hour	25 miles 1,207 yards	Elsy Jacobs (Luxembourg)	Milan	9 Nov.

Amateur unpaced flying start:

200 metres	12.3	Lyubov Razuvayeva (U.S.S.R.)	Irkutsk	17 July
500 metres	32.5	Irena Kirichenko (U.S.S.R.)	Irkutsk	
1,000 metres	1 10.6	Irena Kirichenko (U.S.S.R.)	Irkutsk	

COVERED TRACKS

MEN
Professional unpaced standing start:

1 km.	1 08.0	Reginald Hargreaves Harris (U.K.)	Zürich	19 July
5 kms.	6 05.6	Ferdinand Bracke (Belgium)	Brussels	5 Dec.
10 kms.	12 26.8	Roger Rivière (France)	Paris	19 Oct.
20 kms.	25 18.0	Siegfried Adler (W. Germany)	Zürich	2 Aug.
1 hour	29 miles 162 yards	Siegfried Adler (W. Germany)	Zürich	2 Aug.

Professional unpaced flying start:

200 metres	10.99	Oscar Plattner (Switzerland)	Zürich	1 Dec
500 metres	28.6	Oscar Plattner (Switzerland)	Zürich	17 Aug.
1,000 metres	1 01.23	Patrick Sercu (Belgium)	Antwerp	3 Feb.

Professional motor-paced:

100 kms.	1 23 59.8	Guillermo Timoner (Spain)	San Sebastian	12 Sept.
1 hour	46 miles 669 yards	Guy Solente (France)	Paris	13 Feb.

Amateur unpaced standing start:

1 km.	1 06.76	Patrick Sercu (Belgium)	Brussels	12 Dec.
5 kms.	6 06.0	Xavier Kurmann (Switzerland)	Zürich	28 Nov.
10 kms.	12 26.2	Xavier Kurmann (Switzerland)	Zürich	1 Dec.
20 kms.	25 14.6	Ole Ritter (Denmark)	Zürich	30 Oct.
1 hour	28 miles 575 yards	Alfred Ruegg (Switzerland)	Zürich	16 Nov.

Amateur unpaced flying start:

200 metres	10.72	Daniel Morelon (France)	Zürich	4 Nov.
500 metres	28.89	Pierre Trentin (France)	Zürich	4 Nov.
1,000 metres	1 02.44	Pierre Trentin (France)	Zürich	15 Nov.

WOMEN
Amateur unpaced standing start:

1,000 metres	1 15.5	Elizabeth Eichholz (Germany)	Berlin	4 Mar.

Amateur unpaced flying start:

200 metres	13.2	Karla Günther (Germany)	Berlin	7 Mar.
500 metres	35.0	Karla Günther (Germany)	Berlin	7 Mar.

Most British titles The greatest number of National individual track cycling championships secured by any male rider is 12 by Albert White (1920-25), ranging from the quarter mile to 25 miles. Beryl Burton (b. 12 May 1937) since 1958 won 40 R.T.T.C. 10 track and 10 r titles.

ROAD CYCLING RECORDS
(British) as recognized by the Road Time Trials Council (out-and-home records).

MEN

Distance	hrs. mins. secs.	Name	Course area	Date
25 miles				
30 miles	1 04 56	Dave Dungworth	Derby	10 June
50 miles	1 43 46	John Watson	Boroughbridge	23 Aug.
100 miles	3 46 37	Anthony Taylor	Boroughbridge	31 Aug.
12 hours	281.87 miles	John Watson	Blyth, Nottinghamshire	7 Sept.
24 hours	507.00 miles	Roy Cromack	Cheshire	26–27 July

WOMEN

Distance	hrs. mins. secs.	Name	Course area	Date
10 miles	22 06	Beryl Burton, O.B.E.	Barnet	24 June
25 miles	54 44	Beryl Burton, O.B.E.	Boroughbridge	22 July
30 miles	1 12 20	Beryl Burton, O.B.E.	St. Neots	3 May
50 miles	1 55 4	Beryl Burton, O.B.E.	Catterick	21 Sept.
100 miles	3 55 5	Beryl Burton, O.B.E.	Essex	4 Aug.
12 hours	277.25 miles	Beryl Burton, O.B.E.	Wetherby	17 Sept.
24 hours	427.86 miles	Christine Moody	Cheshire	26–27 July

ROAD RECORDS ASSOCIATION'S STRAIGHT-OUT DISTANCE RECORDS

Distance	days	hrs.	mins.	secs.	Name	Date	
25 miles			47	0	Peter Crofts	10 Oct.	1971
50 miles		1	39	23	Derek Cottington	2 May	1970
100 miles		3	28	40	Ray Booty	28 Sept.	1956
1,000 miles	2	10	40	0	Reg Randall	19–21 Aug.	1960
12 hours			276½ miles		Harry Earnshaw	4 July	1939
24 hours			475¾ miles		Ken Joy	26–27 July	1954

PLACE TO PLACE RECORDS
(British) as recognized by the Road Records Association

	days	hrs.	mins.	secs.	Name	Date	
London to Edinburgh (380 miles)		18	49	42	Cliff Smith	2 Nov	1965
London to Bath and back (210 miles)		9	36	23	Ken Joy	14 June	1953
London to York (197 miles)		8	23	0	Harry Earnshaw	4 July	1939
London to Brighton and back (107 miles)		4	18	18	Les West	3 Oct	1970
Land's End to London (287 miles)		12	34	0	Robert Maitland	17 Sept	1954
Land's End to John o'Groats (879 miles)	1	23	46	35	Richard W.E. Poole	18 June	1965

Tour de France The greatest number of wins in the Tour de France (inaugurated 1903) is five by Jacques Anquetil (b. 8 Jan. 1934) of France, who won in 1957, 1961, 1962, 1963 and 1964. The closest race ever was that of 1968 when after 2,898.7 miles over the 25 days (27 June-21 July) Jan Janssen (Netherlands) (b. 1940) beat Herman van Springel (Belgium) in Paris by 38 seconds. Eddie Merekx (see p 251) equalled Anquetil's record of 4 consecutive wins in 1969-70-71-72.

Most Olympic titles Cycling has been on the Olympic programme since the revival of the Games in 1896. The greatest number of gold medals ever won is four by Marcus Hurley (U.S.A.) over the ¼, ⅓, ½ and 1 mile in 1904.

The Land's End to John o' Groats (879 miles) feminine record is 2 days 11 hours 7 minutes (average speed 14.75 m.p.h.) by Mrs. Eileen Sheridan on 9-11 June 1954. She continued to complete 1,000 miles in 3 days 1 hour.

Roller cycling The greatest recorded distance registered in a 12-hour roller team cycling test is 508 miles 330 yards by Adrian Perkin, John Pugh, Bernard Trudgill and Lindsay Wigby of the Godric C.C. at Bungay, Suffolk on 23 March 1968.

The eight-man 24-hour record is 1,008 miles 1,320 yards by the Barnwell C.R.S. at Cambridge on 9-10 Jan. 1970. The team was Jim Bowyer, Ian Cannell, Colin Chapman, John Day, Bob Sampson, Peter Scarth, Chris Stevens and Richard Voss.

Endurance The greatest endurance feat in cycling was by Tommy Godwin (G.B.) who in the 365 days of 1939 covered 75,065 miles or an average of 205.65 miles per day. He then completed 100,000 miles in 500 days on 14 May 1940.

John Atkins, (Coventry) the professional Cyclo-cross champion.

CYCLO-CROSS
The greatest number of world championships (inst. 1950) have been won by E. de Vlaeminck (Belgium) who took the Open title in 1967 and the professional world titles in 1968-69-70-71-72. British titles (inst. 1955) have been won most often by John Atkins (Coventry R.C.) with 5 Amateur (1961-62-66-67-68) and 4 professional (1968-69, 1969-70, 1970-71 and 1971-72).

DARTS

Origins The origins of darts date from the use by archers of heavily weighted ten-inch throwing arrows for self--defence in close quarters fighting. The "dartes" were used in Ireland in the 16th century and darts was played on the *Mayflower* by the Plymouth pilgrims in 1620. Today there are an estimated 6,000,000 dart players in the British Isles—a higher participation than in any other sporting pastime. No national or international controlling organization for the game has existed which has collated records and conditions of play. The throwing distances and boards vary considerably from one locality to another.

Lowest possible scores The lowest number of darts to achieve standard scores are: 201 four darts, 301 six darts, 501 nine darts, 1,001 seventeen darts. The four and six darts "possibles" have been many times achieved, the nine darts 501 occasionally but never the seventeen darts 1,001

which would require 15 treble 20's, a treble 17 and a 50. The lowest even number which cannot be scored with three darts (ending on a double) is 162. The lowest odd number which cannot be scored with three darts (ending on a double) is 159.

Fastest match The fastest time taken for a match of three games of 301 is 2½ minutes by Jim Pike (1903-1960) at Broadcasting House, Broad Street, Birmingham, in 1952.

Fastest "round the board" The record time for going round the board in "doubles" at arm's length is 14.5 seconds by Jim Pike at the Craven Club, Newmarket, in March 1944. The record for this feat at the nine-feet throwing distance, retrieving own darts, is 2 minutes 24 seconds by Malcolm Duffield at Royal Hotel, Bradford, Yorkshire on 22 Mar. 1972.

Million and one up The shortest recorded time to score 1,000,001 up *on one board,* under the rules of darts, is 9 hours 48 minutes 31 seconds (scoring rate of 28.32 per second) by eight players from the Sergeant's Mess of the 13th/18th Royal Hussars (Q.M.O.) at Munster, West Germany on 15 March 1969.

Most doubles The recorded number of doubles scored in 10 hours is 2,030 (in 8,699 darts) for a percentage of 23.33 by Ray Smith, 27 at the Crosville Bus Depot, Heswell, Cheshire on 25 June 1972.

Marathon record The most protracted recorded darts marathon was one of 150 hours by four boys of the Central Grammar School for Boys, Gressell Lane, Tile Cross, Birmingham in continuous pairs on 24-30 June 1972.

Greatest crowd The largest attendance at any darts match was the 17,000 at the Agricultural Hall, Islington, London, at the finals of the 1939 *News of the World* contest.

Most titles Re-instituted in 1947, the annual *News of the World* England and Wales individual Championships consist of the best of 3 legs 501 up, "straight" start and finish on a double with an 8-feet throwing distance. The only men to win twice are Tommy Gibbons (Ivanhoe Working Men's Club) of Conisbrough, Yorkshire, in 1952 and 1958; Tom Reddington (Derbyshire) in 1955 and 1960; and Tom M. Barrett (Odco Sports Club, London) in 1964 and 1965.

EQUESTRIAN SPORTS

SHOW JUMPING

Origins Evidence of horse-riding dates from an Anatolian statuette dated *c.* 1400 B.C. Pignatelli's academy of horsemanship at Naples dates from the 16th century. The earliest show jumping was in Paris in 1886. Equestrian events have been included in the Olympic Games since 1912.

Most Olympic medals The greatest number of Olympic gold medals is four by three horsemen:- Lt. C. Ferdinand Pahud de Mortanges (Netherlands), who won the individual three-day event in 1928 and 1932 and was in the winning team in 1924 and 1928; by Major (later Col.) Henri St. Cyr (Sweden), who won the individual Grand Prix de dressage event in 1952 and 1956 and who was also in the winning teams; and by Hans Winkler (Germany), who won the Grand Prix jumping in 1956 and was in the winning team of 1956, 1960 and 1964. The most team wins in the Prix des Nations is four by Germany in 1936, 1956, 1960 and 1964. The lowest score obtained by a winner was no faults, by F. Ventura (Czechoslovakia) in 1928 and by Pierre Jonqueres d'Oriola (France), the only two-time winner (1952 and 1964), in 1952.

Jumping records The official *Fédération Equestre Internationale* high jump record is 8 feet 1¼ inches by *Huasó*, ridden by Capt. Alberto Larraguibel Morales (Chile) at Vina del Mar, Santiago, Chile, on 5 Feb. 1949, and 27 feet 2¾ inches for long jump over water by *Amado Mío* ridden by Lt.-Col. Lopez del Hierro (Spain), at Barcelona, Spain on 12 Nov. 1951. *Heatherbloom*, ridden by Dick Donnelly was reputed to have covered 37 feet in clearing an 8-foot 3-inch *puissance* jump at Richmond, Virginia, U.S.A. in 1903. *Solid Gold* cleared 36 feet 3 inches over water at the Wagga Show, New South Wales, Australia in August 1936 for an Australian record. *Jerry M.* allegedly cleared 40 feet over the water at Aintree in 1912.

At Cairns, Queensland, *Golden Meade* ridden by Jack Martin cleared an unofficially measured 8 feet 6

Major Piero d'Inzeo (Italy) co-holder of the record of winning the King George V cup three times.

inches on 25 July 1946. *Ben Bolt* was credited w clearing 9 feet 6 inches at the 1938 Royal Ho Show, Sydney, Australia. The Australian record feet 4 inches by *Flyaway* (C. Russell) in 1939 *Golden Meade* (A. L. Payne) in 1946. The wor unofficial best for a woman is 7 feet 5½ inches by M B. Perry (Australia) on *Plain Bill* at Cairns, Quee land, Australia in 1940. The greatest recorded hei reached bareback is 6 feet 7 inches by *Silver Woo* Heidelberg, Victoria, Australia, on 10 Dec. 1938.

The highest British performance is 7 feet 6¼ inches the 16.2 hands bay gelding *Swank*, ridden by Do Beard, at Olympia, London, on 25 June 1937. On same day, the Lady Wright (*née* Margery A Bullows) set the best recorded height for a Brit equestrienne on her liver chestnut *Jimmy Brown* feet 4 inches. These records were over the now unu sloping poles. Harvey Smith on *O'Malley* cleare feet 3 inches in Toronto, Canada in 1967.

Most titles The most B.S.J.A. championships won is four by A Oliver (1951-54-59-69). The only horses to have w twice are *Maguire* (Lt.-Col. Nathaniel Kindersley 1945 and 1947, *Sheila* (Hayes) in 1949-50 and *Admiral* (Oliver) in 1951 and 1954. The record the Ladies' Championship is 8 by Miss Patr Smythe (born 22 Nov. 1928), now Mrs. Sam Koechlin, O.B.E. (1952-53-55-57-58-59-61-62). was on *Flanagan*, owned by Robert Hanson C.B.E. 1955, 1958 and 1962—the only three time winner.

Marathon The longest continuous period spent in the saddl 42 hours 20 mins by Joseph Roberts of Newp Pagnell, Buckinghamshire, from Brighton, Sussex Bletchley, Buckinghamshire on 6-8 July 1972.

George V Gold Cup Only 3 men have thrice won this premier award (f held in 1911):- the late Lt.-Col. J A Talbot-Ponso (1930-32-34), Lt.-Col. Harry M. Llewellyn C.B (1948-50-53 on *Foxhunter*) and Piero d'Inzeo (Ita (1957-61-62).

FENCING

Origins Fencing was practised as a sport in Egypt as early the 12th century B.C. The first governing body fencing in Britain was the Corporation of Masters Defence founded by Henry VIII before 1540 a fencing was practised as sport, notably in prize figh since that time. The foil was the practice weapon the short court sword from the 17th century. T épée was established in the mid-19th century and t light sabre was introduced by the Italians in the l 19th century.

Most Olympic titles The greatest number of individual Olympic gold medals won is three by Nedo Nadi (Italy) in 1912 and 1920 (2) and Ramon Fonst (Cuba) in 1900 and 1904 (2). Nadi also won three team gold medals in 1920 making an unprecedented total of five gold medals at one celebration. Italy has won the épée team title six times. Hungary have won nine out of the 13 sabre team titles and France five foil team titles. Aladàr Gerevich (Hungary) was in the winning sabre team in 1932-36 1948-52-56-60. Allan Jay, M.B.E. (G.B.) competed in 5 Olympics (1952-68).

Most world titles The greatest number of individual world titles won is four by Christian d'Oriola (France) with the foil in 1947-49-53-54. He also won the Olympic titles in 1952 and 1956. Ellen Müller-Priess (Austria) won the women's foil in 1947 and 1949 and shared it in 1950. She also won the Olympic title in 1932. Italy won the men's foil teams thirteen times; Hungary the ladies' foil teams eleven times; Italy the épée teams ten times and Hungary the sabre teams thirteen times.

t A.F.A. titles The greatest number of Amateur Fencing Association titles have been won as follows:-

Foil	(Instituted 1898)	7	J. Emrys Lloyd	1928, 1930-33, 1937-38
Épée	(Instituted 1904)	5	R. Montgomerie	1905, 1907, 1909, 1912, 1914
Sabre	(Instituted 1898)	6	Dr. R.F. Tredgold	1937, 1939, 1947-49, 1955
Foil (Ladies)	(Instituted 1907)	10	Miss Gillian M. Sheen (now Mrs. R.G. Donaldson	1949, 1951-58, 1960

FIVES

ETON FIVES
A handball game against the buttress of Eton College Chapel was recorded in 1825, but a court existed at Lord Weymouth's School, Warminster, as early as 1773 and a handball game against the church wall at Babcary, Somerset, was recorded in June 1765. New courts were built at Eton in 1840, the rules were codified in 1877, rewritten laws were introduced in 1931 and the laws were last drawn up in 1950.

ost titles Only one pair have won the Amateur Championship (Kinnaird Cup) six times—Anthony Hughes and Arthur James Gordon Campbell (1958, 1965-68 and 1971). Hughes also was in the winning pair in 1963 making seven titles in all.

RUGBY FIVES
As now known, this game dates from c. 1850 with the first inter-public school matches recorded in the early 1870s. The Oxford v. Cambridge contest was inaugurated in 1925 and the Rugby Fives Association was founded in the home of Dr. Cyriax, in Welbeck Street, London, on 29 Oct. 1927. The dimensions of the Standard Rugby Fives court were approved by the Association in 1931.

Most titles The greatest number of Amateur Singles Championships (instituted 1932) ever won is four by John Frederick Pretlove in 1953, 1955-56 and 1958, and by Eric Marsh in 1960-61-62-63. Pretlove also holds the record for the Amateur Doubles Championship (instituted 1925), being co-champion in 1952, 1954, 1956-57-58-59 and 1961. The first person to have held all ten National and Provincial titles during his playing career is David E. Gardner. To 1972 he had won 12 Scottish titles (5 singles and 7 doubles), 14 North of England titles (4 singles and 10 doubles), 7 West of England titles (2 singles and 5 doubles), Lancashire Open (1 singles, 2 doubles), the Amateur Singles in 1964 and the Amateur Doubles in 1960, 1965, 1966, 1970, 1971, and 1972.

FOOTBALL (Soccer)

Origins A game with some similarities termed *Tsu-chin* was played in China in the 3rd and 4th centuries B.C. The earliest clear representation of the game is an Edinburgh print dated 1672-73. It became standardized with the formation of the Football Association in England on 26 Oct. 1863. A 26-a-side game, however, existed in Florence, Italy, as early as 1530, for which rules were codified in *Discorsa Calcio* in 1580. The oldest club is Sheffield F.C., formed on 24 Oct. 1857. Eleven per side was standardized in 1870.

HIGHEST SCORES
Teams The highest score recorded in a British first-class match is 36. This occurred in the Scottish Cup match between Arbroath and Bon Accord on 5 Sept. 1885, when Arbroath won 36-0 on their home ground. The goals were not fitted with nets.

The highest margin recorded in an international match is 17. This occurred in the England v. Australia match at Sydney on 30 June 1951, when England won 17-0. The highest in the British Isles was when England beat Ireland 13-0 at Belfast on 18 Feb. 1882. The highest score in an F.A. Cup match is 26, when Preston North End beat Hyde 26-0 at Deepdale, Preston on 15 Oct. 1887. This is also the highest score between English clubs. The biggest victory in a final tie is 6 when Bury beat Derby County 6-0 at Crystal Palace on 18 April 1903, in which year Bury did not concede a single goal in the five Cup matches.

The highest score by one side in a Football League (Division I) match is 12 goals when West Bromwich Albion beat Darwen 12-0 at West Bromwich on 4 March 1892; when Nottingham Forest beat Leicester Fosse by the same score at Nottingham on 21 April 1909; and when Aston Villa beat Accrington 12-2 at Villa Park on 12 March 1892.

The highest aggregate in League Football was 17 goals when Tranmere Rovers beat Oldham Athletic 13-4 in a 3rd Division (North) match at Prenton Park, Birkenhead, on Boxing Day, 1935. The record margin in a League match has been 13 in the Newcastle United 13, Newport County 0 Division II match in 1946 and in the Stockport County 13, Halifax 0 Division III (North) match in 1934.

Individuals The most scored by one player in a first-class match is 16 by Stains for Racing Club de Lens v. Aubry-Asturies, in Lens, France, on 13 Dec. 1942. The record for any British first-class match is 13 by John Petrie in the Arbroath v. Bon Accord Scottish Cup match in 1885 (see above). The record in League Football is 10 by Joe Payne (b.Bolsover, Derbyshire) for Luton Town v. Bristol Rovers in a 3rd Division (South) match at Luton on 13 April 1936. The English 1st Division record is 7 goals by Ted Drake (b. Southampton, Hampshire) for Arsenal v. Aston Villa at Birmingham on 14 Dec. 1935, and James for Preston North End v. Stoke at Preston on 6 Oct. 1888. The Scottish 1st Division record is 8 goals by James McGrory for Celtic v. Dunfermline Athletic at Celtic Park, Glasgow, on 14 Jan. 1928.

The record for individual goal-scoring in a British home international is 6 by Joe Bambrick for Ireland v. Wales at Belfast on 1 Feb. 1930.

Career The greatest total of goals scored in a career is 1,026 by Edson Arantes do Nascimento (b, Baurú, Brazil, 28 June 1940), known as Pelé, the Brazilian inside left from 1957 to the World Cup final on 21 June 1970. His best year was 1958 with 139 and the *milesimo* (1,000th) came in a penalty for his club Santos in the Maracanā Stadium, Rio de Janeiro on 19 Nov. 1969 when playing in his 909th first-class match.

The best season League records are 60 goals in 39 League games by William Ralph ("Dixie") Dean (b. Birkenhead, Cheshire, 1906) for Everton (Division I) in]1927-28 and 66 goals in 38 games by Jim Smith for Ayr United (Scottish Division II) in the same season. With 3 more in Cup ties and 19 in representative matches Dean's total was 82.

The international career record for England is 49 goals by Robert ("Bobby") Charlton O.B.E. (b. Ashington, Northumberland, 11 Oct. 1937). His first was *v.* Scotland in 1958 and his last on 20 May 1970 *v.* Colombia.

The greatest number of goals scored in British first-class football is 550 (410 in League matches) by James McGrory of Glasgow Celtic (1922-38). The most scored in League matches is 434, for West Bromwich Albion, Fulham, Leicester City and Shrewsbury Town, by George Arthur Rowley (b. 1926) between 1946 and April 1965. Rowley also scored 32 goals in the F.A. Cup and 1 for England "B".

Fastest goals The fastest goal on record was one variously claimed to be from 4 to 13 seconds after the kick-off by Jim Fryatt of Bradford in a Fourth Division match against Tranmere Rovers at Park Avenue, Bradford on 25 April 1964. An 8 second goal was scored by George Jones for Bury *v.* Notts. County at Bury, Lancashire on 12 Dec. 1970. John Scarth (Gillingham) scored 3 goals in 2 minutes against Leyton Orient at Priestfield Stadium, Gillingham on 1 Nov. 1952. John McIntyre (Blackburn Rovers) scored 4 goals in 5 minutes *v.* Everton at Ewood Park, Blackburn, on 16 Sept. 1922. W.G. ("Billy") Richardson (West Bromwich Albion) scored 4 goals in 5 minutes against West Ham United at Upton Park on 7 Nov. 1931. Frank Keetley scored 6 goals in 21 minutes in the 2nd half of the Lincoln City *v.* Halifax Town league match on 16 Jan. 1932.

The international record is 3 goals in 3½ minutes by Willie Hall (Tottenham Hotspur) for England against Ireland on 16 Nov. 1938 at Old Trafford, Manchester.

Largest goal-less streak In Oct.-Dec. 1919 Coventry played 11 successive games without scoring.

MOST APPEARANCES
The greatest total of full international appearances by a British footballer is 106 by "Bobby" Charlton, O.B.E. of Manchester United. His first was *v.* Scotland on 19 April 1958 and his 106th in the World Cup in Mexico City on 14 June 1970. Pelé retired from international play on 18 July 1971 having played for Brazil in 110 matches (95 goals) and scored 12 goals in the World Cup series of 1958-62-66-70.

England The greatest number of appearances for England secured in the International Championship is 38 by William (Billy) Ambrose Wright, C.B.E. (b. Iron-bridge, Shropshire, 6 Feb. 1924) in 1946-1959.

Wales The record number of appearances for Wales in the International Chapionship is 48 by William (Billy) Meredith (Manchester City and United) in the longest international span of 26 years (1895-1920). This is a record for any of the four home countries. Ivor Allchurch, M.B.E., (born 29 Dec. 1929) of Swansea,

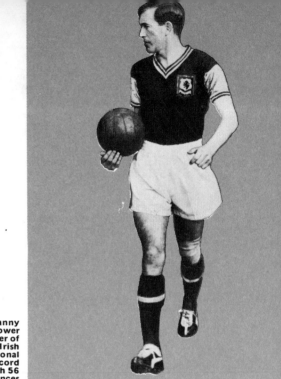

Danny Blanchflower co-holder of the Irish International Cap record with 56 appearances

Newcastle, Cardiff City and Worcester City played times for Wales, including 37 times against the h countries, between 15 Nov. 1950 and Feb. 1968.

Scotland The Scottish record for International Champions matches is 30 by Alan Morton (Queen's Park Glasgow Rangers) from 1920 to 1932. Morton had a single foreign international making a total o caps. George Young (Glasgow Rangers) has a rec total of 53 appearances for Scotland, of which were for International Championship match between 1946 and 1957.

Ireland The greatest number of appearances for Ireland is by Billy Bingham (b. Belfast) (Sunderland, Lut Everton and Port Vale) (1951 to 1964) and by Da Blanchflower (Bransley, Aston Villa and Tottenh Hotspur) (1950 to 1963). The total by Jim McIlroy (Burnley, Stoke City and Oldham Athle was 55 (1951-1966).

Oldest cap The oldest cap has been William Henry (Bi Meredith (1874-1958), who played outside right Wales *v.* England at Highbury, London, on 15 Ma 1920 when aged 45 years 229 days.

Youngest caps *World* The world's youngest international footballer been G. Dorval who played for Brazil *v.* Argentin 1957 while still 15.

British Isles The youngest cap in the British Isles h internationals has been Norman Kernoghan (Bel Celtic) who played for Ireland *v.* Wales in 1936 a 17 years 80 days. It is possible, however, that W Gibson (Cliftonville) who played for Ireland *v,* W in 1894 at 17 was slightly younger. Englar youngest home international was Duncan Edwa (b. Dudley, Staffordshire, 1 Oct. 1936, d. 21 F 1958, 15 days after the Munich air crash) Manchester United left half, against Scotland Wembley on 2 April 1955, aged 18 years 6 mon The youngest Welsh cap was John Cha (b. Swansea, 19 Jan. 1932) the Leeds United cer half, against Ireland at Wrexham on 8 March 19 aged 18 years 1 month. Scotland's young international has been Denis Law (b, Aberde 24 Feb. 1940) of Huddersfield Town, who pla against Wales on 18 Oct. 1958, aged 18 years days. Jacky Robinson played for England *v.* Finla in 1937 aged 17 years 9 months. Research remain be completed on the date of birth of David Black Hurlford, Ayrshire, who may have been 17 when played for Scotland *v.* Ireland in 1889.

Longest match The duration record for first class fixtures was set in the Western Hemisphere club championship in Santos, Brazil, on 2-3 Aug. 1962, when Santos drew 3-3 with Penarol F.C. of Montevideo, Uruguay. The game lasted 3½ hours, from 9.30p.m. to 1.00a.m.

The longest British match on record was one of 3 hours 23 minutes between Stockport County and Doncaster Rovers in the second leg of the 3rd Division (North) Cup at Edgeley Park, Stockport, on 30 March 1946.

Heaviest goalkeeper The biggest goalkeeper in representative football was the England international Willie J. Foulke (1874-1916), who stood 6 feet 3 inches and weighed 22 stone 3 lb. His last games were for Bradford, by which time he was 26 stone. He once stopped a game by snapping the cross bar.

TRANSFER FEES

The world's highest reported transfer fee is more than £400,000 for the Varese centre forward Pietro Anastasi signed by Juventus, of Turin, Italy on 18 May 1968. The British cash record is c. £190,000 for the Burnley forward Ralph Coates (b. Helton-le-Hole, Co. Durham, 1945) paid by Tottenham Hotspur on 5 May 1971. The record as between British clubs is the £220,000 for the Everton player Alan Ball (b. 1945), who was transferred to Arsenal on 22 Dec. 1971.

The British aggregate record is held by the centre forward Tony Hateley (b. Derby, 1942) who in six moves from July 1963 to 28 Oct. 1970 was reportedly valued at £393,500.

Signing fee On 26 May 1961, Luis Suarez, the Barcelona inside forward, was transferred to Internazionale (Milan) for £144,000, of which Suarez himself received a record £59,000. The British record is £10,000 for John Charles (Leeds United to Juventus, Turin on 19 April 1957), for Denis Law (Manchester City to Torino, Italy on 13 June 1961) and Martin Peters (see above).

CROWD AND GATES

The greatest recorded crowd at any football match was 205,000 (199,854 paid) for the Brazil v. Uruguay World Cup final in the Maracanã Municipal Stadium, Rio de Janeiro, Brazil, on 16 July 1950.

The British record paid attendance is 149,547 at the Scotland v. England international at Hampden Park, Glasgow, on 17 April 1937. It is, however, probable that this total was exceeded (estimated 160,000) on the occasion of the F.A. Cup Final between Bolton Wanderers and West Ham United at Wembley Stadium on 28 April 1923, when the crowd broke in on the pitch and the start was delayed 40 minutes until the pitch was cleared. The counted admissions were 126,047. The record gross F.A. Cup receipts at Wembley, Greater London, is £191,917 (excluding radio and television fees) for the final on 6 May 1972.

The Scottish Cup record attendance is an estimated 170,000 when Celtic played Aberdeen at Hampden Park on 24 April 1937. The record for a British inter-club fixture is 143,570 at the Rangers v. Hibernian match at Hampden Park, Glasgow, on 27 March 1948. The highest attendance at a friendly match has been when Glasgow Rangers played Eintracht, Frankfurt at Hampden Park in 1961.

Smallest The smallest crowd at a full home international was 7,483 for the Scotland v. Northern Ireland match of 6 May 1969 at Hampden Park. The smallest crowd at a Football League fixture was for the Stockport County v. Leicester City Match at Old Trafford, Manchester, on 7 May 1921. Stockport's own ground was under suspension and the "crowd" numbered 13.

RECEIPTS

The greatest receipts at any match were £204,805, from an attendance of 96,924 at the World Cup final between England and West Germany at the Empire Stadium, Wembley, on 30 July 1966.

The record for a British international match is £105,000 for the England v. Scotland match at Wembley on 10 May 1969 (attendance 100,000). The receipts for the Manchester United v. Benfica match at Wembley on 29 May 1968 were £118,000 (attendance 100,000).

Most successful National coach The most successful national coach has been George Raynor (b. 1907) for Sweden. His teams won the 1948 Olympic competition and were 2nd in the 1958 World Cup and 3rd in both the 1950 World Cup and in the 1952 Olympic competition.

F.A. CHALLENGE CUP

Wins The greatest number F.A. Cup wins is 7 by Aston Villa in 1887, 1895, 1897, 1905, 1913, 1920 and 1957 (nine final appearances). Of the 6-time winners Newcastle United have been in the final 10 times, as have 5-time winners West Bromwich Albion. The highest scores have been 6-1 in 1890, 6-0 in 1903 and 4-3 in 1953.

The greatest number of Scottish F.A. Cup wins is 22 by Celtic in 1892, 1899, 1900, 1904, 1907-8, 1911-12, 1914, 1923, 1925, 1927, 1931, 1933, 1937, 1951, 1954, 1965, 1967, 1969, 1971 and 1972.

Youngest player The youngest player in the F.A. Cup Final was Howard Kendall (b. 22 May 1946) of Preston North End, who played against West Ham United on 2 May 1964, 20 days before his 18th birthday. Note however, that Derek Johnstone (Rangers) (b. 4 Nov. 1953) was 16 years 11 months old when he played in the Scottish League Cup Final against Celtic on 24 Oct. 1970.

Most medals Three players have won 5 F.A. Cup Winner's Medals:- J.H. Forrest (Blackburn Rovers) (1884-85-86-90-91); the Hon. Arthur Fitzgerald Kinnaird K.T. (Wanderers) (1873-77-78) and Old Etonians (1879-82) and C.H.R. Wollaston (Wanderers) (1872-73-76-77-78).

Longest tie The most protracted F.A. Cup tie in the competition proper was that between Stoke City and Bury in the 3rd round with Stoke winning 3-2 in the fifth meeting after 9 hours 22 minutes of play in January 1955. The matches were at Bury (1-1) on 8 January; Stoke on Trent 12 January (abandoned after 22 minutes of extra time with the score 1-1); Goodison Park (3-3) on 17 January; Anfield (2-2) on 19 January; and finally at Old Trafford on 24 January. In the 1972 final qualifying round Alvechurch beat Oxford City after five previous drawn games.

MOST LEAGUE CHAMPIONSHIPS

The greatest number of League Championships (Division I) is 8 by Arsenal in 1931, 1933, 1934, 1935, 1938, 1948, 1953 and 1971. The record number of points is in Division I 67 by Leeds United in 1969 while the lowest has been 8 by Doncaster Rovers (Division II) in 1904-5. Doncaster Rovers

Jairzinho (Brazil) the only player to score in every round of a World Cup. He got 7 goals in 1970.

scored 72 points from 42 games in Division III (North) in 1947.

The only F.A. Cup and League Championship "doubles" are those of Preston North End in 1889, Aston Villa in 1897, Tottenham Hotspur in 1961 and Arsenal in 1971. Preston won the League without losing a match and the Cup without having a goal scored against them throughout the whole competition. Glasgow Rangers have won the Scottish League Championship 33 times between 1899 and 1964 and were joint champions on another occasion. Their 76 points in the Scottish 1st Division in 1921 represents a record in any division.

Closest win In 1923-24 Huddersfield won the Division I championship over Cardiff by 0.02 of a goal with a goal average of 1.81.

Most durable player The most durable player in League history has been Jimmy Dickinson (b. 1925), who made 764 appearances for Portsmouth F.C. between 1946 and 1965.

WORLD CUP
The *Fédération Internationale de Football* (F.I.F.A.) was founded in Paris on 21 May 1904 and instituted the World Cup Competition on 13 July 1930, in Montevideo, Uruguay.

The only country to win three times has been Brazil in 1958, 1962 and 1970. Brazil was also third in 1938 and second in 1950, and is the only one of the 40 participating countries to have played in all 9 competitions. Antonion Carbajal (b. 1923) played for Mexico in goal in the competitions of 1950-54-58-62 and 1966. The record goal scorer has been Just Fontaine (France) with 13 goals in 6 games in the 1958 competition in Sweden. The most goals scored in a final is 3 by Geoffrey Hurst (b. Ashton-under-Lyne, 1941) (West Ham United) for England *v.* West Germany on 30 July 1966.

EUROPEAN CHAMPIONSHIP
The European F.A. started in 1958 a tournament to be staged every 4 years. Each tournament takes 2 years to run with the semi-finals and final on the same territory. The U.S.S.R. won the first when they beat Yugoslavia 2-1 in Paris on 10 July 1960 followed by Spain (1964), Italy (1968) and West Germany (1972).

EUROPEAN CHAMPIONS CUP
The European Cup for the League champions of the respective nations was approved by F.I.F.A. on 8 May

1955 and was run by the European F.A. which cam into being in the previous year. Real Madrid defeate Rheims 4-3 in the first final in 1956 and went on t win the Cup in the next 4 seasons and in 1966. The took part in all competitions, either as holders Spanish champions up to and including 1969-70.

Glasgow Celtic became the first British club to wi the Cup when they beat Inter Milan 2-1 in th National Stadium, Lisbon, Portugal, on 25 May 196 At the same time they established the record of bein the only club to win the European Cup and the tw senior domestic tournaments (League and Cup) in th same season.

EUROPEAN CUP WINNERS CUP
A tournament for the national Cup winners started 1960-1 with 10 entries. Fiorentina beat Glasgo Rangers on 4-1 aggregate in a two-leg final in Ma 1961. Tottenham Hotspur were the first British clu to win the trophy, beating Atletico Madrid 5-1 Rotterdam on 15 May 1963 and were followed b West Ham United in 1965, Manchester City 29 April 1970, Chelsea in 1971 and Glasgow Range in 1972.

FOOTBALL (Amateur)
Most Olympic wins The only country to have won the Olympic footba title 3 times is Hungary in 1952, 1964 and 1968. Th United Kingdom won the unofficial tournament i 1900 and the official tournaments of 1908 and 1912 The highest Olympic score is Denmark 17 *v.* Franc "A" 1 in 1908.

Highest scores The highest score in a home Amateur International 11 goals in the England *v.* Scotland match (8-3) Dulwich on 11 March 1939. The foreign record wa when England beat France 15-0 in Paris on 1 No 1906.

The highest score in an F.A. Amateur Cup Final is 8 when Northern Nomads beat Stockton 7-1 a Sunderland in 1926, and when Dulwich Hamlet bea Marine (Liverpool) by the same score at Upton Par in 1932.

In the match between Sandygate Youth Club *v.* 1 Burnley Boys' Brigade at Burnley, Lancashire o 10 Sept. 1955, the half time score was 27-0 and afte 80 minutes play 53-0. Sandygate's top scorer was Ro Swift with 14 goals.

Individual The highest individual scores in amateu internationals are 6 by William Charles Jordan fo England *v.* France (12-0) at Park Royal, London, o 23 March 1908; 6 by Vivian J. Woodward for Englan *v.* Holland (9-1) at Stamford Bridge, London, o 11 Dec. 1909; and 6 also by Harold A. Walden fo Great Britain *v.* Hungary in Stockholm, Sweden, o 1 July 1912.

Most caps The record number of England amateur caps is 51 b Mike Pinner of Hendon, the former Pegasu goalkeeper who played for England between 195 and 1963, when he became a professional wit Leyton Orient.

F.A. Amateur Cup wins The greatest number of F.A. Amateur Cup (institute 1893) wins is 10 by Bishop Auckland who won i 1896, 1900, 1914, 1921-22, 1935, 1939, 1955, 195 and 1957.

Largest crowd The highest attendances at amateur matches has bee 100,000, first reached at the Cup Final betwee Pegasus and Bishop Auckland at Wembley o 21 April 1951. The amateur gate record is £29,305 a the final between Bishop Auckland and Hendon o 16 April 1955.

Heading The highest recorded number of repetitions fo heading a ball is 3,412 in 34 minutes 8 seconds by

Colin Jones, aged 15, at Queensferry, near Chester, on 8 March 1961.

Least The goalkeeper of the Victoria Boys' and Girls' Club
successful Intermediate "B" team in the 1967-8 season in the
goalkeeper Association for the Jewish Youth League Under 16
Division 2 in London, England, let through 252 goals
in the 12 league matches, an average of better (or
worse) than 21 per match.

Longest The aggregate duration of ties in amateur soccer have
ties not been collated but it is recorded that in the
London F.A. Intermediate Cup first qualifying round
Highfield F.C. Reserves had to meet Mansfield House
F.C. on 19 and 26 Sept. and 3, 10 and 14 Oct. 1970
to get a decision after 9 hours 50 minutes play with
scores of 0-0, 1-1, 1-1, 3-3, and 0-2.

In the Hertfordshire Intermediate Cup, London
Colney beat Leavesden Hospital after 12 hours 41
minutes play and 7 ties on 6 Nov. to 17 Dec. 1971.

Most In the local Cup match between Tongham Youth
disciplined Club, Surrey and Hawley, Hampshire, England on
3 Nov. 1969 the referee booked all 22 players
including one who went to hospital, and one of the
linesmen. The match, won by Tongham 2-0, was
described by a player as "A good, hard game".

Most Coleridge F.C. of the Cambridgeshire F.A. completed
disciplined 18 years without a single member having been
cautioned, sent off or otherwise disciplined since
formed in 1954.

Longest The longest recorded 11-a-side football match played
marathon under F.A. rules without substitutes has been one of
24 hours 20 minutes, by two teams from
Bournemouth, Hampshire on 1-2 July 1972.

The longest recorded authenticated 5-a-side games
have been:- outdoors: 38 hours 5 minutes by two
teams (no substitutes) from Portishead Youth Centre,
Bristol ending at 10.15a.m. on 15 Nov. 1970, and
indoors: 52 hours 20 minutes by two teams (no
substitutes) from the Knutton Centre, Newcastle,
Staffordshire on 24-26 March 1972.

Table The most protracted game of 2-a-side table football
football on record was one of 170 hours maintained by 8
students from Hatfield Polytechnic, Hertfordshire on
19-26 Feb. 1971.

FOOTBALL (GAELIC)

Earliest The game developed from inter-parish "free for all"
references with no time-limit, no defined playing area nor
specific rules. The formation of the Gaelic Athletic
Association was in Thurles, Ireland, on 1 Nov.1884.

Most titles The greatest number of All Ireland Championships
ever won by one team is 22 by Ciarraidhe (Kerry)
between 1903 and 1970. The greatest number of
successive wins is four by Wexford (1915-18) and
four by Kerry (1929-32).

Highest The highest score in an All-Ireland final was when
scores Cork (6 goals, 6 points) beat Antrim (1 goal, 2 points)
in 1911. The highest combined score was when Kerry
(2 goals, 19 points) beat Meath (no goals, 18 points)
in 1970. A goal equal 3 points.

Lowest In four All-Ireland finals the combined totals have
scores been 7 points; 1893 Wexford (1 goal[till 1894 worth
5 points], 1 point) v. Cork (1 point);1895 Tipperary
(4 points) v. Meath (3 points); 1904 Kerry (5 points)
v. Dublin (2 points); 1924 Kerry (4 points) v. Dublin
(3 points).

Most The most appearances in All-Ireland finals is ten by
appearances Dan O'Keeffe (Kerry) of which seven (a record) were
on the winning side.

Individual The highest recorded individual score in All-Ireland
score final has been 2 goals, 5 points by Frank Stockwell
(Galway) in the match against Cork in 1956.

Largest The record crowd is 90,556 for the Down v. Offaly
crowd final at Croke Park, Dublin, in 1961.

Inter- The province of Leinster has won most champion-
provincials ships (Railway Cup) with 17 between 1928 and 1962.
Sean O'Neill (Down) holds the record of 8 medals
with Ulster (1960-71).

FOOTBALL (RUGBY LEAGUE)

Origins The Rugby League was formed originally in 1895 as
"The Northern Rugby Football Union" by the
secession of 22 clubs in Lancashire and Yorkshire
from the parent Rugby Union. Though payment for
loss of working time was a major cause of the
breakaway the "Northern Union" did not itself
embrace full professionalism until 1898. A reduction
in the number of players per team from 15 to 13 took
place in 1906 and the present title of "Rugby
League" was adopted in 1922.

Most wins Under the one-league Championship system
(1907-1962 and 1965-71) the club with the most
wins was Wigan with nine (1909, 1922, 1926, 1934,
1946, 1947, 1950, 1952 and 1960).

In the Rugby League Challenge Cup (inaugurated
1896-97) the club with the most wins is Leeds with 8
in 1910-23-32-36, 1941-42 (wartime), 1957 and
1968. Oldham is the only club to appear in four
consecutive Cup Finals (1924-27) and Bradford
Northern is the only football club (Rugby League or
Association) to have appeared at Wembley in three
consecutive years (1947-48-49).

Only three clubs have won all four major Rugby
League trophies (Challenge Cup, League Champion-
ship, County Cup and County League) in one season:
Hunslet in 1907-08, Huddersfield in 1914-15 and
Swinton in 1927-28.

In addition to the three "All Four Cup clubs", on
only five other occasions has a club taken the Cup and
League honours in one season: Broughton Rangers
(1902); Halifax (1903); Huddersfield (1913);
Warrington (1954); and St. Helens (1966)

World Cup The record aggregate score in a World Cup match is 60
points, when Great Britain beat the Rest by 33 points
to 27 at Bradford on 10 Oct. 1960.

There have been five World Cup Competitions.
Australia were winners in 1957, 1968 and 1970.
Great Britain won in 1954 and 1960.

Senior The highest aggregate score in Cup or League football,
match in a game where a senior club has been concerned, was
121 points, when Huddersfield beat Swinton Park
Rangers by 119 points (19 goals, 27 tries) to 2 points
(one goal) in the first round of the Northern Union
Cup on 28 Feb.1914.

Cup Final The record aggregate in a Cup Final is 43 points, when
Wigan beat Hull 30-13 at Wembley on 9 May 1959,
and when Wakefield Trinity beat Hull 38-5 at
Wembley on 14 May 1960.

The greatest winning margin was 34 points when

HIGHEST SCORES
The highest aggregate scores in international Rugby League football are:

Match	Points	Score
Great Britain v. Australia (*Test Matches*)	62	Australia won 50-12 (Swinton, 9 Nov 1963)
Great Britain v. New Zealand (*Test Matches*)	72	Great Britain won 52-20 (Wellington, 30 July 1910)
Great Britain v. France (*Test Matches*)	65	Great Britain won 50-15 (Leeds, 14 March 1959)
England v. Wales	63	England won 40-23 (Leeds, 18 Oct 1969)
England v. France	55	France won 42-13 (Marseilles, 25 Nov 1951)
England v. Other Nationalities	61	England won 34-27 (Workington, 30 March 1933)
Wales v. France	50	France won 29-21 (Bordeaux, 23 Nov 1947)
Wales v. Other Nationalities	48	Other Nationalities won 27-21 (Swansea, 31 March 19
Australia v. Great Britain	76	Australia won 63-13 (Paris, 31 Dec 1933)
Australia v. Wales	70	Australia won 51-19 (Wembley, 30 Dec 1933)
Australia v. France (*Test Matches*)	62	Australia won 56-6 (Brisbane, 2 July 1960)
Australia v. New Zealand (*Test Matches*)	74	New Zealand won 49-25 (Brisbane, 28 June 1952)
New Zealand v. France (*Test Matches*)	53	France won 31-22 (Lyon, 15 Jan 1956)

Huddersfield beat St. Helens 37-3 at Oldham on 1 May l915.

Touring teams The record score for a British team touring the Commonwealth is 101 points by England v. South Australia (nil) at Adelaide in May 1914.

The record for a Commonwealth touring team in Britain is 92 points (10 goals, 24 tries) by Australia against Bramley's 7 points (2 goals, one try) at the Barley Mow Ground, Bramley, near Leeds, on 9 Nov. 1921.

Record crowds and receipts The greatest attendance at any Rugby League match is 102,569 for the Warrington v. Halifax Cup Final replay at Odsal Stadium, Bradford, on 5 May 1954.

The highest receipts for a match in the United Kingdom have been £89,262 for the Castleford v. Wigan R.L. Cup Final at Wembley Stadium, Greater London on 9 May 1970.

Most international caps Test Matches between Great Britain (formerly England) and Australia are regarded as the highest distinction for an R.L. player in either hemisphere and Jim Sullivan, the Wigan full-back and captain, holds a Test record for a British player with 15 appearances in these games between 1924 and 1933, though Mick Sullivan (no kin) of Huddersfield, Wigan, St. Helens and York, played in 16 G.B. v. Australia games in 1954-1964, of which 13 were Tests and 3 World Cup matches.

In all Tests, including those against New Zealand and France, Mick Sullivan made the record number of 47 appearances and scored 43 tries.

Most Cup Finals Two players have appeared in seven Cup Finals: Alan Edwards (Salford, Dewsbury and Bradford Northern) between 1938 and 1949, and Eric Batten (Leeds, Bradford Northern and Featherstone Rovers) between 1941 and 1952.

Eric Ashton, M.B.E., Wigan and Great Britain centre has the distinction of captaining Wigan at Wembley in six R.L. Cup Finals in nine years 1958-1966, taking the trophy three times (1958, 1959 and 1965).

The youngest player in a Cup Final was Reg Lloyd (Keighley) who was 17 years 8 months when he played at Wembley on 8 May 1937.

Most goals The record number of goals in a season is 224 by Bernard Ganley (Oldham) in the 1957-58 season. His total was made up of 219 in League, Cup and representative games and five in a "friendly" fixture.

MOST TRIES

Season Albert Aaron Rosenfeld (Huddersfield), an Australian-born wing-threequarter, scored 80 tries in the 1913-14 season.

Career Brian Bevan, an Australian-born wing-threequar scored 834 tries in League, Cup, representative charity games in the 18 seasons (16 with Warringt 2 with Blackpool Borough) from 1946 to 1964.

MOST POINTS

Cup C.H.("Tich") West of Hull Kingston Rovers scored points (10 goals and 11 tries) in a 1st Rou Challenge Cup-tie v. Brookland Rovers on 4 Ma 1905.

League Lionel Cooper of Huddersfield scored 10 tries a kicked two goals against Keighley on 17 Nov. 19.

Season B. Lewis Jones (Leeds) with 505 (197 goals and tries) in 1956-57 and David Watkins (Salford) 503 1971-2 are the only 2 over 500 points. The rec number of points in a single season by a team is 1,2 by Huddersfield (1914-15) and Wigan (1949-50).

Career Jim Sullivan (Wigan) scored 6,192 points (2,955 go and 94 tries) in a senior Rugby League car extending from 1921 to 1946.

Record transfer fees The highest R.L. transfer fee is the reputed £15,0 deal which took Colin Dixon, the Halifax forward, Salford on 19 Dec. 1968. David Watkins (Welsh R. received an £11,000 signing fee at a guarante £1,000 p.a. for 5 years from Salford in Oct. 1967.

Longest kick The longest claimed place kick was one of 80 yards H.H. (Dally) Messenger for Australia v. Hull in Hu Yorkshire in 1908 but this was apparently on estimated. In April 1940 Martin Hodgson (Swinto kicked a goal on the Rochdale ground later measur to be 77¾ yards.

FOOTBALL (RUGBY UNION)

(All point scores are compiled according to curre values)

Origins The game is traditionally said to have originated fro a breach of the rules of the football played November 1823 at Rugby School by William We Ellis (later the Rev.) (c. 1807-72). This handling co of football evolved gradually and was known to ha been played at Cambridge University by 1839. T Rugby Football Union was not founded until 187

MOST CAPPED PLAYERS
The totals below are limited to matches between t seven member countries of the "International Rug Football Board" and France. Michel Craus (b. 7 July 1934) of France has appeared in

internationals of all kinds since 1958.

New Zealand	53	Colin E. Meads	1957-71
Ireland	52	Thomas J. Kiernan	1960-72
Wales	44	Kenneth J. Jones, M.B.E.	1947-57
France	43	Michel Crauste, L.d'H.	1958-66
Australia	42	Peter G. Johnson	1959-72
Scotland	40	Hugh F. McLeod, O.B.E.	1954-62
	40	David M.D. Rollo	1959-68
South Africa	38	Frik C.H. Du Preez	1960-71
England	34	Derek Prior Rogers, O.B.E.	1961-69

HIGHEST SCORES

Internationals The highest score in any full International was when France beat Romania by 72 points (7 goals, six tries and 2 penalty goals) to 3 (1 penalty goal) in the Olympic Games at Colombes, Paris in May 1924.

The above aggregate score also equalled the International Championship record of 75 points when Wales beat France at Swansea in 1910 by 59 points (8 goals, 1 penalty goal, 2 tries) to 16 (1 goal, 2 penalty goals and 1 try).

The highest aggregate score for any International match between the Four Home Unions is 69 when England beat Wales by 69 points (7 goals, 1 drop goal and 6 tries) to 0 at Blackheath, Kent in 1881.

The highest score by any Overseas side in an International in the British Isles is 53 points (7 goals, 1 drop goal and 2 tries) to 0 when South Africa beat Scotland at Murrayfield, Edinburgh on 24 November 1951.

Ian S. Smith (Scotland) has scored most consecutive tries in international matches with 6; 3 in the second half of Scotland *v.* France in 1925 and 3 in the first half against Wales two weeks later.

Tour match The record score for any international tour match is 125-0 (17 goals, 5 tries and 1 penalty goal) when New Zealand beat Northern New South Wales at Quirindi, Australia, on 30 May 1962. Rod Heeps scored 8 tries (32 points) and Don B. Clarke kicked 10 conversions and the penalty goal (23 points).

George Nepia, the Maori full back, played in all 30 of New Zealand's (All Blacks) tour matches of 1924-25 in the British Isles.

Schools Scores of over 200 points have been recorded in club matches, for example Radford School beat Hills

Court by 31 goals and 7 tries (in current values 214 points) to nil on 20 Nov. 1886.

Individual The highest individual points score in any match between members of the International Board is 24 by W. Fergie McCormick—1 drop goal, 3 conversions and 5 penalty goals for New Zealand against Wales at Auckland on 14 June 1969.

In a match in November 1963 between Stucley's and Darracott's in a junior house match at Bideford G.S., Devon the scrum-half, Alan McKenzie, 14, contributed 86 points (13 tries and 17 conversions) to Stucley's winning score.

Longest kicks The longest recorded successful drop-goal is 90 yards by G. Brand for South Africa *v.* England at Twickenham, London, in 1932. This was taken 7 yards inside

Fergie McCormick (N.Z.) who scored 24 points against Wales in 1969.

261

the England "half" 55 yards from the posts and dropped over the dead ball line.

The place kick record is reputed to be 100 yards at Richmond Athletic Ground, Surrey, by D. F. T. Morkell in an unsuccessful penalty for South Africa v. Surrey on 19 Dec. 1906. This was not measured until 1932.

Greatest crowd A crowd of 95,000 has twice been reported: when the British Lions beat South Africa by 1 point at Ellis Park, Johannesburg, on 6 Aug. 1955, and when France met Romania at Bucharest on 19 May 1957, as a curtain raiser for an Association match. The British record is over 76,000 for the Calcutta Cup match (England v. Scotland) at Murrayfield, Edinburgh, on 17 March 1962.

Middlesex Seven-a-Sides The Middlesex Seven-a-Sides were inaugurated in 1926. The most successful side has been Harlequins with 7 wins (1926-27-28-29-33-35-67).

The only players to be in five winning "sevens" have been N. M. Hall (d. 1972) (St. Mary's Hospital 1944-1946 and Richmond 1951-53-55), and J. A. P. Shackleton and I. H. P. Laughland both of London Scottish (1960-61-62-63-65).

Highest posts The world's highest Rugby Union goal posts measure 93 feet 10½ inches and are made of metal. They are at the Municipal Grounds, Barberton, Transvaal, South Africa

Samuel Arthur Doble (b. 9 Mar. 1944) the Moseley player, who scored an English season record of 581 points including scoring in all 44 matches for his club and 47 points for England in South Africa in 1971-2.

ALL TIME SCORING RECORDS – AGGREGATE and MARGIN of VICTORY in the ten annual matches in the 'International Championsh
(All scores are given in terms of current scoring values, e.g. a try at 4 points and a dropped goal at 3 points)

Match	Pts	Match record aggregate of points scored	Pts	Match record margin of victory
1. England v. Scotland	57	Scotland won 34-23 in 1931	21	England won 21-0 in 1924 and 27-6 in 19
2. England v. Ireland	61	England won 43-18 in 1938	27	Ireland won by 27-0 in 1947
3. England v. Wales	69	England won 69-0 in 1881	69	England won 69-0 in 1881
4. England v. France	64	England won 49-15 in 1907	44	England won by 44-0 in 1911
5. Scotland v. Ireland	51	Scotland won 36-15 in 1913	44	Scotland won 44-0 in 1877
6. Scotland v. Wales	55	Scotland won 56-0 in 1887	56	Scotland won 56-0 in 1887
7. Scotland v. France	41	Scotland won 37-4 in 1912	33	Scotland won by 37-4 in 1912
8. Ireland v. Wales	36	Wales won 33-3 in 1920 and 27-9 in 1971	34	Wales won by 34-0 in 1907
9. Ireland v. France	40	France won 33-7 in 1964	30	Ireland won 30-0 in 1913
10. Wales v. France	75	Wales won by 59-16 in 1910	52	Wales won 58-6 in 1909

FOX HUNTING

EARLIEST REFERENCES
Hunting the fox in Britain dates only from the middle of the 17th century. Prior to that time hunting was confined principally to the deer or the hare with the fox being hunted only by mistake. It is now estimated that huntsmen account for 10,000 of the 50,000 foxes killed each year.

PACK
Oldest The oldest pack of foxhounds in existence in England is the Sinnington (1680), but the old Charlton Hunt in Sussex, now extinct, the Mid-Devon and the Duke of Buckingham in the Bilsdale country, Yorkshire, hunted foxes prior to that time.

Largest The pack with the greatest number of hounds has been the Duke of Beaufort's hounds maintained at Badminton, Gloucestershire, since c. 1780. At times hunting eight times a week, this pack had 120 couples.

HUNT
Longest The longest recorded hunt was one led by Squire Sandys which ran from Holmbank, northern Lancashire, to Ulpha, Cumberland, a total of nearly 80 miles in reputedly only six hours, in January or February 1743. The longest hunt in Ireland is probably a run of 24 miles made by the Scarteen Hunt, County Limerick, from Pallas, to Knockoura in

1914. The longest duration hunt was one of 10 hou 5 minutes by the Charlton Hunt of Sussex, which ra from East Dean Wood at 7.45 a.m. to kill over 24 miles away at 5.50 p.m. on 26 Jan. 1736.

Largest fox The largest fox ever killed by a hunt in England was 23¾ lb. dog on Cross Fell, Cumberland, by a Ullswater Hunt in 1936. A fox weighing 28 lb. 2 o measuring 54 inches from nose to tail was shot on th Staffordshire-Worcestershire border on 11 Marc 1956.

BEAGLING
The oldest beagle hunt is the Royal Rock Beag Hunt, Wirral, Cheshire, whose first outing was o 28 March 1845. The Newcastle and District Beagl claim their origin from the municipally-support Newcastle Harriers existing in 1787. The Roy Agricultural College beagle pack killed 75½ brace hares in the 1966-67 season.

GAMBLING

World's biggest win The world's biggest gambling win was £770,000 for bet of 14p in the Brazilian football pools by Eduard Teixeira, 23 on 2 May 1972.

Largest Casino The largest casino in the world is the Casino, Mer d Plata, Argentina with average daily attendances 14,500 rising to 25,000 during carnivals. The Casi has more than 150 roulette tables running simultaneously. The gambling capital of the world is the State of Nevada whose casinos in 1971 removed $662,000,000 from its clients.

BINGO

Origins Bingo is a lottery game which, as keno, was developed in the 1880s from lotto, whose origin is thought to be the 17th century Italian game *tumbule*. It has long been known in the British Army (called Housey-Housey) and the Royal Navy (called Tombola). The winner was the first to complete a random selection of numbers from 1-90. The U.S.A. version called Bingo differs in that the selection is from 1-75. With the introduction of the Betting and Gaming Act on 1 Jan 1961, large scale Bingo sessions were introduced in Britain by Mecca Ltd., which played to more than 250,000 entrants in an average week during the summer of 1962.

Largest house The largest 'house' in Bingo sessions was staged at the Empire Pool, Wembley, Greater London, on 25 April 1965 when 10,000 attended. "Full House" calls have occurred when as few as 41 or as many as 67 of the 90 numbers have been called.

Largest prize Prizes have been controlled since 1 July 1970 by the Betting and Gaming Act 1968. Prior to limitation, prizes in linked games between more than 50 clubs reached £16,000. The largest in a single game was £5,000 won in the Mecca National Rally at the Empire Pool, Wembley on 29 March 1970.

Longest session A session of 60 hours (two callers) was held at St. Mark's Church Hall, London W.1 on 1-3 April 1970 and at the Royal Bingo, Haverfordwest, Pembrokeshire by Ron Taylor and Ron McKenzie (1,255 games and 72,790 calls) later in April 1970.

FOOTBALL POOLS

The winning dividend paid out by Littlewoods Pools Ltd. in their first week in February 1923 was £2.12s.0d. In April 1937 a record £30,780 was paid to R. Levy of London on 4 away wins, and in April 1947 a record £64,450 for a 1d. points pool.

Progressive list of individual record winnings

Amount	Recipient	Date	
£75,000	P.C. Frank H Chivers, 54, Aldershot, Hampshire	6 April	1948
£91,832	George A Borrett, Huyton Lancashire	26 Sept.	1950
£94,335	Thomas A Wood, 42 Carlisle	10 Oct.	1950
£104,990	Mrs Evelyn Knowlson, 43, Manchester	7 Nov.	1950
£75,000 (limit)	(45 limit winners)	from 20 Nov. to 10 Sept.	1951 1957
£205,235	Mrs Nellie McGrail (now Mrs Albert Cooper), 37, of Reddish, Cheshire	5 Nov.	1957
£206,028	W. John Brockwell, 29, Epsom Surrey	18 Feb.	1958
£209,079	Tom Riley, 58, of Horden Co. Durham	1 April	1958
£209,837	Ronald Smith of Liverpool	23 Dec.	1958
£260,104	John Dunn, 45, of Chelsea London	27 Oct.	1959
£265,352	Arthur Webb, 70, of Scarborough, Yorkshire	24 Nov.	1959
£301,739.45	Lawrence Freedman, 54, of Willesden, London	8 Dec.	1964
£316,000	Geoffrey Liddiard	Mar.	1965
£338,356.80	Percy Harrison, 52 of East Stockwith, Lincolnshire	30 Aug.	1966
£401,792	Albert Crocker, 54, of Dobwalls, Cornwall	17 April	1971
£478,062	Cyril Grimes, 62 of Hampshire	4 Mar.	1972

The odds for selecting 8 draws (if there are 8 draws) from 54 matches for and all-correct line are 1,040,465,789 to 1 against.

Shared winnings The largest first dividend ever paid was one of £458,270, paid by Littlewoods and shared between 4,722 people on 1 March 1966. The most paid on one coupon for a first dividend is £331,196 received by Percy Harrison.

Mr. Cyril Grimes the winner of the greatest individual football pool prize, £478,062 (free of tax).

Summer record The greatest amount won in out of season summer pools is £286,962 by Tom Woods, 44 of Blackburn, Lancashire on Littlewoods Treble Chance on 19 May 1971.

HORSE RACING

Highest ever odds The highest recorded odds ever secured by a backer were 560,000 to 1 by A. Stone in the Penny Jackpot Accumulator run by A. Williams Ltd. betting shop branch at Kingston, Surrey, England on 18 April 1970. On the Newbury card he won 6 races and was paid out £2,337.30 for 1 (old) penny. The world record odds on a 'double' are 24,741 to 1 secured by Mr. Montague Harry Parker of Windsor, England, for a £1 each-way 'double' on *Ivernia* and *Golden Sparkle* with William Hill.

Biggest tote win The best recorded tote win was one of £341 2s 6d. to 2s. (£341.12½ to 10p) by Mrs. Catharine Unsworth of Blundellsands, Liverpool at Haydock Park on a race won by *Coole* on 30 Nov. 1929. The highest odds in Irish tote history were £184 7s. 6d. on a 2s. 6d. (£184.37½ on a 12½p) stake, *viz.* 1,475 to 1 on *Hillhead* VI at Baldoyle on 31 Jan 1970.

Most complicated bet The most complicated bet is the Harlequin, a compound wager on 4 horses with 2,028 possible ways of winning. It was invented by Monty H. Preston of London who is reputed to be the fastest settler of bets in the world. He once completed 3,000 bets in a 4½-hour test.

Largest bookmaker The world's largest bookmaker is Ladbroke's of London with a turnover which in 1971/72 reached £100 million. The largest chain of Betting Shops is Ladbroke's with 820 shops plus 12 credit offices in the United Kingdom.

Topmost tipster The only recorded instance of a racing correspondent forecasting 8 out of 8 winners on a race card was at Taunton, Somerset, on 15 April 1969 by Tom Cosgrove of the London *Evening News*.

Greatest pay out The greatest published pay out on a single bet is £69,375. Ladbroke's to Bernard Sunley on the Derby victory of *Santa Claus* in 1964. In 1944 it was said that a backer won £200,000 in an ante post bet on *Garden Path*, which won the 2,000 Guineas.

ROULETTE

The longest run on an ungaffed (*i.e.* true) wheel

reliably recorded is 6 successive coups (in No. 10) at El San Juan Hotel, Puerto Rico on 9 July 1959. The odds were 1 in 133,448,704.

Longest Marathon The longest 'marathon' on record is one of 31 days from 10 April to 11 May 1970 at The Casino de Macao organized by Paddy O'Neil-Dunne, author of 'Roulette for the Millions,' to test the validity or invalidity of certain contentions in 20,000 spins.

ELECTIONS
Ladbroke's biggest turnover on any topic is on General Elections. The highest ever individual bet was £50,000 on Labour to win the 1964 Election by Maxwell Joseph. He made £37,272 on the odds offered.

GLIDING

An ASW-12 which holds the world's distance record.

Emanuel Swedenborg (1688-1772) made sketches of gliders in the 18th century.

The earliest man-carrying glider was designed by Sir George Cayley (1773-1857) and carried his coachman (possibly John Appleby) about 500 yards across a valley near Brompton Hall, Yorkshire, in the summer of 1853; Gliders now attain speeds of 145 m.p.h. and the Jastrzab aerobatic sailplane is designed to withstand vertical dives at up to 280 m.p.h.

Highest standard A Gold C with three diamonds (for goal flig distance and height) is the highest standard in glidi This has been gained by 24 British pilots up to J 1972.

Most titles The British national championship (instituted 19 has been won most often by Philip A. Wills (b. 26 M 1907), in 1948-49-50 and 1955. The first woman win this title was Mrs. Anne Burns of Farnha Surrey on 30 May 1966.

SELECTED WORLD RECORDS (Single-seaters)

			BRITISH NATIONAL RECORDS[1] (Single-seaters)	
Distance	907.7 miles	Hans-Werner Grosse (Germany) in an ASW-12 on 25 Apr 1972 from Lübeck to Biarritz	460.5 miles	P.D. Lane, in a Skylark 3F, Geilen-kirchen to Hiersac, Germany on 1 June 1962
Declared Goal Flight	653.1 miles	Klaus Tesch (Germany) in an LS-1, on 25 Apr 1972 from Hamburg to Nantes.	360 miles	Rear-Ad. H.C.N. Goodhart in a Skylark 3, Lasham, Hants to Portmoak, Scotland on 10 May 195
Absolute Altitude	46,266 feet	Paul F. Bikle, Jr. (U.S.A.) in a Schweizer SGS 1-23E, over Mojave, California (released at 3,963 feet) on 25 Feb, 1961 (also record altitude gain—42,303 feet)	42,520 feet*	Michael Field in a Skylark IV over Oxford—Swindon on 9 May 19
Goal and Return	569 miles	Karl Striedeck (U.S.A.) in an ASW-15 on 7 Nov 1971	385 miles	Edward Pearson in a Standard Cirrus over South Africa on 4 Jan 19
Speed over Triangular Course				
100 km.	96.34 m.p.h.	Walter Neubert (Germany) in a Kestrel 604 over the U.S.A. on 5 July 1970	78.5 m.p.h.	Edward P. Hodge in a Diamant 16.5 over Rhodesia on 1 Nov 1970
300 km.	94.16 m.p.h.	Walter Neubert (Germany) in a Kestrel 604 over Kenya on 3 Mar. 1972	81.00 m.p.h.	Edward Pearson in a Standard Cirrus over South Africa on 1 Jan 19
500 km.	85.25 m.p.h.	M. Jackson (South Africa) in a BJ-3 in South Africa on 28 Dec 1967	69.63 m.p.h.[2]	Conrad M. Greaves in a Standard Cirrus over South Africa on 1 Jan 19

[1] British National records may be set up by British pilots in any part of the world
[2] Mrs Anne Burns (G.B.) holds the women's world record for this event with 64.20 m.p.h. in a Standard Austria, at Kimberley, South Africa on 25 Dec. 196
* Subject to ratification

GOLF

Origins The earliest mention of golf occurs in a prohibiting law passed by the Scottish Parliament in March 1457 under which "golfe be utterly cryed downe". The Romans had a cognate game called *paganica* which may have been carried to Britain before A.D. 400. In February 1962 the Soviet newspaper *Izvestiya* claimed that the game was of 15th century Danish origin while the Chinese Nationalist Golf Association claim the game is of Chinese origin ("the ball hitting game") in the 3rd or 2nd century B.C. Gutta percha balls succeeded feather balls in 1848 and were in turn succeeded in 1902 by rubber-cored balls, invented in 1899 by Haskell (U.S.A.). Steel shafts were authorized in 1929.

CLUBS
The oldest club of which there is written evidence is the Gentlemen Golfers (now the Honourable Company of Edinburgh Golfers) formed in March 1744—10 years prior to the institution of the Royal and Ancient Club at St. Andrews, Fife. The oldest existing club in North America is the Royal Montreal Club (1873) and the oldest in the U.S.A. is the

Foxbury Country Club, Clarion County, Per sylvania (1887).

Largest The only club in the world with 15 courses is t Eldorado Golf Club, California, U.S.A. The club wi the highest membership in the world is the Wandere Club, Johannesburg, South Africa, with 9,1 members, of whom 850 are golfers. The club with t highest membership in the British Isles is the Roy and Ancient Golf Club at St. Andrews, Fife (1,75(The largest in England is Wentworth Club, Virgin Water, Surrey, with 1,702 members, and the largest Ireland is Royal Portrush with 594 full gentlem members.

COURSES
Highest The highest golf course in the world is the Tuctu G Club in Morococha, Peru, which is 14,335 feet abo sea-level at its lowest point. Golf has, however, bee played in Tibet at an altitude of over 16,000 feet.

The highest golf course in Great Britain is one of holes at Leadhills, Lanarkshire, 1,500 feet abo sea-level.

Lowest The lowest golf course in the world was that of t Sodom and Gomorrah Golfing Society at Kallia, the north-eastern shores of the Dead Sea, 1,250 feet below sea-level. The clubhouse was burnt down in 1948 and it is now no longer in use.

Longest hole The longest hole in the world is the 17th hole (par 6) of 745 yards at the Black Mountain Golf Club, North Carolina, U.S.A. It was opened in 1964. In August 1927 the 6th hole at Prescott Country Club in Arkansas, U.S.A., measured 838 yards. The longest hole on a championship course in Great Britain is the sixth at Troon, Ayrshire, which stretches 580 yards. The 9th at Hillsborough Golf Course, Wadsley, Sheffield, Yorkshire is 654 yards.

Largest green Probably the largest green in the world is the 5th green at Runaway Brook G.C., Bolton, Massachusetts, U.S.A. with an area greater than 28,000 square feet.

Biggest bunker The world's biggest bunker (called a trap in the U.S.A.) is Hell's Half Acre on the seventh hole of the Pine Valley course, New Jersey, U.S.A., built in 1912 and generally regarded as the world's most trying course.

LOWEST SCORES

holes and 18 holes
Men The lowest recorded score on any 18-hole course with a par score of 70 or more is 55 (15 under bogey) first achieved by A.E. Smith, the Woolacombe professional, on his home course on 1 Jan. 1936. The course measured 4,248 yards. The detail was, 4, 2, 3, 4, 2, 4, 3, 4, 3 = 29 out, and 2, 3, 3, 3, 3, 2, 5, 4, 1 = 26 in. Homero Blancas (b. 1938, of Houston, Texas) also scored 55 (27 + 28) on a course of 5,022 yards (par 70) in a tournament at the Premier Golf Course. Longview, Texas, U.S.A., on 19 Aug. 1962. The lowest recorded score on a long course (over 6,000 yards) in Britain is 58 by Harry Weetman (1920-72) the British Ryder Cup golfer, for the 6,171-yard Croham Hurst Course, Croydon, on 30 Jan. 1956.

Nine holes in 25 (4, 3, 3, 2, 3, 3, 1, 4, 2) was recorded by A.J. "Bill" Burke in a round in 57 (32 + 25) on the 6,389-yard par 71 Normandie course St. Louis, Missouri, U.S.A. on 20 May 1970.

The United States P.G.A. tournament record for 18 holes is 60 by Al Brosch (30 + 30) in the Texas Open on 10 Feb. 1951; William Nary in the El Paso Open, Texas on 9 Feb. 1952; Ted Kroll (b. August 1919) in the Texas Open on Feb. 20 1954; Wally Ulrich in the Virginia Beach Open on 11 June 1954; Tommy Bolt (b. March 1918) in the Insurance City Open on 25 June 1954; Mike Souchak (b. May 1927) in the Texas Open on 17 Feb. 1955 and Samuel Jackson Snead (b. 27 May 1912) in the Dallas Open, Texas on 14 Sept. 1957. Snead went round in 59 in the 3rd round of the Sam Snead Festival, a non-P.G.A. tournament, at White Sulphur Springs, West Virginia, U.S.A., on 16 May 1959.

Women The lowest recorded score on an 18-hole course for a woman is 62 (30 + 32) by Mary (Mickey) Kathryn Wright. (b. May 1935) of Dallas, Texas, on the Hogan Park Course (6,286 yards) at Midland, Texas, U.S.A., in November 1964.

United Kingdom The British Tournament 9-hole record is 28 by John Panton (b. 1917) in the Swallow-Penfold Tournament at Harrogate, Yorkshire, in 1952; by Bernard John Hunt (b. 2 Feb. 1930) of Hartsbourne in the Spalding Tournament at Worthing, Sussex, in August 1953; and by Lionel Platts (b. 10 Oct. 1934, Yorkshire), of Wanstead in the Ulster Open at Shandon Park, Belfast, on 11 Sept. 1965. The lowest score recorded in a first class professional tournament on a course of more than 6,000 yards in Great Britain was set at 61 (29 + 32), by Thomas Bruce Haliburton (b. Scotland, on 5 Jun 1915) of Wentworth G.C. in the Spalding Tournament at Worthing, Sussex, in

The first green at St. Andrews, Fife, Scotland in 1798.

June 1952. Peter Butler equalled the 18-hole record with 61 (32 + 29) in the Bowmaker Tournament on the Old Course at Sunningdale, Berkshire, on 4 July 1967.

36 holes The record for 36 holes is 122 (59 + 63) by Snead in the 1959 Sam Snead Festival on 16-17 May 1959. Horton Smith (see below) scored 63 + 58=121 on a short course on 21 Dec. 1928. The lowest score by a British golfer has been 61 + 65 = 126 by Tom Haliburton.

72 holes The lowest recorded score on a first-class course is 257 (27 under par) by Mike Souchak (born May 1927) in the Texas Open at San Antonio in February 1955, made up of 60 (33 + 27), 68, 64, 65 (average 64.25 per round).

The late Horton Smith (born 1908), a U.S. Masters Champion, scored 245 (63, 58, 61 and 63) for 72 holes on the 4,700-yard course (par 64) at Catalina Country Club, California, U.S.A., to win the Catalina Open on 21-23 Dec. 1928.

The lowest 72 holes in a national championship is 262 by Percy Allis (G.B.) in the 1932 Italian Open at San Remo, and by Liang Huan Lu (Formosa) in the 1971 French Open at Biarritz. The lowest for four rounds in a British first-class tournament is 262 (66, 63, 66 and 67) by Bernard Hunt in the Piccadilly Stroke Play tournament on Wentworth East Course, Virginia Water, Surrey, on 4-5 Oct. 1966. Kel Nagle of Australia shot 260 (64, 65, 66 and 65) in the Irish Hospitals Golf Tournament at Woodbrook Golf Club, near Bray, Ireland, on 21-23 July 1961.

Eclectic record The lowest recorded eclectic (from the Greek *eklektikos* = choosing) score, i.e. the sum of a player's all-time personal low scores for each hole, for a course of more than 6,000 yards is 33 by the club professional Jack McKinnon on the 6,538-yard Capilano Golf and Country Club course, Vancouver, British Columbia, Canada. This was compiled over the period 1937-1964 and reads 2-2-2-1-2-2-2-2-1 (=16 out) and 2-1-2-2-1-2-2-2-3 (=17 in) =33. The British record is 39 by John W. Ellmore at Elsham Golf Club, Lincolnshire (6,070 yards). This is made up of 2, 3, 2, 2, 2, 2, 2, 3, 2=20 (out) and 3, 1, 2, 1, 2, 2, 3, 3, 2=19 (in).

265

Highest scores The highest score for a single hole in the British Open is 21 by a player in the inaugural meeting at Prestwick in 1860. Double figures have been recorded on the card of the winner only once, when Willie Fernie (1851-1924) scored a 10 at Musselburgh, Midlothian, in 1883. Ray Ainsley of Ojai, California, took 19 strokes for the par-4 16th hole during the second round of the U.S. Open at Cherry Hills Country Club, Denver, Colorado, on 10 June 1938. Most of the strokes were used in trying to extricate the ball from a brook. Hans Merrell of Mogadore, Ohio, took 19 strokes on the par-3 16th (222 yards) during the third round of the Bing Crosby National Tournament at Cypress Point Club, Del Monte, California, U.S.A., on 17 Jan. 1959. It is recorded that Chevalier von Cittern went round 18 holes in 316 at Biarritz, France, in 1888.

Most shots for one hole A woman player in the qualifying round of the Shawnee Invitational for Ladies at Shawnee-on-Delaware, Pennsylvania, U.S.A., in c. 1912, took 166 strokes for the short 130-yard 16th hole. Her tee shot went into the Binniekill River and the ball floated. She put out in a boat with her exemplary, but statistically minded husband at the oars. She eventually beached the ball 1½ miles downstream but was not yet out of the wood. She had to play through one on the home run.

Fastest and slowest rounds With such variations in lengths of courses, speed records, even for rounds under par, are of little comparative value. Using a motor cycle and a Land Rover, Peter Hall, 24, went round the 6,080 yard (par 71) Northcliffe G.C. course, Shipley Yorkshire, on 8 Aug. 1971 in 31 min. 25 secs. in 86.

On 25 June 1971 a golf ball was propelled from the first tee to the eighteenth green (and 18 times holed out) by 45 members of the Dungannon Golf Club (5,818 yards), County Tyrone N. Ireland in 14 minutes 02.2 seconds.

The slowest stroke play tournament round was one of 5 hours 15 minutes by Sam Snead and Ben W. Hogan (b. 13 Aug. 1912) of the U.S.A. v. Stan Leonard and Al Balding (b. April 1924) of Canada in the Canada Cup contest on the West Course, at Wentworth, Surrey, in 1956. This was a 4-ball medal round, everything holed out.

Six Countries In a Day The only golfers to have played 9 hole rounds in six "countries" in a day are Dr Gerry W Donaldson of Newry and Edward S "Skip" Wilson on 21 June 1972. They started at Dundalk G.C. County Louth Republic of Ireland at 4.20 a.m. then flew to Castletown, Isle of Man; Hawarden, Wales; Chester, England; Tarnberry Scotland and finished at Whitehead G.C., Country Antrim, Northern Ireland at 9.05 p.m. On 12 June 1939 the professional Ernest Smith also using an aircraft shot a 70 at Prestwick, Scotland, 76 at Bangor, Northern Ireland, 76 at Castledown, 72 in Blackpool England and a course record 68 at Hawarden.

Most rounds in a day The greatest number of rounds played in 24 hours is 22 rounds 5 holes (401 holes) by Ian Colston 35 at Bendigo G.C. Victoria (6,061 yards) on 27-28 Nov. 1971. He covered more than 100 miles in 23¾ hours play. Edward A. Ferguson of Detroit, Michigan, U.S.A., played 828 holes (46 rounds) in 158 hours from 6.00 p.m. 25 Aug. to 8.00 a.m. 1 Sept. 1930. He walked 327½ miles.

Youngest and oldest champions The youngest winner of the British Open was Tom Morris, Jr. (born 1850, died 25 Dec. 1875) at Prestwick, Ayrshire, in 1868. The youngest winner of the British Amateur title was John Charles Beharrel (born 2 May 1938) at Troon, Ayrshire, on 2 June 1956, aged 18 years 1 month. The oldest winner of the British Amateur was the Hon. Michael Scott at

Ian Colston (Australia) during his record 22 rounds in a day.

Hoylake, Cheshire in 1933, when 54. The old British Open Champion was "Old Tom" Mo (b. 1821), who was aged 46 in 1867. In recent tim the 1967 champion, Robert de Vicenzo (Argenti was aged 44 years 93 days. The oldest United Sta Amateur Champion was Jack Westland (b. 1905) Seattle, Washington, in 1952.

Longest drives In long-driving contests 330 yards is rarely surpass at sea level. The United States P.G.A. record is 3 yards by Jack William Nicklaus (born Columb Ohio, 21 Jan. 1940), weighing 14¾ stone, in J 1963. Bill Calise, 32 won the McGregor contest Wayne on 20 June 1954 with 365 yards. The Ir Professional Golfers Association record is howe 392 yards by their amateur member William Thom (Tommie) Campbell (Foxrock Golf Club) made Dun Laoghaire, Co. Dublin, in July 1964. Under fr conditions of wind, slope, parched or frozen surfac or ricochet from a stone or flint, even grea distances are achieved. The greatest recorded drive one of 445 yards by Edward C. Bliss (1863-1917) 12 handicap player, at the 9th hole of the Old Cour Herne Bay, Kent, in August 1913. Bliss, 6 feet tall a over 13 stone, drove to the back of the green on t left-handed dog-leg. The drive was measured by government surveyor, Capt. L. H. Lloyd, who al measured the drop from the tee to resting place as feet.

Other freak drives include the driving of the 483-ya 13th at Westward Ho! by F. Lemarchand, backed b gale; and to the edge of the 465-yard downhill 9th the East Devon Course, Budleigh Salterton, by T.H. Haydon in September 1934. Neither drive w accurately measured.

Perhaps the longest recorded drive on level grou was one of an estimated 430 yards by Craig Ral Wood (born 18 Nov. 1901) of the U.S.A. on t 530-yard fifth hole at the Old Course, St. Andrew Fife, in the Open Championship in June 1933. T ground was parched and there was a strong followi wind.

Tony Jacklin drove a ball from the roof of the Sav Hotel (125 feet above the pavement) 353 yards splash into the River Thames on 26 Nov. 1969. drive of 2,640 yards (1½ miles) across ice w achieved by an Australian meteorologist named N Lied at Mawson Base, Antarctica, in 1962. On t

Moon the energy expended on a mundane 300-yard drive would achieve, craters permitting, a distance of a mile.

Longest hitter The golfer regarded as the longest consistent hitter the game has ever known is the 6 feet 5 inches tall, 17 st. 2 lb. George Bayer (U.S.A.), the 1957 Canadian Open Champion. His longest measured drive was one of 420 yards at the fourth in the Las Vegas Invitational, Nevada, in 1953. It was measured as a precaution against litigation since the ball struck a spectator. Bayer also drove a ball pin high on a 426-yard hole in Tucson, Arizona, U.S.A. Radar measurements show that an 87 m.p.h. impact velocity for a golf ball falls to 46 m.p.h. in 3.0 seconds.

Longest Putt The longest recorded putt in a major tournament was one of 86 feet on the vast 13th green at the Augusta National, Georgia by Cary Middlecoff in the 1955 Master's Tournament.

The Open The Open Championship was inaugurated in 1860 at Prestwick, Ayrshire, Scotland. The lowest score for 9 holes is 29 by Tom Haliburton (Wentworth) and Peter W. Thomson, M.B.E. (Australia) in the first round of the Open on the Royal Lytham and St. Anne's course at Lytham St. Anne's, Lancashire, on 10 July 1963.

The lowest scoring round is 63 (all in qualifying rounds) by Frank Jowle (b. 14 May 1912) at the New Course, St. Andrews (6,526 yards), on 4 July 1955; by Peter William Thomson, M.B.E. (b. 23 Aug. 1929) of Melbourne, Australia at Royal Lytham and St. Anne's (6,635 yards) on 30 June 1958; and Maurice Bembridge (Little Aston) at Delamere Forest, Cheshire, on 7 July 1967. The best by an amateur is 65 by Ronnie David Bell Mitchell Shade, M.B.E. (b. 15 Oct. 1938) in a qualifying round on the Eden Course (6,250 yards), St. Andrews, on 4 July 1964. The lowest rounds in The Open itself have been 65 by (Thomas) Henry Cotton, M.B.E. (b. Holmes Chapel, Cheshire, 26 Jan. 1907) at Royal St. George's, Sandwich, Kent in the 2nd round on 27 June 1934 to complete a 36-hole record of 132 (67 + 65); by Eric Brown at Royal Lytham and St. Anne's Lancashire in the third round on 3 July 1958: by Christy O'Connor (b. County Donegal, Ireland, 1925) (Royal Dublin) at Lytham in the 2nd round on 10 July 1969; and by Neil C. Coles (b. 26 Sept. 1934) (Coombe Hill) on the Old Course, St. Andrews in the 1st round on 8 July 1970. The lowest 72-hole aggregate is 276 (71, 69, 67, 69) by Arnold Daniel Palmer (b. 10 Sept. 1929) of Latrobe, Pennsylvania, U.S.A., at Troon, Ayrshire, ending on 13 July 1962.

British Amateur The lowest score for nine holes in the British Amateur Championship (inaugurated in 1885) is 29 by Richard

Michael Bonallack, O.B.E., who holds the record for amateur international appearances for England with more than 70 since 1957.

Davol Chapman (born 23 March 1911) of the U.S.A. at Sandwich in 1948.

Michael Francis Bonallack, O.B.E. (b. 1935) shot a 61 (32+29) on the par-71 6,905-yard course at Ganton, Yorkshire, on 27 July 1968 in the 1st round of the English Amateur championship.

U.S. Open The United States Open Championship was inaugurated in 1894. The lowest 72-hole aggregate is 275 (71, 67, 72 and 65) by Jack Nicklaus on the Lower Course (7,015 yards) at Baltusrol Country Club, Springfield, New Jersey, on 15-18 June 1967 and 275 (69, 68, 69 and 69) by Lee Trevino (born near Horizon City, Texas 1940) at Oak Hill Country Club, Rochester, N.Y., on 13-16 June 1968. The lowest score for 18 holes is 64, achieved three times: by Lee Mackey, Jr., at Merion Country Club in Ardmore, Pennsylvania, on 8 June 1950; by Tommy Jacobs on the 7,053-yard course at the Congressional Country Club, Washington D.C., on 19 June 1964; and by Rives McBee at the Olympic Country Club in San Francisco, California, on 17 June 1966.

U.S. Masters The lowest score in the U.S. Masters (instituted on the par-72 6,980-yard Augusta National Golf Course, Georgia, in 1934) has been 271 by Jack Nicklaus in 1965. The lowest rounds have been 64 by Lloyd Mangrum (1st round, 1940) and Jack Nicklaus (3rd round, 1965).

MOST TITLES
The most titles won in the world's major championships are as follows:

The Open	Harry Vardon (1870-1937)	6	1896-98-99, 1903-11-14
British Amateur	John Ball (1861-1940)	8	1888-90-92-94-99, 1907-10-12
U.S. Open	W. Anderson	4	1901-03-04-05
	Robert Tyre Jones, Jr. (1902-71)	4	1923-26-29-30
	Ben William Hogan (b. 13 Aug. 1912)	4	1948-50-51-53
U.S. Amateur	R. T. Jones, Jr. (1902-71)	5	1924-25-27-28-30
P.G.A. Championship (U.S.A.)	Walter Charles Hagen	5	1921-24-25-26-27
Masters Championship (U.S.A.)	Arnold D. Palmer	4	1958-60-62-64
U.S. Women's Open	Miss Elizabeth (Betsy) Earle-Rawls	4	1951-53-57-60
	Miss "Mickey" Wright	4	1958-59-61-64
U.S. Women's Amateur	Mrs. Glenna C. Vare (*née* Collett)	6	1922-25-28-29-30-35
British Women's	Miss Charlotte Cecilia Pitcairn Leitch	4	1914-20-21-26
	Miss Joyce Wethered (born 1901) (now Lady Heathcoat-Amory)	4	1922-24-25-29

NOTE: *Jones won 13 major titles in 1923-30 while Nicklaus is the only golfer to have won 5 different such titles and the Open, U.S. Open, Masters and P.G.A. titles twice.*

Weller Noble (U.S.A.) who has shot his age or better 644 times.

Richest prizes The greatest first place prize money was $60,000 (total purse $300,000 [£125,000]) in the Dow Jones Open Invitational played at Upper Montclair Country Club, Clifton, New Jersey on 27-30 Aug. 1970 won by Bobby Nichols (U.S.) and £25,000 ($60,000) in the John Player Golf Classic at Hollinwell, Nottinghamshire, England on 3-6 Sept. 1970.

Highest earnings The all time professional money-winner is Jack Nicklaus who surpassed Arnold Palmer's record with $1,477,200.86 (then £615,500) on 6 Mar. 1972. His record for official tournaments in a year is $244,490.50 (then £101,871) for 1971. The earnings for a woman have been $332,117 (£127,737) by Kathy Whitworth (U.S.A.) up to 15 Jan. 1972.

Most tournament wins The record for winning tournaments in a single season is 19 (out of 31) by Byron Nelson (b. 4 Feb. 1912) of Fort Worth, Texas, in 1945. Of these 11 were consecutive, including the P.G.A., Canadian P.G.A. and Canadian Open, from 16 March to 15 August. He was a money prize winner in 113 consecutive tournaments. Miss Whitworth (see above) won 54 Ladies P.G.A. tournaments to the end of 1971.

Most club championships The British record for amateur club championships is 20 consecutive wins (1937-39 and 1946-62) by R. W. H. Taylor at the Dyke Golf Club, Brighton, Sussex, who retired unbeaten in July 1963, and by Edward Christopher Chapman (b. 9 April 1909), who won the Tunbridge Wells G.C. Scratch Championship 20 consecutive years from 1951 to 1971.

HOLES IN ONE

Longest The longest hole ever holed in one shot is the 10th hole (444 yards) at Miracle Hills Golf Club, Omaha, Nebraska, U.S.A. Robert Mitera achieved a hole-in-one there on 7 Oct. 1965. Mitera, aged 21, stands 5 feet 6 inches tall and weighs 165 lb. (11 st. 11 lb.). He is a two handicap player who can normally drive 245 yards. A 50 m.p.h. gust carried his shot over a 290-yard drop-off. The ground in front testified to the remaining 154 yards. The feminine record is 393 yards by Marie Robie of Wollaston, Massachusetts, U.S.A., on the first hole at the Furnace Brook Golf Club, western Massachusetts, on 4 Sept. 1949.

The longest hole in one performed in the British Is is the 5th (380 yards) on Tankersley Park course, ne Sheffield, Yorkshire, by David Hulley in 1961.

Most The record total number of "aces" recorded in t United States in a year has been 18,319 (indicati more than 100 on some days) in 1969. The great number of holes-in-one in a career is 37 by Art W. Jr. (b. November 1923) between 1936 and 1967. T British record is 30 by Charles T. Cheval (b. 22 July 1902) of Heaton Moor Golf Club, Stoc port, Lancashire between 20 June 1918 and 17 Ju 1965. Dr. Joseph O. Boydstone scored holes-in-one the 3rd, 4th and 9th holes on the Bakersfield Pub Golf Course, California, U.S.A., on 10 Oct. 1961. T holes measured 210, 132 and 135 yards.

Double albatross There is no record instance of a golfer performi three consecutive holes-in-one but there are at lea 14 cases of "aces" being achieved in two consecuti holes of which the greatest was Norman L. Manle unique "double albatross" on the par-4 330-yard 7 and par-4 290-yard 8th holes on the Del Va Country Club course, Saugus, California, on 2 Se 1964. Three examples by Britons have been by Rog Game at Walmer and Kingsdown, Kent in 196 Charles Fairlie at Gourock in June 1968, and by t professional John Hudson, 25, of Hendon at Roy Norwich (11th eagle and 12th albatross) in t Martini International on 11 June 1971.

Youngest and oldest The youngest golfer recorded to have shot a hole-i one was Tommy Moore (6 years 36 days) Hagerstown, Maryland on the 145-yard 4th at th Woodbrier Golf Course, Martinsville, West Virgini on 8 March 1968. The oldest golfer to have pe formed the feat is Walter Fast, aged 92 years 1 days, at Madison G.C., Peoria, Illinois on the 140-ya 13th hole on 25 June 1971. The Canadian Charl Youngman of the Tam O'Shantar Club, Toronto reputed to have holed-in-one aged 93.

Shooting your age The record for scoring one's age in years over a 18-hole round is held by Weller Noble who betwee 1955 (scoring 64 aged 64) on 13 Dec. 1971 h amassed 644 "age scores" on the Claremont Countr Club, Oakland, California par-68 course of 5,73 yards. The course is provenly harder than many o 6,000 yards or more on which to produce low score

The oldest player to score under his age is C. Arthu Thompson (b. 1869) of Victoria, British Columbi Canada, who scored 96 on the Uplands course o 6,215 yards on 3 Oct. 1966. He was reported to b still in action aged 101 in April 1971.

Largest Tournament The largest golfing tournament in the world has bee the 1971 U.S. Open with 4,349 entrants. The *Dail Mirror* North of England Amateur (Match Play Tournament in 1972 attracted a record 4,267 ama teur competitors.

World Cup (formerly) Canada Cup The World Cup (instituted as the Canada Cup i 1953) has been won most often by the U.S.A., wit eleven victories in 1955-1956-1960-1961-1962-196 1964-1966-1967-1969-1971. The only man to hav been on six winning teams has been Arnold Palme (1960, 62-64, 66-67). Only Nicklaus has taken th individual title 3 times (1963-64-71). The lowes aggregate score for 144 holes is 545 by Australi (Bruce Devlin and David Graham) at San Isidr Buenos Aires, Argentina on 12-15 Nov. 1970. Th lowest individual score has been 269 by Roberto d Vicenzo then 47 (Argentina) also in 1970.

Throwing the golf ball The lowest recorded score for throwing a golf ba round 18 holes (over 6,000 yards) is 84 by Douglas V Shipe at the 6,220 yard A.L. Gustin Course, Univer sity of Missouri, Columbia, Missouri, U.S.A. o 16 Nov. 1971.

Sherry's Prince, **the only dog to win three consecutive English classics.**

GREYHOUND RACING

Earliest meeting In Sept. 1876 a greyhound meeting was staged at Hendon, North London with a railed hare operated by a windlass. Modern greyhound racing originated with the perfecting of the mechanical hare by Oliver P. Smith at Emeryville, California, U.S.A., in 1919. The earliest greyhound race behind a mechanical hare in the British Isles was at Belle Vue, Manchester, opened on 24 July 1926.

Derby The only dog to have twice won the English Greyhound Derby (held since 1928 over 525 yards at the White City Stadium, London) was *Mick the Miller* (whelped in Ireland, June 1926 and died 1939) on 25 July 1929, when owned by Albert H. Williams, and on 28 June 1930 (owned by Mrs. Arundel H. Kempton). This dog won a record sequence of 19 consecutive races from 19 March to 20 Aug. 1930. The highest prize was £10,000 to *Delores Rocket* for the Derby on 26 June 1971. The only dogs to win the English, Scottish and Welsh Derby "triple" are *Trev's Perfection,* owned by Fred Trevillion, in 1947, and *Mile Bush Pride,* owned by Noel W. Purvis, in 1959.

Grand National The only dog to have thrice won the Greyhound Grand National (instituted 1927) over 525 yards and 4 flights is *Sherry's Prince,* a 75 lb. dog whelped in April 1967, owned by Mrs Joyce Mathews of Sanderstead, Surrey. He won in 1970, 1971 (record 29.22 secs) and 1972 when he won by 6¼ lengths.

Fastest 525 yard timings The fastest *photo*-timing is 28.26 seconds or 37.99 m.p.h. by *Rory* on 17 June 1972. The fastest *photo*-time over 525 yard hurdles is 29.10 secs. (36.90 m.p.h.) by *Sherry's Prince* on 8 May 1971.

Fastest dog The highest speed at which any greyhound has been timed is 41.72 m.p.h. (410 yards in 20.1 secs.) by *The Shoe* on the then straightaway track at Richmond, N.S.W., Australia on 25 Apr. 1968. It is estimated that he covered the last 100 yards in 4.5 secs. or at 45.45 m.p.h. The highest speed recorded for a greyhound in Great Britain is 39.13 m.p.h. by *Beef Cutlet,* when covering a straight course of 500 yards in 26.13 seconds at Blackpool, Lancashire, on 13 May 1933.

GYMNASTICS

Earliest references Gymnastics were widely practised in Greece during the period of the ancient Olympic Games (776 B.C. to A.D. 393), but they were not revived until c. 1780.

World Championships The greatest number of individual titles won by a man in the World Championships is 10 by Boris Shakhlin (U.S.S.R.) between 1954 and 1964. He also won 3 team titles. The female record is 10 individual wins and 5 team titles by Larissa Semyonovna Latynina (born 1935, retired 1966) of the U.S.S.R., between 1956 and 1964.

Olympic Games Italy has won most Olympic team titles with four victories in 1912, 1920, 1924 and 1932.

The only man to win six individual gold medals is Boris Shakhlin (U.S.S.R.), with one in 1956, four (two shared) in 1960 and one in 1964. He also was a member of the winning Combined Exercises team in 1956.

The most successful woman has been Vera Caslavska-Odlozil (Czechoslovakia), with 7 individual Gold Medals, three in 1964 and four (one shared) in 1968. She also won a team Silver Medal in 1960, 1964 and 1968 and an individual Silver Medal in 1968. Latynina won six individual Gold Medals and first places in three team events in 1956-64.

British Championship The most times that the British Gymnastic Championship has been won is 10 by Arthur Whitford in 1928-36 and 39. He was also in four winning Championship teams. The women's record is 5 wins by Miss Margaret Bell, 1965-69.

Rope climbing The United States Amateur Athletic Union records are tantamount to world records: 20 feet (hands alone—2.8 seconds, Don Perry (U.S.A.) at Champaign, Illinois, U.S.A., on 3 April 1954; 25 feet (hands alone). 4.7 seconds, Garvin S. Smith at Los Angeles, California, U.S.A., on 19 April 1947.

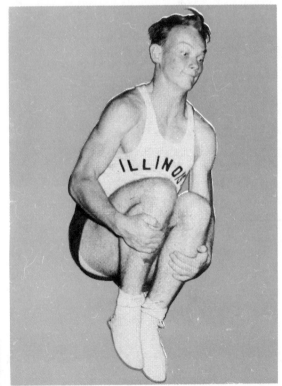

Dick Browning (U.S.A.) the greatest tumbler of all-time.

Chinning the bar The greatest number of chin-ups (from a dead hang position) recorded is 106 by William D. Reed at the Weightman Hall, University of Pennsylvania, U.S.A. on 23 June 1969. The feminine record for one-handed chin-ups is 27 in Hermann's Gym, Philadelphia, Pennsylvania, U.S.A. in 1918 by Lillian Leitzel (Mrs Alfredo Codona) (U.S.A.), who was killed in Copenhagen, Denmark, on 12 Feb 1931. Her total would be unmatched by any male but it is doubtful if they were achieved from a 'dead hang' position. It is believed that only one person in 100,000 can chin a bar one-handed. Francis Lewis (b. 1896) of Beatrice, Nebraska, U.S.A. in May 1914 achieved 7 consecutive chins using only the middle finger of his left hand. His bodyweight was 158 lb.

Press-ups The greatest recorded number of consecutive press-ups is 6,006 in 3 hours 54 minutes by Chick Linster, aged 16, of Wilmette, Illinois, U.S.A. on 5 Oct 1965. Masura Noma of Mihara, Japan did 1,227 press-ups in 37 minutes in January 1968. Jim Slegh of Long Beach, California did 72 one-arm press-ups on 9 Oct 1939.

Sit-ups The greatest recorded number of consecutive sit-ups on a hard surface without feet pinned down is 15,512 in 12 hours 24 mins. by Jonathan C. Mote (b. 1955) on 9 April 1972 at Hamilton Southeastern High School, near Noblesville, Indiana, U.S.A.

Greatest tumbler The greatest tumbler of all time is Dick Browning (U.S.A.) who made a backward somersault over a 7-foot 3-inch bar at Santa Barbara, California, in April 1954. In his unique repertoire was a 'round-off', backward handspring, backward somersault with half-twist, walk-out, tinsica tigna round-off, backward handspring, double backward somersault.

Hand-to-hand balancing The longest horizontal dive achieved in any hand-to-hand balancing act is 22 feet by Harry Berry (top mounter) and the late Nelson Soule (understander) of the Bell-Thazer Brothers from Kentucky, U.S.A., who played at State fairs and vaudevilles from 1912 to 1918. Berry used a 10-foot tower and trampoline for impetus.

Largest gymnasium The world's largest gymnasium is Yale University's Payne Whitney Gymnasium at New Haven, Connecticut, U.S.A., completed in 1932 and valued at $18,000,000 (£7,500,000). The building, known as the 'Cathedral of Muscle', has nine storeys with wings of five storeys each. It is equipped with four basketball courts, three rowing tanks, 28 squash courts, 12 handball courts, a roof jogging track and a 25-yard by 42-foot swimming pool on the first floor and a 55-yard long pool on the third floor.

HANDBALL (COURT)

Handball played against walls or in a court is a game of ancient Celtic origin. In the early 19th century only a front wall was used but gradually side and back walls were added. The earliest international contest was in New York City, U.S.A. in 1887 between the champions of the U.S.A. and Ireland. The court is now a standardized 60 feet by 30 feet in Ireland, Ghana and Australia, and 40 feet by 20 feet in Canada, Mexico and the U.S.A. The game is played with both a hard and a soft ball.

Championship World championships were inaugurated in New York in October 1964 with competitors from Australia, Canada, Ireland, Mexico and the U.S.A. U.S.A. won in 1964; Canada and U.S.A. shared the title in 1967 and Ireland won in 1970.

Most titles In Ireland the most titles (instituted 1925) have be won as follows:

Hardball

Singles	John J. Gilmartin (Kilkerry)	
	10	1936-42, 1945-47
Doubles	John Ryan and John Doyle (Wexford)	
	6	1952, 1954-58

Softball

Singles	Paddy Perry (Roscommon)	
	8	1930-37
Doubles	James O'Brien and Patrick Downey (Kerry)	
	7	1955-56, 1960-64

The U.S. Championship 4 wall singles has been w 6 times by Jimmy Jacobs in 1955-56-57-60-64-6

HANDBALL (FIELD

Handball, similar to association football with substitution of the hands for the feet, was first play c. 1895. It was introduced into the Olympic Games Berlin in 1936 as an 11-a-side outdoor game wi Germany winning, but in 1972 it was an indoor gar with 7-a-side, which has been the standard size team since 1952.

By 1971 there were 41 countries affiliated to t International Handball Federation, a World C competition and an estimated 5 million participan The earliest international match was when Swed beat Denmark on 8 March 1935.

HOCKEY

Origins A representation of two hockey players apparently an orthodox "bully" position was found in Tomb N 16 at Beni Hasan, United Arab Republic (former Egypt) and has been dated to c. 2000 B.C. There i British reference to the game in Lincolnshire in 127 The oldest club is Blackheath, founded in 1861. Th first country to form a national association w England (The Hockey Association) in 1886.

MEN

Earliest international The first international match was the Wales v. Irelar match at Rhyl on 26 Jan. 1895. Ireland won 3–0.

Highest international score The highest score in international hockey was whe India defeated the United States 24–1 at L Angeles, California, U.S.A., in the 1932 Olymp Games. The Indians were Olympic Champions fro the re-inception of Olympic hockey in 1928 unt 1960, when Pakistan beat them 1–0 at Rome. The had their seventh win in 1964. Four Indians have wo 3 Olympic gold medals—Dhyan Chand and Richard Allen (1928, 1932, 1936) and Leslie Claudius an Randhir Gentle (1948, 1952, 1956). The greates number of goals in a home international match wa when England defeated France 16–0 at Beckenha on 25 March 1922. The 1971 World Cup was won b Pakistan at Barcelona.

Longest game The longest international game on record was one 145 minutes (into the sixth period of extra time when Netherlands beat Spain 1–0 in the Olymp tournament at Mexico City on 25 Oct. 1968. Aft Moss Sports had played Symington's in the Count mixed senior competition at Leicester on 22 Marc 1969 for 170 minutes without decision, a coin w tossed and Symington's won.

Most appearances The most by a home countries player is 98 by Harol A. Cahill with 65 for Ireland and 33 for Great Britai won from 1953 to 1972.

England 55, Michael W. Corby (Middlesex) (1961-72 Wales 69, David J. Prosser (1961-72) Scotland 63, Frederick H. Scott (Hounslow) (up t 1971)

Michael Corby holder of the England hockey cap record.

Ireland 68, H.D. Judge (1957-72)
Great Britain 56, John W. Neill (England) (1959-68)

Five brothers In the England *v*. Ireland match of 1904, the Irish team included five brothers, Jack, Cecil, Willie, Walter and Nick Peterson of the Palmerston Club. A sixth brother, Bertie, had played for Ireland *v*. Wales in 1900 and 1902.

Greatest scoring feat M. C. Marckx (Bowdon 2nd XI) scored 19 goals against Brooklands 2nd XI (score 23−0) on 31 Dec. 1910. He was selected for England in March 1912 but declined due to business priorities.

WOMEN

Origins The earliest women's club was East Molesey in Surrey, England formed in *c*. 1887. The first national association was the Irish Ladies' Hockey Union founded in 1894. The All England Women's Hockey Association held its first formal meeting in Westminster Town Hall, London, on 23 Nov, 1895. The first international match was an England *v*. Ireland game in Dublin in 1896. Ireland won 2−0. The 1971 World Championship was won by the Netherlands over New Zealand in Auckland, N.Z.

Highest international score The highest score in a women's international match occurred when England defeated France 23−0 at Merton, Surrey, on 3 Feb. 1923.

Most appearances The England records are 53 caps by Miss Mildred Mary Knott (1923-39) and 17 seasons by Miss Mabel Bryant (1907-1929), who won 39 caps. The Irish record is 58 (46 full caps and 12 touring) by Mrs. Sean Kyle (born Maeve Esther Enid Shankey, 6 Oct. 1928) between November 1947 and 1966.

Highest attendance The highest attendance at a women's hockey match was 65,000 for the match between England and Wales at the Empire Stadium, Wembley, Greater London, on 8 March 1969.

HORSE RACING

Origins Horsemanship was an important part of the Hittite culture of Anatolia, Turkey in the 2nd millenium B.C. The 23rd ancient Olympic Games of 624 B.C. in Greece featured horse racing. The earliest horse race recorded in England was one held in about A.D. 210 at Netherby, Yorkshire, among Arabians brought to Britain by Lucius Septimius Severus (A.D. 146-211), Emperor of Rome. The oldest race still being run annually is the Lanark Silver Bell, instituted in Scotland by William Lion (1165-1214).

The Jockey Club was formed in 1750-51 and the General Stud Book started in 1791. Racing colours (silks) became compulsory in 1889.

RACECOURSES

Largest The world's largest racecourse is the Newmarket course, (founded 1636) on which the Beacon Course, the longest of the 19 courses, is 4 miles 397 yards long and the Rowley Mile is 167 feet wide. The border between Suffolk and Cambridgeshire runs through the Newmarket course. The world's largest grandstand is that opened in 1968 at Belmont Park, Nassau County, Long Island, N.Y., U.S.A. at a cost of $30,700,000 (£12.8 million). It is 110 feet tall, 440 yards long and contains 908 mutuel windows. The highest seating capacity at any racetrack is 40,000 at Atlantic City Audit, New Jersey, U.S.A.

Smallest The world's smallest racecourse is the Lebong racecourse, Darjeeling, West Bengal, India (altitude 7,000 feet), where the complete lap is 481 yards. It was laid out *c*. 1885 and used as a parade ground.

HORSES

Greatest record The horse with the best recorded win-loss record and the only one on which it was safe to bet was *Kincsem*, a Hungarian mare foaled in 1874, who was unbeaten in 54 races (1877-1880), including the Goodwood Cup of 1878. *Camarero* owned by Don José Coll Vidal of Puerto Rico, foaled in 1951, had a winning streak of 56 races from 19 Apr 1953 to 17 Aug 1955. He died 'from a colic' on 26 Aug 1956 the day after his 73rd win in 77 starts.

Tallest The tallest horse ever to race is *Fort d'Or*, owned by Lady Elizabeth (Eliza) Nugent (*née* Guinness) of Berkshire, England. He stands 18 hands 2 inches.

Highest price The highest price ever paid for a stallion is $5,440,000 (£2,666,666) paid after the 1970 season by a 32 share syndicate for the Canadian-bred *Nijinsky* owned by Charles Engelhard of Far Hills, New Jersey, U.S.A.

Greatest winning The greatest amount ever won by a horse is $1,977,896 (then £706,391) by *Kelso* (foaled in 1957) in the U.S.A., between 1959 and his retirement on 10 Mar 1966. He is now the supreme status symbol of the hunt under Mrs. Richard C. du Pont. In 63 races he won 39, came second in 12 and third in 2. The most successful horse of all time has been *Buckpasser*, whose career winnings were $1,462,014 (£609,172) in 1965-66-67. He won 25 races out of 31. The most won by a mare is $783,674 (£279,883) by *Cicada*. In 42 races she won 23, came second in 8 and third in 6. The most won in a year is $817,941 (£340,808) by *Damascus* in 1967. His total reached $1,176,781.

Largest prizes The richest race ever held is the All-American Futurity, a race for quarter-horses over 400 yards at Ruidoso Downs, New Mexico, U.S.A. The prizes in 1971 totalled $753,910 (then £314,129). *Laico Bird*, the winner in 1967 in 20.11 seconds, received $228,300 (£81,535.) The largest single prize ever paid was 1,094,126 francs, plus 78 per cent. of the entry fees, making 1,480,000 francs (then £107,000) to the owner of *Prince Royal II*, winner of the 43rd Prix de l'Arc de Triomphe at Longchamp, Paris, on 4 Oct 1964.

JOCKEYS

The most successful jockey of all time has been Willie Shoemaker (b. weighing 2½ lb. on 19 Aug 1931) now weighing 98 lb. after 23 years in the saddle, beating Johnny Longden's life-time record of 6,032 winners at Del Mar, California, U.S.A. on 7 Sept 1970. Shoemaker, known as The Ice Man, stands 4 feet 11½ inches and rode his 6,223rd winner on his 40th birthday. From 19 March 1949 his winnings have been $46,000,000. His 485 wins from 1,683 mounts in 1953 constitute a record for any one year.

The greatest amount ever won by any jockey in a year is $3,088,888 by Braulio Baeza (b. Panama) in the U.S.A. in 1967. The oldest jockey was Levi Barlin-

271

game (U.S.A.)., who rode his last race at Stafford, Kansas, U.S.A., in 1932 aged 80. The youngest jockey was Frank Wootton (English Champion jockey 1909-12), who rode his first winner in South Africa aged 9 years 10 months. The lightest recorded jockey was Kitchener (died 1872), who won the Chester Cup on *Red Deer* in 1844 at 3 stone 7 lb. He was said to have weighed only 2 stone 12 lb. in 1840.

The greatest number of winners ridden on one card is 8 by Hubert S. Jones at Caliente, California, U.S.A. on 11 June 1944 of which 5 were photo-finishes. The longest winning streak is 12 by Sir Gordon Richards with 12 (last race at Nottingham on 3 Oct, 6 out of 6 at Chepstow on 4 Oct and the first 5 races next day at Chepstow) in 1953.

Trainers The greatest amount ever won by a trainer in one year is $2,456,250 (then £881,519) by Eddie A, Neloy (U.S.A.) in 1966 when his horses won 93 races.

Dead heats There is no recorded case in turf history of a quintuple dead heat. The nearest approach was in the Astley Stakes, at Lewes, England, in August 1880 when *Mazurka*, *Wandering Nun* and *Scobell* triple dead-heated for first place, just ahead of *Cumberland* and *Thora*, who dead-heated for fourth place. Each of the five jockeys thought he had won. The only two known examples of a quadruple dead heat were between *The Defaulter*, *Squire of Malton*, *Reindeer* and *Pulcherrima* in the Omnibus Stakes at The Hoo, England, on 26 April 1851, and between *Overreach*, *Lady Go-Lightly*, *Gamester* and *The Unexpected* at the Houghton Meeting at Newmarket on 22 Oct 1855. The earliest recorded photo-finish dead heat in Britain was between *Phantom Bridge* and *Resistance* in the 5-furlong Beechfield Handicap at Doncaster on 22 Oct. 1947.

Longest race The longest recorded horse race was one of 1,200 miles in Portugal, won by a horse *Emir* bred from Egyptian-bred Blunt Arab stock. The holder of the world's record for long distance racing and speed is *Champion Crabbet*, who covered 300 miles in 52 hours 33 minutes, carrying 17½ stone, in 1920. In 1831 Squire George Osbaldeston (1787-1866), M.P. of East Retford, covered 200 miles in 8 hours 42 minutes at Newmarket, using 50 mounts, so averaging 22.99 m.p.h. In 1967 G. Steecher covered 100 miles on a single horse in 11 hours 4 minutes in Victoria, Australia.

Shortest price The shortest odds ever quoted for any racehorse are 10,000 to 1 on for *Dragon Blood*, ridden by Lester Piggott (G.B.) in the Premio Naviglio in Milan, Italy on 1 June 1967. Odds of 100 to 1 on were quoted for the United States horse *Man o'War* (foaled 29 March 1917, died 1 Nov. 1947) on three separate occasions in 1920., and for the two British horses, *Ormonde* in the Champion Stakes on 14 Oct 1886 (three runners), and *Sceptre* in the Limekiln Stakes on 27 Oct 1903 (two runners).

BRITISH TURF RECORDS

Most expensive horses The highest price ever paid for a horse in the Briti Isles is £250,000, paid in February 1953 for *Tuly* by the Irish National Stud to the Rt. Hon. Aga Sult. Sir Mohammed Shah, H.H. Aga Khan III, G.C.S. G.C.M.G., G.C.I.E., G.C.V.O. (1877-1957) of Ir (Persia). *Sir Ivor* commands a covering fee of £8,00 A sum of £250,000 was also paid for *Ballymoss* by syndicate in September 1958. The French hor *Charlottesville* was bought by a syndicate f £336,000 from H.H. Shah Karim, Aga Khan I (b. 13 Dec 1936), in November 1960. The reco payment for a horse in training is 136,000 guine (£142,800) for *Vaguely Noble* at Park Paddock Newmarket auction sale by Dr. Robert A. Frankly (U.S.) on 7 Dec 1967.

Most successful horses Only fillies are eligible to win all five classics. *Sceptr* came closest in 1902 when she won the 1,00 Guineas, 2,000 Guineas, Oaks and St. Leger. In 186 *Formosa* won the same four but dead-heated in th 2,000 Guineas. The most races won in a season is 2 by *Fisherman* in 1856. *Catherina* won 79 out of 17 races between 1833 and 1841. The only horse to wi the same race in seven successive years was *D Syntax*, who won the Preston Gold Cup (1815-21 The most successful sire was *Stockwell*, whos progeny won 1,153 races (1858-76) and in 1866 set record of 132 races won. The first English horse t win more than £200,000 in prize money on Englis racecourses is *Brigadier Gerard* during the 197 season.

Most successful owners The greatest amount of stake money won £1,025,592 from 784 races by H.H. Aga Khan I (1877-1957) from 1922 until his death. These in luded 35 classics, of which 17 were English classic The record for a season was set by Mr. H.J. Joel, wh surpassed the previous record of £100,668 by wir ning £120,924 in 1967. The most wins in a season 106 by Mr. David Robinson. The most English classic won is 20 by the 4th Duke of Grafton, K.G (1760-1844), from 1813 to 1831.

Most successful trainers Captain Sir Cecil Charles Boyd-Rochfort, K.C.V.C (b. 16 April 1887) has earned more than £1,500,00 for his patrons. The record for a season is £256,89 by Charles Francis Noel Murless (born 1910) in 1967 The most classics won by a trainer is 40 or 41 by Joh Scott, including 16 St. Leger winners between 182 and 1862.

Most successful jockeys Sir Gordon Richards (b. 5 March 1904) retired i 1954, having won 4,870 races from 21,834 mount since his first win at Leicester on 21 March 1921. I 1953, after 27 attempts, he won the Derby, six day after being knighted. He set a record of 12 con secutive wins by winning the last race in which h rode at Nottingham on 3 Oct 1933, all six a Chepstow on the 4th and the first five on the 5th. I 1947 he won a record 269 races. The most classic

SPEED RECORDS

Distance	Time	m.p.h.	Name	Course	Date	
¼ mile	20.8s	43.26	*Big Racket* (U.S.A.)	Lomas de Sotelo, Mexico	5 Feb.	194:
½ mile (straight)	45.0s	40.00	*Gloaming* (N.Z.)	Wellington, New Zealand	12 Jan.	192
½ mile	45.0s	40.00	*Beau Madison* (U.S.A.)	Phoenix, Arizona, U.S.A.	30 Mar.	195
	45.0s	40.00	*Another Nell* (U.S.A.)	Cicero, Ill, U.S.A.	8 May	196
⁵⁄₈ mile	53.6s	41.98	*Indigenous* (G.B.)	Epsom, Surrey	2 June	196
¾ mile	1m 07.4s	40.06	*Zip Pocket* (U.S.A.)	Phoenix, Arizona, U.S.A.	6 Dec.	196
	1m.07.4s	40.06	*Vale of Tears* (U.S.A.)	Ab Sar Ben, Omaha, Neb., U.S.A.	7 June	196
	1m.06.2s	40.78	*Broken Tindril* (G.B.)	* Brighton, Sussex	6 Aug.	192
Mile	1m.31.8s	39.21	*Soueida* (G.B.)	* Brighton, Sussex	19 Sept.	196
	1m.31.8s	39.21	*Loose Cover*, (G.B.)	* Brighton, Sussex	9 June	196
	1m.32.2s	39.04	*Dr. Fager* (U.S.A.)	Arlington, Ill, U.S.A.	24 Aug.	196:
1½ miles	2m.23.0s	37.76	*Fiddle Isle* (U.S.A.)	Arcadia, Cal, U.S.A.	21 Mar.	197
2 miles **	3m.15.0s	36.93	*Polazel* (G.B.)	Salisbury, Wiltshire	8 July	192
3 miles	5m.15.0s	34.29	*Farragut* (Mexico)	Agua Caliente	9 Mar.	194

*Course downhill for two thirds of a mile
**A more reliable modern record is 3m 16.75secs by Il Tempo (N.Z.) at Trentham, Wellington, New Zealand on 17 Jan. 1970.

Six time Derby winner—Lester Piggott.

races won by a jockey is 27 by Frank Buckle (1766-1832), between 1792 and 1827.

Most runners The most horses in a race is 66 (a world record) in the Grand National of 22 March 1929. The record for the flat is 58 in the Lincolnshire Handicap on 13 March 1948. The most runners at a meeting were 214 (flat) in seven races at Newmarket on 15 June 1915 and 229 (National Hunt) in eight races at Worcester on 13 Jan 1965.

THE DERBY

The greatest of England's five classic races, the Epsom Derby, was inaugurated on 4 May 1780 by the 12th Earl of Derby (1752-1834). It has been run over 1 mile 885 yards since 1784 (1½ miles since World War I) on Epsom Downs, Surrey, except for the two war periods, when it was run at Newmarket. Since 1884 the race has been for three-year-old colts carrying 9 stone and fillies carrying 8 stone 9 lb.

Highest prize The highest prize for winning any English race was £74,489.50 for *Charlottown* in the Derby on 25 May 1966.

Most winning owners The only owner with five outright winners was the 3rd Earl of Egremont (1751-1837) with *Assassin* (1782), *Hannibal* (1804), *Cardinal Beaufort* (1805), *Election* (1807), and *Lapdog* (1826). H.H. Aga Khan III (1877-1957) had four winners in *Blenheim* (1930), *Bahram* (1935), *Mahmoud* (1936) and *Tulyar* (1952) and a half-share in *My Love* (1948).

Trainer The only two trainers with seven winners were John Porter with *Blue Gown* (1868), *Shotover* (1882), *St. Blaise* (1883), *Ormonde* (1886), *Sainfoin* (1890), *Common* (1891) and *Flying Fox* (1899), and Robert Robson with *Waxy* (1793), *Tyrant* (1802), *Pope* (1809), *Whalebone* (1810), *Whisker* (1815), *Azor* (1817), and *Emilius* (1823). Fred Darling had seven winners, including two in the war-time meetings at Newmarket (1940-41).

Jockey The most successful jockeys have been Jem Robinson, who won six times in 1817, 1824-25, 1827-28 and 1836 and Lester Piggott (1954-57-60-68-70-72). Steve Donogue (1884-1945) rode six winners (1915-1925) but the first two were war-time races not on the Epsom Course.

Record time The record time for the Derby is 2 minutes 33.8 seconds (average speed 35.06 m.p.h.) by *Mahmoud*, ridden by Charlie Smirke, owned by H.H. Aga Khan III, trained by Frank Butters (1878-1957), winning at 100 to 8 by three lengths from a field of 22 in 1936. The fastest time recorded over the Derby course is, however, 2 minutes 33.0 seconds by the four-year-old *Apelle* in winning the 1928 Coronation Cup.

Dead heats The two instances of dead heats were in 1828, when *Cadland* beat *The Colonel* in the run off, and in 1884 between *Harvester* and *St. Gatien* (stakes divided).

Disqualifications The two disqualifications were of *Running Rein* (race awarded to *Orlando*) in 1844 and of *Craganour* (race awarded to *Aboyeur*) in the 'Suffragette Derby' on 4 June 1913, when Miss Emily Davison killed herself by impeding King George V's horse *Anmer*.

Other records The only greys to have won were *Gustavus* (1821), *Tagalie* (1912), *Mahmoud* (1936) and *Airborne* (1946.) Only two black horses have ever won—*Smolensko* (1813) and *Grand Parade* (1919). The longest odds quoted on a placed Derby horse were 200-1 against for *Black Tommy*, second to *Blink Bonny* in 1857. The shortest priced winner was *Ladas* (1894) at 9-2 on and the highest priced winners were *Jeddah* (1898), *Signorinetta* (1908) and *Aboyeur* (1913), all at 100 to 1 against. The smallest field was four in 1794 and the largest 34 in 1862. The smallest winner was *Little Wonder* (14 hands 3½ inches) in 1840.

GRAND NATIONAL

Most wins Horse The first official Grand National Steeplechase may be regarded as the Grand Liverpool Steeplechase of 26 Feb 1839 though the race was not so named until some years later. The first winner of the Grand Liverpool Steeplechase was Mr Pott's *The Duke* in 1837. The race is for six-year-olds and over (since 1930) and is run over a course of 4 miles 856 yards, with 30 jumps, at Aintree, near Liverpool. No horse has won three times but six share the record of two wins:

Peter Simple	1849 and 1853	*The Colonel*	1869 and 1870
Abd-el-Kader	1850 and 1851	*Manifesto*	1897 and 1899
The Lamb	1868 and 1871	*Reynoldstown*	1935 and 1936

Manifesto was entered eight times (1895-1904) and won twice, came third three times and fourth once. *Poethlyn* won in 1919 having won the war-time Gatwick race in 1918.

Jockey The only jockey to ride five winners was G. Stevens on *Free Trader* (1856), *Emblem* (1863), *Emblematic* (1864) and *The Colonel* (1869-70).

Owner The only owners with three winners, since the race became a handicap in 1843, are Captain Machell with *Disturbance* (1873), *Reughy* (1874) and *Regal* (1876); and Sir Charles Assheton-Smith with *Cloister* (1893), *Jerry M* (1912) and *Covertcoat* (1913).

Il Tempo (N.Z.) the fastest reliably timed 2 miler in turf history.

273

Stan Mellor the first National Hunt jockey to reach 1,000 wins.

Trainer The only trainer with four winners was the Ho Aubrey Hastings with *Ascetic's Silver* (1906), *A Sloper* (1915), *Ballymacad* (1917, Gatwick) a *Master Robert* (1924).

Highest prize The highest prize was £22,334.25 won by *Anglo* 26 March 1966.

Fastest time Times before the 1939-45 War were not official returned. In 1935 the eight-year-old *Reynoldsto* ridden by Mr. F. Furlong won by 3 lengths from field at 27 in times variously reported as 9 minu 21.0 seconds or 9 minutes 20.2 seconds. *Gold Miller*, a seven-year-old ridden by G. Wilson, carryi 12 stone 2 lb., and owned by the Hon. Miss Dorot Paget, won by 5 lengths from a field of 30 in minutes 20.4 seconds (28.82 m.p.h.) in 1934.

Highest jump The 15th jump, known as the 'Open Ditch', is 5 fee inches high and 3 feet 9 inches thick. The ditch on t take-off side is 6 feet wide, and the guard rail in fro of the ditch is 1 foot 6 inches in height.

STEEPLECHASING
Golden Miller won the Cheltenham Gold Cup 14 March 1935 in very heavy conditions carrying stone over 3 miles 3 furlongs in 6 minutes 30 secon so averaging an unsurpassed 31.15 m.p.h.

Jockey The first National Hunt jockey to reach 1,000 win Stan Mellor. This he achieved on *Ouzo* at Nottingh on 18 Dec. 1971.

HURLING

Earliest reference A game of very ancient origin, hurling only became standardized with the formation of the Gaelic Athletic Association in Thurles, Ireland, on 1 Nov. 1884.

Most titles The greatest number of All-Ireland Championships won by one team is 22 by Tipperary in 1887, 1895-96, 1898-99-1900, 1906, 1908, 1916, 1925, 1930, 1937, 1945, 1949-50-51, 1958, 1961-62, 1964-65 and 1971. The greatest number of successive wins is the four by Cork (1941-44).

Highest score The highest score in an All-Ireland final was in 1896 when Tipperary (8 goals, 14 points) beat Dublin (no goals, 4 points). The record aggregate score was when Cork (6 goals, 21 points) defeated Wexford (5 goals, 10 points) in 1970. A goal equals 3 points.

Lowest score The lowest score in an All-Ireland final was when Tipperary (1 goal, 1 point) beat Galway (nil) in the first championship at Birr in 1887.

Most The most appearances in All-Ireland finals is ten shared by Christy Ring (Cork) and John Doyle (Tipperary). They also share the record of All-Ireland medals won with 8 each. Ring's appearances on the winning side were in 1941-42-43-44, 1946 and 1952-53-54, while Doyle's were in 1949-50-51, 1958, 1961-62 and 1964-65.

Individual score The highest recorded individual score was by Nick Rackard (Wexford), who scored 7 goals and 7 points against Antrim in the 1954 All-Ireland semi-final.

Largest crowd The largest crowd was 84,856 for the final between Cork and Wexford at Croke Park, Dublin, in 1954.

Inter-provincials Munster holds the greatest number of inter-provincial (Railway Cup) championships with 32 (1928-1970). Christy Ring (Cork and Munster) played in a record

22 finals (1942-1963) and was on the winning side times.

Longest stroke The greatest distance for a "lift and stroke" is one 129 yards credited to Tom Murphy of Three Castle Kilkenny, in a "long puck" contest in 1906. T record for the annual *An Poc Fada* (Long Puc contest (instituted 1961) in the ravines of the Cool Hills, north of Dundalk, County Louth, is 65 puc (drives) plus 87 yards over the course of 3 miles 3 yards by Fionnbar O'Neill (Cork) in 1966. T represents an average of 84.8 yards per drive.

ICE HOCKEY

Origins There is pictorial evidence that hockey was played ice in the 17th century in The Netherlands. The ga was probably first played in North America in 1860 Kingston, Ontario, Canada, but Montreal and Halif also lay claim to priority.

Olympic Games Canada has won the Olympic title six tim (1920-24-28-32-48-52) and the world title 19 tim the last being at Geneva in 1961. The longest Olym career is that of Richard Torriani (Switzerland) fro 1928 to 1948. The most gold medals won by a player is three achieved by Vitaliy Davidov, Anato Firssov, Viktor Kuzkin and Aleksandr Ragulin of t U.S.S.R. teams that won the Olympic titles 1964-68 and 1972. Davidov and Ragulin had play in 9 World championship teams prior to the 19 Games.

Stanley Cup The Stanley Cup, presented by the Governor-Gene Lord Stanley (original cost $48.67), became e blematic of world professional team suprema several years after the first contest at Montrea 1893. It has been won most often by the Montre Canadiens *[sic]*, with 17 wins in 1916, 1924, 193 1931, 1944, 1946, 1953, 1956 (winning a record games), 1957, 1958, 1959, 1960, 1965, 1966, 196 1969, and 1971. Henri Richard and Jean Belive played in their tenth finals in 1971.

An old 17th century Dutch print evidence of the earliest origins of ice hockey.

goals by Phil Esposito of the Boston Bruins in 1970-71. The most points in a season is 152 (76 goals and 76 assists) by Phil Esposito (Boston Bruins) also in 1970-71. The North American career record for goals is 786 by Gordie Howe. (b. 31 Mar. 1928) (Detroit Red Wings) in 25 seasons ending in 1970-71. He has also collected 500 stitches in his face. Two players have scored 1,000 goals in Great Britain––Chick Zamick (Nottingham Panthers and Wembley Lions) and George Beach (Wembley Monarchs and later Wembley Lions).

Fastest scoring Toronto scored 8 goals against the New York Americans in 4 minutes 52 seconds on 19 March 1938. Bill Mosienko (Chicago) scored three goals in 21 seconds against New York Rangers on 23 March 1952.

Fastest player The highest speed measured for any player is 29.7 m.p.h. for Bobby Hull (Chicago Black Hawks) (born 3 Jan. 1939). The highest puck speed is also attributed to Hull, whose left-handed slap shot has been measured at 118.3 m.p.h.

BRITISH LEAGUE
The highest score on record was when Streatham beat Racing Club de Paris 23-3 in 1949-50. Bud McEachern shot seven goals for Streatham.

Most wins The British League championship (instituted 1934 but ended in 1960) has been won most often by the Wembley Lions with four victories in 1936-37, 1952 and 1957.

Longest match The longest match was 2 hours 56 minutes 30 seconds when Detroit Red Wings eventually beat Montreal Maroons 1-0 in the sixth period of overtime at the Forum, Montreal, at 2.25 a.m. on 25 March 1936.

Most goals Ottawa defeated Dawson City 23-2 at Ottawa on 16 Jan. 1905.

Most National Hockey League goals in a season: 76

ICE SKATING

Origins The earliest reference to ice skating is that of a Danish writer dated 1134. The earliest English account of 1180 refers to skates made of bone. Metal blades date from probably c. 1600. The earliest skating club was the Edinburgh Skating Club formed in 1742. The earliest artificial ice rink in the world was the "Glaciarium" in Chelsea, London, in 1876.

Olympic The most Olympic gold medals won in speed skating is six by Lidia Skoblikova (b. 8 March 1939) of Chelyaminsk, U.S.S.R., in 1960 (2) and 1964 (4).

FIGURE SKATING
World The greatest number of world men's figure skating titles (instituted 1896) is ten by Ulrich Salchow (b. 7 Aug. 1877) of Sweden, in 1901-05 and 1907-11. The only British figure skater to win has been Henry Graham Sharp (b. 19 Dec. 1917) in Budapest on 18-19 Feb. 1939. The women's record (instituted 1906) is ten titles by Frk. Sonja Henie (b. 8 April 1912) of Norway, between 1927 and 1936.

Olympic The most Olympic gold medals won by a figure skater is three by Gillis Graftström (b. 7 June 1893) of Sweden in 1920, 1924 and 1928 (also silver medal in 1932); and by Sonja Henie (see above) in 1928, 1932 and 1936.

WORLD SPEED SKATING RECORDS

	Distance	mins. secs.	Name and Nationality	Place	Date	
MEN	500 metres	38.00*	Leo Linkovesi (Finland)	Davos, Switzerland	8 Jan	1972
		38.00*	Hasse Borjes (Sweden)	Inzell, West Germany	4 Mar	1972
		38.00*	Erhard Keller (West Germany)	Inzell, West Germany	4 Mar	1972
	1,000 metres	1:18.50	Erhard Keller (West Germany)	Inzell, West Germany	4 Mar	1972
	1,500 metres	1:58.70	Ard Schenk (Netherlands)	Davos, Switzerland	15 Feb	1971
	3,000 metres	4:08.30	Ard Schenk (Netherlands)	Inzell, West Germany	2 Mar	1972
	5,000 metres	7:09.80	Ard Schenk (Netherlands)	Inzell, West Germany	4 Mar	1972
	10,000 metres	14:55.96	Ard Schenk (Netherlands)	Inzell, West Germany	14 Mar	1971
WOMEN	500 metres	42.50	Anne Henning (U.S.A.)	Davos, Switzerland	7 Jan	1972
	1,000 metres	1:27.38	Anne Henning (U.S.A.)	Davos, Switzerland	8 Jan	1972
	1,500 metres	2:17.82	Nina Statkevich (U.S.S.R.)	Medeo, U.S.S.R.	17 Jan	1970
	3,000 metres	4:50.30	Ans Schut (Netherlands)	Inzell, West Germany	23 Feb	1969
	5,000 metres	9:01.60	Rimma Zhukova (U.S.S.R.)	Medeo, U.S.S.R.	24 Jan	1953

BRITISH OUTDOOR RECORDS

	Distance	mins. secs.	Name	Place	Date	
MEN	500 metres	40.90	A. John Tipper	Cortina d'Ampezzo, Italy	28 Jan	1970
	1,000 metres	1:23.1	A. John Tipper	Davos, Switzerland	8 Jan	1972
	1,500 metres	2:08.40	A. John Tipper	Cortina d'Ampezzo, Italy	28 Jan	1970
	3,000 metres	4:34.70	John B. Blewitt	Cortina d'Ampezzo, Italy	16 Jan	1968
	5,000 metres	7:51.2	John B Blewitt	Davos, Switzerland	22 Jan	1972
	10,000 metres	16:30.10	Terence A. Malkin	Oslo, Norway	19 Jan	1964
WOMEN	500 metres	51.90	Patricia K. Tipper	Cortina d'Ampezzo, Italy	16 Jan	1968
	1,000 metres	1:44.20	Patricia K. Tipper	Inzell, West Germany	7 Jan	1968
	1,500 metres	2:42.80	Patricia K. Tipper	Cortina d'Ampezzo, Italy	17 Dec	1967
	3,000 metres	5:39.40	Patricia K. Tipper	Cortina d'Ampezzo, Italy	16 Dec	1967

*This represents a speed of 29.43 m.p.h.

British The record number of British titles is 11 by Jack Page (Manchester S.C.) in 1922-31 and 1933, and six by Miss Cecilia Colledge (Park Lane F S.C., London) in 1935-36-37(2)-38 and 1946.

Most Difficult Jump The triple Lutz has been performed by only 3 skaters—by Donald Jackson (U.S.) in Prague, 1962; by Haïg B. Oundjian (G.B.) in the Grand Prix de Saint Gervais in Aug. 1969 and by John Mischa Petkevich, the 1971 U.S. champion.

Longest race The longest race regularly held is the "Elfstedentocht" ("Tour of the Eleven Towns") in the Netherlands. It covers 200 kilometres (124 miles 483 yards) and the fastest time is 7 hours 35 minutes by Jeen van den Berg (b. 8 Jan. 1928) on 3 Feb. 1954.

Skating marathon The longest recorded skating marathon is one of 62 hours 50 minutes by Jean Pierre Lehoux at the Timmins Winter Carnival in Ontario, Canada, from 25 Feb. to 28 Feb. 1972. The fastest time to complete 100 miles is 5 hours 35 minutes by Robert B.

Kerns, on 20 Feb. 1972 at Glacier Falls Ice Rink Anaheim, California, U.S.A.

Largest rink The world's largest indoor ice rink is the Tōkyō Ice Rink, completed in 1960, which has an ice area of 43,000 sq. ft. (or 0.99 of an acre). The largest artificial outdoor rink is the Fujikyu Highland Promenade Rink, Japan opened at a cost of £335,000 in 1967 and with an area of 165,750 square feet (3.8 acres). The largest in the U.K. has been the Crossmy loof Ice Rink, Glasgow, with an ice area of 225 feet by 97 feet.

SPEED SKATING

Most titles World The greatest number of world speed skating title (instituted 1893) won by any skater is five by Osca Mathisen (Norway) in 1908-09 and 1912-14, and Cla Thunberg (b. 5 April 1893) of Finland, in 1923 1925, 1928-29 and 1931. The most titles won by woman is four by Mrs. Inga Voronina, née Artomo nova (1936-66) of Moscow, U.S.S.R., in 1957, 1958 1962 and 1965.

ICE AND SAND YACHTING

Origin The sport originated in The Netherlands from the year 1600 (earliest patent granted) and along the Baltic coast. The earliest authentic record is Dutch, dating from 1768. Land or Sand yatchts of Dutch construction were first reported on beaches (now in Belgium) in 1595. The earliest International championship was staged in 1914.

Record Speeds Ice The largest known ice yacht was *Icicle,* built for Commodore John E. Roosevelt for racing on the Hudson River, New York, in *c.* 1870. It was 68 feet 11 inches long and carried 1,070 square feet of canvas. The highest speed officially recorded is 143 m.p.h. by John D. Buckstaff in a Class A stern-steerer on Lake Winnebago, Wisconsin, U.S.A., in 1938. Such a speed is possible in a wind of 72 m.p.h.

Sand The fastest recorded speed for a sand yacht is 57.69 m.p.h. (measured mile in 62.4 secs) by *Coronation Year Mk.II* owned by R. Millett Denning and crewed by J. Halliday, Bob Harding, J. Glassbrook and Cliff Martindale at Lytham St. Anne's in 1956.

The world's fastest sand yacht *Coronation Year Mk.II.*

JUDO (JIU-JITSU)

Origins Judo is a modern combat sport which developed out of an amalgam of several old Japanese fighting arts, the most popular of which was ju-jitsu (jiu-jitsu), which is thought to be of pre-Christian Chinese origin. Judo has been greatly developed by the Japanese since 1882, when it was first devised by *Shihan* Dr. Jigoro Kano. World championships were inaugurated in 1956. Great Britain has won most consecutive European championships (instituted in 1951) with 3 victories (1957-58-59). France won in 1951-52, 1954-55, and 1962. Britain won again in 1971.

Highest grade The efficiency grades in Judo are divided into pupil *(kyu)* and master *(dan)* grades. The highest awarded is the extremely rare red belt *Judan (10th dan),* given only to seven men. The Judo protocol provides for an *11th dan (Juichidan)* who also would wear a red belt and even a *12th dan* who would wear a white belt twice as wide as an ordinary belt, but these have never been bestowed. The highest British native honorary grade is *7th dan* by Trevor P. Leggett. The world's only blind Black Belt Judoka is Bob Noon, 40 of Newton le-Willows, Lancashire who qualified in October 1971.

Heaviest champion The heaviest world champion was Antonius (Anton J. Geesink (b. 6 April 1934) of the Netherlands, wh won the 1964 Olympic open title in Tōkyō at weight of 17 stone. He was 19 stone in 1965 an stood 6 feet 6 inches tall.

Marathon The longest recorded Judo marathon with continuou action by two of 8 Judoka in 5 minute stints is 1 hours at St. Paul's School, Plumstead, London o 3 July 1971.

KARATE

Origins Based on techniques devised from the 6th centur Chinese art of *Chuan-fa* (Kempo), karate (empt hand) was developed by an unarmed populac in Okinawa as a weapon against armed oppressors Transmitted to Japan in the 1920's by Funakosh Gichin, the founder of modern karate, this method o combat was further refined and organised into a spor with competitive rules. The five major styles of karat in Japan are: *Shotokan, Wado-ryu, Goju-ryu, Shito ryu* and *Kyokushinkai,* each of which place differen emphasis on speed and power etc. *Tae kwan-do* is lethal Korean form of military karate.

276

The Governing Body for the sport in Britain is the British Karate Control Commission on which the major karate styles in this country are represented.

Most Titles The only winner of three All-Japanese titles has been Takeshi Oishi who won in 1969-70-71.

Top exponents The highest dan among karatekas is Yamaguchi Gogen (b. 1907) a 10th dan of the *Goju-ryu* Karate Do.

The leading exponents in the United Kingdom are Tatsuo Suzuki (7th dan, *Wado-ryu*), chief instructor to the United Kingdom Karate Federation; Keinosuke Enoeda (6th dan, *Shotokan*), resident instructor to the Karate Union of Great Britain and Steve Arneil (5th dan, *Kyokushinkai*) British national born in South Africa.

Greatest force Considerably less emphasis is placed on *Tamashiwara* (wood breaking etc.) than is generally supposed. Most styles use it only for demonstration purposes. However, the force needed to break a brick with the abductor *digiti quinti* muscle of the hand is normally 130-140 lb. The highest measured impact is 196 lb. The greatest brick breaking feat was 269 per hour for 13 hours (total 3,500) by Billy Corbett in Kent, Washington, U.S.A. on 18-20 Sept. 1971.

Demolition work Fifteen members of the International Budo Association led by Phil Milner (3rd Dan Karate) demolished a 6-roomed early Victorian house at Idle, Bradford, Yorkshire by head, foot and empty hand in 6 hours on 4 June 1972. On completion they bowed to the rubble.

LACROSSE

Origin The game is of American Indian origin, derived from the inter-tribal game *baggataway,* and was played before 1492 by Iroquois Indians in lower Ontario, Canada and upper New York State, U.S.A. It was introduced into Great Britain in 1867. The English Lacrosse Union was formed in 1892. The Oxford v. Cambridge match was instituted in 1903 and the game was included in the Olympic Games of 1908 and featured as an exhibition sport in the 1928 and 1948 Games.

World championship The first World Tournament was held at Toronto, Canada in 1967 and the U.S.A. won.

Longest throw The longest recorded throw is 162.86 yards by Barney Quinn of Ottawa on 10 Sept. 1892.

Most titles The English Club Championship (Iroquois Cup), instituted in 1890, has been won most often by Stockport with 15 wins between 1897 and 1934.

Highest score The highest score in any international match was Australia's 19−3 win over England at Manchester in May 1972.

The record number of international representations for England is 13 by G. A. MacDonald of Mellor, Cheshire to 1967. (No internationals were played in 1968.)

The record for women is 52 for Scotland by Caro Macintosh (1952−1969)

LAWN TENNIS

Origins The modern game is generally agreed to have evolved as an outdoor form of the indoor game of Tennis (see separate entry). "Field Tennis" is mentioned in an English magazine–*Sporting Magazine*–of 29 Sept. 1793. The earliest club for such a game, variously called Pelota or Lawn Rackets, was the Leamington Club founded in 1872 by Major Harry Gem. The earliest attempt to commercialise the game was by Major Walter Clopton Wingfield, M.V.O. (1833-1912) who patented a form called "sphairistike" in February 1874. It soon became called Lawn Tennis. Amateur players were permitted to play with and against professionals in 'Open' tournaments in 1968.

ALL TIME RECORDS

Greatest domination The grand slam is to win all four of the world's major championship singles: Wimbledon, the United States, Australian and French (on hard courts) championships. The first man to have won all four was Frederick John Perry (G.B.) (born 1909) with the French title in 1935. The first man to hold all four championships simultaneously was J. Donald Budge (U.S.A.) (born 1915) with the French title in 1938. The first man to achieve the grand slam twice was Rodney George Laver (Australia) (born 1938) having won in 1962 as an amateur and again in 1969 when the titles were 'open' to professionals.

Only two women have achieved the grand slam: Maureen Catherine Connolly (U.S.A.) (1934/1969), later Mrs. Norman Brinker with the French title in 1953; and Mrs. Barry M. Court, M.B.E., (*née* Margaret Smith) (Australia) (born 1942) in 1970.

Fastest service The fastest service ever *measured* was one of 154 m.p.h. by Michael J. Sangster (U.K.) in June 1963. Crossing the net the ball was travelling at 108 m.p.h. Some players consider the service of Robert Falkenberg (U.S.A.) the 1948 Wimbledon

Champion as the fastest ever used.

Greatest crowd The greatest crowd at a tennis match was 25,578 at the first day of the Davis Cup Challenge Round between Australia and the United States at the White City, Sydney, New South Wales, Australia, on 27 Dec. 1954.

Youngest champions The youngest ever champion at Wimbledon was Miss Charlotte Dod (1871-1960), who was 15 years 8 months when she won in 1887. The youngest male singles champion was Wilfred Baddeley (b. 11 Jan. 1872) who won the Wimbledon title in 1891 at the age of 19.

Ricardo (Pancho) Gonzalez (U.S.A.) victor in Wimbledon's longest ever match in 1966.

Richard Dennis Ralston (b. 27 July 1942) of Bakers-field, Califonia, U.S.A. was 25 days short of his 18th birthday when he won the men's doubles with Rafael H. Osuna (1938 1969) of Mexico in 1960.

Most appearances Arthur W. Gore (1868-1928) of the U.K. made 36 appearances between 1888 and 1927, and was in 1909 at 41 years the oldest ever singles winner. In 1964, Jean Borotra (b. 13 Aug. 1898) of France made his 35th appearance since 1922. In 1972 he appeared in the Veterans' Doubles aged 73.

Most wins Miss Elizabeth Ryan (U.S.A.) won her first title in 1914 and her nineteenth in 1934 (12 women's doubles with 5 different partners and 7 mixed doubles with 5 different partners).

The greatest number of wins by a man at Wimbledon has been William Charles Renshaw (b. 1861) (G.B.) who won 7 singles titles (1881-2-3-4-5-6-9) and 7 doubles (1880-1-4-5-6-8-9), partnered by his twin brother (James) Ernest. Hugh Lawrence Doherty (1875-1919) won 5 singles (1902-3-4-5-6), 8 men's doubles (1897-8-9-1900-01 and 1903-4-5), partnered by his brother Reginald Frank Doherty (1872-1910), and two mixed doubles (then unofficial) in 1901-02, partnered by Mrs. Charlotte Sterry (*née* Cooper).

The greatest number of singles wins was eight by Mrs. F. S. Moody (*nee* Helen N. Wills), now Mrs Aiden Roark, of the U.S.A. who won in 1927, 1928, 1929, 1930, 1932, 1933, 1935 and 1938.

The greatest number of singles wins by a man was seven by William C. Renshaw (G.B.), as quoted above.

The greatest number of doubles wins by men was 8 by

Laurie Doherty (G.B.) winner of most Wimbledon doubles titles.

the brothers R.F. and H.L. Doherty (G.B.). They wo each year from 1897 to 1905 except for 1902.

The most wins in women's doubles were 12 by Mi Elizabeth Ryan (U.S.A.) between 1914 and 1934 (se above).

The most wins in mixed doubles was 7 by Mi Elizabeth Ryan (U.S.A.) between 1919 and 193. The male record is four wins shared by Elias Victe Seixas (U.S.A.) in 1953-54-55-56 and Kenneth N

MOST GAMES AND LONGEST MATCHES

Note: The increasing option since 1970 by tournament organisers to use various "tie break" systems, which are precisely designed to stop long sets, is reducing the likelihood of these records, which may shortly become of mere historic interest, being broken.

Any match	147	Dick Leach–Dick Dell (Michigan Univ.) bt. Tommy Mozur–Lenny Schloss 3-6, 49-47, 22-20	Newport, Rhode Island. U.S.A. 18-19 Aug.1967
Any singles	126	Roger Taylor (GB) bt. Wieslaw Gasiorek (Poland) 27-29, 31-29, 6-4 (4 hrs. 35 mins.)	King's Cup, Warsaw, Poland. 5 Nov 196
Any women's singles	62	Kathy Blake (USA) bt. Elena Subirats (Mexico) 12-10, 6-8, 14-12	Riping Rock, Locust Valley, N.Y., USA. 196
Any women's match	81	Nancy Richey–Carole Graebner (*née* Caldwell) bt. Justina Bricka–Carol Hanks (all USA) 31-33, 6-1, 6-4	South Orange, New Jersey, USA, 196
Any mixed doubles	71	William F. Talbot–Margaret du Pont (*née* Osborne) bt. Robert Falkenburg–Gertrude Moran (all USA) 27-25, 5-7, 6-1	Forest Hills, N.Y., USA. 194
Any set	96	see middle set of Any match above	
Longest time for Any match	6 hrs. 23 mins	Mark Cox–Robert K. Wilson (UK) bt. Charles M. Pasarell–Ron E. Holmburg (USA) 26-24, 17-19, 30-28	U.S. Indoor Championships, Salisbury, Maryland, USA 18-19 Aug 196
Any Wimbledon match	112	Ricardo Alonzo Gonzalez (USA) bt. Charles M. Pasarell (USA) 22-24, 1-6, 16-14, 6-3, 11-9	First round 24-25 June 1969
Any Wimbledon doubles	98	Eugene L. Scott (USA)–Nicola Pilic (Yugoslavia) bt. G. Cliff Richey (USA) Torben Ulrich (Denmark) 19-21, 12-10, 6-4, 4-6, 9-7	First round 22 June 196
Any Wimbledon set	62	Pancho Segura (Ecuador)–Alex Olmedo (Peru) bt. Abe A. Segal–Gordon L. Forbes (S. Africa) 32-30	Second round June 196
Longest time for any Wimbledon match	5 hrs. 12 mins	see Any Wimbledon match above	
Wimbledon men's final	58	Jaroslav Drobny (then Egypt) bt. Kenneth R. Rosewall (Australia) 13-11, 4-6, 6-2, 9-7	Final July 195
Wimbledon men's doubles Final	70	John D. Newcombe–Anthony D. Roche (Australia) bt Kenneth R. Rosewall–Frederick S. Stolle (Australia) 3-6, 8-6, 5-7, 14-12, 6-3	Final July 196
Wimbledon women's Final	46	Mrs Barry M. Court, M.B.E. (*née* Margaret Smith) (Australia) bt. Mrs L.W. King (*née* Billie-Jean Moffitt) (USA) 14-12, 11-9. (2 hrs. 25 mins)	Final July 197
Wimbledon women's Doubles final	38	Mme. Simone Mathieu (France)–Miss Elizabeth Ryan (USA) bt. Freda James (now Hammersley)–Adeline Maud Yorke (now Eyres) (both GB) 6-2, 9-11, 6-4	Final July 193
		Rosemary Casals–Mrs. L.W. King (*née* Moffitt) (both USA) bt. Maria E. Bueno (Brazil) Nancy Richey (USA) 9-11, 6-4, 6-2	Final July 196
Wimbledon mixed Doubles final	48	Eric W. Sturgess–Mrs Sheila Summers (S. Africa) bt. John E. Bromwich (Australia)–Alice Louise Brough (now Clapp) (USA) 9-7, 9-11, 7-5	Final July 194
Any Davis Cup rubber	95	Wilhelm Bungert–Christian Kuhnke (Germany) bt. Mark Cox–Peter Curtis (GB) 10-8, 17-19, 13-11, 6-3	European Zone Quarter-final, Edgbaston, Birmingham, England 196
Any Davis Cup singles	86	Arthur Ashe (USA) bt. Christian Kuhnke (Germany) 6-8, 10-12, 9-7, 13-11, 6-4	Challenge Round, Cleveland, Ohio, USA. 197
Any Davis Cup tie i.e. 5 rubbers	281	Italy bt. USA 3 rubbers to 2	Inter Zone Final, Perth, Western Australia 196

Fletcher (Australia) in 1963-65-66-68.

Lawn tennis marathons The longest recorded non-stop lawn tennis doubles game is one of 40 hours 6 minutes 44 seconds by 4 players of Giffnock Bowling and Tennis Club, Glasgow ending on 2 July 1972. The duration record for singles by 2 players is 73 hours 25 minutes by Mel Baleson and Glen Grisillo (S.A.), at Reno, Nevada, U.S.A. on 6-9 May 1971.

DAVIS CUP

Most victories The greatest number of wins in the Davis Cup (instituted 1900) has been (inclusive of 1971) the U.S.A., with 23 wins and Australasia/Australia with 22. The British Isles/Great Britain have won 9 times, in 1903-04-05-06, 1912, 1933-34-35-36.

Individual performance Nicola Pietrangeli (Italy) played 161 rubbers, 1954 to 1971, winning 117. He played 110 singles (winning 77) and 51 doubles (winning 40). He took part in 63 ties.

Highest Prize Money The highest prize money won in a year is $292,717 (£121,965) by Rodney George Laver (Australia) in 1971. His career total in nine professional seasons was thus brought to a record $1,006,947 (£419,561). The highest prize money won by a woman in a season is $117,000 (£48,750) by Mrs. Billie-Jean King (*née* Moffitt) (U.S.A.) also in 1971, which was more than any American male player. The biggest single prize won was $50,000 (£20,833) by Kenneth R. Rosewall (Australia) in the World Championship Tennis final playoffs at Dallas, Texas in 1971.

MARBLES

Origins Marbles was played by the Romans who are believed to have introduced it into Britain in the 1st Century A.D. It was organised as a competitive sport with the setting up of the British Marbles Board of Control at the Greyhound Hotel, Tinsley Green, Crawley, Sussex in 1926.

The game is also played in Australia, Brazil (as Gude), Canada, China, France, Germany, India, Iran, New Zealand, Spain, Syria, Turkey and the United States.

Most championships The British Championship (established 1926) has been won most often by the Toucan Terribles with 16 consecutive titles (1957-1972). Len Smith has won the individual title twelve times (1958-65, 1966, 1968-71).

The record for clearing the ring (between 5¾ and 6¼ feet in diameter) of 49 marbles is 2 mins. 57 secs. by the Toucan Terribles at Worthing, Sussex in 1971.

The world's top marbles team—the Toucan Terribles with Len Smith (second from left).

MODERN PENTATHLON

Points scores in riding, fencing, cross country and hence overall scores have no comparative value between one competition and another. In shooting and swimming (300 metres) the scores are of record significance.

The Modern Pentathlon (Riding, Fencing, Shooting, Swimming and Running) was inaugurated into the Olympic Games at Stockholm in 1912. The Modern Pentathlon Association of Great Britain was formed in 1922.

MOST TITLES

World The record number of world titles won is 5 by András Balczo (Hungary) in 1963, 1965, 1966, 1967 and 1969.

British The pentathlete with most British titles is Sergeant Jeremy Robert Fox, R.E.M.E. (b. 1941) with eight (1963-65-66-67-68-70-71-72.)

	World			British		
Shooting	1,066	P. Macken (Australia) and	21 Sept. 1965	1,066	R. Phelps, Leipzig	21 Sept. 1965
		R. Phelps (U.K.), Leipzig				
	1,066	I. Mona (Hungary), Jönköping	11 Sept. 1967			
Swimming	1,260	Robert Vonk (Neths.)	Oct. 1971	1,064	L/Cpl. B. Lillywhite, San Antonio, Texas	Oct. 1971
		San Antonio, Texas				

MOTORCYCLING

EARLIEST RACES

The first motorcycle race was one from Paris to Dieppe, France, in 1897. The oldest motorcycle races in the world are the Auto-Cycle Union Tourist Trophy (T.T.) series, first held on the 15¾-mile "Peel" ("St. John's") course in the Isle of Man on 28 May 1907, and still run in the island, on the "Mountain" circuit (37.73 miles) and, until 1959, on the Clypse circuit of 10.79 miles.

FASTEST CIRCUITS

World The highest average lap speed attained on any closed circuit is 182 m.p.h. by a Kawasaki racer powered by a 748 c.c. three-cylinder two-stroke engine on a banked circuit in Tōkyō, Japan in December 1971.

The fastest road circuit is the Francorchamps circuit near Spa, Belgium. It is 14.10 kilometres (8 miles 1,340 yards) in length and was lapped in 4 minutes 1.4 seconds (average speed 130.658 m.p.h.) by Giacomo Agostini (b. Lovere, Italy, 16 June 1942) on a 500 c.c. three-cylinder M.V.-Agusta on lap 7 of the 500 c.c. Belgian Grand Prix on 6 July 1969.

Duncan Hocking (G.B.) holder of the world's 1 km. standing start record.

United Kingdom The fastest circuit in the United Kingdom is the 10.637-mile Portstewart-Coleraine-Portrush circuit in Londonderry, Northern Ireland. The race lap record is 5 minutes 50.6 seconds (average speed 109.222 m.p.h.) by Ralph Bryans (b. Belfast, Northern Ireland, 7 March 1942) on a 250 c.c. six-cylinder Honda, during the North-West 200, on 18 May 1968. Rodney Alfred Gould (b. Banbury, Oxfordshire, 10 March 1943) lapped in 5 minutes 47.6 seconds (average speed 110.165 m.p.h.) on a 350 c.c. parallel twin-cylinder TR2 Yamaha, in practice, on 22 May 1969.

The lap record for the outer circuit (2.767 miles) at the Brooklands Motor Course near Weybridge, Surrey (open between 1907 and 1939) was 80.0 seconds (average speed 124.51 m.p.h.) by Noel Baddow "Bill" Pope (later Major) (1909-1971) of the United Kingdom on a Brough Superior powered by a supercharged 996 c.c. V-twin "8-80" J.A.P. engine developing 110 b.h.p., on 4 July 1939. The race lap record for the outer circuit at Brooklands was 80.6 seconds (average speed 123.588 m.p.h.) by Eric Crudgington Fernihough (1905-1938) of the United Kingdom on a Brough Superior powered by an unsupercharged 996 c.c. V-twin J.A.P. engine, on 28 July 1935.

FASTEST RACES

World The fastest race in the world was held at Grenzlandring, near Wegberg, Germany in 1939. It was won by Georg Meier (b. Germany, 1910) at an average speed of 134 m.p.h. on a supercharged 500 c.c. flat-twin B.M.W.

The fastest road race is the 500 c.c. Belgian Grand Prix held on the Francorchamps circuit (8 miles 1,340 yards) near Spa, Belgium. The record time for this 13-lap (113.898 miles) race is 54 minutes 18.1 seconds (average speed 125.850 m.p.h.) by Giacomo Agostini, on a 500 c.c. three-cylinder M.V.-Agusta, on 6 July 1969.

United Kingdom The fastest race in the United Kingdom is the 350 c.c. event of the North-West 200 held on the Londonderry circuit (see above). The record time for this 7-lap (74.459 miles) race is 41 minutes 25.0 seconds (average speed 107.868 m.p.h.) by Rodney Gould on a 350 c.c. parallel twin-cylinder TR2 Yamaha on 24 May 1969.

MOST SUCCESSFUL RIDERS

Tourist Trophy The record number of victories in the Isle of Man T.T. races is 12 by Stanley Michael Bailey Hailwood, M.B.E. (b. Oxford, 2 April 1940), now of Durban, South Africa, between 1961 and 1967. The first man to win three consecutive T.T. titles in two events was James A. Redman (Rhodesia) (b. Hampstead, London, 8 Nov. 1931). He won the 250 c.c. and 350 c.c. events in 1963-64-65. Mike Hailwood is the only man to win three events in one year, in 1961 and 1967.

280

World championships The most world championship titles (instituted by the *Fédération Internationale Motorcycliste* in 1949) won are:

12 Giacomo Agostini (Italy)
   350 c.c. 1968, 69, 70, 71, 72
   500 c.c. 1966, 67, 68, 69, 70, 71, 72.

Giacomo Agostini is the only man to win two world championships in five consecutive years (350 and 500 c.c. titles in 1968-69-70-71-72).

Mike Hailwood is the youngest person to win a world championship. He was 21 when he won the 250 c.c. title in 1961.

Giacomo Agostini won 92 races in the world championship series between 1965 and 9 June 1972, including a record 19 in 1970, also achieved by Mike Hailwood in 1966.

Trials Samuel Hamilton Miller (b. Belfast, Northern Ireland, 11 Nov. 1935), won eleven A.-C.U. Solo Trials Drivers' Stars in 1959-69.

Scrambles Jeffrey Vincent Smith, M.B.E. (b. Colne, Lancashire, 14 Oct. 1934) won nine A.-C.U. 500 c.c. Scramble Stars in 1955-56, 1960-61-62-63-64-65 and 1967.

Joel Robert (b. Chatelet, Belgium, Nov. 1943) has won six 250 c.c. moto-cross world championships (1964, 1968-69-70-71-72). Between 25 April 1964 and 18 June 1972 he won a record fifty 250 c.c. Grand Prix. He became the youngest moto-cross world champion on 12 July 1964 when he won the 250 c.c. championship aged 20 years 8 months.

MOST SUCCESSFUL MACHINES
Italian M.V.-Agusta machines won 34 world championships between 1952 and 1971 and 237 world championship races between 1952 and 1971. Japanese Honda machines won 29 world championship races and five world championships in 1966.

SPEED RECORDS
The official world speed record (average speed for two runs over a 1 kilometre course) is 224.569 m.p.h. (average time 9.961 seconds) by Bill A. Johnson, aged 38, of Garden Grove, Los Angeles, California, U.S.A. riding a Triumph Bonneville T120 streamliner, with 667.25 c.c. parallel twin-cylinder engine running on methanol and nitromethane and developing 75 to 80 b.h.p., at Bonneville Salt Flats, Tooele County, Utah, U.S.A., on 5 Sept. 1962. His machine was 1? feet long and weighed 400 lb. His first run was made in 9.847 seconds (227.169 m.p.h.).

Calvin G. Rayborn (b. San Diego, California, U.S.A. 20 Feb. 1940) recorded higher speeds over the measured mile, without F.I.M. observers, at Bonneville on 16 Oct. 1970 riding his 10-foot 3-inch long 1,480 c.c. V-twin Harley-Davidson streamliner running on methanol and nitromethane. On the first run Rayborn covered the mile in 13.494 seconds (266.785 m.p.h.). On the second run his time was 13.626 seconds (264.201 m.p.h.). The average time for the two runs was 13.560 seconds (average speed 265.487 m.p.h.).

Jon S. McKibben, 33, of Costa Mesa, California, U.S.A. covered a measured mile one-way at Bonneville in 12.5625 seconds (286.567 m.p.h.) in November 1971 riding his 21-foot 6-inch long Reactio Dynamics *Honda Hawk* streamliner powered by two turbocharged 736 c.c. in-line four-cylinder Honda engines developing 140 b.h.p. each running on methanol.

The world record for two runs over 1 kilometre (1,093.6 yards) from a standing start is 118.91 m.p.h. (18.81 seconds) by Duncan John Hocking (b. Llanfrechfa, Monmouthshire, 2 August 1944) on h supercharged 648 c.c. twin-cylinder Triumph *Titan* developing 120 b.h.p. using methanol and nitromethane, at Elvington Airfield, Yorkshire on 25 Sept. 1971. The faster run was made in 18.80 seconds.

The world record for two runs over 440 yards from a standing start is 92.879 m.p.h. (9.69 seconds) by David Pierre Lecoq (b. Tunbridge Wells, Kent, 24 April 1940) on the supercharged 1,287 c.c. *Drag-Waye* powered by a flat-four Volkswagen engine developing 150 b.h.p. using methanol, at Elvington Airfield, Yorkshire on 27 Sept. 1970. The faster run was made in 9.60 seconds.

The fastest time for a single run over 440 yards from a standing start is 8.68 seconds by E. J. Potter of Ithaca, Michigan, U.S.A., on his 5,359 c.c. Chevrolet Corvette V8 Special at Castlereagh Airstrip near Sydney, Australia on 26 Jan. 1970.

The fastest terminal speed recorded at the end of a

440 yard run from a standing start is 174.74 m.p.h. (elapsed time 8.87 seconds) by Boris Murray (b. U.S.A., 1936) riding his 1,600 c.c. twin-engined Triumph special in Kentucky, U.S.A., in July 1971.

MISCELLANEOUS

Longest race The longest race is the 24-hour Bol d'Or. The greatest distance ever covered is 1,835.95 miles (average speed 76.498 m.p.h.) by Thomas Dickie (b. Aberdare, Glamorganshire, 22 December 1941) and Paul Anthony Smart (b. Eynsford, Kent, 23 April 1943) on a 741 c.c. three-cylinder Triumph Trident at Montlhéry, Paris, France (3 miles 1,610 yards lap) on 12-13 Sept. 1970.

Longest circuit The 37.73-mile "Mountain" circuit, over which the two main T.T. races have been run since 1911, has 264 curves and corners and is the longest used for any motorcycle race.

MOTOR RACING

EARLIEST RACES

The first automobile trial was one of 20 miles from Paris to Versailles and back on 20 April 1887, won by Georges Bouton's steam quadricycle in 74 minutes, at an average of 16.22 m.p.h. The first "real" race was from Paris to Bordeaux and back (732 miles) on 11-13 June 1895. The winner was Emile Levassor (France) driving a Panhard-Levassor two-seater, with a 1.2 litre Daimler engine developing 3½ horse-power. His time was 48 hours 47 minutes (average speed 15.01 m.p.h.).

The oldest motor race in the world, still being regularly run, is the R.A.C. Tourist Trophy (36th race held in 1972), first staged on 14 Sept. 1905 in the Isle of Man. The oldest continental races are the Targa Florio (56th in 1972), in Sicily, first held on 9 May 1906, and the French Grand Prix (50th in 1972), first held on 26-27 June 1906.

FASTEST CIRCUITS

World The highest average lap speed attained on any closed circuit is 201-399 m.p.h. (35.75 seconds) by Gordon Johncock of Mount Pleasant, Michigan, U.S.A. driving a 2,605 c.c. 900 b.h.p. turbocharged McLaren M16B-Offenhauser on the 2-mile banked oval at Michigan International Speedway, Brooklyn, Michigan, U.S.A. on 2 July 1972.

The highest average race lap speed for a closed circuit is over 195 m.p.h. by Richard Brickhouse (U.S.A.) driving a 1969 Dodge Daytona charger, powered by a 426 cubic inch 600 b.h.p. V8 engine, during a 500-mile race on the 2.66-mile, 33-degree banked tri-oval at Alabama International Motor Speedway, Talladega, Alabama, U.S.A. on 14 Sept. 1969.

The fastest road circuit is the Francorchamps circuit near Spa, Belgium. It is 14.10 kilometres (8 miles 1,340 yards) in length and was lapped in 3 minutes 14.6 seconds (average speed 162.080 m.p.h.) during the Francorchamps 1,000 kilometre sports car race on 9 May 1971, by Joseph Siffert (1936-1971) of Switzerland, driving a 4,998 c.c. flat-12 Porsche 917K Group 5 sports car.

United Kingdom The fastest circuit in the United Kingdom is the ex-aerodrome course of 2.927 miles at Silverstone, Northamptonshire (opened 1948). The race lap record is 1 minute 18.8 seconds (average speed 133.721 m.p.h.) by Stanley Michael Bailey Hailwood, M.B.E. (b. Oxford, 2 Apr. 1940) driving a Formula One 2,993 c.c. Surtees TS9B-Cosworth V8 during the 24th *GKN/Daily Express* International Trophy race on 23 April 1972. The practice lap record is 1 minute 17.0 seconds (136.847 m.p.h.) by

Emerson Fittipaldi (Brazil) holder of the British race average speed record (see p.282).

Frank Gardner (b. Australia, 1927) driving a 7.9 litre Lola T260-Chevrolet Group 7 sports car early in June 1971

The lap record for the outer circuit (2.767 miles) at the Brooklands Motor Course near Weybridge, Surrey (open between 1907 and 1939) was 1 minute 9.44 seconds (average speed 143.44 m.p.h.) by John Rhodes Cobb (1899-1952) in his 3-ton 23,856 c.c. Napier-Railton, with a Napier *Lion* 12-cylinder aero-engine developing 450 b.h.p., on 7 Oct. 1935. His average speed over a kilometre was 151.97 m.p.h. (14.72 seconds). The race lap record for the outer circuit at Brooklands was 1 minute 9.6 seconds (average speed 143.11 m.p.h.) by Oliver Henry Julius Bertram (b. Kensington, London, 26 Feb. 1910), driving a 7,963 c.c. Barnato-Hassan Special (Bentley engine), during the 7-lap "Dunlop Jubilee Cup" handicap race on 24 Sept. 1938.

The Motor Industry Research Association (MIRA) High Speed Circuit (2.82-mile lap with 33-degree banking on the bends) at Lindley, Warwickshire, was lapped in 1 minute 2.8 seconds (average speed 161.655 m.p.h.) by Norman Dewis (b. 20 Aug. 1920) driving a Jaguar development car on an officially undisclosed date prior to 1967.

FASTEST RACES

World The fastest race in the world was the 50-mile event at the NASCAR Grand National meeting on the 2.50-mile, 31-degree banked tri-oval at Daytona International Speedway, Daytona Beach, Florida, U.S.A. on 8 Feb. 1964. It was won by Richard Petty

(b. 2 July 1937) of Randleman, North Carolina in 17 minutes 27 seconds (average speed 171.920 m.p.h.), driving a 405 b.h.p. 1964 Plymouth V8.

The fastest road race is the Francorchamps 1,000 kilometre sports car race held on the Francorchamps circuit (8 miles 1,340 yards) near Spa, Belgium. The record time for this 71-lap (622.055 miles) race is 4 hours 1 minute 9.7 seconds (average speed 154.765 m.p.h.) by Pedro Rodriguez (1940-1971) of Mexico and Keith Jack "Jackie" Oliver (b. Chadwell Heath, Essex, 14 Aug. 1942), driving a 4,998 c.c. flat-12 Porsche 917K Group 5 sports car, on 9 May 1971.

United Kingdom The fastest currently held race in the United Kingdom is the *GKN/Daily Express* International Trophy. The record for this 40-lap (117.08 miles) race is 53 mins. 17.8 secs. (average speed 131.806 m.p.h.) by Emerson Fittipaldi (b. São Paulo, Brazil, 12 Dec. 1946) driving a Formula One 2,993 c.c. Lotus 72 John Player Special-Cosworth V8, at Silverstone, in the 24th race, on 23 Apr. 1972.

The fastest race ever held in the United Kingdom was the Broadcast Trophy Handicap held on the Brooklands outer circuit on 29 March 1937. The 29-mile race was won by John Cobb driving his 23,970 c.c. 12-cylinder Napier-Railton at an average speed of 136.03 m.p.h.

TOUGHEST CIRCUITS
The Targa Florio (first run 9 May 1906) is widely acknowledged to be the most arduous race. Held on the Piccolo Madonie Circuit in Sicily, it now covers eleven laps (492.126 miles) and involves the negotiation of 9,350 corners, over severe mountain gradients, and narrow rough roads. The record time is 6 hours 27 mins. 48.0 secs. (average speed 76.141 m.p.h.) by Arturo Merzario and Sandro Munari (both Italy) driving a 2,995 c.c. flat-12 Ferrari 312 P Group 5 sports car in the 56th race on 21 May 1972. The lap record is 33 minutes 36.0 seconds (average speed 79.890 m.p.h.) by Leo Juhani Kinnunen (b. Tampere, Finland, 5 Aug. 1943) on lap 11 of the 54th race on 3 May 1970 driving a 2,997 c.c. flat-8 Porsche 908/3 Spyder Group 6 prototype sports car.

The most difficult Grand Prix circuit is generally regarded to be that for the Monaco Grand Prix (first run 1929), run round the streets and the harbour of Monte Carlo. It is 3,145 metres (1 mile 1,679 yards) in length and has ten pronounced corners and several sharp changes of gradient. The race is run over 80 laps (156.337 miles) and involves on average more than 2,000 gear changes. The record time for the race is 1 hour 52 minutes 21.3 seconds (average speed 83.487 m.p.h.) by John Young "Jackie" Stewart; O.B.E. (b. Milton, Dunbartonshire, 11 June 1939) driving a 2,993 c.c. Tyrrell-Cosworth V8, on 23 May 1971. The race lap record is 1 minute 22.2 seconds (average speed 85.586 m.p.h.) by Stewart on lap 57 of the above race. The record practice lap is 1 min. 21.4 secs. (average speed 86.413 m.p.h.) by Emerson Fittipaldi driving a 2,993 c.c. Lotus 72 John Player Special-Cosworth V8 on 12 May 1972.

LE MANS
The world's most important race for sports cars is the 24-hour *Grand Prix d'Endurance* (first held 1923) on the Sarthe circuit at Le Mans, France. The greatest distance ever covered is 3,315.210 miles (average speed 138.134 m.p.h.) by Dr. Helmut Marko (b. Graz, Austria, 27 April 1943) and Jonkheer Gijs van Lennep (b. Bloemendaal, Netherlands, 16 March 1942) driving a 4,907 c.c. flat-12 Porsche 917K Group 5 sports car, on 12-13 June 1971. The race lap record (8 miles 650 yards lap) is 3 minutes 18.7 seconds (average speed 151.632 m.p.h.) by Pedro Rodriguez (1940-1971) driving a 4,907 c.c. flat-12

Arturo Merzario (Italy) setting the record for the world's toughest circuit—the Targa Florio.

Porsche 917L on 12 June 1971. The record practice lap is 3 minutes 13.6 seconds (average speed 155.627 m.p.h.) by Jackie Oliver driving a similar car on 18 April 1971. The pre-war record average speed was 86.85 m.p.h. by a 3.3 litre Bugatti in 1939.

Most wins The race has been won by Ferrari cars nine times, in 1949, 1954, 1958 and 1960-61-62-63-64-65. The most wins by one man is four by Olivier Gendebien (b. 1924) (Belgium), who won in 1958 and 1960 61 62.

British wins The race has been won 12 times by British cars, thus: Bentley in 1924 and 1927-28-29-30, once by Lagonda in 1935, five times by Jaguar in 1951, 1953 and 1955-56-57 and once by Aston Martin in 1959.

INDIANAPOLIS 500
The Indianapolis 500-mile race (200 laps) was inaugurated in the U.S.A. in 1911. The most successful drivers have been Warren Wilbur Shaw (1902-1954), who won in 1937, 1939 and 1940, Louis Meyer, who won in 1928, 1933 and 1936, and Anthony Joseph "A.J." Foyt, Jr. (b. Houston, Texas, U.S.A., 1935), who won in 1961, 1964 and 1967. Mauri Rose won in 1947 and 1948 and was the co-driver of Floyd Davis in 1941. The record time is 3 hours 4 mins. 5.54 secs. (average speed 162.962 m.p.h.) by Mark Donohue (b. Summit, New Jersey, U.S.A., 18 March 1937) driving a 2,605 c.c. 900 b.h.p. turbocharged Sunoco McLaren M16B-

Dr. Helmut Marko (Austria) whose Porsche covered 3,315 miles in the Le Mans 24 hour race.

Offenhauser on 27 May 1972. Donohue received $218,767.90 from a record prize fund of $1,011,845.94 for winning this, the 56th race. The individual prize record is $271,697.72 by Al Unser (b. Albuquerque, New Mexico, U.S.A., 29 May 1939) on 30 May 1970. The race lap record is 47.99 seconds (average speed 187.539 m.p.h.) by Mark Donohue on lap 150 of the above race. The practice lap record is 45.76 seconds (average speed 196.678 m.p.h.) by Bobby Unser (b. Colorado Springs, Colorado, U.S.A., 1934) driving a 2,589 c.c. 900 b.h.p. turbocharged Olsonite Eagle 72-Offenhauser on lap 3 of his 4-lap qualification run on 14 May 1972.

DRIVERS

Most successful Based on the World Drivers' Championship, inaugurated in 1950, the most successful driver is Juan-Manuel Fangio y Cia (b. Balcarce, Argentina, 24 June 1911) who won five times in 1951-54-55-56-57. He retired in 1958, after having won 24 Grand Prix races (2 shared). The most successful driver in terms of race wins is Stirling Craufurd Moss, O.B.E. (b. Paddington, London, 17 Sept. 1929), with 167 (11 shared) races won, including 16 Grand Prix victories (1 shared), from 18 Sept. 1948 to 11 Feb. 1962. Moss was awarded the annual Gold Star of the British Racing Drivers' Club in 1950-51-52, 1954-55-56-57-58-59 and 1961, a record total of ten awards.

The most Grand Prix victories is 25 by Jim Clark, O.B.E. (1936-1968) of Scotland between 17 June 1962 and 1 January 1968. Clark also holds the record for Grand Prix victories in one year with 7 in 1963. He won a record 61 Formula One and Formula Libre races between 1959 and 1968.

Oldest and youngest P. winners The youngest Grand Prix winner was Bruce Leslie McLaren (1937-1970) of New Zealand, who won the United States Grand Prix at Sebring, Florida, U.S.A. on 12 December 1959 aged 22 years 104 days. The oldest Grand Prix winner was Tazio Giorgio Nuvolari (1892-1953) of Italy, who won the Albi Grand Prix at Albi, France on 14 July 1946 aged 53 years 240 days. The oldest Grand Prix driver was Louis Alexandre Chiron, O. St-C., L.d'H., C.d'I. (b. Monaco, 3 Aug. 1899), who finished 6th in the Monaco Grand Prix on 22 May 1955 aged 55 years 292 days.

Pike's Peak race The Pike's Peak Auto Hill Climb, Colorado, U.S.A. (instituted 1916) has been won by Bobby Unser 11 times between 1956 and 1969 (9 championship, 1 stock and 1 sports car title). On 30 June 1968 in the 46th race, he set a record time of 11 minutes 54.9 seconds in his 336 cubic inch Chevrolet championship car for the 12.42-mile course rising from 9,402 feet to 14,110 feet through 157 curves.

HILL CLIMBING

Most successful drivers The British National Hill Climb Championship inaugurated in 1947 has been won six times by Anthony Ernest Marsh (b. Stourbridge, Worcestershire, 20 July 1913), 1955-56-57, 1965-66-67. Raymond Mays (b. Bourne, Lincolnshire, 1 Aug. 1899) won the Shelsley Walsh hill climb, near Worcester, 19 times between 1923 and 1950.

RALLIES

Earliest The earliest long rally was promoted by the Parisian daily Le Matin in 1907 from Peking, China, to Paris over a route of about 7,500 miles. Five cars left Peking on 10 June. The winner, Prince Scipione Borghesi, arrived in Paris on 10 Aug. 1907 in his 40 h.p. Itala.

Longest The world's longest ever rally was the £10,000 Daily Mirror World Cup Rally run over 16,243 miles starting from Wembley, London on 19 April 1970 to Mexico City via Sofia, Bulgaria and Buenos Aires, Argentina passing through 25 countries. It was won

on 27 May 1970 by Hannu Mikkola (b. Joensuu, Finland, 24 May 1942) and Gunnar Palm (b. Kristinehamn, Sweden, 25 Feb. 1937) in a 1,834 c.c. Ford Escort. The longest held annually is the East African Safari (first run 1953), run through Kenya, Tanzania and Uganda, which is up to 3,874 miles long, as in the 17th Safari held between 8-12 April 1971. The smallest car to win the Monte Carlo Rally (founded 1911) was an 841 c.c. Saab driven by Erik Carlsson (b. Sweden, 1929) and Gunnar Häggbom of Sweden on 25 Jan. 1962, and by Carlsson and Gunnar Palm (Sweden) on 24 Jan. 1963.

DRAGGING

Piston engined The highest terminal velocity recorded by a piston-engined dragster is 243.90 m.p.h. (elapsed time 6.175 seconds) by Donald Glenn "Big Daddy" Garlits (b. 1932) of Seffner, Florida driving his rear-engined Swamp Rat 1-R AA/F dragster, powered by a 473 c.u. supercharged Dodge V8 engine, during the National Hot Rod Association's 3rd Annual Gator-nationals at Gainesville Dragway, Florida, U.S.A., on 19 March 1972. Earlier he had recorded the lowest elapsed time ever, 6.158 seconds (terminal velocity 228.42 m.p.h.).

Rocket or jet-engined The highest terminal velocity and lowest elapsed time recorded by any dragster is 311.41 m.p.h. and 5.10 secs. by Victor Wilson of Sydney, Australia in the 22-foot long 3-wheeled Courage of Australia, powered by a 6,000 lb. s.t. hydrogen peroxide rocket engine, at Orange County International Raceway, E. Irvine, California, U.S.A., in November 1971.

Terminal velocity is the speed attained at the end of a 440-yard run made from a standing start and elapsed time is the time taken for the run.

LAND SPEED RECORDS

The highest speed ever recorded by a wheeled vehicle was achieved by Gary Gabelich (b. San Pedro, California, U.S.A., 29 Aug. 1940), at Bonneville Salt Flats, Utah, U.S.A., on 23 Oct. 1970. He drove the Reaction Dynamics The Blue Flame, weighing 4,950 lb. and measuring 37 feet long, powered by a liquid natural gas—hydrogen peroxide rocket engine developing a maximum static thrust of 22,000 lb. On his first run, at 11.23 a.m. (local time), he covered the measured kilometre in 3.543 secs. (average speed 631.367 m.p.h.) and the mile in 5.829 seconds (617.602 m.p.h.) On the second run, at 12.11 a.m., his times were 3.554 seconds for the kilometre (629.413 m.p.h.and 5.739 seconds for the mile (627.287 m.p.h.). The average times for the two runs were 3.5485 secs. for the kilometre (630.388 m.p.h.) and 5.784 secs. for the mile (622.407 m.p.h.). During the attempt only 13,000 lb. s.t. was used and a peak speed of 650 m.p.h. was momentarily attained.

The most successful land speed record breaker was Major Sir Malcolm Campbell (1885-1948) of the United Kingdom. He broke the official record nine times between 25 Sept. 1924, with 146.157 m.p.h. in a Sunbeam, and 3 Sept. 1935, when he achieved 301.129 m.p.h. in the Rolls-Royce engined Bluebird.

The world speed record for compression ignition engined cars is 190.344 m.p.h. (average of two runs over measured mile) by Robert Havemann of Eureka, California, U.S.A. driving his Corsair streamliner, powered by a turbocharged 426 cubic inch 6-cylinder GMC 6-71 diesel engine developing 746 b.h.p., at Bonneville Salt Flats, Utah, U.S.A., in August 1971. The faster run was made at 210 m.p.h.

MISCELLANEOUS

Fastest pit stop Jackie Oliver took 9 seconds to load 100 litres (22.0 Imperial gallons) of fuel during the Francorchamps 1,000 kilometre sports car race on 9 May 1971. This time was equalled by A.J. Foyt, Jr. during his first fuel stop (lap 14) in the Indianapolis 500 on 29 May 1971.

Duration record The greatest distance ever covered in one year is 400,000 kilometres (248,548.5 miles) by François Lecot (1879-1949), an innkeeper from Rochetaillée, near Lyon, France, in an 11 c.v. Citroën (1,900 c.c., 66 b.h.p.), mainly between Paris and Monte Carlo, from 22 July 1935 to 26 July 1936. He drove on 363 of the 370 days.

The world's duration record is 185,353 miles 1,741 yards in 133 days 17 hours 37 minutes 38.64 seconds (average speed 58.07 m.p.h.) by Marchand, Presalé and six others in a Citroën on the Montlhéry track near Paris, France, during March-July 1933.

Go-kart circum-navigation The only recorded instance of a go-kart being driven round the world was a circumnavigation by Stan Mott, of New York, U.S.A., who drove a Lambretta engined 175 c.c. "Italkart" with a ground clearance of two inches, 23,300 land miles through 28 countries from 15 Feb. 1961 to 5 June 1964, starting and finishing in New York, U.S.A.

MOUNTAINEERING

Origins Although bronze-age artifacts have been found on the summit of the Riffelhorn, mountaineering, as a sport, has a continuous history dating back only to 1854. Isolated instances of climbing for its own sake exist back to the 14th century. The Atacamenans built sacrificial platforms near the summit of Llullaillaco (22,058 feet) in late pre-Columbian times *c.* 1490. The earliest recorded rock climb in the British Isles was of Stacna Biorrach, St. Kilda by Sir Robert Moray in 1698.

Mount Everest Mount Everest (29,028 feet) was first climbed at 11.30 a.m. on 29 May 1953, when the summit was reached by Edmund Percival Hillary (born 20 July 1919), created K.B.E., of New Zealand, and the Sherpa, Tenzing Norkhay (born, as Namgyal Wangdi, in Nepal in 1914, formerly called Tenzing Khumjung Bhutia), who was awarded the G.M. The successful expedition was led by Col. (later Hon. Brigadier) Henry Cecil John Hunt, C.B.E., D.S.O. (born 22 June 1910), who was created a Knight Bachelor in 1953 and a life peer on 11 June 1966.

Greatest wall The greatest wall in the world is the 14,500-foot-high south face of Annapurna I (26,504 feet) which starts at 12,000 feet. It was climbed by the British expedition led by Christian Bonnington when on 27 May 1970 Donald Whillans, 36 and Dougal Haston, 27 scaled to the summit.

Greatest Alpine Wall Europe's greatest wall is the 6,600 foot North face of the Eigerwand (Ogre wall) first climbed on 20 Aug. 1932 by Hans Lauper, Alfred Zurcher, Alexander Graven and Josef Knubel. The first direct ascent was by Heinrich Harrar and Fritz Kasparek of Austria and Andreas Heckmair and Ludvig Vörg of Germany on 21-24 July 1938. The greatest alpine solo climb was that of Walter Bonatti (Italy) of the South West Pillar of the Dru, Montenvers now called the Bonatti Pillar in 126 hours 7 mins. on 17-22 Aug. 1955.

Rock climbing The world's most demanding XS (extremely severe) rock climb is regarded as the sheer almost totally

Don Whillans co-conqueror of the world's greatest mountain wall—the south face of Annapurna I.

holdless 3,000 foot Muir Wall of El Capitan (7,564 ft.) Yosemite, California, U.S.A. first climbed in November 1958. In 1968 Royal Robbins (U.S.A.) climbed this solo with pitons.

MOUNTAIN RACING

Ben Nevis The record time for the race from Fort William to the summit of Ben Nevis and return is 1 hour 33 mins. 5 secs. by Dave Cannon on 4 Sept. 1971. The feminine record is 1 hour 51 minutes for the ascent only, by Elizabeth Wilson-Smith on 14 Sept. 1909 and 3 hours 2 minutes for the ascent and return by Kathleen Connachie, aged 16, on 3 Sept. 1965. The full course by the bridle path is about 14 miles but distance can be saved by crossing the open hillside. The mountain was first climbed in about 1720 and the earliest race was in 1895.

The Lakeland 24-hour record is 63 peaks achieved by Joss Naylor (b. 10 Feb. 1936) of Wasdale on 24-25 June 1972. He covered 92 miles with 35,000 feet of ascents and descents. Naylor has won every Ennerdale mountain race over 23 miles since it was instituted in 1968 setting a record time of 3 hours 30 mins. 40 secs in 1972. The Yorkshire three peak record is 2 hours 36 mins. 26 secs. by Jeff Norman on 25 April 1971.

The "Three Thousander" record over the 14 Welsh peaks of over 3,000 feet is 5 hours 13 minutes by the late Eric Beard (Leeds A.C.) on 17 June 1965.

Three peaks record The Three Peaks run from sea level at Fort William, Inverness-shire, to sea level at Caernarvon, *via* the summits of Ben Nevis, Scafell Pike and Snowdon was uniquely achieved by the late Eric Beard, 37, of Leeds Athletic Club, in 10 days in June 1969.

Pennine Way The record for traversing the 270 mile long Pennine Way is 4 days 5 hours 10 mins. by Alan Heaton, 4 and Michael Meath, 25 of Clayton-le-Moor Harriers on 30 June to 4 July 1972.

African Two Peaks Record The climbing of Africa's two highest mountains Kilimanjaro (19,340 ft.) and Mount Kenya (17,058 ft.) from summit to summit in 24 hours, was achieved on 9-10 Feb. 1964 by Rusty Baillie (Rhodesia) and Barry Cliff (G.B.). The descent of 15,300 feet, the 250 mile drive and the 8,500 foot ascent of Mount Kenya were achieved in 21 hours 50 minutes.

SUBSEQUENT ASCENTS OF MOUNT EVEREST

Climbers	Date	Climbers	Date
Ernst Schmidt, Jürg Marmet	23 May 1956	Dr. William F. Unsoeld, Dr. Thomas F. Hornbein	22 May 196
Hans Rudolf von Gunten, Adolf Reist	24 May 1956	Capt. A. S. Cheema, Sherpa Nawang Gombu	20 May 196
*Wang Fu-chou, Chu Yin-hua, Konbu	25 May 1960	Sonam Gyaltso, Sonam Wangyal	22 May 196
James Warren Whittaker, Sherpa Nawang Gombu	1 May 1963	C. P. Vohra, Sherpa Ang Kami	24 May 196
Barry C. Bishop, Luther G. Jerstad	22 May 1963	Capt. H. P. S. Ahluwalia, H. C. S. Rawat, Phu Dorji	29 May 196
		Nomi Uemura, Tero Matsuura (Japan)	11 May 197
		Katsutoshi Hirabayoshi (Japan), Sherpa Chotari	12 May 197

Not internationally accepted as authentic.

ell running Bill Teasdale won the Guide's Race at the Grasmere Sports, Westmorland, for the eleventh time in 1966. It involves running to a turning point on Butter Crag (966 feet above sea level) and back, a distance of about 1½ miles.

Greatest fall The greatest recorded fall survived by a mountaineer was when Christopher Timms (Christchurch University) slid 7,500 feet down an ice face into a crevasse on Mt. Elie de Beaumont (10,200 feet), New Zealand on 7 Dec. 1966. His companion was killed but he survived with concussion, bruises and a hand injury.

NETBALL

Origins The game was invented in the U.S.A. in 1891 and introduced into England in 1895 by Dr. Toles. The All England Women's Netball Association was formed in 1926.

World title World championships were inaugurated in August 1963 at Eastbourne, Sussex and were won by Australia. The 1971 world championships at Kingston, Jamaica were also won by Australia. The record number of goals in the World Tournament is 402 by Mrs Judith Heath in 1971.

Highest scores England has never been beaten in a home international. England's record score is 94 goals to 12 *v.* Wales in 1970 and 94 goals *v.* Northern Ireland in Jamaica in January 1971. The highest international score recorded was when New Zealand beat Northern Ireland 112-4 at Eastbourne, Sussex on 2 Aug. 1963.

Most rnationals The record number of internationals is 39 by Anne Miles, of England to 1972.

Marathon A longest netball marathon match lasting 48 hours by 6 teams of 7 girls was played by Bungay 'Shell' Youth Club, Suffolk on 2-4 June 1972.

OLYMPIC GAMES

Note: *The Guinness Book of Olympic Records* (Penguin, 1972) contains a complete roll of all the medal winners in currently contested events and their performances from 1896 to 1968 and the Winter Games at Sapporo in 1972. A roll of Olympic records as they stand after the XXth Games at Munich which closed on 10 Sept. 1972 appears on the back end-papers of the volume.

Origins The earliest celebration of the ancient Olympic Games of which there is a certain record is that of July 776 B.C., when Koroibos, a cook from Elis, won a foot race, though their origin dates from *c.* 1370 B.C. The ancient Games were terminated by an order issued in Milan in A.D. 393 by Theodosius I, "the Great" (*c.* 346-395), Emperor of Rome. At the instigation of Pierre de Fredi, Baron de Coubertin (1863-1937), the Olympic Games of the modern era were inaugurated in Athens on 6 April 1896.

Largest crowd The largest crowd at any Olympic site was 150,000 at the 1952 ski-jumping at the Holmenkollen, outside Oslo, Norway. Estimates of the number of spectators of the marathon race through Tōkyō, Japan on 21 Oct. 1964 have ranged from 500,000 to 1,500,000.

MOST GOLD MEDALS

Individual In the ancient Olympic Games victors were given a chaplet of olive leaves. Milo (Milon of Krotōn) won 6 titles at *palaisma* (wrestling) 540-516 B.C. The most individual gold medals won by a male competitor in the modern Games is eight by Ray C. Ewry (U.S.A.) (see Athletics). The female record is seven by Vera Caslavska-Odlozil (see Gymnastics). The most won by a British competitor is four by Paul Radmilovic (1886–1968) in Water Polo in 1908, 1912 and 1920 and in the 800 metres team swimming event in 1908. The sculler and oarsman Jack Beresford C.B.E. won the three gold and two silver medals in the five Olympics from 1920 to 1936.

National The United States has won most medals in all Olympic events (summer and winter) with (gold, silver, bronze) 572–431½–376½=1,380 with U.S.S.R. (formerly Russia) (did not compete 1920 to 1948 inclusive) second with 199–181–177=557, and the United Kingdom third with a total of 146½–176½–157=480. These figures exclude demonstration sports, art competitions and medals in the unofficial Games of 1906. *Note:* The British total of gold medals 1896–1968 in the Summer Games of 142½ was misprinted 192½ in the first printing of *The Guinness Book of Olympic Records* (1972 edition).

Oldest and youngest competitors The oldest recorded competitor was Oscar G. Swahn (Sweden), who won a silver medal for shooting running deer in 1920, when aged 73. The youngest-ever female gold medal winner is Miss Marjorie Gestring (U.S.A.) (b. 18 November 1922, now Mrs Bowman), aged 13 years 9 months, in the 1936 women's springboard event. Bernard Malivoire, aged 12, coxed the winning French pairs in 1952.

Longest span The longest span of an Olympic competitor is 40 years by Dr. Ivan Osiier (Denmark), who competed as a fencer in 1908, 1912 (silver medal) 1920, 1924, 1928, 1932 and 1948, totalling seven celebrations. He refused to compete in the 1936 Games on the grounds that they were Nazi-dominated. The longest feminine span is 24 years (1932-1956) by the Austrian fencer Ellen Müller-Preiss. The longest span of any British competitor is 20 years by George Mackenzie who wrestled in the Games of 1908, 1912, 1920, 1924 and 1928, and by Mrs Dorothy J. B. Tyler (*née* Odam), who high-jumped in 1936-48-52 and 56. The only Olympian to win 4 consecutive titles in athletics has been Alfred A. Oerter (b. 19 Sept. 1936, Astoria, N.Y.) of the U.S.A. who won the discus title in 1956-60-64-68.

Most Countries and Participants The greatest number of competitors in any summer Olympic Games up to 1968 has been 6,082 from a record 109 countries in Mexico in 1968. The fewest was 285 competitors in 1896. In 1904 only 11 countries participated.

The first Winter Games in 1924 attracted 293 competitors from 16 nations.

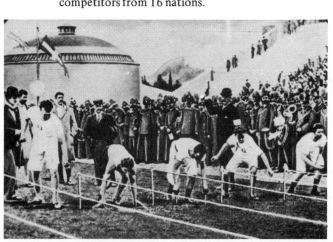

The first modern Olympic Games 100 metres final—note use of starting sticks.

285

Celebrations have been allocated as follows:—

I	Athens	6-15 April 1896
II	Paris	2-22 July 1900
III	St. Louis	29 Aug.-7 Sept. 1904
†	Athens	22 April-2 May 1906
IV	London	13-25 July 1908
V	Stockholm	6-15 July 1912
VI	*Berlin	1916
VII	Antwerp	14-29 Aug. 1920
VIII	Paris	5-27 July 1924
IX	Amsterdam	28 July-12 Aug. 1928
X	Los Angeles	30 July-14 Aug. 1932
XI	Berlin	1-16 Aug. 1936
XII	*Tōkyō, then Helsinki	1940
XIII	*London	1944
XIV	London	29 July-14 Aug. 1948
XV	Helsinki	19 July-3 Aug. 1952
XVI	Melbourne	22 Nov.-8 Dec. 1956
XVII	Rome	25 Aug.-11 Sept. 1960
XVIII	Tōkyō	10-24 Oct. 1964
XIX	Mexico City	12-27 Oct. 1968
XX	Munich	26 Aug.-10 Sept. 1972
XXI	Montreal	18 July-1 Aug. 1976

Cancelled due to World Wars.
† Unofficial or Intercalated Celebration.

The Winter Olympics were inaugurated in 1924 and have been allocated as follows:—

I	Chamonix, France	25 Jan.-4 Feb. 1924
II	St. Moritz, Switzerland	11-19 Feb. 1928
III	Lake Placid, U.S.A.	4-13 Feb. 1932
IV	Garmisch-Partenkirchen, Germany	6-16 Feb. 1936
V	St. Moritz, Switzerland	30 Jan.-8 Feb. 1948
VI	Oslo, Norway	14-25 Feb. 1952
VII	Cortina d'Ampezzo, Italy	26 Jan.-5 Feb. 1956
VIII	Squaw Valley, California	18-28 Feb. 1960
IX	Innsbruck, Austria	29 Jan.-9 Feb. 1964
X	Grenoble, France	6-18 Feb. 1968
XI	Sapporo, Japan	3-13 Feb. 1972
XII	Denver, Colorado, U.S.A.	20-29 Feb. 1976

ORIENTEERING

Origins Orienteering was invented by Major Ernst Killander in Sweden in 1918. World championships were inaugurated in 1966 and are held biennially. Annual British championships were instituted in 1967.

Most titles Sweden won the world men's relay titles in 1966 and
World 1968 and the women's relay in 1966 with Ulla Lindkvist (Sweden) winning the individual titles in both 1966 and 1968.

Britain The most successful British team has been Edinburgh Southern Orienteering Club, which won the Senior Men's title in 1969 and 1970 and the Senior Ladies' title in 1970. Gordon Pirie won the men's individual title in 1967 and 1968 and Carol McNeill won the women's title in 1967 and 1969.

PELOTA VASCA (JAI ALAI)

Origins The game, which originated in Italy as *longue paume* and was introduced into France in the 13th century, is said to be the fastest of all ball games with speeds of up to 160 m.p.h. Gloves were introduced *c.* 1840 and the *chisterak* was invented *c.* 1860 by Gantchiki Dithurbide of Sainte Pée. The long *chistera* was invented by Melchior Curuchage of Buenos Aires, Argentina in 1888. The world's largest *frontón* (the playing court) is that built for $4,500,000 (now £1,875,000) at Miami, Florida, U.S.A.

Longest The longest domination as the world's No. 1 player
Domination was enjoyed by Chiquito de Cambo (*né* Joseph Apesteguy), born 10 May 1881-died 1955, from the

The world's largest frontón at Miami, Florida, U.S.A.

beginning of the century until succeeded in 1938 by Jean Urruty (b. 19 Oct. 1913).

Games played in a *frontón* are *Frontenis, pelote* and *paleta* with both leather and rubber balls. The sport is governed by the International Federation of Basque Pelote.

PIGEON RACING

Earliest Pigeon Racing was the natural development of the use
references of homing pigeons for the carrying of messages—quality utilized in the ancient Olympic Game (776 B.C.-A.D. 393). The sport originated in Belgium and came to Britain *c.* 1820. The earliest major long-distance race was from Crystal Palace, South London, in 1871. The earliest recorded occasion on which 500 miles was flown in a day was by "Motor" (owned by G.P. Pointer of Alexander Park Racing Club) which was released from Thurso, Scotland, on 30 June 1896 and covered 501 miles at an average speed of 1,454 yards per minute (49½ m.p.h.).

Longest The greatest recorded homing flight by a pigeon was
flights made by one owned by the 1st Duke of Wellington (1769-1852). Released from a sailing ship off the Ichabo Islands, West Africa, on 8 April, it dropped dead a mile from its loft at Nine Elms, London, on 1 June 1845, 55 days later, having flown an airline route of 5,400 miles, but an actual distance of possibly 7,000 miles to avoid the Sahara Desert. It was reported on 27 Nov. 1971 that an exhausted pigeon bearing a Hannover label was found 10,000 miles away at Cunnamulla, Queensland, Australia. The official British duration record (into Great Britain) is 1,141 miles by A. Bruce's bird in the 1960 Barcelona Race which was liberated on 9 July and homed at Fraserburgh, Aberdeenshire, Scotland on 5 August.

Highest In level flight in windless conditions it is very
speeds doubtful if any pigeon can exceed 60 m.p.h. The highest race speed recorded is one of 3,229 yards per min. (110.07 m.p.h) in the East Anglian Federation race from East Croydon on 8 May 1965 when the 1,428 birds were backed by a powerful south south-west wind. The winner was A. Vidgeon & Son.

The highest race speed recorded over a distance of more than 1000 km is 2,432.70 yards per minute (82.93 m.p.h.) by a hen pigeon in the Central Cumberland Combine race over 683 miles 147 yards from Murray Bridge, South Australia to North Ryde Sydney on 2 Oct. 1971. The world's longest reputed distance in 24 hours is 803 miles (velocity 1,525 yards per minute) by E.S. Peterson's winner of the 1941 San Antonio R.C. event Texas, U.S.A.

The best 24—hour performance into the United Kingdom is 686 miles by A.R. Hill's winner of the 1952 race from Hannover, Germany to St. Just Cornwall—average speed 1,300 yards per minute (44.31 m.p.h.).

POLO

Earliest games The earliest polo club was the Kachar Club (founded in 1859) in Assam, India. The game was introduced into England from India in 1869 by the 10th Hussars at Aldershot, Hampshire and the earliest match was one between the 9th Lancers and the 10th Hussars on Hounslow Heath, west of London, in July 1871. The first All–Ireland Cup match was at Phoenix Park, Dublin, in 1878. The earliest international match between England and the U.S.A. was in 1886.

The game is played on the largest pitch of any ball game in the world. A ground measures 300 yards long by 160 yards wide with side boards, or as in India, 200 yards wide without boards.

Highest handicap The highest handicap based on eight 7½–minute "chukkas" is 10 goals introduced in the U.S.A. in 1891 and in the United Kingdom and in Argentina in 1910. The most recent additions to the select ranks of the 32 players ever to receive 10–goal handicaps are H. Heguy, F. Dorignal and G. Dorignal all of Argentina. The last (of six) 10–goal handicap players from Great Britain was G. Balding in 1939.

The highest handicap of any of the United Kingdom's 300 players is 7, achieved in the Argentine in October 1966 by Paul Withers and John Lucas. H.R.H. Prince Philip, the Duke of Edinburgh (b. 10 June 1921) has a handicap of 5 at back and thus ranks among the highest handicapped players in the United Kingdom.

Highest score The highest aggregate number of goals scored in an international match is 30, when Argentina beat the U.S.A. 21–9 at Meadow Brook, Long Island, New York, U.S.A., in September 1936.

Most nationals The greatest number of times any player has represented England is four in the case of Frederick M. Freake in 1900, 1902, 1909 and 1913. Thomas Hitchcock, Jr. (1900-44) played five times for the U.S.A. *v.* England (1921-24-27-30-39) and twice *v.* Argentina (1928-36).

Most expensive pony The highest price ever paid for a polo pony was $22,000 (now £7,857), paid by Stephen Sanford for Lewis Lacey's *Jupiter* after the U.S.A. *v.* Argentina international in 1928.

Largest trophy The world's largest trophy for a particular sport is the Bangalore Limited Handicap Polo Tournament Trophy. This massive cup standing on its plinth is 6 feet tall and was presented in 1936 by the Raja of Kolanke.

Largest crowd World record crowds of over 50,000 have watched floodlit matches at a number of Australian agricultural shows.

POWER BOAT RACING

Origins The earliest application of the petrol engine to a boat was Gottlieb Daimler's experimental power boat on the River Seine, Paris, France, in 1887. The sport was given impetus by the presentation of an international championship cup by Sir Alfred Harmsworth in 1903, which was also the year of the first off-shore race from Calais to Dover.

nsworth Cup Of the 25 contests from 1903 to 1961, the United States has won 16, the United Kingdom 5, Canada 3 and France 1.

The greatest number of wins has been achieved by

Don Aronow (U.S.A.) with the world's fastest off-shore power boat—*The Cigarette.*

Garfield A. Wood with eight (1920-21, 1926, 1928-29-30, 1932-33). The only boat to win three times is *Miss Supertest III*, owned by James G. Thompson (Canada), in 1959-60-61. This boat also achieved the record speed of 115.972 m.p.h. at Picton, Ontario, Canada in 1960.

Gold Cup The Gold Cup (instituted 1903) has been won four times by Garfield A. Wood (1917, 1919-20-21) and by Bill Muncey (1956-57, 1961-62). The record speed is 120.356 m.p.h. for a 3-mile lap by Rolls-Royce-engined *Miss Exide*, owned by Milo Stoen, driven by Bill Brow at Seattle, Washington, U.S.A. on 4 Aug. 1965.

Highest off-shore speeds The highest race speed attained is 74.32 m.p.h. by Don Aronow (U.S.A.) in his 32-foot *The Cigarette*, powered by two 475 h.p. Mercruiser engines over 214 miles at Viareggio, Italy on 20 July 1969. The highest average race speed off British shores has been 69.5 m.p.h. by Vincenzo Balastrieri (Italy) and D. Pruett in *Red Tornado* over 184 miles from Southsea Pier, Hampshire to Weymouth, Dorset to Hillhead Buoy, south of the Isle of Wight in the Wills International Race on 14 June 1969. The Countess of Arran drove her off-shore powerboat *Highland Fling* for a feminine record of 85.63 m.p.h. despite fuel trouble on the back-up run on Windermere on 21 Oct. 1971.

Longest race The longest race is the *Daily Telegraph and B.P.* Round Britain event inaugurated on 26 July 1969 at Portsmouth with 1,403 miles in 10 stages west—about England, Wales and across Northern Scotland *via* the Caledonian Canal. The 1969 race (26 July to 7 August) was won by *Avenger Too* (Timo Makinen and Pascoe Watson) in 39 hours 9 minutes 37.7 seconds. Of the 42 starters, 24 finished.

Cowes-Torquay race The record average for the *Daily Express* International Off-Shore Race (instituted 1961) is 66.47 m.p.h. by *The Cigarette* (Don Aronow) (see above) over the 236-mile course from Cowes, Isle of Wight to Torquay, Devon and back in 3 hours 33 minutes.

Dragsters The first drag boat to attain 200 m.p.h. was Sam Kurtovich's *Crisis* which attained 200.44 m.p.h. in California in Oct. 1969 in a one-way run.

Longest journey The Dane Hans Tholstrup, 25, circumnavigated Australia in a 17 foot Caribbean Cougar fibreglass runabout with a single 80 h.p. Mercury outboard motor from 11 May to 25 July 1971.

RACKETS

Earliest world champion The first world rackets champion was Robert Mackay, who claimed the title in London in 1820. The first closed court champion was Francis Erwood at Woolwich in 1860. The first new court built in Great Britain since 1914 was the Second Court opened at Harrow School in 1965.

Longest reign Of the 18 world champions since 1820 the longest reign is held by British—born U.S. resident Geoffrey W.T. Atkins, who has held the title since beating the professional James Dear in 1954 and retired after a fourth successful defence of it in April 1970.

Most Amateur titles Since the Amateur singles championship was instituted in 1888 the most titles won by an individual is nine by Edgar M. Baerlein (1879—1971) between 1903 and 1923. Since the institution of the Amateur doubles championship in 1890 the most shares in titles has been eleven by David Sumner Milford, between 1938 and 1959. He also has seven Amateur singles titles (1930—52), an open title (1936) and held the world title from 1937 to 1947.

RODEO

Origins Rodeo came into being with the early days of the North American cattle industry. The earliest references to the sport are from Sante Fe, New Mexico, U.S.A., in 1847. Steer wrestling came in with Bill Pickett (Oklahoma) in 1903. The other events are calf roping, bull riding, saddle and bare-back bronc riding.

The largest rodeo in the world is the Calgary Exhibition and Stampede at Calgary, Alberta, Canada. The record attendance has been 853,620 on 9-18 July 1969. The record for one day is 127,043 on 15 July 1967.

Most world titles The record number of all-round titles is five by Jim Shoulders (U.S.A.), in 1949 and 1956-57-58-59 and by Larry Mahan (U.S.A.), in 1966-67-68-69-70. The record figure for prize money in a single season is $57,726 (£24,052) in the three riding events by Larry Maham, (born 21 Nov 1943) of Brooks, Oregon, U.S.A. in 1969.

Time records Records for timed events, such as calf-roping and steer-wrestling, are meaningless, because of the widely varying conditions due to the size of arenas and amount of start given the stock. The fastest time recorded for roping a calf is 7.5 seconds by Junior Garrison of Marlow, Oklahoma, at Evergreen, Colorado, U.S.A. in 1967, and the fastest time for overcoming a steer was 2.4 seconds by James Bynum of Waxahachie, Texas, at Marietta, Oklahoma, in 1955.

The standard required time to stay on in bareback events is 8 seconds and in saddle bronc riding 10 seconds. In the now obsolete ride-to-a-finish events, rodeo riders have been recorded to have survived 90+ minutes, until the mount had not a buck left in it.

Champion bull The top bucking bull is *V-61.* an 1,800-lb. Brahma owned by the Henry Knight Rodeo Company of Fowler, Colorado, U.S.A. He was never ridden in 9 years until John Quintana, 23, of Milwaukee, Oregon, succeeded in June 1971, so scoring 94 points—an absolute Rodeo record.

Champion bronc The greatest bucking bronco of all time was *Midnight*, owned by Verne Elliott of Platteville, Colorado. In seven years (1923—1930) he was ridden by only four riders once each, and of these only Frank Studnick (at Pendleton, Oregon, in 1929) was not subsequently thrown because he did not mount him again.

Larry Mahan (U.S.A.) five times all round Rodeo champion of the world.

ROLLER SKATING

Origins The first roller skate was devised by Joseph Merlin of Huy, Belgium, in 1760. Several "improved" versions appeared during the next century, but a really satisfactory roller skate did not materialize before 1866, when James L. Plimpton of New York produced the present four-wheeled type, patented it, and opened the first public rink in the world at Newport, Rhode Island, that year. The great boom periods were 1870-75, 1908-12 and 1948-54, each originating in the United States.

Largest rink The largest indoor rink ever to operate was located in the Grand Hall, Olympia, London. It had an actual skating area of 68,000 square feet. It first opened in 1890, for one season, then again from 1909 to 1912.

Roller hockey Roller hockey (previously known as Rink Hockey in Europe) was first introduced in this country as Rink Polo, at the old Lava rink, Denmark Hill, London in the late 1870s. The Amateur Rink Hockey Association was formed in 1905, and in 1913 became the National Rink Hockey (now Roller Hockey) Association. Britain won the inaugural World Championship in 1936 since when Portugal has won most titles with 11 between 1947 and 1971.

Most titles Leslie E. Woodley of Birmingham won 12 British national individual titles over the three regulation distances (880 yards, one mile and five miles) between 1957 and 1964. Mrs. Chloe Ronaldson of London won 17 ladies' titles over 440 yards, 800 metres and 880 yards in 1958-71.

Records The fastest speed put up in an official world record is 25.78 m.p.h. when Giuseppe Cantarello (Italy) recorded 34.9 seconds for 440 yards on a road at Catania, Sicily on 28 Sept. 1963. The world mile record on a rink is 2 minutes 25.1 seconds by Johnny Ferriti (Italy). The greatest distance skated in one hour on a rink by a woman is 20 miles 1,355 yards by C. Patricia Barnett (G.B.) at Brixton, London on 24 June 1962. The men's record on a closed road circuit is 22 miles 465.9 yards (35 km. 831 m.) by Alberto Civolani (Italy) at Bologna, Italy on 15 Oct. 1967.

Marathon record The longest recorded continuous roller skating marathon was performed by Professor Eckard with 100 hours at Rockhampton, Queensland, Australia in 1913. The longest reported skate was by Clinton Shaw from Victoria, British Columbia to St. John's, Newfoundland (4,900 miles) on the Trans-Canadian Highway *via* Montreal from 1 April to 11 Nov. 1967.

ROWING

Oldest race The earliest established sculling race is the Dogget's Coat and Badge, which was rowed on 1 Aug. 1716 over 5 miles from London Bridge to Chelsea and is still being rowed every year over the same course, under the administration of the Fishmongers' Company. The first English regatta probably took place on the Thames by the Ranelagh Gardens, near Putney in 1775. Boating began at Eton in 1793, 72 years before the "song". The Leander Club was formed c. 1818.

OLYMPIC GAMES

Since 1900 there have been 93 Olympic finals, of which the U.S.A. have won 27, Germany 16 and the United Kingdom 14. Four oarsmen have won 3 gold medals; John B. Kelly (U.S.A.), father of Princess Grace of Monaco, in the sculls (1920) and double sculls (1920 and 1924); Paul V. Costello (U.S.A.) in the double sculls (1920, 1924 and 1928); Jack Beresford, Jr. C.B.E. (G.B.) in the sculls (1924), coxless fours (1932) and double sculls (1936) and Vyacheslav Ivanov (U.S.S.R.) in the sculls (1956, 1960 and 1964). (For 1972 Games see back endpapers).

BOAT RACE

The earliest University Boat Race, which Oxford won, was from Hambleden Lock to Henley Bridge on 10 June 1829. In the 118 races to 1972. Cambridge won 66 times, Oxford 51 times and there was a dead heat on 24 March 1877.

Record time The race record time for the course of 4 miles 374 yards (Putney to Mortlake) is 17 minutes 50 seconds by Cambridge in 1948. Oxford returned 17 minutes 37 seconds in practice on 19 March 1965. The smallest winning margin was Oxford's win by a canvas in 1952. The greatest margin (apart from sinking) was Cambridge's win by 20 lengths in 1900. The record for the distance (rowed on the ebb from Mortlake to Putney) is 17 minutes 24 seconds by the Tideway Scullers School in the Head of the River Race on 21 March 1964.

Intermediate times The record to the Mile Post is 3 minutes 47 seconds (Oxford 1960 and 25 March 1967); Hammersmith Bridge 6 minutes 42 seconds (Oxford 25 March 1967); Chiswick Steps 10 minutes 45 seconds (Oxford 1965, in practice) and Barnes Bridge 14 minutes 39 seconds (Oxford 19 March 1965, in practice).

Oarsman Heaviest The heaviest man ever to row in a University boat has been David L. Cruttenden (b. Hartlepool, 1947) the No. 6 in the 1970 Cambridge boat at 16 st. 0 lb. The 1972 Cambridge crew averaged a record 13 st. 11¼ lb.

Lightest The lightest oarsman was the 1882 Oxford Stroke, A. H. Higgins, at 9 stone 6½ lb. The lightest cox was F.H.

Archer (Oxford) in 1862 at 5 stone 2 lb.

HENLEY ROYAL REGATTA

The annual regatta at Henley-on-Thames, Oxfordshire, was inaugurated on 26 March 1839.

Since 1839 the course, except in 1923, has been about 1 mile 550 yards, varying slightly according to the length of boat. In 1967 the shorter craft were "drawn up" so all bows start level. Prior to 1922 there were two slight angles. Classic Records (year in brackets indicates the date instituted):

Sculling The record number of wins in the Wingfield Sculls (instituted on the Thames 1830) is seven by Jack Beresford, Jr. (see Olympics), from 1920 to 1926. The fastest time (Putney to Mortlake) has been 21 minutes 11 seconds by L.F. Southworth in 1933. The record number of world professional sculling titles (instituted 1831) won is seven by W. Beach (Australia) between 1884 and 1887. Stuart A. Mackenzie (Great Britain and Australia) performed the unique feat of winning the Diamond Sculls at Henley for the sixth consecutive occasion on 7 July 1962. In 1960 and 1962 he was in Leander colours.

Stuart A. Mackenzie who won the Diamond Sculls at Henley on 6 consecutive occasions up to 7 July 1962.

Highest speed Speeds in tidal or flowing water are of no comparative value. The highest recorded speed for 2,000 metres by an eight in the World Championships is 5 minutes 43.61 seconds (13.02 m.p.h.) by Norway at St. Catherine's, Ontario, Canada, on 4 Sept. 1970 and in the Olympic Games 5 minutes 54.02 seconds (12.64 m.p.h.) by Germany at Toda, Japan on 12 Oct. 1964.

Fastest Cross Channel Row The fastest row across the channel has been 4 hours 15 mins. from Sandgate, Kent to Boulogne, France by a coxed four (Jack Hughes (Stroke) Maurice Drummond, Samuel Osborne, George Edwards (bow) and Jimmy Ladlow (cox)) on 27 July 1947.

HENLEY ROYAL REGATTA—Classic Records

				mins. secs.	
Grand Challenge Cup (1839)	8 oars	Ratzeburger Ruderclub (West Germany)		6:16	3 July 1965
Ladies' Challenge Plate (1845)	8 oars	G.S.R., Aegir (Netherlands)		6:42	3 July 1970
Thames Challenge Cup (1868)	8 oars	Isis		6:35	3 July 1965
Princess Elizabeth Challenge Cup (1946)	8 oars	Emmanuel School		6:44	1 July 1965
		Tabor Academy, U.S.A. (twice)		6:44	3 July 1965
Stewards' Challenge Cup (1841)	4 oars	Quintin		6:55	3 July 1965
Visitors' Challenge Cup (1847)	4 oars	St. Edmund Hall, Oxford		7:13	3 July 1965
Wyfold Challenge Cup (1855)	4 oars	Derby R.C.		7:06	3 July 1965
Prince Philip Cup (1963)	4 oars	Leander		7:03	3 July 1965
Britannia Challenge Cup	4 oars	Thame R.C. (coxed)		7:26	6 July 1968
Silver Goblets and Nickalls' Cup (1895)	Pair oar	Peter Gorny and Gunther Bergau (ASK Vorwaerts Rostock, East Germany)		7:35	1 July 1965
Double Sculls Challenge Cup (1939)	Sculls	Melch Buergin and Martin Studach (Grasshoppers Club, Zürich)		7:01	3 July 1965
Diamond Challenge Sculls (1844)	Sculls	Donald M. Spero (New York A.C., U.S.A.)		7:42	3 July 1965

Loch Ness Loch Ness, the longest stretch of inland water in Great Britain (22.7 miles), was rowed by a coxed four jollyboat from Eastern Amateur Rowing Club of Portobello on 11 Oct. 1969 in 4 hours 11 minutes.

Oxford–London The fastest time registered between Folly Bridge, Oxford through 33 locks and 112 miles to Westminster Bridge, London is 15 hours 16 minutes by an eight (no substitutes) from the Wallingford R.C. on 18 Oct. 1970 so beating a military record set in 1824.

Circum-navigation of Ireland Ireland, the world's twentieth largest island, was first circumnavigated by an oarsman when Derek Paul King, 25, of Dartford, Kent, landed at Rosnowlagh, County Donegal on 3 Oct. 1971 having rowed *Louise* 1,500 miles in 108 days since 11 June.

Marathon An eight from the Aramoho Boating Club, New Zealand covered 78 miles in 12 hours a 4 mile long shuttle course on the River Wanganui on 20 Nov. 1971.

SHOOTING

Olympic Games The record number of gold medals won is five by Morris Fisher (U.S.A.) with three in 1920 and two in 1924.

Record heads The world's finest head is the 23-pointer stag head in the Maritzburg collection, Germany. The outside span is 75½ inches, the length 47½ inches and the weight 41½ lb. The greatest number of points is probably 33 (plus 29) on the stag shot in 1696 by Frederick III (1657-1713), the Elector of Brandenburg, later King Frederick I of Prussia.

The record head for a British Red Deer is a 47-pointer (length 33½ inches) from the Great Warnham Deer Park, Sussex in 1892. The record for a semi-feral stag is a 20-pointer with an antler length of $45^3/_8$ inches from Endsleigh Wood, Devon, found in December 1950 and owned by G. Kenneth Whitehead.

Largest shoulder guns The largest bore shoulder guns made were 2 bores. Less than a dozen of these were made by two English wildfowl gunmakers *c.* 1885. Normally the largest guns made are double-barrelled 4-bore weighing up to 26 lb., which can be handled only by men of exceptional physique. Larger smooth-bore guns have been made, but these are for use as punt-guns.

Highest muzzle velocity The highest muzzle velocity of any rifle bullet is 7,100 feet per second (4,840 m.p.h. by a 1937 0.30 calibre, M 1903 Standard U.S. Army Ordnance Department rifle.

Clay pigeon The record number of clay birds shot in an hour is 1,308 by Joseph Nother (formerly Wheater) (born 1918) of Kingston-upon-Hull, Yorkshire, at Bedford on 21 Sept. 1957. Using 5 guns and 7 loaders he shot 1,000 in 42 minutes 22.5 seconds.

BISLEY

The National Rifle Association was instituted in 1859. The Queen's (King's) Prize has been shot since 1860 and has only once been won by a woman—Miss Marjorie Elaine Foster, M.B.E. (score 280) in 1930. Only Arthur G. Fulton, M.B.E. has won 3 times (1912, 1926, 1931).

The highest score (possible 300) is 292 by Capt. C. H. Vernon, with 146 in both the 2nd and 3rd stages, on 15-16 July 1927. The record for the Silver Medal, shot at 300, 500 and 600 yards, is 148 (possible 150) by four marksmen in 1927, C. A. Sutherland on 19 July 1935, Warrant Officer Norman L. Beckett (Canada) on 21 July 1961 and Keith M. Pilcher on 19 July 1963.

Bob Braithwaite (G.B.) who achieved 187 consecutive hits to win the 1968 Olympic Trench gold medal.

Bench rest Shooting The smallest group on record at 1,000 yards is 7.6 inches by Mary Louise De Vito with a 7mm-300 Weatherby in Pennsylvania on 11 Oct. 1970.

Block tossing Using a pair of auto-loading Remington Nylon 66.2 calibre guns, Tom Frye (U.S.A.) tossed 100,0 blocks (2½-inch pine cubes) and hit 100,004—h longest run was 32,860—on 5-17 Oct. 1959.

Biggest bag The largest animal ever shot by any big game hunt was a bull African elephant (*Loxodonta african* shot by J. J. Fénykövi (Hungary), 48 mi north-northwest of Macusso, Angola, on 13 No 1955. It required 16 heavy calibre bullets from 0.416 Rigby and weighed an estimated 24,000 (10.7 tons), standing 13 feet 2 inches at the shoulde In November 1965 Simon Fletcher, 28, a Keny farmer, claimed to have killed two elephants with o 0.458 bullet.

The greatest recorded lifetime bag is 556,000 bird including 241,000 pheasants, by the 2nd Marquess Ripon (1867-1923). He himself dropped dead on grouse moor after shooting his 52nd bird on t morning of 22 Sept. 1923.

Revolver shooting The greatest rapid fire feat was that of Ed. McGive (U.S.A.), who twice fired from 15 feet 5 shots whi could be covered by a silver half-dollar pie (diameter 1.205 inches) in 0.45 seconds at the Le Club Range, South Dakota, U.S.A., on 20 Aug. 193

Quickest draw The super-star of fast drawing and winner of t annual "World's Fastest Gun" award from 1960-19 is Bob Munden (b. Kansas City, Missouri, 8 Fe 1942). His Single shot records include Walk and Dr Level Blanks in 21/100ths sec. and Standing Reacti Blanks (4-inch balloons at 8 feet) in 20/100ths s both at Las Vegas, Nevada on 9 Aug. 1966 and S Start Blanks in 2/100ths sec. at Baldwin Pa California on 17 Aug. 1968. At Las Vegas he got 10 shots in 2.12 secs.

Small Bore On 27 Jan 1956 in the National Inter-Coun Association League at 25 yards prone the Kent te of 20 scored a possible 2,000 *ex* 2,000. The reco score for a round in the British Schools' Small B Rifle Association (B.S.S.R.A.) contest is a te possible of 500 *ex* 500 by Gresham's School, H Norfolk in Lent Term, 1972. S.J. Carter scored 50 *ex* 500 in the 5 rounds in this .22 contest.

WORLD RECORDS

		Possible–Score			
Free Pistol	50 m. 6 X 10 shot series	600–572	G. J. Kosych (U.S.S.R.)	Pilsen	1969
Free Rifle	300 m. 3 X 40 shot series	1,200–1,157	G. L. Anderson (U.S.A.)	Mexico City 23 Oct. 1968	
Small Bore Rifle	50 m. 3 X 40 shot series	1,200–1,164	L. W. Wigger, Jr. (U.S.A.)	Tokyo 20 Oct. 1964	
		1,200–1,164	G. L. Anderson (U.S.A.)	Johannesburg 1969	
Small Bore Rifle	50 m. 60 shots prone	600–599	N. Rotaru (Romania)	Moscow 19 May 1972	
Centre-Fire Pistol	25 m. 60 shots	600–597	T. D. Smith (U.S.A.)	São Paulo 1963	
Rapid Fire Pistol	25 m. silhouettes 60 shots	600–598	G. Liverzani (Italy)	Phoenix, Arizona 1970	
Running Target	50 m. 40 shots	200–171	M. Nordfors (Sweden)	Pistoia, Italy 1967	
Trap	300 birds	300–297	K. Jones (U.S.A.)	Wiesbaden 1966	
Skeet	200 birds	200–200	N. Durney (U.S.S.R.)	Cairo 1962	
		200–200	E. Petrov (U.S.S.R.)	Phoenix, Arizona 1970	

LARGEST BRITISH BAGS

Woodpigeon	550	1 gun	Major A. J. Coates, near Winchester	10 Jan.	1962
Snipe	1,108	2 guns	Tiree, Inner Hebrides	25 Oct.–3 Nov.	1906
Hares	1,215	11 guns	Holkham, Norfolk	19 Dec.	1877
Woodcock	228	6 guns	Ashford, County Galway	28 Jan.	1910
Grouse	2,929	8 guns	Littledale and Abbeystead, Lancashire	12 Aug.	1915
Grouse	1,070	1 gun	Lord Walsingham in Yorkshire	30 Aug.	1888
Geese (Brent)	704*	32 punt-guns	Colonel Russell i/c, River Blackwater, Essex	c. 1860	
Rabbits	6,943	5 guns	Blenheim, Oxfordshire	17 Oct.	1898
Partridges	2,015†	6 guns	Rothwell, Lincolnshire	12 Oct.	1952
Pheasants	3,937	7 guns	Hall Barn, Beaconsfield, Buckinghamshire	18 Dec.	1913
Pigeons	561	1 gun	K. Ransford, Shropshire-Montgomery	22 July	1970

Plus about 250 later picked up.   † *Plus 104 later picked up.*

SKI-ING

Origins The earliest dated skis found in Fenno–Scandian bogs have been dated to c. 2500 B.C. A rock carving of a skier at Rødøy, Tjøtta, North Norway, dates from 2000 B.C. The earliest recorded military competition was an isolated one in Oslo, Norway, in 1767. Ski-ing did not develop into a sport until at Tromsø. Ski-ing was known in California by 1856, having been introduced by "Snowshoe" Thompson from Norway. The Kiandra Snow Shoe Club (founded 1878), Australia, claims it is the world's oldest. Sking-ing was introduced into the Alps until 1883, though there is some evidence of earlier use in the Carniola district. The first Slalom event was run at Mürren, Switzerland, on 21 Jan. 1922. The Winter Olympics were inaugurated in 1924. The Ski Club of Great Britain was founded on 6 May 1903. The National Ski Federation of Great Britain was formed in 1964.

Most Olympic wins The most Olympic gold medals won by an individual for ski-ing is four (including one for a relay) by Sixten Jernberg (b. 6 Feb. 1929) of Sweden, in 1956-60-64. In addition, Jernberg has won three silver and two bronze medals. The only women to win three gold medals are Klavdiya Boyarskikh and Galina Koulakova both of the U.S.S.R., who each won the 5 Km. and 10 Km. and were members of the winning 3 X 5 Km. relay teams at Innsbruck, Austria and at Sapporo, Japan in 1964 and 1972 respectively.

Most world titles The world alpine championships were inaugurated at Mürren, Switzerland, in 1931. The greatest number of titles won is 12 by Christel Cranz (b. 1 July 1914) of Germany, with four Slalom (1934-37-38-39), three Downhill (1935-37-39) and five Combined (1934-35-37-38-39). She also won the gold medal for the Combined in the 1936 Olympics. The most titles won by a man is seven by Anton ("Toni") Sailer (b. 17 Nov. 1935) of Austria, who won all four in 1956 (Giant Slalom, Slalom, Downhill and the non-Olympic Alpine Combination) and the Downhill, Giant Slalom and Combined in 1958.

In the Nordic events Johan Gröttumsbraaten (b. 24 Feb. 1899) of Norway won six titles (two at 18 kilometres and four Combined) in 1931-32. The record for a jumper is five by Birger Ruud (b. 23 Aug. 1911) of Norway, in 1931-32 and 1935-36-37.

The World Cup, instituted in 1967, has been twice won by Jean-Claude Killy (France) (b 30 Aug. 1943) in 1967 and 1968; by Karl Schranz (Austria) in 1969

Jean-Claude Killy (France) winner of the World Cup in 1967 and 1968.

and 1970 and by Gustav Thöni (Italy) in 1971-1972. The women's cup has been twice won by Miss Nancy Greene (Canada) in 1967 and 1968 and by Annemarie Proell (Austria) in 1971 and in 1972 with a record 269 points.

Most British titles The greatest number of British Ski-running titles won is three by Leonard Dobbs (1921, 1923-24), William R. Bracken (1929-31) and Jeremy Palmer-Tomkinson (1965-66-68). The most Ladies Titles is four by Miss Isobel M. Roe (1938-39, 1948-49) and Miss Gina Hathorn (1966-68-69-70). The most wins in the British Ski-jumping Championship (discontinued 1936) is three, by Colin Wyatt (1931, 1934, 1936).

Heaviest Heavyweight Champion The greatest winner of the "World Heavyweight Ski Championship" at Sugarloaf Mountain, Maine, U.S.A. was John Truden (U.S.) who weighed in at 401 lb. (28 st. 9 lb.) in 1972. It has been said that, apart from avalanches, his best event is giant slalom.

Highest speed The highest speed claimed for any skier is 109.14 m.p.h. by Ralph Miller (U.S.A.) on the 62 degree slopes of the Garganta *Schuss* at Portillo, Chile, on 25 Aug. 1955. Since the timing was only manual by two time-keepers standing half a kilometre back from a marked 50-metre section of *piste*, this claim cannot be regarded as reliable. Some error is further indicated by the fact that to achieve such a speed 50 metres would have to be covered in 1.0248 seconds—an accuracy quite impossible on a stopwatch. The highest speed recorded in Europe is 108.589 m.p.h. over a flying 100 metres by Luigi de Marco (Italy) on a 62.8 degree gradient near the Rosa plateau above Cervinia, Italy, on 18 July 1964. The average race speeds by the 1968 Olympic downhill champion on the Chamrousse course, Grenoble, France were Jean-Claude Killy (France) (53.93 m.p.h.) and Olga Pall (Austria) (47.90 m.p.h.).

Duration The longest non-stop ski-ing marathon was one lasting 48 hours by Onni Savi, aged 35, of Padasjoki, Finland, who covered 305.9 kilometres (190.1 miles) between noon on 19 April and noon on 21 April 1966.

Largest entry The world's greatest Nordic ski race is the "Vasa Lopp", which commemorates an event of 1521 when Gustav Vasa (1496-1560), later King Gustavus Eriksson, skied 85 kilometres (52.8 miles) from Mora to Sälen, Sweden. The re-enactment of this journey in reverse direction is now an annual event, with 9,397 starters on 4 March 1970. The record time is 4 hours 39 minutes 49 seconds by Janne Stefansson on 3 March 1968.

Longest jump The longest ski-jump ever recorded is one of 165 metres (541.3 feet) by Manfred Wolf (East Germany) at Planica, Jugoslavia on 23 March 1969.

World

British The British record is 61 metres (200.1 feet) by Guy John Nixon (b. 9 Jan. 1909) at Davos on 24 Feb. 1931. The record at Hampstead, London, on artificial snow is 28 metres (90.8 feet) by Reidar Anderson (b. 20 April 1911) of Norway on 24 March 1950.

Ski-Parachuting The greatest recorded vertical descent in parachute ski-jumping is 2,300 feet by Rick Sylvester, 29, (U.S.) who on 31 Jan. 1972 skied off the 3,200 foot sheer face of El Capitan, Yosemite Valley, California. His parachute opened at 1,500 feet.

Longest run The longest all-downhill ski run in the world is the Weissfluhjoch-Küblis Parsenn course (7.6 miles long), near Davos, Switzerland. The run from the Aiguille du Midi top of the Chamonix lift (vertical lift 8,176 feet) across the Vallée Blanche is 13 miles.

Longest lift The longest chair lift in the world is the Alpine Way to Kosciusko Châlet lift above Thredbo, near the Snowy Mountains, New South Wales, Australia. It takes from 45 to 75 minutes to ascend the 3.5 miles, according to the weather, The highest is at Chactaltaya, Bolivia, rising to 16,500 feet.

SKIJORING
The record speed reached in aircraft skijoring (being towed by an aircraft) is 109.23 m.p.h. by Reto Pitsch on the Silsersee, St. Moritz, Switzerland, in 1956.

SKI-BOB
The ski-bob was invented by Mr. Stevens of Hartford, Connecticut, U.S.A., and patented (No. 47334) on 19 April 1892 as a "bicycle with ski-runners". The Fédération Internationale de Skibob was founded on 14 Jan. 1961 in Innsbruck, Austria. The Ski-Bob Association of Great Britain was registered on 23 Aug. 1967. The highest speed attained is 103.4 m.p.h. by Erick Brenter (Austria) at Cervinia, N. Italy, in 1964

World Championships The only ski-bobber to retain a world championship is G. Schiffkorn (Austria) who won the women's title in 1967 and 1969.

Highest altitude Yuichiro Miura (Japan) skied 1.6 miles down Mt. Everest starting from 26,200 feet. In a run from a height of 24,418 feet he reached speeds of 93.6 m.p.h. on 6 May 1970.

SNOWMOBILE
Ky Michaelson, in the 3,000 h.p. snowmobile *Son Challenger*, was timed at 114.5 m.p.h. over 440 yar on Lake Champlain, Vermont, U.S.A., on 15 Fe 1970.

SNOOKER

Earliest mention Research shows that snooker was originated b Lt.-Gen. Sir Neville Chamberlain (1820-1902) as variation of "black pool", in the Ootacamund Clu Nilgiris, South India in 1875. It did not reach Englan until 1885.

Rex Williams (G.B.) who achieved a world record break of 147 in December 1965.

Highest breaks It is possible if an opponent commits a foul with reds on the table that his opponent can exercise option of nominating a colour as a red and then po this free ball and then goes on to pot the black with reds still on the table, he can score 155. The offici world record break is the maximum possib (excluding handicaps or penalties) of 147 by J Davis, O.B.E. (b. 15 April 1901) against Willie Smi at Leicester Square Hall, London, on 22 Jan. 19 and by Rex Williams (G.B.) against Manuel Francis at Cape Town, South Africa, on 22 Dec. 196 Horace Lindrum "cleared the table" with an u official 147 in Sydney in 1941. The highest officia recognized break by an amateur is one of 122 Ratan Badar (India) in 1964. On 11 Jan. 1970 E Baxter, 45, scored 136 at Wombwell Reform Clu Yorkshire which score is being submitted f ratification.

Most centuries Joe Davis secured his 500th century on 18 Feb. 195 at which time the game's next most prolific scorer w his brother, Fred, with 144 centuries. His record centuries made in public exhibitions reached 6 before he retired in 1965. The highest total centuries logged in public and private is over 2,000 Norman Squire (Australia). Rex Williams record 682 centuries to March 1967.

Marathon The most protracted snooker endurance record cognized by the Billiards and Snooker Contr Council as at July 1972 is one of 168 hours by players in the Melton Country Club, Melt Constable, Norfolk with 315 frames.

SPEEDWAY

Origins Motor cycle racing on large dirt track surfaces h been traced back to 1902 in the United States. T first organized "short track" races were at the We Maitland (New South Wales, Australia) Agricultur Show of 1924. The sport was introduced to Gre Britain at High Beech, Essex, on 19 Feb. 1928. Aft three seasons of competition in southern and northern leagues, the National League was instituted in 1932. The best record is that of the Wembley Lions who won in 1932, 1946-47, 1949-53, making a record total of eight victories. Since the National Trophy knock-out competition was instituted in 1931, Belle Vue (Manchester) have been most successful with nine victories in 1933-34-35-36-37, 1946-47, 1949 and 1958. In 1965 the League was replaced by the British League.

Most world titles The world speedway championship was inaugurated in 1936. The only five-time winner has been Ove Fundin (b. Tranås, 1933) (Sweden), who won in 1956, 1960, 1961, 1963 and 1967. In addition he was second in 1957-58-59 and third in 1962, 1964 and 1965.

Lap speed The fastest recorded speed on a British speedway track is 54.62 m.p.h. on the 470-yard 2nd Division track at Crewe by Barry Meeks. This track was shortened by 40 yards in 1970 and the current fastest track record on a British circuit is 51.19 m.p.h. (433 yards in 69.2 secs.) at Exeter by Bob Kilby on 1 May 1972.

SQUASH RACKETS

(Note: "1971", for example, refers to the 1971-72 season.)

Earliest champion Although rackets (U.S. spelling, racquets) with a soft ball was evolved c. 1850 at Harrow School (England), there was no recognized champion of any country until J. A. Miskey of Philadelphia won the American Amateur Singles Championship in 1906.

World title The inaugural international (world) championships were staged in Australia in August 1967 when Australia won the team title in Sydney and Geoffrey B. Hunt (Victoria) took the individual title, both these titles being retained in 1969 and 1971.

MOST WINS

Open Championship The most wins in the Open Championship (amateur or professional), held annually in Britain, is seven by Hashim Khan (Pakistan) in 1950-51-52-53-54-55 and 1957.

Amateur Championship The most wins in the Amateur Championship is six by Abdel Fattah Amr Bey (Egypt, now the United Arab Republic), later appointed Ambassador in London, who won in 1931-32-33 and 1935-36-37. Norman F. Borrett of England won in 1946-47-48-49-50.

Professional Championship The most wins in the Professional Championship is five by J. St. G. Dear, M.B.E. (Great Britain) in 1935-36-37-38 and 1949, and Hashim Khan (Pakistan) in 1950-51-52-53-54.

Most international selections The record for international selections is held by O. L. Balfour (Scotland) with 45 between 1954 and 1968. The record for England is 40 by J. G. A. Lyon from 1959 to 1968; for Ireland 41 by D. M. Pratt from 1956 to 1971 and for Wales 44 by L. J. Verney between 1949 and 1965.

Longest span of internationals Mrs. Henry G. Macintosh (née Sheila Speight), the 1960 British Champion, played for England v. Wales in April 1949 and in Dec. 1971—a span of 22 years. Among men P. Harding-Edgar first played for Scotland in 1938 and last played 21 years later in 1959.

Longest championship match The longest recorded championship match was one of 2 hours 13 minutes in the final of the Open Championship of the British Isles at the Edgbaston-Priory Club, Birmingham in December

Mrs Heather McKay — eleven-time winner of the Women's Squash Rackets Championship.

1969 when Jonah P. Barrington, M.B.E. (Ireland) beat Geoffrey B. Hunt (Australia) 9-7, 3-9, 3-9, 9-4, 9-4 with the last game lasting 37 minutes.

Most wins in the women's championship The most wins in the Women's Squash Rackets Championship is eleven by Mrs. Heather McKay, M.B.E. (née Blundell) of Australia, 1961 to 1971.

Marathon record The longest recorded squash singles marathon (under competition conditions) has been one of 48 hours 2 minutes by Douglas J. Irvine and George S. Gray at North Berwick Sports Centre, East Lothian, Scotland on 2-4 June 1972. Graham Greer recorded 50 hours (having lost his opponent at 45 hours 40 mins.) at the University of Natal, South Africa on 9-12 Apr. 1972. A 53 hour marathon was maintained at Bunbury, Western Australia by David Morrison, Patricia Viney, Graham Parkin and Aub. Hickey ending on 23 July 1972.

SURFING

Origins The traditional Polynesian sport of surfing in a canoe (*ehorooe*) was first recorded by Captain James Cook, R.N., F.R.S. (1728-79) on his third voyage at Tahiti in December 1771. Surfing on a board (*Amo Amo iluna ka lau oka nalu*) was first described ("most perilous and extraordinary . . . altogether astonishing, and is scarcely to be credited") by Lt. (later Capt.) James King, R.N., F.R.S. in March 1779 at Kealakekua Bay, Hawaii Island. A surfer was first depicted by this voyage's official artist John Webber.

The sport was revived at Waikiki by 1900. Australia's first body surfing events were run by the Bondi Surf Bathers Lifesaving Club, which was formed in February 1906. Australia's most successful champion has been Bob Newbiggin, who won the senior title in 1939-40-45-46-47 and the senior Belt Race in 1940. Hollow boards came in in 1929 and the light plastic foam type in 1956.

Highest waves ridden Makaha Beach, Hawaii provides the reputedly highest consistently high waves often reaching the rideable limit of 30-35 feet. The highest wave ever ridden was the *tsunami* of "perhaps 50 feet", which struck Minole, Hawaii on 3 April 1868, and was ridden to save his life by a Hawaiian named Holua.

Longest ride
Sea wave About 4 to 6 times each year rideable surfing waves break in Matanchen Bay near San Blas, Nayarit, Mexico which make rides of c. 5,700 feet possible.

293

World Champions World Championships were inaugurated in 1964 at Sydney, Australia. The first surfer to win two titles has been Joyce Hoffman (U.S.) in 1965 and 1966.

River bore The longest recorded rides on a river bore have been set on the Severn bore, England. On 18 Sept. 1970 Colin Prior and Charles Williams (G.B.) and Neil Reading and John Ryland (Australia) rode 2 miles in an expedition organized by *Drive* magazine. In 1968 local residents reported a ride of 4 to 6 miles by Rodney Sumpter of Sussex.

SWIMMING

Earliest references It is recorded that inter-school swimming contests in Japan were ordered by Imperial edict of Emperor Go-Yoozei as early as 1603. In Great Britain competitive swimming originated in London *c.* 1837, at which time there were five or more pools, the earliest of which had been opened at St. George's Pier Head, Liverpool in 1828.

Largest pools The largest swimming pool in the world is the sea-water Orthlieb Pool in Casablanca, Morocco. It is 480 metres (1,547 feet) long and 75 metres (246 feet) wide, and has an area of 3.6 hectares (8.9 acres). The largest land-locked swimming pool with heated water is the Fleishhacker Pool on Sloat Boulevard, near Great Highway, San Francisco, California, U.S.A. It measures 1,000 feet by 150 feet (3.44 acres) and up to 14 feet deep, and contains 7,500,000 gallons of heated water. The world's largest competition pool is that at Osaka, Japan, which accommodates 25,000 spectators. The largest in the United Kingdom is the Empire Pool, Cardiff, completed in 1958.

Shane Gould (Australia) holder of all five freestyle world records.

Fastest swimmer Excluding relay stages with their anticipatory start the highest speed reached by a swimmer 4.89 m.p.h. by Stephen Edward Clark (U.S.A.), wh recorded 20.9 seconds for a heat of 50 yards in 25-yard pool at Yale University, New Haver Connecticut, U.S.A., on 26 March 1964. Spitz's 10 metre record of 51.47 secs. required an average 4.346 m.p.h.

Most world records Men, 32, Arne Borg (Sweden) (b. 1901 1921-1929. Women, 42, Ragnhild Hveg (Denmark) (b. 10 Dec. 1920), 1936-1942.

WORLD RECORDS—MEN (at distances recognized by the *Fédération Internationale de Nations Amateur*)

Distance	Time mins. secs.	Name and Nationality	Place	Date
FREE STYLE				
100 metres	51.5*	Mark Spitz (U.S.A.)	Chicago, Illinois, U.S.A.	5 Aug. 1972
200 metres	1:53.5	Mark Spitz (U.S.A.)	Minsk, U.S.S.R.	10 Sept. 1971
400 metres	4:00.1	Kurt Krumpholz (U.S.A.)	Chicago, Illinois, U.S.A.	4 Aug. 1972
800 metres	8:23.8	Brad Cooper (Australia)	Sydney, Australia	12 Jan. 1972
1,500 metres	15:52.9	Rick De Mont (U.S.A.)	Chicago, Illinois, U.S.A.	6 Aug. 1972
BREAST STROKE				
100 metres	1:05.8	Nikolai Pankin (U.S.S.R.)	Magdeburg, East Germany	20 April 1969
200 metres	2:22.8*	John Hencken (U.S.A.)	Chicago, Illinois, U.S.A.	5 Aug. 1972
BUTTERFLY STROKE				
100 metres	54.6	Mark Spitz (U.S.A.)	Chicago, Illinois, U.S.A.	4 Aug. 1972
200 metres	2:01.5*	Mark Spitz (U.S.A.)	Chicago, Illinois, U.S.A.	2 Aug. 1972
BACK STROKE				
100 metres	56.3	Roland Matthes (E. Germany)	Moscow, U.S.S.R.	9 Apr. 1972
200 metres	2:02.8	Roland Matthes (E. Germany)	Leipzig, E. Germany	10 July 1972
INDIVIDUAL MEDLEY				
200 metres	2:09.3* 2:09.3*	Gunnar Larsson (Sweden) Gary Hall (U.S.A.)	Barcelona, Spain Chicago, Illinois, U.S.A.	12 Sept. 1970 3 Aug. 1972
400 metres	4:30.8*	Gary Hall (U.S.A.)	Chicago, Illinois, U.S.A.	6 Aug. 1972
FREE STYLE RELAYS				
4 x 100 metres	3:28.8	Los Angeles S.C., U.S.A. (Don Havens, Mike Weston, Bill Frawley, Frank Heckl)	Los Angeles, California, U.S.A.	23 Aug. 1970
4 x 200 metres	7:43.3	United States National Team Mark Spitz, Jerry Heidenrich, Fred Tyler, Tim McBreen)	Minsk, U.S.S.R.	10 Sept. 1971
MEDLEY RELAY				
4 x 100 metres	3:50.4	United States (Charles Campbell, Pete Dahlberg, Mark Spitz, Jerry Heidenrich)	Leipzig, E. Germany	4 Sept. 1971

Those marked with an asterisk are awaiting ratification.
† = Salt Water   †† = Fresh and Salt Water mixed

Only performances set up in 50 metres or 55 yards baths are recognized as World Records. F.N.A. no longer recognize any records made for distances over non-metric distances.

WORLD RECORDS—WOMEN

Distance	Time mins. secs.	Name and Nationality	Place	Date
FREE STYLE				
100 metres	58.5	Shane Gould (Australia)	Sydney, Australia	8 Jan. 1972
200 metres	2:05.2	Shirley Babashoff (U.S.A.)	Chicago, Illinois, U.S.A.	4 Aug. 1972
400 metres	4:21.2	Shane Gould (Australia)	Sydney, Australia	9 July 1971
800 metres	8:53.8	Jo Harschbarger (U.S.A.)	Chicago, Illinois, U.S.A.	6 Aug. 1972
1,500 metres	17:00.6	Shane Gould (Australia)	Sydney, Australia	11 Dec. 1971
BREAST STROKE				
100 metres	1:14.2	Catharine Ball (U.S.A.)	Los Angeles, California, U.S.A.	25 Aug. 1968
200 metres	2:38.5	Catharine Ball (U.S.A.)	Los Angeles, California, U.S.A.	26 Aug. 1968
BUTTERFLY STROKE				
100 metres	1:03.9	Mayumi Aoki (Japan)	Osaka, Japan	-June 1972
200 metres	2:16.6*	Karen Moe (U.S.A.)	Chicago, Illinois, U.S.A.	6 Aug. 1972
BACKSTROKE				
100 metres	1:05.6	Karen Yvette Muir (South Africa)	Utrecht, Netherlands	6 July 1969
200 metres	2:20.6*	Melissa Belote (U.S.A.)	Chicago, Illinois, U.S.A.	5 Aug. 1972
INDIVIDUAL MEDLEY				
200 metres	2:23.5	Claudia Anne Kolb (U.S.A.)	Los Angeles, California, U.S.A.	25 Aug. 1968
400 metres	5:04.7	Claudia Anne Kolb (U.S.A.)	Los Angeles, California, U.S.A.	24 Aug. 1968
FREE STYLE RELAY				
4 X 100 metres	3:58.1	United States (Kim Peyton, Sandy Nielson, Janice Barkman, Shirley Babashoff)	Tennessee, U.S.A.	19 Aug. 1972
MEDLEY RELAY				
4 X 100 metres	4:25.3	United States (Janice Barkman, Susan Atwood, Ellie Daniel, Lynn Vidali)	Tennessee, U.S.A.	19 Aug. 1972

BRITISH NATIONAL RECORDS
(short course and record equalling performances are *not* recognised)

MEN

Distance	Time mins. secs.	Name	Place	Date	
FREESTYLE					
100 metres	53.4	Robert Bilsland McGregor	Tokyo, Japan	29 Aug.	1967
200 metres	1 57.5	Brian Brinkley	Hanover, West Germany	18 Apr.	1972
400 metres	4 10.0	Brian Brinkley	Leeds, Yorkshire	25 June	1972
800 metres	8 42.6	Brian Brinkley	Leeds, Yorkshire	28 May	1972
1,500 metres	16 39.6	Brian Brinkley	Crystal Palace, London	15 July	1972
BREAST STROKE					
100 metres	1 07.8	Malcolm O'Connell	Hanover, West Germany	18 Apr.	1972
200 metres	2 26.8	David Wilkie	Edinburgh, Scotland	29 July	1972
BUTTERFLY					
100 metres	58.8	Martyn John Woodroffe	Santa Clara, Calif. U.S.A.	11 July	1969
200 metres	2 05.6	Brian Brinkley	Crystal Palace, London	14 July	1972
BACK STROKE					
100 metres	1 00.3	Colin Cunningham	Crystal Palace, London	15 July	1972
200 metres	2 09.5	Colin Cunningham	Crystal Palace, London	13 July	1972
INDIVIDUAL MEDLEY					
200 metres	2 11.9	Ray Terrell	Crystal Palace, London	13 July	1972
400 metres	4 42.7	Ray Terrell	Crystal Palace, London	15 July	1972

WOMEN

Distance	Time	Name	Place	Date	
FREESTYLE					
100 metres	1 00.5	Alexandra Elizabeth Jackson	Mexico City, Mexico	18 Oct.	1968
200 metres	2 12.2	Lesley Allardice	Crystal Palace, London	14 July	1972
400 metres	4 35.4	June Green	Crystal Palace, London	15 July	1972
800 metres	9 31.3	June Green	Crystal Palace, London	14 July	1972
1,500 metres	19 40.0	Standard time not yet achieved			
BREAST STROKE					
100 metres	1 17.0	Dorothy Harrison	Barcelona, Spain	7 Sept.	1970
200 metres	2 44.2	Pat Beavan	Edinburgh, Scotland	28 July	1972
BUTTERFLY					
100 metres	1 06.6	Jean Jeavons	Crystal Palace, London	15 July	1972
200 metres	2 23.6	Jean Jeavons	Crystal Palace, London	14 July	1972

Most Olympic titles **Men** The greatest number of Olympic gold medals won is five shared by John Weissmuller (U.S.A.), born 1904 with freestyle 100 m. (1924-28), 400 m. (1924) and 4 X 200 m. relay (1924-28)and five by Donald Arthur Schollander (U.S.A.), born 1946 with freestyle 100 m. and 400 m., 4 X 100 m. and 4 X 200 m. relays (1964) and 4 X 200 m. relay (1968).

Women The record number for women is four shared by Dawn Fraser M.B.E. (now Mrs. Gary Ware) (Australia), born 1937 with freestyle 100 m. (1956-60-64) and 4 X 100 m. relay (1956) and four by Mrs. Patricia McCormick (*née* Keller) (U.S.A.),

295

SPORTS, GAMES AND PASTIMES

born 1930 with High Diving (1952-56) and Springboard (1952-56).

British The record number of any British swimmer (excluding Water Polo *q.v.*) is three by Henry Taylor (1885-1951) with freestyle 400 m., 1,500 m. and 4×200 m. relay (1908). The claim that John Arthur Jervis (1872-1933) also won three titles with freestyle 100 m., 1,000 m. and 4,000 m. (1900) is disputed in that no official 100 m. event was held. It may be noted that Iain Murray Rose (Australia) winner of four titles in 1956 and 1960 was born in England in 1939.

Other Olympic records Miss Fraser (see above) uniquely won the same event at three successive Olympic celebrations. Miss Deborah Meyer (U.S.A.), born 1952 uniquely won three *individual* titles at the same Games (freestyle 200 m., 400 m. and 800 m., 1968) and D. A. Schollander (see above) uniquely won four medals (2 individual and 2 relay) at the same Games (1964).

Most difficult dives Those with the highest tariff (degree of difficulty 3.0) are the "3½ forward somersault in tuck position from the one metre board, the backward 2½ somersault piked; the reverse 2½ piked and the forward 3½ piked from the 10 metre board". Joaquin Capilla of Mexico has performed a 4½ somersaults dive from a 10-metre board, but this is not on the international tarriff.

LONG DISTANCE SWIMMING
A unique achievement in long distance swimming was established in 1966 by the cross-Channel swimmer Mihir Sen of Calcutta, India. These were the Palk Strait from India to Ceylon (in 25 hours 36 minutes on 5-6 April); the Straits of Gibraltar (Europe to Africa in 8 hours 1 minute on 24 August); the Dardanelles (Gallipoli, Europe to Sedulbahir, Asia Minor in 13 hours 55 minutes on 12 September) and the entire length of the Panama Canal in 34 hours 15 minutes on 29-31 October. He had earlier swum the English Channel in 14 hours 45 minutes on 27 Sept. 1958.

Turkey-Cyprus A team of R.A.F. swimmers covered the 72 miles from Southern Turkey to Cyprus in 2½ days in 1971.

CHANNEL SWIMMING
Earliest Man The first man to swim across the English Channel (without a life jacket) was the Merchant Navy captain Matthew Webb, A.M. (1848-83), who swam breaststroke from Dover, England, to Cap Gris-Nez, France, in 21 hours 45 minutes from 12.56 p.m. to 10.41 a.m., 24-25 Aug. 1875. He swam an estimated 38 miles to make the 21-mile crossing. Paul Boyton (U.S.A.) had swum from Cap Gris-Nez to the South Foreland in his patent life-saving suit in 23 hours 30 minutes on 28-29 May 1875. There is good evidence that Jean-Marie Saletti, a French soldier, escaped from a British prison hulk off Dover by swimming to Boulogne in July or August 1815. The first crossing from France to England was made by Enrique Tiraboschi, a wealthy Italian living in Argentina, who crossed in 16 hours 33 minutes on 11 Aug. 1923, to win the *Daily Sketch* prize of £1,000.

Woman The first woman to succeed was Gertrude Ederle (U.S.A.) who swam from Cap Gris-Nez, France to Dover, England on 6 Aug. 1926, in the then overall record of 14 hours 39 minutes. The first woman to swim from England to France was Florence Chadwick of California, U.S.A., in 16 hours 19 minutes on 11 Sept. 1951. She repeated this on 4 Sept. 1953 and 12 Oct. 1955.

Fastest The official Channel Swimming Association record

Lynne Cox (U.S.A.) holder of the official Channel Swimming Association record time of 9 hours 57 minutes.

time is 9 hours 57 mins. by Lynne Cox, 15 (U.S.A. from Dover to Cap Gris-Nez on 20 July 1972. T fastest crossing ever claimed is one of 9 hou 35 minutes by Barry Watson, aged 25, of Bingle Yorkshire, from Cap Gris-Nez, France, to Margaret's Bay, near Dover, on 15-16 Aug. 196 The fastest crossing by a relay team is one 9 hours 29 minutes by Radcliffe Swimming Club Lancashire, from Cap Gris-Nez to Walmer 13 June 1966.

Slowest The slowest crossing was the third ever made, wh Henry Sullivan (U.S.A.) swam from England France in 26 hours 50 minutes on 5-6 Aug. 192 The slowest from France to England and the slowe ever by a Briton was one of 23 hours 48 minutes Philip Mickman (born Ossett, Yorkshire, 1931) 23-24 Aug. 1949.

Earliest and latest The earliest time in the year on which the Chann has been swum is 6 June by Dorothy Perki (England), aged 19, in 1961, and the latest 14 October by Ivy Gill (England) in 1927. Bo swims were from France to England.

Youngest The youngest conqueror is Leonore Modell Sacramento, California, U.S.A., who swam fro Cap Gris-Nez to near Dover in 15 hours 33 minut on 3 Sept. 1964, when aged 14 years 5 months. T youngest relay team to cross are from the Roy Tunbridge Wells Monson S.C. from England France on 4 Sept. 1968. The team, coached by Jo Wrapson, had an average age of 12 years 4 mont and were David Young, Richard Field, Kim Tayle Peter Chapman, Stephen Underdown and Pe Burns.

Oldest The oldest swimmer to swim the Channel has be William E. (Ned) Barnie, aged 55, when he swa from France to England in 15 hours 1 minute 16 Aug. 1951.

Double crossing First Antonio Abertondo (b. Buenos Aires, Argentina aged 42, swam from England to France in 18 hou 50 minutes (8.35 a.m. on 20 Sept. to 3.25 a.m. 21 Sept. 1961) and after about 4 minutes re returned to England in 24 hours 16 minutes, landi at St. Margaret's Bay at 3.45 a.m. on 22 Sept. 196 to complete the first "double crossing" in 43 hou 10 minutes. Kevin Murphy, 21, completed the fi double crossing by a Briton in 35 hours 10 minut on 6 Aug 1970. The first swimmer to achieve crossing both ways was Edward H. Temr (b. 1904) on 5 Aug. 1927 and 19 Aug. 1934.

Fastest The fastest double crossing, and the second to achieved, was one of 30 hours 3 minutes by Edwa (Ted) Erikson, aged 37, a physiochemist fro Chicago, Illinois, U.S.A. He left St. Margaret's Ba near Dover, at 8.20 p.m. on 19 Sept. 1965 and landed at a beach about a mile west of Calais, after a swim of 14 hours 15 minutes. After a rest of about 10 minutes he returned and landed at South Foreland Point, east of Dover, at 2.23 a.m. on 21 Sept. 1965.

Most conquests Brojan Das (Pakistan) swam the Channel six times in 1958-61. Greta Andersen (U.S.A.) also swum the Channel six times in the period 1957-1965.

Underwater The first underwater cross-Channel swim was achieved by Fred Baldasare (U.S.A.), aged 38, who completed the distance from France to England with Scuba in 18 hours 1 minute on 11 July 1962. Simon Paterson, aged 20, a frogman from Egham, Surrey, travelled underwater from France to England with an air hose attached to his pilot boat in 14 hours 50 minutes on 28 July 1962.

Irish Channel The swimming of the 22-mile wide Irish Channel from Donaghadee, Northern Ireland to Portpatrick, Scotland was first accomplished by Tom Blower of Nottingham in 1947 and repeated by Kevin Murphy in 1970 and 1971.

Bristol Channel The first person to achieve a double crossing of the Bristol Channel is Jenny James who swam from Sully, Glamorganshire to Weston-super-Mare, Somerset in 10 hours 2 minutes on 18 Sept. 1949 and the return course in 8 hours 21 minutes on 9 July 1950.

Solent The fastest time for swimming the Solent (Southsea to Ryde, Isle of Wight) has been 1 hour 13 mins. 3 secs. by Keith Richards (Southsea) in 1970. The greatest number of crossings has been 19 single and 2 non-stop double crossings by Richard Glynn of Cheltenham.

Loch Ness The first person to swim the length of Great Britain's longest lake, the 22¾-mile-long Loch Ness, was Brenda Sherratt of West Bollington, Cheshire, aged 18, in 31 hours 27 minutes on 26-27 July 1966.

Round the Isle of Wight Kevin Murphy of Harrow achieved the first circumnavigation of the Isle of Wight covering the 55 miles in 26 hours 51 mins. on 22-24 Sept. 1971.

Treading water The duration record for treading water (vertical posture without touching the lane markers) is 17½ hours by Peter Strawson of Lawford, Essex on 25-26 July 1967.

Ice swimming Jenny Kammersgård, 53 swam 200 metres in 7 mins. 13 secs. in Denmark on 19 Feb. 1972 in water at a temperature of 1.5°C (34.7°F).

Relays The longest recorded mileage in a 24-hour swim relay (team of 5) is 63 miles 487 yards by a relay team from the Paarl Amateur Swimming Club, South Africa, on 5-6 Jan. 1970. The fastest time recorded for 100 miles by a team of 20 swimmers is 31 hours 35 minutes 21.3 seconds by Piedmont Swim Club, California, U.S.A., on 3-4 Sept. 1970.

Marathon relays In Buttermere, Westmorland, England on 18-28 July 1968 six boys, aged 13 to 15, covered 300 miles in 230 hours 39 minutes.

Underground swimming The longest recorded underground swim is one of 3,402 yards in 87 minutes by David Stanley Gale through the Dudley Old Canal Tunnel, Worcestershire, in August 1967.

Sponsored swimming The greatest amount of money raised in a sponsored swim is £5,101.89 by the Lions Club of Jersey with 936 swimmers covering 254 miles in 21 hours at the Fort Regent Pool, Jersey in January 1972.

Underwater swimming Vladimir Kon covered 100 metres underwater with flippers in 40.6 secs. at Chelyabinsk, U.S.S.R. on 10 Mar. 1972. Nina Avdegeva (U.S.S.R.) recorded 48.2 secs. at the same meeting. A team of eight from the Furness Sub-Aqua Club swam the 10½ mile length of Lake Windermere from Lakeside Hotel Pier to Ambledside public beach in 10 hours 0 mins. 58 secs. on 18 July, 1971. A Champagne bottle was used as the relay baton by the team which claimed a record for self-navigation.

TABLE TENNIS

Earliest reference The earliest evidence relating to a game resembling table tennis has been found in the catalogues of London sports goods manufacturers in the 1880s. The old Ping Pong Association was formed in 1902 but the game proved only a temporary craze until resuscitated in 1921. The English Table Tennis Association was formed on 24 April 1927.

The highest total of English men's titles is 20 by G. Viktor Barna (d. 28 Feb 1972). The women's record is 18 by Diane Rowe (b. 14 April 1933), now Mrs. Eberhard Scholer. Her twin Rosalind (Now Mrs. Cornett) has won 9 (two in singles).

Youngest international The youngest ever international (probably in any sport) was Joy Foster, aged 8, the 1958 Jamaican singles and mixed doubles champion.

Marathon records In the Swaythling Cup final match between Austria and Romania in Prague, Czeckoslovakia, in 1936, the play lasted for 25 or 26 hours, spread over three nights.

The longest recorded time for a marathon singles match by two players is 72 hours by Robert McDuff and Stephen McKee of Ringwood, Victoria, Australia, from 5-8 May 1972. On 20-23 Dec. 1971 Craig Harris, 16 played 77 hours 7 mins against a series of opponents in Davis, California, U.S.A.

The longest recorded marathon by 4 players maintaining continuous singles is 500 hours (20 days 20 hours) by 8 players (all aged 16) (two sets of four players at separate tables) from the Maryborough Boys' High School Interact Club, Queensland, Australia on 30 Nov-21 Dec. 1970. The longest doubles marathon by 4 players is 32½ hours by four members of Goole Youth Centre, West Riding, Yorkshire, on 27-29 May 1972.

Highest speed No conclusive measurements have been published, but Chuang Tse-tung (China) the world champion of 1961-63-65, has probably smashed the 2.5 gramme ball at a speed of more than 60 m.p.h.

Chuang Tse-tung (China) who has probably propelled a table tennis ball at more than 60 m.p.h.

MOST WINS IN WORLD CHAMPIONSHIPS (Instituted 1926-27)

Event	Name and Nationality	Times	Years
Men's Singles (St. Bride's Vasc)	G. Viktor Barna (Hungary)	5	1930, 1932-33-34-35
Women's Singles (G. Geist Prize)	Angelica Rozeanu (Romania)	6	1950-51-52-53-54-55
Men's Doubles	G. Viktor Barna (Hungary) with two different partners	8	1929-35, 1939
Women's Doubles	Maria Mednyanszky (Hungary) with three different partners	7	1928, 1930-31-32-33-34-3
Mixed Doubles (Men)	Ferenc Sido (Hungary) with two different partners	4	1949-50, 1952-53
(Women)	Maria Mednyanszky (Hungary) with three diferent partners	6	1927-28, 1930-31, 1933-3

G. Viktor Barna gained a personal total of 15 world titles, while 18 have been won by Miss Maria Mednyanszky.

MOST TEAM TITLES

Event	Team	Times	Years
Men's Team (Swaythling Cup)	Hungary	11	1927-31, 1933-35, 1938, 1949, 1952
Women's Team (Marcel Corbillon Cup)	Japan	7	1952, 1954, 1957, 1959, 1961, 1963, 1

MOST WINS IN ENGLISH OPEN CHAMPIONSHIPS (Instituted 1921)

Event	Name and Nationality	Times	Years
Men's Singles	Richard Bergmann (Austria, then G.B.)	6	1939-40, 1948, 1950, 1952, 19
Women's Singles	Miss K.M. Berry (G.B.)	3	1923-24-25
	Miss G. Farkas (Hungary)	3	1947-48, 1956
Men's Doubles	G. Viktor Barna (Hungary, then G.B.) with five different partners	7	1931, 1933-34-35, 1938-39, 1
Women's Doubles	Miss Diane Rowe (G.B.) with four different partners	12	1950 56, 1960, 1962-65
Mixed Doubles (Men)	G. Viktor Barna (Hungary, then G.B.) with four different partners	8	1933-36, 1938, 1940, 1951, 19
(Women)	Miss Diane Rowe (G.B.) (now Scholer) with three different partners	4	1952, 1954, 1956, 1960, 1969

TENNIS (REAL OR ROYAL)

Origins The game originated in French monasteries c. 1050.

Oldest court The oldest of the 18 surviving Tennis Courts in the British Isles is the Royal Tennis Court at Hampton Court Palace, which was built by order of King Henry VIII in 1529-30 and rebuilt by order of Charles II in 1660. The oldest court in the world is one built in Paris in 1496. There are estimated to be 3,000 players and 29 courts in the world.

World titles The first recorded World Tennis Champion was Clerge (France) c. 1740. Pierre Etchebaster won the title at Prince's, Paris, in May 1928, last defended it in New York (winning 7-1) in December 1949 and retired undefeated in 1955, after 27 years. Etchebaster, a Basque, also holds the record for the greatest number of successful defences of his title with six.

British titles The Amateur Championship of the British Isles (instituted 1780) has been won 13 times by Edgar M. Baerlein (b. 1879) (1912 to 1930). The greatest number of international appearances has been 18 by Sir Clarance Napier Bruce, G.B.E., 3rd Baron Aberdare (1885-1957).

TIDDLYWINKS

Accuracy The lowest number of shots taken to pot 12 winks from 3 feet is 23, achieved by M. Brogden (Hull University) on 18 Oct. 1962. This record was equalled by A. Cooper (Altrincham Grammar School) in December 1963 and by J. King (Ealing Grammar School) on 2 May 1965.

Speed The record for potting 24 winks from 18 inches is 21.8 seconds by Stephen Williams (Altrincham Grammar School) in May 1966.

Marathon Allen R. Astles (University of Wales) potted 10,000 winks in 3 hours 51 minutes 46 seconds at Aberystwyth, Cardiganshire in February 1966. The m protracted game on record is one of 168 hour minutes by six students from Southampton Univ sity (with at least two participants at all times) 24 Feb-2 Mar. 1972.

TRAMPOLINING

Origins Trampolines were used in show business at least early as "The Walloons" of the period 1910-12. T sport of trampolining (from the Spanish word tramp lin, a springboard) dates from 1936, when prototype "T" model trampoline was developed George Nissen (U.S.A.).

Most difficult manoeuvres The three most difficult manoeuvres yet achieved the triple twisting double back somersault, knowr a Miller after the first trampolinist to achieve i Wayne Miller (b. 1947) of the U.S.A.; four conse tive triple somersaults by Len Ranson (1970 Aust lian champion) and the women's Wills (5½ twist back somersault), named after the five-time wo champion Judy Wills (b. 1948) of the U.S.A.

Most titles The only men to win a world title (instituted 196 twice have been Dave Jacobs (U.S.) the 1967- champion and Wayne Miller (U.S.), who won in 19 and 1970. Judy Wills won the first 5 women's tit (1964-65-66-67-68). Both European men's tit (1969 and 1971) were won by Paul Luxon (G.E Three United Kingdom titles have been won by Da Curtis (1966-67-68) and Paul Luxon (1969-70-7 while Miss Jackie Allen (1960-61), Mary Hunkin (r Chamberlaine) (1963-64) and Lynda Ball (1965-6 have each won twice.

Marathon record The longest recorded trampoline bouncing marath is one of 500 hours, set by a team of 15 membe from the Police and Citizens Youth Club, Harv Western Australia on 27 Sept.-18 Oct. 1971. T record for a 6-man team is 254 hours set in Tow ville, Queensland, Australia on 30 Apr.-11 May 19 The solo record is 44 hours 30 minutes (w 5-minute breaks per hour permissible) by Mar Eastment at Hamilton, New Zealand on 23-25 M 1972.

TROTTING AND PACING

The trotting gait (the simultaneous use of the diagonally opposite legs) was first recorded in England in *c.* 1750. The sulky first appeared in harness-racing in 1829. Pacers thrust out their fore and hind legs simultaneously on one side.

Highest price The highest price paid for a trotter is $3,000,000 for *Nevele Pride* by the Stoner Creek Stud of Lexington,

Kentucky from Louis Resnick and Nevele Acres in the autumn of 1969. The highest price ever paid for a pacer is $2,000,000 for *Bret Hanover* in August 1966.

Greatest winnings The greatest amount won by a trotting horse is $1,300,855 by *Une de Mai* to 31 Aug. 1971. The record for a pacing horse is $1,001,448 by *Rum Customer* which was retired to stud in Jan. 1972.

Most Successful Driver The most successful sulky driver in harness racing history has been Herve Filion of Quebec, Canada who reached a record 3,477 wins at Yonkers, New York in December 1971 after a record 543 wins in the 1971 season.

Records against time	Trotting			Pacing		
World (mile track)	1:54.8	Nevele Pride (U.S.A.), Indianapolis, Indiana	31 Aug. 1969	1:52.0	Steady Star (U.S.A.) Lexington, Kentucky	1 Oct. 1971
Australia	2:01.2	Gramel, Harold Park, Sydney	1964	1:57.3	Halwes, Harold Park, Sydney	1968
New Zealand	2:02.4	Control, Addington, Christchurch	1964	1:56.2	Cardigan Bay, Hutt Park, Wellington	1963

VOLLEYBALL

Origins The game was invented as *Minnonette* in 1895 by William G. Morgan at the Y.M.C.A. gymnasium at Springfield, Massachusetts, U.S.A. The International Volleyball Association was formed in Paris in April 1947. The Amateur (now English) Volleyball Association of Great Britain was formed in May 1955. The ball travels at a speed of 70 m.p.h. when smashed over the net, which measures 2.43 metres (7 feet 11.6 inches). In the women's game the net is 2.24 metres (7 feet 4.1 inches).

World titles World Championships were instituted in 1949. The U.S.S.R. has won six men's titles (1949, 1952, 1960, 1962, 1964 and 1968) in the eight meetings held. The U.S.S.R. won the women's championship in 1952, 1956, 1960, 1968 and 1970. The record crowd is 60,000 for the 1952 world title matches in Moscow, U.S.S.R.

Marathon The longest recorded volleyball marathon is one of 125 hours played by 4. Grace Baptist Church Youth teams of six completed on 31 July 1971.

WALKING

Trans-Continental The record for walking across the United States from San Francisco, California, to New York is 53 days 12¼ hours by John Lees (for details see page 165). The feminine record for the 3,207-mile route is 86 days by Dr. Barbara Moore (b. Varvara Belayeva, in Kalouga, Russia, 22 Dec. 1903), ending on 6 July 1960.

"End to end" The record for walking from John o'Groats to Land's End (route varies between 876 and 891 miles) is 11 days 23 hours 45 minutes achieved by Malcolm Taylor of Milnsbridge, Huddersfield, Yorkshire on 18-30 July 1969. The feminine record is 17 days 7 hours by Miss Wendy Lewis ending on 15 March 1960. End to end and back has twice been achieved. Frederick E. Westcott, aged 31, finished on 18 Dec. 1966 and David Tremayne (Australia), aged 27, finished on 28 May 1971. The Irish "End to End" record over the 376 miles from Mizen Head, Cork to Malin Head, Donegal is 7 days 22 hours 10 mins, set by Tom Casey (b. 1930) on 1-9 July 1972.

London to Brighton The record time for the London to Brighton walk is 7 hours 35 minutes 12 seconds by Donald James

Thompson M.B.E.(b. 20 Jan. 1933) on 14 Sept. 1957. The record time for London to Brighton and back is 18 hours 5 minutes 51 seconds by William Frederick Baker (b. 5 April 1889) of Queen's Park Harriers, London, on 18-19 June 1926.

Walking on crutches David Ryder, 21, a polio victim from Chigwell, Essex, arrived at Land's End from John o'Groats on 18 Aug. 1969 having completed the entire course on crutches. From 30 March to 14 Aug. 1970 he succeeded in walking on crutches 2,960 miles across North America.

Road walking The world's best performances for the two Road Walking events on the current Olympic programme are: 20,000 metres 1 hr. 24 mins. 50.0 secs. by Vincent Paul Nihill (G.B.) on the Isle of Man, 30 July 1972 and 50,000 metres 3 hrs. 52 min. 44.6 secs. by Bernhard Kannenburg (West Germany) 1972.

Most titles The greatest number of national titles won by a British walker is 26 by Vincent Paul Nihill from 1963 to 1972. These are AAA 2 miles/3 kms 1965-70-71; 7 miles/10 kms 1965-66-68-69 and R.W.A. 10 miles 1965-68-69-72; 20 kms 1965-66-68-69-71-72; 20 miles 1963-64-65-68-69-71 and 50 kms 1964-68-71.

OFFICIAL WORLD RECORDS (Track Walking)

(As recognized by the International Amateur Athletic Federation) (*Awaiting ratification)

Distance	Time Hrs mins. secs			Name and Nationality	Place	Date
20,000 metres	1	25	19.4*	Hans-Georg Reimann (East Germany)	Erfurt, East Germany	24 June 1972
	1	25	19.4*	Peter Frenkel (East Germany)	Erfurt, East Germany	24 June 1972
30,000 metres	2	14	45.6	Karl–Heinz Stadtmuller (East Germany)	Berlin	16 Apr. 1972
20 miles	2	31	33.0	Anatoliy S. Vedyakov (U.S.S.R.)	Moscow, U.S.S.R.	23 Aug. 1958
30 miles	3	56	12.6	Peter Selzer (East Germany)	Naumburg, East Germany	3 Oct. 1971
50,000 metres	4	04	19.8	Peter Selzer (East Germany)	Naumburg, East Germany	3 Oct. 1971
2 hours	26,658 metres (16 miles 993 yards)			Peter Frenkel (East Germany)	Berlin	11 Apr. 1971

WATER POLO

Origins Water Polo was developed in England as "Water Soccer" in 1869 and was first included in the Olympic Games in Paris in 1900.

Olympic Games Hungary has won the Olympic tournament five times, in 1932, 1936, 1952, 1956 and 1964. Great Britain won in 1900, 1908, 1912 and 1920. Four players share the record of three gold medals: Paulo (Paul) Radmilovic (1886-1968) and Charles Smith both G.B. in 1908-12-20; and the Hungarians Gyorgy Karpati and Deszo Gyarmati in 1952-56-64. Radmilovic (see Olympic Games) also won a gold medal for the 4 × 200 m. relay in 1908.

A.S.A. championships The club with the greatest number of Amateur Swimming Association titles is Plaistow United Swimming Club of Greater London, with eleven from 1928 to 1954.

Most goals The greatest number of goals scored by an individual in a home international is eleven by Terry C. Miller (Plaistow United), when England defeated Wales 13-3 at Newport, Monmouthshire, in 1951.

Most caps The greatest number of internationals is 168 by Zahan (Romania) to 1970. The British record is 96 by Peter Pass M.B.E. of Chesham Bois, Buckinghamshire in 1955-1969.

WATER SKI-ING

Origins The origins of water ski-ing lie in plank gliding or aquaplaning. A photograph exists of a "plank-riding" contest in a regatta won by a Mr. S. Storry at Scarborough, Yorkshire on 15 July 1914. Competitors were towed on a *single* plank by a motor launch. The present day sport of water ski-ing was pioneered by Ralph W. Samuelson on Lake Pepin, Minnesota, U.S.A., on two curved pine boards in the summer of 1922, though claims have been made for the birth of the sport on Lake Annecy (Haute Savoie), France, in 1920. The first World Water Ski Organization was formed in Geneva on 27 July 1946. The British Water Ski Federation was founded in London in 1954.

Longest jumps The first recorded jump on water skis was made by Ralph Samuelson off a greased ramp, at Miami Beach, Florida, U.S.A. in 1928. The longest jump ever recorded is one of 169 feet by Wayne Grimditch, 17 (U.S.A.) at Callaway Gardens, Pine Mountain Georgia U.S.A. 15 July 1972. The women's record is 111 feet by Barbara Clack, 27 (U.S.A.) at Callaway Gardens on 11 July 1971.

The British record is 47.9 metres (157 ft. 1 in.) by James Carne at Temple-sur-Lot, Bordeaux, France on 30 July 1972. The Irish record is 128 feet by Alan Dagg (Golden Falls W.S.C.) at Dublin on 25 Aug. 1970. The women's record is 106 feet 3½ inches by Jeannette Stewart-Wood (b. 1946) at Ruislip, Greater London on 11 June 1967. This could not be ratified as a world record because a minimum improvement of 8 inches is required.

Buoys and tricks The world record for slalom is 38 buoys (6 passes through the course plus two buoys with the 75-foot rope shortened by 36 feet by Mike Suyderhoud (U.S.) at Ruislip, Middlesex on 6 June 1970 and Roby Zucchi (Italy) at Canzo, Italy on 6 Sept. 1970. The record for tricks is 5,970 points by Ricky McCormick (U.S.) at Bedfont, near London, in August 1970. The British records are 33 buoys by Ian Walker (Ruislip) at Canzo, Italy in September 1970 (5 passes plus 3 buoys with the 75-foot rope shortened by 32 feet)

and 3,765 points by Paul Adlington (Ruislip) Princes in August 1969.

Longest run The greatest distance travelled non-stop is 818.2 mil by Marvin G. Shackleford round McKellar Lak Memphis, Tennessee, U.S.A. in 35 hours 15 minut in September 1960. The British record is 470.67 mil (in 15 hours 1 minute 53.2 seconds) by Charl Phipps, 30, on Lake Windermere from 4.4 a.m. 7.5 p.m. on 4 Oct. 1969.

Highest speed The water ski-ing speed record is 125.69 m.p.h. b Danny Churchill at the Oakland Marine Stadiun California, U.S.A., in 1971. Sally Younger (b. 1953 set a feminine record of 105.14 m.p.h. at Perri California on 17 June 1970.

Water-ski racing The record for the 58-mile Cross Channel race fron Greatstone-on-Sea, near New Romney, England t Cap Gris-Nez, France and back is 1 hour 37 minute 30 seconds by Robin Manwaring of Kent on 13 Au 1972.

Most titles World overall championships (instituted 1949) hav been won twice by Alfredo Mendoza (U.S.A.) i 1953-55 and Mike Suyderhoud (U.S.A.) in 1967-6 and three times by Mrs. Willa McGuire (*née* Worthin ton) of the U.S.A., in 1949-50 and 1955. Mendoz won five championship events and McGuire an Elizabeth Allen (U.S.A.) seven each. The most Britis overall titles (instituted 1953) ever won by a man four by Lance Callingham in 1959-60 and 1962-6 and the most by a woman is three by Mauree Lynn-Taylor in 1959-60-61 and by Jeanett Stewart-Wood in 1963-66-67.

Barefoot The barefoot duration record is 67 minutes ove about 36 miles by Stephen Z. Northrup (U.S.A.) i 1969. The backwards barefoot record is 33 minute 19 seconds by Paul McManus (Australia) in 1969. barefoot jump of 43 feet was reported from Australia The barefoot speed records are 87.46 m.p.h. by Joh Taylor on Lake Ming, California on 28 Mar. 1972 an 61 m.p.h. by Miss Haidee Jones (Australia).

Water ski flying The altitude record is 4,750 feet by Bill Moyes o Sydney, Australia over Lake Ellesmere, New Zealanc on 14 March 1972 towed by a 435 h.p. Hamilton je boat. The duration record is 15 hours 3 mins. by Bi Flewellyn, 29 (N.Z.) over Lake Bonney, Barmera South Australia 1971.

James Carne holder of the British Water Ski jumping record

WEIGHTLIFTING

Origins Amateur weightlifting is of comparatively modern origin, and the first world championship was staged at the Café Monico, Piccadilly, London, on 28 March 1891. Prior to that time, weightlifting consisted of professional exhibitions in which some of the advertised poundages were open to doubt. The first 400 lb. clean and jerk is, however, attributed to Charles Rigoulot (1903-62), a French professional, in Paris, with 402½ lb. on 1 Feb. 1929.

Greatest back lift The greatest weight ever raised by a human being is 6,270 lb. (2.80 tons) in a back lift (weight raised off trestles) by the 26-stone Paul Anderson (U.S.A.) (born 1933), the 1956 Olympic heavyweight champion, at Toccoa, Georgia, U.S.A., on 12 June 1957. The heaviest Rolls-Royce, the Phantom VI, weighs 5,600 lb. (2½ tons). The greatest lift by a woman is 3,564 lb. with a hip and harness lift by Mrs. Josephine Blatt *née* Schauer (1869-1923) at the Bijou Theatre. Hoboken, New Jersey, U.S.A., on 15 April 1895.

Greatest verhead lift The greatest overhead lifts made from the ground are the clean and jerks achieved by super-heavyweights

Paul Anderson lifter of the greatest weight ever by a human being in a back lift.

which now exceed 4½ cwt. (504 lb.) (see table p. 302). The greatest overhead lift ever made by a woman is 286 lb. in a continental jerk by Katie Sandwina, *née* Brummbach (Germany) (b. 21 Jan. 1884, d. as Mrs. Max Heymann in New York City, U.S.A., on 21 Jan. 1952) in *c.* 1911. This is equivalent to seven 40-pound office typewriters. She stood 6 feet 1 inch tall, weighed 220 lb. (15 stone 10 lb.)

OFFICIAL WORLD WEIGHTLIFTING RECORDS

Bodyweight Class	Lift	Lifted lb.	kg.	Name and Nationality	Place	Date	
Flyweight (114½ lb. 52kg.)	Press	265½	120.5	Adam Gnatov (U.S.S.R.)	Riga, U.S.S.R.	11 July	1972
	Snatch	227	103	Zygmunt Smalcerz (Poland)	Constanza, Romania	13 May	1972
	Jerk	291	132	Adam Gnatov (U.S.S.R.)	Riga, U.S.S.R.	11 July	1972
	Total	754¾	342.5	Sandor Holczreiter (Hungary)	Columbus, Ohio, U.S.A.	12 Sept	1970
Bantamweight (123¼lb. 56kg.)	Press	282	128	Rafael Belenkov (U.S.S.R.)	Tallin, U.S.S.R.	11 Apr.	1972
	Snatch	250	113.5	Koji Miki (Japan)	Osaka, Japan	15 Nov.	1968
	Jerk	330½	150	Mohamed Nassiri (Iran)	Mexico City, Mexico	13 Oct	1968
	Total	826½	375	Genmadi Chetin (U.S.S.R.)	Moscow, U.S.S.R.	17 June	1971
Featherweight (132¼lb. 60kg.)	Press	303½	137.5	Imre Földi (Hungary)	Ulm, Germany	4 Mar	1972
	Snatch	276½	125.5	Yoshinobu Miyake (Japan)	Matsuura, Japan	28 Oct	1969
	Jerk	343¾	156	Dito Shanidze (U.S.S.R.)	Constanza, Romania	15 May	1972
	Total	887	402.5	Dito Shanidze (U.S.S.R.)	Tallin, U.S.S.R.	12 Apr	1972
Lightweight (148¾lb. 67.5kg.)	Press	342¾	155.5	Mladen Kuchev (Bulgaria)	Sofia, Bulgaria	15 July	1972
	Snatch	303	137.5	Waldemar Baszanowski (Poland)	Lublin, Poland	23 Apr	1971
	Jerk	389	176.5	Mukharbi Kirzhinov (U.S.S.R.)	Rigo, U.S.S.R.	12 July	1972
	Total	991¾	450	Waldemar Baszanowski (Poland)	Sofia, Bulgaria	22 June	1971
Middleweight (165¼lb. 75kg.)	Press	367	166.5	Alexander Kolodkov (U.S.S.R.)	Bollnäs, Sweden	19 Mar	1972
	Snatch	321¾	146	Mohamed Trabulsi (Lebanon)	Aman, Jordan	30 June	1972
	Jerk	413¼	187.5	Viktor Kurentsov (U.S.S.R.)	Mexico City, Mexico	16 Oct	1968
	Total	1,063¼	482.5	Viktor Kurenstov (U.S.S.R.)	Dubna, U.S.S.R.	31 Aug	1968
Light-heavyweight (181¾lb. 82.5kg.)	Press	393½	178.5	Gennadi Ivanchenko (U.S.S.R.)	Riga, U.S.S.R.	18 May	1972
	Snatch	348¼	158	Valeri Shariy (U.S.S.R.)	Riga, U.S.S.R.)	13 July	1972
	Jerk	436½	198	Boris Pavlov (U.S.S.R.)	Halmstad, Sweden	12 Mar	1972
	Total	1,162½	527.5	Valeri Shariy (U.S.S.R.)	Moscow, U.S.S.R.	14 May	1972
Middle-heavyweight (198¼lb. 90kg.)	Press	436½	198	David Rigert (U.S.S.R.)	Riga, U.S.S.R.	13 July	1972
	Snatch	369¼	167.5	David Rigert (U.S.S.R.)	Riga, U.S.S.R.	13 July	1972
	Jerk	464	210.5	Vasili Kolotov (U.S.S.R.)	Riga, U.S.S.R.	13 July	1972
	Total	1,239¾	562.5	David Rigert (U.S.S.R.)	Riga, U.S.S.R.	13 July	1972
Heavyweight (242½lb. 110kg.)	Press	470½	213.5	Yuri Kozin (U.S.S.R.)	Riga, U.S.S.R.	14 July	1972
	Snatch	385¾	175	Pavel Pervushin (U.S.S.R.)	Tallin, U.S.S.R.	14 Apr	1972
	Jerk	490½	222.5	Yan Talts (U.S.S.R.)	Constanza, Romania	20 May	1972
	Total	1,300¼	590	Valeri Yakubovsky (U.S.S.R.)	Moscow, U.S.S.R.	14 May	1972
Super-heavyweight (Above 242½lb. 110kg.)	Press	521¼	236.5	Vasili Alexeev (U.S.S.R.)	Tallin, U.S.S.R.	15 Apr	1972
	Snatch	396¾	180	Vasili Alexeev (U.S.S.R.)	Moscow, U.S.S.R.	24 July	1971
	Jerk	523½	237.5	Vasili Alexeev (U.S.S.R.)	Tallin, U.S.S.R.	15 Apr	1972
	Total	1,421¾	645	Vasili Alexeev (U.S.S.R.)	Tallin, U.S.S.R.	15 Apr	1972

(As supplied by Mr. Oscar State, O.B.E., General Secretary of the *Fédération Haltérophile Internationale*)

and is reputed to have unofficially lifted 312½ lb. and to have shouldered a cannon taken from the tailboard of a Barnum and Bailey circus wagon which allegedly weighed 1,200 lb.

Power lifts Paul Anderson, as a professional, has bench-pressed 627 lb. and has achieved 1,200 lb. in a squat so aggregating, with an 820 lb. dead lift, a career total of 2,647 lb. The A.A.U. of America record for a single contest is an aggregate of 2,040 lb. by Bob Weaver set in 1967.

The highest recorded two-handed dead lift is 820 lb. by Paul Anderson. Hermann Gorner (Germany) performed a one-handed dead lift of 734½ lb. in Dresden on 20 July 1920. Peter B. Cortese (U.S.A.) achieved a one-armed dead lift of 370 lb. *i.e.* 22 lb. over triple his bodyweight at York, Pennsylvania on 4 Sept. 1954.

Gorner (see above) raised 24 men weighing 4,123 lb. on a plank on the soles of his feet in London on 12 Oct. 1927 and also carried on his back a 1,444 lb. piano for a distance of 52½ feet on 3 June 1921.

The highest competitive two-handed dead lift by a woman is 392 lb. by Mlle. Jane de Vesley (France) in Paris on 14 Oct. 1926.

It was reported that an hysterical 8 stone 11 lb. woman, Mrs. Maxwell Rogers, lifted one end of a 3,600 lb. (1.60 ton) station wagon which, after th collapsing of a jack, had fallen on top of her son a Tampa, Florida, U.S.A., on 24 April 1960. Sh cracked some vertebrae.

Cue levering The only man ever to have levered six 16 oz. billiar cues simultaneously by their tips through 90 degree to the horizontal, is W. J. (Bill) Hunt of Darwer Lancashire at the Unity Club, Great Harwood Lancashire on 25 June 1954.

Olympic Games The U.S.S.R. has won 18, the U.S.A. 14 and France of the 68 titles at stake. Eight lifters have so fa succeeded in winning Olympic titles in successiv Games. Three lifters have won 2 gold and 1 silve medal:-

Louis Hostin (France) Light-heavy: Silver 1928; Gold 1932 and 1936.
Tommy Kono (Hawaii/U.S.A.) Lightweight: Gold 1952; Light-heavy: Gold 1956; Middleweight: Silver 1960.
Yoshinobu Miyake (Japan) Bantam: Silver 1960; Featherweight: Gold 1964 and 1968.

Most Successful British Lifter Louis George Martin M.B.E., born Jamaica 1936, wo four world mid-heavyweight titles in 1959-62-63-65 He won an Olympic silver medal in 1964 and a bronz in 1960.

Tonnage Record The highest reported tonnage lifted in 100 hours i 453.22 tons by Jim Foster at King Alfred's Boys Club, Winchester, Hampshire on 20-24 Oct. 1970.

WRESTLING

Earliest references Wrestling holds and falls, depicted on the walls of the Egyptian tombs of Beni Hasan, prove that wrestling dates from 2000 B.C. or earlier. It was introduced into the ancient Olympic Games in the 18th Olympiad in *c.* 704 B.C. The Graeco-Roman style is of French origin and arose about 1860. The International Amateur Wrestling Federation (F.I.L.A.) was founded in 1912.

Most World Championships The greatest number of world championships won by a wrestler is seven by the freestyler Aleksandr Medved (U.S.S.R.), born 1937 with the Light-heavyweight titles in 1964 (Olympic) and 1966, the Heavyweight 1967 and 1968 (Olympic), and the Extra heavyweight title 1969, 1970 and 1971. The only other wrestler to win world titles in 6 successive years has been Abdullah Movahad (Iran) in the lightweight division in 1965-70. The record for Graeco-Roman titles is five shared by Roman Rurua (U.S.S.R.) with the featherweight 1966, 1967, 1968 (Olympic), 1969 and 1970 and Victor Igumenov (U.S.S.R.) with the Welterweight 1966, 1967, 1969, 1970 and 1971.

Most Olympic titles Two wrestlers have won three Olympic titles. They are:

Carl Westergran (Sweden)

Graeco-Roman Middleweight A	1920
Graeco-Roman Middleweight B	1924
Graeco-Roman Heavyweight	1932

Ivar Johansson (Sweden)

Freestyle Middleweight	1932
Graeco-Roman Welterweight	1932
Graeco-Roman Middleweight	1936

Best record Osamu Watanabe (Japan) won the freestyle featherweight event in the 1964 Olympic Games. This was his 186th successive win and he had never been defeated.

Longest bout The longest recorded bout was one of nearly 11 hours between Max Klein (Russia) and Alfred Asikainen (Finland) in the Graeco-Roman middleweight "A" event in the 1912 Olympic Games in Stockholm Sweden.

GREAT BRITAIN-MOST TITLES

Heavyweight	10	Ken Richmond, 1949-60
Middleweight	7	Thomas Albert Baldwin (b. 27 Sept. 1905), 1942, 1944-46, 1948, 1951-52 (also Welterweight in 1941)
Welterweight	9	Joe Feeney, 1957-60, 1962, 1964-66, 1968
Lightweight	8	Arthur Thompson, 1933-40
Featherweight	8	H. Hall, 1952-57, 1961, 1963 and Lightweight 1958-59
Bantamweight	6	Joe Reid, 1930-35

Longest span The longest span for B.A.W.A. titles is 24 years by G Mackenzie, who won his first title in 1909 and his las in 1933. Mackenzie, also jointly holds (see Fencing the record of having represented Great Britain in fiv successive Olympiads from 1908 to 1928.

Heaviest heavyweight The heaviest heavyweight champion in British wrest ling history was A. Dudgeon (Scotland), who won th 1936 and 1937 B.A.W.A. heavyweight titles, scaling 22 stone.

Cumberland Wrestling The British Cumberland and Westmorland Champion ships were established in 1904. The only 6 tim champions have been J. Badderley (Middleweight i 1905-06-08-09-10-12) and E. A. Bacon (Lightweigh in 1919-21-22-23-28-29).

PROFESSIONAL WRESTLING
Professional wrestling dates from *c.* 1875 in the United States. Georges Karl Julius Hackenschmid (1877-1968) made no submissions in the period 1898-1908. The highest paid professional wrestle ever is Antonio ("Tony") Rocca of Puerto Rico, with $180,000 (£75,000) in 1958. The heaviest eve wrestler has been William J. Cobb of Macon, Georgia U.S.A. (b. 1926), who was billed in 1962 as the 802 lb. (57 st. 4 lb.) "Happy" Humphrey. What he lacked in mobility he possessed in suffocating powers By July 1965 he had reduced to a more modes 232 lb. (16 st. 8 lb.).

Most Successful Ed "Strangler" Lewis (1890-1966) *né* Robert H Friedrich, fought 6,200 bouts in 44 years losing only 33 matches. He won world titles in 1920, 1922 and 1928.

Ken Richmond, winner of ten Heavyweight British titles from 1949-1960.

Britain's greatest professional wrestler has been Bert Assirati (b. 1912) who in 21 years was never once pinned on the mat. At 5 ft 6 ins and 266 lb. he could do a crucifix on the rings, 3 one arm pull-ups and dead lift 800 lb.

Sumo wrestling The sport's legendary origins in Japan were 2,000 years ago. The heaviest ever performer was probably Dewagatake, a wrestler of the 1920s who was 6 feet 5 inches tall and weighed up to 30 stone. Weight is amassed by over alimentation with a high protein sea food stew called *chanko-rigori*. The tallest was probably Ozora, an early 19th century performer, who stood 7 feet 3 inches tall. The most successful wrestler has been Koki Naya (b. 1940), *alias* Taiho ("Great Bird"), who won his 26th Emperor's Cup on 10-24 Sept. 1967. He was first a *Yokozuna* (Grand Champion) in 1967. The highest *dan* is Makuuchi.

YACHTING

Origin Yachting in England dates from the £100 stake race between Charles II and his brother James, Duke of York, on the Thames on 1 Sept. 1661 over 23 miles, from Greenwich to Gravesend. The earliest club is the Royal Cork Yacht Club (formerly the Cork Harbour Water Club), established in Ireland in 1720.

Highest speed A speed of 30 knots was attained in September 1966 by *Lady Helmsman*, the 25-foot C class catamaran built by Reg. White (b. 1936) of Brightlingsea, Essex. The aerodynamic mast accounts for a third of the 300 square feet of sail area permitted. Speed trials by the 32-foot D Clan catamaran *Beowulf V* in Los Angeles Harbor in August 1971 recorded 31.7 m.p.h. (27.56 knots) and momentarily probably attained 35 m.p.h. (30.4 knots).

Most successful The most successful racing yacht in history was the Royal Yacht *Britannia* (1893-1935), owned by King George V, which won 231 races in 625 starts.

America's Cup The America's Cup races, open to challenge by any nation's yachts, began on 8 Aug. 1870 with the unsuccessful attempt by J. Ashbury's *Cambria* (G.B.) to capture the trophy from the *Magic*, owned by F. Osgood (U.S.A.). Since then the Cup has been challenged by Great Britain in 15 contests, by Canada in two contests, and by Australia thrice, but the United States holders have never been defeated. The closest race ever was the fourth race of the 1962 series, when the 12-metre sloop *Weatherly* beat her Australian challenger *Gretel* by about 3½ lengths (75 yards), a margin of only 26 seconds, on 22 Sept. 1962. The fastest time ever recorded by a 12-metre boat for the triangular course of 24 miles is 2 hours 46 minutes 58 seconds by *Gretel* in 1962.

Little America's Cup The catamaran counterpart to the America's Cup was instituted in 1961. The British club entry has won on each annual occasion to 1968 *v.* the U.S.A. (1961-66 and 1968) and *v.* Australia in 1967.

Largest yacht The largest private yacht ever built was Mrs. Emily Roebling Cadwalader's *Savarona* of 4,600 gross tons, completed in Hamburg, Germany, in Oct. 1931, at a cost of $4,000,000 (now £1.66 million). She (the yacht), with a 53-foot beam and measuring 407 feet 10 inches overall, was sold to the Turkish government in March 1938. Operating expenses for a full crew of 107 men approached $500,000 (now £208,000) per annum.

The largest private sailing yacht ever built was the full-rigged 350-foot auxiliary barque *Sea Cloud* (formerly *Hussar*), owned by the oft-married Mrs.

Marjorie Merriweather Post-Close-Hutton-Davies-May (born 1888), one-time wife of the U.S. Ambassador in the U.S.S.R. Her four masts carried 30 sails with the total canvas area of 36,000 square feet.

Largest sail The largest sail ever made was a parachute spinnaker with an area of 18,000 square feet (more than two-fifths of an acre) for Vanderbilt's *Ranger* in 1937.

Olympic Games The first sportsman ever to win individual gold medals in four successive Olympic Games was Paul B. Elvstrom of Denmark in the Firefly class in 1948 and the Finn class in 1952, 1956 and 1960. He has also won 8 other world titles in a total of 6 classes. The lowest number of penalty points by the winner of any class in an Olympic regatta is 3 points (6 wins [1 disqualified] and 1 second in 7 starts) by *Superdocius* of the Flying Dutchman class (Lt. Rodney Pattisson, M.B.E., R.N. and Iain Macdonald-Smith, M.B.E.) at Acapulco, Mexico in October 1968.

Longest Race The longest established race is the 3,751 mile Los Angeles to Tahiti event for which the record time is 8 days 13 hours 9 mins. by Eric Tabarly's *Pen Duick IV* (France) in 1969.

Most Boats The 1971-72 pleasure boat market was estimated at £90 million in Britain. The two largest concentrations are at Shoeburyness, Essex with 3,000 sailing boats and 2,000 power boats and Poole, Dorset also with 5,000 boats but in reverse proportion.

24 Hour Dinghy Race The greatest distance covered in 24 hours in the annual West Lancashire Yacht Club event at Southport is 112 miles by a G.P. 14 from West Kirby Sailing Club on 11/12 Sept. 1968.

Reliance, winner of the 1903 America's Cup, the largest ever racing yacht.

STOP PRESS

CHAPTER 1-THE HUMAN BEING

Page 17

Most children *World* Currently the highest reported figure is a 38th child born to Raimundo Carnauba, 58 and Josimar Carnauba, 54 of Belém, Brazil. She was married at 15 and so far has had 14 sons and 24 daughters at yearly intervals. The mother in May 1972 said "They have given us a lot of work and worry but they are worth it", and the father "I don't know why people make such a fuss".

Page 18

Quadruplets Heaviest *World* The heaviest quadruplets ever recorded are the three girls and one boy born to Mrs. Penny McPherson on 8 July 1972 at Liverpool Maternity Hospital. They aggregated 21lb. 5oz.—Fiona (5lb. 1oz.), Kirsten (5lb. 15oz.), Rachel (4lb. 11oz.) and Guy (5lb. 10oz.).

Page 20

Heaviest baby A report from Dezful, S.W. Iran, that Mrs. Massoumeh Valizadeh, 32, had given birth to a 12 kilogramme (26lb. 6½oz.) boy on 7 Feb. 1972, was later officially stated to be incorrect.

Longest pregnancy The Houghton pregnancy was according to the husband and wife, of 390 days duration.

Page 21

Commonest illness The number of working days estimated to be lost in Great Britain as a result of the common cold between mid-1969 and mid-1970 were 4,044,000. Absences of less than three days are not reported. The greatest loss of working time in Britain is from bronchitis, which accounted for 37,053,000 or 10.83 per cent. of the total of 342,065 working days lost in that period.

Page 21

Longest hair The hair of Jane Bunford (see p.11) which she wore in two plaits, reached down to her ankles, indicating a length in excess of 8 feet.

Most fingers Polydactylism is common in the Urdes district of Spain.

Page 26

Most voracious fire eater Jack Sholomir ignited a bale of straw at a distance of ten feet with a flame from his mouth at Highpoint, Hillbrow, Johannesburg, South Africa on 10 March 1972.

CHAPTER 2-THE ANIMAL AND PLANT KINGDOMS

Page 28

Longest gestation The vivaporous amphibian Alpine Black Salamander (*Salamandra atra*) can have a gestation period of up to 38 months when living above 14,600 feet (1,400 metres) in Switzerland.

Page 31

Smallest deer The smallest example of a true deer (family Cervidae) is the pudu (*Pudu pudu*) of South America which is 13-15 inches at the shoulder and weighs 20 lb.

Page 33

Largest litter "Sheba", a five year old Alsatian bitch, owned by Mr. Michael Hawes of Rushholme, Manchester, produced a litter of 24 live pups in June 1972.

Most valuable dog Mrs. Judith Thurlow of Great Ashfield, Suffolk declined an offer of £14,000 for her record-breaking greyhound "Super Rory" (whelped Oct. 1970).

Page 34

Oldest cats "Mr. Nogs" owned by Mrs. Arthur Baxter of Humbleston Lincolnshire, died aged 31 in May 1972. Mr. Baxter's white cat "Boo Boo" has reached the age of 29.

Largest litter On 23 April 1972 a one-year-old seal point Siamese cat named "Chan-Lass", owned by Mrs. Harriet Smith of Southsea, Hants., gave birth to a litter of 13 kittens, 11 of which survived.

Greatest fall On 15 July 1972 "Fat Olive" a black and white tom cat, survived a fall of 160 feet from a Toronto penthouse, breaking only two legs.

Page 36

Longest flights For 14,000 miles read 12,000 miles.

Page 37

Earliest Cuckoo Mr. W.A. Haynes of Trinder Road, Wantage, Berkshire *heard and saw* a cuckoo on 2 March 1972 under acceptable conditions.

Oldest Canary It was reported in June 1972 that Mrs. Kathleen Leck, 32, still has a 31-year-old canary bartered by her father, Mr. Ross of Hull, in Calabar, Nigeria when she was one.

Page 38

Oldest snake A common boa (*Boa constrictor constrictor*) in the Philadelphia Zoo is "still living in August 1972 after 35½ years in captivity".

Page 41

Deepest fish A 6½ inch long *Bassogigas profundissimus*—only the fifth ever taken—was reported to have been netted at a depth of 27,230 feet in the Puerto Rico trench (-27,488 ft.) in the Atlantic, by Dr Gilbert L. Voss, from the research vessel *John Elliott* in April 1970.

Page 43

Smallest and largest tick The smallest known tick is a male *Ixodes soricis* from a British Columbian shrew, and the largest an engorged female, *Amblyomma varium* from a Venezuelan sloth.

Page 48

Earliest life On 24 Apr. 1972 the Ames Research Laboratory, Mountain View, California, announced a date of 3,300 million years for the earliest photosynthesising plant from the Onverwacht strata of the South Africa-Swaziland border.

Longest roots The roots of a wild fig tree at Echo Caves, near Ohrigstad, East Transvaal are reported to extend for many hundreds of feet.

Page 49

Remotest tree Reports that the world's remotest tree in the Tenere region of the Sahara had been killed by being rammed in February 1960 by a French lorry have proven exaggerated. It is hoped to publish a photograph of the tree in the 20th edition.

Page 50

Daisy chain Longest Nineteen girls of the Upper VI at Trowbridge High School, Wiltshire, made a daisy chain 1,320 feet long on 30 June 1972.

Largest wreath The largest wreath ever constructed was a Christmas wreath of 765 lb. and 19½ feet in diameter by the Oshkosh Warriors of Wisconsin, U.S.A., and hung in the Grand Mall for 25 Dec. 1971.

Largest bouquet The largest bouquet on record is one of 243 Baccara red roses made by Jayne Foster of *The Florist* magazine and presented by the Lord Mayor of London to Madam Mayor of Lancaster on the occasion of the opening of the Midland Link joining these two cities, 243 miles apart, on 23 May 1972.

Page 51

Tallest Brussels The tallest Brussels sprout on record is one grown by Mr. W. Lawrence of Kidderminster, Worcestershire,

sprout which in June 1972 had reached 9 ft. 6½ in.

Tallest lupin The tallest lupin reported is one of 6 ft. 0½ in. grown by Mr. J. Lawlor of New Malden, Surrey in 1971.

Largest strawberry A strawberry weighing 7¼ oz. was grown by Mr. Ted Oxley, 71, at Walton-on-the-Naze, Essex. It was weighed on 4 July 1972.

Tallest sunflower A sunflower 16 feet 2 inches in height was grown by G. E. Hooking of Kington Langley, Wilts., and was cut down in October 1971.

Page 52

Tallest rhododendron The cross-section of the trunk of a *Rhododendron giganteum*, reputedly 90 feet high from the George Forest, Yunnan, China is preserved at Inverewe Garden, Ross-shire.

Most Northerley Vineyard On 6 Apr. 1972, 300 grape vines from Neustadt, West Germany were planted by the Old Bishop's Palace in Lincoln at Lat 53° 15′N.

Page 53

Giant Panda Chi Chi died on 22 July 1972. The San Diego Zoo, California has offered £100,000 for a fertile pair.

CHAPTER 3–THE NATURAL WORLD

Page 58

Swamp Largest The world's largest tract of swamp is in the basin of the Pripet or Pripyat River—a tributary of the Dnieper River in the U.S.S.R. These swamps cover an estimated area of 18,125 square miles.

Page 59

Highest points The highest point in Buckinghamshire is the N.E. corner of Aston Hill. The first person known to have visited the highest point in every English county is Mr. Basil Harris of Gloucester.

Page 64

Snowfall The 365 day fall at Tide Lake north of Stewart, British Columbia, Canada from 16 May 1971 to 15 May 1972 totalled 1,104 in.

CHAPTER 4–UNIVERSE AND SPACE

Page 70-71

Pioneer 10 If Pioneer 10 escapes a lethal hit in the asteroid belt it should fly by Jupiter on 3 Dec. 1973 on its 620 million mile flight path.

CHAPTER 5–SCIENTIFIC WORLD

Page 76

Largest pearl The valuation of the Pearl of Lau-tze in July 1971 at $32 per grain, indicates a total of $4,080,000.

Page 77

Largest Telescope A report from Moscow on 31 May 1972 stated that the 600cm. (236.2 inch) Zelenchukskaya telescope was only then "ready for mounting".

Page 78

Most expensive camera According to the U.K. agents, J.J. Silber of London E.C.1., the cost of the full available range of the Japanese made Canon range is £9,758.82. The cost of the eventual full range will exceed £12,000.

Page 79

Nano-second. For 11.7 inches read 11.80 inches.

Lowest This was achieved in March of 1969.
temperature

Page 80

Most powerful It was reported on 15 July 1972 that the Weston,
particle Illinois accelerator had attained 300 GeV.
accelerator

CHAPTER 6—THE ARTS AND ENTERTAINMENTS

Page 82

By British The highest price for the work of a British artist is the
Artist £280,000 paid by Colnaghi's at Sotheby's for
Gainsborough's painting of the Gravenor Family,
from the estate of Major J. Townshend, on 19 July
1972. It had been insured in 1930 for £1,500.

Page 87

Longest We are advised by a Hungarian correspondent that the
word longest grammatically acceptable word in Magyar is
Engedelmeskedhetetlenségeskedéseitekert meaning
"because of your continued disobedience".

Page 90

Most Miss Ursula Bloom's reported total of book titles by
prolific July 1972 was 468.

Page 91

Best sellers There was increasing evidence that *Quotations from
the Works of Mao Tse-tung* ceased to be mandatory
by July 1972 due to the involvement of Marshal Lin
Piao (k. 13 Sept. 1971) and the De-Piaoization
programme.

Page 92

Largest At the 1954 Mom'n Dads Day festivities at the
cartoon University of Arizona a cartoon 150 feet long and
five storeys (50 feet) high was drawn by Peter C.
Kesling.

Print order The print order for the 47th Automobile
Association Handbook (1972-73) was 5,200,000
copies. The total print since 1908 has been
58,710,000.

Page 93

Library The New York Public Library now closes at 6.00
p.m. and does not open on Sundays or holidays.

Page 98

Longest runs *Fiddler on the Roof* reached the Broadway record
of 3,225 performances on 17 June 1972. Paul
Lipson played in it from the opening in 1964
including Tevye 1,811 times. The world gross
earnings reached $64,300,000 to this date.

Page 100

Top selling The total sales of the double (4 sided) L.P. *Jesus
L.P.* Christ Superstar* by Andrew Lloyd Webber
(b. 22 March 1948) and Tim Rice (b. 10 Nov. 1944)
and released on 10 Oct. 1970 reached 4,000,000
sets by July 1972.

306

Gainsborough's painting of the Gravenor family which reached a record price for the work of a British artist at Sotheby's.

Page 103

Most durable The most durable B.B.C. comedy serial th
serials *Clitheroe Kid* produced by Jim Casey entered it
15th year.

Biggest T.V. The running of *Coronation Street* was 20 days 1
sales hours 44 minutes.

CHAPTER 7—THE WORLD'S STRUCTUR

Page 105

Largest The world's largest cooling tower was completed i
cooling 1972 at the Columbia River Atomic Power Statio
towers near Ranier, Oregon, U.S.A. It stands 499 feet ta
and cost $7,800,000.

Page 110

Public Mr. House of Totterdown, Bristol, surpassed th
Houses 2,000 mark on 16 July 1972.
most

Page 110-111

Tallest Target completion date is now Dec. 1973 and th
Tower weight is 650 tons.

Page 113

Bridge Spans The Hartland Covered Bridge was built in 1899.

CHAPTER 8—MECHANICAL WORLD

Page 124

Ships The *Majestic* ended her career not as a troopship b
as a training ship in the Firth of Forth.

Largest The McMullen Report of 19 July 1972 found th
Ever no fewer than 3 fires were started simultaneous
Liner and thus arson was suspected.

Page 125

Warship The U.S. Navy test vehicle SES-100B built by Be
Fastest of Textron, began trials on Lake Pontchartrai
Louisiana in May 1972 and has a design speed
80-plus knots.

Page 127

Heaviest The *Lord Clyde's* sister ship *Lord Warde
wooden ship* completed in 1867 displaced 7,940 tons.

Oil-drilling Rigs British Petroleum have commissioned two 57,000 ton oil-drilling rigs with 500-foot legs for the Forties Field 115 miles off-shore for completion in September 1973.

Propeller heaviest The weight of the *Globtik Tokyo's* propeller is 58 tons.

Page 131

Amphibious Channel crossing The two Welshmen John Milton and John Powell crossed the Channel from Folkestone to Cape Gris Nez on 24 June 1971 in a 7-ton 32 ft. long Dukw (built in 1943) as a stage in a 13-hour journey from London to Paris.

On 30 July 1963 David Tapp drove a County Sea Horse tractor from Cap Gris-Nez to Kingsdown in 7 hrs. 50 mins.

Page 134

Longest Platform Karagpur is in West Bengal.

Longest tram journey The longest tramway journeys that have ever been possible have been in the Rhein-Ruhr area of West Germany where there have been very extensive networks of standard and meter gauge tramways. The record journeys in the United Kingdom have been by the famous illuminated car from Edgehill Works, Liverpool *via* Knotty Ash, St. Helens, Atherton, Leigh, Salford and then branching off to Ashton-under-Lyne on 13 December 1925 and alternatively to Stockport on 14 November 1926. Both journeys were of some 40 miles in length.

Page 135

Greatest mileage Geoffrey Styles and William Lang established a record by travelling through all the 79 counties in Great Britain which are served by British Rail from 00.55 on 25 July to 22.26 on 31 July 1971. Six counties are unserved.

Page 138

Busiest Airport The O'Hare statistics for 1971 were 641,429 movements—a take-off or landing every 49 seconds.

Helicopter altitude A claim for 40,813 feet has been made by Jean Boulet on 23 June 1972.

Page 144

Watch most expensive The Vacheron et Constantin Minute repeater excluding the bracelet has a retail selling price in the region of £10,000. The perpetual calendar however requires re-setting at the end of most centuries.

CHAPTER 9—THE BUSINESS WORLD

Page 146

Largest Take-Over The largest take-over in commercial history has been the bid of £438,000,000 by Grand Metropolitan Hotels Ltd., for the brewers Watney Mann on 17 June 1972.

Largest U.K. Brewery The £22 million Bass-Charrington Brewery on a 90 acre site at Runcorn, Cheshire due to open in mid-1973 will have a reported capacity of 2,500,000 barrels. The bottling and kegging hall will cover 14 acres.

Page 148

Insurance Company largest Prudential Insurance Co's life insurance in force as at 1 Jan. 1972 was reported at $168,253,000,000 and assets at $31,160 million.

Page 151

Credit Cards The largest reported collection of credit cards is one of 147 all different, by Walter Cavanagh (U.S.) in May 1972. The cost of acquisition was nil.

Page 156

Agricultural Origins Recent work on the Nok Not Tha and Sprit Cave, Thailand, tends to confirm that plant cultivation and animal domestication was carried out by people of the Hoabinhian culture *c.* 11,000 B.C.

Heavyweight cattle Bulls of the Chianina breed may measure up to 7 feet at the shoulder.

Page 157

Sheep shearing The world record for machine shearing sheep in an 8 hour day was raised to 410 by Brian Barney Morrison of Ewroa, Victoria, Australia on 12 Feb. 1972.

Egg laying A Rhode Island red "Penny", owned by Mrs. Treena White of Aston Clinton, Buckinghamshire, laid 20 eggs in a week in August 1971 and 7 in one day, on 11 Sept. 1971.

Page 158

Chicken ranch The world's largest chicken ranch is the 600 acre "Egg City", Moor Park, California, established by Jules Goldman in 1954. Some two million eggs are laid daily by 4.5 million chickens. The manure sale totals $72,000 per annum.

Oldest sheep A case has been reported by Mr. H. Poole from Wexford, Ireland of a sheep, according to flock book records, attaining an age of 26 years.

24 Hour Ploughing Record On 22-23 Nov. 1971 a County Eleven Twenty-Four tractor with a Bamford Kverneland 7 furrow plough at a depth of 6 inches, ploughed 115 acres in 24 hours at North Barn Farm, Dorchester, Dorset.

Page 162

Trans-ocean rowing John Fairfax's (G.B.) east-west solo row across the Atlantic was the earliest in either direction. With Sylvia Cook (the first woman to complete an ocean row) he ended the first trans-Pacific row at Hayman Is., Queensland on 23 Apr. 1972.

Page 164

Deep diving table Patrice Chemin and Robert Gauret in June 1972 descended to a depth of 2,001 feet in a simulated chamber dive.

Page 165

Cycling Ray Reece, 41, of Alverstoke, Hants., circumnavigated the world by bicycle (13,000 road miles) between 14 June and 5 Nov. (143 days) in 1971. Peter Duker of Worthing, Sussex in circumnavigating the world (15,000 miles) in 236 days set a coast-to-coast Trans-America record (Santa Monica, California to New York City) in 18 days 2½ hours in 1970.

Page 167

Balancing on one foot The British duration record for a one foot stand (with 5 minute time intervals for each completed hour) is 3 hours 26 minutes set by Ian Philliskirk of Pingle School, Swadlincote from 12.36p.m. to 4.17p.m. on 13 July 1972.

Page 168

Boomerang throwing On 17 June 1972 Herb A. Smith of Rustington, Sussex threw an 8½oz. boomerang outwards to a distance of 108.4 yards at Littlehampton, Sussex.

CHAPTER 10—HUMAN ACHIEVEMENTS

Page 169

Disc Jockey 205 hours 50 minutes by S.A.C. Mick Buckley, R.A.F. Strike Command, High Wycombe, Bucks. from 6-14 July 1972. Non-stop and without sleep and played 3,914 records, *singles only*.

Page 170-171

Hitch Hiking Peter Gillard of Pwllheli, North Wales hitched a total of 25,024 miles through 22 African countries in 298 days (13 Feb.-8 Dec. 1970).

Page 171

Kite descents Bill Moyes of Sydney, Australia descended to earth from a plane-towed kite from an altitude of 8,610 feet over Amery, Wisconsin, U.S.A. on 14 Oct. 1971.

The greatest free-flight descent from a land take-off is 5,757 feet by Bill Bennett, 40, of Sydney, Australia from Dante's Peak to the floor of Death Valley, California on 24 Feb. 1972.

Page 172

Biggest free fall "Star" The world record was raised to 26 parachutists over Oklahoma, U.S.A. on 19 Aug. 1972.

Page 174

Group Singing 5 members of the Methodist Youth Club, Little Hulton, Walkden, Manchester completed 36 hours 35 minutes between 29 and 30 July 1972. At least four people were singing at any one time.

Page 175

Tightrope walking Franz Burbach, 31, of Germany achieved a British distance record of 800 ft. across the Thames near Southwark Bridge in 13 mins. on 23 Aug. 1972.

Page 176

Tunnel of Fire Dick Sheppard of the "Disaster Squad" negotiated a 65 ft. 7½ in. tunnel of fire at Shanklin, Isle of Wight on 20 Aug. 1972.

Page 177

Yo-yo endurance Dave Farrar and Bryan Mellow both completed 20 hours continuous play on 5-6 Aug. 1972 while taking part in the REHAB Tri-Marathon at Chester.

Page 180

Doughnuts 20 in 15 minutes by a student at Durham, England in December 1971.

Spaghetti 100 yards in 42.0 seconds by Tony Danico, Danny Signor, John Burse and Frank Busato in Sydney, Australia on 11 June 1972.

CHAPTER 11—THE HUMAN WORLD

Page 186

Population A governmental publication issued in August 1972 revealed that the population of the People's Republic of China was some 85 million below the U.N. estimate for mid-1971 or only 681 million.

Page 193

Oldest member Lord Aylmer being the holder of an Irish Peerage is not eligible for a seat in the House of Lords. He was born on 23 April 1880.

Page 194

War fatalities The figures should read 54,800,000 and 9,700,000.

Page 206

Largest Budget *United Kingdom* For second paragraph please read: The greatest annual surplus achieved was £4,610 million in 1970-71, and the greatest deficit was £2,825 million in 1944-45.

Page 210

Most expensive menu The menu for the main 5½ hour banquet at the Imperial Iranian 2,500th Anniversary gathering at Persepolis in October 1971 was probably the most expensive ever compiled. It comprised quail egg stuffed with Iranian caviar, a mousse of crayfish tails in Nantua sauce, stuffed rack of roast lamb with a main course of roast peacock stuffed with *foie gras*, fig ring and raspberry sweet with champagne sherbet washed down with wine including Château Lafite-Rothschild 1945 at £40 per bottle.

Page 213

Longest telephone call A continuous call on a pay-phone between Zimmerman Hall (girls) and Ellsworth Hall (male students) at Western Michigan University Kalamazoo, lasted 691 hours 6 minutes from 23 Oct. to 21 Nov. 1969.

Page 220

Cardinals Oldest Cardinal Paolo Giobbe died in Rome on 14 Aug. 1972. The oldest cardinal is now Cardinal José da Costa Nuñes (b. Candelaria, Portugal 15 Mar. 1880). As at 23 Aug. 1972 the Sacred College of Cardinals had 116 members.

CHAPTER 12.—SPORTS, GAMES AND PASTIMES

Page 225

Angling marathon Miss Lynda Hamilton of Kelvedon and District Angling Club fished for 137 hours at Rivenhall Sand Pit, near Silver End, Essex between 4 and 10 Aug. 1972. Approximately five minutes per hour were used as rest breaks.

Page 232

British 200 m. record 20.3* David Jenkins at Edinburgh on 19 Aug. 1972.

Page 237

Basketball marathon 24 players from the Teen Club, Westchester and Civil Air Patrol Sqn. 43, Westchester, U.S.A. completed 140 hours of non-stop basketball from 30 June to 6 July 1972.

Page 241

Most knock-outs Archie Moore's career figures are 141 from 1936-63 Lamar Clark's consecutive figures are 43 from 1958-1960.

Persepolis— the scene of a 5½ hour banquet at which the guests were offered the most expensive ever menu.

Page 244

Caving Depth A 16 man British expedition began in August 1972 to explore the Ghar Paru cave (entrance altitude 10,300 ft.) in the Zagros Mts., W. Iran below the 2,400 ft. level reached in 1971. A floor at 6,000 ft. below the surface is thought possible.

Page 251

Cycling Bob Addy rode from London to York (197 miles) in 7 hours 4 minutes 13 seconds on 6 Aug. 1972.

Ken Webb of Crawley Wheelers, Sussex claimed to have bettered the 365 day mileage record on 10 Aug. 1972 with an unconfirmed 75,347 miles.

Beryl Burton, 13 times British all-round champion (1959-71) won her 21st track title on 12 Aug. 1972.

Page 253

Darts marathon Barry Figgins, Richard Windsor, Mick Lee and John Hudson played non-stop for 168 hours at the Black Swan Hotel, Todmorden, Yorks. They played on a four hourly shift system, on 15-22 July 1972.

Page 257

Transfer fees The British record transfer fee was raised to £225,000 for the Leicester City player David Nish who was transferred to Derby County in August 1972.

Page 259

Five a side football Indoors: Two teams of five from the 6th Form, Hartlepool Grammar School played for 60 hours non-stop between 5 and 7 Aug. 1972. No substitutes were used.

Outside: Two teams of five from Steyning Grammar School, Sussex played for 38 hours 30 minutes in July 1972. No substitutes were used.

11 a side marathon Two teams of 11 from Downpatrick Summer Activities Scheme played non-stop football for 26 hours on 2-3 Aug. 1972. No substitutes were used.

Page 262

Longest try The longest "try" ever executed was that over 136 miles from Wolverhampton Polytechnic to Twickenham, Middlesex, by fifteen players from the Wolverhampton Polytechnic, R.F.C., in 26 hours 47 minutes. There were no forward passes or knock-ons, and the ball was touched down between the posts in the prescribed manner (Law 12).

Page 266

Fastest round 48 members of Doon Valley Golf Club, Kitchener, Ontario, Canada completed the 18 hole 6,358 yard course there in 10 minutes 58.4 seconds on 16 July 1972.

Page 268

Holes in One A 15th case of consecutive holes in one was achieved by Colin Bice at Nowra, New South Wales on 29 Aug. 1972.

Page 270

Most appearances Harold A. Cahill now has 65 appearances for Ireland and 35 for Great Britain making a total of 100 the first Briton to reach this figure. Mr Cahill holds a British Passport.

Page 295

Most Olympic titles Mark Spitz (U.S.A.) won seven gold medals (4 individual and 3 team) in Munich 1972, (with 2 golds in 1968) thus equalling the record of Paavo Nurmi (Finland) who also won 9 gold medals (see page 229).

Page 296

Cross Channel The England to France record was lowered to 9 hours 44 min. by Lt. Richard Davis Hart (U.S. Army), 26, of New Jersey on 21 Aug. 1972.

Page 299

Volleyball marathon The British record is 86¼ hours by four teams of six from Hillingdon Youth Sports Centre, Hayes, Middx., between 27 and 30 August 1971.

INDEX

BIRD, largest, heaviest, largest wing span, greatest wing area, smallest 37, most abundant 35-36, rarest, longest lived, fastest flying, fastest running, fastest wing-beats, fastest swimmer, longest flights, highest flying, most airborne, most acute vision, largest eggs, smallest eggs 36, shortest and longest incubation 36-37, longest, most feathers, earliest and latest cuckoo, heaviest turkey; domesticated birds: largest caged population, longest lived, most talkative 37; largest extinct 46-47, earliest 47, most expensive stuffed 155
BIRTH RATE, highest, lowest 188
BIRTHS, multiple 17-19, latest post mortem delivery 22
BISHOP, oldest Church of England, Roman Catholic, youngest 220
BISHOPRIC, largest tenure 221
BITTEREST SUBSTANCE, 74
BLACK-OUT, biggest 140
BLADES, penknife with greatest number 154
BLAST FURNACE, largest 141
BLENDING VAT, largest 110
BLIND, 100 yards record 236
BLINDNESS, Colour, highest and lowest rate 23
BLOOD DONOR, life time record 22
BLOOD GROUP, commonest, rarest 22
BLOOD TEMPERATURE, highest and lowest mammalian 22
BLOOM, largest, largest inflorescence, largest blossoming plant 50
BOAT, see Ship
BOBSLEIGH, 238
BODY JUMP, greatest 168
BOILER, largest 140
BOILING POINT, lowest and highest for gases 72, metals 73
BOMB, defusing record 168, heaviest conventional, most powerful atom 198, worst disaster world, U.K. 222
BOMBER, heaviest, most powerful, fastest 137
BOMBING, worst in world, U.K. 222
BOND SIGNING, greatest feat 168
BONE, oldest fragment 15, longest, smallest human 20
BONFIRE, largest 120
BOOK, oldest mechanically printed, largest, largest art, smallest hand-written, smallest printed, most valuable, highest priced 20th century, longest novel; encyclopaedia: most comprehensive, largest; top selling 88; largest dictionary 89, Bible 90; best-sellers: world 91-92, non-fiction, slowest seller 91, fiction 92, most overdue 93, largest single display in one room 146
BOOK SHOP, largest 146
BOOMERANG, greatest throws 168
BORES, River, greatest 61
BORING, deepest world, U.K. 121
BOTTLE, largest, smallest (spirit) 75, fastest bottling line 149, message in 172
BOUNDARY, see Frontiers
BOWLING (Ten Pin), 238-239
BOWLS, 239
BOXING, 239-242
BOX-OFFICE, biggest theatre 98, film 102
BRAIN, (human), largest, smallest 20, (animal), heaviest 29, least 46
BRASS, oldest monumental 221
BRASS INSTRUMENT, largest 94-95
BREACH OF CONTRACT, highest damages 200
BREACH OF PROMISE, highest damages 200
BREAKWATER, longest world, U.K. 118
BREEDER, fastest 29
BREWERY, oldest, largest 146-147
BRIBE, largest 206
BRICK-CARRYING, record for man, woman 168
BRICKLAYING, world record 168
BRICK-THROWING, greatest distance 168
BRICKWORKS, largest 147
BRIDGE, longest natural 62, oldest world, British, longest suspension world, U.K., longest cantilever, longest steel arch 112, largest 112-113, longest floating, railway, highest suspension, railway, widest, progressive records, longest spans (by type) 113
BRIDGE (Contract), 243-244
BRIDGE-TUNNEL, longest 116
BROADCAST (Radio), first advertised, trans-Atlantic, longest 102. **(Television)** first 103
BROADCASTER, fastest 25
BROADCASTING, see Radio
BROADMOOR, longest detention, longest escape 205
BROADSHEET, highest price 89
BUBBLE CHAMBER, largest world 80
BUDGERIGAR, longest lived 37
BUDGET, largest, greatest surplus, deficit 206
BUILDING (see also Structure), largest theatre 98, largest cinema 101, earliest world, U.K., largest manufacturing, scientific 104, administrative 104-105, commercial, office 105, tallest, maximum sway, most storeys, highest, northernmost, southernmost 105, wooden 106, for living 107-108, entertainment 108-110, tallest (progressive records) 111, largest university 216, largest religious 217, oldest religious 219
BUILDING CONTRACTOR, largest 147
BUILDING SOCIETY, largest, oldest 147
BULB, most powerful light, most durable light 81
BULL, heaviest England 156, highest price 157
BULLDOZER, largest 130
BULLFIGHTING, 242
BURIAL ALIVE, record 168
BUS, earliest, largest, longest route 130
BUSH-CRICKET, largest 43
BUSINESS, oldest, greatest assets, sales, profits, losses 145
BUTTER FAT, record lifetime, one lactation, day yields 158
BUTTERFLY, slowest wing beat 43, largest, smallest, rarest, highest 43-44

CABER TOSS, greatest 233
CABLE, Telephone, longest submarine 213
CABLE CARS, largest 142
CABLE SHIP, largest 126
CACTUS, largest 52
CADENZA, longest 96
CAKE, largest 210
CALCULATION, greatest feat 24
CALF, highest birthweight, most at one birth 156
CALORIES, most and least calorific fruit 50, highest, lowest consumption, largest available total 210
CAMERA, earliest, largest, smallest, fastest cine, most expensive 78
CAMP, concentration, largest penal 205
CANAL, earliest 113-114, longest, longest big ship, inland waterway U.K., irrigation, largest cut 114, longest tunnel world, U.K. 115
CANDLE, largest 152
CANNON, largest 197
CANNONBALL, Human, record distance 171
CANOEING, 242-243
CANTILEVER BRIDGE, longest world, U.K. 112
CANYON, deepest, deepest submarine 62
CAPE HORN, earliest rounding 162
CAPITAL CITY, most populous, largest, highest, oldest, northernmost, southernmost 187-188, most and least expensive 189
CAPITAL PUNISHMENT, see Execution
CAR, largest ferry 126-127, earliest, earliest mechanically-propelled, first internal combustion, earliest petrol driven, earliest British, oldest internal-combustion, most durable, earliest registration, fastest rocket-engined, fastest jet driven, wheel driven 128, piston engine 128-129, fastest production, largest, longest, widest, most expensive world, most expensive standard, U.K., vintage, cheapest, longest in production, largest engines 129, petrol consumption 130, longest skid marks 131, largest manufacturer, largest single plant 148, greatest T-bone dive 175
CARAVAN, towing record 131, longest journey 131
CARD HOUSES, largest number of storeys, tallest tower 171
CARD PLAYING, 243-244
CARDINAL, oldest, youngest 220
CAR FERRY, largest 126
CARGO VESSEL, largest 126
CARILLON, largest, heaviest 97
CAR MANUFACTURER, largest, largest single plant 148
CARNIVORE, largest land, smallest 29, largest 40
CAR PARKING METERS, earliest 213
CARPET, earliest, largest, most expensive, most finely woven 152
CARRIER, typhoid, most notorious 21
CARTOON, largest, longest lived strip, most read 92
CASH, most found and returned 179
CASTING, see Angling
CASTLE, earliest world, British Isles 106, Irish, largest world, U.K. and Ireland 108, thickest walls 107
CAT, largest, smallest 29, heaviest, oldest, largest litter, most prolific, greatest fall, most lives, richest and most valuable, rarest breed, ratting and mousing, population 34
CATALYST CRACKER, largest 141
CATHEDRAL, tallest (progressive records) 111, largest 217-218, smallest, longest, longest nave 218, tallest spire 219
CATTLE, longest horns 32, heaviest, highest birthweight, prolificacy record 156, record prices 157
CATTLE STATION, largest 156
CAVE, largest, most extensive system, deepest by countries, longest systems by countries 62, progressive depth, deepest, duration 244
CAVERN, largest 62
CAVING, 244
CELLAR, wine, largest 110
CEMETERY, largest world, U.K. 120
CENTENARIAN, oldest 16
CENTI-MILLIONAIRES, 178
CENTIPEDE, longest, most legs, shortest, least legs 44
CENTRIFUGE, fastest 79
CEREAL, biggest consumers 210
CHAIN STORE, largest department, grocery 147
CHAIR, largest 152
CHAMBER, largest underground 62
CHAMPAGNE, largest bottles, cork flight 75
CHAMPIONS (sports), youngest and oldest, longest reign 225
CHANCELLORSHIP, longest, shortest tenure, most appointments 194
CHANNEL CROSSING, see Cross Channel
CHAPEL, smallest U.K. 219
CHARLESTON, duration record 169
CHEESE, heaviest eaters, biggest producer, oldest, varieties, most expensive largest 158, eating record 180
CHELONIANS, largest, longest lived, slowest moving 38, largest prehistoric 46
CHEMICAL COMPANY, largest 147
CHEMICAL NAME, longest 86
CHEMIST SHOP, largest chain 147
CHEQUE, most bad 206, largest, oldest surviving 208
CHESS, 245
CHEST MEASUREMENT, largest 20
CHESTNUT, greatest girth 49
CHICKEN, eating record 180
CHILDREN'S HOSPITAL, largest U.K. 189
CHIMNEYS, tallest world, U.K. 105
CHINNING THE BAR, 270
CHOCOLATE, largest factory 147
CHORISTER, longest serving 221
CHORUS LINE, longest 99
CHRISTMAS, "white", most recent 64, most cards 92, most expensive present 152
CHURCH, tallest (progressive records) 111, longest Gothic, largest 218, smallest 218-219, oldest, tallest spire 219
CHURCHYARD, largest 219
CIGAR, largest, most expensive, most voracious smoker 152
CIGARETTE, consumption, most expensive, most popular, longest and shortest 152, earliest abstention, most expensive lighter, largest collection 152-153, packets (cartons): largest collection, earliest, rarest; cards: earliest and most valuable 153
CINEMA, earliest, highest film production, most attendances, most per population, largest, oldest, most expensive film, musical, film rights 101, longest film 101-102, longest title, highest box office gross, highest earning actor, most Oscars, most durable newsreel commentator 102
CIRCULAR STORM, worst in world, U.K. 222
CIRCULATION, highest newspaper, periodical 93-94
CIRCUMNAVIGATION, first orbital 71; air: earliest, first solo, fastest, earliest solo circumpolar 136; sea: earliest, first solo with one stop, non-stop, fastest solo, longest voyage, submarine 162
CIRCUS, acrobatic feats, largest 177
CITY, longest name 87, most populous, largest, smallest, highest, oldest, northernmost 187, southernmost capitals, farthest from sea 188

CIVIL WAR, bloodiest 195
CLAMS, eating record 180
CLAPPING, longest continuous 168
CLERGY, largest 217
CLIFFS, highest 62
CLOCK, oldest, largest world, U.K., largest public, longest stoppage, most accurate, most expensive 143
CLOTH, finest 153
CLOUDS, highest, lowest, greatest vertical range 64
CLUB SWINGING, duration record 168
COACHING, 128
COAL CARRYING, record time 167
COAL SHOVELLING, record 168
COASTLINES, U.K. Counties, longest 186
COFFEE, greatest drinkers 211
COIN, swallowing 23, largest robbery 205, oldest, heaviest, smallest 208, highest, lowest denomination 208-209, rarest, most expensive; legal tender: oldest, largest, heaviest, highest current denomination, lightest, smallest, greatest collection, largest treasure trove, largest mint, greatest hoarders, largest pile of pennies 209
COLDEST PLACE, world, U.K., Ireland, annual mean, coldest inhabited 64
COLLEGE, oldest, largest university 215
COLLIERY TIP, largest U.K. 122
COLONY, smallest 185
COLOUR BLINDNESS, highest, lowest rate 23
COLOUR SENSITIVITY, 23
COLUMN, tallest monumental 117, tallest, tallest stone 118
COMA, longest 22
COMET, earliest, speed, closest, largest, shortest, longest period 67
COMIC STRIP, (newspaper), most durable 92
COMMENTATOR, most durable 103
COMMERCE, 145-151
COMMON, largest U.K. 53
COMMUNICATIONS, 211-215
COMMUNIST PARTY, largest 191
COMMUTER, most durable 168
COMPANY, oldest, greatest assets world U.K., sales 145, profit, loss 145-146, most efficient, biggest work force 146, largest manufacturing 148, number of companies registered, most directorships 150, largest investment house 151
COMPENSATION (legal), greatest 199
COMPETITIONS, champion winner, largest single prize 168
COMPOSER, most prolific, most rapid 95
COMPOSITION, longest piano, longest silence 96
COMPUTER, most powerful world, largest U.K. 81
CONCENTRATION CAMP, worst 205
CONCERT, greatest attendance classical, pop festival 95
CONDIMENT, rarest 212
CONSONANTS, language with most, least 85-86
CONSTELLATION, largest, smallest 69
CONSTRUCTION JOB, most massive 119
CONSUMPTIONS, food and drink 210
CONTINENT, largest, smallest 57, area 185
CONTRACT, biggest T.V. 103
CONTRACT, Breach of, highest damages 200
CONTRACT BRIDGE, 243-244
CONURBATION, largest 187
CONVEYOR BELT, longest 144
COOLING TOWERS, largest U.K. 105
COPPER MINE, most productive, largest underground, largest excavation 122
CORK, density 50, champagne distance record 75
CORPORATIONS, greatest sales profit and loss 145-146
CORRESPONDENCE, shortest 92
COSMONAUT, earliest, first woman, oldest, youngest 71, altitude, maximum speed 159
COST OF LIVING, greatest increase 189, worst inflation 208
COSTS, highest legal 200
COUNTRY, total number of, largest, smallest, most frontiers, longest frontiers 185, population, largest, smallest, densest, sparsest 186-187
COUNTY, highest points U.K. and Ireland 57, oldest name, youngest U.K. 88, U.K. largest and smallest areas and populations, longest and shortest coastlines 186
COURSING, 245
COW, prolificacy record 156, record milk yield, record price 157, butterfat yields 158
COW SHED, largest 158
CRAB, largest, smallest U.K., most abyssal 42
CRANE, largest and highest lifting capacity, most powerful, highest, greatest weight lifted, largest floating 144
CRATER, largest volcano 55, meteoric 65-66, largest and deepest lunar 66
CREATURE, largest flying (extinct), most southerly 46, earliest four-legged 47
CREMATION, first legal 120
CREMATORIUM, oldest U.K., first legal cremation, largest Europe 120
CRESTA RUN, records 238
CRICKET, 245-249
CRIME AND PUNISHMENT, 201-206
CRIMINAL ORGANISATION, largest 201-202
CRISPS, potato, eating record 180
CROCODILE, largest and heaviest 37, largest extinct 46, worst disaster 222
CROP YIELD, record wheat, barley 156
CROQUET, 250
CROSS-CHANNEL, first amphibious vehicle 131, earliest flight 135, record trip 162, swimming 296
CROSS-COUNTRY RUNNING, 250
CROSSWORD, first, largest, fastest, slowest 92
CROWD, largest 221, sports, Olympic Games 285
CRUISER, most powerful 125
CRUSTACEANS, largest, smallest, oldest, most abyssal 42, earliest 47
CRYPT, church, largest 218
CRYSTAL, largest 76
CUCKOO, earliest, latest 37
CURLING, 250
CURRENT, greatest, strongest 56, most powerful electric 80
CURTAIN, largest 153
CURTAIN CALLS, most 169
CUT, finest 81, largest canal 114
CUTLER, oldest firm 154
CYCLING, duration 165, sport 251-253
CYCLO-CROSS, 253

DAISY CHAIN, longest 50
DAM, earliest, most massive 114, largest concrete, highest, longest river, sea, world; most massive, highest and longest, U.K.; progressive records 115
DAMAGES, loss of life, highest breach of contract, personal injury, breach of promise, defamation, divorce, greatest patent infringement 200
DAM DISASTER, worst world, U.K. 222
DANCE, largest 169
DANCE BAND, longest playing 169
DANCE COURSE, most expensive 169
DANCING, marathon; ballet: most turns, most curtain calls; ballroom, Charleston, flamenco, go-go, jiving, limbo, twist records, most expensive course, modern marathon 169
DANCING MANIA, worst outbreak 169
DARTS, 253-254
DEATH RATE, highest, lowest 188
DEBT, largest National 207
DECATHLON, world record 230, U.K. 235
DECORATIONS, see Medals 163
DEEP SEA DIVING, record depth 163, progressive records 164
DEER, fastest 28, largest, largest antler span, smallest, rarest 31
DEFAMATION, highest damages 200
DEFENCE, world expenditure, greatest, smallest 195
DEGREES, most honorary 184
DELTA, largest 61
DEMONSTRATION, largest 221
DENTISTS, most dedicated 23, most 189
DEPARTMENT STORE, largest chain, largest U.K., most profitable 149
DEPRESSIONS, deepest, largest 60
DESCENDANTS, most 17
DESCENT, greatest ocean 163, progressive ocean records 164
DESERT, largest 62
DESPATCHES, most mentions 182
DESTROYER, fastest 125

315

316

PHOTOGRAPHIC CREDITS

American Museum of Natural History, 27
T.R. Archibald (Colchester College of Art), 31
Art-Wood Photography, 110
Associated Press, 29, 44, 96, 162, 172, 224 (bottom),
230, 231 (left), 231 (bottom right), 303
Australian News Information Bureau, 85

Bath Academy of Art, 155
E.H. Bath, 17
Beken, 303
Bespix, 273
B.M.H. Photographic, 217 (top)
British Rail, 133 (centre)

Canadian National, 112 (right)
Central Press Photos, 289
R. & H. Chapman, 183
Clarendon Laboratory, 81
Congopresse (C. Lamote), 13
Courier Mail, 168
Crawley & District Observer, 279
Crown Copyright, 43 (top)

Daily Mail, 182 (top)
Daily Mirror Newspapers Ltd., 131 (left), 171 (right)
Daily Telegraph, 212
Detroit Free Press, 10 (top)

Esso Photograph, 106
Evening News, 43 (bottom), 277, 290

Foto Engler, 126 (top)
Foto Spaziani, Rome, 10 (bottom)
Fox Photos Ltd., 38 (bottom), 233 (bottom left)

John Hadland (P.I.) Ltd., 78
Antony Hallas, 271
Harmsworth Photo Library, 296

Imperial War Museum, 125 (top left)

Theodora Jacobalaan, 144 (right)

Keystone Press, 301
W.T. Kirk, 89
Freid. Krupp GmbH, 77

Lancashire Life (C. Lindley), 108
Lehtikuba, 233 (top)
Loffland Bros. Co., 121
London Express, 291
London Art Tech., 281, 282, 282
London Transport Executive, 135
Jack de Lorme Photography Ltd., 288

John McFarlane (Colchester College of Art), 119
Metropolitan Photo Service Inc., 150
Brian Moody, 132
Motor Cycle, London, 280
Mt. Wilson & Palomar Observatories, 69

N.A.S.A., 66 (left)
National Gallery, 83
National Geographic Society, 49, 66 (right)
Neely's Photo Service, 176
Nelson, 151
Nell H. Noel, 153 (right)
Northwest Newfoundland Club, 34

Official U.S. Navy Photograph, 125 (bottom left),
125 (right), 196
Ivan O'Riley, 57
Oxford University Press, 91 (bottom)

Parke-Bernet Galleries, 84
Stephen P. Peltz, 139
Photo-Expo, 104
Photopress, N.Z., 273
Planet News Ltd., 38 (top), 211
Port of New York Authority, 105
Courtesy of the Post Office, 213, 214
Press Association, 284, 293

R.A.C. Tank Museum, 197 (top)
Radio Times Hulton Picture Library, 194, 200
Reuter, 37
Richards Bros., 194
Royal Navy Photographic Dept., 126 (bottom)
C. Ryan (Colchester College of Art), 134

Scottish Farmer, 156
Scunthorpe Evening Mail, 169
Simon Livingstone Studios, 170
Sperryn's Ltd., 154
Sport & General, 229

Stearn & Sons, 218 (bottom)
Syndication International, 294

George Tagg, 136
D.C. Thomson & Co. Ltd., 167
Maurice R. Tibbles, 60
The Times & Journal Series, 143
Trustees of British Museum, 93
Twentieth Century Fox, 102

Universal Pictorial Press, 274, 300
University of Illinois, 101
United Press International, 231 (top right), 233
(right)

U.S. Department of the Interior, 54
U.S.I.S., 163

Georges Vermard, 180

Reg Ward, 253
Western Australian News Ltd., 52
Wiltshire Newspapers, 166 (top)
G.L.Wood, 14
S. Woodriffe, 122

Yugoslav Airlines, 173

Zoological Society of London, 53

CURRENT OLYMPIC RECORDS AFTER

 ## ATHLETICS (TRACK AND FIELD EVENTS)

NWR indicates New World Record
EWR indicates Equal World Record

MEN

Event	Time or Distance	Name and/or Nationality	Date
100 metres	9·9	James Ray Hines (U.S.A.)	14 Oct. 1968
200 metres	19·8	Tommie C. Smith (U.S.A.)	16 Oct. 1968
400 metres	43·8	Lee Edward Evans (U.S.A.)	18 Oct. 1968
800 metres	1:44·3	Ralph D. Doubell O.B.E. (Australia)	15 Oct. 1968
1,500 metres	3:34·9	Hezekiah Kipchoge Keino (Kenya)	20 Oct. 1968
5,000 metres	13:26·4	Lasse Viren (Finland)	10 Sep. 1972
10,000 metres	27:38·4 NWR	Lasse Viren (Finland)	3 Sep. 1972
Marathon	2H 12:11·2	Abebe Bikila (Ethiopia)	21 Oct. 1964
4 x 100m relay	38·2	United States of America	20 Oct. 1968
	38·2 EWR	United States of America	10 Sep. 1972
4 x 400m relay	2:56·1	United States of America	20 Oct. 1968
20Km road walk	1H 26:42·4	Peter Frenkel (East Germany)	31 Aug.1972
50Km road walk	3H 56:11·6	Bernd Kannenberg (West Germany)	3 Sep. 1972
110m hurdles	13·2 EWR	Rodney Milburn Jnr. (U.S.A.)	7 Sep. 1972
400m hurdles	47·8 NWR	John Akii-Bua (Uganda)	2 Sep. 1972
3,000m steeplechase	8:23·6	Hezekiah Kipchoge Keino (Kenya)	4 Sep. 1972

	ft	in	m		
High Jump	7	4¼	2·24	Richard D. Fosbury (U.S.A.)	20 Oct. 1968
Pole Vault	18	0½	5·50	Wolfgang Nordwig (East Germany)	2 Sep. 1972
Long Jump	29	2½	8·90	Robert Beamon (U.S.A.)	9 Oct. 1968
Triple Jump	57	0¾	17·39	Viktor Saneyev (U.S.S.R.)	17 Oct. 1968
Shot Putt	69	6	21·18	Wladyslaw Komar (Poland)	9 Sep. 1972
Discus Throw	212	6	64·78	Alfred A. Oerter (U.S.A.)	15 Oct. 1968
Hammer Throw	247	8	75·50	Anatoliy Bondarcuk (U.S.S.R.)	7 Sep. 1972
Javelin Throw	296	10	90·48	Klaus Wolfermann (West Germany)	3 Sep. 1972
Decathlon		8,454 points NWR		Nikolay Avilov (U.S.S.R.)	7–8 Sep. 1972

WOMEN

Event	Time or Distance	Name and/or Nationality	Date
100 metres	11·0	Wyomia Tyus (U.S.A.)	15 Oct. 1968
200 metres	22·4 EWR	Renate Stecher (East Germany)	7 Sep. 1972
400 metres	51·1	Monika Zehrt (East Germany)	7 Sep. 1972
800 metres	1:58·6	Hildegard Falck (West Germany)	3 Sep. 1972
1,500 metres	4:01·4 NWR	Ludmila Bragina (U.S.S.R.)	9 Sep. 1972
4 x 100m relay	42·8	United States of America	20 Oct. 1968
	42·8 EWR	West Germany	10 Sep. 1972
4 x 400m relay	3:23·0 NWR	East Germany	10 Sep. 1972
100m hurdles	12·6	Annelie Ehrhardt (East Germany)	10 Sep. 1972

	ft	in	m		
High Jump	6	3½	1·92 EWR	Ulrike Meyfarth (West Germany)	4 Sep. 1972
Long Jump	22	5	6·83	Heidemarie Rosendahl (West Germany)	3 Sep. 1972
Shot Putt	69	0	21·03 NWR	Nadyezhda Chizhova (U.S.S.R.)	7 Sep. 1972
Discus Throw	218	7	66·62	Fainia Melnik (U.S.S.R.)	10 Sep. 1972
Javelin Throw	209	7	63·88	Ruth Fuchs (East Germany)	1 Sep. 1972
Pentathlon		4,801 points NWR		Mary Elizabeth Peters (G.B. & N.I.)	2–3 Sep. 1972

 ## CYCLING

1,000m Time Trial	1:03·91	Pierre Trentin (France)	17 Oct. 1968
4,000m Individual Pursuit	4:37·54	Mogens Frey (Denmark)	17 Oct. 1968
4,000m Team Pursuit	4:15·76*	West Germany	20 Oct. 1968

SHOOTING

	Points		
50m Small Bore Rifle (3 positions)	1,166 NWR	John Writer (U.S.A.)	30 Aug.1972
50m Small Bore Rifle (Prone position)	599 NWR	Ho Jun Li (North Korea)	28 Aug.1972
Free Rifle	1,157	Gary Anderson (U.S.A.)	23 Oct. 1972
Free Pistol	567	Ragnar Skanaker (Sweden)	27 Aug.1972
Rapid Fire Pistol	595	Jozef Zapedzki (Poland)	1 Sep. 1972
Olympic Trench (Clay Pigeon)	199 NWR	Angelo Scalzone (Italy)	29 Aug.1972
Skeet	198	Evgeny Petrov (U.S.S.R.)	22 Oct. 1972
Running Boar	569 NWR	Yakov Zhelezniak (U.S.S.R.)	1 Sep. 1972